NEW TESTAMENT COMMENTARY

NEW TESTAMENT
COMMENTARY

By

WILLIAM HENDRIKSEN

Exposition
of the
Gospel According to John

TWO VOLUMES COMPLETE IN ONE

BAKER BOOK HOUSE
Grand Rapids, Michigan

The Gospel According to John

John

VOLUME I

ISBN: 0-8010-4051-5

First printing, September 1954
Second printing, February 1960
Third printing, February 1967
Fourth printing, February 1970
Fifth printing, August 1972
Sixth printing, January 1975
Seventh printing, June 1976
Eighth printing, August 1979
Ninth printing, August 1981
Tenth printing, September 1983

PRINTED IN THE UNITED STATES OF AMERICA

TABLE OF CONTENTS
VOLUME I

INTRODUCTION

In writing this commentary it has been our aim to achieve the following objectives:

(1) A careful *translation* of the text. This translation must be in present-day, idiomatic English and must be true to the original. It should not be a mere paraphrase. On the contrary, it should follow the text very closely, bringing out its emphasis wherever it is possible to do so.

(2) A more thorough discussion of *introductory problems* than is found in many commentaries, with special emphasis on *the problems of authorship*.

(3) A brief *analysis of the text*, entering into its concepts and relationships. Central passages, such as 3:16, should be treated more fully than others.

(4) A *synthesis* at the close of each large thought-unit, so that the main ideas of a section are brought out clearly. *Analysis should always be followed by synthesis*. Exegesis includes both. Otherwise one sees the trees, but not the forest.

(5) A defence of *the conservative position*. We believe that the Gospel of John demands this.

(6) *An up-to-date presentation*. During recent years there has been advance along many lines of New Testament scholarship. Important books treating certain phases of the subject have appeared from time to time; also, excellent articles in religious journals, shedding new light on the meaning of certain words and phrases (e.g., John 2:4; 4:9). Doctoral dissertations have been submitted, dealing with concepts of frequent occurrence in the Fourth Gospel. Such materials have been utilized. We have prepared a *Select Bibliography*, and this we hope to include in the next volume (on John 7-21).

(7) *A complete summary of certain grammatical constructions* which have a high frequency rate in this Gospel. References throughout the text of the commentary to *important points of grammar and syntax*, without overloading the commentary with such material, so that one who is not conversant with Greek would have to lay it aside. An attempt to do justice to the valuable elements in the Aramaic theory, without assuming a written, Aramaic original.

INTRODUCTION

We are well aware of the fact that these objectives have not been *fully* achieved. Nevertheless, the kind reception given to our earlier works encouraged us to make the effort. May the One whose love is set forth in this Gospel receive the glory.

William Hendriksen

LIST OF ABBREVIATIONS

The letters in book-abbreviations are followed by periods. Those in periodical-abbreviations omit the periods. Thus one can see at a glance whether the abbreviation refers to a book or to a periodical.

A. *Book Abbreviations*

A.R.V.	American Standard Revised Version
A.V.	Authorized Version (King James)
B.D.B.	Brown-Driver-Briggs, *Hebrew and English Lexicon to the Old Testament*
D.C.G.	Hastings, *Dictionary of Christ and the Gospels*
Gram.N.T.	A. T. Robertson, *Grammar of the Greek New Testament in the Light of Historical Research*
H.B.A.	Hurlbut, *Bible Atlas* (most recent edition)
I.S.B.E.	*International Standard Bible Encyclopedia*
L.N.T.	Thayer's *Greek-English Lexicon of the New Testament*
N.N.	*Novum Testamentum Graece*, edited by D. Eberhard Nestle and D. Erwin Nestle (most recent edition)
R.S.V.	Revised Standard Version
S.BK.	Strack and Billerbeck, *Kommentar zum Neuen Testament aus Talmud und Midrasch*
Th.W.N.T.	*Theologisches Wörterbuch zum Neuen Testament* (edited by G. Kittel)
W.D.B.	*Westminster Dictionary of the Bible*
W.H.A.B.	*Westminster Historical Atlas to the Bible*

B. *Periodical Abbreviations*

AJTh	*American Journal of Theology*
ChrC	*Christian Century*
ClW	*Classical Weekly*
CQR	*Church Quarterly Review*
CThM	*Concordia Theological Monthly*
EQ	*Evangelical Quarterly*
ExT	*Expository Times*
GThT	*Gereformeerd Theologisch Tijdschrift*

LIST OF ABBREVIATIONS

HJ	*Hibbert Journal*
HThR	*Harvard Theological Review*
JBL	*Journal of Biblical Literature*
JThS	*Journal of Theological Studies*
PThR	*Princeton Theological Review*
RThPh	*Revue de Théologie et de Philosophie*
ThG	*Theologie und Glaube*
VD	*Verbum Domini*
WE	*Watchman-Examiner*
ZNTW	*Zeitschrift fur die neutestamentl. Wissenschaft*

Please Note

In order to differentiate between the second person singular and the second person plural (without reverting to the archaic "thou" and "ye" except where it is proper to do so), we have indicated the former as follows: "you"; and the latter, as follows: "y o u."

Introduction
to the
Gospel According to John

I. Authorship, Date, and Place

The Gospel according to John is the most amazing book that was ever written. "Put off thy shoes from off thy feet, for the place whereon thou standest is holy ground." This may well be the attitude of anyone who steps upon the threshold of the study of this book; for if its testimony is true, the faith in Jesus Christ as the Son of God has received glorious confirmation. The reason for this will become clear immediately.

The book tells us that, evidently in the days of Emperor Tiberius and of the tetrarch Herod Antipas, there was living in the land of Palestine a Jew (4:9), named Jesus, who claimed that he was the Rightful Owner of all things, the Bread of Life, the Living Water, the Good Shepherd who would give his life for his sheep, the One who would raise the dead at the last day, the very Messiah, the Way to God, the proper Object of faith and worship, a person so completely and in every sense divine that he was able to say: "I and the Father are One."

This, indeed, is astounding. But even more marvelous is this: *the writer of the book accepts these claims as being true!* To "the Jesus of history" he gives the most exalted titles. He calls him the Word (Logos) of God, and tells us that this Word had been "with God" from eternity, dwelling in the immediate presence of the Father. Boldly the author even calls him *God*, and he does this in the opening verse! For the writer, Jesus is nothing less than what he claims to be. He is God Incarnate (1:1, 14).

Who is this author who accepts these claims and makes these startling declarations? Is he a total stranger, living in a country far removed from the actual scenes which he describes, so that distance lends enchantment to the view? And is he writing at a time very long after the events, so that the "hero" of the story has by degrees and gradual stages become a miracle-worker, and the latter, in strict obedience to the laws of legend and folklore, has at length been transformed into a god? Quite the contrary! The author of the Fourth Gospel is represented as one who belongs to the same race, stock, and family as does his "hero." He is introduced as a contemporary and eye-witness (21:24; cf. I John 1:1-4). He belongs not only to the wide circle of the Master's followers, but according to tradition he is one of the *twelve,* and within that group of twelve he is one of the *three* (Mark 5:37; 9:2; 14:33). But even if one should object to these references to the Synoptics and should wish to confine himself to the testimony of the Fourth Gospel itself, he would have to grant that the author is here regarded as

3

one of the *two* earliest disciples (1:35, 40). This conclusion naturally follows, unless one should adopt the improbable view that the unnamed disciple in 21:24 is someone else than the unnamed disciple in 1:35, 40. And of these two he is the *one* who represents himself as "the disciple whom Jesus loved" (13:23).

No one knew Jesus better than he did. He walked with him from day to day, so that he had ample opportunity to observe his character-faults and personality-defects, had there been any. In that most sacred of all nights, the night of the Supper, he reclined on his bosom. He stood by his cross. He even entered his tomb (13:25; 19:26; 20:8). Yet, it is this very disciple who, as the author of the Fourth Gospel, does not shrink from proclaiming to all and sundry that this Jesus of history, whom he knew so well, is himself God!

Not only that, but in the very first chapter he introduces other eye-witnesses. He tells us that these men were so deeply impressed when they met Jesus for the very first time that they gave utterance to their thoughts and emotions in the following exclamations:

Andrew: "We have found the Messiah."

Philip: "We have found the One of whom Moses wrote in the Law and of whom the prophets wrote."

Nathanael: "Rabbi, thou art the Son of God; thou art the king of Israel" (1:41, 45, 49).

To this may be added the testimony of John the Baptist, also recorded in this first chapter:

"I am not fit to unloose the straps of his sandals. . . . Look, the Lamb of God who takes away the sin of the world. . . . I have testified that this one is the Son of God" (1:27, 29, 34).

The opponents of the traditional view cannot allow this testimony to stand. They realize that if it remains unchallenged they have lost not only a battle but the war. What has Higher Criticism to offer that would shake this testimony? How do anti-conservatives try to prove that the Fourth Gospel could not have been composed by a contemporary and eye-witness; that it was not written in Asia Minor by the aged apostle John, as tradition says? Their arguments may be summarized as follows:[1]

---

[1] Anyone who reads the following literature — a selection from among hundreds of works written on this subject — will have both the arguments of the critics and the answers given by those who cling to the traditional view with reference to the authorship of the Fourth Gospel. *We acknowledge indebtedness to all of the following:*

Albright, W. F., *From The Stone Age to Christianity*, Baltimore, 1940, especially pp. 298-300.

Andrews, Mary E., "The Authorship and Significance of the Gospel of John," *JBL* 64(1945), 183-192.

INTRODUCTION

(1) *John, the apostle, died too early to have written a Gospel in Ephesus toward the close of the first century A. D.* Evidence: In Codex Coislinianus, Paris 305, which is one of the manuscripts of the chronicles of Georgius Hamartolus, a monk who lived in the ninth century A. D., it is stated that, according to Papias, *the apostle John and his brother James* died a martyr's death. We know that James was put to death not later than 44 A. D. by Herod Agrippa I, and that Peter survived him (Acts 12). Now if also John suffered martyrdom at such an early date, he could not have written the Fourth Gospel. Proof: the author of that Gospel survived even Peter (John 21:18-24). This is the gist of the first argument.

Bacon, B. W., *The Fourth Gospel in Research and Debate*, New York, 1910.

Bernard, J. H., *A Critical and Exegetical Commentary on the Gospel according to St. John*, 2 vols. (in *International Critical Commentary*), New York, 1929.

Burney, C. F., *The Aramaic Origin of the Fourth Gospel*, Oxford, 1922, especially pp. 126-152.

Dods, M., *The Gospel of St. John* (in *The Expositor's Greek Testament*), Reprint Grand Rapids, Michigan (no date), vol. I, especially pp. 655-681.

Gardner-Smith, Percival, *St. John and the Synoptic Gospels*, Cambridge, 1938.

Godet, F., *Commentary on the Gospel of John* (translated by T. Dwight), 2 vols., New York, 1886.

Goguel, M., *Le Quatrième Évangile*, Paris, 1924.

Goodenough, E. R., "John A Primitive Gospel," *JBL* 64(1945), 145-182.

Grosheide, F. W., *Johannes* (in *Kommentaar op het Nieuwe Testament*), 2 vols., Amsterdam, 1950, especially vol. I, pp. 1-42.

Hoskyns, E. C., *The Fourth Gospel*, 2 vols., London, 1940.

Howard, W. F., *The Fourth Gospel in Recent Criticism and Interpretation*, London, 1945.

Howard, W. F., *Christianity According to St. John*, Philadelphia, 1946, especially pp. 11-33; also his review of Hoskyns, The Fourth Gospel, *JThS* 42(1941), 75-81.

Luthardt, C. E., *St. John The Author of the Fourth Gospel*, Edinburgh, 1875.

Menoud, P. H., *L'évangile de Jean d'après les recherches recentés*, Neuchatel and Paris, 1943.

Nunn, H. P. V., "The Fourth Gospel in the Early Church," *EQ* 16(1944), 173-191.

Nunn, H. P. V., *The Fourth Gospel, An Outline of the Problem and Evidence*, London, 1946.

Redlich, E. B., *An Introduction to the Fourth Gospel*, London, 1939.

Roberts, C. H., *An Unpublished Fragment of the Fourth Gospel*, Manchester, 1935.

Robertson, A. T., *John, in Word Pictures*, New York and London, 1932, vol. V., especially pp. ix-xxvii (Introduction).

Robinson, J. A., *The Historical Character of St. John's Gospel*, London and New York, 1908.

Sanday, W., *The Authorship and Historical Character of the Fourth Gospel*, London, 1872.

Sanday, W., *The Criticism of the Fourth Gospel*, Oxford, 1905.

Scott, E. F., *The Fourth Gospel, Its Purpose and Theology*, Edinburgh, 1906.

Strachan, R. H., *The Fourth Evangelist, Dramatist or Historian?*, London, 1925.

Streeter, B. H., *The Four Gospels*, New York, 1925.

Taylor, Vincent, "The Fourth Gospel and Some Recent Criticism," in *Contemporary Thinking About Jesus* (edited by T. S. Kepler), New York, Nashville, 1944, pp. 99-106.

The significant passages in the aforementioned Codex are as follows (note the words which we have italicized):

"After Domitian, Nerva reigned one year. It was he who recalled John from the island and allowed him to live in Ephesus. He was the only one of the twelve Apostles still living at the time and, after composing the Gospel that bears his name, was deemed worthy of martyrdom.* Papias, Bishop of Hierapolis, who knew him personally, says in the second book of his *Oracles of the Lord* that he was put to death by the Jews. In this way, together with his brother, he manifestly fulfilled the prophecy of Christ '. . . The cup that I drink you will drink, and with my baptism you will be baptized.' Naturally, this must be so, for God can utter no falsehood! In his exegesis of Matthew, the very learned Origen also vouches for the martyrdom of John on the strength of information to the effect which he received from successors of the apostles. Besides, the great historian Eusebius says in his *Ecclesiastical History:* 'Parthia fell by lot to Thomas; Asia to John. There he lived, dying at Ephesus.' "

Note first of all that while *this* manuscript states that John according to Papias was put to death by the Jews, *other* manuscripts of this author say that *he rested in peace.*

Secondly, this report does not even state that John and James suffered martyrdom *at the same time.*

And finally, also according to this testimony, the apostle John is represented as dwelling *in Ephesus* after his return from Patmos, and dying there *after he had written the Gospel that bears his name.*

Accordingly, what we find is this, that the critics in their attempt to refute the position according to which the apostle John wrote the Fourth Gospel appeal to a document which explicitly states that at least *this* element in the traditional view is correct!

With reference to the "martyrdom" of John and James there is also a manuscript (Baroccianus 142), which was published by C. De Boor (*Texte und Untersuchungen* V. 2, p. 170), and which represents an epitome of the work of Philippus Sidetus, a church-historian who flourished at the beginning of the fifth century. The manuscript contains the following statement:

"Papias, Bishop of Hierapolis, a disciple of John the Theologian and a companion of Polycarp, wrote five books of oracles of the Lord. . . . In the second book *Papias says that John the Theologian* and James his brother were put to death by the Jews."

There are also ancient church calendars in which James and John are commemorated together as martyrs.

With reference to this the detailed argument of J. A. Robinson, *The Historical Character of St. John's Gospel,* London and New York, 1908, pp. 64-80, still holds. His conclusion is as follows:

"There is no sufficient evidence to cast serious doubt on the universal tradition of the Church that St. John the Apostle died peacefully at Ephesus in extreme old age. The attribution to Papias of the statement that John and his brother James were killed by the Jews rests on very slender authority. It is almost inconceivable that, if Papias really said this, Ireneus, Eusebius, and others who had read Papias should not have referred to it. And it is not difficult to explain the attribution of such a statement to Papias as a mistake due to careless interpretation. Nor can this isolated contradiction of the general tradition find any support either in the occasional description of the Apostle as a martyr, or in the position of his commemoration in the calendars of the Church. The word 'martyr' which is the common Greek word for a 'witness' was not at first restricted to those who had sealed their testimony with their blood."

In this connection it must not be overlooked that in ancient writings various persons named John are sometimes confused. And the same is true with respect to James. If Papias said "John and James," he may have been referring to John the Baptist and either James, the son of Zebedee, or James, the brother of the Lord. The latter, according to Josephus and Eusebius, was, indeed, "put to death by the Jews." We know at least that Sidetus is not quoting Papias correctly, for the title *The Theologian* was not applied to the apostle John until much later. Papias surely did not use it. Hence, the entire "quotation" begins to take on a dubious appearance. Did Sidetus really read Papias, or was his ultimate authority Eusebius, which, however, he had misread? Surely, one cannot dignify with the adjective *scholarly* an inference (regarding the authorship of the Fourth Gospel) drawn from a *corrupt quotation*—if quotation at all—*of the words of a writer (supposedly Papias), reputedly "of small intelligence,"* which quotation the critics have found *in a late epitome of the work of a bungling historian!*

And as to church-calendars, an early Carthaginian martyrology contains the following:

Dec. 25 viii Kal. Jan. Domini nostri Jesu Christi, filii Dei.

Dec. 27 vi Kal, Jan. sancti Johannis Baptistae, et Jacobi Apostoli, quem Herodes occidit.

Here, too, James and John are commemorated together, but the John to whom reference is made is John the Baptist! In an ancient Syriac martyrolgy "John and James the apostles at Jerusalem" are linked. Regarding this we agree with the statement of W. M. Ramsay: "That James and John, who were not slain at the same time, should be commemorated together, is the flimsiest conceivable evidence that John was killed early in Jerusalem." This joint-commemoration may simply be due to the fact that the James and John who were prominent among the Twelve were brothers, and to a misinterpretation of Christ's prophecy with respect to them, found in Mark 10:39.

(2) *Already at the beginning of the fourth century A. D. the view that*

7

the apostle John wrote the Fourth Gospel was rejected; namely, by Eusebius who quotes a sentence from Papias in which the latter mentions two Johns, the second of whom was not the apostle but an elder (presbyter). Eusebius concludes from this that it was the "elder" John who wrote the Gospel. Thus, in substance, E. R. Goodenough, "John A Primitive Gospel," *JBL* 64(1945), p. 148.

But what is stated here with reference to Eusebius is not even true,[2] for that historian never said that the "elder" John (in distinction from the apostle John) wrote *the Gospel! Eusebius definitely believed that the Apostle John was the evangelist.* It must be admitted that it is deplorable that Eusebius invented a fictitious person. We agree with T. Zahn's statement: "Without discussing it at length, it is safe to say that the 'Presbyter John' is a product of the critical and exegetical weakness of Eusebius" (*The New Schaff-Herzog Encyclopedia of Religious Knowledge*, art. "John the Apostle"). There is no historical evidence to indicate that this person ever lived. Yet, the critics have written page upon page about this nebulosity; e.g., B. H. Streeter, *The Four Gospels*, New York, 1925, ch. 14.

The statement of Papias which puzzled Eusebius was the following: "And I shall not hesitate to append to the interpretations all that I ever learned well from the elders and remember well, for of their truth I am confident. For unlike most I did not rejoice in them who say much, but in them who teach the truth, nor in them who recount the commandments of others, but in them who repeated those given to the faith by the Lord and derived from truth itself. But if ever anyone came who had followed the elders, I enquired into the words of the elders, what Andrew or Peter or Philip or Thomas or James or John or Matthew, or any other of the Lord's disciples, had said, and what Aristion and the elder John, the Lord's disciples, were saying" (Eusebius, *Ecclesiastical History*, III, xxxix, 3-4).

The most natural interpretation of these words of Papias would seem to be this, that the reference in both cases is to the same John (who also calls himself "the elder" in two New Testament epistles, commonly known as II John and III John). If it be borne in mind that according to tradition the apostle John lived to a ripe old age, surviving all the other disciples, it will not be difficult to understand why Papias, after having first included John in the group of disciples, now again mentions him: he who *had said* certain things while the other disciples were still alive, *was still saying* them after their death.

But Eusebius is of the opinion that Papias was thinking of two Johns, the first of whom was the apostle and writer of the Fourth Gospel, while the second (the "elder") was the author of the book of Revelation. With

---

[2] Cf. R. P. Casey, "Prof. Goodenough and the Fourth Gospel," *JBL* 64(1945), 535-542.

respect to the authorship of the latter Eusebius was clearly influenced by Dionysius (200-265 A. D.) whose forcefully presented arguments against the traditional view merit careful study even though one should disagree with his conclusions. We happen to disagree with them. Were these conclusions due, in part, to his aversion to chiliasm which was always appealing to Rev. 20? On this see N. B. Stonehouse, *The Apocalypse in the Early Church*, p. 151. But for our present purpose the question is: *According to Eusebius, who wrote the Fourth Gospel?* The answer will become clear from his comments on the words of Papias which we have just quoted. Eusebius interprets them as follows (note the words which we have italicized):

"It is here worth noting that *he twice counts the name of John, and reckons the first John with Peter and James and Matthew and the other Apostles, clearly meaning the evangelist, but by changing his statement places the second with the others outside the number of the Apostles,* putting Aristion before him and clearly calling him an elder. This confirms the truth of the story of those who have said that there were two of the same name in Asia, and that there are two tombs at Ephesus both still called John's. This calls for attention: for *it is probable that the second* (unless anyone prefer the former *saw the Revelation* which passes under the name of John (Eusebius, *op. cit.,* III, xxxix, 5-6)."

Clearly, then, Eusebius regards the second or "elder" John as having probably written the book of Revelation. However, it is important to emphasize that *he regarded John, the Apostle to be the evangelist, the writer of the Fourth Gospel.* He expresses the same conviction in III, xxiv, 5.

Hence, *this* appeal of the critics to Papias fails as completely as did the others. The source to which the critics make their appeal confirms the traditional view!

(3) *The Alogi, a heretical sect in Asia Minor about 170 A. D., ascribed the Fourth Gospel and Revelation to Cerinthus. Hence, it is clear that even at this early date the Johannine authorship was in doubt.*[3]

This argument, too, is not nearly as formidable as it may sound. Ascribing to Cerinthus a Gospel which loudly proclaims both the deity of Jesus and the incarnation of the Word or Logos is absurd, because these were the very articles of faith which this heretic denied. One might as well ascribe *Luther's Commentary on Galatians* to the pope! The *Alogi*, as Epiphanius hinted when he gave them this name, were the *illogical* opponents of the Logos Gospel, the *unreasonable rejecters* of the divine and personal *Reason*.

The theory of these Alogi, though absurd, contains one valuable element: it shows, at least, that this sect recognized the very early date of the origin of the Fourth Gospel, for according to tradition John and Cerinthus were

---

[3] See, e.g., M. Goguel, *Le Quatrième Évangile*, Paris, 1923, pp. 161, 162.

contemporaries. And if the Fourth Gospel is so very early, the critics are still confronted with an insoluble enigma, stated in the opening pages of this commentary.

(4) *The Christology of this Gospel is too high to have been written by a first generation disciple.*[4]

But this is not even an argument. It amounts to begging the question. It is a bold assertion when proof is wholly lacking. Besides, the question may well be asked: Is the Christology of Paul any lower? Read Col. 2:9 or Phil. 2:6 or that very tantalizing passage Rom. 9:5 which, however hard they try, the critics never quite succeed in removing as a proof-text for Christ's deity. And, indeed, is the Christology of the Synoptics any lower? Read Matt. 11:27, 28.

(5) *There is no progress or development in the events as here recorded. From the very beginning Jesus is the Messiah, the Son of God. Almost from the beginning his death is plotted. It is hard to believe that one of the Twelve would have written in this manner. Besides, this is the opposite of what is found in the Synoptics.*

This argument does not do justice to the facts:

a. Not only in the Fourth Gospel but also in the Synoptics Jesus is recognized as the Messiah from the very beginning; in the latter by John the Baptist (Mark 1:7, 8) and by the demons (Mark 1:24, 34; 3:11); in the former by John the Baptist, Andrew, Philip, and Nathanael (chapter 1).

b. The fact that the recognition of Jesus as the Messiah and as the Son of God receives greater emphasis in the Fourth Gospel than elsewhere is due to the purpose which the author has in mind, as stated in John 20:30, 31: "that y o u may continue to believe that Jesus is the Christ, the Son of God" From the mass of facts the writer carefully selects whatever is best suited to the realization of that expressed aim. He often omits that what the Synoptics have already told. (See p. 31.)

c. If Jesus is really the Messiah, the Son of God, and if his appearance from the very beginning was one that could not fail to cause amazement and awe (cf. Mark 1:27, 28), then it is not "hard to believe that one of the Twelve would have written in this manner."

d. There is, nevertheless, progress in the recognition of Jesus as Messiah and as Son of God. The disciples see more of "his glory" in 2:11 than in chapter 1; otherwise why is this mentioned at all in 2:11? May we not also safely assume that at first their conception of the Messanic office was still, to a certain extent, earth-bound and nationalistic? But when, in connection with the miracle of the feeding of the five thousand, Jesus shatters the hopes of the multitudes by clearly showing that he was not their kind of Messiah, so that many "walked no longer with him" (6:66), Simon Peter, in answer

---

[4] Cf. E. F. Scott, *The Literature of the New Testament*, New York, 1940, p. 242.

to the Master's question: "Would ye also go away?" replies: "Lord, to whom shall we go? Thou hast the words of everlasting life. And we have believed and know that thou art the Holy One of God" (6:67-69).

This confession, under these circumstances, is surely to be regarded as a step forward. It shows real progress, though this does not rule out later moments of recurrent ignorance and doubt. An even more significant confession made by the disciples appears in 16:30: "Now we know that thou knowest all things, and needest not that any man should ask thee: by this we believe that thou camest forth from God." Here, for a moment at least, the bright light of day breaks through the clouds of sorrow and ignorance. The disciples begin to recognize Jesus as Son of God in the ontological sense.

In the light of the entire preceding context (20:24-27) in which the risen Christ reveals his omniscience (cf. 16:30) we must view the glorious exclamation of Thomas: "My Lord and my God" (20:28). Yet even this adoration lacks perfection, as 20:29 clearly indicates. The Fourth Gospel shows that a fuller measure of knowledge regarding the person and work of Christ would be given later, on and after Pentecost. We read:

"I have yet many things to say to y o u, but y o u cannot hear them now. But when he, the Spirit of truth, is come, he will guide y o u into all the truth: for he will not speak of himself, but whatever he hears he will speak and he will announce to y o u the things that are to come" (16:12, 13).

In the light of the passage just quoted, it can be truly said *that the Gospel according to John is preeminently the Gospel of progress and development!*

In the light of that same passage it also becomes clear that the very climax in the confession of the deity of Christ is reached in those statements —e.g., the Prologue, 1:1-18—in which the evangelist, looking back from the vantage-ground of the post-Pentecost period, expresses his own belief with reference to the Logos. It is entirely true that no higher Christology is found anywhere in the Fourth Gospel than in 1:1-5, 14, 18. But such passages stand outside of the story as such. They cannot be used to prove the theory that there is no progress in the narrative.

As has been shown, there is, indeed, progress in the narrative, but *four things must be carefully distinguished: a. the Messianic consciousness of Jesus, b. his self-disclosure, c. the disciples' recognition and confession of his Messianic office and deity, and d. the faith of the author of the book.*

Anent the first, *the Messianic consciousness,* no development of any kind is recorded in the Fourth Gospel. It must be borne in mind that this Gospel does not describe the childhood of Jesus. But if, according to the Synoptics (Luke 2:49), at the age of twelve Jesus is already conscious of the fact that God is his own Father, it should not be considered surprising that in John he is introduced as speaking and acting from the very beginning with divine majesty.

With respect to the second, *Christ's self-disclosure*—on which see H. N. Ridderbos, *Zelfopenbaring En Zelfverberging*, Kampen, 1946, pp. 66-69; also G. Vos, *The Self-disclosure of Jesus*, New York, 1926—, the difficulty of the problem must be admitted. It is evident that while in the Synoptics the emphasis is on the concealment, in John, in harmony with the purpose of his Gospel, the stress is rather on Christ's self-disclosure. In the first and second chapters (1:51; 2:19) this self-disclosure may be considered not quite as far advanced as in later chapters. Subsequently Jesus is often pictured in the act of revealing his Messianic office and deity. But *the comprehensive significance* of this doctrine cannot be disclosed until the Holy Spirit has been poured out (16:12, 13). The same is true respecting other doctrines regarding the person and the work of the Lord (13:7).

With respect to the third, *the disciples' confession,* the progress which this Gospel records has already been indicated.

Anent the fourth, *the author's own position,* this naturally remains the same throughout the book.

e. Similarly, with respect to the plan to put Jesus to death there is progress and development in the Fourth Gospel. Also in this connection it must be remembered that the writer enjoys the great advantage of historical perspective. Writing many years after the events which he records he discerns the *end* in the beginning, the *branch* in the bud.

Thus, he sees that the disposition to kill Jesus established itself in the hearts and minds of the Jewish leaders immediately after the supposed breach of the sabbath on his part when he healed the man at Bethzatha and called God his own Father (5:18). At the feast of Tabernacles these leaders make an abortive attempt to arrest Jesus (7:32). Later the Jews actually pick up stones to hurl at him (8:59). The formal meeting of the sanhedrin at which the actual execution of Jesus is urged is still later. It follows the raising of Lazarus and the widespread fame of Jesus which resulted. The plans are actually laid now by an official body at an official gathering (11:47-53; cf. 12:10, 11). The trial follows (chapter 18), and Jesus is by the Jews delivered into the hands of the Gentiles. In all this the narrative shows progress and development.

(6) *If the Synoptics were written by (or based upon the account of) eye-witnesses, then it is impossible to believe that the apostle John or any other eye-witness wrote the Fourth Gospel, for the differences are too many and too great.* We answer:

a. *There is no contradiction in doctrine.*

It has never yet been shown that there are any doctrinal differences between the Synoptics and John. The *approach,* to be sure, is different. The Synoptics indicate that this man Jesus, the prophet of Nazareth, is the

Messiah, the Son of God. The Fourth Gospel teaches that the Son of God became incarnate. These two ideas blend beautifully.

b. *The general scheme of events is also the same in both cases:*

In both we are introduced to the ministry of John the Baptist. In both Jesus is portrayed as the One who addresses large multitudes and performs miracles.

In both he feeds the five thousand and walks upon the water. In both he withdraws from the multitudes who have rejected him and teaches his disciples.

In both he enters Jerusalem in triumph and is anointed at Bethany. In both he is described as partaking of a meal with his disciples, in connection with which he points out Judas, the betrayer.

In both he warns the disciples against desertion, and subsequently enters the Garden. There follows, in both, the arrest and the trial before (Annas, in John, and then) Caiaphas. Also Peter's denial and the trial before Pilate is related in both. Both relate the cross-bearing, the crucifixion, the watch of the women and their visit to the tomb from which the Lord has arisen.

The attempt is made at times to reduce the similarity between the Synoptics and John to two blocks of thought: the material contained in John 6 and the story of the Passion Week beginning with chapter 18. But this is hardly fair. For, first of all, the resemblance between John 1:32, 33 and Mark 1:10 is striking. Then also, the anointing at Bethany and the triumphal entry are related in John 12. Both of these events are also found in the Synoptics (Mark 14; Matt. 21; Mark 11; Luke 19). The historical setting for the events pertaining to the Supper and for the Supper Discourses is given in the Synoptics; cf. Mark 14:12-18. Accordingly, anyone who has not yet closed his mind to the probability that the Synoptics and John are referring to the same Supper will see that the material found in chapters 13-17 of the latter Gospel fits eminently into the framework of the former. And even the Early Judean Ministry, John 2:13-4:42, and the Later Judean Ministry, John 7:1-10:42, are not at all in conflict with anything that is found in the Synoptics. Does not Matt. 23:37-39 even suggest extensive activity in Judea? Does not Luke 4:44, according to the reading that is supported by the best manuscripts, teach that Jesus was preaching in the synagogues of *Judea?* Cf. also Luke 5:17, which presupposes that Pharisees and doctors of the law had become acquainted with Christ's work in Judea. And conversely, do not John 2:12, 4:43-54, and chapter 6, show that the Fourth Gospel leaves room for Christ's activity in Galilee?

c. *The "words of Jesus" as recorded in the Synoptics are not at all inconsistent with those recorded in the Fourth Gospel.*

The Synoptics differ in many respects from the Fourth Gospel, as we indicate below. This is also apparent in the sayings and discourses of Jesus.

But the differences are not fundamental. The tone of the reputed words and speeches in John is not at all inconsistent with the tone of those given in the Synoptics. And it is inconsistency—not merely difference—which the critics must prove if their argument is to stand. Using the A.R.V. for this list, what we actually find is as follows:

JOHN:

3:3: "Jesus answered and said unto him, Verily, verily, I say unto thee, Except one be born anew, *he cannot see the kingdom of God.*"

Matt. 18:3: "Verily I say unto you, Except ye turn and become as little children, *ye shall in no wise enter the kingdom of heaven.*"

3:5: ". . . Except one be born of water and the Spirit, *he cannot enter the kingdom of God.*"

Mark 10:23: "How hardly shall they that have riches *enter the kingdom of God.*"

4:35: "Behold I say unto you, Lift up your eyes and look on the fields, that they are white already unto harvest."

Matt. 9:37: "The harvest indeed is plenteous, but the laborers are few. Pray ye therefore the Lord of the harvest, that he send forth laborers into his harvest."

3:35; 10:15; 14:6: "The Father loveth the Son, and hath given all things into his hand . . . The Father knoweth me and I know the Father . . . I am the way, and the truth and the life: no one cometh unto the Father, but by me."

Matt. 11:27, 28: "All things have been delivered unto me of my Father; and no one knoweth the Son, save the Father; neither doth any know the Father; save the Son, and he to whomsoever the Son willeth to reveal him. Come unto me, all ye that labor and are heavy laden, and I will give you rest."

5:8, 9: "Arise, take up thy bed, and walk."

Mark 2:9 (a different occasion): "Arise, and take up thy bed, and walk."

5:35, 36: "He (John the Baptist) was the lamp that burneth and shineth . . . But the witness which I have is greater than that of John."

Matt. 11:11: "Verily I say unto you, Among them that are born of women there hath not arisen a greater than John the Baptist: yet he that is but little in the kingdom of heaven is greater than he."

14

5:39: "Ye search *the scriptures,* because ye think that in them ye have eternal life; and these are *they which bear witness of me.*"

Luke 24:24, 45: "*All things* must needs be fulfilled, *which are written* in the law of Moses, and the prophets, and the psalms, *concerning me.* Then opened he their mind, that they might understand *the Scriptures.*"

6:20: "It is I; be not afraid."

Mark 6:50: "Be of good cheer: it is I; be not afraid."

6:44-46: "No man can come to me except the Father that sent me draw him: and I will raise him up at the last day . . . Not that any man hath seen the Father, save he that is from God, he hath seen the Father."

Matt. 11:27, 28, quoted above.

8:12; 12:36: "I am the light of the world. . . . While ye have the light, believe on the light, that ye may become sons of light."

Matt. 5:14-16: "ye are the light of the world . . . Even so let your light shine before men; that they may see your good works, and glorify your Father who is in heaven."

12:25: "He that loveth his life loseth it; and he that hateth his life in this world shall keep it unto life eternal."

Luke 9:24: "For whosoever would save his life shall lose it; but whosoever shall lose his life for my sake, the same shall save it."

12:27: "Now is my soul troubled; and what shall I say? Father save me from this hour. But for this cause came I unto this hour."

Matt. 26:37, 38: "And he began to be sorrowful and sore troubled. Then saith he unto them, My soul is exceedingly sorrowful, even unto death." Cf. also Luke 12:50.

13:16, 20: "Verily, verily, I say unto you, A servant is not greater than his lord; neither one that is sent greater than he that sent him. . . . Verily, verily I say unto you, He that receiveth whomsoever I send receiveth me; and he that receiveth me receiveth him that sent me." Cf. also 15:20.

Matt. 10:24, 40: "A disciple is not above his teacher, nor a servant above his lord. . . . He that receiveth you receiveth me, and he that receiveth me receiveth him that sent me."

15

13:38: "Verily, verily, I say unto thee, The cock shall not crow till thou hast denied me thrice."	Matt. 26:34: "Verily I say unto thee, that this night, before the cock crow, thou shalt deny me thrice."

It is true that in the Synoptics Jesus often speaks in parables; not so in the Fourth Gospel. But is it really so strange that he who uttered the kingdom-sayings recorded in John 3:3-5 should speak kingdom-parables? And must the figure of the Good Shepherd, John 10, be regarded as impossible in the mouth of him who spoke the parable of the Lost Sheep, Luke 15?

10:27, 28: "My sheep hear my voice, and I know them, and they follow me: and I give unto them eternal life; and they shall never perish, and no one shall snatch them out of my hand."	Luke 15:3-6: "And he spake unto them this parable saying, What man of you, having a hundred sheep, and having lost one of them, doth not leave the ninety and nine in the wilderness, and go after that which is lost, until he find it? And when he hath found it, he layeth it on his shoulders, rejoicing. And when he cometh home, he calleth together his friends and his neighbors, saying unto them, Rejoice with me, for I have found my sheep which was lost."

d. *Even on minor points it has not been established that the Fourth Gospel is in conflict with the Synoptics:*

On the basis of John 13:1, 29 and 18:28 it has been held that the Fourth Gospel is in conflict with the Synoptics, which clearly teach that Jesus ate the Passover at the regular time (Mark 14:12; Luke 22:7). But it would be very strange, indeed, if the Supper described in John 13, which is distinguished in such a remarkable manner and in connection with which so many important events take place, would not be the regular Passover Supper eaten on Thursday-evening, the fourteenth of Nisan. In fact the combination (verse 1): "before the feast of the passover" followed by (verse 2): "and during supper" would seem to indicate that the supper here indicated is the Passover Supper. When it is argued that this Passover *Supper* is, in harmony with Numbers 28:16, 17, followed by seven days of celebration, particularly by a joyful Passover *Feast* (the Chagigah on the fifteenth of Nisan), a solution has been suggested with reference to the last clause of 18:28 which, whatever be its merit, commends itself as being at least more reasonable than the theory that the Fourth Gospel devotes so much space—five chapters!—and attaches such importance to a meal supposedly eaten the night just before the great Passover Supper.

According to John 19:14 *it was about the sixth hour* when Pilate brought Jesus out, and sat down on the judgment-seat at a place called Gabbatha. According to Mark 15:25 *it was about the third hour* when Jesus was crucified. Here again there need not be a conflict. A reasonable solution is this: John figures time the Roman way, and in counting the hours begins at midnight and at noon, just as we do today (D.C.G., art, "Hour"). Hence, when he says "about the sixth hour," this could mean sometime between 6:00 and 6:30 A. M. On the other hand, the evangelist Mark figures time the Jewish way, and therefore tells us that Jesus was crucified about three hours after sunrise. Not only is there no conflict at all but once this solution is adopted, other passages in the Fourth Gospel become clear. See explanation of 1:39; 4:6, 52, 53.

(7) Minor arguments, generally quite subjective in character and therefore not in need of detailed refutation, are the following:

a. *A native Jew could not have written so disparagingly about the Jews, representing them as being the very enemies of God, 5:18; 7:1; 9:22. Moreover, he would not have employed the third person in referring to them.* Answer: When the apostle John wrote this Gospel, the Jews as a nation had rejected the Christ. Moreover, those who were the first to read this book were Christians from the Gentiles (mostly). It is altogether natural that in writing for them the author would be using the third person in referring to the Jews.

b. *A disciple of Jesus would not have ascribed to Jesus the same style of discourse which he himself employs.* Answer: Though it is sometimes difficult to determine just where Jesus stops and John begins (e.g., 3:16-20; 12:44-50), this should not surprise us. We should bear in mind that the author is the disciple whom Jesus loves. He was so very close to Jesus that he began to think his thoughts after him, to speak like his Master, and to write in that same style.

c. *If the apostle John wrote the book of Revelation, he cannot have written the Gospel, for the two differ very much not only in thought-content but also in linguistic characteristics.*

For suggestions in the direction of an attempt to solve this admittedly difficult problem we refer to our *More Than Conquerors*, Grand Rapids, Mich., 1949, pp. 17-19. See also p. 37. All we wish to say about it here is that, while he was living in Ephesus and writing the Gospel, John may have had helpers who, under the guidance of the Holy Spirit and subject to the final approval of the apostle who assumed sole responsibility, influenced style and diction to some extent. Cf. 21:24. The absence of these helpers when he wrote the Apocalypse may account in part for the linguistic differences (cf. A. T. Roberston, *Word Pictures in The New Testament*,

New York and London, 1932, vol. V, p. xix). At any rate, unless all the circumstances under which each book was written are thoroughly known, it would be precarious to say in such a categorical manner that whoever wrote Revelation cannot have written the Fourth Gospel.

Enough has been said to indicate the inadequacy of the arguments of the critics.

On the supposition that the Gospel of St. John was written last of all and that its purpose differs from that of the Synoptics, the main problem has been solved, at least to a very large extent.

According to the information furnished by the Gospel itself the author was:

(1) *A Jew:*

a. This is evident from his style. See p. 63.

b. It also follows from his thorough acquaintance with the Old Testament, which he is able to quote both according to the Hebrew and from the Septuagint. See the following passages: 2:17; 10:34, 35; 12:40; 13:18; 17:12; 19:24, 28, 36, 37.

c. It is corroborated by his references to Jewish (and Samaritan) religious beliefs, particularly regarding the Messiah: 1:41, 46, 49; 4:25; 6:15; 7:27, 42; 12:34.

d. It is supported by evidence which indicates that the author is acquainted with religious and political conditions in Palestine: 4:9; 7:35; 11:49; 18:13, 28, 31, 39; and also with Jewish feasts and purification-rites: the Passover: 2:13, 23; 6:4; 13:1; 18:28; perhaps also 5:1; the Feast of Tabernacles: 7:2, 37, 38; the Feast of Dedication: 10:22, 23. See also 3:25; 11:55; 12:12; 18:28, 39; 19:31.

e. It explains the easy and natural manner in which he introduces Jewish customs with reference to weddings and funerals: 2:1-10; 11:38, 44; 19:40.

(2) *A Palestinian Jew.*

He has a detailed knowledge of Palestinian topography: 1:28 cf. 11:1; 2:1, 12; 3:23; 4:11, 20; 11:54; 12:21; particularly, of Jerusalem and its immediate vicinity: 5:2; 9:7; 11:18; 18:1; 19:17; and of the Temple: 2:14, 20; 8:2, 20; 10:22, 23; 18:1, 20.

(3) *An eye-witness.*

As such he remembers when the events occurred; sometimes the exact hour: 1:29, 35, 39; 2:1; 3:24; 4:6, 40, 52, 53; 6:22; 7:14; 11:6; 12:1; 13:1, 2; 19:14, 31; 20:1, 19, 26.

He knows that Jesus was weary when he sat down by the well (4:6); he remembers the very words spoken by the neighbors of the man born blind (9:8-10); he himself saw the blood and water issuing from the pierced side of Jesus (19:33-35); he knows by name the servant of the high priest whose right ear was cut off by Peter (18:10); and he is acquainted with the high priest (18:15). These and many other details clearly show that the author was an eye-witness of the events which he records.

(4) *One of the Twelve.*

The fact that he partakes of the Supper with his Lord shows that he must be one of the Twelve (13:23). His close association with Peter would also seem to prove this (1:35-42; 13:23, 24; 18:15, 16; 20:2; 21:20-23). That the writer was, indeed, one of the apostles appears also from his intimate knowledge of their actions, words, and feelings: 2:17, 22; 4:27; 6:19; 12:16; 13:22, 28; and 21:21. And if anyone should argue that it is not clear that in all these cases the disciples whose reactions are recorded belong to the inner group and that therefore the inference which we have drawn is not quite convincing, we call attention to such other passages where the reference is distinctly to "the twelve," (6:66-71; 20:24-29). The author knows exactly what was said within that inner group! The conclusion is inescapable that he belongs to it.

Note also that in 1:35-51 the unnamed disciple is mentioned in connection with Andrew, Simon Peter, Philip, and Nathanael, all of whom belong to the Twelve.

(5) *The Apostle John.*

This surely is the most natural inference to be drawn from all the facts presented. It is to be noted that the author, while mentioning other apostles by name, never indicates in that distinct manner either John or his brother James. That very fact is significant and would seem to point in the direction of the writer's identity.

By a process of elimination it is not too difficult to arrive at an answer to the question: who is the author?

There is an old rhyme which makes it easy to remember the names of the Twelve (cf. Matt. 10:2-4; Mark 3:16-19; Luke 6:14-16; Acts 1:13):

> "Peter and Andrew, James and John,
> Philip and Bartholomew,
> Matthew next and Thomas too,
> James the Less and Judas the Greater,
> Simon the Zealot and Judas the Traitor."

As the Fourth Gospel also speaks about "the Twelve" (6:67, 70, 71; 20:24), it may be assumed that the reference is to the same group of men. *Which of these was the author?*

Obviously we immediately eliminate Judas the Traitor. Whenever the author refers to him, he *names* him (6:71; 12:4; 13:2, 26, 29; 18:2, 3, 5).

From 21:24 in comparison with verse 20 we learn that the writer is the disciple who reclined on the bosom of Jesus at the Supper. He is definitely not Peter, from whom he is distinguished. That still leaves ten to choose from.

Matthew's name, however, can be eliminated immediately, for it is associated with another Gospel. Next, the question may be asked: is it at all likely that the writer of the Fourth Gospel who is a most intimate friend of Jesus (13:23) would be a more or less obscure disciple like James the Less (the son of Alphaeus) or Simon the Zealot? Judas (called "The Greater" in the little rhyme, but "Judas of James," "Lebbaeus," "Thaddaeus," and "Judas not Iscariot" in the scriptural references to him) and also Thomas (called Didymus) are mentioned by name in the Fourth Gospel (14:5, 22). This distinguishes them clearly from the author who is not named.

There remain the names of James, John, Andrew, Philip, and Bartholomew. John relates how Philip brought Nathanael to Jesus, and in the lists of the Twelve in the other three Gospels Philip and Bartholomew are always mentioned together. John never mentions Bartholomew; the Synoptics never mention Nathanael. It is thus altogether probable that the Nathanael of John is the Bartholomew of Matthew, Mark, and Luke—Nathanael being his chief name and Bartholomew indicating his filial relationship, meaning son of Tolmai. (Cf. C. E. Macartney, *Of Them He Chose Twelve*, Philadelphia, 1927, pp. 63, 64.) Now if the unnamed disciple is the same person throughout the Gospel, we meet him also in 1:35-51. Here he is clearly distinguished from Andrew (verse 40), from Simon Peter (verses 41 and 42), whose name we have already eliminated on the basis of information furnished by the twenty-first chapter, from Philip (verses 43 and 44), and from Nathanael (Bartholomew, verses 45-51).

Subtracting also the names of Andrew, Philip, and Nathanael, there remain only James and John. However, it is clearly evident from 21:19-24 that the author of the Fourth Gospel was still alive and bearing witness when it was first published (note present tense in verse 24) though Peter had already gained the martyr's crown (verse 19). And whereas we know that Peter survived James (Acts 12), it is clear that the latter cannot have written the Fourth Gospel. *The apostle John remains.*

It is to be noted that in the argumentation which we have followed we have based our conclusions entirely upon data furnished by the Fourth Gospel itself. A comparison with the Synoptics confirms our conclusion. We learn from John 1:35-40 that the author of the Fourth Gospel was one of Christ's earliest disciples, the other two being Andrew and Simon Peter. The Gospel according to Mark also has a list of earliest disciples (1:16-20, 29). In that list occur four names: Simon and Andrew, James and John. By comparing the two lists it is again apparent that the unnamed disciple of the Fourth Gospel is one of the sons of Zebedee.

Attempts to evade the force of these arguments must be considered a failure. They often center about the fact that in 21:2 there is mention of "two other disciples" (besides Simon Peter, Thomas, Nathanael, and the sons of Zebedee). It is argued that these "two" may not have belonged to the Twelve, and that one of them—perhaps the Elder John?—may have been the author. But all this misses the point completely. It does not take into account *all* the evidence which we have presented in the preceding.

Besides, such argumentations do not help any. For, even if the author were not the apostle John but some obscure disciple referred to in 21:2, the fact remains that he was an eye-witness who, according to the story recorded in John 21, had seen the risen Lord and who proclaims to the Church of all the ages that Jesus is what he claimed to be: God in the highest sense of the term (1:1-18) and that by the very first followers Jesus was immediately recognized as the Messiah, the Son of God. How is this possible? How can it be explained psychologically? There is, in the final analysis, only one fully satisfactory solution of this problem, and it is that Jesus is in reality what he himself claimed and what these men proclaimed him to be: the Messiah, the Son of God, the object of worship. Accept his and their testimony as *the truth,* and the problems begin to disappear!

The testimony of the early church is in harmony with the conclusion which has been derived from the Fourth Gospel itself. Thus Eusebius, having made a thorough investigation in the literature at his command, states:

"But come, let us indicate the undoubted writings of *this apostle.* Let the Gospel according to him be first recognized, for it is read in all the churches under heaven. . . . Thus *John* in the course of his gospel relates what Christ did before the Baptist had been thrown into prison, but the other three evangelists narrate the events after the imprisonment of the Baptist" (*Ecclesiastical History* III, xxiv, 1-13). The famous historian wrote these words at the beginning of the fourth century.

Before him Origen (fl. 210-250) stated that John, the beloved disciple, wrote both the Fourth Gospel and the Apocalypse. Origen wrote a Commentary on the former, in which he states:

"The Gospels then being four, I deem the firstfruits of the Gospels to be that which you (Ambrosius) have commanded me to search into, according to my powers, the Gospel of John. . . ." (*Commentary on John* I, vi). In the same paragraph he indicates that the author of the Fourth Gospel is that John "who lay on Jesus' breast."

From Origen we can go back still farther, to his teacher, Clement of Alexandria (fl. 190-200). He knows only one John; namely, the apostle. He definitely ascribes the Fourth Gospel to him, stating:

"Last of all, John, perceiving that the external facts had been made plain in the Gospels, being urged by his friends and inspired by the Spirit, composed a spiritual gospel" (Eusebius, *Ecclesiastical History* VI, xiv, 7). Clement has preserved a beautiful story about the aged apostle John; for reference see p. 31. Born in the middle of the second century, Clement stood close to the successors of the apostles. He was a person of considerable learning and had traveled widely.

About this same time Tertullian ascribes the Fourth Gospel to the apostle John (*Against Marcion* IV, v).

Clement's contemporary was Ireneus. He was a pupil of Polycarp, who had known the apostle John. In a letter to Florinus, who had also received instruction from Polycarp but had erred from the truth, Ireneus states:

"These opinions, O Florinus, that I may speak with caution, do not pertain to sound doctrine. These opinions are inconsistent with the church, and bring those who believe in them into the greatest wickedness. These opinions even the heretics outside of the church never dared to proclaim. These opinions those who were presbyters before us, they who accompanied the apostles, did not transmit to you. For while I was still a boy I knew you in lower Asia in Polycarp's house when you were a man of rank in the royal hall and were endeavoring to stand well with him. I remember the events of those days more clearly than those which happened recently, for what we learn as children grows up with the soul and is united with it, so that I can speak even of the place in which the blessed Polycarp sat and disputed, how he came in and went out, the character of his life, the appearance of his body, the addresses which he delivered to the people, how he reported his intercourse with John and with the others who had seen the Lord, how he remembered their words and what were the things concerning the Lord which he had heard from them, and about their miracles, and about their teaching, and how Polycarp had received them from the eye-witnesses of the word of life, and reported all things in agreement with the Scriptures" (Eusebius, *Ecclesiastical History* V, xx, 4-7).

Now, Ireneus, who had traveled from Asia Minor to Gaul and had frequent contacts with the church in Rome, not only was acquainted with the Fourth Gospel but definitely ascribed it to the apostle John. This testimony, coming from one who had been a pupil of a pupil of the apostle John cannot be robbed of its force. Moreover, because of his many travels and intimate acquaintance with almost the entire church of his day, what Ireneus says about the authorship of the Fourth Gospel must be considered of great significance. His voice in a matter as important as this may be considered the voice of the church. His words, as reported by Eusebius, are:

"Then John, the disciple of the Lord, who had even rested on his breast, himself also gave forth the gospel, while he was living at Ephesus in Asia" (*Ecclesiastical History* V, viii, 4).

Ireneus even argues that there can be neither more nor fewer than four Gospels (*Against Heresies* III, xi, 8).

INTRODUCTION

The Muratorian Fragment, an incomplete list of New Testament books, written in poor Latin and deriving its name from cardinal L. A. Muratori (1672-1750) who discovered it in the Ambrosian Library at Milan, may be assigned to the period 180-200. It contains the following:

"The fourth book of the Gospel is that of John, one of the disciples. In response to the exhortation of his fellow disciples and bishops he said: 'Fast ye with me for three days, and then let us tell each other whatever shall be revealed to each one.' The same night it was revealed to Andrew, who was one of the apostles that it was John who should relate in his own name what they collectively remembered. And so to the faith of believers there is no discord, even though different selections are given from the facts in the individual books of the Gospels, because in all of them, under the one guiding Spirit, all the things relative to his nativity, passion, resurrection, conversation with his disciples, and his twofold advent, the first in his humiliation rising from contempt, which took place, and the second in the glory of royal power, which is yet to come, have been declared. What marvel is it then if John adduces so consistently in his epistles these several things, saying in person: 'what we have seen with our eyes, and heard with our ears, and our hands have handled, those things we have written.' For thus he professes to be not only an eye-witness but also a hearer and narrator of all the wonderful things of the Lord, in their order."

It is thought that the fragment is a translation from the Greek and that it originated in Rome or at least in the region of Roman influence. For our purpose it is important to notice that the disciple John, who like Andrew is one of the apostles, is here described as the writer of the Fourth Gospel. The interesting story with reference to the exact manner in which that Gospel originated must be considered legendary, as it is certainly improbable and contrary to all tradition that the other disciples lived up to the time when this Gospel was produced. For that very reason it is highly precarious to draw any inferences from that circumstantial tale. This is done at times. First the opening words of the clause *"ut recognoscentibus cunctis Johannes suo nomine cuncta describeret"* ("that it was John who should relate in his own name *what they collectively remembered"*) are rendered: *". . . they all acting as correctors."* Next the conclusion is drawn that, because of all these correctors, the apostle John himself may have played a very minor role in the actual writing of the book. Finally, the wholly fictitious "elder" John crops up once more as the actual author! But this is basing too much upon too little! The only legitimate conclusion which one can draw from the *Muratorian Fragment* is that about the year 180-200 the church at Rome (at least, some person of importance in the region of Roman influence) ascribed the Fourth Gospel to the apostle John.

Polycrates, writing about this same time, was a bishop of the church at Ephesus. The place is significant and so is the date. At Ephesus at this early date (approximately 196) the traditions with respect to the apostle John who had lived here were still fresh. Polycrates remarks: "Seven of my relatives were bishops and I am the eighth." He gives advice anent the Paschal controversy (whether Easter should be celebrated on the fourteenth day of the moon, no matter what the day, or always on a Sunday). In his letter he not only refers to John 13:25 (at least, to the fact affirmed in that passage) but also to the residence and the death of John at Ephesus. He writes:

"John, moreover, who reclined in the Lord's bosom, and who became a priest wearing the mitre, and a witness and a teacher—he rests at Ephesus" (*Letter to Victor and the Roman Church concerning the Day of Keeping the Passover*, preserved by Eusebius, *Ecclesiastical History* V, xxiv).

Writing probably a few years earlier, Theophilus, who according to Eusebius was the sixth bishop of Antioch in Syria from the apostles, names John expressly as the inspired writer of the Fourth Gospel. His statement is:

"And hence the holy writings teach us, and all the inspired men, one of whom, John, says: 'In the beginning was the Word and the Word was with God,' showing that at first God was alone, and the Word in him" (*To Autolycus* II, xxii).

From the preceding a few facts become clear:

(1) Within the orthodox church there is a uniform tradition regarding the authorship of the Fourth Gospel. This tradition can be traced back from Eusebius at the beginning of the fourth century to Theophilus who flourished about 170-180.

(2) According to this uniform tradition the Fourth Gospel was written by John. Generally it is even made clear that this John was the apostle, the beloved disciple who reclined on Christ's bosom. The major witnesses are Eusebius, Origen, Clement of Alexandria, Tertullian, Ireneus, the writer of the Muratorian Canon, and Theophilus.

(3) Ireneus, one of the earliest of these witnesses, was a disciple of Polycarp, who, in turn, had been a disciple of the apostle John. The inference would seem to be legitimate that the tradition of apostolic authorship can thus be traced back to the disciple whom Jesus loved.

(4) Because of his wide travels and intimate acquaintance with the convictions of the entire Church Ireneus may be called a representative witness. He represents the faith of the whole Christian community. Tertullian, Clement of Alexandria, Ireneus, and Theophilus show us that in the last quarter of the second century the Fourth Gospel was known and read throughout Christendom: in Africa, Asia Minor, Italy, Gaul, and Syria, and that it was ascribed to the well-known John.

(5) The external evidence derived from this uniform and very early tra-

dition is in harmony with the internal evidence derived from the Fourth Gospel itself.

(6) The evidence which we have examined proves three important things:

a. *That the Fourth Gospel must have been in existence at a very early time.* Surely when about the year 170 this book is called a *holy writing* composed by one who was *inspired* by the Holy Spirit, and when this sacred Gospel is used to prove certain doctrinal positions that are considered so precious that men are willing to die in their defence, it can be safely inferred that its origin goes back to a date that is even earlier.

b. *That it was regarded as being (at least) equal in value and authority to the other Gospels.*

c. *That it was considered to have been written by the apostle John.*

Among the men who can be classified as heretics we find that Tatian (about the year 170), who became a heretic after the death of his teacher, Justin Martyr, accepts the Fourth Gospel and used it in composing his *Harmony (Diatessaron).* In fact, Tatian's book opens with the first five verses of the Fourth Gospel.

Heracleon, of the school of Valentinus, which existed between 140 and 180, even wrote a commentary on the Fourth Gospel. Ptolemy, also of this school, ascribed it to "the apostle." Marcion, indeed, about the middle of the second century, rejected all the Gospels, and prepared one of his own, using as his source a mutilated version of Luke. But it has not been established that he denied that the apostle John was the author of the Fourth Gospel. His rejection of this Gospel seems rather to have been due to the fact that he regarded its author as a Judaizer. He based this conclusion on Paul's words recorded in Gal. 2:9, 11-13, which he grossly misinterpreted (cf. Tertullian, *Against Marcion*, IV, iii).

Now, the fact to be emphasized is this, that if these heretics, who knew very well that their own teaching was not in harmony with that of the Fourth Gospel, could have ascribed this Gospel to a non-apostolic writer, they would have done so.

Among the orthodox writers who flourished at one time or another during the period 100-170 we find that Justin Martyr (Apology I, 61) quotes from John 3:3-5. He uses a number of expressions from this Gospel. (See also his *Dialogue with Trypho*, ch. 105.) Moreover, his doctrine of the Logos is almost surely derived from the Fourth Gospel. Besides, it must not be forgotten that Justin's pupil, Tatian, included it in his *Harmony*.

With reference to Papias and to Polycarp we refer to what has already been said. Eusebius states that Papias "used quotations from the First Epistle of John" (*Ecclesiastical History* III, xxxix, 17). Whether any argument can be based upon this with reference to his acquaintance with the Fourth Gospel, which is very similar in style, is a matter on which there can be a difference of opinion.

The spirit of the Fourth Gospel is evident everywhere in the *Epistles of Ignatius* (short recension). Though it cannot be proved with absolute certainty that he, when sent to his martyrdom (about 110), actually had seen this Gospel and alluded to it, nevertheless, this would seem to be by far the most natural conclusion. The resemblances have impressed many as being too many and too striking to warrant any conflicting inference. It is true, of course, that these *allusions* are not *exact quotations*, but who expects anything else from a prisoner who is on his way to martyrdom in Rome? The parallel columns furnish the evidence:

IGNATIUS	THE FOURTH GOSPEL A.R.V.
"For if I in a short time gained such fellowship with your bishop as was not human but spiritual, how much more do I count you blessed who are so united with him as the Church is with Jesus Christ, and as Jesus Christ is with the Father, that all things may symphonize in unity" (*To the Ephesians* V, i).	"I in them, and thou in me, that they may be perfected into one" (17:23).
"As then the Lord was united to the Father and did nothing without him, neither by himself nor through the apostles, so you should do nothing without the bishop and the presbyters" (*To the Magnesions* VII, i).	"The Son can do nothing of himself, but what he seeth the Father doing" (5:19).
"I desire the bread of God which is the flesh of Jesus Christ . . . and for drink I desire his blood, which is love incorruptible" (*To the Romans* VII, iii).	"He that eateth my flesh and drinketh my blood hath eternal life; and I will raise him up at the last day. For my flesh is meat indeed, and my blood is drink indeed" (6:54, 55).
"For it (the Spirit) knoweth whence it comes and whither it goes" (*To the Philadelphians* VII, i).	"The wind bloweth where it will, and thou hearest the voice thereof, but knowest not whence it cometh, and whither it goeth; so is everyone that is born of the Spirit" (3:8).

If these and several other expressions which remind one of John indicate that Ignatius knew the Fourth Gospel, its date of origin would be pushed back to *sometime before 110.* This would approach a vindication of the traditional belief that it was written not later than the year 98 and not earlier than the year 80.

However, the traditional belief regarding the date of the Fourth Gospel has received strong confirmation in the actual discovery of a very early Gospel of John fragment of a papyrus codex. This together with other Greek papyri, was found in Egypt and acquired for the John Rylands Library. It is the earliest known fragment of any portion of the New Testament. It may have originated from the Christian community in Middle Egypt. On the basis of paleographical evidence it has been established that this papyrus-scrap belonged to a codex which circulated in that general region *in the first half of the second century.* The fragment contains words from the Gospel of John, chapter 18. On the recto it has part of verses 31-33, on the verso part of verses 37-38.

Now if this Gospel was already circulating in Middle Egypt in the early part of the second century, it must have been composed even earlier. From Ephesus, where according to tradition this Gospel was written, to Middle Egypt, where this codex circulated, is a long distance. Some authorities, accordingly, allow for a time-lag of thirty years between the date of composition and that of circulation in Egypt. The statement of W. F. Albright is significant:

"Meanwhile the sensational publication of a fragment of the Gospel from the early second century and of a roughly contemporary fragment of an apocryphal gospel dependent on John has dealt the *coup de grâce* to all radically late dating of John and has proved that the Gospel cannot be later than the first century A. D." *(From Stone Age to Christianity,* p. 299; see also C. H. Roberts, *An Unpublished Fragment of the Fourth Gospel,* Manchester, 1935).

This means, therefore, that the traditional view with respect to the date of the composition of the Fourth Gospel has at length been confirmed by irrefutable evidence. It means that those negative critics who have long maintained that the conservative position was all wrong have suffered a major defeat! Today more than ever we can endorse the exclamation of Volkmar: "It is very certain that it is all over with the critical thesis of the composition of the Fourth Gospel in the middle of the second century!" [5]

---

[5] Dates assigned to the Fourth Gospel by various critics: F. C. Baur: 160-170: Volkmar: 155; Zeller and Scholten: 150; Hilgenfeld: 130-140; Keim: 130; Schenkel: 115-120; Reuss, Nicolas, Renan, Sabatier, Hase: 110-125; Scott (E. F.): 95-115.

P. H. Menoud, *L'Évangile de Jean d'après les recherches recentés,* Neuchâtel and Paris, 1943, concludes with these remarkable words:

"On peut dire, sans trop s'avancer, que les défenseurs de l'autenticité johannique occupent aujourd'hui des positions plus favorables qu'au début du siècle, par

Moreover, now that we have this external evidence, so that we know that the Fourth Gospel existed in Asia Minor very early in the second (and probably already in the first) century, it begins to look very credible that Ignatius, who wrote his Epistles from Asia Minor, had read it!

It is true that neither Justin Martyr nor Ignatius nor anyone else before the middle of the second century mentions the apostle John by name as the author of this Gospel. This, however, is not at all surprising. These men were living so close to the time of the beloved disciple that it was entirely unnecessary for them, in quoting from his Gospel or in alluding to it, to mention his name. Besides, by Ignatius *the apostles* were held in high honor. He writes:

"I do not order you as did Peter and Paul; they were apostles, I am a convict" (*To the Romans* IV, iii).

It is, therefore, safe to assume that in using expressions which remind one of the Fourth Gospel he is conscious of the fact that no one less than a genuine apostle was responsible for the truths which had endeared themselves to him to such an extent that he wishes to impress them upon the hearts of others.

Another fact which favors an early date for the Fourth Gospel is its strongly Semitic tone. (See pp. 63, 64.)

The earliest attestation of apostolic authorship is found in the Gospel itself. After the divinely guided John had written the first twenty chapters, ending with the beautiful conclusion found in 20:30, 31, and another leader at Ephesus, under the guidance of the Holy Spirit, and with the full approval of John, had added a beautiful story which he had heard so often from the lips of his dear friend and which closed with a distinct reference to *the disciple whom Jesus loved* (21:20-23), the presbyters at Ephesus appended these significant words:

"This is the disciple who is bearing witness to these things and who wrote them down, and we know that his testimony is true" (21:24).

We have seen that both internal and external testimony support this attestation.

As pictured in the Gospels, John was the son of Zebedee and Salome (Mark 1:19; 16:1, 2 cf. Matt. 27:56). Zebedee seems to have been a prosperous fisherman. He employed hired servants (Mark 1:20). It is supposed that Salome was a sister of the virgin Mary (Matt. 27:56, cf. John 19:25). If

---

exemple. Car les recherches recentes tendent à écarter les obstacles que la critique a dressés sur la voie de l' identification du 'Bien-Aimé' avec le fils de Zébédée." By the same author also: "Le problème johannique," *RThPh,* 29(1941), 236-256; 30(1942), 155 ff; 31(1943), 80-101.

And yet in 1927 Vincent Taylor spoke about "the collapse of the traditional position," (!) in "The Fourth Gospel and Some Recent Criticism," *HJ* 25(1927) 725-743.

this be correct, Jesus and John were cousins. John's brother James is usually mentioned first, and was probably the elder of the two.

Before he became a follower of Jesus, the apostle John was a disciple of John the Baptist. In his later years the apostle vividly recalled the moment when he first met Jesus and decided to become his follower. He states: "It was about the tenth hour" (1:39). That first meeting of which we have any record was followed after an interval by the decision to become a regular disciple (Mark 1:16 ff; Luke 5:10); and then, an apostle (Matt. 10:2), sent forth and charged by Jesus.

John and James appear to have been men with pent-up emotions, flashing forth on occasion. Jesus called them "sons of thunder" (Mark 3:17). When Jesus is on his way to Jerusalem, and the inhabitants of a Samaritan village refuse to lodge him, the fiery anger of the sons of Zebedee flashes forth in the words: "Lord, wilt thou that we bid fire to come down from heaven and consume them?" (Luke 9:54). Surely, John was "the disciple of love." Love and flashing anger are not mutually exclusive. It was genuine love for Jesus which manifested itself in this ill-conceived utterance. It was love also which caused John to interfere with the man who, though casting out demons in the name of Jesus, was not a regular disciple (Luke 9:49, 50).

It is a mark of John's genuine humility that he never mentions by name those who belong to the inner circle of his relatives. Although he loved the Master intensely, it is not his love for Christ but the latter's love for the apostle that is emphasized in the Fourth Gospel. John styles himself "the disciple whom Jesus loved" (12:23).

Not only in the Gospels, as already indicated, but also in Acts we often find John in the company of Peter (Acts 3:1; 4:19; 8:14). After the resurrection he is one of the pillars of the church at Jerusalem (Gal. 2:9; Acts 15:6). He probably left Jerusalem at the beginning of the Jewish War. T. Zahn states:

"It is safe, then, to say that the apostle John, with other disciples of Christ, came from Palestine to Asia Minor. If Polycarp, on the day of his death (Feb. 23, 155), was looking back on eighty-six years of life as a Christian, not as a man, and was thus baptized in 69, and if his conversion (according to Ireneus, *Against Heresies* III, iii, 4) was the work of an apostle, this migration to Asia Minor must have occurred before that date, possibly as the result of the outbreak of the Jewish War. John, then perhaps not more than sixty or sixty-five, would thus have been able to devote some thirty years to the fostering of Christian life in the province" ("John the Apostle," in *The New Schaff-Herzog Encyclopedia of Religious Knowledge*).

For several years John lived in Ephesus. But sometime during the reign of Domitian, who ruled from 81-96, he was banished to the island of Patmos.

With the accession of Nerva he was allowed to return to Ephesus, where he died at the beginning of Trajan's reign; i.e., about the year 98.

Now tradition is well-nigh unanimous in maintaining that the place where the apostle wrote his Gospel was Ephesus (Eusebius, *Ecclesiastical History* III, xxiii, 1, 6; V, viii, 4; xxiv, 4; Clement of Alexandria, *Who Is the Rich Man That Shall Be Saved?* XLII, ii).[6] Repeated attempts, also in recent literature, to discredit this strong tradition have not been successful.

The question, however, is this: Was the Fourth Gospel written before or after John's banishment to Patmos? Was it composed earlier or later than the book of Revelation?

It would seem that *the earliest date* for its composition would be about the year 80. We base this upon the following considerations: Peter had received his inheritance, as 21:19 seems to imply; Paul, his crown. The latter nowhere mentions the work of the apostle John in Asia Minor. It is considered probable that the Synoptics had been written and that the author of the Fourth Gospel had read them. The Jews had become the confirmed enemies of the Church. The fall of Jerusalem is no longer mentioned, probably because several years had elapsed since it occurred.

On the other hand, *the latest possible date* for the composition of the Gospel is the year 98, if the testimony of Ireneus and Jerome is trustworthy. The former states:

"Then again, the church in Ephesus, founded by Paul, and having John remaining among them permanently until the times of Trajan, is a true witness of the tradition of the apostles" (*Against Heresies* III, iii, 4).

The date, therefore, must lie between 80 and 98. Is it possible to be more definite and to determine the date more precisely? According to Epiphanius (fourth century) John did not write his Gospel until after his return from Patmos when he was more than ninety years of age. However, nothing resembling this has been found in the writings of the early fathers. There are those who prefer a date much closer to the year 80, giving as their reason that the style of the Gospel is that of a matured but not of an aged writer. There may be an element of truth in this view. However, we must exercise caution at this point. If the apostle came to Ephesus in the year 67 (about the time of Paul's death), and if he was then sixty or sixty-five years of age (Zahn), he must have been between seventy-three and seventy-eight in the year 80. He was, therefore, in any case "an aged writer." The problem can also be approached in this way: if John was twenty-five years of age when Jesus died (about the year 30), then in the year 80 he must have been seventy-five.

But he may still have been young and strong in physical and mental

---

[6] See F. Godet, *Commentaire sur l'Évangile de Saint Jean,* Paris, 1881, vol. I, pp. 354-356.

vigor. Clement of Alexandria tells us that *even after his return from Patmos* the apostle carried on a very active ministry as chief administrator of the churches located in the Ephesus district (*Who Is the Rich Man That Shall Be Saved?* XLII). He must have been over ninety then. But who will wish to maintain that he who at this very advanced age was able to convert a robber-chief, according to the interesting story which Clement has transmitted to us in the reference just given, and who went about "appointing bishops and setting in order whole churches," could not have written a Gospel under the guidance of the Spirit, especially if this project had long occupied his mind? Church History furnishes several examples of men who continued in active ministry, charged with very responsible tasks, until they were well over ninety!

Nevertheless, the opposite view—namely, that John wrote the Gospel first of all; i.e., before his banishment to Patmos; that the composition of this book was followed by the Epistles; and that the Apocalypse came last—continues to have its appeal (cf. Lenski, *Interpretation of St. John's Gospel*, p. 20), perhaps because it would seem to be the natural and logical order. The question cannot be definitely answered either way.

II. Readers and Purpose

What is the purpose which the author had in mind when he composed this Gospel? Some say: *to correct the other three.*[7] Upon the basis of what has already been said this cannot be granted. *Real* conflicts between the Synoptics and the Fourth Gospel do not exist.

Was his purpose to *supplement* the Synoptics? This would seem to be implied in the statement of Clement of Alexandria, quoted earlier: the Gospels dealing with external matters had been written; now the deeper, spiritual background must be shown. Eusebius also defends this view, though in a somewhat different sense: John furnishes the record of the Early Judean Ministry, which the others do not give.

This theory presupposes that the apostle had read the Synoptics; at least, that he was acquainted with their contents, which is probably correct. Thus one can explain why so much of the material that is found in the other three Gospels is omitted here. There is here no story of the childhood of Jesus, no genealogy, no lengthy account of the preaching of John the Baptist, no record of Christ's temptations in the desert, no Sermon on the Mount, no story of John's doubt, no parables, no discourse commissioning the twelve or the seventy, no narrative with respect to the casting out of demons or the healing of lepers, no Retirement Ministry[8] (April-October

---

[7] Thus, for example, F. Torm, *ZNTW* 30(1931) 130.
[8] Exception: *one* verse (7:1).

of the year 29 A. D.), which according to the Synoptics included such events as the healing of the daughter of the Syro-phoenician woman, the healing of the deaf stammerer and of the blind man who saw men as trees walking, the feeding of the four thousand, Peter's confession, the transfiguration, and the healing of the epileptic boy; further, there is here no eschatological address, no discourse of woes addressed to the religious leaders, and no account of the institution of the Lord's Supper.

There are also certain definite passages in the Fourth Gospel which, according to many interpreters, seem to indicate that John presupposed that the readers had read the Synoptics. Worthy of mention in this connection are especially the following:

3:24: "For John was not yet cast into prison." The author does not tell the story of the imprisonment of the Baptist, but one can find it in Mark 6.

11:2: "And it was that Mary who anointed the Lord with ointment, and wiped his feet with her hair, whose brother Lazarus was sick." In the Fourth Gospel this anointing-story is found in the next (twelfth) chapter. Is the evangelist proceeding upon the assumption (here in 11:2) that the readers have already read the account in Mark 14:3-9?

18:13: "And they led him to Annas first." This sounds as if John meant to say: "Of course, you know that Jesus was tried before Caiaphas, for you have read this in Matthew or Mark, but they led him to Annas first, a fact which the others have not recorded."

We realize that such facts do not constitute definite proof for the theory that John had read the Synoptics and that he presupposes that his readers had also read them, but, all things considered, this would seem to be probable.[9]

Nevertheless, in view of John's own statement regarding the purpose of his Gospel (20:30, 31), *supplementing the Synoptics* must be considered merely subsidiary to the realization of the main objective.

Was it the evangelist's purpose to combat erroneous views regarding *John the Baptist?*

It is interesting to observe that it was exactly at Ephesus, the very place where John was living and where he composed this book, that certain men were found who had been baptized *into the* baptism of John Baptist (Acts 19:3). In all likelihood they had actually been baptized into the name of

---

[9] The opposite conclusion is reached by P. Gardner-Smith, *St. John and the Synoptic Gospels*, Cambridge, 1938; see also W. F. Howard, *Christianity According to St. John*, Philadelphia, 1946, p. 17. Dr. Howard was "almost persuaded" by the weight of Dr. Gardner-Smith's arguments. However, he accepts some connection between John and the Synoptics. "Some verbal assimilation to the Marcan and Lucan narratives." Cf. E. R. Goodenough, "John A Primitive Gospel," *JBL*, 64(1945), 145-182. Conclusions of this character are generally based on placing all the emphasis on "contrasts" between John and the Synoptics. But we have already shown that the basic pattern is, after all, the same.

INTRODUCTION

John. Hence, they were rebaptized, this time "into the name of the Lord Jesus" (Acts 19:5). Now in his Gospel the apostle John repeatedly indicates that the Baptist pointed away from himself to his Lord (1:19-23, 25-27, 29, 36; 3:27-36), and that he wanted to bear witness of the Light, that men might repose their trust and confidence in the latter (1:7-9).

Accordingly, even the combating of erroneous views regarding the Baptist may be considered as contributing to the main purpose of the Fourth Gospel. It fixed the attention of the readers upon the transcendent greatness of Christ (20:30, 31).

Is it true that John wrote this Gospel in order *to refute the errors of Cerinthus?* [10]

This heretic taught that Jesus was merely human, the son of Joseph and Mary by natural generation; that he was, however, more just and wise than anyone else; that at baptism the Christ in the form of a dove had descended upon him, but had left him again on the eve of his suffering so that it was not Christ who suffered, died, and rose again but Jesus (Ireneus, *Against Heresies* I, xxvi, 1; Hippolytus, *The Refutation of All Heresies* VII, xxi).

Now Cerinthus lived in the days of the apostle. Ireneus relates that there were those who had heard from Polycarp that John, the beloved disciple, going to bathe at Ephesus, and perceiving Cerinthus within, rushed out of the bath-house without bathing, exclaiming: "Let us flee, lest even the bath-house fall down because Cerinthus, the enemy of the truth, is within" (*Against Heresies* III, iii, 4).

Ireneus also definitely states that John seeks by the proclamation of the Gospel to remove the error which by Cerinthus had been disseminated among men (*Against Heresies* III, xi, 1).

It is entirely probable that the apostle in writing the Gospel had the error of Cerinthus in mind. Thus we can explain why he places such emphasis on the fact that Jesus is the Christ, the Son of God, and that this Christ did not merely hover above Jesus without having ever entered into actual and abiding union with him, but actually assumed the human nature and never laid it aside again. Granted, however, that what Ireneus states as the aim of the Fourth Gospel is true, the fact must still be stressed that also this aim was subsidiary in character: the *negative* purpose (to combat the error of Cerinthus) was subordinate to the *positive,* stated so beautifully in 20:30, 31, to which we shall now turn.

"Many other signs therefore did Jesus in the presence of the disciples, which are not written in this book: but these are written, that y o u may

---

[10] See especially F. Godet, *op. cit.,* pp. 356-368.

continue to believe that Jesus is the Christ, the Son of God; and that believing y o u may have life in his name."

Note in this connection that the best attested reading has "that y o u may continue to believe" (πιστεύητε). The faith of believers was being undermined by the errors of men like Cerinthus, who taught that Jesus was not really God and that Christ had not actually come into the flesh (had not adopted the human nature). The apostle, seeing this danger and being guided by the Holy Spirit, writes his Gospel in order that the church may abide in the faith with respect to Christ.[11]

Accordingly, it is not at all the purpose of John to write a complete biography of Jesus. That would not have been possible: the whole world could not have contained the books if everything had been recorded (21:25). He writes in order to confirm believers in the doctrine which they had received.

Once this purpose is clearly understood, it will not be at all difficult to see why John, from among all the events that had occurred and all the words that had been spoken, selects exactly that *additional* material—i.e., material not found in the other Gospels—which was best suited to bring into clear daylight the glory of the Lord; i.e., his Messianic office and his deity in the most exalted sense of the term. With this in mind, note the following distinctly Johannine accounts:

(a) The wedding at Cana. "This Jesus did as a beginning of his signs in Cana in Galilee, and manifested his glory; and his disciples believed in him" (2:11).

(b) The conversation with Nicodemus. "For God so loved the world, that he gave his Son, the only-begotten, in order that whosoever believes in him should not perish but have everlasting life" (3:16).

(c) The conversation with the Samaritan woman. The woman said to him, "I know that Messiah is coming (he that is called Christ); when he arrives, he will declare everything to us." Jesus said to her, "I, the One who is talking to you, am he" (4:25, 26; cf. also 4:29, 42).

(d) The healing of the man at Bethzatha, and the discourse which follows. "My Father is working until now, and I too am working" (5:17; cf. 5:18: "he also called God his own Father, making himself equal with God").

(e) The feeding of the five thousand and the discourse which follows. "For this is the will of my Father, that everyone who beholds the Son and believes in him should have everlasting life; and I will raise him up at the last day" (6:40).

(f) The discourse about the living water, delivered at the feast of Taber-

---

[11] That this Gospel was written to re-establish the faith of believers is also the position of E. N. Harris, "Why John Wrote His Gospel," *WE* 32(1944) 250, 251.

nacles. "If any one thirsts, let him come to me and drink. He who believes in me, as the scripture says, from within him shall flow rivers of living water" (7:37, 38).

(g) The discourse regarding Abraham's seed, "If therefore the Son shall make y o u free, y o u shall be free indeed. Who of y o u convicts me of sin? . . . I most solemnly say to y o u, if a man keep my word, he shall never see death" (8:36, 46, 51).

(h) The cure of the man born blind. "And he worshiped him" (9:38).

(i) The discourse about the Good Shepherd. "I and the Father are one" (10:30).

(j) The raising of Lazarus. "Jesus said to her, Did I not promise you that if you would believe me, you should see the glory of God?" (11:40).

(k) The washing of the disciples' feet. "Jesus, knowing that the Father had given all things into his hands, and that he had come from God and was going back to God. . . ." (13:3).

(l) Upper Room Discourses and Highpriestly Prayer (chapters 14-17). "I am the way and the truth and the life. No can come to the Father except through me. . . . This is everlasting life, that they should know thee, the only true God, and him whom thou didst send, even Jesus Christ. . . . And now Father, glorify thou me, in thine own presence, with the glory which I had with thee before the world existed (14:6; 17:3, 5).

(m) Certain sections in the story of the Passion and Resurrection. "Thomas answered and said to him, My Lord and my God" (20:28).

Note that all this material which is found only in the Fourth Gospel centers in Jesus as the Christ, the Son of God, and has as its purpose that the church may continue to believe in him unto everlasting life.

The miracles that are recorded in this Gospel also fix the attention upon Christ's divine power. The nobleman's son is healed *from a distance* (4:46 ff); the man at Bethzatha had been infirm *thirty-eight years* (5:5); the blind man at Jerusalem had been *born blind* (9:1); and Lazarus had already lain in the grave *four days* (11:17). (Cf. L. Berkhof, *New Testament Introduction,* Grand Rapids, Michigan, p. 104).

The readers for whom this Gospel was primarily intended (though in the final analysis it was, of course, composed for the Church of all the ages, cf. 17:20, 21) were living in Ephesus and surroundings. They were Christians from the Gentiles mostly. This explains why the evangelist adds explanatory notes to his references to Jewish customs and conditions: 2:6; 4:9; 7:2; 10:22; 18:28; 19:31, 41, 42. It also explains the circumstantial manner in which he locates places that were situated in Palestine: 4:5; 5:2; 6:1; 11:1, 18; 12:1, 21.

III. Characteristics

(1) John's Gospel describes, with few exceptions, Christ's work in Judea. The following may be regarded as a brief Chronological Chart of our Lord's Earthly Sojourn, extending from the Manger to the Mount (Olivet):

a. December of the year 5 B. C.—December of the year 26 A. D.: Preparation. Not in the Fourth Gospel; but cf. the Prologue 1:1-18.

b. December of the year 26—April of 27: Inauguration. John 1:19-2:12.

c. April of 27—December of 27: Early Judean Ministry. John 2:13-4:42.

d. December of 27—April of 29: Great Galilean Ministry. John 4:43-6:71.

e. April of 29—December of 29: Retirement Ministry (April—October) and later Judean Ministry (October—December). John has nothing (except 7:1) on the former. For the latter see John 7:2-10:39.

f. December of 29—April of 30: Perean Ministry. John 10:40-12:11.

g. April-May of 30: Passion, Resurrection, and Ascension. John 12:12-21:25.

In the Gospel according to John little is said with reference to the Galilean Ministry; almost nothing in regard to the Retirement Ministry. On the other hand certain events and discourses in the Early and the Later Judean Ministry receive a great deal of attention. In reality, John devotes more space to Christ's work in Judea than might appear from the Chart; for, the scene of the miracle related in ch. 5 is Judea. Similarly, while the raising of Lazarus occurred during the Perean Ministry it actually took place in Judea, on which John loves to dwell. So also the anointing by Mary occurred when Jesus returned to Judea (Bethany) from his Perean Ministry and was about to enter the agonies of the Passion Week. And, of course, the Ministry described as Passion, Resurrection, and Ascension took place in Judea, all except that which is recorded in chapter 21.

We see, therefore, that with the exception of what is recorded in chapter 1 (see 1:28), in 2:1-11, in 4:43-54, in chapter 6, in 10:40-42, and in chapter 21, everything transpires in Judea (and Samaria, 4:1-42). That this difference of scene does not constitute a conflict between the Synoptics and the Fourth Gospel has already been shown.

(2) The Fourth Gospel is far more definite than the Synoptics in indicating the exact time and place of the events that are related. On the basis of the great feasts that are mentioned in this Gospel the length of Christ's ministry can be determined.

(3) A great deal of material that is found in the Synoptics is here omitted, as has been shown. The general framework of the story as found in the Synoptics is, nevertheless, retained. Much new material has been added. All this is completely in harmony with the specific purpose of the evangelist. It does not imply any conflict between John and the Synoptics.

(4) Christ's teaching predominates in this Gospel, but here this teaching is not in the form of parables, as often in the Synoptics, but in that of elaborate discourses. This simply means that while he was in Judea and addressing the religious leaders of the Jews and also when he spoke to the disciples in the Upper Room, Christ considered the non-parabolic form to be the more appropriate. It certainly does not in any way show that he could not have used the parabolic form in Galilee.

(5) The main topic in John is not the kingdom, as in the Synoptics, but the King himself, the Person of the Christ, his deity. Nevertheless, this difference is by no means absolute. Also in the Gospel of John, Jesus is introduced as speaking about entrance into the kingdom (3:3-5); and also in the Synoptics he reveals the glory of his own divine Person. Hence, also with respect to this there is no real conflict.

(6) In harmony with (5), this is the Gospel of the seven "I Am's." They are found in the following passages: 6:35; 8:12; 10:9, 11; 11:25; 14:6; and 15:5.

(7) This Gospel dwells at great length on the events and discourses which belong to a period of less than twenty-four hours (chapters 13-19).

(8) In connection with many other great truths revealed to the disciples in the Upper Room (chapters 14-17) the promise of the coming and work of the Holy Spirit is here recorded (14:16, 17, 26; 15: 26; 16:13, 14).

(9) The style of the Fourth Gospel differs from that of the Apocalypse, but this does not prove that the same author could not have written both books. Besides, the differences should not be exaggerated. The statement of A. T. Robertson is true: "The Apocalypse has much in common with the Gospel" (*A Grammar of the Greek New Testament in the Light of Historical Research*, New York, 1923, p. 134). The optative is found in neither. ἵνα frequently in a sub-final sense, is very common in both; so is οὖν. The verb δίδωμι occurs in both more frequently than anywhere else in the New Testament. Other interesting resemblances are:

a. Water for the thirsty: cf. John 4:10 with Rev. 22:17. Manna for the the hungry: cf. John 6:49-51 with Rev. 2:17.

b. Authority received from the Father: cf. John 10:18 with Rev. 2:27.

c. Christ, the Logos: cf. John 1:1 with Rev. 19:13. Christ, the Light: cf. John 1:4, 5, 7, 9; 3:19; 8:12; 9:5; etc. with Rev. 22:5. Christ, the Lamb: cf. John 1:29 (Greek ἀμνός) with Rev. 5:6 *et passim* (Greek ἀρνίον). Christ, the Bridegroom: cf. John 3:29 with Rev. 19:7, and the One who redeemed us with his blood: cf. John 6:53-56 with Rev. 1:5; 5:9; 7:14; 12:11.

d. The Church, the Bride: cf. John 3:29 with Rev. 19:7; 22:17.

(10) The phrase *"simple* yet *sublime"* describes the style as represented in this Gospel. Especially in the Prologue and in the Upper Room Discourses we observe a kind of rhythmic flow which is very effective and truly fascinating. The manner in which the clauses are co-ordinated, so that often a

truth is stated first positively, then negatively or vice versa (1:3; 14:6; 15:5, 6; 14:18; 15:16); the way in which a clause which expresses the glorious grace of the Logos is followed by one which shows the ungrateful reaction on the part of those who should have accepted him (1:5, 10, 11); and, above all, the careful, yet thoroughly natural, balancing of sentences so that antithesis is followed by synthesis, brief and pithy clauses by longer sentences: all this makes the Fourth Gospel such a beautiful book.

In the Prologue (1:1-18) the manner in which a clause is added to another by the repetition of a leading word, so that the sentences are joined together like overlapping shingles, reminds one of the Epistle of James, the brother of the Lord. (See our *Bible Survey*, Grand Rapids, Mich., 1949, pp. 329, 332.)

Thus, in John 1:4-14 we notice:

In him was LIFE
  And the LIFE was the LIGHT
    And the LIGHT shines in the DARKNESS
      But the DARKNESS apprehended it not.

He came to HIS OWN
  But HIS OWN RECEIVED him not.
  But as many as RECEIVED him, etc.

Cf. also 1:1 and 1:10.

Among the characteristic words in the Fourth Gospel are the following: ἀγαπάω, ἀλήθεια, ἀληθής, ἀληθινός, ἁμαρτία, ἀμήν ἀμήν, γινώσκω, δίδωμι, δόξα, θεωρέω, ζωή, ζωή, αἰώνιος, Ἰουδαῖος, κρίσις, λόγος, μαρτυρέω, ὁράω, πατήρ, πιστεύω, σημεῖον, σκοτία, φιλέω.

John is rich in contrasts, such as: light, darkness; spirit, flesh; earthly, heavenly; from above, from the earth; life, death; to love, to hate; to rejoice, to lament; to be troubled, to trust; to see, to become blind.

IV. Grammar

It is not our purpose to give a complete Johannine Grammar. This has been done by others; e.g., E. A. Abbot, *Johannine Grammar*, London, 1906. Important points of grammar and syntax are mentioned in the commentary proper as they occur. Moreover, these are also basic to the translation which is presented.

With respect to three types of constructions a special remark is needed, as we see it. These constructions occur with great frequency in John's Gospel. We refer to conditional sentences, ἵνα clauses, and ὅτι clauses. Some commentaries say very little about them. Others—including some of the best—comment on some of these constructions but not on others. At times a really controversial ὅτι clause fails to receive any comment. We can easily see the reason for this: it is simply impossible in a commentary to cover every point of grammar. Were one to attempt it, he would have to write a whole set of books on each of the Gospels.

The method which we shall pursue has certain features which, we trust, will recommend it. Under each of the three aforementioned types of clauses the groups or subdivisions are described. Difficult passages in which the clauses occur are explained. Each clause is assigned to its proper column. We believe that this treatment of these frequently occurring clauses has the following advantages:

1. *Completeness.* An attempt has been made to classify all these clauses, so that at a glance it can be seen where each one belongs.

2. *The Saving of Space.* Why should it be necessary in a commentary to say over and over again: "This is a contrary-to-fact conditional sentence. The protasis has εἰ with the past indicative; the apodosis has the past indicative with ἄν. As the imperfect tense occurs in both clauses, we know that the sentence has reference to present unreality." About a hundred of these short paragraphs in connection with conditional sentences and then hundreds of others in connection with the ἵνα and ὅτι clauses not only can be avoided by a simpler method but they also consume the space that can be used for other important commentary material.

Hence, in this commentary on the Fourth Gospel, whenever a conditional sentence occurs in the translation, there is a brief footnote stating that this conditional sentence belongs to group I D (or III A 1 or whatever the case may be). See pp. 40-64. On the indicated pages one will find an explanation of the group to which the sentence belongs, and also the column in which it is classified. When the meaning of ὅτι or of ἵνα is immediately obvious, it receives no special comment in the text. If it be controversial or if for any reason it is discussed, there is a footnote-reference to the page where it is explained. These footnotes accompany the translations.

3. *Readability.* Though a person be not conversant with Greek, he may not mind an *occasional* Greek word or technical remark. If such a person finds too much material of this nature in a commentary, he will soon give up in despair. Hence, also for this reason it is probably better, to a certain extent to separate the following oft-recurring grammatical material from the commentary proper. Those who read Greek will appreciate the attempt which we have made to give a complete classification. This will facilitate comparison with similar points of grammar in the Synoptics and, for example, in the book of Revelation.

NEW TESTAMENT COMMENTARY

Classification of Conditional Sentences in the Fourth Gospel

Three main groups of conditional sentences occur, as follows:

I. *The Simple or First Class Conditional Sentence*

In this case the condition *is assumed to be* true to fact. Whether it is *actually* a fact has nothing to do with the form of the conditional clause.

In this kind of condition we find εἰ and any tense of the indicative in the protasis. This is entirely in harmony with the idea of the indicative, for that mode is used for assertion of facts (or assumed facts). If the protasis is negative, the negative particle οὐ is used.

The apodosis of such a conditional sentence may be a statement of fact (13:14), expressed by the present indicative; a question (1:25), also indicative (present tense in nearly every case); a prediction (11:12), future indicative; or a command (7:4), imperative.

Accordingly, in the Fourth Gospel, First Class conditional sentences are subdivided as follows:

Protasis		*Apodosis*
A		
		Statement of Fact,
Condition assumed to be true to Fact, Indicative		Indicative
Aorist	3:12a	Present
Present	8:39	Present
Aorist	13:14	Present
Perfect with sense of Present	13:17a	Present
B		
Condition assumed to be true to Fact, Indicative		*Question,* Indicative
Present	1:25	Present
Present	5:47	Future
Present	7:23	Present
Present	8:46	Present
Aorist	10:35, 36	Present
Aorist	18:23b	Present
C		
Condition assumed to be true to Fact, Indicative		*Prediction,* Indicative
Perfect	11:12	Future
Aorist	13:32	Future
Aorist	15:20 (twice)	Future

40

INTRODUCTION

D

Condition assumed to be true	to Fact, Indicative	Command or Prohibition, Imperative
Present	7:4	Aorist
Present	10:24	Aorist
Present	10:37	Present
Present	10:38a	Present
Present	15:18	Present
Present	18:8	Aorist
Aorist	18:23a	Aorist
Aorist	20:15	Aorist

II. *The Contrary To Fact or Second Class Conditional Sentence*

The condition (or premise) *is assumed to be* in conflict with reality. The protasis has εἰ with the past indicative; the apodosis has the past indicative with ἄν (usually). A contrary to fact conditional sentence which has reference to *the present time* takes the imperfect in both clauses (15:19). A contrary to fact conditional sentence dealing with *past time* has the aorist or pluperfect in both (14:7). Sometimes, however, there is a shift from present time in the protasis to past time in the apodosis (14:28); or from past to present (15:22).

In the protasis the negative particle is μή, which is not strange in view of the fact that what is asserted is contrary to fact.

We distinguish the following three groups of Second Class Conditional Sentences:

A

Contrary to Fact Conditional Sentences dealing with *Present Time* εἰ with the Imperfect Indicative in the protasis; the Imperfect Indicative with ἄν in the apodosis.

> 5:46
> 8:19 (pluperfect with sense of imperfect)
> 8:42
> 9:33
> 9:41
> 15:19
> 18:36

B

Contrary to Fact Conditional Sentences deal with *Past Time* εἰ with the Aorist or Pluperfect Indicative in the protasis; the Aorist or Pluperfect

41

Indicative with ἄν in the apodosis. In such sentences ἦν may be regarded as being aorist in meaning, for the aorist form is lacking.

11:21
11:32
14:2
14:7

C

Mixed Contrary to Fact Conditional Sentences

Protasis εἰ with		Apodosis with or without ἄν
Pluperfect as Imperfect	4:10	Aorist
Imperfect	14:28	Aorist
Aorist	15:22	Imperfect
Aorist	15:24	Imperfect
Imperfect	18:30	Aorist
Pluperfect	19:11	Imperfect

III. *The Future More Vivid or Third Class Conditional Sentence*

The condition is conceived of neither as a reality nor as in conflict with reality but as a probable future reality. The protasis, accordingly, uses 'εάν with the subjunctive. In about three-fifths of the cases the Fourth Gospel in the protasis of this kind of a conditional sentence employs the aorist subjunctive; in the remaining two-fifths, the present subjunctive. John has a greater fondness for the latter than do the Synoptists. By way of exception the perfect subjunctive is used in the protasis.

When the protasis has the aorist subjunctive, the apodosis usually has the future indicative; sometimes, the present indicative; at times even the subjunctive or imperative.

When the protasis has the present subjunctive, the apodosis generally takes the present indicative; sometimes, the future indicative; a few exceptions will be noted.

In the protasis the negative particle is μή, as could be expected in connection with a mode of uncertainty.

We distinguish the following groups and sub-groups:

A

Future More Vivid Conditional Sentences, using 'εάν with the Aorist Subjunctive in the Protasis, indicating that the Verb is Viewed as a Single conception

INTRODUCTION

1

With Future Indicative in the Apodosis

        3:12 b
        5:43
        6:51
        8:24
        8:36
        8:55
        10:9
        11:40
        11:48
        12:32
        14:3 b
        14:14
        15:10
        16:7a
        20:25

2

With Present Indicative in the Apodosis

        7:51
        8:31
        8:54
        12:24
        12:47 ?
        13:8
        14:3 a
        19:12

3

All Others:

	Apodosis
8:51	Aorist Subjunctive
8:52	Aorist Subjunctive
9:22	Aorist Subjunctive (after sub-final ἵνα)
15:7	Aorist Imperative
16:7a	Aorist Subjunctive
20:23a	Perfect Indicative

B

Future More Vivid Conditional Sentences, using 'εάν with the Present Subjunctive in the Protasis, indicating that the Verb signifies Continued Action.

1

With Present Indicative in the Apodosis

5.31
8:14
8:16
9:31
10:38b
11:9
11:10
13:17 b
15:14
21:22 (implied)
21:23 (implied)
21:25

2

With Future Indicative in the Apodosis

7:17
12:26 b
13:35
14:15
14:23

3

All Others

	Apodosis
6:62	Must be supplied
7:37	Present Imperative
12:26 a	Present Imperative
20:23b	Perfect Indicative

C

Future More Vivid Conditional Sentences, using 'εάν with the Periphrastic Perfect Passive Subjunctive in the Protasis, indicating that the Verb signifies an Action in the Past which still Continues in Force.

	Apodosis
3:27	Present Indicative
6:65	Present Indicative

Classification of ἵνα Clauses in the Fourth Gospel

The great frequency of ἵνα (rather often in a sub-final or non-final sense but much more often to express purpose) is one of the characteristics of the Fourth Gospel.[12] In order to explain it some maintain that this is simply Koine vernacular, for which the author shows a great fondness; others point to the influence of Aramaic. No doubt both of these factors must be borne in mind. And is it not possible that at the root of both there is another; namely, that in any language there is a fondness for analysis rather than synthesis, a preference which is bound to assert itself in time? Today, for example, the infinitive has just about vanished from the Greek language.

Having made an independent study of the use of ἵνα in the Fourth Gospel, according to the text of *Novum Testamentum Graece,* edited by D. Eberhard Nestle and D. Erwin Nestle, twentieth edition, 1950, we have reached the conclusions that are tabulated in the columns found on the following pages.

Column I contains a reference to all ἵνα clauses which, as we see it, express *purpose*. After each reference in this and in the other columns there is an indication of the tense, voice (for all verbs that may take an object, and are transitive in that sense), and mode of the verb (or verbs) introduced by ἵνα. In the text of the Gospel the verb in question does not necessarily directly follow ἵνα but belongs to it. Thus, in 14:3 the verb which is described in the column is not εἰμί but ἦτε. When the description of the verb is preceded by *neg.* (ative), the text has ἵνα μή. In all cases where ἵνα expresses purpose, it has been rendered *in order that* or *in order to* in our translation. A good illustration of ἵνα introducing a purpose clause is 3:16: "For God so loved the world that he gave his Son, the only-begotten, *in order that* (ἵνα) whoever believes in him should not perish but have everlasting life."

Column II A contains a reference to all ἵνα clauses which function as: a. *subject* (of an entire sentence or of a larger clause within the sentence) or b. *subjective complement* or c. *appositive* (of the subject or of its complement) or d. *modifier of any of these three.*

The ἵνα clause of 4:34 furnishes a good illustration: "My food is *to do* the will of the One who sent me, and *to accomplish* his work" (ἵνα ποιῶ . . . καὶ τελειώσω).

---

[12] C. F. Burney calls it "one of the most remarkable phenomena in this Gospel," *The Aramaic Origin of the Fourth Gospel*, Oxford, 1922, p. 69.

Column II B designates those ἵνα clauses which function as: a. *object* (of an entire sentence or of a larger clause within the sentence or even of a phrase) or b. *its appositive.* Verbs of asking, praying (begging, requesting), ordering, appointing, etc., often take a ἵνα clause as object.

An illustration of this type of clause is found in 17:15: "I do not pray *that thou shouldest take* them out of the world but *that thou shouldest keep* them from the evil one (ἵνα ἄρῃς . . . ἀλλ' ἵνα τηρήσῃς)."

When ἵνα introduces either a subject-clause or an object-clause (columns IIA and IIB), it has usually been rendered *that.* In other cases an *infinitive* has been submitted for the entire ἵνα clause. The rendering "in order that" has never been used in translating these clauses. That the substitution of an infinitive for a ἵνα clause is entirely legitimate is clear from a comparison of 1:27 and Luke 3:16; showing that the latter uses the infinitive where the former has the ἵνα clause; yet, the identical thought is conveyed.

Column IIC indicates the ἵνα *result*-clauses. One of the clearest is 9:2, where if ἵνα were given the full telic force, a hardly possible meaning would result. To be sure, some speak of "pre-ordinance" even in this case (if not human, then divine) but it is surely far more natural and simple to view this ἵνα as indicating simple result; so that we translate:

"Rabbi, who sinned, this man or his parents, *so that* (ἵνα) he was born blind?"

In most cases the sense in which ἵνα is used is immediately clear. There are cases, however, where excellent grammarians and interpreters have reached opposite conclusions. Some authorities (especially in the older school) refuse to admit that ἵνα ever introduces a result-clause. But if ἵνα (cf. Latin *ut*) can have the ecbatic sense in late Greek outside of the New Testament, there is no good reason to hold that it cannot have that meaning within the New Testament. Language, after all, is a living thing. To limit the meaning of words too strictly is never wise. Others, however, go to the opposite extreme and refuse to see purpose even in passages which speak about the fulfilment of prophecy (e.g., 13:18). They would, moreover, greatly extend the list of ἵνα result-clauses. However, over against their opinion stands the fact that the idea of *purpose is predominant in this Gospel:* 1:7, 8; 3:17; 5:23, 34, 36; history (here particularly redemptive history, but the two cannot be separated) is viewed as the realization of the *plan* and *will* of God: 4:34; 5:30; 6:37, 44, 64; 18:37; 19:28; and in that plan the exact time or *hour* when each event in the story of redemption is to take place has been designated: 2:4; 7:6, 30; 8:20; 13:1. This Gospel is predestinarian from start to finish, as is apparent to any unbiased student who reads it from beginning to end at one sitting. Hence, we must allow the prophetic-fulfilment ἵνα clauses their full, telic force.

It is true, of course, that the line between purpose clauses and result clauses is sometimes very hard to draw. Room must be left for honest difference of opinion (for example, in such cases as 5:40; 6:5; 9:36; and 14:29). Some, in order to bridge the gap between purpose and result have spoken of *contemplated result*.

Another problem which confronts us is the fine distinction which must be drawn at times between substantive clauses, on the one hand (whether subject or object; i.e., whether they belong to Column IIA or to Column IIB), and purpose clauses (Column I) on the other. Thus one might ask: Shall we conceive of all three ἵνα clauses of 17:21 as purpose clauses? Or shall we view the first and the second as object clauses, and the third as purpose? Though we favor the latter alternative, because the first two clauses seem to be controlled by a verb of *asking*, while the third differs substantially in form, the former alternative counts among its advocates famous exegetes who can appeal to 17:22b and 23a where clauses similar in content to the first two in verse 21 are generally regarded as purpose clauses. Fortunately, however, the resultant interpretations, whether one adopts the first or the second alternative, do not vary widely.

In view of the aforegoing it will have become evident that what is given in the columns must be regarded as being no more than an honest approach to accuracy. We believe that the classification is, in the main, correct.

As to statistics, note the following:

Final ἵνα *clauses* (Column I) number just over 100, while non-final ἵνα (Columns IIA, IIB, IIC) number about 40. Hence, the ratio of final to non-final ἵνα clauses in the Fourth Gospel is 5-2.

The ratio of aorist to present (and a few perfect periphrastic) subjunctives in the entire group of ἵνα clauses is slightly better than 2-1.

The ratio of positive (ἵνα) clauses to negative (ἵνα μή) clauses is about 7-1. There are also a few mixed clauses (one verb negative, the other positive, as in 3:16).

I. FINAL CLAUSES	II. NON-FINAL CLAUSES		
	A SUBJECT	B OBJECT	C RESULT
		1:7 (a) aor.act. subj. explains μαρτυρίαν	
1:7 (b) aor.act.subj.			
1:8 aor.act.subj.			
1:19 aor.act.subj.			
1:22 aor.act.subj.			

I. FINAL CLAUSES	II. NON-FINAL CLAUSES		
	A SUBJECT	B OBJECT	C RESULT
	1:27 aor.act. subj. explains ἄξιος		
1:31 aor.pass.subj.			
		2:25 aor.act. subj. explains χρείαν	
3:15 pres.act.subj. 3:16 neg.aor.mid.subj. and pres.act.subj. 3:17 (a) aor. (or present)act.subj. 3:17 (b) aor. pass. subj. 3:20 neg.aor.pass.subj. 3:21 aor.pass.subj. 4:8 aor.act.subj. 4:15 neg.pres.subj. and neg.pres.mid.subj.			
	4:34 pres.act. subj.(ποιήσω aor. act.subj. also has strong support) and aor.act.subj.		
4:36 pres.act.subj.			
		4:47 aor.act. subj. and aor. mid.subj. 5:7 aor.act. subj. modifies ἄνθρωπον	
5:14 neg.aor.mid.subj. 5:20 pres.act.subj. 5:23 pres.act.subj. 5:34 aor.pass.subj.			
		5:36 aor.act. subj.	
5:40? pres.act.subj. 6:5? aor.act.subj.			
			6:7 aor.act.subj.

INTRODUCTION

I. FINAL CLAUSES	II. NON-FINAL CLAUSES		
	A SUBJECT	**B** OBJECT	**C** RESULT
6:12 neg.aor.mid.subj. 6:15 aor.act.subj. 6:28 pres.mid.subj.			
	6:29 pres.act. subj. explains τοῦτο		
6:30 aor.act.subj. and aor.act.subj. 6:38 pres.act.subj.			
	6:39 neg.aor.act. subj. or fut.act. indic.; aor.act. subj. or fut.act. indic.; these verbs explain τοῦτο 6:40 pres.act. subj.; explains τοῦτο		
6:50 aor.act.subj. and neg.aor.act.subj. 7:3 fut.act.indic. 7:23 neg.aor.pass.subj. 7:32 aor.act.subj. [8:6 pres.act.subj.]			
		8:56 aor.act. subj.	
8:59 aor.act.subj.			
			9:2 aor.pass. subj.
9:3 aor.pass.subj.			
		9:22 aor.mid. subj.	
9:36? aor.act.subj. 9:39 pres.act.subj. and aor.subj. 10:10(a) aor.act.subj. and aor.act.subj. and aor.act.subj. 10:10(b) present act.			

I. FINAL CLAUSES	II. NON-FINAL CLAUSES		
	A SUBJECT	B OBJECT	C RESULT
subj. and pres.act.			
subj.			
10:17 aor.act.subj.			
10:31 aor.act.subj.			
10:38 aor.act.subj.			
and pres.act.subj.			
11:4 aor.pass.subj.			
11:11 aor.act.subj.			
11:15 aor.act.subj.			
11:16 aor.subj.			
11:19 aor.mid.subj.			
11:31 aor.act.subj.			
		11:37 neg.aor. act.subj.	
11:42 aor.act.subj.			
	11:50 aor.subj. and neg.aor. mid.subj.		
11:52 aor.act.subj.			
11:53 aor.act.subj.			
11:55 aor.act.subj.			
		11:57 aor.act. subj.	
12:7 aor.act.subj.			
(supply: *it was*)			
12:9 aor.act.subj.			
		12:10 aor.act. subj.	
12:20 aor.act.subj.			
	12:23 aor.pass. subj.; modifies ὥρα; has almost temporal force		
12:35 neg.aor.act.subj.			
12:36 aor.subj.			
12:38 aor.pass.subj.			
12:40 neg.aor.act.subj.			
and neg.aor.act.subj.			
and neg.aor.act.subj.			

INTRODUCTION

I. FINAL CLAUSES	II. NON-FINAL CLAUSES		
	A SUBJECT	B OBJECT	C RESULT
and neg.fut.act.indic. 12:42 neg.aor.mid. subj. 12:46 neg.aor.act.subj. 12:47 (a) aor.act.subj. 12:47 (b) aor.act.subj.			
	13:1 aor.act. subj.; modifies ὥρα		
		13:2 aor.act. subj.	
13:15 pres.act.subj. 13:18 aor.pass.subj. 13:19 pres.act.subj. 13:29 aor.act.subj.			
		13:34 pres.act. subj.; explains 'εντολήν	
14:3 pres.subj. 14:13 aor.pass.subj. 14:16 pres.subj. 14:29? aor.act.subj. 14:31 aor.act.subj. 15:2 pres.act.subj.			
		15:8 pres.act. subj.; modifies 'εν τούτῳ	
15:11 pres.subj. and aor.pass.subj.			
	15:12 pres.act. subj.; explains αὕτη		
		15:13 aor.act. subj.; explains ἀγάπην 15:16 (a) pres. subj. and pres. act.subj. and pres.subj.	

I. FINAL CLAUSES	II. NON-FINAL CLAUSES		
	A **SUBJECT**	**B** **OBJECT**	**C** **RESULT**
			15:16 (b) aor.act. subj.
15:17 pres.act.subj. 15:25 aor.pass.subj. 16:1 neg.aor.pass.subj.			
	16:2 aor.act. subj.; modifies ὥρα; has almost temporal force		
16:4 pres.act.subj.			
	16:7 aor.act. subj.		
16:24 periphrastic perf.pass.subj.			
		16:30 pres.act. subj.	
	16:32 aor.pass. subj. and aor. act.subj.		
16:33 pres.act.subj. 17:1 aor.act.subj.			
		17:2 aor.act. subj. (another reading has fut. act.indic.) explains 'εξουσίαν	
	17:3 pres.act. subj.; explains αὕτη		
		17:4 aor.act. subj.	
17:11 pres.subj. 17:12 aor.pass.subj. 17:13 pres.act.subj.			
		17:15 (a) aor.act. subj. 17:15 (b) aor.act. subj.	

I. FINAL CLAUSES	II. NON-FINAL CLAUSES		
	A SUBJECT	B OBJECT	C RESULT
17:19 periphrastic perf.pass.subj.			
		17:21 (a) pres. subj.	
		17:21 (b) pres. subj.	
17:21 (c) pres.act.subj. 17:22 pres.subj. 17:23 (a) periphrastic perf.pass.subj. 17:23 (b) pres.act.subj.			
		17:24 (a) pres. subj.	
17:24 (b) pres.act.subj. 17:26 pres.subj. 18:9 aor.pass.subj. 18:28 neg.aor.pass. subj. and aor.act.subj. 18:32 aor.pass.subj. 18:36 neg.aor.pass. subj. 18:37 aor.act.subj.			
	18:39 aor.act. subj.; explains συνήθεια		
19:4 aor.act.subj. 19:16 aor.pass.subj. 19:24 aor.pass.subj. 19:28 aor.pass.subj. 19:31 (a) neg.aor.subj.			
		19:31 (b) aor. subj. and aor. pass.subj.	
19:35 pres.act.subj. 19:36 aor.pass.subj.			
		19:38 aor.act. subj.	
20:31 (a) pres.act.subj. 20:31 (b) pres.act.subj.			

NEW TESTAMENT COMMENTARY

Classification of ὅτι Clauses in the Gospel of John

In this Gospel ὅτι occurs much more often than in any other. There are three main uses: causal, declarative, and recitative. Approximately one-third of the examples are causal, slightly over one half are declarative, and one-ninth are recitative. Specifically:

1. A *causal* ὅτι may be translated *for, because, since*. See Column I below.

2. A *declarative* ὅτι introduces a clause which is the direct object of a verb of declaring, testifying, saying, seeing, thinking, hearing, remembering, knowing, etc. Such a clause may be called *indirect discourse* (when the term is employed in its wider meaning). The translation is *that*. See Column II below. The list also contains a few examples which are not strictly declarative (thus, 3:19 epexegetical; 14:22 probably consecutive). In 6:46 we probably have the elliptical use: "I do not mean *that*," etc.

3. A *recitative* ὅτι introduces a direct quotation. In the English language it is reproduced by quotation marks (". . . .").

In this Gospel when the author quotes Jesus directly, after the words "he said," he generally omits ὅτι (See 18:5). When other persons are quoted directly, their words are introduced by ὅτι (1:20; 9:9). There are, however, several examples of indirect discourse (Column II), in which Jesus is represented as quoting his own previous sayings. Here declarative ὅτι is used (1:50, 6:36; 8:24; etc.). The present tendency is to regard ὅτι after Ἀμὴν ἀμὴν λέγω as recitative.[13]

In by far the most of the examples the distinct meaning of ὅτι is immediately clear from the context. Thus, in 8:47 (where ὅτι is preceded by διὰ τοῦτο) the *causal* sense is evident. So also after words of saying, seeing, etc., the *declarative* usage is generally discerned without difficulty; see, e.g., 4:20. It is also very clear that in 1:20 ὅτι must be *recitative* (no change from first to third person), and that in 4:51 it is *declarative* (change from second to third person). There are also cases where ὅτι can be either declarative or recitative without affecting the sense; e.g., 4:37.

But at times ὅτι creates problems. Note the following:

---

[13] Thus R.S.V. along with other translations leaves ὅτι in 5:24, 25 untranslated, so that no distinction is shown to the English reader between the construction without ὅτι in 5:19 and with ὅτι in 5:24, 25. The question is legitimate whether, perhaps, the presence of ὅτι after Ἀμὴν ἀμὴν λέγω adds to the resumptive character of the saying which follows the words of solemn introduction. If so, the construction would tend in the direction of indirect discourse, as if Jesus is restating what he has said before but is now saying it in different words, perhaps with a new idea added or with a new emphasis. A good argument can be presented for this position in each of the cases where the introductory words appear *with* ὅτι (3:11; 5:24, 25; 8:34; 10:7; 13:21; and 16:20). N.N. omits ὅτι in all the other cases where Ἀμὴν ἀμὴν λέγω σοι (or ὑμῖν) occurs (1:51; 3:3, 5; 5:19; 6:26, 32, 47, 53; 8:51, 58; 10:1; 12:24; 13:16, 20; 13:38; 14:12; 16:23; and 21:18). However, the situation is complicated by the fact that in some instances the text is disputed.

INTRODUCTION

2:18. Here, it would seem, one will have to go beyond the simple declarative *that* in reproducing the sense of ὅτι. The Jews cannot have meant, "What sign do you show (to prove) *that* you are doing these things?" They did not question *the fact* that Jesus had actually cleansed the temple. What they wanted to know was how he could justify his actions; what good, legitimate reason he was able to advance. This points to ὅτι in the causal sense. We translate: "What sign do you show us for doing these things?"

3:7; 4:27; 5:28. The Greek verb θαυμάζω can be used either absolutely or with accusative of person or thing. Once the latter is understood (namely, the fact that the verb can have an object, and that this object can be a single word or even an entire clause), it is easy to see that the ὅτι which follows the verb can be declarative (introducing a *that* clause). In the manner in which the verb is used in 3:7 and in 4:27 it does not differ greatly from verbs of declaring, testifying, saying, etc. (see under 2), which generally take a similar anticipatory, declarative ὅτι. Therefore, though neither in 3:7 nor in 4:27 does it make much difference in resultant meaning whether one translates "that" or "because," we, nevertheless, prefer the translation "that."

In 5:28 the situation is different. Here the object of the verb (μὴ) θαυμάζετε is not a clause but the pronoun τοῦτο. Moreover, τοῦτο evidently refers to what precedes. It does not (here) anticipate; for if it did, it would mean that Jesus was telling the Jews to *stop* being amazed about something which *he had not yet told them;* namely, the details with respect to the future *physical* resurrection. Hence, the clause μὴ θαυμάζετε τοῦτο is complete in itself and in our editions is properly followed by a comma. The ὅτι clause which follows the comma states the reason for the immediately preceding prohibition. The proper translation, accordingly, is "for."

3:19. Here Chrysosthom and others have taken ὅτι in its causal sense. However, comparison with other similar passages—I John 1:5; 5:9, 11, 14— immediately shows that ὅτι is used epexegetically; that is, as introducing a clause which is in apposition with a preceding substantive and explains it. Thus, I John 5:14 can only be translated: "And this is *the confidence* which we have with respect to him *that* (not *because*) if we ask anything according to his will, he hears us." In form 3:19 is exactly similar, and ὅτι must be rendered "that."

4:35(b). Here either *that* or *because* makes good sense. Nevertheless, the context (verse 35 a) would seem to indicate that Jesus does not intend to say: Scan *the fields* (doing this *because* they are white), but rather: Rivet y o u r eyes on the *whiteness* of *these* fields (in contrast with natural fields). Here we have a verb of *seeing* with a direct object and an object-clause.

8:22. In passages such as this one (and *11:47*) there is an ellipsis; so that the entire question can be paraphrased as follows: "Then said the Jews,

55

'Will he kill himself?' *They said this because* (or *since*, ὅτι) he had said, 'Where I am going, y o u cannot come.'"

14:2. That ὅτι in the sense of *because* is possible and even probable here is shown in our explanation of that passage. We do not agree with those expositors who *insist* on declarative ὅτι, as if the causal sense were entirely out of the question. When ὅτι is taken as *declarative,* there are two possibilities:

a. "If it were not so (i.e., if there were not many dwelling-places in my Father's home), I would have told y o u *that* I go to prepare a place for y o u." This explanation makes Jesus say that if there were no predestined mansions in heaven for God's children, he would go up there and take the necessary steps to change the situation, and that in that case he would have informed his disciples about his plans with respect to it. But surely that interpretation is impossible: Jesus and the Father are not in conflict in John's Gospel.

b. "If it were not so, would I have told y o u that I go to prepare a place for y o u?" This, of course, is possible, and much better than a. Nevertheless, the question has been asked, "When had Jesus ever told his disciples this thing (namely, that he was going to prepare a place for them)?" The *possibility* that there had been such very important teaching of which the Gospel has preserved no record must be granted; the *probability* is not great.

Basically there is not a great difference between b. (ὅτι, *that* in a question) and the position that ὅτι must be regarded as causal. Two very important facts are either specifically taught or at least implied in either view:

a. In the Father's house there is ample room for all of his children.

b. One of the purposes of Christ's ascension to heaven was in order that he might get everything in readiness with respect to the dwelling-places of the elect.

Classification of ὅτι Clauses in the New Testament

I. CAUSAL =*for, because, since*	II. DECLARATIVE (MAINLY) =*that*	III. RECITATIVE ="...."
1:15		
1:16		
1:17		
		1:20
1:30		
		1:32
	1:34	
1:50(a)		
	1:50(b)	

56

INTRODUCTION

I. CAUSAL =*for, because, since*	II. DECLARATIVE =*that*	III. RECITATIVE ="...."
	2:17	
2:18		
	2:22	
2:25		
	3:2	
	3:7	
		3:11
3:18		
	3:19	
	3:21	
3:23		
		3:28(a)
		3:28(b)
	3:33	
	4:1(a)	
	4:1(b)	
		4:17
	4:19	
	4:20	
	4:21	
4:22		
	4:25	
	4:27	
		4:35(a)
	4:35(b)	
	4:37	
		4:39
		4:42(a)
	4:42(b)	
	4:44	
	4:47	
	4:51	
		4:52
	4:53	
	5:6	
	5:15	
5:16		
5:18		
		5:24
		5:25

57

I. CAUSAL = *for, because, since*	II. DECLARATIVE = *that*	III. RECITATIVE = *". . . ."*
5:27		
5:28		
5:30		
	5:32	
	5:36	
5:38		
5:39		
	5:42	
	5:45	
6:2		
	6:5	
		6:14
	6:15	
	6:22(a)	
	6:22(b)	
	6:24	
6:26(a)		
6:26(b)		
	6:36	
6:38		
6:41		
		6:42
	6:46	
	6:61	
6:65		
	6:69	
7:1		
7:7(a)		
	7:7(b)	
7:8		
		7:12
	7:22	
7:23		
	7:26	
7:29		
7:30		
	7:35 (almost resultative: so that)	
7:39		
		[7:40]

INTRODUCTION

I. CAUSAL	II. DECLARATIVE	III. RECITATIVE
= *for, because, since*	= *that*	= *". . . ."*
	7:42	
	7:52	
8:14		
8:16		
	8:17	
8:20		
8:22		
	8:24(a)	
	8:24(b)	
	8:27	
	8:28	
8:29		
		8:33
		8:34
	8:37(a)	
8:37(b)		
8:43		
8:44(a)		
8:44(b)		
8:45		
8:47		
		8:48
	8:52	
	8:54	
	8:55	
	9:8	
		9:9(a)
		9:9(b)
		9:11
9:16		
9:17(a)		
		9:17(b)
	9:18	
	9:19	
	9:20(a)	
	9:20(b)	
9:22		
		9:23
	9:24	
	9:25	

I. CAUSAL = *for, because since*	II. DECLARATIVE = *that*	III. RECITATIVE = "...."
	9:29	
	9:30	
	9:31	
	9:32	
	9:35	
		9:41
10:4		
10:5		
		10:7
10:13		
10:17		
10:26		
10:33		
		10:34
		10:36(a)
10:36(b)		
	10:38	
		10:41
	11:6	
11:9		
11:10		
	11:13	
	11:15	
	11:20	
	11:22	
	11:24	
	11:27	
	11:31(a)	
	11:31(b)	
	11:40	
	11:41	
	11:42(a)	
	11:42(b)	
11:47		
	11:50	
	11:51	
	11:56	
12:6(a)		
12:6(b)		
	12:9	

INTRODUCTION

I. CAUSAL	II. DECLARATIVE	III. RECITATIVE
= *for, because since*	= *that*	= "...." '
12:11		
	12:12	
	12:16	
12:18		
	12:19	
	12:34(a)	
	12:34(b)	
12:39		
12:41		
12:49		
	12:50	
	13:1	
	13:3(a)	
	13:3(b)	
		13:11
	13:19	
		13:21
	13:29	
		13:33
	13:35	
14:2		
	14:10	
	14:11	
14:12		
14:17(a)		
14:17(b)		
14:19		
	14:20	
	14:22	
	14:28(a)	
	14:28(b)	
14:28(c)		
	14:31	
15:5		
15:15(a)		
15:15(b)		
	15:18	
15:19		
15:21		
		15:25

I. CAUSAL = *for, because since*	II. DECLARATIVE = *that*	III. RECITATIVE = *". . . ."*
15:27		
16:3		
	16:4(a)	
16:4(b)		
16:6		
16:9		
16:10		
16:11		
16:14		
	16:15	
16:17		
	16:19(a)	
	16:19(b)	
		16:20
16:21(a)		
	16:21(b)	
	16:26	
16:27(a)		
	16:(27b)	
	16:30(a)	
	16:30(b)	
16:32		
	17:7	
17:8(a)		
	17:8(b)	
	17:8(c)	
17:9		
17:14		
	17:21	
	17:23	
17:24		
	17:25	
18:2		
	18:8	
		18:9
	18:14	
18:18		
	18:37	
	19:4	
19:7		

I. CAUSAL =*for, because, since*	II. DECLARATIVE =*that*	III. RECITATIVE ="...."
	19:10	
19:20		
	19:21	
	19:28	
	19:35	
19:42		
	20:9	
		20:13
	20:14	
	20:15	
		20:18
20:29		
	20:31	
	21:4	
	21:7	
	21:12	
	21:15	
	21:16	
21:17(a)		
	21:17(b)	
	21:23(a)	
	21:23(b)	
	21:24	

Influence of Aramaic upon the Greek of the Fourth Gospel

With respect to the possible influence of Aramaic upon the Greek of the Fourth Gospel it is probably best to avoid extremes.[14] On the one hand, it would seem to be obvious that a book composed in Ephesus for those of

---

[14] See W. F. Albright, "Some Observations Favoring the Palestinian Origin of the Gospel of John," *HThR*, April, 1924; same author, *From The Stone Age to Christianity*, Baltimore, 1940, pp. 299, 300. One should read *at least:* C. F. Burney, *The Aramaic Origin of the Fourth Gospel*, Oxford, 1922; O. T. Allis, "The Alleged Aramaic Origin of the Gospels," *PThR* 26(1928), 531-572; E. C. Colwell, *The Greek of the Fourth Gospel*, Chicago, 1931; G. D. Dalman, *Jesus-Jeshua, Studies in the Gospels* (translated by P. P. Levertoff), New York, 1929, especially pp. 1-38; E. J. Goodspeed, *New Chapters in New Testament Study*, New York, 1937, ch. VI; J. De Zwaan, "John Wrote Aramaic," *JBL*, 57(1938), 155-171; the Riddle-Torrey Debate, *ChrC*, July 18-Oct. 31, 1934; F. W. Filson, *One Lord—One Faith*, Philadelphia, 1943, pp. 31-35; and the works of C. C. Torrey; especially, *The Four Gospels, A New Translation*, New York and London, 1933; *Our Translated Gospels*, New York and London, 1936; and *Documents of the Primitive Church*, New York and London, 1941.

Ephesus and vicinity, a Gospel intended to be read by Greek-speaking Christians from among the Gentiles, must have been written in Greek.[15] But since its author was a Jew whose native tongue was Aramaic and since the primary sources for this Gospel must have been Aramaic, it would seem to be just as obvious that its linguistic peculiarities should often be viewed as Aramaisms; at least, as Semitisms. It is true that for many of these characteristic constructions one can find parallels in Epictetus or the Papyri or both. The question remains, however, whether when one finds *so many* of these peculiarities, some of them with such a high frequency rate, *occurring together in the relatively small compass of one Gospel,* and when, in addition, one knows that the author and also the Person whose discourses he reproduces were Aramaic-speaking Jews, whether under these circumstances it may not be best to give the Aramaic language its due as a formative influence which contributed its share in determining the type of Greek that is found here. Thus, the employment of several Aramaic words, constantly recurring parallelisms (often chiastic), suspended subjects, characteristic expressions (like "answered and said" which also occurs frequently in the Aramaic section of the book of Daniel), καί in the sense of "but" (or "and yet"), clause-co-ordination instead of clause-subordination (parataxis instead of hypotaxis), and abundant (redundant ?) use of pronouns and of the historical present, seem altogether natural when one finds them in a book written by an author with a Jewish name and soul.

V. Theme and Divisions

The *theme* is given in 20:31: *Jesus, the Christ, the Son of God.* There is a clear-cut division at the close of chapter 12: Christ turns away from the multitudes and withdraws himself to the inner circle of his disciples.

Good arguments can be advanced for various subdivisions under each of these two main parts. We prefer the following:

The first six chapters form one large unit. They proclaim the glorious Son of God who became flesh, is shown revealing himself to ever-widening circles, and is then rejected, first in Judea (chapter 5), then in Galilee (chapter 6). These chapters (after the Prologue, 1:1-18) cover various great events and discourses that pertain to a period of approximately two years and four months; i.e., from December of the year 26 to Passover of the year 29. There follows a half-year period (The Retirement Ministry, Passover to Feast of Tabernacles) on which John is silent.

Chapters 7-10 form another unit. They record events and discourses that occurred during the period from October to December of the year 29

---

[15] F. W. Ginrich, "The Gospel of John and Modern Greek," *ClW*, 36(1942-1943), 122-123, has found a similarity between John's Greek and modern Greek.

INTRODUCTION

(Feast of Tabernacles to Feast of Dedication). The conclusion of chapter 10 indicates that here again we have a natural division (see 10:40-42). This subdivision describes the Son of God making his tender appeal to sinners and at the same time rebuking his enemies whose hatred and sinister determination with respect to him gradually increases.

Chapters 11 and 12 constitute the third and final subdivision under the first main division. Here the Word is shown revealing himself clearly by two mighty deeds: the raising of Lazarus and the triumphal entry into Jerusalem. This section takes us to the beginning of the Week of the Passion. As already indicated, the closing paragraph of chapter 12 (see especially verse 37) forms a natural conclusion to the entire first division of the Fourth Gospel.

The second part, chapters 13-21, divides itself very readily into four subdivisions. They are:

Chapter 13 stands by itself, though it forms a natural introduction to the Upper Room Discourses. But here in chapter 13, unlike chapters 14-17, we have narrative material. There is action, interspersed with dramatic conversation. We see the Master and his disciples at the Supper. He issues and illustrates his new commandment that they should love one another even as he loved them. The story regarding Peter's denial, introduced in the closing verses of this chapter (13:36-38, the prediction), is continued afterward (in 18:15-18 and verses 25-27, the fulfilment of the prediction). Between this prediction and its fulfilment stands the block, chapters 14-17.

Chapters 14-17 clearly belong together. They contain the Supper Discourses and the Highpriestly Prayer. The Lord tenderly instructs his disciples and in his prayer commits to the care of his Father: himself, them, and those who would come to believe through their word.

In chapters 18 and 19 the Christ is described in the act of dying as a substitute for his people. It is clear, of course, that this section, too, forms a unit.

The final subdivision comprises chapters 20 and 21: the Resurrection and Appearances.

We have divided the Fourth Gospel into two main divisions and seven subdivisions, three under the first main division, four under the second. Though we claim no greater merit for this outline than that it is natural, as has been indicated, and easy to commit to memory, it is, nevertheless, interesting to observe that the apostle John, the author of the Fourth Gospel and of the Apocalypse, loves this kind of an arrangement. In the Apocalypse he also at times divides his sevens into two groups, placing three units in the first and four in the second or vice versa. (See our *More Than Conquerors*, Grand Rapids, 1952, pp. 30 and 75.) In fact, the book of Revelation, too, divides itself in exactly the same manner. Note the parallel:

NEW TESTAMENT COMMENTARY

Gospel of John *Jesus, the Christ, the Son of God*	*Book of Revelation* *The Victory of Christ and His* *Church over Satan and his* *Helpers*

I. During His Public Ministry
  A. Revealing himself to ever-widening circles, *rejected*
  B. Making his tender appeal to sinners, *bitterly resisted*
  C. Manifesting himself as the Messiah by two mighty deeds, *repulsed*
	I. The Struggle on Earth
	  A. Christ in the midst of the seven Golden Lampstands
	  B. The Book with Seven Seals
	  C. The Seven Trumpets of Judgment

II. During His Private Ministry
  A. Issuing and illustrating his new commandment
  B. Tenderly instructing his disciples and committing them to the Father's care
  C. Dying as a substitute for his people
  D. Triumphing gloriously
	II. The Deeper Spiritual Background
	  A. The Woman and the Man-Child Persecuted by the Dragon and his Helpers
	  B. The Seven Bowls of Wrath
	  C. The Fall of the Great Harlot and of the Beasts
	  D. The Judgment upon the Dragon, followed by the New Heaven and Earth

(For this Outline see *More Than Conquerors*, pp. 22-31)

The Plan of John's Gospel is, indeed, beautiful. The arrangement is superb. We see the Word in his pre-incarnate glory, so that we may appreciate his condescending love in coming to earth in order to save sinners. In his earthly ministry he reveals himself to ever-widening circles, but is rejected both in Judea and in Galilee. Nevertheless, he does not at once destroy those who have rejected him, but instead he makes his tender appeal to sinners, that they may accept him by faith. Meanwhile opposition becomes active and bitter resistance. By two mighty deeds he now manifests himself clearly as the Messiah. But though the Greeks seek him, the Jews, who have seen such clear tokens of his character, love, and power, repulse him. So he turns to the inner circle, tenderly instructs them in the Upper Room, and just before his final suffering and death commits them to the Father's care. In his very death he overcomes the world and by means of his resurrection he reveals the meaning of the cross.

The Gospel According to
John

Commentary on Chapters 1-6

Outline of Chapters 1-6

Theme: *Jesus, the Christ, the Son of God*
During His Public Ministry Revealing Himself
to Ever-widening Circles, Rejected

1:1-18   1. The Glory of the Son, as Word of God
        a. In the beginning
        b. At the creation
        c. After the fall
        d. At the incarnation

1:19-4:54   2. Revealing Himself to Ever-widening Circles
        a. To John the Baptist who testifies concerning him
        b. To his immediate disciples. Their testimony; their faith
           when they witness the first sign
        c. To Jerusalem. The cleansing of the temple; the conver-
           sation with Nicodemus
        d. To Judea. John the Baptist's Recessional
        e. To Samaria. Conversation with the Samaritan Woman
           and ministry among the people of Sychar
        f. To Galilee. Healing of the nobleman's son

5-6   3. Rejected
        a. In Judea, as a result of the sabbath-healing of the man
           at Bethzatha and the claims made in that connection
        b. In Galilee, as a result of the Bread of Life discourse

CHAPTER I

1 1 In the beginning was the Word, and the Word was face to face with God, and the Word was God. 2 He himself was in the beginning face to face with God.

3 All things came into being through him, and apart from him not a single thing that exists came into being.

4 In him was life, and that life was the light of men.

5 And the light shines in the darkness, but the darkness did not appropriate it.

1:1-5

This Gospel opens magnificently. It begins by portraying the life of Christ in eternity, before the world was. That life was rich and glorious, filled with infinite delight and serene blessedness in the presence of the Father. Once this truth is grasped, the condescending love of Christ, in becoming flesh, will be appreciated more fully.

1:1 In the beginning — when the heavens and the earth were created (Gen. 1:1) — the Word already existed. This is another way of saying that he existed from all eternity. He was not what certain heretics claimed him to be, a created being. (See p. 33.)

Was the Word. John and the heretics both spoke of the Word (ὁ λόγος); but though the term was the same, the meaning was different. John's doctrine is not dependent on that of heretics nor on that of speculative philosophers like Philo, a prominent Alexandrian who flourished in the first century A. D. One never knows what to make of Philo's Logos. He employs the term no fewer than thirteen hundred times! but the meaning is never very definite.[16] It is described now as a divine attribute, then again as a bridge between God and the world, identical with neither but partaking of the nature of both. Philo allegorized, which makes it difficult to grasp his meaning. Thus, in his comments on Gen. 3:24 he discusses the Cherubim,

---

[16] Cf. H. Bavinck, *The Doctrine of God* (translated by William Hendriksen), Grand Rapids, Mich., 1951, pp. 260-264; W. F. Howard, *Christianity According to John*, Philadelphia, 1946, pp. 34-56.

equipped with flaming sword, who are placed at Eden's gates to prevent access to the tree of life. As Philo sees it, these Cherubim are two divine potencies: God's loving-kindness and his sovereignty. The sword is the Logos or Reason which unites the two. Balaam, the foolish prophet, had no sword (Reason), for he said to the ass: "If I had a sword, I would have pierced thee" (*On the Cherubim*, XXXII).

Surely, the term as employed by the evangelist cannot derive its meaning from such allegorization. It is rooted not in Greek but in Semitic thought.[17] Already in the Old Testament the Word of God is represented as a Person. Note especially Ps. 33:6: "By the Word of Jehovah (LXX: τῷ λόγῳ τοῦ κυρίου) were the heavens made." What is probably the best commentary on John 1:1 is found in Prov. 8:27-30:

> "When he established the heavens, I was there;
>   When he set a circle upon the face of the deep.
> When he made firm the skies above,
>   When the fountains of the deep became strong,
> When he gave to the deep its bound,
>   That the waters should not transgress his commandment,
> When he marked out the foundations of the earth;
>   Then I was by him, as a master workman;
> And I was daily his delight,
>   Rejoicing always before him."

As a New Testament designation of the Christ, the term *Word* occurs only in 1:1, 14; I John 1:1; and Rev. 19:13. A word serves two distinct purposes: a. it gives expression to the inner thought, the soul of the man, doing this even though no one else is present to hear what is said or to read what is thought; and b. it reveals this thought (hence, the soul of the speaker) to others. Christ is *the Word of God* in both respects: he expresses or reflects the mind of God; also, he reveals God to man (1:18; cf. Matt. 11:27; Heb. 1:3).

And the Word was face to face with God (πρὸς τὸν θεόν).[18] The meaning is that the Word existed in the closest possible fellowship with the Father, and that he took supreme delight in this communion. (Cf. I John 1:2.) So deeply had this former joy impressed itself upon the Logos that it was

---

[17] Cf. R. Harris, *The Origin of the Prologue to St. John's Gospel*, Cambridge, 1917, esp. p. 6; W. F. Albright, *From Stone Age to Christianity*, Baltimore, 1940, p. 285; W. F. Howard, *op. cit.*, p. 47; W. P. Phythian-Adams, "The Logos Doctrine of the Fourth Gospel," *CQR*, 139(1944) 1-23.

[18] The New Testament contains more than 600 examples of πρός with the accusative. It indicates motion or direction toward a place, or as here, close proximity; hence, friendship, intimacy, in this context.

never erased from his consciousness, as is also evident from the high-priestly prayer:

"And now, Father, glorify thou me with thine own self or: in thine own presence, with the glory which I had with thee before the world existed."

Thus, the incarnation begins to stand out more clearly as a deed of incomprehensible love and infinite condescension.

And the Word was God. In order to place all the emphasis on Christ's full deity the predicate in the original precedes the subject. (χαι θεός ἦν ὁ λόγος). Over against every heretic it must be made plain that this Word was fully divine.

2. He himself was in the beginning face to face with God. This fully divine Word, existing from all eternity as a distinct Person, was enjoying loving fellowship with the Father. Thus, the full deity of Christ, his eternity, and his distinct personal existence are confessed once more, in order that heretics may be refuted and the Church may be established in the faith and love of God.

3. All things came into being through him, and apart from him not a single thing that exists came into being. All things, one by one, came into being through this divine Word. Thus, the great truth that Christ created all things (for in the external works all three Persons cooperate) is first of all stated positively and from the viewpoint of the past. Stated negatively and from the viewpoint of the present, it is expressed thus: "Apart from him not a single thing that exists came into being."

Two facts are here stressed: a. that the Christ himself was not created; he *was* eternally (in order to convey that thought the imperfect tense is used four times in verses 1 and 2); and b. that all things (viewed distributively, one by one without any exception) were created by him (here the aorist tense is used).

4. In him was life. Not *through* but *in*, just as in 5:26; 6:48, 53; 11:25. The clause "in him was life" means that *from all eternity and throughout the entire old dispensation* life resided in the Word. Hence, the best reading has *was*, not *is*.

But what is meant by the term *life*, as used here? Does it refer directly to every kind of life, physical as well as spiritual, the life of the butterfly as well as that of the archangel?

Physical life, however, does not reside in the second person of the Trinity. God is not physical in any sense (cf. 4:24). Besides, it is a good rule in exegesis to see whether a term is explained when one reads on and on. When that rule is applied in this case, the result is as follows:

The *life* is characterized as the *light* of men (1:4b). This *light* shines in the darkness and is not appropriated by sinful men (1:5). With reference to this light, the Baptist bears testimony (verses 6, 7). The latter was not the original and perfect light, in whose radiance all other lights seem dim, but he came to bear testimony with respect to the light (verses 8, 9). This light is now identified with the One who is rejected by the world but accepted by God's children (verses 10-13).

From this context it is clear that the terms *life* and *light* belong to the spiritual sphere. Moreover, both in the Fourth Gospel and in the First Epistle the term *life* (ζωή) always (54 times) moves in that realm. At times it is interchanged with the expression "everlasting life" (5:24). When one really possesses this life, he experiences close fellowship with God in Christ (17:3). The meaning is similar in the book of Revelation (book of life, water of life, tree of life, crown of life).

From all this it would seem to be evident that basically the term refers to the fulness of God's essence, his glorious attributes: holiness, truth (knowledge, wisdom, veracity), love, omnipotence, sovereignty. This full, blessed life of God is said to have been present in the Word, and this from all eternity and throughout the entire old dispensation: "In him was life."

But although this *life* as such is wholly spiritual, and nothing of a physical nature pertains to it, nevertheless, it is the cause, source, or principle of *all* life, physical as well as spiritual.[19] The universe owes its existence to it: "All things came into being through him and apart from him not a single thing that exists came into being" (verse 3); hence, so does also mankind (verse 10). It is true, of course, that this light is also the source of general revelation. Nevertheless, the present context does not specifically make mention of this idea. It is implied, of course, but it is not expressed. Here, in the present context (John's Prologue) the life of God in Christ, to which all things and all men owe their existence (creation and preservation), is represented as the source of men's illumination regarding *spiritual* matters and of the everlasting salvation of God's children. What we have here is a *Gospel*-context. Hence, we read:

And that life was the light of men. When life is *manifested,* it is called *light,* for it is characteristic of light to shine forth. Since the fall, which is implied already here in the last clause of verse 4, that light was proclaimed to men. Mankind was characterized by darkness, evil, and hatred, which are the antonyms of light. To them (especially to Israel; see the explanation of verses 10, 11) throughout the old dispensation *the truth and the love* of God in Christ were proclaimed. Truth and love are the synonyms of light. (For both antonyms and synonyms see 3:19-21; I John 2:8-10.) Of course, one should not limit the meaning of the term *light* to just these two attri-

[19] Cf. E. Smilde, *Leven In De Johanneische Geschriften,* a doctoral dissertation submitted to the Free University at Amsterdam, Kampen, 1943; especially pp. 11-15, and the first of the 20 theses or propositions.

butes (truth and love); rather, they represent all God's attributes. In the work of salvation all the divine attributes were displayed. They were proclaimed to sinful men.

5. And the light shines in the darkness. Cf. verse 9: the light *illumines* every man. Note the change from the imperfect to the present tense: not only *was* the light shining throughout the old dispensation; it *is* shining still, for it is the very characteristic of light to shine. Moreover, whereas the Word (Christ) is the One *in* whom the *life* resides and *by* whom it is made to shine forth as *light*, he is also himself called *the light*. (Cf. 1:9; 8:12; I John 2:8.) Like the sun in the sky this light shines forth in the mother-promise (Gen. 3:15), in the book of Exodus with its Passover Lamb and all the other types, in Leviticus with its offerings that point forward to the shedding of Christ's blood, in Numbers with its serpent lifted up (Num. 21:8; cf. John 3:14, 15), yea, in all the historical, prophetical, and poetical books of the old dispensation. See, for example, Gen. 49:10; Deut. 18:15-18; II Sam. 7:12-14; Ps. 40:6, 7; 72; 110; 118; Isa. 1:18; 7:14; 9:6; 11:1 ff; 35:5; 40; 42:1-4; 53; 54; 55; 60; 61; 63; 65; Hos. 11:8; Am. 5:4; Mic. 5:2; 7:18; Hag. 2:9; Zech. 9:9; 13:1; Mal. 1:11. We emphasize, however, that not only in these prophecies, promises, and invitations, is the light shining; rather, throughout the entire old dispensation and in the whole Old Testament it shines; also throughout the entire new dispensation and in the whole New Testament, revealing God in all his glorious attributes. That light is shining even today in the midst of this world's darkness.

The sad response to this communication of the light is stated in the second part of verse 5: **But [20] the darkness did not appropriate it.**

The darkness to which the evangelist refers has a concrete meaning. It refers to fallen mankind, darkened by sin and unbelief. This is not the only case in the New Testament in which an abstract noun acquires a concrete meaning. For other examples see Rom. 11:7 ("the election," meaning *the elect remnant*), Rom. 3:30 ("the circumcision," signifying *the circumcized individuals*). This *darkness* is synonymous with "the world" of verse 10. It is the antagonist of Christ, the light. It is an active, personal darkness: *it did not accept or appropriate* the light.

A translation that is gaining favor takes οὐ κατέλαβεν to mean *did not overcome, did not overpower, did not put out or extinguish.* We believe that this is wrong. Whereas in form the three clauses of verses 5b, 10b, and

---

[20] The fact that καί especially in the Fourth Gospel frequently has the meaning *but* or *and yet* is clear from such passages as 7:19; 16:32; 20:29. Cf. also Matt. 7:23; Mark 4:16, 17; Luke 10:24; 13:17. B.D.B., commenting on *waw*, the Hebrew conjunction which is translated καί, states that it connects contrasted ideas, where in our idiom the contrast would be expressed explicitly by the word *but*. See Gen. 2:17; and for similar usage in Aramaic, see Dan. 2:6; 3:6, 18; 4:4.

11b are very similar, it would seem probable that they are also similar in meaning. We have here a striking illustration of parallelism:

"the darkness αὐτὸ οὐ κατέλαβεν (verse 5b);

"the world *did not acknowledge* him (verse 10b);

"his own *did not welcome* him" (verse 11b).

It is immediately evident that the rendering "did not overpower" (for verse 5b) does not fit into this parallelism. The translation *did not appropriate* (or *did not apprehend,* as in the A.R.V.) is much better. Besides, the usual and also the radical signification of the verb is *to seize, to take* (sometimes in the sense of *to overtake,* 6:17; 12:35), *to apprehend, to take possession of, to lay hold on.* It can also be used of mental apprehension or perception (see Rom. 9:30; I Cor. 9:24; Phil. 3:12).

But even when we correctly translate: *but the darkness did not appropriate it,* the fact must be stressed that we are dealing here with a figure of speech called *litotes.* From passages such as 3:20 (cf. Eph. 6:12) it is evident that this darkness does not merely behave negatively; on the contrary, it *hates* the light. It refers to the world of mankind viewed as a hostile power, which actively resists the light and refuses to accept it. What we have here is a manifestation of the absolute antithesis between light and darkness, kingdom of God and the world, Christ and the forces of the evil one.

Synthesis of 1:1-5

See the Outline on p. 68. *The glory of the Son (or Word):*

a. *In the beginning.* When the universe was created, he already existed; he is from everlasting.[21] He enjoyed an eternity of infinitely close communion with his Father, rejoicing always before him. He was himself God.

b. *At the creation.* All things, one by one, came into being through him. Of all that exists today there is nothing that originated apart from him. In him *from eternity and also*

c. *After the fall,* throughout the entire old dispensation, the full, rich life of God resided. Throughout that same old dispensation that life was made manifest: God's glorious attributes, exhibited in the work of salvation, were proclaimed to mankind. *Life which is made manifest is called light.* Thus, the life was the light of men. But the light is shining still, also during the new dispensation: it is the very nature of light to shine. However, the world did not appropriate the light: it steadfastly refused and actively opposed the message of God's truth and love. It hated the Christ *in* whom the life of God resided and *from* whom as light it shines forth to those in darkness.

---

[21] On the doctrine of the real pre-existence of the Logos see S.BK., p. 353.

6 There came a man named John, commissioned by God. 7 He came for the purpose of testifying, to [22] testify concerning the light, in order that everyone through him might come to believe. 8 He was not the light; he came in order that he might testify concerning the light.

9 The true light, which illumines every man, was in the act of coming into the world: [23] 10 In the world he was, and the world came into being through him, but the world did not acknowledge him. 11 To his own home he came, but his own people did not welcome him. 12 But as many as did accept him, to them he gave the right to become God's children, to those who trust in his name; 13 who were born not of blood nor of the will of the flesh nor of the will of man, but of God.

1:6-13

1:6. There came a man named John, commissioned by God. The Baptist is introduced as an example of the constant shining of the light. From this reference to the herald of the Lord it is again clearly evident that the author is discussing the light (not here explicitly of reason or of conscience but) of God's truth and love as concentrated in Jesus Christ; in other words, he is speaking about the light of salvation. John, whose name means "Jehovah has been gracious," had been sent (ἀπεσταλμένος perfect passive participle, indicating abiding result; from ἀποστέλλω) from — or commissioned by — God. The purpose for which he had been commissioned is stated in verses 7 and 8:

7, 8. He came for the purpose of testifying, that he might testify concerning the light, in order that everyone through him might come to believe. He was not the light; he came that he might testify concerning the light.

The exact nature of the work of the Baptist was in need of clarification, for the reason which has been stated above, under Readers and Purpose. It is as if the evangelist wishes to say: the Baptist never claimed for himself what certain heretics are claiming for him today. He definitely was

---

[22] On ἵνα, see pp. 46, 47.

[23] A good argument can be presented for the translation: "There was the true light — even the light which illumines every man — coming into the world." (Cf. A.R.V.) The difference in meaning between the translation to which the A.R.V. gives the preference and the one given above is negligible. According to the latter (similarly, Berkeley Version, Williams, and R.S.V.) ἐρχόμενον may be regarded as a complementary participle, combining with ἦν to form an imperfect periphrastic. This yields a smooth and unambiguous English sentence. The only objection to this would be that the participle is rather far removed from the verb. But John often employs the periphrastic construction, just as one would expect, for the writer of this Gospel is an Aramaic-speaking Jew. Often words intervene between ἦν and the participle. In this instance, however, an entire clause would intervene. Hence, the choice between the two suggested translations is about even. See also E. A. Abbott, *Johannine Grammar*, London, 1906, pp. 220 and 367.

not the light! He was the witness (verse 8). A careful examination of verses 6, 7, and 8, in comparison with verses 1, 2, 9, reveals the following contrasts between Christ and John:

Christ	John
a. *was* (ἦν) from all eternity;	a. *came* (ἐγένετο);
b. is *the Word* (ὁ λόγος);	b. is a mere *man* (ἄνθρωπος);
c. is himself God;	c. is commissioned by God;
d. is the real light;	d. came to testify concerning the real light;
e. is the *object* of trust.	e. is the *agent* through whose testimony men come to trust in the real light, even Christ.

He (the Baptist) **came** (εἰς μαρτυρίαν): for testimony; i.e., for the purpose of testifying. The term *testimony* is almost confined to the writings of John. It occurs in the Fourth Gospel, in John's epistles, and also in the book of Revelation. See the following passages: 1:7, 19; 3:11, 32, 33; 5:31, 32, 34, 36; 8:13, 17; 19:35; I John 5:9, 10; III John 12; Rev. 1:2, 9; 6:9; 11:7; 12:11, 17; 19:10, 20:4. It is probable that the words *testimony* and *testify* are here used in their primary sense; namely, *(to give) competent testimony concerning that which one has himself seen, heard, or experienced.* This follows from what is stated in 1:29, 32, 34. The clause (verse 7) *that he might testify* repeated for the sake of emphasis in verse 8 explains the preceding, "for testimony."

The purpose of the Baptist's testimony was that *through him* (δι᾽ αὐτοῦ) *everyone might come to believe* (πάντες πιστεύσωσιν). In the original, however, the order of the words is reversed: in order that everyone might come to believe through him. The question has, therefore, arisen: Does *through him* mean *through Christ* or *through John* (the Baptist)? We choose the latter, for the following reasons:

a. Nowhere else does the evangelist use the expression *believe through him* as meaning *believe through Jesus.* Jesus is always represented as *the object* (not as the agent) of faith (cf. 3:16).

b. The subject of verse 7 is John the Baptist, and this is also the subject of verse 8. It is natural to construe the pronoun *he* (ἐκεῖνος) of verse 8, which certainly refers to the Baptist, as referring back to the pronoun *him* (in the phrase *through him*) of verse 7.

That through him everyone *might come to believe* (πιστεύσωσιν first aorist active subjunctive, ingressive). While the noun *faith* (πίστις) is not found at all in the Fourth Gospel, and only once in John's epistles (I John 5:4), the verb *to believe* occurs nearly one hundred times in his Gospel and nine times in his First Epistle, *many times as often as in the Synoptics.* Nevertheless, also in the Synoptics Christ is definitely represented as the object of faith (Matt. 18:6). Synonymous expressions are used at times; such as, *to come to* Jesus, *to receive* or *to confess* him (Matt. 10:32, 40; 11:28). Moreover, how is it ever possible to give meaning to passages like Matt. 7:22, 23; 25:31 ff. without accepting the fact that Christ viewed himself as the legitimate object of faith and trust, so that unwillingness to accept him meant everlasting punishment? Paul, too, proclaims the necessity of faith in the Person of Christ and in his atonement (Rom. 3:22, 25; Gal. 2:16, 20; 3:22, 26; Eph. 1:5; Phil. 3:9; Col. 1:4; 2:5; etc.).

The Baptist's intention was that all those who heard his testimony might embrace Christ by a living faith. On Christ as *light* see under verses 4 and 5; also under verse 9. Christ is *the* light; the Baptist is a reflector. The latter is light in a derived sense. Thus only can he be called *a burning and shining lamp* (5:35). John testifies concerning the Christ like the moon testifies concerning the sun.

9. The true light, which illumines every man, was in the act of coming into the world.

Christ is here called *the true light* (for the reason, see under verse 5). The word which has been translated *true* is ἀληθινός, which means real, ideal, genuine. The Word is the perfect light in whose radiance all other lights seem dim.

This light *illumines every man.* Among the many interpretations which have been given and must be considered are the following:

a. Christ, who is the light, actually grants spiritual illumination, in the highest and fullest sense of the term, to every human being dwelling on earth, without any exception.

b. He grants this spiritual illumination, which renews both heart and mind, to every covenant-child (whether elect or not). Some lose it again.

c. He grants this supreme blessing to every man who is saved; in the sense that not one of the saved receives his illumination from any other source.

d. He bestows upon every human individual, without exception, the light of reason and conscience.

e. He illumines every man who hears the Gospel; i.e., he imparts a degree of understanding concerning spiritual matters (not necessarily resulting in salvation) to all those whose ears and minds are reached by the message of salvation. The majority, however, do not respond favorably. Many who have the light prefer the darkness. Some, however, due entirely to the sovereign, saving grace of God, receive the word with the proper attitude of heart and mind, and obtain everlasting life.

Interpretation a. and b. can be rejected at once. The Fourth Gospel teaches a limited atonement. Not every one is saved, but those who are saved remain saved (10:28). Although d. is favored by eminent conservative exegetes and proclaims an element of truth that must not be denied, we do not believe that in this context — or anywhere in the Fourth Gospel where the term *light* (φῶς) is used — the reference is specifically to the light of reason and conscience.[24] We accept the position that the light of which John speaks is *the life of God in Christ — and therefore Christ himself — made manifest to the world by the preaching of the Gospel.* (See reasons for this position under verse 4.)

As we see it, the only defensible views are c. and e. And of these two we prefer the latter, for the following reasons: *First,* this explanation is in harmony with the *succeeding* context. Note that also verses 10, 11, and 12 refer to a wider and a more restricted circle in which the Gospel operates. In each case it is the same glorious Gospel of salvation, but though "many are called, few are chosen." Thus, in verse 10 we see Christ standing in the midst of mankind which, however, did not acknowledge him, and in verse 11 he is represented as having come to his own home, but his own people did not welcome him. There are, however, exceptions, as verse 12 indicates: some accept him.

Secondly, this explanation is also in harmony with the *preceding* context; see verses 4b and 5: ". . . and that life was the light of men. And the light shines in the darkness, but the darkness did not appropriate it." See our explanation of that passage.

Thirdly, this interpretation accords well with similar passages in the same Gospel. An author should be allowed to explain his own phraseology. We have such an explanation in 3:19 and in 12:46: "And this is the judgment, that the light is come into the world, but men loved the darkness rather than the light; for their works were evil" (3:19), and "I am come a light into the world, that whosoever believes on me may not abide in the darkness" (12:46; cf. 12:35a, 36).

Fourthly, this view is entirely in harmony with Heb. 6:4-8 where the same verb *illumine* (φωτίζω) is used as here in 1:9. In the Fourth Gospel this verb occurs nowhere else. In the rest of the New Testament it is used both intransitively (to shine, give light, as in Rev. 22:5) and transitively. The latter means either: *to bring to light* (I Cor. 4:5; II Tim. 1:10) or *to illumine, enlighten.* In Eph. 1:18 this illumination concerns the eyes of the heart and is given to believers. But in Heb. 6:4 it is said to have been given to those who subsequently "fell away" and could not be renewed to repentance. Accordingly, Heb. 6:4 clearly teaches that there is an illumination which does not necessarily lead to salvation.

Concerning the source whence this illumination proceeds — namely,

---

[24] On this see especially the article by W. J. Phythian-Adams, *CQR,* 139(1944), 1-23.

Christ, the light — we read: The true light . . . was in the act of coming into the world. The phrase *coming into the world* (ἐρχόμενον εἰς τὸν κόσμον) must not be understood as modifying *every man* (πάντα ἄνθρωπον), as the A. V. renders it. The Gospel of John does not contain any undisputed passage in which the expression *coming into the world* refers to the birth of an ordinary human being. On the other hand, it is customary for the apostle to speak of *Christ* as the One who *came into the world:* [25] 3:19; 9:39; 11:27; 12:46; 16:28; and 18:37. Also note that in verse 10 the subject is still the Christ. When the Baptist testified concerning the true light, the latter was on the point of *entering upon his public ministry.* He was in the act of coming into the world, the theatre of human history, the realm of mankind.

10, 11. In the world he was, and the world came into being through him, but the world did not acknowledge him. To his own he came but his own people did not welcome him.

In verse 10 the evangelist summarizes the entire presence of Christ in the world. In a note we point out the various uses of the term *world* (κόσμος) in the Gospel of John.[26] Here (1:10, 11) it indicates the realm of mankind

---

[25] Cf. J. Sickenberger, *"Das in die Welt Kommende Licht,"* *ThG,* 33(1941) 129-134.
[26] Lexicons do not give a complete summary of the uses of the term *world* (κόσμος) in the Gospel of John. The root-meaning (Homer, Plato) is *order,* whence *ornament,* as in I Peter 3:3. This leads to the following significations, as found in the Fourth Gospel:

(1) the (orderly) universe, 17:5; perhaps, the earth, 21:25.

(2) by metonymy, the human inhabitants of the earth; hence, mankind, realm of mankind, human race, theatre of human history, framework of human society. 16:21.

(3) the general public, 7:4; perhaps also 14:22.

(4) ethical sense: mankind alienated from the life of God, sin-laden, exposed to the judgment, in the need of salvation, 3:19.

(5) the same as (4) with the additional idea that no distinction is made with respect to race or nationality; hence, men from every tribe and nation; not only Jews but also Gentiles, 4:42 and probably also 1:29; 3:16, 17; 6:33, 51; 8:12; 9:5; 12:46; I John: 2:2; 4:14, 15. Such passages should be read in the light of 4:42; 11:52; and 12:32. Whereas at least in some of these passages meaning (5) is clear, it seems strange that standard lexicons have apparently missed it entirely. This applies even to the excellent article in Th.W.N.T. Also meaning (3) is often ignored.

(6) the realm of evil. This is really the same as (4) but with the additional idea of open hostility to God, his Christ, and his people 7:7; 8:23; 12:31; 14:30; 15:18; 17:9, 14.

No attempt has been made to classify all the passages in which the term occurs. Besides, the transitions from one meaning into another [especially (4) into (6)] are sometimes very delicate. In each case the context will have to decide. Meaning (5), however, should no longer be ignored.

See also W. Griffen Henderson, "The Ethical Idea of the World in John's Gospel" (unpublished Ph.D. dissertation submitted to the faculty of Southern Baptist Theological Seminary, Louisville, Kentucky, 1945).

which, though created by the Word, became alienated from the life of God. That κόσμος does not here refer to birds and trees is evident from the clause: *but the world did not acknowledge him.*

The clause *and the world came into being through him* is added to show that the world should have acknowledged Christ, the light. (Cf. verse 3.) A pathetic fact is now recorded: *but the world did not acknowledge him.* The verb ἔγνω is constative aorist. As is clear from Matt. 7:23 the verb γινώσκω means not only to know, to come to know, to recognize, to perceive, to understand, but also *to acknowledge* as one's own. So also here: the fact that more than mere intellectual recognition is intended is evident also from the parallelism in verses 5 and 11.

The *world* to which Christ, the light, came, is represented by Israel, which was like a small circle inside a larger circle; as if John were saying, "He was in the world, and the world came into being through him, and yet the world did not acknowledge him; *specifically,* he came to his own home,[27] and yet his own people did not welcome him." [28]

Israel was in a very special sense God's own possession (Ex. 19:5; Deut. 7:6). During the entire old dispensation and also at the beginning of the new dispensation Christ came to his own home. Yet his own people gave him no reception. For the meaning of the verb παραλαμβάνω see 14:3. Isa. 1:2, 3 is the best commentary on the tragedy that is here recorded:

"Hear, O heavens, and give ear, O earth; for Jehovah has spoken. I have nourished and brought up children, but they have rebelled against me. The ox knows his owner, and the ass his master's crib; Israel does not know, my people does not consider."

As has been pointed out (see under verse 5), the clauses "did not appropriate," "did not acknowledge," and "did not welcome," are instances of *litotes.* They indicate that the world — particularly, the Jews, which represented it — utterly disowned the Christ. All rejected him; all, with the exception of those to whom reference is made in verses 12 and 13:

12. But as many as did accept him, to them he gave the right to become God's children, to those who trust in his name.

Note: *as many as . . . to them,* which is a common Aramaic idiom. (See p. 64.) While the world and its representative, the Jewish people, rejected the Savior, individuals accepted him. But these persons receive the greatest spiritual benefit without respect to nationality or physical descent. The expression "as many as" amounts to "whosoever" whether Jew or Gentile.

---

[27] Literally τὰ ἴδια: to his own things. It is the very expression which is used with respect to the action of John, when he took Mary, the mother of Jesus, "to his own home." οἱ ἴδιοι means: those of his own home; cf. 13:1.
[28] Cf. F. W. Grosheide, *op. cit.*, p. 82: "Want we zullen telkens zien dat het ongelovige Israel staat voor dien gevallen κόσμος."

The Jew was very slow to learn that in the new dispensation there are no special privileges based upon physical relationships. And the evangelist is keenly aware of this Jewish trait, as he indicates again and again in his book. It is, therefore, not at all strange that John dwells on this great truth and develops it in some detail in verse 14.

As many as did accept him; i.e., as many as appropriated, acknowledged, and welcomed the light (see verses 5, 10, 11), as many as continue to embrace him by a living faith in his *name* (i.e., in his self-revelation in the sphere of redemption), to them he *gave* — it is ever a gift of God's sovereign grace — *the right,* (cf. 5:27; 10:18; 19:10, 11; the authority, cf. 17:2) to become children of God.

Did the Jews boast about their hereditary rights, and did they *call themselves* the children of Abraham? Believers receive the right *actually to become* children (a typically Johannine comparison, I John 3:1); to become children *not of Abraham only but of God.*

But how is it to be understood that believers *become* children of God? Is it not true that they *are* children of God as soon as (and in a sense even *before*) they consciously accept Christ? We do not believe that the solution of this problem lies in interpreting the sentence as if it should be read: "But as many as did accept him, to them he had previously given the right to become God's children, for otherwise they could not have accepted him." The two aorists (ἔλαβον and ἔδωκεν) are simultaneous: when one accepts Christ, he at that self-same moment receives the right to become a child of God. Nor is the answer found by weakening the sense of the verb *to become* (γενέσθαι), as if it meant no more than *to be called* (or to represent oneself as) a child of God.

As we see it, in order to arrive at a correct interpretation of this clause, we should bear in mind the connotation which John attaches to the term *God's children.* Neither in the Gospel nor in the epistles does this evangelist ever employ the term υἱοί in referring to believers. One becomes a υἱός by adoption, but a τέκνον by regeneration and transformation. Paul uses both terms in describing believers as children of God. The noun which John uses for this purpose comes from τίκτω, to beget. To him salvation is the impartation of life, the being begotten of God, so that one becomes his *child* (I John 2:29; 3:9). By means of being thus begotten of God one is transformed into the likeness of God. And inasmuch as God is *love,* hence, being begotten of God is manifested in loving the brethren (I John 4:7, 8). John, accordingly, dwells at length on love as the mark of the Christian: love is light, but hatred is darkness, and one who hates walks in darkness (I John 2:10, 11). The love that is required of us is of the self-sacrificing kind (I John 3:16).

But this transformation, though beginning with an instantaneous act of God, is, nevertheless, a gradual process. In principle, one becomes a child of God at the very moment when the life from above enters the soul. Even now we are the children of God. The highest realization of this ideal is, however, reserved for the future when, freed from every impurity, the life of God — his holiness and love — shall have become completely manifest in us. If this be understood, it becomes clear why John can say here in 1:13: "to them he gave the right *to become* God's children."

This explanation would seem to be in harmony with John's own teaching. Cf. I John 3:2: "Beloved, now are we the children of God, and it is not yet made manifest what we shall be, but we know that when he is made manifest, we shall be like him; for we shall see him even as he is. And everyone who thus hopes in him purifies himself, even as he is pure." (Cf. also II Cor. 3:18; Gal. 4:19; and II Peter 1:4.)

13. The clause **who were born not of blood nor of the will of the flesh nor of the will of man, but of God** has led to much controversy. Able commentators, both liberal and conservative,[29] following the example of Ireneus, prefer to read: "to him who was born" (instead of "to those who were born"), so that verse 14 would refer to Christ's virgin birth (Ireneus, *Against Heresies,* III, xvi, 2; xix, 2). Some are even willing to accept the theory of Tertullian, that "who were born" is an invention of the Valentinian Gnostics (Tertullian, *On The Flesh of Christ,* XIX). But all the old Greek uncials have the plural. Moreover, the clause is a very fitting explanation of the words "as many as . . . to them" of verse 12. The evangelist teaches that God's true children do not owe their origin to *blood* [30] (physical descent; for example, from Abraham), nor to *the will of the flesh* (carnal desire, the sexual impulse of man or woman), nor to *the will of man* (the procreative urge of the male) but to God alone. Note the climactic arrangement of the three expressions. All three emphasize that in no sense whatever do believers derive their birth or standing from physical or biological causes. Nicodemus needed that lesson; so did most of the Jews, as is very clear from the following passages: 3:6; 8:31-59; Luke 3:8; Gal. 3:11, 28.[31]

---

[29] C. C. Torrey, *Our Translated Gospels,* New York and London, 1936, pp. 151, 152; R. C. H. Lenski, *The Interpretation of St. John's Gospel,* Columbus, Ohio, 1931, pp. 62-68. G. Vos, *The Self-Disclosure of Jesus,* New York, 1926, p. 213, considers the argument for the singular to be strong.

[30] The original has the plural: *bloods.* Various explanations are offered to explain this plural; such as, the blood of two parents, the blood of many distinguished ancestors, etc. One might also ask why the English idiom requires the plural *ashes* where the Dutch has the singular. It depends on how one conceives of an object. Hence, some commentaries suggest that the plural *bloods* may have arisen from the many *drops* of blood which enter into its composition.

[31] See John Calvin, Ioannis Calvini in Evangelium Ioannis Commentarii, Berolini (apud Guilelmum Thome), 1553; vol. III, p. 10: Quod oblique hic parvam Iudaeorum confidentiam perstringi quidam putant, libenter amplector. Habebant illi semper in ore generis sui dignitatem, quasi ex sancta progenie orti, naturaliter sancti essent.

Synthesis of 1:6-13

See the Outline on p. 68. *The glory of the Son after the fall* (continued).
This section shows us that the true light, the object of faith, is far more glorious than John the Baptist. The latter had been commissioned by God to give competent testimony concerning the former. While the Baptist was testifying, the true light whose pure Gospel of salvation is proclaimed to all men, regardless of race or nationality, was at the point of entering upon his public ministry.

The evangelist, looking back, and summarizing the presence of the true light in the midst of this world's darkness, declares:

"In the world he was, and the world came into being through him, and yet the world did not acknowledge him. To his own home he came, but his own people did not welcome him."

However, there have always been exceptions: those who did accept him he qualified to become children of God; i.e., to become transformed more and more into God's image. Such people do not boast about physical ancestors, race, or nationality (as the Jews so often did), but recognize that they are the product of God's sovereign grace.

---

14 And the Word became flesh, and dwelt among us as in a tent, and we beheld his glory, a glory as of the only begotten from the Father, full of grace and truth. 15 John testifies concerning him, and he cried, saying: this was the One of whom I said: he who is coming behind me has gotten ahead of me, for he existed before me. 16 For out of his fulness we have all received grace upon grace. 17 For, while the law was given through Moses, grace and truth came through Jesus Christ. 18 God himself no one has ever seen. The only begotten God, who lies upon the Father's breast, it is he who has made him known.

1:14-18

1:14. The glory of the Word at the incarnation is the theme of 1:14-18. The fact recorded in verse 14 is *not later in time* than what has been described in the preceding verses. Rather, it is *greater in love*. The incarnation — and the realization of its purpose, the crucifixion — is the climax of God's condescending grace. This is clear from the context; note verses 10, 11: "In the world he was . . . but the world did not acknowledge him. To his own home he came, but his own people did not welcome him." And yet in the midst of *this ungrateful world* he manifested his supreme love. From the infinite sweep of eternal delight in the very presence of his Father, the Word was willing to descend into this realm of misery, to pitch his tent for a while among sinful men: "Veiled in flesh the godhead see."

83

And the Word became flesh. (See also I John 4:2; Rom. 1:3; 8:3; II Cor. 8:9; Gal. 4:4; Phil. 2:5-11; I Tim. 3:16; and Heb. 2:14. See on 1:1 for comments on "the Word.") The verb *became* has a very special meaning here. Not "became" in the sense of ceasing to be what he was before. When the wife of Lot *becomes* a pillar of salt, she ceases to be the wife of Lot. But when Lot *becomes* the father of Moab and Ammon, he remains Lot. So also here: the Word *becomes* flesh but remains the Word, even God (see verses 1, 18). The second Person of the Trinity assumes the human nature, without laying aside the divine. John everywhere insists — over against heretics (see p. 33)—that the divine and the human nature of Christ became fully united without being fused. The true human nature of Jesus is taught throughout this Gospel (4:6, 7; 6:53; 8:40; 11:33, 35; 12:27; 13:21; 19:28). The relation of the two natures to one another will forever remain a mystery, far above our comprehension; but a better formulation than that which is found in the Symbol of Chalcedon will probably never be found:

"We, then, following the holy Fathers, all with one consent, teach men to confess one and the same Son, our Lord Jesus Christ, the same perfect in Godhead and also perfect in manhood . . . to be acknowledged in two natures *inconfusedly, unchangeably, indivisibly, inseparably* (ἀσυγχύτως, ἀτρέπτως, ἀδιαιρέτως, ἀχωρίστως); the distinction of natures being by no means taken away by the union, but rather the property of each nature being preserved, and concurring in one Person and one Subsistence, not parted or divided into two persons, but one and the same Son, and only begotten, God the Word, the Lord Jesus Christ; as the prophets from the beginning have declared concerning him, and the Lord Jesus Christ himself has taught us, and the Creed of the holy fathers has handed down to us."

The term *flesh* (σάρξ) has various meanings in the New Testament.[32] In our passage it has reference to human nature, considered not as sinful (8:46), yet for a while with the curse due to sin resting upon it, so that until the ransom had been paid it is subject to weariness, pain, misery, death (4:6, 7; 11:33, 35; 12:27; 13:21; 19:30). It was that kind of "flesh" which the Word assumed in his incomprehensible, condescending love.

And dwelt among us as in a tent. These words (καὶ ἐσκήνωσιν ἐν ἡμῖν) must not be regarded as a mere repetition of that which immediately precedes ("and the Word became flesh"). The idea is rather that the eternal Word which assumed the human nature permanently — though not perma-

---

[32] In the Fourth Gospel the word σάρξ indicates the human nature, without ethical disparagement, 1:13, 14; the human nature regarded as the seat and vehicle of sinful desire; i.e., man as he is by nature, 3:6 (a usage common in Paul); the "flesh" (of Christ) in a mystical sense; i.e., his vicarious sacrifice which one should accept (eat) by faith, 6:51-56; man's external appearance, 8:15. The expression "all flesh" (17:2) is *all men,* a Semitism.

nently in its weakened condition — pitched his tent for a while among men, lived among them.

During that same period **we** — i.e., the evangelist and other eye-witnesses — **beheld his glory.** The verb *beheld* (ἐθεασάμεθα) indicates careful and deliberate vision which seeks to interpret its object. It refers, indeed, to physical sight; yet, it always includes a plus, the plus of calm scrutiny, contemplation, or even wonderment. It describes the act of one who does not *stare* absent-mindedly nor merely *look* quickly nor necessarily *perceive* comprehensively. On the contrary, this individual *regards* an object and *reflects* upon it. He *scans* it, *examining* it with care. He *studies* it, *viewing* and *considering* it thoughtfully (1:32; 4:35; 11:45; Acts 1:11).[33] Thus, while Jesus was walking among them, the eye and mind of the evangelist and of other witnesses had rested on the Incarnate Word, until to some extent they had penetrated the mystery; i.e., they had seen *his glory:* the radiance of his grace and the majesty of his truth manifested in all his works and words (cf. 2:11), the attributes of deity shining through the veil of his human nature.

A glory as of the only begotten from the Father, full of grace and truth. These words of verse 14 lend themselves to various interpretations.

The most natural meaning would seem to be that the glory which the eye-witnesses saw in Jesus was what could be expected with respect to One who is *the only begotten from the Father.* And this same Person — i.e. the only begotten from the Father — is full of grace and truth. The fact that the evangelist is actually thinking of the *fulness of Christ* is very clearly stated in verse 16: for *of his fulness* we all received grace upon grace. Thus, by reading on and on we arrive at the true meaning. We favor this interpretation for the following reasons:

(1) Jesus repeatedly declares that he came forth *from God* (παρὰ τοῦ θεοῦ). See 6:46; 7:29; 16:27; 17:8.

(2) Unless there are sufficient reasons to do otherwise — and, indeed, there sometimes are! — it is a good thing to link a phrase with the substantive that stands closest to it. Hence, we construe *from the Father* as a modifier of *the only begotten.* And for the same reason we consider the words *full of grace and truth* to modify *the only begotten from the Father.* (Cf. Acts

---

[33] Note the following synonyms which John uses:
ὁράω: no one *has seen* God (1:18).
βλέπω: the disciples *were looking* at each other (13:22).
'εμβλέπω: Jesus *looked upon him* (or *looked him over*) and said (1:42).
θεάομαι: we *beheld* his glory (1:14).
θεωρέω: many believed in his name, *observing* the signs which he was performing (2:23). Sir, I *perceive* that you are a prophet (4:19).
These verbs cannot always be distinguished so sharply. Each of them has at least one meaning which it shares with others, and in addition, a specific connotation.

6:3, 8; 7:55; 11:24.) As already pointed out, it is the fulness of this only begotten Son which receives further elaboration in verses 16 and 17, the context. (Objections against this interpretation are answered in a note.[34] Other explanations are discussed in another note.[35])

Accordingly, the glory on which John and others had fixed their adoring gaze is the proper and natural possession of the One whose name is *the only begotten from the Father*.

The question has often been asked: To what sonship does the term *the only begotten from the Father* refer? Is it the purely religious *sonship*, so that Jesus is here considered to have been a child of God in the same sense in which all believers are God's children? This can be dismissed at once, for in that case the modifier "only begotten" would have no meaning. Is it, then, *the Messianic sonship*? But even those who maintain that the word μονογενής has nothing to do with the verb γεννάω and merely signifies that Christ was the "only" Son (the only, μόνος, member of a kin, γένος from γίνομαι), and being the *only* one, was therefore the *beloved* one, will have

---

[34] One objection is that the expression *the only begotten from* (παρά) *the Father* would be unusual in John, who uses the preposition *out of* (ἐκ) whenever he wishes to say *begotten* of God (cf. I John 2:29; 3:9; 4:7; 5:1, 4, 18). This objection cannot be considered very serious: in Koine Greek these two prepositions are sometimes interchanged. Besides, it is possible to regard the phrase as being elliptical for "the only begotten *who is from* the Father" (for which see 6:46; 7:29) or "*who comes forth from* the Father" (for which see 16:27; 17:8). Moreover, it should not be immediately taken for granted that the verbal element in μονογενής is derived from γεννάω. (See p. 87.) Another objection which appears in older commentaries but has been robbed of its force by recent discovery is that πλήρης, being in the nominative case, cannot be construed as modifying a word (μονογενοῦς) that is in the genitive. Of course, the same objection would hold when πλήρης is considered a modifier of δόξαν, which is in the accusative. But any standard lexicon supplies the information that πλήρης is often indeclinable in the Koine.

[35] (1) glory as of *an* only-begotten from *a* father: i.e., glory such as an only-begotten son receives from a father, full (modifying glory) of grace and truth.

Those who accept this interpretation point to the fact that *only-begotten* and *father* are not preceded by the definite article. However, words of this type may be considered definite even when they are not preceded by the definite article. Besides, a father does not always and necessarily bestow glory upon an only (begotten) son.

(2) glory as of the only-begotten, from the Father, he (the only-begotten) being full of grace and truth. Here both *as of the only-begotten* and *from the Father* modify *glory*, but *full of grace and truth* modifies *the only-begotten*. Our main objection to this explanation is that it is unnatural: after having interpreted the first and the second phrases as modifiers of the noun *glory*, the mind does not easily return to the first phrase in order to hang a modifier on it!

(3) glory as of the only-begotten, from the Father, full of grace and truth. All three phrases are considered modifiers of glory. This construction is possible and would be our second choice. However, the concept "glory . . . full of grace and truth," though possible, is not easy. Besides, verse 16 speaks about the fulness of the only-begotten, not the fulness of his glory. Finally, the modifier *full of grace and truth* is rather far removed from the noun *glory*. It stands closer to the title: *the only-begotten from the Father*.

to admit that according to the context (see especially 1:1, 18) the sonship here indicated was present *from eternity;* hence, can have no reference to the Messianic office which was assumed in time. (On the question whether μονογενής should be connected with γίνομαι, to be born [Dutch: *Eenigge-boren* Zoon] or with γεννάω, to beget [English: *only begotten* Son] see G. Vos, *The Self-Disclosure of Jesus,* New York, 1926, pp. 218, 219.)

Is it, perhaps, *the nativistic sonship* that is discussed in this passage? If so, then the meaning would be that Christ's human nature is here ascribed to the supernatural paternity of God. But in that case the evangelist would be thinking of *one* kind of sonship here in verse 14 and of *another* in verse 18, which is not probable. (See under verse 18.)

We conclude that the reference must be to Christ's *trinitarian sonship,* i.e., to the fact that he is the Son of God from all eternity. This is favored by the context (1:1, 18) and by such passages as 3:16, 18, which prove that the Son *was already* the only begotten before his incarnation.

On this subject H. Bavinck states:

"But the name *Son of God* when ascribed to Christ has a far deeper meaning than the theocratic: he was not a mere king of Israel who in time became an adopted Son of God; neither was he called Son of God because of his supernatural birth, as the Socinians and Hofman held; neither is he Son of God merely in an ethical sense, as others suppose; neither did he receive the title Son of God as a new name in connection with his atoning work and resurrection, an interpretation in support of which John 10:34-36; Acts 13:32, 33; and Rom. 1:4 are cited; but he is Son of God in a metaphysical sense: by nature and from eternity. He is exalted high above angels and prophets, Matt. 13:32; 21:27; 22:2; and sustains a very special relation to God, Matt. 11:7. He is the beloved Son in whom the Father is well pleased, Matt. 3:17; 17:5; Mark 1:11; 9:7; Luke 3:22; 9:35; the only begotten Son, John 1:18; 3:16; I John 4:9 ff.; God's *own* Son, Rom. 8:32; the eternal Son, John 17:5, 24; Heb. 1:5; 5:5; to whom the Father gave to have life in himself, John 5:26; equal to the Father in knowledge, Matt. 11:27; in honor, John 5:23; in creative and redemptive power, John 1:3; 5:21, 27; in work, John 10:30; and in dominion, Matt. 11:27; Luke 10:22; 22:29; John 16:15; 17:10; and because of this Sonship he was condemned to death, John 10:33; Matt. 26:63 ff." (*The Doctrine of God,* Grand Rapids, Mich., 1951, p. 270).

Now, with reference to this *only begotten One* we read that he is *full of grace and truth. Of grace,* for when he spoke, his messages were filled with unmerited favor for the guilty (e.g., for publicans and sinners), and the same attributes were revealed in his miracles of healing, yea, in his entire life and death, considered as an atoning sacrifice whose very purpose was to merit for his people the grace of God. *Of truth,* for he himself was *the final reality* in contrast with the shadows that had preceded him. Great, indeed, was the glory of the only begotten!

15. John testifies concerning him, and he cried, saying: this was the One of whom I said: he who is coming behind me has gotten ahead of me, for he existed before me.

It follows, of course, that he outranks John the Baptist. The readers in Asia Minor needed this reminder. (See p. 32.) Between the two (Christ and the Baptist) there is a difference as between the Infinite and the finite, the eternal and the temporal, the original light of the sun and the reflected light of the moon. And this is exactly what the Baptist himself had confessed, as verse 15 indicates. Perhaps immediately after he had baptized Jesus and the latter had departed, John (i.e., the Baptist) had cried out — and the testimony was still resounding — : *"This was* [36] *the one of whom I said: he who is coming behind me has gotten ahead of me, for he was before me."* Upon life's pathway,[37] not only in his birth but also in his public ministry, Jesus had come behind John (Luke 1:36; Mark 1:4-9). Yet he who was behind had gotten ahead: the *rights* of seniority belong not to John but to Jesus (cf. Mark 1:7). He ranks far above the Baptist in power and glory. The reason for this was stated by the latter in these words: *he was before me:* he existed from eternity as the Word of God (contrast 1:1 with 1:6: the evangelist agrees with the Baptist).

16, 17. For out of his fulness we have all received grace upon grace. For, while the law was given through Moses, grace and truth came through Jesus Christ.

In these verses it is not the Baptist but the evangelist who is speaking. The thought of verse 14 is here continued. In that verse *the fulness* of Christ had been confessed. The author now substantiates this by adding that he and all other believers with him had experienced the blessed fruits of this fulness: they had received *grace upon grace* from that infinite plenitude. (For the various interpretations of this verse see my thesis "The Meaning of the Preposition ἀντί in the New Testament" in the libraries of Princeton Seminary, Princeton, N.J., and of Calvin Seminary, Grand Rapids, Mich.) The meaning of verse 16 is that believers are constantly receiving grace *in the place of* grace. One manifestation of the unmerited favor of

---

[36] The imperfect ἦν is in need of explanation. If when John made the statement, "This was the One . . . ," Jesus had just departed, the tense is very natural; just as today a person might enquire, "Who *was* that man with whom you were conversing?" The answer might be, "That *was* Mr. X." Another explanation makes ἦν extend backward indefinitely just like in verses 1 and 2.

[37] Basically the adverbs ὀπίσω and ᾽ἔμπροσθεν refer to place. One may think of a race-track or a pathway. But this pathway itself is a metaphor, being the pathway *of life.* Cf. C. Lindeboom, *GThT* 16(1916) 10.

God in Christ is hardly gone when another one arrives; hence, *grace upon grace*. From our thesis we quote the following:

"We agree with this very common interpretation for the following reasons:

(1) It is in harmony with the usual sense of the preposition ἀντί. That ἀντί indicates substitution has been fully proved in this thesis.

(2) It is in harmony with the context, which pictures *the fulness* which is in Christ, and out of which we have received χάριν ἀντὶ χάριτος. The interpretation which we favor does justice to the unity of the phrase, so that it is regarded as being in its entirety the object of the verb ἐλάβομεν. The concept *grace upon grace,* an incessant supply of grace, harmonizes better with the idea *from his fulness* than does the simple term *grace*. The limitless supply or reservoir indicated by the words *his fulness* would seem to suggest a limitless outflow: *grace upon grace*.

(3) This interpretation is also supported by a (linguistically) similar quotation from Philo: 'Wherefore God ever causes his earliest gifts to cease before their recipients are glutted and wax insolent; and storing them up for the future gives others *in their stead* (ἀντ' ἐκείνων), and a third supply *to replace the second* (ἀντὶ τῶν δευτέρων), and ever new *in place of earlier boons* (ἀντὶ παλαιοτέρων), sometimes different in kind, sometimes the same' (Philo, *The Posterity and Exile of Cain*, CXLV)."

In further corroboration of the thought of verse 14 — that the only begotten one is characterized by a fulness of grace and truth — we read: "For, while the law was given through Moses, grace and truth came through Jesus Christ."

There was nothing wrong with the law, moral and ceremonial. It had been given by God through Moses. It was preparatory in character. It revealed man's lost condition and it also foreshadowed his deliverance. But there were two things which the law as such did not supply: *grace* so that transgressors could be pardoned and helped in time of need, and *truth,* i.e., *the reality* to which all the types pointed (think of the sacrifices). Christ, by his atoning work, furnished both. He *merited* grace and he *fulfilled* the types. Note also that while the law "was given," grace and truth "came" through the Person and work of him, who is here for the first time in the Fourth Gospel, called by his full name *Jesus Christ*.

18. God himself no one has ever seen. The only begotten God, who lies upon the Father's breast, it is he who made him known.

Not only had the law been given through Moses, but the latter enjoyed the great privilege of speaking with God "face to face." Nevertheless, even Moses did not *see* God; i.e., *he did not get to know God in all his fulness* (cf. Ex. 33:18). For him as well as for all others the words of Job 11:7 remain true:

"Canst thou by searching find out God?
      Canst thou find out the Almighty *unto perfection?*
It is high as heaven; what canst thou do?
      Deeper than Sheol; what canst thou know?"

Cf. also Deut. 4:12; John 5:37; 6:46; I Tim. 1:17.

From 6:46 we can draw the inference that the idea of this verse is not: "No one has ever physically seen God, because God is spiritual and therefore invisible." Physical vision of God would have been impossible even for the Son. But the evangelist is thinking of a vision of God which is possible for the Son; for in the very similar passage 6:46 we read: "Not that any one has seen the Father, except he that is from God, *he has seen the Father.*"

Note also the word-order: *God himself* no one has ever seen. We do not see God himself but his revelation in Jesus Christ. (For the meaning of the verb ἑώρακεν both here and in 6:46, see explanation of 1:14, footnote 33.)

The reading *the only begotten God* (μονογενὴς θεός) instead of *the only begotten Son* is supported by the best and oldest manuscripts. Since the concept *God* implies eternity, it is evident that the expression *the only begotten God* must refer to Christ's trinitarian sonship. All other types of sonship imply a beginning in time, irreconcilable with the idea of deity. Besides, the added clause *who lies upon the Father's breast* indicates a relation of abiding closeness between the Father-God and the Son-God. Because Jesus Christ is the Son in the highest sense of the term, he knows the Father thoroughly. Therefore *it is he who made him known.* He alone is qualified to be the Interpreter or *Exegete* (the verb is ἐξηγήσατο) of God. This does not mean that he gives us an adequate knowledge of God, so that, after all, the finite would begin to grasp the Infinite; but that he expounds to us with reference to the being of God whatever is necessary for our complete salvation and for a relative knowledge of his work in creation and redemption, so that we may by means of them glorify our Maker and Redeemer.

Synthesis of 1:14-18

See our Outline on p. 68. *The glory of the Son at the incarnation.*

Verse 14 continues the line of thought begun in verses 10 and 11. Not only did the true light manifest itself to the world, not only did he come to his own home and people, but the climax of his love is indicated in this, that *the Word became flesh;* i.e., he assumed our human nature, weakened for a while by the results of sin, though in itself sinless. In this human nature he became the Immanuel, *and pitched his tent among us.* Hence, *our eyes and minds rested on his glory:* the radiance of his divine attributes shining through the veil of his human nature. This glory was the kind which one could reasonably expect to find in him, for it was *glory as of the only begotten who proceeds forever from the Father, and possesses a fulness of grace and truth.* It was, accordingly, the *glory of one who is far superior to John the Baptist,* as the latter himself openly acknowledged when he uttered those remarkable words: "This was the one of whom I said: he who came behind me (i.e., on life's pathway) has gotten ahead of me, for he existed before me." Our own experience as believers enables us to bear testimony with reference to this plenitude that is in Christ, *for out of his fulness we have all received grace upon grace,* like the waves that follow one another upon the seashore, one taking the place of another constantly. *The law, which was given through Moses, was unable to supply this fulness of grace and truth.* Though good in itself, it was unable to save. It made demands, but did not possess the pardoning and enabling grace needed by sinners who are confronted by these demands. It provided types and shadows (e.g., in its sacrifices) but never the reality (truth). *This grace and this truth came through Jesus Christ,* who by his redeeming life and death merited the grace and furnished the reality (truth) to which the types and shadows of the Mosaic law had been pointing.

And because he is fully divine, *being the only begotten God, who,* according to his divine nature, *rests forever on the Father's breast,* and knows him thoroughly, he alone is able to be the Father's Interpreter. Accordingly, *he made known to us the God whom no one else has ever seen (comprehended).*

For a synthesis of this synthesis read only the words in italics. They form a connected paragraph.

19 Now this is the testimony of John. When the Jews sent priests and Levites to him from Jerusalem in order to enquire of him, "Who are you?" 20 he confessed, and did not deny, but confessed,[38] "I am not the Christ." 21 And they asked him, "What then? Are you Elijah?" And he said, "I am not." "Are you the prophet?" And he answered, "No." 22 They said to him then, "Who are you, (tell us) in order that we may give an answer to those who sent us; what have you to say about yourself?" 23 He said, "I am the voice of one shouting in the desert, 'Make the road straight for the Lord,' as Isaiah the prophet said." 24 Now they had been sent from the Pharisees. 25 And they asked him, saying, "Then why are you baptizing if you are neither the Christ nor Elijah nor the prophet?"[39] 26 John answered them, saying, "I baptize with water. In the midst of y o u stands one whom y o u do not know, 27 my successor,[40] whose sandal-straps I am not worthy to [41] unloose." 28 These things took place in Bethany beyond the Jordan, where John was baptizing.

1:19-28

1:19-23. Now this is the testimony of John. . . .

In verses 6-8, 15 the evangelist has indicated the purpose of the ministry of John the Baptist; namely, to focus the attention of everyone upon the true light, Jesus Christ, as the object of faith. In the paragraph which we are now studying we receive a detailed account of the Baptist's testimony as given before a committee sent by the Sanhedrin. The two paragraphs which follow this one (1:29-34 and 1:35-42) contain a record of his testimony; respectively, before a group of people who are not identified, and before two of his disciples. In the light of the lofty descriptions of the Christ and the exalted titles given to him by the Baptist in 1:27, 29-36 it is easy to see why the evangelist has included *this* material in his book. Its inclusion is in harmony with his main purpose as stated in 20:30, 31. It is not the appearance of the Baptist, his manner of life, his preaching as such, the excitement which he created, or even his baptizing, that is emphasized by the author of the Fourth Gospel. He seems to take for granted that the readers are acquainted with all this from oral tradition and from the reading of the Synoptics. It is very specifically *the testimony of the Baptist with reference to Christ* that forms the theme of these paragraphs. And he points out that this testimony, in turn, rests upon divine revelation (1:31-34).

John the Baptist had made his first public appearance in the summer of the year 26 A. D. His austere mode of life, stern preaching, and emphasis upon the fact that even the sons of Abraham are in need of thorough repentance and spiritual cleansing (symbolized by baptism) caused a mighty stir among the people, so that "there went out unto him all the country of

---

[38] On ὅτι see p. 54, 56.
[39] This conditional sentence belongs to Group I B; see p. 40.
[40] Literally: *the one who is coming behind me;* cf. verses 15 and 30.
[41] On ἵνα see pp. 46, 48.

Judea and all they of Jerusalem; and they were baptized by him in the
river Jordan, confessing their sins" (Mark 1:5).

It would seem that the Baptist, beginning in the vicinity of the Dead Sea,
had gradually ascended the Jordan Valley until he had reached a little
place which in the best manuscripts is called Bethany (1:28). We are distinctly told that this Bethany was *beyond the Jordan,* not to be confused
with the place of identical name where Mary, Martha, and their brother
Lazarus lived. The latter was near Jerusalem.

Although the *exact* location of the Bethany mentioned in our paragraph
is not known, it would seem that those are not far wrong who look for it
just east of the Jordan, about thirteen miles below the Sea of Galilee and
about twenty miles south-east of Nazareth (H.B.A., p. 99; cf. A. Fahling,
The Life of Christ, St. Louis, Mo., 1936, p. 148). On many of the older
maps and also on Plate XIV of W.H.A.B., it is suggested that this Bethany
was located just north of the Dead Sea. However, the entire section, John
1:19-2:1, pleads against a location so far to the south. If it be assumed that
all the events recorded in the first chapter of John (i.e., 1:19-51) took place
near *Bethany beyond the Jordan,* an assumption which is probably correct,
then, if Bethany were situated so far to the south, it is very difficult to see
how Jesus and his disciples could have arrived in Cana of Galilee *on the
third day* (2:1) after these events. Traveling was very slow in those days.
It should also be borne in mind that all the disciples to whom reference
(either direct or indirect) is made in chapter 1 had their home in Galilee.
Peter, Andrew, and Philip were from Bethsaida; James and John, from
Capernaum; Nathanael, from Cana. Accordingly, the scene of the event
recorded in the paragraph which we are going to discuss (1:19-23) is in the
general vicinity of Galilee, but not in Galilee itself (see 1:28, 43).

It was during the last days of December of the year 26 or in the month
of January of the year 27 that Jesus had left Nazareth in order that he might
voluntarily take upon himself the great task assigned to him by the Father.
He had gone to Bethany beyond the Jordan, which, as we have seen, was
located not far away from his home. Here he had been baptized by John
(cf. Matt. 3:13-17; Mark 1:9-11; Luke 3:21, 22; for the story). From the
Jordan Valley Jesus had been led to the heights of the desert, to be tempted
by the devil. This temptation covers a period of more than forty days and
apparently immediately followed the baptism (Mark 1:12). It is probable
that from his victory in the temptation Jesus returned directly to the place
where John was baptizing. His arrival is recorded in 1:29. The event
described in our present paragraph (1:19-28) takes place one day earlier.

Accordingly, *the scene is just east of the Jordan, not far from the Sea of
Galilee, and the time is February (or early March) of the year 27.* The
evangelist tells us what happened during a period of four successive days

93

(see the definite time indications in 1:29, 35, 43) and *on the third day* after that (2:1).

When the Jews sent priests and Levites to him from Jerusalem. We learn that on the first of these four days the Jews sent a committee to investigate John. The term *Jews* in the Fourth Gospel. often carries a sinister connotation: the nation as represented by its religious leaders who were hostile to Jesus (7:1; 9:22; 18:12-14). In this case it was the Sanhedrin (consisting of highpriests, scribes, and elders) which sent the delegation. The reason, though not definitely stated, is easy to surmise. Reports concerning the new preacher and the excitement which he created had been coming in thick and fast. Probably rumor even suggested that he might be the Messiah. There was also his impressive method of urging repentance by uttering heavy threats upon the impenitent, and the fact that he baptized . . . Jews, just as if *they*, children of Abraham, still needed repentance and cleansing. Moreover, it had probably been reported to them that this new revivalist (?) had said certain very unfriendly things about Pharisees and Sadducees (Matt. 3:7). Surely, *an investigating committee* was in order. A false Messiah might do a great deal of damage. Was it not the duty of the venerable members of the Sanhedrin to expose false prophets and would-be Messiahs (cf. Deut. 18:20-22) and to guard the religious interests of Israel?

The committee consisted of *priests and Levites.* The actual questioning was probably done by the former. The latter were sent along to see that the company would have a safe arrival, and to quell any riot which might arise.

In order to enquire of him. Having reached the place of their destination and having found John, the first question of this official enquiry was, **Who are you?** i.e., What important personage do you claim to be? **He** (the Baptist), who had undoubtedly obtained some information concerning the rumors that were afloat, **confessed, and did not deny, but confessed** (let Baptist-glorifiers take note!) **I am not the Christ.** There followed the question, **What then? Are you Elijah?** Now, although John went forth in the spirit and power of Elijah (Luke 1:17), and was, therefore, called Elijah by Christ himself (Matt. 17:12), yet he was not literally Elijah, and it was the literal, personal forerunner Elijah whom the Jews expected, as the result of their erroneous interpretation of Mal. 4:5. Hence, John answers, **I am not.** This reply is immediately followed by the question, **Are you the prophet?** The reference is to Deut. 18:15-18. Some interpreted this passage as having reference to another forerunner of the Messiah; others, as pointing forward to the Messiah himself, which was correct (Acts 3:22; 7:37). The Baptist, accepting this correct explanation, and knowing that he himself was not the Messiah, answers, **No.**

They said to him then, Who are you, (tell us) in order that we may give an answer to those who sent us; what have you to say about yourself? He said, I am the voice of one shouting in the desert, Make the road straight for the Lord, as Isaiah the prophet said. This is a rather free quotation of Is. 40:3. Note that what is elsewhere said *about* John (Matt. 3:3; Mark 1:3; Luke 3:4) is here spoken *by* John himself. Moreover, his quotation from Isaiah serves a twofold purpose: it indicates who the Baptist is, being a reply to the question that had been asked; and it also amounts to an earnest invitation to repent. Every member of the committee — yea, and also every member of the Sanhedrin which will receive the report — must make the road straight so that the Lord may enter. The implied figure is that of a king who is about to visit a province of his realm, just as in Isaiah's prophecy Jehovah had promised to visit with new tokens of his grace those who are pictured as having returned from the Babylonian captivity. Surely, when a king is about to visit his people, the road must be prepared so that he may enter in state, without any difficulties or obstructions. Thus also, the Baptist wishes to say, the Jews, including the members of the investigating committee, should *make straight* the Lord's highway that leads into their hearts. Genuine sorrow for sin and a prayer for mercy and pardon are required; both of these, of course, considered as the product of God's sovereign grace. The Baptist is only *a voice*. Let them realize that the command to repent is issued by the One whom *the voice* represents!

24. Now they had been sent from the Pharisees. The verb ἀπεσταλμένοι ἦσαν is periphrastic past perfect of ἀποστέλλω. Various interpretations can be found in the commentaries. There are two which we reject:

a. That this verse indicates that it was the Pharisees who had sent the Sadducees (A. T. Robertson, *Word Pictures in the New Testament*, New York and London, 1932, vol. V, pp. 18, 21). But why would the Pharisees — who were not even the leading men in the Sanhedrin — *send* Sadducees, and that to enquire about a subject with respect to which the latter were rather ignorant? The Sadducees were the liberals of their day. They constituted the worldly party and busied themselves with the affairs of this present age. The idea that Pharisees, who favored strict adherence to the law and were deeply concerned with problems touching the coming of the Messiah, would actually send worldly-minded Sadducees (cf. Matt. 22:23 ff.) to investigate a possible false Messiah seems unreasonable. The preposition ἐκ surely does not need to indicate agency.

b. That a new paragraph begins here, and that verse 24 must be translated: "And some Pharisees had been commissioned" (R. C. H. Lenski, *op. cit.*, p. 11). According to this view, the Sadducees have completed their investigation. Now a new delegation begins to function.

Our objections to this view are as follows:

95

(1) If this were the case, we would expect to read, "And *also* some Pharisees had been commissioned."

(2) Verse 25 is clearly linked with verses 20-23. John has just confessed that he is neither the Messiah nor the forerunner whom the Jews expected. The question is now asked, "Then why are you baptizing; i.e., why do you perform the work which properly pertains to the Messiah or his special ambassador if you are neither the one nor the other?" It is evident, therefore, that what we have here is the report of a single enquiry conducted by a single delegation.

Accordingly, the best interpretation of verse 24 would seem to be this, that the committee, mentioned in verse 19, and consisting of priests and Levites, had been sent from (ἐκ) the Pharisees, in the sense that they *belonged to the party of the Pharisees.*[42] (For a rather similar use of ἐκ see 1:35, 40; Gal. 2:15; Phil. 3:5.) It has not been proved that every priest in the days of Christ's sojourn was a Sadducee. *These* (1:19), evidently, were not. Moreover, the fact here recorded explains a. why the investigation had been so thorough — Pharisees were very strict! b. why the Baptist had referred to the prophet Isaiah — Pharisees had a much higher regard for the prophets than did Sadducees, and c. why the examination is continued — religiously indifferent Sadducees would probably not have asked any further questions.

25-28. And they asked him, saying, Then why are you baptizing if you are neither the Christ nor Elijah nor the prophet? . . .

It was the *baptizing* rather than the preaching which vexed these priests as they questioned the son of a priest. Priests were supposed to know all about lustrations. They certainly knew that not just anybody was allowed to administer rites of purification. In the final analysis, was not the cleansing of the people a distinctly Messianic act, according to passages like Ezek. 36:25 and 37:23? Why, then, did John baptize if he were neither the Messiah nor the kind of forerunner whom they expected? It is clear from this question that they had not understood the meaning of the Baptist's reference to the herald (1:23). They were not looking for such a deeply spiritual forerunner.

John answered them, saying, I baptize with water. In the midst of y o u stands one whom y o u do not know, my successor, whose sandal-straps I am not worthy to unloose. By saying, *"I baptize with water,"* John points out that there is, after all, a vast difference between what *he* is doing and what the *Messiah* will do. All John can do is administer *the sign* (water); the Messiah — he alone — can bestow *the thing signified* (the cleansing power of the Holy Spirit). (Cf. Mark 1:8.) And that Messiah has actually

---

[42] Thus also F. W. Grosheide, *op. cit.,* p. 127.

arrived. *He is standing right in their very midst;* i.e., he belongs to their own generation and is at the point of beginning his public labors as John's successor. In fact he has already been baptized. Yet, they do not know him and seem not even to be concerned about him. In their eagerness to expose false Messiahs, they are ignoring the true Messiah. The latter, however, is so glorious that *the Baptist considers himself of no account in comparison with him.* In fact, John deems himself unworthy of performing even the humblest service for this Stranger of Galilee; such as kneeling down in front of him in order to unloose his sandal-straps and remove the sandals with a view to washing his feet.

For an explanation of verse 28 — **These things took place in Bethany beyond the Jordan, where John was baptizing** — see above, under verses 19-23.

Synthesis of 1:19-28

See the Outline on p. 68. *The Son of God revealing himself to ever-widening circles: to John the Baptist who testifies concerning him.*

In this section the reference to the testimony of the Baptist in the preceding verses (6-8, 15) is expanded. The place is Bethany beyond the Jordan, probably at a ford, not far from the Sea of Galilee. The time is February or early March of the year 27. What is here recorded takes place on the first of four successive days on which the evangelist comments. It was the day just before Jesus returned from the desert where he had been tempted. The Sanhedrin, having heard much about John and apparently alarmed about the possibility that this might be another false Messiah, sends a delegation having as its purpose to conduct an official enquiry. When questioned, the Baptist answers that he is neither the Messiah nor the forerunner whom the Jews expected (namely, Elijah in person) nor the prophet of Deut. 18:15-18. He identifies himself with *the voice shouting in the desert,* to which Is. 40:3 refers. Then how is it that he, nevertheless, engages in a task which pertains to the Messiah or to his official herald? Why does he baptize? He answers that while he administers *the sign* (water), he does not claim to be able to bestow *the thing signified* (the gift of the Holy Spirit). That is Messiah's high prerogative, and that glorious One has even now arrived upon the scene of Israel's history, though they have not recognized him. In their search for false Messiahs they have missed the true One. So exalted is the latter that the Baptist deems himself utterly unworthy even to unloose his sandal-straps.

29 The next day he saw Jesus coming toward him, and said, "Look, the Lamb of God who is taking away the sin of the world! 30 This is the one concerning whom I said, 'Behind me comes a man who has gotten ahead of me, because he was before me.' 31 And I myself did not know him, but in order that he might be made manifest to Israel, for this reason I came baptizing with water." 32 And John testified, saying, "I beheld the Spirit descending like a dove out of heaven, and he remained on him. 33 And I myself did not know him, but he who sent me to baptize with water, that one said to me, 'He upon whom you see the Spirit descending and remaining on him, he it is who baptizes with the Holy Spirit.' 34 And I have seen and I have testified that this one is the Son of God."

1:29-34

1:29. The next day he saw Jesus coming toward him. Jesus returns from the desert where he has been tempted. As John sees him approaching, he exclaims to his audience, while he looks or points toward Jesus, **Look, the Lamb of God who is taking away the sin of the world!** Is it not true that by his voluntary submission to the rite of baptism and by his victory over satan in the desert of temptation Jesus had, indeed, entered upon his task of vicariously taking upon himself the curse of the law and of rendering perfect obedience? And was he not by these very acts and by those that were to follow *taking away* (present participle) the sin of the world? How fitting were these words of the Baptist just at this moment! The word ἴδε is not to be construed as a transitive verb that has *the lamb* as its object. It is an interjection. Hence, the translation should not be, "Behold the Lamb of God," or "See the Lamb of God." If one wishes to retain either of these, a comma must be placed after the first word. This comma, though generally present in the translations, is not always felt when the words are spoken or sung! To avoid ambiguity we translate as follows, "*Look,* the Lamb of God, who is taking away the sin of the world."

The question is usually asked, "Was the Baptist thinking of the paschal lamb (Ex. 12-13; cf. John 19:36; I Cor. 5:7; I Peter 1:19); of the lamb for the daily offering (Num. 28:4); or of the lamb in Isa. 53:6, 7, 10? Good reasons have been advanced for each of these: for the first, that Passover was approaching; for the second, that the slaughter of these lambs was a daily occurrence and therefore well-known to the people whom John addressed; and for the third, that the Baptist only yesterday had described himself and his task in language borrowed from Isaiah (chapter 40). Matthew, too, was familiar with Isa. 53 (see Matt. 8:17); so was Peter (I Peter 2:22); also the evangelist Philip (Acts 8:32); and the author of the epistle to the Hebrews (Heb. 9:28). But why is it necessary to make a choice? Were not all of these types fulfilled in Christ, and was not he the Antitype to whom they all pointed (cf. I Peter 1:19; 2:22)?

Although it is true that the primary meaning of the verb αἴρω is *to lift*

98

up, raise (8:59), nevertheless, in the types it was the actual *taking away* of sin and/or its consequence that was symbolized by the slaughtered lamb (Ex. 12:13; Isa. 53:5, 8, 11, 12). Hence, it is natural that here in 1:29 we must assign to αἴρω the meaning which has always been assigned to it by the reader of the English Bible; namely, *to take away* (just as in 19:31). According to the Baptist it is the sin *of the world* (men from every tribe and people, by nature lost in sin, cf. 11:51, 52) which the Lamb is taking away, not merely the sin of a particular nation (e.g., the Jewish). All the sins (see I John 3:5 for the plural) which the Lamb removes are spoken of collectively as *the sin*. The passage does not teach a universal atonement. The Baptist did not teach that, nor does the evangelist, nor Jesus himself (1:12, 13; 10:11, 27, 28; 17:9; 11:50-52; notice in the last reference the term "the children of God").

30. It is probable that the Baptist had *often* spoken of the Christ in language similar to that employed in verse 30. Hence, he testifies, **This is the One concerning whom I said, Behind me comes a man who has gotten ahead of me, because he was before me.** (See 1:15 and 27; for comments see under verse 15.)

31. And I myself did not know him. The Baptist means to say, "*I* did not know him any more than y o u did." The verb οἶδα (here ᾔδειν, pluperfect with meaning of the imperfect) indicates a mental process. It refers to a knowledge by intuition or by reflection, as distinguished from γινώσκω which refers to a knowledge by observation and experience. It is, of course, possible that John, a man from Judah, had not become closely acquainted with Jesus, who had spent most of his time in Galilee. Nevertheless, it is clear from the context (verse 33) that the reference here is to something higher than mere physical acquaintance: the Baptist confesses that it had to be revealed to him from above that *this Jesus is the Christ*. In that sense he had not known him. **But in order that he** (Jesus, in *that* capacity) **might be made manifest to Israel, for this reason I came baptizing with water.** Water symbolized the impurity of sin,[43] which gave John the opportunity to point to (or to speak about) Jesus as the Lamb of God who is taking away the sin of the world.

32. And John testified, saying, I beheld the Spirit like a dove descending from heaven, and he remained on him.

Here the evangelist seems to take it for granted that the readers are acquainted with the Synoptics, for in these *the occasion* in connection with which the Holy Spirit descended upon Jesus in the form of a dove is

---

[43] Not directly, of course; but indirectly; just as stated in the Form for the Baptism of Infants, in the Liturgy of *The Christian Reformed Church:* "The dipping in or sprinkling with water . . . whereby the impurity of our souls is signified."

clearly stated (Matt. 3:13-17; Mark 1:9, 10; Luke 3:21, 22) and not merely implied as in verse 33. Hence, the author of the Fourth Gospel does not even take the trouble to inform the readers clearly that this important event took place *when Jesus was baptized.*

For the meaning of the verbs *testified* and *beheld* see, respectively, explanation of 1:7 and of 1:14. Luke 3:22 explains several of the terms which we find in John 1:32-34. Thus, by comparing we discover that what John beheld was the Holy Spirit. Of course, the Spirit himself has no body and cannot be seen with physical eyes. But we are distinctly told that it was under the symbolism of a dove that the third Person of the Trinity manifested himself to the Baptist. What was seen physically was *a bodily form, as a dove,* as Luke 3:22 also explains. It is not clear just why God chose the dove to represent the Holy Spirit. Some commentators point to the *purity* and the *gentleness* or *graciousness* of the dove, which properties in an infinite degree characterize the Spirit. This explanation may be correct. John noticed that the bodily form *remained* (for a while) on Jesus; i.e., it did not immediately disappear. On the basis of passages like 3:34; Luke 4:18 ff., and Isa. 61:1 ff., we may say that what John saw was the visible manifestation of the anointing of Jesus Christ by the Holy Spirit. This anointing, as the references indicate, includes two elements: a. that the Mediator was ordained by God for his specific task, and b. that he was qualified to carry it out.

33. And I myself did not know him. The Baptist repeats that he had had no previous knowledge of Jesus in his quality as Messiah (see verse 31). Hence, his testimony is all the more valuable because it was given to him from above, resting on supernatural revelation. **But he who sent me to baptize with water, that one said to me, He upon whom you see the Spirit descending and remaining on him, he it is who baptizes with the Holy Spirit.** John quotes the words of his divine Sender. On baptizing with water versus baptizing with the Holy Spirit, see explanation of 1:26. Note repetition of pronouns in this verse, and see pp. 63, 64.

34. This verse brings to a close the testimony of the Baptist. **And I have seen and I have testified. . . .** The perfect tenses show clearly that the man who had this wonderful experience wishes to declare in a most solemn manner that he not only saw but that the vision is still before his eyes; that he not only testified but that his testimony still stands. The content of the testimony is: (that) **this one is the Son of God.** By placing the title at the very end of the sentence a striking climax results, in beautiful harmony with the purpose of the Fourth Gospel, as set forth in 20:30, 31. With respect to the meaning of this title we can fall back once more on Luke 3:22. From that passage it becomes clear that the Baptist, in addition to seeing a bodily form as a dove, also heard a voice out of heaven, saying to

Jesus, "Thou art my beloved Son; in thee I am well pleased." Hence, the expression *the Son of God* here in John 1:34 refers to God's own Son in the most exalted sense in which that term can be used. It expresses the peculiar relation which exists eternally between the Father and the Son (1:1, 18; 3:16-18; 5:25; 17:5; 19:7; 20:31).

Synthesis of 1:29-34

See Outline on p. 68. *The Son of God revealing himself to ever-widening circles: to John the Baptist who testifies concerning him* (continued).

This paragraph refers to an event that took place on the day after the delegation from the Sanhedrin had visited the Baptist. The latter sees Jesus returning from the desert of temptation and exclaims, "Look, the Lamb of God, who is taking away the sin of the world." In Christ, God's Lamb, all typical lambs of law and prophecy find their great Antitype. This Lamb was taking away sin. He was doing this throughout his entire earthly sojourn, not only when he died on the cross. His entire life and death under the curse was an atonement which he rendered to God. Moreover, not the sin of Israel only but the sin of the world was being carried away by him, for he saves men from every tribe and nation.

The Baptist repeats the testimony which he had given before, perhaps frequently: "Behind me comes a man who has gotten ahead of me, because he was before me." (For explanation see under verse 15.) "I myself did not know him," says John, continuing his testimony. Yet, the very purpose of his baptizing was this, that the water of baptism, which symbolized the need of spiritual purification, might rivet the attention of Israel on the Lamb of God, who removes sin.

That this Lamb of God was Jesus had been revealed to the Baptist by a direct message from God, as follows, "He upon whom you see the Spirit descending and remaining on him, he it is who baptizes with the Holy Spirit." By this token Jesus had become revealed as being, indeed, the Christ; i.e., the Anointed One, set apart and qualified by the Spirit for his task as redemptive Mediator.

The testimony of the Baptist reaches its glorious climax in the words, "And I have seen and I have testified that this One is the Son of God." The Baptist had heard the voice from heaven: "Thou art my beloved Son; in thee I am well pleased." His testimony is, as it were, the echo of this voice. And that echo never fades.

35 Again the next day John was standing with two of his disciples. 36 and he looked upon Jesus, who was walking, and said, "Look, the Lamb of God." 37 And the two disciples heard him speaking and followed Jesus. 38 And Jesus turned and saw them following and he said to them, "What are y o u seeking?" And they said, "Rabbi (which, translated, means Teacher), where are you lodging?" 39 He said to them, "Come, and y o u will see." Accordingly, they came and saw where he lodged, and they remained with him that day; it was about the tenth hour. 40 Andrew, the brother of Simon Peter, was one of the two who heard John and followed Jesus. 41 He, as the first, found his own brother Simon, and said to him, "We have found the Messiah" (which, translated, is Christ). He led him to Jesus. 42 Jesus looked upon him and said, "You are Simon, son of John. You will be called Cephas" (which, translated, is Peter).

1:35-42

1:35. Again the next day John was standing with two of his disciples. This is the third successive day of the four discussed in 1:19-51. As previously, the Baptist occupies a prominent place near the Jordan and is giving his testimony with reference to Jesus. However, while *yesterday* he had addressed a multitude of undetermined size and character, *today* he is standing *with two of his disciples* (Andrew and the apostle John himself; for proof see pp. 18-21).

36. And he looked upon Jesus, who was walking. Another difference between the two days is this: yesterday Jesus was coming toward the Baptist; today he is evidently walking away from him, toward the place where he was staying for the time being. (See verses 38b and 39).

Also, while on the preceding day the testimony of the Baptist had not brought about any active response on the part of the two disciples, today these two men take a decisive step which they will remember the rest of their days.

We hear once more the same testimony as on the preceding day: **And (he) said, Look, the Lamb of God.** (For explanation see comments on verse 29.) Observe, however, that today the testimony is more concise. Perhaps only the first part of the sentence found in verse 29 was necessary in order to recall that sentence in its entirety.

37. And the two disciples heard him (their teacher John) **speaking, and followed Jesus.**

38. And Jesus, having turned around and having fixed his eyes upon them while they were following, said to them, What are y o u seeking? Notice: not whom (are y o u seeking) but *what*. Was what they were seeking *the removal of sin* by this Lamb of God? Was it, accordingly, salvation full and free, entrance into the kingdom? Whatever it was, he was (and is) able to supply.

In answering, the two disciples of the Baptist use the term of polite address, "Rabbi." This word is derived from an adjective meaning *great;* hence, *master* or *teacher.*[44]

Because John is writing to Christians drawn (mainly) from the Gentile world, he interprets Aramaic terms. Hence, we read, **And they said, Rabbi, which, translated, means Teacher.** The word *translated* is μεθερμηνευόμενον, present passive participle of μεθερμηνεύω, a late compound of μετά and ἑρμηνεύω, where the prefix μετά indicates the *change* from one language into another, while ἑρμηνεύω means to *interpret* or *translate;* hence, to interpret an expression by changing it from one language to another. The simple form of the verb is found in 1:42. The verb is derived from *Hermes,* the god of speech. Acts 14:12 informs us that the people of Lystra called Paul, Hermes, because he was the chief speaker.

The two disciples, accordingly, are asking, **Where are you lodging?**

---

[44] The manner in which the author of the Fourth Gospel uses the term is interesting. It shows that also in this respect there is a degree of progress in his book, and this for the simple reason that there was a degree of progress in the disciples' reverence for Jesus. At first *the Twelve* (also Nicodemus) are represented as saying, "Rabbi," while *others* (the woman of Samaria, the nobleman of Capernaum, the sick man at Bethzatha, the man who was born blind) say κύριε. For "Rabbi" see 1:38, 49; 3:2; 4:31. For κύριε in the sense of "Sir" see 4:11-19, 49; 5:7; 9:36. Many translators prefer "Lord" or "Master" for κύριε in 9:38. At the conclusion of Christ's discourse on The Bread of Life — delivered at the close of the Great Galilean Ministry, — we hear Peter address Jesus as κύριε; here generally translated "Lord" (6:68). The multitude has also changed its "Rabbi" to κύριε (6:25; cf. 6:34). Only twice after this — namely, in 9:2 and 11:8; but see also 20:16 — do we hear the disciples use the term "Rabbi." After 11:8 the disciples of Jesus — i.e., the Twelve and also such friends as Martha and Mary — *are introduced as saying* κύριε, which in the following passages is generally translated "Lord": 11:12, 21, 27, 32, 34, 39; 13:6, 9, 25, 36, 37; 14:5, 8, 22; 20:2, 13, 18, 20, 25, 28; 21:7, 12, 15, 16, 17, 20, 21. They use this term both in addressing Jesus and in referring to him in the third person. However, we cannot build too much on these statistics. It is, perhaps, correct to say that a general trend is here indicated, pointing in the direction of increased reverence and of a gradual substitution of κύριε in the sense of "Lord" for "Rabbi." This, however, does not mean that except in the two passages indicated (9:2; 11:8) the disciples actually never again used the term "Rabbi" in addressing Jesus. A comparison of 13:13 with 1:38 shows that, at least for a considerable time, the two terms — "Rabbi" and κύριε — must have been used interchangeably. If this is borne in mind, it again becomes apparent that also on this minor point — contrary to the opinion of some — there is really no basic difference between the Synoptics and John.

After Christ's resurrection ῥαββί disappears completely and, as already indicated, κύριε is used with great regularity. Also, the latter term has gained in significance. When after 11:8 this title is used, *by those who know him,* with reference to him *whom they know* to be Jesus, the translation "Lord" is generally found in our versions, both old and new. The words in italics also indicate why in 12:21 and in 20:15 the translation "Sir" is required: the Greeks did not know Jesus; Mary did not know that she was addressing *him.* (See further on the meaning of κύριος G. Vos, *The Self-Disclosure of Jesus,* New York, 1926, pp. 117-139; and G. J. Machen, *The Origin of Paul's Religion,* pp. 293-317.)

Whether this temporary abode of Jesus was a home in Bethany beyond the Jordan or a near-by cloth-covered booth, constructed of platted twigs, has not been revealed and is of no particular significance. The important thing to notice is that the disciples desired an opportunity for uninterrupted conversation with Jesus. Because this was rather difficult out in the open, they ask where Jesus is staying just now, clearly implying that they are desirous of receiving an invitation to visit him. Their interest has been fully aroused by the testimony of the Baptist, who, accordingly, proved that he was a true herald and way-preparer.

39. He said to them, Come, and you will see. The answer was better than could have been expected. They are invited to accompany Jesus at once. **Accordingly, they came and saw where he lodged.**[45] The facts are stated as such, by simple, historical aorists. *They came and saw.* They sought and found. Note how the verb *found* in verses 41, 43, 45 corresponds to the verb *seek* in verse 38.

And they remained with him that day; it was about the tenth hour. The really important point in this connection is not, "What is meant by the tenth hour?" but, "Why does the author mention the hour at all?"

The answer is: The author, as has been shown, was himself one of these two disciples. That day with Jesus changed his whole life! It made such a deep impression upon him that he never forgot the exact hour when the invitation had been received and the decision to accept it had been taken.

Commentators will probably never agree on the meaning of the expression *the tenth hour*. Does this mean *the tenth hour after sunrise;* hence, about 4 P. M.? This would be in accordance with the Jewish method of computing time, recognized in the Synoptics. But the same method was frequently used among the Romans. The latter, however, in counting the hours, also started from midnight and from noon, just as we do today. They employed the latter method in order to designate the hours of their *civil* day (e.g., in dating leases and contracts). However, contemporary records do not make clear just where the one method of figuring the hours ended and the other began. Usage probably differed in different regions. Accordingly, the expression "the tenth hour" can mean 4 P. M. or 10 A. M. or even 10 P. M. However, the context makes it quite impossible to think of 10 P. M. As to the choice between 4 P. M. and 10 A. M. we believe (with A. Edersheim, A. T. Robertson, F. W. Grosheide, and many others) that much can be said in favor of the latter:

(1) John is writing at the close of the first century. His readers are Christians from among the Gentiles (mostly). Hence, he does not need to

---

[45] Greek μένει, present active indicative in an indirect question after a secondary tense (εἶδαν). This is normal. See *Gram.N.T.*, pp. 1029, 1043.

use the Jewish method of counting the hours. He *may have* used the Roman civil-day method.

(2) In 20:19 the author *must* mean the Roman day. If there, why not here?

(3) The context would seem to favor this interpretation. We read, "They remained with him *that day*." Had it been 4 P. M., we would have expected, "They remained with him *that evening*." Cf. Luke 24:29. Also if *the tenth hour* means 10 A. M., there is sufficient time *on that same day* for the search which resulted in the bringing in of two more disciples: Simon Peter and (in all probability) James. (See verses 41, 42.)

(4) This method of computing the hours also suits the circumstances better in other passages of this Gospel. (See our explanation of 4:6 and of 4:52.)

(5) This time-calculation brings 19:14 into harmony with Mark 15:25. If in both of these passages the hours are counted from sunrise, there is a hopeless conflict.[46]

40. Andrew, the brother of Simon Peter, was one of the two who heard John and followed Jesus. It is as if the author were saying, "One of the two disciples who followed Jesus that day was Andrew. I mean: the brother of Simon Peter, well-known to y o u." Does he not seem to take for granted that the readers are acquainted with the Simon Peter stories in the Synoptics?

The author does not identify the other disciple, but we have tried to show that this man was he himself; namely, the apostle John. (See Authorship, Date, and Place.)

41. He, as the first, found his own brother Simon. In verse 41 we can read either, "He (Andrew), as the first (adjective πρῶτος), found his own brother Simon," or "He first (adverb πρῶτον) found his own brother Simon." External evidence does not definitely settle the question in favor of either reading.[47] If the *second* reading is correct — as many interpreters believe — then the evangelist wishes to convey one of the following ideas:

(1) Before doing something else Andrew found his own brother Simon; or
(2) Andrew first found his own brother Simon; later he found someone else; or

---

[46] It is strange that commentators who favor the opposite view will at times refer to 11:9 in defence of their theory. But the expression, "Are there not twelve hours in the day?" proves nothing either way. We, too, can use the same proverbial saying. For us also there are, on an average, twelve hours of light in an entire twenty-four hour day. Yet, in indicating the time of day we count from midnight and from noon.

[47] Some old Latin manuscripts favor still another reading: mane, for Greek πρωί, but this reading is very weak.

(3) Andrew and John both set out to find Simon, but Andrew found him first.

Objections have been advanced against each of these interpretations which result from reading the adverb instead of the adjective. Against (1), then why is nothing else reported? Against (2), then who was that other person whom Andrew found? Against (3), then why is it that both of these men set out to find the brother of *one* of them? Remember: John also had a brother who had to be found! Moreover, he actually *was* found, as we learn from Mark 1:16-20, 29.

Though external evidence is slightly in favor of the adverb, the difference is not decisive. The adverb may be correct, but if so, we must confess that we cannot give a satisfactory explanation.

If the *first* reading is correct, all is relatively simple. The meaning then is that two men (Andrew and John), having spent a day with Jesus, have become so impressed with what they have found in him that they become missionaries. Each starts out (perhaps in the evening of that same day) to find *his own* brother. Andrew, as the first, finds his brother Peter. *It is implied that John, as the second missionary, finds his brother James.* However, in thorough keeping with his delicate reserve, John does not say this directly.

When Andrew sees Peter, **he said to him, We have found the Messiah.** The expectation of the coming of the Messiah, the testimony of the Baptist with reference to Jesus (1:29, 36), and especially the day-long visit with the latter at his temporary abode near the Jordan, had paved the way for this joyful exclamation. It must be borne in mind, however, that the conception of the Messiah in the minds of the disciples was still in need of purification. The history of their confession and witness-bearing reveals many ups and downs. Though all in all there is a gradual upward trend in their recognition and understanding of Christ's mediatorial office, nevertheless, even after the Lord's resurrection, nationalistic elements cling to their Messianic hopes and expectations (cf. Acts. 1:6). The joyful discovery which finds expression in the words of Andrew was a good beginning on the path to greater and deeper knowledge. On the parenthetical clause: **which, translated, is Christ,** from χρίω, to anoint, see pp. 35, 103.

He led him to Jesus. Andrew brought Peter to where Jesus was.

42. Jesus looked upon him; i.e., Jesus regarded Simon closely, studied him a moment; literally, *looked upon him* or *looked him over* (ἐμβλέψας).[48]

---

[48] We have in this section — verses 35-43 — several synonyms for vision: verses 36 and 42: ἐμβλέπω; verse 38: θεάομαι; 39: ὄψομαι which is used as the future of ὁράω. The aorist εἶδαν also occurs in this verse. (For the meanings of these synonyms, see Note 33, and explanation of 1:14.)

**And he said, You are Simon, son of John. You will be called Cephas
(which, translated, is Peter).** Jesus functioning in his prophetic office, looks
into the future and sees not so much the impulsive Simon who stood before
him that day as the steadfast Cephas (in Aramaic) or Peter (in Greek): i.e.,
the Rock. Accordingly, Jesus here predicts what divine grace will accomplish in the heart of this disciple. (See also Matt. 16:18.)

Synthesis of 1:35-42

See Outline on p. 68. *The Son of God revealing himself to widening
circles: to John the Baptist who testifies concerning him; to his immediate
disciples: their testimony.*

Next day (the third day) the Baptist was again standing near the Jordan
with two of his disciples: Andrew and John, the author, who, with delicate
reserve, does not mention himself by name. When the Baptist saw Jesus
walking toward his temporary lodging-place, he said to the two disciples,
"Look, the Lamb of God." They followed Jesus.

Jesus turned and having regarded them carefully asked, "What (not
whom) are you seeking?" They answered, "Rabbi (that is, Teacher), where
do you lodge?" They were asking for an invitation to the place where
Jesus was staying, in order that, away from the disturbances of the open
country, they might spend some time with the man who had been pointed
out to them as *the Lamb of God.* Jesus answered, "Come, and you will
see." This answer was even better than they had expected: it meant that
they did not need to wait for some future day but were permitted — *invited*
even — to accompany the Lord at once! From this moment these two men
become the disciples of Jesus.

It was about *the tenth hour* when this happened; i.e., probably 10 A. M.
Because this was a decisive step in the author's life, he remembered the
exact hour ever after. The two men remained that day with Jesus.

Probably in the evening of that same day Andrew finds his brother
Simon and brings him to Jesus. It seems to be implied that John, a little
later, does the same for his brother James. It does not surprise us, therefore, to find these four mentioned together in Mark 1:29. Andrew meets
his brother with the joyful exclamation, "We have found the Messiah."
Apparently both Andrew and Simon had been looking for the Messiah;
i.e., had been eagerly expecting him.

Jesus, having looked upon Andrew's brother, manifests his penetrating
knowledge and ability to predict the future, by saying, "You are Simon, the
son of John. You will be called Cephas" (in Aramaic) or Peter (in Greek),
meaning Rock. However, this was not merely a prediction it was also a
promise, indicating what God's grace would accomplish in the heart and
life of his disciple.

43 The next day he decided to leave for Galilee, and he found Philip, and said to him, "Follow me." 44 Now Philip was from Bethsaida, the town of Andrew and Peter. 45 Philip found Nathaniel and said to him, "The one about whom Moses wrote in the law and about whom the prophets wrote, we have found, Jesus, son of Joseph, the one from Nazareth." 46 And Nathaniel said to him, "Out of Nazareth can any good come?" Philip said, "Come and see." 47 Jesus saw Nathaniel coming toward him, and said of him, "Look, truly an Israelite in whom deceit does not exist." 48 Nathaniel said to him, "How do you know me?" Jesus answered and said to him, "Before Philip called you, when you were under the fig-tree, I saw you." 49 Nathaniel answered him, "Rabbi, thou art the Son of God, thou art the king of Israel!" 50 Jesus answered and said to him, "Because I said to you that [49] I saw you under the fig-tree, you believe. Greater things than these you shall see." 51 And he said to him, "Most solemnly do I say to y o u, y o u shall see the heaven opened, and the angels of God ascending and descending upon the Son of man."

1:43-51

1:43, 44. The next day he decided to leave for Galilee, and he found Philip, and said to him, Follow me. Now Philip was from Bethsaida, the town of Andrew and Peter.

This is the last of four successive days commented on in the first chapter of the Fourth Gospel. Jesus, still at Bethany beyond the Jordan, decided to cross over to the western shores of the Jordan and to proceed from there to Galilee. Perhaps while he was busy with his preparations for this journey, he found Philip. This is not surprising, in view of the fact that Philip came from the town of Andrew and Peter; namely, Bethsaida (House of Fishing), located, it would seem, not far from Capernaum. The exact site is not known, however, and the question whether there was more than one place by that name is still being debated.[50] (See also on 6:1.) We may probably assume that Andrew and Peter had told their friend and townsman about Jesus. It is possible that all three had come to John's baptism. Jesus said to Philip, "Follow me." It is clearly implied that this command was obeyed, so that Philip became a disciple of the Lord. Of all the apostles only Andrew and Philip have Greek names. When long afterward the Greeks desired to see Jesus, they made known their wish to Philip. He and Andrew brought the request of the Greeks to Jesus, 12:20-22.

45. Returning now to the present paragraph (1:43-51): the new disciple, **Philip,** in turn, **found Nathaniel,** who was from Cana (21:2). In all probability Nathaniel of the Fourth Gospel is Bartholomew of the Synoptics, as has been shown on p. 20. Bartholomew is a patronymic (Bar Tholmai,

---

[49] On ὅτι see pp. 54, 56.
[50] See article "Bethsaida," in W.D.B. and in I.S.B.E.

meaning *son of Tholmai*). Nathaniel is a Hebrew name, meaning *God has given,* like the Greek Theodore, which means *Gift of God.*

And said to him . . . What Philip said to Nathaniel is recorded in verse 45. It is important to preserve the word-order of the original. When this is done, it becomes apparent that in his great enthusiasm Philip begins the sentence with a reference to the Messiah, and that the very last word which Nathaniel hears is *Nazareth*. These two concepts (Messiah — Nazareth) seemed to Nathaniel to be utterly self-contradictory.

Filled with enthusiasm Philip exclaims, **The one about whom Moses wrote in the law and about whom the prophets wrote, we have found. . . .** Up to this point Philip is expressing a great truth, for *Moses and the Prophets* (i.e., the entire Old Testament) *can never be understood unless the Christ is seen in them.* As long as one does not perceive this, the Old Testament remains a closed book. As soon as this idea is grasped, the scriptures are opened, as the following passages clearly indicate: Luke 24:32, 44; John 5:39, 46; Acts 3:18, 24; 7:52; 10:43; 13:29; 26:22, 23; 28:23; and I Peter 1:10. When Philip added, **Jesus, son of Joseph, the one from Nazareth,** he was not uttering a falsehood, for legally Jesus was, indeed, the son of Joseph (cf. Matt. 1:16). Moreover, by adding that he was the one from Nazareth, Philip simply indicated that Jesus had spent nearly all of his days in that town. Philip says nothing with reference to the Savior's place of *birth.* It is not fair to accuse him of errors which he did not make. On the other hand, at this early stage Philip had probably not yet arrived at the exalted view of Christ's *divine* sonship which the author of the Fourth Gospel expressed so beautifully in the Prologue (1:1-18), nor at the mountain-peak of Nathaniel's confession (1:49).

46. And Nathaniel said to him . . . The echo of the word *Nazareth* has not yet died when Nathaniel, in complete candor, exclaims, **Out of Nazareth can any good come?** Though some are of the opinion that this scorn for Nazareth must be interpreted as springing from town-rivalry — a possibility which cannot be denied — yet, in view of the immediate context here (see also 7:52), it is more probable that Nathaniel meant to say, "Is it possible, indeed, that *the Messiah* can come out of Nazareth? Have Moses and the prophets predicted that any good thing in the Messianic category would come forth from that town?" **Philip said . . .** Philip gives the best possible answer — one that closely resembles Christ's reply to Andrew and John, recorded in 1:39 —, **Come and see.**

47. Jesus saw Nathaniel coming toward him, and said of him, Look, truly an Israelite in whom deceit does not exist. Jesus says this with respect to Nathaniel, who, accompanied by Philip, was approaching him. Jesus

109

spoke of *deceit* (δόλος, bait for fish; hence, a snare; then: deceit, guile). In the light of the entire context (see verse 51) it becomes apparent that throughout this account of his conversation with Nathaniel, Christ is thinking of the patriarch Jacob. With reference to the latter, father Isaac had complained, speaking to his son Esau, "Thy brother came *with guile,* and has taken away thy blessing" (Gen. 27:35; see also the following verse). The employment of trickery for selfish advantage characterized not only Jacob himself (see also Gen. 30:37-43) but also his descendants (cf. Gen. 34). A really honest and sincere Israelite, a Jew without duplicity, had become such an exception that at the approach of Nathaniel Jesus exclaimed, "Look, truly an Israelite in whom deceit does not exist."

48. A man of lesser integrity might have thanked Jesus for the compliment and kept his real thoughts to himself, but not so Nathaniel. With pleasing candor **Nathaniel said to him, How do you know me?** He desires to become informed about the source of Christ's knowledge. Was it Philip who had supplied the information upon which Jesus had based his judgment? The Lord now shows that this possible inference would be incorrect. **Jesus answered and said, Before Philip called you, when you were under the fig-tree, I saw you.** Nathaniel learns, to his great astonishment, that the penetrating eye of his new Master had entered even the sanctuary of his inner devotions beneath the fig-tree (cf. Ps. 139).

49. Deeply moved, **Nathaniel answered him, Rabbi** (see on 1:38, footnote 44), **thou art the Son of God, thou art the King of Israel!** The context, as has been shown, forbids us to tone down the meaning of this confession. It is not claimed that Nathaniel's consciousness of Christ's exalted character remained on that high level. We do maintain, however, that this confession must be read in the light of the revelation of our Lord's supernatural knowledge which is recorded in the immediately preceding context. To Nathaniel, at the moment when he uttered this exclamation, Jesus was nothing less than God's own Son. (See on 1:14.) How, then, would he not be the King of Israel, the long-expected Messiah? (cf. Ps. 2).

50. **Jesus answered and said to him, Because I said to you that I saw you under the fig-tree you believe. Greater things than these you shall see.**
Jesus says nothing in disparagement of Nathaniel's glorious testimony. It seems best — most fitting in this context — to read verse 50 as a declaration and a promise, and not as a question. The gist of what the Lord tells his new disciple is this, that as a reward for his faith, greater things would be revealed to him.

51. Of what greater things is Jesus thinking? That becomes evident from verse 51, which is introduced by the Aramaic double *Amen* (occurring 25

times in the Fourth Gospel). It may be freely rendered, **Most solemnly.**[51] It often introduces a statement which expresses a conclusion to what has preceded.

The great promise which Jesus now makes is addressed not only to Nathaniel but to all those present: **do I say to y o u.** And the contents of the promise is this, **Y o u shall see the heaven opened, and the angels of God ascending and descending upon the Son of man.**

As in verse 47 so also here in verse 51 the reference is to the story of Jacob, but while verse 47 has Gen. 27 as its background, verse 51 is based on Gen. 28. According to the latter chapter Jacob, resting one evening during his flight from his brother Esau, whom he had deceived, had a dream. He saw a ladder standing on the earth, its top reaching heaven. Ascending and descending upon it were the angels of God. In connection with this dream Jacob hears the voice of God pronouncing upon him a glorious blessing, which was climaxed by these words, "And in thy seed shall all the families of the earth be blessed." Jacob's ladder finds its antitype or fulfilment in Christ. That is the meaning of the words of the Lord to Nathaniel, "Y o u shall see the heaven opened, and the angels of God ascending and descending upon the Son of man." The latter is here represented as *the link between heaven and earth, the bond of union between God and man,* the One who by means of his sacrifice reconciles God to man. With the eye of faith the disciples will be able to see him in that light. They will be able to see the angels of God ascending and descending upon the *Son of man.* For Jesus this mysterious term (Son of man) is as rich in meaning as is the concept Messiah. The term is based on Dan. 7. We discuss it in detail in connection with 12:34.

Accordingly, when the question is asked, "What are these *greater things* which Nathaniel will see?" the answer is as follows:

(1) Has he caught a glimpse of Christ's penetrating knowledge? This disciple — and the others with him — will see that attribute, and all the other attributes, employed in the service of *man's salvation, to God's glory.*

(2) Has Nathaniel confessed Jesus as the *Son of God?* The greater thing which he and others will come to see is this, that the Lord is *both the Son of God* (see verse 49) and the *Son of man* (verse 51), reconciling God with man, the true Ladder between heaven and earth.

(3) Has Bartholomew given expression to his new discovery by exclaiming, "Thou art King *of Israel?*" The greater thing, reserved for the future, is that the followers of the Lord will learn to adore him as standing in relation to Israel not only but to *mankind* in general, for he is the Son *of man!*

---

[51] The Synoptics have the single *Amen.* As an expression which indicates solemn affirmation or confirmation the double *Amen* occurs also in the Old Testament: Num. 5:22; Neh. 8:6; Ps. 41:13; 72:19; 89:52.

Synthesis of 1:43-51

See Outline on p. 68. *The Son of God revealing himself to ever-widening circles: to his immediate disciples, their testimony.*

On the fourth day Jesus, making preparations to depart for Galilee, added another disciple to the little group. He was a man with a Greek name, Philip (meaning *lover of horses*). We are not surprised that it was this disciple who (together with Andrew, the only other disciple with a Greek name, meaning *manly*) introduced Greeks to Jesus. But this happened a long time afterward (12:20-22). The first two disciples were Andrew and John. The third and fourth were Peter and James. Philip was, therefore, the fifth disciple. In every list of apostles he is mentioned as the fifth one (Matt. 10:2 f.; Mark 3:16 f.; Luke 6:14 f.; and Acts 1:13 f.). He came from Bethsaida, the town of Andrew and Peter. It is, therefore, probable that these two disciples had already spoken to Philip about their great discovery. Jesus told Philip to follow him, and he obeyed.

Philip, in turn, found Nathaniel, a man from Cana in Galilee. When he was told that the Messiah was the son of Joseph, the one from Nazareth, Nathaniel, at the sound of the name of this place, exclaimed, "Out of Nazareth can any good come?" He had never connected any Messianic promises with this town. Rather than to argue with him, Philip says, "Come and see."

Jesus, seeing Nathaniel approaching, remarked, "Look, truly an Israelite in whom deceit does not exist," an evident reference to the story of Jacob recorded in Gen. 27. He reveals to this new disciple that his secret devotions under the fig tree had not been concealed from the eyes of the One about whom Moses wrote in the law and about whom the prophets wrote. In the light of this marvelous knowledge Nathaniel exclaimed, "Rabbi, thou art the Son of God, thou art King of Israel."

As a reward for this manifestation of faith Jesus promises that Nathaniel and others with him would see even greater things; namely, "the heaven opened, and the angels of God ascending and descending upon the Son of man," a reference to the story of Jacob's dream about the ladder (Gen. 28). Among these *greater things* we may mention: the recognition that Jesus is not only the Son of God but also the Son of Man; hence, the Ladder between God and man, and that he would use *all* his attributes for the purpose of saving the elect from *every* nation, to the glory of God.

CHAPTER II

1 And on the third day there was a wedding at Cana in Galilee, and the mother of Jesus was there. 2 And Jesus was also invited to the wedding, together with his disciples.

3 And when the wine failed, the mother of Jesus said to him, "They have no wine." 4 And Jesus said to her, "Woman, what have you to do with me? My hour has not yet come." 5 His mother said to the waiters, "Whatever he tells y o u, do."

6 Now six stone water-jars were standing there, in accordance with the Jews' manner of purifying, each holding two or three measures. 7 Jesus said to them, "Fill the jars with water." And they filled them to the brim. 8 And he said to them, "Now dip out, and bring it to the steward of the feast." And they brought it. 9 And when the steward of the feast tasted the water, now become wine, and did not know where it came from, though the waiters who had dipped out the water knew, the steward of the feast called the bridegroom, 10 and he said to him, "Everybody serves the good wine first, and when men have drunk freely, they serve the wine of lesser quality; but you have kept the good wine until now."

11 This Jesus did as a beginning of his signs at Cana in Galilee, and manifested his glory; and his disciples believed in him.

2:1-11

2:1, 2. And on the third day there was a wedding at Cana in Galilee.
It was *the third day* after Jesus had gained two more disciples: Philip and Nathaniel. We may probably assume that on the two preceding days (and perhaps even on part of the third day) the Lord and his first six disciples (Andrew, John, Peter, James, Philip, and Nathaniel) had been traveling afoot toward the place where the event recorded in John 2 occurred. Hence, on the third day we find the little company present at *Cana in Galilee*. The statement that the mother of Jesus, who lived at Nazareth, was also present, may indicate that Cana and Nazareth were not very far apart. There seem to have been several Cana's, however, even in the province of Galilee. The exact location of the one where the wedding was held no one knows. Present-day commentators and geographers favor a spot situated about 8 or 9 miles north of Nazareth.[52] Now if we are right in locating "Bethany

---

[52] See Ch. Kopp, *Das Kana des Evangeliums*, Cologne, 1940.

beyond Jordan" about twenty miles south-east of Nazareth, then two days
(or slightly more than two days) of travel were, indeed, required. We should
also figure with the possibility that 1:43 may imply the departure from
Bethany on the very day when Philip and Nathaniel were called; i.e., there
may have been a few hours of travel also on that day. If Bethany and Cana
were located where we have placed them, no serious travel-difficulty remains.
On the other hand, those who place Bethany far to the south, near the Dead
Sea, get into difficulty when they must account for Christ's presence in Cana
of Galilee "on the third day" after the event recorded in 1:43-51. Though
even this very long journey may have been possible [53] within such a brief
period of time, it must be regarded as improbable. Some of those who,
nevertheless, insist on the seventy mile trip try to get around the difficulty
by bringing Jesus to Cana after the festivities had been in progress a few
days. But this hardly merits comment.

And the mother of Jesus was there. The *mother of Jesus* was also at the
wedding. The author is consistent in not mentioning the name of the lady
who was probably his aunt (the sister of his mother Salome). Throughout
the Gospel he leaves himself and his close relatives anonymous. It is probable that Mary was not an invited guest but rather an assistant at the
wedding. This might explain how it was that she knew about the wine
giving out. **Jesus was also invited, together with his disciples.** As these
disciples had joined the master so recently, the question might occur, "How
could they have been included in the invitation which was extended to
Jesus?" We must leave room for several possibilities, one of which is that
Jesus, on his way to Cana, stopped at Nazareth (which would not have
necessitated a detour of any great extent) and received the invitation for
himself and all who were with him. Another possibility is that Nathaniel,
who was from Cana, was authorized to extend invitations. Some are of the
opinion that he was a relative of the bridegroom, but of this we know
nothing.

The main point, however, is this, that Jesus accepted the invitation for
the entire group. He was not an ascetic. He came eating and drinking
(Matt. 11:19).

3. And when the wine failed. As the wedding proceeded, the wine began
to run short. We have no way of knowing what may have been the reason
for this, and it is better not to speculate.[54] That the deficiency in the wine-
supply was occasioned by the unexpected arrival of Jesus with his six

[53] As F. W. Grosheide contends in *Kommentaar op het Nieuwe Testament, Johannes,* I., p. 167, note 1. Josephus affirms that by rapid travel Jerusalem may be
reached in three days from Galilee (*The Life* LVII).
[54] S.BK., p. 401. A Jewish wedding often lasted a week, and new guests constantly
arrived.

disciples is probably a wrong guess, for their arrival cannot have been altogether unexpected. They had been *invited!* The fact that wine was considered a staple article of food is clear from such passages as Gen. 14:18; Num. 6:20; Deut. 14:26; Neh. 5:18; Matt. 11:19. Because of its intoxicating character its use was definitely restricted: in connection with the execution of certain functions it was forbidden; excessive indulgence was always definitely condemned (Lev. 10:9; Prov. 31:4, 5; Eccl. 10:17; Isa. 28:7; I Tim. 3:8).

In Palestine grapes ripened from June to September. There is, accordingly, no good reason to suppose that wine served at weddings which took place during the period October-May would be anything else but fermented grape-juice, in other words, actual wine. Nevertheless, intemperance, as has been indicated, is contrary to the spirit of both Old and New Testament. There is, therefore, nothing in this account which can in any way give comfort to those who favor the abuse or excessive use of the gifts of God.

The mother of Jesus said to him, They have no wine. Now in these embarrassing circumstances, when the wine failed, Mary comes to the rescue with the remark, addressed to Jesus, "They have no wine." Of all those present no one knew better than Mary who Jesus actually was and what task had been assigned to him. (Cf. Luke 1:26-38.) Did she show a degree of impatience because he did not at once do something about the present embarrassing situation? Note, however, that she did not in so many words *tell* him what to do. She merely mentioned the need, but the hint was clear enough. That Mary expected a miracle seems certain.

4. And Jesus said to her, Woman (here one could almost translate "Lady," for no disrespect of any kind is intended; cf. 19:26), **what have you to do with me?** [55] **My hour has not yet come.** When the Lord said, "Woman," he did not indulge in rudeness. On the contrary, it was very kind of him to emphasize, by the use of this word, that Mary must no longer think of him as being merely her son; for, the more she conceives of him as her son, the more also will she suffer when he suffers. Mary must begin to look upon Jesus as *her Lord.* The words, "My hour has not yet come," clearly indicate Christ's consciousness of the fact that he was accomplishing a task entrusted to him by the Father, every detail of which had been definitely marked off in the eternal decree, so that for each act there was a stipulated moment. (See also 7:6, 8; 7:30; 8:20; 12:23; 13:1; and 17:1.) When Jesus knew that this moment had arrived, he would act, not before.

5. Mary immediately sensed that the reply of Jesus implied his readiness

[55] See M. Smith, "Notes on Goodspeed's 'Problems of New Testament Translation,'" *JBL*, Dec. 1945, pp. 112, 113; also Judg. 11:12, "What hast thou to do with me?" Cf. T. Gallus, "'*Quid mihi et tibi, mulier? Nondum venit hora mea*' (Joh. 2:4)," *VD*, 22(1942), 41-50.

to act at the proper time. In the spirit of complete submission and confident expectation **his mother said to the waiters** (servants, in the sense of
assistants at the wedding), **Whatever he tells y o u, do.** That she regarded
it necessary to speak to the servants should not cause surprise. She was
aware of two things: a. that otherwise it might seem rather strange that
waiters should receive orders from a guest; and b. that what Jesus would
order these attendants to do would, perhaps, even seem foolish, so that they
might not have been willing to do it.

**6. Now six stone water-jars were standing there, in accordance with the
Jews' manner of purifying.** Somewhere in the vicinity of the room where
the feast was held six stone water-jars were standing. These were considerably larger than the one used by the Samaritan woman (4:28). The purpose
of these larger jars is explained in Mark 7:3, "For the Pharisees and all the
Jews do not eat unless they wash their hands, observing the tradition of the
elders."

Each (of the jars) holding two or three measures. A *measure* was the
equivalent of about 8½ gallons; hence, each jar was able to hold between
17 and 25 gallons of water. Accordingly, the six jars had a total capacity
of between 100 and 150 gallons! But why is this fact stated? Obviously, in
order to emphasize the greatness of Christ's gift!

7. Jesus said to them (i.e., to the waiters), **Fill the water-jars with water.
And they filled them to the brim.** Also this detail of the story places the
emphasis on the greatness of the gift. Besides, the phrase *with water* is
added, to show that the jars contained nothing else, and that nothing else
could be added, for they were full to the very top.

**8. And he said to them, Now dip out, and bring it to the steward of the
feast. And they brought it.** Apparently what these men dipped out was
water (see verse 9), but it changed into wine immediately. However, the
author does not intend to convey the idea that only a small portion of the
water was actually dipped out and changed into wine. On the contrary,
the sense seems to be: keep on carrying (φέρετε) wine. They dip out again
and again. And the jars hold between one hundred and one hundred
fifty gallons, all of which, having been dipped out, was immediately changed
into wine.

**9, 10. And when the steward of the feast tasted the water now become
wine, and did not know where it came from, though the waiters who had
dipped out the water knew.** The waiters carry the wine to the steward of
the feast (ὁ ἀρχιτρίκλινος); i.e. literally: to the superintendent of the room
with three couches (usually found on three sides of a low table). Evidently
this banquet-manager had not been present in the hall where the water-jars

116

were standing. Hence, he was greatly surprised to see this wine, and especially was he surprised when he tasted it. It was wine such as he had never tasted before, so excellent in quality. So **he called the bridegroom and said to him, Everybody serves** (lit.: sets on the table) **the good wine first, and when men have drunk freely** (not necessarily: have become drunk), **they serve the wine of inferior quality; but you have kept the good wine until now.** From these words we learn that it was apparently a custom to hold in reserve the inferior wine until the taste of the guests had been dulled sufficiently so that they would not be able to discern the exact flavor and excellence of the wine that was served last of all. The steward, therefore, expressed astonishment that this bridegroom had reversed the usual order. The remark of the banquet-manager has been interpreted as a mild rebuke. However, it is not necessary to draw this conclusion. The exclamation must be regarded as one that expresses surprise. It may even have been intended as a compliment to the groom on the excellence of this wine.

11. This Jesus did as a beginning of his signs. In chronological order this was the first *sign* (σημεῖον).[56] The term is used more often by John than by the other Gospel-writers. It indicates a miracle viewed as *a proof of divine authority and majesty*. Hence, it leads the attention of the spectator away from the deed itself to the divine Doer. Often, too, the *sign,* a work of power in the physical realm, illustrates a principle that is operative in the *spiritual* realm; that which takes place in the sphere of creation points away from itself to the sphere of redemption. Thus, the multiplication of the loaves (a *sign,* 6:14, 26, 30) rivets the attention on Christ as the Bread of Life (6:35); the opening of the eyes of the man born blind (another *sign,* 9:16) centers about the Lord's saying, "I am the light of the world" (9:5) — light in the realm of the spiritual (9:39-41) —; and the raising of Lazarus (also a *sign,* 11:47; 12:18) is immediately connected with Jesus as the Giver of spiritual (as well as material) life (11:23-27). Whether in any particular passage the term *sign* has this deep meaning — namely, a physical illustration of a spiritual principle — will have to be determined by the context. One thing, however, is certain: the *sign* points away from itself to the One who performed it.

This truth receives a particularly striking illustration in the present account. Note that *everything* else remains in the background. Who was the bridegroom? We do not know. Who was the bride? We are not told. In exactly what relation did Mary stand to the wedded pair: was she, per-

---

[56] For synonyms see R. C. Trench, *Synonyms of the New Testament,* pp. 339-344. In 4:48 τέρας (wonder) is linked with σημεῖον, as also often in the book of Acts. On σημεῖον see F. Stagg "ΣΗΜΕΙΟΝ in the Fourth Gospel," unpublished dissertation, submitted to the faculty of Southern Baptist Theological Seminary, Louisville, Kentucky, 1943.

haps, the aunt of bride or groom? Silence again. Did Nathaniel serve as "best man" (friend of the bridegroom)? Also on this score our curiosity receives no satisfaction whatever. *In the full light of day stands the Christ. All the rest is shadow.* What Rembrandt did for art, John, under the Spirit's guidance, does for religion.

In thorough keeping with this fact is the following clause: **and manifested his glory.** (For the term glory see on 1:14.)

Christ stands revealed here as:

(1) The One who honors the bond of marriage. This does not surprise us, for according to John's description (3:29; cf. Rev. 19:7) Christ is himself the Bridegroom, who, by means of his incarnation, work of redemption, and final manifestation, comes to his Bride (the church). How, then, would he not honor that which is a symbol of his own relation to his people?

(2) The One who bestows his gifts lavishly, without stint. Surely One who supplies so abundantly in the physical realm will not be less generous in the spiritual. To his munificence there are no bounds. And all his gifts are of the very best. He helps us even in our embarrassments.

(3) The One whose infinite love is made effective by his equally infinite power.

(4) The One who, accordingly, is the Son of God, full of grace and glory.

And his disciples believed in him. The faith of the disciples, present even before this time, was strengthened by this sign.

Synthesis of 2:1-11

See Outline on p. 68. *The Son of God revealing himself to ever-widening circles: to his immediate disciples, their faith when they witness the first sign.*

Starting out, perhaps, on the very day when Philip and Nathaniel were called, and continuing for two more days, Jesus and his little band of disciples, after journeying for a distance of not much less than thirty miles, finally arrived at Cana in Galilee "on the third day," to attend a wedding to which they had been invited. It is significant that Jesus accepted the invitation. He did not come in order to rob men of their joy and gladness.

As the wedding proceeded, the wine began to run short. Jesus' mother, who may have been a widow by this time, was also present, perhaps in the capacity of general assistant. She may have been a good friend of the young couple. When she noticed the embarrassing situation, she said to Jesus, "They have no wine." In this connection it must be borne in mind that Mary had not only kept in her heart (Luke 2:51) all the wonderful sayings which had come to her in connection with the conception and birth of Jesus, but must also have heard about the wondrous happenings in connection with his baptism (the descent of the Spirit, the voice from above). Hence, she, knowing better than anyone else who he really was, expected a miracle from him. However, she did not fully realize that the mother-son relationship would be replaced by the believer-Savior relationship. She still felt that she must at least hint to her son that he should do something about this deficiency of wine. So she said to him, "They have no wine." Jesus answered, "Woman, what have you to do with me? My hour is not yet come." Jesus knew that all his deeds had been predetermined as to the exact hour of their occurrence. Mary, perceiving that this answer, though cast in the form of a mild (even merciful!) rebuke, contained a promise, said to the waiters (διάκονοι: attendants; in a technical sense, as in Phil. 1:1, it acquired the meaning *deacon*), "Whatever he tells y o u, do," a suggestion which, for obvious reasons, was entirely necessary.

Somewhere, perhaps in a hall or vestibule near the room where the feast was held, six stone water-jars of considerable size and capacity were standing. The water in these jars was for the purpose of ceremonial cleansing, on which the Jews insisted with such rigor (especially after their return from the Babylonian captivity). Together the six jars could hold between 100 and 150 gallons of water. Jesus tells the waiters to fill these jars, and they filled them to the brim. Then Jesus said, "Now dip out and bring it to the steward of the feast." Imagine their surprise when they noticed that "the conscious water saw its God and blushed" (Crashaw).

No natural explanation will suffice. The notion that these same jars had previously been filled with wine and that this wine-sediment explains what happened, deserves no answer at all. The idea that what is here recorded was in reality an acceleration of a natural process which takes place whenever rain-water, having descended into the soil, is drawn up by the roots of the vine, and is thus gradually changed into grape-juice, which, when fermented, becomes wine, explains nothing. It should be borne in mind that *this* water (cf. John 2:7-9) is not in contact with the soil, does not enter into combination with plant-food and minerals, does not come under the influence of the fostering rays of the sun, and is, therefore, in an entirely different condition. There simply is no explanation for what happened here. It is a miracle which one either accepts or denies. There is no third way out of the difficulty.

The steward compliments the bridegroom on the excellent character of this wine. Generally the best wine was served first; in this case, last.

By means of this sign, the first one of a long series, Christ displayed the glory of his power and of his love. We see the Bridegroom honoring the bond of marriage. Here the Bridegroom does not *receive* gifts. He *bestows* them, and in a most liberal manner. Moreover, he stands revealed as being infinite not only in his love but also in his power; hence, as being, indeed, the Son of God. His disciples began to realize this, and believed in him.

Anyone who, failing completely to see the glorious lessons here revealed, should draw from this miracle-account the inference that in the complex, present-day situation (with its heavy traffic, stress and strain) unrestrained indulgence in the use of liquor receives any support should read and take to heart the following passages: I Cor. 8:9; 9:12; 10:23, 24, 32, 33.

---

12 After this he went down to Capernaum, he himself and his mother and his brothers and his disciples, and he stayed there for a few days.

13 And the Passover of the Jews was near, and Jesus went up to Jerusalem. 14 And he found in the temple those who were selling oxen and sheep and pigeons, and the money-changers sitting. 15 So he made a whip out of cords and drove all out of the temple, also the sheep and the oxen, and he scattered the coins of the money-changers, and he threw their tables upside down. 16 And he said to those who sold the pigeons, "Take these things out! Stop making my Father's house a house of merchandise." 17 And his disciples recalled that it is written, "Zeal for thy house will consume me."

18 The Jews, accordingly, said to him, "What sign do you show us for [57] doing these things?" 19 Jesus answered and said, "Break down this sanctuary, and in three days I will raise it up." 20 The Jews then said, "For forty-six years this sanctuary has been in the process of building, and *you*, will you raise it up in three days?" 21 But he was speaking about the sanctuary of his body. 22 When therefore he was raised from the dead, his disciples remembered that he had said this, and they believed the scripture and the word which Jesus had spoken.

2:12-22

2:12. After this he went down to Capernaum, he himself and his mother and his brothers and his disciples, and he stayed there for a few days.

The event recorded in the preceding paragraph probably occurred in late February or early March of the year 27 A. D. Accordingly, when now we read, *After this,* the first thought which occurs to us is that what is about to be recorded took place shortly after the wedding at Cana. This would seem to follow from the very expression that is used, for elsewhere in the Fourth Gospel it indicates an event which followed *soon after* (11:11; 19:28). This inference receives further corroboration from the very next verse where we read, "And the Passover of the Jews was near, and Jesus went up to Jerusalem." Now, all of this is very logical: Jesus in February or early March changes the water into wine; from Cana's wedding he proceeds to Capernaum where he stays a few days; there follows the Passover festival, which was held in early Spring (about April). We cannot agree, therefore with those who are of the opinion that the temple-cleansing here recorded took place at the close of Christ's ministry and is to be identified with the one about which we read in Matt. 21.[58]

---

[57] On ὅτι see pp. 55, 57.

[58] Closely connected with this is the question: Was 2:13-3:21 misplaced? For the reasons given we do not believe this. See E. B. Redlich, "St. John 1-3: A Study in Dislocation," *ExT* 55(1944) 89-92; and G. Ogg, "The Jerusalem Visit of John 2:13-3:21," *ExT* 56(1944) 70-72.

From the higher ground of Nazareth, Jesus, his mother Mary, *his brothers* (James, Joses, Jude, and Simon; see Mark 6:3), and his disciples went down to the lower levels of the lake-side, until they reached *Capernaum*. Here two of the disciples lived: John and James, the sons of Zebedee and Salome. It is not strange, therefore, that the Lord made a brief visit here before journeying to Jerusalem. From what we read in the final clause of verse 12, **and he stayed there for a few days,** it hardly seems to follow that the family *moved* to Capernaum at this time.

13. And the Passover of the Jews was near. Every male Jew, from the age of twelve and up, was expected to attend *the Passover* at Jerusalem, a feast celebrated to commemorate the deliverance of the people of Israel from Egyptian bondage. On the tenth of the month Abib or Nisan (which generally corresponds to our March, though its closing days sometimes extend into our April) a male lamb, of the first year, without blemish, was taken, and on the fourteenth day, between three and six o'clock in the afternoon, it was killed. The elaborate evening-celebration of the feast in the days of our Lord's sojourn included the following elements:

a. A prayer of thanksgiving by the head of the house; drinking the first cup of wine. Other cups were emptied as the feast proceeded.

b. The eating of bitter herbs, as a reminder of the bitter slavery in Egypt.

c. The *son's* enquiry, "Why is this night distinguished from all other nights?" and the *father's* appropriate reply, either narrated or read.

d. The singing of the first part of the Hallel (Pss. 113, 114) and the washing of hands.

e. The carving and eating of the lamb, together with unleavened bread. The lamb was eaten in commemoration of what the fathers had been commanded to do in the night when the Lord smote all the first-born of Egypt and delivered his people. (See Ex. 12 and 13.) The unleavened bread was a memorial of the first days of the journey during which this *bread of haste* had been eaten by the ancestors. It was also an emblem of purity.

f. The continuation of the meal, each one eating as much as he liked, but always last of the lamb.

g. The singing of the last part of the Hallel (Pss. 115-118).

The day on which the lamb was killed was followed by the seven-day Feast of Unleavened Bread, celebrated from the fifteenth to the twenty-first of Nisan.

So very close was the connection between the Passover-meal proper and the immediately following Feast of Unleavened Bread that the term *Passover* is frequently used to cover both.

Thus, in Luke 22:1 — a very significant passage — we read: "Now the Feast of Unleavened Bread drew near, *which is called the Passover.*" Also in

Acts 12:4 (see the preceding verse) the term Passover clearly covers the entire seven-day festival. The Old Testament, too, calls the Passover *a feast of seven days* (Ezek. 45:21).

During this seven-day festival, called Passover, many animals were offered in sacrifice (Num. 28:16-25) to Jehovah. Hence, when in the second chapter of John we read about oxen and sheep that were sold in the temple-court, the conclusion would seem to be warranted that the term Passover, in verse 13, refers also here to the entire one-week festival. **And Jesus went up to Jerusalem,** true in this case even in a literal sense (actually *ascending* from 680 feet below sea-level near the Sea of Galilee to 2,500 feet above sea-level, the altitude of the Holy City), but ever true in the religious sense.

14. And he found in the temple those who were selling oxen and sheep and pigeons, and the money-changers sitting. Now at this occasion Jesus, entering Jerusalem's temple, notices that the court of the Gentiles had been changed into what must have resembled a stockyard. There was the stench and the filth, the bleating and the lowing of animals, destined for sacrifice. It is true, in the abstract, that each worshipper was allowed to bring to the temple an animal of his own selection. But let him try it! In all likelihood it would not be approved by the judges, the privileged venders who filled the money-chests of Annas! Hence, to save trouble and disappointment, animals for sacrifice were bought right here in the outer court, which was called the court of the Gentiles because they were permitted to enter it. Of course, the dealers in cattle and sheep would be tempted to charge exorbitant prices for such animals. They would exploit the worshippers. And those who sold pigeons would do likewise, charging, perhaps, $4 for a pair of doves worth a nickel.[59] And then there were the money-changers, sitting cross-legged behind their little coin-covered tables. They gave the worshipper lawful, Jewish coin in exchange for foreign currency. It must be borne in mind that only Jewish coins were allowed to be offered in the temple, and every worshipper — women, slaves, and minors excepted — had to pay the annual temple tribute of half a shekel (cf. Ex. 30:13). The money-changers would charge a certain fee for every exchange-transaction. Here, too, there were abundant opportunities for deception and abuse. And in view of these conditions the Holy Temple, intended as a house of prayer for all people, had become a den of robbers (cf. Isa. 56:7; Jer. 7:11; Mark 11:17).

15, 16. What Jesus did about this is stated in verses 15 and 16. **Out of pieces of cord** or rope — not difficult to find where so many animals are tied up — **he made a whip. And drove all out of the temple.** But to what

[59] A. Edersheim, *The Life and Times of Jesus the Messiah*, New York, 1897, vol. I, p. 370.

does the word *all* (πάντας) refer? Merely to **the sheep and the oxen?** That is the picture drawn by the A.R.V. However, the A.V. and the R.S.V. favor the idea that Jesus actually drove out all the wicked traffickers together with the sheep and oxen. The latter view is not only better from a grammatical point of view [60] but is also supported by Matt. 21:12. In the second cleansing of the temple, described in that passage, it is definitely stated that the cattle-dealers were themselves driven out. If that happened *then*, we may take for granted that it also took place *now*.

Filled with holy zeal Jesus turned his attention to the money-changers and **he threw their tables upside down** so that **he scattered their coins. And he said to those who sold the pigeons, Take these things out;** i.e., he told those who sold doves to remove the crates in which they were kept. When he added, **Stop making** [61] **my Father's house a house of merchandise,** (cf. Zech. 14:21) he exercised his right as the Father's only-begotten Son (cf. Luke 2:49).

17. And his disciples recalled that it is written, Zeal for thy house will consume me. The disciples, witnessing this manifestation of the zeal of their Lord for the house of his Father, are filled with fear that Jesus may suffer what David had to endure in his day; namely, that this zeal in some way would result in his being consumed.

Now, in expressing this thought use is made of Ps. 69, which is one of six Psalms most often referred to in the New Testament (the others being Pss. 2, 22, 89, 110, and 118). Other echoes of various passages of this Psalm (which is Ps. 68 in the LXX) are heard in Matt. 27:34, 48; Mark 15:36; Luke 23:36; John 15:25; 19:28; Rom. 11:9, 10; 15:3; Heb. 11:26; Rev. 3:5; 13:8; 16:1; 17:8; 20:12, 15; and 21:27. While some of these are quotations, others are allusions, references more or less indirect. Jesus himself (15:25) cites Ps. 69:4, "They hated me without a cause," and refers it to his own experience. In fulfilment of Ps. 69:21 he uttered the word from the cross, "I thirst" (19:28).

From this it appears that Ps. 69 is Messianic. It is possible that the disciples so regarded it even at this time, but that cannot be proved. These men, watching Jesus in the act of cleansing the temple, are reminded of Ps. 69:9. Note, however, that they, fearing that in some way what *once happened* to David, when he suffered reproaches as a result of his burning zeal for the cause of Jehovah, *is going to happen* to Jesus, change the tense from the past (LXX κατέφαγεν) to the future (καταφάγεται).

---

[60] The nearest antecedent of πάντας is τοὺς κερματιστὰς. Besides, if πάντας refers only to the animals, one would have expected τοὺς βόας before τὰ πρόβατα in verse 15 (just as in verse 14).
[61] μή and the present active imperative.

18. The Jews, accordingly, said to him, What sign do you show us for doing these things? The hostile Jewish authorities (perhaps temple-police, scribes, priests) now ask that Jesus vindicate his drastic action. He has taken it upon himself to act in the capacity of a Reformer. Now let him prove that he had the right to act as he did. But this request was *stupid.* The temple-cleansing was itself a sign. It was a definite anticipatory fulfilment of Mal. 3:1-3 ("The Lord whom ye seek will suddenly come to his temple . . . he will purify the sons of Levi") and also — as was shown under verse 17 — of Ps. 69. The majestic manner in which Jesus performed this task, so that none, seeing him, even dared to resist, was proof sufficient that the Messiah had entered the temple and was purging it, as had been predicted. What additional sign could one ask for?

The request for a sign was not only stupid, however; it was also *wicked.* It was the result of unwillingness to admit guilt. The authorities should have been ashamed of all this graft and greed within the temple-court. Instead of asking Jesus by what right he had cleansed the temple, they should have confessed their sins and thanked him.

19, 20. Jesus answered and said (to them). **Break down this sanctuary, and in three days I will raise it up.** We have here another *mashal;* that is, a paradoxical saying, a veiled and pointed remark, often in the form of a riddle. The first one was uttered by John the Baptist (see explanation of 1:15). The one now under discussion requires very careful consideration, for it contains several terms which (probably in Aramaic as well as in Greek) lend themselves to twofold interpretation.[62] Thus, *break down* (λύσατε) is a term which is applicable both to the tearing down of a building and the destruction of the human body. *This sanctuary* (τὸν ναόν τοῦτον) could refer to the sacred shrine (Holy Place and Holy of holies usually, but in verse 20 probably the entire temple, including the courts; otherwise the Jews could not have said *forty-six* years); but it might also indicate man's physical frame viewed as a dwelling-place of the Spirit. And finally, *I will raise up* (ἐγερῶ) is an expression used with respect to both reconstruction of buildings and resuscitation of individuals.

The Jews, instead of jumping at the conclusion that Jesus was referring to nothing else than the physical structure which he had just cleansed, should have pondered this paradox. After all, their own literature was full of just such veiled sayings.

But they completely misinterpreted the mashal (verse 20). Afterward they even twisted it as if Jesus had said that he himself would destroy the temple (Matt. 26:61; cf. Acts 6:14).

What, then, did the Lord really mean? The first part of the saying must

---

[62] Cf. F. W. Gingrich, "Ambiguity of Word Meaning in John's Gospel," *ClW* 37(1943-1944) 77.

not be interpreted as a direct command, as if Jesus were actually ordering them to break down or destroy. The meaning of the entire saying may be paraphrased as follows:

"Even though you, Jews, by your wickedness, are clearly breaking down the sanctuary of my body (see explanation of verse 17) — and even though, as a result, you are also destroying your own temple of stone and the entire system of religious practices connected with it — ; nevertheless, in three days I will raise up that sanctuary (referring to his resurrection from the dead) — and, as a result, I will establish a new temple with a new cult: the Church, with its worship of the Father in spirit and in truth."

The type and the Antitype cannot be separated. Israel's physical temple (or tabernacle) was the place in which God dwelt. Hence, it was the type of Christ's body, which also, and in a far superior sense, was the dwelling-place of God. If anyone destroys the second, Christ's body, he also pulls down the first, the temple of stone at Jerusalem. This is true for two reasons: a. when Christ is crucified, the physical temple and its entire cult cease to have any meaning (when Jesus died, the veil was rent!); also b. the terrible crime of nailing him to the cross results in the destruction of Jerusalem with its physical temple. Similarly, the raising again of the body of Christ (cf. 10:18), so that the resurrected Lord now sends forth his Spirit, implies the establishment of the new temple which is his Church (the sanctuary *made without hands,* cf. Mark 14:58). On the Church as the sanctuary of Christ see also I Cor. 3:16, 17; II Cor. 6:16; Eph. 2:21; and II Thess. 2:4.

The Jews, however, said, For forty-six years this sanctuary has been in the process of building, and *you,* will you raise it up in three days? The Fourth Gospel contains numerous instances of unwarranted, crassly literal interpretation. The enemies of Jesus, the people with whom he came in contact, and frequently even his own disciples, fail to see the Antitype in the type; or, at least, they do not discern that the physical symbolizes the spiritual; see also, in this connection, the following passages: 3:3, 4; 4:14, 15; 4:32, 33; 6:51, 52; 7:34, 35; 8:51, 52; 11:11, 12; 11:23, 24; 14:4, 5.[63]

The Jews see only the literal sanctuary. Had they studied the scriptures with a believing heart, they would have known that the temple, together with all its furniture and ceremonies, was only a type, destined for destruction (cf. especially Ps. 40:6, 7 and Jer. 3:16). Because of their unbelief and darkened minds they now point to the fact [64] that the temple has been in process of building for forty-six years. (For chronology see Fl. Josephus, *Antiquities,* Bk. 15, xi; E. Schürer, *A History of the Jewish People in the*

[63] Cf. D. W. Riddle and H. H. Hutson, *New Testament Life and Literature,* Chicago, Ill., 1946, pp. 192, 193.
[64] Note the aorist. Though it had taken forty-six years, yet the entire building process over all these years is here viewed as one fact.

Time of Christ, sec. ed., I, i, 438; and our *Bible Survey*, pp. 61, 415.)
Herod the Great began to reign in the year 37 B. C., and, according to
Josephus, began building the temple in the eighteenth year of his reign;
hence, in the year 20-19 B. C. So, in the Spring of 27 A. D. the Jews could
say that it had already taken forty-six years to build their temple. It is
interesting to note that this grand structure was not finished until . . . just
a few years before it was destroyed by the Romans!

". . . and *you*,[65] will raise it up in three days?" This was spoken, as is
evident from the very language, in a tone of contempt: it took *us* forty-six
years, and we are not yet finished; but *you* think that you can re-erect it in
just three days!

21. But he was speaking about the sanctuary of his body. The author
added these words, because he realized that even among the readers there
might be those who would fail to understand that, for the reason already
stated (pp. 123, 125), the temple was a type of Christ's body.

22. Because the truth had been cast in the form of a mashal (veiled saying), it lingered in the mind of the disciples. Again and again they turned
it over in their minds. But until the day of Christ's resurrection they failed
to see its meaning. No doubt this was due in part to their unwillingness to
accept the fact that the Messiah would certainly suffer and die. We can
easily see that **when, therefore, he was raised from the dead** *on the third
day,* suddenly **his disciples remembered that he had said this,** *"and in three
days* I will raise it up." So then **they believed the scripture** (all the various
references in the Old Testament to the necessity of Christ's suffering, death,
and resurrection) **and the word which Jesus had spoken** (i.e., 2:19).

Synthesis of John 2:12-22

See Outline on p. 68. *The Son of God revealing himself to ever-widening
circles: to Jerusalem, the cleansing of the temple (outward Reformation).*

Probably in late February or early March of the year 27 A. D. Jesus in
the company of his mother, brothers, and disciples went down to Capernaum, the town of John and James. After a brief visit there he went up to
Jerusalem, to attend the Passover, a religious and harvest festival, lasting
seven days. When, upon entering his Father's house, he observed the terrible traffic that was being conducted in its outer court, the graft connected
with the sale of animals and money-exchange, he made a whip and drove
out of the temple all these thieves, together with their animals. He upset
the little tables of the money-changers so that the coins were poured out
over the floor. To those who sold pigeons he said, "Take these things out!

---

[65] Note the emphatic καὶ σὺ at the very beginning.

Stop making my Father's house a house of merchandise." His disciples saw in this a fulfilment of Ps. 69:9. The Jews, utterly failing to understand that what Jesus had just done was a fulfilment of Mal. 3:1-3 and therefore a proof of his authority as Messiah, asked that he would vindicate his deed by means of a sign. Jesus then uttered the profound mashal, "Break down this sanctuary and in three days I will raise it up." The Jews, because their minds were darkened by unbelief, expressed amazement at the idea that Jesus would raise up *in just three days* a structure which had already been in building for forty-six years and was not yet finished. However, the Lord actually referred to the sanctuary of his body, of which the earthly temple was a type. The very fact that Jesus arose *on the third day* opened the minds of the disciples so that they then understood the veiled saying about raising up the sanctuary *in three days.*

By means of this temple-cleansing Jesus:

(1) attacked the secularizing spirit of the Jews. One should not tamper with holy things;

(2) exposed graft and greed;

(3) assailed the anti-missionary spirit: the court of the Gentiles had been built as an invitation for them to worship the God of Israel (cf. Mark 11:17); but Annas and his sons were using for their own selfish purpose that which had been intended as a blessing for the nations; and

(4) fulfilled Messianic prophecy (Ps. 69 and Mal. 3).

---

23 Now while he was in Jerusalem during Passover Feast, many trusted in his name when they observed his signs which he was doing. 24 But Jesus was not trusting himself to them, because he knew all men, 25 and because he did not need to [66] have anyone bear testimony concerning man, for he himself knew what was in man.

2:23-25

2:23. Now while he was in Jerusalem during Passover Feast. Jesus remained in Jerusalem during the entire Passover Feast (see on 2:13). **Many trusted in his name;** i.e., because of the manner in which his power was displayed they accepted him as a great prophet and perhaps even as the Messiah. This, however, is not the same as saying that they surrendered their hearts to him. Not all faith is saving faith (cf. 6:26).

These people, who had flocked to Jerusalem from every quarter, accepted him (in the sense explained) **when they observed** (θεωροῦντες, see on 1:14; note 33) **the signs** (τὰ σημεῖα, see on 1:11) **which he was doing.** Signs are done in order to strengthen true, saving faith (20:30, 31). Of themselves

---

[66] On ἵνα see pp. 46, 48.

they do not create faith. The Holy Spirit must do this. Moreover, once saving faith is present, one will believe in the word of Jesus even when there is no sign.

24, 25. But Jesus was not trusting himself to them. Note the contrast between *many trusted* (ἐπίστευσαν) and *he was not trusting himself* (οὐκ ἐπίστευεν αὐτόν) to them. Jesus did not look upon all these individuals as being true believers to whom his cause could be entrusted. The reason why he did not do this was **because he knew all men;** i.e., knew just what was in the heart of anyone with whom he would come in contact. This had become amazingly clear when the Lord saw Simon for the first time and when he first met Nathaniel. It would seem, however, that in this verse (2:24) the connection is rather with that which follows: **and because he did not need to have anyone bear testimony concerning man, for he himself knew what was in man;** i.e., it was not necessary for Jesus to listen to *testimony* (for this word see on 1:7); concerning any particular person, for his own penetrating eyes were able to look into the very depths of that person's heart; take, as an example, Nicodemus. So, chapter 3 relates the story of Christ's conversation with this Jewish leader. Hence, though 2:23-25, in a sense, is a continuation of the preceding paragraph (for in both Jesus' work in Jerusalem is described), yet the chapter-division might have been made after verse 22. This becomes evident when the last verse of chapter 2 and the first verse of chapter 3 are read together; thus:

"He himself knew what was in *man*. Now there was *a man* of the Pharisees, named Nicodemus," etc.

For Synthesis see after 3:21.

CHAPTER III

3 1 Now there was a man of the Pharisees, named Nicodemus, a ruler of the Jews.
2 He came to him by night, and said to him, "Rabbi, we know that you are a teacher come from God; for no one can do these signs which you do unless God is with him." 3 Jesus answered and said to him, "I most solemnly assure you, unless one is born anew, he cannot see the kingdom of God." 4 Nicodemus said to him, "How can a man be born when he is old? He cannot again enter into his mother's womb and be born, can he?" 5 Jesus answered, "I most solemnly assure you, unless one is born of water and the Spirit, he cannot enter the kingdom of God. 6 That which is born of the flesh is flesh, and that which is born of the Spirit is spirit. 7 Do not be amazed that [67] I said to you, 'y o u must be born anew.' 8 The wind blows where it wills, and you hear its sound, but you do not know where it comes from and where it goes to. So is everyone who is born of the Spirit."

9 Nicodemus answered and said to him, "How can these things be?" 10 Jesus answered and said to him, *"You* are Israel's teacher, and yet you do not know these things?"

11 I most solemnly assure you,[68] that which we know we utter, and that which we have seen we testify, but y o u do not accept our testimony. 12 If I have told y o u earthly things and y o u do not believe, how shall y o u believe if I tell y o u heavenly things? [69] 13 And no one has gone up into heaven but he who descended from heaven, the Son of man.[70] 14 And as Moses lifted up the serpent in the desert, so must the Son of man be lifted up, 15 in order that whoever believes may in him have everlasting life. 16 For God so loved the world that he gave his Son, the only-begotten, in order that [71] whoever believes in him should not perish but have everlasting life. 17 For God sent his Son into the world, not in order to condemn the world, but in order that the world might be saved through him. 18 He who believes in him is not condemned; he who does not believe is condemned already, because he has not believed in the only-begotten Son of God. 19 Now this is the judgment, that [72] the light has come into the world, but men loved the darkness rather than the light, because their deeds were

---

[67] On ὅτι see pp. 55, 57.
[68] On ὅτι see pp. 54 (and footnote 13), 57.
[69] The conditional sentence belongs to Group IA and IIIA1; see pp. 40, 43.
[70] N.N. omits "who is in heaven." So does F. W. Grosheide, *op. cit.*, p. 226, Note 1. The idea contained in that omitted clause is, however, definitely scriptural (cf. 1:18). See Note on 3:13 in Vol. II.
[71] On ἵνα see pp. 45, 48.
[72] On ὅτι see pp. 55, 57.

evil. 20 For whoever is in the habit of practicing what is wrong hates the light, and does not come to the light, lest [73] his deeds should be exposed. 21 But he who is in the habit of doing what is true comes to the light, in order that it may become clearly evident that his deeds were wrought in God.

3:1-21

This lengthy paragraph may be divided into three sections: the first verse, in which Nicodemus is introduced; verses 2-10, in which he asks three questions and receives three answers; and verses 11-21, in which the dialogue becomes a discourse — Nicodemus having become a silent listener to the words of Jesus—, and information with respect to "earthly things" is supplanted by teaching concerning "heavenly things."

3:1. Now there was a man of the Pharisees, named Nicodemus, a ruler of the Jews.

The Son of God reveals himself to ever widening circles. In 2:23-3:21 (see especially 2:23 and 3:21) he makes himself manifest to the people who are present in Jerusalem on and after the Passover Feast. In 3:22-36 he becomes known to the inhabitants of the country-region of Judea.

3:1-21 is an illustration of Christ's penetrating insight into the secrets of the human soul, an insight to which reference was made in 2:24, 25.

One night, while the Lord was carrying on his work in Jerusalem, he received a visitor. The *name* of that visitor is mentioned, as are also his *religious-party affiliation* and *position*. His *financial standing* would seem to be implied in 19:39. There are commentators who believe that in 3:4 something is said with respect to his *age*, but this is probably an instance of reading too much into a verse.

His *name* was Nicodemus (meaning: victor over the people). It is a Greek name, but that does not mean that the man was a Greek. It must be borne in mind that beginning with the period of the Maccabean rulers who followed Simon one can expect to find an intermingling of Greek personal names among the Hebrew.[74]

Nicodemus belonged to the party of the *Pharisees*. This party seems to have originated during the period preceding the Maccabean wars. It may be looked upon as the crystallization of a reaction against the *secularistic* spirit of Hellenism.[75] During the second century B. C. those people who

---

[73] Literally, "in order that not."

[74] Cf. A. Sizoo, *Uit De Wereld van het Nieuwe Testament,* Kampen, 1946, pp. 183-200.

[75] Nevertheless, the Pharisees in their emphasis on systematic study and on the application of certain hermeneutical rules, clearly showed that Hellenism had not bypassed them. Cf. W. F. Albright, *From the Stone Age to Christianity,* Baltimore, 1940, pp. 272-275.

abhorred the idolatrous customs of the Greeks and who, during the fierce religious persecution led by the monstrously wicked Antiochus Epiphanes, stood firm and refused to abandon the faith, were called ḥasidhim (Pietists or Saints). They were the forerunners of the Pharisees (Separatists), who began to appear under that name during the reign of John Hyrcanus (135-105 B. C.). One is reminded of the fact that in England the 17th century Puritans became the 19th century Non-conformists.

Although the Pharisees were right in many points of doctrine — the divine decree, man's moral accountability and immortality, the resurrection of the body, the existence of spirits, rewards and punishments in the future life — and produced men of high renown — Gamaliel, Paul, Josephus —, they made one basic and very tragic error: *they externalized religion.* Outward conformity to the law was far too often considered by them to be *the* goal of one's existence. In actual practice (though not in theory) the oral law, which via the men of the great synagogue, the prophets, the elders, and Joshua, was traced back to Moses and thus to God himself, was often honored even more highly than the written. The Lord denounced them again and again for their exhibitionism and holier-than-thou attitude (Matt. 5:20; 16:6, 11, 12; 23:1-39: Luke 18:9-14). Their scrupulosity knew no bounds, especially with respect to the observance of man-made Sabbath laws. Thus, some of them held that a woman should not look into a mirror on the sabbath because she might see a gray hair and be tempted to pull it out, which would be working! One was allowed to *swallow* vinegar on the sabbath, as a remedy for a sore throat, but not use it as a gargle. The climax, perhaps, was the rule that an egg laid on the sabbath could be eaten, provided one *intended* to kill the hen.[76] The Pharisees owed their influence upon the people to the antipathy of the masses against the House of Herod.

To this salvation-by-works party Nicodemus belonged. He occupied a very prominent *position*, being a *ruler of the Jews.* Cf. also 3:10 and 7:50 which indicate that he was a member of the Sanhedrin, also that he was a scribe: i.e. a professional student, interpreter, and teacher of the law.

---

[76] *The Babylonian Talmud* (English translation by M. L. Rodkinson), Boston, 1918 Vol. on *Festivals:*, see especially pp. 19, 20, 175, 179, and 327. Cf. A. T. Robertson, *The Pharisees and Jesus,* New York, 1920. S.BK. should be consulted; see its Index, under "Pharisäer." On this subject one cannot afford to ignore Fl. Josephus; e.g., *Antiquities* XIII, x; XVIII, i; for other references see its Index. Especially interesting and delightfully written (should be read with discretion, of course!) is L. Finkelstein, *The Pharisees,* Philadelphia, 1938, two vols. We have also enjoyed the various sections on the Pharisees in W. F. Albright, *From the Stone Age to Christianity.* Other recent writers on this subject are I. Abrahams, H. Danby, P. Fiebig, J. Goldin, R. T. Herford, J. Jeremias, J. Klausner, G. F. Moore, and L. J. Newman. An excellent help for the Jewish point of view on this and related subjects is L. Finkelstein, *The Jews, Their History, Culture, and Religion,* New York, 1945, two volumes; see especially vol. I, chapter 3.

2. He came to him by night. — Nicodemus came to Jesus *by night*. Was he afraid lest, if discovered in conversation with Jesus, he might be criticized by other Sanhedrin-members? Some commentators are of this opinion, which is rather popular and may be correct (cf. 19:38). Others, again, say that at this very early stage of Christ's ministry opposition to his teachings could not have been sufficiently pronounced to produce such fear. Some accept the fear-element but for that very reason assign the entire story to the period immediately preceding Christ's death. And finally, there are those who believe that the only reason why Nicodemus came by night was because Jesus was too busy during the day: at night one could converse at leisure. We just do not know why he came by night.

And (he) said to him, Rabbi (for explanation see on 1:49) **we know that you are a teacher come from God** . . . This amounted to saying, "We — I and other likeminded persons (cf. 2:23; 3:11)—know that you are a prophet." The reason which Nicodemus assigns for this conviction is given in these words: . . . **for no one can do these signs which you do unless God is with him.** (On the meaning of the term *sign* see on 1:11.) Nicodemus is convinced that Jesus must stand in very close relation to God to be able to do these signs.

3. Jesus answered and said to him, I most solemnly assure you (see on 1:51), **unless one is born anew, he cannot see the kingdom of God.** Nicodemus has not asked any question. Nevertheless, Jesus *answers* him, for he read the question which was buried deeply in the heart of this Pharisee. On the basis of Christ's answer we may safely assume that the question of Nicodemus was very similiar to the one found in Matt. 19:16. Like "the rich *young* ruler," so also this Pharisee, who came to Jesus one night and who by some is considered to have been a "rich *old* ruler," wanted to know what good thing he had to do in order to enter the kingdom of heaven (or: in order to have everlasting life, which is simply another way of saying the same thing). However, Nicodemus was never even given the chance to translate into actual words the question of his inner soul.

The answer which Jesus gives is another mashal (see on 2:19). It must have sounded like a riddle to the ears of Nicodemus. This remains true whether the conversation was conducted in Greek or in Aramaic. The Greek text as it lies before us immediately raises a problem. When Jesus said, "Unless one is born ἄνωθεν," what is the meaning of that last word? It can mean "from above" (from the top). In fact, everywhere else in John's Gospel it has that meaning (3:31; 19:11; 19:23). It seems probable, therefore, that also here (in 3:3, 7) it has that significance. Moreover, also in Matt. 27:51, Mark 15:38, and James 1:17; 3:15, 17, it has that sense. Jesus, then, we may believe, was referring to the birth "from above," i.e., from heaven. However, the word can also have a different connotation; namely, "anew," or "again" (Gal. 4:9). And, in the third place, it may mean "from the first," "from the beginning" (Luke 1:3; Acts 26:5). Nevertheless, the third meaning may be dismissed, because it would not be suitable to the present context. Nicodemus, then is faced with the choice between the first and the second connotation.

However, all that has been said so far is true only *on the basis of the Greek*. If it be assumed that the conversation was conducted in Aramaic, which seems probable, the riddle, in slightly modified form, remains. It may be argued that there was no Aramaic word identical in ambiguity to the Greek ἄνωθεν. But even if that should be granted, Nicodemus would still be faced with this great difficulty: how can a man experience *another birth* in any sense whatever? Of course, *we* know what Jesus meant; namely, that in order to see the kingdom of God it is necessary that a person be born from above; i.e., that the Spirit must implant in his heart the life that has its origin not on earth but in heaven. Let not Nicodemus imagine that earthly or nationalistic distinctions qualify one for entrance into this realm. Let not this Pharisee think either that improvement in outward behavior — a conduct more precisely in keeping with the law — is all that is necessary. There must be a *radical* change. And unless one is born from above he cannot even see the kingdom of God; i.e., he cannot experience and partake of it; he cannot possess and enjoy it (cf. Luke 2:26; 9:27; John 8:51; Acts 2:27; Rev. 18:7).

When Jesus speaks about entering the kingdom of God, it is clear that the expression is equivalent to *having everlasting life* or being saved (cf. 3:16, 17). The kingdom of God is the realm in which his rule is recognized and obeyed and in which his grace prevails. Before one can see that kingdom, before one can have everlasting life in any sense, one must be born from above. It is very clear, therefore, that there is an act of God which precedes any act of man. *In its initial stage* the process of changing a person into a child of God precedes conversion and faith. (See also on 1:12.)

4. Nicodemus reveals that he has failed completely to grasp the deep meaning of the divine mashal. He **said to him, How can a man be born when he is old?** This answer certainly does not necessarily imply that Nicodemus was an old man. Jesus had uttered a saying which would apply to any person. Nicodemus, as if to show the absurd character of the saying, takes the most extreme case: one certainly cannot conceive of the idea that an old man would actually have to be born all over again! Nicodemus continues, **He cannot again enter into his mother's womb and be born, can he?** The very suggestion seems utterly impossible to this Pharisee. To his rhetorical question he expects a negative answer. (For other instances of crassly literal interpretation see on 2:19.)

133

5. Jesus answered, I most solemnly assure you, unless one is born of water and the Spirit, he cannot enter the kingdom of God. The key to the interpretation of these words is found in 1:22. (See also 1:26, 31; cf. Matt. 3:11; Mark 1:8; Luke 3:16) where *water* and *Spirit* are also found side by side, in connection with baptism. The evident meaning, therefore, is this: being baptized with water is not sufficient. The *sign* is valuable, indeed. It is of great importance both as a pictorial representation and as a seal. But *the sign should be accompanied by the thing signified:* the cleansing work of the Holy Spirit. It is the latter that is absolutely necessary if one is to be saved. Note, in this connection, that in verses 6 and 8 we no longer read about the birth *of water* but only about the birth *of the Spirit,* the one great essential.

Now it is true that the cleansing work of the Holy Spirit is not finished until the believer enters heaven. In a sense, becoming a child of God is a life-long process (see 1:12), but in the present passage the *initial* cleansing implied in the implantation of new life in the heart of the sinner is meant, as is evident from the fact that we are taught here that unless one is born of water and of the Spirit, he cannot even *enter* the kingdom of God. (For the meaning of *kingdom of God* see on 3:3.)

6. Great stress, accordingly, is placed on the fact that *physical* birth (see on 1:13) does not give one any priority in the sphere of salvation. Hence, Jesus continues, **That which is born of the flesh is flesh, and that which is born of the Spirit is spirit.** (For the various meanings of the term flesh in the Fourth Gospel, see on 1:14.) One could paraphrase as follows: sinful human nature produces sinful human nature (cf. Job 14:4, "Who can bring a clean thing out of an unclean? Not one." Cf. also Ps. 51:5). The Holy Spirit produces the sanctified human nature.

7. Jesus continues, **Do not be amazed** (or: do not begin to wonder) **that I said to you, Y o u must be born anew.** To Nicodemus everything seemed so very, very strange. He was used to the idea of salvation by law-works; i.e., by *an act of man.* Now he is taught that salvation is *a gift of God,* and that, in its initial stage, it is brought about by an event in which man is necessarily passive. A person can do nothing about his own birth. And Jesus had said, "Y o u *must* be born anew." Very often, in present-day preaching, this word *must* is misinterpreted. It should be clearly understood that, in harmony with the entire context, it does not refer to the realm of moral duty, but to that of the divine decree. When Jesus says, "Y o u *must* be born again," he does not mean, *"By all means see to it* that y o u are born again." On the contrary, he means, *"Something has to happen to* y o u: the Holy Spirit must plant in y o u r hearts the life from above." And Nicodemus should have had a sufficiently penetrating knowledge of his own inability and corruption to understand this at once. He should not have shown by his expression or by his words that the teaching of Jesus regarding the absolute necessity and sovereign character of regeneration is so very strange and surprising.

8. The sovereign character of regeneration is clarified by an illustration taken from the action of the wind. That in the first clause of verse 8 the term πνεῦμα means *wind* and not *Spirit* is clear from the last clause, "So is everyone who is born of the Spirit." That clause — particularly, the word *so* — indicates that we are dealing with a comparison here. Jesus, then, says, **The wind blows where it wills, and you hear its sound, but you do not know where it comes from and where it goes to.** Nobody on earth can direct the wind. It acts with complete independence. It cannot even be seen. That it must be there you know, for, in striking any object it makes a sound. Its source and its ultimate goal or destination [77] no one knows. Jesus adds, **So is everyone who is born of the Spirit.** The relation of the wind to your body resembles that of the Spirit to your soul. The wind does as it pleases. So does the Spirit. Its operation is sovereign, incomprehensible, and mysterious. What a lesson this was for a man who had been brought up in the belief that a person could and should *save himself* by perfect obedience to the law of Moses and to a host of man-made, thoroughly analyzable, human regulations.

9. It must have been very difficult for **Nicodemus** to unlearn what he had always believed. So he **answered and said to him, How can these things be?** He is constantly asking that same question: *how can? . . . he cannot, can he? . . . how can?* (3:4, 9). It becomes very clear that this religious leader lacked the most elementary knowledge of the way of salvation. At the outset his Pharisaic training seems to have made him immune to spiritual apprehension. Is he still of the opinion that the words of Jesus must be understood in a crassly literal sense?

10. Jesus answered and said to him, You are Israel's teacher, and yet you do not know these things? Both *Israel* and *teacher* are preceded by the definite article, so that one might paraphrase the exclamation as follows: "And *you*, that widely recognized and very prominent teacher of the highly favored people of Israel, do *you* actually mean to say that you are ignorant with respect to these matters?" Nicodemus had the Old Testament, the teachings of the Baptist, the instruction of Jesus given in 3:3-8, but up to this moment the truth seems not to have penetrated his mind.

11. The dialogue now changes to discourse. Jesus is speaking and Nicodemus is listening. Jesus says, **I solemnly assure you** (see on 1:51) **that which we know we utter, and that which we have seen we testify.** Thus,

---

[77] Jesus does not say that no one knows *the direction* of the wind.

over against the "we know" of Nicodemus (3:2), a knowledge produced by human reflection, the Lord places his own "we know," a knowledge resulting from close communion with the Father (5:20; 14:10). Jesus, accordingly, wants Nicodemus to know that there can be no doubt with respect to the doctrine of baptism and regeneration which he has discussed, nor with respect to the doctrine of God's eternal decree for the salvation of sinners, which he is about to unfold.

In this eleventh verse, corresponding to *that which we know* stands *that which we have seen,* which is stronger. Similarly, *we utter* is explained by *we testify,* which also is the more definite and forceful expression. (For the terms *testify* and *testimony* see on 1:7.) Jesus uses the plural *we* instead of the singular *I.* In all probability he is not referring to himself and the prophets. The reference is in all likelihood to Jesus himself and John the Baptist. The term *testify* immediately reminds one of what was said with reference to the Baptist (cf. 1:7, 8, 34). Besides, 3:5 points to the work of the forerunner.

Jesus adds, **But y o u do not accept our testimony.** Nicodemus had indicated by his questions and his entire expression that he was not ready to accept the teaching of Jesus concerning the necessity of regeneration. Besides, Jesus was able to read what was in his heart (2:25). And Nicodemus was not the only one who hesitated to believe this strange doctrine. Christ uses the plural y o u. The members of the Sanhedrin refused to admit that the Baptist was right when he testified concerning Jesus. This body also refused to believe that Jesus was whatever he claimed to be. Consequently, these chief priests, elders, and scribes rejected Christ's teaching on the subject of regeneration.

12. The Lord continues, **If I have told y o u earthly things** — he implies that he has been doing this — **and y o u do not believe, how shall y o u believe if I tell y o u heavenly things?** Jesus had been speaking of earthly things; i.e., of things which, though heavenly in character and origin, take place on earth; e.g., regeneration. But it is clear from 1:11, 26; 2:4, 9, that such truths, though clearly taught even in the Old Testament, were rejected by men like Nicodemus. At best, such doctrines were regarded as being very strange. They were not *received.*

Now, the point which Jesus stresses is this: if even such earthly matters, which take place within the sphere of man's experience (we did not say *conscious* experience) and whose necessity should be self-evident immediately to any one who reflects upon his own natural inability to please God, are regarded as being incredible, will not heavenly matters — e.g., God's eternal plan for the redemption of mankind by sending his Son into the world (cf. 3:16) — be rejected much more readily? Such heavenly things lie completely outside of the range of man's experience. In their conception and origin they are so majestic and transcendent that they could never have occurred to man's finite mind. If then the earthly things have been rejected, how can it be reasonably expected that the much more mysterious heavenly things will be accepted? The question is at the same time a warning to Nicodemus. Let him ponder and reflect. Let him no longer regard the teachings of Christ as being unbelievable. Is it possible that the further silence of Nicodemus, his failure to come up with another "how can this be" (3:4, 9), shows that the warning was taken to heart?

13. And no one has gone up into heaven but he who descended from heaven, the Son of man. Now, in order to have first-hand information about those heavenly things one must have been present in God's Throne-room when the decisions were made. *But no one has gone up into heaven.* Hence, God's decree concerning the redemption of his people lies completely outside of the range of man's knowledge until it is revealed to him. Was there actually no one present with the Father when the plan was made which centers in the decree to send the Son into the world in order to bear the curse and set man free? Yes, there was One, the One *who descended from heaven* namely, *the Son of man.* (On ὁ ἐκ τοῦ οὐρανοῦ καταβάς, see also p. 237.) On *Son of Man* see 12:34. On *who is in heaven,* see p. 129, footnote 70, Vol. II.

14, 15. The heart and center of this wonderful plan of redemption is stated in verses 14-18. It is stated not as something entirely new, but as something which had been partially disclosed in the types of the old dispensation; particularly, the type with reference to the serpent which by Moses had been set upon a standard, raised up high so that everyone could see it. **And as Moses lifted up the serpent in the desert, so must the Son of man be lifted up.**

The story of *The Serpent Lifted Up* is found in Numbers. In fact that account (chapter 21) furnishes the key to the interpretation of the fourth book of the Pentateuch. The contents of this book may be summarized as follows:

Theme: *Israel's Journey from Sinai to the Plains of Moab: A Lesson Concerning Sin and Grace*

chapters 1-9: I. Preparations for leaving Sinai.
          10-21 II. Journey from Sinai to the plains of Moab: a story of repeated *sin* and resulting *failure* until Jehovah in his *grace* causes *the serpent to be lifted up.* Thereupon mainly,
          22-36 III. Blessing and victory in the plains of Moab.[78]

[78] Cf. *Bible Survey*, Grand Rapids, Mich., 1949, pp. 229, 230.

Israel had been rebellious again. The people had spoken against God
and Moses, saying, "Wherefore have you brought us up out of Egypt to die
in the wilderness, for there is no bread and there is no water; and our soul
loathes this light bread" (Num. 21:5). So Jehovah had sent fiery serpents
among the people, killing many. When the people confessed their sins,
Moses prayed for them. "And Jehovah said to Moses, 'Make thee a fiery
serpent, and set it upon a standard: and it shall come to pass, that every
one that is bitten, when he sees it, shall live.' And Moses made a serpent of
brass, and set it upon a standard: and it came to pass, that if the serpent
had bitten any man, when he looked upon the serpent of brass, he lived"
(Num. 21:8, 9).

Now, in John 3:14 the words *"As* Moses . . . *so* must the Son of man"
clearly indicate that the event recorded in Numbers 21 is a type of the
lifting up of the Son of man. This does not mean, however, that we now
have the right to test our ingenuity by attempting to furnish a long list of
resemblances between type and Antitype, as is often done. In reality, as we
see it, only the following points of comparison are either specifically mentioned or clearly implied in 3:14, 15 (cf. also verse 16):

a. In both cases (Numbers 21 and John 3) death threatens as a punishment for sin.

b. In both cases it is God himself who, in his sovereign grace, provides a
remedy.

c. In both cases this remedy consists of something (or some One) which
(who) must be lifted up, in public view.[79]

d. In both cases those who, with a believing heart, look unto that which
(or: look unto the One who) is lifted up, are healed.

Here, as always, the Antitype far transcends the type. In Numbers the
people are face to face with *physical death;* in John, mankind is viewed as
exposed to *eternal death* because of sin. In Numbers it is *the type* that is
lifted up. This type — the brazen serpent — has no power to heal. It points
forward to *the Antitype,* Christ, who does have this power. In Numbers
the emphasis is on *physical healing:* when a man fixed his eye upon the
serpent of brass, he was restored to health. In John it is *spiritual life —*
everlasting life — that is granted to him who reposes his trust in the One
who is lifted up.

The lifting up of the Son of man is presented as a *"must."* (cf. Mark
8:31; Luke 24:7). It is not *a* remedy; it is *the only possible* remedy for sin,
for in this way only can the demands of God's holiness and righteousness —

---

[79] Many commentators add something like this: as the uplifted serpent was not an
actual serpent but one of brass, so also Christ is not really a partaker of sin but
only "made in the likeness of sinful flesh." But is not this an instance of carrying
typology too far?

and love! — be met. But just what is meant by this lifting up? Here we cannot follow the reasoning of those commentators who would exclude from the meaning of this term any reference to Christ's death. On the contrary, that being lifted up on the cross is certainly included. In fact, in the fourth Gospel the term *to be lifted up* (from ὑψόω) always refers to the cross (cf. 8:28; 12:32, 34). However, it is, indeed, significant that the inspired author employs a term which, while certainly referring to Christ's death on the cross, is elsewhere used with reference to his exaltation (Acts 2:33; 5:31). The cross is never isolated from other great events (such as resurrection, ascension, coronation) in the history of redemption. It is ever the path to the crown. Moreover, where does the glory of all of God's attributes in Christ shine forth more brilliantly than on the cross (cf. 12:28 with 12:32, 33)?

Though Christ is lifted up in the sight of all, he does not save all. We read, **in order that whoever believes may in him have everlasting life.** Just as *in connection with* the serpent of brass the Israelite was healed (for though the serpent had no healing power and was merely a "piece of brass," II Kings 18:4, entirely unworthy of veneration and worship, nevertheless, *God's* blessing was obtained by looking at this serpent), so also *in connection with* Christ, the great Antitype, believers attain everlasting life. As the main concepts of verse 15 recur in the following verse, we shall proceed at once to that most precious of all Bible passages:

16. For God so loved the world that he gave his Son, the only-begotten, that whoever believes in him should not perish but have everlasting life.

God's infinite love made manifest in an infinitely glorious manner, this is the theme of the golden text which has endeared itself to the hearts of all God's children. The verse sheds light on the following aspects of this love: 1. its character (*so* loved), 2. its Author (God), 3. its object (the world), 4. its Gift (his Son, the only-begotten), and 5. its purpose (that whoever believes in him should not perish but have everlasting life).

The conjunction *for* establishes a causal relation between this and the preceding verse. We might paraphrase as follows: the fact that it is only in connection with Christ that everlasting life is ever obtained (see verse 15) is clear from this, that it has pleased God to grant this supreme gift only to those who repose their trust in him (verse 16).

1. *Its character.*

The word *so* by reason of what follows must be interpreted as indicating: *in such an infinite degree* and *in such a transcendently glorious manner*. Great emphasis is placed on this thought.

So *loved*. The tense used in the original (the aorist ἠγάπησεν) shows that God's love in action, reaching back to eternity and coming to fruition in

139

Bethlehem and at Calvary, is viewed as *one,* great, central fact. That love was rich and true, full of understanding, tenderness, and majesty.[80]

2. *Its Author.*

So loved *God* (with the article in the original: ὁ θεός, just as in 1:1 where, as has been shown, the Father is indicated). In order to gain some conception of the Deity it will never do to subtract from the popular concept every possible attribute until literally nothing is left. God is ever *full* of life and *full* of love.[81] Take all human virtues; then raise them to the nth degree, and realize that no matter how grand and glorious a total picture is formed in the mind, even that is a mere shadow of the love-life which exists eternally in the heart of him whose very name is Love. And that love of God ever precedes our love (I John 4:9, 10, 19; cf. Rom. 5:8-10), and makes the latter possible.

3. *Its object.*

Now the object of this love is *the world.* (See on 1:10 and note 26 where the various meanings have been summarized.) Just what is meant by this term here in 3:16? We answer:

a. The words, "that whoever believes" clearly indicate that the reference is not to birds and trees but to mankind. Cf. also 4:42; 8:12; I John 4:14.

b. However, here mankind is not viewed as the realm of evil, breaking out into open hostility to God and Christ (meaning 6, in note 26), for God does not love evil.

c. The term *world,* as here used, must mean mankind which, though sin-laden, exposed to the judgment, and in need of salvation (see verse 16b and verse 17), is still the object of his care. God's image is still, to a degree, reflected in the children of men. Mankind is like a mirror. Originally this mirror was very beautiful, a work of art. But, through no fault of the Maker, it has become horribly blurred. Its creator, however, still recognizes his own work.

d. By reason of the context and other passages in which a similar thought is expressed (see note 26, meaning 5), it is probable that also here in 3:16 the term indicates *fallen mankind in its international aspect:* men from every tribe and nation; not only Jews but also Gentiles. This is in harmony with the thought expressed repeatedly in the Fourth Gospel (including this very chapter) to the effect that physical ancestry has nothing to do with entrance into the kingdom of heaven: 1:12, 13; 3:6; 8:31-39.

4. *Its gift.*

". . . that he gave his Son, the only-begotten." Literally the original reads, "that his Son, the only-begotten, he gave." All the emphasis is on the

---

[80] For difference between ἀγαπάω and φιλέω see comments on 21:15-17.
[81] God is not an abstract, contentless essence, the Absolute of the philosophers. On the contrary, he is an infinite fulness of essence. On this subject see H. Bavinck, *The Doctrine of God,* Grand Rapids, Mich., 1951, pp. 121-124.

140

astounding greatness of the gift; hence, in this clause the object precedes the verb. The verb *he gave* must be taken in the sense of *he gave unto death as an offering for sin* (cf. 15:13; I John 3:16; especially I John 4:10; Rom. 8:32: John's *gave* is Paul's *spared not*). On the meaning of *the only begotten,* see on 1:14. Note that the article which precedes the word *Son* is repeated before *only begotten.* Thus both substantive and adjective receive emphasis.[82] We hear, as it were, the echo of Gen. 22:2, "Take now *thy son, thine only son,* whom thou lovest, even Isaac. . . ." The gift of the Son is the climax of God's love (cf. Matt. 21:33-39).

5. *Its purpose.*

. . . in order that whoever believes in him should not perish but have everlasting life.

God does not leave mankind to itself. He so loved the world that his Son, the only begotten, he gave, with *this purpose:* that those who receive him with *abiding trust and confidence* [83] may have *everlasting life.* Though the Gospel is proclaimed to men of every tribe and nation, not every one who hears it believes in the Son. But *whoever believes* — whether he be a Jew or a Gentile — has everlasting life.

The words ". . . should not perish" do not merely mean: should not lose physical existence; nor do they signify: should not be annihilated. As the context (verse 17) indicates, the perishing of which this verse speaks indicates divine condemnation, complete and everlasting, so that one is banished from the presence of the God of love and dwells forever in the presence of a God of wrath, a condition which, in principle, begins here and now but does not reach its full and terrible culmination for both soul and body until the day of the great consummation. Note that *perishing* is the antonym of *having everlasting life.*

". . . but have everlasting life." (On the meaning of *life* see on 1:4.) The life which pertains to the future age, to the realm of glory, becomes the possession of the believer here and now; that is, in principle. This life is salvation, and manifests itself in fellowship with God in Christ (17:3); in partaking of the love of God (5:42), of his peace (16:33), and of his joy (17:13). The adjective *everlasting* (αἰώνιος) occurs 17 times in the Fourth Gospel, 6 times in I John, always with the noun *life.* It indicates, as has been pointed out, a life that is different *in quality* from the life which characterizes the present age. However, the noun with its adjective (ζωή αἰώνιος) as used here in 3:16 has also a quantitative connotation: it is actually *everlasting,* never-ending life.

---

[82] See Gram.N.T., p. 776.
[83] On πιστεύω see 1:8; 8:30, 31. The present participle of this verb εἰς = *exercising living faith in* the person of Christ. On πιστεύω in the Fourth Gospel see W. F. Howard, *Christianity According to St. John,* Philadelphia, 1946, pp. 151-173.

In order to receive this everlasting life one must believe in God's only begotten Son. It is important, however, to take note of the fact that Jesus mentions the necessity of regeneration before he speaks about faith (cf. 3:3, 5 with 3:12, 14-16). The work of God *within* the soul ever precedes the work of God in which the soul cooperates (see especially 6:44). And because faith is, accordingly, the gift of God (not only with Paul, Eph. 2:8, but also in the Fourth Gospel), its fruit, everlasting life, is also God's gift (10:28). God gave his Son; he gives us the faith to embrace the Son; he gives us everlasting life as a reward for the exercise of this faith. To him be the glory forever and ever!

17. In close connection with 3:16, verse 17 continues, **For God sent his Son into the world, not to condemn the world, but in order that the world might be saved through him.**

As the Jews saw it, the Messiah at his coming would condemn the heathen. *The Day of Jehovah* would mean punishment for the nations which had oppressed Israel, but not for Israel. This misinterpretation of prophecy had been censured most severely by Amos (Amos 5:18-20), but it never subsided. It is against this Jewish exclusivism that the words of Jesus are directed. Verse 17 clearly indicates:

a. That God's redemptive purpose is not confined to the Jews but embraces the world (men from every tribe and nation, considered as a unit);

b. that the primary object of Christ's *first* coming was not to condemn but to save.

It is true that the verb which was translated *to condemn* ($\varkappa\rho\acute{\iota}\nu\eta$ from $\varkappa\rho\acute{\iota}\nu\omega$) has a very wide meaning in the original. Our word *to discriminate,* which is derived from the same stem, points in the direction of the basic idea: *to separate.* From this, in turn, came the idea of *selecting* one thing above another; hence, *judging, deciding.* Whereas in this sinful world *to judge* frequently means *to condemn,* the word employed in the original can also have that connotation, which is expressed more fully by the term $\varkappa\alpha\tau\alpha\varkappa\rho\acute{\iota}\nu\omega$. The fact that here, in 3:17, it actually has (or at least approaches) that meaning is shown by the antonym: *to save.* Salvation, in the fullest sense of the term (deliverance from punishment not only but from sin itself, and the bestowal of everlasting life) was what God had in store for the world into which he sent his Son; not condemnation but salvation.

This raises the question: Shall we say, then, that the purpose of Christ's first coming was to bring salvation, while the purpose of the second coming will be to bring condemnation (or judgment, at least)?

But the matter is not as simple as that, as verse 18 indicates. No one needs to wait for the day of the great consummation to receive his sentence. To be sure, on that great day something very important is going to take place: *the verdict will be publicly proclaimed* (5:25-29). But the decision itself, which is basic to this public proclamation, has already been made long before:

18. He who believes in him is not condemned (or *judged*); **he who does not believe is condemned already.**

Jesus divides all those to whom the message of salvation is presented into two groups, each of which is represented by one individual:

(1) The one who abides in Christ by faith is not judged; i.e., no sentence of condemnation will ever be read against him. Even now he is in the eyes of God without guilt.

(2) The one who rejects Christ by not believing in him as God's only-begotten Son (on this term see 1:14) does not need to wait for the final judgment, as if the verdict would be postponed until then. Already, by the very fact of his obstinate unbelief, he has been (and therefore stands) condemned.

19. With reference to such obstinate rejecters a verdict is announced in verse 19. Very little comment is necessary here, because most of the ideas and concepts of this passage have already been explained. **Now this is the judgment.** The term *judgment* (κρίσις) means (in this context) *divine decision* or *verdict.* (See also under 3:17; on the term κρίνω.) For the clause, **that the light has come into the world,** see on 1:4, 5, 9, 10, 11. On the term *world* see 1:10; Note 26. On *darkness* see 1:5, and on *light,* see 1:4. **But men loved the darkness rather than the light because their deeds were evil.**

We may paraphrase the thought of verse 19 as follows: Now with respect to those who reject the only-begotten Son of God, this is the divine verdict, that the Christ who is himself the Light — the very embodiment of the truth and love of God, yea, ot all his attributes — he, by means of the word of prophecy and especially by means of his own incarnation, came into the realm of fallen mankind; but, though some accepted him, by far the majority preferred the moral and spiritual darkness of sin (spiritual blindness, hatred of the brethren, etc., see especially I John 2:11, but also 8:12; 12:35, 46; and I John 2:8, 9). In fact, they actually loved this darkness; and the reason was not that they were ignorant, having never heard the Gospel, but rather this: their works were evil.

20. To say that these people loved the darkness rather than the light does not mean, however, that, after all, they loved also the light to some extent. On the contrary, **for whoever is in the habit of practicing what is wrong hates the light, and does not come to the light.** Such a person is always avoiding the light; i.e., he will have nothing to do with the Christ, the source and embodiment of God's truth and love. Hence, he never reads the Bible; refuses to attend church, etc. In his heart he really *hates* the light. The reason for this is that he fears **lest** (by this light) **his** (evil) **deeds might be exposed.** People of this type resemble loathsome insects that hide themselves beneath logs and stones, always preferring the darkness, and terribly frightened whenever they are exposed to the light.

21. But while unbelievers may thus be compared to the denizens of the domain of darkness, believers, on the other hand, resemble beautiful house-plants which turn their green parts toward the window and the light of the sun: **But he who is in the habit of doing what is true** (cf. I John 1:6) **comes to the light.** It has been indicated that there is a very close relationship between light and truth; hence, it is not surprising that he who does the truth comes to the light **in order that it may become evident that his deeds were wrought in God.** He desires to show that his deeds, though by no means perfect, were, nevertheless, wrought with God's approval (that they were done, in principle, according to God's law), and that they retain this character forever.

"He . . . comes to the light," said Jesus. Thus, the discourse ends most appropriately with the implied invitation that Nicodemus, too, should leave the realm of darkness and unbelief and should embrace Christ, the true light.

Synthesis of 2:23-3:21

See the Outline on p. 68. *The Son of God revealing himself to ever-widening circles: to Jerusalem; conversation with Nicodemus.*

At Jerusalem, during the Passover-week, many people, having closely observed the signs which Jesus did, accepted him as a divine teacher, a great and powerful prophet, and as such placed their trust in him. However, he knew that this was not saving faith, and he did not entrust himself to them. With his penetrating eye he read the secrets of men's hearts, as he had already shown in the case of Simon and Nathaneal, and as he was about to indicate in the case of Nicodemus.

The latter was a Pharisee, and a member of the Sanhedrin. He was one of those who, having beheld the signs, accepted Jesus as a divine teacher. The latter immediately discerned the unspoken question within the heart of Nicodemus. That question was: "How can I enter the kingdom of God?" In reply, the Lord emphasized the necessity of being born anew. He employed a term which can mean either: *to be born from above* or *to be born again.* Nicodemus assigns to it the most crudely literal connotation. Jesus then points out that he was not speaking about anything physical, and that physical distinctions have no significance for the kingdom of heaven. He emphasizes that regeneration is a work of God over which man has no more control than he has over the wind. Evidently in a tone of protest Nicodemus asks, "How can these things be?"

Jesus traces the surprise of Nicodemus and of those like him to its source: unbelief, and asks, "If I have told you earthly things (baptism, regeneration), and you do not believe, how can you believe if I tell you heavenly things (God's plan of redemption)?" The plan of redemption was even more mysterious than regeneration, for it was made in heaven and can be revealed only by him who was there when it was made and who descended in order to disclose it. The heart of this plan was the decree to send the Son, in order that he might be lifted up upon the cross for man's salvation, just as the serpent had been lifted up in the wilderness for man's physical recovery.

In this connection Jesus sets forth God's infinite love (3:16), making known a. its glorious character, b. Author, c. object, d. gift, and e. purpose. He points out that the purpose of the first coming was not the condemnation but the salvation of the world, and that at the second coming *that* verdict will be revealed, with reference to each person, which corresponds to his present attitude to God's only begotten Son. If anyone rejects the Son, such a rejecter is condemned already. Most of those who hear the Gospel belong to the latter category: the light has come into the world, but men loved the darkness rather than the light, because their deeds are evil. They hate to have their deeds exposed. They shun the light.

The discourse ends with a beautiful, implied invitation to Nicodemus to come to the light. The words of this closing passage are:

"But he who is in the habit of doing what is true comes to the light, that it may become clearly evident that his deeds were wrought in God."

22 After these things Jesus and his disciples came into the Judean country-district, and there he stayed with them and baptized.   23 And John also was baptizing at Aenon near Salim, because there were many waters there, and people came to him and were baptized;   24 for John had not yet been imprisoned.

25 So there arose a dispute between John's disciples and a Jew over purifying. 26 And they came to John and said to him, "Rabbi, he who was with you beyond the Jordan, to whom you bore testimony, look, he baptizes, and all are going to him."   27 John answered and said, "No man can receive anything unless it is given to him from heaven.[84]   28 I call y o u to witness that I said, 'I myself am not the Christ, but I am sent ahead of him.'   29 He who has the bride is the bridegroom. Now the bridegroom's friend who stands and hears him is very happy to hear the bridegroom's voice. Therefore, this joy of mine is now full.   30 He must increase, but I must decrease.   31 He who comes from above is above all; he who springs from the earth belongs to the earth and speaks from the earth; he who comes from heaven is above all.   32 What he has seen and heard, to this he bears testimony; but no one accepts his testimony.   33 He who does accept his testimony attests that God is true.   34 For he whom God has sent speaks the words of God; for it is not by measure that he gives (him) the Spirit.   35 The Father loves the Son and has given all things into his hand.   36 He who believes in the Son has everlasting life; but he who disobeys the Son shall not see life, but the wrath of God remains on him."

3:22-36

3:22. On the meaning of the phrase **after these things** (μετὰ ταῦτα) see also 5:1.

Jesus and his disciples came into the Judean district. After Passover-week and the interview with Nicodemus, Jesus, in the company of his disciples (probably the six mentioned or referred to in 1:35-51), left Jerusalem and came into the country-district of Judea. Because baptism is mentioned in verse 22, it is regarded as probable that the locality here indicated was not far from Jericho, near the fords of Jordan.

And there he stayed with them (i.e. with his disciples). He must have spent a considerable period of time in this neighborhood; probably from May-December of the year 27.[85] **And baptized.** While here, Jesus baptized, not in person but by means of his disciples (4:2). This rite, as here performed, may be regarded as a transition between Johannine and Christian baptism. In both, the water points to the need of spiritual cleansing, brought about by the blood and Spirit of Christ, the Lamb of God. However, by not baptizing in person but through the agency of others, Jesus manifests himself as being greater than John the Baptist. The next step will be the command to baptize into the name of the Father and the Son

---

84 III C; see p. 44.
85 See *Bible Survey*, pp. 59-62.

and the Holy Spirit, Matt. 28:19. That baptism, moreover, will extend to all nations.

23. And John also was baptizing at Aenon near Salim, because there were many waters there. While Jesus, through his disciples, was baptizing in the country-region of Judea, John was continuing his ministry farther to the north. We find him very close to the place where we last met him. He was then in Bethany beyond Jordan (1:28). Now he has crossed the river, so that he is carrying on his task *on this side* (i.e., west) of Jordan. According to many, Aenon (probably from the Aramaic, meaning *fountains*) near Salim was situated a few miles south-west of Bethany. Though its exact location is in doubt, the view that its site was near the juncture of Samaria, Perea, and Decapolis, about eight miles south of Scythopolis, fits all the circumstances and is supported by Eusebius and Jerome. Here there is a group of seven springs. Not far to the north lies Galilee. Hence, this place was centrally located, within easy reach for people of four provinces, and furnished with a goodly supply of water for baptizing. **And people came to him and were baptized.** People came to John from every direction and were baptized. But little by little the crowds left John and resorted to Jesus.

24. Before proceeding with his narrative the author solves a problem. The readers might raise the objection, "How was it possible for John to be engaged in the work of baptizing *at this time?* Is it not true that immediately after our Lord's temptation the Baptist had been cast into prison?" The author senses that some might misinterpret Matt. 4:11, 12 in that sense. Hence, evidently taking for granted that believers in Asia Minor at this relatively late date had read the earlier Gospels (see pp. 31, 32), the author corrects a possible misunderstanding, and shows that between Matt. 4:11 and 4:12 (or between Mark 1:13 and 1:14; or between Luke 4:13 and 4:14; i.e., between Christ's temptation and the arrest of John the Baptist) there was a considerable period of time during which Jesus and John were engaged in a parallel ministry. It is thus that we explain the statement, **For John had not yet been imprisoned.**

25-28. So there arose a dispute between John's disciples and a Jew over purifying. The parallel ministry of Jesus and John resulted in a dispute between admirers of the latter and a Jew who favored the former. The argument was begun by the disciples of John, who probably ascribed superior (or exclusive) *purifying* efficacy to the baptism of their teacher.

Filled with dissatisfaction caused by the constantly increasing multitudes which gathered about Jesus and the gradually dwindling crowds which remained with John, the disciples of the latter ran to their master with the words of bitter complaint. **And they came to John and said to him, Rabbi,**

147

he who was with you beyond the Jordan, to whom you bore testimony, look, he baptizes, and all are going to him. Note the following:

(1) In the spirit of jealousy and anger they purposely avoid even mentioning the name of Jesus. As they see it, Jesus and John are rivals, competitors.

(2) They seem not to have been very pleased with the fact that John had borne testimony to Jesus. Their words probably constitute a veiled rebuke. (With reference to this testimony see 1:6, 7, 8, 15; 1:26-34.)

(3) They make full use of the figure of speech called *hyperbole*, "*All* are going to him," i.e., soon you'll be without any follower.

In harmony with the purpose of the book (see pp. 32, 33), the author now dwells at length on the self-effacing answer of the Baptist. Let those in Asia Minor who follow him take it to heart, so that they may know that when they place John above Jesus they sin not only against the latter but also against the former!

The Baptist's answer was surprising and noble. **John answered and said, No man can receive anything unless it is given to him from heaven.** (Cf. 6:65; 19:11; I Cor. 4:7.) The herald of the Christ meant to say that to every one God has assigned a place in his eternal plan, and that he, the Baptist, has no right to lay claim to an honor which had not been given to him in heaven. Once given, it remains given, as the tense used in the original implies. Similarly, once withheld, it so remains. Instead of complaining about the success of Jesus, John's disciples should have rejoiced in the fact that the task of the Baptist was being fulfilled. And the nature of this task had been clearly indicated. Says John, **I call y o u to witness that I said, I myself am not the Christ, but I am sent ahead of him.** (For the first clause see on 1:8, 20; for the second, on 1:15, 23, 27.)

29. Then John takes an illustration from marriage customs. He says, **He who has the bride is the bridegroom.** The Baptist points out that the bride belongs to the bridegroom, not to the latter's friend. Now Christ is the Bridegroom, and his people are the Bride. The Bride, then, must be brought to the Bridegroom. That is exactly what John has been doing. He is constantly pointing to the Lamb of God, hoping that many will follow the latter. **Now, the bridegroom's friend who stands and hears him is very happy to hear the bridegroom's voice.** So it is with John. Just as the friend of the bridegroom, who stands at his side, listening, rejoices when the bridegroom voices his joy upon receiving the bride, so also the Baptist is very happy when he reflects on the satisfaction in the heart of the real Bridegroom, Christ, upon welcoming his own. He says, **This joy of mine is now full.** He means: when, in connection with the report regarding the dispute çoncerning purifying, I receive further assurance

148

that people are leaving me and are flocking to Jesus, my cup of joy is running over.

30. Summing up the preceding, the way-preparer states, **He must increase, but I must decrease,** i.e., he (Jesus) must continue to grow, while I (John) must continue to diminish. Note the *must,* indicating that this is in accordance with God's eternal plan. Of what use is a herald after the king has arrived? Why should crowds continue to surround the forerunner after his task has been accomplished? When he lays aside his responsibilities, let the multitude depart. Let them follow the king! Let them realize that the latter is glorious in his origin and has a glorious message. It is the Baptist who continues: [86]

31. He who comes from above is above all; he who springs from the earth belongs to the earth and speaks from the earth; he who comes from heaven is above all. The contrast between Jesus and the Baptist is continued. Jesus came from above (cf. 3:13), and, in view of his heavenly origin, is higher than all (cf. Eph. 1:20-23); hence, higher also than "the voice shouting in the desert." In comparison with Jesus, the herald has an earthly origin and character (cf. Matt. 11:11). He even speaks from the earth; for, though when God speaks through him, he is the voice of God, nevertheless, at times, when the herald's own weak and sinful nature asserts itself, fears and doubts begin to manifest themselves (as actually happened in John's case, Matt. 11:2, 3). The Christ, even he who comes from heaven, is above all: sinful doubts and fears never assail him.

32, 33. His testimony is pure and should be accepted, for: **What he has seen and heard, to this he bears testimony** (cf. 1:18; 3:11, 13, 31; cf. 8:40; 15:15). (For the verb *to bear testimony* see on 1:7.)

How has this testimony been received? On the whole, it was rejected: **but no one accepts his testimony.** Nevertheless, there are exceptions: **He who does accept his testimony. . . .** We have the same contrast here as in 1:11, 12. With reference to him who accepts the testimony of Christ it is stated that he **attests that God is true.** The simplest explanation is the following: those who accept Christ's testimony concerning himself (namely, that he is *the Son of God*) thereby set the seal of their approval upon God's own testimony regarding Jesus: "Thou art my beloved Son" (Luke 3:22; cf. John 1:34). They show that they believe that *God is true* in thus addressing Jesus. What is affirmed here in a positive way is stated negatively in I John 5:10, "He who does not believe God has made him a liar; because

---

[86] Many commentators hold that the words from here to the end of the chapter cannot have been spoken by the Baptist. They regard especially the contents of 3:34, 35 too advanced to be ascribed to him. But it is not at all clear that one who had seen and heard what is recorded in 1:32; Mark 1:9-11 (cf. Luke 3:21, 22) would not have been able to utter what is found in 3:34, 35.

he has not believed in the testimony which God has borne concerning his Son."

34, 35. Every one should accept Christ's testimony *not only because* a. he utters that which he has seen and heard (verse 32); *and because* b. his testimony with reference to himself is in perfect agreement with the Father's testimony regarding him (verse 33); *but also* (and in close harmony with the preceding) **because** c. **he whom God has sent** (as his ambassador) **speaks the words of God.** Although it is true that not only Jesus is represented in the Fourth Gospel as having been *sent* by God (in 1:6 and 3:28 it is the Baptist who is said to have been sent), it is, nevertheless, also true that in *nearly* every case this designation is used with reference to *him;* i.e., to the Son (3:17; 5:36, 38; 6:29, 57; 7:29; 8:42; 9:7; 10:36; 11:42; 17:3, 8, 18, 21, 23, 25; 20:21). Hence, we see no good reason to depart from the usual interpretation that in 3:34 the Son is described in the words, "he whom God has sent." Now it is the only begotten Son who, having been sent by God, speaks the words of God. In fact, he never utters anything else, for he is not like an ordinary prophet (e.g., the Baptist) upon whom the Spirit rests in a limited degree. **For it is not by measure** (but in fulness) **that he** (i.e., God; see preceding clause) **gives (him) the Spirit.** The best texts omit the pronoun *him.* Nevertheless, it should be supplied mentally, and it must be considered as referring to Christ, as is clearly indicated by verse 35. (See also 1:33.) Not only did the Father give *the Spirit* to the Son. He gave *all things* into his hand (cf. 5:19-30; 6:37; 12:49; 13:3; 17:2, 4, 11; cf. Matt. 11:27; 28:18). To limit this passage to Christ's Messianic sonship is hardly correct. The language (beginning at verse 31) is too majestic to permit such an interpretation. The Baptist, having witnessed the descent of the dove, and having heard the voice of the Father from heaven, understood that the mediatorial sonship of Jesus rested upon the trinitarian sonship. Thus, too, the gift of all things results from the eternal love-relationship between the Father and the Son: **The Father loves** (see on 21:15-17) **the Son and has given all things into his hand.**

36. In verse 36 the testimony of the Baptist reaches its *final* climax. A kind of climax was also noted in 1:29 and again in 1:34. By combining the three we get the following:

"Look, the Lamb of God who is taking away the sin of the world."

"And I have seen and I have testified that this one is the Son of God."

"He who believes in the Son has everlasting life; but he who disobeys the Son shall not see life, but the wrath of God remains on him."

Whereas *all things* are in the hand of the Son (verse 35), everlasting life too is in his hand. Accordingly, we read, **He who believes in the Son has everlasting life; but he who disobeys the Son shall not see life, but the wrath of God remains on him.**

This passage leads us back to the very similar words of Jesus himself in 3:16-18. (See on 3:16-18.) Christ's climax is also John's. *Everlasting life* is given to those who have an abiding *faith* in the Son. It is not for thrill-seekers (who "believe" in him as a worker of miracles; cf. 2:23) but for trusters.

Over against the destiny of believers Jesus had placed that of unbelievers (cf. 3:16 with 3:18). The Baptist does the same when he closes his remarks by stating that he who disobeys the Son shall not see life, the wrath of God remaining on him. Note that over against abiding faith stands *disobedience;* i.e., refusal to accept Christ by a true and abiding faith. Such base rejection of the Son of God (for explanation of this term see on 1:14) who confronts sinners with the invitation and the demand to "trust and obey," results in the punishment described in the final clause: they shall not *see life;* i.e., they shall not experience its joys and delights. The wrath of God, moreover, abides on them. The Baptist had spoken about this *wrath of God* in another connection (Matt. 3:7; cf. Luke 3:7). Luke refers to God's wrath in his Gospel (21:23). Paul speaks of it again and again (Rom. 1:18; 2:5, 8; 3:5; 4:15; 5:9; 9:22; 12:19; 13:4, 5; Eph. 2:3; 5:6; Col. 3:6; I Thess. 1:10; 2:16; 5:9). The concept is also found in Hebrews (3:11; 4:3), and in the book of Revelation (19:15; cf. 6:16, 17; 11:18; 14:10; 16:19). Upon one occasion this attitude is ascribed to Christ (Mark 3:5), who in his parabolic teaching does not hesitate to ascribe it to the King, Lord, or Householder in heaven (Matt. 18:34; 22:7; Luke 14:21).

Though in the light of Rom. 1:18 and Eph. 2:3 it is surely erroneous to limit this divine disposition too narrowly by defining it as *God's displeasure with those who reject the Gospel* (it also rests on those who have never heard the Gospel!), it is, nevertheless, true that man's impenitent heart, his obduracy and sinister unwillingness to embrace Christ by a living faith, often furnishes the setting for these wrath-of-God passages. That is true also with respect to the passage which we are now studying (3:36). It is the only instance of the use of this word *wrath* (ὀργή) in the Fourth Gospel. It indicates *settled indignation* (sometimes in contrast with *anger,* θυμός, which is then defined as *turbulent commotion,* suddenly blazing up and quickly extinguished, like fire in straw,[87] but especially when applied to God it is probably wrong to press the distinction between the two words).[88]

The mention of man's disobedience, his base refusal to accept the Gospel, causes the mind to travel back to the story of the fall in Paradise. As a result of this fall Adam and Eve had been refused access to the tree of life (Gen. 3:24), and the wrath of God had been visited upon mankind. John

---

[87] Cf. C. Trench, *Synonyms of the New Testament,* Grand Rapids, 1948, pp. 130-134.
[88] See article θυμός, ὀργή in Th.W.N.T.

3:36 now teaches us that this wrath remains on those who disobey the Son. (For further comment see comments on 3:18.)

This conclusion of the Baptist's testimony is beautiful because of its clear implication: *Embrace the Son of God by a living and abiding faith, and have everlasting life. Cf. 3:21.*

Synthesis of 3:22-36

See the Outline on p. 68. *The Son of God revealing himself to ever-widening circles: to Judea; John the Baptist's Recessional.*

After his conversation with Nicodemus in Jerusalem, Jesus retired to the country-region of Judea, near Jordan, where, by means of his disciples, he baptized (probably May-December in the year 27 A. D.).

Farther to the north, at Aenon near to Salim, John — not yet imprisoned — was baptizing. His crowds gradually diminished and went over to Jesus. This resulted in jealousy on the part of the disciples of the Baptist, who, having argued with a Jew who favored Jesus, rushed to their master, complaining, "Rabbi, he who was with you beyond the Jordan, to whom you bore testimony, look, he baptizes, and all are going to him."

In harmony with the purpose of his book the author dwells at length on the self-effacing answer of the Baptist. The latter, having referred to his earlier testimony, maintains that each man should accept with gratitude whatever station in life God assigns him. He points out that just as in natural life the bride belongs to the groom and not to the latter's friend, so it is in the realm of the kingdom. Here, too, it is the duty of the friend to lead the Bride to the Bridegroom. In this case the Bridegroom is Christ. The Bride represents those who are brought to him and accept him by a living faith. The "friend" is John the Baptist. When the latter hears the Bridegroom's voice welcoming the Bride, he rejoices greatly. When the heavenly king arrives, the earthly herald recedes. Let everyone now accept the king, the Spirit-filled Son of God, who speaks the words of God. Those who, in contrast with the great majority, embrace Christ with a living faith, thereby indicate that they have accepted the verdict of the Father with reference to him ("This is my beloved Son"). Their faith in the Object of God's love and generosity will be rewarded with everlasting life. But upon the disobedient God's wrath (settled indignation) remains. Implication: Harden not your heart but accept by faith the Son of God!

CHAPTER IV

JOHN   4:1-26

4 1 Now when the Lord knew that the Pharisees had heard, "Jesus is gaining and baptizing more disciples than John" 2 —although Jesus himself was not baptizing, but his disciples—, 3 he left Judea and went back again to Galilee.

4 Now he had to go through Samaria. 5 So he came to a Samaritan town called Sychar, near the parcel of ground which Jacob had given to his son Joseph. 6 And Jacob's spring was there. So Jesus, travel-weary, was sitting by the spring just as he was. It was about the sixth hour.

7 There came a woman of Samaria to draw water. Jesus said to her, "Give me a drink." 8 For his disciples were gone away into the town in order to buy articles of food. 9 So the Samaritan woman said to him, "How is it that you, a Jew, ask a drink of me, a Samaritan woman?" (For Jews do not use [vessels] together with Samaritans.) 10 Jesus answered and said to her, "If you knew the gift of God, and who it is that said to you, 'Give me a drink,' you would have been the one to ask him, and he would have given you living water." [89]

11 She said to him, "Sir, you have no rope-bucket, and the well is deep; where do you get that living water? 12 Surely, you are not greater, are you, than our father Jacob, who gave us this well, and he himself drank from it, and so did his sons and his flocks?" 13 Jesus answered and said to her, "Whoever drinks this water will get thirsty again; 14 but whoever drinks the water that I shall give him will in no way be thirsty again forever, but the water that I shall give him will become within him a spring of water that keeps on bubbling up unto everlasting life."

15 The woman said to him, "Sir, give me this water, in order that I may not get thirsty nor have to keep on coming so far to draw." 16 He said to her, "Go, call your husband, and come back here." 17 The woman answered and said, "I have no husband." Jesus said to her, "You were right when you said, 'A husband I have not,' 18 for five *husbands* you have had, but the one whom you now have is not your *husband;* this you have stated correctly."

19 The woman said to him, "Sir, I perceive that you are a prophet. 20 Our fathers worshiped on this mountain, but y o u say that [90] the place where one must worship is in Jerusalem." 21 Jesus said to her, "Believe me, woman, the hour is coming when neither in this mountain nor in Jerusalem will y o u worship the Father. 22 y o u worship what y o u do not know; we worship what we know, for salvation is from the Jews. 23 But the hour is coming — yea, has already arrived! — when the genuine worshipers will worship the Father in spirit and truth, for such are the very people whom the Father is seeking as his worshipers. 24 God is

---

[89] II C; see pp. 41, 42.
[90] On ὅτι see pp. 54, 57.

Spirit, and those who worship (him) must worship in spirit and truth." 25 The woman said, "I know that Messiah is coming (the One who is called Christ); whenever he arrives, he will declare everything to us." 26 Jesus said to her, "I, the One who is talking to you, am he."

4:1-26

4:1. Now when the Lord knew that the Pharisees had heard, Jesus is gaining and baptizing more disciples than John. About December of the year 27 A. D. the Baptist was imprisoned (cf. Mark 6:17-20). The religious leaders of Jerusalem who, in the days of John's great popularity, had been filled with jealousy, rejoiced. What were the reasons for their displeasure with him? (See on 1:19.) But this joy was of short duration, for other tidings reached the Pharisees: namely, that the multitudes surrounding Jesus — the disciples whom he was gaining and baptizing — were more numerous than those which had followed the herald. In fact, even before John's imprisonment Jesus had forged ahead of him in popular favor (3:22-26). Hence, from the point of view of the members of the Sanhedrin, matters were becoming worse instead of better.

"Now when *the Lord* (see on 1:38, footnote 44) *knew.*" How did he know? (See on 5:6). The modern Greek New Testament has ἔμαθεν— learned — here; he had *come to know.* Specifically, Jesus had come to know: a. that John had been imprisoned (Matt. 4:12); and b. that the Pharisees had heard that the crowds had gone over to Jesus, who was gaining and baptizing more disciples than John.

2. Although Jesus himself was not baptizing, but his disciples. No one must ever be able to boast, "*I* was baptized by *the Lord himself in person,* whereas *you* were baptized by a mere disciple." (Cf. I Cor. 1:17.) That Jesus, nevertheless, approved of baptism and assumed responsibility for the rite as administered by his disciples is clear from the use of the singular of the verb "to baptize" both here (4:1) and in 3:22. What *they* (his disciples) did, *he* was in reality doing (through his agents).

3. He left Judea. Jesus decides to *leave* (on this verb see 4:28) Judea. Why? Because he was well aware of the fact that his own great "popularity" in the country-region of Judea would bring about such keen resentment on the part of the religious leaders in that southern province that this resentment, in the natural course of events, would lead to *a premature crisis.* Now the Lord knew that for every event in his life there was an appointed time in God's decree. And he also knew that the appropriate moment for his death had not yet arrived. As soon as that moment arrived, he would voluntarily lay down his life (cf. 10:18; 13:1; 14:31). He would do so *then,* but not before then. Hence, he must now leave Judea.

And went back again to Galilee. Jesus went back *again* to Galilee. From this word *again* (πάλιν) it certainly cannot be deduced that he had already been living in Galilee for a considerable period of time, so that the entire story recorded in Chapter 4 must be referred to the close of Christ's earthly ministry. It is much more natural to infer that the author was thinking of the events recorded in 2:1-12. Jesus had been in Galilee in late February or early March. It was there that he had performed his first sign. From Cana and Capernaum he had traveled to Jerusalem at the time of the Passover. And now, after having spent some time in the capital and in the country-region of Judea, he was going back *again* to Galilee.

4. Now he had to go through Samaria. Jesus *had to* go through Samaria. There were several roads leading from Judea to Galilee: one near the sea-coast, another through Perea, and one through the heart of Samaria. Josephus informs us, however, that it was the custom of the Galileans, when they came to the holy city at the festivals, to take their journey through the country of the Samaritans (*Antiquities*, XX, vi, 1). Besides, the shortest distance from the Jerusalem-Jericho region, where Jesus had been carrying on his ministry, to Cana in Galilee, his destination (4:46), was the road through Samaria. It is *possible* that the verb *had to* or *must* (ἔδει) refers merely to this circumstance; namely, that in order to save time and needless steps, a traveler coming from the country-region of Judea *had to* go through Samaria if he desired to reach Cana in Galilee. Nevertheless, in view of the fact that our Lord's consciousness of fulfilling the divine plan is constantly stressed in this Gospel (see 2:4; 7:30; 8:20; 12:23; 13:1; 14:31) and is implied also in the immediate context (4:1-3), it is more *probable* that the meaning here is: he had to go through Samaria *in agreement with the orders of his heavenly Father:* to do the will of the One who had sent him and to accomplish his work (4:34).

5. So he came to a Samaritan town called Sychar. Having entered the province of Samaria, Jesus reached the fork of an old Roman road, just south of Sychar at the site of present-day Askar, with Joseph's tomb near-by. To the w.n.w of Sychar or Askar is Gerizim, the mount of the blessing (Deut. 27:12). Behind Askar and to the n.e. of Gerizim rises the more elevated Ebal, the mount of the curse (Deut. 27:13).[91] Today a modern city of considerable size is situated at the foot and on the slopes of Mt. Gerizim. It is called Nablus, which is an Arabic corruption of Neapolis (new city). On the southern slope of Gerizim one finds the synagogue of the Samaritans that contains the scrolls of the Samaritan Pentateuch, to which the owners ascribe a fantastic antiquity. The biblical city of Shechem

---

[91] See W.H.A.B., Plate IX; also *Viewmaster Travelogue*, Reel Number 4016, The Samaritans, Samaria, Palestine, Scene 4.

was located not far from the present Nablus. On Shechem see Gen. 12; 34; 37:12, 13; Josh. 21:21; 24; Judg. 9; I Kings 12:25; Jer. 41:5.

Jesus stopped at a spot about one-half mile s.s.w. of Sychar, **near to the parcel of ground which Jacob had given to his son Joseph.** According to Gen. 33:19 Jacob, on his return from Paddan-aram, had bought a field from the children of Hamor for a hundred pieces of silver. The ground purchased was probably a rather extensive tract, much larger than the burial-lot which contains Joseph's tomb. It probably included the place where the well was dug, which was therefore *near* the burial-lot of Joseph. However, it would seem that the Amorites failed to honor this business-transaction, and that they acted as if the land had never been sold to Jacob. So Jacob had to regain his property by force of arms. Later he gave it to his favorite son Joseph. We read (Gen. 48:22):

"Moreover, I have given to thee one portion (literally *shoulder* or *mountain-slope*, Hebrew *shechem*, from which the city of Shechem derived its name) above thy brethren, which I took out of the hand of the Amorite with my sword and with my bow."

When Joseph was about to die in Egypt, he requested that when the Lord would visit his people by bringing them back to the land of the fathers (Gen. 50:25, 26) his body would be buried there (Gen. 50:25, 26). This was done, as is recorded in Josh. 24:32:

"And the bones of Joseph, which the children of Israel brought up out of Egypt, buried they in Shechem, in the parcel of ground which Jacob bought of the sons of Hamor the father of Shechem for a hundred pieces of money; and they became the inheritance of the children of Joseph."

6. It was on this piece of land which Jacob once had owned, and not far from the lot where Joseph had been buried, that Jesus stopped in order to rest a while. The place was admirably suited to this purpose, for **Jacob's Spring** (or Jacob's Well) **was there.** Jews, Samaritans, Mohammedans, and Christians agree in associating this spring with the patriarch Jacob. There is not a good reason to doubt the truth of this tradition.

We must distinguish between two terms used in this account: *spring* [92] (πηγή, probably in 4:6 in the sense of spring-fed well) and *well* (φρέαρ). The first term occurs in 4:6, 14. In 4:6 (used twice in that verse) it probably refers to the fact that water was known to be bubbling up at the bottom of the pit. The second term is found in 4:11, 12. It indicates any kind of well, whether spring-fed or not. The shaft of Jacob's Well at the time of this story and again today is more than 100 feet deep. The debris, which collected during the intervening centuries, and which caused so many commentaries to say that the depth is 75 feet, has been removed in

---

[92] Cf. W. R. Hutton, " 'Spring' and 'Well' in John 4:6, 11, 12," *ExT*, 56(1945), 27.

recent years. The well is surrounded by the walls of a convent. The water of Jacob's Spring is very refreshing, not inferior in quality to that of the surrounding springs.

The question has often been asked, Why did Jacob dig a well here, when an unusually copious water-supply was gushing out of the near-by mountains of Samaria? The answer may be that other fountains sometimes were dry in the summer or that he wanted his own well on his own ground for his own flocks. He did not desire to have any trouble with the neighbors regarding water-rights. For the troubles of his father Isaac regarding wells see Gen. 26:15.

So Jesus, travel-weary (fatigued as a result of a long journey), **was sitting by the spring, just as he was;** i.e., tired, dusty, and thirsty. The Fourth Gospel stresses not only the divine but also the human nature of Jesus; see p. 84. The Greek preposition ἐπί, which we have translated *by*, has as primary meaning *upon*. The phrase in which it occurs can, therefore, be rendered *upon* (the curbstone of) *the spring.* Yet, in view of the fact that this preposition (used here with the locative) can also have the secondary meaning *by* or *at,* which is simpler (requiring no mental insertion of words which are not actually found in the text), it is probably better to give it that meaning here, just as in 5:2.

It was about the sixth hour. (For the difficult problem of time-computation in the Fourth Gospel we refer to what has been said on pp. 104, 105.) Here in 4:6 the Roman civil day computation — so that it would be either 6 A. M. or 6 P. M. when Jesus arrived at the spring — can lay claim to many arguments in its favor. However, we must immediately modify this statement, for 6 A. M. is obviously out of the question, in view of the entire context. We are not saying that it is entirely impossible that the Jewish time-reckoning is followed here, so that it was noon when our Lord arrived at the well. Nevertheless, we prefer the theory that it was 6 P. M., and this on the basis of the following considerations:

(1) *This was the usual time for drawing water* (Gen. 24:11). The fact that a woman comes to this well *all alone* does not prove anything to the contrary. Let it be borne in mind that there were several springs in the immediate vicinity, so that it may not have been strictly necessary for all the women of Sychar to go to *this* one.[93] Or the other women may have come a little earlier, not wishing to associate with this particular woman, for obvious reasons (4:16-18).

(2) There would still be plenty of time for the events recorded in verses 27-40. Besides, it is certainly more likely that the Samaritans in great num-

---

[93] A. Edersheim, *The Life and Times of Jesus the Messiah,* New York, 1898, vol. 1, p. 409.

bers would resort to Jesus in the cool of the evening, when the work was done, than at high noon.

(3) If it was toward evening (6 P. M.), we can also understand the request of the people that Jesus *abide with them* (4:40), which reminds one of Luke 24:29: "Abide with us, for it is toward evening, and the day is now far spent." We admit, of course, that a similar request could have been made any time of the day, but it was most appropriate in the late afternoon or evening.

7-10. At Jacob's Spring she sees a stranger. It is Jesus who, in obedience to the will of the Father and in complete harmony with his own inner desire (4:34), is going to direct every effort to manifest his glory in the land of the Samaritans, gathering fruit for eternal life (4:36). By means of this woman the Lord purposes to reach her neighbors. He will prove to be the Savior not only for his elect in Judea but also for those in Samaria.

The contrast between the third chapter of John (Christ's work in Judea) and the fourth (his work in Samaria) is very striking. In the former Jesus was described as dealing with a *man* (Nicodemus); here, in chapter 4, with a *woman;* there with a *Jew,* here with a *Samaritan;* there with a person of *high moral standing,* here with an individual of *low repute.* Nevertheless, the Lord proves himself able to save both.

Now in the process of *winning the soul* (cf. Prov. 11:30; Dan. 12:3; James 5:20) of this woman Jesus appeals to her *sympathy* ("Give me a drink"), to her *curiosity* ("If thou knewest . . ."), to her desire for *ultimate rest and satisfaction* ("whoever drinks the water that I shall give him will in no way be thirsty again forever") and to her *conscience* ("Go, call your husband"). He addresses himself to every phase of her personality in order that the goal may be reached.

And what is the woman doing? One would almost be justified in saying: for a while she is trying her utmost *not* to be saved, as will be shown. Nevertheless, though she opposes the efforts of Christ, the bulwarks of opposition are being broken down one by one, until finally, and in her case perhaps rather suddenly, grace penetrates and achieves the victory. However, that victory of grace over sin in her own life is presupposed (cf. 4:34, 36) rather than explicitly stated. The real topic is not the salvation of this soul, nor even the salvation of many souls in the province of Samaria, but rather the manner in which by means of this work the glory of God in Christ is made manifest.

There came a woman of Samaria. The idea is not that the woman came all the way from *the city* of Samaria, a two hour walk at least! What is meant is that she was a native of *the province* of Samaria. She came **to draw water.** Hence, we can picture her carrying her water-pitcher (4:28) upon her head or, like Rebecca, upon her shoulder (cf. Gen. 24:15), as she walks from her home in Sychar (4:5, 28) in a southerly direction to Jacob's Spring. How many people living today would not consider it rather burdensome to have to walk even this half mile to get water? The Samaritan woman would agree with them (4:15).

Appealing then to her *sympathy* **Jesus said to her, Give me a drink.** It is reasonable to assume that the request was made *after* the woman had drawn the water; see on 4:28. It was an altogether natural request, for Jesus was, indeed, thirsty. At the same time it was also a manifestation of divine strategy and of psychological insight, for if you wish to gain entrance into the heart of another person two methods can be employed: a. do that person a favor; b. give that person an opportunity to do you a favor. Often b. is more effective than a. Rightly considered, however, Jesus combined the two (a. and b.)!

8. The request of Jesus was also very natural **for** this reason that he was alone, there was no one else to serve him; and he had nothing with which to draw water. **His disciples** (see on 2:2) **were gone away into the town in order to buy articles of food,** i.e., to purchase provisions. It would seem that at this time Jews and Samaritans, though mutually hostile, still had dealings with each other to some extent (Jews could buy from Samaritans), which observation should guard us against a wrong interpretation of the parenthetical sentence in 4:9.

9. Nevertheless, the relation between Jews and Samaritans was by no means cordial, as is evident from what the woman now says in answer to the request of this stranger. **So the Samaritan woman said to him, How is it that you, a Jew, ask a drink of me, a Samaritan woman?** Christ's accent and pronunciation probably sufficed to indicate to this woman that the stranger was a Jew.

In order to understand the religious enmity between the two peoples it is necessary to give a brief review of the history of the Samaritans. When Israel's last king Hosea, after first paying tribute to Assyria, transferred his allegiance to Egypt, Samaria, the capital of the northern kingdom, was surrounded by the armies of Shalmaneser and after a long siege was taken by Sargon. This was in the year 722 B. C. Most of the people were driven forth from their country and carried away to Assyria, Halah, and the Habor, the river of Gozan, and the cities of the Medes (II Kings 17:3-6). The very poor were allowed to remain behind in the land of Israel. Foreigners from Babylon and surrounding territories were brought to the devastated region, and these intermarried with the Israelites which had been left behind. To this mixed population was given the name *Samaritans* (after Samaria, the metropolis, founded by Omri). The colonists from foreign lands were not pleased with conditions as they found them. They found the country overrun by wild beasts, and they correctly ascribed this plague to the displeasure of Jehovah whom they had offended. They begged their monarch to send them an Israelitish priest, who would teach them "the law of the god of the land." And so it came about that an adulterated Judaism was grafted on the pagan cult. When a remnant of the Jews returned to the land of the fathers (chiefly, but not exclusively, from those who had been deported in the Babylonian Exile of 586 B. C.), built the altar of burnt-offering, and laid the foundation of the temple, jealous Samaritans and their allies interrupted the work (Ezra 3 and 4). The reason for this was that they had been refused permission to cooperate in the work of rebuilding. They had asked:

"Let us build with you; for we seek your God, as you do; and we sacrifice unto him since the days of Esar-haddon king of Assyria, who brought us up hither."

The answer which they had received was as follows:

"You have nothing to do with us in building a house unto our God." Having received this blunt refusal, the Samaritans hated the Jews (cf. also Neh. 4:1, 2) and subsequently built their own temple on Mt. Gerizim. This was destroyed by one of the Maccabean rulers, John Hyrcanus, about the year 128 B. C. The worshipers, however, continued to offer their adorations on the summit of the hill where the sacred edifice had stood. They do so even today. At Passover the entire community leaves home and camps on top of Gerizim where, when the full moon rises, the highpriest intones the prayers, and the slaughterers cut the throats of the lambs just as they did many, many centuries ago. The Samaritans now number about 270 people. Of the Old Testament they accept only the five books of Moses. It seemed for a while as if the sect was doomed to extinction, owing to their close inbreeding and the great shortage of women among them. Of late, however, they have begun to marry Jewish women.

The unfriendly sentiments of the Jews with respect to the Samaritans may be gathered from such passages as 8:48 and (the apocryphal book) Ecclesiasticus 50:25, 26. The similarly hostile attitude of the Samaritans toward the Jews is shown in Luke 9:51-53. Our Lord's lovingkindness overleaped the boundaries of national hatred as is shown not only here in John 4 but also in Luke 9:54, 55; 17:11-19; and in the Parable of the Good Samaritan (Luke 10:25-37).

Having now briefly reviewed the history of the relation between Jews and Samaritans, we are somewhat better prepared for the woman's question, "How is it that you, a Jew, ask a drink of me, a Samaritan woman?" Nevertheless, unless another factor is taken into account, we might still be tempted to ask, If Samaritans were willing to sell victuals to the Jews (4:8), why should they not be willing to offer them water? Or, the question might be stated thus, If the disciples of Jesus could buy food from the Samaritans, why did the woman consider it so strange that a Jew would ask her for a drink? The explanation is found in the explanatory note (whether added by John himself or another — the textual evidence is indecisive — does not matter):

(For Jews do not use [vessels] together with Samaritans.) The verb which we have translated "(do not) use [vessels] together with" (ουγχρῶνται) in all probability should not be translated "have (no) dealings with." As a matter of fact the Jews did have dealings with the Samaritans, but according to Pharisaic interpretation of the laws of purity (e.g., Lev. 15) Jews and Samaritans were not allowed to use drinking-vessels together.[94] It is for this reason that this woman, realizing that Jesus will have to use her pitcher, is greatly surprised and, perhaps also somewhat pleased that this Jew addresses her and is willing to drink from her pitcher.

10. Our Lord makes use of this aroused feeling of surprise on her part, and fans into flame her *curiosity* in order that her respect for him may increase, and the work of rescuing this soul from the fetters of sin and evil may make further progress. Though he does not answer her question in so many words, he does not ignore it. He shows that the question is based on an erroneous presupposition. She proceeded from the assumption: *you, a Jew,* are needy and helpless. . . . *I, a Samaritan woman* am self-sufficient and therefore able to supply your need. Jesus, by his answer, shows that the very opposite is the case: *she* is the one who needs the water, and *he* is the Fountain that is able to supply it! Cf. Rev. 3:17. Hence, we read: **Jesus answered and said to her, If you knew the gift of God, and who it is that said to you, Give me a drink, you would have been the one to ask him, and he would have given you living water.**[95]

We have in these words another glorious *mashal.* (We refer the reader to what has been said on this subject in connection with 2:19.) The term *living water* lends itself to a twofold interpretation (just as do the mysterious terms in 2:19 and 3:3). A riddle-like character of the saying causes reflection, wonderment. It will make the woman ask questions. And that is exactly what Jesus wants. Even though she does not grasp the significance of his words at once, she will revolve them in her mind, until by and by, with dramatic suddenness, all will become clear. This, as we have said before, is divine pedagogy!

When Jesus spoke about "the gift of God," he meant "living water." But "living water" could mean *spring-water* (Gen. 26:19), which bubbles up by itself, in distinction from rain water, which must be collected in a cistern or reservoir. Of course, it happens at times that a shaft is sunk into

---

[94] Cf. *JBL,* 69(1950), 137-147.
[95] The protasis indicates present unreality, while the apodosis refers to past unreality. But the difference in time is negligible: "If you knew *now.* . . . then a *moment ago* you would not have asked."

the earth until a spring is reached. Jacob's Spring illustrates the point exactly. Hence, when Jesus said, "he would have given you *living water,*" the woman interprets this to mean, "he would have given you not the water which has for some time been standing in the well but the spring-water at the bottom of it.

However, in the mind of Christ fresh and pure and never-ceasing spring-water was a symbol of everlasting life or salvation. As yet the woman does not know *who he is* — namely, the Author of salvation — nor *what is meant by the living water* of which he speaks.

Note also this point: there is a mild rebuke in the words of Jesus; as if he had said, "*I* asked you for *ordinary* water, the lesser gift, but *you* hesitate; if *you* had asked me for *living* water, the supreme gift ("the gift of God"), *I* would not have hesitated but would have *given* it to you at once." However, the rebuke is softened by the clause: "If you knew the gift of God and who it is," implying, "You did not know."

11. She said to him, Sir, you have no rope-bucket, and the well is deep; where do you get that living water?

Jesus had told the woman that to the one who asks him he gives the living water. Thinking that the reference was to the spring-water at the very bottom of the well, the woman answered, "Sir, you have no *rope-bucket*" (from ἄντλος, bilge-water in a hold; hence, ἀντλέω: to bale out, to draw out; and ἄντλημα: the rope-bucket used to draw water out of a well). As the woman sees it, two obstacles make it impossible for Jesus to supply this living water about which he has been speaking:

a. he has no rope-bucket; but even if he had one,

b. the well (τὸ φρέαρ, see on 4:6) is deep (again, see on 4:6).

How then will anyone be able to get at the spring-water that bubbles up at the very bottom of this well, below the standing water? The woman is thoroughly perplexed and mystified. What this stranger is saying seems to be absurd. Meanwhile, however, she keeps on revolving the riddle in her mind!

12. She continues, **Surely, you are not greater, are you, than our father Jacob** (through Joseph the Samaritans traced their descent to Jacob, conveniently forgetting their mixed ancestry), **who gave us this well** (explained in connection with 4:5), **and he himself drank from it, and so did his sons and his flocks** (*flocks,* literally: nurselings, whatever has to be nourished or fed; here the reference is to animals). Though the question anticipates a negative answer, yet the woman shows that she is beginning to ponder the *greatness* of this stranger. Thus, she is being made receptive for the Gospel.

13, 14. Has she questioned the stranger's superior greatness? Jesus now indicates that he is, indeed, greater by far than Jacob, for the gift which he bestows is infinitely more precious than the one bequeathed upon posterity by the patriarch. It is in this sense that Christ's answer must be interpreted: **Jesus answered and said to her, Whoever drinks this water will get thirsty again; but whoever drinks the water that I shall give him will in no way be thirsty again forever, but that water which I shall give him will become a spring of water that keeps on bubbling up unto everlasting life.** Thus Jesus appeals to her *craving for ultimate rest and satisfaction.*

Note the contrast which Jesus draws here:

Physical water from Jacob's Well:	The Living Water which Jesus Bestows:
(1) cannot prevent one from becoming thirsty again . . . and again . . . and again.	(1) makes one lose this thirst for all time to come; i.e., gives lasting satisfaction. Once a believer, always a believer. Once reborn, always reborn. Cf. 6:35; also Is. 49:10; Rev. 7:16, 17; 21:6; 22:1, 17.
(2) remains *outside* of the soul, and is incapable of filling its needs.	(2) enters into the soul and remains *within,* as a source of spiritual refreshment and satisfaction.
(3) is limited in quantity, lessens, disappears whenever we drink it.	(3) is a self-perpetuating spring (the progressive idea; see also on 1:12). Here on earth it sustains a person spiritually, *with a view to* the everlasting life in the realms above ("*unto* everlasting life").

15. The woman by this time has become aware of the fact that Jesus (verse 14) is referring to a very special kind of water. Hence, she **said to him, Sir, give me** *this* **water** . . . Nevertheless, she still believes that this water, no matter how precious it may be, is physical in character. She believes that it can prevent physical thirst: . . . **that I may not get thirsty nor have to *keep on coming so far*** (present subjunctive διέρχωμαι) to draw. Ordinarily, if she wanted the water from Jacob's Well, she would have to walk those ten minutes from her home to this well, and she would have to do this every day, at least once a day. Hence, she yearns for the water which not only quenches but prevents thirst.

"You would have been the one to ask" for this "gift of God," Jesus had said (4:10). Now she actually asks, "Sir, give me this water." Yet, her request is not in compliance with the hint contained in verse 10, for she does not yet recognize the spiritual nature of the gift of God neither does she know the character of the Giver.

16. Many see no connection between the woman's request, "Sir, give me this water," (verse 15) and Jesus' reply. **He said to her, Go, call your husband and come back here.** They are of the opinion that the Lord changes the subject at this juncture. Others, in somewhat similar vein, suggest that what Jesus meant was something like this: "Since you, woman, are so slow of understanding that you do not perceive that in mentioning *living water* I was speaking about a *spiritual* gift, I now consider your case hopeless. Please call your husband. Perhaps, I can succeed better with him."

However, in that case we would have to suppose that Jesus actually did not know that she had no husband; but the context informs us that he *did* know this (4:17, 18). There is, however, a close connection between the woman's request and Christ's command. Does the woman desire living water? Then there must be a thirst for this water. This thirst will not be truly awakened unless there be a sense of guilt, a consciousness of sin. The mention of her *husband* is the best means of reminding this woman of her immoral life. The Lord is now addressing himself to her *conscience*.

17, 18. The woman answered and said, I have no husband.
Very abrupt is the woman's answer. She, who has been so very talkative (note 4:11, 12, 15), suddenly becomes close-mouthed. It is interesting to count the number of words in her various replies: according to the Greek, in verse nine she uses 11 words (Syriac, closely related to Samaritan, also 11 words); in verse fifteen, 13 words (Syriac, 15); in verses eleven and twelve, 42 words (Syriac, 29); but in verse seventeen, only 3 words: "not I-have husband" (οὐκ ἔχω ἄνδρα; Syriac, also only 3 words)! Is she single then? A widow, perhaps? She knows very well that her curt reply does not do justice to the truth! She is throwing up her guard. She refuses to be exposed or unmasked. She is by no means immediately ready to make a full confession of her sins. That is what we meant when we said (see on 4:7-10): One would almost be justified in saying: for a while she is trying her utmost *not* to be saved.

But the Lord does not leave her alone. He finishes what he has begun. **Jesus said to her, You were right when you said, A husband I have not.** Note that Jesus lays all the emphasis on the word *husband*, placing it first in the sentence, whereas in the woman's speech it had been the last word. (This, at least, is true in the Greek, which is of some significance. The fact that some manuscripts have the same order of words in both cases is probably due to harmonistic corruption). The woman *is living with a man*. She has a paramour; not a husband, not even in a loosely legal sense. Jesus continues, **. . . for five husbands you have had, but the one whom you now have is not your husband; this you have stated correctly.** How the

Lord, in this one sentence lays bare her entire past and present life (cf. 4:29)! If even *among the Jews* many people followed the laxer school of Hillel in interpreting the divorce-regulation of Deut. 24:1, so that as a result a husband would divorce his wife if she did not exactly please him, it is easy to see that *among the Samaritans* conditions touching marriage and divorce were not any better. This woman had had five husbands. (It is, of course, *possible* that one or two had died.) Jerome makes mention of a woman who had had no less than twenty-two husbands! There is nothing new under the sun.

How did Jesus know all this? (See p. 191.) In his conversation with this woman the Lord had indicated that she should obtain a saving knowledge of a. the gift of God; i.e., the living water; and b. the Giver of this gift (see 4:10). By exposing her sin Jesus is preparing her heart for the knowledge and reception of *the gift* (4:16-18). By revealing and laying bare her entire immoral present and past life he is revealing the character of *the Giver* (4:17, 18). He manifests himself as One who according to his divine nature is the Omniscient One! Thus he also answers the question of 4:12.

19. The woman said to him, Sir, I perceive that you are a prophet.
The woman does not deny the remarks of Jesus concerning her immoral life. In fact, by calling him *a prophet* (which to her meant one who can read secrets) she really admits her guilt! It is clear from 4:29 that this stranger's résumé of her evil conduct shocked her beyond words. Though she did not see in him the Messiah, nevertheless, such penetrating knowledge ("he told me *all* that I ever did") makes her think of the coming Messiah who will know and will declare *everything*.

20. She continues: **Our fathers worshiped on this mountain** (perhaps pointing to Gerizim), **but y o u say that the place where one must worship is in Jerusalem.**
Some commentators see in this remark the (implied) question of one who is seeking information on a matter in which she was *really* interested. Others look upon it as an artful and clever device to divert the conversation from a very painful topic to one of a much more innocent character.

The following, as we see it, must be borne in mind: a. When Scripture does not reveal inner motives, it is generally best not to speak with the air of *certainty*. One must often be satisfied with *probability*. b. A *probable* answer or solution will be one which does justice to the requirement of *consistent character portrayal*. On this score the theory that the woman, by means of her remark about the proper place of worship, was trying abruptly to break off and change the subject merits consideration, for this is exactly what she had tried once before (4:17). Nothing is more common than for sinners to make an attempt to change the subject in order to avoid painful reminders of sinful conduct. c. Nevertheless, why should it be

165

considered impossible that *both* classes of commentators are correct, except, of course, in so far as an interpreter of the one class definitely rejects the solution favored by the other class? In fact, does not this appear to be the most plausible?

Here, as it seems probable to us, we see a woman who in her anxiety to drop a painful subject proposes a question about which she has heard much and in which she has developed a certain interest. This interest has been stimulated by the stranger at the well, who has shocked her to the very depths of her being. The Holy Spirit is working in her heart. Though she does not cherish the idea of dwelling any longer on the subject of her immoral life, she is beginning even now to regret her condition. But where will she go and what must she do? Must she worship on Gerizim or at Jerusalem? (See what has been said, in our explanation of 4:4, 5, 9, about Gerizim and the worship at that place.) "Our fathers" (e.g., Abraham and Jacob, Gen. 12:7; 33:20) had erected altars at Shechem on or near Gerizim's slopes. And the Samaritan Pentateuch substitutes Gerizim for Ebal in Deut. 27:4. The Jews, on the other hand, placed great stress on Jerusalem as the one, central place of worship.[96] Who was right? is the implied question.

21. Jesus answers that not *where* one worships matters but *the attitude of heart and mind and the obedience to God's truth regarding the object and method of worship* is what matters. It is not the *where* but the *how* and the *what* that is all-important.

Jesus said to her, Believe me. He said this in order to emphasize the startling character of the declaration which he is about to make. The expression **the hour is coming,** is found also in 4:23; 5:25, 28; 16:2, 25, 32. When the Lord continues, **when neither in this mountain nor in Jerusalem will y o u worship the Father,** he predicts that God's elect *from every tribe and nation* will serve him (cf. Zeph. 2:11; Mal. 1:11). The clause may be paraphrased thus: "the hour is coming when neither *exclusively* in this mountain nor *exclusively* in Jerusalem will y o u worship the one and only Father (through Jesus Christ) of the Church Universal." That is his answer with respect to the *where* (which already contains a hint with respect to the *how* and the *what*).

22. With respect to the *what* the Lord continues, **Y o u** (Samaritans) **worship what y o u do not know** — i.e., the creature of your own imagination, having rejected the prophetical and poetical books of the Old Testament; **we** (Jews) **worship what we know** — i.e., God as revealed to us in the entire Old Testament —, **for salvation is from** (ἐκ) **the Jews.** Literally he says *the* salvation; i.e., that specific rescue from the guilt, pollution, and punishment of sin, and that sum-total of every spiritual endowment, which God grants to his people on the basis of the redemptive work of his Son. That this salvation proceeds from the Jews is clear from Ps. 147:19, 20; Isa. 2:3; Amos 3:2; Mic. 4:1, 2; Rom. 3:1, 2; 9:3-5; 9:18.

23. Finally, anent the *how and the what* Jesus states what is found in 4:23, 24. He introduces this great saying by employing an expression that is also found in 5:25, **The hour is coming — yea, has already arrived! —**. In the mind of our Lord the perfected state of the future is foreshadowed in the present. The present is the future in embryo. Thus, the kingdom of heaven is both future and present. This holds also with respect to everlasting life. It is true that the worship of the Father in spirit and truth will not reach perfection until the great day of the consummation of all things; but even now the religion of the old dispensation, which attached so much importance to stipulated seasons, places, and outward observances, is beginning to vanish. Very soon the veil of the temple will be rent in two from top to bottom (Matt. 27:51), and with it the last remnant of the validity of ceremonial worship will cease to exist.

. . . when the genuine worshipers (i.e., those deserving of the name) **will worship the Father in spirit and truth.** The verb *will worship* (fut. indicative of προσκυνέω) in the Fourth Gospel never means merely *will respect;* see also 4:20, 21, 22, 24; 9:38; 12:20. The final phase *in spirit and truth* has been interpreted variously. The context should decide. Jesus has been emphasizing two things: a. worship which is worth the name is not hampered by *physical* considerations; e.g., whether one prays at this place or at that place (4:21); and b. such worship operates in the realm of *truth:* clear and definite knowledge of God derived from his special revelation (4:22). In such a setting, it would seem to us, worshiping *in spirit and truth* can only mean a. rendering such homage to God that the entire heart enters into the act, and b. doing this in full harmony with the truth of God as revealed in his Word. Such worship, therefore, will not only be spiritual instead of physical, inward instead of outward, but it will also be directed to the true God as set forth in Scripture and as displayed in the work of redemption. As some see it, a humble, spiritual attitude means little. According to others, truth or doctrinal soundness is of no importance. Both are one-sided, unbalanced, and therefore wrong. Genuine worshipers worship *in spirit and truth!* **For such are the very people whom the Father is seeking as his worshipers,** not in the sense that there are individuals who have made themselves such worshipers, and that the Father is, as it were, searching for them; but in the sense that he keeps on intensely yearning for his elect in order that he may make them *such* worshipers. His seeking is saving (cf. Luke 19:10). It is ever God who takes the initiative in the work of salvation; it is never man (cf. 3:16; 6:37, 39, 44, 65; 15:16).

24. The necessity for distinctly *spiritual* worship is rooted in the very being of God: **God is Spirit.** In the original (πνεῦμα ὁ θεός) the subject, God, stands last and is preceded by the article. The predicate, Spirit, is the first word of the sentence, and is not preceded by the article. (Cf. our remarks on the grammatical construction of the third clause of 1:1.) The predicate is placed first for the sake of emphasis: *completely spiritual* in his essence is God! He is not a stone-deity or tree-deity, neither is he a mountain-deity so that he has to be worshiped on this or that specific mountain; e.g., Gerizim! He is an independent, incorporeal, personal Being. Hence, **those who worship him must worship in spirit and truth.** Genuine worshipers not only *will* worship the Father in spirit and truth; they *must* do so. Jesus places his own *must* over against that of the woman (cf. 4:24 with 4:20). (See comments on verse 23 for the meaning of "worship in spirit and truth.")

25. The thoughts of the woman have been directed toward the expectation of the coming Messiah. The stranger's penetrating knowledge about her own life (4:17, 18; cf. 4:29) and his deep insight into the essence of God and of all true worship (4:21-24) remind her of certain traditions which, on the basis of Deut. 18:15, 18, had been transmitted to the people of Samaria. Not that she in any way recognized this stranger as being the Messiah. Far from it; but by what he had said he made her think of the Messiah. Hence, we are not surprised to read, **The woman said, I know that Messiah is coming, the One who is called Christ** (an addition by John, the author, for the sake of his readers in Asia Minor); **whenever he arrives, he will declare everything to us.**

The fact that among the Samaritans, too, there was a Messianic expectation (note that the woman even employs the term Messiah as a proper name without preceding article) is clear from this passage, from Act 8:9, and from Josephus, *Antiquities* XVIII, iv, 1. Nevertheless, as to time of fulfilment the hope in the woman's heart was rather vague. She says, "*Whenever* he arrives"; it may be tomorrow, but it may also be several years from now. The fact which should be emphasized, however, is this: she now hopes! She is beginning to yearn for Messiah, the One who will tell her just what to do for her own sinful condition; nay more, the One who will *openly declare* (cf. 16:13, 14, 15) *everything*, not only to her but *also to her people* ("to us").

26. And now the supreme moment of Messianic self-disclosure has arrived. **Jesus said to her, I, the One who is talking to you, am he.** This is the greatest surprise of all! But this is also the *only* solution to all the problems and the only answer to all the questions that have arisen in this woman's heart.

Did this woman accept Jesus as her Lord? If so, why is this not stated in so many words? Anent these questions we refer to what has already been said in our explanation of 4:7-10.

When the further question is asked, How is it that Jesus disclosed himself to *her* as the Christ and not to everyone with whom he came into contact? we answer that it was well-pleasing in the sight of the Father to hide this great fact from the wise and understanding but to reveal it to this predestined child of his (Matt. 11:25, 26). Was it safe for Jesus to reveal himself as the Messiah? In this connection it must be borne in mind that, as far as we know, Jesus performed no miracles in Samaria. Such deeds of power at times resulted in the perversion of the concept of the Messianic office (cf. 6:15). Also, after a stay of only two days (4:40) he again proceeded on his way toward Galilee, so that there was hardly sufficient time in which the declaration, "I am Messiah" could have aroused opposition from the side of the authorities, bringing about a premature crisis.

Synthesis of 4:1-26

See the Outline on p. 68. *The Son of God revealing himself to everwidening circles: to Samaria: the conversation with the Samaritan Woman.*

In order to prevent a premature crisis Jesus left Judea for Galilee. He had to go through Samaria. He reached Sychar, located in this province, and sat down, weary and thirsty, at Jacob's Spring or Well. Here he engaged in a conversation with an immoral Samaritan woman. He asked her for a drink, spoke to her about the living water which he himself was able to supply, told her that this living water would not only quench thirst but would even prevent its recurrence, revealed to her the secrets of her own immoral life, showed her the character of true worship, and finally disclosed himself to her as the Messiah.

The woman's heart rebelled against the disclosure of her sinful state and she tried to change the subject. It seems at first as if the woman is in control of the conversation and as if the Lord allows himself to be sidetracked. However, without realizing it, the woman is being led to the goal established by the Lord himself.

Is this woman, in her attempt to evade the real issue, a symbol of the sinner as he is by nature? Is the manner in which Christ addresses her an example for us to follow in working with the lost?

This section shows a progressive series of surprises. Little by little Jesus reveals who he is; and, in complete correspondence with this gradually ascending self-disclosure, the woman's confession also advances, so that she sees in this stranger first a Jew; then, a prophet, finally, the Christ.

27 And at that moment his disciples came, and were amazed that [97] he was talk-ing with a woman. Yet no one said, "What do you desire (of her)?" or, "Why are you talking with her?" 28 So the woman left her water jar and went back to town, and she said to the people, 29 "Come, see a man who told me all that I ever did. He is not, perhaps, the Christ, is he?" 30 They went out of the town and were coming to him.

31 In the meantime his disciples kept urging him, saying, "Rabbi, eat." 32 But he said to them, "I have food to eat of which y o u have no knowledge." 33 The disciples then were saying to each other, "Surely, no one has brought him food?" 34 Jesus said to them, "My food is to [98] do the will of the One who sent me, and to accomplish his work. 35 Are y o u not saying, 'There are yet four months; then comes the harvest?' I say to y o u, Look, lift up y o u r eyes and scan the fields that [99] they are white for harvesting. 36 Already the reaper receives wages and gathers fruit for everlasting life, in order that the sower and the reaper may rejoice together. 37 For in this is real the proverb,[100] 'One is the sower, and another the reaper.' 38 I sent y o u to reap that for which y o u did not labor. Others have labored, and y o u have entered into their labor."

39 Now many of the Samaritans from that town believed in him because of the word of the woman who testified, "He told me all I ever did." 40 So when the Samaritans came to him, they kept urging him to remain with them. And he remained there two days. 41 And many more believed because of his word. 42 And they were saying to the woman, "It is no longer because of your talk that we believe, for we ourselves have heard, and we know that this is really the Savior of the world."

4:27-42

4:27. And at that moment his disciples came. Note: *at that moment!* The disciples had finished their business in Sychar and *naturally* returned to the well. Jesus had just made his great declaration, reaching a climax in a manner that was wholly natural and unforced. Yet, the divine providence is such that at that exact moment — not earlier, so that the conversation with the woman would have been interrupted; nor later, so that the disciples would have missed this great event (their Lord condescending to a Samaritan woman) with all its missionary implications — the disciples arrived! This is a glorious manifestation and illustration of the operation of God's providence for the furtherance of his kingdom.

They came **and were amazed** (kept on wondering) **that he was talking with a woman.** Was he not a rabbi? Then how could he ignore the rabbinical rule: "Let no one talk with a woman in the street, no not with his own wife"? The disciples were receiving a lesson in the true emancipation of womanhood. Though they continued to wonder at what they saw and

---

[97] On ὅτι see pp. 55, 57.
[98] On ἵνα see pp. 45, 48.
[99] On ὅτι see pp. 55, 57.
[100] On ὅτι see pp. 54, 57.

heard, their reverence for their master was so great that **no one said, What do you desire (of her)?** The answer, had it been given, would have been, To receive from her physical water. Nor did any one ask, **Why are you talking with her?** The answer, had it been given, would have been, To give her living water.

28. So the woman left her water jar and went back to town, and she said to the people. The wonderful news which the woman had just received (and which she just *had to* tell others), as well as the arrival of the disciples, caused her to go back to town. She left her water jar at the well. Very generally this is interpreted to mean that in her excitement because of the strange happenings she *forgot* her pitcher as she hurried back to tell everybody the news. According to many, the story of the woman's water jar is as follows: a. To the well comes this woman equipped with a pitcher to draw water. Before she draws it, a tired traveler — we know that it was Jesus — asks her for a drink. b. The conversation continues, in which she becomes so interested that the water jar remains empty. c. Having heard the stranger's great declaration, she rushes off, forgetting all about the jar.

More natural, however — and also more in keeping with the correct translation of the parenthetical clause of verse 9 — is the following construction:

a. To the well comes this woman equipped with a pitcher to draw water. *She draws water, filling her pitcher.* Viewing the filled jar, a total stranger, whom she recognizes to be a Jew and who is sitting by the well, asks her for a drink.

b. Knowing that it is not customary for Jews *to use vessels together with* Samaritans, she does not immediately offer the requested gift, but asks the stranger to explain his strange request. An increasingly interesting and revealing conversation develops.

c. Having heard the stranger's great declaration, and being now fully convinced that genuine worship is of an entirely spiritual nature and that accordingly there can be no basic objection to the idea of Jews and Samaritans drinking from the same pitcher, *she purposely leaves the jar at the well,* so that Jesus may quench his physical thirst, and so that he may know that she has taken to heart the lesson anent the nature of true religion. Afterward, having led a multitude of people to the well, she can retrieve her pitcher.

In this connection we should remember that 4:28 does not say *she forgot* (ἐπελήσατο cf. Phil. 3:13), but *she left* (ἀφῆκεν, first aorist active indicative of ἀφίημι) her water jar. Exactly the same form of this verb was used earlier, in this same chapter (4:3): *the Lord . . . left Judea* (ὁ κύριος . . . ἀφῆκεν τὴν Ιουδαίαν). He did not *forget* Judea but he purposely *left* it. So

171

here also: she did not *forget* her water jar but she purposely *left* it, left it there for him to use.

29. In Sychar this woman, having gathered a crowd, exclaims, **Come, see a man who told me all that I ever did.** Here she reveals the wisdom of Philip when he spoke to Nathaniel (1:46). Though we have no reason to doubt that in her own heart she is already convinced that Jesus is, indeed, the Christ, she very wisely formulates her question in such a manner that the people will have to arrive at their own answer. She said, **He is not, perhaps, the Christ, is he?**

30. They went out of the town and were coming to him. The crowd rushed off immediately (aorist tense) and is pictured in the act of proceeding toward Jesus (imperfect tense). In verse 35 the disciples are told to lift up their eyes and see these people as they are approaching the well. In verse 40 they have arrived.

31. In the meantime his disciples kept urging him, saying, Rabbi, eat. Genuine concern for the physical needs of Jesus finally overcame the disciples' amazement. So, in the meantime — i.e., from the woman's departure to the arrival of the Samaritans — his disciples kept urging him, saying, "Rabbi, eat." (On the term *Rabbi* see 1:38, footnote 44.) As these men saw it, it was time to eat. Besides, Jesus must be hungry by now. Hence, let him eat.

32. But the Lord replied, **I have food to eat of which y o u have no knowledge.** In the original of verse 32 the term translated *food* is βρῶσις; while in verse 34 it is βρῶμα. John uses the two terms apparently with very little difference in meaning. In its primary sense the first one signifies *eating* (just as Paul employs it in I Cor. 8:4: "Concerning the *eating* of things sacrificed to idols"); and from this it develops into a synonym for food, just as in our English vernacular we speak of *good eating* or *eats*. The second terms means *food, victual(s), anything that is eaten,* and in that sense *meat* (cf. Paul in I Cor. 6:13: "*Meats* for the belly").

33. In verse 34 Jesus himself explains the character of this food; see on that verse. It is *spiritual* nourishment. Because the disciples had not been present during the conversation with the woman, they had no knowledge of this mysterious food to which the Lord referred. As so often in this Gospel — see on 2:19 — the disciples, just like the Samaritan woman (4:11, 15), interpret his words literally. They are pictured as asking each other, **Surely, no one has brought him food?** It is hard for them to imagine that in the land of the Samaritans anyone could have brought food to Jesus!

34. Jesus said to them, My *food* — that which imparts satisfaction to me and in which my soul delights — **is to do the will of my** *Sender* — i.e., the

Father (5:36) (see also 3:34) — and to *accomplish* his work. i.e., to bring this work to its predestined goal; to fulfil and finish it. In the night of the Supper, a few hours before his death on the cross, Jesus, using a participle of the same verb, said, "I glorified thee on the earth, *having accomplished* (τελειώσας) the work which thou hast given me to do" (17:4). The nature of that work is indicated in 17:4, 6 (see in Vol. II). A verb ultimately derived from the same root is used in 19:28, 30, spoken when Jesus bowed his head and gave up his spirit: τετέλεσται, i.e., "It is finished."

35. Are you not saying, There are yet four months; then comes the harvest. The disciples were saying this. The harvest in this region being in April (or early May), it was now December (or early January). For, this is probably not a proverb indicating the usual time-interval between seed-time and harvest. Aside from the fact that *four months* would be incorrect (for the interval is actually longer), and that no such proverb or anything resembling it has been found anywhere, the adverb *yet* would seem to be hardly fitting. In a *proverb* one would expect simply: "There are four months between seedtime and harvest," or simply, "There are four months; then comes the harvest," but not, "There are *yet* four months; then comes the harvest." The words which introduce the chronological indication — "Are you not saying" — prove nothing either way. The disciples had been observing the month-old verdure, and they had just now been saying, ". . . yet four more months; then comes the harvest."

In the mind of Jesus there is a close relationship — though also a contrast (see on 4:36, 37) — between the physical and the spiritual harvest. In the verses which follow, the Lord bases his remarks upon this relationship. We should bear in mind that by this time the procession of Samaritans (4:30) was becoming plainly visible as coming across the fields it approached the well. Pointing at this harvest of faith (4:39) Jesus says to his disciples, **Look, lift up y o u r eyes, and scan** (θεάσασθε; see on 1:14 footnote 33) **the fields, that they are white for harvesting** (4:35). Though the *grain*-harvest may still be four months off, the *soul*-harvest is ripe for the plucking even now! When Jesus tells the disciples to ponder the spectacle of the approaching Samaritans, and to consider them to be fields ready for harvesting, does this not clearly imply that he is sending out his disciples to gather this harvest?[101]

36. The word *already* (ἤδη) belongs to verse 36, not to verse 35, where it would be redundant. **Already** — not four months from now as is true with respect to the physical harvest — **the reaper receives wages,** a reward; **and**

---

[101] Note similar connection between Matt. 9:37, 38 and 10:1. Here Jesus tells the disciples that the harvest is plenteous, the laborers few. He urges them to pray the Lord of the harvest that he may send forth laborers into his harvest. Then he calls them, and sends them out into the harvest.

gathers fruit for everlasting life, he is gathering fruit destined for everlasting life. (For meaning of *everlasting life* see on 1:4 and 3:16.) Thus, the sower and the reaper rejoice together. Generally there is a considerable interval between sowing and reaping. But in this case hardly any time had elapsed between the sowing of the seed and the reaping of the harvest. Hence, **in order that the sower and the reaper may rejoice together.** Christ, the Sower, and the disciples, as reapers, *rejoice together.* The prophecy of Amos 9:13 is fulfilled:

"Behold, the days come, saith Jehovah, that the plowman shall overtake the reaper, and the treader of grapes him that soweth seed; and the mountains shall drop sweet wine, and the hills shall melt."

37, 38. The disciples, therefore, as reapers, will be able to rejoice in a spiritual crop which they themselves have not planted. For, the rule in the realm of the spiritual is that the sower and the reaper are two different persons. Hence, Jesus continues:

For in this the proverb is real — attains its most striking illustration.

In the realm of the natural the proverb **One is the sower and another the reaper** often corresponds to the actual facts of life; e.g., a man may reap where he has not sown (Deut. 6:11; Josh. 24:13), or a sower may never experience the joy of reaping (Deut. 28:30; Job 31:8; Mic. 6:15): someone else gathers in the harvest. But in the realm of the spiritual it is the usual thing that one man reaps where another has sown. Each kingdom-worker is at the same time reaper (of that which has been sown *by others*) and sower (of seed which brings forth a harvest that will be gathered *by others*). Hence, both sower and reaper rejoice in this divine arrangement: there will always be a harvest to reap.

I sent y o u to reap, says Jesus. The question has been asked, "What act of commissioning does this sentence indicate?" It cannot refer to what is recorded in Mark 3:13-19 nor to the contents of Mark 6:6-13 (cf. Matt. 9:35-11:1), for the events there described had not yet taken place. Besides, in these passages the disciples are charged to sow rather than to reap. It is also open to doubt whether Jesus has in mind 4:2 which refers to the work of the disciples in *Judea.* Far more in harmony with the present context, it would seem to us, is the thought that Jesus referred to the commissioning that is so clearly implied in 4:35. (See comments on 4:35.) **I sent y o u to reap that for which y o u did not labor. Others have labored, and y o u have entered into their labor.** *Right here* in Samaria the Lord had *just now* commissioned his disciples to reap that for which they had not labored. Others had labored among these Samaritans, and now the disciples have been commissioned to enter into (i.e., to gather the fruits of) their labor. But who were these *others* who had toiled (worked with much effort)? At this point many introduce Moses, the Old Testament prophets,

John the Baptist, etc. More definitely in harmony with the historical facts and with the immediate context is the inference that the Lord here refers to *himself* — think of the labor of love which he had performed here at the well, as recorded in 4:1-26 — and *the Samaritan woman,* whose preparatory labor is recorded in 4:29, 39. Both Jesus and the Samaritan woman had been laboring among these Samaritans: Jesus indirectly, via the Samaritan woman; she, in turn, directly, among her neighbors. Into this labor the disciples now entered.

39. The story begun in 4:28, 29 is now continued. **Now many of the people of Sychar believed on him because of the word of the woman, who testified, He told me all that I ever did.** i.e., they were deeply impressed by the mysterious powers of one who was able to reveal a person's past.

40. They were, moreover, friendly to Jesus, not hostile. In fact, they were so eager to meet this stranger personally, in order to see for themselves, that **they came to him.** They were also hospitable toward Jesus **and kept on urging him to remain with them.**

Jesus did not evangelize the province of Samaria. In harmony with the will of his heavenly Father (4:4) **he remained there two days** only, and he limited his work to one small village. Therefore, nothing in this account conflicts in any way with the order issued to the disciples in Matt. 10:5. And that order, it must be borne in mind, was of an entirely temporary character. It was set aside and supplanted by the great commission (Matt. 28:18-20). Much fruitful labor was carried on in the city and province of Samaria at a later time (Acts 8).

41. And many more believed because of his word. The attitude of the Samaritans at the well contrasts sharply with those other Samaritan villagers who later refused to receive him because he was on his way to Jerusalem (Luke 9:51-56). Nevertheless, we need not suppose that the faith of all these people of Sychar who went out to see Jesus was saving faith. With some it probably remained on the level of 2:23. (See comments on 2:23.) With others, we may safely assume, it rose to the highest level after they had heard the word of Jesus himself. Also, the number of those who accepted him because of his own word was far larger than the number of those who had believed on him as a result of the woman's testimony.

42. And they were saying. That far larger group of believers now address the woman in these words: **It is no longer because of your talk that we believe, for we ourselves have heard, and we know that this is really the Savior of the world.** Note in this connection:

(1) The *talk* (ἡ λαλιά) of the woman is here (in 4:42) contrasted with the *word* (ὁ λόγος, 4:41) of Christ. However, in 4:39 the woman's testimony (for μαρτυρία and μαρτυρέω see on 1:7) is called her *word* (λόγος).

(2) What these Samaritans say involves a principle that has validity for

175

all time: *personal* contact with Christ is necessary to make faith complete.

(3) The Samaritans call Jesus "the Savior of the world." [102] The Lord had told the Samaritan woman that salvation is *from* the Jews (4:22). In his brief stay among them he must have emphasized that this salvation was, nevertheless, *for* the world. In fact, this glorious truth is already implied in 4:21, 23. Study the following passages for the concept *Savior* as applied to Jesus: Matt. 1:21; Luke 2:11; Acts 5:31; 13:23; Phil. 3:20; Eph. 5:23; Titus 1:4; 2:13; 3:6; II Tim. 1:10; II Peter 1:1, 11; 2:20; 3:2, 18. The full title *Savior of the world* is found not only here in 4:42 but also in I John 4:14. This *world* consists of elect from every nation: from the realm of heathendom (in the present context, from the realm of Samaritans) as well as from that of Judaism. (For the various meanings of the term *world* in the Fourth Gospel see on 1:10, footnote 26.)

As the world's *Savior*, Jesus, on the basis of and by means of his own infinite sacrifice, takes away sin's guilt, pollution, and punishment, and bestows upon the hearts and lives of those whom he so favors all the fruits of the operation of the Holy Spirit.

Synthesis of 4:27-42

See the Outline on p. 68. *The Son of God revealing himself to ever-widening circles; to Samaria: work among the people of Sychar.*

When, at the providential moment, the disciples came back from Sychar, having made their purchases, they were greatly astonished to see the Lord talking with a woman. Thus, quietly and without ostentation, Jesus gives these men a lesson in the true, spiritual emancipation of womanhood. Without changing any creation-ordinance regarding the proper place of woman, the Lord clearly indicates that before God the soul of a woman is not less precious than that of a man.

After the arrival of the disciples the woman, now that Jesus has reached a glorious climax of self-revelation, runs back to town that she may tell her people the great news. In taking her departure she purposely leaves her water-jar at the well, so that Jesus may quench his thirst. Has not the Lord made very clear to her that true worship is essentially spiritual in nature, and that it is the same for all individuals whether they be Jews or Samaritans? Why then should a Jew hesitate to drink from a Samaritan vessel?

In Sychar the woman tells her story and piques the curiosity of her neighbors by asking, "Come, see a man who told me all that I ever did. He is not, perhaps, the Christ, is he?"

In her absence the disciples, gathered with their Master at the well, learn

---

[102] Romans called their emperors *Savior of the world*. See A. Deissmann, *Light From The Ancient East* (translated by L. R. M. Strachan) New York, 1922, pp. 364, 365.

that his need for physical food is superseded by the intense satisfaction
which he received in bringing this woman out of the darkness into the
light, thereby carrying forward the accomplishment of the will of his
heavenly Sender. On the approach of the Samaritans Jesus exhorts his
disciples to look upon this arriving procession as a spiritual harvest. Only
a few moments ago the seed had been sown — first, by Jesus himself in the
heart of the woman, then by her in the hearts of her people —, and now
harvest-time has already arrived! How different it is in the physical realm
where at this moment the harvest was still four months away. And how
wonderful that the disciples, viewed as reapers, are privileged to harvest
that which they have not sown.

In accepting Jesus by faith the *Samaritans* form a striking and pleasing
contrast with most of the *Jews*. If the entire story (4:1-42) be taken into
account, definite progress in faith is clearly noticeable, so that Jesus is regarded as a mere Jew, then as a prophet, next as Messiah, and finally as the
Savior of the world.

The omniscience which the Lord reveals marks him as being, indeed, the
Christ, the Son of God. Hence, the author of the Fourth Gospel has again
reached his goal (20:30).

---

43 Now after the two days he departed from that place and went to Galilee.
44 For Jesus himself had testified, "A prophet has no honor in his own fatherland."
45 So when he came to Galilee, the Galileans welcomed him having seen all that
he had done in Jerusalem at the feast; for they too had attended the feast.
46 Now he came again to Cana of Galilee, where he had turned the water into
wine. And at Capernaum there was a courtier whose son was ill. 47 When he
heard that Jesus had come from Judea to Galilee, he went and begged him to
come down and heal his son, for he was at the point of death.
48 Jesus therefore said to him, "Unless y o u see signs and wonders, y o u will
definitely not believe." 49 The courtier said to him, "Sir, come down before my
dear child is dead." 50 Jesus said to him, "Go your way, your son lives." The
man believed the word which Jesus had spoken to him and he went on his way.
51 Now while he was still going down (to Capernaum), his servants met him,
saying that [103] his child was living. 52 So he asked them at what hour he had
begun to improve, and they said to him, "Yesterday, at the seventh hour, the fever
left him." 53 The father therefore knew that this was the very hour when Jesus
had said to him, "Your son lives." And he himself believed, and so did his whole
household. 54 Now this was the second sign that Jesus performed after he had
come from Judea to Galilee.

4:43-54

**4:43-45. Now after the two days he departed from that place and went
to Galilee. 44 For Jesus himself had testified, A prophet has no honor in**

---

[103] On ὅτι see pp. 54, 57.

his own fatherland. 45 So when he came to Galilee, the Galileans welcomed him, having seen all that he had done in Jerusalem at the feast;
for they too had attended the feast.

This paragraph presents a problem. We are told that *Jesus returned to
Galilee because "a prophet has no honor in his own fatherland."* Just what
does this mean? From the list of explanations that have been offered we
select the following:

(1) Some contend that *Jesus clings to his plan to go to Galilee in spite of
the fact that he knows that a prophet has no honor in his own fatherland*
(i.e., in Galilee).[104]

We cannot accept this explanation. The passage clearly states that Jesus
went to Galilee *because* he knew that a prophet has no honor in his own
fatherland; not *in spite of* this knowledge but *because of* it. The word
which connects verse 43 and verse 44 is the particle *for* (γάρ) in its *causal*
sense.

(2) Others say that *Jesus proceeds from Sychar to Galilee because he
knows that in his fatherland* — i.e., the land of his birth, Judea — *his labor
had been fruitless.*[105]

This explanation we also reject, for the simple reason that everywhere
else in the Gospels the term *his fatherland* clearly points to Galilee, never
to Judea. See Matt. 13:54, 57; Mark 6:1, 4; Luke 4:16, 24. In these passages
we find the same proverb, but the country to which it refers is that in
which Nazareth is located. Although Jesus was born in Bethlehem of
Judea, nevertheless, his parents had their home in Galilee, and it was in
Galilee that he grew up to manhood. Galilee was, accordingly, *his own
country.*

(3) Then there are those who claim: *Jesus goes to Galilee, but not until
he has won esteem in Jerusalem, for he knew that a prophet has no honor
in his own country* (i.e., in Galilee). *Having won esteem in Judea, he finds
that Galilee is now also ready to honor him.*[106]

It is claimed that verse 45 proves this theory to be correct. There we
read:

"So when he came to Galilee, the Galileans welcomed him, having seen
all that he had done in Jerusalem at the feast; for they too had attended
the feast."

In favor of this explanation it must be admitted that a. It does justice to

---

[104] Cf. F. W. Grosheide, *Kommentaar op het Nieuwe Testament, Johannes,* Amsterdam, 1950, vol. 1, p. 324. He maintains that the sense of the passage is that Jesus
takes no account of the fact, well-known also to him, that a prophet is not honored
in his own fatherland.
[105] Thus C. Bouma, *Het Evangelie Naar Johannes, in Korte Verklaring,* Kampen,
1927, p. 69.
[106] Cf. R. C. H. Lenski, *The Interpretation of John,* Columbus, Ohio, 1931, pp.
332-335.

the meaning of the particle *for* (causal relationship), b. It correctly interprets the term *his fatherland* as referring to Galilee, and c. It takes the context into consideration to some extent.

Nevertheless, we are not ready to accept this theory. Our objections are as follows: a. It reads too much into the text. To say, "Jesus departed . . . and went to Galilee, for he himself testified, 'A prophet has no honor in his own fatherland,' " is not at all the same as it would be to say: "Jesus did not go to Galilee until he had first won fame in Jerusalem, for he himself testified, 'A prophet has no honor in his own fatherland.' " In the first case (the text as it actually reads) a reason is given to show why Jesus proceeded on his way to Galilee. In the second case a reason is given to indicate why he worked in Jerusalem before going to Galilee. These are two different propositions, and it will never do to assume that the reader already knows the contents of verse 45 before he has even come across verse 44! b. This view assumes that the text intends to indicate that Jesus received honor in Galilee. But in the other passages in which the same proverb occurs the very opposite is clearly taught (Matt. 13:54-58; Mark 6:1-6; Luke 4:16-30: instead of honoring him, the people made an attempt to kill him). Moreover, when 4:45 states that the Galileans welcomed him, because they had seen his miracles, this must not be interpreted to mean that they *honored* him (4:48 teaches the opposite). Outward enthusiasm, often for selfish purposes, is not honor.

(4) There is still another explanation: *Jesus went to Galilee because here he did not need to fear such honor as would bring him into immediate collision with the Pharisees, creating a premature crisis.*[107]

We accept this explanation for the following reasons:

a. *It is by far the most simple and obvious.* Not only does it do full justice to the term *his own fatherland* (interpreting it in the light of the parallel passages in the other Gospels) and also to the causal connection expressed by the particle *for*, but it accepts verses 43 and 44 at face value, just as they stand, without any attempt to encumber them with mental insertions or preconceived historical constructions. The contents of the two verses may then be briefly analyzed as follows: After the two days Jesus departed from Sychar. He went to Galilee, his fatherland. He did this because he knew that a prophet has no honor in his own country, as he himself had also testified.

b. *It is entirely in harmony with the preceding context.* In this connection it must be borne in mind that verses 43 and 44 resume the thought that was expressed in verses 1-3. The account of Christ's conversation with the Samaritan woman and of his work among the Samaritans (4:4-42) is, in

---

[107] Cf. M. Dods, *The Gospel of St. John*, in *The Expositor's Greek Testament*, pp. 732, 733.

reality, an interlude. The reasonable nature of the explanation will appear when 4:1-3 and 4:44 are read consecutively; as follows:

"Now when the Lord knew that the Pharisees had heard, 'Jesus is gaining and baptizing more disciples than John' — although Jesus himself was not baptizing, but his disciples —, he left Judea and went back again to Galilee. . . . For he himself testified, 'A prophet has no honor in his own fatherland.' "

c. *It is entirely in harmony with the succeeding context.* Though the Galileans were, of course, happy to receive into their midst a miracle-worker (4:45), they did not thereby honor him (4:48). By and by they begin to grumble about him (6:41); they finally leave him in great numbers (6:66).

46. Now he came again to Cana of Galilee.

The Great Galilean Ministry begins at this point. It covers the period December of the year 27 — April of the year 29 A. D., about sixteen months in all. After the death of Herod the Great in the year 4 B. C. his kingdom had been divided among his sons in the following manner:

Archelaus had become ethnarch of Judea, Samaria, and part of Idumea, ruling over these regions from 4 B. C. to 6 A. D. When he was deposed, his territory was placed under procurators, who succeeded each other. One of them was Pontius Pilate, the procurator who ordered Christ's crucifixion. He ruled from 26 — 36 A. D.

Philip had been made tetrarch of the region east and northeast of the Sea of Galilee, a tetrarchy to which the evangelist Luke gives the name "the region of Iturea and Trachonitis" (Luke 3:1).

To *Herod Antipas* has been assigned Galilee and Perea, over which he reigned as tetrarch, in which capacity he continued from 4 B. C. — 39 A. D. He was a full brother of Archelaus.

Hence, during the Great Galilean Ministry Jesus labored in the domain of Herod Antipas. This is the Herod of the Gospels (except Matthew 2 and Luke 1).

A very large portion of the Gospels of Matthew and Mark is devoted to this Great Galilean Ministry; also a considerable portion of Luke's Gospel (Matt. 4:12-15:20; Mark 1:14-7:23; Luke 4:14-9:17).

Whereas it is the purpose of John's Gospel to select only those events from the life of our Lord in which his deity becomes most strikingly evident (see pp. 33-35) and whereas its author presupposes that his readers are acquainted with the contents of the other three Gospels (see pp. 31, 32), it is not surprising that the record of the Great Galilean Ministry is here confined to two events: the healing of the courtier's son (4:46-54) and the multiplication of the loaves (chapter 6). The miracle recorded in chapter

5, though occurring *during* the Great Galilean Ministry, actually took place *in* Judea.

The main point, however, is this: Jesus, the Christ, the Son of God, is revealing himself to ever-widening circles. He has now again reached Cana of Galilee. Here he performs a miracle in which his divine majesty and power are exhibited in a most remarkable manner.

Where he had turned the water into wine. The Cana to which Jesus came was the one where he had performed his first sign (see our comments on 2:1-11). Nathaneal lived here (21:2). The news of the Lord's arrival at Cana reached Capernaum, located about two and one-half miles south-west of the point where the Jordan River, coming from the north, enters the Sea of Galilee. This was the town of James and John, the sons of Zebedee and Salome. It was a tax-collecting center and probably the seat of a Roman military post. See also on 2:12.

And at Capernaum there was a courtier. A royal officer (τις βασιλικός) is introduced at this point. He was probably one of the courtiers of the tetrarch Herod Antipas. His name is not given. Hence, to identify him with Chuza (Herod's "steward," Luke 8:3) or with Manaen (Acts 13:1) is pure guess-work. It would seem that this courtier was a Jew, for in 4:48 he is included in the multitude of Jews (cf. 2:23) who were interested in Jesus chiefly as a miracle-worker. It is not impossible that this man had attended the Passover at Jerusalem and while there had seen some of the miracles which Jesus had performed. At any rate, he recognized that the new prophet had power to heal, for there had been ample time for the fame of Jesus to spread throughout Galilee.

Whose son was ill . . . at the point of death. We learn that this man had a son who was ill. Whether the son was an only child (which some infer from the expression ὁ υἱός in 4:46, 50) cannot be established. It is not even absolutely certain that the son was still a very young child. The Fourth Gospel uses the term παιδίον in the sense of *a little one* (16:21) and as *a term of endearment* or *familiarity*, like our "lad" (21:5).

We *do* know, however, that the sickness of this son was very severe. He was *at the point of death* (4:47, 49).

When he heard that Jesus had come from Judea to Galilee, he repeatedly **begged him to come down and heal his son.**

The sick child's father, having traveled from Capernaum to Cana, committed at least two errors. (1) He took for granted that in order to effect a cure Jesus would have to travel from Cana to Capernaum and would have *to come* to the bedside of the boy. In this respect he does not compare favorably with the centurion whose servant was ill (Luke 7:1-10), and with whom, nevertheless, he has been confused. (2) He also was convinced that

181

Christ's power did not extend beyond death. *Jesus must come at once, for the child is at the point of death.* If there be any delay so that the boy dies before the healer arrives, all will be lost. Such was his "faith."

Basic to these two errors was a third one that is pointed out in the next paragraph:

48-50. Jesus therefore said to him, Unless y o u see signs and wonders, y o u will definitely not believe. Jesus complains that this man, who had already heard (and, perhaps, seen) so much of the Christ, is still standing on the lowest rung of faith's ladder. His confidence, and that of others like him, has to be constantly fed by signs and wonders. He does not believe in *the divine person* of Christ nor even in *his word* if the latter be unaccompanied by a miracle.

When Jesus spoke of *signs and wonders,* he was not referring to two kinds of supernatural works. Rather, the same deed of power is a *sign* when it is viewed in one way, and a *wonder* (τέρας) when it is viewed in another way. (For the meaning of the term "sign," σημεῖον, see on 2:1-11.) A *wonder* is something startling. The term views the mighty deed not, like *sign,* from the point of view of the light which it sheds upon the person and work of the Lord, but from the aspect of the effect which it has upon the spectators. These spectators were always looking for something sensational or exciting! So Jesus says, "Unless y o u see signs and wonders, y o u will *definitely* not (οὐ μή) believe."

This arrow of tender rebuke hit the mark. The man takes to heart the word of earnest warning and serious complaint, as is shown in 4:50. At the same time his heart is all wrapped up in the condition of his son. **The courtier** therefore pours out his soul in this one, brief word of urgency: he **said to him, Sir, come down, before my dear child is dead.**

Jesus, who at this very moment is healing both the son's body and the father's soul, **said to him, Go your way, your son lives.** This last expression must not be toned down to something like "is going to live." It indicates that by a deed of omnipotence performed at this moment the child is now fully restored and is, therefore, enjoying complete health and vigor.

The man whose faith had been resting completely upon miracles now advances to a higher stage: he **believed the word which Jesus had spoken.** Accepted *the word* though he saw no *deed.* The next day (cf. 4:52), probably at dawn, the father **went on his way** back to Capernaum.

51. Now while he was still going down (to Capernaum), his servants met him, saying that his child was living. In Capernaum the servants have noticed the sudden and remarkable recovery. Filled with rejoicing they cannot wait for the arrival of their master. Between the lines we can easily discern the fact that in this household the relation between master and servants was ideal. The servants, on their way to meet their master with the glad news, shout the message of cheer as soon as they see him. The phrase which they in all probability [108] employed was almost identical to that which had been used by Jesus himself: "Your child lives." Note: Jesus had used the term *your son* (ὁ υἱός σου); the father had said *my dear child* (τὸ παιδίον μου) but cf. 4:47; the servants now say *your child*.

52. Very natural, indeed, is the father's further question. **He asked them at what hour he had begun to improve** (literally, *to do nicely, handsomely,* an idiomatic expression). **And they said to him, Yesterday, at the seventh hour, the fever left him.** Here again we are confronted with the problem of time-computation in the Fourth Gospel. And now also, as before, the Roman civil-day computation would seem to offer the most natural explanation. If *the seventh hour* means one o'clock in the afternoon (by Jewish time-reckoning), we would have to suppose that the courtier, having heard from the lips of Jesus that his son was restored, decided to stay right in Cana for the rest of that day, not leaving for home until the next morning; or else, that, having walked a few miles, he spent the rest of the afternoon, evening, and night at some village along the road, before proceeding on his way to see his son. Now this is certainly very unnatural. The explanation which is at times advanced by those who, nevertheless, favor the Jewish time-computation, is this: the father deliberately delayed his journey back to Capernaum, knowing that "he that believeth shall not make haste" (Isa. 28:16). But would not the love of the father for his child, now fully restored, have impelled him to proceed on his way immediately; and this in view of the fact that, if the Jewish time-reckoning applies here, there would still have been ample time to reach home long before midnight? Must we, indeed, suppose that both the father and the servants acted in a most leisurely fashion? On the other hand, if the cure was effected at 7 P. M., according to the Roman civil-day computation, we can understand that the father could not reach Capernaum until the following day. Although the distance between Cana and Capernaum is only sixteen miles, much of this is hilly country, so that not much less than seven hours is required to cover it. (For other instances of Roman civil-day time-computation see pp. 104, 105, 157, 158.)

53. When the servants answered, "Yesterday, at the seventh hour, the fever left him," their master immediately recognized the hour: **the father therefore knew that this was the very hour when Jesus had said, Your son lives. And the father himself believed and so did his whole household;** i.e., all those dwelling in this house; perhaps (in addition to the

---

[108] We cannot be entirely certain, because we are dealing here with indirect discourse.

father) the mother, the servants, this healed child and other children, if there were any who had arrived at the years of discretion. Of course, it is *not necessary* to assume that there were other children. On the other hand, it is not necessary either to take for granted that this was the only child.

54. Now this was the second sign that Jesus performed after he had come from Judea to Galilee. Having returned from Judea to Galilee, this was the second sign which the Lord performed there. Both occurred in Cana. In both the Lord had manifested his glory. First, by turning water into wine, he had indicated his absolute control over the physical universe. And now, by means of this second sign, he had shown that distance presents no real obstacle to the manifestation of his power and love. Accordingly, in both instances, the Savior had made himself known as the Son of God (20:31). And finally, both of these miracles were used by the Lord as means (in conjunction with his words) to bring about faith in the hearts of his children. After the first sign the disciples believed. After the second, not only the official at the royal court believed but so did his entire household. This is the usual way in the kingdom. God is the God of the covenant. His promise is to bless believing parents and their seed (Gen. 17:7; Ps. 105:8-10; Acts 2:39).

Synthesis of 4:43-54

See the Outline on p. 68. *The Son of God revealing himself to ever-widening circles; to Galilee: healing of the nobleman's son.*

Having gathered fruit unto everlasting life in Samaria, Jesus now resumes his journey toward Galilee. He does not at this time return to Judea where the rapid increase in the number of his disciples was tending in the direction of a premature crisis (4:1-3), but he continues on his way to the north, knowing that the immediate danger in his home-country of Galilee is not as great as in Judea: "a prophet has no honor in his own fatherland."

Arrived in Cana — the place where he had performed his first miracle — a Jew of noble rank urged him to come to his home at once. This man seems to have been a courtier in the service of "king" Herod Antipas, who was really a tetrarch (Luke 3:1; 3:19; 9:7; literally, ruler over a fourth part of the kingdom; later, ruler over any part of the country; hence, petty king). The courtier's son lay ill at home in Capernaum. The father kept urging Jesus to come down to Capernaum to heal this child.

Not only did Jesus grant physical healing to the child but he also imparted spiritual healing to the father, whose faith he transformed; as follows:

(1) from a mere belief in Christ's miracle-working *power* (4:47, 48);
(2) to faith in the *word* of Jesus (4:50); and finally

(3) to faith in the *person* of Christ, in which faith this father was joined by his entire household.

In this second sign at Cana the glory of Christ was made manifest in a most remarkable manner. At times Jesus imparted healing by touching the sick (Mark 1:41), or by taking them by the hand (Mark 1:31), or by issuing a command to them (Mark 2:11). Here, however, there is nothing of the kind. The Son of God asserts his will. Result? *Instantly* healing power enters the body of a boy, restoring him *completely* . . . at a distance of sixteen miles!

CHAPTER V

5 1 After these things there was a feast of the Jews, and Jesus went up to Jerusalem. 2 Now in Jerusalem by the sheep-gate there is a pool, called in Hebrew Bethzatha, which has five porticoes. 3 In these lay a crowd of invalids, blind, lame, shriveled up. 5 Now there was a certain man there who had been afflicted with his illness for thirty-eight years. 6 When Jesus saw this man lying there, and when he knew that he had been in that condition for a long time, he said to him, "Do you want to get well?" 7 The sick man answered him, "Sir, I have no one to [109] put me into the pool when the water is disturbed; and while I am coming, another steps down ahead of me." 8 Jesus said to him, "Get up, pick up your mat and walk." 9 All at once the man was healed, and he picked up his mat and was walking.

That day was sabbath. 10 So the Jews were saying to the healed man, "It is sabbath; it is against the law for you to carry your mat." 11 But he answered them, "The man who healed me, it was he who said to me, 'Pick up your mat and walk.' " 12 They asked him, "Who is the man that said to you, 'Pick up (your mat) and walk?' " 13 Now the healed man did not know who it was, for Jesus had slipped out of the crowd that was in that place.

14 After these things Jesus came across him in the temple, and said to him, "See here, you have been healed. No longer continue in sin, or something worse may happen to you." [110] 15 The man went back and told the Jews that it was Jesus who had healed him. 16 And for this reason the Jews were persecuting Jesus, because he was doing these things on the sabbath. 17 But he answered them, "My Father is working until now, and I too am working." 18 So for this reason the Jews tried all the harder to kill him, because not only did he break the sabbath, but he also called God his own Father, making himself equal with God.

5:1-18

5:1. The phrase **after these things** (μετὰ ταῦτα, which occurs in 3:22; 5:1, 14; 6:1; 7:1; 13:7; 19:38; and 21:1) does not necessarily indicate *a long time afterward* (in 19:38 that cannot even be the meaning). It is, however, distinguished from the expression *after this* (μετὰ τοῦτο, which is found in 2:12; 11:7, 11; 19:28 and in all these passages refers to events that occurred *shortly* afterward) in being more indefinite. It simply gives no hint with

---

[109] On ἵνα see pp. 46, 48.
[110] Literally: "in order that something worse may not happen to you."

respect to the length of the period which elapsed since the events took place that were last recorded.

Hence, we do not know just when the great miracle on which our attention is fixed in this chapter occurred. We do know that it was when **there was a feast of the Jews;** but this indication, too, is rather indefinite. To which feast does the author refer?

In discussing this question the following Table of Jewish Festivals which require consideration in this connection may be helpful. The names of the months are, of course, approximate; i.e., they do not correspond exactly to those of the Jewish religious calendar. The period covered extends from Christ's baptism to the outpouring of the Holy Spirit.

MARCH	APRIL	MAY	OCTOBER	DECEMBER
During the Year 26 A. D.				
				Dedication
During the Year 27 A. D.				
Purim	Passover 2:13, 23	Pentecost	Tabernacles	Dedication cf. 4:35
During the Year 28 A. D.				
Purim	Passover 5:1?	Pentecost	Tabernacles	Dedication
During the Year 29 A. D.				
Purim	Passover 6:4	Pentecost	Tabernacles 7:2, 37	Dedication 10:22, 23
During the Year 30 A. D.				
Purim	Passover 12:1; 13:1; 19:14	Pentecost Acts 2:1		

By glancing at this Table it is immediately obvious that the feast indicated in 5:1 cannot belong to the year 26 A. D. or even to the year 27 A. D., for 4:35 already carried us to December of 27 A. D.

It has been suggested that the Passover mentioned in *6:4* is that of 28 A. D., and that, accordingly, the feast of 5:1 is Purim of that year.

Against this view we present the following objections:

(1) Having left Judea for the reason stated in 4:1-3, 43, 44, Jesus would

not have returned to that region so soon afterward unless it would be for the purpose of attending one of the three pilgrim feasts.

(2) Purim was not a pilgrim feast. It was celebrated in the local synagogues where for that occasion the book of Esther was read amid great joy.

(3) The Passover mentioned in 6:4 carries us to the *close* of the Great Galilean Ministry. Now if that Passover occurred in 28 A. D., this entire lengthy ministry, during which so very many events occurred, would be crowded into a period of four months. This will never do.

Now if the feast of 5:1 was not Purim of 28 A. D., and if (as is clear from 6:1: *after* these things) it cannot be the Passover of 6:4, then *the latter* must be dated in the year 29 A. D.

We arrive at the conclusion, therefore, that the feast of 5:1, if it was one of the three Jewish pilgrim feasts,[111] must have been either Passover or Pentecost or Tabernacles of the year 28 A. D.

Of these three the term *feast of the Jews* (5:1) is used elsewhere in the Fourth Gospel to indicate either Passover (6:4) or feast of Tabernacles (7:2). In both cases, moreover, the original has the definite article preceding the noun *feast*. Accordingly, the omission of that article here in 5:1 according to the best textual evidence, does not decide the question either way.

We conclude, therefore, by stating as our opinion that this unnamed feast a. was one of the three pilgrim feasts; b. must be dated in the year 28 A. D.; and c. was, *in all probability,* either Passover or feast of Tabernacles (without ruling out the possibility that it was Pentecost). In favor of the Passover two additional arguments are sometimes presented: 1. this is supported by the tradition of Ireneus, and 2. this was the only feast which the Israelites were required to attend. However, the evidence is not entirely conclusive.

We read that it was Jesus who attended the feast: **And Jesus went up to Jerusalem.** Nothing is said in this entire chapter with reference to his disciples. But this does not prove that they did not accompany him. It is possible that here as elsewhere (e.g., in 3:22 cf. 4:2) the entire group went up, though the name of the leader alone is mentioned. (Anent the expression "he *went up* to Jerusalem" see 2:13.)

2. Now in Jerusalem by the sheep-gate there is a pool, called in Hebrew Bethzatha, which has five porticoes. Not far from the *sheep-gate* (St. Stephen's?), probably called thus because through it many sheep were led for the purpose of being sacrificed in the near-by temple-court, there was a *pool*. Popularly, this pool is known as Bethesda (*house of mercy*), but the

---

[111] It is hard to believe that *at this time* Jesus would have gone to Jerusalem to attend one of the lesser feasts, such as that of Wood-offering or even that of Trumpets, though these too are favored by some commentators.

reading *Bethzatha* (Aramaic: *house of the olive-tree?*) has better textual attestation.

After much guess-work with respect to the identity of this pool, its site has finally been established to the satisfaction of most scholars. The pool (or, in reality, the reservoir which formed it) was laid bare in the year 1888 in connection with the repair of the church of St. Anne, in n.e. Jerusalem. A faded fresco on the wall pictures an angel "troubling" the water. It appears, therefore, that by the early church this pool was viewed as Bethzatha. In the time of our Lord it had *five porticos* or covered colonnades where the sick could rest, protected from inclement weather.[112]

3. Now in these five porticoes or wards **lay a crowd of invalids** of every description; particularly, **blind, lame, and shriveled up;** i.e., withered or paralyzed (ξηρός; literally *dry;* hence, shrunken by disease; cf. Mark 3:3; Luke 6:6). Apparently the sick man whom Jesus cured was one of these *withered* ones. It is worthy of note that not only cripples and paralytics but also blind people sought healing at this pool. Did any blind person ever receive his sight at the Pool of Bethzatha, or was it thus, that the benefit which the *lame* man received caused the *blind* man to imagine that for him too there might be a cure?

After 5:3 of the A.R.V., the A.V. has the following: Verse 3 b: ". . . waiting for the moving of the water." Verse 4: "For an angel went down at a certain season into the pool, and troubled the water; whosoever then first after the troubling of the water stepped in was made whole of whatsoever disease he had."

None of the best and most ancient manuscripts have these words which, accordingly, have not been retained in the A.R.V.[113] On the other hand, Tertullian (about 145-220 A. D.) already shows that he knows this passage; for he states:

"An angel, by his intervention, was wont to stir the pool at Bethsaida. They who were complaining of ill health used to watch for him; for whoever was the first to descend into these waters, after his washing ceased to complain" (*On Baptism* V).

The following, it would seem to us, is a reasonable position with respect to the entire story and particularly with reference to the words that are omitted in the best ancient manuscripts and also in the A.R.V.:

(1) It is probably much more difficult to explain how it came about that these words were omitted from all the best manuscripts if they were really a part of the original text than to account for the manner in which they

---

[112] See J. Jeremias, *Die Wiederentdeckung von Bethesda,* Göttingen, 1949. Also W.H.A.B., p. 99 and Plate XVII B.

[113] See further on this subject A. T. Robertson, *An Introduction to the Textual Criticism of the New Testament,* New York, 1925, pp. 154, 183, 209.

may have crept into the text (e.g., as a marginal gloss which was intended as an explanation of the disturbance of the water, mentioned in 4:7, and which ascribed this "troubling" to the periodic visit of an angel).

(2) On the basis of the text as it is found in the best manuscripts and in the A.R.V. (hence; with 4:3b and 4 omitted) *there is no necessity* to believe that the agitation that occurred in the water was actually due to any supernatural cause. Also, the idea that whoever, after such a disturbance, was the first man to step into the pool was healed is not presented here as being necessarily the belief of the author of the Fourth Gospel nor as the teaching of the Holy Spirit but as the implied opinion of the sick man (4:7b).

(3) On the other hand, it is certainly true that *the possibility* of supernatural, angelic activity must not be ruled out. It should never be forgotten that an interpolation from the margin into the text *may be correct*. In the days of our Lord's earthly ministry angels come into prominence again and again, and unusual powers and energies play an important role.

(4) It must be stressed, however, that the miracle which occurs here when *this sick man* is cured is ascribed not to any medicinal virtue inherent in this particular pool, nor to any angelic activity, but to the power and the love of Jesus! In fact, when the Lord heals this man *he does not even make any use of the pool* (contrast 9:7; II Kings 5:10, 14). And it is on *this miracle* that we should place all the emphasis; not on the question whether or not miracles were constantly taking place at this pool.

5. Now there was a certain man there, i.e., among the invalids there was one man who more than any other attracted the attention of Jesus. He was the man **who had been afflicted with his illness for thirty-eight years.** This, of course, does not mean that he had been here at this pool for that length of time. The reason why John has selected *this* miracle for inclusion in his Gospel has already been stated (see pp. 33-35).

6. When Jesus saw this man lying there, and when he knew that he had been in that condition for a long time. Jesus *saw* this man; undoubtedly he looked upon him with an eye of sympathy (cf. Mark 8:3; 10:21), probing his very soul. The Lord *knew* that the invalid had been in that lamentable condition for a long time. Where did Jesus obtain this knowledge? There are three possibilities, none of which should be ruled out in this connection:

(1) Someone may have given him this information in a perfectly natural and human manner. In that case we should translate, "And when he was informed. . . ."

(2) The Father may have revealed it to him.

(3) Christ's divine nature may have imparted this knowledge to his human nature in a manner which we do not understand.

Knowing, then, that this man had been in this condition for a long time, Jesus addressed him. **He said to him, Do you want to get well?** Does this question imply that the soul of this man had actually descended to that morbid state where he had lost the very will to be cured? Whether or not this was the case, in all probability these words were spoken in order to bring him to an open acknowledgment of his deep misery and of his inability to deliver himself from it; so that, in turn, this confession might cause the miraculous recovery to stand out in bolder relief. The question of Jesus also contains a promise of help.

7. The sick man answered him, Sir, I have no one to put me into the pool when the water is disturbed; and while I am coming, another steps down ahead of me.

It seems that the rule at this pool was, "Everyone for himself." No one had ever helped this invalid whose power of locomotion, due to his physical affliction, was very limited. He was never able to proceed fast enough: someone always stepped down into the pool ahead of him. And if, in this connection, it be remarked that today matters are different — there would be someone to help: an attendant or a nurse —, it should not be forgotten that such improved present-day conditions, wherever they occur, can be largely traced back to the influence of the loving and sympathetic heart of Christ, as revealed in Scripture, including the present chapter.

As has already been remarked, the cause of *the water's disturbance* may have been supernatural or natural. If natural, then it would seem that the sudden bubbling up was caused by an intermittent spring by which the pool was fed. In general it may be stated that it is never uncommon for people, afflicted with various illnesses, to gather around mineral springs. Think of the springs around Tiberias or, in our own country, of the waters of Hot Springs, Arkansas, which long before the Spaniards arrived were already being credited with healing virtues.

8. When the sick man complained, in utter hopelessness, that someone always stepped down into the pool ahead of him, did the light of sympathy and encouragement that was shining in the eyes of the Lord revive hope to some extent, especially in view of the question which Jesus had asked: "Do you want to get well?" Did it occur to the invalid that, perhaps at the next disturbance of the water-surface, this stranger might be willing to put him into the pool? What a welcome surprise he received when suddenly the Healer addresses him in never-to-be-forgotten words: **Jesus said to him, Get up, pick up your mat, and walk.**[114] What a challenge this was to a man who had just now confessed his own complete inability! The *mat* to which Jesus refers (κράβαττος, cf. the Latin *grabatus*) was a camp-bed, pallet,

---

[114] Of the three imperatives the first is aoristic present; the second aorist; the third, continuative (durative) present: go on walking.

pad, or thin mattress. The man was told to pick this up and to start walking.

9a. All at once the man was healed. He obeyed and was healed *all at once* (εὐθέως). The very fact that the author of the Fourth Gospel, in contrast with Mark, seldom uses the expression *all at once, straightway,* or *instantly* (also in 6:21 and 18:27; for εὐθύς see 13:30, 32; 19:34) indicates that he wishes to place special stress on this sudden and complete character of the cure. Once more the glory of the Son of God stands revealed. *This* recovery is neither gradual nor partial; nor, we may well add, was the sickness faked (as some, nevertheless, have supposed). All so-called "faith-healers" should make a close study of this wonderful account. At the word of Jesus new strength and vigor surged through this man's whole body; **and he picked up his mat and was walking!**

9b, 10. That day was sabbath. So the Jews were saying to the healed man.

The day on which Jesus healed this man was a sabbath. So a controversy develops between Jesus and *the Jews* (for the specific meaning of this term in the Fourth Gospel see on 1:19). The Pharisees had superimposed upon the law of God their own hair-splitting distinctions and rabbinical restrictions. This was true particularly with reference to the sabbath, as has been shown in connection with 3:1. Instead of looking upon it as a day of special consecration unto works of gratitude for the salvation which God had given, they viewed it as a day of cessation from all (common) work with a view to the salvation which man must merit. For them the sabbath meant idleness; for Christ it meant work. Nevertheless, for them it constituted hardship; for him, rest. As they saw it, man was made for the sabbath; as he knew it, the sabbath was made for man.

Hence, the Jews said to the healed man, **It is sabbath; it is against the law for you to carry your mat.** They referred, undoubtedly, to Ex. 20:10 and more specifically to Jer. 17:19-27 ("Thus said Jehovah, Take heed to yourselves, and bear no burden on the sabbath day, nor bring it in by the gates of Jerusalem; neither carry forth a burden out of your houses on the sabbath day. . . .") and to Neh. 13:15 ("In those days saw I in Judah some men treading winepresses on the sabbath, and bringing in sheaves, and lading asses therewith; as also wine, grapes, and figs, and all manner of burdens, which they brought into Jerusalem on the sabbath day: and I testified against them in the day wherein they sold victuals"). In these passages the reference is, however, clearly to that type of burden-bearing which was connected with the performance of ordinary labor for gain, with trading and marketing. By forbidding a cured man to pick up his mat — as if that were comparable to a burden which he was carrying to the marketplace in order to sell it at a profit! — they were making a caricature of the law of God.

11. The reply of the cured one was to the point. **He answered them, The man who healed me, it was he who said to me, Pick up your mat and walk.** His reasoning was as follows: one who performs so glorious a deed — instantaneously granting complete recovery to a shriveled up individual whose body had been in that atrophied condition for thirty-eight years! — has a right even on the sabbath to tell that healed person what to do.

12. **They asked him, Who is the man** (i.e., the fellow, in a tone of derision) **that said to you, Pick up and walk?** They do not ask, "Who healed you?" They are not at all interested in this man's glorious recovery. They are interested only in their hair-splitting man-made regulations. In their great zeal for the maintenance of the latter they even forget to see the utterly ridiculous character of their complaint: they do not seem to realize that, after all, it was only a *mat* (see p. 192) that the man was carrying. Hence, they omit even this word. As they saw it, the sin which the man was committing was this, a. that he had *picked up* something, anything, it hardly mattered what it was, and b. that he was *walking* away with it! They are logical, however, when they attempt to trace the awful deed to the one who had commanded it to be done.

13. **Now the healed man did not know who it was, for Jesus had slipped out of the crowd that was in that place.** The healed man had not learned the identity of his Benefactor, for immediately after performing the miracle Jesus had slipped away from the crowd of sabbath-sick-visitors. Was it in order to avoid a public demonstration that Jesus had slipped away? Or, perhaps, in order that he might face the religious leaders themselves rather than their followers? Or, as others have thought, in order that he might give this healed person an opportunity to be strengthened in his convictions by being compelled to express them without help from anyone? Whatever may have been the reason or combination of reasons, the fact remains that the healed man was unable to point out who it was that had changed his sadness to gladness.

14. **After these things Jesus came across him in the temple, and said to him, See here, you have been healed. No longer continue in sin, or something worse may happen to you.**

On the phrase *after these things* see on 5:1. *Jesus came across the healed man in the temple;* probably in the court of the Gentiles. Whether this meeting occurred the same day or the next day or still later cannot be established from the text. Neither is there anything in the text or context that indicates the purpose for which the healed man had gone to the temple. There were many reasons — strictly or not so strictly religious — why Jews, in great numbers, would enter the house of God and spend a while there. Hence, it is not at all certain that the man's presence in the temple at this particular occasion was in order to bring a thank-offering to God for his recovery.

On the other hand, the reason why Jesus continued to work with him would seem to be far more obvious. In the entire account of the healing of this man (5:1-13) nothing at all was said with respect to a change in his *spiritual* condition. His body had been healed. So it is no wonder that the Healer now restores the soul.

Jesus, accordingly, addresses him in these words, *"See here, you have been healed. No longer continue in sin, or something worse may happen to you."* In our interpretation of this passage we disagree with those commentators — and there are many! — who draw the conclusion that the Lord meant to say, "More than thirty-eight years ago you committed a sin. As a result, you became physically deformed and paralyzed. Now I warn you not to sin again, or something worse may happen to you." On the contrary, the present tense of the verb (μηκέτι ἁμάρτανε), so that we translate, "No longer continue in sin," rather shows that Jesus is referring not to what supposedly happened more than thirty-eight years ago but to *the present* condition of the man.[115] Right now he was in the state of being unreconciled with God. Jesus knew this. Hence, he warns him not to continue in this condition. Otherwise there is in store for him something worse than the physical illness from which so recently he had been delivered. Is it not probable that by "something worse" Jesus meant to indicate eternal punishment? From this it is clear that the account does not contain a single word with reference to the cause of the man's physical illness. This explanation also harmonizes with the words of Christ in 9:3.

15. With gratitude in his heart **the man went back and told the Jews that it was Jesus who had healed him.** However, we note an interesting difference between the question of the Jewish religious leaders, and the answer given by the man. *They* had asked, "Who is the man that said to you, 'Pick up and walk'?" But *he* answered, "It is Jesus who *healed* me." He places the emphasis where it belongs; namely, on the *healing*, in which the Jews had shown so little interest.

16. So intense is the anger of the Jewish authorities when their attention is fixed upon Jesus that they determine in their hearts to persecute him even unto death. **And for this reason the Jews were persecuting.** The verb refers to continued hostile activity. It became more and more definite and determined until it finally nailed Christ to the cross. On the progressive

---

[115] Cf. F. W. Grosheide, *op. cit.*, pp. 352, 353. We agree with him.

character of this persecution see p. 236. The reason for the hatred is stated in these words: **because he was doing these things** (healing the man and telling him to pick up and walk) **on the sabbath.**

17. Did the Jews at this moment begin to address Jesus personally, accusing him of violating the sabbath? Or did the Lord, reading their hearts, address them first? Either way, in defence Jesus points out that in performing this work of mercy on the sabbath he had acted in conformity with the example of his own Father (note *my* Father; and see on 1:14, the nature of Christ's sonship) and in conformity with the mandate which he had received from him. Do the Jews really mean to say that the essence of the sabbath is idleness, and that all work on that day is wrong? But then would they not be accusing God himself of sabbath-violation? If up to this very moment the Father of Jesus is carrying on the work of preservation and redemption, how should not the Son, who stands in the closest possible relation to him (5:19-23), do the same? In the final analysis, Father and Son are engaged in *one* task. Hence, we read: **But he answered them, My Father is working until now, and I too am working.**

18. **So, for this reason** (διὰ τοῦτο, just as in 4:16) **the Jews tried all the harder to kill him;** i.e., they were already determined to bring him to death **because not only did he break the Sabbath,** (in their estimation he was a sabbath-violator), but now this determination became even more intense, active, and energetic; the added reason being: **but he also called God his own Father, making himself equal with God.**

By the words, *he also called God his own Father, making himself equal with God,* the author once more brings into clear view the purpose of his Gospel. That purpose was to strengthen believers so that they might continue to believe that Jesus is the Christ, *the Son of God,* and that believing they might continue to have life in his name (20:30, 31).

In addition to his stand with respect to the sabbath it was his claim of being *equal with God* that nailed Christ to the cross. When the Jewish authorities heard Jesus call God "my (own) Father," they did not do what many moderns have done. They did not try to tone down the character of Christ's sonship. They immediately understood that Jesus claimed for himself deity in the highest possible sense of that term. That claim was either the most wicked blasphemy, to be punished with death; or else, it was the most glorious truth, to be accepted by faith. The very character of the sign which Jesus had just now performed should have caused these religious leaders to adopt the latter alternative. Instead, they chose the former.

196

Synthesis of 5:1-18

See the Outline on p. 68. *The Son of God Rejected in Judea, as a Result of Healing the Man at Bethzatha on the Sabbath, and of Claiming Equality with God.*

For fully eight months Jesus had been carrying on his teaching and healing ministry in Jerusalem and Judea. Then, after a stay of only two days in Samaria, he had entered Galilee. Here, too, he had already performed many miracles, one of them being the cure of the courtier's son, a very remarkable sign, especially in view of the fact that it was performed *at a distance* of about sixteen miles from the abode of the sick child. The Great Galilean Ministry had already been in progress for at least four months. During the course of this ministry the Lord was fulfilling the prophecy of Isa. 9:1, "In the former time he brought into contempt the land of Zebulum and the land of Naphtali; but in the latter time hath he made it glorious, by the way of the sea, beyond the Jordan, Galilee of the nations."

Galilee was full of excitement and enthusiasm, but not of true, saving faith. Now it was during the course of this work in the northern province that Jesus decided to attend one of the three pilgrim feasts in Jerusalem. This was during the year 28 A. D. In Jerusalem he visited the pool of Bethzatha, where he healed a man who had been in his paralytic condition for thirty-eight years.

It was on the sabbath that Jesus said to this sick man, "Get up, pick up your mat, and walk." The man obeyed and instantly received complete physical recovery. Spiritually also the Lord provided for him, by warning him as he met him in the temple, "No longer continue to sin, or something worse may happen to you."

When the Jewish authorities saw the man carrying his mat on the sabbath, in obedience to Christ's command, they criticized both him and his Benefactor. Jesus, however, answered, "My Father is working until now, and I too am working." The religious leaders at Jerusalem therefore instigated a plot to put Jesus to death, and this for two reasons: a. sabbath-violation, b. blasphemy (making himself equal with God).

197

19 Jesus answered and said to them, "I most solemnly assure y o u, the Son can do nothing whatever of himself, but only what he sees the Father doing; for whatever he does, that the Son does likewise. 20 For the Father loves the Son, and has shown him all that he himself is doing, and greater works than these will he show him, in order that y o u may be amazed. 21 For even as the Father raises the dead and imparts life to them, so also the Son imparts life to whom he wills. 22 For the Father judges no one, but has committed all judgment to the Son, 23 in order that all may honor the Son even as they honor the Father. He who does not honor the Son does not honor the Father who sent him.

24 "I most solemnly assure y o u,[116] he who hears my word and believes him who sent me has everlasting life, and does not come into condemnation, but has passed out of death into life. 25 I most solemnly assure y o u,[116] the hour is coming — yea, has already arrived! — when the dead will hear the voice of the Son of God, and those who hear will live. 26 For just as the Father has life in himself, so he has granted to the Son also to have life in himself, 27 and he gave him authority to function as Judge, because he is the Son of man. 28 Stop being surprised about this, for [117] the hour is coming when all who are in the tombs will hear his voice 29 and will come out: those who have done good, for the resurrection of life, and those who have practised evil, for the resurrection of condemnation. 30 I can do nothing whatever of myself; as I hear I judge, and my judgment is just, because I do not seek my own will, but the will of him who sent me."

5:19-30

5:19. Instead of in any way seeking to moderate his earlier statement (verse 17) which had aroused the anger of the Jews, Jesus strengthens it by means of a. the majestic introductory formula **I most solemnly assure y o u** (see on 1:5) and b. the rest of the contents of verses 19-23. The passage under discussion may be paraphrased as follows.

"Do y o u Jews accuse me of transgressing the Father's sabbath-ordinance and of blaspheming his name by claiming equality with him? The charge is absurd, for in that case the will of the Son would be separate (not merely distinct) from the will of the Father and would even oppose the latter. But as a matter of fact **the Son can do nothing whatever** (οὐ δύναται . . . ποιεῖν . . . οὐδέν) **of himself, but only what he sees the Father doing; for** here, indeed, is the perfect pattern of that which is so often seen on earth; namely, that **whatever he** (the Father) **does that the Son does likewise** (here, indeed, there is flawless correspondence).

20, 21. "I have a right to say this, **for** (γάρ), being myself the Son, I know that **the Father loves** (φιλεῖ; see comments on 21:15-17) **the Son, and has shown him all that he himself is** (constantly) **doing** in working out his eternal plan of redemption. The performance of miracles — e.g., the

---

[116] On ὅτι in verses 24 and 25 see pp. 54 (also footnote 13), 57.
[117] On ὅτι in verse 28 see pp. 55, 58.

healing of this man at the Pool — also belongs to the working out of this eternal plan; **and greater works than these** wonders of healing the sick **will he** (the Father) **show him** (the Son) — namely, bringing to life those who are dead, and pronouncing judgment with reference to all — **in order that y o u,** already astonished because of the miracle at the Pool, **may** really **be amazed. For even as the Father raises the dead and imparts life to them** (both to those spiritually dead, and to those physically dead, the latter in the day of judgment) **so also the Son,** for he is equally sovereign, **imparts life to whom he wills.**

22, 23. For the Father judges no one, but has committed all judgment to the Son, that is, the Father never acts alone (in separation from the Son) in pronouncing judgment, but has committed all judgment to the Son (both for the present, in the sense of 3:18b, 19; and with respect to the future, in the sense of Matt. 25: 31 ff). Thus, the Father always works through the Son, **in order that all may honor the Son even as they honor the Father;** that is, in order that those two persons who are equal in *essence* (5:17, 18) and in *works* (5:19-22) may also be equal in *honor.* Y o u unbelieving Jews, who have determined in y o u r hearts to put the Son to death (5:18) should not imagine that y o u can honor the Father: **he who does not honor the Son does not honor the Father who sent him.**

24-30. *Quickening the dead* and *pronouncing judgment* were the two *greater* works which the Father had assigned to the Son (see verses 20b, 21, 22 above). *As the terms "to judge" and "judgment" are used in verses 24, 27, 29, we refer to our explanation of 3:17-19 for further comment.* In the present paragraph we are told:

a. How the Son performs this work *at present* in the *spiritual* sphere — (verses 24, 25); and

c. How he is going to accomplish this task *in the future* in the *physical* realm (verses 28, 29). Between these two passages there is one which shows

b. *How it is to be explained* that the Son is able to carry out this double assignment (quickening the dead and pronouncing judgment) *in the present and in the future, and this in both spheres* (verses 26, 27).

d. The closing passage (verse 30), on the basis of a, b, and c, reaffirms the Son's perfect unity with the One who sent him.

Subdivisions a. and c. (verses 24, 25 and verses 28, 29) are clearly distinguished by the words "the hour is coming, *yea, has already arrived*" of verse 25, and the words "the hour *is coming*" (but not: "has already arrived") of verse 28. The first passage, accordingly, deals with *the first resurrection;* namely, that of the soul; the second subdivision describes *the second resurrection;* namely, that of the body. We meet exactly the same sequence of events in another work by the same author (John); namely, in the book of

Revelation, where the former is discussed in 20:4-6; the latter in 20:11 ff.[118]
Note the parallel:

Fourth Gospel	*Revelation:*
A. *First Resurrection*	A. *First Resurrection*
I most solemnly assure y o u, he who hears my word and believes him who sent me has everlasting life . . . has passed out of death into life. I most solemnly assure y o u, the hour is coming — yea, has already arrived! — when the dead will hear the voice of the Son of God, and those who hear will live.	". . . and I saw *the souls* of them that had been beheaded . . . and such as worshiped not the beast, neither his image, and received not the mark upon their forehead and upon their hand; and *they lived* and reigned with Christ a thousand years. . . . *This is the first resurrection.*
. . . and (he) does not come into condemnation. (For the solemn introductory formula see on 1:51.)	"Blessed and holy is he who has part in the first resurrection: over these the second death has no power."
B. *Second Resurrection* (unto judgment)	B. *Second Resurrection* (unto judgment)
Stop being surprised about this, for the hour is coming when all who are in the tombs will hear his voice and will come out: those who have done good, for the resurrection of life, and those who have practised evil, for the resurrection of condemnation.	"And I saw a great white throne and him who sat upon it. . . . And I saw the dead, the great and the small, standing before the throne; and books were opened: and another book was opened, which is the book of life: and the dead were judged out of the things which were written in the books, according to their works: And the sea gave up the dead that were in it; and death and Hades gave up the dead that were in them: and they were judged every man according to their works. . . . And if any was not found in the book of life, he was cast into the lake of fire."

On the basis of this comparison a few conclusions are warranted:

1. Though it is often maintained that the Fourth Gospel contains no teaching with reference to *the last things,* this is not true, as the present

---

[118] See our *More than Conquerors,* sixth edition, Grand Rapids, Mich., 1952, pp. 231, 232.

paragraph shows. See also 6:39, 40, 44, 54; 11:24; 12:48; 14:3, 28; 15:18 ff.; 16:1 ff.; 16:19 ff.[119]

2. The first resurrection has nothing to do with the body; it concerns the soul. As soon as the word of Christ is accepted by faith ("he who hears my word and believes") one "has everlasting life (on this see 1:4; 3:16) and has passed out of death into life"; and what else is this but *the first resurrection,* which, though beginning here on earth, culminates in the life of the soul with Christ in heaven? In the passage from Revelation it is especially the latter phase of this first resurrection which receives the emphasis.

3. One who takes part in the first resurrection (i.e., one who has embraced Christ by a living faith) need not fear the coming day of judgment. In the language of the Fourth Gospel "he does not come into condemnation" (εἰς κρίσιν); in the language of Revelation "over these the second death (in which the sentence of condemnation is executed) has no power."

4. The second resurrection is physical in character.[120] It pertains to the great day of the consummation of all things. It is universal: *all* will be raised: both believers and unbelievers.

5. Neither the Fourth Gospel nor Revelation teaches that a period of a thousand years will intervene between the physical resurrection of believers and the physical resurrection of unbelievers: "the hour is coming when all who are in the tombs will hear his voice and will come out." "And I saw the dead, *the great and the small* . . . books were opened and another book was opened. . . . And the sea gave up *the dead* that were in it; and death and Hades gave up the dead that were in them." It is all as general as possible. Calvin is right when he remarks that here in John's Gospel (5:28) the expression *"all who are in the tombs will come out"* certainly does not imply that those who were devoured by wild beasts or were drowned or burned to death are excluded from the number of those who will arise. When that great hour arrives *all arise* and *all* are judged! See also Matt. 25:46; Acts 24:15; II Cor. 5:10; II Thess. 1:7-10. No time-difference is indicated anywhere, not in John's writings, nor in Paul's. (I Cor. 15:22, 23; I Thess. 4:13-18 teach nothing of the kind, as we have pointed out elsewhere.) [121]

6. Although as concerns *time* there is but *one,* universal physical resurrection, nevertheless, as concerns *quality* or *character* we may, indeed, speak of two future resurrections. (See also Dan. 12:2.) In other words, the one, universal resurrection has two phases, as is taught clearly both in the Fourth Gospel and in the Apocalypse. There is a "resurrection of life," on the one

---

[119] See on this subject W. F. Howard, *Christianity According to St. John,* Philadelphia, 1946, pp. 106-128.
[120] M. Goguel, *Le Quatrième Évangile,* Paris, 1924, vol. II, p. 536 is in error when he states: "L'eschatologie est, comme nous l'avons vu, entièrement spiritualisée."
[121] See our *Lectures on the Last Things,* Grand Rapids, Mich., 1951, pp. 31-49.

hand (qualitative genitive: this resurrection is in harmony with the character of everlasting life; hence, is glorious, etc.), and a "resurrection of condemnation," on the other hand (same genitive: this resurrection is in harmony with the idea of condemnation; hence, is unto shame and derision). *Believers* are raised in order to reign forever and ever with Christ, as to both body and soul (heretofore only as to the soul); *unbelievers* are cast into the lake of fire.

In addition to these remarks which are based on a comparison between the *Gospel* and the *Revelation* of John, the following points with reference to John 5:24-30 require attention:

With respect to a. (verses 24, 25):

Spiritual quickening does not occur apart from the word. Nevertheless, the mere hearing of the word is not enough; it must be accepted by faith: "he who hears my word and believes." This faith must have as its object Jesus as *the Son of God:* "believes him who sent me." Such a one "has everlasting life." The idea that a sinner is by nature *dead,* so that when the great change takes place he actually passes "out of death into life," is found not only here but also in Luke 15:32; Eph. 2:1; 5:14. Regeneration and conversion are basic changes, radical transformations. They are not to be confused with moral improvements whereby, for example, a drunkard renounces the use of liquor. Of course, when the entire personality is regenerated, the morals too are changed.

The expression "the hour is coming, yea has already arrived" refers to this entire new dispensation, which when Jesus spoke these words was both present and future. The Lord is thinking about the hosts of converts that will be drawn out of the darkness into the light, and out of death into life, from the realm of both Jew and Gentile until the day of his second coming. "The dead will hear the voice of the Son of God, and those who hear will live."

With respect to b. (verses 26, 27):

For just as the Father has life in himself, so he has granted to the Son also to have life in himself, and he gave him authority to function as judge, because he is the Son of man. Just as the Father is self-sufficient, having within himself *eternal* life, so also the Son has been given to have this life (inherent) in himself; and this explains the fact (note γάρ) that he is able to grant *everlasting* life to his elect. In passages of this nature it must be borne in mind that our Lord's mediatorial sonship in which he carries out his task on earth rests upon his eternal, intra-trinitarian sonship. When Jesus spoke these words, the Jews must have asked, "Whence does this man derive the right to utter such language? Is *he* actually going to judge?" Jesus points out that this authority to judge (as well as the power to impart life) has been given to him because he is *the Son of man.* More-

202

over, the two ideas *judging* and *Son of man* always go together in Scripture. (On the title *Son of man* and its connection with the judgment see our comments on 12:34.) Many commentators suggest that the absence of the article before *Son of man* here in 5:27 (so that we have υἱὸς ἀνθρώπου) is very significant. On the basis of this absence a host of interpretations of this verse have been offered; *especially* these two:

a. The authority to function as judge had to be *given* to Jesus because it is as *man*, and not as God, that he performs this task.

b. The authority to function as judge of *men* was given to him because he too is a *man*, thoroughly acquainted, therefore, with human thoughts, words, and actions. In order to be a good judge one must share the nature of those who are to be judged.

But with all due respect for the ability of those commentators who base their whole exegesis of this passage on the omission of the article, we cannot go along with them in their conclusions. It is, indeed, very doubtful whether the absence of the article should be pressed. It is a well-known fact that official titles have a tendency to lose the article. It would, indeed, be very strange if in this one instance the title had a different meaning than it does in all the other cases. Besides, as was pointed out, the idea that the right to judge was given to him as (the) *Son of man,* in the messianic meaning of the term, renders excellent sense. It is an eminently scriptural thought, whereas this cannot be said with the same emphasis with respect to either of the other interpretations.

With respect to c. (verses 28, 29):

The idea of judgment (condemnation and acquittal; with consequent retribution and remuneration) did not take the Jews by surprise. However, what did cause them to be filled with amazement was the claim of Jesus (verses 22 and 27) a claim utterly preposterous and intolerable, as *they* saw it — that *he himself* had received the right to judge, and that men were being judged and were going to be judged on the basis of their attitude to *him.*

Therefore Jesus says, "Stop being surprised about this, for (what I have affirmed is true, as will be shown by the fact that) the hour is coming when all who are in the tombs will hear his voice and will come out. . . ." The statement, *all who are in the tombs will hear his voice* would seem to indicate that instead of being in any sense secret or silent, the second coming is going to be public and audible (as well as visible). Cf. I Cor. 15:52.[122] Note also that both in the spiritual and in the physical realm the voice of Christ is *creative.* If it were not, the *dead* would not be able *to hear* it! For further comments on this passage (verses 28, 29) we refer to what has already been said on pp. 199-202.

---

[122] See our *Lectures on the Last Things,* Grand Rapids, Mich., 1951, pp. 26, 33, 34.

With respect to d. (verse 30):

In this verse Jesus sums up the entire argument. He has arrived at the conclusion which was already *stated* at the beginning (see verse 19), but is now *emphasized* by the use of the pronoun, first person singular; namely that the Jews have no right to judge and condemn him as if what he had done to this man at the Pool on the sabbath (or, in general, as if whatever act he performed) were something for which he alone — and not he *and the Father* — was responsible. Says he, **I can do nothing of myself.** The Jews must know that in criticizing the Son of God they are opposing God himself. The Son as Mediator has received definite information (as to standards of judgment) from the Father. Moreover, inasmuch as his Mediatorial sonship rests upon his eternal sonship, it is clear that he himself desires to do the *wholly righteous* will of the Father, with whom he is united in essence: **as I hear I judge, and my judgment is just, because I do not seek my own will, but the will of him who sent me** (τοῦ πεμψαντός με; little if any difference between πέμπω and ἀποστέλλω in John's usage; see also on 1:6 and 3:34).

Synthesis of 5:19-30

See the Outline on p. 68. *The Son of God Rejected in Judea, as a Result of Healing the Man at Bathzatha on the Sabbath, and of Claiming Equality with God* (continued).

In this section Jesus sets forth his claims with respect to his relation to the Father. He does this in answer to the unbelief and hatred of the Jews who are determined to put him to death. The Lord's defence may be summarized as follows:

1. In attacking me, the Son, you are attacking the Father himself, for the Son does what he sees the Father doing; he judges as the Father judges. He cannot do otherwise. Neither does he desire to do otherwise.

2. Are you amazed because of this act of healing a sick man? This was, indeed, a *great* work, but *greater* works will follow: imparting life to those who are dead (yes, both to the spiritually dead and, at the last day, to those physically dead) and judging all men (both now and at the Return in glory).

3. Do you question how it is possible for me a. to impart life and b. to pronounce and execute judgment? I can do the former because the Father has granted me to have life in myself (just as he also has life in himself); and the latter, in my capacity as Son of man.

4. The proper reaction to my words and works is not base unbelief and hatred, nor even the attitude of mind that fails to rise above amazement, but faith which honors the Son even as it honors the Father.

5. Those who exercise this faith do not come into condemnation but have even now passed out of death into life. In the great day of judgment

they — together with all the dead — will also arise physically. But though all will be raised, there will be a great difference in the quality or character of their resurrection: those who have done good will come out of their tombs for "the resurrection of life"; those who have practised evil, for "the resurrection of condemnation." Implication: "Therefore, embrace by faith the Son of God!" Cf. purpose of the Gospel (20:30, 31).

---

31 "If I testify concerning myself, my testimony is not true.[123] 32 It is another who testifies concerning me, and I know that the testimony which he bears concerning me is true. 33 Y o u, on y o u r part, have sent to John, and he has testified to the truth. 34 But I, on my part, do not accept (mere) human testimony, but I say these things in order that y o u may be saved. 35 He was the lamp burning and shining. And y o u were willing to rejoice for a while in his light. 36 But I have testimony that surpasses that of John, for the works which the Father has given me to [124] accomplish, these very works in which I am engaged testify concerning me that the Father has sent me. 37 And the Father who sent me, he himself has testified concerning me. But his voice y o u have never heard, his form y o u have never seen; 38 and y o u do not have his word abiding within y o u, because in the One whom he sent, in him y o u do not believe. 39 Y o u are searching the Scriptures, because y o u think that in them y o u have everlasting life, and yet it is they that testify concerning me. 40 But y o u do not want to come to me in order that [125] y o u may have life.

41 "Praise from men I do not accept, 42 but I know y o u, that y o u do not have the love of God within y o u. 43 I have come in my Father's name, but y o u do not accept me. If another comes in his own name, him y o u will accept.[126] 44 How can y o u believe, y o u who accept praise from one another, while the praise that comes from the only God y o u do not seek? 45 Do not think that I shall accuse y o u before the Father. Y o u r accuser is Moses, on whom y o u have set y o u r hope. 46 For if y o u believed Moses, y o u would believe me, since he wrote about me.[127] 47 But if his writings y o u do not believe, how will y o u believe my words?" [128]

5:31-47

5:31. Jesus has made majestic claims. But who is he to make them? It does not surprise us, therefore, that in the present paragraph the claims are supported by testimonies regarding himself. The Lord begins by saying, **If I testify concerning myself, my testimony is not true.** Commentators agree, of course, that these words cannot be taken literally, as if he meant that what he said with reference to himself was not true to fact. If that were the

---

[123] III B 1; see pp. 42, 44.
[124] On ἵνα see pp. 46, 48.
[125] On ἵνα see pp. 46, 47, 48.
[126] III A 1; see pp. 42, 43.
[127] II A; see p. 41.
[128] I B; see p. 40.

11

correct interpretation, Jesus would cease to be the sinless One. Other attempts to explain these words are as follows:

1. The meaning is, "If I should be testifying concerning myself, my testimony would not be true." Objection: a glance at the form of these words in the original immediately shows that this cannot be correct, for we do not have a contrary-to-fact conditional sentence here, but one that belongs to group III B 1.

2. What Jesus means is, "If I present *lone, unsupported* testimony concerning myself, my testimony is not true." But if that be the meaning *here,* then why should we not give the *same* interpretation to the *same* words in 8:14, "Even though I do testify concerning myself, my testimony *is true"?* Jesus says nothing about lone, unsupported testimony.

3. The word *true* has a different meaning here. The sense of the passage is, "If I testify concerning myself, my testimony is not *admissible in a court of law* (usually with an appeal to Matt. 18:16; II Cor. 13:1; I Tim. 5:19). But this reasoning would imply that in 8:14 Jesus states that such testimony regarding oneself *is* admissible in a law-court. Hence, we would have a flat contradiction.

The true solution, as we see it, will be found when we realize that Jesus is speaking the language of the people, the vernacular. One of the characteristics of this type of discourse is that it is marked by figures of speech, abbreviated expressions, allusions, overtones, implications which the hearers will immediately catch, etc. We should never lose sight of the fact that those to whom these words were addressed not only heard the actual words, but also saw our Lord's eyes, and took notice of his tone of voice and of the words on which he placed the accent. Bearing all this in mind, we believe that from a certain point of view the situation in which our Lord finds himself as he utters these words can be compared with that of someone who today is addressing a group of people who are not too friendly toward the speaker. Let us say that the latter is an enthusiastic Republican and that he is talking to a group of Democrats. He might address them as follows, "If I tell you that Mr. E. (Republican candidate for President) is the best man this country could ever elect as President, then, of course, I'm a liar." The hearers would then immediately interpret his words to mean this: "If I tell you that Mr. E is the best man the country could ever elect as President, then, of course, I'm a liar *in your estimation."*

The same, as we see it, holds with respect to our present passage (5:31). Jesus simply means, "If I testify concerning myself, my testimony is not true *in your estimation."* In other words, "You will then immediately raise the objection, 'You are testifying concerning yourself; hence, your testimony is not true.' " This interpretation is certainly supported by the fact that this very thing happened a little later, as indicated in 8:12, 13. There Jesus is recorded as testifying concerning himself, and saying, "I am the light of the world." Immediately the Pharisees shout their objection, "You are testifying concerning yourself; your testimony is not true."

32, 33. Jesus continues, **It is another who testifies concerning me, and I know that the testimony which he bears concerning me is true.** Without in any way admitting that his own testimony with reference to himself would not be reliable, Jesus now introduces *another* witness, who is constantly bearing witness to him. Jesus — by virtue of the fact that he is himself the Son of God — *knows* that the testimony of this *other* one is true. He does not say, however, who this other witness is. *We* know from verses 36, 37 that the reference is to the Father. Meanwhile *the Jews,* who did not know, are guessing, wondering whom Jesus has in mind. Is he referring, perhaps, to John the Baptist? Perceiving what is going on in the minds of his audience, Jesus continues, **You, on your part, have sent to John, and he has testified to the truth.** The reference is to the testimony of John which is found in 1:19-28, given to a delegation that had been sent to him. (See explanation on 1:19-28.) The Baptist's testimony to the truth, however, is found not only in that paragraph but also in 1:29-36 (see explanation), and in 3:22-36 (see explanation). In brief it amounted to this: "I (John) am not the Christ; Jesus is the Christ; he is the Lamb of God who is taking away the sin of the world; it is upon him that I saw the Spirit descending and remaining; he is the Bridegroom; he is the One who came from above and is above all; he speaks the words of God, and is himself the Son of God."

34. Why did Jesus mention this testimony of the Baptist? Was it because he needed it for himself? No! After all, he says, **I, on my part, do not accept (mere) human testimony.** So it was not at all his intention, on his own behalf and in his own defence, to appeal to the testimony of man and to rest his claim upon it. On the contrary, he said these things because this testimony regarding him was true, and in order that they might accept it, take it to heart, *and be saved.* Says Jesus, **I say these things in order that you may be saved.**

35. The Lord continues, **He (John) was the lamp burning and shining.** While Jesus calls himself the light (τό φῶς), he calls John, the lamp (ὁ λύχνος). A lamp must be lit, and its wick must be fed with oil; moreover, it illumines a very limited space. Though we believe that the choice of the word was intentional, nevertheless, it is doubtful whether the contrast between *lamp* and *light* is the idea which predominates in the mind of the Lord. After all, Jesus himself is also a *lamp* (same term in a book by the same author, Rev. 21:23). He is *the* lamp of the new Jerusalem. The *emphasis* in 5:35 is rather on the fact that the Baptist, as lamp, was burning and shining (for the latter term see on 1:5), so that, as a result, *it attracted people!* The context clearly shows that it was this characteristic of the

207

lamp (rather than its contrast with Christ, the light, though this contrast is not excluded) which Jesus wishes to stress; for he continues, . . . **and y o u were willing to rejoice for a while in his light.** *That* was the point: just as a lamp attracts moths, so the Baptist attracted crowds of people. Did not even Herod Antipas hear him *gladly* (Mk. 6:20); that is, *for a while?* When Jesus says, "He *was* a lamp . . . you *were* willing to rejoice," he is evidently referring, by implication, to the fact that the Baptist had been removed from the public scene, and was now in prison! The main purpose of his remark was, however, to point out that though thrill-seekers had been willing enough *to rejoice for a while* in the light of the Baptist's lamp; they had not been willing to accept his testimony regarding Christ unto salvation.

36. Nevertheless, the remark of Jesus "It is another who testifies concerning me" (verse 32) did not have reference to John the Baptist. This is very clear from what follows, as Jesus continues, **But I have testimony that surpasses that of John, for the works which the Father has given me to accomplish** (ἵνα τελείωσω; for this see on 4:34) **these very works in which I am engaged testify concerning me that the Father has sent me.** The Father's own testimony by means of the works of Christ certainly surpasses the indirect testimony given by John the Baptist. (On references to John the Baptist in this Gospel see pp. 32, 33.) The works in which Jesus *is engaged* are his miracles, including the healing of the man at the Pool. These works, to be sure, do not of themselves produce faith. They are never as important as are the *words* of our Lord. Nevertheless, they must not be ignored. They should serve to strengthen faith. Also, they have evidential value, for there was truth in the remark of Nicodemus, "No one can do these signs which you do unless God is with him." These signs were a seal of the Father's approval; specifically, of the fact that the Father had *commissioned* him (ἀπέσταλκεν, see on 1:6; 3:34; cf. 5:30).

37. Jesus continues, **And the Father who sent me, he himself has testified concerning me.** There had been the voice from heaven at baptism (Mark 1:11) to which the Baptist alludes in 1:34. Then, there is also the witness of the Father in the hearts of believers (I John 5:9, 10). Nevertheless, here in this passage (5:37), as is clearly indicated by the immediately following context, it is especially the Father's testimony in the Old Testament Scriptures that is meant. The Father *has testified;* that is, though he bore witness in the past, this testimony has validity for all time to come: it is there to stay. Jesus adds a word of sharp rebuke, however. Says he, **But his voice y o u have never heard; his form y o u have never seen.** The *voice* of God is, of course, the Christ himself (5:19; 14:19, 24); the *form* of God, too, is the Christ (see especially II Cor. 4:4, εἰκών — likeness, image — τοῦ θεοῦ; here in John 5:37 the term used is εἶδος — external form). The hostile Jews have failed to see in Jesus the voice and the form of God. They have failed through unbelief.

38. That the reference in verse 37 is distinctly to the hostile attitude of the hearers is evident from the following verses (38-40). Jesus does not deny that in a sense the Jews have the word of God. What he does say is that they do not have this word in their hearts as an abiding possession, the reason being that they had not placed their confidence in the One commissioned unto his Messianic task by the Father — **y o u do not have his word abiding in y o u, because in the One whom he sent, in him, y o u do not believe.** They were not able to see, because the veil of unbelief was lying upon the eyes of their hearts (II Cor. 3:15). On "the One whom he sent" see 3:34; cf. 1:6. What follows in verse 39 is very closely connected with this.

39. Says Jesus, **Y o u are searching the Scriptures, because y o u think that in them y o u have everlasting life, and yet it is they that testify concerning me.** Having read all the arguments of those who insist that the verb ἐρευνᾶτε must be read as an imperative, so that with the A.V. we must read "Search the Scriptures," we cannot agree. We take the verb as a present indicative of continued action. Reasons:

a. This, as has been shown, is entirely in line with the preceding verse (you have the word, but you do not have it in your heart; so here: you search the scriptures, but you do not find the Christ in them);

b. The imperative "Search the Scriptures" forms a strange introduction to the clause "because y o u think." If the imperative is intended, we would have expected, "because you *have*" or "because you *will obtain*" everlasting life by searching. On the other hand, the sentence, "Y o u are searching the Scriptures because y o u think that in them y o u have everlasting life," makes excellent sense.

c. The succeeding context also clearly indicates that it is not at all the intention of Jesus to tell his opponents that their sin consists in this, that they do not search the Scriptures. On the contrary, he desires to rivet their attention upon this important truth: "Though you have the books of Moses and though you have even set your hope on them, nevertheless, they will not profit you, will rather testify against you because *you do not see me in them*" (see verses 45, 46).

Jesus does not deny that in the Old Testament Scriptures men have *everlasting life* (for this see on 3:16). If the Jews think (note: "because y o u think") of their sacred writings as being potentially means of grace, they are right. What the Lord wishes to impress upon them, however, is this: Y o u fail to see me revealed in these scriptures, and yet "it is they that testify concerning me." This same truth — the Christ in all the Scriptures! —, which unlocks the mysteries of the Old Testament (as well as the New), and apart from which the Bible remains a closed book, is also emphasized in the following passages: Lk. 24:32, 44; John 5:46; Acts 3:18, 24; 7:52; 10:43; 13:29; 26:22; 28:23; and I Pet. 1:10.

40. Back of this blindness is the unwilling heart: **Y o u do not want to come to me in order that y o u may have life.** In the light of this passage such expressions as "y o u have never heard," "y o u have never seen," "y o u do not believe" (5:37, 38) must be regarded as examples of litotes. The real meaning is: in your hardness of heart you have basely *rejected* the Son of God.

41, 42. What was the reason for the clash between Jesus and the Jews? *Their* answer to this question would probably have been, "He is irked because we criticized him for breaking the sabbath and for implying that he is equal with God; if we had only praised him because of what he did to the man at the Pool, he would have been satisfied."

Jesus, who knew them thoroughly and was able to read their very hearts, answers by saying, **Praise from men I do not accept.** He does not seek it, and is not even willing to receive as valid the praise of unbelievers. Then Jesus gives his own answer to the question respecting the reason for his controversy with the Jews. The real reason is not *his* yearning for praise but *their* lack of love toward God. Says the Lord, **I know y o u** (how did he know them? see on 5:6) **that y o u do not have the love of God** (that is the love *for* God, objective genitive, as the following context clearly shows) **within y o u.** Had there been this love in their hearts, they would, of course, have accepted the Father's testimony concerning his Son.

43. It was easy for Jesus to prove that his statement "Y o u do not love God," was true. The proof consisted in this: **I have come in my Father's name, but y o u do not accept me.** Though he had come *in the name* of the Father — i.e., not only at his behest, but definitely to reveal him by word and deed — yet they had *not accepted* him. Here is another instance of litotes. They had stubbornly *rejected* him, and this in spite of all the powerful testimonies enumerated in 5:31-40. **If another comes in his own name, him y o u will accept.** This prophecy was fulfilled over and over again. One false Messiah was Theudas; and another, Judas of Galilee (Acts 5:36, 37). Then came Barkochba (132-135 A. D.), whom such a distinguished rabbi as Akiba called *The Star of Jacob* (Num. 24:17). There have been several scores of others since their days. The last one will be the antichrist himself (II Thess. 2:8-10). All of these present themselves without proper credentials: they come "in their own name." Yet people yield their all to them. They lead many astray.

44. Not only is it true that the Jews *do not* believe; they actually *cannot* believe either, inasmuch as they are constantly seeking praise from men, not praise which comes down from (παρά) God. Jesus voices this truth in the following words, **How can y o u believe, y o u who accept praise from one another, while the praise that comes from the only God y o u do not seek?** The very name *Jew* — from Judah, meaning *praised* — constantly reminds them of praise, glory, honor; but it is the wrong kind of honor, springing from the wrong source, which they are seeking. Cf. Rom. 2:29 where Paul reminds his readers that a true Jew is one whose *praise* is not of men but of God.

These Jews whom Jesus is addressing may intone their petitions twice each day, addressing them to *the Only God* — on the basis of Deut. 6:4, 5 — yet they do not seek the praise that comes from *the Only God,* neither do they *love* him, as commanded in the Deuteronomy passage. Lack of love always has a blinding effect. It was not lack of evidence but lack of love which caused these men to reject the Christ.

45, 46. The Jews had listened to this sharp rebuke. Perhaps they drew the conclusion that the words recorded in 5:34, "I say these things in order that y o u may be saved," were not true. Perhaps they were beginning to regard Jesus as an accuser, after the fashion of satan who stood at the right hand of the Angel of Jehovah in order that he might accuse Joshua, the highpriest, because of his filthy garments (Zech. 3:1-5). Nevertheless, that was not the purpose of Jesus (cf. 3:17). In fact, it was not even necessary. With words of terrible import the Lord flings this final challenge before his hostile audience, **Do not think** (or: do not be thinking μὴ δοκεῖτε, pres. imperative) **that *I* shall accuse y o u before the Father. Y o u r accuser is Moses, on whom y o u have set y o u r hope.** Again and again the Jews would appeal to Moses and would boast, "We are disciples of Moses," (9:28). Now Jesus tells them that Moses, the constant object of their hope, to whose scriptures they were always appealing, whose instructions they debated and analyzed with hair-splitting casuistry, would actually prove to be their accuser; the reason being that, in spite of all their boasting about being his followers, they, in reality, did not believe him: **For if y o u believed Moses, y o u would believe me, since he wrote of me.** "Moses wrote of me," said Jesus. Here we refer first of all to the list of references given in our comments on 1:5 showing that Christ is, indeed, the heart of the writings of Moses and of the entire Old Testament. In the Pentateuch — which, as to its essence, must be ascribed to the authorship of Moses, and this upon the testimony of no one less than Christ himself in this verse — there are certain passages which very definitely refer to Christ; e.g., Gen. 3:15; 9:26; 22:18; 49:10; Num. 24:17; and Deut. 18:15-18. But what Moses wrote about Christ is certainly not limited to these passages. The *entire* Pentateuch — and not only the Pentateuch but the entire Old Testament — points forward to the coming of Christ, and definitely prepares the way for his arrival. There are four lines which, running through the whole Old Testament, converge at Bethlehem and Calvary; namely, the historical, typological, psychological, and prophetical.

By the *historical* preparation we mean that again and again the forces of evil direct their attack against the people of God, endeavoring to render impossible the fulfilment of God's promise with respect to the coming Christ; and that whenever the need is highest, help is nighest: man's extremity is God's opportunity. The Pentateuch and the rest of the books of the Old Testament are full of examples.

By the *typological* preparation we mean that the character of the coming Messiah and of salvation in him is pictured in types that are either material or personal. We think, for instance, of the water from the smitten rock, the manna, the Passover, the pillar of fire, the tabernacle with its furniture, the entire sacrificial ritual, the serpent lifted up; of Adam, Melchizedek, Joshua, David, Solomon, etc. The books of Moses are full of Christ-centered types.

The *psychological* preparation points to the fact that during the entire Old Dispensation — certainly also in the books of Moses! — one truth is brought home with increasing clarity; namely, that in his own strength man can never achieve true happiness and salvation. The bringing about of this conviction was one of the chief objectives of the giving of the law on Sinai. If ever man is to be saved, Another will have to save him. That Other One is the Christ.

Finally, the *prophetical* preparation indicates that by means of direct prophecies the coming of Christ, his work, suffering, and consequent glory had been announced.

Truly, "Moses wrote of me." Properly understood, whatever Moses wrote concerned the Christ! [129]

47. Jesus concludes his address to the Jews with this rhetorical question, **But if his writings y o u do not believe, how will y o u believe my words** (ῥήμασιν, speech, discourse)? (Cf. Luke 16:31.) It has become fashionable to accept the position that in this verse a contrast is drawn between *his* and *my*, but not between *writings* and *words*. We are inclined, however, to agree with A. T. Robertson and others who see a contrast not only between the pronouns but also between the nouns: *his writings* is contrasted with *my words*. If Jesus actually intended to place merely the pronouns over against each other, then he would probably have caused the *same* noun (for example, *teachings, words, commandments*) to follow both pronouns; thus: "But if *his* words y o u do not believe, how will y o u believe *my* words?" By this device the intended contrast between *his* and *my* is immediately made clear. But now in this

---

[129] We have written a summary of Old Testament History, which centers around that theme; see *Bible Survey*, third edition, Grand Rapids, Mich., 1949, pp. 79-130.

conditional sentence, we have *his writings* in the protasis, and *my words* in the apodosis. Moreover, the contrast between these two concepts (each consisting of a noun and its modifier) makes good sense. As we see it, what Jesus meant was this: "Y o u Jews *are always saying* that nothing is as sacred as *the written Torah* (though in actual practice y o u often seem to esteem the oral law above the written). Y o u place that *written* Law above everything else, certainly above any words which anyone might utter. Also, y o u regard Moses as y o u r chief leader, and vie with one another in praising his memory. As y o u see it, no one living today could possibly compare with him. Therefore, if *his writings* y o u do not believe, how will y o u believe *my words?*" The chiastic sentence-structure of the original, which we have tried to reproduce in our translation, confirms the idea that this is, indeed, the contrast which Jesus intended. — The question which Jesus asked was unanswerable. Deny the sacred writings, and all is lost. The Jews needed this lesson; so do we today.

Synthesis of 5:31-47

See the Outline on p. 68. *The Son of God Rejected in Judea, as a Result of Healing the Man at Bethzatha on the Sabbath, and of Claiming Equality with God* (concluded).

The section on the Claims of Jesus is followed by this one which deals with his Witnesses. These may be summarized as follows:

(1) His witness concerning himself (5:31; cf. 8:14).

This is true, but its reliability is denied by the Jews.

(2) The witness of John the Baptist (5:33-35).

He testified to the truth concerning Christ, calling him the Lamb of God, the Son of God, etc. This testimony should be accepted by faith, unto salvation.

(3) The witness of his works (5:36).

These have evidential value, proving that Jesus was sent by the Father to accomplish his mediatorial task.

(4) The witness of the Father (5:37, 38).

He had testified by means of the voice from heaven but especially by means of:

(5) The witness of the Scriptures (5:39-47).

The Jews have been blinded by their lack of love for God, so that they cannot read these writings as they should be read. Hence, Moses, in whom they boast, will testify against them.

It is sometimes added that the Fourth Gospel proclaims two additional witnesses:

213

(6) The witness of individual believers (15:27).
(7) The witness of the Holy Spirit (14:16, 26; 15:26).

Here, however, we should exercise caution. As has been shown in the exegesis, these seven are hardly to be regarded as so many separate witnesses. Rather, it is the Father who testifies by means of all the others.

CHAPTER VI

6 1 After these things Jesus went to the other side of the Sea of Galilee, which is the Sea of Tiberias. 2 And a vast crowd was following him, because they were viewing the signs which he was performing upon the sick. 3 So Jesus went up the hill, and there he was sitting with his disciples. 4 Now the Passover, the feast of the Jews, was approaching. 5 So when Jesus lifted up his eyes and observed that a vast crowd was coming toward him, he said to Philip, "How are we to buy bread-cakes that [130] these may eat?" 6 This he was saying to test him; for he himself knew what he was about to do. 7 Philip answered him, "Bread-cakes for two hundred denarii would not be sufficient for them so that each might get a little something." 8 One of the disciples, Andrew, the brother of Simon Peter, said to him, 9 "There is a young lad here who has five barley-cakes and two fishes, but what are these for so many?" 10 Jesus said, "Make the people sit down." Now there was plenty of grass in that place. So the men sat down, in number about five thousand. 11 Jesus, therefore, took the bread-cakes, and when he had given thanks, he distributed them among those that were seated; similarly the fishes as much as they wanted. 12 Now when they had eaten their fill, he said to his disciples, "Pick up the pieces that are left, in order that nothing be wasted." 13 So they picked them up, and from the five barley-cakes they filled twelve baskets with pieces that were left over by those who had partaken of the food. 14 So when the people saw the sign which he had done, they were saying, "This is really the prophet who is to come into the world." 15 Now when Jesus knew that they were about to come and take him by force in order that they might make him king, he went away again to the hill by himself.

16 And when evening fell, his disciples went down to the sea, 17 and having embarked in a boat, they were proceeding across the sea toward Capernaum. Now it was already dark,[131] and Jesus had not yet come to them. 18 And the sea was getting rough, as a strong wind was blowing. 19 Now when they had rowed about three or four miles, they saw Jesus walking upon the sea and approaching the boat, and they were frightened. 20 But he said to them, "It is I, stop being frightened." 21 Then they were willing to take him aboard, and all at once the boat was at the land where they were going.

6:1-21

6:1. The story opens with the familiar phrase **After these things.** This has been explained in connection with 5:1. The miracle recorded in this

---

[130] On ἵνα see pp. 46, 47, 48.
[131] Literally, "darkness had already come to be."

paragraph occurred six months to a year after the events of chapter 5. It took place, in all probability, in April of the year 29 A. D.; see on 5:1. This was a year before Christ's death.

The Gospel of John seems to take for granted that the readers are familiar with the contents of the Great Galilean Ministry as found in the Synoptics (Matt. 4:12-15:20; Mark 1:14-7:23; and Luke 4:14-9:17). Having recorded the miracle which occurred at the very opening of this ministry (4:43-54), the evangelist now proceeds at once to the one which marked its close. The miracle of the feeding of the five thousand is recorded in all four Gospels (Matt. 14:13-23; Mark 6:30-46; Luke 9:10-17; John 6:1-15). John's purpose in telling the story is clearly to set forth the majesty of Christ (cf. 20:30, 31). In doing this he furnishes certain details which are not found in the other accounts. Also, he draws a striking parallel between chapters 5 and 6: in the former he has shown how Jesus was rejected in Judea; in the latter he will now indicate how he was rejected in Galilee (compare especially 5:18 with 6:66). The account of this double rejection is necessary in order to furnish a background for the next few chapters, in the sense that it causes the tender love of the Savior to stand out sharply against the background of human ingratitude.

The present chapter also reveals, more clearly perhaps that any other portion of Scripture, the kind of Messiah the people wanted; namely, one who would be able and willing to provide for their physical needs. When it seemed to them that Jesus would actually fulfil this expectation, they were anxious to lead him in triumph to Jerusalem, if need be by force, in order to crown him king. But as soon as it was made clear to them that their hero was not at all what they had imagined him to be, but a spiritual Messiah, who had come to save people from the guilt, pollution, and misery of sin, they turned their backs upon him and walked no longer with him. Hence, one and the same chapter pictures Jesus, first of all, at the very zenith of his popularity; then, suddenly, proceeding with rapid strides toward the nadir of public scorn. But in the midst of the fickle multitude his glory stands revealed, especially in *this* respect: that, though he knew these people so thoroughly, he was, nevertheless, willing to lavish his kindness upon them!

We are told that **Jesus went to the other side of the Sea of Galilee.** Luke 9:10 informs us that the place of its occurrence was in the general vicinity of Bethsaida. Although there is no certainty with respect to the question whether there was more than one city by that name near the Sea of Galilee (see also explanation of 1:44) nevertheless, having studied the arguments on both sides, we feel inclined to answer in the affirmative. Our reasoning is as follows:

1. According to the Synoptics, before crossing the sea of Galilee Jesus had been laboring in the western part of the country, in and around Caper-

naum, Nazareth, etc. Also, as we have seen, the miracle recorded in the fifth chapter of John took place west of the Jordan (in Jerusalem, at the Pool). For both of these reasons it would seem that the expression "Jesus went to the other side of the sea" could have only one intelligible meaning for those who had read the Gospel-stories up to this point; namely, that he now crossed over to the east (or north-east) of the sea. And that is exactly where Bethsaida *Julias* was located, just south-east of the point where the Jordan River, coming from the north, flows into the sea of Galilee.

2. After the miracle of the feeding of the five thousand the disciples re-crossed the sea. Their boat was now headed toward Capernaum (6:17), but according to Mk. 6:45 it was proceeding toward Bethsaida. Certainly, the explanation which lies ready at hand is that this was another Bethsaida, situated somewhere in the vicinity of Capernaum.

3. This conclusion is also supported by the fact that *this* Bethsaida (of Mark 6:45) was located in the plain of Gennesaret (Mark 6:53), which stretches north-west from the sea of Galilee.[132]

4. The very fact that when the home-town of Philip (also of Andrew and Peter, 1:44) is mentioned (12:21) it is called Bethsaida *of Galilee* may point in the direction of a distinction between that Bethsaida and another Bethsaida which was *not* in Galilee; namely, Bethsaida Julias, a town which had been recently rebuilt by Philip the tetrarch, and had been named after the beautiful but profligate daughter of Emperor Augustus.

5. The argument which is sometimes advanced against the supposition that there were two Bethsaidas is this: the existence of two towns of the same name on the same lake must be considered unlikely. But is not this the answer: a. there were many identically named towns and villages in biblical Palestine, and some of them were not far apart; and b. in view of the abundance of fish in the sea of Galilee it would almost seem strange if only one coast-town were named "House of Fish" (i.e., Bethsaida).

Jesus then crossed the Sea of Galilee and stepped ashore in the vicinity of Bethsaida Julias. The Sea of Galilee is here designated also by one of its other names. It had many names: Sea of Chinnereth (Num. 34:11; Deut. 3:17; Josh. 13:27; 19:35), Sea of Chinneroth (Josh. 12:3; I Kings 15:20), Lake of Gennesaret (Luke 5:1), and Sea of Tiberias (here in John 6:1). The latter name, which in modified form is used to this very day, was derived from the city (Tiberias) which was founded on its western shores by Herod Antipas in the year 22 A. D. Probably the readers in Asia Minor were better acquainted with that name than with any of the others. Therefore the explanation **which is the Sea of Tiberias** is added to the older designation.

---

[132] A vivid, three-dimension full-color view of The Plain of Gennesaret is furnished by *Viewmaster Travelogue*, Reel Number 4009, The Sea of Galilee, Scene 7.

The reason why Jesus, together with his disciples, crossed the sea is told in Mark 6:30-32 and Matt. 14:12, 13: the disciples had just returned from a missionary tour, and needed rest and an opportunity to be alone with Jesus. On the busy, western shores — especially, in Capernaum — there was no opportunity for leisure. Then also, the shocking intelligence of the Baptist's cruel death had just reached Jesus. This, too, required reflection and quiet meditation.

2. And a vast crowd was following him, because they were viewing the signs which he was performing upon the sick. In picturesque language — note the three imperfects — the crowds that followed Jesus while he labored in Galilee are here described: they *were following* him because they *were viewing* the signs which he *was performing* upon the sick. From Matt. 14:13 (cf. Mark 6:33; Luke 9:11) we learn that the people, noticing that Jesus had gone on board a boat and was heading for Bethsaida Julias, ran around the lake, from the various towns and villages, in order to be with him once more. Not that they were interested in a *Savior from sin,* but they were definitely impressed by a *Worker of miracles.* Now these miracles were in reality *signs* (see on 2:11) but this was not understood by the crowds.

3. So while the people were walking around the lake, Jesus was crossing it.[133] He reached the lonely region near Bethsaida Julias. Here **Jesus went up** (into) **the hill** (εἰς τὸ ὄρος). Here A.V. has "into a mountain," A.R.V.: "into the mountain." But if the term "mountain" be used for any height 2000 ft. or more above sea-level, and any lower conspicuous elevation be called a "hill," then we cannot speak of a *mountain* in this vicinity. It is not necessary, however, nor even advisable, to use the plural ("into the hills") as if a hilly region or chain were indicated. A little study of the territory around Bethsaida Julias will make this clear. On the north-eastern shore of the sea, about a mile south of the town, there is a little plain of rich silt soil. As it was Spring-time when Jesus and his disciples landed here, we are not surprised to read that there was plenty of green grass here. A hill actually rises up just behind this plain, so that all the requirements of the account as found in the Gospels are fully met. Accordingly, when the evangelist writes that Jesus *went up (into) the hill,* those acquainted with the surroundings would know exactly what hill was indicated; those unacquainted could easily guess that there was a hill behind a level stretch of territory along the sea-shore.

Here, then, we can picture Jesus. He had ascended the slope of the hill

---

[133] Who arrived first, Jesus or the crowd? Many find a conflict between Mark 6:33b and John 6:5a. There is, however, no good reason to assume any conflict. The term προῆλθον in the Marcan passage must be given the proper interpretation, and harmony results. In support of John 6:5a see also Matt. 14:13, 14 and Luke 9:11.

for a certain distance, and **there he was sitting with his disciples.** From the Synoptics the readers in Asia Minor (and elsewhere) have learned that by this time the Lord has twelve disciples. Some of them are named in this very chapter: Philip (6:5, 6), Andrew (6:8), Simon Peter (6:68), and Judas Iscariot (6:71). Their reactions to the work and the words of Jesus are recorded. What the Lord did was for them a test, revealing what was in their heart.

4. Now the Passover was approaching. It is here called **the feast of the Jews,** a name given to the feast of Tabernacles in 7:2. The nearness of Passover is probably added to explain 6:15. Passover was a reminder of the deliverance from the bondage of Egypt. Hence, it was especially on this day that the thoughts of the Jews revolved about the question, "When shall we be delivered from the bondage of Rome?"

5. From his elevated position it was easy for Jesus to see from afar the approach of a great multitude. **So when Jesus lifted up his eyes and observed** (θεασάμενος, just as he had done when the vast crowd of Samaritans approached him, see 4:35) **that a vast crowd was coming toward him,** the Lord, far from regarding them as a cause of unwelcome disturbance, started out down the slope to meet them, for he was filled with compassion with respect to them (Matt. 14:14). **He then said to Philip, How [134] are we to buy bread-cakes that people may eat?** In this connection note the following:

1. The reason why the Lord turned to *Philip* has not been revealed. Commentators make various guesses; such as, a. because Philip came from Bethsaida, was therefore well acquainted with the region, and could be expected to know where bread-cakes could be obtained (but here, to mention no other objections, the two Bethsaidas are probably being confused); b. because Philip was slow of understanding and more in need of being tested than the others (usually with a reference to 14:8, 9); c. because he was the matter-of-fact, coldly-calculating type of person; d. because he had just asked a question; or e. because he was standing closest to Jesus.

We do not have the answer. There is nothing in the context that suggests why Jesus selected Philip as the man to whom the question was addressed. To be sure, Philip's faith needed to be proved (6:6), but was not this true also with respect to the faith of the other disciples?

2. For "bread" the original employs a term which should not be rendered "loaves," as this English word has a meaning that is entirely foreign to the

---

[134] The word πόθεν (whence) need not mean "from which town or village." It could also mean "from what pecuniary resources." In fact, Philip seems to take it in the latter sense (see verse 7). The translation "how" covers either idea.

sense of the original. An ἄρτος was flat and round, resembling a pan-cake rather than a loaf. At times the term simply means *bread*.

6. The reason for *this* question is given in the following words: **This he was saying to test him; for he himself knew what he was about to do.** The word used in the original may mean either *to tempt* (as in Jas. 1:13) or *to test, to prove, to try* (as in Jas. 1:2: trials). Here, of course, the meaning is that the Lord wished to give Philip an opportunity to reveal whether he was moved with sympathy for these people, and whether he had taken to heart the lesson which the miracles as signs were intended to teach; namely, that they pointed to the majesty, power, and glory of the Lord, his ability and willingness to supply every need. The purpose of the question was not at all to obtain needed information regarding the places where bread might be obtained; nor was the question an indication that the Lord was at a loss what to do; for we read, "He himself knew what he was about to do."

7. Philip sees the vast crowds, and immediately begins to calculate, forgetting entirely that the power of Jesus surpasses any possibility of calculation. He **answered him, Bread-cakes for two hundred denarii** (genitive of price) **would not be sufficient for them so that each might get a little something.** The silver *denarius* was, perhaps, the most used Roman coin in New Testament times. Literally the name *denarius* means *containing ten*. It was called thus in relation to the *as,* a bronze coin having the value of 1/10 denarius. However, when it is said, as is done in many commentaries, that the denarius is equal to 16 or 17 or even 20 American cents, and that Philip, who mentioned two hundred denarii, was therefore thinking of a total amount of $32, $34 or $40, this is misleading. The value of the dollar and of the humble penny is constantly fluctuating. It is therefore better to point out, on the basis of Scripture (Matt. 20:2, 9, 13), that a denarius represented the wages paid to a laborer for one day's work; hence two hundred denarii means the amount of remuneration which one man receives for two hundred days of work. This amount would not have bought enough bread so that each might have *a little something* (βραχύ τι). Moreover, it is doubtful whether Judas, the treasurer, actually had as much as two hundred denarii in his bag!

Philip had time to reflect on the answer which he had given, and (more important!) on the question that had been asked. Jesus began to speak to the multitude about the kingdom of God. Moreover, those who needed healing he healed (Luke 9:11). Nevertheless, in spite of these manifestations of power, it seems not to have occurred to Philip that the Lord who at Cana had manifested his ability to supply wine when it failed would be just as able at Bethsaida to furnish bread.

8, 9. And so the day wore on, until evening fell. By this time the people, who had been with Jesus several hours, had become hungry. What happened next is recorded in Mark 6:35-37: "And when the day was now drawing to its close, his disciples came to him and said, 'This is a lonely place, and the day is drawing to its close; send the people away, so that they may go to the country and the villages round about and buy themselves something to eat.' But he answered them, '*Y o u* give them something to eat.' They answered, 'Shall we go and buy bread for two hundred denarii, and give it to them to eat?' "

It is clear from this that the faith of the rest of the disciples was not any stronger than that of Philip. The power of Jesus seems not to have occurred to any of them. They all *calculated,* but failed *to exercise faith.*

Mark informs us that Jesus asked the disciples: "How many bread-cakes do you have? Go and see" (Mark 6:38). The answer (Mark 6:38b; Matt. 14:17; Luke 9:13b) was: "five bread-cakes and two fishes." The author of the Fourth Gospel, himself an eye-witness, adds certain interesting details. We read, **One of the disciples, Andrew, the brother of Simon Peter** (see on 1:40) **said to him, There is a young lad here who has five barley-cakes and two fishes, but what are these for so many?**

It is interesting to notice that not only here but also in 12:20-22 we find Philip and Andrew mentioned together. We know, of course, that they came from the same town, and that both were numbered among the six earliest disciples of our Lord (see on 1:41-43). Andrew, in answer to the question which Jesus had asked, points to a *young lad,* παιδάριον, not necessarily a very small child; diminutives in Greek as well as in other languages have a tendency to lose something of their original, diminutive force. Andrew informs the Lord that this boy has five cakes of barley bread and two fishes (ὀψάρια here and also in 21:9-13, not ἰχθύας as in the Synoptics), the latter to cover the bread as a relish, or to be eaten with it as a side-dish.

Many sermons have been preached about this lad. With reference to him information has been supplied of which we find no hint in Scripture nor anywhere else; e.g., that this boy had been sent on an errand, and was returning to his mother with the bread-cakes and the fishes which she had ordered; or, that he was on an outing, had taken his lunch along, and that Andrew must have used some very persuasive language to deprive this boy of his lunch; or (not much better) that this boy was simply carrying on his usual business as a vender of refreshments (just like today!). It has not pleased the Lord to supply any additional information. The light is focussed on the *Lord,* not on the *lad.* Suffice it to know that Jesus was willing to make use of this boy. The fact that barley-bread was considered in certain circles to be "the poor man's bread," and that Josephus even speaks of a certain barley-cake as being "too vile for man's consumption," [135] has little or nothing to do with the present story. A cake of barley-bread is good, wholesome food. Food eaten by the poor is not necessarily poor food! When Andrew thinks of the five bread-cakes — only *five!* — and the two fishes — only *two!* —, of the vast and hungry crowd, *but not of Jesus and his power and love,* he exclaims, "What are these for so many?" And as Andrew *spoke* so *thought* they all.

10. Without administering any verbal rebuke for their *little faith,* **Jesus said, Make the people sit down.** The command was easy to obey, as about this time of the year **there was plenty of grass in that place,** growing on the slopes of the hill. **So the men sat down** (ἀνέπεσαν, fell back; i.e., reclined against the hillside). For ease of counting and serving, the people sat down in groups of hundreds and fifties constituting a very charming picture, like so many *garden-beds* (cf. Mark 6:40 in the original). One can readily visualize this multitude dressed in bright Oriental garments, reclining under the blue vault of heaven, upon the green grass, with the Sea of Galilee not very far away: "a sapphire in a setting of emerald." Were they expecting a miracle to happen? And is that the reason why no one hesitated to obey the command to sit down in orderly fashion? Is it possible that the *men* were counted because there were many more men than women and children? At any rate, there were **about five thousand** men, besides the women and children.

11. With wonderful simplicity the miracle is now recorded: **Jesus, therefore, took the bread-cakes, and when he had given thanks, he distributed them among those that were seated; similarly the fishes as much as they wanted.** Note that the thanksgiving comes first, then the miracle, just as in 11:41, 42. (For prayer *after* meals see Deut. 8:10.) In this connection it is often said that Jesus must have used a customary table-prayer. This is barely possible; nevertheless, the best answer is that we just do not know. It must be borne in mind in this connection that our Lord's addresses delivered to the multitudes were always characterized by freshness and originality — he never spoke like the scribes, merely copying the words of former rabbis. Is it probable, then, that when he addressed his Father in heaven he borrowed a formula-prayer?

Jesus *distributed the bread-cakes among those that were seated.* Notice how John abbreviates here. He seems to take for granted that the readers have learned the further details from the other Gospels. From them (Mark 6:41; Matt. 14:19; Luke 9:16) we learn that after the Lord had given

---

[135] F. Josephus, *Jewish Antiquities,* in H. St. J. Thackeray and R. Marcus, Josephus with an English Translation, The Loeb Classical Library, London and Cambridge, 1934, vol. V, pp. 100, 101.

thanks, he took the bread-cakes and began to break off fragments (of edible size) which he then gave to the disciples, who carried them (in baskets collected here and there from the crowd?) to the people. With the fishes the procedure was somewhat similar. The point that is emphasized is that those present received *as much as they wanted.* Some even took more fragments than they were able to consume. Thus, with majestic simplicity, the miracle is related. Did the bread multiply in the hands of the Savior? Just at what point did the miracle occur? All we know is that a great miracle took place, a sign which was transformative in character. Just as Jesus at Cana did not simply create wine, but changed water into wine, so here he does not just create bread, but changes bread into more bread. This was entirely in line with the purpose of his coming to earth. He had come not to create but to transform, and in the process of this glorious work he shows his (and therefore also the Father's) amazing generosity: whenever he gives, he gives lavishly.

12. Nevertheless, infinite resources are no excuse for waste. Wastefulness is sinfulness. Besides, were there not others who needed something to eat; for example, that young lad, the disciples, the poor on the day of tomorrow; last but not least, Jesus himself? So we are not surprised to read, **Now when they had eaten their fill, he said to his disciples, Pick up the pieces that are left, in order that nothing be wasted.** Note: *the pieces* or *fragments,* not scraps or crumbs.

13. **So they picked them up, and from the five barley-cakes they filled twelve baskets with pieces that were left over by those who had partaken of the food.** The idea is that some people had taken too many pieces when they were being distributed by the disciples. These pieces are now collected. Not less than twelve stout *wicker-baskets* (κόφινος-οι; contrast σφυρίς) were needed, and these were actually *filled* with the left-overs.

14, 15. The miracle was not appreciated in its true character. Its lesson was not understood. **Now when the people saw the sign** (for the term *sign* see 2:11) **which he had done, they were saying, This is really the prophet who is to come into the word.** They identified Jesus with *the prophet* of Deut. 18:15-18. So far so good. It is even possible (see p. 94) that in this prophet they saw the Messiah, for it must not be overlooked that to characterize this prophet they employ a phrase which elsewhere in the Fourth Gospel indicates the Christ; namely, the phrase, "who is to come (or; who is coming) into the world" (ὁ ἐρχόμενος εἰς τὸν κόσμον; see p. 79). But even if they viewed him as the Messiah, it was the earthly, political Messiah of Pharisaic hope whom they imagined to see in him, as is clear from verse 15: **Now when Jesus knew that they were about to come and take him by force in order that they might make him king, he went away again to the hill by** himself. Filled with enthusiasm, the type of fervor which takes hold of a Jewish mob at the season of Passover, they were ready to proceed post-haste to Jerusalem, holding in their midst their *strong man,* who was able to effect cures and to provide bread and prosperity for everybody — if he refused to come along of his own accord, they actually intended to kidnap him, thus forcing him to go with them — in order that, arrived in the Holy City, they might crown him king, throwing off the yoke of the Romans and establishing the kingdom of God on earth. But he, *whose kingdom is not of this world* (18:36), went away again to the hill (cf. 6:3 and Matt. 14:14); i.e., he proceeded farther toward the top, in order that he might be by himself. But first, by the power of his word, he frustrated the design of the mob: he simply dismissed the vast throng, meanwhile ordering the disciples to go into a boat in order to row back to the other side of the sea of Galilee.

16-21. And when evening fell, the disciples went down to the sea, and having entered a boat, they were proceeding across the sea toward Capernaum. Now it was already dark, and Jesus had not yet come to them. And the sea was getting rough, as a strong wind was blowing.

The disciples, having been ordered by Jesus to "go before him to the other side" (Matt. 14:22) went down to the sea. The evangelist pictures them as, having embarked in a boat, they proceed across the sea in the direction of Capernaum, on the north-western shore. The idea of some that they waited a long time before starting out, expecting that Jesus would join them, is a plain contradiction of Matt. 14:22, and certainly does not follow from 6:17.

The manner in which John uses the Greek tenses in verses 17 and 18 is very instructive.[136] He employs the imperfects "were proceeding" (ἤρχοντο) and "was getting rough" or "was rising" (διηγείρετο) to picture the condition, respectively, of the men in the boat and of the sea. But between these imperfects he makes use of the pluperfects (darkness) "had come (to be)" (ἐγεγόνει) and (Jesus) "had not yet come" (οὔπω ἐληλύθει), to indicate what had (or had not yet) happened before the disciples had reached the opposite shore. Moreover, when the author says, "Now darkness had already come (or: "now it was already dark"), and Jesus had not yet come to them," he is writing from the point of view of one who himself had been in that boat and now, many years later, is writing the story. As he wrote, he knew, of course, that before the night was over and the opposite shore had been reached, the Lord had joined the little group; he is also aware of the fact that the readers know this from Mk. 6 or Matt. 14. Hence, his words may be paraphrased as follows: "Now it was already dark, and Jesus had not yet

---

[136] Cf. *Gram.* N.T. pp. 904, 905.

come to them; that coming of Jesus about which you have read in the other Gospels happened later during this same night. But even a long time before Jesus appeared upon the scene, the sea was getting rough (or: was rising), as a strong wind was blowing."

From the ravines (deep and narrow valleys or gorges between the hills to the west) strong blasts of wind came rushing down, and suddenly struck the lake whose surface lies 682 ft. below the level of the Mediterranean. Soon the storm was increasing in intensity. The night deepened. Hour upon hour the disciples, used to the sea, were plying the oars. As they did so, *they* were facing Bethsaida Julias, while *their boat* faced (was headed in the direction of) Bethsaida of Galilee. They found themselves in a situation of real danger; that is, from the human point of view. Actually it was not so, as will become evident when two verses in Matthew 14 are seen in their relation to each other. These verses form, as it were, a composite picture. Famous artists [137] have painted Part I of this picture (Jesus alone in prayer) or Part II (the disciples in the midst of the storm), but what we should have is the one *composite* picture, just as Matthew shows it to us in the following words:

"And after he had sent the crowds away, he went up into the hills by himself to pray; and when evening fell, he was there alone. But the boat was now in the midst of the sea (or: many stadia distant from the land) beaten by the waves, for the wind was from the opposite direction" (Matt. 14:23, 24).

While the storm was raging, and the darkness enveloped the little group of men, they were, nevertheless, perfectly safe, for upon the hill the Lord was interceding for them. A beautiful picture, indeed, one which has many present-day applications.

The disciples had been rowing now for several hours. They had left the eastern shores when darkness fell or very shortly afterward. And now it was 3:00 A. M. or later (Matt. 14:25: the fourth watch of the night; hence, between 3:00 and 6:00 A. M.). So fierce was the storm that the boat had covered only twenty-five to thirty stadia. A stadium is $\frac{1}{8}$ of a mile; hence, the meaning is that the boat had proceeded a distance of from $3\frac{1}{8}$ to $3\frac{3}{4}$ miles; i.e., translated into our modern way of speaking "about three or four miles." Now if the distance between the point from which they started to the place where they landed was fives miles, as seems probable, then it is clear that the disciples were now, indeed, "in the midst of the sea" (Mk. 6:47). Besides, the possibility must not be discounted that they were driven somewhat off their course by the violence of the wind or that they had

---

[137] I am thinking, for example, of the famous painting by Hofmann, *Christ in Gethsemane* (which, though the scene is not that of John 6, shows Jesus in the act of prayer) and of Jalabert, *Storm on Galilee*.

attempted for a while to hug the shore. At any rate they still had a long way to go before reaching their destination. **Now when they had rowed three or four miles, they saw Jesus walking upon the sea and approaching the boat, and they were frightened.**

Then suddenly it happened! Facing east (while their boat faced west) these rowers through the enshrouding darkness discerned the outlines of a form walking on top of the angry billows. The winds and the waves did not seem to bother this man-shaped form in the least. It was walking right into the gale, and walking so fast that it was gradually catching up with the boat, until for a moment it seemed as if it were going to pass on alongside of it. Thoroughly alarmed, the storm-weary disciples cried out, "A ghost, a ghost!" (Mark 6:48, 49). These details which are furnished by Matthew and Mark are omitted by John, who simply says, "Now when they had rowed three or four miles, they saw Jesus walking upon the sea and approaching the boat, and they were frightened." The reason for this fear was that at first the men did not know that it was Jesus. **But he said to them, It is I, stop being frightened** (μὴ φοβεῖσθε present imperative). According to Matthew and Mark the words "It is I" were preceded by "Take heart" (or "Be of good cheer"). In Matthew (14:28-31) the story of Peter's attempt to walk upon the waters to Jesus is told next.

Returning now to the Fourth Gospel (6:21), when the disciples were convinced that what they saw was not a ghost but the Lord himself, they *were willing* to take him aboard, which they actually did. Then the wind ceased (Matt. 14:32). And *all at once* (εὐθέως) the boat, which when Jesus went aboard was still a long way from shore, was at the land where they were going. This, too, is represented as a miracle. The One who had manifested his power over sickness (ch. 5) had absolute control over winds and waves. He proved himself to be *the Son of God* (20:30, 31; cf. Matt. 14:23).

Synthesis of 6:1-21

See the Outline on p. 68. *The Son of God Rejected in Galilee (the two miracles).*

The two sub-divisions are 6:1-15, which suggests the lines, "Come, for the feast is spread . . . Come to the Living Bread," and 6:16-21, "On the Stormy Sea He Speaks Peace to Me."

Under the first theme we have:

A. *The Bankruptcy of Human Calculation*

The place (a plain about a mile south of Bethsaida Julias, north-east of the Sea of Galilee) was lonely. And the time? It was getting dark. Furthermore, there were more than five thousand mouths to feed. The disciples did

226

not have enough money to buy even "a little something" for each person. And the young lad who appeared upon the scene had only five bread-cakes and two fishes! The situation, in brief, appeared hopeless; that is, on the basis of human calculation, apart from faith in the love and power of Christ. The disciples (not only Philip and Andrew, but all of them) were men of *little* faith. It seems that they had not yet sufficiently learned to know Jesus as the Son of God, whose resources are infinite.

B. *The All-Sufficiency of Divine Provision*

Jesus was never at a loss what to do. From the very beginning he knew just how he was going to provide. His heart was filled with love. Did this mob spoil his need for rest and quiet? Were they earthly-minded thrill-seekers? Did Jesus know that they were yearning for a political Messiah, and that they would reject the true Messiah? Of course, he knew! Nevertheless, he provided bread for them, as much as they wanted. When one studies this miracle, the question occurs: which virtue shines forth most gloriously: Christ's love or his power?

For Old Testament stories which foreshadow this miracle we refer to Num. 11:13; I Kings 17:16, and II Kings 4:42.

Although the miracle is told in all four Gospels, yet as John tells it, it is different: in his Gospel it is distinctly a *sign* (see on 1:11), and forms the introduction to Christ's Discourse on *The Bread of Life*.

It is foolish to try to *explain* what happened here. One of the most absurd examples is this: Jesus and the disciples had taken some food with them, and they started to share this with others who had none. When the people saw this, each man who had taken something with him from home, ashamed of his own selfishness, began to do the same. Hence, there was enough for all. — This miracle-story should be accepted by faith. If one does not believe it, however, let him *not* try to explain it away. Let him be honest and say, "I do not believe it."

The miracle on the sea is really four miracles in one: a. Jesus walks upon the sea (without *suspending* the laws of gravity, he *controls* them in the interest of the kingdom); b. he causes Peter to walk upon the sea (but this story is not found in the Fourth Gospel); c. he reveals himself as master of the storm, for when he enters the boat the storm ceases (not in John); and d. he conquers even space, for when he enters the boat, it is on the shore *all at once.*

The story as told by John may be divided into these three parts:
A. The Disciples without Jesus

B. The Disciples and the Unknown Jesus

C. The Disciples and the Lord whom they know and who speaks peace to them.

---

22 The next day the crowd which had remained on the other side of the sea perceived that no other boat had been there except one, and that Jesus had not embarked with his disciples in that boat but his disciples had departed by themselves. 23 However, boats from Tiberias came near to the place where they ate the bread after the Lord had given thanks. 24 So when the crowd saw that Jesus was not there nor his disciples, they embarked in the boats and came to Capernaum, seeking Jesus.

25 And when they found him on the other side of the sea, they said to him, "Rabbi, when did you come here?" 26 Jesus answered and said to them, "I solemnly assure y o u, y o u seek me not because y o u saw signs, but because y o u ate of the bread-cakes and were filled. 27 No longer work for food that perishes, but work for food that endures for everlasting life, which food the Son of man will give y o u, for on him God the Father has set his seal."

28 So they said to him, "What must we do in order that we may be working the works of God?" 29 Jesus answered and said to them, "This is the work of God, that [138] y o u believe in him whom he has sent." 30 So they said to him, "Then what are you doing as a sign, in order that we may see and believe you? What are you working? 31 Our fathers ate the manna in the wilderness, as it is written, 'Bread out of heaven he gave them to eat.' "

32 Jesus then said to them, "I most solemnly assure y o u, it was not Moses who gave y o u the bread out of heaven, but it is my Father who is giving y o u the real bread out of heaven. 33 For the bread of God is that which comes down out of heaven and gives life to the world." 34 So they said to him, "Lord, always give us this bread." 35 Jesus said to them, "I am the bread of life. He who comes to me will in no way get hungry, and he who believes in me will in no way ever get thirsty. 36 But I said to y o u that [139] although y o u have seen (me), yet y o u do not believe. 37 All that the Father gives me will come to me, and him who comes to me I will in no way cast out, 38 for I am come down from heaven, not in order to do my own will but the will of him who sent me. 39 Now this is the will of him who sent me, that [140] of all that he has given me I should lose nothing but should raise it up at the last day. 40 For this is the will of my Father, that [140] everyone who sees the Son and believes in him should have everlasting life, and I myself will raise him up at the last day."

6:22-40

6:22, 23. Jesus and his disciples had landed on the western shore of the Sea of Galilee sometime between 3 and 6 A. M. It was now **the next day** — that is, the morning *after* the feeding of the "five thousand," which is the same as saying: the morning *of* the arrival of Christ and his disciples on

---

[138] On ἵνα see pp. 45, 49.
[139] On ὅτι see pp. 54, 58.
[140] On ἵνα see pp. 45, 49.

the Plain of Gennesaret. You will recall **the crowd which had remained
on the other side of the sea.** Those people who, having been dismissed by
Jesus, had not yet returned to their homes but had remained overnight on
the eastern shore, began to realize something. They **perceived:**

a. **That no other boat** (πλοιάριον a diminutive; one might translate "a
little sea-going vessel" hence, a boat) **had been there** (i.e., here at the
landing-place south of Bethsaida Julias) **except one;** namely, the one with
which the Lord and his disciples had come to this northeastern shore, **and**

b. **That Jesus had not embarked with his disciples in that boat, but his
disciples had departed by themselves in** *that* boat. Jesus had gone to the
top of the hill to pray; and his disciples at his command, as we know from
Matt. 14:22, had departed by themselves.

So the people began to search for Jesus, thinking that he was still in the
neighborhood of Bethsaida Julias. This is implied in 6:24 a. They discovered, however, that Jesus, too, had disappeared, however mysteriously.
They drew the correct conclusion that he had gone back to the western
(Capernaum) region; though, of course, with no other boat in sight to take
him back, they could not figure out *how* he got back. Did he walk *around*
the sea? But in that case would they not have seen him? They never
thought for a moment that he might have walked *across!* [141]

The crowd wanted to be with Jesus. Besides, the people desired to return
to their homes on the western shore. Of course, it was possible once again
to walk the whole distance around the sea (as many, perhaps, had already
done), about ten miles for those who lived in or near Capernaum. This,
however, due to all the marshes north of the sea, and especially in view of
the fact that just yesterday these same people had made that trip, was not
easy. However, intelligence had reached the boat-owners in Tiberias [142]
(the capital-city on the south-western shore, south of the Plain of Gennesaret) to the effect that there was business for them across the sea: a large
crowd of people was waiting to be carried across to their towns and villages.
So we are not surprised to read: **However, boats from Tiberias came near
to the place where they ate the bread after the Lord had given thanks**

---

[141] The sentence contained in verse 22 does not dangle in the air for a while, without a proper conclusion, as it does in the A.V., which treats verse 23 as a parenthesis, and then in verse 24 makes an awkward attempt to catch the sentence begun
in verse 22. We call this a rather awkward attempt, because while verse 24 makes
perfect sense as a new statement which adds to the preceding, it does not form a
proper *conclusion* to the sentence which, supposedly, began in verse 22. The
mistake which the A.V. makes is due to the weakly attested variant ἰδών instead of
the correct εἶδον.
[142] A vivid, three-dimension full-color view of The Plain of Gennesaret is furnished
by *Viewmaster Travelogue*, Reel Number 4009, Ancient Tiberias, Scene 6.

(the last words: *after the Lord had given thanks,* are added to show that this had not been an ordinary meal).

24. So when the crowd saw that Jesus was not there nor his disciples, they embarked in the boats and came to Capernaum, seeking Jesus. We are not surprised to learn that these vessels brought their cargo of passengers to *Capernaum;* for a. this was Christ's headquarters during the Galilean Ministry; and b. this must have been centrally located as far as the passengers were concerned, the most convenient landing place for them. Arrived in Capernaum, the crowd started to search for Jesus.

6:25-27

25, 26. And when they found him on the other side of the sea . . . In view of what is known about the location of the Plain of Gennesaret and of the time when Jesus and his disciples had arrived there — sometime between 3 and 6 A. M. — it does not at all surprise us to read that these people actually found Jesus. We cannot see any good reason for assuming, with certain commentators, that Jesus could not have covered the distance from the place where he landed to Capernaum in such a brief span of time. There was ample time even if Jesus proceeded in ordinary fashion, without a further miracle, and even if it be taken for granted that *the entire* discourse from verse 28 on was delivered in the Synagogue at Capernaum (see 6:59). And there was ample time even for the events mentioned in Matt. 14:35, 36.

Having found Jesus, these people, who have just been carried across the sea by boats whose owners lived in Tiberias, exclaimed to him, **Rabbi** (on this term see 1:38, footnote 44), **when did you come here?** The reason for their surprise has already been stated. Instead of answering their question, which might have strengthened them in their conception that Jesus was, first and most of all, a miracle-worker, powerful enough to lead a revolution and to provide prosperity for all, the Lord sharply reprimands them. The motive of their search for Jesus was all wrong. Says he, **I solemnly assure y o u, y o u seek me not because y o u saw signs, but because y o u ate of the bread-cakes and were filled.** (For the words of majesty which introduce this sentence see on 1:51.) What Jesus meant was that though these people had seen his miracles (especially the healing of the sick and the feeding of the "five thousand," but, in a more general way, all the wonders which he had performed), they had not understood them in their quality as *signs* which pointed to him as the spiritual Messiah, the Son of God. (For the term *sign,* σημεῖον, see on 2:11.) The people's chief interest in Jesus was this, that they had eaten the bread-cakes which he had provided, and that thus their stomachs had been filled (ἐχορτάσθητε: "and were filled," a word is selected which in its primary meaning refers to the kind of eating that is

230

done by animals; e.g., when they eat grass: χόρτος, from which this verb is derived).

27. There follows another beautiful mashal (see on 2:19): **No longer work** (or "stop working," the verb is present imperative) **for food that perishes, but work for food that endures for everlasting life, which food the Son of man will give y o u, for on him God the Father has set his seal.**

This veiled saying should be compared with the very similar one in 4:14; and the answer, especially that contained in verse 34, should be compared with the one in 4:15. The Jews did not understand Christ's saying about food (i.e., *bread;* see verses 31-35) any better than the Samaritan woman grasped his saying about *water.* Both gave a literal interpretation to his mashal, and both were wrong! In the light of the explanation which follows in verses 32-35 (cf. for the last clause also 5:31-37) we know that the saying has the following meaning:

The Mashal	*Its Meaning*
"No longer work for food that perishes,	Stop yearning for bread-cakes and the like, as if physical food would ever be able to fill the void in y o u r *heart.* Realize that this food perishes, has no abiding value.
"but work for food that endures for everlasting life,	Instead, render to God the work of faith in the One whom God has sent, the *real* food, which produces and sustains everlasting life;
"which food the Son of man will give y o u,	which food, I, the Son of man, will give; i.e., I will give *myself* for those among y o u who believe in me;
"for on him God the Father has set his seal."	for, by means of the testimony of the Son himself, of John the Baptist, of the many works or *signs,* of the Father (directly), and of the Scriptures, God the Father has certified that I am the real Messiah, the Son of God.

For the term βρῶσις see on 4:32. For *Son of man* see on 12:34. For everlasting life see on 3:16.

28, 29. Of the true, spiritual meaning of the mashal the audience understands nothing. When Jesus mentions "works," this term is immediately

231

taken in its crassly literal sense, as indicating law-works which one performs in order to earn a place in the kingdom. The Pharisees weighed and counted such works. **So they (the people) said to him, What must we do in order that we may be working the works of God? Jesus answered and said to them, This is the work of God, that y o u believe in him whom he has sent.** (On Jesus as the One *sent* see 3:34; cf. 1:6.) But in this passage does not Jesus call the exercise of faith a *work?* And if it be a work *which man must render,* then is it true that man is saved by *grace?* Cf. Eph. 2:5, 8. We answer:

a. The teaching of Christ as recorded in the Fourth Gospel, including chapter 6, leaves no room for doubt that salvation is entirely by grace. It is the work of God and of his Christ; it is a *gift:* 1:13, 17, 29; 3:3, 5, 16; 4:10, 14, 36, 42; 5:21; 6:27, 33, 37, 39, 44, 51, 55, 65; 8:12, 36; 10:7-9, 28, 29; 11:25, 51, 52; 14:2, 3, 6; 15:5; 17:2, 6, 9, 12, 24; and 18:9.

b. But this does not exclude the idea that man must render to God the *work* of faith. An illustration will make this clear. The roots of a tall oak perform a well-nigh unbelievable amount of work in drawing water and minerals from the soil to serve as nourishment for the tree. Nevertheless, these roots do not themselves produce these necessities but *receive them as a gift. Similarly, the work of faith is the work of receiving the gift of God.*

30, 31. When Christ demanded faith in himself as the One sent by the Father, the Jews asked to see his credentials (cf. Deut. 18:20-22). **They said to him, Then what are you doing as a sign, in order that we may see and believe you?** But had not Jesus performed many signs? And was not the multiplication of the bread-cakes on the preceding day a glorious sign? How is it possible that these people dare to say, **What are you working?** Verse 31 explains what they have in mind: **Our (fore)fathers ate the manna in the wilderness, as it is written, Bread out of heaven he gave them to eat.** The phrase "out of heaven" modifies the noun *bread* (as is clear from verse 32), not the verb *he gave.* The quotation is from Ps. 78:24 (see, however, also Neh. 9:15; Ex. 16:4, 15; and Ps. 105; 40). In the Old Testament passages it is distinctly stated that it was Jehovah who had given this wonderful bread. Nevertheless it is true that the passage from Nehemiah mentions Moses in the preceding verse (i.e., in Neh. 9:14); similarly Ex. 16. From the reply of Jesus it can be inferred that the Jews were reasoning in the following trend:

"If he is even greater than Moses, let him perform a sign that is greater than the one which Moses did when he gave us bread *from heaven.* To be sure, yesterday Jesus multiplied the bread-cakes. He had bread, and from it he made more bread. But he had something to begin with (five bread-cakes, two fishes); and besides, he gave us *earthly* bread, but Moses gave us bread straight *out of heaven!"*

32, 33. Jesus said to them, I most solemnly assure y o u, it was not Moses who gave y o u the bread out of heaven, but it is my Father who is giving y o u the real bread out of heaven. For the bread of God is that which comes down out of heaven and gives life to the world.

After another solemn introduction (see on 1:51) Jesus in verses 32 and 33 annihilates the contrast which the Jews had drawn, and in its stead presents his own comparison. It is as follows:

1. *Moses,* as God's agent, merely gave directions to the people regarding the manner in which manna was to be collected, Ex. 16.

2. Even if Moses be considered the giver, it remains true that he did not give the *real* bread out of heaven. The manna was a type; it was not the Antitype.

3. What the manna provided, as it descended from the visible heaven, was *nourishment* (τροφή).

1. *The Father in* heaven is ever the real Giver.

2. The Father is giving the *real* bread out of heaven. That real bread is Jesus, the Antitype.

3. What Jesus, the real bread of life, gives, is *life* (ζωή). (For meaning of the term *life* see on 1:4; 3:16.)

34. In the spirit of 4:15 they (the Jews), totally blind with respect to the spiritual meaning of the words of Christ, **said to him, Lord** (for this see 1:38, footnote 44) **always give us this bread,** i.e., never fail to supply us with this wonderful, physical bread, which not only sustains but even imparts (physical) life.

35-38. Jesus explains his mysterious saying. He **said to them, I** (myself) **am the bread of life;** i.e., I am the One who both imparts and sustains life. According to the form of the sentence in the original, Jesus completely identifies himself with this bread of life; really, *of the life* (τῆς ζωῆς, qualitative genitive, referring not to any kind of life but to *spiritual, everlasting* life). It is through faith, i.e., through intimate union with him, assimilating him spiritually as physical bread is assimilated physically, that man attains to everlasting life. When Jesus continues, **He who comes to me will in no way get hungry, and he who believes in me will in no way get thirsty,** he is, of course, speaking about *spiritual* hunger and *spiritual* thirst. Note also that here *believing* in Jesus is defined as *coming* to him; i.e., coming as one who has nothing (but sin) and needs everything; turning to him as plants

233

turn their green parts toward the sun. (On the meaning of *believing* see also 3:16, and note 83.) He who comes to Jesus with a believing heart will in no way get hungry nor ever get thirsty. This is, of course, another example of the figure of speech called *litotes* (affirmation produced by the denial of the opposite). The meaning is that such a person will receive complete and enduring spiritual satisfaction, perfect peace of soul. But the Jews have not accepted Jesus by a living faith. According to verse 30 they had asked *to see a sign,* and had stated that if their request were granted, they would *believe* in him. But Jesus, entirely in the spirit of verse 26, to which in all probability verse 36 refers, states, **But I said to y o u that although y o u have seen (me), yet y o u do not believe.** The Lord, therefore, clearly places the blame upon these unbelievers themselves as persons who are fully responsible for their actions. Does this mean, therefore, that he who does accept Jesus with a believing heart can give himself the credit for this excellent deed? By no means: salvation is ever by grace, and faith is ever the work of God in the heart of the sinner. Hence, immediately following a statement in which human responsibility is emphasized (verse 36) we have one in which divine predestination is stressed (verse 37): **All that the Father gives me will come to me, and him who comes to me I will in no wise cast out.** A person cannot be saved unless he comes to Jesus; he cannot come unless he is given (cf. especially 6:44). But "all that" is given, certainly comes. The expression "all that" (see also 6:39; 7:2, 24; I John 5:4) views the elect as a unity; they are all *one* people. The clause, "And him who comes to me I will in no way cast out," places the emphasis once more on human responsibility; as if to say, "Let no one hesitate, saying, 'Perhaps I have not been given to the Son by the Father.' Whoever comes is welcomed heartily" (*I will in no way cast him out* is another example of litotes). Note that verse 37 also teaches: a. that in working out the plan of redemption, so that salvation is bestowed upon the elect individuals and upon the entire elect race, there is complete harmony and cooperation between the Father and the Son: those whom the Father gives, the Son welcomes; and b. that the work of redemption cannot be frustrated by the unbelief of the Jews of which mention was made in the preceding verse: there is an elect race; a remnant will most certainly be saved. The reason why it is so certain that the Son will not cast out those given to him by the Father is stated in verse 38: **for I am come down from heaven, not in order to do my own will but the will of him who sent me.** This cannot mean, of course, that the two wills ever clash; the contrary is explicitly taught in 4:34; 5:19; and 17:4. It does mean, however, that the Jewish unbelievers who have questioned the authority of Jesus must understand that whenever they oppose his will they are also opposing the will of the Father.

39, 40. That will is defined in the two closing verses of this paragraph: Now this is the will of him who sent me, that of all that he has given me I should lose nothing, but should raise it up at the last day. For this is the will of my Father, that everyone who sees the Son and believes in him should have everlasting life, and I myself will raise him up at the last day. Here in verse 39 something is added to what was stated in the preceding verses with reference to the will of the Father which is carried out by the Son. *There,* by means of a litotes, it was stated that the latter would *welcome* those given to him by the Father; *here* it is added that he will *guard* them to the very end. Again we have a litotes: "I should lose nothing." This addition is, indeed, very comforting. The doctrine of *the perseverance of the saints* is taught here in unmistakable terms; first negatively, then positively. The *last day* is the judgment day; see on 5:28, 29. The idea is: the elect will be kept and guarded *to the very end.* This doctrine is also taught in 10:28; Rom. 8:29, 30, 38; 11:29; Phil. 1:6; Heb. 6:17; II Tim. 2:19; I Pet. 1:4, 5; etc. In these and many other passages Scripture teaches a counsel that cannot be changed, a calling that cannot be revoked, an inheritance that cannot be defiled, a foundation that cannot be shaken; a seal that cannot be broken, and a life that cannot perish. The doctrine of the preservation (hence, perseverance) of the saints is surely implied in the very term *everlasting life* (on which see 3:16). A further definition of the will of the Father (which is at the same time a reason for the act of raising believers at the last day) is given in verse 40. Everyone who with the eye of faith *sees* in Jesus the Son of God, and who, accordingly, believes in him, has everlasting life. Jesus himself will raise him up at the last day. In this verse the matter which in the preceding verse was viewed from the point of view of divine predestination is described from the aspect of human responsibility (cf. the two clauses of 6:37). Note also that πᾶν of verse 39, where believers are viewed collectively, is here individualized, so that we have πᾶς. For the sense in which Jesus is *the Son of God* in the Fourth Gospel see on 1:14. Note also the very emphatic "I myself."

For Synthesis see p. 249.

41 So the Jews were murmuring about him, because he said, 'I am the bread which came down from heaven,' 42 And were saying, "Is not this Jesus, the son of Joseph, whose father and mother we know? How is it that he now says, 'I have come down out of heaven.'?" 43 Jesus answered and said to them, "Stop murmuring among y o u rselves. 44 No one can come to me unless the Father who sent me draw him, and I will raise him up at the last day. 45 It is written in the prophets, 'And they shall all be taught of God.' Everyone who listens to the Father and learns of him will come to me. 46 Not that [143] anyone has seen the Father, except the One who comes from God, he has seen the Father, 47 I most solemnly assure y o u, he who believes has everlasting life. 48 I am the bread of life. 49 Y o u r fathers ate the manna in the wilderness, and died. 50 This is the bread which comes down out of heaven, in order that a man may eat of it and not die. 51 I myself am the living bread which came down out of heaven. If anyone eat of this bread he will live forever.[144] And the bread which I shall give for the life of the world is my flesh." [145]

52 The Jews, therefore, were wrangling among each other, saying, "How can this man give us his flesh to eat?" 53 So Jesus said to them, "I most solemnly assure y o u, 'Unless y o u eat the flesh of the Son of man, and drink his blood, y o u have no life in y o u rselves. 54 He who eats my flesh and drinks my blood has everlasting life, and I will raise him up at the last day. 55 For my flesh is food indeed, and my blood is drink indeed. 56 He who eats my flesh and drinks my blood remains in me, and I in him. 57 As the living Father sent me, and I live because of the Father, so also he who eats me, he, indeed, will live because of me. 58 This is the bread that came down out of heaven, not such as the fathers ate, and died. He who eats this bread will live forever." 59 These things he said in the synagogue, as he was teaching in Capernaum.

6:41-59

6:41. So the Jews were murmuring about him. For the contrast "ordinary bread versus manna from heaven," which antithesis the Jews had proposed, Jesus had offered a far better one: "bread" (or manna) considered as a type versus the real bread, even "I myself," the Antitype. People do not like to see their carefully constructed argument shattered so completely. So they were *murmuring* about him. The original has ἐγόγγυζον. The verb is an imitative word. It does not necessarily carry a sinister implication. It could refer to mere speaking in whispers. However, in view of verses 42, 52, and of the prohibition in verse 43, it is probably better to see in this type of reaction a kind of dissatisfied grumbling or muttering, a speaking in low, sullen tones. In this connection it must not escape notice that it was *the Jews* who did the murmuring (see on 1:19). In the Fourth Gospel these are

---

143 On ὅτι see pp. 54, 58.
144 III A 1; see pp. 42, 43.
145 This translation is based on the best reading. The one on which the A.V. rests has late textual support. However, whether on this point one accepts the A.V. or the A.R.V. makes very little difference in resulting idea.

generally represented as being hostile to Jesus. According to some commentators the reference is here to Sanhedrin representatives from Jerusalem; this on the basis of Mark 3:22. But there is no intimation of this in the present context. Besides, verse 42 seems to indicate that these Jews belonged to Galilee, and were well acquainted with the family in whose midst Jesus had grown up. We do better therefore to think of such men as the leaders of the Capernaum synagogue and those who were of similar mind.

What the Jews objected to most strenuously was the Lord's statement concerning himself (cf. the parallel in 5:17, 18). Hence, we read, **because he said, I** (myself) **am the bread that came down from heaven.** *He himself,* and not the vaunted manna of their forefathers, was the real bread, which both sustained *and imparted* life. (These glorified ancestors, by the way, had not always held this manna in such high esteem; cf. Numbers 11:6, "But now our soul is dried away; there is nothing at all save this manna to look upon!" It is so easy to enclose the past in a halo.) Jesus is called the bread "which came down out of heaven" (ὁ καταβὰς ἐκ τοῦ οὐρανοῦ). Note that here the aorist participle is used, though Jesus himself in verse 33 had used the present when he had spoken about "that which comes (or: is coming) down out of heaven" as being the true bread of God. Some commentators make a point of it that Jesus subsequently accommodated himself to the phraseology employed by the Jews, for in verses 51 and 58 he also uses the aorist. However, it must not be forgotten that not the Jews but Jesus, in his conversation with Nicodemus (3:13) had been the first to use the aorist. As to the difference in meaning: a. the *present* (6:33, 50) indicates quality; showing that even during his sojourn on earth the Lord in many respects retains the character of One who belonged to the sphere of heaven; b. the *aorist* (3:13; 6:41, 51, 58) fixes the attention on the incarnation as such conceived as a single act; and c. the *perfect* (6:38, 42) pictures him as one whose act of humiliation performed in the past has abiding significance.

42. It is very clear from 6:42 that when Jesus spoke of himself in this fashion, the Jews did not interpret his language as referring only to his Messianic mission. They realized that the Lord denied that he was born like any other human being. Nowhere does Jesus say or imply that *in reaching this conclusion* they had misinterpreted his words. The inference is clear, therefore, that what Jesus taught here was the counterpart or complement of the doctrine of the *virgin birth.* One who is born of a virgin — and who, accordingly, never had a human father (in the ordinary sense of the term), and is not a human person (though he has a human nature) — must have come down out of heaven! The Synoptics and John are in beautiful harmony. (See also pp. 12, 13, 34.) And, of course, we are not surprised to find indirect reference to the doctrine of the virgin birth in a Gospel written by the great opponent of Cerinthus! (See p. 33.)[146]

And were saying. They raise a question. This question of the Jews, **Is not this Jesus, the son of Joseph, whose father and mother we know?** expects an affirmative answer. The question does not necessarily imply that Joseph was still alive. The words have a scornful ring. One could almost translate the first part as follows: "Is not *this fellow* (οὗτος) Jesus. . . . ?" They regard Jesus as being guilty of base presumption, if not outright blasphemy. It is in this spirit that the next question is uttered: **How is it that he now says, I have come down out of heaven?** Their argument was: "We have known him since the days of his childhood; his father, his mother, his family. Yet *now* that he is grown up, look what happens! He makes extravagant claims. Does he actually expect us to believe them?"

43, 44. In view of the testimonies that had been given (see on 5:30-47) there was no excuse for this scornful attitude on the part of the Jews. If everything was not immediately clear, they could have asked questions *in a polite and humble manner*. The questions which they actually asked were wrong both in content and in spirit. Hence, Jesus does not enter into them. He realizes that this would have been useless. In a passage (verse 43, taken in its entirety) which again places side by side human responsibility and divine predestination, **Jesus answered and said to them, Stop murmuring among yourselves.** Here human responsibility is stressed. Then, taking up again one of his own main points (see 6:37), Jesus continues, **No one can come to me unless the Father who sent me draw him, and I will raise him up at the last day.** Here the emphasis is on the divine decree of predestination carried out in history. When Jesus refers to the divine *drawing* activity, he employs a term which clearly indicates that more than *moral influence* is indicated. The Father does not merely beckon or advise, he *draws!* The same verb (ἕλκω, ἑλκύω) occurs also in 12:32, where the drawing activity is ascribed to the Son; and further, in 18:10; 21:6, 11; Acts 16:19; 21:30; and Jas. 2:6. The *drawing* of which these passages speak indicates a very powerful — we may even say, an *irresistible* — activity. To be sure, man resists, but his resistance is ineffective. It is in that sense that we speak of God's grace as being irresistible. The net full of big fishes *is actually drawn* or *dragged* ashore (21:6, 11). Paul and Silas *are dragged* into the forum (Acts 16:19). Paul *is dragged* out of the temple (Acts 21:30). The rich *drag* the poor before the judgment-seats (Jas. 2:6). Returning now to the Fourth Gospel, Jesus *will draw* all men to himself (12:32) and Simon *drew* his sword, striking the high priest's servant, cutting off his right ear

---

[146] Cf. J. Orr, *The Virgin Birth of Christ*, New York, 1924, pp. 108-113. Also J. Gresham Machen, *The Virgin Birth of Christ*, New York, 1930, pp. 254-259.

(18:10). To be sure, there is a difference between the drawing of a net or
a sword, on the one hand, and of a sinner, on the other. With the latter
God deals as with a responsible being. He powerfully influences the mind,
will, heart, the entire personality. These, too, begin to function in their
own right, so that Christ is accepted by a living faith. But both at the
beginning and throughout the entire process of being saved, the power is
ever from above; it is very real, strong, and effective; and it is wielded by
God himself!

The question may be asked: Why is it that in the teaching of Jesus
(12:32) this drawing activity is ascribed to the Father (6:44) and to the Son
(12:32) but not to the Holy Spirit? We answer: a. As long as the Holy
Spirit has not been poured out, we cannot expect detailed teaching with
reference to him; b. nevertheless, in the night of the betrayal Jesus did refer
to the drawing power of the Holy Spirit, though the words used are different (14:26; 15:26; 16:13, 14; see esp. the thirteenth verse of that chapter);
and c. the work of regeneration which is specifically ascribed to the Spirit
(3:3, 5) is certainly included in this process of drawing a sinner from death
to life! — In connection with the work of the triune God in drawing sinners
to himself see also Jer. 31:3; Rom. 8:14; and Col. 1:13.

The one drawn, actually gets there: he whom the Father draws is raised
to life by the Son. Moreover, the powerful operation affects both soul and
body. Jesus says, "And I will raise him up at the last day." The *last day*
is again the judgment day. On Jesus as the One sent by the Father see 3:34;
cf. 1:6.

45, 46. It is not true that 6:45 cancels or at least weakens 6:44. The
expression, **It is written in the prophets, And they shall all be taught of
God,** does not in any sense whatever place in the hands of men the *power*
to accept Jesus as Lord. Here is more — much more! — than mere intellectual advancement. Here, too, is more than that plus moral suasion.
Here is the transformation of the entire personality! The reference to the
prophets is very general, indicating that it was the prevalent teaching of
that section of the Old Testament which is called "the prophets" that in
the Messianic age all the citizens of the true Israel would be taught of God.
The following passages immediately occur to the mind: Isa. 54:13; 60:2, 3;
Jer. 31:33, 34; Joel 2:28; Mic. 4:2; Zeph. 3:9; and Mal. 1:11. Clearest is Isa.
54:13, as is evident when we place side by side

THE LXX VERSION   and   JOHN 6:45

καὶ πάντας τοὺς υἱούς σου διδακτοὺς   καὶ ἔσονται πάντες διδακτοὶ θεοῦ.
θεοῦ.

In the LXX the quoted words are in the accusative as object of the verb
239

θήσω; in the passage from the Fourth Gospel the words form a complete sentence. The idea, however, is the same.

Here again the divine and the human activities in the work of salvation are juxtaposed, for immediately after "And they shall all be taught of God" there follows, **Everyone who listens to the Father and learns of him will come to me.** *In this connection, however, it should be emphasized that in showing how sinners are saved Scripture never merely places side by side the divine and the human factors, predestination and responsibility, God's teaching and man's listening. On the contrary, it is always definitely indicated that it is God who takes the initiative and who is in control from start to finish.* It is God who draws before man comes; it is he that teaches before man can listen and learn. Unless the Father draws, no one can come. That is the negative side. The positive is: everyone who listens to the Father and learns of him will come. Grace always conquers; it does what it sets out to do. In that sense it is irresistible. The absolute character of the cooperation between Father and Son, which, in turn, is based upon unity of essence, is stressed once more as in so many other passages in this Gospel: he who listens to *the Father* (not merely in the outward sense but so that he actually learns of him) comes to *the Son*, "will come to me." Such a person will embrace Christ by a true and living faith. This listening and learning, however, does not indicate that any human being would ever be able to comprehend God (or to have an immediate knowledge of him apart from his revelation in Christ). Such fullness of knowledge is the prerogative of the Son. Hence, we read: **Not that anyone has seen the Father, except the One who comes from God, he has seen the Father.** (On this see also 1:18. On the use of παρά in 6:46 cf. 1:14.)

47-51. But the knowledge which one does attain by listening to the Father and learning of him is not to be disparaged. It results in the greatest possible blessing: **I most solemnly assure y o u** (on this see 1:51), **he who believes has everlasting life.** (For the verb *to believe* and on *everlasting life,* see on 3:16.) Note: the believer already has it; he has it here and now. This life is the gift of Jesus as "the bread of life." Hence, this thought is repeated: **I am the bread of life** (for which see 6:35). This bread does what no other bread, including even the manna from heaven, has ever done or can ever do: it imparts and sustains life, and it banishes death. It imparts and sustains *spiritual* life; it banishes *spiritual* death. However, it even affects the body, raising it up in the last day so that it may be conformed to the glorious body of him who is *the bread of life* (cf. Phil. 3:21). In sharp contrast with this is the manna which the (fore)fathers had gathered: **Y o u r fathers ate the manna in the wilderness, and died. This** (did Jesus point to himself as he spoke this word?) **is the bread which comes down out of heaven** (see 6:32), **in order that a man may eat of it and not die.** Not only

240

is Jesus *the bread of life* (imparting and sustaining life) but he is this because he is *the living bread* (cf. 4:10), having within himself the source of life (5:26): **I myself am the living bread which came down out of heaven. If anyone eat of this bread, he will live forever.** For ὁ ἐξ οὐρανοῦ καταβάς see on 6:41. One must *eat* this bread, not merely *taste* it (Heb. 6:4, 5). To eat Christ, as the bread of life, means *to accept, appropriate, assimilate* him — in other words, to believe in him (6:47) —, so that he begins to live in us and we in him. One who does this *will live forever* (the truth of verse 51 now stated positively). The words *will live forever* clearly indicate that one cannot dissociate the quantitative idea from the concept of "everlasting life." When one has ζωὴν αἰώνιον, he actually ζήσει εἰς τὸν αἰῶνα. Of course, the meaning of "everlasting life" is not exhausted in this quantitative concept. (See on 3:16 and cf. 1:4).

A new thought is now added. Up to this point Jesus has been stressing the fact that not the manna but he himself is the true bread from heaven. He now gives a further definition of the term *bread*, showing in which sense he is the bread: **And the bread which I shall give for the life of the world is my flesh.** (On the meaning of the term σάρξ see 1:14; also the note at the bottom of that page.) What Jesus means here is that he is going to give *himself* — see 6:57 — as a vicarious sacrifice for sin; that he will offer up his human nature (soul and body) to eternal death on the cross. *The Father gave the Son; the Son gives* himself (10:18; Gal. 2:20; Eph. 5:2). Note: "the bread which *I myself* — in distinction from the Father — shall give!" The future tense — "I shall give" — clearly indicates that the Lord is thinking of one, definite act; namely, his atoning sacrifice on the cross, which, in turn, represents and climaxes his humiliation during the entire earthly sojourn. This, and this alone, is meant when he calls himself flesh. The meaning cannot be that Jesus is for us the bread of life in a twofold sense: a. *entirely apart from* his sacrificial death; and b. *in* his sacrificial death. On the contrary, the words are very clear: "And the bread which I shall give for the life of the world *is my flesh.*" To believe in Christ means to accept (appropriate and assimilate) him *as the Crucified One.* Apart from that voluntary sacrifice, Christ ceases to be bread for us in any sense. That Jesus actually thought of his death is clear from 6:4, 53-56, 64, 70, and 71, which should be studied in this connection.

This bread is given "for the life of the world." Its purpose is, accordingly, that the world may receive everlasting life. The concepts *life* and *world* are used here as in 3:16. (See commentary on 3:16.)

52. The Jews had drawn the correct conclusion: what Jesus wanted is that men should eat his flesh. Jesus had not said that in so many words, but the implication was very clear. Jesus had said:

a. "I am the bread of life" (6:35, 48).

241

b. Men should eat this bread (6:50, 51).

c. "The bread . . . is my flesh" (6:51).

The obvious conclusion was: men should eat my flesh. I *give* it for that very purpose (6:51).

However, as so often (see pp. 125, 133) so also now, the Jews interpret the words of Jesus literally, as if the Lord had intended that in some way or other men must partake of his physical frame. But how? To some this must have seemed an utter impossibility. Others probably tried to show in which sense, always physical, Jesus might have meant this saying. None of the answers given seemed to satisfy. The more they argued, the more impossible the whole thing appeared to be. Hence, we read: **The Jews, therefore, were wrangling among each other, saying, How can this man give us his flesh to eat?** This "how can?" reminds us of 3:4, 9; 4:11, 12; and 6:42. Unbelief never understands the mysteries of salvation. Moreover, it is ever ready to scoff, and to say, "This or that is a sheer impossibility."

53-58. In his answer Jesus does not try to tone down his earlier statements. He strengthens them, so that what seemed impossible at first seems absurd now. Instead of speaking merely about the necessity of *eating his flesh,* Jesus now speaks about the necessity of eating his flesh *and drinking his blood.* To the Jews drinking blood was very repulsive; cf. Gen. 9:4; Lev. 3:17; 17:10, 12, 14. Nevertheless, had they known their scriptures thoroughly, they would also have recognized the symbolism which Jesus employed. They would have known that the blood, viewed as the seat of life, represents the soul and is without intrinsic value for salvation apart from the soul. The language of Lev. 17:11 is very clear on this point: "For the life of the flesh is in the blood; and I have given it to y o u upon the altar to make atonement for y o u r souls; for it is the blood that maketh atonement *by reason of the life.*" It is clear, therefore, that when Jesus speaks about eating his flesh and drinking his blood he cannot have reference to any physical eating or drinking. He must mean: "He who accepts, appropriates, and assimilates my vicarious sacrifice as the only ground of his salvation, remains in me and I in him." As food and drink are offered and accepted, so also is Christ's sacrifice offered to believers and accepted by them. As *those* are assimilated by the body, so is *this* sacrifice assimilated by the soul. As *those* nourish and sustain physical life, so *this* nourishes and sustains spiritual life. Here is the doctrine of the voluntary shedding of Christ's blood as a ransom for the salvation of believers. The same doctrine is either explicitly taught or implied in such passages as the following:

1:29, 36; Matt. 20:28; Mark 10:45; Luke 22:20; Acts 20:28; Rom. 3:25; 5:9; I Cor. 10:16; 11:25, 26; Eph. 1:7; 2:13; Col. 1:20, 22; Heb. 9:14, 22; 10:19, 20; 10:20; 13:12; I Pet. 1:2, 18, 19; I John 1:7; 5:6; Rev. 1:5; 7:14; 12:11.

In the history of theology attempts have been made again and again to conceive of this eating of the flesh of Christ and drinking of his blood in a physical manner. Such interpretations crumble before the following arguments:

a. The passage in which Jesus, by implication, urges the eating of his flesh and the drinking of his blood is clearly a *mashal*. Such veiled sayings always require a spiritual interpretation; see pp. 124, 125.

b. If these words be interpreted in a strictly literal fashion, the only logical conclusion would be that Jesus advocated cannibalism. No one dares to draw this conclusion.

c. Verse 57 clearly indicates that the phrase "eating my flesh and drinking my blood" means "eating *me*." It is, accordingly, an act of personal appropriation and fellowship that is indicated. Cf. also 6:35 which shows that "coming to me" means "believing in me."

d. We are told that those who eat Christ's flesh and drink his blood *remain in him and he in them* (verse 56). This, of course, cannot be true literally. It must be given a metaphorical interpretation (intimate, spiritual union with the Lord). Similarly, the result of such eating and drinking is said to be *everlasting life*. This, too, is a spiritual concept. If the result be spiritual, it would seem reasonable that the cause, too, be conceived of as being spiritual.

The section 6:53-58 is a summary of Christ's teaching with reference to the bread of life. Nearly every clause and phrase appears elsewhere in this Gospel. Hence, to avoid repetition we shall not again comment on that which is explained elsewhere in this book; but instead, shall limit ourselves to two things: a. we shall reproduce the passage in full, giving in each instance the reference to the passage where the identical (or a very similar) clause or phrase is explained; and b. we shall give a paraphrase of the entire passage.

So Jesus said to them, I most solemnly assure y o u (see on 1:51), **unless y o u eat the flesh** (see on 1:14) **of the Son of man** (see on 12:34), **and drink his blood, y o u have no life in y o u rselves** (see on 4:14). **He that eats my flesh and drinks my blood has everlasting life** (see on 3:16), **and I will raise him up at the last day** (see on 5:28, 29; 6:39, 40). **For my flesh is food indeed, and my blood is drink indeed** (see on 6:32, 35). **He who eats my flesh and drinks my blood remains in me and I in him** (see on 15:4). **As the living Father** (see on 5:26) **sent me** (see on 3:17, 34; cf. 1:6) **and I live because of the Father** (see on 5:26), **so also he who eats me, he, indeed, will live because of me** (see on 14:19). **This is the bread that came down out of heaven** (see on 6:41), **not such as the fathers ate** (see on 6:31) **and died** (see on 6:49). **He who eats this bread will live forever** (see on 6:50, 51).

This passage may be paraphrased as follows: So Jesus said to them, I most solemnly assure y o u, unless by a living faith y o u accept, appropriate, and assimilate the Christ, trusting in his sacrifice (broken body and shed blood) as the only ground of y o u r salvation,[147] y o u do not possess ever-lasting life (the love of God shed abroad in the heart, salvation full and free). On the other hand, he who does accept my sacrifice with a believing heart, digesting it spiritually, has everlasting life for the soul, and I will raise up his body gloriously at the last day, the great day of judgment. For my sacrifice (broken body and shed blood) is the real spiritual food and drink. He who spiritually digests this food remains in the closest and most vital union with me. As the Father, the Ever-living One, commissioned me, and is for me the fountain of life, so also he who spiritually digests me, he, indeed, will find in me the source of life for himself. (Pointing to himself?) *This* is the real bread, the genuine source of spiritual life and nurture, even the One who does not owe his origin to this earthly sphere but came down from heaven. And *this* bread is far better than that mere shadow and type — namely, the manna in the wilderness — which y o u r fathers ate, but which could not keep them alive in any sense whatever, not even physically, for they died. He who spiritually digests me as the true bread of life will live forever (first, with respect to the soul, afterward also with respect to the body which on the last day will be raised gloriously).

59. We are informed that this discourse on The Bread of Life was a synagogue-sermon. The translation, **These things he said in the synagogue** is not necessarily wrong. Though it is true that the original does not have the article, this was probably not necessary in order to make the word defi-nite. *We* also say "in church," "in town," "at home." Yet, these phrases are definite, even without the article. The synagogue in which Jesus delivered this discourse was at **Capernaum.** The ruins of a structure which was prob-ably similar to it in many respects have been excavated in recent years. That ancient synagogue was built about the third century A. D.

From the fact that Jesus delivered his discourse in the synagogue it does not necessarily follow that the day on which it was spoken was a sabbath. There were also services on Monday and on Thursday.[148]

For Synthesis see p. 249.

---

[147] At the communion-table this "eating and drinking" comes to clear expression. Cf. 6:53 with Lk. 22:17-20. Nevertheless, the spiritual activity here indicated is not limited to the eucharist. We agree entirely with F. W. Grosheide, *op. cit.,* p. 468.
[148] L. Finkelstein, *The Jews: Their History, Culture, and Religion,* two volumes, New York, 1949, vol. II, p. 1359.

60 So, many of his disciples, having heard it, said, "Hard (to accept) is this message. Who can listen to it?" 61 Now when Jesus knew within himself that his disciples were murmuring about it, he said to them, "Does this ensnare y o u? 62 Then what if y o u shall see the Son of man ascending where he was before? [149] 63 The spirit is that which makes alive; the flesh does not help at all. The words which I have spoken to y o u, spirit are they and life are they. 64 But there are some of y o u who do not believe." For Jesus knew from the beginning who those were that did not believe, and who he was that would deliver him up. 65 And he was saying, "Therefore I said to y o u that no one can come to me unless it is given to him by the Father." [150]

66 As a result of this, many of his disciples drew back and were no longer walking with him. 67 So Jesus said to the twelve, "Y o u, surely, do not also wish to go back, do y o u?" 68 Simon Peter answered him, "Lord, to whom shall we go? Thou hast the words of everlasting life. 69 And we have believed and know that thou art the Holy One of God." 70 Jesus answered them, "Have I not chosen y o u, the twelve, yet one of y o u is a devil?" 71 Now he was referring to Judas, (son) of Simon Iscariot, for he, one of the twelve, was going to deliver him up.

6:60-71

6:60. So, many of his disciples, having heard it, said. . . . Those who heard Jesus deliver this discourse on The Bread of Life are by the author divided into three groups: "the Jews" (hostile leaders and their followers), "the disciples," and "the twelve." The last two groups in reality overlapped; or may be represented by concentric circles, the larger of which represents the "disciples" (6:66), the smaller "the twelve" (6:67). The reaction of *the Jews* has been stated: they asked questions which originated in hearts of unbelief, self-satisfaction, and glorying in tradition (6:28, 30, 31); they muttered and belittled (6:41, 42); they even wrangled among each other (6:52). The present section (6:60-65) describes the reaction of *the disciples*. This is the group of more or less regular followers of the Lord, as 6:66 clearly indicates. There were probably scores, if not actually hundreds, of them in Galilee.

When the sermon was over, these disciples appear not to have been pleased with it. They said, **Hard is this message. Who can listen to it?** It is clear from the answer of Jesus (6:61-65) and from their own final reaction (6:66) that they did not merely mean that the sermon was difficult to understand, but that it was hard to accept. We translate, "Who can listen to *it?*" Though it is true that "Who can listen to *him?*" is also a possible rendering, nevertheless, the *verb* employed certainly permits either translation (cf. also 10:16, 27; Acts 9:7; 22:7, 10 in the original), the antecedent of the pronoun is, no doubt, "this message," to which also the immediately following con-

---

[149] III B 3; see pp. 42, 44.
[150] III C; see pp. 42, 44, 45.

text (verse 61) clearly refers. These disciples of Jesus were clearly offended by his words. To say that they were disgusted is probably correct. Their hearts were rebellious. It is in that light that we can understand the Lord's question which immediately follows.

61-65. When Jesus knew within himself (how? see on 5:6) **that his disciples were murmuring about it, he said to them, Does this ensnare you?** The verb translated *ensnare* (σκανδαλίζει from σκάνδαλον, the bait-stick in a trap or snare; this crooked stick springs the trap) does not merely signify *offend,* nor, on the other hand, does it mean *kill;* it means: *cause to fall into a trap,* here in the figurative sense; hence, *cause to sin.* Jesus, therefore, is asking whether by his sermon these hearers have actually been seduced or led into sin. Yet, it was not the hardness of the sermon but rather the hardness of their own hearts that had brought about this unfavorable reaction on their part (as Calvin [151] and many commentators after him have correctly pointed out). Just what did they object to in Christ's discourse? No doubt the answer is: they were displeased with the sermon *in its entirety.* The Lord had pointed out that not the manna about which they had heard so much, but *he himself* was the true bread that had come down from heaven; that in his quality as the true bread he was offering his flesh; and that in order to have everlasting life (i.e., to be saved) one had to eat his flesh and drink his blood. This was too much for these people to take. Had they only been willing to accept the evidence of the witnesses regarding Jesus (see 5:30-47), they would have asked, "Is it possible that these words have a deeper sense?" As it was, they regarded the sayings of the Lord as lacking in spirit and void of life. They attached to them the most rigidly literal interpretation. When Jesus mentioned the word "flesh," they thought of his body *not as an instrument of* the soul but merely *in distinction from* the soul. When he said "blood," they did not ponder the possibility that he might be referring to his own voluntary sacrifice even unto the shedding of his blood. No, they saw only the actual drops of blood, and shuddered to think of *drinking* it! What! was this man, whose parents they knew (or had known) so well, was *he* bread that had come down from heaven? Jesus answers: **If you shall see the Son of man ascending where he was before?** The apodosis is probably: **What will you say then?** Will not the Son of man's ascension to heaven prove that he had really *come down from heaven?* (On the term *Son of man* see our comments on 12:34). Jesus continues, **The spirit is that which makes alive; the flesh does not help at all.** The sense, it would seem, is perfectly clear in the light of the entire pre-

---

[151] John Calvin, *op. cit.,* p. 130: *Durus est hic sermo.* Quin potius in illorum cordibus erat durities, non in sermone.

ceding context. What Jesus meant was this: "My flesh as such cannot benefit y o u; stop thinking that I was asking y o u literally to eat my body or literally to drink my blood. It is my *spirit,* my *person,* in the act of giving my body to be broken and my blood to be shed, that bestows and sustains life, even everlasting life." Turning now to the blunder of the misinterpretation of his words, Jesus says, **The words which I have spoken to y o u, spirit are they and life are they.** These words are full of his own spirit and his own life. They are not dead letters. On the contrary, not only are they rich in metaphors, as Jesus expressly declared (16:25), but when accepted by faith, these words in their deep, spiritual meaning, become instruments of salvation for his people. The Lord continues: **But there are some of y o u who do not believe.** Unbelief was the root of intellectual lethargy; and this, in turn, was the cause of failure to grasp Christ's words and of attaching a crassly literal interpretation to them. The evangelist adds the comment: **For Jesus knew from the beginning who those were that did not believe, and who he was that would deliver him up.** The last clause is explained by 6:70, 71. Jesus *knew* all this from the beginning of his work as Mediator. (On this knowledge of Jesus see on 5:6.) Now this unbelief, though inexcusable, was to be expected, for faith is a gift of God, and it is not given to all men: **And he was saying, Therefore said I to y o u that no one can come to me unless it is given to him by the Father.** The reference is to such passages as 6:37, 44 (see our comments on 6:37, 44).

6:66-71

66. In view of the immediately preceding context, we translate ἐκ τούτου **as a result of this,** rather than simply "after this." As a result, then, of the discourse of Jesus on The Bread of Life, but more especially as a result of Christ's accusation "There are some of y o u who do not believe, **many of his disciples drew back, and were no longer walking with him.** They went back *to the things which they had left behind* (εἰς τὰ ὀπίσω), not only their ordinary daily pursuit but also their former way of thinking and living, not intending ever to return to Jesus. They proved by this action that they were not fit for the kingdom of God (Luke 6:62). This was the real crisis. Now not only the masses left him, but even many (possibly the majority, cf. verses 66, 67) of *his disciples,* i.e., of those who had been much more closely and regularly associated with him.

67. Jesus now intends that this desertion of so many of his regular followers shall become for the innermost circle a reason for testing themselves, an opportunity for confessing their faith. **So Jesus said to the twelve** — here designated by that name for the first time in the Fourth Gospel — , **Y o u, surely, do not also wish to go back, do y o u?** The form of the question, as it is found in the original, shows that a negative reply is expected.[152] Do they really *wish* to remain his followers? Do they make this conscious choice after listening to the discourse on the Bread of Life? Have they fully made up their minds to remain with Jesus, regardless of the fact that the great masses have left him, including even many of his regular followers?

68, 69. **Simon Peter** is the man who gives the answer, and a glorious answer it was! He uses the plural, showing that he was the spokesman for all, though not in reality the spokesman for Judas. Peter **answered him** by asking him a question: **Lord** (on this see 1:38; footnote 44) **to whom shall we go?** Man is so constituted that he must go to someone. He cannot stand by himself. What Peter means is clearly this: "There is no one else to go to; no one who satisfies the yearning of the heart." He continues: **Thou hast the words of everlasting life.** The reference is clearly to what Jesus himself has said (6:63). Peter knows that the words of Jesus are more than mere sounds or dead utterances. They are vital and dynamic, full of spirit and life, means unto salvation, means of grace (on *everlasting life* see 3:16; cf. 1:4). Peter adds: **And we have believed and know** — i.e., we have begun to believe and we still believe; we have come to realize, and we still are convinced — **that thou art the Holy One of God.** Jesus is confessed to be the Holy One; i.e., *consecrated* unto God to fulfil his Messianic task; he is *set apart* and *qualified* to perform whatever pertains to his office (cf. 10:36; Acts 3:14; 4:27; Rev. 3:7). He is *God's* Holy One, belonging to God and appointed by God. — It was a most meaningful and glorious confession!

70, 71. Jesus knows, however, that this confession did not represent the inner convictions of *every* one of the twelve; there was *one* exception. So, in order that the man who forms this exception may never be able to say that he was not warned, and in order that the others will never be able to think that their Lord was taken unawares, **Jesus answered them, Have I not chosen y o u, the twelve, yet one of y o u is a devil?** (On *the twelve* see p. 19.) That these twelve men had been chosen to be Christ's special disciples and apostles they knew, of course. The readers of this Gospel also knew it, both from oral tradition and from the Synoptics. Jesus says, ". . . yet one of y o u is a devil." The term διάβολος means slanderer, false accuser. This one man is the servant, the instrument of the devil. His

---

[152] Some commentators see significance in the fact that Jesus uses the verb ὑπάγω (6:67), and not ἀπέρχομαι, the verb which John employs in verse 66. They insist that the prefix ὑπό in ὑπάγω must be given its full, primary force. However, the conjunction καί in the question of Jesus clearly indicates that he regards the verb to be applicable also to the many deserters mentioned in verse 66. Also, if any particular importance is to be attached to the verb in Christ's question *because of its prefix,* Peter seems to have missed this point (see verse 68).

devilish character appears especially from this fact that while others, ever so many of them, *had deserted* the Lord when they felt that they could not agree with him and when they rebelled against the spiritual character of his teaching, this one individual *remained* with him, *as if he were in full accord with Jesus!* (He reminds one of those people who, while they hate the distinctive doctrines of the denomination to which they belong, remain right in it, preferring to drag it along with them to utter ruin.) The evangelist, writing so many years later, adds a note of explanation: **Now he was referring to Judas, (son) of Simon Iscariot, for he, one of the twelve, was going to deliver him up.** The father of Judas was Simon. This Simon was called Iscariot; i.e., a man of Kerioth; probably in Judah (Josh. 15:25), though there was also a place of that name in Moab (Jer. 48:24). The traitor is here so carefully described in order to distinguish him from another Judas, who also belonged to the twelve. The appositive "one of the twelve," was probably added to show the enormity of his sin (though a highly favored one, yet he was going to commit this terrible deed) and to justify the remark of Jesus in verse 70, "Have I not chosen y o u, *the twelve.*" The *manner* in which Judas was going to *deliver up* the Lord is not described here (but see 13:2, 30; 18:2, 3; Mark 14:43-45). It is enough that the terrible deed has been indicated.

Synthesis of 6:22-71

See the Outline on p. 68. *The Son of God Rejected in Galilee* (concluded).

On the day after the miraculous feeding of the five thousand, the crowds embarked in ships from Tiberias and found Jesus on the western shore. The Lord criticized them for their thoroughly materialistic motive in seeking him. Jesus told them to work for the food that endures. When they compared his miracle to the one which had taken place many centuries earlier, in the wilderness, where their forefathers had received manna *from heaven,* while Jesus had merely given them *earthly* bread, he shattered their argument by telling them that he himself was "the true bread from heaven," of which the manna was merely a shadow. In a beautiful and meaningful discourse on The Bread of Life he declared himself to be the real gift of the Father. He said that he, in turn, would give his flesh and blood for the life of the world, and that in order to be saved, one had to eat his flesh and drink his blood.

Although Jesus, of course, had in mind the necessity of *spiritual* acceptance, appropriation, and assimilation, many of his hearers not only interpreted his words literally, but in their unbelieving hearts rebelled against him and his message. Jesus emphasizes that only those can come to him who have been drawn by the Father.

The reaction of the audience to this discourse was fourfold: a. The masses and their "religious" leaders, utterly rejected the message and belittled the speaker. Their sentiment is summarized in 6:42: "Is not this Jesus, the son of Joseph, whose father and mother we know? How is it that he now says, 'I have come down from heaven?'" b. The large group of rather regular followers (called "disciples" here) considered the discourse hard to accept; and when Jesus showed that unbelief was the root of this reaction, they, in large numbers, turned away from him. c. The innermost group of disciples (called "the twelve") by mouth of Peter, made a glorious confession, recognizing Jesus as God's Holy One. d. Judas, though in rebellion against the divine speaker and his words, in typical traitorous fashion decided to remain in the company of Jesus!

The Gospel According to
John
VOLUME II

PRINTED IN THE UNITED STATES OF AMERICA

TABLE OF CONTENTS

Volume II

Commentary on Chapters 7-21

The Gospel According to
John

Commentary on Chapters 7-21

Outline of Chapters 7-10

Theme: *Jesus, the Christ, the Son of God*
During his Public Ministry Earnestly Exhorting Sinners to Repent,
Bitterly Resisted

ch. 7 1. At the Feast of Tabernacles in Jerusalem He exclaims, "If anyone thirsts, let him come to me and drink." His Enemies Regard Him as a Demon-possessed Pretender.

ch. 8 2. At This Same Feast (or immediately afterward) He Exhorts the Woman Taken in Adultery: "Go and from now on sin no more"; and the Multitudes: "I am the light of the world." His Enemies Are Ready to Stone Him.

ch. 9 3. He Heals the Man Born Blind, to Whom in Love He Reveals Himself as the Son of Man. His Enemies Have Decided to Unsynagogue Those Who Accept Him.

ch. 10 4. He Reveals Himself as the Good Shepherd and also (at the Feast of Dedication) as the Christ, One with the Father. His Enemies Again Seek to Stone Him.

CHAPTER VII

7 1 And after these things Jesus was going about in Galilee, for he did not wish to go about in Judea because the Jews were seeking to kill him. 2 Now the feast of the Jews, that of Tabernacles, drew near. 3 So his brothers said to him, "Leave here and go to Judea, in order that your disciples also may view the works which you are doing. 4 For no one does anything in secret when he seeks to be known to the public. If you do these things, show yourself to the world." [1] 5 For even his brothers did not believe in him.

7:1-5

7:1. And after these things. The events which occurred during the period April-October of the year 29 A. D. are by John summarized in one verse: "And after these things Jesus was going to Galilee, for he did not wish to go about in Judea because the Jews were seeking to kill him" (7:1). In Matthew, Mark, and Luke we have the detailed account of the happenings which belong to this half year of Christ's ministry. We may call it the Retirement Ministry; see Mark, Chapters 7-9. John says that during these months **Jesus was going about in Galilee.** This is in harmony with the account as given in the Synoptics, which indicates that the Lord went from Capernaum in Galilee to the borders of Tyre and Sidon, traversing a large section of Galilee; then departing from Galilee in crossing over to Decapolis; went back again to Galilee (Dalmanutha); left it again for the region of Cesarea Philippi; and finally, covering another large stretch of Galilean territory, went on his way back to Capernaum. Here and there, however, it is not immediately clear whether these various journeys are described in chronological order (cf. e.g., Mk. 8:1: "in those days"). A glance at the map would seem to indicate that they are. What characterizes the period is that to a large extent Jesus *withdrew himself* (hence, *Retirement* Ministry) from the Capernaum multitudes, to be with his disciples. **For he did not wish to go about in Judea because the Jews were seeking to kill him.** Here is a continuation of the plot which was mentioned for the first time in 5:18; see Vol. I, p. 196. Now although the Lord had come

---

[1] I D; see Vol. I, pp. 40, 41.

from heaven for the very purpose of laying down his life, he knew that the exact moment when in accordance with the eternal counsel of God this must take place had not yet arrived. Hence, he remained in the northern regions of the country during this period. It is also true, of course, that a positive motive guided the steps of the Master: he wanted to reveal his glory unto the salvation of sinners in this northern territory, and he desired to avail himself of this opportunity of relative retirement to instruct his disciples with reference to his coming suffering.

2. Now the feast of the Jews, that of Tabernacles, drew near.

But when October was finally approaching, a question must have occurred to the minds of those who knew Jesus; namely, was it his plan to go to Jerusalem in order to attend the very important pilgrim-feast of Tabernacles (Dwelling in Booths)? On this feast see Lev. 23:33-44 and Numbers 29. It was celebrated from the fifteenth to the twenty-first or twenty-second day of the seventh month, which approximates our October. It was a feast of thanksgiving for the vintage. But besides being a harvest-festival it was also a joyful commemoration of the divine guidance granted to the forefathers in their wilderness-journey. Following hard upon the day of Atonement, the idea of joy after redemption was naturally very prominent. In a decreased daily scale a special sacrifice of seventy bullocks was made. The temple-trumpets were blown on each day. There was the ceremony of the outpouring of water, drawn from Siloam, *in commemoration* of the refreshing stream which had come forth miraculously out of the rock at Meribah (Ex. 17:1-7), and *in anticipation* of blessings both for Israel and for the world. There was the illumination of the inner court of the temple, where the light of the grand candelabra reminded one of the pillar of fire by night which had served as a guide through the desert (Num. 14:14). There was a torch-parade. And above all, everywhere in and around Jerusalem, in the street, the square, and even on the roofs of the houses booths were erected. These leafy dwellings provided shelter for the pilgrims who came from every direction to attend this feast. But most of all they too were reminders of the wilderness-life of the ancestors (Lev. 23:43).

It is rather generally assumed that John mentions this feast because he is about to report certain sayings of Jesus that were connected with its ceremonies (7:37; 8:12; 9:7).

3-5. When it appears that Jesus is not in a hurry to attend the feast, his brothers — James, Joseph, Simon, and Judas (or Jude), Matt. 13:55 — begin to criticize him. They view his present behavior as being inconsistent. On the one hand, so they reason, Jesus is aiming at a high public office. Yet, on the other hand, he remains behind in Galilee, while "the public" is already on its way to Jerusalem. **So his brothers said to him,**

4

Leave here and go to Judea, in order that your disciples also may view the works which you are doing. For no one does anything in secret when he seeks to be known to the public. If you do these things, show yourself to the world. In Jerusalem Jesus will be in the limelight. His followers, having gathered in Jerusalem from every direction, will thus receive an opportunity to see his miracles. If Jesus is doing these mighty works, which fact as such these brothers do not call into question, then let him show himself to the world. Jesus must attain to glory and fame *by means of a mighty demonstration of power.* That is the way they see it.

The reason why they see it that way is, as stated in verse 5, **For even his brothers did not believe in him.** It is certain that they did not see in him the Messiah who was to prove himself as such by means of suffering and the cross! Their Messianic conception was, in a sense, similar to that of the crowd which had partaken of the bread-cakes (6:15). It was thoroughly earthly and materialistic. Strictly speaking, it does not even follow that these brothers took Jesus to be the Messiah in any sense whatever. The story merely shows that they were charging him with inconsistency, and that they, in common with so many others, harbored secular ideas with reference to the coming and office of the Messiah. After Christ's resurrection the attitude of these brothers changed completely (Acts 1:14).

---

6 Jesus then said to them, "For me the proper time is not yet here, but for y o u the time is always suitable.[2] 7 The world cannot hate y o u, but me it hates because I testify concerning it, that its works are wicked. 8 Go up to the feast yourselves. I am not yet going up to this feast, because for me the proper time has not yet arrived.[3] 9 Having said these things to them, he remained in Galilee. 10 But after his brothers had gone up to the feast, then he also went up, not publicly but as it were in secret. 11 Now the Jews were looking for him at the feast, and were saying, "Where is he?" 12 And there was much murmuring about him among the crowds. Some were saying, "He is a good man," but others were saying, "No, on the contrary, he is leading the people astray." 13 Nevertheless, for fear of the Jews no one was speaking publicly about him.

7:6-13

7:6. Jesus then said to them, For me the proper time is not yet here, but for y o u the time is always suitable.

Jesus speaks about the "proper time" (καιρός in distinction from χρόνος; even in the Koine this distinction has not entirely vanished). He says that the proper moment has not yet arrived for him. However, the question may be asked: "The proper moment to do what: to go up to the feast, or:

---

[2] Literally: "but y o u r proper time is always ready."
[3] Literally: "because my proper time has not yet been made full."

to manifest himself to the world?" The preceding context permits either interpretation. However, the succeeding context permits only *one* explanation. When Jesus says (verse 6b), ". . . but for y o u the time is always suitable" (literally, "y o u r proper time is always ready"), he can only mean, "Y o u can go up *to the feast* at any time." Therefore, it is certainly very probable that also in verse 6a what he means is this: "For me the proper time *to go up to the feast* is not yet here." This conclusion is also in harmony with verse 8 (second clause) where, regardless of the reading one adopts (whether οὐκ or οὔπω) Jesus speaks twice about going up to the feast. Hence, verse 6 definitely shows that for *every* deed and action of the Lord (not only for his death on the cross) there is a definite moment, determined from all eternity in the plan of God. See also vol. I, p. 115. The will of Jesus being in complete accord with this eternal counsel of God, he naturally waits for the proper moment to arrive. For the brothers of Jesus there were no such considerations. They had no such conscious contact with the clock of God's eternal counsel. Besides, they were as yet unbelievers. Hence, Jesus says, ". . . but for y o u the time is always suitable."

When the further question is asked; namely, "Why was it that Jesus delayed going up to the feast?" the answer probably lies in this direction: had he gone up at once, with the firstcomers, there would have been ample time for the Sanhedrin to plan his arrest *at this time,* so as to put him to death *now.* But Jesus knew that his death as the Lamb of God must take place at the time of the next Passover, not during this feast of Tabernacles. Hence, he delays.

7. The brothers had said, "Show yourself to the world." From *their* point of view that is understandable, as Jesus also now says, **The world cannot hate y o u, but me it hates. . . ."** The *world* (ὁ κόσμος; see Vol. I, p. 79) is here the realm of evil, mankind alienated from the life of God, and manifesting open hostility to God and his Anointed. This world is represented by Jerusalem's religious hierarchy. Inasmuch as the brothers of Jesus at this time "did not believe in him" (7:5), the world, of course, could not hate them. Cf. 15:18, 19; 17:14. It hated the Christ; the reason being: **because I testify concerning it, that its works are wicked.** For that testimony see 2:14-16; 3:19, 20; 5:30-47.

8, 9. Jesus continues: **Go up to the feast yourselves. I am not yet going up to this feast, because for me the proper time has not yet arrived** (literally, has not yet become full: the lower compartment of the hourglass of God's providence is not yet filled). Jesus differs by a whole heaven from his brothers. In going up to the feast, their purpose, however "religious" it may be, is yet altogether worldly. So, let them go up by themselves. On *going up* to Jerusalem see Vol. I, p. 122. For the reason already stated, the proper time has not yet arrived for Jesus to go up. He will go, but not immediately.

This explanation is very simple, and suits the entire context. However, a real difficulty has been created by reading "not" instead of "not yet" in verse 8. We are then confronted with this puzzle: Jesus says, "I go not up unto this feast" (so, e.g., A.R.V.); yet a little later he does go up (verse 10). Once having established this as the reading to be followed, all kinds of explanations are attempted. According to some, when Jesus said, "I go not up," he meant, "I am not going up *in order to manifest myself as the Messiah. That I will do at a later feast.*" According to others, verse 8 must be interpreted on this fashion: "I am not going up *publicly*, but secretly." These commentators appeal to verse 10. Still others believe that Jesus changed his mind or that the Father changed his mind for him. All of these unnatural explanations can be avoided by simply adopting for this verse the reading upon which the A.V. is based: "I go not up *yet* unto this feast." The textual evidence is about equal.[4] The context (verses 6, 9, 10) is certainly all in favor of the reading which has "not yet" (οὔπω) instead of "not." Jesus has already indicated (verse 6) that the proper time to attend the feast has "not yet" arrived for him. Hence, **having said these things he remained** a little while longer **in Galilee.** But after his brothers had gone up, he goes up also (verse 10). Into this context the reading "not yet" in verse 8 fits beautifully. Why create a difficulty when there is no need for one? There certainly are problems enough in exegesis without creating additional ones.

10. **So Jesus remained in Galilee for a while. But after his brothers had gone up to the feast, then he also went up, not publicly but as it were in secret.** Just how did Jesus go up to Jerusalem *in secret?* The answers vary. Some are of the opinion that this was the only possible way Jesus was able

---

[4] The external evidence for οὔπω is by no means less than that for οὐκ. A. T. Robertson, who in his *Introduction to the Textual Criticism of the New Testament,* New York, 1925, pp. 162, 169, 173, 176, 180, 182, 198, and 209, defends οὐκ, admits that, if there be any difference, the balance of textual support is in favor of οὔπω, which is favored by B, W, L, T, etc.; οὐκ by Aleph, D, K, M, etc. The oldest versions are divided. So, with no appreciable help from textual evidence, those who, nevertheless, support οὐκ resort to internal evidence; particularly, to the rule:

"*That* reading is to be preferred which best explains the origin of the others." In practice this usually amounts to accepting the more difficult reading. It is argued that a scribe would more likely substitute οὔπω for the difficult οὐκ than vice versa, and that, accordingly, οὐκ is probably right. However, others have felt — we believe correctly — that the rule, though of great value, should not be pressed too far. When the less difficult word — in this case οὔπω — has the clear support of the context, as we have shown, the argument based upon internal evidence loses its force. Hence, with Westcott and Hort, Nestle until (and including) the edition of 1936, and Grosheide, *Het Heilig Evangelie Volgens Johannes,* Kommentaar op het Nieuwe Testament, Amsterdam, 1950, vol. I, p. 501, footnote 1, we accept οὔπω in the second (as well as in the third) clause of 7:8.

7

to go, because the roads were deserted by this time, seeing that the busy caravans of pilgrims, including the brothers of Jesus, had already arrived in the capital. But if the explanation is so altogether obvious, then why is the fact mentioned at all? Others are inclined to think that Jesus was accompanied only by his disciples, chose the less traveled roads, journeyed only or mainly by night, and did not publicly announce his departure from Galilee or his arrival in Jerusalem. Something on that order, no doubt, is what is meant by the statement that Jesus went up *in secret*.

11. Now the Jews, consisting mainly or exclusively of the religious leaders of Jerusalem who were hostile to Jesus, had been expecting him earlier. **They were looking for him at the feast and were saying** again and again, **Where is he?** Their intentions, in view of 5:18 and 7:25, cannot have been friendly. Yet 9:22 and 11:49-53 are still future.

12. And there was much murmuring about him among the crowds. Among the crowds which had been streaming into the city from every direction the opinion was definitely divided, just as it was in Galilee (note 6:66: *many*, not all, had deserted him), though the present multitudes, coming not only from Galilee but from every section of the Holy Land and from all the countries of the Diaspora, were perhaps more evenly divided in their sentiments. **Some** people **were saying, He is a good man,** aiming to do good, morally upright, not a deceiver. **Others,** however, differed very sharply (note οὔ, ἀλλά), and **were saying, No, on the contrary, he is leading the people astray.** Cf. Lk. 23:2, 5. They saw in Jesus a mere demagogue, a man to be shunned, a false prophet, one who was interested in getting the crowd or mob (τὸν ὄχλον) on his side, ingratiating himself with the multitudes for selfish purposes.

13. Nevertheless, for fear of the Jews, no one was speaking publicly about him. These contrasting opinions, however, were uttered in whispers. As long as the Sanhedrin had not yet pronounced an official verdict, no one dared to speak out openly. Cf. 9:22. No one dared to "stick his neck out." Saying the wrong word in public might mean expulsion from the synagogue. Very powerful was the dreaded hierarchical "machine" in Jerusalem. It was fast becoming a curse for the religious life of Israel. There have been somewhat similar curses since that day. Great was the muttering and the mumbling among the crowds. The whereabouts and the character of Jesus were the center of interest.

---

14 Now when the feast was already half over, Jesus went up to the temple and started to teach.   15 The Jews therefore were amazed and said, "How can this fellow know letters without an education?"   16 So Jesus answered them, and said, "My teaching is not mine but his who sent me.   17 If anyone is willing to do his

8

will, he shall know concerning the teaching whether it is of God or whether I am
(merely) expressing my own views.[5] 18 He who (merely) expresses his own views
is seeking his own glory. He who seeks the glory of him who sent him, this one
is truly reliable, and there is in him nothing false. 19 Did not Moses give y o u
the law? Yet none of y o u keeps the law. Why are y o u seeking to kill me?"
20 The crowd answered, "You have a demon! Who is seeking to kill you?" 21
Jesus answered and said to them, *"One* deed I did, and y o u are all amazed.
22 It is for that reason (that I say to y o u), Moses gave y o u the rite of circumcision — not that it originated with Moses but with the fathers — and on the sabbath y o u circumcize a person. 23 If a person receives circumcision on the sabbath
in order that the law of Moses may not be broken, are y o u angry at me because
I made a man completely well on the sabbath?[6] 24 Stop judging superficially,
but render just judgment."

7:14-24

**7:14, 15. Now when the feast was already half over, Jesus went up to
the temple and started to teach.**

All of a sudden Jesus appeared in the temple. The feast which lasted
fully a week (Lev. 23:26) was already half over (ἤδη δὲ τῆς ἑορτῆς μεσούσης,
"already half-way the feast"). With so many pilgrims present in Jerusalem,
many of whom were sufficiently interested in Jesus and sympathetic toward
him that harming him might have led to difficulties for those in charge,
really *adequate* preparations for his arrest were no longer possible. Clumsy,
last-minute efforts in this direction led to nothing, as we shall see (7:32,
45-52). Jesus then, having found a convenient place for himself (perhaps
in the court of the Gentiles?) sat down, as was the customary posture of
those who taught (cf. Matt. 5:1, 2; but cf. 7:37). A crowd of listeners
quickly gathered, whom he started to instruct. This time there was no
miracle, as on the previous (recorded) occasion (chapter 5). But the people
will soon discover that whatever the Lord does is amazing, his teaching as
well as his miracles.

Presently some of the hostile leaders joined the audience. They listened
for a while. Then, startled by the character and contents of the words
which they heard, these men, who were never ready to admit any true
greatness on the part of the Lord, were able to contain themselves no
longer. **The Jews therefore were amazed** about his audacity. Their anger
exploded in a vituperative exclamation concerning Jesus, **and they said
to the crowd: How can this fellow know letters without an education?**
Jesus had never received instruction in any of the rabbinical schools. In
present-day language, one might say that he had failed to receive his degree
at an accredited institution. Therefore, whatever he said must be wrong!

---

[5] Literally: "or whether I speak of myself. IIIB2; see Vol. I, p. 44.
[6] IAB; see Vol. I, p. 40.

He did not know "letters" (γράμματα, a. actual *letters* of the alphabet, Gal. 6:11; b. an *epistle*, Acts 28:21; c. *Scriptures*, II Tim. 3:15; finally, as here, *learning;* however, Jewish learning was mainly focussed on the sacred writings and their interpretation). The implication was that Jesus was simply uttering his own private opinions about religious matters; and, therefore, that one should refuse to listen to him any longer.

16. In his answer Jesus shows that the critics had failed completely to think of the possibility that the contents of his teaching might have been derived from another source, far superior to any Jewish seminary. As the *critics* saw it, there were only two possibilities: either, Jesus must have been enrolled as a regular student in a rabbinical school; or else, he is simply spouting his own ideas. And whereas they knew that the first of these alternatives was definitely "out," the second must be the truth. **So Jesus answered them and said, My teaching is not mine, but his who sent me.** Not taught by man, nor self-taught, but instructed by God himself, that was his answer. On Jesus as the One *sent* by God see vol. I, pp. 142, 150, 208. Not only had he derived the contents of his teaching from his Father in heaven, but he had also been divinely commissioned to convey it to the people on earth. Let his enemies take note of this fact; namely, that in rejecting him and his message they are rejecting God himself (cf. 4:34; 5:23, 24, 30; Matt. 10:40).

17, 18. Jesus then lays down a basic principle: he stipulates the qualifications which one should possess before he is able, in a measure, to evaluate Christ's teaching. Anyone who wishes to do this must a. have the proper disposition (verse 17); b. aim at the proper ideal (verse 18).

He must have the proper disposition of heart and mind: **If anyone is willing to do his will, he shall know concerning the teaching whether it is of God or whether I am (merely) expressing my own views.** If there be no true desire to obey the will of God as expressed in his Word, true knowledge (both intellectual and experiential) will not be found. This introduces the interesting question: Just how are the various elements of Christian experience related to each other? In general it may be said that, according to the teaching of Christ and the apostles, *knowledge* (concerning Christ and the facts of redemption: implying, of course, a knowledge of misery) comes first. When we try to trace our love for God in Christ to its source, we discover that it resulted from the contemplation of the facts of the Gospel and from our interpretation of the significance of these facts. Nevertheless, we hasten to add: knowledge as such never produces love. It results in love when the Holy Spirit applies this knowledge to the heart; i.e., when he creates in the heart a response to the love of Christ, the knowledge of which is already present in the mind. Now this love, in turn, expresses itself in deeds of obedience: "If y o u love me, y o u will

10

keep my commandments." The fundamental relation between the three is, therefore: a. knowledge, b. love, c. obedience. Cf. John 17:26; 14:15.

Yet, this representation is in need of qualification. Each of the elements (knowledge, love, obedience), once present in any slight degree, enriches, intensifies, deepens the others. There is a constant interaction, each influencing the other two. In fact, the three are so closely related that none is complete in and by itself alone. Thus, not only does knowledge, applied by the Holy Spirit, lead to love; but love, in turn, is the indispensable prerequisite of full-grown knowledge. Hence, at times we find the opposite order: instead of *knowledge . . . love,* we find *love . . . knowledge.* Cf. Eph. 3:17. Similarly, instead of the order according to which obedience is last (as in 14:15), we also find the order in which it is first. This, of course, is the way in which the sequence is expressed in the passage which we are now studying (7:17): "If anyone is willing to do his will, he shall know concerning the teaching whether it is of God or whether I am (merely) expressing my own views." Here we have: 1. obedience (willingness to do God's will) and 2. knowledge.

The only logical conclusion, in view of these various and (at first glance) seemingly (though never *really*) conflicting representations, is this: when we speak of *knowledge, love and obedience,* we are not thinking of three altogether separate experiences, but of one single, comprehensive experience in which the three are united in such a manner that each contributes its share, and all cooperate unto man's salvation and God's glory. This experience is *personal* in character. Hence, we can no longer speak of the primacy of the intellect or of the primacy of the emotions or of the primacy of the will, but of the primacy of the sovereign grace of God influencing and transforming the entire personality for the glory of God.

Knowledge, therefore, will never be sanctified to the heart and lead to true discernment of the divine character and origin of Christ's teaching unless the willingness to do God's will is present first of all. When the latter is present, one will immediately perceive that the base charge of the Jews — namely, that Jesus was merely expressing his own private opinions — is utterly false.

Now one who has the proper disposition (verse 17) will also aim at the proper ideal (verse 18): **He who (merely) expresses his own views is seeking his own glory. He who seeks the glory of him who sent him, this one is truly reliable, and there is in him nothing false.** On this passage see 5:41-44. If this glory of God be the listener's ideal, he will also be able to detect whether it is the speaker's ideal. Would a self-appointed prophet do what Jesus is always doing (cf. 5:19; 7:16; 17:4); i.e., would he show in all his words and actions that he is seeking the glory of his Sender? Would not one who is merely uttering his own private opinions be doing the exact opposite; i.e., would he not seek his own glory? These words

11

serve a double purpose: a. they show the utter groundlessness of the scoffing remark of the leaders, "How can this fellow know letters without an education?" and b. they expose the sin of these leaders. *They* were the very people who were always seeking to promote their own glory, even to such an extent that six months after this feast of Tabernacles their envy caused them to deliver up Jesus to be crucified (Matt. 27:18). They just could not "take it" that there was such an interest in Jesus on the part of the crowds. Hence, while *he* was the truly reliable (ἀληθής) One, in whom there was no deceit of any kind, *they* were the ones whose religion, in spite of all their outward show of zeal for the law, was nothing but a false pretense.

19. Jesus exposes this hypocrisy even more thoroughly when he asks the rhetorical question: **Did not Moses give y o u the law?** Indeed, these very men were constantly boasting about being disciples of Moses (9:28), and sitting in Moses' seat (cf. Matt. 23:2). They had received the Torah (the whole law: civil, ceremonial, moral, with emphasis on the latter as summarized in the Ten Commandments) through the mediation of Moses. Jesus continues: **Yet none of y o u keeps the law. Why are y o u seeking to kill me?** The offended One is now taking the offensive. The double denunciation, aimed at the leaders, comes like a thunderbolt and a lightning flash. It shows that Jesus was at this very moment reading the hearts of these men. He knew that while they tried to pose as the guardians of the law of Moses, a law which is summarized in the one word *love,* they had hatred and murder in their hearts (cf. 5:18). But the terrible charge, the devastating accusation, is aimed not only (though especially) at the leaders. Jesus knows that the citizens of Jerusalem are going to join with them by and by, and so will others (7:30, 44), until finally, a half year from now, the entire mob, gathered in Jerusalem from everywhere, will shout, "Let him be crucified." To be neutral with respect to Christ is not even possible. Hence, the question "Why are y o u seeking to kill me?" is, in a sense, meant for the entire audience.

20. The crowd answered, You have a demon! Who is seeking to kill you?

Nevertheless, among the assembled multitudes — which consist of hostile leaders (Pharisees, scribes), pilgrims from everywhere, and citizens of Jerusalem (cf. verses 14, 20, 25, respectively, for the three classes) — there are those who have no conscious desire at this present moment to put Jesus to death. We can imagine how they, consisting, no doubt, mostly of people who had come from afar, felt themselves aggrieved by the question of Jesus. While their cheeks are glowing with indignation, they burst out with the exclamation, "You have a demon! Who is seeking to kill you?" They feel certain that an evil spirit must have taken possession of his mind, and must have made him insane. This crowd of pilgrims evidently did not know that the leaders at Jerusalem had already in their hearts planned to put him out of the way. People are usually slow to catch on to the plots of "religious" leaders for whom they have high respect. The story enacted here in Jerusalem has, on a smaller scale, been repeated many times in history. For example, a few leaders, holding high office, filled with envy, plot the ruin of this or that person. Very cleverly they lay their plans. Their plot succeeds. The people in general never realize what has happened. If the intended victim of the leaders' envy would ever have told them in plain language, "These leaders are plotting my ruin," they would have replied: "Man, you have a demon or at least a persecution-complex! Nobody is trying to harm you in any way."

21-24. Jesus, however, proves his point. The plot to kill him had entered the hearts and minds of the leaders in connection with the healing of the man at the pool, as is definitely stated in 5:18. **Jesus answered and said to them, One deed I did, and y o u are all amazed.** To be sure, Jesus had also performed other deeds of healing in Jerusalem (2:23; 4:45); but this *one* deed — the cure of the paralytic at Bethzatha (5:1-18; see vol. I, pp. 187-197) — , performed on the sabbath, had been the immediate occasion for the plot against his life. The miracle itself, but especially the attendant circumstances (that it was done on the sabbath and that on the sabbath the man had been ordered to carry his mat), had caused general amazement. It must be borne in mind that neither here nor in verse 15 of this chapter does amazement necessarily imply approbation.

Now in view of the fact that the reaction of the people had not been one of true, living faith but rather of adverse criticism (especially among the leaders), the Lord continues: **It is for that reason that I say to y o u** (διὰ τοῦτο is probably elliptical here [7]), **Moses gave y o u the rite of circumcision — not that it originated with Moses but with the fathers — and on the sabbath y o u circumcise a person.** To show them the weakness of their criticism of his deed, as if it had been sabbath-violation, this circumcision-ordinance is here introduced. Though this rite became an ordinance for Israel by virtue of its inclusion in the Mosaic legislation (Lev. 12:1-3), yet it was practised long before Moses, in the days of the "fathers" who preceded him (Gen. 17:9-14, 23-27; 21:4). The Jews, in their zeal for the law of Moses, were prone to forget that certain important religious practices were in vogue long before his time; hence, Jesus adds the parenthetical clause.

---

[7] The phrase would be redundant if construed with verse 21. Besides, it generally occurs *at the beginning* of a clause (1:31; 5:16, 18; 6:65; 8:47; 9:23, 10:17; 12:18, 27, 39; 13:11; 15:19; 16:15; and 19:11); and in the sense of "therefore" (or: "for that reason") as here it is not always followed by causal ὅτι (cf. 1:31; 9:23; 12:27; 19:11). Ellipsis is not uncommon in the Fourth Gospel.

Now according to the law which governed this religious rite, a male child had to be circumcised *on the eighth day* after its birth. The point which Jesus stresses is this: even if that eighth day happens to be a sabbath, the child is, nevertheless, circumcised. He continues, bringing home his argument in such a manner that its cogency is immediately clear: **If a person receives circumcision on the sabbath in order that the law of Moses may not be broken, are y o u angry at me because I made a man completely well on the sabbath?** If *ceremonial cleansing* of *one member* of the body (the procreative member) is permitted on the sabbath, then would *actual healing* of *the entire body* (yes, of the entire man, body and soul) be forbidden on the sabbath, giving the people righteous cause for anger against the Healer? The argument is, of course, unanswerable. "The sabbath was made for man; not man for the sabbath" (Mk. 2:27).

What the people (both the leaders and the rest) should do is this: they should calmly reflect on these matters. They should cease being so rash in their judgments. Hence, Jesus said, **Stop judging superficially** (χατ' ὄψιν; literally: according to appearance), **but render just judgment.** Compare the somewhat similar thought expressed so beautifully in I Sam. 16:7 b: "For Jehovah sees not as man sees; for man looks on the outward appearance, but Jehovah looks on the heart."

---

25 Some of the people of Jerusalem therefore were saying, "Is not this the man whom they are seeking to kill? 26 Now look! He is speaking openly, and they say nothing to him. Surely, the rulers have not really become convinced that he is the Christ, have they? 27 Yet we know where this man is from; but when the Christ comes, no one will know where he comes from." 28 So Jesus cried out, teaching in the temple and saying, "So y o u know me; and y o u know where I am from! But I have not come of my own accord; on the contrary, he who sent me is the Real One, but him y o u do not know. 29 I do know him, because I am from his presence, and he sent me."

7:25-29

7:25-27. The reaction of the Sanhedrin-members has been recorded in 7:15; that of the crowd (mostly pilgrims) in 7:20. We now hear from the citizens of Jerusalem (7:25-27). These were better informed with respect to the real intentions of the leaders, who had their headquarters in their own city. Also, they were not as friendly to Jesus as were many of the pilgrims from afar. The Jerusalemites were greatly surprised about the fact that no one had tried to stop Jesus when he had flung his terrible accusations in the teeth of his opponents (verse 19), and, in addition, had charged them and their followers with most glaring inconsistency (verses 21-24). To be sure, there had been a momentary interruption, an ejacula-

14

tion of anger (verse 20), but that was all. Jesus had been allowed to continue his "revolutionary" teaching.

In this light we can understand the statement: **Some of the people therefore said, Is not this the man whom they are seeking to kill? Now look! He is speaking** *openly* (παρρησία from πᾶς and ῥῆσις; hence, telling all, keeping back nothing, a term which in the form of μετὰ παρρησίας has a beautiful meaning in Heb. 4:16), **and they** (those in charge of the temple, its ritual, services, etc.) **say nothing to him.** A possibility flashes across their minds, but is almost immediately dismissed: **Surely, the rulers have not really become convinced that he is the Christ, have they? Yet we know where this man is from; but when the Christ comes, no one will know where he is from.** The opinion of the rulers! That was the all-important thing, for these men had the right to cast dissenters out of the synagogue, a most terrible punishment (cf. 7:13; 7:48; 9:22; 9:34; and 12:42). But how can it be explained that, in the face of such dreadful accusations which Jesus had hurled against them, they allowed him to proceed as if nothing had happened? Could it be that *they had really come to know* (ἔγνωσαν, actually become convinced) that he is the Christ? But no, that could not be. Hence, the question is cast in a form which expects a negative answer, even though the door of doubt is kept slightly ajar (μήποτε ἀληθῶς). The idea of some to the effect that these people of Jerusalem are asking the question in the attitude of ridicule hardly seems to harmonize with the calm manner of discourse — the weighing of arguments pro and con — which appears in verse 27. The suggestion of the Jerusalemites that the rulers might have arrived at the conclusion that this was really the Christ vanishes before the objection that the place of origin of this man, Jesus, is well-known; but that the whence of the genuine Messiah would be unknown.

Did not everybody know that Jesus came from Nazareth in Galilee, and that he was a son of Joseph and Mary! We find something similar in 6:42 and in 7:41, 42. Hence, the possibility that he might be the Christ was immediately ruled out. According to the present chapter of John's Gospel there were two opinions among the Jews regarding the origin of the expected Messiah: a. according to some, no one would know where he came from (7:27); b. according to others, he would be born in Bethlehem (7:41, 42; cf. Matt. 2:3-5).

The first of these ideas — that Messiah would appear very suddenly, as if from nowhere — seems to have been a piece of popular theology, probably based upon inferences from certain passages in the Apocrypha (although we do not find it *clearly* stated in any of those books).[8] The second idea

[8] See, however, A. T. Robertson, *Word Pictures in the New Testament*, New York and London, 1932, vol. V, p. 127.

(as the given references indicate) was correct, and was the official position of the Sanhedrin. On either score, however, since everybody "knew" where Jesus came from, namely, from Nazareth in Galilee, he could not be the true Messiah!

28. How thoroughly wrong they were! And how this woeful ignorance concerning his real origin must have pained the Lord! Stirred to the very depths of his being, Jesus **cried out** (ἔκραξεν) — this too belonged to his teaching in the temple — : **So, y o u know me, and y o u know where I am from!** One can also read the exclamation as a question; thus: "So y o u know me, and y o u know where I am from?" Either way, the meaning is the same. Jesus ridicules the very idea that these biased, legalistic materialistic citizens of Jerusalem would actually *know* him and his origin! And when he now says "So, y o u know me, and y o u know where I am from!" he means, "That is what y o u *think!*" We do not accept the interpretation of those who exclude the idea of irony, and who believe that Jesus actually meant to say that these citizens of the capital knew him and his origin inasmuch as they knew that he came from Nazareth in Galilee. We cannot accept this, for the following reasons:

a. In that case would not the Lord be hiding his *real* origin (namely, that he came from heaven and was born, according to prophecy, in Bethlehem); and would he not, therefore, become partly responsible for the notion that he could not be the Christ? Besides, his childhood in Nazareth does not constitute a cogent argument either for or against his exalted character and origin. Hence, we cannot believe that *Jesus* would in all seriousness bring up that subject.

b. Jesus himself again and again declares, either explicitly or by implication, that the people *do not* know him or his origin (8:19, 42, 43; see also 3:11; 5:18, 37, 38; 6:42, 60-62; 8:55-59; and cf. 14:9). Would he then say the very opposite here (7:28)? Also, notice that in the last clause of verse 28 Jesus tells these people that they do not know God. Is it logical then to suppose that he would say in the same verse: "But y o u do actually know me"? Cf. 8:19!

c. Failure to see the sparkling, lively character of our Lord's conversation — the notion, for example, that it would have been far below his dignity and glorious majesty ever to use irony or ridicule — has led to mistakes in exegesis again and again. See what has been said about this in connection with 5:31; vol. I, pp. 205, 206.

d. The fact that when Jesus spoke these words, he was deeply stirred, so that he *cried out*, harmonizes beautifully with the idea that what we have here is not a calm statement of fact but an exclamation of the character: "So y o u know me, and y o u know where I am from!" In the

16

light of this stinging ridicule it is not too difficult to understand that the persons addressed were anxious to have Jesus arrested (7:30).

e. Finally, we must bear in mind that the leaders and some of the Jerusalemites regarded Jesus as a deceiver, an impostor; as one who most certainly *could not be* the Messiah (7:12, 27, 41, 42). Is it logical, then, to assume that Jesus would say to such people that they actually knew him and knew where he came from?

With John Calvin (and many others: Godet, Weizsäcker, Lücke, Lenski) we believe, therefore, that Jesus here employs irony.[9]

These same people who were so certain that Jesus could not be the promised Messiah regarded him as a self-appointed prophet. Hence, in refutation Jesus says, **But I have not come of my own accord; on the contrary, he who sent me is the Real One, and him y o u do not know.** Instead of having come of his own accord, Jesus was the divinely commissioned One, having been sent by the Father, as is taught in many a passage of the Fourth Gospel (5:30; 8:28; 12:49; 14:10). Moreover, the people must not think that the Sender is a mere figment of the imagination, a subjective notion; on the contrary, he is the Real One (ἀληθινός), but he is the very One whom the people do not know (cf. 8:19, 55), although they imagine that they know him very well.

29. Jesus continues: *I do know him, because I am from him* (or: from his presence), **and he sent me.** There is some doubt about the correct reading, whether this be "I am *from* him" or "I am *with* him." However, the context clearly shows that the question that was in the minds of all was this: "Who is Jesus, and where is he *from?*" Thus in verse 27 and again in verse 28. Besides, the idea that Jesus is the One who came *from* God is rather common in John (1:14; 6:46; 16:27; 17:8). Of course, the One who came *from* God was at one time (and in a sense is *always)* *with* him. And because the Son was with the Father and came forth from him, he knows him thoroughly (cf. 1:18; 8:55; 17:25; Matt. 11:27). Let there be no doubt about this in the minds of the hearers. On the side of the Jerusalem critics there is conceit and error, all of this born of unbelief. Their syllogism was as follows:

Major Premise: No one will know where the real Messiah comes from.
Minor Premise: We know where Jesus comes from.
Conclusion: Hence, Jesus cannot be the real Messiah.

Given the major and the minor premise, the conclusion follows logically.

---

[9] John Calvin. *Ioannis Calvini in Evangelium Ioannis Commentarii,* Berolini (apud Guilelmum Thome), 1553; vol. III, p. 145: Acerbis verbis in corum temeritatem invehitur, quod superbe sibi in falsa opinione placentes a veri notitia se excluderent, acsi diceret, Vos omnia cognoscendo nihil tandem cognoscitis . . . . . Ironice loquitur quum dicit *me nostis, et nostis unde sim, a me ipso non veni.*

But the major premise was false; the minor premise was false: the conclusion was false. Over against their delusions Jesus, who comes straight from God and was commissioned by him, proclaims the truth; namely, that he is, indeed, the Christ, and that he, he *alone*, knows the Father thoroughly.

---

30 Therefore they were anxious to arrest him, but no one laid a hand on him, because his hour had not yet come. 31 But many of the people believed in him, and said, "When the Christ comes, he surely will not do more signs than this man has done, will he?"

7:30, 31

7:30. Jesus had made the loftiest claims with respect to his own person and origin, had exposed to ridicule the pretended knowledge of the Jerusalemites, and had told them in blunt, unmistakable language that they did not even know God (7:28, 29)! So we are not surprised to read: **Therefore they were anxious** [10] **to arrest him.** Why did they not carry out their wish? Did fear of those pilgrims who were favorably disposed to Jesus restrain them? Verse 31 seems to point in that direction (see also 7:12 a). The deeper reason for this failure to capture Jesus at this time is stated in words which have a familiar ring in the Fourth Gospel: **But no one laid a hand on him** (cf. Matt. 26:50) **because his hour had not yet come.** For this last clause see on 2:4. Though surrounded by danger — the anger of these Jerusalemites, the hostile desire and power of the leaders —, Jesus was in reality free from all danger, because it was not the will of God that he should die at this time.[11]

31. But many of the people (no doubt, mostly pilgrims) **believed in him.** This does not necessarily indicate true, living faith, however. They probably were ready to accept Jesus as the political Messiah of their dreams. They based their attitude upon the miracles which they had seen or about which they had been hearing such glowing reports. Cf. 2:23; 4:45, 48; Acts 8:13. They expected that the Messiah at his coming would perform miracles (cf. Is. 35:5, 6; Matt. 11:2-5) and that he would restore the kingdom to Israel (Acts 1:6). In the light of what Jesus has all along been doing they are ready to accept him as being this kind of a Messiah. **And they were saying, When the Christ comes, he surely will not do more** (or possibly:

---

10 Probably conative (ἐζήτουν).
11 John Calvin, *op. cit.*, p. 146: Res difficilis creditu, quod tot fortuitis casibus obnoxii, tot hominum ferarumque inuriis et insidiis expositi, tot obsessi morbis, simus tamen extra omnem periculorum aleam nisi quum evocare nos Deus volet: sed cum diffidentia nostra luctandum.

greater) **signs than this man has done, will he?** A negative answer is expected.

---

32 The Pharisees heard the crowd mumbling these things about him; so the chief priests and Pharisees sent officers in order that they might arrest him. 33 So Jesus said, "Yet a little while am I with y o u, and then I go to him who sent me. 34 Y o u will seek me, but y o u will not find me, and where I am y o u cannot come." 35 The Jews therefore said to one another, "Where does this fellow intend to go, that we shall not find him? He surely does not intend to go to the Diaspora among the Greeks, and teach the Greeks, does he? 36 What does he mean by saying, 'Y o u will seek me, but y o u will not find me,' and 'Where I am y o u cannot come'?"

7:32-36

7.32. The Pharisees heard the crowd mumbling these things about him; so the chief priests and Pharisees sent officers in order that they might arrest him.

As the Pharisees saw it, things were beginning to look very serious. People were actually beginning to regard this impostor as the true Messiah. The mumbling of voices which expressed these sentiments had been heard. Intervention was necessary. It could not be delayed any longer. So these guardians of the law reveal their anxiety to the members of the priestly families (mostly Sadducees). Agreement is soon reached. Mutual arch-enemies — Pharisees and Sadducees — are entirely willing to unite in their common opposition to Jesus (cf. Lk. 23:12; Acts 4:27). Whether an actual Sanhedrin-session was held at *this* time (as in 7:45-52, and in 11:47) we do not know. The agreement may have been of a less formal character. At any rate, the opposition against Jesus reaches a new stage here: the sinister desire, expressed in 5:18, begins to be put into effect. The men who should have been most zealous in their defence of Christ and his kingdom actually send officers (ὑπηρέτας: under-rowers; hence, servants, officers) to arrest the Messiah!

33. But Jesus shows that the counsel of God must be carried out. **So, with serenity and majesty, calm and unperturbed, Jesus said** (addressing himself to the entire assembled multitude, but especially to the leaders who are present): **Yet a little while I am with y o u, and then I go to him who sent me.** Cf. 16:16-19. Jesus knows that he will be on earth a little while longer; i.e., one half year (from October of the year 29 to April of the year 30; from feast of Tabernacles to feast of Passover). He will then return to his Sender, having fully accomplished the task that had been entrusted to him.

34. In a statement full of mystery the Lord continues: **Y o u will seek**

19

me, but y o u will not find me. Cf. 13:33-36. The Jewish nation, in its despair, will seek deliverance, but it will then be too late. Think of the despair of Esau (Gen. 27:30-38; Heb. 12:17); of the men regarding whom Amos writes his prophecy of woe: "Behold, the days come, saith the Lord Jehovah, that I will send a famine in the land, not a famine of bread, nor a thirst for water, but of hearing the words of Jehovah. And they shall wander from sea to sea, and from the north even to the east; they shall run to and fro to seek the word of Jehovah, and shall not find it" (Am. 8:11, 12). Cf. also Prov. 1:24-28. Not finding him, they will die in their sins (8:21).

When Jesus adds: **And where I am y o u cannot come,** he means this: "I am going to the Father; but y o u have rejected the Father by rejecting me. Hence, where I am y o u cannot come." In the presence of the Father there is no room for those who have refused to accept the Son.

The warning implied in these words is, of course, very clear. It is the warning of Ps. 95:8-11.

Thus Jesus clearly showed that, regardless of whatever the Jews might be planning, he would die at the appointed time, and that in his death the divine purpose, far from being frustrated, would be carried out: by means of the cross he would attain unto the crown; he would reach the glory that awaited him in heaven after the accomplishment of his mediatorial task on earth.

35, 36. But as in all previous cases so also now: this significant mashal was given a crassly literal interpretation. From the reaction of **the Jews** it appears immediately that they have failed to see in the words of Jesus a disclosure of their own dreadful state of sin and its inevitable consequences. Lightheartedly casting aside the implied warning, they therefore said to one another: **Where does this fellow intend to go, that we shall not find him? He surely does not intend to go to the Diaspora among the Greeks, and teach the Greeks, does he? What does he mean by saying, Y o u will seek me, but y o u will not find me, and Where I am y o u cannot come?**

They were mocking. Was it the intention of Jesus, after his work in Judea had ended in disappointment, to go to the Dispersion (διασπορά from διασπείρω, to scatter abroad; cf. Acts 8:1, 4; Jas. 1:1) of the Jews among the Greeks? In various regions of the earth Jews were living among the Greeks and other heathen peoples (cf. Acts 2:9-11). When the evangelist mentions *Greeks,* he does not mean Greek-speaking Jews (Hellenists; see Acts 6:1; 9:29) but people who belong to the Hellenic stock. Was the intention of Jesus to work among the scattered Jews, and when also this work issued in failure, then to labor among the Greeks themselves?

They do not realize that what they are saying in derision contains a

20

glorious prophecy. Indeed, the Greeks will take an interest in the Gospel (see 12:20). And the tidings of salvation will be spread throughout the earth, and the kingdom of the Lord will be established, and . . . the scoffers will seek . . . in vain!

---

37 Now on the last, the great day of the feast, Jesus was standing and cried out, saying, "If any one thirsts, let him come to me and drink. 38 He who believes in me, as the scripture says, 'From within him shall flow rivers of living water.' " 39 Now this he said about the Spirit, which those were to receive who believed in him. For as yet the Spirit was not present, because Jesus was not yet glorified.

7:37-39

7:37-38. Now on the last, the great day of the feast, Jesus was standing and cried out, saying, If any man thirst, let him come unto me and drink. He who believes in me, as the scripture says, From within him shall flow rivers of living water.

From midway the feast (7:14) the story now advances to its last day. It is not certain whether this "last day" indicates the seventh or the eighth day (i.e., whether it refers to the twenty-first or to the twenty-second of the seventh month). There were seven days of regular feasting which were characterized, among other things, by dwelling in booths, by bringing offerings on a diminishing scale (on the first day, in addition to other sacrifices, *thirteen* young bullocks; on the second day, *twelve* young bullocks; on the third day, *eleven;* etc.; see Num. 29:12-34), and by fetching water from the pool of Siloam. The eighth day was a day of rest, of "solemn assembly" or "holy convocation."

Although many commentators show preference for either the seventh or eighth day, on the basis of the available evidence it would seem to be the part of wisdom to leave this question undecided.

In favor of the eighth day as being the one to which reference is made here in 7:37 the following arguments have been presented:

1. Not only do the Old Testament passages mention this eighth day, but during the intertestamentary period and afterward it became customary to speak of this feast as one of *eight* days. Thus, II Macc. 10:6: "And they kept (the feast) eight days with gladness," and Flavius Josephus, *Antiquities of the Jews* III, x, 4: "And keep a festival for eight days."

2. The designation "the last, the great day of the feast" accords better with the eighth than with the seventh day; for the eighth day marked the close not only of the feast of Tabernacles but of the entire great cycle of annual, religious festivals. The LXX (e.g., in Lev. 23:36) calls this day the ἐξόδιον, i.e., the finale or closing festival.

3. As the water-pouring ceremony took place on each of the seven regular

21

feast-days *but not on the eighth* [this, however, is not admitted by all], this very lack which characterized that eighth day furnished a most fitting reason for Christ's exclamation, "If any man thirsts, let him come to me and drink."

Those who favor the opposite theory — that 7:37 refers to the seventh day — argue as follows:

1. It may be confidently assumed that the language of 7:37 is rooted in the soil of the Old Testament rather than in that of the Apocrypha and of Josephus. Now in the Old Testament the eighth day is always reckoned separately, while the feast itself is said to last *seven* days: "Y o u shall keep the feast of Jehovah seven days" (Lev. 23:39); "And y o u shall keep a feast unto Jehovah seven days" (Num. 29:2); "And they kept the feast seven days" (Neh. 8:18). The last day *of the feast* (7:37) is, therefore, the seventh day.

2. This was *the great day* of the feast. The seventh day was, indeed, great, for: a. On this one day there were seven processions around the altar; on preceding days only one per day. b. In these processions the priests chanted, "O then, work now salvation, Jehovah! O Jehovah, send now prosperity" (Ps. 118:25). Hence, the seventh day, when this passage was chanted so many times, is called the day of *The Great Hosannah*.

3. Not only was this the last day of the regular series of diminishing sacrifices, and the last day of drawing water from Siloam, but it was also the last day of dwelling in booths. On the afternoon of this day the booths were dismantled, and the feast ended. The holy convocation on the eighth day was not a part of the feast proper. The last day of the feast is, therefore the seventh day.

What is far more important to remember in connection with the events of this day — whether it be regarded as the seventh or as the eighth day of the feast — is the fact that the Lord, far from turning himself away from the multitudes, many of whom in one way or another had rejected him, extended his gracious invitation: "If any one thirst, let him come to me and drink."

Prophecy was being fulfilled in a most remarkable manner. About five and one half centuries earlier Haggai had been urging the returned remnant to resume the work of rebuilding the temple. In order to encourage those who deplored the insignificant look of the new building even in its very beginnings, this prophet was used as the vehicle for the utterance of the following message of Jehovah, a word full of comfort and cheer:

"Yet once, it is a little while, and I will shake the heavens, and the earth, and the sea, and the dry land; and I will shake all nations; and the desire of all nations shall come; and I will fill this house with glory, saith Jehovah of hosts. The silver is mine, and the gold is mine, saith Jehovah of hosts. The latter glory of this house shall be greater than the former,

22

saith Jehovah of hosts; and in this place will I give peace, saith Jehovah of hosts" (Hag. 2:6-9).

This passage, which in its deepest implications is a glorious Messianic prophecy, must have been uttered not far away from *the very place* where Jesus stood now; i.e., more than five centuries later. The *time* when it was spoken is also most remarkable. Haggai delivered this message of encouragement *"in the seventh month, on the twenty-first day of the month."* And when Jesus in a measure fulfilled this prophecy and sought to persuade the thirsty ones to come to himself and drink, it was again *the seventh month, the twenty-first or twenty-second day of the month!*

Although it cannot be demonstrated with mathematical certainty, it must be regarded as very probable that the invitation uttered by Jesus (7:37) had some connection with the drawing of water from the pool of Siloam. On each of the seven feast-days a priest would fill a golden pitcher with water from this pool. Accompanied by a solemn procession, he would return to the temple and amid the sounding of trumpets and the shouting of rejoicing multitudes he would pour it through a funnel which led to the base of the altar of burntoffering. The people were in a jubilant mood. Not only did this ceremony remind them of the blessings granted to the forefathers in the wilderness (the water from the rock), but it also pointed forward to the spiritual bounties of the Messianic age. Their minds, hearts, and voices were occupied with such passages as Is. 12:3, "Therefore with joy shall y o u draw water from the wells of salvation." In their right hand they held a branch of myrtle, a willow-twig, and a bough of the palm-tree; in the left, a citron or similar fruit. The desert-life of the ancestors passed in review. The festival resembled a historical pageant. And the citrons, though not intended for that purpose, came in handy when a worldly highpriest would try to improve upon the established ritual of the feast, as Alexander Janneus (104-78 B. C.) discovered to his dismay when he was pelted with them.

Now it may have been immediately after the completion of the symbolic rite of water-pouring and the chanting of the familiar lines from Ps. 118, or else it may have been on the day when, according to many, no such ceremony took place, that the voice of Jesus was heard loud and clear: "If any one thirst, let him come to me and drink." It was as if he wanted to say, "Do y o u not realize that this water points to me, and that all these reminders of the life of your fathers in the wilderness lose their most vital significance apart from me?"

At this point we should pay some attention to a departure from the usual translation of verses 37 and 38. In reality, this is a matter that concerns the punctuation of the Greek, and the supposedly wrong vocalization of the original Aramaic. That the words of 7:37, spoken by Jesus to a large gathering of Jews in the temple, were actually uttered in Aramaic is granted. This, of course, does not necessarily imply that what is given in our Greek New Testament rests upon a *written* Aramaic original. Certain Aramaic scholars — among whom we wish to mention especially C. F. Burney and C. C. Torrey [12] — have assailed the passage as found in the Greek New Testament, and, by implication, the translations that are based upon it. Torrey speaks of the text as it has come down to us as being "miserable nonsense." He refers to "the absurd reading of our Greek version." For 7:37, 38 Torrey proposes the following:

"Whoever thirsts, let him come to me, and let him drink who believes on me. As the scripture says, Out of the midst of Her (i.e., Jerusalem) shall flow rivers of living water."

We have carefully studied Torrey's argument, but we cannot agree. Our objections to it and our reasons for clinging to the Greek text are as follows:

1. *In the original* (though not in Torrey's English translation) the two subjects of this supposed parallelism are dissimilar in structure ($\tau\iota\varsigma$ . . . $\acute{o}$ $\pi\iota\sigma\tau\epsilon\acute{u}\omega\nu$).

2. It would seem to follow from Torrey's translation that "whoever thirsts" and "who believes" are synonymous. But according to 6:35 the believer is exactly the one who "will in no way ever get thirsty." The believer is the person who has quenched his thirst by coming to Christ, the True Fountain. He is the one who has stilled his hunger by coming to Christ, the True Bread.

3. As to the latter part of verse 38, it is true that in the Old Testament the river of life is found in "the city of God" (Ps 46:4) and issues forth "out from under the threshold" of its temple (Ezek. 47:1); but that in the Greek text of John 7:38 these waters are pictured as flowing from the hearts of individual believers. However, is it not true that Old Testament passages are often given a slightly different application in the New? Besides, if these waters stream forth from "the city of God," do they not necessarily issue from the hearts of individual believers? Do not the latter collectively constitute the true "city of God"?

4. That the Greek text which requires "from within *him*" (and not: "from within *her*") is correct, so that the reference is to the individual believer, also agrees with the immediately following context, which is still speaking about "those . . . . who believed in him."

5. The Greek text and the translation based upon it are in exact accord with 4:14: "But whoever drinks the water that I shall give him will in no way be thirsty again forever, but the water that I shall give him *will be-*

---

[12] C. F. Burney, *The Aramaic Origin of the Fourth Gospel,* Oxford, 1922, p. 109; C. C. Torrey, *Our Translated Gospels,* New York and London, 1936, pp. 108-111; same author, *The Four Gospels, A New Translation,* New York and London, 1933, pp. 200, 201.

*come within him a spring of water that keeps on bubbling up unto ever-
lasting life."* We have heard (4:14) about the spring of water within the
believer's heart. We are now told (7:38) that from within him the rivers
of living water flow forth. What could be more consistent? The Lord, in
complete consistency with the very figure which he himself introduced
previously, gives it a new application.

For the reasons given we abide by the Greek text as it is. In a land where
water is not always within reach and the heat can at times make one feel
very uncomfortable, water is "the one thing needful" in the physical
realm.[13] It is, therefore, a fit symbol of salvation, everlasting life. Metaphorically speaking, in a sense *all men* are thirsty; i.e., by nature all lack
the water of life. In another sense, *those only* are thirsty who have been
regenerated and have received the inner call. As a result of the operation
of God's sovereign grace within their hearts, these feel the need of the
spiritual water. Though, accordingly, the well-meant invitation leaves
all the listeners responsible, only those *given* to Jesus by the Father will
actually come and drink. In the words "let him come to me and drink,"
we have two imperatives which should be regarded as aoristic presents.
When a person drinks of the Fountain, Christ, he never thirsts again
(4:14; 6:35). This has been expressed beautifully in the following lines
of the familiar hymn:

"I heard the voice of Jesus say,
'Behold, I freely give
The living water, thirsty one,
Stoop down and drink, and live.'
I came to Jesus, and I drank
Of that life-giving stream!
My thirst was quenched, my soul revived,
And now I live in him."

With this passage (7:37, 38) should be compared Is. 55:1, 2; Rev. 22:17.
The nominative absolute, so that we have in verse 38: *"He who believes
in me . . .* from within him" is not at all unusual in the writings of John
(cf. Rev. 3:12, 21). Since these words were originally spoken in Aramaic,
we can expect constructions of this nature. See vol. I, pp. 63, 64. Although
there is not any Old Testament passage which is the exact equivalent of
what is found here, it is certainly not difficult to discover the basic idea —
waters flowing forth from Zion (or from its citizens) as a blessing to others —
expressed in several passages: Prov. 11:25; 18:4; Ezek. 47:1-12; Zech. 8:14.
Particularly, the last two passages are very clear in this respect, and may

---

[13] See G. Dalman, *Jesus-Jeshua;* translated by Paul P. Levertoff; New York, 1929,
pp. 208, 209.

have been in the mind of Jesus when he uttered the contents of John 7:38. There are also other passages which show certain similarities to this one. The resemblance may be in the presence of the river within Zion, or in the emphasis on the abundance of the waters, or in the connection that is established between the waters (as the symbol) and the Spirit (as the One signified): Ps. 46:4, 5; Is. 58:11 (cf. also Is. 55:1); and Is. 44:3. Taking all these passages together, the clause *"As the scripture says"* is entirely justified.

The general idea of the passage is, of course, perfectly clear: not only do those who drink from the Fountain, Christ, receive lasting satisfaction *for themselves* — everlasting life, salvation full and free — (the idea expressed in 4:14), but in addition, life in a bounteous manner communicates itself *to others. The blessed one becomes, by God's sovereign grace, a channel of abundant blessings to others.* The church proclaims the message of salvation to the world, so that the elect from every clime and nation are gathered in.

39. This, as is clear from the entire New Testament — particularly from the book of Acts — became a reality in a special sense on and after the outpouring of the Holy Spirit on the day of Pentecost. For the meaning of *Spirit* see on 13:21. When that Spirit, as a Person, made the new Zion his central dwelling-place, the church became international. Hence, we are not surprised to read: **Now this he said about the Spirit, which those were to receive who believed in him.** To be sure, the third person of the Trinity *existed* from all eternity, and caused his influence to be felt long before Pentecost (cf. 3:3, 5); but **as yet the Spirit was not present** (ἦν is equal to παρῆν here), in the sense already indicated; the reason being **because Jesus was not yet glorified.** Just as believers cannot become the greatest possible blessing to the world until the Holy Spirit comes upon them (Acts 1:8), so also that Spirit could not come until Jesus was glorified (see on 16:7). The Old Testament connects the issuing forth of streams of blessing with the coming of the Spirit. Clearest is Is. 44:3.

---

40 So some of the people, having listened to these words, said, "This is indeed the prophet." 41 Others said, "This is the Christ." But some said, "Surely, the Christ does not come out of Galilee, does he? 42 Has not the scripture said that the Christ comes out of the seed of David and from Bethlehem, the village where David lived?" 43 So there was a division among the crowd because of him. 44 Some of them wanted to arrest him, but no one laid hold on him.

7:40-44

7:40-42. So some of the people, having listened to these words, said, This is indeed the prophet.

The effect of the words of tender invitation varied. Some said, "This is indeed the prophet." Whether they saw in this prophet (of Deut. 18:15-18) the Christ, is not certain. See also on 1:21. **Others,** however, were far more definite. **They said, This is the Christ.** They accepted Jesus as the promised Messiah. But again, this does not mean that all of those who said this accepted him with a living faith as the One who came to save his people from their sin! A third group is convinced that Jesus cannot be the Christ at all. We read, **But some said, Surely, the Christ does not come out of Galilee, does he?** It was a question which anticipated a *negative* answer. It was followed by a corresponding one, expecting a *positive* reply: **Has not the scripture said that the Christ comes out of the seed of David and from Bethlehem, the village where David lived?** Note the following:

1. The objection raised by these people was the same as in 6:42 and 7:27. The objectors should have presented their difficulty to Jesus. Failing to do so, they must be accounted as guilty of rejecting him.

2. *The major premise* — namely, that the Christ comes out of the seed of David and from Bethlehem, the village where David lived — was entirely correct. Although certain orthodox commentators deny the former and believe (on the basis of what we regard as an erroneous interpretation of Lk. 1:5, 36) that Jesus (according to his human nature) and his mother Mary did not descend from David, this is, nevertheless, the uniform teaching of Scripture: II Sam. 7:12, 13; Acts 2:30; Rom. 1:3; II Tim. 2:8; Rev. 5:5.[14] It is also true, of course, that the Messiah was to be born in Bethlehem, according to prophecy (Mic. 5:2). This was the official Sanhedrin interpretation of that famous prophecy, and it was correct! See Matt. 2:6. But *the minor premise* — this man, Jesus, though probably of Davidic lineage, was not born in Bethlehem but in Galilee — was wrong. Hence, *the conclusion* — he cannot be the Christ — was also wrong.

43, 44. So there was a division among the crowd because of him.

The result of the expression of these three opinions was a division or *schism* (σχίσμα) among the people. **Some of them wanted to arrest him** — cf. 7:30 — **but no one laid hold on him.** For this see on 7:32. But officers had already been sent to arrest Jesus; which introduces us to the next paragraph:

---

[14] See discussion of the Genealogy of Jesus in my *Bible Survey*, Grand Rapids, Mich., third edition, 1952, pp. 135-139.

45 So the officers came back to the chief priests and Pharisees, who said to them, "Why did y o u not bring him?" 46 The officers answered, "Never did a man speak as this man speaks." 47 The Pharisees, therefore, answered them, "It surely cannot be that y o u also have been led astray? 48 None of the rulers or of the Pharisees believed in him, did they? 49 But this rabble that does not know the law, accursed are they!" 50 Nicodemus, one of their number, the one who had come to him previously, said, 51 "Our law does not judge a man before giving him a hearing and learning what he is doing, does it?" [15] 52 They answered and said to him, "You are not also, perhaps, from Galilee, are you? Search and see that out of Galilee there arises no prophet."

7:45-52

7:45-49. So the officers came back to the chief priests and Pharisees, who said to them, Why did y o u not bring him?

The officers now return. What is described in this closing paragraph must have taken place in an official meeting of the Sanhedrin. What immediately arrested the attention of the council was that the officers returned *empty-handed;* i.e., without Jesus. Thoroughly perplexed the superiors exclaimed: "Why did y o u not bring him?" In their reply **the officers** show a. that they had been deeply impressed by the words of Jesus (perhaps, because he emphasized the grace of God, as in 7:37, rather than the work of man); and b. that they had the courage to admit this. They **answered, Never did a man speak as this man speaks.** In a state of violent agitation the Pharisees, when they notice that Jesus has overawed those who had been sent to arrest him and that he has cast a spell over them, burst out with an exclamation full of scorn, an accusation character-ized by sarcasm:

The Pharisees, therefore, answered them, It surely cannot be that y o u also have been led astray? None of the rulers or of the Pharisees believed in him, did they? But this rabble that does not know the law, accursed are they! Note the following:

1. When the officers said, "Never did a man speak as this man speaks," they meant: *so divinely,* with such unaffected grace and truth and therefore so convincingly and so effectively. But the Sanhedrists change this into: *so cleverly,* with such a sinister purpose *to lead astray.*

2. The Pharisees try to impress upon these "underlings," who had not made a special study of the law, that it was wrong for them to have a mind of their own. Questions touching the identity and character of the Mes-siah should have been left entirely to *the experts!*

3. With disdain these Jewish leaders, who see their power slipping away

---

[15] Conditional sentence in 7:37 is IIIB3! see Vol. I, p. 44; the one in 7:51 is III A 2; see Vol. I, pp. 41, 43.

from them, look down upon the unlettered crowds, the "people of the soil," the mere rabble, the riffraff. The basic idea of the Pharisees was that the study of the law is able to make one wise and pious. Hence, the crowd must be ignorant and wicked.

50-52. Opposition arises, however, within their own camp: **Nicodemus, one of their number, the man who had come to him previously** — see on 3:1-21 —, **said, Our law does not judge a man before giving** (or: "if it does not first give") **him a hearing and learning what he is doing, does it?** It is remarkable that immediately after the Pharisees have asserted by implication that surely none of the leaders have believed in Jesus as the Christ, one of their own number speaks favorably about him. Perhaps even more noteworthy is the fact that the men who have just a moment before denounced the "rabble" because of their ignorance of the law now have their own ignorance exposed! Or if not ignorance, then something worse: *unwillingness* to obey the law in this one, particular case; namely, the case of Jesus. The hasty verdict of the Sanhedrists, a judgment which implied that in their eyes he was a deceiver (7:47), worthy of arrest (7:32) and even of death (5:18), was a gross violation of a basic human law — observed even among pagans — confirmed by a Mosaic ordinance (Ex. 23:1; Deut. 1:16, 17), to the effect that Justice must be impartial and must always give a man a fair hearing before condemning him! It has been said that Nicodemus acted rather weakly in this instance. He merely asked a question. But it must be noted that Nicodemus was being opposed by a large and very powerful machine in the religious world. Nicodemus showed great courage, though it is true that he had not yet risen to the pinnacle of Christian confession.

It is with evident scorn and indignation that **they** (the Pharisees) **answered and said to him, You are not also, perhaps, from Galilee, are you? Search and see that out of Galilee there arises no prophet.** The accusation implied in the question of Nicodemus — namely, that these men who pride themselves on being the guardians of the law are themselves breaking the law — was unanswerable. A defence was simply impossible. The leaders should have admitted it. But instead of admitting the charge of one of their number they chose to ignore it and to give him an answer which implied that they regarded him as being insincere. It must be that he, too, hailed from Galilee! Out of Galilee came Jesus, and out of Galilee came some of the people who regarded him as being at least the prophet of Deut. 18:15-18. And in Galilee the law was not studied as in Jerusalem! A curse upon those Galileans!

In their deep-seated wrath, a wrath born of jealousy, the Pharisees even commit a rather serious error. They challenge Nicodemus to search the Scriptures. If he does this, he will soon discover that Galilee never produces any prophet (hence, certainly not the Messiah). They forgot about Jonah (II Kings 14:25; cf. Jonah 1:1) and perhaps also about Hosea and Nahum (cf. Capernaum; according to some: village of Nahum, the prophet), and about the fact that Scripture simply does not reveal the place of origin of every prophet. Thus, the Christ was again rejected. In fact, the attitude of the leaders, moved by envy, had become even more bitter than before. But the attempt of the Sanhedrin to arrest him at this time failed completely.

Synthesis of Chapter 7

See the Outline on p. 2. *The Son of God Earnestly Exhorting Sinners to Repent. At the Feast of Tabernacles in Jerusalem He Exclaims to the Multitudes in the Temple: "If any one thirsts, let him come to me and drink." He is Bitterly Resisted by His Enemies.*

The Galilean Ministry is ended. Then came six months of relative withdrawal (called the Retirement Ministry), spent in the northern regions of the country. With 7:2 begins the account of the Later Judean Ministry, which lasted from October to December of the year 29 A.D., and which included Christ's appearance in Jerusalem at the feast of Tabernacles and at that of Dedication. Under the general theme:

"The Son of God, attending the feast of Tabernacles at Jerusalem, makes his urgent appeal, but is bitterly resisted by his enemies" we have the following subdivisions:

1. His deliberate delay in attending the feast

2. The divided sentiment at the feast among the people who were expecting him to attend

3. The reaction to his sudden appearance; reaction of:

a. *The leaders.* Already filled with anger against him because of the happenings at Bethzatha, their hostility increases in bitterness when they notice that he not only confirms his earlier exalted claims but also exposes their inconsistent reasoning anent the sabbath, and that within the crowd there is considerable sentiment in his favor. Hence, they make an abortive attempt to arrest him.

b. *Some of the citizens of Jerusalem.* These reject him because they "know where he comes from."

c. *Many of the pilgrims.* On the basis of his signs they regard him as being the Messiah.

4. His urgent appeal (tender invitation, earnest exhortation).

a. Its contents (verses 37, 38, with explanatory remark in verse 40).

b. Its reception:

(1) *By the crowds.* The sentiment was divided. Some said: "This is the prophet"; others, "This is the Christ"; still others, "Surely, the Christ does not come out of Galilee, does he?"

(2) *By the officers* who had been sent to arrest him: "Never did a man speak as this man speaks."

(3) *By the Pharisees,* in an official Sanhedrin-session. In a sneering criticism addressed to the officers who had failed to arrest him, these Pharisees show that they regard him as one who leads astray "the accursed rabble (riffraff) that does not know the law."

(4) *By Nicodemus.* In an appeal to the law he defends Jesus' right to a full and fair hearing.

CHAPTER VIII

8 53 And they went each to his own house; 1 but Jesus went to the Mount of Olives. 2 And early in the morning he came again to the temple, and all the people came to him. And having seated himself, he began to teach them. 3 So the scribes and Pharisees brought a woman who had been caught in adultery; and having set her in the midst, 4 they said to him, "Teacher, this woman was caught in the very act of adultery. 5 Now in the law Moses commanded us to stone such. So what do you say?" 6 This they were saying to tempt him, in order that they might have some charge to bring against him. But Jesus bent down and wrote [16] with his fingers on the ground. 7 And as they kept on questioning him, he stood up and said to them, "Let him who is without sin among y o u be the first to cast a stone at her." 8 And again he bent down and wrote [16] on the ground. 9 But when they heard it, they went away, one by one, beginning with the eldest, and he was left behind alone, and the woman in the midst. 10 Jesus raised himself and said to her, "Woman, where are they? Has no one condemned you?" 11 She said, "No one, Lord." So Jesus said, "Neither do I condemn you. Go and from now on sin no more."

7:53 — 8:11

Preliminary Comments

Much has been written with respect to the authenticity of this story. Is it to be considered a genuine part of the Fourth Gospel written (or at least dictated) by the apostle John? Also, regardless of whether John himself wrote it, does it belong in the Bible, or should it be removed from Scripture? In answer to the first question it should be clearly stated that the facts at our disposal do not enable us to declare definitely that the apostle himself wrote or dictated this account. As to the second, it is our conviction that these same facts indicate that no attempt should be made to remove this portion from Holy Writ.

The facts, then, are as follows:

1. The story contains several words which do not occur elsewhere in any of John's writings. This, however, is not entirely decisive.

---

[16] Respectively κατέγραφεν (verse 6) and ἔγραφεν (verse 8), here perhaps *traced* (figures or letters). There are variants, but not strongly supported.

2. The oldest and best manuscripts (Aleph, A, B, L, N, W) do not have this story. It makes its first appearance in Codex Bezae. It is found in the later uncials (the so-called Koine text) and the cursives based upon them. Thus it found its way into the A.V. The A.R.V. has the story, but places it between brackets, and states in the margin: "Most of the ancient authorities omit John 7:53-8:11. Those which contain it vary much from each other." Some manuscripts place it at the close of the Fourth Gospel and some (the Ferrar cursives) after Luke 21:38.

3. Some of the old Latin witnesses (a, f, g) and also the Syriac sin., Syriac cur., Peshito, as well as the Sahidic (Upper Egypt), Armenian, and Gothic translations omit this portion. Moreover, the Greek expositors Origen, Cyril of Alexandria, Chrysostom, Nonnus, and Theophylact fail to comment on it. It is found *here* (i.e., between 7:52 and 8:12) in some Old Latin witnesses (b, c, e, ff, j), in the Vulgate, and in the Palestinian Syriac translation.

Now, if there were no additional information with respect to this paragraph, the evidence in its favor would be very weak, indeed. We are not at all surprised that A. T. Robertson regards it as a marginal gloss which through a scribal error crept into the text.[17] Lenski expresses himself in no uncertain language, regards it as spurious, and omits it completely from his exposition. E. J. Goodspeed considers it an anecdote which should be omitted.

4. However, the matter is not simple by any means. There are facts which point in the opposite direction:

The story fits very well into the present context. It can be viewed as serving to prepare for and to elucidate the discourse of the Lord in 8:12 ff. Let it be borne in mind that this woman had been walking in moral *darkness*. It is probable that Jesus dispelled her darkness. So, we are not surprised to read in verse 12: "I am the *light* of the world."

5. The Christ as pictured here (7:53-8:11) is entirely "in character": as he is described here so he is also pictured elsewhere. Here is the Savior who came not to condemn but to save, and who actually did save such persons as the woman of Lk. 7, the Samaritan woman, publicans, sinners. Here the One who told the touching parable of "the prodigal *son*" is shown in the act of revealing his tender mercy to a prodigal *daughter*. And the scribes and Pharisees, too, are "in character." These men who had shown very clearly that they cared more for their own sabbath-regulations than for the total recovery of the paralytic at the pool (ch. 5) reveal their utter lack of human consideration in the case of this woman.

6. Papias, a disciple of the apostle John, seems to have known this story

---

[17] A. T. Robertson, *Introduction to the Textual Criticism of the New Testament*, New York, 1925, p. 154.

and to have expounded it. Says Eusebius: "The same writer (Papias) has expounded another *story about a woman who was accused before the Lord of many sins,* which the Gospel according to the Hebrews contains" (*Ecclesiastical History* III, xxxix, 17). It would seem, therefore, that Papias already knew this story, that he regarded it of sufficient importance for exposition, but that he did not find it in *John's* Gospel. Was it never there, or had it been removed for certain reasons?

7. Augustine has stated definitely that certain individuals had removed from their codices the section regarding the adulteress, because they feared that women would appeal to this story as an excuse for their infidelity (*De adulterinis conjugiis* II, vii). Closely connected with this is the fact that asceticism played an important role in the sub-apostolic age. Hence, the suggestion that the section (7:53-8:11) was at one time actually part of John's Gospel but had been removed from it cannot be entirely dismissed.

Our final conclusion, then, is this: though it cannot now be proved that this story formed an integral part of the Fourth Gospel, neither is it possible to establish the opposite with any degree of finality. We believe, moreover, that what is here recorded really took place, and contains nothing that is in conflict with the apostolic spirit. Hence, instead of removing this section from the Bible it should be retained and used for our benefit.[18] Ministers should not be afraid to base sermons upon it! On the other hand, *all* the facts concerning the textual evidence should be made known!

7:53, 8:1. And they went each to his own house: but Jesus went to the Mount of Olives.

The men who had been sent to arrest Jesus had returned empty-handed. So the Sanhedrin-session adjourns and the members go home. The multitude in the temple also betake themselves to their dwellings. Jesus retires for the night to the Mount of Olives, perhaps to lodge in Gethsemane, or else at the hospitable abode of Mary, Martha, and Lazarus in Bethany (located just over the ridge, to the east of the mount). Cf. Luke 21:37; 22:39. Did Jesus withdraw from the city in order to avoid the danger of arrest, knowing that the appropriate time for his arrest and crucifixion had not yet arrived?

2. However that may be, **early in the morning he came again to the temple.** Whether this was the eighth day of the feast or the day after

---

[18] Cf. John Calvin, *op. cit.,* p. 156; Satis constat historiam hanc olim Graecis fuisse ignotam. Itaque nonnulli coniiciunt aliunde assutam esse. Sed quia semper a Latinis Ecclesiis recepta fuit et in plurimis vetustis Graecorum codicibus reperitur, et nihil Apostolico Spiritu indignum continet, non est cur in usum nostrum accommodare recusemus. — The opposite view is defended by E. J. Goodspeed in *Problems of New Testament Translation,* Chicago, 1945, pp. 105-109.

we do not know, as has been pointed out; see explanation of 7:37-39. **As usual, all the people came to him. And having seated himself** (contrast 7:37) **he began to teach them.**

3. So the scribes and Pharisees brought a woman who had been caught in adultery.

Presently some pharisaic scribes — men who copied, interpreted, and taught the law — enter and create a disturbance. They are bringing a woman who had been caught in the very act of adultery. From the use of the term μοιχεία it may be inferred that she was a married woman. Her arrest may have been ordered by the temple-police. It is just *possible* that the men who brought her before Jesus belonged to the Sanhedrin, and that they were intending to take her before that official body to be sentenced. However, the story rather leaves the impression that these religious leaders are merely using this woman as a tool, and that they are not interested in bringing her before the Sanhedrin. So, as if they really thought that Jesus had authority to judge such cases, they push her through the crowd that had gathered around the Master until she is right *in front of* him. **And having set her in the midst** of the staring multitude,

4, 5. they said to him: Teacher, this woman was caught in the very act (ἐπ' αὐτοφώρῳ: literally, in the very act of *thievery*, but later on *in the very act* of *any* gross sin) **of adultery. Now in the law Moses commanded us to stone such. So what do you say?** Note the following:

1. The feast of Tabernacles, as it was actually celebrated, was a gay festival. It is not surprising that immoral acts occurred when so many people were crowded together amid such hilarity and merry-making.

2. Many commentators argue that this cannot have been a married woman, because "the law of Moses" specifies death *by stoning* only in the case of a *betrothed girl* who is guilty of adultery (Deut. 22:23 f.), but commands that the *married woman* who commits such a sin be put to death, without stating the manner in which this punishment is to be carried out (whether by stoning, strangulation, or in some other way). But over against this stands the fact that the term "adultery" points definitely to one who is already married. Besides, Ezek. 23:43, 44, 47 seems to indicate that — whatever may have been prescribed subsequently in the Talmud (death by *strangulation* for married women) — it was the original intention of the Mosaic law that also married women who committed such acts of infidelity were to be *stoned* to death.

3. The question has been asked: "What purpose did these scribes and Pharisees have in bringing this woman before Jesus and in asking him this question?" Various answers have been suggested; such as:

a. To bring him into the dilemma of showing disrespect either for the law of Moses (if he would answer: "Do not stone her") or for the Roman law (if he would demand that this woman be stoned to death, while according to the Roman law the Jews were not permitted to execute anyone);

b. to make him face the alternative of becoming either an enemy of the law of Moses (if he would advise that she be not stoned) or else an enemy of the common people whose defender he was reputed to be.

But in the present instance the answer to the question is clearly stated in verse 6.

6. This they were saying to tempt him, in order that they might have some charge to bring against him. The verb πειράζω is here used in its evil sense (contrast 6:6), *to lead into sin.* Their purpose clearly was this: to cause Jesus to give an answer which would be in violation of the law of Moses; next, to place this as an official charge against him; then on the basis of this charge, to have him condemned by the Sanhedrin at an official session; and finally, by branding him as a transgressor, to destroy his influence with the people.

This purpose may also explain why the *man* who was involved in this transgression was not brought before the Lord. For the fabrication of a charge against Jesus the arrest of one party was sufficient. In this connection it is not at all certain that the scribes and Pharisees *actually* meant to have this woman stoned. They were not primarily interested in *her;* they were simply using her *case* in order to get at Jesus, who was their real intended victim! And in order to carry out their diabolical purpose against him, they threw kindness and diffidence to the winds. The shame or fears of this woman, in being thus publicly exposed, meant nothing to them as long as their purpose was being achieved. Such were the "religious" leaders in Jerusalem! It is only when in our thoughts we enter somewhat into the tragically perverse condition of hearts so steeped in wickedness that we can appreciate the reaction of Jesus, which is now recorded:

But Jesus bent down and wrote with his finger on the ground. Jesus stooped down (cf. Mark 1:7), bowing his head toward the ground. Then with his finger he wrote on the ground or traced figures in it. Various explanations have been given; as follows: a. Jesus wrote down the names and sins of the men who had brought this woman to him; b. Jesus wrote a word of warning that was aimed at these scribes and Pharisees; c. Jesus doodled, as one does when he is day-dreaming, showing that he simply was not interested in questions such as these, for his purpose in coming into the world was not to judge but to save (with this last clause we are, of course, in hearty agreement); d. Jesus was at a loss what to say; hence, he merely scribbled something in the sand.

It has not pleased the Lord to reveal to us whether Jesus wrote certain words or traced figures; and if the former, *what* he wrote, *for whom* he wrote, or *why* he wrote. Nevertheless, if an explanation is to be attempted at all, it should be in thorough keeping with the context, which, as we have seen, pictured the depths of human depravity, the depravity not so much of this woman but rather of these self-righteous and wicked scribes and Pharisees, these men with murder in their hearts, willing to use this woman as a mere tool to carry out their sinister plot against Jesus. It is in keeping with this context that we believe there is much to say in favor of the explanation that Jesus was so thoroughly shocked by the brazen hardness of his enemies that for a long time he remained silent, simply scribbling figures or letters in the sand. This was a silence that spoke louder than words. It reminds one of Rev. 8:1.[19] In both passages it is a symbol of horror. The silent scribbling in the sand, which both precedes and follows the words which Jesus spoke at this occasion, imparts to them a setting of majesty and awe.

7, 8. And as they kept questioning him, he stood up and said to them, Let him who is without sin among y o u be the first to cast a stone at her. And again he bent down and wrote (or: traced figures or letters) **on the ground.**

Unabashed by the first silence, the persecutors kept on pressing for an answer. We can imagine that their conversation was on this order, as they stood there, crowding the Lord: "Well, what do *you* say . . . do you agree with Moses . . . what do you say . . . shall we stone her, as the law of Moses requires . . . or shall we release her . . .what do *you* say . . . what do *you* say?"

To add weight to his answer (cf. 7:37) Jesus arose. He then gave a reply such as only he was able to give. He did not make light of her sin. Neither did he either expressly or by implication abolish the seventh commandment. He did not even in so many words set aside the law which demanded the death-penalty for offences such as these. On the contrary, without in any way implying that he personally desired her death, he proceeded upon *their presumed* assumption, as if the law of Moses were to be literally applied in this given case — which even they themselves, of course, did not *really* want —; but then he showed them that they were not fit to execute the very law which *ostensibly* they were so eager to carry out! What caused his cheeks to burn with indignation was the fact that these men, intent upon committing the sin of murdering the very Messiah, posed as if they were shocked by the infinitely lesser (though still grievous) offence of this woman! Hence, he said: "Let him who is without sin among y o u be the first to cast a stone at her." The reference is to Deut. 17:7: "The hand of the witnesses shall be the first upon him to put him to death, and

---

[19] Cf. *More Than Conquerors*, sixth edition, Grand Rapids, Mich., 1952, p. 141.

afterward the hand of all the people." These scribes and Pharisees were acting in the capacity of witnesses and accusers. Yet the sin of the accused was as nothing in comparison with *their* perverseness.

9. But when they heard it, they went away, one by one, beginning with the eldest, and he was left behind alone, and the woman in the midst. One can almost see the accusers slink away, one by one, beginning with the eldest, until this entire crowd of scribes and Pharisees had melted away. Why did they withdraw? Was it because they had become ashamed of their own sinful condition? Or was it because they had been outgeneraled (and were now at a loss what to say or what to do), having completely failed to elicit from the lips of Jesus an answer which could form the basis of a charge against him? There is nothing in the context which suggests the former alternative. They had suffered a humiliating defeat, and the eldest among them were also the first to see this; hence, they were the first to disappear. The rest followed.

The words, "He was left behind alone, and the woman in the midst," have caused considerable difficulty. It has been asked: "If he was left behind *alone* with this woman, how could she still be described as being 'in the midst'?" The simplest and truest answer is probably this: though the inner circle (consisting of scribes and Pharisees) had vanished, the outer circle (the multitude) was still present; hence, the woman is still "in the midst" of the crowd.

10. Jesus raised himself and said to her, Woman, where are they? Has no one condemned you? Not as if Jesus did not know! But he wished to impress upon her the great favor he had bestowed upon her. Let her revolve this in her mind and let her give expression to it; namely, that the sentence of condemnation, though demanded by the law of Moses, had not been pronounced against her by anyone.

11. She said, No one, Lord. Jesus in a tone of gentle reassurance and earnest admonition **said to her: Neither do I condemn you. Go, and from now on sin no more.** In thorough conformity with 3:17 and Luke 12:14 Jesus did not cast this woman aside or condemn her as unfit for the kingdom. For adulterers and adulteresses there is, indeed, a place in that kingdom, *if they discontinue to live in adultery* (Luke 7:47).

Synthesis of 7:53 — 8:11

See the Outline on p. 2. *The Son of God Exhorting the Woman Taken in Adultery: "Go and from now on sin no more."*

Though it cannot be proved that this story formed a part of the Fourth Gospel (as originally written by John), neither is it possible to establish the opposite. The story should be retained and used for our benefit.

The members of the Sanhedrin, their attempt to arrest Jesus having failed, have gone home. The multitude has left the temple. Jesus has retired for the night to the Mt. of Olives. When early next morning he returns to the temple, all the people come to him and he teaches them.

Pharisaic scribes cause an interruption. To Jesus they bring a woman caught in the act of adultery, and they ask him: "In the law Moses commands to stone such. So what do you say?" In order to undermine his influence with the people they are trying to expose him as an opponent of Moses.

This readiness on their part to use even the most sordid means to carry out their wicked plot against him causes him to remain silent for a considerable length of time as, shocked beyond words, he scribbles figures or letters in the sand. He then says: "Let him who is without sin among y o u be the first to cast a stone at her."

Sensing their defeat, they begin to slink away one by one, the eldest being the first to do so. The woman is left behind in the midst of the gathered multitude. With characteristic tenderness Jesus addresses her in these memorable words: "Woman, has no one condemned you?" Her negative answer is followed by his reassuring remark: "Neither do I condemn y o u. Go, and from now on sin no more."

---

12 Again, therefore, Jesus spoke to them, saying, "I am the light of the world. He who follows me will not walk in the darkness, but will have the light of life." 13 In reply the Pharisees said to him, "You are testifying concerning yourself; your testimony is not true." 14 Jesus answered and said to them, "Even if I testify concerning myself, my testimony is certainly true, because I know where I came from and where I am going [20]; but y o u do not know where I came from and where I am going. 15 Y o u judge according to the flesh, I judge no one. 16 Yet, even if I do judge, my judgment is true, for I am not alone but I and the One who sent me.[21] 17 And in y o u r law it is written that the testimony of two men is true. 18 I am the One who is bearing testimony concerning myself, and One bears testimony concerning me; namely, my Sender [22], the Father. 19 They were saying therefore to him, "Where is your Father?" Jesus answered, "Y o u know neither me nor my Father; if y o u knew me, y o u would know my Father also." [23] 20 These words he spoke in the Treasury as he was teaching in the temple. And no one arrested him, because his hour had not yet arrived.

8:12-20

8:12. Again, therefore, Jesus spoke to them saying, I am the light of the world.

---

20 IIIB1; see Vol. I, p. 44.
21 IIIB1; see Vol. I, p. 44.
22 Literally: "he who sent me."
23 IIA; see Vol. I, p. 41.

According to many this is the continuation of 7:37-52. It must be granted that such a connection is, indeed, possible. One might reason as follows: he who according to 7:37, 38 represents himself as being *living water* for the thirsty one, reveals himself here (in 8:12) as *light* for those who sit in darkness. So rich and glorious is he that not a single name can describe him, and not a single metaphor can do justice to his greatness. He is life, light, bread, water, etc.

Others, however, see a very close connection between the story of the adulteress (7:53—8:11) and the present paragraph (8:12 ff.). They reason that Jesus, by dispelling the moral *darkness* which reigned in the heart of this woman (if, indeed, it was dispelled!), gave an illustration of his work as the *light* of the world. We do not have sufficient information to make a definite choice between these alternatives. The decision would depend on the authenticity of 7:53—8:11, which has been discussed.

Jesus is again addressing the people in the temple. To them he says, "I am the light of the world." This is the second of the seven great "I Am's." For the entire list see Vol. I, p. 37. This second "I Am" is similar in grammatical structure to the first (see our explanation of 6:35). Hence, also in this case subject and predicate (the latter preceded by the article) are interchangeable. Jesus is the light of the world; the light of the world is Jesus. He himself in person is that light. *He* — no one else beside him — is that light, for it is only in and through him that God's glorious attributes shine forth most brilliantly in the midst of the world.

The meaning of Christ as light has been set forth in connection with 1:4 and 1:9. That Jesus represents himself (here in 8:12) as the light of *the world* indicates that in the midst of sin-laden mankind, exposed to the judgment and in need of salvation, mankind in *all* its phases (both Jew and Gentile, young and old, male and female, rich and poor, free and slave), he stands forth as the source of men's illumination regarding spiritual matters and of the everlasting salvation of God's children. To all who come within hearing he proclaims the Gospel of deliverance from sin and never-ending peace. On the concept *world* (κόσμος) see the explanation of 1:10.[24]

Jesus is the *light* of the world; i.e., to the ignorant he proclaims wisdom; to the impure, holiness; to those in sadness, gladness. Moreover, to those who by sovereign grace are drawn (6:44) to the light and follow its guidance he not only *proclaims* but actually *imparts* these blessings.

---

[24] Instructive with respect to the meaning of this term is what H. Bavinck says in his *Gereformeerde Dogmatiek*, third edition, Kampen, 1918, Vol. III, p. 527; and what L. Berkhof states in his *Vicarious Atonement Through Christ*, Grand Rapids, Mich., 1936, p. 167. Both of these authors point out that in certain passages of the New Testament (including the Gospel of John) the word has reference to *all nations*, and that it lays stress on the fact that the Gospel is not limited to the Jews.

But not all follow where the light leads. There is a separation, a parting of the ways, an absolute antithesis, as is clear from the words, "He who follows me will not walk in the darkness, but will have the light of life." Some follow the light; many do not. Many are called; few are chosen.

To *follow* the light, Christ, means to trust and obey him. It means to believe in him and out of gratitude to keep his commandments. Man must follow where the light leads: he is not permitted to ,map out his own course through the desert of this life. In the wilderness the forefathers had followed the pillar of light. The symbolism of the feast of Tabernacles (now in progress or just ended) reminded the audience of this light which the ancestors had enjoyed as a guide. Those who had followed it and had not rebelled against its guidance had reached Canaan. The others had died in the desert. So it is here: the true followers not only will not walk in the darkness of moral and spiritual ignorance, of impurity, and of gloom, but will reach the land of light. Nay more: they will *have* the light! The Antitype is ever richer than the type. Physical light — for example, that of the pillar of light in the desert or that of the candelabra in the Court of the Women — imparts *outward* illumination. *This* light, Jesus Christ as the object of our faith, becomes our *inner* possession: we *have* him, and this abidingly; cf. 4:14. He is, moreover, the light *of life* (τὸ φῶς τῆς ζωῆς). In harmony with what was said in connection with 1:4b we regard this as a genitive of apposition: the light is itself the life, when the latter is made manifest.[25]

13. Jesus had made a majestic claim. In reply, **the Pharisees said to him, You are testifying concerning yourself; your testimony is not true.** In connection with this verse and those that follow see our comments on 5:31. The Pharisees certainly cannot have meant, "Though your testimony with reference to yourself may be true, it is not legally valid or acceptable." What they actually meant was this: "When you call yourself the light of the world, you are just boasting. No one confirms your testimony with reference to yourself; hence, it cannot be *true*."

14. When **Jesus answered and said to them, Even if I testify concerning myself, my testimony is certainly true,** he is not in any way contradicting what he had said previously (see on 5:31). In corroboration of the true character of his own testimony, as contrasted with the false character of Pharisaic assertions, the Lord points to: a. his heavenly origin and destination (verse 14b); b. his intimate union with the Father (verses 15, 16); and c. the perfect agreement between his own testimony and that of the Father (verses 17, 18).

With respect to a. Jesus says, . . . **because I know where I came from**

---

[25] Cf. on 8:12 the article by J. L. Koole, in *GThT*, XLIII (1942), 406-408.

and where I am going. What he means is this: *I know myself.* This knowledge, moreover, is not only immediate, intuitive, and reflective (οἶδα) but also complete: I know the facts about myself, where I came from (from heaven, from God) and where I am going (to heaven, to God). Hence when I say that I am the light of the world, this declaration is based upon my perfect self-consciousness and should, accordingly, be accepted. Y o u, on the contrary, have no such knowledge respecting myself: **but y o u do not know where I came from and where I am going.** Hence y o u r denial of my testimony regarding myself is worthless.

15, 16. With respect to b. Jesus continues, **Y o u judge according to the flesh. I judge no one. Yet even if I do judge, my judgment is true, for I am not alone but I and the One who sent me.**

Note that b. naturally follows a. What the Lord means is this: though y o u lack the necessary knowledge to judge, yet y o u are constantly judging me. Y o u are doing this, moreover, according to earthly standards, according to external appearance (on σάρξ see the explanation of 1:14). So judged, I am not the light of the world but merely a countryman from Galilee, the son of Joseph. See the explanation of 6:42, 7:24, 41, 42, 52. On the other hand, I, though (because of my perfect knowledge of self and of others) able to judge, judge no one. See the explanation of 3:17-19. I did not come to judge but to save. Yet, even if judgment is rendered inevitable because of the hardness of men's hearts, so that though I came to save I still must judge some people, my judgment is true, genuine, the real thing (ἀληθινή), for, far from being contrary to the divine will, it is a judgment in which the Father and the Son unite. On "I and the One who *sent* me" see 3:34; 5:19, 30, 36, 37; cf. 1:6. It is not the judgment of a mere man, as y o u think, but of God.

17, 18. With respect to c. (the perfect agreement between his own testimony and that of his Father) Jesus continues, **And in y o u r law it is written that the testimony of two men is true.** The reference is to such passages as Deut. 17:6 ("At the mouth of two witnesses or three witnesses, shall he that is to die be put to death; at the mouth of one witness he shall not be put to death"), cf. Num. 35:30. *Y o u r* law, because y o u claim to regard it so highly. The reasoning is this: surely, if this rule holds wtih respect to men, it holds *even more* with respect to God. The argument is from the minor to the major. The testimony (ἡ μαρτυρία; see the explanation of 1:6) of two witnesses was considered *true,* not merely "legally on the table" or "valid" (legally acceptable). That the translation "true" is correct here — and that its meaning must not be toned down in any way — follows also from the fact that, according to the law of Moses to which reference is made, when two such witnesses agreed, the man concerning whom they agreed *had to be put to death!* The testimony was regarded as entirely

43

reliable, a proper basis for drastic action. Of course, the witnesses had to be trustworthy persons, not false or unrighteous. This, too, was plainly stipulated in the law (Deut. 19:16-19). Surely, the Father and the Son are both reliable! Hence, their witness with respect to Jesus must be accepted. It is a testimony in which the two (Father and Son) — each being a reliable witness — completely agree. In our translation of verse 18 we have preserved the chiastic sentence-structure of the original. Note that the names of the two witnesses occur at the very beginning and at the very end of the sentence, to emphasize the independent character of each. Each, standing by himself, is thoroughly reliable (on .this cf. verse 14, "Even if I testify concerning myself, my testimony is certainly true"); both agreeing, the argument becomes doubly unanswerable. **I am the One who is bearing testimony concerning myself, and One bears testimony concerning me; namely, my Sender, the Father.** For the testimony of the Father concerning the Son see on 5:31-40.

19. The Jews, who had rejected the testimony of the Son, now also reject the testimony of the Father. **In reply, they were saying to him, Where is your Father?** These words were probably accompanied with a gesture of disdain. They clearly indicate that Christ's teaching with reference to the Father had fallen on deaf ears. The Pharisees were engaged in the most dangerous activity found among men: they were hardening their hearts! Such hardening results in total blindness and ignorance. Hence, **Jesus answered, Y o u know neither me nor my Father; if y o u knew me, y o u would know my Father also.** The one and only way to the Father is the Son; cf. 5:38; 14:7, 9; Matt. 11:27.

20. These words he spoke in the Treasury, as he was teaching in the temple. Against the wall in the Court of Women stood thirteen trumpet-shaped chests in which the people deposited their gifts for various causes. Hence, taking the part for the whole, this court was sometimes called the Treasury. Here Jesus was teaching, in the immediate proximity of the hall in which the Sanhedrin held (or: used to hold) its sessions. **And,** though it is possible that this august body, so thoroughly hostile to Jesus, could almost hear the echo of his voice, **no one arrested him, because his hour had not yet arrived.** On the meaning of these words see 7:30.

---

21 So he said again to them, "I am going away, and y o u will seek me, but y o u will die in y o u r sin. Where I am going y o u cannot come." 22 The Jews, therefore, were saying, "He is not going to kill himself, is he, since [26] he says, 'Where I am going y o u cannot come'?" 23 So he was saying to them, "Y o u are from below, I am from above; y o u are of this world, I am not of

---

[26] On ὅτι see pp. 55, 56, 59.

this world." 24 Did I not say to y o u that [27] y o u would die in y o u r sins? For if y o u will not believe that I am he, y o u will die in y o u r sins." [28] 25 In reply, they were saying to him, *"You,* who are *you?"* Jesus said to them, "Exactly what I am telling y o u." 26 I have many things to say concerning y o u and to judge. But he who sent me is true, and whatsoever I have heard from him, these things I speak to the world." 27 They did not recognize that he spoke to them of the Father. 28 So Jesus said, "When y o u will have lifted up the Son of man, then y o u will know that I am he, and that of myself I do nothing but speak thus as the Father taught me. 29 And he who sent me is with me. He has not left me alone, because I always do the things that are pleasing to him."

8:21-29

8:21. So he said again to them, I am going away, and y o u will seek me, but y o u will die in y o u r sin. Where I am going y o u cannot come.

Because of the derisive manner in which the Jews had treated the testimony of Jesus, he again announces their doom. He said *again* what he had declared earlier (see 7:33, 34). The words, "Yet a little while I am with y o u," are now omitted, perhaps because this time no one is attempting to arrest him. The going away to which Jesus refers indicates his departure to the Father (see on 7:33, 34). When it is added, "And y o u will seek me," to what does Jesus refer? To the seeking in repentance and faith? But this is excluded by the next clause. To the search for a deliverer in connection with the terrible events accompanying the destruction of Jerusalem in the year A. D. 70? It is probably better to interpret this seeking as that of despair at the moment of death. We adopt this interpretation in view of the words: "but y o u will die in y o u r sin." In their death they will experience no comfort and no peace of any kind, only dark despair. The One whom they have rejected will not be present to help them in their need. In their *sin* — all their sins viewed collectively, but separately in verse 24 *(sins)* — they will die. The wrath of God resting upon them, they will go to the place of everlasting perdition. They cannot go where Jesus is going; namely, to the Father.

22. The Jews, therefore, were saying, He is not going to kill himself, is he, since he says, Where I am going y o u cannot come?

The Jews, stung by the announcement of their coming doom, act as if they have not even heard the words of Jesus with reference to themselves. They reflect only on the last clause in his remarks; i.e., on that which pertained to his plans with reference to himself: that *he* would soon take his departure to a place to which *they* could not come. Sneering, they ask, "He is not going to kill himself, is he?" As if by killing himself he would

---

[27] On ὅτι as used here see Vol. I, pp. 54, 59.
[28] IIIA1; see Vol. I, pp. 42, 43.

be going to a place where they (as they saw it) could not come! At a previous occasion (7:35, 36) when Jesus uttered similar words, they had ventured another guess, also uttered in mockery, "He surely does not intend to go to the Diaspora among the Greeks, and teach the Greeks, does he?"

The present taunting insinuation that he was possibly contemplating suicide (very prevalent in those days!) was, unbeknown to them, a bitter caricature of the truth; namely, that he was going *to give his life as a ransom for many* (10:11, 18; cf. Matt. 20:28).

23, 24. So he was saying to them, Y o u are from below, I am from above; y o u are of this world, I am not of this world. Did I not say to y o u that y o u would die in y o u r sins? For if y o u will not believe that I am he, y o u will die in y o u r sins.

This reply of Jesus serves both as a continuation of verse 21, giving the reason (as if he had said, "Where I am going y o u cannot come, for y o u are from below, I am from above"), and as a fitting response to the sneering question of the Jews (as if he had said, "Y o u r mockery indicates that y o u are from below," etc.). What Jesus means is that the thoughts and motives of these Jews were hell-inspired; his own, were heaven-inspired. Jesus then repeats the words of verse 21 ("Y o u will die," etc.) with a slight change (see on that verse). This death in sins will be the result of not believing *that I am he;* literally, *that I am* (ἐγώ εἰμι), the predicate must be supplied mentally, as in 4:26; 6:20; 9:9; 13:19; 18:5, 6, 9. Basic to the expression are passages such as Ex. 3:14; Deut. 32:39; Is. 43:10. The meaning is: that I am all that I claim to be; the One sent by the Father, the One who is from above, the Son of man, the only-begotten Son of God, equal with God, the One who has life in himself, the very essence of the scriptures, the bread of life, the light of the world, etc. The fact that rejection of the Son — failure to believe in him and to obey him — results in everlasting death is expressed not only here in 8:24 but also in 3:36 (see on that verse), which may be viewed as an explanation of 8:24.

25, 26. In reply, they were saying to him, *You, who are you?* Once again, as in verse 22, the Jews act as if they have not heard the remarks of Jesus with reference to themselves. Probably thinking that the best defence is an offense, they attack him with an expression of scorn and ridicule: *"You, who are you?"* (σὺ τίς εἶ;) **Jesus said to them, Exactly what I am also telling y o u.**[29] **I have many things to say concerning y o u and to judge.**

---

[29] There are various interpretations of the phrase τὴν ἀρχήν. The following should be noted:

(1) *from the beginning.* Cf. A.R.V.: "Even that which I have also spoken unto you from the beginning." Cf. A.V. and R.S.V. (in the text). The use of the present

Clearly, Jesus is not going to be sidetracked. He answers their derisive question very pointedly and very briefly, and then immediately continues the attack upon them begun in verses 21, 23, and 24. Their question (*You, who are you?*) was not only wicked; it was also entirely uncalled for and superfluous, for Jesus had been telling them all the while who he was (see on verse 24) and he was engaged in doing that very thing now. Hence, he immediately shifts back to the attack, as if he wanted to say, "I am not yet through with y o u." When Jesus says, "I have yet many things to say concerning y o u and to judge," he implies that the *utterances* (note the verb λαλέω both here and in the preceding verse) of his mouth are *judgments*. Moreover, the verb used is also especially appropriate in such cases as this, where someone *utters* or speaks the mind (not of himself alone but also) *of Another* (here, the Father). It is clear from 8:15, 16 (cf. on 3:17, where the verb κρίνω is discussed) that when Jesus judges these men he *condemns* them.

The Lord continues: **But he who sent me is true.** It has been argued by some that the conjunction ἀλλά (translated *"But"*) is here not adversative in meaning. It is, however, not at all necessary to depart from the more usual meaning of the word. What we have here — and in so many other places — is an instance of abbreviated style, an ellipsis, on which we have commented in another connection (see on 5:31). It is very difficult for us today to supply what was omitted. Perhaps the thought of verse 26 fully expressed might be reproduced in these words: "I have many things to say concerning y o u and to judge. But, in spite of y o u r vehemently uttered rejections and y o u r manifestations of unbelief, what I shall say is true because he who sent me is true, and whatsoever I have heard from him, these things I speak to the world."

On "he who sent me," see 3:17, 34; 5:30, 36, 37; cf. 1:6. The Sender is, of course, the Father. The Sender is *true* in all his declarations and

---

tense (λαλῶ) is not an insuperable objection to this translation. Nevertheless, this rendering is beset with difficulties, chief of them being: a. In that case one would expect ἀπ' ἀρχῆς, as in 15:27 or ἐξ ἀρχῆς, as in 16:4; and b. the phrase would stand closer to λαλῶ.

(2) *at all.* Thus several Greek fathers render it; see also R.S.V., footnote. Thus rendered, the sentence would amount to an exclamation: "That I should even speak to y o u at all!" But if Jesus is not sure whether he should speak *at all* to the Jews, how then can he say in the next breath, "I have *many things* to say concerning y o u and to judge"? If the answer be that what is said *concerning* a person is not said *to* him, this hardly satisfies, for Jesus continues to talk both *concerning* and also *to* the Jews and their followers. Besides, the rendering is also objectionable from a theological point of view. It would amount to a kind of self-accusation, which is in conflict with Christ's sinless nature.

(3) *altogether, nothing else than, exactly.* This rendering, which is adopted by Melanchton, Luther, Dods, and many others, makes excellent sense, is in keeping with the word-order, is not without parallel elsewhere, and is easy to explain. Cf. our expression: *from first to last* (hence, altogether, exactly).

judgments, for he is true in his inner nature. Cf. on 3:33. **And whatsoever I have heard from him, these things I speak to the world.** In every word of Jesus the mind of the Father is expressed. Hence, when the Jews reject the One who now addresses them, they thereby reject the Father! The same (or a very similar) thought is expressed in 3:11; 5:19, 30, 32, 37; 7:16. What Jesus has heard (from all eternity) from the Father, these things he utters not only to the Jews but to Jew and Gentile alike; they are meant for all, for the entire world (on meaning of κόσμος see 1:10, footnote 26, here probably meaning number 5).

27. They did not recognize that he was speaking to them of the Father. Even though Jesus had frequently told the Jews in clear language that the Sender was the Father (cf. 5:36, 37; 8:18), yet this fact had failed to register. So blinding is the power of infidelity and prejudice! We do not know by what means they indicated this ignorance. Perhaps they showed it by raising an objection or asking a stupid question or staring vacantly.

28. So Jesus said, When y o u will have lifted up the Son of man, then y o u will know that I am he, and that of myself I do nothing but speak thus as the Father taught me. The gist of the remark is certainly this: "having nailed me to the cross (hence, having indirectly led me to the crown) the awful truth will dawn on y o u that I am in reality the One I have always claimed to be, and that in my words and works I reveal and represent the Father."

For the meaning of the verb *to lift up* see on 3:14. For *Son of man* see on 12:34. By saying "y o u will *know* (γνώσεσθε fr. γινώσκω)" Jesus meant "y o u will recognize or perceive." This verb occurs fifty-six times in John's Gospel, while its synonym (οἶδα) occurs eighty-four times in the same book. See further on 1:10, 31; 3:11. For the clause "that I am he" see on 8:24. For the meaning of the clause "and that of myself I do nothing but speak thus as the Father taught me" see on 8:26 (last clause) which expresses the same thought.

The clause "then y o u will know that I am he" is not a prediction of salvation for the Jews. The knowledge here indicated is not a saving knowledge and does not refer to the conversion of the three thousand on the day of Pentecost (Acts 2:36, 41). The present context does not allow that interpretation (see especially verses 21 and 24). What Jesus means is that having refused to accept him by faith and having nailed him to the cross (which, in turn, led to the crown), they would one day awaken to the terrifying realization that this One whom they despised was, nevertheless, whatever he claimed to be. Too late this truth would crash in upon them, in the hour of death and at the final judgment.

29. And he who sent me is with me. He has not left me alone, be-

48

cause I always do the things that are pleasing to him. "He who sent me" is, of course, the Father (5:36, 37; 8:18, 27) who is constantly indicated as the Sender; i.e., as the One who commissioned his Son to be the Mediator (see on 3:17, 34; cf. 1:6). In the two statements: a. *he is with me,* and b. *I always do the things that are pleasing to him* we have a beautiful expression of the close and intimate nature of the cooperation between the One who commissions and the One who is commissioned. See also on 3:11; 5:19, 30, 32, 37; 7:16; and 8:26. The absolute obedience of the Son, always doing what is pleasing to the Father, assures the continuation of the Father's love for him. "He has not left me alone," has not rejected the Son or cast him off. Even Matt. 27:46 cannot mean that the Father would reject him as a disobedient Son, for that is forever impossible. In that passage the Son is *forsaken* in a twofold sense: a. all alone he bears the burden of God's wrath against sin, no one shares his punishment; and b. while experiencing within himself that indescribable torture, he must forego the consoling sweetness of the Father's fellowship. Nevertheless, because of his voluntary acceptance of this eternal death the Father loves him all the more! We hasten to add that this spiritual closeness rests, of course, upon the ontological or trinitarian relationship between Father and Son.

---

30 While he was saying these things, many believed in him. 31 So Jesus was saying to those Jews who had believed in him, "If y o u remain in my word, y o u are truly my disciples, 32 and y o u will know the truth and the truth will set you free.[30] 33 They answered him, "Seed of Abraham are we, and to no one have

---

[30] This section — verses 30-59 — contains no less than nine conditional sentences, distributed among the three groups as follows:
  IA verse 39; see vol. I, p. 40.
  IB verse 46; see vol. I, p. 40.
  IIA verse 42; see vol. I, p. 41.
  IIIA1 verses 36 and 55; see vol. I, pp. 42, 43.
  IIIA2 verses 31 (in thought verse 32 is included in the apodosis), 54; see vol. I, pp. 42, 43.
  IIIA3 verses 51, 52 (the second conditional sentence repeats the first, with very slight change); see vol. I, pp. 42, 43.
Thus each of the three main groups is represented in this section. In connection with the conditional sentences found in verses 31, 36, 39, 54, and 55, the statement of A. T. Robertson should be borne in mind: "The point about all the four classes to note is that the form of the condition has to do only with the *statement,* not with the absolute truth or certainty of the matter" (Gram. N.T., p. 1006). Thus, in verse 55 the form of the sentence does not imply that Christ actually considered it probable that he would say, "I do not know him (the Father)." Jesus merely points out the logical conclusion which would follow if what is stated in the protasis is deemed probable. One might translate: *"Suppose I say. . . ."* Similarly, the form of the conditional sentence proves nothing with respect to the genuine character of the faith of those who are referred to in verse 31. And the form of the sentence does not prove that Jesus regarded his Jewish opponents as being *actually* Abraham's children, verse 39.

we been enslaved ever. How is it that you say, 'Y o u will become free'?" 34 Jesus answered them, "I most solemnly assure y o u [31], every one who commits sin is the slave of sin. 35 Now the slave does not remain in the house permanently, but the son remains permanently. 36 If therefore the Son will make y o u free, y o u will be free indeed.[32] 37 I know that y o u are the seed of Abraham, yet y o u are seeking to kill me, because my words find no room in y o u. 38 The things which I have seen at the Father's side I speak, and so also the things which y o u have heard at y o u r Father's side y o u do."

8:30-38

8:30, 31a. While he was saying these things, many believed in him. So Jesus was saying to those Jews who had believed in him . . .

During the course of the discourse discussed in the preceding verses, now one, then another became convinced that Jesus was (at least to some extent) what he claimed to be, until those who reacted in this manner formed a considerable group ("many"). *Was this conviction genuine faith?* Was it merely a mental persuasion or was it also wholehearted personal surrender? This question, which has caused so much discussion and controversy among commentators, becomes even more acute when it is borne in mind that the verses which follow show a swift change from belief to violent hostility. Not only does Jesus encounter verbal *opposition* (verse 33) but even verbal *abuse* (verse 48: "You are a Samaritan and have a demon"; cf. 52). At last there is even an attempt to stone him (verse 59).

The various views of commentators may be summarized as follows:

(1) Verse 30 (ἐπίστευσαν, believed) refers to those who embraced Jesus by genuine faith. Verse 31 (πεπιστευκότας, had believed) refers to those who had not made the full surrender of faith. Hence, the transition is between verses 30 and 31.[33]

(2) Verses 30, 31, and 32 refer to genuine believers, those who have experienced a real change of heart and life. The transition is between verses 32 and 33. The objectors in verse 33 (and the verses which follow) are the unbelieving Jews.[34]

(3) Verses 30-36 refer to genuine believers. The transition is between verses 36 and 37.[35]

(4) The entire section is an uninterrupted story: those who in verse 30 are described as having believed in him are the same as those who oppose

---

[31] On ὅτι see Vol. I, p. 54.
[32] On this conditional sentence, see Note 30.
[33] Cf. W. F. Howard, *The Interpreter's Bible,* New York, 1952, vol. VIII, p. 600.
[34] Cf. R. C. H. Lenski, *Interpretation of St. John's Gospel,* Columbus, Ohio, 1931, pp. 607-613.
[35] Cf. F. W. Grosheide, *Kommentaar op het Nieuwe Testament, Johannes,* Amsterdam, 1950, vol. II, p. 42.

him vehemently in the verses which follow. There is no transition from one group to another. The people who are described in verses 30 and 31 do not have *genuine* faith, as the subsequent verses also clearly indicate.[36]

In connection with the first three views the following is clear:

a. All regard the people who are described in verse 30 as being genuine believers.

b. All accept the theory that we are dealing here with two different groups, and that there is a transition (rather abrupt, it would seem) between the genuine *believers* of verse 30 and the genuine *unbelievers* who appear on the scene subsequently (whether at verse 31 or verse 33 or verse 37).

But, as to a., there is nothing that compels us to view the men described in verse 30 as being genuine believers. The finite verb *believed* (ἐπίστευσαν) followed by *in him* (εἰς αὐτόν) or *in his name* does not always indicate a change of heart. See on 2:23; 7:31; 12:42. See especially the context of 2:23 and 12:42. What is true is that the *present participle* (πιστεύων, -οντες) in such cases always indicates genuine faith (3:16, 18, 36; 6:35, 40, 47; 7:38; 11:25, 26; 12:44, 46; 14:12; 17:20). See also on 3:16. But the present participle is not used here in 8:30. Hence, whether the faith here indicated is genuine or not will have to be indicated by the following verses (the context).

As to b., no transition of any kind *from one group of men to another sharply contrasted group* is apparent to the ordinary reader of the Greek text or of the English translation. Thus, it is very difficult to see why the men indicated by the participle (τοὺς πεπιστευκότας) in verse 31 would have to be a completely different group than those to whom reference is made by the finite verb in verse 30. They believed while Jesus was still speaking; some of them perhaps after Jesus had spoken only a few minutes. They continued to believe (note force of the perfect participle) to the very end of the discourse (i.e., until Jesus again addresses them in verse 31).

As to the transition beginning at verse 33 or at verse 37, neither of these verses indicates a transition *from one group to another group*. Verse 33 begins with the words, "*They* answered him." Naturally, the "they" refers to the people addressed in verse 32. Verse 36 reads, "If therefore the Son will make y o u free, y o u will be free indeed." Then verse 37 continues, "I know that y o u are the seed of Abraham, yet y o u are seeking to kill me." The conclusion which one naturally draws in such cases is that the

[36] John Calvin, *op. cit.,* p. 167: Caeterum fidem Evangelista improprie nominat, quae solum erat quaedam ad fidem praeparatio. Nihil enim altius de illis praedicat quam quod propensi fuerunt ad recipiendam Christi doctrinam, quo etiam spectat proxima admonitio. This is his comment on verse 30. In similar vein C. Bouma, M. Dods, J. P. Lange, A. T. Robertson, and M. C. Tenney (see Bibliography for titles).

"y o u" of verse 36 indicates the same group as the "y o u" of verse 37. Otherwise the entire paragraph becomes unintelligible.

We, accordingly, accept the view of Calvin and most other commentators (number 4 above) as being by far the most natural.

All this does not mean that there is no transition. There is, indeed, a transition; but it is not from one group to a totally different group. The transition is from one attitude to another attitude *within the same group of people*. That transition is very clear. It is, in fact, a striking change. As soon as Jesus shows these people that mere mental acceptance (as to Jesus being the Messiah of their dreams, for instance) is not enough, but that they must surrender themselves to him as their personal Deliverer from bondage to Satan and to sin, they become furious and no longer *believe* in him in any sense.

31b, 32. If y o u remain in my word, y o u are truly my disciples, and y o u will know the truth and the truth will set y o u free.

One abides in the word of Christ by making it the rule of one's life. In other words, *obedience* is the same thing as abiding in the word. This makes one a true disciple of Jesus and leads to genuine knowledge of the truth (God's special revelation which has its heart and center in the work of Christ). Such knowledge, born of revelation and experience, sets one free. For the meaning of the two most familiar Greek words for *to know* see on 1:10, 31; 3:11; 8:28. Jesus himself furnishes a commentary on the meaning of freedom. One is free when sin no longer rules over him, and when the word of Christ dominates his heart and life (see verses 34, 35, 37). One is free, therefore, not when he can do what he wishes to do but when he wishes to do and can do what he should do. See also on 7:17, 18 (discussion of the order of the elements in Christian experience).

33. They answered him, Seed of Abraham are we, and to no one have we been enslaved ever. How is it that you say, Y o u will become free?

The people who answer Jesus are the same as those who have just been addressed (see on 8:30, 31a). The *attitude*, however, changes. The word of Jesus, implying that spiritually they were not freemen but slaves, has shocked and angered them. They deeply resented his remark. In their pride of heart they exclaimed, "Seed of Abraham are we, and to no one have we been enslaved ever." Obviously they are not thinking of their *political* condition when they say this. They surely could not conveniently forget their past bondage to Egypt, Babylonia, Medo-Persia, and Syria, nor their present bondage to Rome! Nor are they thinking about their *social* condition: many Jews had been slaves. *Religiously*, however, they deem themselves freemen, being seed (descendants) of Abraham, with whom God had made his covenant of grace (Gen. 17:7). Thus *as a people or nation* (the line of physical descent; see on 1:13) they enjoy a unique religious

52

standing. Are they not an elect race, royal priesthood, holy nation, people for God's own possession (Ex. 19:6; Deut. 7:6; 10:15; cf. I Pet. 2:9)? Amos 3:2 (the first part of the verse) is ever before their mind, but they conveniently forget Amos 3:2 (the last part of the verse)! Their line of reasoning is on this order: heathen are in bondage; they serve idols; but surely we are not in bondage. We are no heathen; we are not even Samaritans (cf. 8:48). How, then, is it that Jesus can say, "Y o u will become free?"

34. Jesus answered them, I most solemnly assure y o u, every one who commits sin is a slave of sin.

For the meaning of the words of solemn introduction see on 1:51. This is one of the most remarkable sayings ever uttered by our Lord. He immediately wipes out the distinction between Jew and Gentile with respect to their standing before God and his holy law. He says, *"Every one . . . . is a slave of sin."* The subject is qualified by *who commits sin* (ὁ ποιῶν τὴν ἁμαρτίαν); i.e., who is constantly doing sin; present continuative; one might render it: who lives in sin. One is reminded of the continuative force of the present in I John 3:6. Such a sinner has not seen the Lord, and does not know him. John does not teach that a man is able to live without sinning; far from it (see I John 1:8). But the man who is *constantly missing the mark* of God's glory (cf. the use of διαμαρτάνοντες in LXX Judg. 20:16), and delights in this is definitely a *transgressor of God's law* (I John 3:4).

Such a man is here called a slave of sin (cf. Rom. 6:16; 11:32; II Pet. 2:19). He is a slave, for he has been overcome and taken captive by his master, sin, and is unable to deliver himself from this bondage. He is as truly (nay, *more* truly) chained as is the prisoner with the iron band around his leg, the band that is fastened to a chain which is cemented into the wall of a dungeon. He cannot break the chain. On the contrary, every sin he commits draws it tighter, until at last it crushes him completely. That is the picture which Jesus draws here of sinners as they are by nature. Do the Jews regard themselves as free men? In reality they are slaves without any freedom at all. They are prisoners in chains.

35, 36. Now the slave does not remain in the house permanently, but the son remains permanently. If therefore the Son will make y o u free, y o u will be free indeed.

Jesus has been picturing his enemies as slaves in chains, lacking all true freedom. Now — changing the figure slightly — he dwells upon another aspect of this condition of slavery: a slave may enjoy the privileges of his master's house *for a while,* but not forever. At any moment he may be dismissed or sold. The Jews, who pride themselves upon their descent from Abraham, must bear this in mind. The old dispensation with its special privileges for Israel has ended. Abraham's *true* children will remain in his household and enjoy its privileges permanently, but Abraham's slaves (think of Hagar, and cf. Gal. 4:21-31) will be driven out. Only a son enjoys freedom. If therefore the Son of God — see on 1:14 — will make them free, they will be free indeed. The conditional sentence leaves *the responsibility* with them, but *the action* (that of making free) with him! The expression *free, indeed* probably refers to the fact that the freedom given by Christ is the only real freedom:

a. It is freedom from slavery to sin, in contrast with the freedom of which the Jews were thinking (such as freedom from bondage to idols, freedom from the darkness of heathen polytheism).

b. It is always freedom *plus*. When an accused man is declared not guilty, he is free. Likewise when a slave has been emancipated, he is free. But the judge or the emancipator does not, as a rule, adopt the freed individual as his own son. But when the Son makes one free, he will be free indeed, rejoicing in the glorious freedom of sonship. And how does the Son make one free? Answer; see 18:12; cf. Is. 53:5; II Cor. 3:17; Gal. 4:6, 7.

37. I know that y o u are the seed of Abraham. Jesus continues to address the same group of people as in the preceding verse (see on 8:30, 31a). He grants that they are in the physical sense the descendants of Abraham. But this relationship, which entailed so many advantages (see Rom. 3:1, 2; 9:4, 5) only served to increase their responsibility (cf. Amos 3:2). It made their present sinful attitude toward the Christ of God stand out all the more clearly, in all its heinousness. Hence, Jesus continues: **yet y o u are seeking to kill me.** The seed of Abraham seeking to kill the very One to whom Abraham looked forward with joyful anticipation (8:56)! That the Jews were actually bent on murdering Jesus is clear from the following passages: 5:18; 7:19, 25; cf. 7:30, 32, 45; 8:59. That in this plan to put Jesus to death a progressive development is noticeable in John's Gospel has been shown in vol. I, p. 12. When Jesus here emphasizes that the very seed of Abraham is seeking to kill him, he is beginning to show them that, after all, Abraham is not their father in the *spiritual* sense. Who then are the real children of Abraham? *All* true believers. See Rom. 4:11, 12; Gal. 3:7, 29. To be sure, Jesus does not state this in so many words; yet, this truth, proclaimed by Paul, is clearly implied in the words of the Lord.

Why are the Jews seeking to kill Jesus? The answer is: **because my word finds no room in y o u.** Murder-plots occupy such a large space in the hearts of these Jews that there is no space (χώρα; hence, here the verb χωρεῖ) left for the word of Jesus! We have here another instance of litotes. The real meaning is: y o u completely reject my word!

54

38. The things which I have seen at the Father's side I speak, and so also the things which y o u have heard at y o u r father's side y o u do.

The meaning is briefly this:

a. There is a contrast between *the* (meaning *my*) Father and y o u r father. My father and y o u r father are not the same. My Father is the first person of the Trinity; y o u r s is . . . . . . let them guess! By and by Jesus will tell them who is their real, spiritual father (see 8:44).

b. There is a contrast between my relation to my Father, and y o u r relation to y o u r father. At my Father's side (for I was in his very presence from eternity; see also 1:14; 6:46; 7:29; 16:29; 17:8; and cf. 1:1) I not only heard but saw certain things; at y o u r father's side (for y o u are very close to him) y o u have heard certain whisperings; e.g., the instigation to kill me.

c. My emphasis (at present) is on *uttering* (the verb is λαλῶ) what I have seen; I am the great Prophet, who came to reveal the Father's will. Y o u r emphasis is on *acting*, on doing, without fully penetrating what this implies, whatever y o u r father whispers into y o u r ears.

Y o u have heard the whisperings of y o u r father, and y o u are ready to act; I have actually seen the glory of my Father, and I am giving expression to that which I have seen.

The sequel indicates, however, that the basic contrast is that between *the* (i.e., *my*) Father and y o u r father.

---

39 They answered and said to him, "Our father is Abraham." Jesus said to them, "If y o u are Abraham's children, y o u are doing the works of Abraham. [37] 40 But now y o u are seeking to kill me, a man who has been telling y o u the truth which I heard from God. This Abraham did not do. 41 Y o u are doing the works of y o u r father." They said to him, "We were not born of fornication; [38] one Father have we, even God." 42 Jesus said to them, "If God were y o u r Father, y o u would love me, for I came forth from and am come from God, for I do not come forth of myself, but he sent me.[39] 43 Why do y o u not understand my utterances? It is because y o u cannot bear to hear my word. 44 Y o u are of y o u r father, the devil, and y o u desire to carry out the wishes of y o u r father. He was a murderer from the beginning, and does not take his stand in the truth, for there is no truth in him. When he speaks the lie, he speaks of himself, for he is a liar, and the father of the lie. 45 But because I speak the truth, y o u do not believe me. 46 Who of y o u convicts me of sin? If I speak the truth, why do y o u not believe me? [40] 47 He who is of God hears God's utterances. Y o u do not hear, because [41] y o u are not of God."

48 The Jews answered and said to him, "Are we not correct in saying, 'You are a Samaritan and have a demon'?" 49 Jesus answered, "I do not have a demon;

---

[37] On this conditional sentence see Note 30.
[38] For the meaning of *fornication* see N.T.C. on I Thess. 4:3.
[39] On this conditional sentence see Note 30.
[40] On this conditional sentence see Note 30.
[41] On ὅτι see Vol. I, pp. 54, 59.

on the contrary, I am honoring my Father, but y o u are dishonoring me. 50 But I do not seek my own glory; there is One who does seek (it), and he judges. 51 I most solemnly assure y o u, if anyone keeps my word, he will certainly never see death." [42] 52 The Jews said to him, "Now we know that you have a demon. Abraham died, as did the prophets; yet you say, 'If anyone keeps my word, he will certainly never taste death.' [43] 53 Surely, you are not greater than our father Abraham, who died? The prophets also died! Whom are you making yourself?" 54 Jesus answered, "If I glorify myself, my glory is nothing.[44] My Father, whom y o u call 'Our God,' is the One who glorifies me; 55 yet y o u do not know him, but I do know him. And if I say, 'I do not know him,' I will be a liar just like y o u.[44] But I know him, and his word I keep. 56 Abraham, y o u r father, was extremely happy that he was to see my day, and he saw it and rejoiced." 57 The Jews therefore said to him, "You have not even (lived) fifty years, and have y o u seen Abraham?" 58 Jesus said to them, "I most solemnly assure y o u, before Abraham was born, I am." 59 So they picked up stones in order to hurl them at him. But Jesus hid himself, and went out of the temple.

8:39-59

8:39a. They answered and said to him, Our father is Abraham. The very fact that Jesus had not stated in clear language whom he had in mind when he said "Y o u r father" angered these Jews. The implication (namely, that he meant *the devil*) was going to become clear, but was still veiled. However, whatever he means or implies they thrust aside by saying, "Our father is Abraham." They mean, of course, Abraham is our father in every sense of the term, not only physically but also spiritually; hence, we are spiritually free and we have no need of being delivered from bondage. They regard themselves as the spiritual *offspring* of Abraham.

39b, 40. Jesus said to them, If y o u are Abraham's children, y o u are doing the works of Abraham. See also Note 30 above. Jesus, for the sake of the argument, assumes for a moment that the Jews are correct in calling Abraham their (spiritual) father. Now on that presupposition, says Jesus, y o u are doing the works of Abraham. It cannot be otherwise. Abraham's children do Abraham's works. Like Abraham of old they obey God's commands, fully trusting that God will make all things well; they welcome his messengers; and, last but not least, they rejoice in the day of Christ (see on 8:56). These were the works of Abraham. (See, e.g., Gen. 12:1-4; 17:17; 18:1-8; ch. 22). From the entire context (see especially verses 37 and 40), the tone of voice, the look in his eyes, the Jews can easily infer that Jesus is merely assuming, for the sake of the argument, that these

---

[42] On this conditional sentence see Note 30.
[43] On this conditional sentence see Note 30.
[44] On this conditional sentence see Note 30.

people are Abraham's offspring and are therefore doing Abraham's works.[45]
Figures of speech, including irony, abound in the lively discourse which
we find here and everywhere in the Gospels. See what has been said about
this in connection with 5:31. Stripped of irony, the intent of the statement
is, of course, this: "If y o u were really Abraham's children,[46] y o u would
be doing the works of Abraham."

Jesus continues: **But now y o u are seeking to kill me, a man who has
been telling y o u the truth which I heard from God. This Abraham did
not do.** In sharp contrast with Abraham, who received God's messengers
most cordially (Gen. 18:1-8) and who looked forward with rejoicing to the
coming of the Christ (see on 8:56), these Jews were seeking to kill the latter.
They were plotting the downfall of mankind's greatest Benefactor, a *man*
(Christ's human nature comes to the fore here) who is, nevertheless, also
God, having come from the very presence of God, so that he can say: *I
have been telling y o u what I have heard from God.* Note the first personal
pronoun used in the original; literally: "a man who the truth to y o u I
have been telling." For evidences of the fact that the Jews were really
plotting to kill Jesus see on 8:37 (the references listed there). For the
meaning of the statement, "I have been telling y o u the truth which I
heard from God," see on 5:30; 7:16; and 8:26; and cf. 3:11; 5:19, 32, 37.
For the meaning of the term *the truth* see on 8:32. The little sentence,
"This Abraham did not do," is again litotes: Abraham did the very opposite (see especially 8:56).

41. Y o u are doing the works of y o u r father. This essentially is a

---

[45] I agree here with the text of N.N. Failure to see the irony in the statement is,
perhaps, the reason why attempts were made to change ἐστε to ἦτε, and ποιεῖτε to
ἐποίειτε. This may also account for the fact that some commentators, while retaining ποιεῖτε, would interpret it as an imperative. It must be granted that the support for the reading ἐποίειτε is by no means inconsiderable. See the textual apparatus in N.N. The reading retained in the text of N.N. also has strong support, and
the change from the present to the imperfect is easily explained. It is true, of
course, that whether one looks upon the conditional sentence in 8:39 as a mixed
condition, with an apodosis indicating unreality, or as a straight First Class condition, with ironical implication, the resultant idea is the same. In either case what
Jesus means is that these Jews are not really the children of Abraham, and that this
is proved by the fact that they are not doing Abraham's works.
[46] It is true that Jesus uses σπέρμα in verse 37, but τέκνα in verse 39. However, it
is probably incorrect to press this point, as if the *term* σπέρμα as such meant physical seed, and the *term* τέκνον-α spiritual seed. A reference to Rom. 9:7 (as if also
there the latter term had the more spiritual connotation) is based on the assumption
that the usual rendering of that passage is correct. However, it is very evident from
the context there (in Rom. 9:7) that this usual rendering is incorrect and confusing,
and that actually the term σπέρμα is the more exclusive one ("in Isaac shall thy
seed be called . . . . . the children of the promise are reckoned for the *seed*"). In
our present passage (8:39) the term *children* has the same meaning as the term *seed*
(8:37): *physically,* these Jews are, indeed, the seed or the children of Abraham;
spiritually, they are not the seed or the children of Abraham.

repetition of Jesus' words recorded in verse 38; only, it is beginning to become clearer who this *father* of the Jews is: he is the kind of father who encourages them to kill God's only Son! So much is now clear from verse 40. The very fact that Jesus still does not indicate specifically whom he has in mind when he speaks about their father makes the Jews all the more indignant and impatient. Hence, they blurt out the name of the One whom *they* regard as their spiritual Father, their one and only, unmistakable Father. **They said to him, We were not born of fornication.** Had they been born of fornication (πορνεία; the noun, used only here in *John's* Gospel — but see Matt. 5:32; 15:19; 19:9; Mk. 7:21 — occurs frequently in the epistles and in Revelation), i.e., of unlawful sexual intercourse, there would undoubtedly be legitimate questions with respect to their parentage. *Several* persons are often pointed out as the possible fathers of one who was born of fornication. These Jews, however, are sure that they know the identity of their Father: **one Father have we, even God.** It is not at all impossible that a sinister insinuation is implied in the words of these enemies of the Lord, and that what they really meant was this, "*We* were not born of fornication, but *you* were! With respect to *our* parentage there is no reasonable doubt, but it is different with *you!*" Cf. 8:48. At any rate such stories circulated among the Jews later on, and in their literature Jesus is often represented as the bastard son of Mary.[47]

When the Jews call God their one and only Father, they may have been thinking of Mal. 2:10, "Have we not all one father? hath not one God created us?"

42. Jesus said to them, If God were y o u r Father, y o u would love me, for I came forth from and am come from God, and I do not come forth of myself, but he sent me. Thus Jesus demolishes the claim of the Jews. Their very actions and their attitude belie their boast. If God were their real, spiritual Father, they would, of course, love him. Loving him, they would also love his Son, Jesus. Him they hate; hence, they also hate the Father and are not his true children. I John 5:1 is the best commentary on the first part of Christ's answer. See also what we have said in connection with 7:17, 18, on the elements in Christian experience.

We do not believe that the words *I came forth from God* and the words *and am come from God* should be separated in such a manner that the former expression refers to Christ's incarnation, the latter to his Messianic mission. Both undoubtedly refer to his mission (or commission); but this, of course, cannot be thought of apart from his incarnation. And basic to both is the eternal generation of the Son from the Father.

Now, in the incarnation Jesus *came forth from* God in order to ac-

---

[47] Cf. T. Walker, *Jewish Views of Jesus,* New York, 1931, pp. 14-23.

complish his mediatorial task on earth. But the contact between the Sender and the One Sent remains intact; the latter still truly and fully represents the Father in all he does. Hence, we read *and am come from God*. The Son is not the kind of ambassador who must return to his country and to his superiors in order to receive new instructions and to see whether, perhaps, he has lost true contact with the views and attitudes of those who sent him. For the meaning of *I came forth from* (or: *out of*) *God* or *heaven* see also on 6:41, where the delicate shading in the meaning of different tenses is discussed.

The Jews were always looking upon Jesus as a vain pretender; one who came forth *of himself* or *of his own accord*. See on 7:28. Jesus again emphatically denies this when he states, "And I do not come forth of myself." The words *he sent me* are explained by the parallelism *I came forth from him* (God). See above; and see also on 1:6; 3:17, 34; 5:36, 37; 8:18, 27, 29; 10:36; 11:42; 12:49; 14:10; 17:3, 8.

43. Why do y o u not understand my utterance? It is because y o u cannot (bear to) hear my word.

The Jews have given repeated indications of spiritual obtuseness. That is particularly striking in this chapter, as is evidenced from 8:27; from the many stupid questions which they are constantly asking, such as: "Where is your father?" (8:19), "He is not going to kill himself, is he?" (8:22), *"You, who are you?"* (8:25), "How is it that you say, 'Y o u will become free'?" (8:33); and particularly from the fact that they do not seem to understand whom Jesus has in mind when he speaks about their real, spiritual father. The language which Jesus employs, his terms and phrases, his entire utterance (λαλιά) or manner of speaking, is a mystery to them. They do not *understand* it. For the meaning of the verb see on 1:10, 31; 8:28.

Jesus explains this spiritual dulness. He says that it arises from the fact that they cannot hear his *word* (τὸν λόγον), i.e., his message. In the given context it is clear that Jesus holds them accountable for this inability. Hence, the words *y o u cannot* mean *y o u cannot bear to*. Their *will* is evil, as is shown in the next verse. The question and its answer do not form a tautology; on the contrary, the answer states the reason for the fact which is stated in the question. The whole might be paraphrased as follows: "Why do y o u not recognize the meaning of my phrases, as y o u r constant questions and exclamations and insults so clearly indicate? It is because, through ill will, you cannot bear to hear the truth or message conveyed by these phrases." Their minds are beclouded through bias! Y o u cannot—y o u cannot—y o u cannot (see 3:3, 5; 5:44; 6:44; and now also 8:43), that is the sad state of the sinner; especially, of that man who hardens himself against God's oracles.

44. Y o u are of y o u r father, the devil, and y o u desire to carry out the wishes of y o u r father.

Suddenly Jesus speaks out openly; i.e., he no longer hints but plainly *names* their father. The word which he now utters is like the dropping of a bomb: "Y o u are of y o u r father, the devil." Cf. Matt. 13:38; 23:15; I John 3:8; and Rev. 12:9. Physically these Jews, to be sure, are children of Abraham; but spiritually and morally — and *that* was the issue — they are the children of the devil. In passing, it may be observed that the rendering "Y o u are the children of the devil's father" is, of course, so completely foreign to the context that it deserves no further comment.

Jesus not only makes this charge but also proves it. Identity of inner passions and desires establishes spiritual descent: they are *constantly* desiring (present continuative tense) to carry out the wishes (desires, yearnings) of the devil; so he must be their father. The devil desires *to kill* and *to lie*, and so do they. Jesus dwells a moment on each of these desires:

He was a murderer (literally *man-slayer*) **from the beginning.** From the very beginning of the history of the human race the devil had murder in his heart, and he actually plunged the human race into the ocean of death, physical, spiritual, and eternal; cf. Rom. 5:12; Heb. 2:14; I John 3:8. The fall of man together with all its results points back to him as its author. **And (he) does not take his stand in the truth, for there is no truth in him.** It was through a lie that the devil brought about death (see Gen. 3:1, 4). Hence, Jesus links these two: the devil is both murderous and mendacious. By saying that satan does not take his stand in the truth, and immediately adding that there is no truth in him, the Lord stresses in the strongest possible manner the idea that between the devil and the truth there is absolutely no connection: the two are opposites. Note, however, that the second statement is introduced as the reason for the first: what satan *is* determines his stand.[48]

---

[48] The rendering, "And (he) *stood* not in the truth," though adopted by many commentators on textual grounds, furnishes a very difficult sentence. Some attempts at explanation, once that rendering has been adopted, are in this direction:

(1) The perfect angel, satan, did not remain standing in the truth but fell. — Objection: did he fall because there *is* (at present) no truth in him? But then the effect precedes the cause. Did he fall, perhaps, because *essentially* there is no truth in him (there is not and never was)? But then how can one speak of a *fall* at all?

(2) After the fall the devil was not standing in the truth. — Though this is better, we would still have expected the following clause to read, "for there *was* no truth in him."

The difficulties are removed and we get a beautifully balanced sentence, with the tenses in perfect correspondence, by adopting the rendering which we prefer: "and (he) does not take his stand in the truth, for there is no truth in him." The sentence which immediately follows also indicates that Jesus emphasizes what the devil is doing *at this present time* (in continuation of his activity from the very beginning). The textual evidence for the reading which is the basis for the rendering

Whenever he speaks the lie, he speaks of himself. The devil, then, is the very wellspring of lies, the creator of falsehoods (see Gen. 3:1, 4; Job 1:9, 10, 11; Matt. 4:6, 9; Acts 5:3; II Thess. 2:9, 10, 11). When he lies, he is original. When he does not lie (Acts 16:16, 17), he quotes or even plagiarizes; but even then he gives the borrowed words a false setting, in order to create an illusion. He ever strives to lie and deceive, and this he does in order to murder. **For he is a liar, and the father of the lie.** We may render either: . . . and the father *of it* (i.e., of the lie), or . . . and the father *of him* (i.e., of the liar); however, the logical connection here favors the former.

As is clearly evident from this entire passage, Jesus believes that the devil actually exists and that he exerts a tremendous influence on earth. To our Lord the prince of evil was not a figment of the imagination but a grim reality!

45. But because I speak the truth, y o u do not believe me. The term *the truth* is here used in the sense of that universe of ideas which corresponds with reality as revealed to the Son by the Father (see 8:40). It is the truth concerning spiritual matters; such as man's total depravity and natural inability, the plan of God for his salvation, the sending of the Son to merit that salvation, the punishment for those who reject the Son, etc. Man's proud heart does not welcome this truth, for it reveals his damnable character and lost condition. Besides, it must be borne in mind that those addressed are the children of him who is called *the father of the lie.* Hence, because Jesus speaks the truth he is rejected. Cf. on 8:43.

46, 47. Jesus anticipates the objection: "You do not speak the truth; hence, you cannot expect us to believe you." But in that case, he would be a sinner, and they should be able to prove it. Can they? Says Jesus, **Who of y o u convicts me of sin?** To convict means here to charge and then to prove that charge. The question clearly implies that Jesus not only was not conscious of any sin in himself but that he actually had no sin. The inescapable conclusion is, of course, that he ever speaks the truth. Today's radical theologian is inconsistent when on the one hand he loudly proclaims the moral perfection of Jesus; yet on the other hand rejects his majestic claims! If Jesus is sinless, his claims should be accepted. Any other course is positively wicked: **If I speak the truth, why do y o u not believe me?** The question stuns them. They have no answer. The true answer would have been: "Because we are not of God." **He who is of God**

("And he *stood*") cannot be considered conclusive. We grant immediately that the "best" texts support the reading οὐκ ἔστηκεν (instead of οὐχ ἔστηκεν) but two closely related facts must be borne in mind: a. the preferred text can also be a form of the perfect; b. gradual de-aspiration is characteristic of Koine Greek.

hears God's utterances. Just as those who are of the devil are inflamed
with his lusts (8:44), so also those who are of God give heed to his utterances. The Jews, by not giving heed to them, also in this manner prove
their spiritual kinship and descent.

48. Unwilling to admit their defeat, the Jews now resort to vicious,
stinging insults: **Are we not correct in saying, You are a Samaritan and
have a demon?** Bitter was the hatred between Jews and Samaritans! See
on 4:9, where this point is proved and explained. Hence, the biting remark, "You are a Samaritan," was about the meanest thing the Jews could
think of. To make the insult even more deadly they tell Jesus that this
is a common saying among them. And as if this were not enough they add
(for their *question* is put in such a form that a positive answer is deemed
to be so obvious that it is not even necessary): "and (you) have a demon!"
Cf. also 10:20 and Matt. 12:24. An evil spirit possesses him and is causing
him to denounce those good people who acknowledge no Father but God!

**49, 50, 51. Jesus answered, I do not have a demon; on the contrary, I am
honoring my Father, but y o u are dishonoring me.**

Jesus' emphatic denial that the Jews had a right to claim God as their
Father was not satan-inspired; on the contrary, it was called forth by his
zeal for the Father's honor (cf. 7:18); for, by calling God *their* Father
(8:41), a Father of such (!) children, and by heaping monstrous insults upon
the Son (8:48) they are dishonoring the Father. They also dishonor the Son,
directly by saying, "You are a Samaritan and have a demon," and indirectly,
by dishonoring the Father (cf. 5:23).

However, it is not necessary for the Son to vindicate his own honor;
the Father will take care of that and will judge a righteous judgment:
**But I do not seek my own glory; there is One who does seek (it), and he
judges.** On the contrary, **I most solemnly assure y o u** (on this see 1:51),
if (instead of dishonoring me) **any one keeps my word, he will certainly
never see death.** The enemies will not be able to say that they never had
an opportunity to listen to the proclamation of the Gospel! *To keep* the
word of Christ means to: a. accept it by faith, b. obey it, and c. stand
guard over it. See also 8:55; 14:23, 24; 15:20; 17:6; and 1 John 2:5. Any
one (whether Jew or Gentile, it does not matter in the least!) who does
this will certainly never *see* (i.e., experience; cf. on 3:3) death. As is evident from parallel passages in this Gospel, death, as here used, is separation from the love of God, and experiencing the crushing weight of his
wrath and condemnation, and that forever. Cf. also Matt. 25:46; II Tim.
1:9. The entire expression is, of course, a litotes. The real meaning is that
the person who keeps the word of Christ will, indeed, see (everlasting)
life and will partake of it in all its sweetness and beauty, as described so

exquisitely in 14:23; 17:3; and Rev. 3:20. See also on John 3:16. With
this passage (8:51) also compare 3:36; 5:24; and 11:25, 26.

**52, 53. The Jews said to him, Now we know that you have a demon.
Abraham died, as did the prophets; yet you say, If anyone keeps my word,
he will certainly never see death. — Surely, you are not greater than our
father Abraham, who died? The prophets also died! Whom are you
making yourself?**
The terrible insult (cf. 8:48) is now repeated with added emphasis. It
has become a wicked, exulting jeer: "Now we know that you have a demon."
The meaning of this expression should not be toned down to, ". . . that
you are insane." The reality of demon-possession was accepted on every
side (cf. Matt. 12:24). Again, as so often before, Christ's sublime saying
(8:51) is given a most literal, earthly interpretation, as if he had been
talking about physical death. They said, "Abraham died, as did the
prophets." The biography of each of these great men ended with the terse
comment, "And he died." One seems to hear the echo of Gen. 5: "and he
died . . . and he died . . . and he died." Of course, even on the merely
physical plane there was also Gen. 5:24 and II Kings 2:11, and these
prophets (Enoch and Elijah) had not died, not even physically! But Jesus
had not been speaking about physical death. Hence, when these hostile
Jews now repeat and by implication vehemently reject the Lord's majestic promise as if it were a palpable absurdity, they are simply proving
the truth of his saying recorded in 8:43.
The exclamation, "Surely, you are not greater than our father Abraham . . ." immediately recalls a somewhat similar one which proceeded
from the lips of the Samaritan woman (4:12). However, soon afterward
her heart gave an affirmative answer to her question. With *them* it was
different. Theirs was a case of progressive hardening: "Whom are you
making yourself?" As if Jesus were trying to glorify himself! Of course,
8:49 ("I am honoring my Father") had not even registered. Accordingly,

54. Jesus answered, If I glorify myself, my glory is nothing. The glory
of a vain pretender or usurper, a braggart or megalomaniac, is empty. It
has no substance or merit. But Jesus definitely does not belong to this
class: **My Father, whom you call *Our God*, is the One who glorifies me.**
For the claim of the Jews that God was their Father, and for Christ's refutation of this claim, see on 8:41, 42. The very One who by these base and
wicked vilifiers is proudly called "Our God" glorifies the Son whom they
reject! This proves how empty was their claim and how wicked their attack. The Father is *ever engaged in* (notice continuative force of the present participle) the glorification of the Son. He does this by enabling the
Son to perform mighty works (11:4; cf. Acts 2:22), by causing his virtues to
stand out in connection with his suffering and rewarding him for it (12:16;

13:31; 17:1, 2, 5; cf. Phil. 2:9-11); and at times even by a direct voice from heaven (see on 1:34). "This Father y o u call *Our God*," says Jesus, and he continues:

55. Yet y o u do not know him, but I do know him. And if I say, I do not know him, I will be a liar just like y o u. But I do know him, and his word I keep. Though y o u boastfully monopolize him, calling him *Our God,* y o u do not *know* him. But I do *know* him. In the original the first verb is ἐγνώκατε (from γινώσκω); the second is οἶδα. Accordingly, unless the transition from one verb to the other is merely for the sake of variation (which is improbable), the meaning is this: Y o u have not learned to recognize him, have not become acquainted with him (though he revealed himself to y o u), but I do know him intuitively and directly (having been in his very presence from all eternity; cf. 1:18). It is fair to add, however, that the wicked Jews possessed neither the one nor the other kind of knowledge (cf. 8:55 with 7:28); and that Jesus possessed both; i.e., he knew the Father both intuitively and by experience (cf. 8:55 with 10:15; 17:25).

Observe that by means of the conditional sentence (on which see Note 30, under our discussion of 8:32) Jesus calls these men liars right to their face. This was already implied in 8:44; see explanation of that verse.

For the rest, the ideas contained in 8:55 must be regarded as repetitious. For "Y o u do not know him," see on 7:28; 8:19; cf. on 3:11; 5:37, 38; 6:42. For "I do know him," see on 7:29; cf. on 3:11, 32, 34; 6:46; 10:15; 17:25. For "his word I keep (or guard)" see on 8:29, 46, 49. For the meaning of the verb *to keep* or *to guard* see on 8:51.

56. Abraham, y o u r father, was extremely happy that he was to see my day, and he saw it and rejoiced.

The Jews have been priding themselves in the fact that Abraham was their father (8:33). But Jesus shows that this self-gratulation is unwarranted. Abraham was of an entirely different spirit (8:39, 40). He would have been unspeakably displeased with them, had they been living in his day, for his attitude with respect to the Christ was the very opposite, as Jesus declares: "Abraham, y o u r father (physically yes, but spiritually only in your imagination) was extremely happy (for the verb see also 5:35; Matt. 5:12; Lk. 1:47; 10:21; Acts 2:26; 16:34; I Pet. 1:6, 8; 4:13; Rev. 19:7; and note its association with *rejoiced* in a few of these passages as also in the present passage, 8:56) that he was to see my day." He yearned for that day, looking forward to it with eager anticipation. And when it arrived, "he saw it and rejoiced."

What seems to us to be the most reasonable explanation of this saying is the following: Abraham exultantly rejoiced when God promised to give him a son. He could hardly wait until the promise was fulfilled. And

when for the centenarian that happy day actually arrived, the child was
called Isaac; i.e., laughter. The promise of the birth of that son (and also
the realization of that promise) meant everything to Abraham; for not only
were many *temporal* blessings connected with it but also *the one great
spiritual* blessing, namely, that all the families of the earth would be
blessed through this birth. Did Abraham, even in his day, understand that
not Isaac himself would be the Hope of mankind but that Isaac's birth
would pave the way for the coming of the real Messiah? He certainly must
have confidently expected that God would accomplish his designs through
Isaac, for when God ordered him to sacrifice his son, he was thoroughly
convinced that death would not have the last word, but that God, if necessary, would raise Isaac back to life (Gen. 22; cf. Heb. 11:17-19). And why
was his heart so filled with joy in connection with Isaac's birth? Isaac was
his own son, the son *of Sarah.* But was there still a deeper reason? Yes,
and it was this: he interpreted God's promise (Gen. 15:4-6; 17:1-8; cf. 22:18)
as meaning that in the line of Isaac that Blessed One would at length arrive through whom God would bless all the nations. Thus, as is stated
specifically in Heb. 11:13, he (and others before and after him) died in
faith, not having received (the fulfilment of) the promises, but having
greeted them from afar. It was thus that Abraham saw the day of Christ
and rejoiced.

We accept this explanation on the following grounds:

(1) It rests upon the solid foundation of inspired historical tradition:
the *rejoicing* of Abraham (and Sarah, though in her case it was mingled
with sin) in connection with the birth of Isaac was a well-known fact to
which there are many references (Gen. 17:17; 21:3, 6; cf. Gen. 18:12-15 and
Heb. 11:17). Anyone who listened to the words of Jesus and was acquainted with the story of Abraham would naturally connect his reference
(to Abraham's rejoicing) with the well-known passages from Genesis.

(2) By the Aramaic Targum of Gen. 17:17 the Hebrew word "laughed"
is rendered "rejoiced." [49]

(3) The fact that during the old dispensation and right up to the days
of Christ's sojourn on earth there was a Messianic expectation is clearly
taught in Scripture (see besides Heb. 11:13; also Gen. 3:15; 49:10; Deut.
18:15-18; II Sam. 7:12, 13; Ps. 2:8, 16; 22; 40; 45; 48; 69; 89; 95; 102; 109; 110;
118; Is. 7:14; 9:6; 42; 53; Dan. 7:9; Mic. 5; Zech. 6:9; Mal. 3; Matt.
11:1-3; Lk. 2:25, 26, 38; 3:15; John 1:19-28, 41; 4:25, 29, 42; Acts 10:43;
I Pet. 1:10-12); and although most of the given references are later than
Abraham, who will deny the possibility that this expectation of a personal
Deliverer could have arisen already in Paradise and could certainly have

---

[49] See E. Nestle, "Abraham Rejoiced," *ExT*, 20 (1909), 477.

enshrined itself in the heart of Abraham? — For explanations which we reject see the Note.[50]

57. The Jews therefore said to him, You have not even (lived) fifty years, and have you seen Abraham?

The Jews, with their materialistic, earthly, and literalistic bent of mind, were not able to figure out how there could ever have been any contact between Abraham and Jesus. The idea of *a seeing (and greeting) from afar by faith* was, of course, foreign to them. Now Jesus had said that Abraham had seen him (his day). Hence, one would expect them to say, ". . . and has Abraham seen you?" And this is exactly the way one important reading has it. That reading may be correct. On the other hand, it may also be a very natural scribal error arising from the fact that the text which the scribe was copying contained the question in the *unexpected* form: "And have you seen Abraham?" The question thus put (which has strong textual support), though somewhat surprising as to its form, can be explained as the result of the following reasoning process: "If, as he says, Abraham has seen him, then he must have seen Abraham; but to have seen Abraham, who lived about two thousand years ago, he must be a very old man, indeed." Hence, they said, "You have not even (lived) fifty years, and have you seen Abraham?" To their infidel minds it was an absurdity that Jesus could have seen Abraham. Why, he was not even forty years; but to be very generous they are willing to make it "not even *fifty*." In any event (so they reason) Jesus could not have seen Abraham. — In passing, it should be remarked that their question of unbelief implies nothing whatever as to the exact age of Jesus or as to his outward appearance (whether he looked as if he were almost fifty).

58. Jesus said to them, I most solemnly assure y o u, before Abraham was born, I am. The Jews had committed the error of ascribing to Jesus a merely temporal existence. They saw only the historical *manifestation*, not the eternal *Person;* only the human, not the divine. Jesus, therefore, reaffirms his eternal, timeless, absolute essence. For the introductory clause ("I most solemnly assure y o u") see on 1:51. The appropriate character

---

[50] We cannot agree with the following explanations of 8:56:

(1) He rejoiced when he saw Jesus as one of the three men to whom reference is made in Gen. 18. — But, aside from other objections, the term rejoicing or laughing is not used in that account in connection with Abraham. Also, why would this interview be called "my day"?

(2) As Abraham saw it, the day of Christ in which he rejoiced actually arrived in connection with the birth of Isaac. — But thus a strange meaning is given to the term "my day." Also, Heb. 11:13 does not receive its due.

(3) Abraham's soul in heaven rejoiced when Jesus was born in Bethlehem. — But this explanation impresses us as carrying into the text a foreign element, a novelty of which there is no record anywhere in Scripture.

of this clause, as being used here to introduce a very sublime truth, is immediately evident.

Over against Abraham's fleeting span of life (see Gen. 25:7) Jesus places his own timeless present. To emphasize this eternal *present* he sets over against the aorist infinitive, indicating Abraham's birth in time, the present indicative, with reference to himself; hence, not I *was,* but I *am.* Hence, the thought here conveyed is not only that the second Person always existed (existed from all eternity; cf. 1:1, 2; cf. Col. 1:17), though this, too, is implied; but also, and very definitely, that his existence *transcends time.* He is therefore exalted infinitely above Abraham. See also on 1:18; and cf. 1:1, 2. The "I am" here (8:58) reminds one of the "I am" in 8:24. Basically the same thought is expressed in both passages; namely, that Jesus is God! Moreover, what he states here in 8:58 is his answer not only to the statement of the Jews recorded in 8:57 but also to that found in 8:53.

59. So they picked up stones in order to hurl them at him. But Jesus hid himself, and went out of the temple. The opposition against Jesus here reaches a new height. Unable to restrain themselves and their wrathful indignation any longer, and apparently viewing Christ's statement (8:58) as horrible blasphemy which must be punished with death by stoning (Lev. 24:16), the Jews run to a place in the large temple-area where building-operations are still being carried on. See on John 2:20. Stones are lying all around. These they pick up in order to hurl them at Jesus, thus to put him to death without due process of law or trial by court.

In the meantime, however, Jesus — knowing, of course, that the proper moment to lay down his life had not yet arrived — hid himself (perhaps, amid a crowd of friends) and went out of the temple. It is probable that this last sentence of 8:59 must be regarded as hendiadys, so that the resultant thought is on this order: he went secretly (concealed by the crowd) out of the temple.

Synthesis of 8:12-59

See the Outline on p. 2. *The Son of God Exhorting the Multitudes: "I am the light of the world." His Enemies Are Ready to Stone Him.*

Again exhorting the multitude in the temple (hostile religious leaders, Pharisees, citizens of Jerusalem, and some lingering pilgrims perhaps) Jesus once more reveals who he is. This section contains: a. his exalted claims, and b. their reaction. In verses 12-20 we have the record of the reaction on the part of *the Pharisees.* Some of these, no doubt, were members of the Sanhedrin. In verses 21-30 the attitude of *the Jews* is described. In all probability, however, the terms *Pharisees* and *Jews* overlap (as would seem to be evident from a comparison between verses 13, 20, 21, and 22). The term *Jews* generally indicates the hostile ruling class and their followers. In this large group there were, of course, many Pharisees. From verse 30 to the end of the chapter the conversation is carried on between Jesus, on the one side, and on the other: *many* of the assembled multitude. By and large, however, we are still dealing with the same crowd of people: note the expression "the Jews" in verses 48, 52, and 57. In fact, it would seem that throughout the entire chapter those addressed are, on the whole, the same; though, of course, not everybody is making a vocal response to the words of Jesus.

Christ's self-revelation, on the one hand, and the reaction of those addressed and responding, on the other, may be briefly summarized as follows:

Jesus:	The Jews:
The Bringer of light: "I am the light of the world."	1. *Flat contradiction:* "Your testimony is not true."
The Reliable One: "My testimony is certainly true. . . . It is I bearing testimony concerning myself, and the Father who sent me."	2. *Slanderous insinuation:* "Where is your father?"
The One who is going to the Father: "Where I am going you cannot come."	3. *Sneering sarcasm:* "He is not going to kill himself, is he?"
The Rightful Object of faith: "If you will not believe that I am he, you will die in your sins."	4. *Scornful disdain:* "You, who are *you?*"
The One sent by the Father: "He who sent me is true, and whatsoever I have heard from him, these things I speak to the world."	5. *Ignorance born of prejudice:* "They did not recognize that he spoke to them of the Father."
The Son of man who was going to be "lifted up" by them: "When you will have lifted up the Son of man, then you will know that I am he."	6. *Merely mental concurrence:* "While he was saying these things, many believed in him."
The Truth, able to set men free: "If you remain in my word, you are truly my disciples, and you will know the truth, and the truth will set you free."	7. *Arrogant surprise:* "The seed of Abraham are we, and to no one have we been enslaved ever. How is it that you say: 'You will become free'?"

Jesus:	The Jews:

The One who reveals God:

"If y o u are Abraham's children, y o u are doing the works of Abraham. But now y o u are seeking to kill me, a man who has been telling y o u the truth which I heard from God. This Abraham did not do. Y o u are doing the works of y o ur father."

The One without sin:

"Y o u are of y o u r father, the devil. . . . Who of y o u convicts me of sin?"

The Prince of life:

"I do not have a demon. . . . If any one keeps my word, he will certainly never see death."

Abraham's Delight:

"Abraham, y o u r father, was extremely happy that he was to see my day, and he saw it and rejoiced."

The Eternal One:

"Before Abraham was born, I am."

8. *Slanderous insinuation (again) and blind boastfulness:*

"We were not born of fornication; one Father have we, even God."

9. *Scurrilous abuse:*

"Are we not correct in saying, 'You are a Samaritan and have a demon'?"

10. *Blustering infidelity:*

"Now we know that you have a demon. . . . Whom are you making yourself?"

11. *Scathing ridicule:*

"You have not even (lived) fifty years, and have *you* seen Abraham?"

12. *Open violence:*

"So they picked up stones in order to hurl them at him."

69

CHAPTER IX

9 1 And as he was walking along, he saw a man blind from his birth. 2 And his disciples asked him saying, "Rabbi, who sinned, this man or his parents, so that [51] he was born blind?" 3 Jesus answered, "Neither did this man sin nor his parents, but (this happened) in order that the works of God should be displayed in him.[52] 4 We, while it is day, must work the works of him who sent me. Night is approaching when no one can work. 5 As long as I am in the world, I am the light of the world. 6 Having said these things he spat on the ground and made mud with the saliva and daubed its mud on his eyes 7 and said to him, "Go, wash in the pool Siloam (which, interpreted, means Sent). So he went away and washed and came (back) seeing.

9:1-7

9:1. And as he was walking along, he saw a man blind from his birth.

As Jesus *walked along* or *passed by*, he saw a man afflicted with congenital blindness. This was rather common among the ancients, just as it is even today among those who do not use the necessary precautionary measures in connection with childbirth.[53]

Neither the time nor the place of the event related in the present paragraph is recorded. There is, nevertheless, an interesting comparison between the man afflicted with congenital blindness and the one who was handicapped by congenital paralysis (see for the latter Acts 3). Both were beggars (cf. 9:8 with Acts 3:3). The latter was laid daily at the temple-gate called *Beautiful*. In view of the fact that many of the devout passed in and out of this gate, it was a natural place for the objects of pity and charity. Now also the present paragraph (9:1-7) establishes a close connection between the temple (8:59) and this beggar who had been blind from his birth. Hence, some are of the opinion that Jesus in leaving the temple found this man sitting at one of the temple-gates, begging. Others, how-

---

[51] On ἵνα see Vol. I, pp. 46, 49.
[52] Or: "but in order that the works of God may be displayed in him we must work the works of him who sent me, while it is day." See W. H. Spencer, "John 9:3" *ExT*, 55 (1944), 110.
[53] See article *Blindness,* in D.C.G.

ever, point to the fact that the blind man was cured on a sabbath (9:14), and they consider it improbable that the Jews would have tried to stone the Lord (8:59) on that sacred day. However, it is probably not wise to limit too rigidly the number of crimes which Jews, beside themselves with anger and jealousy, permitted themselves to commit on the sabbath (cf. Matt. 27:62-66). We simply do not know whether the events recorded in chapters 8 and 9:1-34 happened on the same day. But if the blind man was not cured on the day when Jesus escaped being stoned to death, the miracle must have taken place very soon afterward (perhaps, the next day). Incorrect is the view that it occurred at the feast of the Dedication (in December). The time of that feast is not reached until 10:22.

We are not told how Jesus or his disciples discovered that this man had been blind *from his birth*, but this may have been a matter of common knowledge. See also on 5:6.

2. And his disciples asked him saying, Rabbi, who sinned, this man or his parents, sothat he was born blind? It appears from this verse that the disciples had accompanied their Master to Jerusalem. To them this blind man presents a theological puzzle. They probably reasoned somewhat as follows: "Back of every physical affliction or defect lies a sin, generally the sin of the afflicted one. But how can this be true if the man *is born* with a defect? In that case he cannot have brought it upon himself through his own misconduct, can he? Is he being punished, then, for the sin of his parents? And if so, is this fair? But no, there is another possibility: the individual who was born with a defect may, after all, be the cause of his own misfortune; for he may have committed acts of sin while he was still in the womb!"

Weighing the two possibilities, the disciples ask the question, "Rabbi — for this term see on 1:38 —, who sinned, this man or his parents, sothat he was born blind?"

According to Scripture (and the apocrypha) physical afflictions (defects, hardships, suffering, "accidents," sickness, death) can be traced to various moral causes; such as:

(1) The sin of Adam, in whom all have fallen and are by nature guilty before God. This is implied in Rom. 5:12-21 (cf. also Gen. 3:17-19; Rom. 8:20-23; I Cor. 15:21, 22; Eph. 2:3; and the apocryphal book Ecclus. 25:24).

(2) The sins of the parents (Ex. 20:5; 34:7; Num. 14:18; Deut. 5:9; 28:32; Jer. 31:29; Ezek. 18:2. Cf. the apocryphal books Wisdom of Sol. 4:6; Ecclus. 41:5-7).

(3) One's own personal sins (Deut. 28:15-68; Jer. 31:30; Ezek. 18:4).

Cause (1) is ever presupposed by and qualifies causes (2) and (3). Hence, no one ever has a right to charge God with injustice.

The Jews, however, had a tendency to exaggerate the importance of (2) and (3) out of all proportion to revealed truth. They traced each particular sorrow to a particular sin. Thus the friends of Job traced his afflictions to the sin of cruelty to the widow and the fatherless (Job 4:7; 8:20; 11:6; 22:5-10); and in Jesus' own day that kind of reasoning was still very prevalent (see, for example, Lk. 13:2-5). That Jesus himself did not approve of this disproportionate emphasis is clear from the last-mentioned reference and is not contradicted by John 5:14 (see on that verse).

When the disciples mentioned as one of their alternatives that the man, though *born* blind, was perhaps reaping the fruits of *his own* sin, they were probably not thinking of metempsychosis (transmigration of souls), though this construction is placed upon their question by Calvin and Beza, nor of the purely spiritual pre-existence of the soul (cf. Philo, *On the Giants,* III, 12-15; some would add Wisd. of Sol. 8:20; however, this passage does not necessarily imply that doctrine), but of the rabbinic (overemphasis upon the) idea that babies are able to sin in the womb. From Gen. 25:22-26 (cf. Ps. 58:3 and Lk. 1:41-44) the rabbis concluded that in the womb Esau had tried to kill Jacob.[54]

The other alternative which occurred to the minds of these disciples was that this unfortunate individual was the victim of parental transgression, perhaps the sin of a dissolute father (as is at times actually the case, even today).

3-5. Jesus answered, Neither did this man sin nor his parents, but (this happened) in order that the works of God should be displayed in him. In this answer Jesus immediately rules out the man's personal sins and the sins of his parents as causes to which his blindness can be traced. If a cause must be mentioned, the sin of Adam, our representative head, would be the answer. However, Jesus is not even interested in this at the present time. For the backward look of the disciples he substitutes the forward look. They had asked, "How did it come to be?" He answers, "It happened with a purpose; namely, that the works of God (miracles in which he shows his power and his love) should be displayed in him." *All* things — even afflictions and calamities — have as their ultimate purpose the glorification of God in Christ by means of the manifestation of his greatness (cf. 1:14; 5:19, 20). **We, while it is day, must work the works of him who sent me** (the textual evidence furnishes no adequate reason to depart from this reading). **Night is approaching when no man can work.** To the disciples a glance at this man suggested a theological puzzle. To Jesus a look in his direction presented a challenge, an opportunity for work. *They* reasoned: "How did he get that way?" *He* answered: "What can we do for him?" So there were two ways of looking at this man, and the latter was by far the better.

---

[54] See S.BK. II, pp. 527-529.

Note the emphatic position of the pronoun "we" in the answer which Jesus gives: *"We,* while it is day, must work the works of him who sent me." This "we" refers, of course, to Jesus himself and his disciples, the men who have just asked the question. For Jesus and for these followers (and, in a sense, for *all* his followers) the rule holds: while it is day we must work the works of God. Essentially these works are *one* (cf. 5:17, 20; 14:12); they are kingdom-works, whose oneness is clearly evident from the phrase which Jesus uses in calling them "the works of him who sent me." On "sent" see below, verse 7.

This teaching of our Lord is very striking, especially in the present connection. It is as if he intends to say: When someone crosses y o u r path, y o u can react in a threefold manner:

(1) If he excites y o u r envy, *y o u can pelt him with brickbats.* — Just now (or very recently) the Jews had tried to do that with reference to Jesus (8:59). The history of the world — and, sad to say, also to some extent of the visible church — furnishes examples of this general attitude. Some people never do anything constructively. Their life, from day to day, is a constant attempt to annihilate the object of their jealousy. The "Jews" are still with us. The "sanhedrin" also (at least its spirit) has not completely disappeared.

(2) If he arouses your desire for additional information, *y o u can try to gratify y o u r curiosity* by asking questions about him, in order, perhaps, to solve a theological puzzle. The disciples were occupying themselves with that, as has just been shown (see on 9:2). Now curiosity has its legitimate place, and questions of a theological nature should be encouraged rather than discouraged. But there is a limit. One should not *only* ask questions; one should *also* perform deeds ("works") of love! In fact, that is where the emphasis should rest. Hence,

(3) *Y o u should love him and help him!* "That," says Jesus, as it were, must be *our* attitude: "We, while it is day, must work the works of him who sent me."

The expression "while it is day" is explained in the very next verse by "when I am in the world." When Jesus, having said "It is finished," breathes his last, his *day* is done, his work of rendering an atonement for sin has been accomplished. Though it is true that even after his resurrection there were "appearances," he is not "in the world" any more as he was formerly. The same holds with respect to the disciple: for him too there is a divinely-appointed time; namely, his life-time here below. Let him make the most of his opportunities. The mandate is urgent, for "Night (that is, death) is approaching when no one can work." **As long as I am in the world, I am the light of the world.** The particle which we have rendered "as long as" (ὅταν) here, as in most other instances, refers to a rather indefinite time-relationship (Jesus is not saying just how long he will be in the world). It would appear from the present context that in this case the best translation is not "whenever," as if Jesus wanted to refer to more than one act of coming into (and being in) the world, an idea wholly foreign to the present paragraph. The rendering "as long as" is suggested by the parallel in verse 4 "while." For the meaning of the solemn declaration "I am the light of the world," see on 8:12. It is true that here in 9:5 the definite article does not precede the noun *light*, but it is very doubtful whether any special significance must be attached to this omission. If a designation of the character of our Lord begins to be thought of as a proper name or title, the article is not always felt to be necessary. There is a certain latitude of usage.

It is clear that the saying "I am the light of the world" furnishes the key to the interpretation of what follows. The cure of the man born blind, about to be related, is an illustration of what Jesus is constantly doing in his capacity as the light of the world.

6. Having said these things he spat on the ground and made mud with the saliva and daubed its mud on his eyes. Just why the Lord chose this particular method we do not know. The answers usually given fail to satisfy; for example, that he did this in order to impress upon the man that the healing power came from Jesus (but would not the *word* of Jesus take care of this?); or in order to make use of the healing qualities of saliva or of mud; or to make this blind man even more thoroughly blind (!) sothat he might appreciate the cure even more deeply; or to symbolize the fact that man was made from the dust of the earth; etc., etc. If an answer must be given, it may be said that the Lord probably used this method in order to induce the proper attitude of heart and mind; i.e., to bring about perfect obedience, that type of submission which carries out a seemingly arbitrary command. Cf. Gen. 2:16, 17. According to this answer, the mud had nothing whatever to do with the physical cure; it had no medicinal qualities, not any more than did the waters of Jordan into which Elisha bade Naaman to plunge himself seven times (II Kings 5:10) in order to be healed of his leprosy. In both cases the command was a test of obedience. It must be borne in mind that *he* is at work here who calls himself *the light of the world,* and that in this particular case light is imparted not only to the body but also to the soul (9:35-38).

7. And (he) said to him, Go, wash in the pool Siloam [55] **(which interpreted means Sent).** This pool reminds one of the one at Bethzatha ("Bethesda"), but while the latter was located to the north-east of Jerusalem —

---

[55] The genitive is either appositional (the pool Siloam) or possessive (the pool of — i.e., belonging to — Siloam). In the latter case the name Siloam designates the entire water-system: spring, tunnel, pool; and we are told that the pool in which the blind man must wash belonged to this system.

see on 5:2 — the Siloam pool was just inside the south-east portion of the city-wall. King Hezekiah had built a tunnel to carry the water of the Gihon Spring (now Virgin's Fount), located outside the wall, in a south-south-westward direction to just within the wall. The purpose had been to guarantee a water-supply in case of a siege. The original name of the pool was probably *Shiloah,* a proper name derived from the Hebrew passive participle meaning "sent" or "conducted," given to it because through its tunnel water was (and *is* even today) *conducted* from the intermittently flowing fountain to the pool; cf. our word "aqueduct." [56]

Some commentators reject the idea that Jesus attached symbolical significance to the meaning of the name of this pool. Nevertheless, three facts should be borne in mind:

(1) This miracle is certainly symbolical, picturing Jesus as *the light of the world* (8:12; 9:5).

(2) In this Gospel Jesus constantly presents himself as the One who is *sent* by the Father (see on 3:17, 34; 5:36, 37; 6:57; 7:29; 8:18, 27, 29; etc.). Now the name of the pool is also Shiloah (changed to Siloam); i.e., *Sent.* Is it not very natural to connect the water of this spring and pool with the One who is the water of life (see 4:10; 7:37)?

(3) The waters of Shiloah flow from the temple-hill and are even in the Old Testament regarded as symbolical of the spiritual blessings which issue forth from God's dwelling-place (see Is. 8:6 and cf. Ezek. 47:1).

Accordingly, when the man is told to go and wash in the pool Siloam, though it is certainly true that this must be taken in the most literal sense sothat he was actually expected to wash his eyes in that literal pool, the deeper meaning is surely this: that for spiritual cleansing one must go to the true Siloam; i.e., to the One who was *sent* by the Father to save sinners.

So he went away and washed and came (back) seeing. In spite of the strange character of the command, the man does not copy the example of Naaman. He does not protest but he immediately obeys. To the pool he goes and with his hand he dips up some water. With this he washes the mud off his eyes. (The passage in no way implies that he jumped into the pool or bathed. We are dealing here with a blind man, not with a leper.) His obedience is immediately rewarded: he came back seeing.

---

[56] See further W.H.A.B., pp. 50, 98, and Plate XVII B. Also II Kings 20:20; II Chron. 32:4, 30; 33:14; Neh. 3:15; Is. 8:6; Luke 13:4; John 7:2, 37; Josephus, *Antiquities,* VII, xiv, 5. For the Siloam Inscription see article *Siloam,* in W.D.B., and also art. *The Siloam Tunnel,* in M. S. & J. L. Miller, *Encyclopedia of Bible Life,* New York and London, 1944, p. 430.

8 The neighbors, therefore, and those who had seen him before as a beggar[57] were saying, "Is not this the one who used to sit begging?" 9 Some were saying,[58] "This is the one"; others were saying, "No, but he resembles him." He was saying,[58] "I am the one." 10 In reply, they were saying to him, "How then were your eyes opened?" 11 He answered, "The man who is called Jesus made mud and daubed my eyes and said to me, 'Go to Siloam and wash.' So I went and washed and received (my) sight." 12 They said to him, "Where is he?" He said, "I do not know."

9:8-12

9:8, 9. The man was now able to see everything: the sun, the sky, the houses, and — most interesting of all — the people. It does not surprise us that, in all likelihood, he went to his home. When the neighbors saw him, they were looking at a man who seemed to differ very much from the familiar mendicant, known to almost everybody. The miracle had produced a change in his entire appearance and bearing.

The neighbors, therefore, and those who had seen him before as a beggar were saying, Is not this the one who used to sit begging? Some were saying, This is the one; others were saying, No, but he resembles him. He was saying, I am the one.

At this point the story becomes very graphic. (Notice the many instances of the use of the imperfect tense: "were saying." Cf. 7:11-13.) Opinions were divided. One would say, "Is not this man the one who used to sit begging?" An affirmative answer was expected, though there is in the question a tiny element of doubt borne of surprise. Another would answer with absolute certainty, "This is the one." But a third person, unable to believe that one who was born blind could be cured, would again and again forcefully declare, "No, but he resembles him." Perhaps the last speaker was somewhat deceived by the change that had taken place in the man's bearing and demeanor. The cured man put an end to the controversy by repeatedly declaring, "I am the one."

10-12. The neighbors are no longer in doubt with reference to the identity of the man. It is altogether natural that **in reply, they were saying to him, How then were your eyes opened?"** The man gives a slightly condensed account of what had happened (cf. this with verses 6, 7 above), a report which was true in every detail. **He answered, The man who is called Jesus made mud and daubed my eyes and said to me, go to Siloam and**

---

[57] Literally, "*that* he was a beggar." — Declarative ὅτι is not unusual after this verb of seeing; cf. 4:19; 12:19. It is not necessary, therefore to view this ὅτι is causal in the present instance.
[58] On ὅτι in both of these instances see Vol. I, pp. 54, 59.

wash. So I went and washed and received my sight. He even mentions the name of his benefactor — someone must have told him — but apparently does not realize that this miracle-worker is the world's Redeemer. In his report of his own actions ("So I went and washed and received my sight") a word is used (ἀνέβλεψα) which means "I recovered my sight"; but since this man had never enjoyed the blessing of sight, we may translate rather freely, "I received (my) sight." The desire to see the man who had performed so great a miracle is altogether natural. **They said to him, Where is he?** (just like in 7:11). **He answered, I do not know.** In the nature of the case, he could not have known the whereabouts of Jesus. Remember also 8:59 in this connection. Just now and for good reasons Jesus was not showing himself to the public.

---

13 They brought to the Pharisees the man formerly blind. 14 Now the day when Jesus had made the mud and had opened his eyes was a sabbath. 15 Again, therefore, the Pharisees also were asking him how he had received (his) sight. So he said to them, "Mud he put on my eyes and I washed and I see." 16 In reply, some of the Pharisees were saying, "This man is not from God for he does not keep the sabbath." Others were saying, "How can a man who is a sinner do such signs?" And there was a division among them. 17 Then they again said to the blind man, "What do you say about him, seeing that he opened your eyes?" He said, "He is a prophet."

9:13-17

9:13. They brought to the Pharisees the man formerly blind.

The section 9:13-34 contains the record of the man's examination by the Pharisees. The first question which occurs is this: *By whom* was this man examined: by a group of men meeting informally or by an official body in a formal examination? With respect to this question commentators are divided into two groups. On the one hand, there are those who defend a view which, barring minor variations, may be described as follows:

The man is brought before a group of Pharisees, *meeting informally,* perhaps in the home of one of them. These religious leaders, angered by the fact that Jesus had again violated their sabbath-regulations and even more by his increasing influence among the people try to discredit the miracle. They suspect that a fraud has been perpetrated. When they do not succeed in persuading the man to admit his guilt and when they come out second best in the argument, their anger flares up. Thoroughly enraged by what they regard as the man's brazen impudence they throw him out of the house or hall.

In support of their position (that the entire examination is informal and that no formal sentence of excommunication from the religious life of

78

Israel is pronounced) these interpreters declare that the individual in question, a mere beggar, would have been considered too unimportant for any formal action, and also that the verb used in 9:34 ("and they threw him out") is not the one employed in 9:22 ("would be unsynagogued"; i.e., expelled from the synagogue).

On the other hand, there are those who look upon this incident as far more formal. We believe that they are right. It is true, of course, that the evangelist is not describing a plenary session of the great Sanhedrin (cf. 9:13), but this does not mean that the meeting and the sentence which was carried out were of an informal nature. In all likelihood these Pharisees were acting under orders from the Sanhedrin and knew that in expelling the man they were acting in accordance with the decision of that body. Either they had received power to act in this particular case, or else, having been appointed to examine this man, they knew that their action with respect to him would subsequently be approved by the Sanhedrin. We regard the verb in 9:34 to be a synonym for the one used in 9:22.

We base this conclusion upon the following grounds:

(1) It is clear from 1:24 (see on that verse) that the Sanhedrin would at times delegate a group of Pharisees to examine matters touching those who by some of the people were regarded as the Messiah. If in that case, why not in this? Surely, the Pharisees would not only examine the alleged claimant but also those who by their stories of his miraculous deeds might seem to be in danger of bolstering that claim.

(2) The fact that authority to act was sometimes given to a group of religious teachers seems to be borne out by the records.[59] Is it not possible that we are dealing here with the minor Sanhedrin or synagogue-court, of which there are said to have been two in Jerusalem?

(3) According to 9:22 the Sanhedrin had agreed upon expulsion from the synagogue for those who confessed Jesus to be the Christ. According to 9:28 the group of Pharisees which examines this man regards him as a disciple of Jesus; hence, a candidate for expulsion. It is true that at this point the man had not yet actually confessed Jesus to be the Christ (see 9:38), but it does not seem probable that the enemies of Jesus, in their exasperation, would make generous allowance for this difference. The man, after all, had confessed Jesus to be a prophet (9:17), a genuine miracle-worker, in a sense altogether unique (9:32), and a person who performed his miracles because of the extraordinary favor and power of God which rested upon him (9:33). Accordingly, when 9:34 now states, "And they cast him out," it is altogether natural to regard this as actual expulsion from the synagogue. What is recorded in 9:22, 28, 32, 33 has certainly prepared the reader to expect nothing less than excommunication for this man.

---

[59] S.BK. IV, p. 298.

(4) The manner in which this group of Pharisees summons individuals (9:18, 24), the legal formality of its method of inquiry (9:19), and also the extreme caution exercised by the parents (9:21, 22), a caution resulting from fear, pleads in favor of a formal meeting before a group of authorized representatives of the Sanhedrin.

(5) The importance which 9:35 ascribes to his expulsion also points in the same general direction.

For the reasons given we shall, therefore, in our exegesis proceed from this point of view.

Who brought this man to the Pharisees? Perhaps, the neighbors (see context, 9:8, 12). On the other hand, it is also possible that the third person plural active verb, followed by the object-pronoun ("they brought him") should simply be regarded as the same in meaning as our third person singular passive verb preceded by the subject-pronoun ("he was brought"), according to a familiar Aramaic style-characteristic (cf., for example, Dan. 4:25 in English and in Hebrew. The reference in the Hebrew Bible is Dan. 4:22). In that case if we wish to retain the third person plural active construction, the pronoun "they" must be regarded as indefinite, like the German *man* (Dutch *men* or French *on*).

When was he brought? Probably not on the sabbath but a little later.

Why was he brought before the Pharisees? Was it because he had violated the sabbath-regulations which were esteemed so highly by the religious authorities? That is possible, but nothing with reference to the sabbath is mentioned before the time of the judicial inquiry. From the connection between verses 13 and 14 it would seem as if the Pharisees themselves bring up this point.

Another reason suggests itself: the Pharisees had been telling the people that Jesus was a deceiver. In fact, already the people were aware of the fact that a decision had been made by the Sanhedrin that anyone who should confess Jesus to be the Christ would be expelled from the synagogue (9:22). But what were the Pharisees going to say now? Did not this great miracle speak louder than any verdict of the Sanhedrin? Let the man in question be brought before the Pharisaic judges, so that they can hear the story from his own lips. Then will they still persist in their opinion about Jesus? Or has some fraud been committed which they are able to uncover and expose?

We are not sure that the suggested reason was the real one. It would, nevertheless, furnish a very natural explanation.

14, 15a. Now the day when Jesus had made the mud and had opened his eyes was a sabbath. To make mud on the sabbath and on that day to cover a person's eyes with this mud was a violation of the regulations. Also, on the sabbath it was not permissible to practice the art of healing, except in cases of extreme emergency. With respect to the Pharisaic attitude toward the sabbath see on 3:1 and 5:9b-13. So the Pharisees (not by any means *all* of them, however; see on 9:16) probably reason somewhat in the following trend: a. Even if he did not actually perform a miracle, Jesus has in any case violated the sabbath; hence, b. he is an open sinner; but, c. *God* would never enable *open sinners* to effect a *real* cure; hence, d. this whole case looks very suspicious and requires thorough investigation. Is it a fraud perhaps? Cf. 9:18.

Again, therefore, the Pharisees also were asking him how he (had) received his sight. Indeed, *again*, for this was not the first time the question had been asked. He had been bombarded with it. First it had come from the lips of the neighbors, who had voiced it again and again (9:10). And now *also* the Pharisees confront him with it.

15b. So he said to them, Mud he put on my eyes and I washed and I see. Already the man appears to be wary. He weighs his words. Note how the report of the miracle is becoming more and more concise; cf. verses 6, 7; then 11; then 15b.

16. *The Battle of the Syllogisms* follows. It is continued to the end of the story. We have first: the syllogism of the predominant group of Pharisees (verse 16a); and next, the syllogism vaguely suggested by the question of the minority. This second syllogism is going to be used with telling force by the cured man himself (see on 9:31-33). Accordingly, we shall speak of *Syllogism A* and *Syllogism B*.

In reply, some of the Pharisees were saying, This man is not from God, for he does not keep the sabbath. Here we have what we shall refer to as:

Syllogism A

Major Premise: All people who are from God keep the sabbath.
Minor Premise: This man (Jesus) does not keep the sabbath.
Conclusion: This man is not from God.

On the surface this looks like excellent reasoning. As a syllogism its validity must be granted. But this does not mean that the conclusion is *true.* There may be no flaw in logic in deriving a conclusion from a major and a minor premise, but if either of these premises be contrary to fact, the conclusion is no longer legitimate. In the present case *what these men mean in their* major premise is wrong. The Pharisees have identified their own trifling, hair-splitting sabbath-regulations with the law of God. Hence, their *real* major premise is, "All people who are from God observe *our sabbath-regulations.*" The minor premise is also wrong, and for the same reason: confusion of concepts. And because these premises are false, the conclusion ("This man is not from God") is no longer *dependable*. Whether in itself it is true or false is still another matter. But we know that the statement which forms the conclusion is wholly false, the very opposite of the truth.

Others were saying, How can a man who is a sinner do such signs? Here we have:

Syllogism B Unimproved

Major Premise: Only people who are from God (or: who are not sinners) can open the eyes of those born blind (or: can do "such" signs).

Minor Premise: This man, Jesus, has opened the eyes of one born blind (or: has done "such" a sign).

Conclusion: This man is from God (or: this man is not a sinner).

Note, however, that this syllogism is cast in the form of a *question*. At best, it is merely suggested, but not definitely stated. These more mild-tempered Pharisees are confronted with a problem and they seek a solution. The problem is, "How can a man who is a sinner do such signs?" Even among this group there were probably several who would have rejected the proposition: "Perhaps Jesus is not a sinner." For *them* Jesus is definitely a sinner. Hence, for *them* the whole matter is a profound mystery. For *them* Syllogism B has no reality whatever. Others, however, are beginning to see the light. The syllogism, then, is *the very most* that can possibly be derived from the question, and even then *it is only suggested* by the question. It is not a positive statement.

Is the vaguely suggested syllogism valid? As an exercise in logic (note the exclusive character of the major premise: the word "only") its validity must be granted. The reasoning is as sound as a silver dollar fresh from the mint. But is the major premise *correct*? If not, then the conclusion — though ever so correct as a historical fact — is not legitimate.

To answer this question it must not be forgotten that those whose question suggests this syllogism (here in verse 16) are, after all, *Pharisees*. Call them the better, milder class of Pharisees, they remain Pharisees all the same. The type of reasoning that is here suggested fits into their scheme of thinking. One finds something resembling it in the following syllogism:

Major Premise: Only the wicked suffer physical affliction.
Minor Premise: This man suffers physical affliction.
Conclusion: This man is wicked.

That such reasoning is out of harmony with reality has been shown in connection with 9:2. Hence, if among these Pharisees there are those who adopt *Syllogism B Unimproved* because they believe that the ability to perform *a* miracle (*any* miracle) is, in and by itself, always proof of divine approval, they are wrong, as is very clear to anyone who reads Matt. 7:22. But we must be fair to them. As actually stated, the situation is slightly different. Among these milder Pharisees there must have been a considerable number who stressed *the exceeding greatness of this miracle.* Read the syllogism. They *had* something there, as is clear from 15:24. Jesus himself was going to say, "If I had not done among them *the works which no one else did,* they would have no sin." From this it is clear that he himself viewed his own miracles as being (from a certain aspect) in a class by themselves, signs of his deity and of his divine mission.

One more element must be added, however, for Jesus himself added it. It is this, that not only were his miracles *unique in character* ("works which no one else did") but also they were done *in answer to prayer;* hence, *with the purpose of glorifying God.* When *Syllogism B* is severed from its Pharisaic context and is given a distinctly Christian context, it is entirely valid. See on verses 31-33; also on 10:37, 38; 11:39-44; 15:24; and 20:30, 31. Jesus himself supplied this context when he said: "This happened *in order that the works of God should be displayed in him.* We, while it is day, must work the works of him who sent me." This gives us:

Syllogism B Improved

Major Premise: Only people who are from God (or: who are not sinners) can open the eyes of those born blind, *in order that by doing this they may display the works of God.*

Minor Premise: This man, Jesus, *with that purpose in mind,* has opened the eyes of one born blind.

Conclusion: This man is from God (or: this man is not a sinner).

And there was a division among them. That is, among the Pharisees a sharp division or *schism* arises between the supporters of *Syllogism A* and the suggesters of *Syllogism B* Unimproved. The former, after a brief *direct* thrust at the conclusion of *Syllogism B,* a thrust in the form of a question (see verse 17), begin their *indirect* attack. Verses 18-26 contain the record of their attempt to demolish the conclusion by rejecting the minor premise. If they can show that this man, Jesus, has not done a great sign, they will have overthrown the suggested conclusion of their opponents.

In their embarrassment, unable to agree among themselves, the Pharisees turn again to the man who had just been cured of his blindness.

17. Then they again said to the blind man, What do you say about him, seeing that he opened your eyes? It is clear from verse 18 that those who favored *Syllogism A* (Christ's bitter opponents) were in the majority, as we also could have expected. In the light of that fact it is clear, of course, that when the Pharisees (probably both parties) now ask the man, "What do you say about him?" the causal modifier — "seeing that he opened your eyes" — does not imply any admission, on the part of the majority, as if *they* now were willing to grant that Jesus had actually performed this astounding miracle. The clause is elliptical for "seeing that *you have declared that* he opened your eyes."

He said, He is a prophet. The man is advancing in knowledge. He also shows courage. He knew that, through Jesus, God had revealed himself to him by means of this miracle. And surely one who in such a remarkable manner reveals God must be a prophet!

---

18 However, the Jews did not believe concerning him that he had been blind and had received (his) sight, until they called the parents of him who had received (his) sight, 19 and asked them, saying, "Is this y o u r son whom y o u say was born blind? How then is it that he now sees? 20 Then his parents answered and said, "We know that this is our son and that he was born blind. 21 How it is that he now sees we do not know, and who opened his eyes we do not know. Ask him; he is of age; he will speak for himself." 22 His parents said these things because they were afraid of the Jews, for already the Jews had agreed that anyone who should confess him to be the Christ would be expelled from the synagogue.[60] 23 It was for that reason that his parents said, "He is of age; ask him."

9:18-23

9:18, 19. However, the Jews did not believe concerning him that he had been blind and had received his sight, until they called the parents of him who had received his sight, and asked them, saying, Is this y o u r son whom y o u say was born blind? How then is it that he now sees?

In their attempt to destroy the conclusion of suggested *Syllogism B* the Pharisees had failed to receive the co-operation of the man most directly concerned. Well, then if the direct method fails, they will try the indirect method: destroying the conclusion by attacking the minor premise. Moreover, if *the son* will not help them in their efforts to produce this result, they will seek the aid of *his parents!*

The opponents of Jesus are here called "the Jews" (see on 1:19). How is it to be explained that they (the Pharisaic majority) did not believe that this man had been blind and had received his sight? There are, of course, several possibilities: a. the mendicant may not have been as well-known

---

60 Literally: "that if anyone should confess him to be the Christ, he would be expelled from the synagogue." IIIA3; see Vol. I, pp. 42, 43.

to the religious leaders as he was to the common people; b. they may have doubted that *this* was that familiar beggar. Perhaps they thought that the *really* blind man had been kidnapped and that his "double" (in every respect except blindness) had been substituted for him; c. or, finally, they may have concluded that the well-known mendicant had been fooling everybody by acting as if he were blind.

Ill-will toward Jesus played its role, of course. To believe that this man had been blind and had been cured of his blindness would have been *the first step* toward crediting Jesus with a remarkable miracle. This step they did not want to take. Just as one often believes what he wishes to believe, so also one often disbelieves what he wishes to disbelieve.

They disbelieved that this man had been blind and had received his sight, *until they called his parents*. Did they believe these two facts afterward? It is true that the word "until" does not necessarily imply this. Nevertheless, it is hard to believe that even after the parents had given their testimony, the disbelief (with respect to the aforementioned two facts) continued. Verse 34 certainly implies that they then believed that this man had been born blind (as a punishment for sin). That he had been cured of his blindness was so evident that it could not be denied.

But it is one thing to accept the fact that this man was cured of his blindness. It is another thing to ascribe this cure to Jesus. To do justice to the truth the hostile Jews would have had to take *four steps.* They would have had to admit. a. This man was cured of congenital blindness. b. It was Jesus who cured him. c. The cure was effected through the power and love of God, *resting upon Jesus,* and not through the power of the prince of demons, working in Jesus. d. This shows that Jesus is, indeed, "a man from God." In fact, it indicates that he is all he claims to be. Now verse 18 simply teaches that before the parents had been summoned, the hostile Jews had not even taken step Number 1.

Verse 19 implies that the Jewish leaders had heard a rumor to the effect that these parents had been talking about the cure of their son. On the basis of this information the examiners now ask *two* questions.[61] First, they wish to know whether this is that widely discussed son who by the parents was said to have been born blind; secondly, they desire information with reference to the fact and manner of his cure.

---

[61] Many commentators are of the opinion that there are essentially *three* questions, though only two are definitely expressed. These three, as they see it, are the following: a. Is this your son? b. Was he born blind? c. How is it that he now sees? — But we cannot agree with this view. Rather, the Jews are saying, in substance, "Is this that son of y o u r s about whom y o u are telling everybody that he was cured of congenital blindness? If so, how is it that he now can see?" It is true that in the *answer* given by the parents there are *three* (or four!) parts. But one should not confuse the question with the answer.

20, 21. Then his parents answered and said, We know that this is our son and that he was born blind. By this open declaration identifying this man as their son and testifying that he was, indeed, born blind, these parents are forcing the Jews to take that dreaded *first step* (see on 9:18, 19) toward crediting Jesus with a remarkable miracle. Whether they (the majority, the men who evidently take the leading part) ever took the second step, admitting even mentally that it was Jesus who cured him, is debatable. Verse 26 does not necessarily imply this. *Openly* they never took this step but opposed it (see on 9:24). They definitely never took steps three and four.

How (it is that) he now sees we do not know, and who opened his eyes we do not know. Ask him; he is of age. He will speak for himself. The parents shy away from the second question. They also lie. They *do* know how it is that their son now sees. He has certainly told them all about the miracle. Verse 22 implies that they also knew who had performed it. It was lack of courage, selfish cowardice, which caused them to say, "We do not know . . . we do not know . . . Ask him; he is *of age* (at thirteen years and one day a Jew was considered *of age*); he will speak for himself." At a decisive moment, when they should have spoken, they were guilty of "passing the buck." Nevertheless, we must not be too hard on them. The question must always be asked, "What would we have done in similar circumstances?" The threatened punishment was most terrible! See on verses 22, 23. — It is possible that the intimate knowledge which these parents had with respect to the talents and character of their son — his ability to defend himself, ready wit, and courage — had something to do with their desire *to let him speak for himself.* The main reason why they spoke as they did is, however, stated in the passage which follows:

22, 23. His parents said these things because they were afraid of the Jews, for already the Jews had agreed that anyone who should confess him to be the Christ would be expelled from the synagogue. It was for that reason that his parents said, He is of age; ask him.

Fear of the Jews is a common theme in John's Gospel; see on 3:2 and 7:13. Already (long before Jesus was *formally* condemned as being worthy of death) the hostile Jewish authorities had agreed (i.e., made a formal Sanhedrin-decision) that anyone of his followers who would recognize in him the Messiah, God's Anointed, should be unsynagogued (ἀποσυνάγωγος γένηται). To read back into this account the later regulations regarding the minor ban (for thirty, sixty, or ninety days) and the major ban (for all time) is probably not warranted. The account surely reads as if the excommunication here intended was final and terrible. For other references to the application of this rule see 12:42; 16:2. Note that in the last reference expulsion from the synagogue and killing are juxtaposed. The one who was unsynagogued was virtually cut off from the religious and social life of Israel (cf. Lk. 6:22). From every point of view — social, economic, religious — the results were frightening, and this especially for people who were so poor that their son had to make his living by begging! Hence, although we cannot *justify* these parents in shirking their duty, we can *understand* them. How often has not courage been lacking in the case of those who should have shown it when the Sanhedrin or its equivalent under some other name threatened to *put out* those who were defending the truth of God! Church History is full of examples!

---

24 So for the second time they called the man who had been blind, and said to him, "Give glory to God; we know that this man is a sinner." 25 He answered, "Whether he is a sinner I do not know. One thing I do know: that though I was blind, I now see." 26 In reply they said to him, "What did he do to you? How did he open your eyes?" 27 He answered them, "I already told y o u, but y o u did not listen. Why do y o u wish to hear it again? It surely cannot be that y o u too wish to become his disciples?" 28 And they reviled him and said, "*You* are this fellow's disciple, but *we* are disciples of Moses. 29 We know that God has spoken to Moses; but as for this fellow, we do not know where he hails from." 30 The man answered and said to them, "Why this is an astonishing fact, that y o u do not know where he hails from, and yet he opened my eyes! 31 We know that God does not listen to sinners, but if anyone is God-fearing and does his will, to him he listens.[62] 32 Since the world began it was never heard of that anyone opened the eyes of a man born blind. 33 If this man were not from God, he could do nothing." [63] 34 They answered and said to him, "You were wholly born in sin, and you would teach us?" And they threw him out.

9:24-34

9:24. So for the second time they call the man who had been blind, and said to him, Give glory to God; we know that this man is a sinner.

The Jews were trying in every possible way to prove that Jesus was not the One who had opened the eyes of the man born blind. They were engaged in an attack on the minor premise of *Syllogism B* Unimproved (see on verse 16), in order to annihilate the conclusion: "Jesus is from God." But in this attempt they had failed to receive any help from the parents, who, driven by fear, had refused to commit themselves in any way with respect to the manner in which their son had received his sight.

In fact, the parents' testimony had made the case even more difficult for the Pharisees, for it had left them without any excuse for thinking that there had been no miracle at all. And they fear lest within a very short

---

[62] IIIB1; see Vol. I, pp. 42, 44.
[63] IIA; see Vol. I, p. 41.

time in the mind of everyone the name of Jesus will be linked with this miracle. And that must be prevented by all means.

Hence, these leaders decide to resummon the man formerly blind, in order to exact from him a promise that he will never again give Jesus the credit for the great benefit which he has received. They say to him: "Give glory *to God; we* know that *this man* is a sinner." The most simple explanation of this declaration is the following: "Glorify God by ascribing the miracle to *him,* and not to anyone else. Do not give that man (Jesus) the credit for it, for we have his number: *we know* that he is an open sinner. Surely, such a man could not have performed so great a deed!"

Notice how, in this argumentation, *Syllogism A* is beginning to bear fruit! Its conclusion has become the minor premise of another syllogism, on this order:

Syllogism A (2)

Major Premise: Only people who are from God can open the eyes of those born blind.

Minor Premise: This man (Jesus) is not from God.

Conclusion: He cannot have opened the eyes of one born blind.

Let it be granted then, so reason these Pharisees, that Jesus did actually cover the eyes of this man with mud and that he sent him to Siloam. When the man came to Siloam and washed the mud off his eyes, it was *God* — not Jesus — who performed the miracle. Hence, the man should give *God* the glory!

This explanation is in harmony with the entire context. Note how the words *God* and *this man* are contrasted! Not this man but God must receive the honor.

There is another interpretation on which we wish to comment briefly. It is to this effect, that the expression, "Give glory to God," is a kind of standard phrase, meaning "Glorify God by confessing your sin." According to these commentators, the Pharisees have not yet given up the idea that the whole thing is a fraud, which they now ask the man to confess. These interpreters usually refer to Josh. 7:19 in defence of the position that also here in John 9:24 the disputed expression has this meaning. However, one can *glorify God* in more ways than one: a. by acknowledging one's sins, to be sure; but also by bringing a conciliatory offering (cf. I Sam. 6:5); or, as here in 9:24, by giving God the thanksgiving and the praise for the inestimable privilege of physical eyesight. We, therefore, abide by the interpretation of 9:24 as we gave it.

25. As the story progresses it becomes increasingly clear that this man is not an ordinary individual. He is not easily shaken. Evidently the vaunted *knowledge* of these eminent judges has failed to impress him.

He answered, **Whether he is a sinner I do not know. One thing I do know: that though I was blind, I now see.** Boldly he places both his "I do not know" and his "I do know" over against their "we know." We say "over against," for instead of assenting to the proposition "This man is a sinner," he openly declares that *he,* the one formerly blind, is not aware of this; but that he is very definitely aware of the fact that, though blind, he is now fully able to see! Between the lines of his terse saying one can surely read this much: "Over against y o u r *mere say-so* I place this *one great fact of experience:* though I was blind, I now see. *Facts* are more stubborn than unsupportable *opinions.*"

26. Clearly, the Pharisees are being crowded against the wall. Having come out second best in their interview with the parents, they have failed even more wretchedly in their conversation with the son! They seem to be in a quandary. So, **In reply, they said to him, What did he do to you? How did he open your eyes?** Having exhausted their mental resources, they now return to the questions asked previously (see on 9:15), perhaps because they can think of nothing else to do. It is also possible that they were trying by means of this procedure to weary the man, so that by forcing boredom upon him they might cause him, in an unguarded moment, to make an inconsistent statement. How often the man had heard those questions: from the lips, first, of the neighbors, and that repeatedly; then, of the Pharisees; and now *once more,* of the Pharisees! It was the same thing over and over again: "What did he do to you? How did he open your eyes?"

27. **He answered them, I already told y o u, but y o u did not listen.** Clearly, the man is losing his patience. He is becoming disgusted with this stalling procedure. That, in itself, is not at all surprising. What *is* surprising is the fact that he is not at all afraid to express his marked displeasure in words that are clear and forceful. He had not inherited his parents' timidity. Moreover, he brandishes the weapon of irony — so delicious to him, but so distasteful to them — and he does it in such a manner that the intended victims would never forgive or forget. Says he, **Why do y o u wish to hear it again? It surely cannot be that y o u too wish to become his disciples?** The last words constitute a skillfully expressed question which anticipates a negative answer, to be sure, but leaves the door slightly ajar for a positive one; as if one were saying, "This is, of course, impossible . . . yet, one can never tell what y o u Pharisees might do!" If this is not scorching satire, it is at least the next thing to it. How some commentators can imagine that this man was *actually* of the opinion that the Pharisees (especially those who predominated) were seriously considering the idea of becoming disciples of Jesus is more than we can understand.

28, 29. And they reviled him and said, *You* are that fellow's disciple, but *we* are disciples of Moses. We know that God has spoken to Moses; but as for this fellow, we do not know where he hails from.

Under the circumstances this reaction of the Jewish leaders is entirely understandable. They were not the kind of people who would admit defeat. Moreover, they feel deeply insulted and humiliated. A mere beggar has defied their authority. He has made sport of their dignity and superior position. What, *they* about to become disciples of Jesus? His very *name* is poison to them, so that they refuse to take it upon their lips. They prefer to call him "that one" or "that fellow."

"You are that fellow's disciple," they say. They seem to regard the title *disciple of Jesus* to be a crowning insult. They can think of nothing worse to call the beggar. They do not even dream that they are bestowing upon him the highest possible honor. With self-satisfied arrogance they refer to themselves as "disciples of Moses" (see on 5:45, 46; 6:32; 8:5), not realizing that Moses was going to condemn them! They know that God spoke to Moses. Yes, they know the divine origin of the laws and ordinances which Moses instituted. What they do not know is that the One whom they hate with such devilish hatred has the right to say, "Moses spoke *of me.*"

When, in this connection, they affirm, "But as to this fellow, we do not know where he hails from," they are not denying what they (or their friends) have said previously with respect to the parentage of Jesus (6:42; 7:27). What they mean is: "We do not know from what source *he,* in distinction from Moses, derives his authority." Now Jesus had answered that question again and again. But they had refused to accept his answer.

30. The man answered and said to them, "Why, this is an astonishing fact that y o u do not know where he hails from, and yet he opened my eyes! And, it was, indeed, astonishing to hear these dignified men say, "We do *not* know." They were so used to saying, "We *know*" (9:24, 29; and cf. 6:42; 7:27), that it came as a shock that here for once they actually admitted ignorance with respect to a certain matter; and such an important matter! It concerned the One who had bestowed the blessing of vision upon a man *born* blind! About this most remarkable miracle-worker these wise men know almost nothing. They do not even know the source of his authority. The man born blind takes full advantage of the situation. To use a colloquialism, *he rubs it in!* Says he, "Why,[64] this is an astonishing fact (literally, *in this is the marvel*) that y o u (who pretend to know so much) do not know where he hails from (literally, *where he is from*), and yet (see on 1:5, footnote with respect to καί) he opend my eyes!"

---

[64] Note emphatic sense of ἀλλά in exclamations, like our *why!, but really!, indeed!* See the following passages for this use of the particle: Acts 4:16, 34; 8:31; 16:37; 19:35; I Cor. 5:3; 11:22; II Tim. 2:7.

31, 32, 33. The healed man continues, **We know that God does not listen to sinners, but if anyone is Godfearing and does his will, to him he listens.** Since the world began it was never heard of that anyone opened the eyes of a man born blind. If this man were not from God, he could do nothing.

Here *Syllogism B* returns in strengthened form *(essentially* the same as *Syllogism B Improved)*. Verse 31 is the major premise; verse 32, the minor; verse 33, the conclusion. See on 9:16.

Major Premise: Only people who are from God — i.e., who are God-fearing (literally, "God-worshipping") and do his will — are heard by God, so that they can open the eyes of those born blind.

Minor Premise: This man, Jesus, was heard by God, so that he opened the eyes of one born blind, and thus performed a miracle so great that since the world began (literally, "from the age," "from of old") it was never heard of.

Conclusion: This man is from God. If he were not, he could do nothing. He is definitely not a (flagrant) sinner.

Note that by speaking as he does this man is employing the Pharisaic type of argumentation. He is defeating the Pharisees with their own syllogistic reasoning. This in itself is very remarkable: *a beggar defeating a Pharisee with the Pharisee's own weapon!* But the man is doing even better than that: he takes the Pharisaic syllogism, and improves it, not only by stating positively what before was only a hint (cf. 9:31-33 with 9:16b) but also by giving it a definitely scriptural setting. The man regards the miracle as *an answer to prayer!* He says, "If anyone is God-fearing and does his will, to him he (God) listens." That position is entirely correct. It is Scriptural. The idea that God hears the prayers of the righteous but rejects the prayers of the wicked is found everywhere in the Bible: I Sam. 8:18; Job 27:9; 35:12; Ps. 18:41; 66:18; Prov. 1:28; 15:29; Is. 1:15; 59:2; Jer. 11:11; 14:12; Ezek. 8:18; Mic. 3:4; Zech. 7:13; John 8:21; Acts 10:35. Moreover, miracles (especially *such* miracles; see on 15:24) performed in answer to prayer and in order to display the works of God, do have evidential value (see on 10:37, 38; 11:39-44; 20:30, 31; cf. Acts 2:22; 4:31; II Cor. 12:12).

The Pharisees have suffered a humiliating defeat. They have been driven into a corner. Meanwhile, the beggar has made definite progress in his confession. He is no longer saying, "Whether he (Jesus) is a sinner, I do not know" (9:25). By this time he *knows* that Jesus is not a sinner, but the recipient of God's favor in a very high degree.

34. Having lost the argument, the Pharisees resort to arrogant, glaring abuse. **They answered and said to him, You were wholly born in sin, and you would teach us?** But even this abuse contains the evidence of their defeat, for by implication they now admit that this man who stands before them clear-sighted was born blind. The position recorded in verse 18 ("Now the Jews did not believe concerning him that he had been blind and had received his sight") has been abandoned. The miracle has actually occurred. So much is now clear to all. The very idea, however, of ascribing it to Jesus, as the One on whom the favor of God rests, is so obnoxious to them, that they regard the one who entertains it as "wholly born in sin" (his blindness being regarded by them as a punishment for sin; see on 3:2). That such a base fellow would actually take it upon himself to teach such worthies as themselves is disgusting! **And they threw him out;** i.e., out of the building and out of the religious fellowship of Israel. See on 9:13.

---

35 Jesus heard that they had thrown him out, and having found him he said, "Do *you* believe in the Son of man?" 36 He answered and said, "And who is he, sir, (tell me) in order that [65] I may believe in him?" 37 Jesus said to him, "You have seen him; in fact the One who is speaking to you is he." 38 He said, "I believe, Lord," and he worshiped him.

9:35-38

9:35. Jesus heard that they had thrown him out, and having found him he said, Do *you* believe in the Son of man? Jesus, the Good Shepherd (see chapter 10), is interested not only in the body but also in the soul of those whom he saves (see also on 5:14). So, having heard that this man had been expelled from the synagogue, the Lord seeks and finds him. Having located him, Jesus asks, "Do *you* believe in the Son of man?" It is probable that the pronoun *you* received a certain emphasis, so the import of the question is, "Do *you*, like a true disciple and in distinction from the unbelieving Jews, believe . . . ?" [66] The context clearly shows that the expression *believe in* in the present instance indicates true faith; in other words, "Do you rely entirely — for life and death — on the Son of man? Do you trust him, and do you entrust yourself wholly to him with reference to the present and the future, for your physical and for your spiritual needs?" For πιστεύω see also on 1:8; 3:16; 8:30, 31a. Jesus asked whether this man believed in *the Son of man*. For this term see on 12:34. The textual support for the reading *the Son of God* is definitely weaker; in fact, there are no good reasons to accept that reading.

---

[65] On ἵνα see Vol. I, pp. 46, 47, 49.
[66] We base this probability not on the presence of the pronoun (see Vol. I, pp. 63, 64) but on its position at the very beginning of the question.

36. He answered and said, And who is he, sir, (tell me) in order that I may believe in him? Before being able to answer the question, the man feels the need of knowing who this Son of man — this Messiah — might be. Hence, the question begins with the conjunction *And*, which anticipates additional information. Note that the Greek word κύριος has been translated *sir* here (verse 36) but *Lord* in verse 38. The reason is, of course, that in the present verse the once blind man is addressing someone whose identity has not yet been clearly revealed, though he may have surmised that it was Jesus; but in verse 38 the man is worshiping the One whom he now fully recognizes for what he is. See also on 1:38. On *believe in him* see verse 35.

37. Jesus said to him, You have seen him; in fact, the One who is speaking to you is he. Literally the answer of Jesus is, "You have both seen him, and the One who is speaking to you is he," but we believe that in English the translation which we have given is a little clearer without changing the sense in any way. In words that are almost identical to those found in 4:26 (see on that passage) Jesus reveals himself to this man as the true Messiah, even the Son of man.

38. He said, I believe, Lord, and he worshiped him. Being now fully aware of the fact that the One who has addressed him is the very One who has also healed him, namely, Jesus, on whom with wide-eyed wonder he fixes his gaze (what a privilege it is to be able to see!), and recognizing in Jesus the Messiah, the very Son of man, who is also Son of God and therefore the proper object of worship, the man falls down on his knees and renders religious worship (not merely respect or even reverence) to his Benefactor. In the Gospel of John the verb always indicates divine worship (see also 4:20, 21, 22, 23, 24; 12:20).

---

39 And Jesus said, "For judgment I came into this world, in order that those who do not see may see, and that those who see may become blind." 40 Some of the Pharisees near him heard these things, and they said to him, "Certainly, we too are not blind, are we?" 41 Jesus said to them, "If y o u were blind, y o u would have no sin;[67] but now that y o u say, 'We see,' y o u r sin remains."

9:39-41

9:39. And Jesus said, For judgment I came into this world. When Jesus sees this man on his knees in the attitude of genuine worship, and compares this humble and confiding condition of heart and mind with the

---

[67] IIA; see Vol. I, p. 41.

hostility and stubbornness of the Pharisees, he sees that his coming into this world has two diametrically opposed effects. Some receive him with joy and are rewarded. Others reject him and are punished. This reward and this punishment is his judgment (κρίμα; see on 3:17) upon those who come in contact with him. It is for that reason that he can say, "For judgment I came into this world." See on 3:18-21. He came with the very purpose of pronouncing and carrying into effect this authoritative verdict upon these two sharply contrasted groups. On the expression "came into this world" as a characterization of the Messiah see 1:9.

The rewarding aspect of this judgment is expressed in the words: **in order that those who do not see, may see;** i.e., in order that those who lack the light of salvation (who are without true knowledge of God, righteousness, holiness, joy), and regretting their condition have by God's preparatory grace been made anxious to receive the light, may be placed in full possession of it. The man who had been blind from his birth but was now able to see both physically and spiritually illustrates the point. — Then follows the punitive aspect of this judgment: **and that those who see may become blind;** i.e., and in order that those who are constantly saying, "We see" (9:41), but who deceive themselves by rejecting the light, may at last be completely separated from it (cf. on 7:34). Think of the Pharisees, who harden themselves more and more.

40, 41. Did some of the Pharisees (see on 1:24) gather around him in order to find fault? It seems so, for we read **Some of the Pharisees near him heard these things. And** with arrogant scorn and disdain **they said to him, Certainly, we too are not blind, are we?** Does Jesus mean to place them in the category of the accursed rabble that knows not the law (see on 7:49)? Are *they*, the devout disciples and interpreters of Moses, in a class with *the people of the soil* who know nothing? **Jesus said to them, If y o u were blind, y o u would have no sin;** i.e., if y o u were not only without the light (the true knowledge of God, holiness, righteousness, joy) but also conscious of this deplorable condition and anxiously yearning for God's salvation, no charge could be brought against y o u. He continues: **But now that y o u say, We see, y o u r sin remains.** In other words, "If y o u do not see the greatness of your sins and miseries, y o u cannot enjoy true comfort." Y o u r *sin* remains, for y o u have rejected God's *salvation*.

Synthesis of Chapter 9

See the Outline on p. 2. *The Son of God Healing the Man Born Blind, to Whom in Love He Reveals Himself as the Son of Man. His Enemies Have Decided to Unsynagogue Those Who Accept Him.*

The story may be outlined as follows:

I. *A Jerusalem beggar is healed of his congenital blindness* (9:1-7).

Jesus, on leaving the temple or shortly afterward, saw a man born blind. The disciples asked whether the man's own sin or that of his parents had caused this blindness. Jesus by implication criticized the question, and substituted the forward look for the backward, the deed of mercy for the merely theoretical speculation. He said, "Neither did this man sin nor his parents, but (this happened) in order that the works of God should be displayed in him." Thus *moral and spiritual insight* was given to the disciples by him who called himself *the light of the world* (9:5). He then further illustrated this light-giving activity by imparting *physical light* to the eyes of this blind man. He did this after covering the man's eyes with mud and sending him to the pool Siloam to wash it off.

II. *He is questioned by the neighbors* (9:8-12).

Among the neighbors opinions were divided: some were sure that this was the man who was born blind; others were almost sure; still others saw close resemblance. The man himself put an end to all this by stating definitely, "I am the one." In answer to their further questions he related the manner of his cure and declared that he did not know the whereabouts of his benefactor.

III. *He is interrogated and expelled from the synagogue by the Jewish leaders* (9:13-34).

In an official interview the man was questioned. When he related what had happened to him, there arose a division among the Pharisees: both factions drawing logically valid conclusions from false premises! When the parents were called in, they damaged the cause of the enquirers by answering in such a manner that only one conclusion was possible: a miracle had really occurred. For fear of the authorities who had already decided that those who accepted Jesus as the Messiah must be expelled from the synagogue, the parents refused to say how or by whom their son had been healed. The once blind man, resummoned, refused to answer the questions which he had answered before. With ill-concealed humor he asked whether the Pharisees possibly wished to become disciples of Jesus. With a slur upon his birth the authorities expelled him from the room and from religious fellowship.

IV. *He is found by Jesus, who, in his capacity as the Son of man, reveals himself to him* (9:35-38).

In this connection Calvin's commentary contains a beautiful thought. It is this: if the man had been allowed to remain in the synagogue, he would in course of time have become estranged from Christ. The very fact that he was cast out made him more receptive for the grace of God. Similarly, when the pope expelled Luther and others from the Roman synagogue, and thundered his anathemas upon them, Christ reached out his hand, and revealed himself fully to them. Hence, the best thing for us is to be as far as possible removed from the enemies of the Gospel, in order that Christ may draw so much closer to us.[68]

With tenderness the Good Shepherd asked him, "Do *you* believe in the Son of man?" Salvation is ever a *personal* matter. When, in answer to the man's question, Jesus revealed himself as being the Son of man, the full light of heaven shone into the soul of the beggar. He said, "I believe, Lord," and he worshiped him. Thus, the "works of God" (his power, love, grace) were displayed in this man (cf. 9:3).

V. *He is contrasted with the willfully blind Pharisees* (9:39-41).

Jesus, in this connection, reveals the twofold purpose of his coming into the world "in order that those who do not see may see, and that those who see may become blind." Some Pharisees, standing near, resented what they felt to be an uncomplimentary reference to themselves. They said, "Certainly, we too are not blind, are we?" Jesus rebuked their smug complacency by saying, "If y o u were blind, y o u would have no sin; but now that y o u say, 'We see,' y o u r sin remains."

Thus, "the light shone in the darkness, but the darkness did not appropriate it. . . . To his own home he came, but his own people did not welcome him. But as many as did accept him, to them he gave the right to become God's children."

---

[68] John Calvin, *op. cit.*, p. 192: Si retentus fuisset in synagoga, periculum erat ne paulatim a Christo alienatus in idem eum impiis exitium mergeratur . . . Hoc idem et nostro tempore experti sumus. Nam quum Lutherus et alii similes initio crassiores Papae abusus reprehenderunt, vix tenuem habebant puri Christianisimi gustum. Postquam in eos fulminavit Papa ac terrificis bullis a Romana synagoga eiecti sunt, manum illis porrexit Christus ac penitus illis innotuit. Ita nobis nihil melius quam ab Evangelii hostibus longissime abesse, ut ipse propius ad nos accedat.

CHAPTER X

10 1 I most solemnly assure y o u, he who does not enter the sheepfold by the door but climbs over from another place, that man is a thief and a robber; 2 but he who enters by the door is shepherd of the sheep. 3 To him the door-keeper opens, and the sheep listen to his voice, and he calls his own sheep by name and leads them out. 4 Whenever he has put out all his own, he goes on ahead of them, and the sheep follow him, for they know his voice; 5 but a stranger they will in no way follow but will run away from him, for they do not know the voice of strangers.

Discussion of Certain Basic Points in connection with the Allegory of the Good Shepherd

In the interpretation of this sublime allegory commentators differ widely. The solution which one adopts with respect to the various problems that are presented here determines, in a measure, the explanation of individual passages. It is for this reason that we discuss some of the more important points and problems before entering upon a detailed exegesis.

I. *Its Connection with the Preceding Context (if any)*

Was 10:1-18 spoken on (and does the entire section 10:1-21 belong to) the day on which Jesus found the excommunicated man? We have the first record of what happened on that day in 9:35-41. Is 10:1-21 to be regarded as the logical and chronological continuation?

A. Those who do not see this close connection argue as follows:

1. The style is altogether different: 9:35-41 is polemical; 10:1-18 is allegorical.

2. The Good Shepherd discourse is continued in 10:26-28, but the latter passage was spoken at the feast of Dedication (10:22) in December; hence, a few months later than 9:35-41. It is clear, therefore, that either the entire Good Shepherd discourse belongs to that feast or else we simply do not know where to place it; the time when it was delivered is completely uncertain.

B. Those who see this close connection (between 9:35-41 and 10:1-21) answer as follows, and with this answer we agree:

97

1. Though the style is different, the thought-connection is very close. Jesus describes himself as the good shepherd over against false shepherds. The good shepherd lays down his life for the sheep; the Pharisees, on the other hand, as evil shepherds, are not concerned about the sheep, and cast them out. The man born blind, a true sheep, had been excommunicated by the Jewish authorities; but Jesus, as the good shepherd, had sought and found him. What matters is this connection in thought. Once this is seen, it becomes evident that 10:1-21 is the logical and chronological continuation of 9:35-41 (and, in a sense, of chapter 9, in its entirety).

2. Why should it be considered impossible for Jesus (in 10:26-28) to refer to a theme (the good shepherd's care) which a few months earlier had been the subject of an extensive discourse? Note how the miracle at Bethzatha (5:2) is taken up again many months later (7:23). Besides, the present section (10:1-21) shows very clearly that it is closely connected with the preceding (i.e., with chapter 9), for verse 21 reads: "A demon cannot *open the eyes of the blind,* can he?" The opening of the eyes of the blind was the subject of chapter 9.

3. This section is not introduced by a fresh note of time. On the contrary, it begins with the familiar expression, "I most solemnly assure y o u," which nowhere else in this Gospel begins a new section. N.N. does not even begin a new paragraph at this point.

II. *Its Old Testament Background*

The audience which listened to this allegory was the same as in 9:35-41: Christ's disciples, the man who had been healed of his blindness (unless he had already left), the Pharisees, and probably other Jews, see on 10:6. They did not understand it. Had they been better students of the Word, they would have understood it at least to some extent, for this discourse is rooted in Old Testament symbolism, which Jesus used for his own purpose.

The following are some of the most striking parallels in the Old Testament:

A. *Jehovah is the shepherd of Israel and of individual believers, who are regarded as the sheep.* "Jehovah is my shepherd; I shall not want," etc. (Ps. 23). "So we thy people and the sheep of thy pasture will give thee thanks forever" (Ps. 79:13). "Give ear, O Shepherd of Israel, thou that leadest Joseph like a flock" (Ps. 80:1). "For he is our God, and we are the people of his pasture, and the sheep of his hand," (Ps. 95:7). "I myself will be the shepherd of my sheep, and I will cause them to lie down, saith the Lord Jehovah" (Ezek. 34:15; see the entire beautiful chapter). That sheep have a tendency to wander, and are, therefore in need of a guiding shepherd, is clear from Ps. 119:176; Is. 53:6.

B. *He is a very good, a very tender-hearted and loving shepherd.*

This is clear from the passages referred to under A (above), and also from Is. 40:11: "He will feed his flock like a shepherd, he will gather the lambs in his arm,. and carry them in his bosom, and will gently lead those that have their young." Cf. II Sam. 12:3; Luke 15:3-6.

C. *There are, nevertheless, evil shepherds:* "Woe unto the shepherds that destroy and scatter the sheep of my pasture! saith Jehovah" (Jer. 23:1 ff). "Son of man, prophesy against the shepherds of Israel, prophesy and say unto them, even to the shepherds, Woe unto the shepherds of Israel that do feed themselves! should not the shepherds feed the sheep?" (Ezek. 34:1, 2). Semitic people (e.g., the Assyrians) often refer to their rulers (kings, princes, religious leaders, etc.) as *shepherds.* "Woe to the worthless shepherd that leaves the flock!" (Zech. 11:17).

D. *Forsaken by the shepherd, the sheep become a prey of wild beasts: lions, bears, especially wolves.* ". . . that the congregation of Jehovah be not as sheep which have no shepherd" (Num. 27:17). "And David said unto Saul, Thy servant was keeping his father's sheep; and when there came a lion or a bear, and took a lamb out of the flock, I went out after him, and smote him, and delivered it out of his mouth; and when he arose against me, I caught him by his beard, and smote him and slew him. Thy servant smote both the lion and the bear" (I Sam. 17:34-36). "I saw all Israel scattered upon the mountains, as sheep that have no shepherd" (I Kings 22:17). "And the wolf shall dwell with the lamb" (Is. 11:6, implying, of course, that heretofore the wolf has been the lamb's greatest enemy). "Therefore they go their way like sheep, they are afflicted because there is no shepherd" (Zech. 10:2). "Smite the shepherd, and the sheep shall be scattered" (Zech. 13:7).

E. *The great Son of David (the Messiah) will be the one shepherd of the reunited remnant (Israel and Judah, but now no longer regarded as separate):* "And I will set up *one* shepherd over them, and he shall feed them, even my servant David; he shall feed them, and he shall be their shepherd" (Ezek. 34:23; cf. Jer. 23:5 where the righteous Branch is contrasted with the evil shepherds).

The allegory recorded in John 10:1-18 may be regarded as the fulfillment of Ezek. 34:23. Jesus is himself the good shepherd, just as had been predicted!

III. *Its Character as an Allegory*

A. What Is an Allegory?

The discourse about the good shepherd is called a *paroimia.* In general a παροιμία (literally, wayside saying) is a *figurative* saying (16:25, 29). Here in chapter 10 it is an *allegory* rather than a *parable.* The Gospel of John does not contain any parables. The very term *parable* occurs only in the Synoptics (and in Heb. 9:9; 11:19), while παροιμία occurs only in the Fourth

Gospel (and in II Pet. 2:22). In the N. T. there is some overlapping in the meaning of the terms *parable* and *paroimia:* each may refer to a *proverb* (II Pet. 2:22; cf. Luke 4:23), but this is the exception rather than the rule. Similarly the Hebrew *mashal* has a very wide connotation: proverb, parable, poem, riddle (veiled and pointed remark). See on 2:19.

Essentially the difference in meaning between a παροιμία in the sense of *allegory* (as here in chapter 10) and a *parable* amounts to this, that the former partakes of the nature of a *metaphor;* the latter is more like a *simile.* A metaphor is an *implied* comparison ("Tell that fox," meaning Herod); a simile is an *expressed* comparison ("his appearance was *as* lightning). An *allegory* may be defined as an *extended metaphor;* a *parable,* as an *extended simile.*

B. How Must an Allegory be Interpreted?

The following rules should be observed:

1. *No attempt should be made to explain every trait or feature of the symbol. When, however, Jesus himself or the concrete historical situation, supplies the interpretation, that elucidation should receive its due.*

One should not ask at *every* point, "What does this represent and what does that represent?" Over-analysis leads to misinterpretation. The *main idea* must be grasped (see IV below). In harmony with this main idea, certain objects that are mentioned have parallels in the kingdom-sphere or in the sphere of the enemies of the kingdom. In the present allegory that is true with respect to the following: door, fold, sheep, shepherd, flock; and also the following: thief and robber, stranger, hireling.

But the question is legitimate: How do we know that *these* terms have symbolical significance? We answer:

a. As to the first list (door, fold, sheep, shepherd, flock), it is interpreted by Jesus himself. We should not hesitate to permit a term to have the symbolical meaning which its author attaches to it! Note the following:

Verse 1:

Symbol:	Meaning:
the door	Jesus himself (verses 7 and 9)
the fold	Israel (clearly implied in verse 16)
sheep	those for whom Christ died,
	those destined to be saved;
	those who obtain eternal life;
	those who heed the voice of Jesus
	and follow him (10:4, 9, 11, 14, 28).

Verse 2:

shepherd	Jesus (the good shepherd, 10:11, 14)

Verse 16:

flock   the entire company of the saved
                                    (*one* flock, 10:16).

b. As to the second list (thief and robber, stranger, hireling) see under
3 (below). The concrete, historical situation out of which the allegory
arises is all that is necessary to explain these symbols.

When we follow this rule, certain terms will remain, to which we cannot
with any degree of certainty ascribe symbolical significance; such as *door-
keeper*. These terms are necessary to round out the symbol. For *the wolf*
see on 10:29.

2. *Not every predication must be referred to the symbol.*

We have reached a crucial point in the interpretation of the present
allegory. As we see it, it is here that many interpreters go astray. Often
the reality (in the sphere of the kingdom) is more prominent than *the figure. This means that in certain cases the sentence has as its subject (or implied subject) a metaphor, but the predicate applies not to the metaphor
itself but only to the person to whom the metaphor refers.* Thus, when in
Ps. 79:13 the poet says, "So we, thy people and the sheep of thy pasture,
will give thee thanks forever," it is immediately clear that this giving of
thanks lies outside of the sphere of animals (sheep, for instance). Sheep
(in the literal sense) cannot give thanks. Sheep-like *people,* however, do
give thanks. (In this particular instance the reference is made very clear
by the word "thy people" which explains "the sheep of thy pasture." The
two expressions are mutually interpretive.)

Once this point is grasped, there will be no further difficulty in explaining the last part of 10:9: "By me if anyone enters, he will be saved, and
will go in and out, and will find pasture." It is, of course, perfectly true
that one cannot say with reference to animals that they are "saved," but
this can be said, nevertheless, with respect to *people* who have received the
characteristics of certain animals (in this case sheep). Hence, we cannot
agree with commentators who argue that the entire interpretation is upset
by the theory that in verse 9 Jesus is thinking of sheep. Their argument
is that inasmuch as the subject of the sentence (*anyone*) is masculine, it
cannot refer to a sheep, the word for which (in the original Greek) is
neuter. Also, that it would be foolish to speak about a sheep entering the
door, for how else but by the door would it enter the fold? They continue
that the entire conception of a sheep going in and out of the fold at pleasure is wrong, as no sheep does that; and that a sheep does not find pasture
for itself. But all this, as we see it, is the result of a failure to grasp the
important rule in symbol-interpretation which we printed in italics at
the head of this paragraph: *"Not every predication must be referred to the
symbol."*

The subject (*anyone*) can very well refer to a sheep; i.e., to a person with sheep-like character (one who really follows the shepherd, Christ). Again, it is not at all foolish to speak about a sheep entering by the door, for the reference also in this case is to the person who by faith in Christ enters the kingdom. Now it so happens that many *people* try to enter by some other way; for example, by trusting in their own good works. Also, a sheep — i.e., a sheep-like person — does, indeed, go in and out and find pasture, rejoicing when he finds it (e.g., in the Word). Moreover, both the preceding context (verse 8) and the succeeding context (verse 10) clearly show that our own interpretation is on the right track, for these passages speak about *people,* not about animals (see our explanation of these verses). A text should always be explained in the light of its context (in the present case, verse 9 must be explained in the light of verses 8 and 10). Besides, verses 26-29 also speak about *sheep;* but it is very clear that *these sheep are people,* the true followers of Jesus.

Once Rule 2 is understood, so-called "mixed metaphors" will not be so disturbing. Accordingly, we turn now to the next rule:

3. *So-called "mixed metaphors" (really, sudden changes of metaphors) do not present any real problem if it be borne in mind that what may be impossible as far as the symbol is concerned, is often entirely reasonable and true with respect to the reality to which the symbol refers.*

In the present allegory the difficulty which has baffled so many interpreters consists in the fact that Jesus is referred to both as *the door* (10:7, 9) and as *the good shepherd* (10:11, 14). How can he be both? Feeling that this is impossible, some have resorted to the idea that we have here a corruption of the text. But for this there is no solid evidence. Instead, the solution must be sought in the direction of the application of Rule 2 (above). So great is Jesus that his significance can never be fully expressed. No symbol, taken by itself, can do justice to his fulness. He is, indeed, both door and shepherd. We encounter exactly the same phenomenon in the book of Revelation. John expects to see a lion (Rev. 5:5), but he sees . . . a lamb (Rev. 5:6). The lamb *stands, as having been slaughtered!* John expects to see a bride (Rev. 21:9); but he sees a city (Rev. 21:10). — Yet when we begin to study these seeming irregularities, we see a good reason for every one of them. *To be sure, a bride cannot at the same time be a city, but the church of God (to which both bride and city refer) can be (and is) both! Christ is both lion and lamb.*[69] *So also here is John 10, though it is entirely true that a door cannot at the same time be a shepherd, it is also true that Jesus is both at the same time!*

And just as Jesus is both *door* and *good shepherd,* so also his enemies

---

[69] See for other examples the author's *More Than Conquerors,* Grand Rapids, Mich., sixth edition, 1952, p. 268, note 43.

(the Pharisees) are represented as thieves, robbers, strangers, and hirelings. It is not at all necessary nor advisable to regard each of these terms as referring to a different category, sothat, for example, the thieves and robbers would indicate false Messiahs; the strangers, Pharisees; and the hirelings, covetous ministers. *One must have an eye for the concrete, historical situation.* In the entire context nothing at all is said about false Messiahs or about money-mad preachers. *The Pharisees,* on the other hand, are very much in evidence. It is to these that Jesus refers as being in one respect thieves and robbers; in another respect strangers; and in still another respect, hirelings! This interpretation does not inject *foreign* elements into the exegesis.

IV. *Its Main Idea*

The main theme throughout is Jesus as the good shepherd, contrasted with the evil shepherds. To be sure, Jesus is also *the door.* But this thought is secondary. It is a very beautiful and very necessary element in the entire picture, but it is subordinate to the *main* idea. It is introduced, first, to show who the false shepherds are. They are those who try to enter the fold illegitimately; i.e., not by the door (faith in Jesus and appointment by him) but by some other way (intimidation, for instance, 9:22). The true shepherd is not at all like that. He has the right of entrance ("to him the door-keeper opens"). The idea of Jesus as *the door* also does duty in stressing the fact that he furnishes rest, safety (salvation even!), and food for his (spiritual) sheep. Being the good shepherd, he is naturally the door!

The fact that the idea of the good shepherd is indeed predominant is apparent to anyone who counts the many references to him in this capacity. Notice: in the capacity of good shepherd Jesus:

1. enters by the door and is welcomed by the door-keeper (10:3).
2. calls the sheep by name (10:3); knows them thoroughly (10:14, 15; cf. 10:27, 28).
3. leads them out (10:3).
4. goes on ahead of the sheep (10:4).
5. is recognized and followed by the sheep ("they know his voice") (10:3, 4).
6. furnishes *access* to every blessing (10:7-9); is "the door."
7. provides life and abundance (10:10; cf. 10:27, 28).
8. lays down his life for the sheep (10:11, 14).
9. guides his sheep (cf. 10:4), gathering also other sheep, sothat all become *one* flock with *one* shepherd (10:16).
10. is loved by the Father (10:17).

In harmony with all that has been said in the aforegoing we are now ready to interpret the allegory:

103

10:1-5

He who does not enter the sheepfold by the door but climbs over from another place, that man is a thief and a robber.

10:1, 2. For the words of solemn introduction **I most solemnly assure y o u,** see on 1:51. The underlying symbol here is a sheepfold. The original uses a term (αὐλή from ἄω to blow) whose meaning in certain passages of the Gospels is disputed. See on 18:15. But here (in 10:1) the meaning is clear. It is a sheepfold. It was a roofless enclosure in the open field. It consisted of a wall made of rough stones and provided with a sturdy door. Sometimes caves served the same purpose, but that is not the idea here. A thief (one who is determined to deprive another of his property) and robber (one who uses violence in order to obtain the coveted goods) would not choose to enter by the door, for a. it was locked, had to be opened; and b. it was guarded by a door-keeper. Hence, such a man, in order to get in, would climb over from another place. Thus also the religious leaders, hostile to Jesus, were trying illegitimately to gain the mastery over the people of Israel (see verse 16). They tried to gain the people through intimidation (see 9:22). They avoided *the door,* the Lord Jesus Christ (did not believe in him, were not appointed by him). By means of threats (expulsion from the synagogue) they wanted to deprive Jesus of his disciples. They were thieves and robbers, therefore. On the other hand, *Jesus,* who had been definitely appointed and sent by his heavenly Father, appears here in the quality of legitimate shepherd (see 10:11, 14).[70] That is implied here, **but he who enters by the door is shepherd of the sheep,** and expressed in 10:11, 14.

3. To him the door-keeper opens, and the sheep listen to his voice, and he calls his own sheep by name and leads them out. We can picture it thus. During the night the door-keeper has been with the sheep. He is acquainted with the shepherd. Hence, when in the morning he hears the shepherd's voice, he opens the door. The sheep also immediately recognize the voice of their own shepherd. They not only *hear* (more or less unconsciously) but *listen.* They obey. This is true with respect to actual sheep (the animals). But in a higher sense it holds with respect to all true

---

[70] In the abstract it is possible that the subject "he who enters by the door" has reference to *all* divinely appointed (hence, legitimate) ambassadors (prophets, apostles, ministers, etc.). Yet, in his own explanation of this allegory Jesus refers only to himself as the shepherd (10:11, 14). Though he speaks of *many* thieves, robbers, etc., he refers to only *one* shepherd. It is for this reason that we explained verse 2 as we did. Though the underlying *symbol* may presuppose several shepherds, each having *his own* sheep (10:3, 4), only *one* shepherd has symbolical meaning! — Nevertheless, it is true that to a limited extent the work of *the chief shepherd* (I Peter 5:4) is reflected in that of the under-shepherds (John 21:15-17).

disciples of Jesus. And it must be borne in mind that the reality in the kingdom of God predominates the symbol here! Just as an Oriental shepherd, even in our own day and age, often calls his own sheep *by name* (cases have been reported of shepherds who had been blindfolded but who even with that handicap recognized their individual sheep), so also (in fact, much more so!) Jesus, as the good shepherd, has an intimate, personal knowledge of all those whom he intends to save. And just as the shepherd leads his own sheep out of the fold, so also the tender and loving shepherd, Jesus, gathers his flock, leading them out of the fold of Israel (10:3; cf. 1:11-13; Mic. 2:12) and of heathendom (10:16).

4, 5. Whenever he has put out all his own, he goes on ahead of them, and the sheep follow him, for they know his voice; but a stranger they will in no way follow but will run away from him, for they do not know the voice of strangers.

The shepherd returns every morning. So also Jesus is constantly gathering his sheep. Hence, we read "whenever." In an Oriental fold several flocks would at times be kept together for the night. In the morning each shepherd would lead out *his own* sheep. His own sheep, and they *alone,* would respond to his call. The others, belonging to other shepherds, would pay no attention. The shepherd, Jesus, *puts out* all his own. He overcomes all their objections. Sometimes sheep have to be pushed out! In any event, not a single one of his own is left behind. Note the word *all.* See on 6:37, 39.

The shepherd, having put out all his own, goes on ahead of them, and the sheep *follow.* That is the custom in the Orient. Elsewhere the shepherd drives the sheep ahead of him. We see immediately that the Oriental custom is better adapted to illustrate the relation between Christ and his disciples. Jesus *leads;* he does not *drive!*

The reason why the sheep follow their own shepherd is given in the words: "for they know his voice." In the Word of God the true shepherd addresses his sheep. They recognize his voice, and follow — i.e., trust and obey — him.

In no way (note the strong negative) will the sheep follow a stranger! When Jesus is thinking of the faithful and ever-watchful loving-care which he extends to his own and wishes to contrast this with the selfishness of the Pharisees, who are ever seeking to promote their own glory and to rob him of his followers (9:22), he calls himself the good shepherd, and he calls them *thieves and robbers.* But when he reflects on the intimate knowledge which he has with respect to his own disciples and wishes to contrast this with the ignorance of the Pharisees — for they know neither the Lord nor his people —, though he again thinks of himself as the good shepherd (for both tender care and thorough knowledge are bound up with the idea of being a true shepherd), he calls them *strangers*.

A normal sheep does not follow a stranger even though the latter may put on the shepherd's garb, and may try to imitate the shepherd's call. It has been tried again and again. So also (and much more so!) the true disciple of the Lord "does not know" (refuses to acknowledge) the voice of strangers (cf. II John 10), who come to him with strange philosophy, strange theology, and strange ethics; and, therefore, he does not follow them. He is resolutely determined to follow only the *one* true shepherd, Jesus, as he speaks in his Word. All others he shuns; in fact, he runs away from them in horror.

---

6 This allegory Jesus told them; but they did not understand what it meant that he was telling them. 7 So Jesus said again, "I most solemnly assure y o u,[71] "I am the door of the sheep. 8 All who came before me are thieves and robbers; but the sheep did not listen to them. 9 I am the door: by me if anyone enters. he will be saved, and will go in and out and will find pasture.[72] 10 The thief comes only in order to steal and kill and destroy; I came in order that people may have life, and may have abundance. 11 I am the good shepherd. The good shepherd lays down his life for the sheep. 12 He who is a hireling and not a shepherd, whose own the sheep are not, sees the wolf coming and deserts the sheep and runs away. And the wolf snatches them and scatters (the flock). 13 (He runs away) because he is a hireling and not concerned about the sheep.

14 I am the good shepherd, and I know my own, and my own know me, 15 just as my Father knows me and I know the Father, and I lay down my life for the sheep. 16 I also have other sheep which do not belong to this fold; them also I must lead, and they will listen to my voice, and become one flock, one shepherd. 17 For this reason the Father loves me because I lay down my life in order that I may take it again. 18 No one has taken it away from me; on the contrary, I lay it down of my own accord. I have the right to lay it down and I have the right to take it again. This charge I received from my Father."

19 There was again a division among the Jews on account of these words. 20 Many of them were saying, "He has a demon and raves; why do y o u listen to him?" 21 Others were saying, "These are not the remarks of a demon-possessed (person). A demon cannot open the eyes of the blind, can he?"

10:6-21

10:6. This allegory Jesus told them. It is hard to see how some interpreters can maintain that this allegory was spoken only to the disciples, and that these disciples — they alone — did not understand what it meant. That these words were spoken not only to the disciples (9:2) but also to the Pharisees and perhaps other Jews would seem to be clear from a careful

---

[71] On ὅτι see Vol. I, pp. 54, 60.
[72] IIIA1; see Vol. I, pp. 42, 43.

examination of the following passages: 9:40, 41 (continued into 10:1 ff); 10:7; and especially 10:19-21. For the meaning of the term *allegory* (παροιμία) and the rules of interpretation that apply to it see what has been said on pp. 100-103 above.

The Jews did not understand the allegory; **they did not understand what it meant that he was telling them.** Had they known their Old Testament more thoroughly, they would not have experienced this difficulty. See what was said on pp. 98, 99 above. However, here one should distinguish carefully. Although the idea of shepherd and sheep (Jehovah the shepherd, his people the sheep) can be found on *so* very many pages of the Old Testament that total ignorance regarding this figure is almost unimaginable, the additional thought conveyed here in 10:1-6, namely, that the good shepherd (here not Jehovah but Jesus) would separate the true Israel from the national Israel (would lead *his own* out of *the fold*) was probably not so well known. However, even this idea should not have sounded so *very* strange. The outgathering or election of a remnant is taught in many Old Testament passages: Jer. 3:14; 23:3; Am. 3:12; 5:15; Mic. 2:12; 5:3, 7, 8; 7:18-20; Hab. 2:4; Zeph. 3:12, 13; Hag. 1:12, 14; Zech. 8:6, 12; 13:8, 9. In Mic. 2:12 this outgathering of the remnant is even associated with the idea of the shepherd. Cf. Am. 3:12.

7. So Jesus said again, I most solemnly assure y o u, I am the door of the sheep.

Because his audience had failed to understand the allegory, Jesus explains it in the present paragraph. Nevertheless, what we have here is more than explanation. Certain details are added, so that we may speak of *explanation and amplification.*

When Jesus says, "I — emphatic; i.e., I *alone* — am the door of the sheep," he means that he is *the only One* through whom anyone obtains legitimate access. There simply is no other entrance. Cf. 14:6.

Now this basic idea is given a twofold application. Once that is seen, the question whether Jesus is the door *to* the sheep or whether he is the door *for* the sheep has been answered. In verse 8 Jesus appears as the door *to* the sheep; in verse 9 as the door *for* the sheep. He, and he alone, is, and is always, the door. For the true shepherd he is the door. For every true sheep he is also the door. For the shepherd he is the door to the sheep. For the sheep he is the door to all the blessings of salvation. The figure is very appropriate: a door leads both in and out: it gives the shepherd access to his sheep that are inside. It gives the sheep access to the fold, and to the pasture which is outside.

8. All who came before me are thieves and robbers, but the sheep did not listen to them.

Verses 7 and 8, taken together, give a beautiful explanation of verses

107

1 and 2. In the light of this interpretation, supplied by Jesus himself, verses 1 and 2 may now be paraphrased as follows:

"I most solemnly assure y o u, he who does not enter the sheepfold by faith in me and appointment by me but enters illegitimately, that man is a thief and a robber. Thus, all who came before me are thieves and robbers. But he who enters legitimately is shepherd of the sheep."

Jesus, as the one and only good shepherd, contrasts himself very sharply with all who had come *before* him. But what does the preposition *before* (πρό) mean here? In the New Testament this little word has the following recognized meanings: a. "in front of" (*before* of place), as in Acts 12:6: "guards *before* the door"; b. "earlier than" (*before* of time), as in Matt. 8:29: "Art thou come hither to torment us *before* the time"; c. "more than," or "above" (*before* of preference), as in I Pet. 4:8: *"before* all things." Of other meanings that have been ascribed to this word (such as "in the interest of" or even "in the room of" and "in the name of") there are no undisputed instances in the New Testament.[73] By far the most common is meaning b. *before* of time. In fact, in *all* other places in which the Fourth Gospel uses this preposition it has that meaning (1:49; 5:7 — where the idea of place seems to blend with that of time — ; 11:55; 12:1; 13:1; 13:19; 17:5, 24). It surely is the natural signification also here in 10:8. If the temporal force is not *basic* here, it must at least be regarded as the *resultant* meaning. But we cannot even accept the interpretation of *all* who give the preposition its temporal sense. For example, it would seem to us that the idea that the Lord is referring here to the prophets of the Old Testament period and to John the Baptist, as if these had been thieves and robbers, is hardly worthy of comment. Again, to think in this connection of false Messiahs who had arisen before the beginning of Christ's ministry is equally unrealistic. The context says nothing about them. Without any question, it would seem to us, Jesus is thinking here of the men who are standing right in front of him as he is speaking, namely, the religious leaders of the people, the members of the Sanhedrin, Sadducees and Pharisees, but especially the latter (see 9:40; 10:19). *They* were the ones who were trying, by means of intimidation (9:22), to steal the people, and thus to gain honor for themselves in an illegitimate manner. If threats were insufficient, they would use violence. They were, indeed, both thieves and robbers. Moreover, they were already on the scene when Jesus came into

---

[73] I cannot agree here with H. E. Dana and J. L. Mantey who, in their excellent work (a little gem for class-room use!) *A Manual Grammar of the Greek New Testament,* New York, 1950, pp. 109, 110, ascribe the meaning "in the room of" or "in the name of" to the preposition as used here in 10:8. W. D. Chamberlain, who also wrote a most worth-while book on N.T. Grammar, *An Exegetical Grammar of the Greek New Testament,* New York, 1941, pp. 127, 128, recognizes only the three meanings which we have given above. (We are not here discussing the meaning of πρό-in composition). With this agrees Gram. N.T., pp. 620-622.

the world (see on 3:1). Hence, it is easy to understand why Jesus says that
they had come *before* him. It is also understandable that Jesus says, *"are*
(not *were*) thieves and robbers." They had not disappeared, were still
present.

Now there were many people who listened to these selfish religious leaders. But *the sheep* — Christ's true disciples — did not listen to them! Instead of heeding them, the sheep obeyed the true shepherd, Jesus (cf.
10:3, 14).

9. I am the door. For the meaning of the statement, "I am the door,"
see on 10:7.

Not only is Jesus the door *to* the sheep; he is also the door *for* the sheep.
To some extent we have already explained verse 9. See pp. 101, 102. A few
thoughts must be added. Jesus has just stated that his true followers refuse
to listen to thieves and robbers. It is logical, therefore, to assume that
when he now says, **by me if anyone enters,** he is still thinking of these
same true followers. Note emphatic position of the phrase *by me.* There is
no other entrance! Let 3:16 serve as commentary: faith in Christ as the
Son of God is the only entrance-door. And this faith is full, personal trust
in him and in his substitutionary atonement.

Jesus says, "By me if anyone enters, **he will be saved.** What does he
mean when he says that such a person will be *saved.* This term is explained
in verse 10. It means *will be given life.* The terms *to be saved* and *to have
life* are used together here, just as in 3:16 and 3:17. From 3:16 we know
that everlasting life is meant. See on that verse. And even if we did not
have 3:16, 17, we would still have the commentary furnished us by 10:28.
These sheep receive freedom from the guilt, the misery, and the punishment of sin. Abundance — the love of God shed abroad in their hearts,
the peace of God that passes all understanding — is their portion, here in
principle, by and by in perfection. — There is no good reason to restrict
the meaning of the verb in this passage, as if it meant no more than, "he
will be safe." To be sure, safety is implied also in the words, **and will go in
and out;** but this is only part of the meaning. Not only will he go in and
out, i.e., experience perfect freedom from all real harm and danger, and
this even in the small affairs of every-day living, and feel himself entirely at
home in the daily routine of God's people (see especially the beautiful
words of Ps. 121:8), but in addition, he **will find pasture;** i.e., life and abundance, as the following verse indicates. The pasture which the true sheep
finds in the study of the Word is certainly included.

**10, 11. The thief comes only in order to steal and kill and destroy; I
come in order that people may have life, and may have abundance.** The
thief is the Pharisee, as has been explained (see on 10:1). Note the climactic arrangement: steal, kill, destroy. That these religious leaders spiritually

killed and destroyed the people whom they had stolen is clear from Matt. 23:15. The exact opposite of killing and destroying is *making alive.* And the exact opposite of the thief is the good shepherd, Christ. So Jesus says, "I came in order that they (i.e., people; here *the sheep*) may have *life* (see on 3:16) and may have *abundance* (of grace, 1:16; cf. Rom. 5:17, 20; Eph. 1:7, 8; of joy, II Cor. 8:2; of peace, Jer. 33:6). See also 2:6, 7; 4:14; 6:13, 35. These passages show that Jesus always provides an *overflowing* measure, a surplus.

Jesus continues, **I am the good shepherd,** really: *the shepherd, the good one.* The adjective is stressed! This adjective, however, is not ἀγαθός but καλός. The basic meaning of this word is *beautiful.* Here it indicates *excellent.* This shepherd answers to the ideal both in his character and in his work. And he is *the only one* in his class. (See footnote 70 above.) The predicate of this great *I AM* has the article, and is therefore interchangeable with the subject. The statement *"I am the good shepherd"* explains 10:2, 3, 4. We now know whom Jesus had in mind when he spoke about the shepherd to whom the sheep give heed.

The excellent character of this shepherd is shown especially in this, **The good shepherd lays down his life for the sheep.** In the sense in which this is meant it cannot apply to an ordinary sheep-herder, no matter how good he may be. Such a shepherd may, indeed, risk his life in the defence of his sheep (I Sam. 17:34-36), but he does not really *lay down* (τίθησι) his life; i.e., he does not yield his life as a voluntary sacrifice. Also, in ordinary life the death of the herder means loss and possible death for the herd. In *this* case the death of the shepherd means *life* (ζωή) for the sheep! The good shepherd "pours out his soul (note τὴν ψυχὴν αὐτοῦ both here in 10:11 and also in Is. 53:12, the LXX translation) unto death." He gives *himself!* The idea is *not* that this shepherd gives merely his natural life. No, ψυχή which rests on an Aramaic original (whether oral or written) is the full equivalent of the *self,* the *person.* See also the same phrase, "his life," in Matt. 20:28; Mark 10:45, while I Tim. 2:6 has *himself.* It is probable that ψυχή has this meaning wherever it occurs in John's Gospel (10:11, 15, 17, 24; 12:25, 27; 13:37, 38; and 15:13).

The good shepherd lays down his life *for* the sheep. The preposition is ὑπέρ, a word which has the root-meaning *over.* In the Fourth Gospel it is always used with the genitive.[74] Thus used, its meaning pendulates all the way from the colorless *concerning* (1:30), through *for the benefit of* and the closely related *for the sake of* (6:51; 11:4; 17:19), to the very meaningful *instead of* (see 10:11, 15; 11:50, 51, 52; 13:37, 38; 15:13; 18:14). However, it is probably incorrect to say that this preposition *in itself* ever means

---

[74] The possible exception (ὑπέρ with acc.) is 12:43, but here what is probably the better reading has ἤπερ.

instead of. That is its resultant connotation when it is used in certain contexts. The good shepherd lays down his life *for the benefit* of the sheep, but the only way in which he can benefit the sheep, saving them from everlasting destruction and imparting everlasting life to them, is by dying *instead of* them, as we learn from Matt. 20:28; Mark 10:45, where the preposition ἀντί (*instead of, in exchange for*) is used. It is easy to see how by a very gradual transition *for the benefit of* or *in behalf of* may become *instead of.* Thus, in the papyri the scribe who writes a document in behalf of someone who cannot write is writing it instead of that unlettered individual.[75] Cf. also II Cor. 5:21; Gal. 3:13.

It is for *the sheep — only* for the sheep — that the good shepherd lays down his life. The design of the atonement is definitely restricted.[76] Jesus dies for those who had been given to him by the Father, for the children of God, for true believers. This is the teaching of the Fourth Gospel throughout (3:16; 6:37, 39, 40, 44, 65; 10:11, 15, 29; 17:6, 9, 20, 21, 24). It is also the doctrine of the rest of Scripture. With his precious blood Christ purchased his church (Acts 20:28; Eph. 5:25-27); his people (Matt. 1:21); the elect (Rom. 8:32-35).

Nevertheless, the love of God is wide as the ocean. The sheep are found everywhere. They are not confined to *one* fold (10:16; see also on 1:10, 29; 3:16; 4:42; 6:33, 51; 11:52).

On Jesus as the good shepherd see also Ezek. 34:23; Luke 15:3-6; Heb. 13:20; and I Pet. 2:25; 5:4; see especially on John 10:14, 15.

12, 13. Jesus had already compared his enemies to strangers and thieves. They are *strangers* because they do not know the sheep. *Thieves* are they because they seek to gain possession of the sheep in an illegitimate manner. And now Jesus adds the figure of the hireling. Yes, the Pharisees are also hirelings. **He who is a hireling and not a shepherd, whose own the sheep are not.** They are *hirelings* because they have no concern, no love,

---

[75] See on ὑπέρ A. T. Robertson, *The Minister and his Greek New Testament,* New York, 1923, pp. 35-42. Also W. Hendriksen, *The Meaning of the Preposition ἀντι in the New Testament,* doctoral thesis in the Princeton Seminary Library, especially pp. 77, 78, from which I quote the following: "The fact that ἀντί may be called in a sense, and in one of its meanings, a synonym of ὑπέρ, does not mean that the two prepositions are exactly alike in connotation. Whether in a given case ὑπέρ may approach the strictly substitutionary sense depends upon the context." See also E. H. Blakeney, "ὑπέρ with Genitive in the New Testament," ExT 55 (1944), 306.

[76] See on this subject L. Berkhof, *Systematic Theology,* Grand Rapids, Mich. 1949, pp. 394-399. The same author also wrote *Vicarious Atonement Through Christ;* Grand Rapids, 1936; see pp. 151-178. C. Bouma, *Geen Algemeene Verzoening;* Kampen, 1928. The entire book is devoted to a discussion of the limited character of the atonement and to an attempt to answer the objections advanced against this doctrine. A. A. Hodge, *The Atonement,* Philadelphia, 1867, pp. 347-429

for the sheep. That is typical of the hireling. He is not the equivalent of *any* hired man. Some hired men may have the shepherd's heart. But these *hirelings* have not. They are merely working for wages. They had just given a very telling example of their utter lack of concern for the true sheep (9:34). They were the kind of people who would devour widows' houses!

The hireling **sees the wolf coming.** (About this *wolf* see on verse 29) **and deserts the sheep and runs away.** He immediately forgets about the sheep. Says he to himself, "What do I care about the sheep, as long as they are not mine anyway?" So in the spirit of cold selfishness he flees. Jesus could never have chosen a better figure than that of the hireling. Had the Pharisees — these religious leaders of the people — shown the least interest in the lame man at Bethzatha (see on 5:10, 12)? Had they manifested even a speck of pity for the woman taken in the very act of adultery (see on 8:3, 6)? And see how they treated the man whom Jesus had cured of his congenital blindness (9:34). Instead of in any way defending Israel against the spiritual dangers which surrounded it, they riveted all their attention upon themselves and their own ease. They were exactly like the hireling who, when he sees the wolf coming, abandons the sheep, **And the wolf snatches them and scatters the flock. (He runs away) because he is a hireling and not concerned about the sheep.** That hireling, therefore, is the exact opposite of the good shepherd who takes care that no one ever snatches the sheep out of his hands (see on 10:28, 29). Moreover, instead of *scattering* his sheep, the good shepherd *gathers* them (cf. 10:16).

14, 15. I am the good shepherd, and I know my own, and my own know me, just as my Father knows me and I know my Father, and I lay down my life for the sheep.

Here we have an emphatic repetition and amplification of the preceding. Jesus says, "I am the good shepherd." This is a repetition of 10:11 (see explanation of that verse). Here (in verse 14 and 15), however, the matter is not merely stated but fully set forth. Jesus — and he *alone* — is the *good* shepherd, for:

a. in distinction from the Pharisees viewed as *strangers* (10:5), *he knows* his sheep. Note: "I know." See 10:27; II Tim. 2:19. He knows the name (10:3) and nature of each sheep, and the sheep have an experiential knowledge of their shepherd (10:3, 4).

b. in distinction from the Pharisees viewed as *thieves and robbers* (10:1, 8, 10), *he owns* his sheep. He calls them: "my own." See 6:37, 39; 17:6, 24.

c. in distinction from the Pharisees viewed as *hirelings* (10:12, 13), he *loves* his sheep, even to the point of offering himself as a sacrifice in their behalf and in their stead. He says, "I lay down my life for the sheep." For explanation of this sublime statement see on verse 11. (Note, however,

112

the difference: in verse 11 the third person is used; here in verse 15 the first person; hence verse 15 explains verse 11).

Note also the chiastic arrangement of the parallelism which we have in these verses:

>   a. I know my own
>   b. my own know me
>   c. (just as) my Father knows me, and
>   d. I know the Father.

In a. and d. Jesus, the good shepherd, is *the subject:* the action proceeds from him. In b. and c. he is *the object:* the action proceeds from the sheep and from the Father.

What Jesus states in these verses cannot mean that the fellowship which is found on earth (between good shepherd and sheep) is just as close as is that which is found in heaven (between the Father and the Son), but that the former is patterned after (is a reflection of) the latter. For the closeness of the fellowship between the Father and the Son see 10:30, 38; 14:11, 17, 21; also Matt. 11:27.

Four times in these two verses the verb *know* (γινώσκω) occurs. See on 1:10, 31; 3:11; 8:28. It is here a knowledge of experience and of loving fellowship. Jesus acknowledges his own (as his true disciples); they acknowledge him (as their Lord). Nothing could be more wonderful! Thus also the Father acknowledges the Son; the Son acknowledges the Father.

16. I also have other sheep which do not belong to this fold; them also I must lead, and they will listen to my voice, and become one flock, one shepherd.

Not all the sheep belong to the fold of Israel. The good shepherd also has other sheep. He *has* them even now because they have been given to him by the Father in the decree of predestination from eternity (6:37, 39; 17:6, 24). That is also the reason why even before they are gathered out they can be called his *sheep.*[77]

A very great truth is proclaimed here, namely, that the flock of Christ will no longer be almost confined to believers from among the Jews. A new period is dawning. During the old dispensation all the nations — with the exception of the Jews — were under the thraldom of satan. Not, of course, in the absolute sense of the term, for God always reigns supreme, but in the sense of Acts 14:16: *"God . . . who in the past generations suf-*

---

[77] John Calvin, *op. cit.,* p. 202: nec vero tantum hoc nomine quales futuri sint docet, quin potius ad arcanam Patris electionem hoc refert, quia iam oves sumus Deo, antequan ipsum sentiamus nobis esse pastorem; quemadmodum alibi dicimur fuisse inimici quo tempore nos amabat (Rom. 5:10); qua ratione etiam Paulus dicit nos prius a Deo fuisse cognitos, quam illum cognosceremus (Gal. 4:9).

fered all the nations to walk *in their own ways."* But that is going to change now. The church is going to become international.[78] Through the labors of Paul and other great missionaries who were to follow him believers from among the Gentiles would be added to the church. The great blessing of Pentecost and the Gospel Age which followed it is here predicted. It is a wonderful theme. In a sense it was predicted even in the Old Testament: Gen. 12:3; Ps. 72:8, 9; 87:4-6; Is. 60:3; Joel 2:28; Zeph. 2:9; Mal. 1:11. But there the idea that elect from among the Gentiles will come in *on the basis of equality* with the elect of Israel does not receive emphasis. The usual representation is that Israel's tent will be enlarged so as to have room also for the nations (Is. 54:2, 3); that the nations shall go to the mountain of Jehovah in Jerusalem (Mic. 4:1, 2). The idea that the Gentiles would be fellow-heirs, and fellow-members of the body, and fellow-partakers of the promise in Christ Jesus, in other words that they would enter into the kingdom on the basis of equality with the Jews, this idea (though not excluded by the prophets) is not stressed in the Old Testament. Hence, Paul could speak of it as a *mystery* (Eph. 1:9, 10; 3:1-6).

But that very idea is here proclaimed by Jesus. Note that he does not lead the sheep of heathendom into the *fold* of Israel; but he gathers together the sheep of Israel and the sheep of heathendom as one *flock!*

This passage may be regarded as a key to the explanation of the term *world* in 1:29; 3:16, 17; 4:42; 6:51; 8:12; 9:5; 11:52; 12:46. See on 1:10; cf. 12:32.

The good shepherd *must* lead them. This is the must of predestination, of prophecy, and of inner compulsion, rolled into one. The shepherd *leads* or *guides* them (going on ahead of them, so that they follow him; see on 10:4), and they *heed* his voice (see on 10:3), as it comes to them in the Word applied to the heart by the Spirit. Thus all become one *flock* (not one *fold,* as the A.V. has, on the basis of the Vulgate), with one *shepherd.* Cf. 17:20, 21; Ezek. 34:23.

17, 18. For this reason the Father loves me because I lay down my life in order that I may take it again. No one has taken it away from me; on the contrary, I lay it down of my own accord. I have the right to lay it down and I have the right to take it again. This charge I received from my Father.

Jesus has been speaking about laying down his life (verses 11, 15). It is sometimes said that Jesus does what any good shepherd does for his sheep. This is true only in the sense that neither flees when the wolf comes. But the Antitype is always better than the type. Christ's action differs in two

---

[78] See W. Hendriksen, *More Than Conquerors,* Grand Rapids, Mich., sixth edition, 1952, pp. 223-229. What we find in John 10:16 harmonizes beautifully with Rev. 20:1-3 ("that he should deceive the nations no more").

respects from that of a shepherd who risks his life in behalf of the flock:
a. it is a voluntary sacrifice (when the proper moment arrives, Jesus will
not try to cling to life, like the shepherd who, in his struggle with the wolf,
tries to save himself); and b. it actually saves the sheep. We now (verses 17
and 18) note still a third difference: c. Jesus lays down his life *in order to
take it again*. See on 2:19. No ordinary shepherd is able to do that.
Christ's death (as also his birth) is purposeful. Had he not *given* his life
(i.e., had he resisted death) he would not have been able to take it again.
So he gives in order to take back, and he does both in obedience to the
divine will and in the interest of his people.

The fact that Christ's death is an act of free volition must be stressed
in order that when death occurs the enemies who have brought it about
may have no right to boast as if this were *their* victory, and also in order
that the disciples may have no reason to despair as if this were *his* defeat.

The dying and the rising again are *deeds,* not merely *experiences*. They
are deeds of perfect and purposeful obedience and love. *For this reason*
(the phrase points *forward* here) the Father loves the Son (for the meaning
of the verb ἀγαπάω see on 21:15-17) "because," says Jesus, "I lay down my
life in order that I may take it again." The Father will show his love by
the reward described in Phil. 2:9.

Prophetically viewing his entire atoning sacrifice from the aspect of one
who has already accomplished it, Jesus says, "No one *has taken* (the better
reading) it away from me; on the contrary, I lay it down of my own accord." Thus, the voluntary character of the deed is again emphasized.
Apart from that voluntary nature, Christ's death would not have had any
saving value. Apart from the steadfast, resolute face when he was on his
way to Jerusalem and the cross, the pleasure of Jehovah would not have
prospered in his hands. See 18:4-11; Matt. 26:52-54; 27:50; Rom. 5:8;
Heb. 9:14; and cf. Is. 53:10.

No one has a *right* to lay down his life, but Jesus did have that right.
He had the right both to lay it down and to take it again. The exact
translation of the term ἐξουσία (see also on 1:12) is not easy, however. In
fact, it is doubtful whether anything in English is the full equivalent of
the Greek term. It has been rendered "right," "authority," "freedom,"
"power." The fact that Jesus has the ἐξουσίαν probably means that nothing
in the realm of what is *proper* nor in the realm of what is *possible* could
stop him from doing what he wanted to do. He is *free* in every respect
to do what he intends. In the present case he is not only free but he also
even received a definite *charge* or *commission* from the Father, a charge
to do what he himself wanted to do! (For the meaning of the term *charge*
see also on 13:34.) Here again the will of the Son as Mediator harmonizes
completely with that of the Father. The Father *gave* the Son unto death

115

(3:16); the Son *gave* himself. The Father *would raise* the Son; the Son *would take back* his own life.

19-21. There was again a division among the Jews on account of these words. Many were saying, He has a demon and raves; why do y o u listen to him? — Others were saying, These are not the remarks of a demon-possessed (person). A demon cannot open the eyes of the blind, can he?

It is not difficult to understand that to the mind of the natural man the words of Jesus appeared to be foolishness. Why would a man lay down his life *in order to take it back again?* True, some people desire to commit suicide, but surely not with the intention of coming back to life once more even if they could! *Many* (perhaps, the majority; see also on 9:16) were reasoning in this manner. Hence, they said, "He has a demon and raves." See on 7:20, 49, 52; 8:48. They did not mean to identify insanity with demon-possession, but intended to convey the idea that Jesus, being definitely under the control of an evil spirit, was uttering sheer nonsense. So, why should anyone continue to listen to him?

With this sentiment not everyone was in agreement. So there was *again* a division (schism) among the Jews. For other instances of a sharp clash of opinion see on 6:52; 7:43; 9:16. Those who disagreed with the majority revolved in their minds the entire beautiful allegory of the good shepherd who in contrast with strangers *knows* his sheep, in contrast with thieves and robbers *owns* his sheep, and in contrast with hirelings *loves* his sheep. Perhaps they could not understand everything, but of one thing they were certain: "These are not the remarks of a demon-possessed (person)." Besides, they have not forgotten the great miracle which Jesus had performed so very recently. As they see it, this miracle has evidential value (see on 9:16, 31-33). They are not now interested in debating the question, "Does this opening of the eyes of the man born blind indicate that Jesus is *from God?*" They take a position which, even on the surface, seems unassailable: "A demon cannot open the eyes of the blind, can he?" The implication is: "Certainly not!" Note how impressive and dramatic is this closing sentence of the account in which the Fourth Gospel reproduces the good shepherd discourse. Jerusalem has had a great Visitor. With respect to him no one can be neutral!

Synthesis of 10:1-21

See the Outline on p. 2. *The Son of God Revealing Himself as the Good Shepherd. His Enemies Regard Him as a Demon-possessed Maniac*

In this delightful allegory Jesus describes himself as the good shepherd, in contrast with evil shepherds who harm the sheep (having, no doubt, in mind the Pharisees who had cast out the man whom Jesus had healed of his blindness).

The figure which underlies the allegory is that of an Oriental shepherd, who in the morning seeks to enter the fold where his sheep are kept. The door-keeper opens to him, and the shepherd then puts out his own sheep, calling them by the pet-names which he has given them. Hence, a little later in the day we see this shepherd leading his sheep to pasture-grounds, and by his call assuring them of his constant presence. At nightfall the shepherd returns with his flock and protects them against wolves. He is willing, if need be, to risk his own life in their defence. Being a real shepherd he is deeply interested in his sheep.

We must distinguish between the symbol and the reality which is indicated by the symbol. Sometimes — as in 10:1-5, 12, 13 — *the symbol* itself "rises above the surface," as it were. It is so conspicuous that we must remind ourselves again and again that *these things mean something.* At other times — as in 10:6-11, 14-18 — *the* actual *realities (Jesus,* caring for his own, laying down his life for them; *humble believers,* trusting in him and obeying him; the *Pharisees* hating Jesus and his followers) are much more clearly evident.

As indicated, there are, in the main, three realities that require attention, as is also shown by the three main points in the following summary:

The Allegory of the Good Shepherd

I. *The Friend of the Sheep: the Good Shepherd*

Everything in the way of rightful, complete, protective *ownership,* amazing, intimate, intuitive *knowledge,* and limitless, devoted, self-sacrificing *love* is wrapped up in this term. The actions of the good shepherd have been summarized on p. 103. The main thought is this, that whatever of goodness an earthly sheep-herder may possess is but a dim reflection of the transcending "beauty" (remember the Greek adjective: καλός) of the great Antitype Jesus, the real, the genuine good shepherd, the only one in his class! He owns, he knows, he loves his own, and he does all this in such a wonderful manner!

Although there is only *one* good shepherd, namely, Jesus, nevertheless, there are lessons here for every under-shepherd, for every minister. He too should exercise protecting care with reference to his flock, should know each member, and should tenderly love each and all. In this connection the question was a burning one in the early church: "May a shepherd ever leave his sheep; for example, if the shepherd's life is in danger?" Extreme statements were made by the opponents on either side of this debate. Some hold that this action is permissible only if a. there be another under-shepherd who can take over immediately; and if b. by leaving the sheep who belong to one section of the fold, the shepherd's life is saved for service in another section and for possible return at a later time to his former post. Others simply emphasize that he should do whatever will promote the greatest good for the greatest number. Let every under-shepherd and every denomination which sends him out study this question in the light of whatever lessons may be legitimately derived from the present allegory. — Meanwhile, the *main* idea is certainly not the under-shepherd, but the one and only good shepherd, who never leaves his sheep!

II. *The Foe of the Sheep: Thieves and Robbers, Strangers, Hirelings*

Thieves and robbers are they, for they do not *own* the sheep; strangers, for they do not *know* the sheep; hirelings, for they do not *love* the sheep. Thus, in everything they are the exact opposite of the good shepherd (see above, first sentence under I).

By means of *intimidation* they try to acquire possession of the sheep: they climb over the wall to get into the fold! By means of *imitation* (false philosophy, false religion, false ethics) they try to entice the sheep. When danger approaches, they run away from the sheep. They are thoroughly selfish, a fit symbol of the Pharisees of Jesus' day and of many false leaders in every age of history.

III. *The Sheep*

These have the following characteristics:

1. They listen to the shepherd's voice, but they do not heed the voice of strangers (10:3-5).

2. They follow the shepherd, but they run away from strangers (10:4, 5).

3. They enter by the door (true faith in Jesus and his righteousness), are saved, go in and out and find pasture (10:9). They obtain life and abundance (10:11).

4. They do not all belong to the same fold, but they will all become one flock, with one shepherd, Jesus (10:16).

The absolute dependence of sheep upon the shepherd is everywhere implied. The sheep are dependent on him for provision, direction, and protection. The shepherd is "all things" to them. And they place all their confidence in him. Blessed sheep that have such a shepherd! No foe will ever molest them.

---

22 Then came the feast of Dedication in Jerusalem. It was winter, 23 and Jesus was walking inside the temple, in Solomon's portico. 24 So the Jews gathered around him and said to him, "How long will you keep us in suspense? If you are the Christ, tell us plainly." [79] 25 Jesus answered them, "I *did* tell y o u, but y o u do not believe. The works which I am doing in my Father's name, these bear wit-ness concerning me; 26 but y o u do not believe because y o u are not of my sheep.

---

[79] I D; see Vol. I, pp. 40, 41.

27 My sheep listen to my voice, and I know them, and they follow me, 28 and I give them everlasting life, and they shall certainly never perish, and no one shall snatch them out of my hand. 29 That which my Father has given me is more excellent than all, and no one is able to snatch (it) out of the Father's hand. 30 I and the Father, we are one." 31 The Jews carried stones again in order to stone him. 32 Jesus answered them, "Many good works I showed y o u from the Father. For which of these works are y o u trying to stone me?" 33 The Jews answered him, "Not for a good work are we trying to stone you but for blasphemy, because you, being a man, make yourself God." 34 Jesus answered them "Is it not written in y o u r law, 'I said, y o u are gods'? 35 If he called them gods to whom the Word of God came, and scripture cannot be broken, 36 do y o u say of him whom the Father conse- crated and sent into the world, 'You are blaspheming,' because I said, 'I am the Son of God'? [80]   37 If I am not doing the works of my Father, then do not believe me; [81] 38 but if I do them, then even though y o u do not believe me, believe the works,[82] in order that y o u may come to realize and may continue to realize that the Father (is) in me, and I in the Father." 39 So they were again trying to arrest him, but he escaped out of their hand.

40 And he went away across the Jordan, to the place where John at first was baptizing, and he was staying there. 41 And many came to him and they were saying, "John did no sign; yet everything John said about this man was true." 42 And many believed in him there.

10:22-24

10:22a. From the events that belong, in general, to the feast of Taber- nacles the evangelist proceeds at once to the feast of Dedication. **Then came the feast of Dedication in Jerusalem.** But where was Jesus in the interval between these two festivals? Where was he between October and December of the year 29 A. D.? Opinions vary. Some say, "He spent this period at 'the place where John at first was baptizing.'" They base this upon 10:40 (on the word *again*), but it is certainly not difficult to see that this conclusion by no means follows. Others make Jesus travel back to Galilee. Still others hold that he kept himself in seclusion within the city, that he spent the time at nearby Bethany, or that he was "somewhere" in Judea (cf. Lk. 10:1-13:21). John simply does not give us any definite information with respect to this point.

At the feast of Dedication in the latter part of December Jesus is still (or: *is again*) in Jerusalem. This feast was (and *is* even today) the com- memoration of the purification and rededication of the temple by Judas the Maccabee in the year 165 B. C. (on the twenty-fifth day of Kislev, which approximates our December), exactly three years after it had been defiled by the wicked Antiochus Epiphanes. See I Macc. 1:59; 4:52, 59;

---

[80] I B; see Vol. I, p. 40.
[81] I D; see Vol. I, pp. 40, 41.
[82] I D and IIIB1; see Vol. I, pp. 40, 41; 42, 44.

Fl. Josephus, *Antiquities* XII, vii, 7; L. Finkelstein, *The Jews, Their History, Culture, and Religion,* two volumes, New York, 1949, vol. II, p. 1373; cf. also Dan. 8:14. It is an eight-day, joyous festival, marked by illumination of the dwellings (hence, also called "feast of Lights") and family-reunions. Though it is not one of the three great pilgrim-feasts, it nevertheless, drew many people to Jerusalem.

10:22b, 23. It was winter, and Jesus was walking inside the temple, in Solomon's portico. The rainy season had arrived. Hence, it does not cause surprise that Jesus was walking in the *covered* colonnade that ran along the eastern wall of the temple. This portico is said to have been the only remnant of the original temple. Because it was so regarded it was called *Solomon's* portico (see also Acts 3:11; 5:12). It lasted until the destruction of the temple by Titus, A. D. 70 (Fl. Josephus, *Antiquities* XX, ix, 7).

24, 25a. So the Jews (see on 1:19), still smarting as a result of the verbal lashing which Jesus had given them when he, by implication, had called them thieves and robbers, strangers, and hirelings (10:1-18), **gathered around him** in order to obtain from his lips a statement on the basis of which they would be able to bring about his doom.

So they confront him with the question, **How long do you keep us in suspense?** Literally what they say is, "Until when do you lift up (or: *take away)* our soul?" That the *lifting up of the soul* has here the meaning *keeping the person in suspense* is clear from the sentence which immediately follows: **If you are the Christ, tell us plainly** ("do not keep us on tenter-hooks" or "do not keep us hanging in the air"). For the meaning of ψυχή see 10:11.

The question may be asked, "Why had not Jesus told them *plainly* (i.e., in so many words), 'I am the Christ'? He had revealed himself as such to the Samaritan woman (4:25, 26); why had he not used the same clear language in speaking to the Jews?" Although various answers have been given to this question, the best, it would seem to us, is the traditional one; namely, that to the mind of the Jews (particularly, the Jewish religious leaders, hostile to Jesus) *being the Christ* meant being *the political* (even more than spiritual) *king of Israel, in rebellion against the Roman govern-ment.* Cf. Matt. 26:63 and Luke 23:2. Had Jesus used the plain language which they now demanded, it would have been completely misunderstood. See also on 6:15. In this connection it must be borne in mind that even to the Samaritan woman Jesus did not make himself known as the Christ until he had given her a much needed lesson in the *spiritual* character of religion.

But although Jesus had not used the very words which the Jews were now trying to extract from his lips, he had, nevertheless, employed phraseology which clearly implied the fact that he regarded himself as the

Messiah; in the strictly *spiritual* sense, however. See also on 8:25; and then on 8:23, 24. Hence, 25a. **Jesus answered them, I** *did* **tell y o u, but y o u do not believe.**

If the Jews had been willing to approach the words of Jesus with a believing heart, they would have known that Jesus was, indeed, the Messiah, the Son of God, sent by the Father to accomplish his mediatorial task. The declaration, "I *did* tell y o u," is entirely justified, as anyone can see by rereading the following passages: 5:17-47; 6:29, 35, 51-65; 7:37-39; 8:12-20, 28, 29, 42, 56-58; and 10:7-18. Jesus explains that unbelief has a blinding and stultifying effect: lack of faith (resulting from ill-will toward Jesus) means lack of spiritual understanding. In 8:43 the Lord expressed the same idea in these words: "Why do y o u not understand my utterance? It is because y o u cannot (bear to) hear my word." See on that verse.

25b, 26. Jesus continues, **The works which I am doing in my Father's name, these bear witness concerning me.** Not only has Jesus *told* them about his exalted origin and character, but he had also *proved* it! The *words* had been accompanied by *works*. Think of the paralytic at the pool of Bethzatha ("Bethesda") and of the man born blind (see on chapters 5 and 9). Jesus was constantly doing works *in the name of* his Father; i.e., by his direction, in co-operation with him, especially: with the purpose of revealing his power, love, and glory. That these works had evidential value — clearly indicating that Jesus is the One commissioned by the Father to carry out the plan of salvation — had been stated previously (see on 5:20, 36; and cf. on 9:31-33; for the meaning of the term *bear witness* or *testify* see on 1:7).

The Jews, however, had ignored the meaning of these signs. Worse even, they were doing all in their power to paralyze the effect which they might have among the people. So Jesus says to the Jews **Y o u do not believe** what these works so clearly teach. That failure to believe, that open hostility, is *their sin*. For this they — *and they alone* — are fully responsible. Nevertheless, there is also the factor of divine predestination: "**y o u do not believe because y o u are not of my sheep.**" The sheep of the good shepherd are those who had been *given* to him by the Father (10:29; cf. 6:39, 44). They listen to the shepherd's voice and follow him (10:3,4).

Returning to the angle of the divine decree, note the following: Whereas all men have sinned in Adam, lie under the curse, and are deserving of everlasting death, no one can ever charge God with injustice for having left some to perish, while he chose others out of this mass of corruption to be his own. We confess, of course, that it is not possible for us to harmonize the two lines which run parallel in Scripture (and sometimes, as here, even in one verse: 10:26!): human responsibility, on the one hand, and divine predestination, on the other. To deny either is foolish. Both lines are clearly drawn by Jesus, by John (and by Scripture in general; cf. Luke 22:22; Acts 2:23), and this again and again. Not only that, but the factor of divine predestination is more basic than that of human responsibility; more basic in this sense, that those who listen to Christ's voice and follow him (trust in him and obey him), do so *because* they were *given and drawn;* and those who are not able to listen to him and to follow him remain in this state of inability *because* it has not pleased God to rescue them from the condition into which they, by their own guilt, have plunged themselves. Note the causal connection: "but y o u do not believe *because* y o u are not of my sheep." God is not obliged to save those who have brought destruction upon themselves! Besides, it must ever be borne in mind that on their part *inability* and *ill will* go hand in hand! Hence, in this entire representation God remains holy as well as sovereign, and it is man upon whom all the blame rests.

27, 28. My sheep listen to my voice, and I know them, and they follow me, and I give them everlasting life, and they shall certainly never perish, and no one shall snatch them out of my hand. Looking at this sublime sentence from a merely formal point of view we notice six parts, arranged in beautiful reciprocal relationship. This may be represented as follows:

My sheep		*I*
1. listen to my voice	&	2. know them;
3. follow me	&	4. give them everlasting life;
5. shall certainly never perish	&	6. will take care that no one shall snatch them out of my hand.

However, it must be stressed that this is true only from a *formal* point of view. It is certainly not fair to base wrong doctrinal conclusions upon this rhetorical arrangement, and to say, for example, that *in actual fact,* the six elements are all simultaneous. Very clearly, people cannot make themselves sheep (6:39, 44; 10:29); sheep do not hear a voice unless that voice has gone forth first of all; and sheep do not follow unless the shepherd has first pushed them out of the fold and has gone on ahead of them (10:3, 4). Again, it is because the good shepherd gives to the sheep everlasting life that they never perish and that no one snatches them out of his hand. The sheep are not passive. Indeed not! They listen; they follow. But the action results from the gift. They themselves are *the gift* of the Father to the Son. That thought is stressed in this very context (verse 29).

With slight variation all of these six elements have been mentioned before. Hence, for the explanation we simply refer to the passages where the same truths were expressed previously. Kindly turn to the indicated references:

1. My sheep listen to my voice. See on 10:3, 8, 16.
2. And I know them. See on 10:3, 14.
3. And ˙they follow me. See on 10:4, 5.
4. And I give them everlasting life. See on 10:10 and on 3:16.
5. And they shall certainly never perish. See on 3:16.
6. And no one shall snatch them out of my hand. See on 10:12.

What is stated here, accordingly, amounts in brief to this: "My sheep — having become such because they were given to me by my Father (10:29) — put forth an effort to catch the sound of my voice. They do this constantly. They eagerly obey me, placing their full confidence in me. I know them, acknowledging them as my very own. They follow *me*, but turn away from strangers. I give to them here and now (as well as in the future) that life which is rooted in God and which pertains to the future age, to the realm of glory. In principle it becomes their possession even before they reach the shores of heaven. That life is salvation full and free, and manifests itself in fellowship with God in Christ (17:3); in partaking of the love of God (5:43), of his peace (16:33) and of his joy (17:13). Hence, it differs in quality from the life which characterizes the present age, being its very opposite. And it never ends. The sheep shall certainly never perish; i.e., they shall never enter the state of wrath, the condition of being banished forever from the presence of the God of love. And no one shall snatch them out of my hand (symbolizing my power)."

Some commentators insist that when Jesus states, "They shall certainly never perish, and no one shall snatch them out of my hand," he does not really mean this. They are so sure that believers may, after all, be lost, that they are unwilling to do justice even to the plain sense of Scripture. But it must be borne in mind, as has been shown previously (see Vol. I, p. 46; see also on 4:4; 6:39, 44) that in the Fourth Gospel the idea of predestination (and at times also its corollary: the perseverance of the saints, their being guarded by the power of God, so that they keep clinging to him to the very end) is constantly stressed (see 2:4; 4:34; 5:30; 6:37, 39, 44, 64; 7:6, 30; 8:20; 13:1; 18:37; 19:28). Hence, it is utterly futile to deny this or to seek refuge in a passage which, considered merely on the surface, may seem to be in conflict with this consistent teaching. Thus, 15:6 is often pressed into service by those who deny what John so clearly emphasizes; but see on that verse. The basis of man's salvation rests forever in God, not in man! That point is not grasped by those who teach that man is able, after all, to tear himself loose from the power of God. Thus, in essence, God is dethroned, and the comfort of the assurance of salvation is lost.

29. That which my Father has given me is more excellent than all, and no one is able to snatch (it) out of the hand of the Father.

This verse presents a well-known textual problem. The original offers two different readings, and each of these has minor variations in the separate manuscripts. When the readings differ, the translations based upon them differ. The one which we favor is also adopted by such commentators as F. W. Grosheide, C. Bouma, and others. Cf. the margin of A.R.V. As the reading (hence, also the translation) which we favor has the stronger support, makes excellent sense, and is in complete harmony with the context, we shall discuss the arguments which have been raised against it (and in favor of the weaker reading) in a note.[83]

Note that Jesus uses the expression *my Father* (not *our* Father). He does this because his sonship is altogether unique (see on 1:14).

Viewing all the sheep as *one* flock, Jesus refers to them as "that which my Father *has given* me." On this gift of the Father to the Son see also 6:37, 39, 44. One holds on to a gift, especially if it be a gift from One so

---

[83] The following objections are raised:

(1) Some interpreters claim that the textual support for the reading which we have followed is, after all, rather weak; at least insufficient. But at this point one should be very careful. An examination of the evidence — see, e.g., N.N. — convinces one that the true situation is this: the reading which we have followed, and which makes the *real* subject of the first clause refer to the flock, has definitely the stronger textual support, but within this group of manuscripts there are variations on points of lesser importance.

(2) It is said that the grammar is irregular, the syntax strange, especially because the sentence begins with the words "my Father" (literal translation: "My Father, that which he has given me," etc.) But the Aramaic (which in any event lies back of the Greek) loves "hanging nominatives." See Vol. I, pp. 63, 64. Besides, it is not at all strange, in the present context, that the sentence should place emphasis on the words *my Father*. See point (3). And on the other hand, the grammatical difficulties that surround the other reading are at least just as formidable. For example, while it is not at all out of the ordinary to omit *one* pronoun (to be supplied mentally), it is surely a bit strange in such a brief compass to omit *two* expected pronouns. Literally, the sentence, according to the reading which we reject, would read as follows: "The Father who gave to me is greater, and no one is able to snatch out of his hand." Who gave *what?* To snatch *what?*

(3) The question has been asked, "In which respect are the sheep (here taken collectively, the flock; hence *that which*) more excellent (literally *greater*) than all?" The answer is: exactly in this respect, that they constitute *the Father's present to the Son* in the eternal decree of predestination. *All men* are the object of God's special providence, but only the sheep are the object of God's *very special providence* (see Rom. 8:28).

(4) It is claimed that the reading (and translation) which we prefer is out of line with the context. We are convinced, on the contrary, that it fits the context most beautifully. Note that according to verse 28 Jesus has just said, with reference to the sheep, "And no one shall snatch them out of my hand." The question naturally arises, "Why not?" The answer (verse 29) is, in substance, "Because they are so very precious to both the Father and myself, having been given to me by the Father." We see no good reason, therefore, to depart from what must be considered the better text.

dear as is the Father to the Son. That explains verse 28: "no one shall snatch them out of my (the Son's) hand." But it also explains verse 29: a father will certainly cherish and protect that which he, in incomprehensible love, has given to his son. Note also that in *this* case what the Father gave to the Son *remains the possession of the Father* (is now the possession of both). This gift, then, being more excellent (literally, *greater;* hence, more precious) than all other creatures (see note 82, point 3) can never perish. True believers are never lost. They are the objects of God's very special care, which rests upon his

Predestinating Love

"I sing the gracious, fixed decree
Passed by the great, eternal Three,
The counsel held in heaven above,
The Lord's predestinating love.

"All that concerns the chosen race
In nature, history, or grace:
Where they shall dwell, and when remove
Fixed by predestinating love.

"Their calling, growth and robes they wear;
Their conflict, trials, daily care
Are for them well arranged above
In God's predestinating love.

"In this let Zion's sons rejoice:
Their God will not revoke his choice;
Nor sin nor death nor hell can move
His firm predestinating love.

"This is our bulwark of defence;
Nor foe nor friend can drive us hence.
In life, in death, in realms above
We'll sing predestinating love."

"No one is able to snatch." This *no one* (think of the *wolf* of 10:12) must be permitted to stand in all its absoluteness. Neither satan, nor the clever false prophet, nor the powerful persecutor, nor anyone else shall ever be able to snatch any sheep of the flock out of the hand of the Father! Cf. I Pet. 1:4, 5. See also on verse 28.

30. In verse 28 Jesus has spoken about his own love for the sheep; in verse 29 about his Father's love. No one shall snatch them out of the Son's hand nor out of the Father's hand, for they are more precious than all others. Hence, with respect to this protecting care, Son (verse 28) and Father (verse 29) are *one*. Therefore Jesus says, **I and the Father, we are one.**

However, inasmuch as in other passages it is clearly taught that the oneness is a matter not only of outward operation but also (and basically) of inner essence (see especially 5:18 but also 1:14, 18; 3:16), it is clear that also here nothing less than this can have been meant. Certainly if Son and Father are *one* essentially, then when Jesus states, "I and the Father, we are one," he cannot merely mean, "We are one in providing protective care for the sheep." The economic trinity rests forever upon the essential trinity (see on 1:14 and 1:18).

Note how carefully both the diversity of the persons and the unity of the essence is expressed here. Jesus says, "I and the Father." Hence, he clearly speaks about *two* persons. And this plurality is shown also by the verb (one word in Greek) *"we-*are" (ἐσμεν). These two persons never become one *person*. Hence, Jesus does not say, "We are *one person*" (εἷς), but he says, "We are one *substance* (ἕν). Though two *persons,* the two are one *substance* or *essence.* It has been well said that ἕν frees us from the Charybdis of Arianism (which denies the unity of essence), and ἐσμεν from the Scylla of Sabellianism (which denies the diversity of the persons). Thus in this passage Jesus affirms his complete equality with the Father.

31. The Jews (see on 1:19) thoroughly understood that Jesus by saying, "I and the Father, we are one," had affirmed his absolute equality with the Father. See on 5:17, 18. Now *if* Jesus had not been God, these Jews would have been absolutely right in regarding such a statement as being blasphemy. That they so regarded it is stated in verse 33. Moreover, they were right again when they proceeded upon the assumption that the blasphemer must be put to death by stoning, for the law had so prescribed (Lev. 24:16). Their reasoning may be expressed in the form of a syllogism, as follows:

> Major Premise: A blasphemer must be stoned to death.
> Minor Premise: This man is a blasphemer.
> Conclusion: This man must be stoned to death.

The reasoning was very logical, but the minor premise was wrong! Hence, the conclusion was wrong and . . . wicked! (We are not forgetting, of course, that even the major premise was right only from the point of view of the Old Testament theocracy, and not legally possible in the present political situation.) It was wicked because Jesus had furnished abundant proof of his divine Sonship.

The Jews **carried stones again in order to stone him.** Note that the Jews *carried* stones. The verb is ἐβάστασαν from βαστάζω which means: to bear, carry or carry away, take or take away. Thus in 12:6 Judas is said

126

to have *taken (away)* what was put into the money-box; in 16:12 Jesus tells the disciples that they cannot at this time *bear* to hear the many things which he must tell them; in 19:17 Jesus is pictured as *bearing* his own cross; and in 20:15 Mary Magdalene says to the one whom she regarded as the gardener, "Sir, if you have *carried* him *away*," etc. In the present context the idea seems to be that the Jews, wishing to execute the sentence which the law prescribed in the case of blasphemers, ran to that part of the temple in which building operations were still going on, and having picked up some stones started *to carry* them to Solomon's Porch. The word *again* refers to the fact that this was not the first time that they had tried to stone Jesus (see on 8:59 and cf. 11:8).

32. Jesus answered them, Many good works I showed y o u from the Father. Many works beautiful in intention and execution (for the adjective see on 10:11) had been performed by Jesus. They had been performed at the direction of the Father, and they manifested his glory (power, wisdom, grace); hence, "from (out of) the Father." These works should have convinced the Jews that this was, indeed, the Son of God. There had been *many* (see chapters 5, 6, 9, also 2:23, and those works which are mentioned in the Synoptics) great works that were designed to save or sustain life whether physical or spiritual or both. Now Jesus asks, **For which of these works are y o u trying to stone me?** What Jesus means is this, "For *what kind* of work (the quality is stressed) are y o u *trying* (conative present active indicative) to stone me?" The works which Jesus had performed, being works *from the Father,* showed that Jesus and the Father are one; hence, that he is not a blasphemer, and should not be stoned but worshiped!

33. The Jews answered him, Not for a good work are we trying to stone you, but for blasphemy, because you, being a man, make yourself God. The remark of Jesus with reference to his good works was completely lost upon the Jews. To them what Jesus *said* in 8:30 was far more important than what he *did*. In fact, as they saw it, what he said concerning himself contaminated whatever he did, rendering the latter of no significance and value. That they fully grasped the fact that he claimed for himself full equality with God is clear from the following comparisons:

5:17, 18: "But he answered them, 'My Father is working until now, and I too am working.' — So for this reason the Jews tried all the harder to kill him, because not only did he break the sabbath, but he also called God his own Father, making himself equal with God."

8:58, 59: "Jesus said to them, 'I most solemnly assure y o u, before Abraham was born, I am.' — So they picked up stones in order to hurl them at him."

10:30, 31, 33: " 'I and the Father, we are one.' — The Jews carried stones again in order to stone him . . . (They said) 'Not for a good work are we trying to stone you but for blasphemy, because you, being a man, make yourself God.' "

The Jews regarded Jesus as a mere man who committed the terrible sin of trying to make others believe that he was God. This was blasphemy, to be punished with death.

34-36. Jesus answered them, Is it not written in y o u r law, I said, y o u are gods? If he called them gods to whom the Word of God came, and the scripture cannot be broken, do y o u say of him whom the Father consecrated and sent into the world, You are blaspheming, because I said, I am the Son of God?

The argument which Jesus employs is unanswerable. It is based on Ps. 82:6 which pictures God in the act of entering the assembly of the judges and condemning them because of their unfairness. Now the argument, in brief, amounts to this:

1. Scripture cannot be broken. It is absolutely indestructible, no matter how man may regard it. The Old Testament, *as it lies there in written form!* is inspired, infallible, authoritative. (Note that the days of Karl Barth had not yet arrived.)

2. Now Scripture (y o u r law, y o u r because y o u make so much of it, cf. on 8:17, *law* because the entire Old Testament is *the law,* or else because this passage implies a divine ordinance) calls men *gods.* It uses this title with reference to *judges,* because they represent *divine* justice: the Word of God had come to them. Think of the moral law of Moses, which was (at least, should have been) the basis for their decisions in concrete cases.

3. Y o u have never protested this use of the term. Y o u have never said that God (or Asaph) committed an error by calling these judges *gods.*

4. Then *all the more* (the argument proceeds from the less to the greater, from the minor to the major) y o u should refrain from protesting when I call myself the Son of God. Note the differences:

a. The Word of God (in written form) *had come to* the judges, but Jesus *is* himself, in very person, the Word of God (the Word Incarnate)!

b. The judges were born, just like other men, but Jesus *was sent into the world* (having come from above).

c. The judges were sons of God in a general sense only, Jesus is God's only-begotten (see on 1:14, 18; 3:16).

d. The judges received an important but, as compared with Jesus, an inferior task, but Jesus was *consecrated* (set aside and qualified, cf. 17:19) and *sent* (from ἀποστέλλω; see on 3:17, 34; 5:36-38) into the world to be the Savior.

Hence, the Jews have no right whatever to say to Jesus, "You are blaspheming," when he says, "I am the Son of God."

37, 38. If I am not doing the works of my Father, then do not believe me; but if I do them, then even though y o u do not believe me, believe the works, in order that y o u may come to realize and may continue to realize that the Father (is) in me, and I in the Father.
Tender and earnest is the appeal of Jesus, urging men to place their confidence in him. Was this invitation fruitless? In view of the fact that most of the listeners were enemies of the truth, an affirmative answer might seem to be correct. But it must be borne in mind that even among the (present) enemies God in all probability has his elect who will ultimately turn to him.

The alternative which Jesus presents to his audience is this: a. If I am not doing the works of my Father (not as if Jesus actually believes that this is possible — 5:19, 30, 36; 6:38; 8:29; 9:31-33 are clear enough! —, but he proceeds from this assumption for *their* sake), then do not believe me; but b. If I do them (and, of course I do), then even though y o u do not believe *me* (note the type of condition; see footnote 82), believe the works; that is, even if y o u should not directly accept me as y o u r Savior and Lord, continue to ponder my works in order that at last, by seeing that these are the very works of the Father, y o u are brought to genuine abiding faith in me: i.e., "in order that y o u may come to recognize and may continue to recognize (γνῶτε καὶ γινώσκητε; see also on 1:10, 31; 8:28) that the Father is in me, and I in the Father. There is identity of works; for there is *one essence;* and *the persons* exist in and through each other (glorious reciprocal relationship!) as moments in one divine, self-conscious life. The Father is not subordinate to the Son, and the Son is not subordinate to the Father. They are identical *in essence,* yet distinct *in person.*

39. So they were again trying to arrest him, but he escaped out of their hand. They have given up the attempt to stone him, but (as in 7:30; cf. 7:45) they now try to arrest him, in order to deliver him to the San-hedrin for condemnation and punishment. However, as his time had not yet arrived, he (miraculously?) escaped out of their hand (i.e., their power).

40. And he went away again across the Jordan, to the place where John at first was baptizing, and he was staying there.
The Later Judean Ministry — 7:1-10:39 (October-December of the Year 29 A. D.) — has ended, though not the work in Judea. See Vol. I, p. 36. Jesus goes again *across* (πέραν) the Jordan. The Perean Ministry — 10:40-12:11 (December of the year 29-April of the year 30 A. D.) — begins. To what does the expression *again across the Jordan* refer? Some are of the opinion that Jesus spent the interval between the feast of Tabernacles

and that of Dedication (the interval presupposed between 10:21 and 10:22) across the Jordan, and that he now *again* retires to that region. This possibility must be granted. However, there is no evidence whatever in the text that Jesus actually went across the Jordan between the feasts. This hypothesis is entirely based on the use of the word *again* here in 10:40.

It appears more probable that the expression *again across the Jordan* must be interpreted in the light of what immediately follows, namely, "to the place where John at first was baptizing." The meaning then is this: Jesus goes again to the place where he had been before, namely, at the time that John was baptizing: he goes again to the place across the Jordan.

Which place is indicated? John had been baptizing "in all the region round about the Jordan" (Luke 3:3). It may probably be assumed that the Baptist, having begun in the vicinity of the Dead Sea, (cf. Matt. 3:1; Mark 1:4, 5), had gradually ascended the Jordan Valley, until he had reached Bethany (John 1:28), just east of the Jordan, about thirteen miles below the Sea of Galilee and about twenty miles south-east of Nazareth. Later on (3:23) we find John at Aenon, near the junction of Samaria, Perea, and Decapolis.

It is therefore natural that the author, having previously reported *two* places where John baptized, and now saying that Jesus went to the place where John *at first* was baptizing, is thinking of the first-mentioned place, namely, Bethany across the Jordan (1:28). See on 1:19. This place was about fifty miles (probably a few more by actual travel) from Bethany near Jerusalem. If on the day when Lazarus died, the place from which Jesus started out was trans-Jordanic Bethany (but this is not actually stated in John 11), it would not be strange at all that when he reached Judean Bethany, Lazarus "had been in the tomb four days already" (11:17). Jesus *stayed for a while* in the place where John at first was baptizing.

41, 42. And many came to him and they were saying, John did no sign; yet everything John said about this man was true. It stands to reason that here, in the very district where John had been baptizing and where Jesus himself also was baptized, many people remembered the Baptist and his ministry of preparation. They recalled what John had said about Jesus (see on 1:19-36; 3:22-36; and 5:33), and when they heard the words of Jesus as they flocked around him and saw his signs (in contrast with John who had not performed any signs), they exclaimed, "John did no *sign* (see on 2:11); yet (even though he did no sign to confirm his message) everything John said about this man was true (cf. 5:33)." **And** the result was that **many believed in him there.** This *believed in him* is the same expression as in 8:30. It does not necessarily mean that *all* these believers embraced him with a *living* faith (see on 8:30). It is possible that the word *there,* by its position in the sentence, draws a contrast between what happened here at Bethany across the Jordan and what had occurred elsewhere, but in view of 8:30 we cannot be too sure about this.

Synthesis of 10:22-42

See the Outline on p. 2. *The Son of God Revealing Himself as the Good Shepherd (continued) and also as the Christ, One with the Father. His Enemies Again Seek to Stone Him.*

During the feast of Dedication, December of the year 29 A. D., Jesus was walking in what was probably the only remnant of Solomon's ancient temple; hence called Solomon's Portico. The Jews demanded that if he were the Christ, he would say this in so many words. Jesus, in answering them, points to his previous declarations (which implied his spiritual Messiah-ship), and to his miracles viewed as signs. He declares that the reason for their disbelief was the fact that they were no sheep. Had they been sheep belonging to the Shepherd, Jesus, they would have listened to his words, would have obeyed him, and would have obtained everlasting life. Sheep are never finally lost. Being most precious to both the Father and the Son, no one can snatch them out of the hand (or power) of either Father or Son. These two are one, one not only in the ministry of protective care but also in very essence.

This assertion of perfect equality with God is resented by the Jews who, regarding it as blasphemy, begin to run to the place where there is a pile of stones. They are seen in the act of carrying stones in order to hurl them at Jesus, as the Mosaic law required in cases of blasphemy. On the basis of Ps. 82:6 Jesus, arguing from the minor to the major, reveals the unwarranted character of their conclusion. If earthly judges are called gods because they represent divine justice, does not he, who comes from heaven and was consecrated by the Father for his Messianic task, have the right to this designation? Let them make a diligent study of the works of Jesus, in order that they may accept him by faith. Abandoning their attempt to stone him, the Jews now seek to arrest Jesus, but he withdraws from them.

The Later Judean Ministry having ended, Jesus departs to Perea, to the place where John at first baptized, probably Bethany (cf. 1:28), where many people, remembering what the Baptist had said about Jesus and seeing everything fulfilled in him, believe in him.

Thus, another section (chapters 7-10) of the first main division of John's Gospel (chapters 1-12) ends. See the Outline on p. 2 and see also Vol. I, p. 66.

What is particularly striking is the fact that this section (chapters 7-10) which, on the one hand, shows the progress of hostility, on the other hand

131

is also so full of earnest exhortation and. tender appeal. Sometimes these admonitions are clearly expressed (7:37; 8:11; 10:38); at other times they are just as clearly implied (7:17, 38; 8:12, 31, 32, 36, 51; 9:35-37; 10:1-18; 10:27-30). Such passages as are mentioned in the latter group are not really grasped until one understands that by showing the greatness of the blessings which are bestowed upon true believers Jesus earnestly invites sinners to come to him and to embrace him by a living faith. *Thus, though in actual form the language may not be that of invitation, in essence it surely is an invitation, and, by holding forth blessings, it in reality, speaks even louder.*

Outline of Chapters 11, 12

Theme: *Jesus, the Christ, the Son of God*
During his Public Ministry Manifesting Himself as the Messiah by
Two Mighty Deeds
Anointed by Mary, Sought by the Greeks, but Repulsed by the Jews

ch. 11   *He Raises Lazarus of Bethany.* The Sanhedrin Plans His Death.

ch. 12   He Is Anointed by Mary, *Makes His Triumphal Entry into Jerusalem,* Is Sought by the Greeks, but Repulsed by the Jews.

CHAPTER XI

11 1 Now a certain person was ill, Lazarus from Bethany, of the village of Mary and Martha her sister. 2 Now it was the Mary who anointed the Lord with ointment and wiped his feet with her hair, whose brother Lazarus was ill. 3 So the sisters sent to him, saying, "Lord, listen!,[84] the one whom thou lovest is ill." 4 But when Jesus heard it, he said, "This illness is not unto death; on the contrary, it is for the glory of God, in order that the Son of God may be glorified by means of it."

5 Now Jesus was holding in loving esteem Martha and her sister and Lazarus. 6 So when he heard that he was ill, he then remained two days in the place where he was. 7 Then after this he said to the disciples, "Let us go into Judea again." 8 The disciples said to him, "Rabbi, the Jews just now were seeking to stone you, and are you going there again?" 9 Jesus answered, "There are twelve hours in the day, are there not? If anyone walk about during day-time, he does not stumble, because he sees the world's light;[85] 10 but if anyone walk about during the night, he stumbles, because the light is not in him."[86] 11 These things he spoke, and after this he said to them, "Our friend Lazarus has fallen asleep, but I go in order to wake him up." 12 The disciples said to him, "Lord, if he has fallen asleep, he will recover."[87] 13 But Jesus had been speaking about his death; they however, thought that he spoke about the repose of sleep. 14 Then Jesus said to them plainly, "Lazarus died, 15 and for y o u r sake, that y o u may believe, I am glad that I was not present; but let us go to him." 16 Thomas, the one called the Twin, said to the disciples, "Let us go too, in order that we may die with him."

Preliminary Remarks
on the Raising of Lazarus

I. *Its Significance*

This is threefold:

A. It is a *sign* pointing to Jesus as the Son of God; specifically, as *the resurrection and the life* (11:25). Just as the miraculous multiplication of the bread-cakes was an illustration of Jesus as *the bread of life,* and the cure of the man born blind (as well as the pardon granted to the adulterous

---

[84] Literally, *look!*
[85] IIIB1; see Vol. I, pp. 42, 44.
[86] IIIB1; see Vol. I, pp. 42, 44.
[87] I C; see Vol. I, p. 40.

woman) made him manifest as *the light of the world,* so this miracle points to him as *the resurrection and the life.*

B. In connection with A. (above) it revealed Jesus to be the Messiah who was to die for his people, the fulfilment of prophecy (See on 11:51, 52; 12:14, 15).

We should never lose the thread of the entire story. In his early ministry Jesus revealed himself to ever-widening circles, but was rejected (chapters 1-6). At the feast of Tabernacles and at the feast of Dedication he made his earnest appeal to sinners, inviting them again and again, not only by direct appeal but also indirectly by showing the rewards of discipleship. He also performed a great miracle. But he was bitterly resisted (chapters 7-10). And now, by means of two deeds which in greatness excelled all the others (the raising of Lazarus and the triumphal entry into Jerusalem) he more than ever before manifests himself as being, indeed, the Messiah.

C. It directly led to the formal decision to put Jesus to death, and to the execution of that plot. See 11:47-55; and cf. Vol. I, pp. 12.

II. *The Parts of the Story*

There are four divisions, as follows:

A. The report of Lazarus' illness; his death (11:1-16).

B. The arrival of Jesus (and his disciples) in Bethany near Jerusalem (11:17-37).

C. The miracle itself (11:38-44).

D. Its results (11:45-57).

A good argument can be advanced for the position that verses 55-57 really begin a new chapter. However, one may also argue that the tension in Jerusalem (cf. the somewhat similar tension after the miracle of the multiplication of the loaves, chapter 6; then 7:11) was caused in part by the raising of Lazarus, and therefore can be regarded as one of the results.

III. *The Place and Time of Occurrence*

A. Place

The place where Jesus received the report concerning Lazarus' illness is not mentioned in chapter 11. It may have been Bethany across the Jordan (see on 10:40). The place where Lazarus and his sisters lived was Bethany near Jerusalem (see on 11:18).

B. Time

The last-mentioned time-indication that is definite is found in 10:22, feast of Dedication; hence, December (probably of the year 29 A. D.). The present miracle occurs a little later. Jesus has been staying a little while at the place where John was at first baptizing (10:40). Perhaps he stayed there a few weeks or a month (during which he may have made a journey), but not much longer (see 11:8). There is, however, also a considerable span of time between the raising of Lazarus and the Passover of 30 A. D.

(11:54, 55). This again allows for events not recorded by the apostle John.

On the basis of all these indications we cannot be greatly in error if we state as our belief that Lazarus was raised from the dead in January or early February of the year 30 A. D. The anointing at Bethany takes place six days before the Passover (12:1); hence, at the very close of the Perean Ministry, to which the raising of Lazarus also belongs. The triumphal entry (12:12-19) belongs to the Passion Week (April of the year 30 A. D.), and so does the request of the Greeks to see Jesus (12:20-36).

It is clear from this that the apostle John does not really give us a full description of the ministries of Jesus; say, the Perean Ministry. He simply records a few happenings within a ministry. All in all these events actually occupy only a few days. Hence, there is no real conflict with the accounts as we find them in the Synoptics (particularly in Luke's Gospel). The Perean Ministry, for example, lasted long enough (December of 29 – April of 30 A. D.) to allow for many other events and journeys. By many what is recorded in Luke 13:22-19:27 is assigned to this ministry. There is, at any rate, no conflict.

IV. *The Sequence of Events within the Story*

There are two views which we reject as being too speculative:

A. The first takes for granted that it took the messenger only *one* day to travel from Judean Bethany to the place where Jesus was; that when he arrived, Lazarus had already died; that *after Lazarus' death* Jesus remained where he was for *two* more days, and that Jesus then in *one* day journeyed to the home of Mary and Martha; thus accounting for the fact that when he arrived, Lazarus had been in the tomb *four* days (11:17, 39).

But the story itself contains no hint that this construction is the true one. In fact, if any inferences are warranted at all, they are in the opposite direction. There would seem to be some basis for believing that when the messenger arrives Jesus knows only that Lazarus is *ill* (11:4, 6), and that Lazarus actually died two days later, when his death was immediately reported to the disciples by Jesus (11:11, 14). They then immediately start off on their journey to Judean Bethany (11:15). That it was, nevertheless, the fourth day (three days after the day of the death and burial) when the company arrived would seem to indicate that the place from which Jesus traveled was some distance removed. This would harmonize very well with the idea that Jesus had been staying far to the north, in Bethany across the Jordan, exactly as 10:40 would seem to indicate.

B. The second view, which is the very opposite of the first, proceeds upon the assumption that Lazarus was still alive, and this not only when the messenger (sent by the sisters to report his illness) *reached Jesus,* but also when he *returned again;* and that he then found Lazarus still fully conscious, and intimated to him that he would be raised from the dead, so that he knew about this and was comforted by it before he died! But all this is highly speculative. The account says nothing about it; seems, in fact, to contradict this construction (see under A. above). We should adhere to the story as given in Scripture.

11:1-16

11:1, 2. Now a certain person was ill, Lazarus from Bethany, of the village of Mary and Martha her sister. Now it was the Mary who anointed the Lord with ointment and wiped his feet with her hair, whose brother Lazarus was ill.

The occasion of the miracle was the illness of Lazarus. His name is an abbreviation of Eleazar, meaning "he whom God helped." In order to distinguish him from other persons by the same name (cf. Lk. 16:20) he is called Lazarus *from Bethany,* a native and resident of that village. And in order to distinguish this Judean Bethany (see on 11:18) from the one on the east bank of the Jordan (see on 1:19) it is here called "the village of Mary and Martha her sister." This suggests that it is taken for granted that the readers are acquainted with the beautiful story recorded in Luke 10:38-42, where Mary and Martha are named together. When in the next sentence the Mary referred to is even more definitely indicated as the one "who anointed The Lord with ointment," she is not only distinguished from other Marys — a very necessary distinction, for there were so many bearers of this name — , but she is also designated as being the one whom the readers have met before, namely, in the story recorded in Mark 14:3-9 (Matt. 26:6-13). See Vol. I, pp. 31, 32. However, neither in Matthew nor in Mark is there mention of the *name* of the woman who anointed Jesus. Hence, John mentions the name here. In 12:1-8 he is going to give his own version of the anointing (see on that paragraph). He will add certain details not mentioned in the other Gospels; for example, the one noted even here in 11:2: "and wiped his feet with her hair."

The mention of Mary here *before* Martha (though the latter was probably the elder sister), and of Martha simply as Mary's sister (contrast the order of the names in 11:5, 19; Luke 10:38, 39) may be due to the fact that in both of the stories as recorded earlier (the reception and the anointing) it is *Mary* (whether named or not named), who does something that makes her famous for all time to come. In Luke 10:38-42 it is Mary in distinction from Martha; but see especially Matt. 26:13. Moreover, it is not improbable that it was the raising of Lazarus, recorded here in John 11, which led to *Mary's* deed of gratitude, chapter 12.

3. So the sisters sent to him saying, Lord, listen! the one whom thou lovest is ill.

While the condition of Lazarus was becoming more serious every day,

138

the sisters were ardently wishing that Jesus, the close friend and great healer, were present (11:21, 32). They feel sure that with him present their brother would be healed, and would certainly not die. We can picture them saying again and again, "Were Jesus only here!" In this frame of mind it is altogether natural that they despatch a messenger to Jesus. How long it took him to reach his destination we do not know. If (as seems probable) the Lord was still at Bethany across the Jordan, far to the north, it may have taken the messenger considerable time, perhaps three days, certainly not less than two if he traveled fast.

The message which the sisters sent was very beautiful: "Lord (for this word see on 1:38, the footnote) listen! (see note 84 above), the one whom thou lovest is ill." Note the following:

a. The urgent character of the appeal, which is brought out by the word *listen!*

b. The fact that they do not tell Jesus what to do, but leave it all to him, simply stating the fact: "the one whom thou lovest is ill." They do not even ask Jesus to come and heal him.

c. The fact that they base their plea not on their brother's love or their own love for the Lord, but only on *the Lord's love* for their brother. They know that in the heart of Jesus there is a warm, personal affection for Lazarus. Probably at previous occasions they had noticed this. Jesus may even have told them in so many words. By and by others are going to make remarks about Jesus' love for Lazarus (11:36). For the possible distinction between the two words for *love* used in this account see on 21: 15-17.

4. But when Jesus heard it, he said, This illness is not unto death; on the contrary, it is for the glory of God, in order that the Son of God may be glorified by means of it.

The answer which Jesus gave indicates that he was looking beyond death. When he said, "This illness is not unto death," he did not mean, "Lazarus is not going to die," but "Death will not be the final outcome of this illness." The culmination will be "the glory of God," i.e., the manifestation of the power, love, and wisdom of God, sothat men may see and proclaim these virtues. One should compare this with 9:3. See also on 1:14; 2:11; 5:41, 44; 7:18; 8:50, 54; 11:40; 12:41, 43; and 17:5, 22, 24. When the Son is glorified through the exhibition of his brilliant virtues in works of might and grace, the Father, too, is glorified. These two cannot be separated (10:30; then 5:23). And in order that this glory may shine forth most brilliantly Lazarus must first die (see on 11:6). The illness is *for* (in the interest of) the glory of God.

When Jesus says, *"This illness* is not unto death," the inference would seem to be legitimate that Lazarus had not yet died, and that Jesus knew this. But when he adds, "It is for the glory of God," it is clear that he already knew exactly what was going to happen, namely, that Lazarus would die and that he would raise him.

If we assume an interval of at least two (probably three) days between the delivery of the message ("The one whom you love is ill") and the messenger's re-entrance into the home of Mary and Martha, then, in all probability, Lazarus had already died when the round-trip was completed. But in the midst of the sisters' deepest gloom the words of the Lord, conveyed to them by the messenger upon his return, would continue to resound in their ears: "This illness is not unto death; on the contrary it is for the glory of God, in order that the Son of God (for this term see on 1:14) may be glorified by means of it." The message must have baffled the sisters. Yet, at times it may even have caused a ray of hope to shine across their path. How else can we account for Martha's mysterious saying recorded in 11:22?

When Jesus said, "This illness is not unto death" *the disciples* must have thought that he meant, *"Lazarus will not die* as a result of this illness."

5, 6. Now Jesus was holding in loving esteem Martha and her sister and Lazarus. So when he heard that he was ill, he then remained two days in the place where he was.

For the verb *was holding in loving esteem* (note the imperfect of continued action) see on verse 3 above; then on 21:15-17. For the reason why Martha is now mentioned first, see on 11:1, 2.

According to verse 4 the ultimate goal of the amazing miracle which is going to take place is the advancement of the glory of God. But this final goal does not exclude subsidiary objectives in harmony with it. One of them was the strengthening of the faith of the members of this family and of the disciples (11:15). Now what was the most effective means of accomplishing this end? *Was it the healing of a sick man or the raising of a dead man?* Naturally, the latter. Hence, when Jesus heard that Lazarus was *ill,* he remained two days longer in the place where he was; i.e., he probably did not depart for Judea until Lazarus had died. And he did not want to arrive in Judean Bethany until Lazarus had been in the grave four days, in order that the miracle and the glory might be all the greater. Hence, what may have looked like cruel delay was in reality the tenderest concern for the spiritual welfare of true disciples. The ways of God are sometimes very strange! Moreover, the more faith was strengthened, so much the more the glory of God would be extolled! Accordingly, there is perfect harmony between the subsidiary and the ultimate goal.

> "God moves in a mysterious way
> His wonders to perform;
> He plants his footsteps in the sea,
> And rides upon the storm.

"Ye fearful saints, fresh courage take;
The clouds ye so much dread
Are big with mercy, and shall break
In blessings on your head.

"His purposes will ripen fast,
Unfolding every hour;
The bud may have a bitter taste,
But sweet will be the flower."

7-10. Then after this he said to the disciples, Let us go into Judea again. The disciples said to him, Rabbi, the Jews just now were seeking to stone you, and you are going there again? Jesus answered, There are twelve hours in the day, are there not? If anyone walk about during daytime, he does not stumble, because he sees the world's light; but if anyone walk about during the night, he stumbles, because the light is not in him.

The two days are over, and Lazarus has died. So Jesus said to the disciples, "Let us go into Judea again." They, certain that Lazarus is on the way to recovery (see on 11:4), wonder whether the Lord intends to enter upon a new task in the province of his most bitter enemies. They did not yet understand that Jesus *had to* suffer (cf. Matt. 16:21, 22). Viewed in this light, their reply is not surprising, "Rabbi (for this term see on 1:38), the Jews (see on 1:19) just now were seeking to stone you, and are you going there again?" We disagree with those commentators who deny that the word *now* (νῦν) followed by the imperfect has the temporal force here. That is certainly the most natural meaning in the present context (as also in 21:10). Thus construed it accounts for the puzzled surprise on the part of the disciples: they cannot understand why Jesus wishes to return to a territory which *so very recently* made an attempt to stone him (10:31 cf. 10:39).

The answer which Jesus gives, like so many of his sayings, has a deep meaning.

A figure is used in order that it may illustrate a beautiful and comforting spiritual truth. However, just as even today certain people in a minister's audience will listen to the illustrative story but will fail completely to grasp the point which it intends to bring home, so also the audiences addressed by our Lord during his earthly sojourn very often saw the figure but missed the real lesson, the underlying truth (see on 2:19; 3:3; 4:10; 6:52; and also verses 11-13 of the present chapter).

The figure which Jesus used, in its literal meaning, was as follows:

The Jewish day has twelve hours. Whether it be winter or summer it always has exactly twelve hours, though the length of the hour differs, ranging all the way from (what with us would be) 9 hours and 48 minutes to 14 hours and 12 minutes. Thus the Jewish hour, being stretchable, differs from ours which is always of the same duration. Yet even with us

141

there are, on an average, twelve hours in the day, sothat the saying of Jesus remains true for all time. Now if anyone walk about during daytime he does not stumble, the reason being that though there are obstacles which of themselves might easily cause him to stumble, he sees them clearly, for shining from above is the world's light, the sun. Hence, the obstacles can be avoided or else surmounted. However, if anyone walk during the night (especially in a country with hardly any artificial light), he stumbles, because the light of the sun does not illumine his eyes (there is no light in him).

Now if Jesus simply meant, "Let us take our journey by daytime, and hide during the night," this saying would be out of line with his otherwise highly symbolical style; see this very chapter, verses 11-13. In harmony with similar expressions which abound in John's Gospel (see on 2:4; 7:30; 8:20; 12:23; 13:1; 17:1) what he meant was this:

The time allotted to me, to accomplish my earthly ministry, is definitely fixed (just like day-time is always exactly twelve hours). See on 9:4, 5. It cannot be lengthened by any precautionary measure which y o u, my disciples, would like to take, nor can it be shortened by any plot which my enemies would like to execute. It has been definitely fixed in the eternal decree. If we walk in the light of this plan (which was known to Jesus), willingly submitting to it, we shall have nothing to worry about (we cannot suffer *real* injury); if we do not, we shall fail. — For Jesus himself rebellion against the plan of his heavenly Father (which was also *his own* plan) was, of course, unthinkable. With the disciples it was different. They needed this instruction.

11-13. These things he spoke, and after this he said to them, Our friend Lazarus has fallen asleep, but I go in order to wake him up. — The disciples said to him, Lord, if he has fallen asleep, he will recover. — But Jesus had been speaking about his death; they, however, thought that he spoke about the repose of sleep.

Jesus now reveals the purpose of his plan to go to Judea. It has to do with Lazarus. The Lord calls the brother of Mary and Martha *our friend Lazarus*. From this the disciples can infer that it was not lack of love which caused Jesus to permit Lazarus' death. The Lord addresses his disciples in these words, "Our friend Lazarus has fallen asleep, but I go in order to wake him up." How did Jesus know that Lazarus had departed from this life? See on 5:6 [method (2) or (3)].

The death of believers is often compared to sleep: Gen. 47:30, "When I (Jacob) sleep with my fathers . . ." II Sam. 7:12, "When thy (David's) days are fulfilled and thou shalt sleep with thy fathers . . ." Matt. 27:52, "Many bodies of the saints that had fallen asleep were raised." Acts 7:60, "And when he (Stephen) had said this, he fell asleep." I Thess. 4:13, "But we would not have y o u ignorant, brothers, concerning those that fall asleep." The comparison is, of course, very appropriate: believers expect a glorious awakening on the other side. In the case of Lazarus the figure is still more striking: as a man rises from sleep, so Lazarus was about to rise again from death.

In this connection it is instructive to observe the beautiful and comforting manner in which Scripture everywhere speaks about the death *of believers. That* death is "precious in the sight of Jehovah" (Ps. 116:15); "a being carried away by the angels into Abraham's bosom" (Luke 16:22); "a going to Paradise" (Luke 23:43); "a going to the house with many mansions" (John 14:2); "a (blessed) departure" Phil. 1:23; II Tim. 4:6), in order "to be with Christ" Phil. 1:23), "to be at home with the Lord" (II Cor. 5:8); "a gain" (Phil. 1:21); "very far better" (Phil. 1:23); and, as here, "a falling asleep" in the Lord.

The passages which speak of believers falling asleep do not teach an intermediate state of unconscious repose (soul-sleep, psychopannychy). Though the soul is asleep to the world which it has left (Job 7:9, 10; Is. 63:16; Eccl. 9:6) it is awake with respect to its own world (Luke 16:19-31; 23:43; II Cor. 5:8; Phil. 1:21-23; Rev. 7:15-17; 20:4).

When Jesus told his disciples that he was going to Bethany "to wake up" Lazarus, they should have realized, by the length of the journey (perhaps three days), that the reference was not to the repose of natural slumber. For the readers in Asia Minor (and everywhere) the evangelist makes it very clear that Jesus had been speaking about Lazarus' *death.* The disciples, taking his words (about Lazarus having fallen asleep) in the most literal sense (here as so often; see on verses 7-10 above) showed that they were still not very good at exegesis. They were doing what so many today want us to do: they were taking everything *literally.* They said, "Lord, if he has fallen asleep, he will recover"; i.e., sleep itself will have its restorative effect on him. Though this may look like a very stupid remark on their part.— and to a certain extent it was stupid! — it is only fair to note that the idea that Lazarus would recover from his illness was a natural inference from the words of Jesus recorded in 11:4, *as* (in all probability) *interpreted by them.* The one mistake simply led to another. — When John writes, *"The disciples* said to him, '. . . he will recover,'" this does not necessarily imply, "but *I (John)* knew better." Such exegesis reads too much into the text.

14, 15. Then Jesus said to them plainly, Lazarus died, and for y o u r sake, that y o u may believe, I am glad that I was not present; but let us go to him.

Jesus waited until now to tell the disciples *plainly* (see on 7:26), "Lazarus died." By waiting until now they would be enabled to reflect on this announcement *in the light of* that other very striking statement (spoken only a few moments previously), "Our friend Lazarus has fallen asleep, but I go in order to wake him up." Thus the *waking up* begins to be interpreted. It is the waking up of a man who has just fallen asleep; i.e., who has just died! But the fact that this *should have* cleared up matters in the minds of the apostles does not mean that it actually had that effect. In the case of Thomas we know that it did not (see on verse 16). Had the disciples forgotten the great event that is recorded in Luke 7:11-17? And had Peter, James, and John forgotten about the raising of the daughter of Jairus when Jesus had used similar (not identical) language with respect to death ("The child is not dead but is sleeping")?

Had Jesus been *present,* a healing miracle would have been expected of him; but, as pointed out previously (see on 11:5, 6), the raising of a dead man would naturally be a more effective means of strengthening faith than the healing of a sick man. It is for this reason that Jesus said, ". . . and for y o u r sake, that y o u may believe, I am glad that I was not present." Since the miracle which is going to be performed is (among other things) for the benefit of *the disciples,* it is not surprising that Jesus says, "But let *us* go to him."

16. Thomas, the one called the Twin, said to the disciples, Let us go too, in order that we may die with him.

One of the disciples had a name which both in Aramaic (Thomas) and in Greek (Δίδυμος) meant Twin. We do not know anything about his twin-brother or twin-sister, and it is useless to add to the theories. John, writing for Greek readers, adds the Greek equivalent of the Aramaic name.

Elsewhere Thomas is merely mentioned in the list of apostles (Matt. 10:3; Mark 3:18; Luke 6:15; cf. Acts 1:13). The Fourth Gospel *describes* him, indicates his character. *Despondency* and *devotion* (to Jesus) mark the man (cf. 11:16; 14:5; and 20:24-28). He is ever afraid that he may lose his beloved Master, or that some evil will befall the latter. He expects evil, and cannot believe the good when it occurs.

In the spirit of devotion and despondency he says, "Let us go too, in order that (or: sothat) we may die with him." He does not think first of all of Lazarus nor of himself but of his Lord, who must not be permitted to die *alone!*

We believe that the phrase "with him" (in "Let us go too, in order that we may die with him") means *with Jesus.* As the disciples see it, going to Judea means danger, possibly death, *for Jesus* (see the context, verse 8). Certain able commentators argue that the clause "that we may die with him" cannot mean "that we may die with Jesus," in view of the fact that in the hour of crisis "all the disciples (including Thomas) left him and fled" (Matt. 26:56). But how often does it not happen that a person's intentions are better than his actions? Thomas was probably very sincere in his intention to die with his Lord, but his courage failed him when death actually seemed to threaten. And may it not be safely assumed that Peter, too, was sincere when he affirmed with vehemence that he would never deny the Master? Nevertheless, we know what happened!

We see no reason, therefore, to interpret the clause, "that we may die *with him,*" as if it meant "that we may die *with Lazarus.*" When Thomas said, "Let us go too," he meant, "Let us go *with Jesus.*" Hence, when he added, "that we may die *with him,*" he must have meant "that we may die *with Jesus.*" Similarly Peter said, "Even if I must die *with thee*" (i.e., with Jesus, Matt. 26:35).

---

17 So when Jesus came, he found that he had been in the tomb four days already. 18 Now Bethany was near Jerusalem, about two miles off, 19 and many of the Jews had come to Martha and Mary in order to console them about their brother. 20 Now when Martha heard that Jesus was coming, she went out and met him; but Mary continued to sit in the house. 21 So Martha said to Jesus, "Lord, if thou hadst been here, my brother would not have died.[88] 22 And even now I know that whatever thou wilt ask God, God will give thee." 23 Jesus said to her, "Your brother will rise again." 24 Martha said to him, "I know that he will rise in the resurrection on the last day." 25 Jesus said to her, "I am the resurrection and the life; he who believes in me, though he die, yet shall he live,[89] 26 and everyone who lives and believes in me shall never, never die; do you believe this?" 27 She said to him, "Yes, Lord, I have believed that thou art the Christ, the Son of God, the One coming into the world."

28 And when she had said this, she went back and quietly called Mary, her sister, saying, "The teacher is here and is asking for you." 29 So she, when she heard it, hurriedly arose and was coming to him. 30 Now Jesus had not yet entered the village, but was still at the place where Martha had met him. 31 Now when the Jews, who were with her in the house and were consoling her, noticed that Mary had arisen hurriedly and had gone out, they followed her, supposing that she was going to the tomb in order to weep there. 32 Then Mary, when she arrived at the place where Jesus was, at sight of him fell at his feet, saying to him, "Lord, if thou hadst been here, my brother would not have died." 33 So Jesus, when he saw her weeping, and the Jews who had come along with her also weeping, was deeply moved in the spirit and was agitated, 34 and he said, "Where have y o u laid him?" They said to him, "Lord, come and see." 35 Jesus burst into tears. 36 So the Jews were saying, "See how he (constantly) loved him! 37 But some of them said, "Could not he who opened the eyes of the blind man have kept also this man from dying?"

11:17-37

11:17. So when Jesus came, he found that he had been in the tomb four days already. Jesus arrived at the outskirts of Judean Bethany. The

---

[88] IIB; see Vol. I, pp. 41, 42.
[89] IIIA1; see Vol. I, pp. 42, 43, and re-insert in list on p. 43.

words *he found* probably mean that he had enquired about Lazarus, and had been told that the brother of Martha and Mary had been in the tomb four days already. The soul of Jesus was able to gain information in more ways than one. See on 5:6. In the present instance someone seems to have given him the information in a perfectly natural and human manner.

The news which the Lord received was that Lazarus had been *in the tomb* (μνημεῖον, memorial, monument, Luke 11:47; then, as here, a sepulchre, tomb) four days already. In all probability having started out immediately after Lazarus had died and had been buried (death and burial having taken place on the same day, as was customary; see Deut. 21:23; Acts 5:5, 6, 9, 10), Jesus had arrived at the village-limits of Bethany after three days of travel; i.e., on the *fourth* day (counting the day of death and burial as the *first*). See on 10:40; also above, under *Preliminary Remarks*, III. The evangelist makes special mention of this *fourth* day in order to stress the magnitude of the miracle. According to a rabbinical tradition the soul of a deceased person hovers around the body for three days in the hope of reunion, but takes its final departure when it notices that the body has entered the state of decomposition.[90] *Scripture* nowhere teaches this; rather, the very opposite: the soul goes immediately to its eternal state (see on 11:11-13); but it is *possible* that the people of Jesus' day were deluded by this bit of superstition. We say *possible* (not *certain*), for the written form of the tradition dates from the early part of the third century A. D. If such a belief was current in the days of Jesus' sojourn on earth, the greatness of the miracle, about to be performed, would naturally be enhanced. However, even entirely apart from this, the fourth day in this instance certainly meant decomposition (see on 11:39); hence, this note of time prepares the reader for a most remarkable manifestation of power.

18, 19. Now Bethany was near Jerusalem, about two miles off, and many of the Jews had come to Martha and Mary in order to console them about their brother. This topographical note is added so that the readers living far away from Palestine may be able to visualize the happening. Does the verb *was* mean that the Judean Bethany of Jesus' day had ceased to exist when this Gospel was written? Probably not: the past tense fits into the narration of a past event. Literally John locates Bethany as follows: "about off stadia fifteen" (ὡς ἀπὸ σταδίων δεκαπέντε); which is an idiomatic way of expressing distance, taking the more distant place (in this case Jerusalem) as the basis of computation. A stadium is $\frac{1}{8}$ of a mile; hence, fifteen stadia is slightly less than two miles. See also on 6:19. The closeness of Bethany to Jerusalem is mentioned to explain why so many Jews from the capital had come to console the sisters. For the meaning of the term *Jews*

---

[90] S. BK. II, pp. 250, 251.

see on 1:19. From the fact that Martha and Mary were disciples of Jesus it must not be inferred that the Jews who had come to pay their respects were all friendly to the Lord. Fact is that before the occurrence of this miracle these Jews were critical of Jesus, and did not believe in him in any sense. Many changed their attitude after seeing the miracle. Some, however, persisted in their unbelief, which broke out into open and determined hostility. Such is the picture as the evangelist himself draws it (11:36, 37, 42, 45, 46).

20. Now when Martha heard that Jesus was coming, she went and met him. It would seem that the approach of Jesus had not been announced to the company of mourners at the home of Martha and Mary. Had Jesus sent a special messenger (perhaps, one of his disciples) to convey the news to Martha, to her alone? We are not told, in so many words, that Jesus called Martha. In any event, it seems that the Lord wished to talk to Martha, and that he desired to do this in the absence of the busy crowd. He wanted to speak to her alone and undisturbed. So he remained at the outskirts of the village. There may have been an additional reason why Jesus stopped here instead of proceeding to the house of mourning. See on verse 30.

But Mary continued to sit in the house. The beautiful correspondence between the Gospels (in this case Luke and John) is shown by the character-portraiture of the two sisters. Compare Luke 10:28-32 (busy Martha, overly active; quiet and contemplative Mary, remaining at the Master's feet) and the present story in John. Jesus, understanding the nature of each sister, allows Mary to remain for a while in the house, while he holds a conversation with Martha just outside the village.

21, 22. So Martha said to Jesus, Lord, if thou hadst been here, my brother would not have died. When Martha met Jesus, she repeated, in substance, what, in all probability, she had been saying so often during the illness of her brother. Then she — and also Mary (see on 11:32) — had been uttering the sigh of near-despair: "If only Jesus were here." So now Martha says, "*Lord* (for this see on 1:38), if thou hadst been here, my brother would not have died." This remark must not be viewed as an expression of reproach or resentment, as if Martha were saying, "Why did you have to dawdle for two whole days, remaining where you where when you knew very well that we needed you so badly?" It is not the utterance of disappointment with Jesus. Martha knew very well that it would have been very difficult (if not actually impossible, except by means of a miracle) for Jesus to have reached the home at Bethany in time to heal Lazarus. *Humanly speaking* the message had arrived too late. Accordingly, we must look upon Martha's words as the expression of poignant grief.

147

Martha adds, **And even now I know that whatever thou wilt ask of God, God will give thee.** The striking character of this added statement must receive its full due. It is unrealistic to say that by means of these words Martha cannot have hinted that possibly Jesus might even bring Lazarus back to life. It is true that, on the surface, 11:24, 39 seem to point in the direction of the abandonment of present hope. But it must be borne in mind that a few days ago (day before yesterday?), Lazarus being already in the tomb!, the messenger had returned from his interview with Jesus. And this was his message, quoting the words of the Lord: "This sickness is not unto death; on the contrary it is for the glory of God, in order that the Son of God may be glorified by means of it." See on 11:4. We can imagine how again and again Martha, now that her brother was dead, had been repeating these strange, these very mysterious words, "This sickness is *not* unto death." It is in that light that the words of verse 22 assume meaning: God will grant Jesus *whatever* he asks. In the mind of Martha, the raising of Lazarus is not excluded from this *whatever.*

Nevertheless, although Martha's words imply the possibility of the great miracle which is about to occur, with her this was only a glimmering hope. She did not dare to express it openly and in so many words. She was afraid of her own inference. When Jesus stated in very plain language (see 11:23) what Martha had merely hinted, then she, having transferred her attention from Christ's glorious promise (in 11:4) to the present state of her dead brother, concealed her hope (11:24). Perhaps we may even say that for the moment its spark had been extinguished within her soul, so that it had to be rekindled. In verse 39 we have a similar instance of momentary defeatism experienced by Martha.

We believe that this psychological explanation is the right one. In the heart of Martha the darkness of grief and the light of hope were engaged in deadly combat. Sometimes her lips gave expression to her near-despair; then again to her optimism. Hence, it is wrong, as we see it, to say that, in view of 11:24, 39, the words recorded in 11:22 must not be interpreted as the expression of half-revealed and half-concealed hope. Here is *a woman,* deeply emotional. Her soul is overcome by grief over the death of a brother whom she loved very dearly. But, here is also a *disciple of Jesus,* her soul filled with reverence for her Lord. Here is, consequently, a heart, stirred to its very depths, and swaying between grief and hope.

Martha looked upon the works of Jesus as done in answer to prayer. That was correct (see on 9:31). Nevertheless, when she said, "And even now I know that whatever thou wilt *ask* God, God will give to thee," she used a word for prayer (αἰτέω: to ask) which Jesus never employed with reference to his own requests. The term which Martha used is proper upon the lips of an inferior asking a favor of a superior (4:9, 10; 14:13; 15:7, 16; 16:23, 24, 26). The term which Jesus employed with respect to his own requests generally implies the equality of the two persons (the one who makes the request and the one to whom it is made). The latter term (ἐρωτάω) means *to make request,* see on 14:16, 17:9, 15, 20; but also simply: *to question* or *to inquire* (in which sense it is proper on the lips of anyone), see on 16:19, 23. We might say, therefore, that Martha, who was about to make a beautiful confession with respect to Jesus, did not understand the full meaning of the relation between the Father and the Son. Nevertheless, the important fact to be emphasized is this, that in verse 22 the light of Martha's faith, though still obscured by rising doubts, momentarily dispels the darkness of near-despair.

23, 24. Jesus said to her, Your brother will rise again. Martha said to him, I know that he will rise again in the resurrection on the last day.

In the simplest possible manner Jesus predicted what was about to occur: "Your brother will rise again." Martha, *suppressing* (perhaps even *extinguishing?*) for the moment her flickering hope, as if it were too good to be true, and as if *keeping* a firm grasp on the promise of Jesus would be too bold a stroke, replied plaintively, "I know that he will rise again in the resurrection on the last day." If *suppressing* — and not *extinguishing* — should be the right word here, one might ask further: Was she trying by means of her reply to draw Jesus out, in order to get him to say just what he meant? But more probable is the opinion that, for the moment (see on 11:21, 22) grief and despondency had once more gained the victory. She was probably thinking: "Jesus refers, of course, to the resurrection at the end of history." This reference to the resurrection at the great consummation was perhaps a kind of conventional consolation, frequently poured forth by professional mourners who were at a loss what else to say. — But that was *not* what Jesus had in mind when he said, *"Your brother* will rise again."

It must not remain unnoticed that in what she said Martha took for granted, as entirely indisputable, the resurrection on the last day. Personal belief in individual resurrection is expressed in many Old Testament references (Ps. 16:9-11; 17:15; 49:16; 73:24, 26; perhaps also Job 19:25-27). Collective resurrection is implied in Ezek. 37:1-14; Hos. 6:2; and clearly expressed in Is. 26:19 and Dan. 12:2. Besides, it must be remembered that Martha was not merely a Jewess; she was a disciple of Jesus. We may assume that she had accepted by faith such teaching as that which we find in 5:28, 29 (see on those verses).

25, 26. Jesus said to her, I am the resurrection and the life; he who believes in me, though he die, yet shall he live, and everyone who lives and believes in me shall never, never die; do you believe this?

Here follows another great I AM, the fifth one. There are seven. For the others see on 6:35; 8:12; 10:9; 10:11; 14:6; and 15:5. Subject and predicate are again interchangeable. Jesus is the resurrection and the life; the resurrection and the life, *that* is Jesus. Both the resurrection and the life are rooted in him (cf. Rom. 6:8, 9; I Cor. 15:20, 57; Col. 1:18; I Thess. 4:16). Note the order: first resurrection, then life; because resurrection opens the gate to immortal life.

Jesus is the resurrection and the life *in person* (see on 1:3, 4), the full, blessed life of God, all his glorious attributes: omniscience, wisdom, omnipotence, love, holiness, etc. As such he is also the cause, source, or fountain of the believers' glorious resurrection and of their everlasting life. Because he lives we too shall live. With him removed, nothing but death is left. With him present, resurrection and life is assured. The Prince of life is *ever* the conqueror of death. Not only is he this by and by in the resurrection on the last day; he is this *always*. That is exactly the truth which Martha failed to grasp. Hence, Jesus placed emphasis upon it here, in order that the spark of hope might be kindled once more in Martha's breast, and that it might be fanned into a briskly burning, open flame. What Martha scarcely dared to hope was about to become *real,* for he, who was the Prince of life *also at this moment,* was victor over death, over death in every form.

The remainder of this glorious I AM is a systematic development of the opening words. Jesus is *the resurrection;* hence, "he who believes in me, *though he die, yet shall he live.*" Jesus is *the life;* hence, "everyone *who lives* and believes in me *shall never, never die.*" This is beautiful parallelism, synthetic in character. The second clause reinforces the first, but does not merely repeat it!

First, the believer is pictured *at the moment of death.* One naturally thinks of Lazarus, but what is said is true of every believer who dies physically. The words are: "He who believes (abidingly) in me (note present participle ὁ πιστεύων followed by εἰς; and see on 1:8; 3:16; and especially on 8:30, 31a), though he die (physically), yet shall he live (possessing everlasting life in glory).

Next, the believer is pictured as he lives here on earth, *before death.* We read: "And everyone who lives (spiritually; see on 1:3, 4; 3:16) and believes (abidingly) in me, shall never, never die (shall most certainly never taste everlasting death; shall never, never be separated soul and body from the presence of the God of love)." See also on 3:15-17; 6:47. Even physical death fails to quench the believer's *real* life; on the contrary, such death is gain, for it introduces him into the full enjoyment of life.

In the first clause *believing* is followed by *living.* The life of heaven is meant. It is true, of course, that even here on earth the believer has a foretaste of this heavenly life (3:36; cf. 3:16). — In the second clause *living and believing* (a kind of hendiadys: *living by faith*) is followed by *never dying.* We have here an instance of *litotes: shall never, never die* really

150

implies: *shall most certainly live forever, yes forever.* Note the strong negative: *shall never, never die (*οὐ μὴ ἀποθάνῃ εἰς τὸν αἰῶνα*).*

The whole is beautiful *parallelism,* in which the second clause confirms
and strengthens the first. The arrangement, moreover, is *climactic.* This
will be seen immediately: that the believer at death enters upon life in the
state of perfection is comforting, but not unfamiliar; that the believer
residing here on earth is given the assurance *that he will never, no never
die,* is astounding! Cf. also Rom. 8:10; II Cor. 4:16.

Thus gloriously the miracle itself (11:38-44) is introduced and illumined,
sothat when it occurs it shall be viewed not as an end in itself but as an
illustration of what Christ is and wishes to be for all those who trust in
him. Thus, the miracle will be seen in its true character, namely, as a
sign, pointing away from itself, to Christ, and making him manifest in all
his glory.

An unbeliever rejects both propositions of this glorious I AM (i.e., both
11:25b and 11:26a), and also the statement in which the two are rooted
(11:25a). He is of the opinion that death ends all. Hence he cannot
accept the statement: "He who believes in me, though he die, yet shall he
live." He also conceives of physical death as being the *real* thing, the grim
reaper; hence, for him the idea that this death could ever be robbed of
its real power is nonsense. It is *by faith,* by faith alone, that these great
truths are accepted. Hence, Jesus demanded that Martha should personally
appropriate what she had just now heard from his lips, namely, that *as a
result of what he is* — namely, the resurrection and the life — the life of a
believer ever conquers death. "Do you believe this?" says Jesus to Martha.
There follows a beautiful confession:

**27. She said to him, Yes, Lord, I have believed that thou art the Christ,
the Son of God, the One coming into the world.** Martha's confession here
is positive, heroic, and comprehensive. It is, indeed, very touching, all the
more remarkable because it was made under such trying circumstances.
The I AM of Jesus had helped her considerably. We now see her at her
best; rather, we see God's grace displayed in her, as we hear her say, "Yes
(assenting to the statement that Jesus is the resurrection and the life, and
to the two propositions which followed it), Lord (see on 1:38), I have
believed (perfect tense: it has become a settled conviction with me) that
thou art the Christ (see on 10:25), the Son of God (see on 1:14, 34; 20:31;
Vol. I, pp. 33-35), the One coming into the world" (a fixed title for the
One who willingly came from heaven to earth, Phil. 2:5-8; II Cor. 8:9;
see on 1:9).

To say, as is sometimes done, that Martha did not intend to confess the
Lord's full deity, involves one in hopeless inconsistency. Martha must have
heard Jesus speaking about himself as the Son of God. Now if *others*

understood this to mean that he claimed full equality with the Father (see on 10:30-33; cf. on 5:18), *why not Martha?* She had heard the claims of Jesus, and *she* believed them. Note. *"I* have believed." The pronoun *I,* because it is expressed and because of its position in the sentence, must probably be regarded as emphatic here (but see vol. I, pp. 63, 64). *Others* had heard the same claims, but had rejected them, calling Jesus a blasphemer.

For other notable confessions, recorded in preceding chapters of John's Gospel, see the one by John the Baptist ("Look, the Lamb of God, who is taking away the sin of the world," 1:29), by Andrew ("We have found the Messiah," 1:41), by Philip ("The One about whom Moses wrote in the law and about whom the prophets wrote, we have found," 1:45), by Nathaniel ("Rabbi, thou art the Son of God, thou art King of Israel," 1:49), by the Samaritans ("We know that this is really the Savior of the world," 4:42), and by Simon Peter ("Lord, to whom shall we go? Thou hast the words of everlasting life. And we have believed and know that thou art the Holy One of God," 6:68, 69; cf. also his confession recorded in Matt. 16:16).

That a little later (see on 11:39) Martha wavers again, sothat she then for the moment does not see the full implications of her previous confession, is understandable. Martha's eyes were not always fixed on Jesus. Sometimes they were turned in the direction of a corpse. When that happened, her spiritual vision became obscured. Peter had a somewhat similar experience (see Matt. 14:28-31).

28-30. And when she had said this, she went back and quietly called Mary, her sister, saying, The teacher is here and is asking for you. Having made her glorious confession Martha went back to the house of mourning. We can picture her re-entering and whispering to her sister, Mary. Why did she call Mary quietly? Was it because she did not desire to have the Jews (generally hostile to Jesus) know about the nearness of Jesus? Was she afraid, perhaps, that otherwise a controversy would arise between Jesus and the Jews, and did she wish to give also Mary an opportunity to converse with the Master in private? That is probable.

The reason why she called Mary *at all* was (in addition to her own desire) that Jesus had requested her to do this. That is surely the most natural explanation of the words: "The teacher is here and *is asking for you* (or: *is calling you*)."

So she, when she heard it, hurriedly arose and was coming to him. Now Jesus had not yet entered the village, but was still at the place where Martha had met him. When Mary heard this, she jumped up and hurried out of the house. Presently she *was coming* (imperfect tense, very graphic) to Jesus. The latter had not yet entered the village proper but was still at the place where Martha had met him. Commentators suggest several possible reasons to account for the fact that Jesus remained there even after his conversation with Martha. One suggested reason is: to give Mary the same opportunity for a private interview which her sister had enjoyed. But in this connection it must be remembered that in actual fact *Mary's* interview can hardly be called private. Perhaps the solution must be sought in an entirely different direction, which has also been suggested by several commentators; namely, that the place where the conversations with Martha and (later) with Mary occurred was in the close proximity of the "cemetery." Although we cannot be sure about this, the account, nevertheless, leaves this impression upon us (cf. verses 30, 32, 33, 34, 38). Now if this was the case, it is not hard to understand why Jesus, whose business was not in the house of mourning but at the tomb, would have remained right where he was.

31. Now when the Jews, who were with her in the house and were consoling her, noticed that Mary had arisen hurriedly and had gone out, they followed her, supposing that she was going to the tomb in order to weep there.
For the meaning of the expression "the Jews with her in the house consoling her" see on verse 19 above. It would seem that Mary was the most emotional of the two sisters, as especially verse 32 appears to indicate (and see also 12:3). It is possible that this trait also accounts for the hurried manner in which she got up and left the house, although it must be borne in mind that we are distinctly told that Jesus, through Martha as messenger, *had called Mary*. We do not read that he had called Martha, though this is probable (see on verse 20).
Was it this *hurried manner* of rising which caused the Jews to arrive at the conclusion that Mary was going to the tomb to weep there, sothat they followed *her* though they had not followed Martha? Certain commentators are of this opinion, which may be correct, but we do not know positively.
It should not escape us that also this decision on the part of the Jews, namely, to follow Mary to the tomb, was in the plan of God. He wanted the Jews to see the miracle! The word for *weep* here in verse 31 is not the same as that in verse 35; see on that verse.

32. Then Mary, when she arrived at the place where Jesus was, at the sight of him fell at his feet, saying to him, Lord, if thou hadst been here, my brother would not have died. When Mary saw Jesus, at that very moment she fell weeping (see verse 35) at his feet. In the attitude of reverence and worship she repeated what Martha had said, "Lord, if thou hadst been here, my brother would not have died." For the meaning of this exclamation see on 11:21. Note that while Martha did not fall down at Jesus' feet (11:20; 21), Mary did not add (as Martha had done), "And

153

even now I know that whatever thou wilt ask of God, God will give thee." That seems to even the score. In any event, on the basis of what is found here in John 11 there is insufficient evidence to declare that Mary's faith was more excellent in quality or degree than Martha's. But see also chapter 12:1-8; then Luke 10:38-42. In the latter story it surely was Mary who "chose the good part."

33, 34. So Jesus, when he saw her weeping, and the Jews who had come along with her also weeping, was deeply moved in the spirit and was agitated, and he said, Where have y o u laid him? They said to him, Lord, come and see.

When Jesus saw Mary weeping and the Jews who had come along with her — many of whom were going to accept him by faith (11:45) — also weeping, he *was deeply moved* in *the spirit* (see on 13:21). The *verb* here used has the root-meaning *to snort* (of a horse); then, to be moved with anger (Mark 14:5), to charge sternly (Matt. 9:30; Mark 1:43). The question arises, therefore, "Does this verb as used here in verse 33 (see also verse 38) have the same meaning?" Many commentators believe that it does. Jesus, according to their interpretation, *was filled with indignation.* But why was he angry? Certainly not because Mary and the Jews were weeping. He himself was about to burst into tears (verse 35). Why then? The answer that is generally given is this: Jesus was concentrating his attention upon sin, as the underlying cause of all suffering, grief, and sorrow. He was filled with indignation against sin. It would seem to us that this explanation contains a considerable element of truth. The very fact that the verb employed generally (i.e., in other passages) refers to a feeling of indignation would seem to point in this direction. Besides, it is inconceivable that Christ would think of sorrow and grief and not at the same time of sin as its cause. Nevertheless, we believe that this explanation, though correct as far as it goes, fails to go far enough. The intense emotion which surged in the heart of the Lord comprised at least one other element besides indignation. It went beyond *anger* and included more than this. The entire setting clearly indicates that it also included *sympathy.* In fact the immediate context does not even mention sin. It speaks only about the weeping of Mary and of the Jews, and we are given the impression that it was *this* weeping which led to *his* weeping (cf. 11:33, 34 with 11:35). The context, therefore, is one of sympathy rather than one of anger. Also the verb *and was agitated* or *was troubled* (here literally *troubled himself, shook himself*) which is used in connection with the verb in question, suggests inward *disturbance* (as it does also in 12:27; 13:21; 14:1, 27) of whatever nature, rather than purely indignation. For the meaning of the second verb (ταράσσω) see also on 14:1.

It would seem, therefore, that the translation *was deeply moved in the spirit* is the best. Thus rendered, the verb is sufficiently comprehensive to include both indignation and sympathy. The intense upsurge of emotion was probably visible in Christ's look, tone of voice, and (perhaps *especially*) in his constant sighing. For the meaning of the term *spirit* (πνεῦμα) see on 13:21.

Indignant with sin as the root of all suffering and sorrow, but also taking to heart the sorrow of those about him, Jesus, thus deeply moved in the spirit and visibly agitated, said, "Where have y o u laid him?" Although he was able to obtain information in various ways (see on 5:6), he used the most human method here: he enquired of those who were standing around him. They (perhaps those among them who were most favorably inclined toward him) answered, "Lord (see on 1:38), come and see." The aoristic present is used for the first verb, simple aorist for the second; both are imperatives, with little if any distinction here in the meaning of the tenses.

35. Jesus burst into tears. This is the only place in the New Testament where this *verb* occurs. It is probably ingressive aorist (ἐδάκρυσε). However, the *noun* (tear, tears) whose root enters into the formation of this verb, is found also in Heb. 5:7 in connection with Jesus: "who in the days of his flesh, having offered up prayers and supplications with strong crying and tears unto him that was able to have him from death, and having been heard for his godly fear," etc. See also Mark 9:24; Luke 7:38, 44; Acts 20:19, 31; II Cor. 2:4; II Tim. 1:4; Heb. 12:17; Rev. 7:17; 21:4. In all these passages (beginning with Mark 9:24) the tears are shed by others, not by Jesus. However, there surely is a connection between 11:35 ("Jesus burst into tears") and Rev. 7:17 ("God shall wipe away every tear from their eyes"): because of his tears ours shall be wiped away.

Note the difference, which cannot have been unintentional: in 11:31, 33 another verb is used (κλαίω) than here in 11:35. Mary and the Jews *wept*. In Mary's case such weeping was, of course, genuine, the expression of real, inner sorrow over the loss of a dear brother. In the case of the Jews it was, in many cases, probably tantamount to *wailing*. See on 16:20. The verb κλαίω does not necessarily or always mean *to wail* (hence, in the sense of weeping, not wailing, it can be used even with reference to Jesus, Luke 19:41: Jesus wept over Jerusalem) but can have that meaning (Mark 5:38, 39). The verb δακρύω, used here in 11:35 does not mean *to wail*. These tears were the expression of love, love not only for Lazarus (as the Jews thought, 11:37) but also for Mary, Martha and others (see on 11:33). They were tears of genuine sympathy (Heb. 4:15; cf. Rom. 12:15).

In connection with these tears the remark is often made that they prove Jesus' true humanity. This is certainly correct (see also Vol. I, p. 84). The Fourth Gospel (the very book which stresses Christ's *deity*, Vol. I, pp. 33-35) describes him as being not only absolutely divine but also truly human. It must be stressed, however, that these tears of our Lord were unaccompanied by sin. They were not the tears of the professional mourner, nor those of the sentimentalist, but those of the pure and holy, sympathizing Highpriest! They proceeded from the most genuine love for man found in the entire universe, the love which gave itself.

36, 37. So the Jews were saying, See how he (constantly) loved him! But some of them said, Could not he who opened the eyes of the blind man have kept also this man from dying?

The Jews gave a rather limited interpretation to these tears of Jesus, as if they had been shed only in grief over the death of Lazarus and not also (as the context clearly teaches) in genuine sympathy with the tears of others. Among these Jews, as already remarked, there were those who were going to accept Christ by faith (cf. 11:45). The Jews (see on 1:19) were deeply moved by Christ's *love,* just as a little later they are going to be deeply impressed by his *power.* In their exclamation they refer to the tender affection of Jesus for Lazarus. (For the meaning of the verb for *love* and its synonyms see on 21:15-17). The form here used is vivid (the imperfect: ἐφίλει): *he was loving* (in the past and up to the moment of Lazarus' death) or *he constantly loved.*

The Jews regarded the case of Lazarus to be closed. The matter was hopeless now. After all, Lazarus was dead! But why had not Jesus prevented this death? Some asked in criticism, others in sheer perplexity: "Could not he who opened the eyes of the blind man (the last great miracle at Jerusalem, about which the people were still talking; see on chapter 9) have kept also this man from dying?" This question reminds one of the exclamation of regret recorded in 11:21 and 11:32, but does not convey exactly the same thought. Moreover, it does not rise to the height attained by Martha in 11:22 (see on that verse). It seems that the news of the raising of Jairus' daughter and of the widow's son had not reached Jerusalem, or if it had, *this* death was altogether different: it was now the fourth day! This case was hopeless!

For Synthesis see pp. 167-169.

---

38 So Jesus, again deeply moved within himself, came to the tomb. It was a cavern, and a stone was lying against it. 39 Jesus said, "Take away the stone." Martha, the sister of the deceased, said to him, "Lord, by this time there is an odor, for he has been dead four days." 40 Jesus said to her, "Did I not say to you that if you would believe, you would see the glory of God?" [91] 41 So they took away the stone. And Jesus lifted up his eyes and said, "Father, I thank thee

---

[91] IIIA1; see Vol. I, pp. 42, 43.

that thou hast heard me.   42 I knew that thou dost always hear me, but on account of the multitude that is standing around I said (this), in order that they may believe that thou hast sent me."

43 And having said these things, he shouted with a loud voice, "Lazarus, come out."   44 Out came the dead man, bound hand and foot with grave-bands, and his face was bound about with a sweat-band. Jesus said to them, "Untie him, and let him go."

11:38-44

11:38. So Jesus, again deeply moved within himself, came to the tomb. It was a cavern, and a stone was lying against it. Jesus came sighing to the tomb. For the verb *deeply moved within himself (in the spirit,* verse 33) see on 11:33. The tomb was in the form of a cavern or chamber hewn into a rock. We picture the rock as rising from the ground, perhaps slanting back somewhat. In order to ward off wild animals a slab of stone was lying against it.

39. In performing miracles Jesus did not waste his power. Only God can raise the dead, but men can move a stone away from a tomb. So Jesus bade them do this. Note the brevity of the command, **Jesus said, Take away** (aorist active imperative) **the stone.**

At this point **Martha, the sister of the deceased,** riveting her attention upon her brother's corpse and not upon death's Conqueror (see on 11:21, 22), **said to him, Lord** (see on 1:38), **by this time there is an odor** (or: by this time he stinks), **for he has been dead four days.** The evangelist records this objection of Martha in order to emphasize the greatness of the miracle (see also on 11:17). It is not at all necessary nor even advisable to translate the original as if it read, "Lord, by this time *there will be an odor"* (See R.S.V.). The idea back of that rendering may have been that with the stone still in front of the tomb there could be no odor. Hence, it is argued that Martha could not have meant: there *is* an odor. But even today there is sometimes an odor around a properly sealed tomb! [92] When Martha adds, "for he has been dead four days" (literally, "for he is a fourth-day man"; cf. Acts 28:13), she ascribes the odor to the body's decomposition. The preparation of the body for burial was not nearly as thorough in Palestine as it was in Egypt. *Embalming* was a custom foreign to the Hebrews, but practised with great thoroughness among influential Egyptians (cf. Gen. 50:2, 26). The *anointing* that was customary among prominent Jews was less effective. See further on 11:44.

Martha's faith wavered momentarily. So

---

[92] F. W. Grosheide, *op. cit.,* p. 176, Note 1.

40, 41a. Jesus said to her, Did I not say to you that if you would believe, you would see the glory of God?

In order to strengthen Martha's faith Jesus summarized what he had told her before, whether by means of a messenger (11:4) or directly (11:23, 25, 26); note especially the following words:

11:4: "This illness is not unto death; on the contrary, *it is for the glory of God,* in order that the Son of God may be glorified by means of it."

11:23: "Your brother shall rise again."

11:25, 26: "I am the resurrection and the life, he who believes in me, even though he die, yet shall he live, and everyone who lives and believes in me shall never die; *do you believe this?*"

All this is briefly summarized in the words: "Did I not say to you that if you would believe, you would see the glory of God?"

Of course, Jesus cannot have meant that the performance of the miracle was dependent upon Martha's exercise of faith. What he intended to convey was this, that if Martha would only stop thinking about that corpse and would rivet her attention on Jesus, trusting completely in him (his power and his love), she would see this miracle as a true sign, an illustration and proof of the glory of God reflected in the Son of God. For the meaning of the concept *glory* see on 1:14.

Martha became silent, **So they took away the stone.**

41b, 42. And Jesus lifted up his eyes and said, Father I thank thee that thou hast heard me. I know that thou dost always hear me, but on account of the multitude that is standing around I said (this), in order that they may believe that thou hast sent me.

Before actually performing the miracle Jesus offered a prayer, beautiful because of its trustfulness, simplicity, and sincerity. He prayed as the One sent by the Father (see on 3:17, 34; 5:36, 37; 8:18, 27, 29); i.e., he prayed as the Mediator, being himself the Son of God. He *lifted up* his eyes, the throne of God being *in heaven,* and said, "Father (not *our Father;* God is his Father in a unique sense; see on 1:14; 3:16), I thank thee that thou *hast heard* me." Jesus was able to say this, speaking as if the miracle had already been performed, for he felt in his heart *the certainty* of its near occurrence. For the sake of the audience Jesus spoke these words audibly, and it is for their sake that he added, "I know that thou dost always hear me." That the Father *always* hears the Son follows naturally from 5:30 and 10:30 (see on these passages). When the man born blind (and later when Martha) viewed Christ's miracles as answers to prayer (9:31; 11:22), they were right.

The purpose of the prayer, in which, of course, the close relation between the Father and the Son appears, was this, that the surrounding multitude *might come to believe* (ingressive aorist: πιστεύσωσι) that Jesus is the Sent One, the true Messiah, divinely commissioned to carry out his mediatorial task. See above under *Preliminary Remarks* I B.

43, 44. And having said these things — having placed the miracle, which was about to be performed, in its proper setting — , **Jesus shouted with a loud voice.** On the *loud* voice see also Matt. 27:46, 50; Luke 23:46; I Thess. 4:16; and cf. John 5:28, 29. In order to awaken the dead a *loud* voice, a penetrating shout, was not at all necessary (see Mark 5:41; Luke 7:14). But Jesus cried out so forcibly in order that everyone in the crowd might be aware of the fact that the dead would respond to *his* call!

What Jesus shouted was, **Lazarus, come out** (literally, "Lazarus, hither, out!" two adverbs). It was this voice of Jesus, the expression of his omnipotent will, which caused the dead man to come to life and to obey the command. How this happened we do not know, for it was a miracle, and a miracle transcends human understanding. With majestic simplicity the marvelous work is recorded: **Out came the dead man.** Lazarus is here described as the *dead* man, *dead* not in the sense of "having been dead and still dead," which would reduce everything to nonsense, but *dead* in the sense that he had been dead and was at this instant called back to life.

A vivid picture is drawn of Lazarus stepping out of the grave. He was **bound hand and foot** (literally, *bound with respect to the feet and the hands*) **with grave bands,** strips of linen wrapped around the limbs. Nothing is said here about a white, winding sheet around the body. It seems that though bound hand and foot, Lazarus was able to walk, though perhaps with difficulty. **And his face was bound about** (or: *wrapped around*) **with a sweat-band** or napkin. The word used (σουδάριον) is derived from the Latin *sudarium,* from *sudor,* to which our English word *sweat* is directly related; hence, we translate *sweat-band.* See also on 20:7; cf. Luke 19:20; Acts 19:12.

The glory of God, the revelation of his wonderful attributes (power, love, etc.), was there for all to see. And it is *that* point which the evangelist wishes to emphasize, because Jesus himself stressed it (11:4). Hence, the Lord discouraged all vain curiosity. He did not want Lazarus to stand there a while, in order to be gaped at or to answer ever so many questions; for example, "Where was your soul?" "How does it feel to come back to earth?" To prevent all this and to help Lazarus, who was still handicapped by the grave-bands and the sweat-band, Jesus now issued a brisk command (probably to those standing nearest): **Jesus said to them, Untie him and let him go** (two aorist imperatives, the last one followed by the present infinitive).

45 Many of the Jews, therefore, who had come to Mary and had observed what he had done, believed in him.   46 But some of them went off to the Pharisees and told them the things which Jesus had done.

47 So the chief priests and the Pharisees called a Sanhedrin-session and were saying, "What are we doing, for [93] this fellow is performing many signs?   48 If we let him alone thus, everybody will believe in him, and the Romans will come and take away from us both our place and our nation." [94]

49 But a certain one of them, Caiaphas, being highpriest of that year, said to them, "Y o u do not know anything,   50 neither do y o u take into account that it is expedient for y o u that one man die for the people, and that the whole nation perish not."   51 Now this he said not (merely) of his own accord, but being highpriest that year he prophesied that Jesus was about to die for the nation, 52 and not for the nation only, but in order that he might also gather into one the children of God who are scattered abroad.

53 Now from that day they plotted in order that [95] they might put him to death. 54 So Jesus was no longer walking about openly among the Jews, but departed from there to the country near the desert, to a town called Ephraim, and there he stayed with the disciples.

55 Now the Passover of the Jews was approaching, and many went up to Jerusalem from the country before the Passover, in order that they might purify themselves.   56 So they were looking for Jesus, and were saying to each other, while standing in the temple, "What do y o u think, that he will certainly not come to the feast?"   57 Now the chief priests and the Pharisees had given orders that if anyone knew where he (Jesus) was, he should report (it),[96] in order that they might arrest him.

11:45-57

A fourfold effect is either clearly implied or definitely recorded: (1) The miracle caused many of the Jews, who had previously been unfriendly to Jesus, to come to believe in him (11:45). (2) It added to the bitterness of his enemies, who now, in an official Sanhedrin-session, began to plot his death (11:46-54; cf. verse 57). See *Preliminary Remarks*. (3) It caused great excitement among the Passover-crowds at Jerusalem (11:55-57). (4) It strengthened the faith of Mary and Martha and of the disciples (except Judas, of course, who had none; cf. 12:4). This strengthening of their faith is not recorded in so many words, but may be inferred from 11:4, 15, 26, 40. Moreover, in the case of Mary it manifested itself in a deed of glorious love (12:1-8). These four points are taken up, in that order, in the verses which will now be explained:

11:45. The miracle caused many of the Jews, who had previously been unfriendly to Jesus, to come to believe in him. The words are: **Many of**

[93] On ὅτι see Vol. I, pp. 55, 60.
[94] IIIA1; see Vol. I, pp. 42, 43.
[95] Or simply: "they plotted to put him to death."
[96] IIIA3; see Vol. I, p. 42. The conditional clause is part of a ἵνα object clause, listed as such on p. 50. Cf. 9:22.

the Jews, therefore, who had come to Mary and had observed what he had done, believed in him.

For the character of the Jews who had come to impart consolation see on 1:19; then on 11:19. We take the clause "who had come to Mary and had observed what he had done" to modify its closest antecedent *Jews*. By implication it also modifies the *many* who came to believe in Jesus. Only Mary is mentioned here, perhaps for the same reason that caused her to be mentioned *before* Martha in 11:1 (see on 11:1, 2).

We read that many of these Jews who had visited the home of Mary to pour out their grief had *observed* what Jesus had done. They had not only physically witnessed the miracle but they had studied it, reflected on it, pondered it. The verb is θεάομαι; see on 1:14. The result was that they came to *believe* in Jesus. Although the expression *believed in him* (ἐπίστευσαν εἰς αὐτόν) does not in itself necessarily refer to genuine faith (see on 1:8; 3:16; 8:30, 31a), and although, as the following verses indicate (especially verses 48, 49, 50), the rulers interpreted this faith as loyalty to Jesus as an earthly ruler, nevertheless, in the light of 11:4, 52, it can hardly be doubted that many sincere believers in Jesus Christ as the spiritual Savior were added to the flock on the day of the miraculous resurrection of Lazarus.

46. The miracle added to the bitterness of his enemies, who now, in an official Sanhedrin-session, began to plot his death. **But some of them went off to the Pharisees and told them the things which Jesus had done.** Some of the Jews, having witnessed the miracle and having noticed its effect upon the people, became even more embittered against him. Although grammatically it is possible to take *some of them* to mean *some of the many Jews who believed*, this is obviously incorrect. The idea, here as so often, is simply this, that the Jewish witnesses divide themselves into two classes: *many* believe (in whatever sense this may have been true), *others* become even more hostile than heretofore. With sinister intention the latter group went off to *the Pharisees* (see on 3:1), not in order to tell them that they were all wrong about Jesus, but in order to convince them that drastic action had to be taken against the miracle-worker. This interpretation is in harmony with what follows in verses 47, 48:

47, 48. So the chief priests and the Pharisees called a Sanhedrin-session and were saying, What are we doing, for this fellow is performing many signs? If we let him alone thus, everybody will believe in him, and the Romans will come and take away from us both our place and our nation. Alerted by the Pharisees, a Sanhedrin committee consisting of *chief priests* (ex-highpriests and members of highpriestly families, mostly Sadducees) and *Pharisees*, called a Sanhedrin-session. They explained to the assembled members that the reason why the session had been called was to consider the question: "What are we doing (or: *what must we do*), for this fellow is performing *many signs?*" They were probably thinking especially of those signs recorded in chapters 9 (healing of the man born blind) and 11 (raising of Lazarus), possibly also those recorded in chapters 5 and 6 and others not found in the Fourth Gospel. Note that here they openly admitted that Jesus was performing many signs. What they were afraid of is expressed in the following words: "If we let him alone thus — the very advice which Gamaliel was going to give them a few years later with respect to Christ's disciples! see Acts 5:38 — everybody will believe in him, and the Romans will come and take away from us both our place and our nation."

As the Sanhedrin's committee saw it, everybody would soon accept Jesus as political Messiah. This would happen unless something were done about it. If no action was taken, the Romans, hearing about the new Messiah who was about to lead the rebellion against the constituted government, would come and take away from the Jews (particularly, from the Sanhedrin) both their *place* (the city of Jerusalem with its temple, perhaps with special reference to the latter; cf. Acts 6:13) and their *nation,* putting an end to their national existence, scattering them all over the earth. The Greek word τόπος sometimes means *position* (our position as rulers), but the concrete meaning *place,* in the sense of *city* or *temple,* harmonizes better with what follows: *and our nation.*

49, 50. But a certain one of them, Caiaphas, being highpriest of that year, said to them, Y o u do not know anything, neither do y o u take into account that it is expedient that one man die for the people, and that the whole nation perish not.

When no one could suggest a solution, the president of the meeting presented one. It is clear that *this* chairman was not merely a parliamentarian who kept order. On the contrary, he himself did most of the talking. In the patchwork of his personality the strands of brazen impudence, insane ambition, rancorous jealousy and consummate cleverness were interwoven. He knew all the answers, and he knew how to make others see things his way. He was the kind of individual concerning whom a Dutch proverb says, "The saucy person owns half the world."

His name was *Caiaphas* ("Joseph who was called Caiaphas," says Josephus). The exact meaning of the name Caiaphas is not known, though it has been interpreted as *physiognomist* (expert in the art of reading character in the lineaments of a person's face or form) or, by a slight modification of this interpretation, fortune-teller, prophet. If that explanation of the meaning of his name be correct, it would be particularly fitting (see on 11:51). Having been appointed to the highpriesthood by Valerius Gratus, the predecessor· of Pontius Pilate, in the year A. D. 18, he was

162

going to be deposed by Vitellus, the successor of Pontius Pilate, in the year A. D. 36 Caiaphas was the son-in-law of Annas, who was highpriest from A. D. 6-15.

That Caiaphas was a rude and sly manipulator, an opportunist, who did not know the meaning of fairness or justice and who was bent on having his own way "by hook or by crook," is clear from the passages in which he is mentioned (Matt. 26:3, 57; Luke 3:2; John 11:49; 18:13, 14, 24, 28; Acts 4:6). He did not shrink from shedding innocent blood. What he himself ardently craved, for selfish purposes, he made to look as if it were the one thing needful for the welfare of the people. In order to effect the condemnation of Jesus, who had aroused his envy (Matt. 27:18), he was going to use devices which were the product of clever calculation and unprecedented boldness (Matt. 26:57-66). He was a hypocrite, for in the final trial, at the selfsame moment when he was filled with inner glee because he had found what he considered a ground for Christ's condemnation, he tore his priestly robe as if overcome by profound sorrow! Such was Caiaphas. See also Josephus, *Antiquities* XVIII, iv, 3.

Now, according to the passage under study during *that memorable year,* when Lazarus was raised from the dead and when subsequently Jesus was condemned and crucified, Caiaphas was highpriest, and therefore president of the Sanhedrin. Having listened to the presentation of the problem (see verses 47, 48) and having taken notice of the fact that no one came out with a ready solution, he blurted out, "Y o u do not know anything." The extreme rudeness of the remark reminds one of the manner in which Josephus describes the Sadducees. That famous Jewish historian, who at the age of nineteen had himself joined the Pharisees and was somewhat prejudiced in their favor, states, "The Pharisees are affectionate to each other and cultivate harmonious relations with the community. The Sadducees, on the contrary, are, even among themselves, rather savage in their conduct, and in their intercourse with their peers are as ungentle as they are to aliens" (*Jewish War* II, viii, 14). The boorishness of Caiaphas' remark at this occasion seems to confirm the statement of Josephus with respect to the Sadducees.

Caiaphas continues: ". . . neither do y o u take into account that it is expedient that one man die for the people, and that the whole nation perish not." Under the guise of noble patriotism this unscrupulous scoundrel was trying to get rid of an obstacle to his own popularity and glory!

The alternative which Caiaphas presented was false because it was based upon a presupposition which was the exact opposite of the truth. His reasoning was: Follow Jesus, and the nation perishes; put Jesus to death, and the nation is saved. Conclusion: Jesus must be put to death, — By the irony of history the exact opposite was to happen: when the Jews murdered

Jesus, they sealed their own doom. The Romans came, indeed, and destroyed the city (with its temple) and the nation! See on verse 48.

"One man for the people," said Caiaphas. The meaning of *for* (ὑπέρ) has been explained in connection with 10:11; see on that verse.

51, 52. Now this he said not (merely) of his own accord, but being highpriest that year he prophesied that Jesus was about to die for the nation, and not for the nation only, but in order that he might also gather into one the children of God who are scattered abroad.

The words of Caiaphas had a deeper meaning than he himself realized. The prophets of old, too, often spoke words which they themselves did not fully understand. Cf. I Pet. 1:10-12. Caiaphas poured *one* meaning into his words; God, *another*. The clause, "Now this he said not of his own accord," cannot mean that Caiaphas had been *forced* to say, "It is expedient that one man die for the people, and that the whole nation perish not." He said what he wanted to say, and the responsibility for the wicked meaning which his words conveyed remains entirely his own. Yet, in God's wonderful providence, the choice of words was so directed that these same words were capable of expressing the gist of God's glorious plan of salvation. Just as of old God had spoken through the wicked prophet Balaam, so now he spoke once more, this time through the wicked highpriest Caiaphas. That God chose a highpriest for this was, of course, peculiarly appropriate, for it was he who stood between God and the people. For the moment Caiaphas was not only highpriest but also prophet ("he prophesied"). This passage affords a glimpse into the mystery of the wonderful relationship between the divine counsel and providence, on the one hand, and the exercise of human responsibility, on the other; Caiaphas was left entirely free, was not prevented in any way from saying what his wicked heart urged him to say. Nevertheless, God's will, without becoming even in the least degree defiled, so directed the choice of phraseology that the words which issue from the lips of this coldblooded murderer were exactly the ones that were needed to give expression to the most sublime and glorious truth regarding God's redemptive love. Without becoming aware of it the villain had become the prophet!

Yes, Jesus was, indeed, to die *for the nation;* i.e., for the "holy nation" of Ex. 19:6 (ἔθνος ἅγιον according to the LXX), for the "all Israel" of Rom. 11:26. For Caiaphas the term "the nation" (as he uses it in the clause, "and that the whole nation perish not") had one meaning, namely, the people of Israel viewed as a political unit; for God it had another meaning, as is very clear from the immediately following context (verse 52). The meaning, in the divine mind, surely cannot be "Jesus is about to die for Israel as a political unit, and not for this political entity only, but also for the children of God who are scattered abroad." You cannot join a *political* with a *purely spiritual* concept ("the children of God"). The correct explanation — one that is also in harmony with the consistent teaching of the Fourth Gospel — requires that the expression "not for the nation only" be interpreted in the light of "but . . . also (for) the children of God *who are scattered abroad."*

There are, then, two groups. *All* of those included in these two groups are *children of God* (τέκνα τοῦ θεοῦ; for the meaning of this phrase see on 1:12). But the first group consists of those children of God *who are not scattered abroad;* that is, it consists of Jews, and Jews only, the fold of Israel (see on 10:1); while the second group consists of those children of God *who are scattered abroad;* that is, it consists of Gentiles, and Gentiles only, those elect children of God (whether already born or not yet born) who are not of the fold of Israel (see on 10:16). That the last-mentioned reference (10:16) is in the mind of the author here is clear from the striking similarity between the closing words of that passage and the closing words of the verse now under study. Note the resemblance:

10:16. "And they will listen to my voice, and become *one* flock, *one* shepherd."
11:52. ". . . in order that he might gather into *one* the children of God who are scattered abroad."

The meaning, accordingly, is this: the children of God *(ideally,* namely, according to God's decree from eternity) who are scattered abroad in the *heathen* world, throughout history, will be united with those children of God who constitute "all *Israel"* (all elect Jews, conceived as an organic unit, "holy nation"), so that they will form *one church.* And this church is gathered by *him* (Jesus). Note the words "that *he* might also gather into one." Thus, the Lamb of God was taking away the sin *of the world* (1:29; see also on 1:10).

53, 54. Now from that day they plotted in order that they might put him to death. So Jesus was no longer walking about openly among the Jews, but departed from there to the country near the desert, to a town called Ephraim, and there he stayed with the disciples.

With respect to the plan to put Jesus to death there is progress and development in the Fourth Gospel, as has been pointed out in Vol. I, p. 12. The *official agreement* has now been reached in an official Sanhedrin-session, though the mock-trial, with the sentence fixed in advance, has not yet been conducted. Whether one translates "they plotted in order that they might put him to death," or "they plotted to put him to death" (in other words, whether ἵνα is regarded here as introducing a final clause or as introducing an object clause) makes very little difference in resultant meaning. Either is possible.

So Jesus, knowing that the time designated in God's eternal plan for his death had not yet fully arrived, was no longer walking about (preaching from place to place) *openly* (παρρησία; see on 7:4, 13, 26; 10:24; 11:14; 16:25, 29; 18:20) among the Jews (the hostile leaders and their followers; see on 1:19), but departed from there (i.e., from the environs of Bethany and Jerusalem) to the country near the desert (in all probability the desert *of Judea*), to a town called Ephraim. The exact location of Ephraim has not been determined. W.H.A.B. (see Plate IX) suggests that it might possibly be identical with Ophrah. We can conceive of this place as a kind of small, out-of-the-way, brown-mud wilderness-village. W.H.A.B. locates Ophrah in the territory originally allotted to the tribe of Ephraim (see Plate VI). If this village be the Ephraim to which 11:54 refers, it was about fourteen miles N.N.E. of Jerusalem, about the same distance west of the Jordan River, and about eighteen miles south of Jacob's Well. A few miles to the southwest of it was Bethel. Cf. II Chron. 13:19.

In this remote village of Ephraim Jesus stayed in seclusion with his disciples.

55. Now the Passover of the Jews was approaching, and many went up to Jerusalem from the country before the Passover, in order that they might purify themselves.

The miracle (of the raising of Lazarus) caused great excitement among the Passover-crowds of Jerusalem.

Verses 55-57 introduce the reader to what must have transpired in Jerusalem about March of the year A. D. 30. The Passover was approaching. For the feast of Passover see on 2:13. It was a seven or eight day festival, one of the three great pilgrim-feasts. From all over the country (i.e., the region outside the capital) the people began to wend their way toward Jerusalem, "going up" (see on 2:13) to the holy city. Many of the pilgrims wanted to reach their destination *before* the Passover in order to comply with the regulations regarding purification. See Ex. 19:10-15; Num. 9:9-14; II Chron. 30:17, 18; and cf. John 18:28.

56, 57. So they were looking for Jesus, and were saying to each other, while standing in the temple, What do y o u think, that he will certainly not come to the feast? Now the chief priests and the Pharisees had given orders that if anyone knew where he (Jesus) was, he should report (it), in order that they might arrest him.

Just as once before, at the feast of Tabernacles, the Jews, filled with curiosity and excitement, had been asking, "Where is he?" (see on 7:11), so now the question, "What do y o u think, that he will certainly not come to the feast?" was being bandied back and forth by the Jews who were standing group by group in the temple-courts. Note that the form of the question is such that the questioner already assumes that it is far more likely that Jesus will not come to the feast. Of course, everyone regretted this, being anxious to see the man who had raised Lazarus. Cf. 12:9.

The reason which caused these early pilgrims to conclude that, in all likelihood, Jesus would not come was the recently issued decree of the Sanhedrin ("chief priests and Pharisees"): "If anyone knows where Jesus is, he shall report (it)." The purpose of this was: ". . . that they might arrest him." In view of 11:53 this is not surprising. The Sanhedrin was now fully determined to put Jesus to death. From 11:57 it appears that the prevailing sentiment (due to the advice of the Pharisees within the chief council?) was to give the proceedings the semblance of legality: *to arrest him.*

Synthesis of Chapter 11

See the Outline on p. 134. *The Son of God raises Lazarus of Bethany. The Sanhedrin Plans His Death.*

I. *The Report* (11:1-16).

"Lord, listen! the one whom thou lovest is ill." The sisters (Mary and Martha) of the sick man (Lazarus) simply told Jesus the situation, trusting that he would do the best thing. And he did, though not what they had expected.

They based their implied plea upon Christ's love for Lazarus, not vice-versa.

Jesus, by means of the messenger, informed the sisters, "This illness is not unto death; on the contrary, it is for the Glory of God, that the Son of God may be glorified by means of it." Reasoning back, the steps were as follows:

1. God (and the Son of God, Jesus Christ) must be glorified.

2. He is glorified when unbelievers accept him by faith, and when the faith of believers is strengthened.

3. Such faith can be brought about (or strengthened if it is already present) by means of a great miracle; i.e., when its meaning is applied to the heart by the Spirit.

4. Bringing Lazarus back to life, especially after he has been dead for some considerable time, is a greater miracle than preventing his death.

5. But if Lazarus is to be brought back to life, the sickness must be allowed to have its full course: Lazarus must die.

It was in this way that Lazarus' illness was unto the glory of God. Illness, death, bringing back to life, faith, the glory of God: these were the steps. Jesus saw them all from the very start. He ever sees the end from the beginning. We see only one step ahead, and sometimes not even that one. Hence, the attitude of humble trust is the only proper one. That is what is meant by "walking in the day."

II. *The Arrival* (11:17-37).

First, there is a conversation between Jesus and *Martha.* Whenever she rivets her attention on Jesus, his power, wisdom, and love, she expects great things (see especially verses 22 and 27). Whenever she looks away from Jesus, and dwells on the power of death, she becomes pessimistic (see especially verses 24 and 39).

In his fifth great I AM Jesus shows Martha that he is *always* the Resurrection and the Life, *ever* victorious over death. Hence, *real* death (separation from the love of God in Christ) does not exist for the believer, neither now nor in the hereafter, and even *physical* death is never such that it cannot be set aside by him. Martha must not think that the only hope for her brother is in connection with the resurrection at the last day. — In answer to Christ's question Martha confesses Jesus as the Messiah, the One who was to come into the world, the Son of God.

Secondly, there is a conversation between Jesus and *Mary.* She (as her sister had done a little earlier) exclaims sorrowfully, "Lord, if thou hadst been here, my brother would not have died." Just as Martha and Mary had been perplexed as a result of Christ's absence during the illness of their brother (an absence for which they, however, did not criticize Jesus), so the Jews are perplexed by his tears at Lazarus' tomb. All interested persons seem to be sure that things would have been far better if only Jesus had been near-at-hand when Lazarus became ill. *All* interested persons feel that way about it, *except Jesus,* who saw the end from the beginning! See under I. above.

When Jesus sees Mary and others weep, he himself bursts into tears. These are the tears of *genuine* sympathy. Jesus does not despise sympathy as Nietzsche did, neither does he permit it to deteriorate into a kind of weak sentimentality. On the contrary, he reveals himself here as the One who "bears our griefs and carries our sorrows," who is "afflicted in all our afflictions." He *takes to heart* the suffering of his friends. These sorrows cause him to be deeply moved in spirit. He hates the agonies that torment the souls of his friends, hates them enough to do something about them. What we have here in John 11 is not Schopenhauer or Wagner, who glory in a kind of sympathy that is based upon a mystic philosophy of the identity of all that exists, and who fail to figure sufficiently with the reality of sin as the root of sorrow. What we do have here is the Highpriest Jesus Christ, who as the Lamb of God is taking upon himself the *sin* of *the world* (the elect from every nation), and therefore also its *suffering and woe.* Moreover, the sympathy that expresses itself in the tears of our Lord as he weeps at the tomb of Lazarus is in sharp contrast with that caricature of sympathy which was revealed that day by *many* (we did not say by *all*) professional mourners.

III. *The Miracle* (11:38-44).

Having waved aside the objection of Martha ("Lord, by this time there is an odor, for he has been dead four days"), Jesus bids some of those who were standing around to take away the stone. After a touching prayer to his Father in heaven, Jesus shouts, "Lazarus, come forth." The dead man begins to stir. He actually arises and walks out of the tomb. Freed from the encumbrances of grave-bands at the command of Jesus ("Untie him and let him go"), he disappears from the crowd, in all probability returning to that dwelling which now no longer is a house of mourning.

The significance of this miracle has been pointed out (see under Preliminary Remarks I. at the beginning of this chapter). It is necessary to dwell for a moment on the second of the three points mentioned there: the Miracle reveals Jesus as the Messiah who was to come. This is evident from the following:

(1) It is clearly implied in the prayer of Jesus at the tomb: "I know that thou dost always hear me, but on account of the multitude that is standing around I said (this), *in order that they may believe that thou hast sent me.*"

(2) It is also clearly implied in 10:24, 25: "So the Jews surrounded him, and said to him, 'How long will you keep us in suspense? If you are the Christ, tell us plainly.' Jesus answered them, 'I did tell y o u, but y o u do not believe. *The works which I am doing in my Father's name, these bear witness concerning me.*'" See also 10:28. Surely among all these works the raising of Lazarus is one of the greatest, if not the greatest. Cf. 20:30, 31.

(3) By bringing Lazarus back to life Jesus (more than) fulfilled prophecy with respect to the Messiah and his glorious works (cf. Is. 35:5, 6; Matt. 11:2-4).

IV. *The Results* (11:45-57).

For the fourfold effect of the miracle see p. 160.

CHAPTER XII

12 1 Now six days before the Passover Jesus came to Bethany, where Lazarus was, whom Jesus had raised from the dead. 2 So they made him a supper there, and Martha was serving, while Lazarus was one of those reclining with him.

3 Mary, therefore, took a pound of very precious ointment of pure nard, and anointed the feet of Jesus, and with her hair wiped his feet; and the house was filled with the fragrance of the ointment.

4 But Judas Iscariot, one of his disciples, who was about to betray him, said, 5 "Why was not this ointment sold for three hundred denarii, and given to the poor?" 6 Now this he said, not because he was concerned about the poor, but because he was a thief; and as he had the money-box, he used to take away what was put into it. 7 Jesus therefore said, "Let her be, (it was) in order that she might keep it for the day of my burial; 8 for the poor y o u have always with y o u, but me y o u have not always."

9 The great multitude of the Jews learned that Jesus was there, and they came, not only on account of Jesus, but also in order that they might see Lazarus, whom he had raised from the dead. 10 So the chief priests planned to put Lazarus to death also, 11 because on account of him many of the Jews were going away believing in Jesus.

This chapter has four sections: a. Jesus is anointed at Bethany (12:1-11). b. He makes his triumphal entry into Jerusalem (12:12-19). c. He is sought by the Greeks (12:20-36). d. He is repulsed by the Jews (12:37-50).

12:1-11

12:1. Now six days before the Passover Jesus came to Bethany. That is, six days before the *final* Passover Jesus came *again* to Bethany. Whether he came directly from Ephraim where the Fourth Gospel last located him (11:54) or whether he now came from Jericho (from the home of Zaccheus; cf. Luke 18:35-19:10), as seems possible, the Fourth Gospel does not say. If Jesus withdrew to Ephraim in the early part of February and remained there two or three weeks, there would be sufficient time for other journeys before Passover in April. Accordingly, there is certainly no conflict here between John and Luke.

In order to establish what is meant by "six days before the Passover," the day when Passover began must be determined first of all. This question will be discussed in detail in connection with 13:1 (see on that verse). Anticipating the conclusion arrived at in the discussion of that passage, we shall here assume that the week of Passover began on Thursday, the fourteenth of Nisan. From Ex. 12:6 it is probably safe to conclude that it began officially in the afternoon of that day. Hence, it is not necessary to inquire whether John had in mind the Roman or the Jewish day, for if the feast began in the afternoon before sunset, it would be the same day according to either system of reckoning.

However, even with this assumed, it is not easy to determine the exact day when Jesus arrived in Bethany. Does the expression *six days before Passover* exclude the first day of the Passover-week or does it include this? If Passover began on Thursday, then *six days before Passover,* according to the inclusive method of computation, would bring us to the preceding Saturday; the exclusive method would fix the date of arrival one day earlier (Friday). Which is correct? [97]

We would be ready to leave the question unsettled and to confess our ignorance were it not for the information furnished in 12:9-11. Believing, as we do (see on 13:1), that the Triumphal Entry (12:12-19) occurred on Sunday, it is clear from 12:9-11 that on the day preceding (cf. 12:12), i.e., on Saturday, a great multitude of people came to Bethany to see both Jesus and Lazarus whom he had raised from the dead. It would seem that this big crowd came from Jerusalem (see on 12:9), having been informed about Jesus' whereabouts by the caravan which had passed through Bethany (and had left Jesus there) on its way to the feast. The question, accordingly, arises, *"If Jesus did not arrive in Bethany until Saturday-evening* (the evening just before the Triumphal Entry), then would there have been enough time for all of the following events to happen that evening?"* Study the list:

a. The caravan, with Jesus in its midst, has started out after sunset, i.e., after the conclusion of the sabbath (from Jericho? but that is a distance of fourteen miles!) and has reached Bethany.

---

[97] Other New Testament passages which contain time-notes do not help any. Those who favor the inclusive interpretation of the expression *six days before the Passover* point to 20:26, where *after eight days* means *a week (seven days) later.* (One might also refer to Mark 8:31). But this use of *after* (μετά) does not determine how we should count the days (or years, cf. II Cor. 12:2) when the preposition *before* (πρό) is used. The author recalls how in the district where he was born the expression "eight days from today" was an idiom for "a week from today" *(inclusive* phraseology). Nevertheless, if a person's birthday were on November 18, the phrase "three days *before* your birthday" would certainly mean November 15 (exclusive phraseology). It looks as if we have a similar usage in the Fourth Gospel. Also, if the inclusive method is applied to 12:1, then Jesus arrived at Bethany on Saturday. Is it reasonable to assume that he would be traveling on the sabbath? When the answer is given, "Yes, a sabbath-day's journey," is not this a subterfuge?

b. Jesus leaves the caravan in order to spend some time with his friends in the village.

c. The rest of the caravan proceeds to Jerusalem, a distance (on the average) of about two miles (11:18, though for some, who camped between Jerusalem and Bethany, it was a little shorter).

d. The people who had belonged to the caravan now begin to spread the news about Jesus' whereabouts.

e. After a while, a big crowd gathers and travels from Jerusalem to Bethany to see both Jesus and Lazarus, whom Jesus had raised from the dead.

f. Many people, having seen Jesus and Lazarus, believe.

g. This news travels back to Jerusalem, where the priests meet and decide to put Lazarus to death also.

Is it not more probable that items, *a, b, c,* and *d* occurred on Friday, while *e, f,* and *g* took place on Saturday? Otherwise there would seem to be too much crowding of events in *one* evening. We shall assume, therefore, that Jesus arrived at Bethany before sunset on Friday, and that on the sabbath (Friday sunset to Saturday sunset) he enjoyed the sabbath-rest with his friends, the very last sabbath before his body rested in the tomb. Meanwhile in Jerusalem the news is spreading that Jesus is in Bethany; and the people are making their plans for Saturday-evening. (See on 12:9-11.)

In Bethany on that same Saturday-evening, a supper is given in honor of Jesus.

John's Gospel begins to run parallel with the Synoptics at this point. See Matt. 26:6-13; Mark 14:3-9. There is no conflict. The time-indications in Matt. 26:2 and Mark 14:1 do not say that *the supper at Bethany* was given two days before the Passover, but that two days before the Passover the following happened: a. Jesus predicted that he would be delivered up to be crucified *after two days,* and b. the rulers resolved that he should not be put to death at the feast.

In order to show the connection between the story recorded in chapter 11 and the present account (12:1-8), the evangelist writes: Bethany, **where Lazarus was, whom Jesus had raised from the dead.**

2. So they made him a supper there, and Martha was serving, while Lazarus was one of those reclining with him.

Instead of reporting Jesus for the purpose of arrest (11:57), the friends at Bethany gave a dinner in his honor. As it was not considered proper for women in public to be reclining along with men, we must assume that the guests were exclusively men. There were at least fifteen of them: Jesus, the Twelve, Lazarus, and a certain Simon, who is mentioned only in the Synoptics (Matt. 26:6; Mark 14:3).

The question, "Why is Lazarus singled out for special mention?" (12:2), has received various answers. Some say, "Because he was an honored guest." Others, "Because his public appearance, after having been raised from the dead, was unusual." Still others, "Because his resurrection was the reason, or one of the reasons, for this festive meal." We do not know the answer, though to us the last seems the most probable. The idea readily suggests itself that this supper (or "dinner" if one prefers) was prompted by love for the Lord, specifically by gratitude for the raising of Lazarus (and perhaps also for the healing of Simon who had been a leper, and who is still called "Simon the leper" in Matthew and Mark). It was given at the home of Simon.

Though not reclining along with the invited guests, both Martha and Mary figure prominently in this story. Martha, as usual (cf. Luke 10:40), had taken upon herself the responsibility of serving. Had she agreed to do this at the request of Simon, the reason being that he was unmarried? We do not know. Whether Mary also helped along is not recorded. Nevertheless, the story concerns her and her Lord more than it concerns any other:

3. Mary, therefore, took a pound of very precious ointment of pure nard, and anointed the feet of Jesus, and with her hair wiped his feet; and the house was filled with the fragrance of the ointment.

It is claimed by many interpreters that, in describing the beautiful deed of Mary, the evangelist borrowed from Luke 7:36-50, and that the Mary mentioned in John 12:3 is the same as the sinful woman of Luke 7; or, that, while the two events are distinct, the author of the Fourth Gospel got his sources mixed and simply added to the story which he had found in Matthew 26:6-13 and Mark 14:3-9 the detail concerning the wiping of Jesus' feet, which feature he had found in Luke 7. We completely reject this theory. See the footnote.[98]

---

[98] There is hardly any resemblance between the two accounts. Note the following differences:

Luke 7:36-50 / John 12:1-8

The Occasion

The dinner was in all probability occasioned by the desire of a certain unfriendly Pharisee to examine this famous rabbi, perhaps in order to confirm his suspicions with respect to Jesus. Note the unfriendly manner in which he treated the Lord. See Luke 7:44-46.

The dinner is in all probability occasioned by the desire of a group at Bethany, friendly to Jesus, to honor him and to express their gratitude.

The Place

The house of a Pharisee

The house of Simon the leper, according to Matt. 26:6.

"Lazarus was one of those reclining with him. Mary therefore. . . ." It is possible that the connective οὖν must here be given its full meaning *therefore;* i.e., because Lazarus had been raised from the dead and was now reclining, hale and hearty, with Jesus, *therefore* Mary performed her noble deed.

Mary took a pound of ointment (twelve ounces). For *ointment* the original has the term μύρον; cf. our *myrrh.* A girl's name *Muriel* is from the same root, and means *perfume.* For the distinction between oil (ἔλαιον) and *ointment* (μύρον) see Luke 7:46.[99] The ointment which Mary bought was *very precious* (πολύτιμος-ον, cf. βαρύτιμος-ον, in Matt. 26:7). Mark 14:3 has *very costly* or *very expensive,* πολυτελής-ές; but this word is sometimes used metaphorically with about the same connotation as πολύτιμος-ον; cf. I Pet. 3:4. However, in view of Mark 14:5 (cf. John 12:5) it is probable that in Mark 14:3 πολυτελής-ές actually means *very costly.*

The essence of this ointment was derived from pure *nard,* which is an aromatic herb grown in the high pasture-land of the Himalayas, between Tibet and India.[100] In view of the fact that it had to be procured in a region so remote, and carried on camel-back through miles and miles of mountain-passes, it was very high-priced. Note, moreover, that *this* nard was no substitute. On the contrary, it was the *genuine* article. The ointment was extracted from *pure* nard.[101] Moreover, the Synoptics point out

---

The Main Female Character

A woman who was in the city, a sinner. Even according to Luke this woman was not Mary, the sister of Martha, for these sisters are subsequently introduced as new personages (in Luke 10:38, 39).

Mary of Bethany, a devout disciple of Jesus. She is mentioned in connection with her sister Martha and her brother Lazarus.

The Act

This woman wept. Her tears dropped on Jesus' feet. She then proceeded to wipe off these *tears.* She also kissed and anointed them.

Mary did not weep. She did not wet Jesus' feet with her tears. She anointed these feet with ointment, and then wiped off the excess *ointment.*—It is clear, therefore, that even the detail concerning the wiping of the feet is completely different in the two accounts.

The Result

Jesus sharply rebuked the Pharisee. He praised the woman and dismissed her with a friendly and encouraging word.

Jesus rebuked Judas Iscariot for criticizing Mary. He defended Mary's deed in the light of its purpose.

[99] See also R. C. Trench, *Synonyms of the New Testament,* Grand Rapids, Mich., 1948 (reprint), pp. 135-137.
[100] M. S. and J. L. Miller, *Encyclopedia of Bible Life,* New York and London, 1944, pp. 204, 205.
[101] On the meaning of the adjective πιστικός-ή-όν see the entry in J. H. Moulton and

that this ointment was in an *alabaster* jar; i.e., in a jar of white (or perhaps delicately tinted) fine-grained gypsum.

One can picture the scene. Her heart overflowing with love and gratitude for her Lord, Mary has occupied the position behind Jesus, as the guests, according to Oriental custom, are reclining on couches arranged in inverted U-shaped fashion around a low table (see on 2:9, 10; 13:23, 24). Suddenly she breaks the jar which she is holding in her hand, and she pours its sweet-smelling contents over Jesus. According to Matthew and Mark she pours it upon his *head* (cf. Ps. 23:5); according to John she anoints his *feet*. There is no conflict, for Matthew and Mark clearly indicate that the ointment was poured over the *body* of Christ (Matt. 26:12; Mark 14:8). Evidently there was enough for the entire body: head, neck, shoulders, and even for the feet. (Cf. Ps. 133:2, but here in John the ointment does not merely flow down, but is actually *poured out* upon the feet.) In complete disregard of Oriental rules of propriety, which viewed with definite disfavor the action of a woman who would loosen her tresses in the presence of men, Mary, allowing her heart to speak freely, not only unbinds her hair but (worse even, from the point of view of the Oriental) *with her hair wipes* his feet! Clearly, even the feet (a comparison with Luke 10:39 is significant here!) are covered with an amount of ointment so abundant that they have to be dried. A pound of ointment is a very large quantity! And Mary, having broken the jar, pours out all of this upon Jesus. She *empties* the contents of the alabaster cruse. Hence, the house of Simon is literally filled with fragrance. It floats in every direction, and, for a while, continues to spread and spread. — One hardly knows what to admire most, the irrepressible character of Mary's devotion or the lavish nature of her sacrifice. The former, of course, produced the latter.

It is wrong to detract in any way from Mary's generosity. Nevertheless, this is sometimes done. In that case the *reconstruction* of the narrative is on this order: the sisters had bought some ointment for the burial of Lazarus, but had not used all of it. What was left was by Mary poured upon the head and feet of Jesus. — But this is erroneous. What Mary had in her hand was a new, alabaster jar or vase. In order to pour its contents on Jesus, she *broke* it here and now (Mark 14:3).

4, 5. But Judas Iscariot, one of his disciples, who was about to betray him, said, Why was not this ointment sold for three hundred denarii, and given to the poor?

The contrast between the generosity of Mary and the selfishness of Judas is striking. The evangelist, writing so long after the event and looking

---

G. Milligan, *The Vocabulary of the Greek New Testament*, New York, 1945. The evidence seems to favor the translation *pure* or *genuine* rather than *liquid* or *spiked*. Cf., however, E. Nestle, *ZNTW* 3 (1902), 169 ff.

back, describes the traitor as follows: "Judas Iscariot, one of his disciples, who was about to betray him." For the meaning of the expression see on 6:71.

Judas says in his heart, "What a waste!" That the native language of love is eager generosity was something which Judas could not comprehend. The selfish person cannot understand the unselfish individual. So Judas said, "Why was not this ointment sold for three hundred denarii, and (the proceeds) given to the poor?" Judas is the type of man who has money on his mind all the while. He views everything from the aspect of pecuniary value. He has already estimated the price of this alabaster jar filled with the most precious ointment. He reckons that it must be worth three hundred denarii. See on 6:7. The sum represents the wages which an ordinary laborer would receive for three hundred days of work.

The wages of three hundred days for a single jar of ointment! To Judas this looks like unjustifiable extravagance under any circumstance, even if Mary herself were well-to-do (which was probably true) and did not have to work for a living. How much better — as Judas sees it — it would have been if Mary had sold her ointment and had given the proceeds to . . . to whom? Well, to *Jesus and the Twelve, % Judas, Treasurer;* but it will hardly do for Judas to say that; hence, what he actually says is: "to the poor." A noble individual, this Judas! How deeply concerned about the poor is he!

Because Judas was master in the art of dissimulation and of stating his case very persuasively, others (Mark 14:4) immediately chimed in. The disciples "had indignation" (Matt. 26:8). Wherever Mary looked she met angry glances, looks of shocked disapproval. Only *one* comes to her defence, but that One was the greatest of all! See on 12:8, 9.

Here in verse 5 there follows an explanatory remark, such as John is in the habit of making. It sheds light on the character of Judas. Either by the course of events which followed (for example, the actual betrayal of Jesus by Judas for thirty pieces of silver), or by direct revelation, or both, the evangelist subsequently gained an insight into the soul of the traitor. Writing long afterward, he reveals to the readers the information which he had gained:

6. Now this he said, not because he was concerned about the poor, but because he was a thief, and as he had the money-box he used to take away what was put into it.

Judas was, in reality, a thief. He was the kind of thief who as yet was undiscovered. He still enjoyed the confidence of all. He had been made treasurer of the common fund. He, accordingly, had the money-box (γλωσσόκομον, originally a box containing the "tongues" or mouth-pieces of flutes; later, extended to indicate any box-like receptacle). From this box he would, off and on, pilfer a small amount. That the verb βαστάζω has here the meaning to take away (i.e., to steal) is clear from the fact that it is immediately preceded by the information that Judas was a *thief*. For the meaning of this verb in various passages of John's Gospel see on 10:31.

7, 8. Jesus therefore said, Let her be, (it was) in order that she might keep it for the day of my burial; for the poor y o u have always with y o u, but me y o u have not always.

When Mary is being criticized by all, Jesus comes to the rescue. The words which he speaks in her defence have been reproduced and interpreted in various ways. Among these the most prevalent are as follows:

(1) "Suffer her to keep it against the day of my burial" (A.R.V.). Or: "Let her be, in order that she may keep this for the day of my burial." Or: "Let her be, let her keep it for the day of my burial."

When rendered in this manner, the usual explanation (if one is given) is this: Mary had not used all the ointment. There was some left in the jar. Now Jesus says, in substance, "Let her *keep* what is left. Do not take it away from her. Neither force her to sell it, in order to give the proceeds to the poor. By and by she will need what is left of the ointment. She will need it for my burial."

The one great objection against this interpretation is that the Gospel of Mark states definitely (14:3) that Mary *had broken the cruse!* She had broken it in order to empty its contents on the *head* (Matthew and Mark) and *feet* (John) of Jesus. There was nothing left. Those who, nevertheless, wish to cling to the theory that there was some ointment left in the jar, and that according to John 12:7 Jesus defended her right to keep this for a future day, have only one *logical* way out. It is the way followed by W. F. Howard in *The Interpreter's Bible* (p. 655), namely, to declare definitely that the version of the story as presented in the Fourth Gospel is *contrary to the Synoptic statement.* According to W. F. Howard, John contradicts Mark. That is consistent reasoning. But that conclusion cannot be accepted by anyone who believes in the infallibility of Scripture. Besides, nowhere — not in Matthew, nor in Mark, nor in John — is there any indication that Mary had used only a little of the ointment. On the contrary, even John, who does not mention the breaking of the jar, nevertheless stresses the *lavish* character of the gift: "The house *was filled* with the fragrance of the ointment." It is, accordingly, entirely impossible for us to accept this interpretation.

(2) "Let her alone: against the day of my burial hath she kept this" (A.V.). This is much better. As it stands, the statement is true and in complete harmony with the account as found in Matthew and Mark. Nevertheless, though true in itself, this reproduction of the Lord's statement does not rest upon the best reading. The better and older manu-

scripts insert the word *in order that* (ἵνα) and have the aorist active subjunctive (τηρήσῃ) form of the verb instead of the perfect active indicative (τετήρηκε). Therefore, literally what the best text says is not, "Let her alone . . . she kept it," but "Let her alone . . . in order that she may (or: might) keep it."

(3) "Let her be, (it was) in order that she might keep it for the day of my burial." This is the rendering which, with slight variations, is followed by many (including the margin of the A.R.V.). We believe that it is the best. It is immediately apparent that here, as so often, we have an instance of abbreviated style. See what was said about this in connection with 5:31 (Vol. I, p. 206). Words are left out which have to be mentally inserted. In the present case we have to supply "it was." To show that these words are not actually in the text we have placed them between parentheses. Strictly speaking, also verse 5 of this chapter is a condensed expression. Judas did not literally mean, "Why was not *this ointment* sold for three hundred denarii, and *given to the poor?*" He did not mean that *the ointment* be given to the poor, but that *the proceeds of the sale of the ointment* be donated to them. Hence, also in connection with that verse, one (perhaps even unconsciously) supplies a few words that are necessary to complete the thought. There is nothing strange about this. Our daily conversation is full of shortened expressions.

In order to arrive at what is probably the meaning of the words of Jesus in 12:7 the preceding context must be kept in mind. Judas (as spokesman for the rest) has criticized Mary. If Mary had come into possession of this costly jar filled with most precious ointment (whether by purchase, inheritance, or gift, Judas does not enquire), why did she not sell it and give the proceeds to the poor? Jesus now reveals the reason why Mary (who had, of course, *purchased* the ointment) had *not* followed the course indicated by her critics: "It was in order that she might keep it for the day of my burial."

Mary knew what she was doing. She actually believed that before long Jesus would be put to death by his enemies. Would his friends be given the opportunity to anoint his body? Yet, this honor must not be withheld. Mary owes so much, so very much, to Jesus! To him she owes her salvation, and . . . the recovery of her brother Lazarus from the very realm of the dead. Hence, she had decided to keep the ointment for the day of her Lord's burial. Not, however, in the sense that she literally wanted to keep the jar tightly closed until that day had actually arrived, for that might be too late; but thus, that she would keep it until a good opportunity would present itself, and then she would anoint him *in anticipation of his burial.* It was now or never! Contrast 19:39, 40.

We believe that this interpretation is the probable one, and for the following reasons:

(1) It is in harmony with the clear statement found in Matthew 26:12: "She has done it *to prepare me* for burial," and in Mark 14:8, "She has anointed my body *in advance* for burial."

(2) It is also in harmony with the fact that Mary, perhaps more than any other disciple of Jesus, must have been convinced that the day of Christ's death and burial was rapidly approaching. Note in this connection:

a. Jesus had often predicted his approaching death; sometimes publicly, sometimes privately. See Matt. 9:22; 16:21; Mark 8:31, 32; 9:12; 10:32-34; John 6:52-56; 7:33; 8:21-23; 10:11, 15. Some of these predictions must have reached Mary's ears.

b. The events of the last few months clearly pointed in the direction of the fulfilment of his predictions. See 8:58; 9:22; 10:31; 10:45-57; cf. 12:10. Gradually the wrath of the enemies was being translated into action.

c. Mary was, perhaps, the best listener Jesus ever had. The one who now *anointed* the Lord's feet was the same one who previously had been *sitting* at the Lord's feet (Luke 10:39). Between these two facts there is a close connection.

Mary had embraced her opportunity, and that opportunity would soon be a thing of the past. Hence, very significantly, Jesus, in defending her action, adds: ". . . for the poor y o u have always with y o u, but me y o u have not always." Note the fact that *y o u* is plural. Those translations which (like the R.S.V.) have substituted *you* for *ye* read as if Jesus were telling *Judas* that the latter always had the poor with him. By spacing the letters of the pronoun *y o u* whenever the original has the plural, the distinction is retained, and the true meaning is conveyed. Jesus, then, is speaking not only to Judas but to all the disciples; in fact, to all those who listen to him that day. He is telling them that *just now* anointing him in anticipation of his burial is more important than the care of the poor. By implication, however, he is saying to the church of all the ages that the care of the poor is its responsibility and privilege. Jesus loves the poor who trust in him. Cf. Mark 10:23; Luke 16:19-31. He wants them to be the objects of the constant care of the church (Mark 14:7). Let Judas, the man who seems to champion the cause of the poor but who on the sly is robbing them, take this to heart!

As a reward for Mary's golden deed Jesus adds a beautiful promise. See Matt. 26:13 Mark 14:9.

9. The great multitude of the Jews learned that Jesus was there, and they came, not only on account of Jesus, but also in order that they might see Lazarus, whom he had raised from the dead.

For the explanation of verses 9-11 see also on 12:1. It is logical to assume that *the great multitude* (ὁ ὄχλος πολὺς: the people in large numbers) *of the Jews* consisted mainly of those very people who, having arrived early at the capital, had been inquiring about Jesus (see on 11:55, 56). From the caravan that had just entered the city, and that had come by way of Bethany, they received an answer to their oft-repeated question: "What do y o u think, that he will certainly not come to the feast?" Friday-evening and Saturday, in the midst of great excitement, people are telling each other, "Have you heard the latest? Jesus is actually coming. He has already arrived at Bethany."

And so on Saturday-evening they came flocking out of the city on their way to Bethany. (Those who were lodging less than a sabbath-day's journey away from Bethany may have come a little earlier.) Their purpose, of course, is to see both Jesus, who just recently raised Lazarus from the dead, and also Lazarus himself.

These *Jews* of whom mention is made here are not the religious leaders, hostile to Jesus (the sense in which the term is so often used in the Fourth Gospel; see on 1:19), but the common people, the thrill-seekers.

10, 11. So the chief priests planned to put Lazarus to death also, because on account of him many of the Jews were going away believing in Jesus.

The chief priests (see on 11:47) were absolutely ruthless. In order to gain their objective they were willing to kill not only Jesus but also Lazarus. The latter, too, was an offence to them, and this for two reasons: a. the reason definitely stated here: "on account of him many of the Jews were going away believing in Jesus" (literally: *were going away and were believing,* but this is clearly hendiadys); and b. Lazarus had been raised from the dead, and the chief priests, being Sadducees, did not believe in the resurrection! — So they plotted to kill him also, hoping in all probability that he might not rise again. It would seem that the decision with respect to *Lazarus* was never carried out.

Lazarus, enjoying excellent health, walking around as usual, left an indelible impression upon the multitude, for they knew that this same man had been dead and in his tomb for four days! As a result of what they had now seen with their own eyes many, in departing from Bethany, *were believing in him* (the imperfect is used here ἐπίστευον, followed by εἰς). For the meaning of πιστεύω εἰς see also on 1:8; 3:16; 8:30, 31a. In view of 12:37 where the same form is used in the original (the imperfect of the verb followed by εἰς), and where genuine faith is indicated, it must be considered probable that these believers had become disciples in the best sense of the term; at least, that this was true with respect to many among them.

181

Synthesis of 12:1-11

See the Outline on p. 134. *The Son of God Is Anointed by Mary of Bethany. Mary's Noble Act.*

I. Its Character.

A. *It was prompted by thankfulness.*

The difference between Mary and Judas was this: Judas failed to complete the circle; Mary (by the sovereign grace of God) completed it. Fellowship (even though only outward) with the Lord from day to day should have resulted in gratitude on Judas' part, but it did not, for he was a thoroughly selfish person, a coldly calculating thief, a base pretender. Mary, on the other hand, understood that when love descends from heaven in deeds of might and mercy — such as, the raising of Lazarus — , it must be returned in the form of gratitude. *Heaven* had spoken: "Lazarus, come out." Earth answered, and the sweet fragrance of its deed was wafted back to *heaven*. Thus love answered love, and the circle was completed. Woe to the man or the woman who fails to complete the circle! Cf. Eph. 1:3, 12.

B. *It was unique in its understandingness.*

Jesus had often mentioned his approaching suffering and death (also his resurrection, but even Mary seems not to have grasped this). These predictions were disbelieved. Peter had said, "This shall never happen to thee." But Mary understood, at least to some extent. She believed, and she anointed Jesus in anticipation of his burial.

C. *It was regal in its lavishness.*

There was nothing measured or carefully calculated about this gift. Mary broke the jar and emptied it completely! Her devotion was unrestrained in its expression. The jar was of the costliest alabaster. The ointment was very precious. Its essence was the *genuine* article: real nard, obtained with great difficulty from a remote region. And the quantity of the ointment was a whole pound, enough to anoint not only the head but even the feet, and the latter so lavishly that they had to be dried! The entire house was filled with fragrance!

D. *It was beautiful in its timeliness.*

The very presence of Lazarus, raised from the dead (and of Simon, cured of his leprosy) made the deed timely. Also, Jesus was about to enter the deep waters and the dark night of the Passion Week. *Now* was the proper time for Mary's noble act (her καλὸν ἔργον: beautiful deed; see Mark 14:6).

II. Its Evaluation.

A. By Judas: "To what purpose is this waste?" (Matt. 26:8).

B. By Jesus: "She has performed a noble deed" *(a beautiful work, Mark 14:6).*

"And I solemnly declare to y o u, wherever the gospel is preached in the whole world also what this woman has done will be told for a memorial of her" (Matt. 26:13).

---

12 The next day the vast multitude that had come to the feast, on hearing that Jesus was coming to Jerusalem, 13 took the branches of palm-trees and went out to meet him. And they kept on shouting:
"Hosanna!
Blessed is he (who is) coming in the name of the Lord,
Even the King of Israel!"
14 Now Jesus found a young donkey and mounted it, as it is written:
15 "Stop being afraid, daughter of Zion,
    Look, your king is coming, mounted on the colt of an ass."
16 These things his disciples did not understand at first, but when Jesus was glorified, then they recalled that about him these things had been written, and that these things had been done to him.
17 And the crowd that had been with him when he called Lazarus out of the tomb and raised him from the dead kept on testifying. 18 And for this reason the multitude went out to meet him, because they had heard that he had performed this sign.
19 So the Pharisees said to each other, "Y o u see that y o u are gaining nothing. Look, the world has gone after him!"

Preliminary Remarks
on the Triumphal Entry into Jerusalem

A. *Significance.*

This is an event of outstanding significance. The following points should be noted:

1. *Jesus by means of his Triumphal Entry definitely indicates that he lays down his life; i.e., that he dies voluntarily.* He takes matters into his own hands. He is forcing the issue. He deliberately plans a demonstration, fully realizing that, as a result, the enthusiasm of the masses will enrage the hostile leaders at Jerusalem to such a degree that they will desire more intensely than ever to carry out their plot against him.

2. *Jesus forces the members of the Sanhedrin to change their time-table (with respect to his execution) sothat it will harmonize with his (and with the Father's) time-table.* Originally it had not been the plan of the Sanhedrin to put Jesus to death at this particular time. But the excitement over Jesus aroused by the Triumphal Entry was one of the factors which, considered from the human point of view, hastened the crisis.

3. *Jesus sets himself forth as the Messiah.*

By means of this Triumphal Entry he fulfils the Messianic prophecy of Zech. 9:9. Moreover, when the multitudes hail him as the Messiah, he does not in any way deny the clear implication of their Hosannas.

4. *He also shows the multitudes what kind of a Messiah he is,* namely,

not the earthly Messiah of Israel's dreams. He enters Jerusalem mounted upon a colt, the foal of an ass, an animal associated not with the rigors of war but with the pursuits of peace. He enters as the Prince of Peace.

B. *Sources.*

The *story* is found in all four Gospels, but the *accounts* differ, even though they do not conflict in any way. One might compare this with the miracle of the feeding of the five thousand. There, too, the *story* was found in all four Gospels (as we pointed out in Vol. I, pp. 13, 216); but the *accounts* differed to such an extent that of the more than fifty verses which John devotes to the Feeding of the Five Thousand and the Sermon on the Bread of Life (which followed) only a very few have a parallel in the Synoptics. The *accounts* are so very different that we included John 6 (the miracle and the discourse taken together) in the list of *distinctly* Johannine material (Vol. I. pp. 34, 216, and 227).

We have something similar in John 12. John presents a summary. Nevertheless, even in this account one finds several details that are not recorded in the Synoptics. Also, whereas the Synoptists (as Edersheim observes) "accompany Jesus from Bethany," John, on the other hand, "seems to follow from Jerusalem that multitude which, on tidings of his approach, hastened to meet him." [102]

In order to be able to appreciate the Johannine account of the Triumphal Entry it is probably best first of all to see the whole story, in outline-form. Piecing together the different accounts (Synoptics and John) we obtain the following:

1. Matt. 21:1-3, 6, 7; Mark 11:1-6; Luke 19:29-34:

As Jesus takes his departure from Bethany, very soon after starting out (perhaps on approaching the eastern slope of the mount of Olives) he sends two of his disciples into a small village (probably Bethphage, which has been called a suburb of Jerusalem), in order to fetch from there a donkey on which he plans to enter the capital. In reality (as Matthew points out) there were *two* animals (a colt and its dam), but it appears later that Jesus makes use of the colt, the other animal either trotting by its side or else being held back by the disciples.

The disciples find everything exactly as Jesus had predicted: they find the ass and its colt tied to a stake at the entrance of the village. There are some people standing around. "Why are y o u untying them (or *it*)?" ask the owners. "The Lord needs them (it)," is the answer. The owners, who were probably disciples of Jesus, comply immediately, and the disciples bring the animals to Jesus.

2. Matt. 21:4, 5; Mark 11:7; Luke 19:35; John 12:14, 15:

---

[102] A. Edersheim, *The Life and Times of Jesus the Messiah,* New York, 1898, Vol. II, p. 364.

The disciples throw their outer garments upon both of the animals (not knowing at first which one Jesus will choose), and when it has become clear that he wishes to ride upon *the colt,* they assist him in mounting this animal. Jesus starts out toward Jerusalem.

Both Matthew and John see in this event a fulfilment of the prophecy of Zechariah 9:9. "Stop being afraid, daughter of Zion, Look, your king is coming, mounted on the colt of an ass" (or ". . . meek, and riding upon an ass, even upon a colt, the foal of an ass").

3. Matt. 21:8; Mark 11:8; Luke 19:36:

Most of the people who accompany Jesus from Bethany spread their garments in the way. Others cut branches from the trees and with these they pave the way before him.

4. John 12:1, 12, 13a, 18:

Meanwhile the multitude of pilgrims who had previously arrived in Jerusalem and had heard a. that Jesus had raised Lazarus from the dead, and b. that he was on his way toward the city, come pouring out of the eastern gate on their way to meet him. They cut fronds from the palm-trees that line the road, and with these they proceed on their way to welcome the Messiah.

5. Matt. 21:9; Mark 11:9, 10; Luke 19:37, 38; John 12:13b:

As the two throngs meet, the enthusiasm mounts. This large multitude consisting of those who (having turned around as soon as they met him) are going ahead of him and of those who follow, includes the following elements: the Twelve, a throng from Bethany (many of whom had witnessed the miracle, which, however, had also been witnessed by some from Jerusalem), a host of pilgrims from Galilee (who had reached their destination, Jerusalem), and even some hostile Pharisees.

Descending the western slope of the mount of Olives, and drawing near to Jerusalem, the combined throngs, with the exception of the hostile Pharisees, start to shout:

> "Hosanna!
> Blessed is he (who is) coming in the name of the Lord,
> Even the king of Israel!
> Blessed is the kingdom that is coming,
> The kingdom of our father David.
> Peace in heaven,
> And glory in the highest."

6. John 12:17:

That part of the multitude which had been with Jesus when Lazarus was raised from the dead continues to bear testimony with reference to this astounding deed. As a result, the excitement and the enthusiasm reaches a climax.

185

7. Luke 19:39, 40:

The Pharisees, beside themselves with envy as they listen to this mad cheering, appeal to Jesus to stop it: "Teacher, rebuke your disciples!" Jesus answers: "I tell y o u, if these were silent, the very stones would cry out."

8. Luke 19:41-44:

When, of a sudden, the city comes into view, Jesus, fully realizing that much of the praise which he had been receiving is shallow and is based upon the identification of himself with the expected earthly, political Messiah, breaks into loud weeping. Before his prophetic eyes there arises the vision of Jerusalem as a besieged city, a city surrounded by Roman legions. In a wail of bitter lamentation he cries:

"Would that even today you, yes you yourself, had known the things that pertain to peace! but now they are hidden from your eyes. For the days shall come upon you, when your enemies will cast up earthworks around you and surround you and besiege you from every direction, and will dash to the ground you and your children within you, and will not leave one stone upon another within you, because you did not know the time of your visitation."

9. Matt. 21:10, 11

As Jesus enters Jerusalem, the entire city is stirred. Everybody who had remained behind, on seeing someone surrounded by a great multitude and riding into the city on a donkey, asks, "Who is this?" The answer comes back, "This is the prophet, Jesus, from Nazareth of Galilee."

10. Matt. 21:14; Mark 11:11a

Arrived in the temple, Jesus heals the blind and the lame.

11. Matt. 21:15, 16

The children in the temple begin to shout, "Hosanna to the son of David." The chief priests and the scribes, in their fury, ask Jesus: "Do you hear what these are saying?" Jesus answers, "Yes, have y o u never read:

'Out of the mouth of babes and sucklings thou hast perfected praise'?"

12. John 12:19

The Pharisees, filled with the spirit of frustration, envy, and rage, say to each other, "Y o u see that y o u are gaining nothing. Look, the world has gone after him."

13. Matt. 21:17; Mark 11:11b

When evening falls, Jesus and the Twelve retire to Bethany for the night.

14. John 12:16

Not until Jesus had been glorified did the disciples, looking back and revolving all these things in their minds, realize that the Triumphal Entry was the fulfilment of prophecy.

12:12-19

Of the fourteen elements that enter into the composition of this harmonized story John has six (items 2, 4, 5, 6, 12, and 14). The first three he has in common with the Synoptics; the last three are new material. In listing the fourteen items we are not claiming that the order in which we gave them is correct. All we can reasonably claim is that the sequence which we have presented is probably not far removed from the facts of history as they occurred.

12:12, 13a. The next day the vast multitude that had come to the feast, on hearing that Jesus was coming to Jerusalem, took branches of palm-trees and went out to meet him.

This is item 4 in the list as given in the Preliminary Remarks on this section. Hence, if the order which we have suggested is correct, Jesus, riding upon a young donkey, is even now proceeding from Bethany toward Jerusalem. The multitude that is coming from Jerusalem toward the mount of Olives has heard about the raising of Lazarus (12:18) and about the approach of Jesus (12:12). The news that Jesus was actually planning to attend the feast (see on 12:9), in spite of the decision of the Sanhedrin (see on 11:57), had come first; and now the cry is heard: "He is on the way!"

It was a large crowd, a Passover-multitude, that came pouring out of Jerusalem's eastern gate that Sunday-morning. At the sight of Jesus the people, having cut fronds from the palm-trees (literally: palm-branches of palm-trees), which in those days lined the road from Jerusalem to the mount of Olives, probably begin to wave these in token of rejoicing.

In Scripture the palm-tree, with its perpetual verdure and remarkable longevity (constantly replenished with fresh vigor from deep-set roots), majestic growth and stately appearance (its trunk rising straight up from the earth, its magnificent crown of fronds), is a symbol of the righteousness and spiritual vigor of God's children (Ps. 92:12).

Holding in one's hand the *lulav* — palm with myrtle and willow branch on either side of it —, according to the divine commandment (Lev. 23:40), and shaking it, was the way in which Israel during the feast of Tabernacles expressed its *joy*. Here in John 12 the symbolism was the same. The multitude waved palm-branches in token of *rejoicing* and of *triumph*. Now at last *victory* (prosperity, "salvation," conceived along earthly lines) seemed assured, for if this Jesus was able to raise from the dead a man who had been in the tomb four days, where were the limits to his power? Under such a leader one could even shake off the yoke of the Romans!

The fact that not only today but also at *that* time palm-branches were considered to be an emblem not only of rejoicing but also of victory and prosperity has been called in question by certain commentators. Nevertheless, the sources point in the direction of this twofold meaning. Or, we might say, combining the two concepts, "The waving of the palm-branch was the manifestation of *the joy of victory,* of the feeling: everything is going to be better from now on." When Simon, the Maccabee, entered Jerusalem, in *triumph,* it is recorded that he entered "with thanksgiving and *branches of palm-trees* and with harps and cymbals and with viols and hymns and songs, because there was destroyed a great enemy out of Israel" (I Macc. 13:51). And when his brother, Judas the Maccabee, defeated the Syrians, it is said: "the people carried branches and fair boughs, *and palms also,* and sang psalms" (II Macc. 10:7).

In the present context not only the carrying of palm-branches but also the raising of a mighty shout, which echoed from hill to hill, and began with the exclamation "Hosanna!," certainly lends support to the view that it was *the joy of victory* and *prosperity* to which the people were giving expression.

13b. And they kept on shouting:
Hosanna!
Blessed is he (who is) coming in the name of the Lord,
Even the King of Israel!

This is item 5 in the *Preliminary Remarks* on this section. The two crowds — the one from Bethany and the other from Jerusalem — are now united. The procession is descending the western slope of the mount of Olives. The cheering grows louder and louder. For this tumultuous jubilation and enthusiasm there were the following reasons:

(1) Passover was near at hand, in commemoration of the deliverance from the bondage of Egypt. At such occasions deliverance from foreign subjugation was always one of the main themes of conversation.

(2) To liberate the Jews from Roman domination required a mighty deliverer. Jesus had already demonstrated his extraordinary power, especially by raising Lazarus from the dead. Hence, it looked as if now at last the ancient dream of the re-establishment of the Davidic dynasty would attain fulfilment. See also on 6:15.

What the Jews kept on shouting, as they paved the way for Jesus by strewing branches, and as they shook their palm-fronds, was:

"Hosanna!" This is derived from the imperative form of the verb *to save,* and means "save now," or "save, pray." It is a supplication addressed to Jehovah by the worshipper, who is convinced that the proper time for full deliverance has now at last arrived. In the spirit of joy and of approaching triumph he prays that Jehovah may no longer delay the promised salvation. It amounts to: "We beseech thee, O Jehovah, save now." We wish to stress that this expression had not deteriorated into a mere exclamation of elation like our "Hurrah!," but that it still retained (at least some of) its original sense: "Save now. . . . Send now prosperity." [103] Proof: it has this supplicatory sense in Ps. 118:25, and the words which follow (here in John 12) indicate that the people were thinking of that Hallel Psalm.

Accordingly, the shout continues with these words (taken from Ps. 118:26):

"Blessed is he (who is) coming in the name of the Lord."

Ps. 118 is one of six Psalms most often referred to in the New Testament. (For the others see Vol. I, p. 123). It is a distinctly Messianic Psalm, a Psalm which speaks about the stone which the builders rejected and which became the head of the corner (Cf. Ps. 118:22, 23 with Matt. 21:42; Mark 12:10; Luke 20:17; Acts 4:11; and I Pet. 2:7). Clearly, according to Ps. 118 (in the light of its New Testament interpretation), the One who is *coming in the name of the Lord,* and who is called *Blessed* is the Messiah. Note the verses quoted in John 12 as they appear in their Ps. 118 context:

> *"The stone which the builders rejected*
> *Is become the head of the corner,*
> This is the day which Jehovah has made;
> We will rejoice and be glad in it.
> *Save now, we beseech thee,* O Jehovah;
> O Jehovah, we beseech thee, send now prosperity.
> *Blessed is he that cometh in the name of Jehovah."*

Psalm 118 was one of the Hallel Psalms sung at Passover.[104]

But did *the Jews* regard Ps. 118 to be Messianic? From Mark 11:8, 9 it is clear that the vast multitude proclaimed Jesus to be *the Messiah-king.* According to John 12:13b they regarded him as the Blessed One, who had come to them in the name (revelation) of the Lord Jehovah.

However, it is also clear that very many of those people who cheered so loudly and who supplicated with such enthusiasm were hoping that this Messiah would answer their *earthly* expectations. They hailed him as *the King of Israel,* the One who was about to re-establish "the kingdom of our father David." To them he was the mighty miracle-worker (Luke 19:37). In the light of all this it does not surprise us that when Jesus saw the city, he wept over it. See Point 8 in the *Preliminary Remarks.*

**14, 15. Now Jesus found a young donkey and mounted it, as it is written: Stop being afraid, daughter of Zion,
Look, your king is coming, mounted on the colt of an ass.**

---

[103] See Eric Werner, *"Hosanna* in the Gospels," *JBL* 65 (June, 1946), 97-122.
[104] Cf. Vol. I, p. 121; also A. Edersheim, *The Temple,* London (no date), pp. 223-225, 262, 279, 334.

Here the story, as John tells it, leaves the multitude, and turns to Jesus, coming from Bethany.

Having *found* and *mounted* a donkey (see points 1 and 2, *Preliminary Remarks,* for the commentary which is provided by the Synoptics) Jesus is proceeding toward Jerusalem.

What he did was a clear fulfilment of prophecy, and the people of Jerusalem should have seen this immediately. The prediction which he fulfilled is found in the book of Zechariah (9:9). See point 2, *Preliminary Remarks.* That book has as its theme:

The Future Glory of Zion and of Its Shepherd-King

Its four divisions are:
I.   Visions (1:1-6:8)
II.   A Symbolic Act (6:9-15)
III. An answer to a Question (chapters 7, 8)
IV. Predictions and Promises (chapters 9-14)

Especially the second and the fourth division are clearly Messianic, though several sections of Part I are in the same category. Division IV comprises predictions and promises regarding the future of Zion, and the rejection and subsequent glory of its Shepherd-King.[105]

The prophecy quoted is taken from the fourth division. With the version as given in Matthew 21:5 one should compare that found in the LXX. John abbreviates still more, and changes *Rejoice greatly* to *Stop being afraid.* However, this is not serious, the underlying thought is exactly the same: when one rejoices *greatly,* he will also, in course of time (not always immediately, cf. Matt. 28:8), stop being afraid. John also omits the line "just and having salvation, lowly," (reduced in Matthew to the one word *meek),* and for the animal on which Jesus rode he simply has *the colt of an ass* (not the more complicated version found in Matt. 21:5, which has given rise to various interpretations).

When Zion receives *its own king,* there is no reason to fear. This time no *foreign* king is approaching Jerusalem; hence, let the daughter of Zion cease being fearful. This king, in harmony (as has been indicated) with the entire fourth division of Zechariah's prophecy, is the Shepherd-King, Messiah himself. Even the Talmud applies this prophecy to the Messiah.

The daughter of Zion, who is here addressed, is Zion itself, i.e., Jerusalem and its inhabitants.[106]

---

[105] See my *Bible Survey,* Grand Rapids, Mich., fourth edition 1953, pp. 283-286.
[106] There is much confusion with respect to the meaning of the term *Zion* in Scripture. The following meanings should be distinguished:
(1) Originally Zion was (or *became*) the city of David, located in the s.e. of later Jerusalem (see II Sam. 5:7; I Chron. 11:5). It was lower than the area where the

The daughter of Zion is told that *its king,* its spiritual Messiah, the One who will open a fountain for sin and for uncleanness (Zech. 13:1), is coming. To emphasize the *peaceful* character of his approach and of his reign it is added that he is mounted upon *the colt of an ass.* He comes as the Prince of Peace, not as a war-lord. Hence, the daughter of Zion should stop being afraid.

The ass or donkey is commonly associated with the pursuits of peace (Judg. 10:4; 12:14; II Sam. 17:23; 19:26; Is. 1:3); *the horse,* with warfare (Ex. 15:1, 19, 21; Ps. 33:17; 76:6; 147:10; Prov. 21:31; Jer. 8:6; 51:21; Zech. 10:3; and Rev. 6:4). This king is *meek* (πραΰς), *peaceful, gentle.* He comes to bring salvation. O that the people would understand it! But even the disciples did not understand it *at the time,* as the following verse indicates:

16. These things his disciples did not understand at first, but when Jesus was glorified, then they recalled that about him these things had been written, and that these things had been done to him.

See point 14, *Preliminary Remarks* on this section. Due to ignorance of the Scriptures and little faith (cf. Luke 24:25) even the Twelve did not immediately understand that the act of Jesus was the fulfilment of the prophecy of Zech. 9:9, and that by means of it he was proclaiming himself to be the spiritual Messiah. When Jesus was glorified by means of his cross and resurrection, and had sent forth his Spirit (16:12, 13), all this became clear to them. They recalled everything, and saw what it meant. They understood that Zech. 9:9 referred *to him,* and that these things had been done *to him.* (One should not insist on the translation: "that *they* had done these things to him," and then start to wonder what is meant by *they.* This is a simple Aramaism; for the active we substitute the passive; cf. Vol. I, pp. 63, 64). *These things* means: the waving of palm-branches, spreading of branches in the way, the cheering, etc.

---

temple was subsequently built, and also lower than the s.w. sector of the city (cf. II Sam. 24:18; I Kings 8:4).

(2) From this city of David (II Sam. 6:16) the ark was brought *up* to Solomon's temple (II Chron. 5:2). It is possible that thereafter Moriah (the temple-hill, located north of the city of David; hence, in the n.e. section of later Jerusalem) became identified with Zion. We might say: Zion's location changed with the transfer of the ark (see Is. 10:12; 24:23), but according to some interpreters the change was directly from (1) to (3).

(3) By a very natural semantic change the term began to indicate the entire city of Jerusalem and its inhabitants (Is. 10:24; Jer. 3:14).

(4) Finally, it attained a more spiritual meaning: those loyal to Jehovah, his elect, the church (whether on earth or in heaven). For this spiritual meaning see Is. 40:9; 52:1; Zech. 2:7. Cf. also Is. 1:27.

The error of Eusebius and Jerome, who identified Zion with the southwestern hill (an impossible location, because from there the Israelites could not have *gone up* to the place of the ark) has not been removed from H.B.A., p. 105.

17, 18. And the crowd that had been with him when he called Lazarus out of the tomb and raised him from the dead kept on testifying. And for this reason the multitude went out to meet him, because they had heard that he had performed this sign.

John returns once more to *the multitude.* See points 4 and 6, *Preliminary Remarks.* The translation as we give it here is based upon the best reading (ὅτε instead of ὅτι), and makes excellent sense. Bear in mind that the large multitude consisted of several component elements, mentioned under point 5, p. 185. As the large multitude proceeded on its way, those who had been with Jesus when he raised Lazarus from the dead kept on testifying to the others. It was such an unheard of and wonderful deed that they just had to tell it again and again. They *testified* what they had seen with their own eyes! For the meaning of *testify* see on 1:7.

In thorough harmony with 12:9 we read that the vast multitude of pilgrims which had come to Jerusalem from every quarter had gone out to meet Jesus *because they had heard* that he had performed this (great) sign, namely, raising Lazarus from the dead.

19. So the Pharisees said to each other, Y o u see that y o u are gaining nothing. Look, the world has gone after him.

See point 12, *Preliminary Remarks.* The *more radical* Pharisees said to the *milder* party — this seems probable, though not stated in so many words —: "Y o u see that y o u are gaining nothing," by y o u r delay. Something has to be done, and done quickly, or it will be too late. "Look," they add, "the *world* (see on 1:10, note 26; here probably meaning 3: the public in general, "everybody") has gone (away from us) after him." The Pharisees are frantic! The *world,* in a different sense, was indeed going after him: the Greeks were coming! See the next section (12:20-36a).

Synthesis of 12:12-19

See the Outline on p. 134. *The Son of God Makes His Triumphant Entry into Jerusalem*

The *Preliminary Remarks* on this section form a Synthesis.

20 Now of those who were accustomed to go up in order that they might worship at the feast there were some Greeks. 21 So these came to Philip, the one from Bethsaida of Galilee, and they were requesting him, saying, "Sir, we wish to see Jesus." 22 Philip went and told Andrew. Andrew and Philip went and told Jesus.
23 Then Jesus answered them, saying, "It has come, the hour in which [107] the Son of man must be glorified. 24 Most solemnly I declare to y o u, unless the grain of wheat falls to the earth and dies, it remains alone; but if it dies it bears

[107] for ἵνα see Vol. I, pp. 45, 50.

much fruit.[108]   25 He who loves his life loses it, and he who hates his life in this world keeps it with a view to everlasting life.   26 If anyone serves me, let him follow me,[109] and where I am there also shall my servant be. If anyone serves me, him will the Father honor.[110]   27 Now is my soul troubled, and what shall I say? Father, save me from this hour! But for this purpose I came to this hour.   28 Father, glorify thy name."

So there came a voice out of heaven, "And I have glorified it, and again I will glorify it."   29 However, the multitude that were standing (there), when they heard it, were saying that it had thundered. Others were saying, "An angel has spoken to him."   30 Jesus answered and said, "Not for my sake has this voice occurred, but for y o u r sake.   31 Now is the judgment of this world. Now shall the prince of this world be cast out.   32 And I, when I am lifted up from the earth, will draw all men to myself." [111]   33 This he was saying, signifying by what kind of death he was about to die.

34 So the multitude answered him, "We heard from the law that the Christ remains forever; how then do you say that the Son of man must be lifted up? Who is this Son of man?"

35 So Jesus said to them, "Yet a little while is the light with y o u. Walk while y o u have the light, lest the darkness overtake y o u. He who is walking in the darkness does not know where he is going.   36 While y o u have the light believe in the light, in order that y o u may become sons of light."

12:20-36a

12:20. Now of those who were accustomed to go up in order that they might worship at the feast there were some Greeks.

From the Jews the story now for a moment turns to the Greeks. The passage does not refer to Hellenists (cf. Acts 6:1) or Greek-speaking Jews, but to Hellenes (Greeks). We do not believe that the meaning which the author wishes to convey is that these Greeks were *among* the regular *Jewish* worshippers. On the contrary, the meaning is this, that these Greeks were *of* (ἐκ, the partitive idea, as in 1:24, 35, 40; 7:48) *those who were accustomed to go up in order that they might worship at the feast;* in other words, these Greeks belonged to the large group of worshippers whom we commonly call *proselytes* (here most likely proselytes *of the gate* or *Godfearers,* Acts 10:1, 22, 35; 13:16, 26, 43, 50; 17:4, uncircumcised converts to the monotheistic religion of the Jews). In the original we have the present participle of the verb *to go up* (hence, *those going up* or *those accustomed to go up*). The concept *going up* to Jerusalem is explained in connection with 2:13. For *at the feast* (of Passover) see also on 2:13.

These Greeks, then, were Gentiles who had given up their worship of

---

[108] A compound conditional sentence. The two protases are parallel in construction, and so are the two apodoses. IIIA2; see Vol. I, pp. 42, 43.
[109] IIIB3; Vol. I, p. 44.
[110] IIIB2; Vol. I, p. 44.
[111] IIIA1; see Vol. I, pp. 42, 43.

many gods and had been won over to the worship of the one God, the God
of Israel. The fact that such people were allowed to render religious
worship in the temple is clear from I Kings 8:42; Is. 56:7; Mark 11:17.
They were not permitted to proceed any farther than the Court of the
Gentiles. For the meaning of the verb translated *worship* see on 4:23 and
9:38.

**21, 22. So these came to Philip, the one from Bethsaida of Galilee, and
they were requesting him, saying, Sir, we wish to see Jesus. — Philip went
and told Andrew. Andrew and Philip went and told Jesus.**

These Greeks desire to have an interview with Jesus. It is not surprising
that they hesitate to approach the Lord directly. It is not clear to them
whether he will welcome an interview. So they ask Philip to act as inter-
mediary. Of course, not the deacon and evangelist (of Acts 6 and 8) is
meant, but one of the Twelve, the apostle Philip who was from Bethsaida
of Galilee (on this see the discussion in connection with 1:44 and 6:1;
Vol. I, p. 108 and especially pp. 216, 217), the town of Andrew and Peter.

Why did they single out Philip? And why did he, in turn, consult
Andrew? Did these two men speak Greek better than the rest? Is it more
than a mere coincidence that among the Twelve these are the only disciples
that appear from the outset with Greek names? (But one must be careful
in drawing an inference from this; see on 3:1.) Or was there a totally
different reason why these two men are in the foreground in this story?
We do not have the answer. See also Vol. I, pp. 102-105, 108, 112.

The Greeks address Philip very politely, They say, "Sir." [112]

The expression, "We wish to see Jesus," cannot mean, "We wish to see
how he looks, in order that our curiosity with reference to him may be
satisfied, and we may be able to tell our friends that we have feasted our
eyes on this celebrity." Nor does it necessarily mean, "We wish to place

---

[112] In some Bible-translations no distinction is made between the Greek title (κύριος)
as used here and the same word as used in 20:28 ("My *Lord* and my God"). These
translations use the term *Lord* in both cases, as the English equivalent. Thus, for
example, *Concordant Version of the Sacred Scriptures*, Los Angeles, 1927. This,
however, is confusing, for though the *one* Greek term (κύριος) has a wide latitude
of meaning, so that it can be used: a. as a title of respect, proper in addressing
any gentleman, b. as a divine proper name, c. as equivalent to our "master," and
d. as a title which expresses the deity of Christ, this same latitude of meaning does
not pertain to the English word "Lord," in its present-day connotation. The argument which is advanced at times, to the effect that the Greeks so addressed Philip
because they held that he, being a disciple of Christ, participated in the latter's
glory and should accordingly be addressed with the same title, lacks merit, for the
simple reason that these Greeks *did not know Jesus*. And because they did not
know him nor his glory, they were not able to inject this deep meaning into the
term when they addressed his disciple Philip. They were speaking to *Philip*, not to
Jesus. They were presenting their request to a mere man. Hence, the correct translation here is "Sir," and not "Lord." See also Vol. I, p. 103, Note 44.

before Jesus the proposal that he forget about the rebellious Jews and from now on preach the Gospel to us, Greeks." That interpretation reads too much into the text.

With a view to what follows (see especially verses 24 and 32) it would seem that the desire of the Greeks had something to do with the great subject of *salvation*. Did they wish to see Jesus: a. because the wisdom of the Greeks had suffered shipwreck, having failed to satisfy the deepest longings of the soul? And b. because on the basis of what they had heard about Jesus they had become hopeful that he might be able to supply that spiritual peace of mind which they had not been able to find anywhere else? That is not at all improbable.

To Philip — and later to Philip and Andrew — the request of the Greeks presented a double problem: a. In view of what Jesus had said on other occasions (Matt. 10:5; 15:24), could he consistently welcome Greeks into his presence? — But, on the other hand, had he not spoken about "other sheep, not of this fold," whom he must also gather? See also Matt. 8:5-13. Just what was the attitude of Jesus toward Greeks: would he welcome them or would he refuse to give them audience? b. Would not Jesus by granting audience to the Greeks invite the wrath of all the Jewish people, especially if the interview were to be held anywhere in the temple? (See Acts 21:28).

The problem being too big for Philip, he consults his friend and fellow-townsman, Andrew. Andrew and Philip, hesitating *to offend* the Greeks, also hesitating *to encourage* them, place the request of the Greeks — before Jesus.

23, 24. Then Jesus answered them, saying, It has come, the hour in which the Son of man must be glorified. Most solemnly I declare to y o u, Unless the grain of wheat falls to the earth and dies, it remains alone; but if it dies it bears much fruit.

Jesus answered Andrew and Philip. They, in turn, could convey the answer to the Greeks. A multitude of Jews was standing around when Jesus made his reply (12:29).

In the request of the Greeks Jesus sees *his seed, i.e.,* numerous spiritual posterity. This had been promised to the Messiah as the fruit of his voluntary sacrifice: "When his soul shall make *an offering for sin, he* shall see *his seed"* (Is. 53:10, A.R.V., margin). Apart from this voluntary sacrifice Jesus could do nothing for these Greeks. Did they understand that? Did they realize that an *earthly* Messiah, no matter how famous (think of the praise he received at the occasion of the Triumphal Entry!) would avail them not at all? Did they fully understand that it was only by means of his substitutionary atonement that he, as *spiritual* Messiah, would be able to save them?

195

To stress this thought Jesus immediately speaks of his *death*. He says, "It has come, the hour in which the Son of man must be glorified." Previously he had indicated that the decisive moment, the time of most bitter suffering, had *not yet* arrived (see on 7:30; 8:20).[113] Now, it has come! The term *hour*, it is hardly necessary to point out, must not be taken too literally, as if it referred to a period of exactly sixty minutes. It is the designated time, the season in which the Lord entered the valley of most intense suffering, followed by the just and promised reward: the resurrection, ascension, and coronation. In this climax of humiliation followed immediately by glorious exaltation *the Son of man* (see on 12:34) is *glorified:* the radiance of his grace and the majesty of his truth is made to stand out. The Father, in giving up the Son to die on the cross, and in granting him the promised reward, exhibits the divine attributes (love, justice, omnipotence, faithfulness, etc.) in all their majestic and indescribable beauty. They are displayed publicly for all who have eyes to see.

With a view to *the absolute necessity* of his death Jesus adds, "Most solemnly I declare to y o u (for this introductory phrase see on 1:51), Unless the *grain of wheat* (or the kernel of grain, any kind of grain, cf. Mark 4:28; Luke 12:18) falls to the earth and dies, it remains alone; but if it dies, it bears much fruit." Apart from the cross there is no spiritual harvest. (On the *necessity* of Christ's substitutionary death see also Gen. 2:16, 17; Luke 24:26; Rom. 3:23-25; 5:12-21.)

The illustration was very clear, especially at the moment when it was spoken, not more than a few days before the (religious and) *harvest* feast of Passover. The kernels or seeds had been entrusted to the soil. As seeds they had died. But by means of this very process of dissolution they had brought forth an abundant harvest. If a seed is not sown, it remains alone, producing no fruit. So also if Jesus does not die, he will remain alone, without spiritual fruit (souls saved for eternity). His death, however, will result in a rich, spiritual harvest.

25, 26. He who loves his life loses it, and he who hates his life in this world will keep it with a view to everlasting life. If anyone serves me, let him follow me, and where I am there also shall my servant be. If anyone serves me, him will the Father honor.

The solemn truth stated in verse 24 applies to Christ, to him alone! He alone dies *as a substitute,* and in doing so bears much fruit. Neverthe-

---

[113] In several commentaries reference is also made to 2:4 and 7:6 in this connection, as if also these passages convey the idea that the appointed time of Christ's *death* had not yet arrived. But, as we have shown in discussing them, the indicated passages do not refer to that subject. Hence, in commenting on 12:23 a reference to 2:4 and 7:6 is appropriate only in so far as also these statements prove that *for everything* in the mediatorial program of the Lord there was a designated, preordained moment.

196

less, there is an analogous principle which operates in the sphere of men. It is the one stated in verses 25, 26. The relation between the two laws (the one applying to Christ, the other to his disciples) may be summarized as follows:

1. *As to Christ:* If there is to be fruit, he must die (verse 24).

2. *As to his disciple:* he must be willing to die for the cause of Christ (verses 25, 26). Of course, he cannot do this in his own strength.

In view of the present context and of the parallel passages in the other Gospels, the meaning of the important statement (verses 25, 26) is as follows:

He who when the issue is between me and my gospel, on the one hand, and whatever has been dearest to him (father, mother, son, daughter, material things, the whole world, his own life, Matt. 10:37; 16:26; Luke 17:32) on the other hand, chooses (here in 12:25; "has affection for," see footnote 306, pp. 494-501) the latter, will perish everlastingly. I will at my coming be ashamed of him (Mark 8:38; Luke 9:26). But he who, in this *world* — that is, in the midst of the present adulterous and wicked generation (Mark 8:38; and see Vol. I, p. 79, footnote 26, meaning 6) — is willing to sacrifice his life [114] for me and my gospel (Mark 8:35) will guard and preserve it (Luke 17:33), sothat it will blossom forth into everlasting life in the mansions above (see on 4:14). If anyone serves me, let him follow me all the way, even though it be the way of self-denial and the cross (Matt. 16:24; 10:38; Mark 8:34), bearing in mind that the way of the cross leads to the crown. He will share with me the glory of heaven, abiding forever in my presence. Besides, also the Father, who loves me, will honor him, for he honors those who honor me.

That this is, indeed, the meaning becomes clear when the passage, after having been studied in its own context, is compared with its parallels. Using the A.R.V., note the following.

Matthew 10:37-39. "He that loveth father or mother more than me is not worthy of me; and he that loveth son or daughter more than me is not worthy of me. And he that doth not take his cross and follow me, is not worthy of me. He that findeth his life shall lose it; and he that loseth his life for my sake shall find it."

Matthew 16:24-26. "If any man will come after me, let him deny himself, and take up his cross and follow me. For whosoever would save his life shall lose it; and whosoever shall lose his life for my sake shall find it. For what shall a man be profited, if he shall gain the whole world, and forfeit his life? Or what shall a man give in exchange for his life?"

Mark 8:34-38. "If any man would come after me, let him deny himself,

---

[114] The *life* in such passages is the *self:* the terms *himself* and *his life* are used interchangeably; see Luke 9:23, 24; also on John 10:11.

and take up his cross, and follow me. For whosoever would save his life shall lose it; and whosoever shall lose his life for my sake and the gospel's sake shall save it. For what doth it profit a man, to gain the whole world, and forfeit his life? For what shall a man give in exchange for his life? For whosoever shall be ashamed of me and my words in this adulterous and sinful generation, the Son of man shall be ashamed of him, when he cometh in the glory of his Father with the holy angels."

Luke 9:23-26. "If any man would come after me, let him deny himself, and take up his cross daily, and follow me. For whosoever would save his life shall lose it; but whosoever shall lose his life for my sake, the same shall save it. For what is a man profited if he gain the whole world and lose or forfeit his own self? For whosoever shall be ashamed of me and of my words, of him shall the Son of man be ashamed."

Luke 17:32, 33. "Remember Lot's wife. Whosoever shall seek to gain his life shall lose it, but whosoever shall lose his life shall preserve it."

27, 28a. Now is my soul troubled, and what shall I say? Father, save me from this hour! But for this purpose I came to this hour. Father, glorify thy name.

Jesus has been speaking about his approaching death — *eternal* death — as an absolute necessity. But the contemplation of this terrible ordeal fills his soul with nameless anguish. He cries out, "Now (at this moment; see verse 23: it has come, the hour!) is my soul troubled." The expression *my soul* is simply *I*, as if he had said, "Now am I troubled." The two are frequently interchanged; e.g., cf. Matt. 20:28 with I Tim. 2:6 ("to give *his soul* or his life a ransom" is the same as "to give *himself* a ransom"). The verb *troubled* or *agitated* (on which see also 5:7; 11:33; 13:21; 14:27; especially 14:1), here perfect passive indicative, indicates that this mighty disturbance in the soul of Christ had been going on for some time and has now become very intense. The horrors of the impending cross were felt now as never before.

So far there is not much difference in interpretation. However, with respect to "Father, save me from this hour!" the opinions vary. From a host of explanations we select the following:

(1) "And what shall I say? Father, save me from this hour? (note *the question-mark*). But no — for this purpose I came to this hour."

Even among those who accept this presentation, and who, accordingly, believe that Jesus did not offer a prayer but merely raised a question, there are differences of opinion. Some think that he actually wavered for a moment in his obedience, that for an instant he rebelled against the idea of having to suffer on the cross. — Our answer would be, "Perish the very thought!" — Others, however, accept the double question in a much more innocent sense: Jesus, as they see it, is simply asking a rhetorical question.

It is as if he had said, "What shall I say? Do y o u suppose that I would say, 'Father, save me from this hour?' But that is entirely impossible, because for this very purpose I came to this hour."

We reject this double question in any form. We do this not only because this entire representation, even when interpreted in the best and most sensible way (as, for example, by Zahn and Lenski) impresses us as an attempt to get rid of a difficulty, but especially because in the comparable agonies of Gethsemane, which occurred only a little while later, *Jesus did not ask, "Shall I say,* Father save me from this hour?" *but he actually prayed:* "My Father, if it be possible, let this cup pass away from me: nevertheless, not as I will, but as thou wilt" (Matt. 26:39); "Abba, Father, all things are possible unto thee; remove this cup from me: howbeit not what I will, but what thou wilt" (Mark 14:36). Cf. also Luke 22:42. It is not true that the double-question construction is the only one which does justice to the word *but* which begins the following sentence. See under (4) below.

(2) "And what shall I say? Father, save me from this hour." According to this interpretation the first clause is a question; the second is a positive request. So far we are in full agreement. But then this second view presents an explanation which is most interesting and merits close scrutiny, namely, that what Jesus meant was: "Father, grant that, after I have endured this hour of bitter agony and woe, I may emerge from it triumphantly." As one author puts it, "Save me out of all the affliction and death of this hour." [115]

This interpretation may be the right one. Grammatically it is possible. The preposition *from* or *out of* (ἐx), can have that meaning. See Rev. 3:10. Thus conceived, this prayer is a request for the resurrection. Now it must be granted that the exaltation (resurrection, etc.) of the Lord as a result of his voluntary suffering and death is mentioned in this very context (12:23; cf. also verse 32; even verse 28, which speaks of the glory of the Father's name implies the glory of the Son). Hence, much can be said in favor of this exegesis.

The reasons why we, nevertheless, are not certain that it is the correct explanation are:

a. In the analogous passages (Matt. 26:39 and Mark 14:36, quoted above) the idea is not that the Lord is asking to receive a reward *after* he has emptied the cup of bitter suffering, but definitely *that, if possible,*

---

[115] H. Hoeksema, *The Amazing Cross,* Grand Rapids, Mich., 1944, p. 117. The books of this author on the Passion of our Lord make worth-while reading. He has written: *The Royal Sufferer, Rejected Of Men,* and *The Amazing Cross,* all of these published by Wm. B. Eerdmans Publishing Co., Grand Rapids, Mich. He is the author of many other works.

he may not even have to drink this cup at all! See Matt. 26:42: "My Father, if this cannot pass away, except I drink it, thy will be done."

b. Both in Heb. 5:7 and in Jas. 5:20 the phrase *from death* (ἐκ θανάτου) means *from entering and experiencing death.*

(3) "And what shall I say? Father, save me from this hour."

According to the third theory Jesus actually rebelled, being unwilling to go to the cross. But this disinclination lasted for only a little while. — Needless to say, we reject this view without any further comment.

(4) "And what shall I say? Father save me from this hour." The vivid realization of the inexpressibly dreadful character of his impending descent into hell shook the human soul of Jesus to its very depths. This does not imply disobedience. A man may shrink from an experience which he, nevertheless, wants to undergo; e.g., an operation. So it is also with Christ. Though his soul is filled with horror, he did not even for a single moment rebel against the will of the Father. To accomplish that will was his inmost desire both now and in Gethsemane. But he asks that *if there be some other way* in which the Father's will can be carried out, some other form of voluntary and substitutionary death, this way may be opened, sothat he may be saved from the terrible agony of the cross.

All in all, we believe that this very common interpretation is probably the correct one. It is in complete harmony with the Gethsemane account. It is hard to believe that words that are so similar (John 12:27, 28; cf. the Gethsemane passages quoted above) would have an entirely different meaning. The only possible objection that we can see would be this, that here in 12:27, 28 Jesus does not add some such expression as, "If it be possible" (Matt. 26:39) or "If it be according to thy will." But is it not reasonable to interpret 12:27, 28 in the light of the Gethsemane passages? In other words, even though the conditional clause is not added here in 12:27, 28, is it not clearly implied? Although we do so with a measure of hesitation (because of the merits of the second theory, discussed above), we, nevertheless believe that this fourth explanation has the greatest plausibility. Now, if this be correct, what the passage means is this:

"Father, save me from this hour of most bitter suffering on the cross." But while he speaks these *words,* this *thought* is implied, ". . . if this be possible and in accordance with thy holy will, for I wish to do thy will."

Jesus adds, "But for this purpose I came to this hour." The adversative *but* should not be surprising. It occurs frequently where one does not immediately expect it. Its occurrence is altogether natural in abbreviated conversation.[116] See Vol. I, p. 206. The entire idea of the prayer may,

---

[116] No matter which interpretation one adopts, it is clear that we are dealing here with abbreviated style, for Jesus says, "For *this purpose,*" without definitely indicating the purpose. The audience, however, was able to complete the thought, in view of what Jesus had said earlier, i.e., in verse 24.

perhaps, be paraphrased as follows (and this also shows why the conjunction *but* is used):

"Father, save me from this hour, if it be possible and in accordance with thy holy will, but do not save me from this hour if this would mean that I would lose the spiritual harvest (12:24), for to obtain this harvest by means of voluntary death is the very purpose of my coming into the world. Hence, Father, grant that through my perfect obedience to thy holy will, wherever that will may direct me (especially in my suffering and death), *thy name may be glorified.*"

28b, 29, 30. So there came a voice out of heaven, And I have glorified it, and again I will glorify it. — However, the multitude that were standing (there), when they heard it, were saying that it had thundered. Others were saying, An angel has spoken to him. — Jesus answered and said, Not for my sake has this voice occurred, but for y o u r sake.

Jesus had asked that the Father would glorify his name; i.e., that the Father by means of his revelation in the Son would cause the radiance of his majestic attributes to become publicly displayed, in order that men might ascribe to him the honor due unto his name. The *name* of the Father is his revelation; here, his revelation in Christ. Immediately there came a voice from heaven, saying, "And I have glorified it, and again I will glorify it." By means of direct voices from heaven (at baptism, Mark 1:11; at the transfiguration, Mark 9:7) and by means of the mighty miracles which Jesus performed, the Father had already glorified himself in the Son. Here he promises that in and by means of the further humiliation and subsequent exaltation of the Son he will do this again.

Just as in the case of Paul's experience on the road to Damascus those who were with him, though hearing a sound, failed to hear the distinct words (Acts 9:7; 22:9), so also here the multitude hears a noise coming from above but is unable to understand the message. Accordingly, most of the people standing around were saying that it had thundered. Perhaps they knew better but were trying to give a natural explanation to a supernatural happening, like the skeptics of today! Others, however, were willing to admit that what had occurred was of an extraordinary nature. These said, "An angel has spoken to him."

Jesus answered and said, "Not for my sake has this voice occurred, but for y o u r sake." This statement has caused considerable difficulty. The question has been asked, "Does not the very nature of the message from heaven — which, after all was a direct answer to Christ's prayer — indicate that it was spoken *for his sake,* to encourage him in his impending bitter suffering?" It seems reasonable that here as elsewhere in similar expressions (see on 4:21; 12:44) the meaning is: "Not *exclusively* for my sake has this voice occurred, but *also* for y o u r sake."

Another question which suggests itself but is easily answered is this: "If the multitude was not even able to understand the words, how can it be said that the voice had occurred *for their sake?*" The answer is: the sound coming *from above* (even though it was not understood) and coming *immediately upon the prayer,* was a clear indication that the Father had heard the Son's request (namely, the request that the Father might be glorified in the Son). If anyone still refused to admit this, it was his own fault.

Jesus continues:

31-33. Now is the judgment of this world. Now shall the prince of this world be cast out. And I, when I am lifted up from the earth, will draw all men to myself. — This he was saying, signifying by what kind of death he was about to die.

By saying *now* Jesus speaks of his descent into hell as if it is already happening. When Jesus died on the cross it seemed as if the world was victorious and the Christ defeated. The *world* appeared to be the winner! We take the term *world* here as indicating the Jewish people who rejected him, their leaders who condemned him, Judas who betrayed him, the soldiers who mocked him, Pilate who sentenced him — in brief, this whole society of evil men, alienated from God and having the devil as its prince (see Vol. I, p. 79, footnote 26, meaning (6)). It had tried the Christ, and had cast him out. *Little did the world realize that by means of this very action it had condemned itself.* As the context indicates, the term *judgment* is here the divine decision with reference to the world. That decision amounts to a condemnation. For the meaning of *judgment* see on 3:17, 19.

"Now shall the prince of this world be cast out." This prince (or *ruler*) is clearly satan. Elsewhere the author of the Fourth Gospel and of the book of Revelation describes him symbolically as being the "red dragon, having seven heads and ten horns, and upon his heads seven diadems" (Rev. 12:3). Cf. also Luke 4:6; II Cor. 4:4; Eph. 2:2; 6:12. The casting out of the prince of this world must be explained in the light of the immediately following statement: "And I, when I am lifted up from the earth, will draw all men to myself." The drawing of all men to the Christ is the casting out of the devil. He loses his power over the nations. A moment ago the Greeks had requested to see Jesus. That is definitely the context. These Greeks represented the nations — elect from every nation — that would come to accept Christ by living faith, through the sovereign grace of God. Hence, through the death of Christ the power of satan over the nations of the world is broken. During the old dispensation these nations had been under the thraldom of satan (though, of course, never in the absolute sense of the term). With the coming of Christ a tremendous change takes place. On and after Pentecost we begin to see the gathering of a church from among all the nations of the world (cf. Rev. 20:3).[117] That is what Jesus sees so clearly when these Greeks approach him.

Jesus promises to draw *all men* to himself. This *all men,* in the given context which places Greeks next to Jews, must mean *men from every nation.* That idea is found in the Fourth Gospel again and again: salvation is not dependent upon blood or race (1:13; cf. 8:31-59); Jesus is the Savior not only for the Jews but also for the Samaritans; hence, he is the Savior *of the world* (4:42); he has other sheep which are not of this (Jewish) fold, those *others* being from the Gentile-world (10:16); he will die not for the (Jewish) nation only, but that he may also gather into one the children of God who are scattered abroad (11:51); in brief, he is the Lamb of God who takes away the sin of *the world* (1:29).

Jesus will draw all men to himself when he is *lifted up from the earth.* This being lifted up has been explained in connection with 3:14; see Vol. I, pp. 138, 139. By means of his crucifixion, resurrection, ascension, and coronation Jesus attracts to himself (i.e., to abiding faith in himself) all of God's elect, from every age, clime, and nation. He draws them by means of his Word and Spirit. This activity of the Spirit is the reward for the Son's being lifted up. From this work of drawing sinners to Christ the operation of the Holy Spirit in the heart in *regeneration* must not be excluded. It precedes even our God-given faith. See further on this drawing activity and on the meaning of the term used in the original Vol. I, pp. 238, 239 (explanation of 6:43, 44).

"This he was saying, signifying by what kind of death he was about to die," i.e., this he was saying in order to indicate that his death would be a being lifted up on the cross, as a means of glory for himself and for the elect from all the nations.

34. So the multitudes answered him, We heard from the law that the Christ remains forever; how then do you say that the Son of man must be lifted up? Who is this Son of man?

The Jewish multitudes, acquainted to a certain extent with the law, were surprised that Jesus had spoken about the necessity of being "lifted up." From *the law* — probably taken in the most comprehensive sense here; i.e., what we today call the Old Testament — they had heard that the Christ would remain forever. The passages which they had in mind were probably the following: Ps. 110:4; Is. 9:7; Ezek. 37:25; Dan. 7:14. These they interpreted literally, as if they taught that the Messiah would remain on earth forever as king of the Jews.

---

[117] See our *More Than Conquerors,* Grand Rapids, Mich., sixth edition 1952, pp. 223-229.

They now ask, "How then do you say that the Son of man must be lifted up? Who is this Son of Man?" What kind of a Son of man is he anyway who, instead of remaining with us forever, is going to be taken away from us? Who is this person, the Son of man (τίς ἐστιν οὗτος ὁ υἱὸς τοῦ ἀνθρώπου)?

The remark is made at times that the evangelist must have made a mistake in reporting this conversation between Jesus and the Jews. This conclusion is drawn from the fact that in the immediate context Jesus never even mentioned the term *Son of man*. He is reported to have said, "And *I*, when *I* am lifted up from the earth, will draw all men to myself." *They* answer: "How do you say that *the Son of man* must be lifted up? Who is this *Son of man?*" The question asked by the Jews, it is said, cannot have arisen from the statement of Jesus. But the critics are wrong. The multitude mentioned in verse 34 is already present in verse 29, and must have been standing around from verse 20 on. Hence, it was only a few moments ago that this multitude had heard Jesus speak about *the Son of man*. The very term occurs in verse 23. The people readily understood that in the mind of Jesus *the Son of man* (of verse 23) and *I* (of verse 32) were one and the same person. This accounts for the form in which their question is presented. Hence also, when they ask, "Who is this Son of man?" they do not mean, "Please point him out to us," but "What kind of person is this anyway, this Son of man who, strange to say, must be lifted up?" It is also clear from their question that they identify *the real Son of man* (as *they* conceive of him) with *the Messiah*. They are aware of the fact that Jesus considers himself to be the Son of man, i.e., the Christ, but they are amazed about the statement which he has just made with reference to this Christ or Son of man, a statement which, so it seems to them, is in sharp conflict with the teaching contained in the law.

"Who is this Son of man?" This is the proper place for a brief discussion of the term.[118]

As to stastistics, the term occurs at least eighty times in the Gospels. In

---

[118] The literature on this subject is very extensive. We mention only a few titles:
Aalders, G. Ch., *Korte Verklaring, Daniel,* Kampen, 1928, pp. 133-135.
Bavinck, H., *Gereformeerde Dogmatiek,* Kampen, 1918, third edition, Vol. III, pp. 259-264.
Berkhof, L., *Systematic Theology,* Grand Rapids, Mich., 1949, fourth edition, pp. 313, 314.
Bouman, J., art. "Son of man," in *ExT* 59 (1948), pp. 283 ff.
Campbell, J. Y., "Son of man," in *A Theological Word Book of the Bible* (edited by A. Richardson), N. Y., 1952, pp. 230-231.
Greijdanus, S., *Het Evangelie naar de Beschrijving van Lukas,* Amsterdam, 1940, Vol. I, p. 253 (and the literature indicated on that page).
Stalker, J., art. "Son of man," in I.S.B.E.
Stevens, G. B., *The Theology of the New Testament,* New York, 1925, pp. 41-53.
Vos, G., *The Self-Disclosure of Jesus,* N. Y., 1926, pp. 42-55; 228-256.
Young, E. J., *The Prophecy of Daniel,* Grand Rapids, Mich., 1949, pp. 154-156.

the Fourth Gospel it is found thirteen times (or eleven times if its controversial occurrence in 5:27 and in 9:35 is excluded).[119]

The instances of its use in John are the following:

(1) 1:51. "Y o u shall see the heavens opened, and the angels of God ascending and descending upon the Son of man."

(2) 3:13. "And no one has gone up into heaven but he who descended from heaven, the Son of man."

(3) 3:14. "And as Moses lifted up the serpent in the desert, so must the Son of man be lifted up."

(4) 5:27 (disputed). "For just as the Father has life in himself, so he has granted to the Son also to have life in himself, and he gave him authority to function as judge, because he is υἱὸς ἀνθρώπου." See Vol. I, pp. 202, 203.

(5) 6:27. "No longer work for food that perishes, but for food that endures for everlasting life, which food the Son of man will give y o u, for on him God the Father has set his seal."

(6) 6:53. "So Jesus said to them, I most solemnly assure y o u, unless y o u eat the flesh of the Son of man, and drink his blood, y o u have no life in yourselves."

(7) 6:62. "If y o u shall see the Son of man ascending where he was before (what will y o u say then?)."

(8) 8:28. "So Jesus said, When y o u will have lifted up the Son of man, then y o u will know that I am he, and that of myself I do nothing but speak thus as the Father taught me."

---

[119] I count 83 instances of its use in the Gospels, or 81 without John 5:27 and 9:35. This figure includes the 13 (or 11, if 5:27 and 9:35 are omitted) in John. I base these figures upon W. F. Moulton and A. S. Geden, *A Concordance to the Greek Testament*, Edinburgh, third edition, 1950 (reprint). J. Y. Campbell (see footnote above for the reference) arrives at the same result (he mentions the figure 81). However, R. C. H. Lenski in his *Interpretation of St. John's Gospel*, Columbus, Ohio, 1931, p. 172, states that the designation *the Son of man* is found *nine* times in John's Gospel and *over fifty-five* times in all the Gospels. In part his lower figure is due to the fact *that he does not include* John 9:35, nor John 5:27 (definite articles omitted). But, according to our count, that still leaves 81 instances in the four Gospels, including 11 in John. We get the following figures:

Matthew:	31	
Mark:	14	
Luke:	25	
John:	13	
Four Gospels	83	
Acts:	1	(Acts 7:56)
Revelation:	2	(these "like unto a Son of man" passages should certainly be included: Rev. 1:13; 14:14).
Total for the N.T.	86	(or 84, when the two controversial instances in John are excluded).

(9) 9:35 (disputed). "Jesus heard that they had thrown him out, and having found him he said, Do *you* believe in the Son of man?"

(10) 12:23. "It has come, the hour in which the Son of man must be glorified."

(11) and (12) 12:34 (two occurrences). "So the multitude answered him, We heard from the law that the Christ remains forever; how then do you say that the Son of man must be lifted up? Who is this Son of man?"

(13) 13:31. "Now the Son of man has been glorified, and God has been glorified in him."

In the Gospels, with the sole exception of 12:34, the term *the Son of man* is never used by anyone else than by Jesus himself. It is his self-designation. That he used this title with reference to himself is clear from 6:53, 54; 8:28; 9:35 (best reading) 37; cf. also 12:34 in the light of what precedes. That the people understood it to refer to the Christ has already been indicated (the present passage, 12:34). The derivation of the term from Dan. 7:13, 14 is scarcely debatable. A comparison between that passage and Matt. 26:64 hardly leaves room for honest doubt on that score. It is not true that the "one like unto a son of man" in Daniel represents the Hebrew people, and that the transference of the title from a collective body to an individual was mediated through post-canonical literature (e.g., the book of Enoch). The *one like unto a son of man* appears on the clouds of heaven, but the *holy ones* are found on earth. (See detailed argument in G. C. Aalders and in Young; for titles see footnote 118.) Also in the book of Revelation which employs the same expression ("one like unto a son of man") the reference is very distinctly to *one person,* namely, the exalted Christ. Too much is often made of the fact that we read "one like unto," as if this meant that the designated individual is not really the Son of man himself but some vague, symbolic, representative figure. But that inference is incorrect. The figure, as it appears in the vision, *resembles* the man for the simple reason that *it designates and describes him.* The *description* in Daniel becomes the *title* in the New Testament, but the same *person* is indicated in both.

Jesus probably used this self-designation in order to indicate his own heavenly, transcendent nature. He is the One who comes from above, the One to whom the final judgment has been committed, who will come with the clouds in great glory. He is, accordingly, not at all the political, earthly, nationalistic Messiah of Jewish expectation. He is not only king of Israel but king of kings. He stands in connection with the whole human race, being *the Son of man.* Nevertheless, he is altogether unique among men. He is not *a* son of man, but *the* Son of man. As a *man* he suffers and treads the path of humiliation. He is *the man of sorrows.* But this very path of suffering leads to the crown, to glory. Moreover, this glory is revealed not only eschatologically, when he comes with the clouds, but reaches back, as it were, through his entire life on earth and through every redemptive act. He is *always* the glorious Son of man!

Specifically, as the passages quoted above show, in the Gospel of John the Son of man is the One who descended from heaven (3:13), speaks the language of his heavenly Father (8:28), is the link between heaven and earth (1:51), fulfils a heaven-inspired mission (suffering and dying for his people, 3:14), has authority from heaven to function as judge both in the present and in the future (5:27), is himself the bread from heaven, which man must eat (6:27, 53), is, accordingly, the object of faith (9:35), and displays the glory of heaven both in and as a reward for his suffering and death (3:13; 12:23, 34; 13:31).

35, 36. So Jesus said to them, Yet a little while is the light with y o u. Walk while y o u have the light, lest the darkness overtake y o u. He who is walking in the darkness does not know where he is going. While y o u have the light believe in the light, in order that y o u may become sons of light.

When the people, by means of their more or less slurring remark, "What kind of a person is this Son of man (who is going to be lifted up, in spite of the fact that the law says that he, the Christ, will remain forever)?" clearly indicated that they did not receive his words in the proper and reverential frame of mind, Jesus, as recorded in verses 35 and 36, reminded them of their grave responsibility. Hence, although the passage which we are studying may not be a direct answer to the question which they had asked (neither is it called *an answer*), it is, indeed, a reply to the spirit in which they had asked it. Jesus said, "Yet a little while is the light with y o u." See on 7:33 (cf. 8:21). It was only a matter of hours now, at very most a few days (probably from Tuesday afternoon to Thursday night). For Christ as light see on 1:4, 5, 9; 3:19, 20, 21; 8:12; 9:5; 11:9, 10. Jesus continues, "Walk while y o u have the light lest the darkness overtake y o u." *This saying sheds light on the meaning of 1:9. See our remarks on that passage.* The Jews have the light, indeed!

To be sure, natural man, even though the Gospel be preached to him, does not have an inner, experiential, spiritual insight into the mysteries of God and of redemption. *Such knowledge is wholly reserved for the children of God* (I Cor. 2:14). Nevertheless, any man to whom the Gospel is proclaimed receives a certain amount of illumination, namely, in the sense that he gets to know the will of God for his life (Luke 12:47). Much is given to him (Luke 12:48; cf. Rom. 3:2). He may even prophesy by the name of Jesus (Matt. 7:22). He knows the way of righteousness and in that sense he has the knowledge of the Lord and Savior Jesus Christ (II Pet. 2:20, 21). Think of Balaam, King Saul, Judas, Demas, and others. But in spite of all this, ever so many people who hear the Gospel do not *walk* in the light, i.e., they do not *show by their daily conduct* that they have accepted and appropriated the truth as proclaimed by Christ, the light.

Those who do not walk while they have the light, are *overtaken* (the verb is explained in detail in connection with 1:5) by the monster, *darkness*. "He who is walking in the darkness does not know where he is going." Perhaps, he is living in the midst of heathendom. He is thoroughly confused. Or again, he may be living in a city that is noted for its many churches. Imagining himself to be a man of superior culture, he is forever talking Plato and Aristotle, and looks down with an eye of pity on those who try, with God's help, to make a thorough study of Scripture. The divine verdict is that, in spite of all this acquaintance with the philosophers (not bad in itself), such a person *does not know where he is going*. He is completely in the dark, having no guide, no star, no compass. The text has many up-to-date applications. Cf. I John 2:11.

The closing admonition is very touching and beautiful: "While y o u have the light (Christ in y o u r midst, as the source of truth and salvation), *believe* — exercise saving faith, by God's sovereign grace; see on 1:8; 3:16; 8:30, 31a — in the light, in order that y o u may become *sons of light,* i.e., *lights* (a Semitism; cf. Matt. 5:14), having the light of Christ not only round about y o u but within y o u r hearts and minds (cf. Eph. 5:8; I Thess. 5:5).

Synthesis of 12:20-36a

See the Outline on p. 134. *The Son of God Is Sought by the Greeks.*

In this story six parts or movements are discernible:

I. *The Request of the Greeks.*

Among the proselytes of the gate who were accustomed to attend the feast of Passover there were some Greeks. Not having found soul-satisfaction anywhere else, they approach Philip with the request, "Sir, we wish to see Jesus." Philip, probably wondering how Jesus will react and how the public will react if the requested audience should be granted, consults his fellow townsman Andrew, and together they inform Jesus. It seems probable that the event related in this paragraph occurred on Tuesday of the Passion Week. See on 12:36b.

II. *The Reaction of Jesus.*

A. The Principle he lays down:

1. In order that there may be spiritual fruit, his own death is absolutely necessary. This is clarified by means of an illustration from the realm of nature (the grain of wheat which must die before it can bear fruit).

2. Those who would participate in the benefits of his death must be willing, if need be, to die for his cause.

B. The Prayer he offers:

"Now is my soul troubled, and what shall I say? Father, save me from this hour! But for this purpose I came to this hour. Father, glorify thy name."

III. *The Father's Answer to Christ's Prayer.*

"And I have glorified it, and again I will glorify it."

IV. *How This Answer Was Interpreted.*

1. By the majority of the people standing around: "They were saying that it had thundered."

2. By some: "They were saying, 'An angel has spoken to him.'"

3. By Jesus: this answer definitely seals the world's doom. *The world, in condemning me, condemns itself.* Its prince (satan) shall be cast out, shall lose his hold on the nations. The coming of the Greeks is the promise of a rich harvest from among the Gentiles: "And I, when I am lifted up from the earth, will draw all men to myself."

V. *How the Multitude Reacted to Christ's Interpretation.*

They were not willing to accept his interpretation. They regard it as being in conflict with the teaching of the law: "We heard from the law that the Christ remains forever; how then do you say that the Son of man must be lifted up? Who is this Son of man?"

VI. *The Resulting Warning Which Jesus Issues.*

"While y o u have the light, believe in the light, in order that y o u may become sons of light."

36b These things said Jesus, and having departed he hid himself from them. 37 But though he had performed so many signs in their presence, they were not believing in him; 38 in order that the word spoken by the prophet Isaiah might be fulfilled:

> "Lord, who has believed our report?
> And the arm of the Lord, to whom was it revealed?"

39 for this reason they could not believe, for Isaiah said again:
40   "He has blinded their eyes and hardened their heart,
>   Lest they should see with their eyes and perceive with their heart,
>   And should turn, and I should heal them."

41 These things said Isaiah because he saw his glory, and he spoke of him. 42 Nevertheless, even of the rulers many believed in him, but because of the Pharisees they were not confessing (it), in order that they might not be put out of the synagogue; 43 for they loved the glory of men rather than the glory of God.

12:36b-43

12:36b. These things said Jesus, and having departed he hid himself from them.

"These things" covers the entire public ministry among the Jews. Having completed his work among them, he departed. From the Synoptics we gather that Tuesday of the Passion Week was a busy day for him. He was teaching in the court of the temple. In the evening of that day, however, he has withdrawn himself. He is with his disciples now, on the Mount of Olives (on his way to Bethany), teaching them about the coming destruction of Jerusalem and the end of the world. Hence, it seems probable that his final departure from the Jewish multitude, his withdrawal from the nation of Israel, took place when he left the temple on Tuesday-afternoon.[120]

We emphasize that this departure was the *final* one. He departed and *hid himself* (ἐκρύβη aor. passive indicative of κρύπτω; literally, was hidden, but the verb has the reflexive meaning here) from them. Verse 37 also clearly shows that this was, indeed, the end; i.e., the end of his *public* ministry. The public will not appear again until he is being led away to (and is standing before) Pilate who will sentence him to be crucified. During his trial, however, he never addresses the public. With 12:36b his public ministry is entirely finished. What we have in verses 44-50 was not spoken afterward but is a summary of all his public teaching.

37. But though he had performed so many signs in their presence, they were not believing in him.

By and large (12:11 is an exception!) the people's response to Christ's ministry had been that of unbelief. This reason was, however, inexcusable, for Jesus had performed ever so many *signs*. See on 2:11 for the meaning of the term; for references to these signs see on 2:11; 2:23; 3:2; 4:48; 4:54; 6:2; 6:14; 6:26; 7:31; 9:16; 10:41; 11:47; and 12:18. These references also show that many more signs are presupposed in the Fourth Gospel than are actually related. Cf. 21:25. After 12:37 the term *sign* does not occur again until we come to the summarizing statement in 20:30.

The imperfect tense "they were not believing" (for the verb see on 1:8; 3:16; 8:30, 31a; 12:11) indicates that there was a constant and progressive unwillingness to accept Jesus with a genuine, living faith. The signs, which so clearly testified to the exalted character of the One who performed them and which should have been an aid to the development of genuine faith, were not considered in their true significance. Though there were exceptions here and there, and though all of these exceptions taken together constituted a sizable group (12:11), on the whole Israel grew more and more callous spiritually, insensitive to the works and the words of Christ. Though many were convinced that he was, indeed, the Messiah, even this knowledge did not issue in genuine faith.

38. . . . in order that the word spoken by the prophet Isaiah might be
     fulfilled:
     Lord, who has believed our report?
     And the arm of the Lord, to whom was it revealed?

---

[120] See our *Bible Survey*, pp. 167-181.

Attempts to weaken the sense of ἵνα (whether by reference to assumed Aramaic written original or to the non-final use of ἵνα elsewhere) cannot be considered successful. See Vol. I, p. 46. In order that the divine moral order, as decreed from eternity and as described by the prophets, might be fulfilled, the Jewish multitudes, *through their own fault,* failed to accept Christ by genuine faith. That divine order demands that those who wilfully harden themselves shall be hardened. When Pharaoh hardens his heart, God carries out his plan (Rom. 9:17) with respect to him, and hardens his heart even more. This entire process had been clearly foreseen by Jehovah. He not only *foresaw* it but he had actually *planned* to harden Pharaoh's heart (Ex. 7:3); to harden it in response, of course, to the latter's own hardening (cf. Ex. 8:32 and 9:12). Man never sins cheaply. Nevertheless, the responsibility and the guilt remains entirely on *his* side. And as it was with Pharaoh, so it was also with Israel.

This purpose clause is, after all, very comforting. It shows that Israel's rejection of the Christ was not a frustration of God's plan. Actually — but again, in such a manner that the guilt remains entirely on the side of Israel! — Israel's hardening served as a means whereby that plan was carried out. It led to Christ's cross and thus to his crown; to his humiliation and thus to his exaltation. Only those (like Isaiah) who are by God's grace privileged to see the end from the beginning, *the glory* of Christ in the shame, can accept this without a protest.

The clause "in order that the word spoken *by the prophet Isaiah* might be fulfilled," indicates that the traditional view of the authorship of Is. 53 is correct, for it is clear that here (John 12:38, 39, 41) the author is not speaking about *the book* of Isaiah but about *the prophet himself* who saw the glory of the Lord and wrote about it in his scroll.

The quotation is from Is. 53:1, according to the LXX rendering. The king of all the prophets prophetically pictures the Christ and his faithful ambassadors as exclaiming, "Lord, who has believed *our report* (literally, *that which was heard from us,* from our lips), and *the arm* of the Lord — the power of Almighty God (cf. Is. 40:10; 52:10; 63:5) made manifest in the signs which Jesus performed — to whom was it revealed; i.e., who understood and took to heart its significance?" Exactly that prophecy had now been fulfilled, for nearly everybody failed to accept Christ with genuine faith.

39-41. For this reason they could not believe, for Isaiah said again:
    He has blinded their eyes and hardened their heart,
    Lest they should see with their eyes and perceive with their heart,
    And should turn, and I should heal them.
These things said Isaiah because he saw his glory, and he spoke of him.
The present quotation (really "adaptation") is from Is. 6:9, 10:

"And he said, Go and tell this people,
Hear ye, indeed, but understand not;
And see ye indeed, but perceive not.
Make the heart of this people fat, and make their ears heavy, and
  shut their eyes;
Lest they see with their eyes, and hear with their ears, and under-
  stand with their heart,
And turn again, and be healed."

Cf. the use that is made of this passage in Matt. 13:14, 15; Mark 4:12; Luke 8:10; Acts 28:26; see also Rom. 11:8.

In adapting this passage to present circumstances, the evangelist changes the imperatives of Isaiah to past indicatives (has blinded, has hardened), because the prophecy has now reached its fulfilment in the Messianic Age. In the clause, "He has blinded their eyes," he omits any reference to the ears and to hearing, perhaps because in that clause he is not reflecting on the *preaching* of Jesus but on the *signs* which he performed. The blinding of the eyes had as its purpose that the people might not be able to see Christ's mighty deeds as signs, pointing to him as the Son of God, the Christ.

Also, just as in the days of Isaiah, so also now the Lord had hardened the people's heart, with this purpose in mind, namely, that they might not perceive the meaning of his preaching.

The reason why the Lord had blinded their eyes and hardened their hearts was in order that they might not turn to him and, as a result, be healed!

To try to get rid of the *purpose*-idea in all this is entirely unwarranted. Any attempt to change the clear meaning of a text in order to bring it into harmony with one's particular theology is reprehensible. We should let the passage stand just as it is, and not tamper with it in any way.

The terrible consequence of hardening ourselves against the solemn admonitions and warnings that come to us is here pointed out. Again, as made clear in the discussion of verse 38, *the fault lies not in any sense with God!* He is the God of love. He is not a cruel monster who deliberately and with inward delight prepares people for everlasting damnation. On the contrary, he earnestly warns, proclaims the Gospel, and states — as Jesus did repeatedly during his earthly ministry — what will happen if people believe, also what will happen if they do not. He even *urges* them to walk in the light. But when people, of their own accord and after re-peated threats and promises, reject him and spurn his messages, then — and not until then — he hardens them, *in order that* those who were *not willing* to repent may *not be able* to repent.

Vain people, who are always ready to charge God with injustice and cruelty, may not be able to see the righteousness of God's dealings with the children of men. But *because* (ὅτι is the best reading here) Isaiah, in the glorious vision recorded in the same chapter from which the quotation was taken (chapter 6, verses 1-5 the vision; verses 9 and 10 the quoted words), saw the glory, the transcendent majesty (not restricted to but certainly including the moral quality of *holiness*) of the Lord Jesus Christ (in whom the glory of Jehovah reflects itself) and was conscious of the fact that he was speaking *of him,* he did not criticize or protest, but recorded faithfully what he had seen and heard. Yes, Isaiah had seen not only the *suffering* of the Servant of Jehovah (Is. 53:1-10a) but also his *glory* (Is. 6:1-5; 9:6, 7; 52:13-15; 53:10b-12). On Christ as the heart and center of Old Testament prophecy see Vol. I, pp. 73, 209-212.

42, 43. Nevertheless, even of the rulers many believed in him, but because of the Pharisees they were not confessing (it), in order that they might not be put out of the synagogue; for they loved the glory of men rather than the glory of God.

Though totally unwilling to accept him by a true and living, personal faith, nevertheless, even of the rulers (think of such men as Nicodemus, Joseph of Arimathea; and cf. Acts 6:7: "a great company of priests") many believed in him (the aorist tense is used; see the discussion on 8:30, 31). However, due to fear of *the Pharisees* (see on 3:1), who were envious of their "competitor" Jesus, and who (though seemingly very religious!) were his chief enemies, these rulers did not dare to confess what they believed. *Day in, day out* (note imperfect tense: *were not confessing*) they kept their opinion to themselves. How did *John* get to know about it then? Perhaps Nicodemus or Joseph of Arimathea told him about it afterward. The fear was inspired by the decision that anyone who should confess Jesus to be the Christ would be banished from the synagogue (see on 9:22).

These men were just like so many Jews in the days of Antiochus Epiphanes (and like so many people today), always ready to get on the bandwagon and to join the majority (cf. Dan. 11:32, 34). How they love to stand well in the opinion of the leaders! "They loved the glory of men — e.g., the flatteries of the members of the Sanhedrin! — rather than the glory of God." For explanation see on 5:44. They were unwilling to take to heart the teaching of Jesus recorded in 12:25 (see on that passage).

---

44 And Jesus cried out and said, "He who believes in me does not believe in me but in him who sent me.   45 And he who observes me observes him who sent me.   46 I have come as a light into the world, in order that no one who believes in me may remain in the darkness.   47 And if anyone hears my sayings but does

not keep them, it is not I that judge him,[121] for I did not come in order to judge the world but in order to save the world. 48 He who rejects me and does not receive my sayings has one that judges him: the word which I have spoken, that will judge him on the last day. 49 For I have not spoken on my own authority, but the Father who sent me, he himself has given me instruction what I should say and what I should utter. 50 And I know that his instruction is everlasting life. Indeed, the things which I utter, even as the Father has told me so I utter (them).

12:44-50

Whereas what follows is a summary of previous public teaching (and to some extent also of subsequent private instruction), sothat the various passages are interpreted elsewhere, we shall refer to the places where an explanation can be found:

12:44. And Jesus cried out and said, He who believes in me, does not believe in me but in him who sent me. As more often in statements of this nature (see on 4:21; 12:30) the sense is: "He who believes in me does not exclusively believe in me but believes also in him who sent me." See especially on 13:20, but also on 7:16; 8:19, 42. *Knowing Christ* means *knowing the Father. Loving Christ* means *loving the Father. Receiving Christ* means *receiving the Father.* Christ and the Father are one (10:30).

45. And he who observes me observes him who sent me. When one is looking intently and constantly upon Jesus (θεωρῶν from θεωρέω; see Vol. I, p. 85, the footnote), and notices how in his words and works the glory of the Father is reflected, then with the eye of faith, one is looking upon his Sender. See especially on 14:9, but also on 8:19; 10:38.

46. I have come as a light into the world, in order that no one who believes in me may remain in the darkness. God's promises are for those who believe (cf. 3:16). To be sure, the Gospel is proclaimed to a wider circle, but the illumination of those who do not accept Jesus by faith is merely outward. In their hearts the darkness remains. In fact, it becomes even more intense. See also on 1:4, 5; 1:9; 8:12; 9:5; and 12:35, 36.

47. And if anyone hears my sayings but does not keep them, it is not I that judge him, for I did not come in order to judge the world but in order to save the world. The main purpose of Christ's first coming was not to bring condemnation but salvation. See on 3:17 and on 8:15, 16. With respect to keeping the sayings of Christ see on 8:51. On hearing but not keeping cf. Matt. 7:24-26; James 2:14-26.

---

[121] IIIA2; see Vol. I, pp. 42, 43. In the light of the following context the verb κρίνω is probably indicative.

JOHN   12:50

48. He who rejects me and does not receive my sayings has one that judges him: the word which I have spoken, that will judge him on the last day. With respect to *the word as judge* see on 5:24; 5:45-47; 8:31, 37, 51; and 14:23, 24. Cf. Matt. 7:21-27; Luke 11:28. For *the last day* see Vol. I, pp. 200, 201, 235, 239.

49. For I have not spoken on my own authority, but the Father who sent me, he himself has given me instruction what I should say and what I should utter. Exactly the same thought is found in 7:16. See also on 3:11; 8:26, 28, 38; and 14:10. In order to stress the idea that absolutely everything in the teaching of the Son is based upon the instruction of the Father, the synonymous clause "and what I should utter" is added to "what I should say." It is probably best not to distinguish between the meaning of these two verbs (*say* and *utter*) in the present connection. For the meaning of the term translated *instruction* (ἐντολή) see also on 13:34.

50. And I know that his instruction is everlasting life. Indeed, the things which I utter, even as the Father has told me so I utter (them). The instruction given to Jesus was to procure, to reveal, and to proclaim everlasting life. Hence, that instruction issues in everlasting life for his people. See on 3:16, 6:63. Cf. I John 2:25. Perish the idea that between the Father and the Son there is a wide gulf (Angry Judge versus Loving Savior). On the contrary, Jesus utters only that which the Father has given him, and he utters it *exactly* as he received it.

Synthesis of 12:36b-50

See the Outline on p. 134. *The Son of God is Repulsed by the Jews.*
I. *The Rejection of Jesus by the Jews* (12:36b-43).
A. Was Inexcusable
1. The Jews have seen many signs.
2. They, *of their own accord,* seek their own glory, not God's.
B. Had been predicted
1. God was not taken unawares; his plan was not defeated by the unbelief of the Jews.
2. On the contrary, the unbelief of the Jews was the fulfilment of definite prophecies (Is. 53:1; 6:9, 10).
C. Was the result of divine hardening
1. God actually blinds the eyes and hardens the hearts of certain people, sothat they cannot turn and be converted.
2. This hardening is, however, a punishment for their own sin. God is love. His invitations, warnings, and admonitions are always sincere and earnest. However, when man rejects him and his word, dire punishment results. God hardens the man who has hardened himself.

II. *The Supreme Importance of Genuine, Personal Faith in Jesus as the Christ* (12:44-50).

A. It is impossible to believe in God if one does not believe in Jesus Christ and in his word, by which one will be judged in the last day.

B. Genuine Faith in Jesus leads one out of the darkness.

C. Genuine Faith in Jesus (his person, his word) brings everlasting life.

Outline of Chapter 13

Theme: *Jesus, the Christ, the Son of God*
During his Private Ministry Issuing and Illustrating His New
Commandment
Predicting the Betrayal and the Denial

13:1-20   He Illustrates His New Commandment by Washing the Feet of
His Disciples, Explaining to Them That He Has Given Them
an Example to be Followed.

13:21-30 He Startles the Disciples by Telling Them that One of Their
Number Is Going to Betray Him. Judas Leaves.

13:31-38 He Issues His New Commandment and Predicts Peter's Denial.

CHAPTER XIII

13 1 Now Jesus, knowing before the feast of the Passover that his hour to [122] depart out of this world (and to go) to the Father had arrived, having loved his own in the world, loved them to the uttermost.   2 And at supper,[123] the devil having already put it into the heart of Judas Iscariot, Simon's son, to betray him, 3 Jesus, knowing that the Father had given all things into his hands, and that he had come from God and was going to God, 4 rose from the supper, laid aside his garments, and having taken a towel, tied it around his waist.[124]   5 Then he poured water into the wash-basin, and began to wash the disciples' feet, and to dry them with the towel which was tied around his waist.[125]

6 So he came to Simon Peter, who said to him, "Lord, dost *thou* wash *my* feet?"   7 Jesus answered and said to him, "What I am doing you do not know now, but hereafter you will understand."   8 Peter said to him, "By no means shalt thou wash my feet ever." Jesus answered him, "If I do not wash you, you have no share with me." [126]   9 Simon Peter said to him, "Lord, not my feet only but also my hands and my head!"   10 Jesus said to him, "He who has bathed has no need of washing anything except his feet, but is clean altogether. And y o u are clean, but not all of y o u are."   11 For he knew the one who was betraying him. It was for this reason that he said, "Not all of y o u are clean."

12 So when he had washed their feet, had taken his garments, and had resumed his place, he said to them, "Do y o u know what I have done to y o u ? 13 Y o u call me 'Teacher' and 'Lord,' and y o u say (this) correctly, for (that is what) I am.   14 If, therefore, *I*, y o u r Lord and Teacher, have washed y o u r feet, y o u also ought to wash *each other's* feet,[127] 15 for I have given y o u an example, in order that just as *I* did to y o u so also y o u should do.   16 Most solemnly do I assure y o u, the servant is not greater than his lord, neither is he who is sent [128] greater than he who sent him.   17 If y o u know these things, blessed are y o u if y o u do them.[129]

---

122 On ἵνα see Vol. I, pp. 45, 51.
123 Or "And at supper-time" (literally: supper arriving).
124 Or "girded himself around" (literally).
125 Or, "with which he was girded around" (literally).
126 IIIA2; see Vol. I, pp. 42, 43.
127 I A; see Vol. I, p. 40.
128 Or "an apostle" (which means: one who is sent or commissioned).
129 This is a conditional sentence with a double protasis. There is a condition within a condition. The protasis of the larger condition (i.e., of the entire sentence) is: "If y o u know these things." The apodosis which corresponds to this is: "blessed are y o u if y o u do them." The protasis of the included condition is: "If y o u do them." The corresponding apodosis is: "blessed are y o u." Hence,

18 Not of y o u all am I speaking. I know the ones I have chosen; but
(it is) in order that [130] the scripture may be fulfilled:

> 'He who eats my bread
> Has lifted his heel against me.'

19 From now on I am telling (this) to y o u before (it) takes place, in
order that when it does take place y o u may continue to believe that I am (he).
20 I most solemnly assure y o u, he who receives anyone whom I send receives
me; and he who receives me receives him who sent me."

13:1-18

**13:1. Now Jesus, knowing (already) before the feast of the Passover that
his hour to depart out of this world (and to go) to the Father had arrived,
having loved his own in the world, loved them to the uttermost.**

The fact that he was now about to depart out of this realm of mankind
(for the meaning of κόσμος see Vol. I, p. 79, footnote 26; here in 13:1 meaning 2 seems probable), and that he was about *to go home*, that is, *to go back
to the Father* (see also on 5:24; 8:23; 14:12, 28; 16:10, 28; and 17:5) did
not suddenly dawn upon Jesus. Even in his human nature (see Vol. I,
p. 191) he had known it long before this feast of Passover of the year 30
A. D. It was in the full and reassuring [131] knowledge of this fact that he
approached the momentous events of Passover-week. On Christ's fore-
knowledge see also 2:4; 7:6; 12:23; 13:11, 18; 18:4; 19:28.

---

the clause common to both apodoses is "blessed are y o u." The verb of this
clause is present indicative. Due to the double protasis (or, one may also say,
due to the two protases), the sentence belongs to two groups (IA and IIIB1); see
Vol. I, pp. 40, 42, 44. This fact is full of meaning. Thus, while the disciples'
knowledge of the proper attitude and conduct toward one another *is assumed to
be true to fact* (hence, conditional sentence of the first class), the question whether
these disciples are acting in accordance with this knowledge is more or less left in
the middle, is conceived of neither as a reality nor as in conflict with reality but
at best as a hopeful expectation (hence, conditional sentence of the third class).
The responsibility is left entirely with the disciples. By refusing to be more definite
Jesus leaves room for what he states in verse 18.

130 On ἵνα see Vol. I, pp. 45, 46, and 51.

131 Verse 1 has its commentary in verse 3: for Jesus to depart out of this world
and to go to the Father meant that he was returning to the One who had given
all things into his hands. Hence, we speak about Christ's *reassuring* knowledge.
He was able to see not only the cross but also the crown. This inner conviction
gave him (in his human nature) that rest and stability of mind which made it
possible for him, in spite of the fact that he was standing on the threshold of
Gethsemane, Gabbatha, and Golgotha, to condescend to the disciples in an act
of infinite love and tenderness. We believe, therefore, that Calvin is entirely correct when he says (commenting on the similar words in verse 3):

Hoc ideo additum fuisse interpretor, ut sciamus unde Christo tam composita
animi quies, nempe quod iam mortis victor animum ad triumphum, qui mox
sequuturus erat, extulit (Ioannis Calvini *in Evangelium Ioannis Commentarii*,
Berolini, 1553, vol. III, p. 254).

Hence, he who all along had loved *his own disciples* (*his own* not merely in the sense of 1:11, but in the full and comprehensive sense of 17:6, 9, 11, 20) considered this to be the appropriate time for the manifestation of his love *to the uttermost* (εἰς τέλος, probably as in I Thess. 2:16). In all that follows — that is, in the feet-washing, farewell address, highpriestly prayer, crucifixion, etc. — that love-motive is operating. For the meaning of the term *the feast of the Passover,* see Vol. I, pp. 121, 122; and see on 13:29.

That briefly is the meaning of 13:1, as we see it, in the light of its own context. Our translation of this verse indicates that we take the phrase *before the feast of the Passover* to modify the nearest verbal form, which in this case is the participle *knowing.* That would seem to be the most natural. We admit, however, that it is grammatically possible to construe this phrase with the main verb *he loved.* If this is interpreted to mean that at the very beginning of Passover-week Jesus exhibited his love most gloriously (by means of the feet-washing), the resulting explanation is not far removed from ours. Hint: those readers of this book who are not interested in the discussion of critical problems are advised to proceed at once to verses 2, 3, 4.

The Origin of a Problem

However, among the interpreters who believe that the phrase *before the feast of the Passover* modifies *he loved* there are those who inject an entirely different idea into the text. Their interpretation is as follows:

"Now *twenty-four hours before the Passover Supper,* Jesus, having all along loved his own who were in the world, showed his love in the most glorious manner by eating a meal with them, in connection with which he washed their feet."

Proceeding upon this assumption, it is further argued that, *as John sees it,* the meal of chapter 13 cannot have been a Passover. — Others, however, are of the opinion that *John* wishes it to be viewed as a Passover Supper which Jesus and his disciples ate a day in advance of the regular time. In either case, as these interpreters see it, it was *John's* intention to picture the Lord as the true Passover Lamb who died when the paschal lambs were sacrificed in the temple-court. He dies while the Jews have not yet eaten their Passover lamb. Or, as others see it (cf. Proposed Solutions (4)), he dies while many Jews — for example, the Sadducees — have not yet had their Passover Supper (as will be explained).

Further support for this idea, namely, that the meal of John 13:2 *as viewed by the author of the Fourth Gospel,* precedes by one day the (or *a*) Passover Supper, is by some interpreters found in 13:29: ". . . buy what we need for the feast," which clause is then interpreted to mean, ". . . buy what we need for the Passover Supper." It is argued that this passage clearly shows that at the time of the meal referred to in 13:2, the food necessary for the Passover Supper had not even been bought. — Here again some would modify the last sentence so as to read, "At the time of the meal referred to in 13:2, the food necessary for the Passover Supper *as observed by many* had not even been bought."

One more passage which is considered to be a strong bulwark in support of this theory is 18:28, which shows, according to these interpreters, that, *as John sees it,* on the very morning of the crucifixion the Passover lamb had not yet been eaten by anybody. With reference to the men who led Jesus from Caiaphas to the praetorium we read, "They themselves did not enter the praetorium, in order that they might not be defiled *but might eat the passover."* — And here once more certain interpreters (cf. Proposed Solutions (4)) would say that 18:28 shows that, *as John sees it, by many Jews* on the very morning of the crucifixion the Passover lamb had not yet been eaten. But, as far as possible, we shall leave 18:28 out of consideration in the present discussion. See, however, on that verse.

The Problem Stated

The problem that results is as follows: *Matthew, Mark, and Luke* (Matt. 26:17; Mark 14:12; Luke 22:7) clearly teach that Jesus and his disciples ate the Passover Supper at the prescribed time; and that he died on (what we would call) the following day (Mark 15:1 ff.). But, if the interpreters whose view we have described are correct, then *John* teaches that Jesus died *before* the Jews ate their Passover lamb. — Or, according to some, Jesus died before many of the Jews ate it.

Did Jesus die *after the Passover Supper* (thus the Synoptics), or did he die *before the Passover Supper* (thus, *say some,* John)? That is the question.

The Proposed Solutions

With respect to a possible answer or solution the following opinions have been expressed:

(1) "A true solution which takes into account all the data of Scripture has not yet been proposed. The problem is very difficult." — Often those who express this opinion purposely avoid saying anything that might create the impression that they believe that John and the Synoptics cannot be harmonized. They believe that somehow there *is* a solution, but that it has not yet been discovered. — This is honest, and we have the highest respect for the men who give this answer. They are usually careful scholars of the orthodox persuasion. Others, however, believe that there is no solution, that the sources simply leave us completely in the dark, and that all we know is that Jesus died about the time of the feast of Passover.

(2) "The Synoptics and John contradict each other. The Synoptics are right. John is wrong." This is the general trend of the answer as given by G. Dalman, *Jesus — Jeshua,* New York, 1929; pp. 88, 106. As he sees it, the supper of John 13 is not a Passover meal. Jesus is by John represented as dying *before* the Passover. The Synoptics are more objective than the Fourth Gospel with respect to this subject. Siding with the Synoptics against John (though with individual variations) are also F. C. Baur, D. F. Strauss, W. Bauer and many others.

(3) "The Synoptics and John contradict each other. John is right. The Synoptics are wrong." Thus, J. H. Barnard, M. Dibelius, E. Hoskyns, A. E. J. Rawlinson, H. Windish, etc. — M. Dods simply states that according to John, though not in agreement with the Synoptists, Jesus suffered as the Paschal Lamb on the day of the Passover.

(4) "The problem is solved by bearing in mind that Jesus and his disciples ate the Passover Thursday-evening, when most of the Jewish people including the Pharisees also ate it; and that the Sadducees celebrated Passover the next evening (Friday). In John 13:2 the supper is the Passover of the Synoptics. In 18:28 the Passover is that of the Sadducees. Hence, when the Synoptics indicate that Jesus died *after* the Passover Supper, they are right, and when the Fourth Gospel (in 18:28) teaches that he died *before* the Passover Supper, it is also right."

Various reasons for eating the Passover Supper on *two* days are given by different authors. Some say that when the fifteenth of Nisan coincided with the sabbath, the Pharisees, fearing that they might otherwise desecrate the sabbath by carrying out the elaborate Passover-ritual, would celebrate it a day earlier; while the Sadducees were not so scrupulous. Others point out that there were sometimes differences of opinion with respect to the day when the month was supposed to begin; or that so very many lambs had to be sacrificed in the temple-court that they could not all be killed in a single afternoon.

In one form or another this theory is advocated by D. Chwolson in *Das Letzte Passamahl Jesu-Christi und der Tag seines Todes nach den in Uebereinstemmung gebrachten Berichten der Synoptiker und des Evangeliums Johannis,* St. Petersburg, 1892; S. BK, pp. 812-854; J. H. Bavinck, *Geschiedenis der Godsopenbaring,* Kampen, 1949, pp. 419, 420; C. Bouma, W. M. Christie, P. A. E. Sillevis-Smit, J. Th. Ubbink, etc.

In the Light of Its Origin Has This Problem a Right of Existence here in chapter 13?

Any attempt at *solving* the problem presupposes that there *is* a legitimate problem. But, *as far as chapter 13 is concerned,* is there? Is it not clear that the problem arose out of two assumptions: (a) *that the supper of 13:2 is not the same as the Passover Supper described in the Synoptics (ex-*

ception: those who favor Proposed Solution (4) consider it to have been the same); and (b) that the term *feast* in 13:29 (". . . buy what we need for the feast") has reference to the Passover Supper and the lamb eaten at that supper?

Were it not for these two assumptions, there would be no problem here in chapter 13. But see also on 18:28; 19:14, 31, 42. Are these assumptions warranted?

As to the first assumption, it has already been shown that it rests not only upon a construction of the Greek text which is by no means certain (the view that the phrase *before the feast of the Passover* modifies *he loved* in 13:1) but upon an even more uncertain interpretation which is superimposed upon this uncertain construction, as if the text read, "Now twenty-four hours before the Passover Supper Jesus . . . showed his love by eating a meal with his disciples," namely, the meal of 13:2.

For the rest, we can safely leave it to the reader to decide whether or not John and the Synoptists are discussing the same Supper. Here is the evidence. Please compare the two accounts:

The Meal as Described by Matthew, Mark, and Luke:	*The Meal as Described by John:*

"And when the hour was come, he sat down, and the apostles with him. And he said to them, With great desire have I desired to eat this passover with you before I suffer — And there arose also a dispute among them, which of them was to be regarded as the greatest. And he said to them . . . he that is greatest among y o u, let him become as the youngest, and the leader as one who serves. For who is greater, one who sits at the table, or one who serves? Is it not the one who sits at the table? But I am in the midst of y o u as one who serves." (Luke 22: 14, 15, 24-27). — The dispute about greatness (Luke) is the natural background for the feetwashing (John).

After washing the feet of his disciples Jesus said: "Most solemnly do I assure y o u, the servant is not greater than his lord, neither is he who is sent greater than he who sent him. If y o u know these things, blessed are y o u if y o u do them." (13:16, 17).

"And as they . . . were eating, Jesus said, I solemnly assure y o u,

"I am not speaking of y o u all. I know whom I have chosen; but it is

One of y o u shall betray me, one who is eating with me." This is followed by a detailed account of the reaction (to this startling announcement) on the part of the disciples (Mark 14:17-21; Matt. 26:20-25).

in order that the scripture may be fulfilled:

'He who eats my bread
Has lifted his heel against me.'
. . . I most solemnly assure y o u, one of y o u will betray me." This is followed by a detailed account of the reaction (to this startling announcement) on the part of the disciples (13:18, 21-30). The details (as given by the Synoptists and by John) differ, but do not conflict.

"Jesus said to him (i.e., to Peter), I solemnly assure you, that this night before the rooster crows, you will thrice deny me" (Matt. 26:34; cf. Mark 14:30; Luke 22:34). The actual denial follows during the same night. *It has to follow,* for it was going to occur before the rooster crows.

"Jesus answered, Will you lay down your life for me? I most solemnly assure you, the rooster will not crow until you have thrice denied me (13:38). The actual denial follows during the same night. *It has to follow,* for it was going to occur before the rooster crows.

Must we, indeed, assume that these three identical incidents—the lesson with respect to true greatness, the startling announcement about the betrayer, and the prediction of Peter's denial, followed shortly afterward by the actual denial — occurred in connection with two different meals on two different evenings? Did Peter deny the Lord on two successive nights? Is it not clear that the Synoptics and John are describing the same supper, and that John, having read the accounts of the others, adds certain details?

Having established that it was *the same supper* we now have the right to go to the Synoptics to ask what kind of supper it was. From such passages as Matt. 26:17; Mark 14:12, 14; and Luke 22:11, 14, 15 it becomes clear that it was the Passover Supper.

That this supper was eaten at the regular time, that is, during the evening which followed the afternoon when according to the law of Moses the lambs had been killed, is clear from Luke 22:7. Jesus was crucified the next day (cf. Luke 22:66-23:33). That the day of Christ's death was a Friday, the day before the sabbath, is expressly stated in Mark 15:42 (cf. Luke 23:54). It was *Preparation Day* (παρασκυή), which has long been the regular term for *Friday* in the Greek language (as my Greek calendar also indicates).

Now John is in complete harmony with this. He also relates that Jesus died on Friday (19:14; 19:31; 19:42).

One can also arrive at this result from another angle. According to the Fourth Gospel Jesus arose on the first day of the week; hence, on Sunday (20:1, 19). Beginning from there and paging backward in the New Testament, the chronology of John becomes clear. On the day preceding this Sunday his body rested in the tomb (19:31). On Friday he was crucified (19:30, 31). Since 18:28 — note the expression "It was early" — clearly begins a new day (namely, Friday), it is evident that the events related in 18:1-27 refer to the *preceding* day; i.e., to Thursday. But 18:1 — "When Jesus had spoken these words, he went out" — indicates that the Farewell Discourse and Highpriestly Prayer belong to the same Thursday. And a comparison between 13:38 — "The rooster will not crow until you have thrice denied me" — and 18:25-27 — Peter's actual denial shows clearly that the events recorded in chapter 13 of John's Gospel occurred on this Thursday-evening.

We are, therefore, in hearty accord with S. BK., p. 841, in believing that there is complete agreement between John and the Synoptics in this respect, namely, that the supper of 13:2 is the Passover Supper of the Synoptics, and that it took place on Thursday-evening, the evening before Christ's death.

This leads to the discussion of the second *assumption* mentioned on p. 224. Does the term *feast* in 13:29 (". . . buy what we need for the feast") have reference to a Passover Supper and to the lamb eaten at that supper?

The following should be noted:

The Jewish people were fully aware of the fact that the law had stipulated *one* particular day for the slaughtering of the lambs.

Two separate evenings for the eating of the lamb would have caused the wildest and most hopeless confusion. The Sadducees, who regulated the affairs of the temple, would certainly not have permitted it. See M. Goguel, *op. cit.,* p. 433.

Besides, does the disputed term in 13:29 refer at all to a Passover Supper? It has already been shown — see Vol. I, pp. 121, 122 — that the Old Testament calls the Passover *a feast of seven days* (Ezek. 45:21). The New Testament evidences the same usage. Thus, Luke 22:1 applies the name *Passover* to the entire seven-day feast of unleavened bread.

Now, with respect to the term *feast* in 13:29, what does this term (when applied to Passover) mean elsewhere in the Fourth Gospel? The remarkable fact is that in all probability it *everywhere* has the meaning *seven-day festival.*

It was "while Jesus was at *the feast* of Passover" that many trusted in his name when they observed the signs which he was doing (2:23). Surely, Jesus did not perform these signs during the eating of the Passover *Supper?* The *feast* here is evidently the entire seven-day celebration.

According to 4:45, "the Galileans welcomed him, having seen *all that he had done in Jerusalem at the feast,* for they too had attended the feast."

It is clear that here again *the feast* cannot refer to anything else than the seven-day festival.

The next clear reference to the feast of Passover (the identity of the feast in 5:1 is disputed, as has been explained, Vol. I, pp. 187-189) is 6:4: "Now the Passover *was approaching, the feast of the Jews."* We find exactly the same expression in 7:2. There, too, *the feast is approaching,* but this time it is the feast of Tabernacles. However, 7:37 — "the last day, the great day of the feast" — clearly shows that the reference is to the entire seven- (or eight-) day feast. If this is true with respect to 7:2, why not with respect to 6:4, where the same author uses the identical expression?

The next reference to *the feast* of Passover is in 11:56 — "What do y o u think, that he will certainly not come to *the feast?"* This cannot mean ". . . to the Supper."

In 12:12 the expression "the vast multitude that had come to *the feast"* the reference is, of course, to the seven-day festival. The Jews did not come from all over Palestine and from the regions outside of it in order to spend just *one* evening (and to partake of just *one* supper) in Jerusalem.

Similarly, the supper of 13:2 which belongs to *the feast* (13:1) indicates the Passover Supper which was part of the seven-day celebration.

Now if wherever (outside of 13:29) John employs the term "feast" with respect to the Passover, he always without exception refers to the entire seven-day festival, why would he not use the term in the same sense in 13:29? It is, therefore, entirely logical that the term *feast* in the expression ". . . buy what we need for the feast" be given the interpretation which must be attached to it everywhere else in John's Gospel. To assign any different meaning to it would be unwarranted.

It has become evident that the supper of chapter 13, which occurred on the first evening of *the feast of the Passover,* was the regular Passover Supper, of which Jesus partook at the regular time, Thursday-evening. It has also become evident that there is nothing in chapter 13 which contradicts the idea that he was crucified on Friday, the fifteenth of Nisan. See further on 18:28.

In the full consciousness of the fact that he was about to return to the Father, Jesus, who had loved his own all along, knew that the proper time had arrived to reveal to them his love to the uttermost.

3, 4. And at supper, the devil having already put it into the heart of Judas Iscariot, Simon's son, to betray him, Jesus, knowing that the Father had given all things into his hands, and that he had come from God and was going to God, rose from the supper, laid aside his garments, and having taken a towel, tied it around his waist.

It is Thursday-evening. The sun has gone down. It is supper-time. The translation "supper being ended" of the A.V. must be rejected. It is based

upon an inferior reading (γενομένου instead of γινομένου), but even that reading does not necessarily mean "supper being *ended*." [132] The washing of
the feet would naturally occur not at the end of a supper but at the beginning.

The situation as pictured here is as follows:

Jesus and the disciples have come from Bethany. The feet, protected
only by sandals, had become partly exposed to sand and dust. They were
dirty, or at least uncomfortable. In such circumstances, the washing of the
feet was customary. The host, though not himself performing this service
(cf. Gen. 18:4; Luke 7:44), would generally see to it that it was performed.
It was, after all, a *menial* task, that is, a task to be discharged by a *servant*.
When John the Baptist desired to give expression to his feeling of un-
worthiness in comparison to Christ, he could think of no better way to
express this than to say that he deemed himself unworthy of kneeling down
in front of Jesus in order to unloose his sandalstraps and remove the sandals
(with a view to washing the Master's feet). See Vol. I, pp. 96, 97. Cf. I Sam.
25:41: "And she (Abigail) arose, and bowed herself with her face to the
earth, and said, Behold, thy handmaid is a servant to wash the feet of the
servants of my lord (David)."

But here in the Upper Room there was no servant. Hence, one of the
disciples should have performed this task. But none was willing. These
men were too proud. A few moments ago (probably in connection with
the order in which they would recline around the table) they had been
arguing among themselves about the question of *greatness* (Luke 22:24).
And this was not the first time that they had been squabbling about it. The
question, "Who among us is the greatest?" seems to have occupied their
minds and hearts again and again. The fact that greatness is measured with
the yardstick of service had not registered with them.

In the Upper Room everything was ready. Here stood the pitcher and
the wash-basin; and there lay the long linen cloth. There was water in the
pitcher. Yet no one stirred. Each disciple was hoping that someone else
would make the first move. And among these disciples there was one man
so indescribably low in character that even at this very moment he was fully
determined to betray the Lord, yes, fully resolved actually to deliver him
up by treachery into the hands of his enemies, and to do this for thirty
pieces of silver! *Not one of the other disciples knew about this or suspected
it.*

It was the devil who had injected this vile purpose into the heart of Judas

---

132 Thus, for example, in Matt. 27:1 πρωΐας γενομένης does not mean morning having *ended,* but morning having *dawned;* and γενομένου σαββάτου in Mark 6:2 is
simply *on a sabbath.* We have already seen that in John 10:22 the clause ἐγένετο
τότε τὰ ἐγκαίνια means, "Then *came* the feast of Dedication." It does not mean,
"Then *was ended* the feast of Dedication."

Iscariot, Simon's son. Having discovered at length that being a disciple of Jesus would not *pay off,* and being a thoroughly greedy individual, he was determined not to be put out of the synagogue (see on 9:22) but instead to cultivate the favor of the authorities by "showing them where Jesus was" (11:57). See further on 6:71 and on 12:4-6.

It was in the midst of such men — men with the *So Big* attitude of heart, men with Judas the traitor in their midst — that Jesus was about to set an example of humility and service. This reference to Judas, accordingly, makes the deed stand out in all its true greatness. Yes, the Master even washed the feet of Judas!

Another wonderful circumstance which adds glory to the deed was the fact that when Jesus performed it, he did it *in the full consciousness* (εἰδώς, probably modal participle; not causal, nor merely concessive) that he was God's only begotten Son; hence, the rightful heir of all things. He knew "that the Father had given all things into his hands — cf. Psalm 2:8 and see Vol. I, pp. 14, 150 —, and that he had come from God and was going to God (see above, on verse 1).

Jesus waited a long time. The disciples had already occupied their places around the U-shaped table. The food was on the table, and the meal was about to begin. Still no one offered to perform the duty of the servant. The water-pitcher, the wash-basin, and the apron-towel, placed there in the plain sight of all, frowned upon them. These utensils constituted a silent accusation against these men! Still no one moved.

It was then that Jesus acted. With calmness and majesty (see on verse 1 above) he rose from the supper and laid aside his *garments* (ἱμάτια). Note that the evangelist uses the plural "garments" both here and in verse 12. In 19:2 and 5 ("purple garment") he uses the singular. In 19:23, 24 (the distribution of the garments among the soldiers, in connection with the crucifixion) he employs the plural once again. It seems, therefore that John makes a careful distinction. Hence, if the word garments in 13:2, 5 has the same meaning as in 19:23, 24, which seems probable, Jesus is pictured here as if he were an Oriental slave, wearing nothing but a loin-cloth. Phil. 2:7 "taking the form of a servant" comes to our mind immediately. Both the flowing outer garment and the tunic (as well as the belt, of course) had been laid aside.

Then Jesus took a long, linen cloth (λέντιον, from the Latin, *linteum*), and tied it around his middle, sothat with the end of this towel he would be able to dry the disciples' feet after he had washed them with his hands. Truly, the Lord of glory had "girded himself with humility" (cf. I Peter 5:5).

5. Then he poured water into the wash-basin, and began to wash the

disciples' feet, and to dry them with the towel which was tied around his waist.

The details of the action are pictured one by one. The scene had left an indelible impression on the mind of the evangelist John, who was present. Hence, the record is very graphic, and rightly so, the purpose being that the reader's mind may ponder this manifestation of wonderful condescension. The heart must linger here a while, until the lesson has been learned. Jesus poured water from the pitcher into the wash-basin. He placed the latter on the floor right behind one of the men whose feet projected from the couch on which he was reclining. With this water the Lord now proceeded to wash this disciple's feet. Then he dried them with the end of the towel which was tied around his waist.

We have purposely used the terms "wash-basin" and "wash" in order to convey the similarity which in the original exists between the corresponding terms νιπτήρ and νίπτω.

We do not know whose feet Jesus washed first of all. The words *"he began* to wash" probably serve to prepare the reader for the fact that there is going to be an interruption. (As this explanation agrees with the context, it would seem to be the most probable. But those commentators who discuss this point are not in agreement). The interruption is recorded in verses 6-11.

6. So he came to Simon Peter, who said to him, Lord, dost thou wash my feet? The reactions of all but one of the disciples are not recorded. They probably kept their thoughts to themselves. Being *perplexed* and (let us hope) *ashamed* (exception: Judas, of course) of the fact that Jesus was doing for them what they should have done for him and for each other, they were at a loss what to say. However, with Peter it was different. Impetuous and impulsive Peter! He was the man who could not keep still. He did his thinking *aloud.* "Lord" (for the term see on 1:38, footnote 44; also on 12:21), says Peter, "dost *thou* wash *my* feet?" Peter sees the incongruity of what is happening. *The Lord of glory,* on the one hand, and *Peter's dirty feet,* on the other; what a contrast! To this disciple the very idea of *the Lord washing Peter's feet* was intolerable. According to the original, the contrast between the words *thou* and *my* is brought out by placing them next to each other. In order to retain the flavor of the original we should really render Peter's protest as follows: "Lord, dost *thou my* feet wash?" Peter was shocked!

7. Jesus answered and said to him, What I am doing you do not know now, but hereafter you will understand.
For "answered and said," see Vol. I, p. 64. Peter had raised his emphatic objection to what Jesus was beginning to do just now. Such an act of humiliation for the physical comfort of Peter was too much! He completely

failed to realize that what the Lord was trying to do at this moment was part and parcel of *all* the events of this memorable night and of the hours that were to follow it. Peter simply did not know what he was saying; for if he demurs to the need of *partial* humiliation for his physical comfort, will he not have to reject the deed of *absolute* humiliation that has as its purpose his complete (spiritual as well as physical) salvation? In reality the two go together: when Jesus washes the feet of his disciples, that too is a necessary constituent of his suffering from conception to burial, whereby he merits salvation for his people.

It was for this reason that Jesus, who saw not only a part but the whole, said to Peter, "What I am doing *you do not know* now, but hereafter *you will understand.*" For the difference in meaning between the two verbs here used (οἶδα and γινώσκω) see on 1:10, 31; 3:11; and 8:28. For the meaning of the expression *hereafter* (literally, "after these things," μετὰ ταῦτα) see on 5:1. Of the many explanations of this expression here in 13:7 there are two which we reject: "in the Hereafter," that is, after you have entered heaven; and b. "as soon as I have washed the feet of all of y o u, and have added a few words of explanation." In harmony with 16:12-14 we must interpret the expression to mean "after my death, resurrection, ascension; particularly, after the outpouring of the Holy Spirit. Then the meaning not only of this feetwashing but of my entire work of humiliation will become clear to y o u."

8. Peter said to him, By no means shalt thou wash my feet ever. — Jesus answered him, If I do not wash you, you have no share with me.

As already explained — see on verse 7 — Peter sees *the part,* not the whole. He is thinking only about what is happening just now, and even that he does not see in its true setting. Jesus, however, is constantly thinking about *the whole* work of humiliation, of which this feet-washing is only a part. It is necessary to keep this distinction in mind. Otherwise it will be impossible to explain the dialogue.

Peter, conscious of the incongruity of the present situation, but completely unaware of the incongruity of a disciple telling his Lord what to do and what not to do, shouts: "By no means shalt thou wash my feet ever!" Note the strong double negative οὐ μή. Had Jesus drawn a contrast between *now* and *hereafter?* Well, no matter how long a time might elapse before *hereafter* would arrive, *never, no, not in all eternity* (οὐ μή . . . εἰς τὸν αἰῶνα) would Peter allow Jesus to wash his disciple's feet! We must probably imagine that Peter, his feet already partly washed, suddenly drew them back in emphatic protest.

Jesus answered, "If I do not wash you, you have no share with me." The meaning is simple, yet very deep: "Peter, unless by means of my entire work of humiliation — of which this feet-washing is only a part — I cleanse you from your sins, you do not share with me in the fruits of my redemptive merits." Jesus, he alone, is the Son, the true Heir. To him all things were promised. He also earned them all by his work of humiliation. In principle he even now possesses them all (see on 13:1 and 3). But what he *has* he *shares* with his own, a thought which is brought out beautifully in Rom. 8:17. Believers are *joint-heirs with Christ*. But if Christ does not wash Peter, the latter will not *share with* the former.

9. Simon Peter said to him, Lord, not my feet only but also my hands and my head!

Peter had completely missed the meaning of the words of his Lord. Jesus certainly had not meant to stress *the physical*, as if in some mysterious manner physical cleansing made one a sharer in the bounties which Jesus provided, and as if the greater the area washed, so much the more numerous would be the blessings received. Proceeding upon his mistaken assumption, Peter blurts out, "Lord, not my feet only but also my hands and my head!"

Note how this disciple turns from one extreme to another. That was characteristic of Simon Peter. In the Gospels he is pictured as a man who again and again loses his balance. Now you see him walking courageously on the waters (Matt. 14:28); a little later you hear him utter the cry for help, "Lord, save me" (Matt. 14:30). At one moment he makes a glorious confession, "Thou art the Christ, the Son of the living God" (Matt. 16:16); hardly have the echoes of this wonderful declaration faded, when he begins to *rebuke* the very Christ whom he has just confessed (Matt. 16:22). Just a little while after the feet-washing — hence, during this selfsame night which is discussed here in John 13 — Simon definitely promises to lay down his life for Jesus (John 13:37; and cf. Matt. 26:33, 35). But a few hours later he is saying again and again, "I am not his disciple" (John 18:17, 25); and cf. Matt. 26:69-75. After Jesus has arisen victoriously, Simon Peter and John are running to the tomb, Simon being outdistanced by John. Once at the tomb Peter enters it before John does (20:4-6). And later on, at Antioch, he first throws aside all ideas of racial segregation and eats with the Gentiles. Nevertheless, soon afterward he withdraws completely from the converts of the pagan world.

We believe that in Peter's case grace gradually won the victory, as is clearly evident from his epistles. But what we have here in John 13 is the typical·Simon, the man who reminds one of a farmer's son who is very unsteady in carrying the bucket of milk. While he is walking, the milk splashes from the pail, now from this side, then from that. Such was Simon.

Peter's reply here in 13:9 recalls the Samaritan woman's answer recorded in 4:15. See Vol. I, p. 163.

10, 11. Jesus said to him, He who is bathed has no need of washing anything except his feet, but is clean altogether. And y o u are clean, but

232

not all of y o u are. — For he knew the one who was betraying him. It was for this reason that he said, Not all of y o u are clean.

Jesus, continuing to use words in their deepest and most comprehensive sense — see on verses 7 and 8 above — answers Simon's request (that not only his feet but also his hands and his head be washed) by saying, "He who is bathed — that is, he who has been cleansed by my blood (justified) — has no need of washing anything *except his feet* (on the basis of internal evidence — the entire context here — the words in italics must be regarded as genuine) — that is, such a person being cleaned altogether (all his sins having been forgiven) needs only *one* thing, namely sanctification, here especially (though not exclusively) that work of God within the heart whereby the believer attains constantly renewed and ever-growing humility and day by day willingness and eagerness to render service to others in gratitude for all the benefits received.

It is true, of course, that a very appropriate symbol is basic to this great saying of the Lord. In the sphere of everyday life in the Orient a person who had taken a bath before leaving for a supper did not need to take another upon arrival at the banqueting-hall. The washing of the feet was all that was necessary. But as in all other instances (see our explanations of chapters 3, 4, and 6), so also here, Jesus is not speaking about the physical but about the spiritual. He who in chapter 3 speaks about *spiritual* rebirth, in chapter 4 about *spiritual* water, and in chapter 6 about the *spiritual* nourishment which he as bread of life provides, is here in 13:10 speaking about *spiritual* cleansing. This follows also from verse 11, "And y o u are clean, but not all of y o u are." The interpreter who explains verse 10 as having reference to *physical* cleansing must be consistent when he arrives at the explanation of verse 11. Logic requires, that he then interpret the verses as follows: "Jesus said to him, He who has taken a physical bath has no need of washing anything except his feet, but is physically altogether clean. And y o u are physically clean, but not all of y o u are. *On the face of Judas I see some dirt.*" That shows how absurd a conclusion can be, even though it be ever so logical, *if the premise be false.*

"And y o u are clean," Jesus adds; that is, "Y o u are sharers in the redemption which my humiliation merits for y o u." In order to indicate for all time to come that he is not taken unawares by Judas but is in complete control of the situation, and in order to make the traitor solely responsible for his actions, Jesus appends this significant exceptive clause: "but not all of y o u are." Judas was not spiritually clean. And Jesus *knew* (ἤδει pluperfect of οἶδα, with sense of imperfect, *knew all the while*) the one who even now was in the process of betraying him. Yet, he did not name Judas. He did not even say in what respect this one man was not clean. The disciples are placed before a riddle. And for this there was a good reason. See on 13:22.

12-15. So when he had washed their feet, had taken his garments, and had resumed his place, he said to them, Do y o u know what I have done to y o u? Y o u call me Teacher and Lord, and y o u say (this) correctly, for (that is what) I am. If, therefore, *I* y o u r Lord and Teacher, have washed *y o u r* feet, *y o u* also ought to wash *each other's* feet, for I have given y o u an example, in order that just as *I* did to y o u so also *y o u* should do.

Peter's objection having been answered, Jesus finished washing his feet, and then the feet of the others until the entire task was done. Then the Lord redressed and resumed his place at the table.

In order to understand what follows it must be borne in mind that the feet-washing was a. *an essential element* in Christ's humiliation; b. *a symbol* of that humiliation (the water that washed away physical filth was a true symbol of Christ's suffering during his entire life on earth and especially on the cross, whereby he not only *atones for the guilt* of his people but also *merits for them the sanctifying work of the Holy Spirit*); and c. *a lesson* in humility; in other words, *an example.*

Ideas a. and b. are very closely related. With respect to them Jesus has already told Peter that he would understand *hereafter,* not now. Nevertheless, Jesus had prepared his mind — and the minds of the others — by saying to him, "If I do not wash you, you have no share with me."

But even though the disciples were able, at this moment, to catch but a glimpse of the deep meaning that was wrapped up in the feet-washing, *the moral* has instantaneous significance for them. How they needed *the lesson* (item c. above) which Jesus meant to teach them by means of this act! Bear in mind Luke 22:24!

So Jesus said to his disciples: "Do y o u know what I have done to y o u?" Do y o u grasp the positive, practical teaching which I have just now imparted to y o u? — Note that the Lord does not scold these men. He does not say, "Shame on y o u! Y o u should have washed each other's feet instead of waiting for me to do it." This rebuke is certainly *implied* in the exhortation, but the words of Jesus go much farther. He is never satisfied with being merely negative. It is as if he were saying, "The past was bad enough; we shall say nothing further about that; *for the future, copy my example.*" The *implied* rebuke, concealed in words of loving, positive exhortation, often does more good than the *expressed* reprimand. In this positive atmosphere Jesus continues:

"Y o u call me Teacher and Lord, and y o u say (this) correctly, for (that is what) I am."

Indeed, the disciples were right in addressing [133] Jesus as *Teacher* (ὁ

---

[133] Certain commentators object to the idea of regarding the terms "Teacher" and "Lord" as *vocatives.* As they see it, Jesus did not mean, "When y o u *address* me,

διδάσκαλος, probably to be regarded as a translation of the Aramaic *Rabbi;*
as 1:38 seems to indicate), for his teaching "with authority and not as the
scribes" was the greatest that was ever heard on earth. Also they were right
in addressing him as *Lord* (ὁ κύριος); and the deeper the meaning they
poured into this concept, the more right they were. He was, indeed, the
owner of all things (see on 13:1, 3); moreover, he was equal in essence and
authority with God, the Father. See Vol. I, p. 103, footnote 44, for the
gradual displacement of *Rabbi* by *Lord.* And see on 12:21.

When Jesus adds, "Y o u say (this) correctly, for (that is what) I am,"
he is making a statement that is entirely in line with his great declaration
in 10:30: "I and the Father, we are one." Those who claim that Jesus never
represented himself as the rightful object of worship are clearly wrong. See
also on 1:7, 8.

Now comes the application. It is an argument from the greater to the
lesser: "If, therefore, *I*, y o u r Lord and Teacher — the terms are reversed
now, for it is especially as *Lord* that Jesus can claim the right to obedience
— have washed y o u r feet (and the very form of the conditional sentence
indicates that this act is here rightly assumed to have *actually* occurred),
y o u also constantly (present tense) ought to wash *each other's feet.*" Surely,
if the Lord of glory is willing to be "girded around" with a towel, having
taken the form of a servant, actually washing and drying the feet of those
who are so very far below him, it ought to be easy for mere disciples to
render loving service to one another in the spirit of genuine humility!
Note the emphatic position of the pronouns in the original. We have tried
to preserve something of the flavor of the original by using italics.

Is Jesus instituting a new ordinance here, that of feet-washing? No, he is
not commanding the disciples to do *what* (ὅ) he has done; but he has given
them an *example* in order that they, of their own accord, may do *as* (καθώς)
he has done. Hence, significantly he adds: "For I have given y o u an
example (ὑπόδειγμα here only in John, but found also in Heb. 4:11; 8:5;
9:26; James 5:10; and II Peter 2:6), in order that just as *I* did to y o u so
also y o u should constantly do." Jesus has *shown* (cf. the verb δείκνυμι)
his humility *under* (ὑπό) their very eyes (hence, ὑπόδειγμα).

---

y o u call me 'Teacher' and 'Lord' " What he meant was, "When y o u *talk about*
me to others, y o u are in the habit of calling me *the* Teacher and *the* Lord."
These commentators base this view upon the fact that the Greek here uses the
definite article in connection with the terms *Teacher* and *Lord.* Their argument
is presented very forcefully by R. C. H. Lenski, *op. cit.,* pp. 901, 902. We do not
share this view. Even in Greek, apart from Aramaic influences, the use of the
articles with the vocative, is not unfamiliar. When, in addition, Aramaic influence
is present (see Vol. I, pp. 63, 64), the usage is not at all surprising. Study also the
following in the original: 20:28; Rev. 4:11; 6:10; 15:3; and compare Matt. 11:26;
Mark 5:41, 9:25; Luke 8:54; 12:32. See Gram. N.T., pp. 465, 466. The verb φωνέω
(φωνεῖτε) does not in any way conflict with our interpretation. Cf. its use in 1:49;
4:16; Acts 16: 28.

But although no sacrament has been instituted to be literally copied [134] this does not remove the fact that under certain conditions those who may wish to show their hospitality in this manner are doing the proper thing (cf. I Tim. 5:10). It should, however, be stressed that what Jesus had in mind was not an *outward rite* but an *inner attitude,* that of humility and eagerness to serve.

16. Most solemnly do I assure y o u, the servant is not greater than his lord, neither is he who is sent greater than he who sent him.

For the words of solemn introduction see on 1:51. In all probability Jesus added these words in order to prevent anyone from saying: "It is below my dignity to wash the feet of another believer." If it was not below the dignity of the Lord, it surely should not be considered below the dignity of the "servant." This remains true even then when the servant is *sent* or divinely *commissioned* to function *in a high office* or to carry out an important task in the Church. If humility is the proper attitude for the Lord and Sender, how unremittingly should not the servant and commissioned individual exercise himself in this grace and grow in it. See also 15:20; Matt. 10:24; Luke 6:40; 22:27.

17. If y o u know these things, blessed are y o u if y o u do them.

See what has been said about this verse above, in footnote 129. The words of Jesus are very clear. Faith without works is dead. See also Matt. 7:17, 24-27; 11:30; I Cor. 4:20; and James 1:22-27; 2:14-26. It must not escape us that we have here not a commandment but a very loving and tender declaration. It has been called a *promise,* but it is even more than that. It is the statement of a *fact: the practice of humility imparts blessedness.* When Jesus says, "If y o u know these things," etc., he means, according to the context, "If y o u know that a. he who is Lord and Teacher is willing to minister to the needs of those who are his subjects and pupils, even though in doing so he has to stoop very low; and if y o u know that b. *all the more,* those who were thus benefited should be willing to serve one another in humility of spirit; if y o u know these things, *blessed* are y o u if y o u do them."

---

[134] It has been thus understood, nevertheless, by many sincere believers throughout the history of the Church. Foot-washing was practised on Maundy Thursday by the Church of Augustine's day. It was recommended by Bernard of Clairvaux in one of his sermons. The practice, moreover, was continued by the pope at Rome and by emperors (of Austria, of Russia) and kings (of Spain, Portugal, Bavaria). For a while it was practised by the Church of England and by the Moravians. It has been continued to this very day by certain Baptist and Adventist bodies. It was roundly condemned by Luther and by his followers as "an abominable papal corruption." See P. Tschackert, "Foot-washing" in *The New Schaff-Herzog Encyclopedia of Religious Knowledge,* reprint, Grand Rapids, Mich., 1950, Vol. IV, pp. 339, 340.

The term *blessed* (μακάριοι) does not necessarily refer to those who are considered happy by others; nor even primarily to those who consider themselves happy, but to those who *are* indeed the objects of God's favor, whether or not they are considered such by other men or even by themselves. The *blessed* ones may be poor and may even be mourning (cf. Matt. 5:1-12, The Beatitudes). The blessedness here spoken of is a matter not (at least, not primarily) of feeling, but of inner spiritual condition or state. The Christian who practises humility possesses this felicity whether he is at all times conscious of it or not. *Before God,* in *his* eyes, he is blessed. The Aramaic word which Jesus probably employed both here in 13:17 (see also 20:29) and in The Beatitudes (also in several other New Testament passages) resembles the Hebrew word found in many passages of the Psalms (1:1; 2:12; 31:1; 32:2; 33:12; 34:8; 40:4; 41:4; etc.). It means superlatively blessed, most blessed. It is true, of course, that the smile of God which is upon such a person who is *constantly* doing these things (note present continuative tense), sothat humility is of the very essence of his character, will sooner or later be reflected in his heart, sothat he will possess the peace of God which passes all understanding.

18. **Not of y o u all am I speaking. I know the ones I have chosen; but (this happened) in order that the scripture may be fulfilled:**
>   He who eats my bread
>   Has lifted his heel against me.

In order to show the probable connection between verses 17 and 18 and to state more fully the thought of this condensed saying, we paraphrase verses 17 and 18 as follows:

"If y o u know these things, blessed are y o u if y o u do them. But not of y o u all am I speaking in holding out this prospect of blessedness. I know the ones I have chosen for myself to be my apostles. There is one who, though chosen, is not blessed. But as to the fact that I also chose him, this happened in order that the scripture may be fulfilled:
>   'He who eats my bread
>   Has lifted up his heel against me.' "

In our *translation* we have placed the words "this happened" between parenthesis because we inserted them. We accept an elipsis at this point. There are certain commentators who do not grant this ellipsis and whose translation and consequent interpretation is quite different. See the footnote in which we state the reasons for not being able to accept their view.[135]

---

135 We refer to such interpreters as Zahn and Lenski (see the latter's argumentation on p. 908 of his *Interpretation of St. John's Gospel*). These men cannot see how a reference to "him" (Judas) can be drawn from τίνας. We answer: a. This "him" (in our paraphrase as given above: "As to the fact that I also chose *him*") is clearly

"Not of y o u all am I speaking." Judas should have pondered this statement. He should have taken to heart the clear implication. The saying serves to fix the responsibility for his act entirely on himself. It also serves to fortify the faith of the other disciples. When, after a little while, they receive the surprise of their lives with respect to Judas, they will begin to realize that Jesus had known it all along, and that what was happening was not a frustration but a fulfilment of the divine plan.

"I know *the ones* (τίνας) I have chosen" (or: I have chosen *for myself*, if the middle voice retains its distinctive flavor). Jesus knows them now. He knew them from the very beginning (see on 1:42; 1:47; 2:24, 25). He knew *what kind* (probably implied in τίνας) of men they were. That was true also with respect to Judas. Yet, when from among many disciples (in a general sense) Jesus had chosen the Twelve (Luke 6:13), he had also chosen Judas (not unto salvation but) to be one of the apostles. Thoroughly aware of what he was doing, he had included in his selection the man who was going to betray him. Explaining this, he continues: "But (this happened) in order that the scripture may be fulfilled, 'He who eats my bread has lifted his heel against me.' " For this use of ἵνα see not only footnote 130 but also on 12:38.

---

implied in the sentence: "Not of y o u all am I speaking." Besides, whether or not one is willing to.admit an ellipsis, one involuntarily fills out the statement as it stands. Something *has to be* supplied. For if this is not done, there is no thought-sequence: Jesus of a sudden turns from the plural to the singular: "I know *the ones* . . . but in order that the scripture may be fulfilled: *he*," etc.

Our objections to the theory of Zahn and Lenski, who, denying that there is here an ellipsis, consider "in order that the scripture may be fulfilled" to be a kind of parenthesis, and who believe that *but* should be construed with "he who eats my bread," are as follows:

1. The conjunction *but* (ἀλλά) is most naturally joined with the words that stand closest to it.

2. In the Fourth Gospel an ellipsis occurs frequently in connection with *but:*

a. 1:8: "He was not the light, *but* . . . in order that he might testify concerning the light." Something on the order of "he came" will have to be inserted between *but* and *in order that.*

b. 9:3: "Neither did this man sin nor his parents, but . . . in order that the works of God should be displayed in him." Insert: "this happened."

c. 15:25: "But . . . in order that the word may be fulfilled that is written in their law." Insert "this happened."

Very similar to 15:25 is the passage which we are discussing (13:18); hence:

d. 13:18: "But . . . in order that the scripture may be fulfilled." Insert "this happened."

3. The translation and interpretation as given by Zahn and Lenski fails to place the emphasis upon the predestination-idea. It is exactly *that* thought which John here (as so often; see Vol. I, p. 46) wishes to stress. In that respect the present passage is entirely in line with 12:38-40. Judas, in a manner such that it leaves him, and him alone, completely responsible for his deed, must fulfil prophecy; he must carry out God's plan with respect to the Christ and himself.

4. The translation and interpretation which we are criticizing fails to figure sufficiently with the concise and abbreviated character of conversational style. See Vol. I, p. 206.

The scripture-passage which was in the process of attaining its final fulfilment was Ps. 41:9, which is quoted here according to the Hebrew. It stresses the reprehensible character of the sin of betraying one's benefactor. *Eating* another person's bread (τρώγων, originally *gnawing, chewing,* but here the same as ἐσθίων, as is clear from the LXX version of Ps. 41:9, and from a comparison of Matt. 24:38 and Luke 17:27), and then suddenly *kicking* him (lifting the heel against him, like a horse which without warning attacks its owner, kicking him violently), is the sin here described and condemned.

Thus David had been betrayed by Ahithophel. Read II Sam. 15:12; 16:23. In the quoted passage (Ps. 41:9) the Psalmist refers to Ahithophel or to a person similar to him. See also Ps. 55:12-14. It is entirely true that the Oriental considers an attack upon a person by whom one has been entertained at dinner to be well-nigh unthinkable. But — especially in the light of Ps. 55:12-14 — an action such as that of Ahithophel merits strong disapproval and revulsion regardless of any regional etiquette. And if this be true with respect to Ahithophel, it is *certainly* true with respect to Judas, who kept up appearances of friendship to the very last! Not one of the disciples suspected Judas. He was two-faced. A double-crosser deserves to be despised.

19. From now on I am telling (this) to y o u before (it) takes place, in order that when it does take place y o u may continue to believe that I am (he).

Here Jesus reveals his very heart. He shows what a kind Savior he is. He displays his affectionate and personal concern for the spiritual welfare of his own, and he does this in a marvelous manner. He knows that the treachery of Judas will have a tendency to upset the disciples and to undermine their faith. They might even begin to think of their Master as having become the victim of the plotting of that very shrewd fellow, Judas. This will happen unless the Lord is able to convince them that whatever befalls him, far from taking him by surprise, was included in God's eternal and all-comprehensive plan. And in order that *when* (ὅταν, *whenever,* the exact moment is not stipulated) it happens they may be strengthened in this comforting conviction, he mentions and describes the deed *in advance.* Not only this, but he even tells them in so many words that this is the reason why he is making the prediction at this time and *from this point on* (ἀπ' ἄρτι, the prediction becomes more definite in 13:21, 26). He is dealing with his disciples like a mother deals with her child, lovingly explaining why she is following a certain course.

When Judas by and by betrays the Master with a kiss, and the latter has seemingly suffered a defeat, when the Messiah experiences the bitter agonies of Gethsemane, Gabbatha, and Golgotha, the disciples must *continue to be-*

lieve (πιστεύητε).[136] See Vol. I, pp. 33, 34; also on 20:30, 31. They must continue to believe that "I am (he)," that is, that Jesus is whatever he claimed to be. See on 8:24.

20. I most solemnly assure y o u — see on 1:51 — , **he who receives anyone whom I send receives me; and he who receives me receives him who sent me.**

When the prediction of verse 18 begins to be fulfilled, Jesus remains the Messiah, the Son of God, clothed with authority to send out his ambassadors. Hence, when the disciples see their Lord delivered into the hands of his enemies, let them not despair. Let them not think, "Now it is all over, not only with him but also with us, his followers." On the contrary, everything continues just as it was. Nay rather, the very facts of the humiliation confirm *his* authority and the validity of *their* commission. An ambassador of "Christ Betrayed, Condemned, and Crucified," is still a true ambassador; in fact, he is *the only* true ambassador.

It follows, of course, that "he who receives anyone whom I send [137] receives me; and he who receives me receives him who sent me." Christ and his Sender are *one* (10:30). It is impossible to accept the one and reject the other. The two are inseparable. And when the plan of God is carried out, and Judas betrays the Lord, delivering him into the hands of the enemy, the disciples must remain conscious of the dignity of their calling. They will remain ambassadors for Christ. And when they say to anyone, "We beseech you, on behalf of Christ, be reconciled to God," God himself through their preaching will be making his appeal to the sinner. If anyone, whether Jew or Greek, rejects such an appeal, he will be rejecting Christ; and if anyone rejects the Christ, he will be rejecting his Sender, God. The statement applies to all time, and to every *true* ambassador for Christ (i.e., to every ambassador who truly represents *him* and truly pro-

---

[136] In the explanation we are proceeding upon the assumption that N.N. is right in the text. The textual apparatus indicates, however, that the variant πιστεύσητε also has strong support. See also on 14:29. The fulfilment of the predictions must indicate to the disciples that Jesus is the very One in whom these *predictions* were destined to be fulfilled.

[137] This is *basically* a conditional sentence. It is as if Jesus had started out to say, "If I send anyone (protasis), the one who receives him receives me, and the one who receives me receives him who sent me (apodosis)." This would be IIIA2; see Vol. I, pp. 42, 43. Yet, in actual form and meaning the statement has departed from the original conditional sentence: Jesus certainly does not mean to say that he *may* send someone, or even that he *will probably* send someone. The idea of indefiniteness lies not in the predicted sending activity of the Lord, but in the *object* of this divine, commissioning activity. The thought is that *no matter who it is* that is sent by Jesus, he must be accepted; and this for the simple reason that he was thus divinely commissioned. Hence, ἄν may be viewed as a particle which purposely adds to the indefiniteness of the pronoun τίνα, thus stressing the thought, "Whom*soever* I send, let him be welcomed!" See also H. E. Dana and J. R. Mantey, *A Manual of the Greek New Testament,* New York, 1950, pp. 259, 260.

claims *his* Word). Hence, it is even more general in its application than the similar one in Matt. 10:40.

---

21 When he had said these things, Jesus was troubled in the spirit, and he testified and said, "Most solemnly do I say to y o u ,[138] one of y o u will betray me." 22 The disciples kept looking at each other, being at a loss (to know) of whom he spoke. 23 There was reclining next to the bosom of Jesus one of his disciples, one whom Jesus (constantly) loved. 24 So Simon Peter nodded to this one and said to him, "Say who it is of whom he speaks." 25 Accordingly, having leaned back on the breast of Jesus, he said to him, "Lord, who is it?" 26 So Jesus answered, "He it is to whom I shall give the morsel after I have dipped it." Having dipped the morsel, he took it and gave it to Judas, the son of Simon Iscariot.
27 Then, after the morsel, Satan entered into him. So Jesus said to him, "What you are doing, do more quickly." 28 Now no one of those reclining knew why he had said this to him. 29 For some were thinking, since Judas had the money-box, that Jesus was telling him, "Buy what we need for the feast," or (that he had said it) in order that Judas might give something to the poor. 30 So, having taken the morsel, he went out immediately; and it was night.

13:21-30

13:21. When he had said these things, Jesus was troubled in the spirit, and he testified and said, Most solemnly do I say to y o u, one of y o u will betray me."

The exact order in which the happenings in the Upper Room followed one another has not been revealed in such a clear and definite manner that all interpreters are agreed. As we see it, the sequence as given by A. T. Robertson (*A Harmony of the Gospels,* New York, 1922, pp. 190-196) is as good as any that has been proposed and better than some. Now if this be correct, the order of events was as follows:

1. Jesus washes the feet of his disciples and explains to them that he has given them an example to be followed (13:1-20).

2. He startles the disciples by telling them that one of their own number is going to betray him. Judas leaves (13:21-30).

3. He issues his "new commandment" and predicts Peter's denial (13: 31-28).

4. He institutes the Lord's Supper (Matt. 26:26-29; Mark 14:22-25; Luke 22:17-20; I Cor. 11:23-26). This important event, having been fully covered by the Synoptists and by Paul, John does not repeat.

5. He tenderly instructs his disciples and commits them to the Father's care (Farewell Discourse and Highpriestly Prayer, chapters 14-17 of John's Gospel).

---

[138] On ὅτι see Vol. I, pp. 54 and 61.

Note that, with the exception of item 4 which John omits, this is the order in which *the man who himself was there* relates the events. But was not Matthew also present? Indeed, but there is this difference between John's account and that of the Synoptists (including Matthew) that, on the whole, John's notes of time are here (and often; see Vol. I, p. 36, item (2)) more numerous and more definite than are theirs. While the Synoptists (especially Luke) do not seem to have any intention of giving us a strictly chronological account, John creates the impression that he is giving us such an account, as appears from the following notes of time:

a. 13:2 *"Now supper arriving . . ."* The account of the feet-washing follows (see 13:1-20).

b. 13:21 *"When he had said these things,* Jesus was troubled in the spirit, and he testified and said . . ."* There follows the announcement with respect to Judas' betrayal (13:21-30).

c. 13:30 *"So, having taken the morsel, he went out immediately; and it was night.*

d. 13:31: *"So when he (Judas) had gone out,* Jesus said . . ."* There follows the new commandment and the prediction concerning Peter's denial (13:31-38).

We turn now to 2, the announcement regarding (and dismissal of) the traitor. It took place "while they were engaged in eating" (Matt. 26:21; Mark 14:18). This probably places it at point f. in the order of the Passover Supper as described in Vol. I, p. 121.

Jesus had said certain things which reflected and increased his grief. He *was troubled.* For the meaning of this verb see on 11:33, 34; 14:1. He had said, "And y o u are clean, but not all of y o u are" (13:10); and "He who eats my bread has lifted his heel against me" (13:18). By saying, "Not all of y o u are clean," he had even given a hint that the wicked conspirator whom he had in mind was one of the twelve. But they had probably failed to catch this hint.

Jesus knows that the time has now arrived to speak more plainly about this painful subject. Hence, it does not surprise us to read, "When he had said *these things* (referring, perhaps, to all that he had said in verses 6-20), he was troubled *in the spirit.*" For *spirit* the original has πνεῦμα. This is the higher element in man viewed in its relation to God. It is the same immaterial substance as that which in the LXX and in the New Testament is sometimes designated the *soul* (ψυχή, Mark 12:30; Acts 14:2; Phil. 1:27, the seat of the will, desires, and affections); but contemplated from a different point of view. Sometimes, however, the terms are used interchangeably (cf. Luke 1:46, 47; Acts 7:59 with Acts 15:26).[139] Jesus was troubled

---

[139] In the Fourth Gospel the term πνεῦμα has the following meanings: a. wind (3:8a); b. the human spirit (4:23, 24b; 6:63a; 6:63b; 11:33; 13:21; 19:30); c. an

because of what he had just said, and *in view of* what he was about to say. "And he testified," that is, in an impressive manner he made an open declaration. It could even mean: he bore witness of that which with the prophetic eye of his soul he had already seen. For the verb *to testify* see on 1:51. He testified and said, "Most solemnly do I say to y o u (see on 1:51), one of y o u will betray me."

One of *y o u!* It came as a bolt from the blue. It was a stunning blow. What! Did the Lord actually mean to say that one of their own number was going to *hand him over* (παραδώσει) to the authorities, for them to deal with as they pleased?

22. The disciples kept looking at each other, being at a loss (to know) of whom he spoke.

In order to see the entire picture one should also read the Synoptics on this (Matt. 26:21-25; Mark 14:18-21; Luke 22:21-23). They inform us that when Jesus said, "One of y o u will betray me," he added, "one who eats with me" (Mark 14:18; Luke 22:21; cf. on John 13:18). They show that in this connection Jesus characterized the act of the betrayer as being: a. a deed which did not take him by surprise, but had been fully determined in the eternal counsel of God; and b. one for which the doer was, nevertheless, fully responsible (see Luke 22:22; cf. Matt. 26:24; Mark 14:21).

The vivid description of the reaction among the disciples shows that the author of the Fourth Gospel was one of the company. He never forgot that dramatic moment. As he was writing, it was as if the soul-terrifying words of Jesus regarding the betrayer were still resounding through the Upper Room. That look of overwhelming consternation, serious misgiving, and painful surprise, on the face of John's fellow-disciples as he had seen them that night, flashed once more upon the screen of his memory. Again he saw it all, just as if it had taken place (not a half century or more but only) a few minutes ago. And as he had seen *them,* so *they* had seen *him!* He writes:

"The disciples — including himself, of course — *kept looking* (see Vol. I, p. 85, footnotes 33) at each other" in startled dismay. They *were at a loss* to know (saw *no way* of knowing; note ἀπορούμενοι, without a way, without resource) of whom he spoke. They were thoroughly *perplexed.*

Christ's shocking announcement evoked three responses; and these responses came in the form of questions, as follows:

1. A question of *wholesome self-distrust,* "Surely not I, Lord?" That was

incorporeal being (4:24); and d. the Holy Spirit (1:32; 1:33a; 1:33b; 3:5, 6, 8b, 34; 6:63; 7:39a; 7:39b; 14:17, 26; 15:26; 16:13; and 20:22). In the case of some of the passages listed the words that are used in association with the noun change the meaning slightly (e.g., 4:23, 24b; 6:63a; 6:63b). Hence, in each case we refer to the exegesis of the passage in which the term occurs. — In the Gospel of John ψυχή is the *person* or *self.* See on 10:11.

the reaction on the part of all the disciples with the exception of Judas (Matt. 26:22).

2. A question of *loathsome hypocrisy*, "Surely not I, Rabbi?" That, probably after considerable hesitation, was Judas' response (Matt. 26:25).

3. A question of *childlike confidence*, "Lord, who is it?" And that, as we shall see, was the way in which John, prompted by Peter, expressed himself.

When the disciples asked, "Surely not I, Lord?" Jesus did not immediately allay their fear or cure their self-distrust. Nor did he at once satisfy their suddenly-aroused curiosity. He gave a very general answer: "He that dipped his hand with me in the dish, the same man will betray me" (Matt. 26:23). But Judas surely was not the only man who was dipping his hand with Jesus in the dish. Hence, this answer did not identify the betrayer. What it did accomplish was the following:

a. It emphasized the low-down character of the betrayer's deed, and in so doing it served as a warning. Think of it: dipping his hand with the Master in the same dish, and then betraying him! Let Judas ponder what he is doing. "I know your designs, Judas," the Master seems to be saying. The revelation of this detailed knowledge was intended as an earnest warning. Yes, in God's incomprehensible and all-comprehensive decree there is room even for solemn admonitions given to those who ultimately are lost. You ask, "How is that possible?" I answer: "I do not know, but the fact remains, nevertheless." If one does not want to accept the idea of warnings even for reprobates, he misses something of the meaning of this account. The serious character of the implied admonition increases the guilt of Judas. It also affords a better and truer insight into the soul of Jesus. Before one is ready to deny the possibility of earnest warnings even for the reprobate, he should study Gen. 4:6, 7; Is. 5:1-7; Ezek. 3:18-21; 18:30-32; 33:11; Prov. 29:1; Luke 13:6-9; 13:34, 35; Acts 20:31. Many similar passages could be added.

b. It rivets the attention upon the depth of Christ's suffering. In a treacherous and humiliating manner he, the Lord of glory, is being handed over to his enemies. It is very important that we see this. Our reflection on the account of Christ's Passion should not become lost in all kinds of details regarding Judas and Peter and Annas and Pilate. It is, after all, the story of *his* suffering. It centers in *him,* and we must never forget to ask how all these things affected *him!*

c. It showed, once again, that Jesus was in full control of the situation. He was not taken by surprise. He knew exactly what was happening and what was going to happen, the very details. See on 13:19.

d. It furnished an opportunity to the disciples *to examine themselves.* This point is often passed by. It is, nevertheless, very important. By giving the answer that is recorded in Matt. 26:23 (see above) Jesus did not identify the betrayer, and exactly by not identifying him the Lord was actually doing all a favor. He knew that self-examination would be the very best exercise for men such as these (remember Luke 22:24!). Let each disciple be caught with a certain dread of himself. Let him be filled with grave misgivings, with wholesome self-distrust. These men need time for self-examination. And so, for a few moments at least, the work of introspection has its free course. Did anyone pray the prayer of Ps. 139:23, 24?

> "Search me, O God, and know my heart;
> Try me, and know my thoughts;
> And see if there be any wicked way in me.
> And lead me in the way everlasting."

23, 24. For one of them (Peter, of course) the suspense soon became unbearable. John tells what happened, for he himself was involved in the following incident: **There was reclining in the bosom of Jesus one of his disciples, one whom Jesus (constantly) loved. So Simon Peter nodded to this one and said to him, Say, who it is of whom he speaks.**

The occupants of the Upper Room were reclining on couches, divans, or mattresses around a low table. On entering the room one would be able to see these divans arranged in inverted U-shaped fashion, with the guests reclining at the opposite end of the table and on the two sides. Each man, facing the table, would be lying slantwise, with his feet extended toward the floor. He would be stretched out on his left side and leaning on his left arm, in order to keep the right arm and hand free to handle the food. Naturally, the person on the right would have his back turned to his neighbor, and his head would be resting in front of (*or upon*) his neighbor's breast, i.e., "in" his *bosom:* that part (or *fold*) of the garment which covers the breast.

Thus, there was reclining in the bosom of Jesus — hence, to his right — one of his disciples, *the one whom Jesus (constantly) loved.* For a discussion of the possible distinction in meaning between two different verbs meaning *to love* see on 21:15-17.

Who was this *disciple whom Jesus loved?* See 13:23; 19:26; 20:2 (ἐφίλει); 21:7, 20. The attempts to identify him have been numerous.[140] For the reasons stated in Vol. I, pp. 18-21 we adhere to the traditional view that this beloved disciple was John, the author of the Fourth Gospel. Now it is clear that Jesus loved *all* his true disciples (13:1; 14:21; 15:9; 17:9, 12). Nevertheless, the name "the disciple whom Jesus loved" had been given to this *one* disciple, to him alone. Is it not possible that the others had be-

---

[140] Two attempts of recent date are that by Floyd V. Filson, "Who Was the Beloved Disciple?" *JBL* 68 (June, 1949), 83-88; and that by Eric L. Titus, "The Identity of the Beloved Disciple," *JBL* 69 (December, 1950), 323-328. Filson identifies him with Lazarus. Titus thinks that a real possibility has been overlooked in the person of Matthias.

stowed this honorable title upon him when they noticed the intimate character of the fellowship between him and the Master? If this be correct, John is simply making use of the name which others had given him. And is it not possible that this unique relationship between Jesus and John was rooted in the fact that, due to God's sovereign distribution of endowments and talents, *John understood Jesus better* than did any of the rest? Moreover, when the evangelist styles himself "the disciple whom Jesus loved," he is not boasting of his own love for the Master; on the contrary, he is glorying in the Master's love for him. Such glorying is not sinful.

"Simon Peter nodded to this one." Attempts have been made to indicate the places occupied respectively by Jesus, John, Peter, and Judas.[141] But, aside from the fact that John was lying *in* ("next to," "close to," "in front of") the bosom of Jesus, we know very little. The information given us in this account is insufficient to lead to any precise results, as is evident from the conflict in the opinions of the interpreters. One well-known expositor places Peter next to — and to the right of — John (why, then, would Peter have to signal to John?); another views him as stretched out behind — that is, to the left of — Jesus (would not this have made conversation between John and Peter rather awkward, with Jesus between them?); and several, probably following Edersheim, place Peter directly across the table from John (which is better, but is not the only possibility). Those who adopt the latter view often add that Simon, thoroughly ashamed of himself because of the lesson which Jesus had taught him in the feet-washing, had rushed off to take the lowest place. But all this is conjecture.

Peter signaled to John. He gave the latter credit for knowing more than he actually knew. Simon was convinced that John knew whom Jesus had in mind when he said, "One of y o u will betray me." Why was John keeping this information to himself? So, having gained his attention, Peter demands of him, *"Say* who it is of whom he speaks." [142]

25. Accordingly, having leaned back on the breast of Jesus, he said to him, Lord, who is it? This is the question of quiet, child-like confidence. See above on 13:22. John addresses Jesus as his divine Lord. See on 1:38 and 12:21. It was very easy for John, who was lying so close to the breast of Jesus, to tilt his head back a little so as to be looking straight into the

---

[141] See, for example, the wood-cut in A. Edersheim, *The Life and Times of Jesus, the Messiah,* New York, 1898, Vol. II, p. 494.

[142] The rendering of the A.V., "Simon Peter therefore beckoned to him, that he should ask who it should be of whom he spake," rests upon a definitely weaker reading. Peter did not tell John to ask Jesus who it was. On the contrary, he proceeded upon the assumption that John, lying so close to Jesus and being on such intimate terms with him, already knew. "Let him then *say* what he knows." It is not necessary to insert the pronoun *me* or *us* ("Tell *me* — or tell *us* — who it is").

eyes of the Master! With adorable frankness and simplicity, entirely convinced that Jesus will not disappoint him, John asks, "Lord, who is it?"

26. So Jesus answered, He it is to whom I shall give the morsel after I have dipped it. Having dipped the morsel, he took it and gave it to Judas, the son of Simon Iscariot.

It would seem that even before John had asked his question, Jesus had broken off a piece of unleavened bread from one of the flat cakes lying on the table. Holding it in his hand, he whispers to his beloved disciple that the traitor is that man to whom he is going to give this morsel after having dipped it. So having dipped it into a vessel filled with bitter herbs, vinegar, and salt, or into one which contained a sauce made of mashed fruit (probably dates, figs, and raisins, representing the fruits of the land), water, and vinegar — the two (bitter herbs and mashed fruit) may even now have been combined in one bowl, as was the practice in later years —, he took it out again and gave it to Judas, the son of Simon Iscariot (see on 6:71).

Now John knew that Judas was the traitor. We may, perhaps, assume that he quickly conveyed this intelligence to Peter (by sign-language?), but this is not in the record.

But why did Jesus use this method to answer John's question? Why did he not simply whisper back, "It is Judas"? It was in order to impress upon the latter the enormity of his crime, that it might serve as an additional warning. See on 13:22. Judas was ready to betray the One out of whose very hand he had been fed! [143]

27. Then, after the morsel, Satan entered into him. The devil had put *an evil suggestion* into the heart of Judas (see on 13:2). Judas had acted upon that suggestion. Now the devil — here called Satan, i.e., the adversary — puts *himself* into Judas' heart. That is his usual method of procedure with those who do not resist him. Satan takes full possession of the betrayer's soul. (How the evangelist discovered this has not been revealed.) Judas is now a completely hardened individual. The warnings of Jesus had not been heeded. Now they will no longer be issued. Jesus is through with Judas.

So Jesus said to him, What you are doing, do more quickly (or: "What you are doing, do it *faster*"). The same word which we have translated *more quickly* or *faster* (τάχιον) occurs also in 20:4, "The other disciple ran ahead, *faster* than Peter."

Thus tersely Jesus dismissed Judas, and at the same time revealed that

---

[143] Handing Judas the morsel was not an act of *friendship*, as is sometimes claimed with an appeal to Ruth 2:14. In the light of *the context* (13:18 and 26a) — and that, after all, is important! — what Jesus does when he hands the morsel to Judas must be viewed as a. an answer to John's question, and b. a warning for Judas.

he, as Lord of all, was complete Master of the situation. All the details of his Passion, including the time-schedule, were in *his own* hands, not in the hands of the traitor. In the plan of God it had been decided that the Son of God would make himself an offering for sin by his death on the cross, *and that this would happen on Friday, the fifteenth of Nisan.* That was not the moment which had been selected by the Sanhedrin or by Judas. Hence, Judas must work *faster*. And Judas *does* work faster, probably because he now knew (Matt. 26:25) that he had been "discovered." He was probably afraid lest the whole plot would fail if he did not act quickly.

28, 29. Now no one of those reclining knew why he had said this to him. For some were thinking, since Judas had the money-box, that Jesus was telling him, Buy what we need for the feast, or (that he had said it) in order that Judas might give something to the poor.

By this time three or four people at the table knew the identity of the traitor: Jesus, who had known it all along, Judas (of course), John, and probably Peter. It is certainly not necessary to suppose that the conversation between Jesus and John, recorded in 13:25, 26, had been heard by all. We know that the mouth of Jesus was very close to the ear of John, and vice versa. Why then should these two have spoken to each other in anything but a low voice? However, the words, "What you are doing, do more quickly," were heard *by all*. It is easy to understand that to the *other* disciples (all except Judas, John, and probably Peter) these words were a riddle, but why should they have been unintelligible to John and Peter? How is it that the evangelist says that *no one* knew why Jesus had issued his terse command? The answer is probably to be sought in this general direction: when one is deeply shocked by a piece of thoroughly unexpected news, it takes time for the mind to adjust itself to the new situation. Probably neither John nor Peter, nor any of the others, had ever thought ill of Judas. Hence, they could not at the spur of the moment, "put two and two together." They were not immediately able to connect the words of dismissal (13:27b) with the symbolic action of identification (13:26b).

Afterward, when, looking back upon this never-to-be-forgotten scene, the disciples exchanged notes, the evangelist discovered that on that memorable evening *some* of them, revolving in their minds the riddle-like saying of Jesus to Judas, "What you are doing, do more quickly," had arrived at conclusions as to what these words might mean. They had been of the opinion that since Judas was in charge of *the money-box* (see on 12:6), he was being directed to buy whatever was necessary for the seven-day festival (see on 13:1); or that the treasurer had received the veiled instruction *in order that* [144] he might give something to the poor. This incidentally indicates

---

[144] After *why* ("No one knew *why* he had said this"), ἵνα to express purpose ("in order that") seems natural. The idea seems to be that some thought that by say-

that the disciples considered it to be *natural* for Jesus to promote Christian charity and benevolence! — Against the idea that this was the night of the Passover Supper the objection has been advanced, "How could Judas be expected to purchase anything *that night?*" Now the inference drawn by the disciples indicates at least that not *everything* in Jerusalem was closed *every* night. In our large cities certain food-stores are open all night. And if things could be purchased during *other* nights, why not during Passover-night? It is hard to see why in Jerusalem during that night provisions would be *absolutely unobtainable anywhere.* It must be borne in mind that exactly *then* there was much activity all over the city. The pilgrims lodging outside of Jerusalem were returning to their quarters after the Passover Supper. The great temple-doors were opened at midnight to begin early preparations for the offering of the Chagigah (festive sacrifice). And *the poor* naturally were in evidence near the temple and wherever people gathered in groups. The burden of proof certainly rests on those who seek to establish that on such a night nothing whatever could be purchased, either on the temple-precincts or anywhere else in the city. See A. Edersheim, *op. cit.,* pp. 508, 568; G. Dalman, *op. cit.,* p. 95.

30. Judas appears throughout as *a pretender*. He cannot be trusted. When, at the close of the Galilean Ministry, "many of the disciples drew back and were no longer walking with him," (6:66) Judas, by remaining with Jesus, *pretended* to be a true disciple (see on 6:70, 71). When Mary of Bethany anointed Jesus, Judas *pretended* to be concerned about the poor (see on 12:4-6). When, during this very night of the Passover Supper, the Master's startling announcement, "One of y o u will betray me," had elicited the quick response from many lips, "Surely not I, Lord?" Judas, too, had chimed in with, "Surely not I, Rabbi?" This, too, was merely *pretense*. And now, a few moments later, when Jesus reaches out toward Judas, and hands him the morsel, the latter brazenly takes it, as if he had a right to accept food out of the hand of One on whose destruction he was bent. If ever there was a man with a seared conscience, it was Judas!

Judas was, *of course* (see on 13:27), very glad to comply with Christ's request to do more quickly what he was doing. **So, having taken the morsel, he went out immediately and it was night.** He went out *imme-*

---

ing, "What you are doing, do more quickly," Jesus *meant,* "Hurry to purchase provisions for the festival," or that he had spoken these words *in order to* rush aid to the poor. According to certain interpreters, on the contrary, the meaning is on this order: "Some were thinking that Jesus *had actually said* 'Buy what we need for the feast,' or that he had expressly told Judas *to* (ἵνα) give something to the poor." In that case ἵνα would be sub-final. But the objection to this interpretation is that verse 28 definitely implies that the remark of Jesus *had been clearly heard by all.* All knew *what* Jesus had said to Judas. No one knew *why* he had said it. Hence, we give ἵνα its full final force here.

diately to confer with the authorities as to the place and the time of the arrest. It is *now or never!* The plot had been "discovered." Hence, lest it be foiled, the rulers must act at once! . . . It was night when Judas left that room, night outside; night also inside the heart of Judas!

---

31 So when he had gone out, Jesus said, "Now the Son of man has been glorified, and God has been glorified in him. 32 If God has been glorified in him, God will also glorify him in himself, yes, immediately will he glorify him.[145] 33 Little children; yet a little while am I with y o u. Y o u will seek me, and as I told the Jews so I tell y o u now, 'Where I am going y o u cannot come.' 34 A new precept I give y o u, that[146] y o u keep on loving one another; just as I loved y o u, that y o u also keep on loving one another. 35 By this everybody will recognize that y o u are my disciples, if y o u keep on having love for one another."[147]

36 Simon Peter said to him, "Lord, where art thou going?" Jesus answered, "Where I am going you cannot follow me now, but you will follow me afterward." 37 Peter said to him, "Lord, why cannot I follow thee right now? My life for thee I will lay down." 38 Jesus answered, "Your life for me you will lay down? I most solemnly assure you, the rooster will certainly not crow until you have denied me three times."

13:31-38

13:31. So when he had gone out, Jesus said, Now the Son of man has been glorified, and God has been glorified in him.

With the dismissal of Judas the die was cast. Not as if there had ever been any uncertainty with respect to the divine plan that Jesus was to die for his people. God's eternal decree is absolutely unchangeable and is sure to be realized. But *now,* with the dismissal of Judas, the realization of this plan in history has reached another decisive stage. When Jesus dismissed Judas with the words, "What you are doing, do it faster," he thereby again decisively manifested his willingness to enter the deep waters and the dark night of eternal death for his own. The Lord knew that it was *with a purpose in mind* that Judas had left the room, namely, to reveal to the rulers the whereabouts of Jesus and to show them how they might seize him. In the full knowledge of this fact, the Master had just now told this hardened sinner to go ahead and to do more quickly what he was in the process of doing. This shows that the Son desired to be obedient to the will of the Father, and that he desired to make manifest his glorious love to the elect by suffering and dying for them.

By means of this *obedience* and *love* Jesus, as the Son of man — see on 12:34 — was glorified. He was glorified *just now,* in speaking these words to

---

[145] I C; see Vol. I, p. 40.
[146] On ἵνα see Vol. I, pp. 46, 51.
[147] IIIB2; see Vol. I, pp. 42, 44.

the traitor, and the glory was still upon him.[148] He had seen the coming of the storm but instead of avoiding it he had walked right into it. Like a hen which, being in the act of spreading its wings protectingly over its chicks, thereby permitting the rain to come down upon its own back in torrents, while its brood is perfectly safe, elicits expressions of admiration from the lips of those who have been watching, so also, and far more so, the Lord, in the act of dismissing Judas, reflects glory on himself; for in doing this he allows the storm, not of *rain* but of wrath, to descend upon himself, while he shelters his own. This was his glory. See on 1:14.

Hence, just now, at this very moment which seems to spell defeat, dishonor, and disaster for him, the Son of man is in reality glorified!

And, due to the infinite closeness existing between the Sender and the One Sent (cf. 10:30), God was glorified in him. The two are inseparable. Whenever we think of Christ's suffering, we never know what to admire most: whether it be the voluntary self-surrender of *the Son* to such a death for such people, or the willingness of *the Father* to give up such a Son to such a death for such people.

32. What had just now occurred is a pledge for the future: **If God has been glorified** *in* **him** (notice *in,* not merely *by;* just like a parent is honored not only *by* his son, but also *in* his son's character and behavior), **God will also glorify him in himself.**

Father and Son glorify each other, for though they are two persons, they are *one* in essence. By means of the passion, resurrection, ascension, and coronation, God will glorify the Son in intimate union with himself (so that the Son's glory reflects glory on the Father, and vice versa). **Yes, immediately will he glorify him.** *Immediately,* indeed, for Gethsemane, Gabbatha, and Golgotha are just around the corner! . . . . It was night (13:30). In a few hours the Son of man would be entering Gethsemane!

33. Little children, yet a little while am I with y o u. Y o u will seek me, and as I told the Jews so I tell y o u now, Where I am going y o u cannot come.

Knowing that in a few more hours the daily association with his disciples would end, never to be resumed in that earthly fashion, the Lord addresses them very affectionately as "little children." This is the only place in the Gospels where the word *little children* (τεκνία) occurs. In the New Testament it is used once by Jesus and several times by "the disciple whom he loved" (John).[149] The latter employs it in the following passages: I John

---

[148] ἐδοξάσθη, dramatic aorist, used of actions that have just happened and whose effect reaches into the present. See Gram. N.T., pp. 841-843.
[149] In Gal. 4:19 the better reading is probably "children" instead of "little children."

2:1, 12, 28; 3:7, 18; 4:4; and 5:21. By using this form of address here in 13:33 Jesus implies that the disciples, though spiritually immature, are, nevertheless, very dear to him.

For the thought contained in this verse see also on 7:33; 8:21; 12:35; 14:19; and 16:16-20. At the feast of Tabernacles, a half year earlier, Jesus had told the Jews that he would be with them only a little while longer. The months have become weeks; the weeks days; the days hours. Only a few more hours now and the day-by-day (and in a sense physical) fellowship between the Master and his disciples will cease forever. By his death Jesus will go to the Father. The hopes of the disciples will be blasted. They will miss him, i.e., his physical nearness. It is in that sense that they will seek him, i.e., his visible presence, and this both after his death and after his ascension. See Luke 24:21; Acts 1:11. Such seeking is very similar to the utterance of the sigh, heard so often since that time, "Oh that Jesus were still on earth!"

Not only will they not be able to bring Jesus back to earth, but also they will not be able to go to the place where he is: "Where I am going y o u cannot come." He goes to the Father. They cannot come to the Father, that is, not until *afterward* (13:36), not until they die. In connection with *death* the great difference between Christ's true disciples and the Jewish enemies will be revealed. These last will not go to the Father, but will die in their sin (8:21).

But although the disciples will no longer be able to rejoice in the visible presence *of Jesus,* they will still be able to enjoy *one another's* visible presence. Hence, Jesus continues:

34. A new precept I give y o u, that y o u keep on loving one another; just as I have loved y o u, that y o u also keep on loving one another.

In the Fourth Gospel the term which we have translated *precept* here (ἐντολή) is used in three connections; as follows,

a. with respect to a legal *commandment* or *order* issued by the Sanhedrin (11:57);

b. with respect to the *charge* or *instruction* given to Jesus by the Father (10:18; 12:49, 50; 14:31);

c. with respect to the *precept* given by Jesus to his disciples (13:34; 14:15, 21; 15:10, 12).

Although these three meanings are very closely related, nevertheless, it is probably best to distinguish among them. A legal *commandment* or *order* is issued by men who may or may not have a warm, personal interest in those who are required to obey it. There is certainly no evidence to show that the Sanhedrin was filled with affection for the people! When used in that sense the word has the flavor of that which is outward, official, and codified. The *charge* or *instruction* given by the Father to the Son is the

252

direction which the Sender in his love gives to the Sent, in complete harmony with the eternal plan on which they have agreed. The *precept* is a rule, made by Jesus and illustrated by his own example, for the regulation of the conduct and inner attitude of the disciples, toward Christ, one another, and the world. Although we do not object to the popular term *the new commandment,* and use it ourselves, yet here in verse 34 the word is employed in the sense of *precept.* Both the *charge* and the *precept* spring from love; hence, when necessity demands (to show that the same term is used in the original in both clauses of a sentence), either term can be used to cover both ideas (as in 15:10). The precept here given is *new* (χαινή, not νέα).[150] It is characterized by the freshness and the beauty of the dawn. It is altogether desirable.

It is true, indeed, that the commandment which required love for the neighbor, for "the children of thy people," is found already in the Old Testament (Lev. 19:18; Prov. 20:22; 24:29). In fact, love for God and for the neighbor is the summary of the law (Mark 12:29, 31). But the *newness* of the precept here promulgated is evident from the fact that Jesus requires that his disciples shall love one another *as he loved them! His* example of constant (note: *keep on loving*), self-sacrificing love (think of his incarnation, earthly ministry, death on the cross) must be the pattern for *their* attitude and relation toward one another. Because voluntary obedience to this precept is of paramount importance for the spiritual welfare of the disciples (and, in fact, of the entire Church), and because his own heart is filled with love, Jesus repeats this precept.

35. By this everybody will recognize that y o u are my disciples, if y o u keep on having love for one another.

Genuine, deep-seated, constant, and self-sacrificing love for one another is the distinguishing trait of the Christian. It is by the outward manifestation of this glorious quality that disciples of the Master can expect to exert an influence upon the world, sothat men will begin to recognize (γνώσονται; see on 1:10, 31; 3:11; 8:28) that *to Christ* (note ἐμοί emphatic) and to no

---

150 Cf. R. C. Trench, *Synonyms of the New Testament,* Grand Rapids, Mich. (reprint), 1948, pp. 219-225. Νέος means *lately sprung up, young.* It contemplates that which is new from the aspect of *time;* χαινός means *not outworn or marred through age.* It views that which is new from the aspect of *form or quality.* It refers at times to that which has not been used before (John 19:41; cf. Matt. 27:60). Hence, the tomb in which the body of Jesus rested, though it may have been hewn out long before, and may not have been νέον, was, nevertheless, χαινόν. Whether the two adjectives are *always* distinct in meaning or tend at times to be used interchangeably, with little, if any, difference in meaning (as is true with respect to many words, especially when they become "old") is debatable. Trench maintains the distinctness in meaning throughout, even between διαθήκη νέα (Heb. 12:24) and διαθήκη χαινή (Heb. 8:8, 13). He may be right! In each separate case the context will have to decide,

one else these believers belong. Thus, everybody will begin to see "the Christ in the Christian."

> "How can you lead to Christ your boy
> Unless Christ's method you employ?
> There's just one thing that you can do —
> It's let that boy see Christ in you.
>
> "Have you a husband fond and true?
> A wife who's blind to all but you?
> If each would win the other one,
> That life must speak of God's dear Son.
>
> "There is but one successful plan
> By which to win a fellow man;
> Have you a neighbor old or new?
> Just let that man see Christ in you.
>
> "The Church that hopes to win the lost
> Must pay the one unchanging cost;
> She must compel the world to see
> In her the Christ of Calvary."
>   — *Author unknown.*

In striking historical confirmation of the words of Jesus recorded here in 13:35, Tertullian (fl. about 200 A. D.) wrote:

"But it is mainly the deeds of a love so noble that lead many to put a brand upon us. 'See,' they say, 'how they love one another,' for they themselves are animated by mutual hatred; 'see how they are ready even to die for one another,' for they themselves will rather put to death" (*Apology XXXIX*).

36. Peter had been disturbed by the remark of Jesus, "Yet a little while am I with y o u . . . Where I am going y o u cannot come" (13:33; see on that verse).[151] He wants to keep Jesus with him here on earth. But if Jesus is going to depart from the company, Peter at least desires to go with him. So **Simon Peter said to him, Lord, where art thou going?**

---

[151] The narrative from verse 1 to the end of chapter 13 is so closely-knit that it is very difficult to find room for the institution of the Lord's Supper anywhere. Thus, those who would wedge it in between verses 35 and 36 forget that verse 36 is a reflection on verse 33. All in all, it would seem that those who prefer to keep the chapter-division (between chapters 13 and 14) exactly where it is now, and to insert the institution of the Lord's Supper at that point (as having occurred between the prediction concerning Peter's denial and the discourse which begins in chapter 14) may be right. Certainty is, however, entirely lacking. See also on 13:21.

Jesus answered, Where I am going you cannot follow me now, but you will follow me afterward.

Jesus, through death by crucifixion, is going to the Father. Peter cannot follow him *now*. Why not? We answer: a. because, according to God's eternal decree, the exact moment for Peter's departure had not yet arrived; and b. because Peter (as is very evident from what follows) was not yet spiritually ready.

Afterward, however, Peter will go the way of Christ. He, too, will go to the Father. He will go to the Father, moreover, by means of death by crucifixion! See on 21:18, 19. (It is hardly necessary to add that, of course, Peter's death on a cross had no atoning, substitutionary value.)

37. Being blissfully unaware of his own weaknesses. **Peter said to him, Lord, why cannot I follow thee right now?** He furnishes, perhaps, the best illustration found anywhere in Scripture of the problem of The Unknown Self. His question, "Lord, why cannot I follow thee *right now* (ἄρτι Jesus had used νῦν)" shows three things:

a. his devotion to the Master; he wants to be where Jesus is;

b. his impatience ("right now"); and

c. his self-reliance; he thinks that he is ready to follow Jesus even into death, as he clearly indicates by continuing:

My life for thee I will lay down.

A comparison with parallel passages in the Synoptics shows that Peter's boast contained the following elements: a. I will be braver than the other disciples. *I will not be ensnared.* "Even though all are ensnared because of thee, yet will I never be ensnared." b. *I will not deny thee either,* no matter what happens: "Even if I must die with thee, yet I will certainly not deny thee." c. *I will go the limit for thy benefit:* "My life for thee I will lay down." Peter is willing, if necessary, to die for Christ.

In connection with this boast a few additional facts must be noted:

a. Peter spoke these words both *before* and *after* Christ's prediction which is recorded in 13:38, as is clear from Matt. 26:33-35; Mark 14:29-31. Evidently, *at the time,* the words of Jesus, telling Peter that in spite of his boasting he would do the very thing which he promised so emphatically not to do, failed to register. *Peter was too sure of himself.*

b. He used *very emphatic* language. Note the double negative in Matt. 26:35, sothat the boast may be rendered: "I will *certainly* not deny thee." And compare: "I will *never* be ensnared."

c. He spoke *with great vehemence* (Mark 14:31), evidently not at all pleased with the fact that Jesus had a different opinion.

d. The passage here in John indicates that Peter's boast was *not only negative* ("I will not be ensnared," "I will *not* deny") *but also positive:* "My life for thee I will lay down." *Luke 22:33 supplies the commentary.*

e. His self-reliant exclamation *was copied by the others:* "Likewise also said all the disciples." Not a single one among these disciples knew his own heart. Notice the three "all's": "Y o u will *all* be ensnared (Mark 14:27), said Jesus. They *all* said, "Impossible" (for exact words see Matt. 26:35). "Then *all* the disciples left him and fled" (Matt. 26:56).

Though not one of the disciples knew his own heart, yet while *all* were ensnared, *Peter* went much farther: he denied that he even knew the Master at all; see on 18:15-17; 18:25-27; cf. Matt. 26:69-75.

38. Jesus answered, Your life for me you will lay down? Jesus knew, of course, that the exact opposite was going to happen within a few hours, and this in two respects:

a. *Not Peter* would lay down his life for Jesus, *but Jesus* would lay down his life for Peter.

b. Peter *would not lay down his life* for Jesus, *but would deny* him.

Hence, Jesus continues: **I most solemnly assure you** (see on 1:51), **the rooster will certainly not crow until you have denied me three times.**

Rooster-crowing served as a time-indication. Mark 13:35 indicates that it marked the third of the four "watches." These four were as follows: "evening": 6-9, "midnight": 9-12, "rooster-crowing": 12-3, "morning": 3-6. Hence, what Jesus means seems to be that before 3:00 A. M. Peter will deny him three times. That the reference is to the second part of this 12-3 period is clear from Mark 14:30. But the mention of the crowing of the rooster refers not only to the time, but also to the actual crowing which would indicate the time. Peter was actually going to hear this crowing.

With reference to this prediction three facts stand out:

a. We see Jesus as *the great Prophet.* Though Peter did not know his own heart, Jesus not only knew it but also revealed it. Note the detailed character of this knowledge and revelation: *three times.* See also its emphatic character: *certainly not* (οὐ μή).

b. We see Jesus as *the great Sufferer.* How the very fact that he saw it all in advance must have pained him!

c. We see Jesus as *the great Savior.* The reference to the crowing of the rooster does double duty: 1. It indicates the shallowness of Peter's boast. *Within just a few hours, yes, even before dawn,* Peter will publicly disown the Master! 2. It is a means of bringing Peter back to repentence. In his subconscious mind the reference to the crowing of the rooster becomes firmly fixed. When the proper moment arrives, this hidden memory will suddenly pull the rope that will ring the bell of Peter's conscience. See 18:15-17; 18:25-27 and parallel passages in the Synoptics.

Synthesis of Chapter 13

See the Outline on p. 218. *The Son of God Illustrating and Issuing His New Commandment, Predicting the Betrayal and the Denial.*

I. He Illustrates His New Commandment by Washing the Feet of His Disciples, Explaining to Them That He Has Given Them an Example to be Followed (13:1-20).

A. Its Circumstances.

Jesus performed this deed in the bracing knowledge, acquired long before the feast of the Passover, that his hour to return to the Father had arrived. The sense of urgency was upon him, for the devil had already put it into the heart of Judas Iscariot to betray him. When he now stoops down to wash the feet of his disciples, he does this in the full consciousness of the fact that the Father had given all things into his hands.

B. Its Progress.

Having waited until the very last moment, Jesus finally rises, lays aside his garments (plural), having taken the form of a servant. He takes a long towel, and having tied it around his waist, pours water into a wash-basin. He begins to wash the feet of his disciples and to dry them with the end of the towel. Peter protests: "Lord, dost thou wash my feet? . . . By no means shalt thou wash my feet ever."

C. Its Significance.

In connection with Peter's protest and also after the entire task was completed, Jesus explains its significance as follows: a. It is *a symbol* of his entire humiliation: "What I am doing you do not know now, but hereafter you will understand." b. It is *an essential element* in Christ's humiliation, apart from which no one, not even Peter, can be saved: "If I wash you not, you have no share with me." c. It is *a lesson* in humility and service, *an example* to be followed: "I have given y o u an example, in order that just as I did to y o u so also y o u should keep on doing." This should be compared with the very similar verse 34: "Just as I loved y o u, y o u also (should) keep on loving one another." By comparing these two passages (verses 15 and 34) it becomes clear that in verses 1-20 Jesus illustrates the new commandment which he issues in verse 34.

II. He Startles the Disciples by Telling Them that One of Their Number Is Going to Betray Him. Judas Leaves.

A. The Shocking Prediction.

Although Jesus had already given a broad hint to the effect that among the twelve there was *one* man who could not be trusted (not being inwardly cleansed; see 13:10, 18), yet the terse declaration, "One of y o u will betray me," had a startling effect on the little company: "The disciples kept looking at each other, being at a loss (to know) of whom he spoke."

B. The Three Responses.

Only the third is recorded in the Fourth Gospel. For all three see p. 243, 244. John, prompted by Peter, asked, "Lord, who is it?"

C. The Lord's Reaction to John's Question.

"He it is to whom I shall give the morsel after I have dipped it," said Jesus. By giving it to Judas, he identified him as the traitor, sothat John (and probably Peter) now knew who it was. And Judas also knew that he had been "discovered" (or: so he thought; in reality, Jesus had known it all along). When Judas takes the morsel, Jesus dismisses him with, "What you are doing, do faster," a remark variously interpreted by the rest.

D. The Departure of Judas.

Judas, having been duly warned, leaves. It was night.

III. He Issues His New Commandment and Predicts Peter's Denial.

A. Jesus explains that by means of the dismissal of Judas he has been glorified (and God in him), and that God will glorify him again, (crucifixion, resurrection, ascension, coronation); yes, *immediately* (Gethsemane, Gabbatha, Golgotha). In Christ's humiliation and exaltation the radiance of God's glorious attributes (justice, faithfulness, love, etc.) shines forth. Such is *the glory*.

B. In view of his imminent departure to a place where he cannot now be followed, Jesus issues his "new commandment" (better: *precept*) that his disciples should show constant and self-sacrificing love to one another, ever looking to him as the One who gave the example. (It was only through the power of the Holy Spirit that they would be enabled to carry it out. Cf. Rom. 5:5; Gal. 5:22; II Tim. 1:7.)

C. Peter answers, "Lord, why cannot I follow thee right now? My life for thee I will lay down." Thus Peter indicates his devotion, impatience, self-reliance.

D. Jesus contradicts Peter by declaring: "Your life for me you will lay down? I most solemnly assure you, the rooster will certainly not crow until you have denied me three times."

Outline of Chapters 14-17

Theme: *Jesus, the Christ, the Son of God*
During His Private Ministry Tenderly Instructing His Disciples
and Committing Them to the Father's Care

ch. 14 A Word of Comfort
Ten grounds; see Synthesis of chapter 14

ch. 15 A Word of Admonition
1. "Abide in me" (verses 1-11): the believers' relation to *Christ*
2. "Love one another" (verses 12-17): the believers' relation to *one another*
3. "Also testify" (verses 18-27): the believers' relation to *the world* (in answer to the world's attitude to the believer: "the world hates y o u")

ch. 16 A Word of Prediction
1. Persecution is in store for believers. *The Holy Spirit* will come. He will perform his task in the world (verses 1-11), and in the Church (verses 12-15)
2. The sorrow of the disciples will be turned into joy by the return of *the Son,* at Easter, Pentecost (verses 16-24)
3. Concluding Remarks: *"The Father* loves y o u . . . Y o u will have peace . . . Be of good courage" (verses 25-33)

ch. 17 The Prayer of the Highpriest
1. For *himself* (verses 1-5)
2. For *his immediate disciples* (verses 6-19)
3. For *the Church at large* (verses 20-26)

Note: Although this is the general Outline of these chapters, there are no clear-cut divisions. Ideas mentioned in one subdivision frequently recur in the next. There is much overlapping.

CHAPTER XIV

14 1 "Let not y o u r hearts any longer be troubled. Continue to trust in God, also in me continue to trust. 2 In my Father's house there are many dwelling-places. If it were not so, I would have told y o u;[152] for [153] I go to prepare a place for y o u. 3 And when I go and prepare a place for y o u, I come again and will take y o u to be face to face with me,[154] in order that where I am y o u may be also. 4 And to the place where I am going y o u know the way."

5 Thomas said to him, "Lord, we do not know where thou art going; how can we know the way?" 6 Jesus said to him, "I am the way and the truth and the life; no one comes to the Father but by me. 7 If y o u had come to know me, y o u would have known my Father also.[155] From now on y o u do know him and have seen him."

8 Philip said to him, "Lord, show us the Father, and we shall be content." 9 Jesus said to him, "So long a time have I been with y o u, and yet you have not learned to recognize me, Philip? He who has seen me has seen the Father. How can you say, 'Show us the Father'? 10 Do you not believe that I am in the Father, and the Father in me? The words that I speak to y o u I do not speak of myself, but the Father who dwells in me is performing his works. 11 Believe me, that I am in the Father, and the Father in me; but if not, then believe me because of the works themselves."

Preliminary Remarks on Chapters 14-17

These chapters contain the Supper Discourses and the Highpriestly Prayer. There is a close connection between chapter 13 and chapter 14. The comfort imparted in the latter chapter has little meaning apart from *the teaching* (in connection with the washing of the disciples' feet) and *the predictions* (concerning Christ's imminent departure, the betrayal by Judas, and the denial by Peter) contained in the former. Without so much as an introductory formula [156] such as, "Jesus said," the Lord is at once repre-

---

152 II B; see Vol. I, pp. 41, 42.
153 On ὅτι see Vol. I, p. 56.
154 IIIA2, IIIA1; see Vol. I, pp. 42, 43.
155 II B; see Vol. I, pp. 41, 42.
156 The reading, "And he said to his disciples," is weakly attested, Western interpolation.

sented as being still in the company of the disciples, addressing them and preparing them for the events that lie ahead.

It is, therefore, not surprising that some have spoken about an unfortunate chapter-division. Nevertheless, we cannot agree. We too would have placed the chapter-division exactly where it is found. For, now that the close relation between chapters 13 and 14 has been pointed out, it is only fair also to mark the differences:

1. Chapter 13 ended with a word of Jesus addressed to Peter, to him alone. Chapter 14 begins with words addressed to the entire company. The *you* in 13:38 is singular; the *y o u r* in 14:1 is plural (a fact which is obscured by modern English translations).

2. Chapter 13 contains a *narrative and a dialogue;* chapters 14-16 contain *discourses.* This is immediately evident from the fact that while in the *thirty-eight* verses of chapter 13 Jesus is interrupted no less than *six* times, in the *ninety-one* verses of chapters 14-16 he is interrupted only *four* times.

3. The subject-matter of chapter 13 is of a miscellaneous nature. On the contrary, chapters 14, 15, 16, and 17 have each one central theme.

Although, to be sure, these discourses of chapters 14, 15, and 16 are in the form of conversations rather than formal addresses, and although at first glance the thoughts may seem to overlap (and actually do overlap) to a certain extent, sothat some have even spoken of a "divine confusion" (whatever that may be!), nevertheless, upon closer study it becomes clear that a certain organic and logical connection runs through the entire three chapters: the predominant note of chapter 14 is *comfort* ("Let not y o u r hearts any longer be troubled"); of chapter 15 *admonition* ("Abide in me . . . love one another . . . also bear witness"); and of chapter 16 *prediction* ("They will make y o u outcasts from the synagogue"); while chapter 17 contains the Prayer of the Highpriest, famous for its simplicity and tenderness.

14:1-17

14:1. Let not y o u r hearts any longer be troubled. We prefer this translation because it reproduces both the meaning and the cadence of the original. First, *the meaning,* for the thought is not, "Do not begin to be troubled," but "Stop being troubled," or "Do not be troubled *any longer.*" And secondly, *the cadence.* In the original the line has a rhythmical flow, a soothing and consoling tenderness, which can be reproduced in English by stressing the words and syllables that have been printed in italics:

"Let not y o u r *hearts* any *long*er be *trou*bled."

Note that Jesus is not merely telling the disciples that they must not be sad any longer; he exhorts them not any longer to be troubled, tempest-

262

tossed, agitated, thrown into a state of confusion and perplexity. The verb used is ταρασσέσθω, third person singular present imperative passive of ταράσσω. See also on 5:7; 11:33; 12:27; 13:21. The original has *y o u r heart* where English idiom prefers *y o u r hearts* (but see A.V. and A.S.V.). The *heart* is here the fulcrum of feeling and faith as well as the mainspring of words and actions, as is evident from such passages as 16:6, 22; cf. Matt. 12:34; 15:19; 22:37; and Rom. 10:10. John seldom uses the term (only in 13:2; 14:1, 27; 16:6; and in 12:40, which, however, is a quotation from Is. 6:10).

The hearts of the disciples were filled with a medley of emotions. They were *sad* because of the gloomy prospect of Christ's departure; *ashamed* because of their own demonstrated selfishness and pride; *perplexed* because of the prediction that one of their own number would betray the Master, that another would deny him, and that all would be ensnared because of him; and finally, they were *wavering* in their faith, probably thinking: "How can one who is about to be betrayed be the Messiah?" Yet, at the same time, they love this Master. They hope against hope. All this is implied in the words, "Let not y o u r hearts any longer be troubled."

The exhortation is based on love of the most tender and self-forgetful character, for when Jesus uttered it he was himself troubled in the spirit (13:21; and compare also Matt. 26:38; Luke 22:28, 44). The agonizing shepherd, facing the cross, comforts others. He consoles the very men who have just demonstrated their selfishness and who are going to be "offended in him." "Was there ever kinder shepherd, half so gentle, half so sweet?"

Moreover, what Jesus is expressing is not merely a pious wish, like our cheering (but often empty) phrase: "Just do not worry. Everything will be all right." When Jesus says, "Let not y o u r hearts any longer be troubled," he fortifies this with solid grounds. See the Synthesis at the end of the chapter.

In this connection there is an interesting superficial resemblance between Christianity and Epicureanism. The latter also stressed the necessity of remaining calm and untroubled in all circumstances of life. In fact this school even used a term which is derived from the same root as is the verb which Jesus employs here in 14:1, 27. They spoke of *ataraxia* (ἀταραξία), the state of being unperturbed. And yet, upon a closer view, the difference between Christianity and Epicureanism, as brought out strikingly in John 14, is great. The reasoning of Epicureanism and of its present-day equivalents is this: "Do not be disturbed, for the gods, if they exist at all, do not take notice of you." — On the contrary, the teaching of Jesus is this: "Do not be disturbed, for the God whom you trust does take notice of you. He hears your prayers. He loves you. And so does the Son of God." Hence, Christianity — or, if you prefer, Christ — furnishes the only adequate grounds for the exhortation of 14:1, 27.

Continue to trust in God, also in me continue to trust.

There is much to be said in favor of the position that both of these verbs (πιστεύετε . . . πιστεύετε) are imperatives, precepts.[157] The imperative form is in harmony with the entire discourse (14:11; 15:4, etc.). It is also in harmony with the first line, for "Let not y o u r hearts any longer be troubled," is also imperative. The old argument, which one can find in many books, to the effect that the first clause cannot be a command because Jesus knew that the disciples already trusted in God, hence, could not order them to do so, has little value. Though they had faith, that faith was beginning to waver. Hence (using the continuative present imperative) Jesus says, "*Continue to* trust!"

Though the disciples still *loved* the Master, their *faith* in him as Messiah-Savior was beginning to waver. Jesus knows that when within a matter of hours he dies on the cross and is buried, that faith will be undermined even more (16:20; cf. Matt. 26:31; Mark 14:27; 16:13; Luke 24:21). He knows also that the only remedy for the troubled heart is the assurance that Jesus is and remains the Savior even though — rather, by virtue of the very fact that — he suffers and dies. That is why he tells them, according to the original, "Keep on trusting in God, also in me keep trusting." The verb may also be rendered *keep on believing*. It makes little difference. We chose *keep on trusting* because it is especially the *trust*-element in faith which is on the foreground in a context which concerns *the troubled heart*.

Jesus does not, in this connection, fully explain *why* he must die on the cross, though there had been some teaching along this line previously (10:11, 14, 28; Mark 10:45); neither was a *full* explanation possible as yet (16:12). He demands *abiding* trust or faith in God and in himself even then when mysteries multiply. Jesus asks that the disciples shall continue to rest in God and in himself with their entire being, sothat their heart, soul, mind, and strength will continually go out to the source of their salvation, the goal of their existence. For the verb see also on 1:8; 3:16; 8:30, 31a.

The clear implication is that Jesus is himself God. This is brought out beautifully by means of the inverted word-order in the second exhortation, sothat the phrases *in God* and *also in me* are placed right next to each other.

2. In my Father's house there are many dwelling-places.

In addition to what has already been said elsewhere on this passage (see Vol. I, p. 56), the following must suffice:

---

[157] In Greek the second person plural indicative and imperative are identical in form. Hence, the word here used may be either. F. W. Ginrich, "Ambiguity of Word Meaning in John's Gospel," *CTW*, 37 (1943-1944), 77, thinks that this is a case of *deliberate* ambiguity. But this is not a mashal in the sense of 3:3.

According to the context, Jesus was comforting the disciples, who dreaded to think of the coming separation. Now it is in this connection that the Lord assured them that his going away to the Father's house had as its purpose a *reunion,* and was not a permanent separation. In the place to which he is going there is room for them also! In fact, his very going away (think of his death on the cross and his ascension which will enable him to send the Spirit) would make this reunion possible, sothat what appeared to be a calamity was in reality a blessing. Apart from Christ's death and the work of the Holy Spirit there would have been no place in heaven for the disciples.

The Father's house is heaven (cf. Ps. 33:13, 14; Is. 63:15). It is a very roomy place. In it there are entire dwelling-places, permanent *homes, abodes* or *mansions* for *all* God's children. The Father's house does not resemble a *tenement-house,* each family occupying one room. On the contrary, it is more like a beautiful *apartment-building,* with *ever so many* completely furnished and spacious apartments or dwelling-places, and no crowding of any kind! Inside the *one* house there are *many mansions!* "Plenty room in heaven, room for me but also room for y o u," is the *one* idea conveyed here. (The idea of variety, degrees of glory, though true in itself, is foreign to the present context.)

If it were not so, I would have told y o u, for I go to prepare a place for y o u. This rendering, which retains the conjunction *for* (in "for I go") yields an excellent meaning: "If in my Father's house there were not plenty room for all God's children, I certainly would have known all about it and would have told y o u so, *for,* by means of my humiliation and exaltation, I prepare a place for y o u. This is my mission. Without my death there would be no place for y o u; without my ascension and the sending forth of the Spirit, y o u would not be made ready for the place."

3. And when I go and prepare a place for y o u, I come again and will take y o u to be face to face with me, in order that where I am y o u may be also.

The coming again of which Jesus speaks in this verse is the counterpart of the going away. Cf. Acts 1:9-11. That fact explains its character. In all probability, therefore, it refers to the second coming, and its purpose is to enable Christ to receive the disciples into his loving presence, to abide with him forever.

Observe that instead of saying what one might expect him to say, namely, "And when I go and prepare a place for y o u, I come again and will take y o u *to that place,*" Jesus says something that is far more comforting: "I will take y o u *to myself*" (or: *to be face to face with me;* for the meaning of πρός see on 1:1). So wonderful is Christ's love for his own that he is not satisfied with the idea of merely bringing them to *heaven*. He must needs take them into his own embrace.

The verb translated, "and will take y o u" (παραλήμψομαι, root-idea: to take over *from* another), with a wide variety of shades of meaning, has here the sense of *welcoming* someone. A. Deissmann has shown that the comfort contained in this passage (14:3) was by the early Christians applied to the *death* of dear ones. Although Jesus himself probably did not directly refer to this, but rather to the meeting again in connection with the second advent, nevertheless, the *application* to death is legitimate. Hence, in ancient letters of consolation the phraseology of 14:3 is often found.[158]

On the expressed purpose of this welcoming, namely, "in order that where I am y o u may be also," see Rev. 14:1; 19:14; 20:4. Wherever the Christ is, there too are the believers.

4. And to the place where I am going y o u know the way. *The way* is the means by which the disciples are brought to the Father. Jesus means, "Y o u know *me; I* am the way." But he does not yet definitely say that *he* is the way. For this see on 14:6. He was able to say, "Y o u *know*," for he had previously revealed himself as the way to the Father (8:19; 10:1, 7, 9, 37, 38; 12:26, 44, 45, 49, 50; cf Matt. 11:27, 28).

The statement is a veiled invitation: "Come to the Father by means of this way." Up to this moment (14:1, 2, 3) Jesus had spoken about what he was going to do for his disciples (prepare a place for them, and come again to receive them to himself). They must not think, however, that *they* have nothing to do. *They must go* to the house where a place is prepared for them (cf. Ps. 84:7; Heb. 11:13-16).

5. Thomas said to him, Lord, we do not know where thou art going; how can we know the way? In saying this Thomas may probably be regarded as the spokesman of the group, the one who actually said what most or all were thinking (cf. 13:36, 37). As to his character see on 11:16. His objection, although involving an element of weakness and sinfulness as it always does, a slowness to understand because one has not paid sufficient attention, nevertheless also reveals his devotion to the Master. He cannot bear the thought that Jesus is leaving. It is for that reason that he makes his protest. Note how Da Vinci in *The Last Supper*, with fine tact, places the *devoted* and *despondent* Thomas very close to Jesus at the supper-table! He is pictured by the artist as a very emotional type, with his finger raised almost in the face of Jesus as he says, "Surely not I, Lord?" — Now in the present passage Thomas means to say:

---

[158] A. Deissmann, *Light From the Ancient East* (translated by L. R. M. Strachan), New York, 1927, pp. 177, 178.

"How can we be expected to know *the way* when we do not even know the *destination?*" He committed two errors:

a. He may have thought that Jesus was referring to his departure in death, or else he may have opined that the Master was leaving for another place on earth. In the latter case *the way* would be an ordinary road, and his error would be similar to that of the Jews in 7:35 (see on that passage).

b. He imagined that the Lord was speaking about the way which *he* was about to take, whereas Jesus was actually referring to the way *the disciples* must take to reach their destination, as is evident from 14:6b.

Nevertheless, the objection raised by Thomas contains an element of truth. He who does not know the destination will not know the way. See verse 7 for the distinction in meaning between the two customary verbs for knowing.

6. Jesus said to him, I am the way and the truth and the life.

This is another of the seven great I AM's of John's Gospel (for the others see on 6:48; 8:12; 10:9; 10:11; 11:25; and 15:1). In the predicate each of the words *way, truth,* and *life* is preceded by the definite article.

"I am the way." Jesus does not merely *show* the way; he *is* himself the way. It is true that he *teaches* the way (Mark 12:14; Luke 20:21), *guides* us in the way (Luke 1:79), and *has dedicated* for us a new and living way (Heb. 10:20); but all this is possible only because he *is* himself the way.

Christ is God. Now God is equal to each of his attributes, whereas he "possesses" each attribute in an infinite degree. Hence, not only does God *have* love (or *exercise* love), but he *is* love, nothing but love; he *is* righteousness, nothing but righteousness, etc. So also Christ *is* the way: in every act, word, and attitude he is the Mediator between God and his elect.

Notice also the pronoun *I.* In the last analysis we are not saved by a principle or by a force but by a person. In the school the pupil is educated not primarily by blackboards, books, and maps, but by the teacher who makes use of all these means. In the home he is brought up by father and mother. So also the means of access to the Father is Christ himself. We are persons. The God from whom we have been estranged is a personal God. Hence, it is not strange that apart from living fellowship with the person, Jesus Christ, who exists in indissoluble union with the Father, there is no salvation for us (cf. Rom. 5:1, 2).

Now Jesus is the way in a twofold sense (cf. also on 10:1, 7, 9). He is the way *from God to man* — all divine blessings come down from the Father through the Son (Matt. 11:27, 28) — ; he is also the way *from man to God.* As already indicated, in the present context the emphasis falls on the latter idea.

"I am . . . the truth."

Much of what has been said in connection with "I am the way" applies here also. Jesus is the very embodiment of the truth. He is the truth in person. As such he is the final reality in contrast with the shadows which preceded him (see on 1:14, 17). But in the present context the term *the truth* seems to have a different shade of meaning. It is that which stands over against the lie. Jesus is the truth because he is *the dependable source of redemptive revelation*. That this is the sense in which the word is used is clear from verse 7 which teaches that Christ reveals the Father. Cf. Matt. 11:27.

But just as the way is a living way, so also the truth is living truth. It is active. It takes hold of us and influences us powerfully. It sanctifies us, guides us, and sets us free (8:32; cf. 17:17). Basically, not *it* but *he* is the truth, he himself in person. Pilate asked, "What is truth?" (18:38). Jesus here in 14:6 answers, *"I am the truth."*

"I am . . . the life."

Jesus is not referring here to the breath or spirit ($\pi\nu\epsilon\tilde{\upsilon}\mu\alpha$) which animates our body. He is not thinking of the *soul* ($\psi\upsilon\chi\acute{\eta}$), nor of *life as outwardly manifested* ($\beta\acute{\iota}o\varsigma$), but of *life as* opposed to death ($\zeta\omega\acute{\eta}$). All God's glorious attributes dwell in the Son of God (see on 1:4). And because he has the life within himself (see on 5:26), he is the source and giver of life for his own (see on 3:16; 6:33; 10:28; 11:25). He has the light of life (8:12), the words of life (6:68), and he came that we might have life and abundance (10:10). Just as death spells separation from God, so life implies communion with him (17:3).

All three concepts are active and dynamic. The way *brings* to God; the truth *makes* men *free;* the life *produces* fellowship.

How are these three related? As more or less separate, wholly coordinate entities? Or, as forming a single concept: "the true and living way"? It is not necessary to choose either of these alternatives. *Truth* and *life* are nouns, not adjectives. Christ *is* the truth and the life, just as well as he *is* the way. Nevertheless, the context indicates that the idea of *the way* predominates. The meaning appears to be: "I am the way because I am the truth and the life." When Jesus reveals God's redemptive truth which sets men free from the enslaving power of sin, and when he imparts the seed of life, which produces fellowship with the Father, then and thereby he, as the way (which they themselves, by sovereign grace, have chosen), has brought them to the Father. Hence, Jesus continues: **No one comes to the Father but by me.**

Since men are absolutely dependent upon Christ for their knowledge of redemptive truth and also for the spark that causes that truth to live in their souls (and their souls to become alive to that truth), it follows that no one comes to the Father but through him. With Christ removed there can be no redemptive *truth,* no everlasting *life;* hence, no *way* to the Father.

Cf. Acts 4:12. Both the absoluteness of the Christian religion and the urgent necessity of Christian Missions is clearly indicated.

7. If y o u had come to know me, y o u would have known my Father also. Jesus had said, "Y o u know the way." Thomas had answered, "How can we know the way?" Jesus was able to say, "Y o u know," because the way had been clearly revealed. But in one sense it was true that the disciples did not know: they had not paid sufficient attention to the words of Jesus! They did not know the Lord as fully as they would have known him had they given closer heed to all his words and admonitions. Moreover, had they done so, they would have had a fuller and richer perception of the Father also. They had failed too often to see in Jesus the only and absolute way to the only and absolute goal. They had failed, to some extent, to see in him the only Son of God who, because he is the Son, reveals the Father. So Jesus says, as it were, "If by daily listening to me, pondering my words and works, if by means of this personal, day-by-day experience, *y o u had learned to know* me (ἐγνώκειτε is probably the best reading) *y o u would have known* (ἤδειτε, gained an insight into by mental reflection) my Father also." [159] Note *my Father,* which indicates Christ's unique sonship (see on 1:14).

From now on, says Jesus, **y o u do know him and have seen him.** The most obvious explanation would seem to be this: "Y o u know (recognize) him from now on because of these very words, for I have now clearly told y o u that I myself am the way (and the truth and the life) to the Father, sothat there is even less excuse for ignorance than heretofore. *Y o u have seen the way* with y o u r very eyes, physical and spiritual."

8. Philip said to him. For Philip see on 1:43-46; 6:5-7; and 12:20-22. He was one of the earliest disciples, a man with a Greek name. He came from Bethsaida in Galilee, the town of Andrew and Peter. It was he who had been instrumental in bringing Nathaniel to Jesus. To him, long ago, Jesus had addressed the question, "How are we to buy bread-cakes that people may eat?" He had given an answer which revealed his *little faith* (which, however, was characteristic not only of him, but of all). To him the Greeks had come with the request, "Sir, we wish to see Jesus."

It was this Philip who said to Jesus, **Lord, show us the Father, and we shall be content.** With his physical eyes Philip (probably representing the

---

[159] In verses 4 and 5 the verb οἶδα is used. In verse 7 there seems to be a deliberate transition from γινώσκω to οἶδα, and then back again to γινώσκω. It is hardly possible to be satisfied with the idea that the change in the use of words at this point is simply due to a desire for variation for the sake of euphony. Giving the verbs their full, distinctive sense yields a good meaning, which is also in complete harmony with the context. See also on 1:10, 31; 3:11; 8:28. Also in verse 9 γινώσκω fits the context exactly.

others; note: show *us*) evidently desired *to see* the Father; not, to be sure, that he denied God's spirituality and essential invisibility, but he was asking for a theophany: a visible manifestation of the Father's glory, such as had been granted to Moses and other believers in the old dispensation (Ex. 24:9-11; 33:18). He did not seem to realize that a far greater privilege than that which Moses enjoyed while on earth, had been given to *him!* For "Lord" see on 1:38; 12:21.

9. Jesus said to him, So long a time have I been with y o u, and yet you have not learned to recognize me, Philip? Philip had failed to listen carefully to the words spoken to Thomas, to the effect that the Father had become manifest in the Son. Moreover, had not the Master revealed this truth again and again from the very beginning of his ministry? Since his first public appearance more than three years had elapsed: *"so long* a time." One may well ask, "Was there any truth which Jesus had emphasized so repeatedly as this one, that he, the Mediator sent by God, had come to speak the words and to perform the works of God; that in these words and works he was revealing the Father; and that this manifestation of the Father in him as Mediator rested upon the eternal, intra-trinitarian relationship between the Father and himself, the only-begotten Son? See the following passages: 1:18; 3:33-36; 5:17, 18, 19-32; 6:29, 38, 57; 7:29; 8:16, 19, 28, 29, 42, 54, 55; 10:15, 30, 33, 37, 38; 12:45; 13:31. Surely Philip and the others have heard some of this teaching! Hence, Jesus administers a tender rebuke when he says, *"So long* a time have I been with *y o u* (note the plural), and yet *you* (note the singular) have not learned to recognize me?" The plural *y o u* refers to all the disciples present in the Upper Room (i.e., the Eleven, Judas having left); the singular *you* refers to Philip alone. Note also the verb, on which see footnote 159, and the reference there indicated. The kind of recognition which Jesus has in mind is spiritual in character. It amounts to seeing by faith the Father in the Son; for Jesus continues: **He who has seen me has seen the Father. How can you say, Show us the Father?**

In the light of the abundant teaching of the Lord on this subject (see on verse 9 above), the remark, "How can you say, 'Show us the Father'" requires no further comment.

The three perfects (ἔγνωκας, ἑωρακώς, ἑώρακε; respectively: you *have* not learned to recognize; he who *has* seen; he *has* seen) show that once this spiritual knowledge or vision has been obtained, it has abiding results. The entire passage indicates that redemptive revelation apart from Christ is impossible. In the Son we have God's *final* revelation. As true as it is that he who has seen the Son has seen the Father, so true it is that he who has *not* seen the Son has *not* seen the Father. What the disciples lacked, however, was not genuine faith *as such* but genuine faith *in full measure.*

They had seen but, due to their own sinfulness, they had not seen clearly enough. Hence Jesus continues, addressing himself first to Philip alone:

10. Do you not believe that I am in the Father and the Father in me? This passage shows that all knowledge with respect to the facts of redemption is based on *genuine, Christian faith.* Thus we get a sound foundation for a truly Christian epistemology. *Reason* cannot penetrate these mysteries. *Jewish monotheism* refuses to accept the possibility that the divine essence can unfold itself in more than one divine person. Only *Christian faith* will do.

The expression "I am in the Father and the Father in me" makes sense only if Father and Son are one in essence, that is, in all their divine attributes. The Father and the Son (also the Spirit, mentioned in 14:16, 17, 26) "do not exist apart as human individualities do, but in and through each other as moments in one divine, self-conscious life.[160]

The Jews did not make the mistake of thinking that when Jesus made statements of this character (see also 5:17; 10:30) he referred merely to moral unity or ethical harmony. They clearly understood that nothing less than *essential equality* with God was intended (see on 1:1).

Nevertheless, the ontological trinity is reflected in the economical: **The words that I speak to y o u** (note change from singular to plural here) **I do not speak of myself, but the Father who dwells in me is performing his works.**

Whenever Jesus speaks, the Father works by means of this speaking. Every *word* of Jesus is a *work* of the Father! This, however, does not mean that the Father is acting like a ventriloquist who speaks through his dummy. On the contrary, the Son speaks the mind of the Father *because this is also his own mind.* It is in that sense that when the Son speaks, the Father's redemptive deeds are being accomplished. However, the *works* of the Father are not limited to the words of the Son. They also include his *miracles* or *signs.* These serve to confirm faith, to strengthen it, to assist it in becoming strong. Therefore Jesus says:

11. Believe me, that I am in the Father, and the Father in me; but if not, then believe me because of the works themselves. The disciples were wavering in their faith (14:1), a faith which had never been strong (14:7). But whatever of faith is present in their hearts must be kept there and strengthened, especially *now,* with the Master about to leave. It is for this reason that Jesus again exhorts his disciples *to believe* (or, as we may also

---

[160] See J. Orr, *The Christian View of God and the World,* third edition, New York, 1897, p. 268. Also H. Bavinck, *The Doctrine of God* (translated by W. Hendriksen), Grand Rapids, Mich., 1951, pp. 255-334. Cf. L. Berkhof, *Systematic Theology,* Grand Rapids, Mich., 1949, pp. 82-99.

render the original: *to keep on believing*) that he is in the Father, and the Father in him (see on verse 10). They are urged to take Jesus at his word! This is ever the highest type of faith. But if this be difficult for them, let them then believe because of *the works considered by themselves*. These works have evidential value. On this see 9:31-33; 10:37, 38; 11:39-44; 20:30, 31; cf. Acts 2:22; 4:31; II Cor. 12:12.

---

12 "I most solemnly assure y o u, he who believes in me, the works that I do will he do also, and greater (works) than these will he do, because I am going to the Father. 13 And whatever y o u ask in my name, that I will do, in order that the Father may be glorified in the Son. 14 If y o u will ask me anything in my name, I will do it.[161] 15 If y o u love me, y o u will keep my precepts[162] 16 And I will pray the Father, and he will give y o u another Helper, in order that he may be in y o u r midst forever, 17 even the Spirit of truth, whom the world cannot receive, because it neither sees nor knows him. Y o u do know him, because he dwells by y o u r side, and will be within y o u. 18 I will not leave y o u orphans: I am coming to y o u. 19 Yet a little while, and the world no longer sees me, but y o u see me; because I live, y o u too will live. 20 In that day y o u will recognize that I am in my Father, and y o u in me, and I in y o u. 21 He who has my precepts and keeps them, he it is who loves me. And he who loves me will be loved of my Father, and I too will love him, and I will manifest myself to him."

22 Judas (not Iscariot) said to him, "Lord, what has happened that[163] thou wilt manifest thyself to us, and not to the world?" 23 Jesus answered and said to him, "If a man loves me, he will keep my word, and my Father will love him, and we will come to him and make our home with him.[164] 24 He who does not love me does not keep my words; and the word which y o u hear is not mine but the Father's who sent me."

14:12-24

14:12. I most solemnly assure y o u, he who believes in me, the works that I do will he do also, and greater (works) than these will he do, because I am going to the Father.

For the words of solemn introduction see on 1:51. The disciples need not fear that Christ's physical absence will mean loss of power to perform miracles. From heaven Jesus will continue to supply them with this power. A glorious promise is here given to the one who *keeps on believing* in him (see on 1:8; 3:16; 8:30, 31a for the meaning of the verb πιστεύω, and of its present participle followed by εἰς). Such a person will do the works which Jesus is doing, and this not *in spite of* the fact that he is going to the

---

161 IIIA1; see Vol. I, pp. 42, 43.
162 IIIB2; see Vol. I, pp. 42, 44.
163 On ὅτι see Vol. I, pp. 54, 61.
164 IIIB2; see Vol. I, pp. 42, 44.

Father but *because of* that fact. The very departure of the Lord will benefit the disciples. How this can be true is explained in 14:16 ff. As a result of this departure the disciples will perform not only the works which Jesus has been doing all along (miracles in the *physical* realm), but even *greater works than these*, namely, miracles in the *spiritual* realm. See on 5:20, 21, 24. Christ's works had consisted to a considerable extent of miracles in the physical realm, performed largely among the Jews. When he now speaks about *the greater works*, he is in all probability thinking of those in connection with *the conversion of the Gentiles*. Such works were of a higher character and vaster in extent. That Jesus actually has this great task in mind seems to follow from the fact that he referred to it just a few days before (12:23-32), and also definitely during this very night (17:20).

Now this conversion of (God's elect from among) the Gentiles, this work of Peter in the home of Cornelius and of Paul on all his missionary journeys, could not have been done *before* Christ's death and ascension for the simple reason that at that time the Holy Spirit had not yet been poured out. For that very reason the wall of separation was still in existence. All this was going to change presently, that is, in connection with Christ's death, resurrection, ascension, and coronation. Hence, Jesus is able to say, "Greater works than these will he do *because I am going to the Father.*"

Two additional remarks are necessary before we leave this passage:

(1) Let no one say that the work of conversion can never in any sense be ascribed to *man.* Cf. Jas. 5:20, *"He who converts a sinner* from the error of his way." See also Prov. 11:30 and Dan. 12:3. This is, of course, a very relative way of speaking. The real Author of conversion is ever God himself, but he uses man as an agent. The disciples are viewed as *reapers* (see on 4:35-38).

(2) It is certainly worthy of notice that, according to this great saying of our Lord, the *greater* works are the *spiritual* works. The miracles in the physical realm are subservient to those in the spiritual sphere: the former serve to prove the genuine character of the latter. Does Jesus, perhaps, by means of this very comparison, which places the spiritual so far above the physical, hint that miracles in the physical sphere would gradually disappear when they would no longer be necessary?

13, 14. And whatever y o u ask in my name, that I will do, in order that the Father may be glorified in the Son. If y o u will ask me anything in my name, I will do it.

The word *whatever* comprises much territory. It refers to both the *great* works and the *greater* works (of verse 12). Accordingly, in this passage the relation of these works to prayer is pointed out. Jesus very clearly teaches that there is this connection. In the book of Acts miracles in both realms

273

are again and again linked with prayer (Acts 1:14 followed by the great miracles of ch. 2; 4:31; 6:6, 7; 9:40, 41; 10:4, 9; 12:5; 13:3; 16:25-34).[165]

Only such prayers, however, are answered which are *in Christ's name.* Such prayers, of course, are not selfish but in the interest of God's kingdom. They proceed from faith, are in accordance with God's will — ever implying, "Not our will, but thy will be done" —, and to his glory. A prayer in Christ's name is a prayer that is in harmony with whatever Christ has revealed concerning himself. His name is his self-revelation in his works; here particularly, his self-revelation in the sphere of redemption.

It is not difficult to see that such a prayer will *always* and *most certainly* be answered, for the one who utters it does not ever want anything that Christ does not want! And when such a prayer is answered, the Father, who abides forever in the Son, will do his works. Hence, the Father will be glorified in the Son. The resplendent attributes of God will shine forth in all their beauty in and by means of these works.

Not only will the believer receive the very thing asked — that is, if it be asked *in Christ's name,* which covers every condition of answered prayer —, but *Christ himself in person* will grant this humble petition of his disciple; note the words, "*I will do it.*" For the meaning of the verb *ask* and its synonym see on 11:22, and below, on 14:16.

Because of the far-reaching character of the promise contained in verse 13 it is repeated in the next verse. However, there is a difference, for now the disciples are told that they must not only pray *in the name of* Christ but *to Christ,* "If y o u will ask *me* anything in my name," etc. Hence, by taking the two verses together we see that Christ here represents himself as:

a. The One in whose name prayer must be offered.

b. The Object of prayer.

c. The Hearer of prayer.

15. If y o u love me, y o u will keep my precepts.

We do not agree with those commentators who claim that there is no connection between this and the preceding. This very night — perhaps an hour or more ago — Jesus had issued his "new commandment" (*precept*); see on 13:34. Similar precepts were added in 14:1 and 14:11. Besides, does not the immediate context (verses 12-14) clearly imply that the Lord wants his disciples ·to keep on believing in him, to pray in his name, and to pray to him? Are not these statements *implied precepts*?

But they must be *kept* if they are to be a blessing. In the conditional sentence, "If y o u love me, y o u will keep my precepts," there are three words that predominate: *love* (ἀγαπάω), *keep* (τηρέω), and *precept* (ἐντολή).

---

[165] Hence, I cannot agree with Lenski who denies this emphatically; *op. cit.,* pp. 966, 967.

For the first see on 21:15-17; for the second, on 8:51; and for the third, on 13:34.

Summarizing the results of these word-studies, the sentence may be paraphrased as follows:

"If with love that is both intelligent and purposeful y o u love me, y o u will accept, obey, and stand guard over the rules which I have laid down for the regulation of y o u r inner attitudes and outer conduct."

The passage implies that from a certain aspect love precedes obedience. Hence, in this connection we refer to what has been said with reference to the order of the elements in Christian experience; see on 7:17, 18.

16. And I will request the Father, and he will give y o u another Helper, in order that he may be in y o u r midst forever . . .

Those who keep Christ's precepts will receive a great blessing. Jesus, as Mediator, will make a request in their interest. We prefer the translation "I will request" to the more indefinite "I will pray." Since Jesus has just used the verb *ask* in speaking of the prayers of the disciples (see on verses 13 and 14), and now shifts to the verb *request* when he is thinking of his own prayer in their interest, it is obvious that the change in verbs was intentional. The disciples are not on a level with God's only begotten Son. *They* must implore; *he* has a right to ask on terms of equality. Only once (I John 5:16) in the New Testament is the term *request* (ἐρωτάω) used with respect to the petitions which man addresses to God, and that *one* exception is easily explained. On the other hand, in speaking of his own prayers, Jesus *always* uses *request*, never *ask* (αἰτέω). See also on 11:22.

Jesus promises that in answer to his request the Father will give to the disciples *another* Helper. In the next verse this Helper is called the Spirit of truth.

The passage clearly indicates that the Holy Spirit is not merely a power but *a person*, just like the Father and the Son. He is *another* Helper, not a *different* Helper. The word *another* indicates *one like myself*, who will take my place, do my work. Hence, if Jesus is a person, the Holy Spirit must also be a person. Moreover, personal attributes are everywhere ascribed to him (14:26; 15:26; Acts 15:28; Rom. 8:26; I Cor. 12:11; I Tim. 4:1; Rev. 22:17). His relation to the Father and the Son is described as of such a character that if these are persons, he too must be a person (Matt. 28:19; I Cor. 12:4-6; II Cor. 13:14; I Pet. 1:1, 2).

For the same reason, if Jesus is divine, the Spirit, too, must be divine. This too is taught throughout the New Testament, to say nothing of the Old. Thus, divine names are given to him (Acts 5:4; 28:25; Heb. 10:15, 16); divine attributes are ascribed to him; such as, eternity, omnipresence, omnipotence, omniscience (I Cor. 2:10; 12:4-6; Heb. 9:14); and divine works are predicated of him (Matt. 12:18; Luke 4:18; John 14:16; I Cor.

12:2-11; II Thess. 2:13; I Pet. 1:12). Passages such as Matt. 28:19 and II Cor. 13:14 clearly indicate that the three persons are completely equal. One and the same divine essence pervades all.

According to the passage which we are studying, the Holy Spirit is given by the Father, in answer to the request of the Son. He proceeds from both Father and Son. The Father gives him; the Son sends him (15:26). He is the Spirit of the Father; he is also the Spirit of Christ (Matt. 10:20; Rom. 8:9; I Cor. 2:11, 12; and Gal. 4:6). The Holy Spirit is the person in whom the Father and the Son meet one another. Moreover, here as elsewhere the economical trinity rests upon the ontological: the Spirit's outpouring on the day of Pentecost, to which the present passage refers, rests upon his eternal procession. Both of these are the works of the Father and the Son.

The Spirit is here called another *Paraclete* (παράκλητος). The term indicates that he is a person who is *called to the side* (in this case, of the disciples) *in order to help.* Two errors, as we see it, should be avoided in this respect:

(1) The fact that by derivation the word is a verbal adjective derived from the passive (perfect) form of the verb παρακαλέω must not be interpreted to mean that therefore the resulting word *remains forever passive in meaning.* The *derivation* of words is one thing, the *history of their meaning in actual usage* (to which the science of semantics devotes its attention) is a different matter. To be sure, there is a relation between the two, but they are by no means the same. The context must decide. In John it is the *active* idea that is stressed, as every reference to him indicates (see next paragraph). The Paraclete *does* certain things for the disciples (and, of course, for the Church).

(2) The meaning of the word must not be too narrowly restricted. The Holy Spirit is a Helper in ever so many respects: he *comforts,* indeed, and since the main theme of chapter 14 is *comfort* it is probable that Jesus had this in mind more than anything else. But the Spirit also (and in close connection with the work of imparting comfort) teaches, guides in the truth (16:13, 14); brings the teaching of Christ home to the recollection of the disciples (14:26); and dwells within them as a source of inspiration and life (14:17). The Father and the Son call the Spirit to the side of the disciples in order to comfort, admonish, teach, and guide them; in other words, in order that in any given condition the Paraclete may furnish *whatever help is necessary.* Hence, we know of no better translation than the term *Helper.*[166]

---

[166] For an up-to-date discussion of the term παράκλητος consult the following:

Deissmann, A., *Light from the Ancient East* (translation by L. R. M. Strachan), fourth edition, New York, 1922, p. 336.

Goodspeed, E. J., *Problems of New Testament Translation,* Chicago, 1945, pp. 110, 111.

In I John 2:1 Jesus Christ is himself called Paraclete. He is the Helper in the sense of being Advocate or Intercessor with the Father in the interest of believers who commit sin.

The sense of 14:16 is, accordingly, this: instead of becoming poorer, the disciples are actually going to become richer. To be sure, *one* Helper is leaving, but he leaves with the purpose of sending *another*. Moreover, the first Helper, though physically absent, will remain a Helper. He will be their Helper *in heaven*. The other will be their Helper *on earth*. The first pleads their case with God. The second pleads God's case with them. This second Helper, moreover, having once arrived (at Pentecost), will never depart from the church in any sense whatever. Hence, Pentecost is never repeated. (See on the next verse for the distinction between *the prepositions* used in verses 16 and 17 with reference to the Holy Spirit's relation to the church.)

17 . . . even the Spirit of truth, whom the world cannot receive, because it neither sees nor acknowledges him.
The Paraclete is here called the Spirit *of truth* (qualitative genitive). This, according to 16:13, means that he, being the truth in person, guides his people into that realm of truth which is embodied in Christ and his redemption.

In view of the fact that *the world* (κόσμος; see Vol. I, p. 79, footnote 26, probably meaning 6) follows Satan's lie (see on 8:44, 45; 14:30), lacks an organ of spiritual discernment (it does not *perceive* the Spirit and his actions, I Cor. 2:12-14) and fails *to acknowledge* the Spirit (Matt. 12:22-37; Acts 2:12-17), ascribing the influences of the third person of the Holy Trinity to "Beelzebub" or to "new wine," it *cannot* (see on 3:3, 5) receive him. (For the meaning of θεωρέω see Vol. I, p. 85, footnote 33; and for γινώσκω see on 1:10, 31; 3:11; 8:28.)

Y o u do know him, because he dwells by y o u r side, and will be within y o u. Note the difference in the verbs and prepositions (according to what is probably the best reading):
14:16. "in order that *he may be in y o u r midst or with y o u* (μεθ' ὑμῶν)."
14:17. "because *he dwells by y o u r side* (παρ' ὑμῖν)."
14:17. "and *will be within y o u* (ἐν ὑμῖν)."

Johnston, G., article "Spirit, Holy Spirit," in *A Theological Word Book of the Bible* (edited by A. Richardson), New York, 1952, p. 245.
Moulton, J. H., and Milligan, G., *The Vocabulary of the Greek New Testament Illustrated from the Papyri and Other Non-Literary Sources,* London, New York, Toronto, second edition, 1915, the entry on this word.
Sasse, H., "Der Paraklet im Joh. Evang." *ZNTW,* 24 (1925), 261.
Snaith, H., "The Meaning of 'The Paraclete,'" *ExT,* 57, Number 2 (Nov. 1945), 47 ff.

The matter of interpreting these clauses is not easy. As has been said before, *one should read on and on* (see Vol. I, p. 71, on 1:4). Unless this is done, we could easily arrive at the following explanation:

"Right now the Holy Spirit is already dwelling within the heart of the Spirit-filled *Savior,* and thus *by their side.* As a result of this, they even now, at least in principle and in moments of spiritual clarity, recognize and acknowledge the Paraclete. But by and by the Spirit will establish an even closer relationship. He who had all along been at their side (παρά) would, on the day of Pentecost, come to be *in their midst* or *with* them (μετά) and *within* (ἐν) them."

Though such an interpretation is tempting, it does not work out, and this particularly in view of verse 23: "and we will come to him, and make our home *by his side* (or: *with* him)." Here the "by his side" relationship is definitely ascribed to the dispensation of the Spirit (note close connection between verse 23 and verses 25, 26). Hence, one is not justified in making any sharp distinction between the present *by y o u r side* relationship and the future *in the midst of* and *within* relationship. Also, one is not justified in ascribing a too restricted meaning to the preposition "by the side" (παρά), as if it necessarily indicated a less close relationship. For the real meaning of παρά in such contexts see on verse 23.

In view of this difficulty some commentators have interpreted the passage now under study (14:17) as if Jesus meant to say, "Even now y o u already have the Spirit in y o u r hearts. By and by, at Pentecost, y o u will know more about him." But this amounts to an underestimation of the significance of Pentecost.

While agreeing that there is a difference in the meaning of the prepositions, it is probably much better to seek the solution in the direction of the following paraphrase:

"The Father will give y o u another Helper (verse 16), in order that he may be in y o u r midst (or, in that sense, *with* y o u) forever, even the Spirit of truth, whom the world cannot receive, because it neither sees nor knows him. Y o u, on the contrary, *once the Spirit has arrived, will know* him, because *he will dwell* at y o u r side (or *with* y o u, in the sense explained below in connection with verse 23) and will be within y o u" (verse 17). This reading of a present tense as if it were future is fully justified in such a context. Jesus is simply projecting himself into the future, having clearly used the future tense in verse 16 ("will give," and cf. "that he may be"). With the future period already *present* to his mind, he can now use the present tense, "Y o u *know him,* because he *dwells* at y o u r side," where we would use the future. That he has this future period in mind is again clearly shown by his use of the future tense in the very next clause, "And will be within y o u" (if the reading of N.N. in the text is correct).

On the day of Pentecost, therefore, the Holy Spirit would come to dwell *in the midst of, by the side of,* and *within* the disciples. He would enter personally into the church, which would become his temple, his permanent dwelling-place (see on 7:39; cf. I Cor. 3:16; II Cor. 6:16; Eph. 2:21). As a result, the church would throw away the swaddling clothes of infancy and would become spiritually of age. It would become a nation of prophets, a kingdom of priests, the Body of Christ (cf. I Pet. 2:9; Joel 2:28; I Cor. 12:7 ff.; Eph. 1:22, 23; 2:21, 22; 5:23-33). As a second result, on that day the church would become international. Broken down and destined to be broken down more and more would be the middle wall, the partition between Jew and Gentile (Is. 54:2, 3; Acts 2:9-11).

18. I will not leave y o u orphans: I am coming to y o u. What Jesus means is: "My departure will not be like that of a father whose children are left orphans when he dies. In the Spirit I am myself coming back to y o u." The Spirit reveals *the Christ,* glorifies *him,* applies *his* merits to the hearts of believers, makes *his* teachings effective in their lives. Hence, when the Spirit is poured out, Christ truly returns.

Here in verse 18 the reference is not primarily to the second coming but to the return of Christ in the Spirit at Pentecost. Reasons for adopting this position:

a. The immediately preceding context refers to the outpouring of the Spirit.

b. So does the immediately following context.

c. Thus only can it be explained that the disciples are not left orphans.

d. At the consummation of the age Jesus will come to *the world* as well as to the church. In the Spirit, poured out at Pentecost, he chooses as his abode the church *only.*

e. One of the results of the coming referred to here in verse 18 is that the disciples will know that "I am in the Father, and y o u in me, and I in y o u." The knowledge of the believers' intimate union with Christ was a fruit of Pentecost: Rom. 6:3-11; 8:1; 12:5; 16:2, 3, 7, 11, 12, 13; I Cor. 1:30; 4:10, 15, 17; 7:39; 9:1; 11:11; 15:31, 58; 16:19, etc.

On the other hand, it is also true that Christ's abode through the Spirit in his church is a type of God's indwelling in the hearts of his people (in heaven and ultimately) in the restored universe. Note the following:

a. In this very context the words of verse 23, "And we will come to him and make our home with him," find their echo in Rev. 21:3, where the reference is to the perfect communion of God with his people in the new heaven and earth.

b. The expression "in that day" (verse 20) often refers to a long period of time in which one event is typical of another (and still future) happening.

c. Prophetic foreshortening, according to which great events seem to be compressed together so as to be seen at a single glance, is not unusual in Scripture. Thus Christ's first and second coming are seen together in Mal. 3:1, 2. The destruction of Jerusalem and the end of the world appear side by side (and the first viewed as foreshadowing the second) in Christ's eschatological address (Matt. 24 and 25; Mark 13; Luke 21). Thus also here in 18-21 the return of Christ in the Spirit holds within its bosom the promise of the return which the church is still awaiting.

19. Yet a little while, and the world no longer sees me, but y o u see me; because I live y o u too will live. For the meaning of the expression "a little while" see also on 7:33; 12:35; 13:33; and 16:16-19. Note, however, that the connotation of this phrase is climactic: the *little while* is shrinking more and more. It is now no longer a half year or even a few days. It is now the night between Thursday and Friday. On Friday Jesus will die on the cross. After that *the world* (κόσμος defined by Jesus himself in verse 24 as referring to those who do not love him; see Vol. I, p. 79, footnote 26, meaning (6)) will no longer see him. Not even physically will they be able to *observe* him. In the Spirit, however, the disciples will indeed *observe* Jesus. (The verb is θεωρέω; see Vol. I, p. 85, footnote 33), for that Spirit, from Pentecost on, will bring Christ's teachings concerning himself home to the hearts of these men and their followers, sothat what the Lord from heaven is doing on earth day by day will *pass in review* (note the verb once more) before their eyes.

Now in order to see Jesus as he carries out his victorious program in the church through the Spirit, one must be fully alive spiritually. The disciples will be able to see or observe Jesus, for they will be alive. They will live because Christ lives. He, being in his own person the way and the truth and the life, is ever the cause of their spiritual life. Yes, *ever,* for he is unchangeable; but as far as *they* are concerned, this life will blossom forth most abundantly on and after Pentecost; hence, with respect to *them* the future tense is used: y o u too *will live.*

20. In that day y o u will recognize that I am in my Father, and y o u in me, and I in y o u.

In the new dispensation, beginning with the outpouring of the Holy Spirit, the disciples (and those who afterward embrace the Christ by living faith) will recognize and joyfully acknowledge the closeness of the relationship between the Father and the Son (as has been shown in connection with verse 18). They will then also understand that this union is in turn the pattern for the relationship between Christ and his followers. To be sure, these two relationships are not identical. Between the Father and the Son there is *basically* (as the root of the unity in outward operation) a unity of *essence.* This unity is *absolute,* incapable of growth. On the other hand, between the Son and believers there is an *ethical and spiritual* unity. We *love* him because he first *loved* us. *This* unity is capable of growth. Nevertheless, in view of the fact that Christ by means of the Spirit actually lives in the hearts of believers, the former is truly a pattern for the latter.

So close is the relation between Christ and believers that while he is the vine, they are the vine-branches. He is the shepherd; they the sheep. They are the members of the body of which he is the head (see on 10:11, 14; 15:5; cf. I Cor. 12:27). One of the most striking passages in this connection is certainly Rev. 3:21, which shows not only *the closeness* and *tenderness* of the relationship between Christ and believers, but also indicates, as does the passage which we are studying (14:20), that this relationship is a reflection of the everlasting and ontological union between the Father and the Son. — This prediction has an anticipatory and an ultimate fulfilment, as has been shown in connection with verse 18 (see above).

21. He who has my precepts and keeps them, he it is who loves me. The joyful and obedient recognition of Christ's sovereignty — hence, the *keeping* (see on 8:51) of his *precepts* (see on 13:34) — is the proof of genuine discipleship. The grammatical structure of the sentence is such that one can turn it around and retain the truth, now viewed from the opposite angle: "He who loves me, he it is who has my precepts and keeps them." One can also put it this way: Verse 21, as it stands (with "he who has my precepts and keeps them" as subject and "he it is who loves me" as predicate) is the obverse of verse 15 ("If y o u love me, y o u will keep my precepts"). But why does Jesus, having spoken about the dispensation of the Spirit in verses 16-20, return to the thought of verse 15, the keeping of his (Christ's) precepts? Probably because apart from the Spirit, no keeping of precepts is possible. Note that the mere *possession* of these precepts is not enough. One must *have them and keep them.* Cf. Matt. 7:24; Jas. 2:14-26.

Now the one who *constantly* keeps the precepts which he has as an *abiding* possession, he (*he alone,* the pronoun ἐκεῖνος is emphatic) shows thereby that he *constantly* loves the Lord Jesus Christ (note the three present participles). For the meaning of the word rendered *loves* (in ἐκεῖνός ἐστιν ὁ ἀγαπῶν με; literally, "that one is the one loving me") we refer to the discussion of this verb and its main synonym, in connection with 21:15-17.

And he who loves me will be loved of my Father, and I too will love him, and will manifest myself to him. Note the future tense. But does not the Father's love *precede* ours? Is it not true that the whole of our love is but the answer to his love? True not only, but that is also exactly what the apostle John remembered of the teaching of Jesus (I John 4:19). But why cannot God's love *both* precede and follow ours? That is exactly what it does, and that is the beauty of it: first, by *preceding* our love, it creates in us the eager desire to keep Christ's precepts; then, by *following* our love, it rewards us for keeping them! Nothing could ever be more glorious

281

than such an arrangement! For a commentary on the love of the Father for his people see Rom. 8:28-32. Note also that in that famous chapter Paul shifts the emphasis, sothat having spoken of the love of *God* (in the verses indicated), he follows this up immediately by riveting the attention on the love of *Christ* (Rom. 8:35-37). He concludes by indicating that in reality the two are one and the same (though the two divine persons remain forever distinct), sothat they can be summarized in the beautiful expression "the love of God which is in Christ Jesus our Lord" (Rom. 8:39).

Similarly, Jesus here, having mentioned the love of the Father, immediately adds, "And *I too* will love him." This intelligent and purposeful love is made manifest by the Spirit. The expression, "and will manifest myself to him" takes on reality in the lives of believers again and again (see on 15:26; 16:13, 14; cf. I Cor. 2:10, 11; 12:3-7), sothat they can say, "But the Lord stood by me and strengthened me" (II Tim. 4:17, 18). See also Ps. 23 and Rev. 3:20. This manifestation of Christ to the believer is ever in the Spirit and through the Word.

22. Judas (not Iscariot) said to him, Lord, what has happened that thou art about to manifest thyself to us, and not to the world? The Judas who interrupts the Lord was not the man who had just left the house (13:30), that is, he was not Iscariot (see on 6:71).[167] This is added for the sake of clarity and for the protection of the memory of "Judas the Greater" (see Vol. I, pp. 19, 20). On the contrary, he was *Judas* the *Thrice*-named, the one who is called *Lebbaeus,* whose surname was *Thaddaeus* (probably *courageous, lion-hearted*). He was "Judas of James" (Luke 6:16; cf. Acts 1:13). In the four lists of the apostles this Judas is placed next to Simon (the Zealot), from which some have inferred that the two were brothers or very close friends. (Note the striking resemblance between these disciples as pictured by Da Vinci in his *Last Supper.*) Although in apocryphal writings his name occurs again and again, the New Testament records no other incident with respect to him than the one here described.

As often in the Fourth Gospel (see on 3:4; 4:11, 15, 33; 6:52; 8:22, 57; 11:12; 13:9) so also in this case a listener takes up a word or phrase which Jesus has uttered, and misinterprets it. Upon this misinterpretation the listener bases his question.

The particular expression to which Judas gave the wrong interpretation was, "Yet a little while, and *the world no longer sees me . . .* and *I will*

---

[167] It is well to distinguish carefully between the seven men mentioned in the New Testament who bear this name (Judas). a. a brother of Jesus, the author of a canonical epistle (Matt. 13:55; Mark 6:3; Jude 1). b. an ancestor of Jesus (Luke 3:30). c. a Galilean who stirred up rebellion in the days of the enrolment (Acts 5:37). d. one with whom Paul lodged in Damascus, whose house was on Straight Street (Acts 9:11). e. Judas Barsabbas (Acts 15:22 ff.). f. Judas Iscariot, the traitor. g. the Judas mentioned in our passage, who also was one of the Twelve.

manifest myself to him (that is, to the one who loves me)" (14:19, 21). Jesus had clearly spoken about a manifestation *in the Spirit,* and therefore *spiritual* in character. Judas, however, was probably thinking of a public manifestation by means of mighty miracles or by means of a kind of Messianic theophany, as on the coming judgment day (cf. 5:27-29). Did he still cherish the hope that powerful works displayed in public would convince the world? (The question of Judas reminds us strongly of the advice given by the brothers of Jesus; see on 7:3, 4.) Moreover, the fact that some weeks later, at the very moment when Jesus was about to ascend to heaven, the disciples were still dreaming earthly, nationalistic dreams (Acts 1:6) causes us to think that what Judas meant here in 14:22 was this, "Lord, what has happened (in other words, *why is it*) that, in a dramatic manner, thou art about to display thy great power to *us* alone, and not also to *the public in general?* Would not the latter policy be far better and more effective?" For the meaning of κόσμος here see Vol. I, p. 79, footnote 26, meaning (3).

We do not believe that the question of Judas was merely theoretical, as if he were asking, "How, in the abstract, is it possible for thee to reveal thyself in such a manner that only thy disciples will be able to see thee?" The occasion was far too serious for purely speculative questions. "Show thyself — thy great power — to the world. It may not be too late. Make an impression. Get into the limelight. Win applause. Overthrow the opposition." There seems to have been something of *that* spirit in Judas. He is somewhat dissatisfied with the words spoken by Jesus (14:19, 21).

In view of the fact that basically the error of Judas concerned the character of Christ's promised *manifestation,* Jesus, while seemingly simply continuing from where he left off in verse 21, gives a further explanation of this concept in the words of verses 23 and 24:

23. Jesus answered and said to him, If a man loves me, he will keep my word, and my Father will love him.

For the meaning of the first part of this conditional sentence see on verse 15. There the plural was used; here the singular. The form of the sentence and the use of the singular emphasizes the responsibility of each disciple to ask himself whether he personally loves Jesus. The term *my word* here in verse 23 is explained by *my precepts* in verse 15.

Such love, having Jesus as its object, receives a rich reward: "My Father (note *my,* and see on 1:14) will love him," etc. The question, "Which love is first?" has been answered in connection with verse 21b. Note that the *active* expression "and my Father will love him," corresponds to the *passive* "he will be loved of my Father" in verse 21; hence, see also on that verse.

And we will come to him and make our home with him. In the Spirit (see preceding context) both the Father and the Son will come *to* (πρός, *face to face with;* see on 1:1) the one who loves the Lord, and will make their home with (παρά: *by the side of*) him.

This presence is very real. Its operation can be felt. The Spirit will convict of sin, lead to daily repentance, impart assurance of salvation, bestow the peace of God that passes all understanding, admonish, comfort; all of this in connection with *the Word.* It is in that way that Christ has promised to manifest himself to *the disciples,* but not to the world (see on 14:21, 22).

The clause, "and make our home with him," (home is μονή; see on 14:2) indicates a very close and intimate relationship. Father and Son, in and through the Spirit, are ever *by the side of* (παρά) those who love their Lord, ready to comfort, ready to cheer, ready to extend any and all necessary help.[168]

That the promise of this coming, though primarily referring to Pentecost and the present dispensation, receives its ultimate fulfilment at Christ's return and in the new heaven and earth has been shown (see on 14:18).

24. He who does not love me does not keep my words; and the word which y o u hear is not mine but the Father's who sent me. For the meaning of this passage see on 14:15, 21, and 23. Jesus has repeatedly shown that both of the following propositions are true: (a) He who loves me keeps my words. (b) He who keeps my words loves me. It follows logically that "He who does not love me does not keep my words." These *words* can be

---

[168] A close study of the use of παρά in John's Gospel is rewarding. The root-meaning is *alongside* or *by the side of* (cf. our *parallel*). Though in the New Testament it often occurs with the accusative (as was to be expected), it is never found with that case in any of John's writings. Followed by the ablative it may indicate agency (1:6), in a context in which agency and origin are very closely related, but usually denotes origin, source. Thus, Jesus is the only begotten *from* (the side of) the Father, *from* whom he has received instructions, has heard words, etc. (1:14; 5:44; 8:40; 9:16, 33; 15:15, 26). See also 1:41; 4:9, 52; 5:34, 41; 6:45, 46; 7:29, 51; 8:26, 38; 10:18; 16:27; 17:7, 8.

With the locative it occurs in the following passages: 1:40; 4:40; 8:38 (first clause); 14:17, 23, 25; 17:5; and 19:25. Except in 19:25 ("standing *by* or *near* the cross of Jesus") the word which follows the preposition indicates a *person* (or persons). This construction (παρά with locative) probably comes closest to retaining the original, etymological sense of the preposition: *at* (or *by*) *the side of.* Nevertheless, it is clear that this must not be taken too literally: *at the side of,* by an easy transition, becomes *in the company of, at the home of* (1:40); *in the presence of, among* (cf. Latin, *apud,* 4:40; 8:38; 14:25; 17:5). It seems probable, in view of the context, that the idea of *helpfulness* is implied in the use of this preposition in 14:17 and 14:23. The Holy Spirit is the *Para*-clete (note the preposition παρά, now in composition), the *Helper,* called to the side of the disciples in order to help them in every possible way. He remains *by their side,* and through him, in glorious mystic union, both Father and Son make their home *by their side,* ready at any time to render assistance and to reveal their love. We do not object in any way to the translation *with* for παρά, if it be understood in this sense. See also *Gram. N.T.,* pp. 612-616.

viewed severally, as so many precepts. They can also be viewed as a unit: Christ's *word*, his *teaching*, as the rule for doctrine and life. Note that here in verse 24 we first have the plural, then the singular.

The last part of the verse has been explained in connection with 7:16, which embodies the same thought. Rejecting the precepts of Christ is a very serious matter, for: a) Such a person is not rejecting the word of a mere man, but of God (Father and Son being one in essence; see on 10:30). (b) To such a person the Lord will not manifest himself in his love (see on 14:21, 23).

---

25 "These things I have told y o u while still remaining with you. 26 Moreover, the Helper, the Holy Spirit, whom the Father will send in my name, he will teach y o u everything, and will remind y o u of everything that I myself said to y o u. 27 Peace I leave with y o u; my peace I give to y o u; not as the world gives do I give to y o u. Let not y o u r hearts any longer be troubled, nor let them remain fearful. 28 Y o u heard that I said to y o u, 'I go away and am coming to y o u.' If y o u loved me, y o u would have rejoiced that I am going to the Father,[169] for the Father is greater than I. 29 And now I have told y o u before it happens, in order that [170] when it does happen, y o u may believe. 30 No longer will I discuss many things with y o u, for the prince of this world is coming. And yet, in me he has nothing; 31 but in order that the world may know that I love the Father, (even so) I do as the Father has commanded me. — Get up and let us go away from here."

14:25-31

14:25, 26. These things I have told y o u while still remaining with y o u. Moreover, the Helper, the Holy Spirit, whom the Father will send in my name, he will teach y o u everything, and will remind y o u of everything that I myself said to y o u.

Jesus seems to linger with his disciples as long as possible. Again and again he seems to bid them farewell; nevertheless, again and again he remains a little longer. There is a tone of departure in the words, "These things I have told y o u while still remaining with y o u." Yet, the Master lingers. Cf. 14:31; 15:11; 16:1, 4, 25, 33. *These things*, in view of *while still remaining with y o u*, which is surely very general, cannot be restricted to the words spoken that night, but obviously indicate *all* his teaching up to this very moment. Now Jesus draws a *distinction* (notice, he does not present a *contrast*; δε should here be translated *moreover* or *and* or *now*, not *but*) between his own teaching during the days of his humiliation, on the one hand, and his own teaching through the Spirit in the glory of his

---

[169] II C; see Vol. 1, pp. 41, 42.
[170] or *sothat* (result); on ἵνα see Vol. I, pp. 46, 47, 51.

exaltation, on the other. The central idea of verses 25, 26 may be summarized as follows:

"While yet abiding physically with y o u I have given y o u certain teachings which after my physical departure from y o u I, through the Spirit, will make much clearer to you (cf. I Cor. 2:13). Moreover, I will then teach y o u *everything* which y o u need to know in order to perform the work of witnessing which is assigned to y o u."

Note the names given to the third person of the Trinity: the Helper (παράκλητος); see on 14:16; the Holy Spirit, *holy* because, he is not only himself completely sinless and in possession of all the moral attributes in an infinite degree — which, of course, is true also with respect to the Father and the Son —, but also because it is *he* [171] who takes the leading part in the work of making others holy (sanctification). He is also characterized as the One "whom the Father will send in my (Christ's) name." Cf. Acts 2:33. The sending of the Holy Spirit and also his work on earth is in complete harmony with Christ's name, that is, with his self-revelation in the sphere of redemption. A comparison between 14:26, "whom the Father will send in my name," and 15:26, "whom I will send from the Father," makes it very clear that the historical sending of the Holy Spirit on the day of Pentecost (see Acts 2) is ascribed to both the Father and the Son. Does not this historical *effusion* imply that also the eternal, super-historical *procession* of the Spirit must be viewed as an act in which the Father and the Son cooperate?

Note that the promise contains *two* elements, and that in all probability the first *everything* (or *all things: πάντα*) is more comprehensive than the second. First, the Spirit will teach y o u *everything* that is necessary (not only for y o u r own salvation, but here specifically) for the work of witnessing (cf. Matt. 10:10; I John 2:27). This includes certain things which Jesus had not specifically taught during the days of his humiliation, having omitted them for a very wise reason (see on 16:12). Secondly, the Spirit will remind y o u of *everything* that I myself said to y o u. As already indicated, by means of both of these Jesus Christ is fulfilling his prophetic office, first on earth, then from heaven.

The two *everythings* may be viewed as concentric circles, for also by means of recalling the old ("everything that I myself said to y o u"), the Spirit would be teaching the new. It must be borne in mind that between the time when Jesus uttered these words and the moment when the Holy Spirit was poured out there occurred the following significant events:

---

[171] Notice "even the Holy Spirit . . . he" The fact that the Holy Spirit is a person is here emphasized, for although πνεῦμα is neuter, the masculine pronoun ἐκεῖνος is used to introduce his activities. Moreover, we are told that this Spirit teaches, reminds, testifies, comes, convinces, guides, speaks, hears, predicts, etc. All these activities are personal.

Christ's crucifixion, resurrection, ascension, and coronation. In the light of these great events the work of the Holy Spirit in reminding the disciples of the former teachings of Jesus would naturally imply new teaching, or if one prefers, it would imply the impartation of a deeper understanding of that which when it was first heard had hardly registered. As proof we offer the following passages: 2:22; 12:16. Even then, of course, the special guidance of the Spirit was necessary in order to convey to their minds the exact meaning of Christ's words in the light of his atonement and glorification.

27. Peace I leave with y o u; my peace I give to y o u; not as the world gives do I give to y o u. By means of all the words of comfort which precede verse 27 Jesus aims to instill peace in the hearts of the disciples. "This peace," says Jesus as it were, "is both *a legacy* which *I leave behind* (ἀφίημι) and *a treasure* which *I give* (δίδωμι)." It is true, of course, that Jesus establishes this peace by his atoning death on the cross, whereby he brings about reconciliation. Nevertheless, to say that the word *peace* as used here in verse 27 is purely objective and has nothing to do with the subjective feeling within the heart of the believer is going too far. That the peace here indicated implies absence of the troubled and fearful feeling is clear from the words which immediately follow, namely, **Let not y o u r hearts any longer be troubled, neither let them be fearful.** As stated repeatedly in this commentary, in order to establish the meaning of terms, phrases, and clauses, one must read on and on. That applies also to this case. But that which *precedes* also has significance in determining meanings. In the light of the entire chapter we believe that the word *peace* here in 14:27 indicates *that absence of spiritual unrest and that assurance of salvation and of God's loving presence under all circumstances which results from exercising faith in God and in his Son (14:1) and from the contemplation of his gracious promises* (see especially 14:1, 2, 3, 12-14, 16-21, 25, 26). It is the peace of which Paul speaks in Phil. 4:6, 7. When Jesus says, "Not as the world gives do I give to y o u," the context makes clear that what he means is, "I give *my* peace," which the world can never bestow, no matter how often it may say, "Peace to y o u," or "Go in peace." The contrast is in the gift itself rather than merely in the manner in which the gift is bestowed. The world may give outward pleasure, physical rest and enjoyment, honor, wealth, but never that inner assurance which is the reflection of the smile of God in the heart of his child.

For the meaning of, "Let not y o u r hearts any longer be troubled," see on 14:1. When the peace bestowed by Christ (and merited for us by his atonement) enters the heart, anxiety is driven out. "Neither let them *be fearful*" (literally, "neither let *it* — y o u r *heart,* where our idiom prefers: y o u r *hearts* — be fearful). It is the only instance of the use of this verb

287

in the New Testament (but see II Tim. 1:7 for the noun). It does occur in Aristotle, in the papyri, and rather frequently in the LXX. It means *to be cowardly, timid, or fearful.* In distinction from φόβος, which is often used in a good sense (pious fear), δειλία to which the verb δειλιάω is related, is never used in a good sense.

28, 29. Y o u heard that I said to y o u, I go away and am coming to y o u. If y o u loved me, y o u would have rejoiced that I am going to the Father, for the Father is greater than I. And now I have told y o u before it happens, in order that when it does happen, y o u may believe.

Again and again Jesus had been saying, "I go away" (see 14:2, 3, 12) and also, "I am coming to y o u" (see 14:3, 18, 19, 21, 23). If the disciples had made more progress in love for their Master, they would not have been so filled with anxious fears. They would have rejoiced in the fact that this departure of the Lord was, after all, *for him a going home to the Father.* Although, to be sure, as the only-begotten Son he was fully equal to the Father as to essence (10:30), nevertheless, as the Mediator between God and man, himself *man,* he was inferior. Hence, when as a reward upon his work, the man of sorrows and acquainted with grief proceeds on his way to the One who was greater than himself — for God is ever greater than man — this is for him a rich reward. Cf. also II Cor. 8:9; Phil. 2:8-11; Hebrews 12:2. For the meaning of 14:29 see on 13:19. Here in verse 29 *the application* is slightly different. The clause, "when it does happen," refers now to Christ's going away (death, resurrection, ascension) and coming again (in the Spirit on Pentecost; as meant for the church in general this has another application in connection with the Parousia).

In their thoughts and meditations the disciples had been concentrating too much on themselves. Had they loved *him* sufficiently, they would have realized that this departure would bring glory *to him!* Seeing this, they would have rejoiced.

30. Much, very much, had happened this evening. The Master and his disciples had been in the Upper Room for a long time, perhaps for several hours. The washing of the disciples' feet, the eating of the Passover Supper, the predictions regarding Judas, Peter, and the Eleven, the institution of the Lord's Supper, the words of chapter 14, all this (and perhaps much more that has not been recorded) belongs to the first part of the night of the betrayal.

And now the time of departure from the room has almost arrived, as Jesus may be indicating by saying, **No longer will I discuss many things with y o u.** The very fact, however, that he says, "No longer . . . many things," implies that he still has a few things to discuss, whether here in the Upper Room or on the way to Gethsemane. The reason why the time for further conversation is short is given in the clause, **for the prince of this world** (for the meaning of this title see on 12:31) **is coming.** Jesus was aware of the footsteps of Judas, Roman soldiers, temple-police, members of the Sanhedrin, all of them inspired by Satan. They were starting out even now and were on their way to capture Jesus. Of course, they had no right to do this. They were proceeding with swords and sticks (Luke 22:52), with "lanterns, torches, and weapons" (18:3), as if their object were to search out and catch a dangerous criminal. **And yet** — for this meaning of χαί see on 1:5b — , **in me he has nothing,** says Jesus; indeed, nothing at all, for there was no guilt in him. See on 18:38; cf. Is. 53:9. In view of this fact, is Jesus going to resist this attempt to capture him? The answer is given in the next verse:

31. But in order that the world may know that I love the Father, (even so) I do as the Father has commanded me.[172] Jesus here says that he will not resist, but instead will go forth boldly, on his way to meet Satan's representatives. He will do this because he lays down his life voluntarily (10:11). This was in accordance with the Father's commandment (see on 10:18). And the world is going to see this. Deep down in their hearts these wicked men will know that this behavior of his — so very strange and uncommon, walking boldly into the hands of his captors! — results from

---

[172] It makes little difference whether we follow the punctuation as given in the text of N.N. (which is also our preference), sothat, "Get up, and let us go away from here," becomes a separate sentence, or do as others prefer (see the textual apparatus in N.N.), that is, place a comma or semi-colon after "has commanded me," thereby making all of verse 31 *one* sentence. In either case the entire passage comprises one central thought, "Let us not flee, but let us go forth to meet Satan's representatives, for by doing this I wish to show the world that I love the Father." It may be objected that the conjunction χαί requires that the entire verse be read as one sentence, and that otherwise it would be "hanging in the air," somewhat as follows: "But in order that the world may know that I love the Father, *and* (χαί) as the Father has commanded me, (that) thus I do. . . ." This would require a conclusion, which those who favor this view find in the words, "Get up, and let us go away from here." Objections:

a. The transition from the first (*"I* love, *I* do") to the second person ("Get up") is not normal in such a connection. One would expect the *first* person (whether sing. or plural), hardly the *second* person.

b. This interpretation seems to be based on the erroneous notion that χαί must mean *and,* and that every Greek χαί must be translated into English. But this is not true at all. Where Greek is influenced by Hebrew or by Aramaic we must ever be on the lookout for χαί's which should be rendered by an English conjunction other than *and* (which is often true even regardless of Semitic influence) *or should be left entirely untranslated.* Failure to see this has led to all manner of confusion, for example, in the interpretation of Rom. 9:23 (note the χαί at the beginning of that verse). In John 14:31, we prefer either to render χαί *even so,* or else to omit it entirely in translating.

the fact that he loves the Father, as he has so often declared. They will know it, but, of course, they would never *admit* it!

In harmony with this expressed determination — namely, to meet the foe — Jesus adds: **Get up, and let us go away from here.** This command has led to endless controversy among interpreters. The difficulty lies in the fact that according to 18:1 Jesus and his disciples did not actually leave until after he had spoken the words of chapters 15, 16, and 17. For solutions which we regard as less probable see the note.[173] But is this difficulty really so great? Why not assign to these words their most natural meaning, and interpret them as actually amounting to a command that the disciples *get up* from their couches, coupled with an exhortation meaning, "And let us go away *from here,* that is, from this Upper Room; hence, from this house"? That still would not imply that the little company now *immediately* rushes out of the house! How often does it not happen even among us Westerners that between the exhortation, "Now let us be going," and the actual departure there is a period of ten minutes? During that ten minutes a great deal can be said. Now, the following must be borne in mind:

a. In this very context Jesus clearly implies that there are still certain things which he wishes to say to the disciples (14:30).

b. Speaking calmly and deliberately, without any attempt to rush himself, Jesus may have uttered the contents of chapters 15, 16, and 17 within a period of *ten minutes!* When a company has been together for several hours, what is ten minutes?

---

[173] We note the following:

(1) What Jesus means here in 14:31 is, "Get up, let us go away from the Upper Room (or: from the house)." *He left immediately.* The words of chapters 15 and 16 were spoken *outside.* Also the prayer of chapter 17 was uttered *outside.* The little company stopped along the way.

Objection: Nowhere do we find any mention of this supposed stopping along the way. And if they did not stop somewhere, it is difficult to see how the prayer could have been uttered while Jesus and his disciples were *walking.* It is surely far more natural to assume that the teaching of all these chapters (14-17) belongs to the Upper Room.

(2) The meaning is, "Get up, let us go away *from the table.*"

Objection: Though we do not claim that this explanation is impossible, yet it would seem that the getting away *from the table* is already implied in the command, "Get up."

(3) The Greek has misconstrued the Aramaic written original, which had, "In order that the world may know that I love the Father, and that as the Father gave me commandment even so I do, *I* will arise and go hence."

Objection: It is not necessary to assume any mistranslation at this point. Besides, "*I* will arise and go hence," is somewhat unnatural when an entire company is about to arise and leave. — We adhere to the Greek text.

(4) There has been a misplacement. Thus, e.g., T. Nicklin, "A Suggested Dislocation in the Text of St. John XIV-XVI," *ExT*, 44 (May, 1933), 8.

Objection: Nothing in the text as it has reached us proves a literal *displacement.* Topical arrangement is possible, however.

c. Besides, the possibility of *topical* (instead of strictly *chronological*) arrangement must not be ruled out. Thus, chapter 15, "I am the real vine," may have been spoken a little earlier, in connection with the institution of the Lord's Supper (the drinking of "the fruit of the vine"). In that case the original author, John, simply inserted the material of ch. 15 because it was spoken *that night*. In Luke topical (instead of chronological) arrangement occurs again and again. John's arrangement is more chronological, but the *possibility* of merely topical arrangement must not be entirely ruled out. We believe, therefore, that chapter 15 was spoken either during or very shortly after (but with distinct reference to) the institution of the Lord's Supper.

Accordingly, we shall proceed upon the assumption that the contents of chapters 14-17 comprise a unit, and that all of this was spoken that night in the Upper Room.

Synthesis of Chapter 14

See the Outline on p. 260. *The Son of God Tenderly Instructing His Disciples. A Word of Comfort.*

We recognize *ten grounds of comfort*, which may be summarized as follows:

I. Verse 1. Continue to trust in God; also in me continue to trust. (This implies: I will continue to provide for y o u in every need. Let not y o u r hearts any longer be troubled).

II. Verse 2. My departure is for the purpose of preparing everything with a view to a blessed reunion in the Father's house with its many mansions.

III. Verse 3. I am coming again and will take y o u to be face to face with me. Then y o u will always be where I am.

IV. Verses 4-11. Although my visible presence will be withdrawn, I will ever remain for y o u the (only) way to the Father ("the way and the truth and the life").

V. Verses 12-14. As a result of my going to the Father y o u will not only do great works but even greater works. If y o u ask anything in my name, I will do it.

VI. Verses 15-17. My physical departure is for the purpose of sending y o u another Helper who will never leave y o u, namely, the Spirit of truth. The Father will give him to y o u in answer to my request.

VII. Verses 18-24. In that other Helper I will myself return (spiritually) to *y o u*, that is to all those who love me, not to the world.

VIII. Verses 25, 26. This other Helper, the Holy Spirit, will teach y o u everything, and will remind y o u of everything which I myself said to y o u.

IX. Verse 27. I leave behind as the greatest present of all (a gift far greater than the world can ever bestow) *my* peace.

X. Verse 28. I am going to the Father. If y o u loved me sufficiently, that would cause y o u to rejoice.

Verses 29-31 (see comments on these on pp. 288-291) form a conclusion to the entire chapter.

CHAPTER XV

JOHN   **15:1-11**

15 1 "I am the real vine, and my Father is the vine-dresser. 2 Every branch in me that bears no fruit he takes away, and every one that does bear fruit he cleanses, in order that it may bear more fruit. 3 Already y o u are clean because of the word which I have spoken to y o u. 4 Abide in me, and I (will abide) in y o u. Just as the branch cannot bear fruit of itself unless it abides in the vine, so neither can y o u unless y o u abide in me.[174] 5 I am the vine, y o u are the branches. He who abides in me, with me abiding in him, he it is that bears much fruit, for apart from me y o u can do nothing. 6 If a man does not abide in me, he is thrown away as a (mere) branch and withers; [174] and such branches are picked up, thrown into the fire, and burned. 7 If y o u abide in me, and my words abide in y o u, ask whatever y o u will, and it will take place for y o u.[174] 8 By this my Father is glorified that [175] you bear much fruit, and so y o u will become my disciples. 9 Just as the Father has loved me, so have I loved y o u; abide in my love. 10 If y o u keep my precepts, y o u will abide in my love,[176] just as I kept my Father's precepts and abide in his love. 11 These things I have spoken to y o u, in order that my joy may be in y o u, and in order that y o u r joy may be full."

Discussion of Certain Basic Points in connection with the Allegory of the Vine and the Branches

We can begin by repeating what was said in connection with the Allegory of the Good Shepherd: "In the interpretation of this sublime allegory commentators differ widely."

It is probably best to read these verses through, from beginning to end, several times before attempting any explanation. The earlier verses cannot be properly understood unless they are seen in the light of all that follows and, we may add, of that which preceded during this same night.

---

[174] The compound conditional sentence in 15:4 is IIIB1; conditional sentence in 15:6 is IIIB3 (with conclusions: aorist passive indicative gnomic, followed by third person plural present active indicative συνάγουσιν; again third person plural present active indicative Βάλλουσιν; and third person *singular* — because αὐτά is *neuter plural* — passive indicative καίεται). These two (15:4 and 15:6) should be reinserted in the lists, Vol. I, p. 44. Conditional sentence in 15:7 is IIIA3; see Vol. I, pp. 42, 43.
[175] On ἵνα see Vol. I, pp. 46, 51.
[176] IIIA1; see Vol. I, pp. 42, 43.

Hence, in order that we may not in studying *the trees* (individual passages) lose sight of *the forest* (the thrust of the entire allegory) we deem a "look at the whole" to be very advisable. *Only then when one reads on and on does the meaning of individual passages become clear.*

I. *The Occasion for This Allegory.*

The fact that before his trial and crucifixion this was the last opportunity which Jesus had to warn the disciples not to be like Judas but to remain in the faith, to manifest in their lives not the work of Satan but the *fruits* of the Holy Spirit, and the additional fact that the fertility of the vine (a very common plant in the Palestine of that day) readily suggested *spiritual fruit-bearing*, explains why Jesus spoke this allegory. Moreover, the illustration was not entirely new or strange. It was natural that the Israelite, acquainted with the Old Testament, would associate *fruitfulness* both natural and spiritual, with the idea of a *vine* (Ps. 80:8, 14; 128:3; Is. 5:1-7; Ezek. 17:8; Joel 2:22; Zech. 8:12; Mal. 3:11). That at times vines failed to bring forth desirable fruit was also well known, as was also the application of this truth to *spiritual* fruit-bearing (Is. 5:4; Jer. 2:21). *All this must be borne in mind in any attempt to interpret John 15:1-11.*

However, it is almost certain that there was an *additional* reason for the use of this allegory.[177] Its main metaphor was in all probability suggested by "the fruit of the vine" to which Jesus referred while instituting *the Lord's Supper.* See on 15:1.

II. *Its Central Meaning.*

The emphasis should be placed where it rightly belongs. Although Jesus speaks about several things, such as the true vine, the vine-dresser, the branches, bearing fruit, the taking away and burning of unfruitful branches, etc., yet there is *one* main lesson:

Just as a vine-offshoot bears fruit only when it abides in the vine, so also believers will bear spiritual fruit only when they abide in Christ. Hence, the precept which underlies the entire section is *Abide in me in order that y o u may bear fruit abundantly.* That this is, indeed, the main idea is clear from the frequent occurrence of the words *bear fruit* and *abide.*

III. *The Two Groups Here Indicated.*

A. These two groups are (metaphorically):

1. Branches that bear fruit (15:2b, 5, 8).

2. Branches that do not bear fruit (15:2a, 6).

B. They are treated as follows:

1. Branches that bear fruit are cleansed (15:2b).

---

[177] A. T. Robertson, *Word Pictures in the New Testament.* New York and London, 1932, Vol. V., p. 257.

2. Branches that do not bear fruit are taken away, allowed to wither, picked up, thrown into the fire, and burned (15:2a, 6).

C. Who are represented by these two groups?

Again and again in the Fourth Gospel those to whom the good tidings are proclaimed and who therefore, in a certain sense, "have the light," are divided into two groups: a. those who accept the message; and b. those who reject it (see on 1:9; 12:35, 36). Do we have something similar here? The historical background certainly points in that direction. Judas had left. His relation to Jesus has been (*outwardly,* to all appearances) very close (see on 13:18). But now Judas was on the way to destruction. Would it not seem natural then that, in speaking of branches that do not bear fruit, are taken away, allowed to wither, picked up, thrown into the fire, and burned, Jesus was thinking of men who, like Judas, had once stood in very close connection with him, had left him, and were on their way to everlasting destruction? And again, would it not seem natural that, in speaking of branches that bear fruit, he was thinking of the other disciples, and in general, of all those who by remaining in him produced much spiritual fruit?

This conclusion as to the meaning of the two metaphors (branches that bear fruit, branches that do not bear fruit) is greatly strengthened by an identical passage found in two accounts, both of which describe the happenings of this same night. Here in chapter 15 this passage is not explained; but in chapter 13, where it is also found, the explanation is added to it.

The passage to which we refer is:

"Y o u are clean" (ὑμεῖς καθαροί ἐστε 13:10; 15:3).

In 13:10, 11 this is amplified as follows: " 'And y o u are clean, but not all of y o u are.' For he knew the one who was betraying him. It was for this reason that he said, 'Not all of y o u are clean.' " — That would seem to settle the question with respect to the identity of the two groups. Group a. (branches that bear fruit and are cleansed) represents all those who not only come into close contact with Christ and the Gospel but also (by God's sovereign grace and through faith) accept it. Group b. (branches that do not bear fruit and are taken away and burned) represents all the others who have come into close contact with Christ and the Gospel.

The two groups have in common their close contact with Christ and the Gospel. Speaking in terms of the metaphor, both groups of branches were *in the vine* (see, however, footnote 179). That this relation of having been *in the vine* (or, dropping the metaphor, *in Christ*) does not have to refer to the spiritual, saving union with Christ is easy to see. Not all those who are *in* the covenant are *of* the covenant. Not all those who were baptized *into* Moses were saved (I Cor. 10:1-5). That in speaking of men who have at one time been *in* him, but subsequently forsook him, Jesus had in mind not a merely hypothetical possibility but an oft-repeated situation in actual

295

life, is apparent from 15:6, "If a man does not abide in me, he is thrown away as a (mere) branch and withers; and such branches *are picked up, thrown into the fire* (literally, "and they pick them up and throw them into the fire") and *burned";* where the indicatives show that it is assumed that these things actually happen.

In no sense whatever do such passages as 15:2 and 15:6 suggest that there is a falling away from grace, as if those who were once actually saved finally perish. *This allegory plainly teaches that the branches which are taken away and burned represent people who never once bore fruit, not even, when they were "in" Christ.* Hence, they never were true believers; and for them the in-the-vine relationship, though close, was merely outward. There is, accordingly, nothing here (in 15:1-11) that clashes in any way with 10:28 (see on that passage). The true believers of chapter 15 are represented by those branches which, abiding forever in the vine, bear fruit, more fruit, much fruit. *These never perish!*

15:1-11

15:1. I am the real vine. Bear in mind that this was spoken during the night of the Passover meal; more specifically either *during* or *very shortly after* the institution of the Lord's Supper. That night one could see on the table (among other things) *the lamb, the bread,* and *the fruit of the vine,* namely, the wine. Now in this very room there was present One apart from whom these things had little real significance (except historical). Did the disciples fail to see this? Yet, as to *the lamb,* had not the Baptist said, while pointing to Christ, "Look, the Lamb of God who is taking away the sin of the world?" Similarly, Jesus now bids these men to look away from the symbols of merely physical bread and wine and to see *in him* the reality, the fulfilment, the great Antitype. Having taken in his hand a piece of bread he said, "This is *my body* . . . do this in remembrance *of me"* (Luke 22:19; I Cor. 11:24). And with reference to the fruit of the vine he said, "This cup is the new covenant in *my blood.* Do this, as often as y o u drink it, in remembrance *of me . . . I* am the *real* vine" (I Cor. 11:25 and the passage now under study, namely, John 15:1). In this connection see also Matt. 26:29; Mark 14:25; Luke 22:18, which clearly show that during the institution of the Lord's Supper Jesus spoke about "the fruit of the vine." [178]

---

[178] Many expositors see no connection whatever between Luke 22:14-19 and John 15:1-11. However, those among them who believe that the words of John 15 were spoken during the night of the Lord's Supper — the very supper in connection with which Jesus spoke about the fruit of the *vine* and about "the cup of the new covenant in my blood" — will have difficulty in explaining why they nevertheless conceive of the "I am the *real* vine" discourse as bearing no relation whatever to the newly instituted sacrament. Such a representation which wholly separates what

Not the vine from which the communion-wine had been derived, nor even Israel (which on the coins of the Maccabean period was represented by a vine), but Christ himself, present with the disciples that memorable night, was the *real* vine. Do the branches attain their unity in the vine? Does the vine sustain them? Do they owe their fruit-bearing capacity to the vine? Thus also — only *in a far higher degree* — does the church find its *unity*, its *life*, and its *fertility* in Christ. We must place the emphasis upon this phrase "in a far higher degree." If we do not do so, we are not doing justice to the lesson which Jesus stressed in this great I AM. He said, "I (or I myself) am the vine, the *real* one." To be sure, the *unity* which an earthly vine imparts to the branches is very close and organic. Were it not so, this metaphor could not have been employed. But the oneness of believers with one another and with Christ is far more glorious. They are the body of which he is the head. This unity is moral, mystical, and spiritual. It is a union founded on love. Again, the *life* which the branch receives from its parent, the vine, is highly appreciated by the owner of the vineyard, for apart from this there would be no vintage. But, after all, this life merely amounts to physical sustenance. It is but a dim shadow compared with the *everlasting* life which Jesus, by means of his death, gives to all those who accept him by a true faith. And so also the *fertility* of the vine, sothat its branches hang their many purple clusters in the sunlight, though ever so glorious, is nothing at all in comparison with the abiding fruitfulness with which the Son of God adorns those who love him; for the fruits of his Spirit are love, joy, peace, patience, kindness, goodness, faithfulness, gentleness, self-control (Gal. 5:22, 23; see also on John 15:16). Yes, indeed, Jesus has the right to say,

"I am the vine, the *real* (or *genuine*) one."

And my Father is the vine-dresser. To Jesus the first person of the Holy Trinity is *my* Father, never *our* Father (see on 1:14). Here the Father is represented as the One who tills the ground (ὁ γεωργός), or, in the present connection, who tends the vine, by busying himself with its branches. These branches need much care in order that they may *bear fruit* (which, as has been shown, is the important point in this allegory). The men represented by the branches need much *fatherly* care. In this connection it must not be forgotten that the cleansing is *first of all* (though not exclusively; see on 13:10) *justification*, a work in which the *Father* takes the

---

almost certainly belongs together, seems unrealistic. On the other hand, it must be admitted that anyone who seeks *absolute proof* that the discourse of John 15 has something to do with the Lord's Supper will not find it. We have presented what we believe, for the reasons given, to be *the most probable* reconstruction. — We are undecided with respect to the question, "Was the allegory of John 15:1-11 spoken *during* the institution of the Lord's Supper or a little later, say: immediately after the words of chapter 14?" It makes no real difference.

leading part. Besides, it was *the Father* who gave the Son (3:16) in order that the forensic foundation for the entire work of cleansing might be established. It is *the Father* who, in answer to the request of the Son, sends the Holy Spirit (14:16). And it is *the Father* who is pre-eminent in those providential events of life whereby, when they are applied to the heart by the Spirit, the believer is cleansed more and more.

We are not saying that Jesus had *all* (or *only*) this in mind when he said, "And *my Father* is the vine-dresser." We merely mean to imply that there was more than sufficient reason why he calls *the Father* (not the Son, nor the Spirit, though in the outgoing works all three cooperate) the vine-dresser. One more item must not be forgotten: it is also the Father who takes away the vine-offshoots that bear no fruit!

What is implied already in verse 1 is stated specifically in verse 2:

2. Every branch in me that bears no fruit he takes it away, and every one that does bear fruit he cleanses it, in order that it may bear more fruit.

Just as a vine-dresser will take away the branches that bear no physical fruit, so the Father rejects those people who bear no spiritual fruit. For the nature of this fruit see especially Gal. 5.22 (quoted on p. 297); also Matt. 3:8-10; 7:16-20; 12:33; 13:8; 13:23; Rom. 1:13; 7:4; II Cor. 9:10; Eph. 5:9; Phil. 4:17; Col. 1:6; Heb. 12:11; 13:15; and Jas. 3:18. These fruits are good motives, desires, attitudes, dispositions (spiritual virtues), words, deeds, all springing from faith, in harmony with God's law, and done to his glory.

Those who bear good fruit are cleansed more and more. Having been justified, they now receive the grace of daily renewal, until *finally* (the last stage is the most *incisive* of all), completely sanctified, they reach the shores of heaven. The purpose of this daily cleansing in the life of God's child is to make him ever more fruitful. The one who has brought forth thirty can probably bring forth sixty or even a hundredfold.

Thus, all who are brought into close contact with Christ are compared with branches that are in the vine. Some bear fruit; others do not.[179] The responsibility is wholly theirs.

---

[179] There is another explanation which is possible grammatically, but we have not seen our way clear to adopt it. According to that view we would have to translate verse 2 as follows: "Every branch that bears no fruit in me (instead of, "Every branch in me that bears no fruit") he takes it away, and every one that does bear fruit (supply: *in me*) he cleanses it, in order that it may bear more fruit." The idea then would be this: besides the branches that are in the vine, *Christ,* there are also branches that are offshoots of *other* vines. These bear no fruit in him. See F. W. Grosheide, *op.cit.,* Vol. 11, p. 335. But, as we see it, this makes the matter too complicated. If that were the meaning, then besides the branches that bear good fruit there would also be those that do not bear such fruit, and these would again be divided into two categories: a. *some* do not bear good fruit

3. Already y o u are clean because of the word which I have spoken to y o u. By *faith* (3:16; 12:37; Acts 10:43; Rom. 3:22) in the *word* (3:34; 5:47; 12:48; Acts 2:41) of Christ, the eleven had become *clean* (see on 13:10), that is, had been *justified* (Rom. 5:1). This grace they had received *already*. The process of gradual cleansing (sanctification) would be continued.

4. Abide in me, and I (will abide) in y o u. In the process of bringing salvation to the hearts of men God is ever first! See on 3:3, 5. By his Spirit he invades the heart of the sinner. Thus the sinner, who has now become, in principle, a saint, has received power to abide in Christ. The more he does so, the more will he experience Christ's loving-presence (see also on 14:21). That is the promise. Hence, the words, "Abide in me," do not constitute a condition which man must fulfill in his own power before Christ will do his part. Far from it. It is sovereign grace from start to finish, but *the responsibility of abiding in Christ is placed squarely upon man's shoulders, exactly where it belongs. Without exertion there is no salvation.* But the power to exert oneself and to persevere is God-given! What is meant by abiding in Christ is explained in verses 7 and 9.

This precept, *even if it had been intended only for the eleven,* is by no means in conflict with the assurance given in 10:28, to the effect that the sheep will never perish. On the contrary, there is beautiful harmony, for exactly by means of obedience to this "command" the promise of 10:28 is fulfilled! The admonition, "Abide in me," is in agreement with numerous exhortations addressed to believers, warning them against apostasy and bidding them to abide in the faith. These warnings regard the matter from the side of man. They move on the plane of human responsibility (Col. 1:23; Heb. 2:1; 3:14; etc.). It is certainly true that once a man is truly saved, he remains saved forever; yet, God does not keep a man on the way of salvation without exertion, diligence, and watchfulness on man's part. And the strength thus to persevere in the faith is ever from God, from him alone!

By way of illustration, one might point to an incident in the life of Paul. In connection with a storm and shipwreck in which Paul was involved God had given him the definite promise, "There will be no loss of life among y o u" (Acts 27:22). Nevertheless, Paul says to the centurion and to the soldiers, "Unless these men remain in the ship, y o u cannot be saved" (Acts 27:31). The word of warning did not in any way contradict the certainty that the men would actually be saved. The men heeded the warning and no life was lost.

---

because they belong to a different vine; *others,* because they do not remain in the vine, Christ. Verses 4 and 6 seem to teach clearly enough that the reason (the *only* reason as far as this allegory is concerned) why some branches do not bear fruit is that they do not *remain* in *the* vine (Christ).

But on the basis of 14:21 (notice the very general character of this declaration) and 17:20 we may believe that the words spoken that night were meant not only for these eleven men, but also for many others who would follow them, in fact for all those who would be brought into close contact with Christ and the Gospel. And among these many there would also be several who would turn away from Christ. Hence, from every point of view the warning was altogether timely and necessary. Judas, let it be remembered, had turned away already!

Just as the branch cannot bear fruit of itself unless it abides in the vine, so neither can y o u unless y o u abide in me. One *cannot* enter the kingdom without birth from above (see on 3:3, 5). Once in the kingdom, one *cannot* bear fruit unless he remains in Christ, the vine. These are laws that allow no exceptions. To expect that fruit-bearing would be possible for the man who does not remain in Christ is even more foolish than to expect that a branch that has been severed from the vine can bring forth grapes! See also verse 5 (last clause).

5. I am the vine, y o u are the branches. First 15:1 is repeated: Jesus is the vine. Next, the thought already clearly implied in 15:2-4, is expressly stated, namely, "Y o u are the branches." A word is used for branch which literally means *vine*-branch or *vine*-twig (κλῆμα).

He who abides in me, with me abiding in him (literally, "He who abides in me, and I in him," but this is hardly good English), **he it is that bears much fruit, for apart from me y o u can do nothing.**
Note: *more fruit* (verse 2), *much fruit* (verses 5 and 8). The vitality of the vine, Jesus Christ, is stressed. This vine enables those who remain in him to produce *fruit* not only but *much* fruit. For the character of this fruit see on 15:1, 2.
On the other hand, those who are out of relation to Christ can do literally nothing, *nothing whatever* (οὐ ... οὐδέν). That holds not only for the drunkard, the thief, the murderer, the immoral person, but also for the poet, the scientist, and the philosopher who has not embraced Christ with a living faith. He can render no work that is acceptable before God. Then why is it that some — even among those who like to pass as Christians and who seek the place of leadership in the church — are ever engaged in ascribing the highest possible honors to such "outsiders," as if one could better afford to do without Paul than without Plato?
The passage certainly teaches the inability of man to do that which is good in the sight of God. It is entirely in line with Rom. 14:23, just as the preceding clause ("He who abides in me .... he it is that bears much fruit") is entirely in line with Phil. 4:13. — Pelagianism and semi-Pelagianism of every description stands condemned here!

300

6. If a man does not abide in me, he is thrown away as a (mere) branch and withers; and such branches are picked up, thrown into the fire, and burned.[180]

Note the *five* elements in the punishment of the man who rejects the light:

a. "He is thrown away as a (mere) branch." He is condemned already (3:18). He is cast out (6:37).

b. "and withers" (or: "and is dried up"). Though such an individual may linger on in this life for a while longer, he has no peace (Is. 48:22), no joy (Joel 1:12: "joy is withered away"). He is like "an autumn tree without fruit, twice dead, plucked up by the roots" (Jude 12; see also Is. 40:24; Mark 4:6; 11:21). The unforgettable example is Judas (Matt. 27:3-5).

c. "And such branches are picked up" (or "are gathered"). Cf. Matt. 13:30: "And in the time of the harvest I will say to the reapers, 'Gather up first the tares, and bind them in bundles to burn them.'" See also Matt. 13:41 and Rev. 14:18.

d. "thrown into the fire." Cf. Matt. 13:41, 42: "The Son of man will send his angels, and they will gather out of his kingdom . . . all evil-doers, and throw them into the furnace of fire." See also Matt. 7:19; 13:50; Rev. 20:15.

e. "and burned." Cf. Matt. 25:46: "And they will go away into everlasting punishment." That this being burned does not mean annihilation is also clear from such passages as Mark 9:43 ("unquenchable fire"), 48 ("where their worm does not die"); cf. Rev. 20:10 ("they will be tormented day and night for ever and ever," said with respect to the devil, the beast, and the false prophet, and compare Rev. 20:15).

On teaching with reference to *the last things* in John's Gospel see Vol. I, pp. 200, 201. Note the instructive change from the singular to the plural here in 15:6. First we have the singular: "If *a man . . . he* is thrown away . . . and withers." This stresses the responsibility of each individual who is brought into close contact with Christ and his Gospel. If he rejects the light, there will come a time when all further work with him as an individual ceases. He is regarded as being simply one of the mass of those who are rejected and cast into hell. Hence, now we have the plural: "And *such branches* are picked up," etc. (The active voice in the original, so that we literally read, "And *they pick them up and throw them* into the fire," where we would use the passive, is probably due to Aramaic influence upon grammar; see Vol. I, pp. 63, 64).

7. If y o u abide in me, and my words abide in y o u, ask whatever y o u will, and it will take place for y o u.

---

[180] The two gnomic aorists followed by three timeless presents, to represent what always happens in such cases, should cause no trouble.

The spoken words or utterances (τὰ ῥήματα) of Jesus had been rejected by many (5:18, 38; 6:66; 12:37-43). These men, in turn, were rejected, etc. (verse 6 above). For those who abide in Christ, on the other hand, there is a great promise. Here the thought of positively abiding in Christ (see 15:4, 5) returns and is explained. We learn that it means to heed the utterances of Christ, sothat they become the dynamic of one's life, taking complete control over a person (note: here not only "y o u abide in my words," but "my words abide in y o u"), sothat he both believes them and acts in accordance with them. In the lives of such individuals the effective-prayer promise of 14:13 is realized (see on that passage). Note:

"*I* will do it" (14:13).

"*He* will give it" (16:23). Hence, it is double sure that:

"It will take place for y o u" (thus here in 15:7).

It stands to reason that a person who abides in Christ and in whose heart Christ's utterances (including the precepts, of course) are in complete control, will ask nothing that is contrary to Christ's will, for he will always ask in the spirit of, "Not my will but thine be done," and in complete harmony with all that Christ has revealed concerning himself (that is, he will always ask "in his name"). Hence, it is not hard to understand that such a person will receive whatever he asks. All the same, this is a glorious promise which becomes an even more glorious reality in the lives of all God's true children whenever they, by God's sovereign grace, truly measure up to the stipulation mentioned in the if-clause.

Abiding in Christ has glorious results: a. effectual prayer (15:7); b. the bearing of much fruit (15:8); c. fulness of joy (15:11). Having discussed a., Jesus now turns to b.

8. By this is my Father glorified that y o u bear much fruit, and so y o u will become my disciples. The spiritual graces or fruits (see on 15:1, 2) which adorn the children of God reflect his own being. Accordingly, seeing himself (his communicable attributes) reflected in their lives, he is thereby glorified, and this especially when the fruits are bountiful ("much fruit"). Thus those who, by God's grace, are already disciples *become* disciples more and more. To weaken the sense of the verb *become* (γενήσεσθε) is neither necessary nor justifiable. It takes a disciple to become a disciple. It takes a child of God to become a child of God. See on 1:12.

9. Just as the Father has loved me, so have I loved y o u; abide in my love. "I have loved y o u," says Jesus. The best commentary on this is 13:1, which see. In this sacred night, the most sacred of all, the Lord looks back on all his experiences with his disciples from the day when he first chose them to discipleship, and then back once more to the eternity which "preceded" the foundation of the world, when in his sovereign goodpleasure he (together with the Father and the Holy Spirit) had elected them. He puts all this together in one word, "I have loved y o u."

This love, moreover, was pure, wholehearted, deep, personal, intelligent, enduring; hence, in all of these respects it was exactly like the Father's love for the Son. *"Just as* the Father has loved me, *so* have I loved y o u" (or simply, "Just as the Father *loved* me, so I *loved* y o u). The Father had spoken of his love for the Son at the baptism: "This is my beloved Son, in whom I am well pleased" (Matt. 3:17), and also in connection with the transfiguration (Matt. 17:5). Very precious to the heart of the Son was this love of the Father. Hence, he makes mention of it in the high-priestly prayer (17:23, 24). Here too the comparison holds, for Jesus specifically mentions that this love of which he himself was the object was a reality even "before the foundation of the world."

Since the love of Christ for the disciples is very, very precious — for it is like the love of the Father for the Son —, hence all the more the disciples should exert themselves to abide in it. For the order in which God's love for us and our love for him follow one another see on 14:21. For the reciprocal relationship of the elements in Christian experience see on 7:17, 18. *"Once for all abide* (note μείνατε, constative aorist active imperative) *in this my love,"* says Jesus. Here too (as in verse 7) we have a clarification of the precept, "Abide in me" (verse 4). In complete harmony with the thought of verse 7, Jesus now reiterates how the disciples may continue in his love:

10. If y o u keep my precepts, y o u will abide in my love, just as I have kept my Father's precepts, and abide in his love.

The believer is surrounded by cords of love, which draw him closer and closer to his Savior:

a. *His* love is always *first,* "We love because he *first* loved us" (I John 4:19). Now *our* love begins to operate. How does it manifest itself? Answer:

b. We show our love by keeping his precepts, "If y o u love me, ẏ o u will keep my precepts" (14:15).

c. This keeping of his precepts results, in turn, in our abiding in his love, "If y o u keep my precepts, y o u will abide in my love, just as I have kept my Father's precepts, and abide in his love." This is 15:10, the passage which we are studying.

So now we are back at the point from which we started, namely, to the station called "my love." It is hardly necessary to add that this love was never absent. It was operating during every instant of our exercise of love. It *precedes* our love. It *accompanies* our love. It *follows* our love, and in the very process of doing this, *creates* more love toward him in our hearts, sothat, as it were, another love-cycle begins, this one even better than the first. Thus, the believer feels himself drawn ever closer to God in Christ. He ever *abides* in that love. — Inasfar as that love is *an answer* to *our obedience* (and also from the point of view of its *everlasting* character) it is an echo or replica of the Father's love for the Son: *"just as* I have kept my Father's precepts, and abide in his love." For the idea of the Son's perfect obedience to the Father's "instructions" see on 8:29; 10:17, 18; 12:49, 50; 14:31; 17:4. The Son's voluntary sacrifice to the bitter death on the cross is certainly the most glorious manifestation of this obedience. Note how Jesus, looking back upon his entire life of obedience, says, "I *have kept"* (τετήρηκα, this reaches from the past to the present and implies that the accomplished obedience has abiding significance) "and *am* (forever) *abiding"* (μένω). For "precepts" see on 13:34. For "keeping" these precepts see on 8:51. See also on 7:17, 18; 14:21.

11. These things have I spoken to y o u, in order that my joy may be in y o u, and in order that y o u r joy may be full. These words (15:1-10), by means of which Jesus has told his disciples how through abiding in him and bearing much fruit they will obtain the blessing of answered prayer and will abide forever in his love, Jesus has spoken in order that *his* joy may *be* (may abidingly remain) in them. Note: *my* joy (not the kind of joy or pleasure which the world promises), and compare *my* peace (14:27). Just as *my* peace means the peace which *I* give, so also *my* joy is the joy which *I* impart, a joy that is spiritual, based on peace with God, neverending. Jesus wants to see this inner delight, this incomparable rejoicing in the hearts of his disciples. They needed this, for at present they were troubled and filled with sorrow (14:1, 27; 16:6). Moreover, not until the cup of joy has at length been filled to the very brim (cf. 16:24; 17:13; I John 1:4) will Jesus be satisfied. On this fulness of spiritual joy see also Luke 2:10; Rom. 14:17; Phil. 2:17, 18; and especially I Peter 1:6, 8.

---

12 "This is my precept, that y o u keep on loving one another as I have loved y o u. 13 Greater love has no man than this, that [181] a man lay down his life for his friends. 14 Y o u are my friends if y o u do what I bid y o u.[182] 15 No longer do I call y o u servants, for the servant does not know what his master is doing; but I have called y o u friends, for all that I have heard from my Father I have made known to y o u. 16 Y o u did not choose me, but I chose y o u and appointed y o u that [183] y o u should go and bear fruit and that y o u r fruit should abide, sothat [183] whatever y o u ask the Father in my name, he may give it to y o u. 17 These things I bid y o u (to do) in order that y o u may keep on loving one another."

---

181 On ἵνα see Vol. I, pp. 46, 51.
182 IIIB1; see Vol. I, pp. 42, 44.
183 On ἵνα in 16a see Vol. I, pp. 46, 51. On ἵνα in 16b see Vol. I, pp. 46, 52.

15:12-17

15:12. This is my precept, that y o u keep on loving one another as I have loved y o u. From the precept "Abide in me" (15:1-11) Jesus now proceeds to the next one, "love one another." It is only when we abide in Christ — in his words, in his love — that we shall be able to keep on loving one another! *For the explanation of 15:12 see on 13:34,* where this is called a new precept.

13. Greater love has no man than this, that a man lay down his life for his friends. When we combine verses 12 and 13, we notice that the thought is this: "Y o u must continue to love each other with that same love which I exercise when I lay down my life for all those who are truly my friends." Cf. I John 3:16.

It is true, of course, that this love of Christ cannot *in every sense* be a pattern for our love toward one another. As far as its *infinite value, substitutionary character,* and glorious *redemptive consequences* are concerned, *his act* of love, whereby he determined to lay down his life for us, can never be a pattern for *our* love of the brethren. In these respects that love is completely unique and cannot be copied. To attempt to copy it with respect to these particulars would be blasphemous. Nevertheless, there is one characteristic of this love which should be reflected in the attitude of one brother to another, namely, its *self-sacrificing nature.* "In y o u r love for one another y o u must be willing to deny yourselves," is what Jesus meant. That this is actually what he had in mind is clear from such passages as 13:15 (viewed in its entire context) and Mark 8:34.

Now, in ordinary life there surely is no greater manifestation of self-denying love for one's friends than this, that a man would even be willing to die for them. In the sphere of redemption Jesus did just that. He died for his friends. Moreover, he died for them when they were his friends only in the sense that he had made them such. In themselves and by nature (apart from God's grace) they were "weak," "ungodly," "sinners," "enemies" (cf. Rom. 5:6-10). A friend of Jesus is one: a. whom he has chosen out of this world (that is always basic); see on 15:19; and therefore b. who does what Jesus wants him to do; see on 15:14.

For these friends Jesus "lays down his life," that is, not only does he *physically* die *for their benefit,* but *in their stead* he even experiences *the torments of hell* on the cross (eternal death). The use of the preposition for (ὑπερ) has been explained in connection with 10:11.

14. Y o u are my friends if y o u do what I bid y o u. This comforting and reassuring statement is much like that found in verse 10; see on that verse. By constantly doing the will of Christ his disciples obtain for themselves the assurance that they are his friends, that is, that they will abide in his love. In the light of the manner in which these men had displayed their character-deficiencies even this very night (see on 13:2, 3, 4; cf. Luke 22:24), it was surely an act of glorious, condescending love for Jesus to say, "Y o u are my friends." Stress must be laid on the qualifying clause, "if y o u do what I bid y o u." This expression places all the stress on *human responsibility.* Verse 19 ("I chose y o u out of the world"; see also verse 16) emphasizes *divine election.* Both receive their due, which is not always the case in the writings of theologians.

15. No longer do I call y o u servants, for the servant does not know what his master is doing; but I have called y o u friends, for all that I have heard from my Father I have made known to y o u.

The disciples are no longer called servants (as probably implied in 13:16) but *friends.* When a superior tells his *servant* [184] to do this or that, the latter receives no minute explanations as to the why and the wherefore. With a *friend* the case is different. A friend is a confidant. By this time Jesus had told the disciples all that he had heard from the Father (see on 8:26; cf. 3:11; and note *"my* Father; see on 1:14, 18); such things as, why he was sent to earth by the Father, why he was going to lay down his life, why he had to leave this earth, what he would do at his return, and how a man could be saved (see such passages as 3:16; 10:11; 14:2, 3; then 3:3, 5, 36). Hence, *when emphasis is to be placed on the closeness of the fellowship between the Master and his disciples,* the name *servants* is no longer the proper term.

Moreover, the task which a servant must perform is often arduous, but

---

[184] I have read but have not been convinced by the arguments of E. J. Goodspeed, who prefers *slave* to *servant* as a translation of the Greek δοῦλος. I admit, of course, that in certain contexts the rendering *slave* is the only proper one (I Cor. 7:21, 22; Philemon 16), but it is hardly true that there is always an "enormous" difference between "slave" and "servant," as Goodspeed maintains. Thus, for example, in Luke 7:2 the centurion's "slave" (δοῦλος) is by his master called "my boy" (ὁ παῖς μου, verse 7). Surely when a "slave" becomes "dear" to the master (Luke 7:2), the ideas which we commonly associate with the concept *slave* drop into the background, and "servant" becomes the better translation. It is interesting to note that R.S.V. has not followed Goodspeed in this constant preference of "slave" to "servant" in translating. Dr. O. T. Allis points out that R.S.V. renders δοῦλος by "servant" nearly eighty times, by "servant" with marginal reading "slave" eighteen times, and by "slave" only thirty times. See O. T. Allis, *Revision or New Translation?,* Philadelphia, 1948, p. 75. For Goodspeed's argument see his *Problems of New Testament Translation,* Chicago, 1945, pp. 139-141. Certainly, in the present context "servant" is all that is needed. A "servant" is not a confidant; a "friend" is.

It remains true, of course, that when the emphasis is placed not on the intimacy of fellowship and confidence but on the fact that Christ redeemed a person by his blood, and therefore *owns* him, the term δοῦλος referring to the ransomed individual, is entirely appropriate (e.g., Rom. 1:1). Thus, when the proper third of comparison is kept in mind, it is felt to be entirely correct that, on the one hand, *Jesus calls his disciples* φίλους; yet, on the other, *Paul introduces himself* as being a δοῦλος.

the yoke which Jesus laid on his disciples was easy, the burden was light (see Matt. 11:25-30), especially in comparison with the load of human ordinances and traditions which pressed down heavily upon the Jews (see Matt. 23:4; Acts 15:10). *They* were servants, *slaves* even. But these disciples were *friends*.

Clearly implied in these words of Jesus is the thought that he is not satisfied with merely servile obedience. His friends are motivated by friendship when they do his bidding. Obedience is an expression of their love.

16. Y o u did not choose me, but I chose y o u and appointed y o u that y o u should go and bear fruit and that y o u r fruit should abide sothat whatever y o u ask the Father in my name, he may give it to y o u.

Though the disciples are Christ's friends, this does not mean that they are on an equal footing with him. On earth friends generally choose each other, but the friendship of which Jesus speaks is different. It is one-sided in its origin. It was not brought about by gradual approach from both sides, as is often the case among men, but by Jesus alone! The words, "Y o u did not choose me, but I chose y o u," emphasize the free, independent, and spontaneous character of Christ's love. The ground of God's love for us never lies in us, always in himself, for even apart from his love for us *God is love*. In his very essence he is love.

The unconditional and sovereign nature of this divine love is shown also by such passages as the following:

"Jehovah did not set his love upon y o u, nor choose y o u, because y o u were more in number than any people; for y o u were the fewest of all peoples, but because Jehovah loves y o u . . . he has brought y o u out with a mighty hand" (Deut. 7:7, 8).

"For mine own sake, for mine own sake will I do it" (Is. 48:11).

"O Lord, hear; O Lord, forgive; O Lord, hearken and do; defer not, for thine own sake, O my God, because thy city and thy people are called by thy name" (Dan. 9:19).

"I will heal their backsliding; I will love them freely" (Hos. 14:4).

"But God commends his own love toward us, in that, while we were yet sinners, Christ died for us" (Rom. 5:8).

"He chose us in him before the foundation of the world, in order that we should be holy" (not: "because he foresaw that we were going to be holy," Eph. 1:4).

"Herein is love, not that we loved God, but that he loved us, and sent his Son to be the propitiation for our sins" (I John 4:10).

"We love, because he first loved us" (I John 4:19).

It was Christ who had elected these men *for himself* out of a *world* of darkness (see on verse 19), in order that they might be his followers and as such might bear fruit, and this not merely for a time or by spurts but

307

abidingly. Unto that purpose he had also *appointed* them; that is, he had set them apart from the world and had promised to give them the required qualification. As has been indicated before, fruit-bearing refers to the bringing forth of such products of divine grace as those mentioned in Gal. 5:22 — love, joy, peace, patience, kindness, goodness, faithfulness, gentleness, self-control —; Eph. 5:9; Col. 1:6; Heb. 12:11; and James 3:18. But in view of 4:36 and 12:24, passages in which the term "fruits" indicates souls saved for eternity, it is certainly not amiss to point out that the good works of which Jesus is thinking are mentioned not as an end in themselves but as a means unto the conversion of others, and thus unto the glory of God, via the avenue indicated in Matt. 5:16 ("that they may see y o u r good works, and glorify y o u r Father who is in heaven").

We agree entirely with Dr. F. W. Grosheide that the election of which the present passage speaks is not that unto office but that which pertains to every Christian.[185] All believers are chosen *out of the world* (verse 19) *to bear fruit* (verses 2, 4, 5, 8). Though this is an act which takes place in time, it has its basis in election "before the foundation of the world" (Eph. 1:4; cf. John 17:24).

Abiding in Christ is rewarded by fruitbearing, and via fruitbearing, also by answered prayer. A true disciple prays for fruits, for these fruits are pleasing to God. He asks God to give whatever is in accordance with his will. He asks this, not as if he (the disciple) himself had any merit, but solely on the basis of Christ's merits and in complete harmony with *his* revelation (hence, in Christ's *name*). Accordingly, verse 16 concludes with the words: **sothat whatever y o u ask the Father in my name, he may give it to y o u.** Here the thought of 15:7 recurs; see on that verse. In verse 16, however, we do not find the impersonal *"it* shall be done for y o u," but the very personal, *"He . . .* gives it." The Father loves the Son; hence, he loves those who do the Son's bidding.

17. These things I bid y o u (to do) in order that[186] **y o u may keep on loving one another,** says Jesus. The thought of verse 12 recurs here, but this time in a slightly altered form. Jesus now shows that in telling the disciples to abide in him (verses 1-11), and especially in reminding

185 F. W. Grosheide, *op. cit.,* pp. 352, 353. The occurrence of the same verb ("elected") here as in 6:69, 70; 13:18, does not necessarily imply that the meaning in these various passages is everywhere exactly the same. In each concrete case the specific context must decide.
186 In the abstract it is possible to construe ἵνα as being non-final (so, for instance, Lenski). In that case we would have a simple repetition of verse 12. But it must be noted that the form of verse 17 differs from verse 12 in one important respect. It presents itself as a summing up of all that precedes — note ταῦτα, "these things" (contrast with the singular antecedant both in 15:12 and in 13:34). After such an introduction ἵνα in the full telic sense seems more natural. Christ's love for me is basic to my love for the brother.

them of his great elective love for them (the immediate context, verse 16 cf. verse 9), he had one great purpose in mind, namely, "in order that y o u may keep on loving one another." The logic here is simple and clear. I, being in myself unlovable, cannot keep on loving my brother, who also is often very unlovable (at least as *I* see him), unless I constantly reflect on (and remain in) the love of Christ for myself. Not only do we love *him* because he first loved us, but we also love *one another* because he first loved us. Our love for one another is an extension of Christ's love for us. It is "the love of God shed abroad in our hearts" *so copiously that it overflows into the lives of others.* Cf. Rom. 5:5.

For Synthesis see p. 316.

---

18 "If the world hates y o u, know that it has hated me before it hated y o u.[187] 19 If y o u were of the world, the world would have affection for its own;[188] but because y o u are not of the world, but I chose y o u out of the world, therefore the world hates y o u. 20 Remember the word which I spoke to y o u, 'A servant is not greater than his lord.' If they persecuted me, they will also persecute y o u. If they kept my word, they will keep y o u r s also.[189] 21 But all these things will they do to y o u for my name's sake,[190] because they do not know the One who sent me. 22 If I had not come and spoken to them, they would have no sin.[191] But now they have no excuse for their sin. 23 He who hates me hates my Father also. 24 If I had not done among them the works which no one else did, they would have no sin;[192] but now they have seen and hated both me and my Father. 25 But (this happened) in order that the word written in their law might be fulfilled, 'They hated me without a cause.' 26 When the Helper comes, whom I will send to y o u from the Father, even the Spirit of truth which proceeds from the Father, he will testify concerning me. 27 And y o u must also testify[193] because y o u have been with me from the beginning."

15:18-27

15:18. If the world hates y o u, know that it has hated me before it hated y o u.

Jesus has admonished his disciples to abide in him (verses 1-11), and to love one another (verses 12-17). He now exhorts them to bear witness to the world (verses 18-27). This witness is to be the disciples' answer to the hatred which they receive from the side of the world. Hence, the present section may be divided into two parts:

---

[187] I D; see Vol. I, pp. 40, 41.
[188] II A; see Vol. I, p. 41.
[189] Both conditions belong to group I C; see Vol. I, p. 40.
[190] Or: "on my account."
[191] II C; see Vol. I, pp. 41, 42.
[192] II C; see Vol. I, pp. 41, 42.
[193] Or: "and y o u are also testifying."

a. The disciples hated by the world (verses 18-25);

b. The disciples (following the example of the Holy Spirit, hence) witnessing to the world (verses 26, 27).

The first of these two sections may, in turn, be subdivided as follows: verses 18-23 state the reasons why the disciples are hated by the world; verses 24 and 25 show why this hatred is very sinful and thoroughly inexcusable.

The disciples are hated because they are not of the world and because they belong to the One whom the world hates, namely, the Christ.

The words, "If the world hates y o u," cannot indicate (in the present connection), "Let us assume that the world hates y o u, whether or not this be actually true." On the contrary, as verse 19 clearly indicates by its very form (in the original), the hatred of the world is a fact, not merely an assumption. The disciples had experienced this hatred. They cannot have been ignorant with respect to the decree of the Sanhedrin, recorded in 9:22. Besides, in the future this hatred against them would manifest itself again and again and would even increase, as the book of Acts indicates.

This hatred proceeds from *the world,* the realm of evil, the society of wicked men who have set themselves against Christ and his kingdom. See Vol. I, p. 79, footnote 26, meaning 6. In the early days of the apostles this cruel and sinister world was represented by the Jews, especially by their leaders.

To comfort his disciples Jesus now adds, "know that it has hated me before it hated y o u." What he means is, "Constantly bear in mind that y o u are in excellent company. When the world hates y o u because y o u confess me, this shows that y o u belong to me and therefore experience, to a certain extent, what I have been experiencing right along."

The fact that the world had hated Jesus, and that this hatred had been present almost from the very beginning of his public ministry and had never subsided, is evident from the following passages: 1:5, 10, 11; 3:11; 5:16, 18, 43; 6:66; 7:1, 30, 32, 47-52; 8:40, 44, 45, 48, 52, 57, 59; 9:22; 10:31, 33, 39; 11:50, 57; 12:37-43.

19. If y o u were of the world, the world would have affection for its own. If y o u owed y o u r spiritual origin to the world; hence, if y o u were like the world in inner being and character, the world would have affection for y o u, for it cherishes its own people. The implication is: "Y o u are definitely not of the world." For the meaning of the verb *to have affection for* (φιλέω) see on 21:15-17. For abbreviated style see on 5:31. Jesus continues: **But because y o u are not of the world, but I chose y o u out of the world, therefore the world hates y o u.** What was already implied in the first clause of verse 19 is now specifically stated, namely, that these disciples (Judas has left!) are not of the world. However, the reason why they are not of the world lies not in them; on the contrary, it is this, that out of the world of darkness the Lord had elected these men for himself. The deed which Jesus has in mind refers not to eternity but to time. Either directly, as in some cases, or indirectly (for example, through the instrumentality of John the Baptist or of another disciple; see chapter 1) these men had been drawn away from *the world* (see on verse 18) into the kingdom of heaven. The act which took place in time was based upon an act which occurred in eternity (Eph. 1:4).

Now this act of drawing love had made these men to differ from the world. Hence, their very existence, manner of life, conversation, as well as actual witness-bearing (in whatever degree it was present) constituted an accusation against the world of evil men. Besides, the world had lost them.

20. Remember the word which I spoke to y o u, A servant is not greater than his lord.

In support of the statement just made (verse 19) with reference to the fierce and continuous opposition which the disciples are enduring and can expect to endure from the side of the world, Jesus now quotes his own previous saying, a saying that had been uttered this selfsame night; see on 13:16. As spoken the first time the meaning was: "A servant is not greater than his lord; hence, he must not consider himself exempt from the obligation to render service in the spirit of humility." As repeated now it means: "A servant is not greater than his lord; hence, he must not consider himself immune to persecution." In both cases we are dealing with litotes (affirmation by means of negation), sothat the real meaning is: "If the lord must be humble, his servant should certainly be humble (13:16); if the lord is persecuted, the servant will surely also be persecuted." (15:20). In fact this implication is stated in so many words: **If they persecuted me, they will also persecute y o u.** For proof of the fact that the world persecuted Jesus see on 15:18. The principle here laid down, namely, that servants can expect the same treatment as their lords, operates in two directions: unfavorably (similar persecution) and favorably (similar obedience). Hence, Jesus continues: **If they kept my word, they will keep y o u r s also.** "Assume," says Jesus, as it were, "that they have kept my word." The result then is invariably: "they will keep y o u r s also." [194] For the meaning of *keeping* the word (precepts) of Christ, see on 8:51.

---

[194] Also in this second conditional sentence the protasis is assumed to be true to fact, for the sake of argument, that is, to illustrate the operation of the principle. That it is not *actually* a fact, is, of course, entirely true. Those who persecute Christ and his disciples do not *actually* keep his word. But the principle as such works in both directions; hence, the same form of conditional sentence is used twice in this passage. See Vol. I, p. 40.

21. But all these things will they do to y o u for my name's sake. Here again the thought appears in abbreviated form. The meaning is probably: "But this fact, that the world treats y o u like it treats me, is not surprising, for they will do all these things to y o u for my name's sake." "All these things," that is, the things mentioned in the preceding: they will hate y o u (verse 18), will not have affection for y o u (implied in verse 19), will persecute y o u (verse 20). They will do all this "for my name's sake," which, as a comparison of parallel passages indicates, is tantamount to, "for my sake," or "on my account." Cf. Mark 13:9 with Luke 21:12. Christ's name is Christ himself, as he reveals himself. When Jesus has departed from the earth, his *name* (revelation, the Gospel that centers in him) will still be there. The enemy will hate this name and will persecute the disciples when they proclaim it. That this is what actually happened is clear from such a passage as Acts 4:18: "And they called them (Peter and John) and charged them not to speak or teach at all in the name of Jesus."

And why were they filled with such bitterness because of this name? The answer is: **because they do not know the One who sent me.** Had they known him, they would have known Jesus as his only-begotten Son; hence, they would not have persecuted him. For Jesus as the One sent by the Father see on 3:17, 34; 5:36, 37; 8:18, 27, 29. This lack of knowledge, moreover, was inexcusable. They should have known both the Father and the Son. Note the next verse:

22. If I had not come and spoken to them, they would have no sin. That Jesus had indeed made his appearance among the ancient covenant people and had indeed spoken to them is clear from the entire Fourth Gospel; see especially on 1:5, 10, 11; chapter 3; 5:17-47; 6:25-59; 7:16-38; chapter 8; chapter 10; and 12:37-50. Had he not done this, they would not have been guilty of the great sin of rejecting him. **But now they have no excuse for their sin.** Any reason which the Jews might still offer in justification of this rejection is mere pretense. They know better.

23. He who hates me hates my Father also. The Jews were in the habit of thinking that they could claim God as their Father (8:41), while at the same time they regarded Jesus as demon-possessed (8:48). They claimed that they loved the Father, though they evidently hated the Son (see on 15:18). But, in view of the fact that the Father and the Son are one in essence (10:30), such an attitude is impossible. A person may *imagine* that he loves the Father while he hates the Son, but he deceives himself. Whoever hates the one necessarily hates the other also. And this holds also with respect to the present day and age. Men who scoff at blood-atonement and reject the vicarious death of Christ do not love God!

24. If I had not done among them the works which no one else did, they

312

would have no sin; but now they have seen and hated both me and my Father. In connection with 9:16 and 9:33 it has been shown that the miracles which Jesus performed have evidential value. See on these passages; see also on verse 22 above, which is similar. A moment ago (verse 22) Jesus had spoken about his *words;* now he adds the *works,* that is, signs. Surely, the terrible hatred of these Jews was unexcusable. The thought of verse 24, completely expressed, would be as follows: "If I had not done among them the works which no one else did, they would have no sin; but now, in and by means of these works, they have seen both me and my Father (for my works reveal *him,* are also *his* works: 5:17, 36; 10:25; 14:9, 11); yet, in spite of this they have hated (and still hate; note perfect tense for both verbs) both me and (therefore) my Father." For the expression *"my* Father" (unique sonship of Christ) see on 1:14.

25. But (this happened) in order that the word written in their law might be fulfilled, They hated me without a cause. That is, in and by means of all this hatred, God is fulfilling his plan of redemption. The hatred of men *must* result in Christ's crucifixion, in order that men (his people) may be saved. Yet the eternal decree is being fulfilled in such a manner that the guilt rests on man, not on God!

The experience of the psalmist is attaining final fulfilment:

"Let not them that are my enemies wrongfully rejoice over me;

Neither let them wink with the eye *that hate me without cause"* (Ps. 35:19).

And again:

"They that hate me without a cause are more than the hairs of my head" (Ps. 69:4).[195]

The author of Ps. 35 had bestowed many favors on those who now were his enemies. *Their* suffering had been *his* suffering; *their* sorrows *his* sorrow. He had treated them like brothers (Ps. 35:13, 14). But they had rewarded evil for good. For the background of Ps. 69 and the use which is made of that Psalm in the New Testament see Vol. I, p. 123. According to Ps. 35 the enemies are those who love to forget past favors; according to Ps. 69 they are people who cannot bear to be witnesses of the burning zeal which David manifests for the cause of Jehovah. Surely, in both cases the Psalmist himself is being mistreated. His enemies are hating him *without a cause.* So also (only *much more so!*) when the enemies of the Christ rejected him, in spite of all his words of grace and miracles of love, they were hating him *without a cause!* For the meaning of the expression "their law" see on 10:34.

---

[195] In both cases the LXX has οἱ μισοῦντες με δωρεάν (see LXX on 34:19; 68:5). This is equivalent in sense to the original in 15:25, here finite verb (aorist) in indirect discourse.

Now what is to be the attitude of the disciples with respect to this *world*, represented by the God-defying, Christ-hating, Church-persecuting Jews? In the midst of this world they must bear witness, just like the Spirit also bears witness:

26. When the helper comes, whom I will send to y o u from the Father, even the Spirit of truth which proceeds from the Father, he will testify concerning me.

Jesus has been speaking about the hatred which the disciples will have to endure from the side of the world, which hates the Father and the Son. Hence, it is not surprising that in this connection he again comforts these men by reminding them of his previous promise (see on 14:16, 17, 26) with respect to the coming of the Spirit, the Helper. *Jesus himself* will send this Helper. He will be sent *from the Father*. Essentially, though with difference in emphasis, this is the same as saying: "I will request the Father, and he will give y o u another Helper" (14:16); "the Helper, the Holy Spirit, whom the Father will send in my name" (14:26). Here in 15:26 the emphasis is on the activity of *the Son* in *the sending* of the Spirit, and on the fact that this Spirit *proceeds eternally* from *the Father*. The *sending* of the Spirit was a matter of the future. Pentecost had not yet arrived. Hence, the future tense is used: "I will send." The *procession* was taking place at the very moment when Jesus was speaking (if matters which in reality transcend time may be viewed from the aspect of time); hence, the present tense is used.[196] Were we to say, "The fact that 15:26 states that *the Son* will send the Spirit proves that the Father does not send him," we would be wrong (see 14:26). Thus also, were we to say, "The fact that 15:26 states that the Spirit proceeds *from the Father* proves that he does not proceed from the Son," we would be wrong (see Acts 5:9; Rom. 8:9; II Cor. 3:17; Gal. 4:6; Phil. 1:19; I Pet. 1:11; where the Spirit is called *the Spirit of Christ*). After all, is it so strange that Jesus, speaking as *Mediator* between God and man, himself man, would, during his period of humiliation, speak of the Spirit as proceeding from *The Father?*

The Holy Spirit is here called *the Spirit of truth,* just as in 14:17; see on that passage. That Spirit *will testify* (see on 1:7, 8). In the midst of the wicked world he will testify against the world (16:8, 9). In the midst of mankind he will bear witness concerning mankind's need. In the midst of the Church he will comfort the Church. The sphere of his testimony must not be restricted. Whenever a true servant of God bears witness against the world, this witness is the work of the Spirit. Whenever a simple believer, by word and example, draws others to Christ, this too is the work

---

[196] Not improperly in such a connection this present tense has been called *timeless present.* The inter-trinitarian relationship which is indicated here — the procession of the Spirit — is *eternal,* that is, it transcends time.

of the Spirit. That Spirit always testifies in connection with the Word, the Word of Christ (14:26; 16:14, 15). By and large, the world that is openly hostile to Christ will not receive him (14:17). Nevertheless, there are exceptions. From among those who *today* are openly hostile some will be drawn. They will be transferred from the kingdom of darkness to that of everlasting light. Was there ever a fiercer persecutor than Saul (or Paul) of Tarsus? The Spirit was going to change him (and others like him) to become a zealous missionary for Christ! See also on 16:7-11.

Now in this work of witnessing the Holy Spirit employs means, as the next verse indicates.

27. And y o u must also testify, because y o u have been with me from the beginning. The verb that is used in the original can be read either as present *indicative* ("Y o u are testifying") or as present *imperative* ("Testify," or "Continue to testify," or simply, "Y o u must testify"). In defence of the indicative the following arguments have been used:

(1) Acts 1:8 (cf. 5:32) teaches that the disciples were actually testifying.

(2) The reason given — namely, "for y o u have been [197] with me from the beginning" — sounds strange after an imperative, "Testify."

But one might answer:

(1) Acts 1:8 (cf. 5:32) does not teach that the disciples were testifying *at this time*, but that they were going to bear witness after the Spirit had been poured out.

(2) Taken in the sense, "Y o u must testify, because y o u are qualified to do so, since y o u have been with me from the beginning," the logic of the sentence, far from being strange, is very clear.

Other arguments in favor of the imperative are as follows:

a. After the future, "He will testify," the imperative *"Also* testify," or "Y o u must *also* testify," seems more natural than the indicative. The meaning seems to be, "Y o u must also do what the Spirit is going to do."

b. It is very logical that the precept, "Abide in me" (15:4), which indicates what should be the disciples' relation to *Christ,* and the precept, "Love one another" (15:12), which shows what must be their attitude to *one another,* should now be followed by, "Also testify" (15:27), which describes their duty with respect to *the persecuting world.* Moreover, in a context replete with *precepts,* expressed or implied, in a setting which makes so much of the disciples' *duty* (see 15:4, 7, 8, 10, 12, 14, 16, 17, 20) *the imperative* seems very natural.

---

[197] No legitimate argument (for the position that the form of the verb *testify* is *indicative*) can be derived from the fact that Jesus uses the present tense ἐστε. This is simply *the present of duration,* associated with an adverb of time. It indicates that which has begun in the past, and continues into the present. The sentence should be rendered, "Y o u *have been* with me from the beginning"; not: "Y o u *are* with me from the beginning."

(3) There is little in the immediate context that indicates that the disciples were even now doing their duty with respect to the work of bearing witness. On the contrary, during this selfsame night they failed to testify; they were "offended" in him. — Therefore, with E. J. Goodspeed (see his translation) we construe this verb as being imperative: "Also testify!"

Certainly upon the eye-witnesses (those who had been with Christ from the beginning of his ministry) rests the duty of testifying concerning the things which they have seen. To be sure, the Holy Spirit's work of bearing witness *is not limited* to the witness-bearing of the disciples. Nevertheless, the latter is a very important means whereby the former achieves its purpose.

Synthesis of Chapter 15

See the Outline on p. 260. *The Son of God Tenderly Instructing His Disciples. A Word of Admonition.*

I. "Abide in me" (verses 1-11): the believers' relation to Christ.

In the night when the Lord's Supper was instituted — the supper with its bread and *wine* — it was natural for Jesus to speak about *the vine* as a symbol of spiritual fruitfulness. He admonished the disciples not to follow the example of Judas (though the latter's *name* is not mentioned here), but to remain in the vine, that is, in Christ, in his word and in his love.

He called himself *the genuine vine,* described his Father as *the vine-dresser,* and designated all those who come into close contact with himself as *branches.*

These branches are divided into two groups: those which bear fruit, and those which do not bear fruit. In order to bear fruit it is absolutely necessary to remain in the vine. Glorious results of abiding in Christ are: a. effective prayer, b. bearing much fruit to the glory of God, and c. fulness of joy. In such cases *each cycle of love* (in which *his* love precedes, accompanies, and follows *theirs*) produces another, better than itself. — Branches that do not bear fruit are thrown away, allowed to wither, picked up, thrown into the fire, and burned.

II. "Love one another" (verses 12-17): the believers' relation to one another.

Christ's self-sacrificing love for believers is the pattern for mutual love among believers. This love manifests itself in self-denial, to the point of being willing to lay down one's life for one's friends. Jesus was in the process of doing just that. It was for his *friends* that he offered his life. No longer were they to be termed *servants* but *friends,* for *he* had told them his secrets, and *they* are glad to please him by keeping his precepts. This friendship is rooted in sovereign, electing love, the kind of love that

316

produces fruitbearing and effective prayer. In order to be able to love one another it is necessary to abide in, and to constantly meditate on, that love of Christ for his friends.

III. "Also testify" (verses 18-27): the believers' relation to the world, in answer to the world's attitude to believers:

A. "The world hates y o u."

1. Reasons for this hatred:

a. Believers are not "of the world"; and

b. Believers belong to Christ, whom the world hates.

2. Inexcusable character of this hatred:

By means of his *words* and *works* Jesus had revealed himself and his Father to the world (not in the sense in which he discloses himself to the heart of the believer, but) to such an extent that the world's hatred was completely inexcusable: they hated him without a cause. Thus, an ancient prophecy was being fulfilled.

B. "The Helper, the Spirit of truth, will testify concerning me . . . And y o u must also testify."

1. The testimony of the Spirit.

This Helper, who proceeds eternally from the Father, and who is sent by Jesus from the Father, will bear testimony with respect to the Son. He is qualified to do this because of his intimate relation to the Son, the two being *one* in essence.

2. The testimony of the disciples.

Who could be better qualified to bear witness than an eye-witness? Because from the very beginning of Christ's ministry these disciples have been eye-witnesses, they too must testify. *Their* testimony, moreover, will serve as a means which the Holy Spirit employs to bring *his* testimony.

CHAPTER XVI

16 1 "These things have I spoken to y o u, in order that y o u should not be caught unawares. 2 They will make yo u outcasts from the synagogue; indeed, the hour is coming when [198] whoever kills y o u will think that he is offering service to God. 3 And these things will they do because they have not come to acknowledge the Father nor me. 4 But these things have I spoken to y o u in order that when their hour arrives, y o u may remember that I told y o u about them. And these things I did not say to y o u from the start, because I was with y o u. 5 But now I am going away to him who sent me; and none of y o u asks me, 'Where art thou going?' 6 But because I have spoken these things to y o u, sorrow has filled y o u r hearts.

7 "Nevertheless, I am telling y o u the truth; it is to y o u r advantage that I go away; for if I do not go away, the Helper will not come to y o u; [199] but if I go, I will send him to y o u. [199] 8 And when he is come, he will convict the world with respect to sin and righteousness and judgment: 9 with respect to sin, because they do not believe in me; 10 with respect to righteousness, because I go away to the Father, and y o u observe me no longer; 11 with respect to judgment, because the ruler of this world is judged.

12 "I have yet many things to say to y o u, but y o u cannot bear them now. 13 But when he is come, the Spirit of truth, he will guide y o u into all the truth; for he will not speak of himself, but whatever he hears he will speak, and he will announce to y o u the things that are to come. 14 He will glorify me, because he will take from what is mine, and will announce (it) to y o u. 15 All that the Father has is mine; therefore I said, 'He will take from what is mine, and will announce (it) to y o u.' "

Preliminary Remarks on Chapter 16

No one who carefully reads the sixteenth chapter will fail to notice the change in the character of the discourse. There is a gradual transition from admonition to prediction. Just as in the fourteenth chapter the tone of *comfort* was predominant, and in the fifteenth that of *admonition*, so in the sixteenth that of *prediction* prevails. The future tense (or its equivalents in meaning), indicating what is going to happen, is definitely in the foreground. Note the following examples (verses 1-14):

---

[198] On ἵνα see Vol. I, pp. 45, 52.
[199] 16:7a is IIIA3; see Vol. I, pp. 42, 43. 16:7b is IIIA1; same reference.

"They *will make* y o u outcasts from the synagogue . . . The hour *is coming* when whoever kills y o u *will think* that he is offering service to God. All these things *will they do* . . . I *will send* him (the Helper) to y o u. He *will convict* the world. He *will guide* y o u into all the truth. He *will glorify* me. He *will take* from what is mine, and *will announce* it to y o u." This continues to the end of the chapter; see verses 15, 16, 20, 22, 23, 24, 25, 26, 32.

Nevertheless, there is no abrupt or mechanical division between chapters 15 and 16. On the contrary, the transition is very gradual. Themes introduced in the preceding chapters are taken up again, such as the sorrow because of Christ's departure (cf. 14:1, 18 with 16:7, 22), and the comfort of effective prayer (cf. 15:7, 16 with 16:23). Also, the same subject which Jesus discussed at the *close* of chapter 15 is dealt with here, namely, the persecution which the disciples will have to endure from the side of the world. But there is a difference in degree of emphasis. Whereas in chapter 15 *the disciples were told what they should do,* in chapter 16 *Jesus predicts what the triune God is going to do for the disciples* in view of this spirit of hatred and persecution. Something to this effect had already been stated in 15:26. Now this theme is expanded. *The Holy Spirit* will convict *the world,* and will lead *the Church* into all the truth. *The Son* will impart joy to the hearts of his disciples (by his glorious resurrection and by sending the Spirit). *The Father* will continue to love them. Hence, the victory is certain.

16:1-15

16:1. These things have I spoken to y o u, in order that y o u should not be caught unawares. *These things* — things pertaining to the hatred which the disciples would experience from the side of the world (15:18-27) — Jesus has spoken in order to forewarn his "friends." If he had not made these predictions, they would have been *caught unawares* (or: *ensnared;* see on 6:61). In the midst of fierce persecution they would have become disappointed with their Lord. They would have begun to wonder whether it were really true that the reins of the universe were in his hands. They would have said, "We had expected so much from him, but we received so little"; just as happens when a bird gets caught in a *snare:* it had expected a delicious morsel, but has become thoroughly disillusioned.

In order to prevent such grievous disappointment which would tend to undermine their faith, the Lord told them all these things ahead of their occurrence. Thus they will know that not only the treachery of Judas (see on 13:19) and the departure of Jesus (see on 14:29) but also the hatred of the world was included in God's plan for their own progress in salvation (cf. Rom. 8:28).

2. They will make y o u outcasts from the synagogue; indeed, the hour is coming when whoever kills y o u will think that he is offering service to God. The fierce hatred which the hostile Jewish leaders would focus upon the disciples would reveal itself in expulsions from the synagogue (see on 9:22, 23). The followers of the Nazarene would be excommunicated from the religious and social life of Israel. They would be cut off from the hopes and prerogatives of the Jews. They would be viewed by their former friends as worse than pagans. They would lose their jobs, would be exiled by their families, and would even lose the privilege of honorable burial. Worse than this even, they would actually be killed. The *hour* (indefinite, one might translate: "the time"; cf. 4:21, 23; 5:25, 28; 16:25, 32) was coming when men would regard the putting to death of a Christian to be a meritorious act, a deed by means of which one "offered service to God." The line of reasoning might be as follows: "Have we not been taught from the days of our childhood that there is only *one* true God, and that we must worship him alone? Now these followers of *Jesus* claim that he too is God. This is blasphemy, and must be punished with death." One immediately thinks of the persecutor Paul, who subsequently testified: "I myself was convinced that *I ought to do* many things contrary to the name of Jesus of Nazareth" (Acts 26:9). It was a principle which had the value of a dogma among the Jews: "Whoever sheds the blood of the wicked is equal to one who brings a sacrifice."

3. And these things will they do because they have not come to acknowledge the Father nor me. The hostile Jews have created their own God. The true God as revealed in Jesus Christ they did not serve. This failure was not due to excusable ignorance. They could have known (see on 15:22, 24). It was the result of refusing to *acknowledge* (for the meaning of the verb see on 1:10) both the Sender and the Sent, and this in spite of all the signs! Of course, when one rejects the Son, he rejects the Father also, and vice versa (see on 10:30).

4. But these things have I spoken to y o u in order that when their hour arrives, you may remember that I told y o u about them. Here the thought of verse 1 is resumed. Lovingly the Master provides for his disciples. When "the fiery trial" arrives, they must never be able to say, "How strange and unexpected! Why did not the Lord prepare us for this? Why did he not warn us?" (cf. I Peter 4:12). Now that they have been warned beforehand, their very suffering (when it arrives) will confirm their faith in Jesus. They will *remember* his words. Hence, they will then say, "If his predictions with respect to *woe* are being realized, those with respect to *weal* will also be fulfilled." Jesus continues: **And these things I did not say to y o u from the start, because I was with y o u.** To be sure, there had been predictions of coming persecution (Matt. 5:10-12; 10:16-39). But *these* *things* (15:18-16:3) — the fact that the world hates the disciples because Jesus has chosen them out of the world, that this hatred was in reality directed against Jesus *and against the Father,* that it was absolutely inexcusable and was rooted in the sinister condition of the heart which deliberately refused to acknowledge the true God, that the time was actually coming when men would regard the putting to death of Christ's followers to be tantamount to an act of worship altogether pleasing to God — *these* things, with *that* emphasis and in *that* forthright manner, had never been revealed before. One does not find "these things" in Matt. 5:10-12, which speaks only of persecution in general and of slander in particular — , nor in Matt. 10:16-39, which describes the outward forms of persecution (arrest, flogging, death, name-calling), but says very little about the hidden root from which this persecution springs (only Matt. 10:22, 24, 25, 40; cf. John 15:20, 21). The reason why Jesus had not said these things from the beginning was that it had not been necessary then, because he was still with them. As long as he was physically present, the brunt of the attack was directed against *him,* not against his disciples. From now on there would be a change. With Jesus crucified, the Sanhedrin would begin to vent its wrath upon his followers. One is reminded of Rev. 12:4, 13, 17: first the dragon seeks to devour the child; next he pursues the woman who had borne the child. Angry with the woman, he makes war on the rest of her seed. The book of Acts shows that this prophecy (15:18-16:4) was fulfilled in every detail.

5. But now I am going to him who sent me; and none of y o u asks me, Where art thou going? Shortly previous to this, when as yet Jesus had not fully explained the purpose of his departure, there had been many questions with respect to his leaving. Peter had asked, "Lord, where art thou going?" (13:36) and Thomas had asked something similar (14:5). But these questions issued from a crudely literal conception of Christ's departure. Then Jesus had given a full explanation. He had clearly indicated that he was not leaving for some other place on earth but was going to the Father (14:28), that this return to the Father should have filled their hearts with rejoicing (also 14:28), and that from there he would send another Helper, namely, the Spirit of truth (14:16, 17, 26; 15:26). *This* was the proper moment for questions, questions as to what that return to the Father would mean for *him,* and for *them.* But there were no questions. There was not even a request that he repeat that very instructive information about the place where he was going. In this failure to ask questions there was an element of selfishness. So deeply concerned were these men with the thought of their own impending loss that this sorrow had crowded out every other consideration. Bitterly Jesus complains, And none of y o u asks me, "Where art thou going?" He continues:

6. But because I have spoken these things to y o u, sorrow has filled y o u r hearts. Jesus had spoken about his departure. The disciples concentrated on *the fact* of this departure, and upon what *they* thought this would mean *for them*. They failed to pay sufficient attention to *the nature* of this departure, and upon what *he* had said this would mean *for them and for himself!* So, sorrow had filled their hearts (cf. 14:1, 27); and this in spite of all the grounds of comfort which Jesus had presented (chapter 14), and in spite of the instruction he had imparted with reference to the fruits of *abiding* in him even after his physical departure (chapter 15). The disciples conceive of their Master's departure as a great loss. So Jesus continues:

7. Nevertheless, I am telling y o u the truth: it is to y o u r advantage that I go away for if I do not go away, the Helper will not come to y o u; but if I go, I will send him to y o u. Here, in plain words Jesus expressed what he had been implying right along. Had he not told his disciples that his departure would be for the purpose of preparing a place for them (14:2); enabling them to do greater works (14:12); imparting richer knowledge to them (14:20); and, in reality, drawing closer to them, namely, in the Spirit (14:28)? Was it not very plain then that the Master's going away would be an advantage for the disciples? Again, as long as the disciples see Jesus in the body, are they able to understand that their relation to him must be of a spiritual character?

Strange, indeed, are the ways of God! Christ and his great enemy Caiaphas are both saying the same thing, namely, that it is expedient that Jesus die (see on 11:50). Of course, Caiaphas himself did not mean what Christ meant. The intention of the Spirit, however, was the same in both cases.

The basic reason why Christ's departure means triumph and not tragedy, the reason why it is a help and not a hindrance for these men (and for the Church in general) is this, that otherwise *the Helper* (see on 14:16), namely, the Holy Spirit, will not come to them. Jesus does not explain why the Spirit cannot come unless the Son departs from the earth and returns to his home above. Suggestions which probably point in the right direction are these: the Son's *going away* is a departure via *the cross*. By his going away he merits redemption for his people. Now the Holy Spirit is the One whose special task it is to apply the saving merits of Christ to the hearts and lives of believers (Rom. 8; Gal. 4:4-6). But the Spirit cannot apply these merits when there are no merits to apply. Hence, unless Jesus *goes away,* the Spirit cannot come. Also, it must be borne in mind that the gift of the Holy Spirit is a reward upon Christ's work (Acts 2:33). But a reward is not given until the task for which it is given has been accomplished. Hence, the Holy Spirit cannot be sent until Jesus has finished his task on earth. We are not saying that Jesus had these reasons in mind when he said, "For if I do not go away, the Helper will not come to y o u, but if I go, I will send him to y o u." We simply do not know just what he had in mind. The reason why we, nevertheless, offer a few suggestions is to show that this statement of Jesus is entirely in harmony with the body of revelation which we find elsewhere in the New Testament. Note: *"I* will send," here and also in 15:26; but 14:26: *"The Father* will send in my name." There is perfect cooperation in the outgoing works! The Father sends; the Son sends; the Spirit goes. Moreover, the Spirit is sent "to y o u." He chooses the Church as his abode. Nevertheless, his influence is also felt by the world:

8. And when he is come, he will convict the world with respect to sin and righteousness and judgment.

The Spirit's work in the world is described in the verses 8-10. Through preaching and the work of the disciples (II Tim. 3:16; 4:2; Tit. 1:9, 13; 2:15) that Spirit, having established his residence in the hearts of believers (see Acts 2; II Cor. 6:16), *will convict* [200] the world.

---

[200] But just what does the term *convict* mean? *Convince* and *convict* are not always nor necessarily identical in sense. A man is *convinced* of a doctrine or of a duty; he is *convicted* of a crime. Nevertheless, when the context or universe of discourse is *human guilt,* the two verbs may approach each other very closely in meaning. However, the English verb *to convict* is rather ambiguous because it may mean either: a. *to prove guilty,* without implying that the person whose guilt is proved is ready to admit and confess his guilt; and b. *to awaken to consciousness of guilt.* Surely, when the Holy Spirit *convicts* the world through the preaching of the Gospel, both of these results are achieved, but not in each individual to whom the Word is proclaimed. The Gospel immediately proves *the whole world* to be guilty. In the case of *many* this guilt is brought home to the conscience, sothat they feel it. And among these, again, there are some (God's elect) who not only are *convinced* of it in their soul, but also *admit* it openly, truly repent, and, *confessing* the wrong which they have committed, cast themselves upon the mercy of God in Christ. Hence, the verb to *convict* does not have the same meaning for all. By and large the wicked *world* continues in open hostility to God, his Christ, and his people (see Vol. I, p. 79, footnote 26, meaning 6). Though its guilt has been *exposed* or *proved* (hence, though in that sense it has been *convicted*), it does not repent.

The term employed in the original (ἐλέγχω) is at least just as elastic in meaning as is the English word *to convict.* That it means more than merely *to rebuke* has been shown by R. C. Trench, *op. cit.,* pp. 13-15. However, as his summary is not complete and as he seems to build his case on some (and not on all) the uses of the term, the value of his discussion is somewhat limited. In the passages which he mentions the verb implies *to rebuke with good effect,* that is, *to bring sin home to the conscience.*

The divergence of views with respect to the proper translation of the term is evident from the following Table, which lists all the seventeen instances of its use in the New Testament. (In this summary no mention is made of John 8:9 and of Jude 22, where the textual support is weak.)

	A.V.	A.R.V.	R.S.V.
Matt. 18:15	tell him his fault	show him his fault	tell him his fault
Luke 3:19	reprove	reprove	reprove
John 3:20	reprove	reprove	expose

He will publicly *expose its guilt and call it to repentance*. He will convict it with respect to three particulars: sin and righteousness and judgment. The result of this operation of the Spirit is not indicated here. From Acts 2:22-41; 7:51-57; 9:1-6; I Cor. 14:24; II Cor. 2:15, 16; Tit. 1:13, we learn that in some cases the result will be conversion; in others, hardening and everlasting punishment.

9. with respect to sin, because they do not believe in me.

Through the work of witnessing, which will be carried on by the apostles and their followers (15:27), the Holy Spirit will not only *lay bare* the world's sin but in the case of *some* will *awaken a consciousness of guilt* which leads to true repentance (cf. I John 3:8). There will be genuine sorrow and a fleeing to the Savior for refuge and pardon. There will be many instances of true conversion. Though the world in general will continue to persecute the Church (Acts 7:51 ff.), there will be millions of people who in the course of history are awakened to the consciousness of their guilt. As a result of the operation of God's sovereign grace, men from every clime and nation will accept Jesus as their Lord and Savior.

When the Holy Spirit, through the preaching of the Gospel, convicts men of their sin, a considerable number will cry out, "Brethren, what shall we do?" (Acts 2:37). They will feel that *the essence* of their sin (*the one great sin* which embraces all others for those who have heard the Gospel) is this: that they have not accepted Jesus as their Lord and Savior but have rejected him (see on 3:18; 12:37, 48). For the meaning of the verb πιστεύω see on 1:8; 3:16; 8:30, 31a.

10. with respect to righteousness, because I go to the Father, and y o u observe me no longer.

	A.V.	A.R.V.	R.S.V.
John 8:46	convince	convict	convict
John 16:8	reprove	convict	convince
I Cor. 14:24	convince	reprove	convict
Eph. 5:11	reprove	reprove	expose
Eph. 5:13	reprove	reprove	expose
I Tim. 5:20	rebuke	reprove	rebuke
II Tim. 4:2	reprove	reprove	convince
Tit. 1:9	convince	convict	confute
Tit. 1:13	rebuke	reprove	rebuke
Tit. 2:15	rebuke	reprove	reprove
Heb. 12:5	rebuke	reprove	punish
James 2:9	convince	convict	convict
Jude 15	convince	convict	convict
Rev. 3:19	rebuke	reprove	reprove

Moulton and Milligan, *op. cit.*, on this verb, prefers the translation *convict* (in the sense of "bring to light the true character of a man and his conduct") for all three instances of its use in the Fourth Gospel; and renders it *expose, set forth* in I Cor. 14:24; Eph. 5:11, giving papyri support for both uses.

The expression "will convict the world with respect to righteousness" must be explained in the light of what follows immediately: "because I go to the Father, and y o u observe me no longer."

The world, represented by the Jews, was about to crucify Jesus. It was going to say, "He *ought to* die" (19:7); hence, in the name of *righteousness* it was going to put him to death. It proclaimed aloud that he was anything but righteous. It treated him as an evil-doer (18:30). But the exact opposite was the truth. Though rejected by the world, he was welcomed by the Father, welcomed home via the cross, the cross which led to the crown. No longer were the disciples going to observe his day-by-day activities as he went in and out among them. He was about to die, and he was about to receive his reward (Phil. 2:9-11). By means of *the resurrection* the Father would place the stamp of his approval upon his life and work (Acts 2:22, 23, 33; Rom. 1:4). He, the very One whom the world had branded as *unrighteous,* would by means of his victorious going to the Father be marked as *the Righteous One* (8:46; Acts 3:14; 7:52; II Cor. 5:21; I Peter 3:18; I John 2:1; and cf. Luke 23:47). Thus, the world would be convicted with respect to righteousness. And this conviction would result in the world's condemnation (that is, in the condemnation of Satan and of all those men who refused to repent):

11. with respect to judgment, because the ruler of this world is judged. Already the prince of this world stood condemned (see on 12:31; 14:30; cf. Col. 2:15). In condemning the Christ (the One welcomed by the Father!) he condemned himself. At the last day this sentence will be made manifest to the entire universe "when the devil that deceived them is cast into the lake of fire and brimstone" (Rev. 20:10). Hence, the world, by clinging to the advice of Satan in condemning Jesus, stands convicted.

Summing up, it has become evident that through the preaching of the Gospel, the Holy Spirit helps the Church, and that he does this by convicting the world with respect to *its own sin* of not believing in Christ, with respect to *the righteousness of Christ,* who by his going to the Father is fully vindicated, and with respect to *the judgment of God* pronounced on the prince of the world.

Note how this prophecy of Jesus was actually fulfilled. Peter's sermon on the day of Pentecost (Acts 2) deals exactly with these three subjects: a. *sin,* the sin of rejecting the Christ ("y o u by the hand of lawless men crucified and killed him" . . . "this Jesus whom y o u crucified"); b. *righteousness,* the righteousness of Christ ("Jesus of Nazareth, a man *approved* by God"); and *judgment,* the judgment of those hostile to Christ ("Sit thou on my right hand, until I make thine enemies the footstool of thy feet . . . Save yourselves from this crooked generation"). The result was: "Now when they heard this, they were pricked in their heart, and said, 'Brothers, what shall we do?' . . . And there were added to them that day about three thousand souls."

12. I have yet many things to say to y o u, but y o u cannot bear them now.

Having spoken about the Spirit's work in the midst of *the world,* Jesus now proceeds to enlighten the minds of the disciples with respect to the Spirit's influence within the bosom of *the Church.* The home-base is just as important as the mission-field. Some people make the mistake of emphasizing the importance of the latter while they pay scant attention to the former. But if by giving heed to heresies, by following dishonest practices, or by permitting itself to be governed by clever manipulators, any section of the visible Church is no longer being led into all the truth, how can it expect a blessing upon its mission-fields? Church History furnishes examples. How can those who think lightly of sin serve as the agents of the Holy Spirit in the work of bringing others "under conviction" of sin?

The *true* Church of God, however, sees the danger, and exercises unceasing vigilance. In its enthusiasm for the glorious cause of missions it does not neglect the home-base! And the Holy Spirit makes use of this God-given watchfulness, and guides the Church into all the truth, strengthening it, sothat it can bear witness to the world.

The disciples were sorely in need of this spiritual strengthening. Picture the scene. Jesus is tenderly looking at these men. During this selfsame night they had revealed their sinful pride (13:14; Luke 22:24); within a few hours they were going to be "offended" in him (16:32; Matt. 26:31); right now, while the Master was uttering these words of life and beauty, they manifested their slowness of mind (13:36, 37; 14:8, 9, 22; 16:5, 6). Indeed, the great Physician of souls knew how frail and how carnally minded they were. He knew and understood all. Yet, he does not rebuke them; but in tender love he says, "I have yet many things to say to y o u, but *y o u cannot bear them now."*

"Mindful of our human frailty
Is the God in whom we trust;
He whose years are everlasting,
He remembers we are dust."

See also Matt. 13:12; I Cor. 3:1, 2; Heb. 5:11-14.

They could not *bear* (see on 10:31) to hear more now. Jesus has almost finished his discourse. In one or two more minutes he will be through. (16:12-33 is all that remains; chapter 17 is addressed to the Father, not to the disciples.) Now for this inability to bear more at this time they were not *entirely* to blame. There were also factors which involved no blame on the part of anyone. There was, for example, the simple fact that *redemp-*

tive acts generally precede full redemptive revelation. Thus, the doctrine with respect to the cross does not attain to full development until Jesus has been crucified; the full significance of the work of the Holy Spirit is not made known until the Holy Spirit has been poured out; etc. And this very fact, namely, that the Holy Spirit had not yet taken up his personal abode in the Church, made it impossible to give any further revelation at *this* time, during *this* night.

When Jesus now states, "*I* have yet many things to say to y o u," he clearly shows that the *later* revelation (which was going to be deposited in written form in Acts, the epistles, and the book of Revelation) was *his own* work. Hence, it is a great error to speak about *Paul's* Gospel as being opposed to *Christ's* Gospel!

The later revelation, moreover, does not contain truths that are "brand-new." On the contrary, springing from the same source, it is the same old truth, gloriously *clarified and amplified*.

13. But when he is come, the Spirit of truth, he will guide y o u into all the truth.

Jesus does not indicate the exact time when the Spirit is going to come. He says, "When" or "whenever." Though the word for Spirit is neuter in the original, the pronoun which refers to this Spirit is masculine. Hence, it is clear that the Spirit is thought of as a person. See also on 14:16. For the meaning of the expression "Spirit of truth," see on 14:17.

The function of the Holy Spirit in the Church is described as that of *guiding,* literally: "leading the way." The Spirit does not use external weapons. He does not *drive;* he *leads.* He exerts his influence upon the regenerated consciousness of the child of God (and here, in particular, of the office-bearers), and enlarges upon the themes which were introduced by Jesus during his earthly sojourn. Thus, he guides into all the truth, that is, into *the whole* (with emphasis on this adjective) body of redemptive revelation. The Holy Spirit never rides a hobby. He never stresses *one* point of doctrine at the expense of all the others. He leads into *all* the truth. Moreover, in the carrying out of this task he stands in intimate relationship to the other persons of the Trinity. We read: **For he will not speak of himself, but whatever he hears he will speak.** Father and Spirit are one in essence. What the Spirit hears from the Father he, in and through the Word, whispers into the hearts of believers. He is ever searching the depths of God. He comprehends them and reveals them to God's children (I Cor. 2:10, 11). In saying *what he hears* the Spirit is just like the Son, for the latter also speaks what he has heard from (and seen while with) the Father (3:11; 7:16; 8:24; 12:49; 14:10, 24). **And he will announce to y o u the things that are to come.** The Spirit *will come* (16:8); he *will lead into all the truth* (16:13a); and he *will announce the things that are*

328

to come (16:13b). For the first, see the book of Acts (particularly chapter 2); for the second, see the epistles; for the third see the book of Revelation. Not as if these three could be so sharply divided. Epistles and Revelation constantly assume the presence of the Spirit; the epistles contain much revelation with respect to the things that are to come (for example, I Cor. 15; II Thess. 2). But by and large the distinction which was made is a good one. Of course, when the Spirit declares the things that are to come, he does not begin to enumerate a long list of specific, day-by-day occurrences, but he predicts *the underlying principles.*[201]

14, 15. He will glorify me, because he will take from what is mine, and will announce (it) to y o u. All that the Father has is mine; therefore I said, He will take from what is mine, and will announce (it) to y o u.

While the world is busily engaged in the work of *rejecting* the Christ and persecuting his Church, the Holy Spirit, through the preaching of the apostles, will *glorify* Christ. He will cause the virtues of Christ to be proclaimed, showing forth his power, holiness, love, etc., and causing these to become respendently manifest among the nations. Thus, the Spirit will glorify the Son. He will take that which is Christ's — the very substance of his teaching regarding the purpose of redemption, manner of salvation, etc. — and will enlarge on it. Whatever Christ has done, is doing, will do (for the Church) is the theme of the Holy Spirit's teaching. Jesus has a right to call this teaching which is based upon the facts of redemption *his very own,* for as he has himself declared again and again (see on verse 13), he has received it from the Father; sothat he is able to say, "All that the Father has is mine," a passage which receives a most striking and beautiful commentary in the words of Matt. 11:27:

"All things have been delivered to me by my Father; and no one knows the Son, except the Father; neither does any one know the Father except the Son, and anyone to whom the Son chooses to reveal him."

There exists between the persons of the Trinity an eternal, voluntarily assumed relationship of love and friendship, each working for the glory and honor of the others (14:13; 16:14; 17:4, 5).

---

16 "A little while, and y o u will observe me no longer, and again a little while, and y o u will see me." 17 Some of his disciples said to each other, "What does he mean by saying to us, 'A little while, and y o u will observe me no longer, and again a little while, and y o u will see me'; and 'because I go away to the Father'?" 18 Accordingly, they kept saying, "What does he mean by the little while? We do not know what he means."

19 Jesus knew that they were desiring to inquire of him. So he said to them, "Are y o u searching among each other about this, that I said, 'A little while, and

---

201 On this see W. Hendriksen, *More Than Conquerors, An Interpretation of the book of Revelation,* Grand Rapids, Mich., sixth edition, 1952, pp. 14, 15, 73.

y o u will observe me no longer, and again a little while and y o u will see me'?
20 I most solemnly assure you,[202] Y o u will weep and wail, but the world will
rejoice; y o u will be sorrowful, but y o u r sorrow will turn into joy. 21 Any
woman, whenever she is in labor, is in pain because her hour has arrived; but
whenever she has given birth to the little one, she no longer remembers her anguish, because of her joy that a human being is born into the world. 22 And,
indeed, y o u too are now in sorrow, but I will see y o u again, and y o u r hearts
will rejoice, and that joy of y o u r s will no one take away from y o u. 23 And
in that day y o u will not inquire of me with respect to anything. I most solemnly
assure y o u, whatever y o u ask the Father he will give y o u in my name.[203] 24
Thus far y o u have not asked anything in my name. Ask and y o u will receive,
in order that y o u r joy may be full."

16:16-24

**16:16. A little while, and y o u will observe me no longer, and again a
little while, and y o u will see me.**

Jesus has been speaking about the work of the Holy Spirit in the world
and in the Church. The prediction found in verses 16-24 concerns the
Son. Nevertheless, there is the closest possible relation between the two
sections. Jesus is coming again. He is coming again *in the Spirit*.

What Jesus says in the present passage about the "little while" reminds
us of 7:33; 12:35; 13:33; and especially of 14:19: "Yet a little while, and
the world no longer sees me, but y o u see me; because I live y o u too will
live."

Now it is remarkable that both here in 16:16 and also in 14:19 (see on
that verse) the expression with reference to the little while occurs in a
context which speaks about the Holy Spirit. The saying recorded in 14:19
(see on that verse) was preceded by, "I will not leave y o u orphans: I am
coming to y o u." It was pointed out that this coming is the return in the
Spirit on the day of Pentecost. And 16:16 (as has just been shown) was
preceded by an entire section setting forth the work of the Spirit in the
world (16:7-11) and in the Church (16:12-15). Hence, it would seem to be
a safe inference that when Jesus states, "And again a little while, and y o u
will see me," he has in mind the dispensation of the Spirit during which
the latter would mightily display his works on earth, sothat with the eye of
faith the Church would be able to see their Author, namely, the promised
Helper, and in the background would discern the Savior who had sent
him. Of course, this dispensation of the Spirit, during which the Church
by means of him sees the Christ, was a direct result of the latter's going
to the Father, as Jesus has clearly set forth. Crucifixion, resurrection, and

---

[202] On ὅτι see Vol. I, p. 54, and footnote 13 on that page.
[203] This may be read like a conditional sentence (IIIA1), and translated: "If y o u
ask anything of the Father, he will give it to y o u in my name."

the outpouring of the Holy Spirit must never be separated. Jesus himself
has shown that they are inseparably linked, sothat the one means nothing
without the other. He had said, "It is to y o u r advantage that I go away;
for if I do not go away, the Helper will not come to y o u; but if I go,
I will send him to you." (16:7). Hence, the question, "When Jesus says,
'A little while, and y o u will see me,' is he thinking of his bodily resurrection *or* of his return in the Spirit?" is not entirely proper. In the thinking (and speaking!) of Jesus these two are not so sharply separated. Calvary
has no meaning apart from Easter, and Easter has no value apart from
Pentecost, which in turn points forward to the coming at the last day. (See
also what was said with respect to prophetic foreshortening, in connection
with 14:18).

Bearing all this in mind we would paraphrase verse 16 as follows:

"A little while — a few more hours! — , and I will be taken away from
y o u, for I will be put to death and buried. Hence, y o u will observe me
no longer. But I will not remain away from y o u. Rising gloriously on
the third day, I will usher in the dispensation of the Spirit. In and by
means of the mighty works which he will perform on earth, y o u will see
me." [204]

**17, 18. Some of his disciples said to each other, What does he mean by
saying to us, A little while, and y o u will observe me no longer, and again
a little while, and y o u will see me, and Because I go away to the Father?
— Accordingly, they kept saying, What does he mean by *the little while?***

Some of [205] his disciples are confused. They are not able to understand
how on the one hand Jesus can say, ". . . Again, a little while, and y o u
will see me," *as if his absence would be very brief,* yet on the other hand
can talk about going to the Father sothat they will see him no more, *as if
his departure would be definite and final.* Note that the words, "Because
I go away to the Father," are literally quoted from the statement of Jesus
in verse 10 (cf. also verse 5: "I am going away to him who sent me"; and
14:12, 28).

But though these men are puzzled, they fear to ask Jesus to help them
out of their difficulty; perhaps because he had again and again hinted
at the sinful ignorance and carnal-mindedness that came to light in their

---

[204] The position that "Again a little while, and y o u will see me," refers to *Christ's
physical resurrection* is defended by, among others, A. T. Robertson (commenting
on this verse in *Word Pictures,* Vol. V, p. 269); C. Bouma *(op. cit.,* p. 199); W. F.
Howard *(The Interpreter's Bible,* Vol. VIII, p. 734, though he thinks that there
is probably a remoter reference to the Parousia); M. Dods in *The Expositor's Bible*
(Vol. 1, p. 836). The opposite view — that it refers to Christ's return in the Spirit
— is very ably defended by F. W. Grosheide *(op. cit.,* pp. 380-385). For a possible
distinction in the meaning of the two verbs *(observe, see)* see on 16:19.
[205] On ἐκ see also 1:24.

questions (13:37, 38; 14:5-10, 22, 23); or perhaps because he had just re-marked, "I have yet many things to say to y o u, *but y o u cannot bear them now*" (16:12).

So, with muffled voices and in low tones, they kept asking *each other* what might be the meaning of this mashal (see on 2:19, 20).

19. Jesus knew that they were desiring to inquire of him.

The evangelist paints a vivid picture. He says that the disciples *were desiring* (imperfect tense) to ask a question, but did not venture to express this desire. He points out that Jesus knew this. He knew both their desire and their hesitancy. But he knew even more than this. His omniscience penetrated not only the hidden corners of the minds but also the secret recesses of the heart. He saw the still continuing and very painful *sadness*. For the knowledge of Jesus see on 1:42, 47, 48; 2:24, 25; 5:6; 6:64; 16:30; and 21:17. He knew that *the solution of the puzzle could wait.* Events about to transpire would take care of that. What the disciples did not understand now they would grasp later. But the pressing need of the mo-ment was to dispel *their gloom. There must be no waiting here.* **So,** in his tender mercy, taking the initiative in order to help his friends in their em-barrassment, **he said to them, Are you searching among each other** [206] **about this, that I said, A little while, and y o u will observe me no longer, and again a little while and y o u will see me?** [207]

20. I most solemnly assure y o u, Y o u will weep and wail, but the world will rejoice; y o u will be sorrowful, but y o u r sorrow will turn into joy.

For the words of solemn introduction see on 1:51. In order that the comfort which he imparts may be very real, Jesus first pictures to the dis-ciples their very deep grief in connection with his death. The more poig-nant the grief, the more exultant will be the joy that follows it. Jesus

---

[206] It is just possible that the phrase "among each other" implies a tender rebuke, as if Jesus meant to say, "Why do y o u search for the answer *among each other?* Why do y o u not ask *me?*" But this cannot be proved.

[207] It must not be considered impossible that the two verbs (first θεωρεῖτε, then ὄψεσθε) are used purposely, with a slight distinction in meaning in the present context. A little while, and the disciples will no longer *observe* Jesus day by day. Death and burial will take him away from their view. But after the second little while they will *see* him, namely, as the risen Savior who ushers in the dispensation of the Spirit. Although it is true that no sharp line of demarcation can be drawn between the two verbs — either can be used for physical as well as for mental and spiritual vision —, it is, nevertheless, also true that in the Fourth Gospel θεωρέω is more often used with reference to physical vision (observing signs, works, a beggar, a wolf, linen bandages, Jesus as he stood) than is the future of the verb ὁράω, which oftener (perhaps *always* in John) refers to mental or spiritual vision (at least a vision that is not exclusively physical). For the first verb see 2:23; 6:2; 7:3; 9:8; 10:12; 20:6, 12, 14 (but also 4:19; 6:40, 62; 8:51; 12:19, 45; 14:17; 17:24); for the second (future tense) see 1:39, 51; 3:36; perhaps even 19:37. See on 1:14; Vol. I, p. 85, footnote 33.

predicts that when he is crucified, the wicked *world* (see Vol. I, p. 79, footnote 26, meaning 6) — think especially of the hostile Jewish leaders — would rejoice. It would look upon the death of Jesus as a "good riddance," worthy of a celebration. But its joy will be premature. Moreover, the disciples' sorrow will not be of a permanent nature. While it is present, it will, indeed, be very painful. The friends of Jesus are going to *weep and wail* (or: "weep and lament"). For the fulfilment of this prophecy see on 20:11, 15; cf. Mark 16:10; Luke 24:38. For the meaning of the verb translated *weep* see on 11:35. In the Fourth Gospel that verb is found in 11:31, 33; 16:20; 20:11, 13, 15. For the meaning of the verb rendered *wail* (or *lament*) see Matt. 11:17 (cf. Luke 7:32): "We wailed but y o u did not mourn," and Luke 23:27, which speaks about "women who bewailed him." This *sorrow* will, however, *turn into joy*.

The illustration which Jesus employs in verse 21 seems to indicate that the meaning of the statement here in verse 20 is not merely this, that grief would be followed by joy, but rather this, that the very event which would cause overwhelming grief would afterward be viewed as a sound reason for superlative rejoicing. In the light of Easter and of Pentecost, the source of mourning, namely *the cross,* becomes the source of exultation, sothat Paul can exclaim, "Far be it from me to glory, save in the cross of our Lord Jesus Christ" (Gal. 6:14; cf. Luke 24:41, 52, 53).

21. Any woman, whenever she is in labor, is in pain because her hour has arrived but whenever she has given birth to the little one, she no longer remembers her anguish, because of her joy that a human being is born into the world.

The illustration fits the case exactly. Just as the birth of a child, into "the world" (realm of mankind), at first produces sorrow and anguish (cf. Gen. 3:16; Is. 26:17), but that selfsame event after a short interval brings about abundant joy; so also one and the same happening, namely, the death of Christ, would first cause the disciples to weep and wail, but in view of Christ's glorious resurrection and in the light of the Holy Spirit's interpretation, would ever afterward be the source of the greatest and most triumphant joy on the part of all God's children.

22. And, indeed, y o u too are now in sorrow, but I will see y o u again, and y o u r hearts will rejoice, and that joy of y o u r s will no one take away from y o u.

At this moment the disciples are sorrowing (cf. 14:1, 27; 16:6). They cannot reconcile themselves to the idea of their Master's imminent departure. However, Jesus declares that he will see them again. This is the counterpart of verse 19, "Y o u will see me." That this "seeing-one-another-again" refers to the entire dispensation of the Spirit (the fruit of Christ's crucifixion and resurrection), and not merely to the physical resurrection.

is very clear from the fact that we are distinctly told that, as a result, the hearts of the disciples will rejoice with a joy *which no one will ever be able to take away.* Besides, the opening words of verse 23 remove any doubt on this score. When Jesus says, "And *in that day* y o u will not question me with respect to anything," he certainly is not thinking merely of the *one* day of twenty-four hours when he arose from the grave! The *day* of verse 23 has already lasted almost two thousand years! To be sure, the rejoicing would *begin* on the very day of Christ's resurrection, but that day ushers in (and must not be thought of as separate from) the entire dispensation of the Spirit. Why this is true has been explained in connection with 16:7.

23. And in that day y o u will not inquire of me with respect to anything.

In order to grasp the meaning of this passage we must first of all connect it with verse 19 where the same verb *inquire* is used. See on 11:22. The disciples had been searching each other to find an answer to Christ's dark saying anent *the little while.* They had been filled with a desire to inquire of him, but they had not dared to interrupt him again. Now, in verse 23 Jesus declares that in the dispensation of the Spirit these men would no longer be at a loss what to do, desiring to ask questions and yet not having the courage to do so. In the light of Christ's resurrection, as interpreted by the Holy Spirit poured out on the day of Pentecost and present with the Church ever afterward, the meaning of *all* such matters would become perfectly clear. *Then* these men would know why Jesus had to die, why his death was advantageous for the Church, in what manner the source of gloom had been turned into a source of joy, etc. Peter would no longer have to ask, "Where art thou going?" (13:36); nor Thomas, "How can we know the way?" (14:5); nor Philip, "Show us the Father," (14:8); nor Judas the Greater "Lord, what has happened that thou art about to manifest thyself to us and not to the world?" (14:22); nor any of them, "What is *the little while?*" (16:18).

In this same dispensation of the Spirit the disciples will also receive an answer to *the petitions* which they send up to the Father. Hence, Jesus continues: **I most solemnly assure y o u, whatever y o u ask the Father he will give y o u in my name.** For the words of solemn introduction (so very appropriate because the prediction is so amazing!) see on 1:51. The transition from an *inquiry* (16:23a) to a *petition* (here in 16:23b) is not as abrupt as it may seem. When one is deeply concerned about a matter, yearning most ardently to receive an explanation of a mystery, *the request for information* readily turns into *the asking for a favor.*

The words of this promise remind one of 14:13, 14; 15:7; and especially 15:16. See on these passages for the explanation. There is, however, one important difference. We now learn that not only the *asking* is in Christ's name, but so is also the *giving*. The Father will give in harmony with his entire redemptive revelation which centers in the Son, and on the basis of his love for the Son and of the latter's sacrifice. The believers' union with Christ has two practical results: on the one hand, the friends of Jesus *are persecuted* for his sake (15:21); on the other hand, they *are blessed* for his sake.

24. Thus far y o u have not asked anything in my name. That is, up to this time the disciples, in their prayers, had addressed themselves directly to God, without making mention of the name of Jesus. Not as if the mere mentioning of the name would help any. Certainly, when a believer concludes his prayer by saying, "All this we ask in Jesus' name," he is not using a magic formula. What he means is, "We ask all this on the basis of Christ's merits and in harmony with his redemptive revelation." The disciples had not been basing their petitions upon this ground. According to some this was an error on their part, for which Jesus here, by implication, reprimands them. According to others, there had been no fault on their part, inasmuch as the full work of redemption had not yet been accomplished. The text (16:24) does not settle this question in either direction. The main point is this, that from now on there must be a change. So Jesus continues: **Ask and y o u will receive.** "Keep on asking," says he. According to the statement which precedes, he means, "Keep on asking *in my name.*" The promise, "and y o u will receive," is the same in substance as that found in the Sermon on the Mount (Matt. 7:7). Anyone who asks in the spirit of Christ's revelation — hence, according to God's will, for the furtherance of his glory, on the basis of Christ's merits — will receive. — And the purpose which the Lord has in mind is this: **that y o u r joy may be full.** Through constant fellowship with God in prayer and through receiving answers to prayer, whatever was lacking in the disciples' joy will be supplied, until the cup of joy is filled to the brim.

Thus Jesus here repeats the wonderful statement made earlier (15:11; see on that passage). What a glorious Savior! The cross with all its agonies is just around the corner. A few more hours, and Jesus will give his life as a ransom for many. He knows what is coming. Already he sees the nails that will pierce his hands and feet. He hears, as it were, the jeers and taunts of the leaders, their hellish laughter. Yet — O love divine and beyond all comprehension! — his ardent desire is this: *"that y o u r joy may be full."*

25 "These things have I spoken to y o u in veiled sayings; the hour is coming when I shall no longer speak to y o u in veiled sayings but shall inform y o u openly about the Father. 26 In that day y o u will ask in my name; and I do not say to y o u that I shall make request of the Father for y o u; 27 for the Father himself loves y o u, because y o u have loved me and have believed that I

came out from the Father. 28 I came out from the Father, and am come into the world; again I am leaving the world and am going to the Father."

29 His disciples said, "Ah, now thou art speaking openly, not in any veiled saying. 30 Now we know that thou knowest all things, and dost not have need of anyone to inquire of thee. For this reason we believe that thou didst come from God."

31 Jesus answered them, "Do y o u now believe? 32 Note well, there comes an hour — yes, it has arrived! — when y o u will be scattered, each to his own home, and y o u will leave me alone; yet I am not alone, for the Father is with me. 33 These things have I spoken to y o u, in order that in me y o u will have peace. In the world y o u have tribulation; but be of good courage, I have conquered the world."

Having shown how in the future *the Spirit* would convict the world and guide the Church (verses 7-15), how *the Son,* by means of his resurrection and in the Spirit, would see them again, turning sorrow into joy (verses 16-24), Jesus now indicates how *the Father* will continue to love his own (verses 25-27). Notice that there are no less than eight references to "the Father" ("God" in verse 30) in this brief paragraph (verses 25-33).

16:25-33

16:25. These things have I spoken to y o u in veiled sayings.

The expression "these things" refers to all the words which Jesus spoke that memorable night, and (in the light of what follows) probably even to all his previous teaching. There had been veiled saying upon veiled saying, mashal upon mashal. In fact, it can even be said that the dark utterance was the very heart of Christ's teaching. The discourse often centers in (or grows out of) the veiled saying. In the body of such a discourse there are many statements of sufficient clarity to remove every excuse for rejecting Jesus as the Son of God.

Perhaps because we have become used to these mashals we often forget how they must have baffled those who first heard them. Nevertheless, this bewilderment was very real. A common reaction was, "How can this be? How can that be?"

Jesus had spoken about raising up the temple in three days, being born again, living water which quenches thirst once and for all, rivers of this water flowing from within believers, people who would never see death; also *about himself,* as the One whose flesh the believer must eat and whose blood he must drink, as having preceded Abraham in time, as the good shepherd who lays down his own life; *about a mysterious betrayer* (whose identity remained undisclosed for a considerable period of time); and *about an enigmatic "little while,"* which was to be followed by another equally puzzling "little while" (see on 2:19; 3:3, 5; 4:10, 14; 6:35, 50, 51,

53-58; 7:37, 38; 8:51, 56, 58; chapter 10; 13:18, 21; 16:16-19). For the meaning of the term *veiled saying (paroimia)* see also chapter 10 (Basic Points III; and 10:6).

Now Jesus reveals that a new era is about to dawn: **The hour is coming when I shall no longer speak to y o u in veiled sayings but shall inform y o u openly about the Father.**

At present Jesus is still prevented from speaking fully and openly, He is held back by the incapacity of the hearers (16:12), by the fact that he had not yet given his life as a ransom for many, and by the additional fact that the Spirit had not yet been poured out (16:13). Until the Man of Sorrows has actually suffered and died on the cross and until he is risen, this cross cannot be fully revealed. Until the Helper has arrived, the Father cannot be fully declared. The revelation of the Father's love in delivering up his own Son and in sending the Spirit must for a while remain veiled. But a great change is coming. In the era of the Spirit this revelation (although of necessity adapted to the finite, human mind) will be clear, free, unrestricted, full. It will no longer be characterized by veiled utterances.

This promise was fulfilled. Anyone who turns from the teaching of Jesus, as recorded in *the Gospels,* to the teaching of Jesus (through the apostles), as recorded in *the epistles,* is immediately aware of the difference. To be sure, the epistles contain many problems with which the interpreter has to wrestle. "Our beloved brother Paul" is not always easy to grasp (II Peter 3:15, 16). But this teaching is, nevertheless, more direct, open. There is here no longer a purposeful choice of words with more than one meaning. Didactic declaration and explanation more and more take the place of truth set forth by means of mysterious utterances and seeming contradictions. The *seed* of the Gospel has become the fully developed *plant.* *Openly* the teaching with reference to the Father's plan of redemption is set forth in such wonderful passages as Rom. 3:21-25; chapter 5; chapter 8; Eph. 1:3-14; Phil. 2:9, 10; I Peter 1:3-12; I John 3; etc. For the meaning of the word *openly* (παρρησία) see on 7:26.

26, 27. In that day y o u will ask in my name; and I do not say to y o u that I shall make request of the Father for y o u; for the Father himself loves y o u because y o u have loved me, and have believed that I came out from the Father.

In the dispensation of the Spirit the disciples are going to do what they have not yet done (16:24). They are going to pray "in Jesus' name," that is, in harmony with his redemptive revelation and on the basis of his accomplished atonement. Verse 26b and verse 27 may be paraphrased as follows:

"And I do not say to y o u that I shall continue to regard y o u like very small children who are not yet able to pray, sothat for that reason others have to pray *for* them. On the contrary, in that new era y o u yourselves

will pray to the Father; and he will hear y o u, for he himself constantly
loves y o u. The reason why he loves y o u is this, that y o u have loved
me, with a love which still continues, and have believed, with a faith that
never ceases, that I came from the Father (as his only-begotten Son)." For
the meaning of "in that day" see on 16:23. For the distinction in meaning
between the verbs *ask* and *make request* see on 11:22. The verb for *love*
here in verse 27 is φιλεῖ. However, either verb (φιλέω or ἀγαπάω) is used in
the Fourth Gospel to express the love of the Father for the disciples, and
the love of the disciples for Jesus. In such contexts the verbs are probably
almost identical in meaning. See on 21:15-17. Does the statement, "the
Father himself loves y o u because y o u have loved me," indicate that *our*
love is first, and *his* love last? Does it mean that *our* love is the source of *his*
love? This question has been answered in connection with 7:17, 18; 14:21b;
and 15:10; see on those passages.

The prediction contained in these two verses does not mean that in the
dispensation of the Spirit all intercession for the disciples is going to cease.
Far from it! That intercession of the Highpriest, Jesus Christ, will never
cease. "In short, the believer's entire communion with God . . . as well
the spiritual blessings which he must have from God, as what he brings to
God, must and can only be through the mediation of the interceding Highpriest in heaven. The living, exalted Christ is still as he was on earth, the
only way to the Father." [208] Accordingly, we do not agree with R. C. H.
Lenski when he states that after Pentecost the petitions directed by the
disciples to the Father in Jesus' name *will not need the support and intercession of Jesus in order to be granted by the Father.*[209] As we see it, such
passages as 14:6; Heb. 7:24, 25; 13:15 clearly teach the opposite. What
John 16:26, 27 does teach is this, that, in the dispensation of the Spirit,
the disciples will reach maturity so that *they themselves also,* in the name
of the Son, *will approach the Father.* Putting it differently, if the question
be asked, "Is Jesus going to pray for them?" the answer is a definite "No"
if by *praying for them* is meant a request presented to the Father in their
behalf because they themselves do not pray and because the Father would
not accept their prayer if one were offered. But the answer is a clear "Yes,"
if by *praying for them* is meant the unceasing intercession of the Highpriest
in heaven for his people, on the basis of his atonement.

**28. I came out from the Father, and am come into the world; again I
am leaving the world and am going to the Father.**
Truly beautiful and full of majesty is the finale of Christ's Farewell to

[208] H. H. Meeter, *The Heavenly Highpriesthood of Christ,* doctoral dissertation
submitted to the Free University at Amsterdam, published in Grand Rapids, Mich.
(no date), p. 186.
[209] R. C. H. Lenski, *op. cit.,* p. 1082.

his disciples. The note of victory prevails. We behold the Son of man in the full consciousness of his triumph. Every word spells exultation over the accomplishment of the task which had been assigned. Every clause is filled with resolute determination to carry out the Father's will. In principle the battle has already been fought. See especially verse 33: "I have conquered the world."

Note the close connection between this and the preceding passage. *There* Jesus asserted, "Y o u . . . have believed that I came out from the Father." *Here* he continues by saying (according to the original), "I came out . . . out of the Father," etc.

The passage stresses the fact that the work of redemption is Christ's own work. *To save his people* was not only a task laid upon him. It was just as emphatically the result of his own free choice. Hence, *"I came out . . . I am come . . . I am leaving . . . I am going."* It is as if Jesus said, *"I myself* do all this. The Father does not compel me to do it. Satan and the world cannot prevent me from doing it."

The passage records *three* central facts or movements in the history of redemption, but due to the fact that the third is viewed from two aspects we have in reality *four* parts, as follows:

First, "I came out from the Father." This refers to Christ's perfect deity, his pre-existence, and his love-revealing departure from heaven in order to dwell on the sin-cursed earth. Cf. II Cor. 8:9. (Here we have the aorist tense, *one* act.)

Secondly, "I . . . am come into the world." That describes Christ's incarnation and his ministry among men. (Here the perfect tense is used, indicating the past act together with its present result.) The term *world* has the same meaning here as in verse 21.

Thirdly and fourthly, "Again I am leaving the world and am going to the Father." Note the present tense of both verbs. The path of suffering, crucifixion, resurrection, ascension is, from one aspect, a departure from the world; from another point of view, it is a journey to the Father. On the basis of this voluntary obedience which Jesus is in the process of rendering, the Father (in the Spirit) exercises loving fellowship with those who are his own.

29, 30. His disciples said, Ah, now thou art speaking openly, not in any veiled saying. Now we know that thou knowest all things, and dost not have need of anyone to inquire of thee.

So impressed are the disciples by the directness and clarity of Christ's words and by his evident knowledge of the whole plan of God, that they imagine that the time has even now arrived in which plain, unhampered, full, and free speaking would take the place of speaking in veiled utterances. In this opinion they were mistaken. Yet, Jesus does not try to correct them. They will correct themselves when the future hour arrives.

All in all, however, the answer given by the disciples does credit to them. They have advanced in knowledge. The Upper Room discourses have not been in vain. The experiences of this "night of all nights" have left their mark on these men. They have begun *to reflect* on the teaching of Jesus. The result is that they now *know* (the verb indicates this knowledge of *reflection*) that Jesus *knows* (same verb but not same reason: Jesus *knows* because he is divine; his knowledge is antecedent, not merely subsequent) *all things* (cf. 21:17). They have once again caught the vision of Christ's deity shining through the veil of his humanity. For the moment at least they *are convinced* — it is the conviction of faith; cf. II Cor. 5:1 — that Jesus is omniscient. The light is shining brightly now, more brightly, perhaps, than ever before. Within a few hours it will be obscured once more. Yet, the confession which is here made will linger on in the realm of the subconscious, until by and by, when the Lord arises in triumph from the tomb and (a little later) pours out his Spirit, it will bear the fruit of calm and stedfast assurance, and this fruit will abide forever.

The key to the interpretation of the words, "and dost not have need of anyone to inquire of thee" is found in the immediately preceding clause ("Now we know that thou knowest all things") and in verse 19: "Jesus knew that they were desiring to inquire of him." He knew it even though they never asked him any question! He had read their secret thoughts. He knew exactly what they were mumbling to each other. In fact, even before any word had been on their tongue, he had known it altogether. And such knowledge had been "too wonderful" for them (Ps. 139:4). Hence, verse 30a may be paraphrased as follows:

"Now we know that thou knowest all things, and that thou dost not have need of anyone to inquire of thee, in order that by means of *his* questions *thou* mayest discover what he has on his mind. Thou knewest it before he even asked."

The disciples draw the only logical conclusion: **For this reason we believe that thou didst come from God.** Only God is omniscient. Jesus is omniscient. Hence, Jesus must be God. Being God, he must have come *from God.* For the latter phrase see on 14:23, footnote 168. For the knowledge of Jesus see on 1:42, 47, 48; 2:24, 25; 5:6; 6:64; and 21:17.

This was the last confession which the disciples made before Christ's death. It reminds us of the earlier confession by Nathaniel (1:49), by Peter (Matt. 16:16), and the later one by Thomas (20:28).

31, 32. Jesus answered them, Do y o u now believe? Note well, there comes an hour — yes, it has arrived! — when y o u will be scattered, each to his own home, and y o u will leave me alone.

It makes little difference whether we read, "Y o u now believe," or, "Do y o u now believe?" Either rendering is possible according to the original. If the question-form is adopted, it *could* mean that Jesus calls into question the genuine character of their faith. Nevertheless, there is another possibility which, in the present connection and in view of the definite statement in 17:8 ("They have really come to acknowledge that I came from thee"), is far more probable, namely, that the Lord, though accepting their confession at face-value, wishes to put them on guard against overconfidence. It is as if he were saying, "I believe that y o u r confession is genuine and that y o u r faith is real; but is it full-grown? Has it reached maturity? Will y o u r anchor hold in the storms of life? Are y o u sure that y o u can stand y o u r ground when the foe suddenly makes his appearance?" That, more or less, is the sense in which these words have generally been interpreted. We have not found any good reason to depart from this common explanation. Nothing better has been offered.

For "there comes an hour" see on verse 25. For the entire expression, "There comes an hour, yes it has arrived," cf. 5:25. The designated season is close at hand. In a way it is still future, for Jesus and the disciples have not yet crossed the brook (in fact, as we see it, are still in the Upper Room), and have not yet encountered the foe (Judas and his band). Yet, in another sense, this season has already arrived, for a. Judas is even now on the way, and b. so *certain* is it that the predicted event will occur that to the mind of Christ it is already *present*. Hence, the expression, "Note well, there comes an hour, yes it has arrived!" describes the situation exactly. And because the prediction is so startling, it is preceded by the exclamation, "Note well!" (literally, "Look!").

The contents of the prediction is twofold: a. "Y o u will be scattered, each to his own home." With this should be compared:

10:12: "And the wolf snatches them and scatters (the flock)." See on that verse.

Matt. 26:31: "Y o u will all be ensnared on account of me this night; for it is written, 'I will strike the shepherd, and the sheep of the flock will be scattered.'" This was spoken after Jesus and his little company had left the Upper Room.

The prophecy which was fulfilled when this happened (see Mark 14:27) is found in Zech. 13:7:

"Strike the shepherd, that the sheep may be scattered;
And I will turn my hand against (or *upon*) the little ones." [210]

---

[210] The background of Zechariah's prophecy is as follows:
After the remnant of the Jews had returned from captivity, they built the altar of burnt-offering and laid the foundations of the temple (Ezra 3:1-10). Jealous Samaritans and their allies interrupted the work (Ezra 4). Discouragement gained the upper hand. But in the second year of Darius—i.e., about the year 520 B. C.—

The phrase "to his own home" here (John 16:32) in the sentence, "And y o u will be scattered, each to his own home" occurs also in 1:11 and 19:27. Jesus came "to his own home, but his own people did not welcome him" (see Vol. I, p. 80, footnote 27). John took Mary "to his own home" (19:27). We see no reason to depart from this sense in the present instance. When, in connection with the arrest of Jesus, the disciples were scattered, each man went to his own home (in this case, to his own place of lodging in or near Jerusalem). It is true, of course, that in the case of John and Peter the going home was delayed a little while. Nevertheless, by and by Mary Magdalene knows exactly where she can find Peter, and also where she can find John. Each had gone to his own home (see on 20:2). The prediction probably implies more than this, however. It seems to indicate that united effort would cease; hope would be lost, kingdom-work would be stopped; and *fishing* (in the ordinary sense of the term) would take the place of *preaching* (see on 21:3).

We turn now to b. "And y o u will leave me alone" (literally: "And *me* y o u will leave alone," with all the emphasis on the pronoun *me*). These words may be viewed as Christ's own commentary on the disciples' confession of a moment ago, "Now *we know* . . . for this reason *we believe*" (verse

---

Haggai urged the rebuilding of the temple. Zechariah joined him in this exhortation and predicted the future glory of Zion; also the coming, suffering, and exaltation of the Branch. The theme of Zechariah's prophecies and the division are as follows:

The Future Glory of Zion and of Its Shepherd-King

   I. Visions (1:1-6:8)
  II. A Symbolic Act (6:9-15)
 III. An Answer to a Question (chapters 7, 8)
 IV. Predictions and Promises (chapters 9-14).

It is particularly this last section that interests us here, in connection with John 16:32, "Y o u will be scattered." It is at least probable that among the events predicted in Zech. 9-14 are the following:

a. The further progressive return of the captives from the lands of the captivity (10:8-12).

b. The defeat of the countries which surround Judah in a day when Judah itself will be protected (9:1-8).

c. The victories of the Maccabees over Antiochus Epiphanes (9:11-17; 12:1-9).

d. The coming of the Righteous King, the true Shepherd (9:9); *also his rejection* (chapter 11; *13:7*); see Matt. 21:5; 26:14-16.

e. The election of the remnant throughout the New Dispensation (13:8, 9).

f. The outpouring of the Spirit, and the blessings of the Messianic Age, with the total disappearance of the dispensation of shadows and ceremonies (most of chapter 14).

The prediction found in John 16:32 (the passage now under study) has to do with d.: the Shepherd's rejection. There is considerable difference of opinion with respect to the words, "And I will turn my hand against (or *upon*) the little ones." Some view this as a prophecy of woe (the more probable view, it would seem to us), some, of weal. — For this material on Zechariah, in more expanded form, see W. Hendriksen, *Bible Survey*, pp. 120, 121; 283-286.

30). The Master does not in any way deny the presence of genuine faith in the hearts of his friends (see also on 17:7); but he stresses the imperfect character of that faith. Perfect faith casts out fear and "working through love" shows real courage at the critical moment. It never forsakes, never winces, never fails! Such was not the faith of these men.

Moreover, by saying, "And me y o u will leave alone," Jesus places the emphasis where it truly belongs, on the theme of his own suffering. More and more he will enter the region of isolation. He will be forsaken by his friends, and at last forsaken by his Father in heaven! But that climax of woe has not yet arrived. At this moment Jesus is still able to say, **Yet I am not alone, for the Father is with me.** This had been his comfort right along, as is clearly indicated by 8:29: "And he who sent me is with me. He has not left me alone, because I always do the things that are pleasing to him." See on that passage. (Although at times reference is also made to 8:16b, yet the sense there is slightly different. See on that verse.)

33. These things have I spoken to y o u, in order that in me y o u may have peace. "These things" includes whatever Jesus told his disciples that night. He had told them about himself, informing them (as he had done so often) that he had come from the Father, had entered the world, was leaving again, and was about to go back to the Father. He had pointed out that he would be betrayed by a man who ate at his table; that he would be denied three times, and this by no one less than Peter; that he was being hated; that *the world* would rejoice in his death; and that *his own disciples* would leave him alone in the hour of crisis. The fulfilment of these prophecies would naturally strengthen their faith in him (see on 16:1, 4). And through faith they would obtain the greatest of all blessings, namely, *peace.* The nature of that peace has been indicated in connection with the explanation of 14:27. It is both objective (reconciliation with God, Rom. 5:1, 2; II Cor. 5:20b) and subjective (the quiet and comforting assurance of justification and adoption, Rom. 8:16 ff.). In view of the context, the emphasis both here and in 14:27 seems to rest on the subjective side of this peace. It is contrasted with *tribulation.* Jesus continues, **In the world y o u have tribulation; but be of good courage. I have conquered the world.**

In Christ they have peace; in the world, *tribulation* (or *anguish;* cf. 16:21). *The world,* as the term is here used, forms a striking antithesis with *the Christ.* It is the world which persecutes the Church (see Vol. I, p. 79, footnote 26, meaning 6). The term which is correctly rendered *tribulation* has the primary meaning (both in Greek and in English): *pressure.* See Rom. 2:9; cf. also Matt. 24:9; Acts 7:11; 11:19; Rom. 2:9; 12:12; II Cor. 1:4, 8; 4:17; 6:4; 7:4; 8:2; II Thess. 1:6; Rev. 1:9; 2:9, 22; 7:14, etc. The world ever tries to *crowd out* the true believer. The disciples can expect tribulation from the side of the world (cf. 16:2) because of their relation to the Master (15:21). But this very principle — namely, that *what happens to the Master will happen to the disciple* — also applies in the opposite direction: the disciple can expect to conquer because of his relation to the Master. The words, "But be of good courage. I have conquered the world," clearly imply, "And therefore y o u, my followers, will also conquer."

Say that a mountain-climber and his guide are trying to ascend a steep cliff. With the skill that results from long experience in mountaineering the guide makes the ascent, and shouts to the man who is at the lower end of the rope, "Do not be afraid, for I have made it." Similarly, the pressure that comes from the side of the world will never succeed in causing the disciples to lose their foothold, for Jesus (with whom they are united) has reached the top; hence, *so* will they.

In view of all that has preceded in this chapter — the promise of the Holy Spirit's coming and work, the prediction of the Son's glorious return, the assurance of the Father's abiding love — it is not surprising that the chapter ends with a note of victory. Having just about reached the end of the path, Jesus can look back, and can say, "I *have* conquered." [211] However, the past tense (*perfect*, for abiding result) also indicates *certainty* with respect to the impending battle. The victory is sure. Jesus had fully committed himself. Hence, he is able to speak as if Calvary even now lay behind him. See also on 12:31; 16:11.

It is certainly remarkable that at the very moment when the Man of Sorrows concludes his final discourse in the Upper Room, just before he treads the valley of deepest gloom, he addresses his disciples with these remarkable words, "Be of good cheer!" As far as the record is concerned, with a single exception, he was the only one who employed that heartening verb (θάρσει, θαρσεῖτε). One finds it in the following passages: Matt. 9:2, 22; 14:27; Mark 6:50; 10:49 (the one exception); John 16:33; and Acts 23:11. Surely, the man who conquers along with Christ has reason to be cheerful! And this even *in the midst* of tribulation; yes, even *because of* tribulation, as is shown beautifully in Acts 5:41.

---

[211] In the Fourth Gospel John uses the verb *to conquer* only once, and then in a quotation, sothat it is really Jesus (not John) who utters it. In the book of Revelation this verb occurs again and again. In fact "More Than Conquerors" may be called the theme of that book. See the author's *More Than Conquerors*, Grand Rapids, Mich., sixth edition, 1952, pp. 12-14, 114, 115. According to the book of Revelation, Jesus has conquered, is conquering, is going to conquer. Hence, those who are with him are also conquerors. This is essentially the same idea as here in 16:33.

Synthesis of Chapter 16

See the Outline on p. 260. *The Son of God Tenderly Instructing the Disciples. A Word of Prediction.*

I. Persecution in Store for Believers. *The Holy Spirit's* Coming and Work.

A. Persecution in Store for Believers (16:1-6)

Jesus predicts what the believer can expect, in order that when persecution arrives his faith may be strengthened instead of weakened. The persecutor will be motivated by religious zeal, imagining that by afflicting believers he is rendering a service to God. Actually, he does not even know God (in Christ). Out of love for his disciples Jesus has delayed as long as possible this prediction with respect to coming tribulation. Now that he is ready to depart (by way of the cross, the resurrection, the ascension), he must tell them about it, in order that they may not be taken unawares. Besides, from now on the attacks will no longer be directed against *him* but against *them*. Although in broad outlines Jesus has explained the purpose of his departure, the disciples seemed more concerned about the departure as such (considering it a loss for themselves) than with its glorious objective. Jesus complains about the fact that dismal gloom on their part has crowded out further questions.

B. The Holy Spirit's Coming and Work (16:7-15)

1. In the world (verses 7-11)

Christ's departure is in the interest of the disciples; for unless he returns to the Father, the Helper will not come. This Helper will *convict* the world. He will not try to *destroy* man's sense of guilt (as is the vogue today — twentieth century) but will *awaken* the sinner's conscience to the evil and heinousness of sin. By means of the work which he, through the preaching of the Gospel, performs in the world, he will drive home three truths: *the world's* own sin, *Christ's* perfect righteousness, and *God's* judgment.

2. In the Church (12-15)

The Holy Spirit *will come* (see the book of Acts, especially chapter 2); will *lead into all the truth* (see the Epistles; the Holy Spirit never rides a hobby; always proclaims *the whole* counsel of God); and *will declare the future* (see the book of Revelation). It is Jesus himself who is speaking when the Spirit speaks. The latter enlarges on the truths which the former taught while here on earth. The persons of the Holy Trinity always glorify each other. Due to lack of fully developed faith and due to the fact that two great events in the history of redemption had not yet occurred (Christ's resurrection and the outpouring of the Spirit), the disciples were not able to bear more teaching during this memorable night.

II. *The Son's* Return (16:16-24)

A little while — just a few hours now — and the disciples will no longer be able to see their Master, for by means of the cross and burial he will be removed from their sight. Again, a little while — that is, from the burial to the resurrection and the outpouring of the Holy Spirit — and the disciples will see their Master again. They will see who he really is. The fact of the resurrection will be an eye-opener for them. The descent of the Spirit will complete the work of making everything clear.

To the startled disciples, who experience great difficulty in explaining the sayings about "the little while," Jesus predicts that the very cause of their great sorrow — namely, his death — will become the source of their supreme joy; just like the birth of a child first produces pain, then gladness. In the dispensation of the Spirit questions such as have been on the minds of the disciples during these past hours (and also previously) will no longer be asked. All will be plain then. And all God-glorifying petitions will be granted, on the basis of Christ's atonement. Thus, their joy will be made full.

III. *The Father's* Love (16:25-33)

The Father loves those who love the Son. These men have accepted Jesus as the One who came from and returns to the Father. They confess their faith. Jesus corrects their over-confidence. He tells them that when the hour of crisis arrives, they will leave him alone. However, the Father is with him.

In a statement unparalleled for beauty and spiritual uplift Jesus climaxes his discourse. He says, "These things have I spoken to y o u, in order that in me y o u may have peace. In the world y o u have tribulation; but be of good courage, I have conquered the world." Implication: "Y o u most certainly will *also* conquer."

CHAPTER XVII

17 1 These things spoke Jesus, and he lifted up his eyes to heaven and said, "Father, the hour has arrived; glorify thy Son in order that the Son may glorify thee, 2 even as thou hast given him authority over all flesh, that [212] to all whom thou hast given him he might give everlasting life. 3 And this is everlasting life, that [213] they should know thee, the only true God, and Jesus Christ whom thou didst send. 4 I glorified thee on the earth, having accomplished the work which thou gavest me to do. 5 And now, Father, glorify thou me in thine own presence with the glory which I had with thee before the world existed."

Introductory Remarks on Chapter 17

I. *Its Close Connection with the Preceding Discourses*

The apostle John himself indicates this connection when he combines the discourse and the prayer in the words: "These things spoke Jesus, and he lifted up his eyes to heaven and said." The prayer may be viewed as *the consummation* of the discourses. It shows that the firm and solid basis for all the grounds of comfort, admonitions, and predictions is in heaven. It links all the promises to the throne of God. Here all is certain. The chapter contains not one conditional sentence.

II. *Its Unique Character*

Is this prayer a model for our prayers? In a certain sense it is; for example, this prayer indicates that the glory of God should be the purpose of our petitions; also, it shows that we should pray not only for ourselves but also for others.

Nevertheless, in an even deeper sense, this prayer of the great Highpriest, Jesus Christ, can never become a model for our prayers. It is altogether unique. Of *this* prayer Jesus never said, "After this manner y o u must pray." It is unique in the following respects:

A. Its Author is the second person of the Trinity, who has assumed the human nature (17:5).

---

[212] On ἵνα see Vol. I, pp. 46, 52.
[213] On ἵνα see Vol. I, pp. 45, 52.

B. It is addressed to Christ's *own* holy and righteous Father, the first person of the Trinity (17:1, 5, 11, 21, 24, 25; cf. 1:18; 3:16; 20:17).

C. It does not contain a single confession of sin; rather, the exact opposite. The prayer is characterized by the Son's consciousness of perfect obedience to the will of the Father (17:4). Contrast this with the prayer which Jesus taught his disciples to pray (Matt. 6:12).

D. This prayer contains *requests* rather than *petitions*. See on 11:22.

III. *Its Parts*

The prayer is *one*. The mission of Jesus Christ and of his followers on earth, unto the glory of God, is the theme throughout. Yet, though the prayer reveals a wonderful unity, a unity so organic and real that commentators are not agreed as to where one part ends and another begins, three movements are discernible. First, Jesus makes request with respect to *himself* (verses 1-5; according to others: 1-8); secondly, with respect (chiefly) to *the apostles* (verses 6-19; according to others: 9-19); thirdly, with respect to *the Church Universal* (verses 20-26).

17:1-5

17:1. These things spoke Jesus, and he lifted up his eyes to heaven and said, Father, the hour has arrived.

The fact that Jesus lifted up his eyes *to heaven* does not prove that he and his disciples were outside (cf. Acts 7:55). In all probability the little group was still in the Upper Room (see on 14:31). To lift up the eyes to heaven was the common posture in prayer, and very proper too, inasmuch as the One who is addressed has his Throne in heaven.

The expression, "The hour has arrived" shows once more that Jesus is conscious of the fact that for every event in the mighty drama of redemption (yes and for every event that ever takes place in history) there is a stipulated moment in the eternal decree (see also on 2:4; 7:6, 8, 30; 8:20; 12:23; 13:1; and Vol. I, p. 46). It is clear from the context that Jesus was thinking of the hour of his *death* not only but of the entire *consummation* of his earthly ministry: *death, resurrection, ascension, and coronation,* his entire *going to the Father.* In the thought of Jesus, suffering and consequent glory go together (12:32; 14:3, 4; 16:20 ff.; cf. Matt. 16:21; 20:19; 26:28, 29). Christ's death was of such a character that his resurrection, ascension, and coronation *had to follow;* hence, *the hour* refers to all four. This was not the first time that Jesus had referred to this hour. The difference was that previously he had said that it had not yet arrived, now it had arrived (cf. 7:30; 8:20).

This hour was the moment of crisis. It was the hour in which the Son of man would terminate his labors by rendering the one and only atoning sacrifice for the sin of mankind; the hour of fulfilling prophecies, types, and symbols; the hour of triumph over the prince of the world; the hour of dismissing the old and of ushering in the new dispensation.

Jesus continues: **Glorify thy Son in order that the Son may glorify thee.** The meaning is: "Grant that by means of my entire going to thee (death, resurrection, ascension, coronation) I may be glorified, and thou mayest be glorified by me." Jesus is glorified when the radiance of his attributes is displayed. Surely, in *the cross* of Christ and also in *the crown* we see this glory. In the cross, viewed as the culmination and climax of the entire work of redemption by which he saves his people, the Son manifests his perfect obedience, his infinite love for sinners, and his power over the prince of this world. This obedience, love, and power reflects *glory* on himself. So does also the saved multitude's gratitude for the gift of everlasting salvation. That this aspect of glory is not forgotten is clear from the immediately following verse: ". . . that to all whom thou hast given him he might give everlasting life." Not only the cross, however, but also the crown, viewed as the reward upon his suffering, displays his glory. That this too is in the mind of Christ is clear from verse 5. For the concept *glory* see also on 1:14.

But why does Jesus say, "Glorify *thy Son?*" We answer, because in that word, "Thy Son" there is a wonderful plea. The Father loves the One who is *his only-begotten Son.* He loves him with a love that is infinitely deep and tender, a love from eternity. Surely, he will grant the request of *his own, only-begotten Son!* Moreover, being the Son, was he not the rightful heir? And had not the Father given ever so many promises to the Son? (cf. Ps. 2:7 ff.; 72:15 ff.; 84:4 ff.; 110:1 ff.; 118:22, 23; II Sam. 7:12-14).

When Jesus adds, "that the Son may glorify thee," he shows that his prayer is not a selfish prayer. Jesus wants to be glorified in order that by means of this glory he may glorify the Father. The cross and the crown reveal not only the Son's but also the Father's virtues. *All* the divine attributes come to full expression here. From among them all let us single out just one: the Father's *righteousness.* Had he not been righteous, he certainly would not have delivered up his only-begotten Son. Again, had he not been righteous, he would not have rewarded the Son for his suffering. And also, by means of the praises of the saved multitude, the Father (as well as the Son) is glorified.

2. Even as thou hast given him authority over all flesh that to all whom thou hast given him he might give everlasting life.

When the Father, by bestowing upon the Son the power to save his people and by rewarding him for this task, glorifies him, this action is *in harmony with* (note "even as") the gift to the Son of authority over *all flesh*. This is clear from the fact that those who are saved are gathered from every tribe, tongue, people, and nation, as is the consistent teaching of the Gospel according to John (hence, of Christ himself). See on 1:13, 29; 3:16; 10:16; cf. Rev. 5:9. The phrase *all flesh* is a Hebraism, indicating *all people*. It emphasizes man's weakness, as he is by nature. Not only are the elect gathered out of all the nations, but in order to gather them Jesus actually has received authority over *everybody,* without exception. See Matt. 11:27; 28:18. The human race is a unit. In order to save *some* (out of every nation) the One who saves them must have absolute authority over *all.* (For the meaning of the term *flesh* in John's Gospel see also Vol. I, p. 84, footnote 32. For the meaning of *authority* see also on 1:12; 10:18.)

That the scope and design of the atonement is, nevertheless, limited is clear from the words, "that *to all whom thou hast given him* he might give everlasting life." See also on 6:37, 39, 44; 10:29. Jesus is thinking of all those who have been given to him in the eternal decree of election. For the meaning of *everlasting life* see on 1:4; 3:16.

3. And this is everlasting life, that they should know thee, the only true God, and Jesus Christ whom thou didst send. The *everlasting life* by means of which both the Father and the Son are glorified *manifests itself* in the true knowledge of the Sender and of the Sent. Verse 3 does not give *a definition* of everlasting life, but shows how it reveals itself and how wonderful it is. *To know* the Father and *Jesus Christ* (for he is the *only* way to the Father; see on 14:6) refers not to merely abstract knowledge, but to joyful *acknowledgment* (see on 1:10) of his sovereignty, glad *acceptance* of his love, and intimate *fellowship* with his person (through Scripture, that is, through his Word to us; and through prayer, that is, through our word to him). Note the words, "the only true God" (cf. I Thess. 1:9), not the figment of Jewish imagination, which tried to worship a Father who had *not* revealed himself in the Son; nor the object of pagan worship, which was directed to the creature rather than to the Creator; but the Father as revealed in the Son. For the concept "Jesus," as the One *sent* from above" see on 3:17, 34; 5:36, 37; 8:18, 27, 29 (cf. 1:5). Note also the full title *Jesus Christ* (as in 1:17). When one experiences everlasting life, he has fellowship with God in his only-begotten Son, who as the *Christ* or *Anointed* (set apart and qualified for his task) is *Jesus,* the Savior.

4. I glorified thee on the earth, having accomplished the work which thou gavest me to do. In sharp contrast with the wicked world, represented by the Jewish leaders, Jesus is able to say that *he* (the pronoun *I* is emphatic) glorified the Father. To do the will of his Father had been his chief delight (4:34; 5:30; 6:38; 8:50). He had accomplished the mission which the Father had assigned him. He had brought this task to its predestined goal. He had fulfilled and finished it (see on 4:34). To be sure, historically speaking, he had not yet suffered on the cross, but he has a right to speak *as if* also this suffering has already been endured, so *certain* is it that he will endure it! It must have given comfort to the disciples to hear Jesus say in his prayer that in the accomplishment of the mission *to save sinners* the Father is glorified! In this work all his glorious "excellencies" are displayed most radiantly (cf. I Pet. 2:9).

5. And now Father, glorify thou me in thine own presence with the glory which I had with thee before the world existed.

Here the thought of verse 2 is resumed. Jesus is again requesting that the Father glorify him. This time he is thinking especially of the reward upon his mediatorial work. He yearns to go home to his Father. The erstwhile glory which had been his delight before the foundation of the *world* (orderly universe; see Vol. I, p. 79, footnote 26, meaning 1) had never been absent from his mind. Throughout his ministry of suffering he, the Man of Sorrows, longed to regain that which he, in the interest of sinners, had voluntarily surrendered (the serene enjoyment of the Father's presence, unmixed with suffering; cf. Phil. 2:7). "To return again to the very presence of the Father so as to be *face to face* with him" is what he now requests. See on 1:1. In this connection Heb. 12:2 immediately occurs to the mind: "For the joy that was set before him he endured the cross." The meaning is that he endured the cross in order that he might exchange it for the crown.[214] For the meaning of the preposition παρά in the phrase "in thine own presence" see on 14:23, footnote 168. It is hardly necessary to add that in this yearning for future *glory* (17:5) or for future *joy* (Heb. 12:2) there was not even a trace of vulgar selfishness (cf. 17:1). To be sure, whatever *God* does he does for *his own glory*, and Jesus is God! Even in his mediatorial capacity it is the divine *person* who is speaking his words and performing his deeds. Nevertheless, when we remember that "God *is love*," that (according to the Fourth Gospel) the persons in the Holy Trinity glorify *one another*, and that the glory and the joy of the exalted Mediator includes also this element that "he ever lives to make intercession for those who draw near unto God through him" (Heb. 7:25), the problem has been solved. Here in 17:5 the Son is looking forward to the glory of

---

214 In my doctoral dissertation "The Meaning of the Preposition ἀντί in the New Testament" (submitted to Princeton Seminary, 1948) I have proved that the meaning of Heb. 12:2 cannot be, "In exchange for the heavenly glory which he possessed from eternity, he endured the cross" (the interpretation favored by several exegetes). On the contrary, the joy of which Heb. 12:2 speaks is definitely *future* joy, which came when the race had been run (see Heb. 12:1), and which included Christ's sitting down at the right hand of the throne of God (Heb. 12:2b). *With a view to* obtaining this joy, Jesus paid the price of the cross with its shame; just as in Heb. 12:16 *with a view to* obtaining the food, Esau paid the price of his birthright. The preposition has the same meaning in both instances.

It is true, of course, that this *future* joy which was the reward upon his suffering was at the same time (though not exclusively) a return to that condition of glory (in the presence of the Father) which Jesus had possessed before the world existed. This is the thought expressed here in 17:5.

rejoicing in the joy of his saved people, the very people whose salvation he (together with the Father and the Spirit) had planned from eternity, before the world existed. God ever delights in his own works. The Son glories in the Father's glory, and rejoices in the joy of all the redeemed. When *they* sing, he sings! (cf. Zeph. 3:17).

---

6 "I have manifested thy name to the men whom thou gavest me out of the world; thine they were, and thou gavest them to me, and they have kept thy word. 7 Now they have come to acknowledge that all things which thou hast given me are from thee; 8 for the words which thou gavest me I have given them, and they received them, and really acknowledged that I came from thee; and they believed that thou didst send me. 9 I am making request for them; not for the world am I making request, but for those whom thou hast given me, for they are thine. 10 And all things are thine, and thine are mine, and I am glorified in them. 11 And now I am no longer in the world, but they are in the world, and I am coming to thee. Holy Father, keep them in thy name which thou hast given me, in order that they may be one, even as we are one. 12 While I was with them, I kept them in thy name which thou hast given me; I have guarded them, and not one of them perished but the son of perdition, in order that the scripture might be fulfilled. 13 But now I am coming to thee; and these things I speak in the world, in order that they may have my joy made full in themselves. 14 I have given them thy word; and the world has hated them because they are not of the world, even as I am not of the world. 15 I do not make request that [215] thou shouldest take them out of the world, but that [215] thou shouldest keep them from the evil one. 16 They are not of the world, even as I am not of the world. 17 Consecrate them in the truth; thy word is truth. 18 Just as thou didst send me into the world, so have I also sent them into the world. 19 And for their sake I consecrate myself, in order that they also may be truly consecrated."

17:6-19

17:6. I have manifested thy name to the men whom thou gavest me out of the world.

There is a fine, organic transition between the request with reference to himself and the request with reference to the disciples. The development of the one request into the other is natural and very gradual, like the colors of the rainbow which seem to blend where they touch. The glory of Jesus is the salvation of *his followers*. So, directing his attention to *his work for them* the Son declares that to them he has *manifested* or *made known* the Father's name. For the meaning of the verb *manifested* see on 21:1. The Son is the Father's Exegete (see on 1:18). Apart from him no one ever gets to know spiritual matters in their real, inner essence and value. The Father's *name* — that is, the Father *himself*, as he displays his glorious attributes in the realm of redemption — is not appreciated apart from the

---

[215] On ἵνα see Vol. I, pp. 46, 52.

words and works of the Son (see on 14:6; cf. Matt. 11:27 and I Cor. 2:14). This knowledge concerning the Father means *everlasting life* (see on 17:3).

Not to everyone was this name made known; only to those who in the eternal decree of election had been *given* (hence, subsequently *drawn*) to the Son by the Father (see on 6:37, 39, 44; cf. 17:9, 24). Out of *the world* (see on 15:19) they had been chosen by the Father as a gift to the Son. Probably the best commentary is that which is found in The Canons of Dort (First Head of Doctrine, Article 7, my translation): [216]

"Now election is the immutable purpose of God, whereby, before the foundations of the world were laid, he has, according to the most free goodpleasure of his own will, of mere grace, chosen out of the whole human race, fallen by its own fault from its primeval integrity into sin and destruction, a certain number of persons, neither better nor more deserving than others but with them involved in a common misery, unto salvation in Christ; whom even from eternity he had appointed Mediator and Head of all the elect and the foundation of salvation; and therefore he has decreed to give them unto him to be saved . . ."

Jesus continues: **Thine they were, and thou gavest them to me.** He is thinking of all the elect, but here particularly of the disciples who are with him in the Upper Room, as verse 12 shows. By virtue of the divine decree these men belonged to the Father. In order that this eternal counsel might become effective in their lives, they had been *given* to Jesus, sothat he by means of his atoning sacrifice might save them. The fruit upon his labor is stated in these words of tender affection: **and they have kept thy word.** For the meaning of *keeping God's* (hence, Christ's) *word* see on 8:51. It should be noted that the same Master who just a moment ago when he addressed *his disciples* had pointed out the weakness of their faith (16:31, 32), now in addressing *the Father* has not a word to say with reference to this condition of imperfection. As the real Highpriest, whose heart is filled with love for his own, he simply describes these "men of little faith" — within a few hours all would forsake him, and one would deny him! — as *those who have kept* the Father's word (have guarded his precepts). Truly, "love takes no account of evil" (I Cor. 13:5).

7, 8. Now they have come to acknowledge that all things which thou hast given me are from thee; for the words which thou gavest me I have given them, and they received them, and really acknowledged that I came from thee; and they believed that thou didst send me.

[216] Years ago I served on a committee to which had been assigned the task of making a new and more faithful (close to literal) translation of the Canons. The committee requested me to do the actual work of translating. I translated from the Latin as found in P. Schaff, *Creeds of Christendom,* Vol. III, pp. 550-580. In the course of the years the assignment was apparently forgotten by the authorizing body. Hence, this translation (though completed) has remained in my private file.

As all of the concepts contained in this sublime passage have occurred previously, we shall not again explain them, but simply paraphrase the whole and give the proper references. What Jesus meant was this:

"As a result of the words which I spoke to them and which I had received from thee, these men have come to acknowledge that whatever thou hast given me — the radiance of thy glory reflected in myself, my words, and my works — is from thee. My words (*utterances*), which thou gavest me and I gave to them, they *received* (believed and kept); and they acknowledged with genuine acknowledgment that I came from thee, from thy very presence, sothat in my entire mission I truly represent thee; yes, they believed that thou didst commission me."

Passage with references: "Now they have come to acknowledge" (see on 1:10) "that all things which thou hast given me are from thee" (see on 16:30; cf. Matt. 11:27); "for the words which thou gavest me I have given them" (see on 3:11, 32; 8:28, 38; 12:49; 14:10), "and they received them, and really acknowledged that I came from thee" (see on 1:12; 16:30); "and they believed" (see on 1:8; 3:16; 8:30, 31a) "that thou didst send me" (see on 3:17, 34; 5:36, 37; 8:18, 27, 29; 9:7; cf. 1:5).

Note also that there is very little difference between the verbs *to acknowledge* and *to believe*. Although it is true that the first verb stresses the idea of *true knowledge,* while the second emphasizes that of *trust,* yet this *knowledge* is not abstract but vital, personal experience; and this *trust* is no mere emotion but is based on joyful and genuine acceptance of certain basic truths concerning God as revealed in Christ. See also on 7:17, 18 (elements in Christian experience).

9. I am making request for them; not for the world am I making request, but for those whom thou hast given me, for they are thine.

It is *with reference to* (περί) the elect that Jesus is making request, in order that the full merits of his redemption may be applied to them, namely, to *the given ones* (see on 6:37, 39, 44; 17:6). It is for these given ones that he lays down his life (see on 10:11, 14); hence, it is also *for them* — for them *alone* — that he makes (is constantly making) this request. See also Rom. 8:34 ("he makes intercession *for us*"); Heb. 7:25 ("he ever lives to make intercession *for those who draw near to God through him*") 9:24 ("Christ entered into heaven itself, now to appear before the face of God *for us*"); and I John 2:1 ("*We* have a Helper with the Father, Jesus Christ, the righteous").

All this is particular, not universal.[217] Nevertheless, the prayer of the

---

[217] This does not necessarily mean that Jesus never in any sense prayed for those who in their ignorance afflicted him (considered as a group). Did he not pray with reference to those who crucified him, in order that the thunderbolts of God's wrath might be held in abeyance? See Luke 23:34.

Highpriest looks beyond the men who were in the Upper Room that night, as is clear from verses 20 and 21. It is wrong, moreover, to say (as is sometimes done) that Jesus prayed only for *believers*. Rather, he prayed for *all* his people, also for those who as yet did not believe in him, but were going to accept him by true faith later on (again, see verses 20, 21), as the result of sovereign grace.

However, the prayer *for spiritual safeguarding, sanctification, and glorification* (see on 17:11, 15, 17, 24) is not for those who until the end of their life basely reject the Savior. The words, "Not for the world am I making request" are very clear. Between the purpose of *the atonement* and the purpose of *Christ's Highpriestly prayer*, there is perfect agreement. And this oneness of divine purpose includes also the decree. In fact, that eternal counsel is the basis of all that follows. Hence, we read, "for *they* (the given ones) are thine (by virtue of election from eternity)." Not all were given. Jesus did not die for all. He did not pray that the saving merits of the cross might be applied to all. Here the logic is perfect. We are reminded of "the unbreakable chain" (Rom. 8:29, 30): "For, whom he foreknew, he also foreordained to be conformed to the image of his Son . . . and whom he foreordained, them he also called; and whom he called, them he also justified; and whom he justified, them he also glorified." *All* those —and *only* those! — who were foreknown and foreordained unto salvation reach heaven at last! (On the other hand, the Gospel must be earnestly proclaimed *to all*; Christ's death is sufficient *for all*; God draws his people *from among all* the nations of the world; he exercises authority *over all*; and is glorified *in all*.)

10. And all my things are thine, and thine are mine.

Jesus is making request with reference to the disciples because they belong not to him alone but also to the Father. It is natural to expect that the Father will cherish that which belongs both to himself and to his beloved Son! So in verse 9 Jesus said, "I am making request concerning them (i.e., concerning those given *to me*) . . . for they are *thine*." He now adds that this double ownership pertains to *whatever* the Son possesses.

Note that he says not only, "And all *my* things are *thine*," but also "and *thine* are *mine*." This last statement is astounding. It makes sense only if the Father and the Son are one in essence (cf. 10:30). For a creature to say to the Creator — or even for a believer to say to God — "All *my* things are *thine*," is not marvelous. But for any one lower than God to add, "All *thy* things are *mine*," would require explanation. Even this last statement is true in the sense that "to him that loves God *all things* work together for good" (Rom. 8:28; cf. I Cor. 3:21). But Jesus has in mind not only the fact that all things promote his glory, but also that he is actually the owner of all and as such has authority over all (cf. 17:2). The One who is here

355

addressing the Father is the same One who was face to face with the Father from eternity (17:5). All things in the entire universe belong both to the Father and to the Son. Hence, what is of interest to the One is of interest to the Other. This is the reason why Jesus is able to pray so fervently for his disciples. They are his, his very own. Hence, he loves them. But whatever is his, is also the Father's. This mutual *ownership* implies mutual *interest,* and this mutual interest assures mutual *action.*

It is very difficult — perhaps even impossible — to make any clearcut distinction in this connection between Jesus as Mediator and Jesus as the eternal Son of God. The *character* of the ownership may differ (by virtue of his eternal generation and position all things *naturally* belong to Jesus as Son of God; by virtue of his office, all things have been *given* to him as Mediator); its *scope* does not differ. Moreover, whether we view him as Mediator between God and man, or as the eternal Son of God, in either case the "I" that speaks is the same. Nevertheless, when Jesus adds, **And I am glorified in them,** he is thinking primarily of the glory which he as Mediator (who is here speaking as if he had already completely finished his task) derives from the salvation of his disciples. The graces which adorn those who have been drawn out of the darkness and into the light reflect *his* redeeming love and power. Surely, if Paul can call the church at Philippi "my joy and crown" (Phil. 4:1), and can speak of the brethren at Thessalonica as "our glory and our joy" (I Thess. 2:20), and this because these congregations display the fruits of his work, Jesus all the more has a right to say that in *all things* — particularly, in those who from eternity are his own — he is glorified.

11. And now I am no longer in the world, but they are in the world, and I am coming to thee. Jesus here speaks as if Calvary is past; so certain is Calvary! In his thought he is even now on his way to the Father. With this ideal standpoint as a basis for his request, Jesus makes mention of the fact that, as far as his own visible presence is concerned, he is leaving the disciples behind in a wicked world. Hence, the request follows very naturally: **Holy Father, keep them in thy name which thou has given me.** The *wicked* world is contrasted here with the *holy* Father. The power of the latter is surely more than sufficient to offset the influence of the former. Being *holy,* the Father is *exalted* far above the creature (cf. Is. 6:3: that *Holy One* is the *all-glorious* One), particularly above the creature's sin. Jesus makes an appeal to the moral and spiritual qualities which characterize the Father, and by virtue of which he is the cause of these same qualities (however dimly present) in the hearts of believers. He asks the Father *to stand guard* (see also on 8:51) over these men, and to keep under his divine surveillance whatever might harm them spiritually. He asks that they be kept in the Father's *name,* his revelation by means of words and works in the sphere of redemption, the very revelation which *Jesus* had transmitted to them and *they* had accepted (17:6, 8). And the purpose of this *keeping* is: **in order that they may constantly be one, even as we (are one).** The meaning of this much disputed passage is, after all, rather clear if it be seen in the light of its context. Jesus is not requesting that some day all denominations may become one mammoth-denomination (however excellent church-union may be when it can be achieved without sacrificing any basic principle). When he offered this prayer, there were no denominations. Neither is he praying that in some vague manner the essential (or ontological) oneness of the Father and the Son may be *duplicated* in the lives of the disciples (true though it be that the mystic union between believers and Christ results from and is a reflection of the relation between the persons of the Holy Trinity). The meaning, as we see it, is this: Jesus requests that the disciples *may constantly* (note the force of the durative present subjunctive) be *one* in their stand over against the world; in other words, that they may remain united in love and in the defence of the truth, just as also the Father and the Son are constantly *one* . . . . and here we probably expect to read: "in their relation to the world, in all their outgoing works"; but Jesus, knowing that *this* unity is even deeper, means . . . one in *essence*. True, the logic here requires that unity *of cooperation* be meant. Well, that *is* meant, but *more* also. In God the unity *of essence* is basic to the unity of manifestation (the ontological trinity lies back of the economic trinity). That nothing less than unity of essence is indicated follows from 17:21; see on that passage; see also on 10:30.[218]

12. While I was with them, I constantly kept them in thy name which[219] thou hast given me. That is, during his entire ministry, by means of his teaching and by means of his miracles, Jesus had fulfilled his task as the good shepherd of the sheep. Thus from day to day he *himself* had kept them, holding before them constantly the things which he had heard from the Father (the Father's *name* which had been given to Jesus; see on verse 11) **and I guarded them, and not one of them perished but the son of perdition, in order that the scripture might be fulfilled.**

By means of this constant spiritual keeping Jesus had guarded his own, having protected them against apostasy. The result had been: not one of

---

[218] Attempts have been made repeatedly in the history of doctrine to sever the economic trinity from its metaphysical foundation. On the basis of Scripture all such attempts stand condemned. See H. Bavinck, *The Doctrine of God* (translated by William Hendriksen), Grand Rapids, Mich., 1951, pp. 317-321. See also L. Berkhof, *Systematic Theology*, Grand Rapids, Mich., fourth edition 1949, p. 83.

[219] I see no reason why the reading "whom thou hast given to me" as if Jesus is here referring to *the disciples* and not to *the name* should be substituted. I disagree here with Lenski and others. The reading to which they give the preference is very weak. There are no internal grounds of sufficient weight to set aside the textual evidence. The established text makes excellent sense.

them perished. When Jesus says, "And not one of them perished but the son of perdition," he does not mean that *with the exception of Judas* all those whom the Father had given to the Son had been guarded. He certainly does not intend to convey the thought that in the case of Judas he had failed miserably to carry out the assignment given to him. On the contrary, what we have here is another instance of abbreviated expression. See on 5:31. More fully stated what Jesus means is this:

"And I guarded them, and not one of them perished. But the son of perdition did perish. However, far from proving that in this one instance the plan from eternity was defeated and prophecy left unfulfilled, this happened in order that the scripture might be fulfilled."

The son of perdition (a Semitism; cf. Matt. 23:15; II Thess. 2:3) is the utterly lost one, designated unto perdition. That Judas was meant is clear from a comparison of passages: 6:71; 13:2, 18, 26, 30; 15:2, 6. Certainly, the Father, who is addressed here, knew who was meant; so did the Son; so did the readers of the Fourth Gospel. And that is sufficient. Whether every disciple in the Upper Room had also *finally* caught on that this man was Judas is not important in this connection. See, however, on 13:28, 29.

Though, on the one hand, Judas was fully responsible, on the other hand, this deed was included in the divine decree from eternity, and in prophecy. See on 13:18. Hence, when the disciples hear Jesus speaking to the Father about the accomplishment of his task with respect to *them,* and the fulfilment of prophecy *even in the case of the son of perdition,* they are strengthened in their faith, and begin to realize that nothing and no one ever defeats the divine purpose! Thus, as Calvin so aptly remarks, that which might otherwise have caused feeble hearts to waver was taken away.[220] See also on 16:1, 4.

13. But now I am coming to thee; and these things I speak in the world, in order that they may have my joy made full in themselves.

---

[220] How certain commentators are able to distil from this text (or from anything else) the idea that at one time Judas, too, possessed genuine faith is hard to understand.

Calvin comments beautifully, stressing the fact that neither God nor prophecy can be blamed for the sin of Judas. That disciple had not been *compelled* to sin. He sinned of his own accord. Says Calvin:

Excidit Iudas, ut impleretur Scriptura. Caeterum perperam quispiam inde colligeret, defectionem Iudae Deo potius quam illi esse imputandam: quia necessitas ei ex vaticinio imposita fuerit. Neque enim rerum eventus ideo vaticiniis ascribi debet, quia illic praedictus fuerit . . . Fateor quidem nihil accidere nisi divinitus ordinatum: sed nunc tantum de Scriptura quaestio est, an eius praedictiones et vaticinia hominibus necessitatem afferant, quod iam falsum esse monstravi. Nec vero Christi consilium est, causam exitii Iudae in Scripturam transferre, sed tantum offendiculi materiam tollere voluit, quod infirmas animas concutere poterat (*op. cit.,* pp. 318, 319).

Jesus is conscious of the fact that the hour has come that he must now depart from the earth and go to the Father. Here again, just as in verse 11, the meaning is not: "I am coming to thee *with a request*," but (as also the immediate context indicates): "I am leaving the world; hence, I am on my way to thee." That this is the correct interpretation is also seen when this statement is compared with the one in verse 11. Note the sequence: "I am no longer in the world. . . . I am coming to thee."

Jesus is speaking these things *in the world* (or, as we would say, *while still on earth*; see Vol. I, p. 79, footnote 26, probable meaning 1; see also on 21:25) in order that the disciples may possess in full measure the joy which he imparts. See on 15:11; cf. 14:27. Certainly, the thoughts expressed in the immediately preceding context would have the effect of filling to the very brim their cup of spiritual joy. They would now be able to sing the first century A. D. equivalents of lines which have endeared themselves to our hearts:

"I am in my Father's keeping" (cf. 17:11)
    Also:
"That soul, though all hell should endeavor to shake,
I'll never, no never, no never forsake" (cf. 17:12a)
    And:
"How firm a foundation, ye saints of the Lord,
Is laid for your faith in his excellent word!" (cf. 17:12b).

14. I have given them thy word, says Jesus. He himself has given to these men an abiding (note the tense) and incomparable gift, namely, the Father's own word, his *message*. See on 17:6, 8. That word fills the heart with joy unspeakable and full of glory (see 17:13b). But it also has another effect: **And the world hated them because they are not of the world, even as I am not of the world.** It would be entirely superfluous to give any further *explanation* of these words. There is nothing new in *what* Jesus is here saying. It has been said before. See on 15:19, 20. The new and very comforting element is this, that what Jesus had previously said *to them* he now says *about them, to the Father.* What a joy must have streamed into the hearts of these men to hear their Master say with reference to themselves, "They are not of the world." But it must have taken all of that comfort to offset the terrible truth: "And the world hated them." Not so much what the disciple *thinks* or *speaks* or *does* (taken by itself) causes wicked men to hate them, but what (by means of his attitudes, words, and deeds) he proves himself *to be* turns them into persecutors. The world hates the disciple because he *is so totally different.* He is not "of the world," just as also Jesus does not belong to (has not derived his character from) the world.

15. I do not make request that thou shouldest take them out of the world, but that thou shouldest keep them from the evil one.

For the verb *to make request* see on 11:22. On the surface, one might have expected that the mention of the intense hatred which the disciples would have to endure from the side of the world would have been followed by a request that the Father remove them from the world. Yet, Jesus refuses to make this request. The reason is that the disciples have a task to perform. The nature of that task is not clearly indicated here, not even in verse 18, unless we take that passage in connection with all that precedes it. It was, however, clearly indicated in 15:27: "And y o u must also testify, because y o u have been with me from the beginning" (see on that verse). Naturally, therefore, Jesus cannot now pray that the witnesses be removed!

What he does request is this, that the Father keep the disciples *from the evil one,* or *from evil.* Both translations are possible. We prefer the former, for the following reasons:

(1) Again and again, during this night, Jesus has spoken about Satan, the prince of this world (12:31; 13:27; 14:30; 16:11): that he would be cast out; that he had entered into Judas; that he was on his way; and that he had been judged. Judas had fallen a prey to the evil one. Why, then, is it unreasonable to suppose that Jesus would pray that the others might be protected against the wiles of Satan?

(2) I John 5:18 is, to a certain extent, a parallel passage. Here the keeping has as its result, that *the evil one* does not touch the man who is born of God.

(3) It is almost impossible to suppose that Jesus, in speaking of *keeping* his (and the Father's) own, was not thinking of the allegory of the shepherd watching over and guarding his sheep. Hence, 10:29 ("and *no one* is able to snatch it out of the hand of the Father") occurs to the mind immediately. Now the enemy referred to in 10:29 is definitely personal; it is not just evil in general, but Satan, the false prophet, the persecutor, etc. Hence, also here in 17:15 we think of the evil one, Satan.

(4) The fact that back of all sinister influences stands Satan himself, so that it is especially against *him* that the believer needs protection is the prevailing New Testament view (both in the teaching of Jesus and in that of the apostles); see in addition to the passages listed under (1) and (2) above, also: Matt. 4:1; 13:19, 38, 39; John 8:44; 13:2; Acts 5:3; II Cor. 12:7; Eph. 2:2; 4:27; 6:11, 12; I Thess. 2:18; Jas. 4:7; I Peter 5:8; Rev. 12:3; 20:2.[221]

16. They are not of the world, even as I am not of the world. Here the thought of verse 14 is repeated. See on 15:19, 20. The difference is that

---

[221] I do not believe that the preposition ἐx makes it necessary that a neuter must follow. In I Cor. 9:19 the object after the preposition is personal.

it is now no longer a dependent clause but a sentence that stands by itself. Literally, we read: "Of the world they are not, even as I am not of the world." All the emphasis is, accordingly, on this phase which both begins and ends the sentence, namely, *of the world.* In connection with what precedes we may now interpret the entire request as follows: "Grant that these disciples may not enter the domain of Satan, for they definitely do not belong to his domain. They are thine and mine; they do not belong to the wicked world."

17. Sanctify them in the truth; thy word is truth. Here is the *positive* side of the request. It is as if Jesus said, "Not only keep them from the evil one, but also consecrate them in the truth. Keep them from the one, and confirm them in the other."

In the original the adjective *holy* (in the expression *Holy Father,* verse 11) and the verb *to sanctify* are derived from the same root. Hence, by combining these two ideas one might translate: *"Holy* Father, *make them holy in the truth."* More fully stated, the verb here employed means *to set apart from the world by actual sanctification of life, so that in heart and mind, in thought, words, and deeds, one begins to live more and more in accordance with the law of God.*

This sanctification can take place only if the entire personality is desirous of being governed by the truth; i.e., by God's redemptive revelation in Christ, as the ultimate standard of life and doctrine. This truth is embodied in Christ, in him alone. He is *the truth* (see on 14:6). However, *the word* of the Father, which had been given to the disciples, must be the source of truth for these men when Jesus is no longer personally with them. That word is truth. It is wholly infallible. Without it the work of sanctification is entirely impossible. Jesus requests, therefore, that the Father may cause these men, in an ever increasing degree, to love *that word,* and to live according to the truth of God revealed in *this message* which *they* had received from him, and which *he,* in turn, had received from the Father.

18. Just as thou didst send me into the world, so have I also sent them into the world.

Jesus is still thinking of *the word,* the message of redemption in Christ to the glory of God. It is in this connection that he makes a double comparison; that is, between the Father as Sender and himself as Sender; and between himself as Sent and the disciples as having been sent. The two comparisons blend into one idea, which is this: just as the Father has sent Jesus into the world *with a message,* so also Jesus has sent the disciples into the world *with a message.* The message, moreover, is the same, that of redemption in Christ.

By comparing the present passage with verse 20 it becomes clear that here in verse 18 Jesus is thinking particularly of the little company of eleven men whom he is addressing. They had been divinely commissioned. They had received a charge, a task with the authority to carry it out. They had been made Christ's *apostles* (a term which has the same root as the verb which is used in this verse). For the term *world* as here used see Vol. I, p. 79, footnote 26, meaning 4 (in all probability).

19. And for their sake I consecrate myself, in order that they also may be truly consecrated ones. If the disciples are going to perform their task in a worthy manner, they must offer themselves up willingly. Basic to this is the consecration of Christ *for their sake* (for the meaning of the preposition see on 10:11). Although the verb in verses 17 and 19 is the same, there seems to be a slight difference in meaning. With reference to Christ it cannot indicate a gradual process of spiritual cleansing (a dying to sin and increasing in every spiritual virtue). It must refer to his self-offering (cf. 1:29), more precisely, to his self-dedication to the sacred task for which he had been set apart by the Father, namely, the task of rendering active and passive obedience, thereby obtaining for his people (and here particularly, for his disciples) complete salvation, which also includes that work of the Holy Spirit whereby they are consecrated. See on 10:36. Hence, one act of consecration (that of the Highpriest) is intended to produce another (that of the disciples). Jesus offers himself willingly in order that the disciples may be *truly* (not merely ceremonially or outwardly) set apart and qualified for the exalted task of proclaiming the Gospel to a world lost in sin; in other words, in order that they may be *truly consecrated persons* (literally, "in order that they also may be consecrated ones in truth").

The nature of the task assigned to the disciples is set forth in 15:27 (see on that passage). The disciples must testify, so that those given to the Son by the Father may be brought in, and God may receive all the glory.

20 Neither concerning these only do I make request, but concerning those also who believe in me through their word, 21 that [222] they all may constantly be one; even as thou, O Father, art in me, and I in thee, that [222] they also may constantly be in us, in order that [222] the world may believe that thou didst send me. 22 And the glory which thou hast given me I have given them, in order that they may constantly be one even as we are one. 23 I in them and thou in me, in order that they may become perfectly one, in order that the world may acknowledge that thou didst send me and lovedst them even as thou lovedst me. 24 Father, I desire that they also, whom thou hast given me, be constantly with me where I am,[223] in order that they may gaze on my glory which thou hast given me, for thou lovedst me before the foundation of the world. 25 O righteous Father, though the world has not acknowledged thee, yet I have acknowledged thee; and these men have come to acknowledge that thou didst send me; 26 and I made known to them thy

222 For the three instances of ἵνα in verse 21 see Vol. I, pp. 47, 53.
223 Or, more literally, "Father, that which thou hast given me, I desire that where I am also they be constantly with me."

name, and I will make it known, in order that the love with which thou hast loved me may be in them, and I in them."

17:20-26

17:20. Neither concerning these only do I make request, but concerning those also who believe in me through their word.

In this, the third division of the prayer, Jesus makes request for the Church Universal. Even in the verses that have preceded we found statements so general in character that, as far as their form and contents were concerned, they were applicable not only to the eleven but also to others. It was only in the light of the entire context (particularly, in the light of the key-passage which we are now discussing, 17:20) that we viewed them as having reference (at least mainly) to the apostles. But engraved upon the breastplate of the great Highpriest are the names not only of those chosen out of the tribes of Israel but also of those drawn from the world of heathendom. In addition to the sheep that are led out of the fold of the Jews there are also "other sheep" (see on 10:16; cf. 3:16). All must become *one* flock, with *one* shepherd (see on 17:21). Because of the resemblance in phraseology between the last statement of 10:16 and 17:21a it is hard to believe that this distinction (between Jews and Gentiles) was completely absent from the mind of the Lord when he spoke the words of 17:20.

But although that distinction may have influenced the form and sense of the present request, it is not *exactly* what is meant by the present passage. Nor is it *entirely* correct to say (as is often done) that Jesus is differentiating here between two groups, namely, on the one hand, those already saved, and on the other, those who were going to be saved through their word. Strictly speaking, the distinction is between the eleven, on the one hand, and on the other, all those who *are* brought to genuine faith in Jesus Christ through their word. Some had already been "gathered" by them (see on 4:38). In times to come (down through the entire new dispensation) ever so many others were going to be converted through their word and the word of those who were to follow them. The eye of Jesus scans the centuries, and presses to his loving heart *all* his true followers, *as if they had all been saved even at this very moment.* Also here, in the third division of the prayer, the standpoint of the prayer is *ideal,* viewing future events as if they had already happened.

For the distinction between *requesting* and *asking* see on 11:22. Literally what Jesus requested was: "Neither concerning (note the preposition) these only do I make request, but also concerning the ones believing through their word in me." The form of the expression *believing in me* indicates that genuine faith is meant, the fruit of saving grace (as has been shown in connection with 8:30, 31a; see also on 1:8; 3:16).

363

The means that is used in order to bring about faith is, as always, *the word (their* word, not as if they had invented it, but because *they* heard it, accepted it, preach it), *the message* of salvation (whether oral or written; cf. Eph. 2:20). It is when the Spirit applies this Word to the heart that a person obtains faith unto salvation, faith in the person of Jesus Christ and in the facts of redemption which center in him. Cf. Acts 4:4; Rom. 10:14, 15.

The contents of the request for the Church Universal is stated in the next verse:

21. That they all may constantly be one even as thou, O Father (are) in me, and I (am) in thee, that they also may be in us, in order that the world may believe that thou didst send me.

Carrying upon his heart *all* the members of the Church Universal, those born and those not yet born, and viewing them all as already really existing, Jesus prays that spiritually they may all be (and may all continue to be) *one.* See on 17:11. What in verse 11 was the purpose of a request is here the request itself: the unity of all believers.

The unity for which Jesus is praying is not merely outward. He guards against this very common misinterpretation. He asks that the oneness of all believers resemble that which exists eternally between the Father and the Son. In both cases the unity is of a definitely *spiritual* nature. To be sure, Father, Son, and Holy Spirit are one *in essence;* believers, on the other hand, are one in mind, effort, and purpose. See also on 17:22, 23. These two kinds of unity are not the same. Nevertheless, there *is* a resemblance. *God is love.* What is true with respect to each divine attribute holds also with respect to love: it constitutes the very essence of God (I John 4:8). Now it is exactly in *loving one another* that the oneness of all believers comes to expression (cf. 13:34; 15:12, 17). Hence, we now understand how Jesus can say ". . . that they may all be one, *even as* thou, O Father (art) in me, and I (am) in thee."

Moreover, there is more here than a mere *comparison* between the oneness of all God's children, on the one hand, and the oneness of the persons of the Holy Trinity, on the other. The latter is not merely *the model;* it is *the foundation* of the former; it makes the former possible. Only such men as have been born from above, and are *in* the Father and *in* the Son, are also spiritually one, and offer united opposition to the world.

Now this oneness of all believers which, in turn, has its root in their oneness with the Father and the Son, and which is patterned after (but not identical with) the oneness which exists eternally between these two divine persons, has as its glorious purpose "that the world may believe that thou didst send me." When believers are united in the faith and present a common front to the world, they exert power and influence. When they are torn asunder by strife and dissension, *the world* (ethical sense: mankind in need of salvation) will not know what to make of them, nor how to interpret their so-called "testimonies." Believers, therefore, should always yearn for peace, *but never for peace at the expense of the truth,* for "unity" which has been gained by means of such a sacrifice is not worthy of the name.

When believers show in their lives that they have been with the Lord, their actions and attitudes, which speak even louder than words, will point to Christ as the source of their moral and spiritual strength. Thus, those on the outside, who formerly despised the Christ, will begin to think highly of *him!* When this changed thinking on the part of men who heretofore belonged to the world is applied to their hearts by the Holy Spirit, they will believe that the wonderful stories anent the character and mission of Jesus Christ are really true. The world will then believe "that thou didst send me." For the meaning of Jesus as the One sent by the Father see on 3:17, 34; 5:36, 37; 8:18, 27, 29; 9:7; cf. 1:5.

22, 23. And the glory which thou hast given me I have given them, in order that they may constantly be one even as we are one. I in them and thou in me, in order that they may become perfectly one, in order that the world may acknowledge that thou didst send me and hast loved them even as thou lovedst me.

When believers are *in Christ* (cf. "that they also may be in us," verse 21), then Christ is *in them.* This is their *glory.* By "the glory which thou hast given me" Jesus refers to the fact that the Father manifested himself in the Son ("thou in me," verse 21). By "I have given them" he means that *he* (i.e., Jesus) manifested himself in the lives of believers. To be able to say, "Christ only, always, living in us," is their glory.

Believers become partakers of Christ, and in that sense, of the divine nature (cf. I John 3:2; II Cor. 3:18; Heb. 12:10; II Pet. 1:4). The glory which Jesus gives to believers means that they have become one plant with him; that *he* cannot be conceived of apart from *them;* that he is the source of all the blessings which they will ever receive; and that they, in turn, earnestly desire and strive to do everything to please him.

When God dwells in the Son, and he (through the Spirit) dwells in those who have placed their trust in him, then, naturally, these believers become partakers of all the riches that are in Christ: pardon, righteousness, love, joy, knowledge, wisdom, etc. And when *all* the members of the Church Universal have become partakers of these blessings, the Church, of course, will be *one,* just as Father and Son are *one* (see on verse 21). And this is the very reason why Christ gave all this *glory* to believers, namely, "in order that they may become perfectly one" (literally, "in order that they may have been brought completely to oneness").

The oneness for which Christ makes request is more than an ethical unity. It is a oneness so intimate, so vital, so personal that it is patterned after, and based on, the relations which exist between the persons of the Holy Trinity: it is a oneness not only of faith, hope, and love but of life itself. Together, believers constitute one Body, of which Christ is the exalted (organic and ruling) Head. Cf. Eph. 1:22, 23; 4:4-6.

The Church, thus united by means of Word and Spirit, exerts a powerful influence upon the world. In speaking of this influence Jesus virtually repeats [224] the words of verse 21 (see on that verse), and then adds: ". . . and lovedst them even as thou lovedst me." Hence, the additional purpose which Jesus has in mind when he prays for oneness is that the world may regard it to be the product of the Father's love, a love which, barring differences in the objects loved, is the same as that which the Father has for the Son. For a discussion of the possible difference in meaning of verbs meaning *to love* see on 21:15-17.

24. Father, I desire that they also, whom thou hast given me, be with me where I am, in order that they may gaze on my glory which thou hast given me, for thou lovedst me before the foundation of the world.

Can anything equal the ineffable tenderness of this final request? "Father (see on 1:14), I *desire* . . . it is my *pleasure,* my *delight.*" [225] This type of *desiring* is not weaker than *willing.* It is useless to object to the translation "I desire" of the A.R.V. and the R.S.V., and to say that "I will" of the A.V. is better.[226] The Greek θέλω *as here used,* combines the *delight* element in the verb *I desire* with the *deliberation and determination* element in the verb *I will.*

The desire of Jesus is: "that they also whom thou hast given me, be constantly with me where I am." A strictly literal translation might be: *"that which* thou hast given me, I desire that where I am, also *they* be

---

[224] There is no *essential* differences between "in order that the world *may believe"* (verse 21) and "in order that the world may *acknowledge"* (verse 23).

[225] On the distinction in meaning between θέλω, here used, and βούλομαι see L.N.T., p. 286. According to that authority the former designates the will which proceeds from *inclination;* the latter, that which follows *deliberation.* The classic example of the two words used side by side, probably with that difference in meaning, is Matt. 1:19. The fourth Gospel does not offer a sufficient number of examples to warrant any definite conclusion. The verb βούλομαι is used only once (18:39). The verb θέλω occurs in the following passages: 1:44; 3:8; 5:6, 21, 35, 40; 6:11, 21, 67; 7:1, 17, 44; 8:44; 9:27; 12:21; 15:7; 16:19; 17:24; 21:18 (twice), 22, 23. A careful examination of these passages would seem to indicate that, if any distinction can be made, it is the one which L.N.T. suggests. Cf. also H. Bavinck *(op. cit.,* p. 342) on the noun βουλή which he defines as "the will of God based upon counsel and deliberation." He defines θέλημα "the will of God as such, cf. Eph. 1:11: *counsel of his will."*

[226] I do not share the objection of R. C. H. Lenski. Personal wishing or desiring is often expressed by the verb θέλω. See J. H. Moulton and G. Milligan, *op. cit.,* p. 286 for numerous examples. When F. W. Grosheide, *op. cit.,* p. 431 translates, "Ik begeer," he is right.

constantly with me." This sounds rather awkward in English. Nevertheless, this more literal translation must not be ignored. It brings out one point, namely, the Highpriest's deeply rooted love for *his own,* viewed first as a unit *(that which),* then severally *(they),* just as in 17:2, for in the original this clause is placed at the very beginning of the sentence, for the sake of emphasis.

This request puts a foundation under the promise of 14:3. Rather, the foundation was always there, but now it is revealed to the disciples in the Upper Room. The Son requests that the Father cooperate with him in carrying out the promise which had been made to the disciples, and which is now extended so as to include *all the given ones.*

Jesus is fond of that expression: *the given ones;* see on 6:39; 17:2, 9, 11; cf. 6:44. From eternity they had been *entrusted* to him, in order that in time they might be *the reward* for his atoning sacrifice. Hence, he desires that all these given ones shall dwell forever in his immediate presence, in order that they may delight forever in the vision of *the glory* of God in Christ, a vision which begins here on earth (II Cor. 3:18), and reaches its climax in heaven.

The glory of which Jesus speaks is his own. He calls it "the glory which thou hast given me." The Son desires that all believers shall *gaze forever* (θεωρῶσιν) on him, that is, on the radiance of his divine attributes as these are reflected in his exalted human nature (though, of course, they never become a part of that human nature) and in the transformed character, the inexpressible joy, the unquenchable love, and the perfect peace of all those who enter into the rest that remains for the people of God. This is the glory which the Father has given to the Son.

This vision of God in Christ is the transporting bliss of all the people of God. See Ps. 17:15; 27:4; 90:16; and I John 3:2; cf. also II Cor. 3:18. As they gaze upon him, they, like perfect prisms, refract the light which beams forth from his glorious countenance, and show its exquisite beauty of color in lives wholly dedicated to him. Truly, the lamp of the new Jerusalem is the Lamb (Rev. 21:23).

> "How blessed, Lord, are they who know the joyful sound,
> Who, when they hear thy voice, in happiness abound!
> With stedfast step they walk, their countenances beaming
> With brightness of the light that from thy face is streaming;
> Exalted by thy might from depths of desolation,
> They praise fore'er thy name, thy justice and salvation."

> "Father of Jesus, Love Divine,
> What rapture will it be,
> Prostrate before thy throne to lie,
> And gaze and gaze on thee!"

Like a sublime musical composition which, after having stirred the innermost depths of the soul, finally comes to rest in an unforgettable climax, so the final request of this touchingly beautiful prayer of the great Highpriest reaches its zenith of infinite tenderness in the words, ". . . for thou lovedst me before the foundation of the world."

It is natural and altogether fitting to regard this clause as a modifier of the immediately preceding clause.[227] It was because the Father loved the Son from before the foundation of the world (i.e., from eternity) that he gave him this glory. Cf. 17:5 and Eph. 1:4. For the verb *to love* and its chief synonym see on 21:15-17 (see the Chart on p. 498, which shows the exact verb which is used in each passage; also read the discussion for the meaning of this verb).

25, 26. O righteous Father, though the world has not acknowledged thee, I have acknowledged thee; and these men have come to acknowledge that thou didst send me; and I made known to them thy name, and I will make it known, in order that the love with which thou hast loved me may be in them, and I in them.

The requests are ended. What follows in verses 25 and 26 may be considered the ground or plea upon which the final request (and in a sense, the entire prayer) is based. But it is even more than that. It breathes the spirit of confidence and assurance, the Son's conviction that the Father will hear him.

"O righteous Father." Because the Father is righteous, he will certainly apply the full merits of the Son's redemption to the hearts and lives of the given ones.

"Though the world has not acknowledged thee, yet I have acknowledged thee; and these men have come to acknowledge that thou didst send me.[228]

The acknowledgment by the disciples (see on 16:30) of the fact that Jesus was, indeed, the One sent by the Father (as also the acknowledgment of the Father by the Son) was all the more striking because it was in open defiance of the uncompromising opposition from the side of the wicked *world* (for the meaning of the latter term see on 1:10, 11; Vol. I, p. 79, footnote 26, meaning 6). For the idea *Jesus as the One who was sent by the Father* see on 3:17, 34; 5:36, 37; 8:18, 27, 29; 9:7; cf. on 1:5.

"I have acknowledged thee." This acknowledgment (for the verb employed see on 1:10) is elucidated by the clause, "And I made known to

---

[227] See R. C. H. Lenski on this passage, for a different interpretation.
[228] We translate ϰαί . . . ϰαί: "though . . . yet." It is best to regard this as a Semitism. Note, for example, the use of *waw* in Judg. 16:15. See L. Koehler, *A Dictionary of the Hebrew Old Testament in English and German*, Leiden, The Netherlands, and Grand Rapids, Mich., 1951, Vol. I, p. 246.

them thy name, and will make it known." See on 17:6 for the meaning of the first clause; and for the meaning of the second, see on 16:12-15.

Jesus will declare the Father's *name* (his revelation in the sphere of redemption), in order that the infinite love with which the Father loved the Son may be "shed abroad" (cf. Rom. 5:5) in the hearts of the disciples (and, of course, in the hearts of all believers). And, when both the Son and all those who place their trust in him are comprehended in the same love (namely, *the Father's* love), the Son himself will be living *in* them. See also on 17:23: "I in them." This is the hope of glory, fully realized (Col. 1:27).

Synthesis of Chapter 17

See the Outline on p. 260. *The Son of God Committing Himself and His Disciples to the Father's Love and Care*
The Prayer of the Highpriest

I. For Himself: glorification (verses 1-5)
II. For His Immediate Disciples (verses 6-19):
   A. Preservation
   B. Sanctification
III. For the Church at Large (verses 20-26):
   C. United Contemplation of Christ's glory, in loving fellowship
with him.

Although there is progress in the prayer, and although it does advance from one theme to the next as indicated, nevertheless, there are no definite boundaries between the three parts. So, for example, verse 24, which belongs to the prayer for the Church Universal, is also a request with respect to the Son himself, and with respect to the immediate disciples. The reason why there are no clearly-drawn dividing lines is because the interests of the one are also those of the other: so close is the unity between and among them.

Hence, the best (not *perfect*) way to represent the relation of the parts to each other is by means of three concentric circles. The mission and eternal destiny of Jesus Christ and his followers is *the center of these circles.* Jesus prays that, as a reward upon the accomplishment of *his* mission, he himself may be glorified, and that in connection with this the disciples, in carrying out *their* mission, may be "kept" and sanctified, and, together with all other members of the Church Universal, may abide everlastingly in his company, in order to "gaze upon" his glory.

The *inner* circle represents Christ's request with respect to *himself.* The *middle* one represents his request for his *immediate disciples,* but includes constant references to himself (see verses 10, 11, 13, 16, 18, 19). Hence, the middle circle is larger than the inner one and includes the latter. The *outer* circle represents Christ's request for *the Church Universal,* but this is the largest circle of all, and includes the other two, as has already been shown.

Accordingly, we get this Diagram of the Contents of Chapter 17:

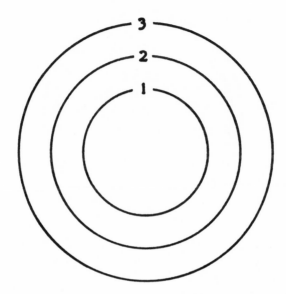

Contents of Circle 1 = verses 1-5; contents of circle 2 = verses 6-19; contents of circle 3 = verses 20-26.

The diagram is not perfect; for example, as has been shown in our exegesis, when the Son prays for himself, he is not forgetting his people!

We proceed now to the discussion of an entirely different circle, one that concerns not the *form* (division into parts) of this prayer but its *contents.* When love runs its full course, it represents a circle, as is very clear from the opening verse of chapter 17: "Glorify thy Son in order that the Son may glorify thee." More fully stated this means: "Do *thou* glorify thy Son in order that the Son may glorify *thee*." The glory which proceeds *from* the Father returns *to* him again, having done its work. See also verses 4 and 5 for a similar circle.

Thus also when the love of God descends *from* heaven to dwell in the hearts of men, it should be returned *to* him again in the form of thanksgiving. Woe to the man who, having received blessings from the Lord, fails to return them in the form of praise and gratitude. *Woe to the man who breaks the circle!* The first chapter of Ephesians contains three complete circles. Try to find them.

This idea of love running its full course may be represented by the following:

Diagram of the Circle of Blessing and Thanksgiving:

Prominent in chapter 17 are the following: *the Father, the Son,* and *believers* (for the present we shall not distinguish between *immediate* disciples and all other followers of Christ in the Church Universal). In the background, but constantly present to the mind of the Son, as he prays, is the wicked world and its evil prince (verses 9, 16, 25). Against these the disciples must be guarded.

Now, in a striking manner the Highpriestly Prayer brings out the *oneness* which characterizes these three: *the Father, the Son, believers,* the bond which unites them, their intimate fellowship with one another.

In the abstract six love-relationships are possible; as follows:

I (the Son) love thee	Thou (the father)	They (believers)
(the Father)	lovest me	love me
I love them (the believers)	Thou lovest them	They love thee

Now, it is striking that in this chapter *all six* actually occur, though often, in the place of the term *love,* another verb is found, one which shows how this love makes itself felt. If that be borne in mind, we obtain the following:

Diagram of the Course of Love:

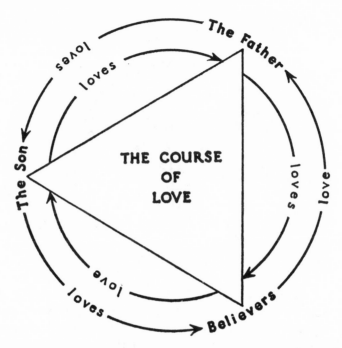

I *love thee:* "I glorified *thee* on the earth" (17:4)

I *love them:* "I have manifested thy name to *the men* whom thou gavest me out of the world" (17:6a)

Thou lovest me: "the love with which *thou* hast loved *me*" (17:26b)

Thou lovest them: "(*thy*) love . . . in *them*" (17:26c)

They love me: "*they* acknowledge that *I* came from thee" (17:8c)

They love thee: "and *they* have kept *thy* word" (17:6d).

372

Outline of Chapters 18, 19

Theme: *Jesus, the Christ, the Son of God*
During His Private Ministry: *Dying As A Substitute for His People*

I. 18:1-11 The Arrest

II. 18:12—19:16 The Trial and The Denial
   A. Before Annas (18:13-17), trial and denial
      1. Jesus is *led* before Annas (18:13, 14)
      2. Peter's first denial (18:15-18)
      3. Jesus is *tried* before Annas; is sent to Caiaphas (18:19-24)
      4. Peter's second and third denial (18:25-27)
   B. Before Pilate (18:28—19:16), trial
      1. Jesus is called an evil-doer. Pilate's first attempt to rid himself of responsibility with respect to Jesus: "Take him yourselves, and judge him according to y o u r own law" (18:28-32)
      2. Jesus "kingship" is examined. Pilate's second attempt to rid himself of responsibility: "Y o u have a custom that I release a man for y o u at the Passover" (18:33-40)
      3. Jesus is scourged. Pilate's third attempt to evade the issue: in an endeavor to arouse the pity of the people he exclaims, "Look! The man!" (19:1-7)
      4. After further attempts on the part of Pilate (to release Jesus if it could be done without discomfort to Pilate!), he succumbs to intimidation, and hands Jesus over to be crucified (19:8-16)

III. 19:17-37 The Crucifixion
   A. Jesus carrying the cross; nailed to a cross between two criminals (verses 17 and 18)
   B. The dispute about the superscription (verses 19-22)
   C. The division of the garments (verses 23 and 24)
   D. The word to Mary and to John (verses 25-27)
   E. Jesus' thirst; his death (verses 28-30)
   F. The piercing of his side (verses 31-37)

IV. 19:38-42 The Entombment

CHAPTER XVIII

18 1 When he had said these things, Jesus together with his disciples went out across the winter-brook Kedron, where was a garden, into which he went, he and his disciples. 2 Now also Judas, who was betraying him, knew this place; for Jesus often met [229] there with his disciples. 3 So Judas took the cohort and some officers from the chief priests and the Pharisees, and went there with torches and lanterns and weapons. 4 Then Jesus, knowing all that was going to happen to him, came out and said to them, "For whom are y o u looking?" 5 They answered him, "For Jesus, the Nazarene." He said to them, "I am he." Now Judas also, the one who was betraying him, was standing (there) with them. 6 Then when he said to them, "I am he," they lurched backward and fell to the ground. 7 So he again requested of them, "For whom are y o u looking?" And they said, "For Jesus, the Nazarene." 8 Jesus answered, "I told y o u that I am he. Therefore, if y o u are looking for me, let these men go their way.[230] 9 (This happened) in order that the word which he had spoken might be fulfilled, "Of those whom thou hast given me, I have lost none."

10 Then Simon Peter, who had a short sword, drew it and struck the servant of the highpriest, and cut off his right ear. Now the servant's name was Malchus. 11 Jesus, however, said to Peter, "Put the sword into the sheath. The cup which my Father has given me, shall I not drink it?"

18:1-11

18:1. When he had said these things, Jesus together with his disciples went out across the winter-brook Kedron, where was a garden, into which he went, he and his disciples.

At the conclusion of the prayer Jesus and the little company of eleven left the house (see on 14:31). Proceeding in an easterly direction, they went *out of the city* (which is probably meant here in 18:1) across the winter-brook Kedron. The valley of the Kedron is located between Jerusalem's eastern wall and the Mount of Olives. During the hot season the channel is dry. Only during the winter — and even then only after a heavy shower — does anything resembling a "brook" actually appear. Hence, it is called (literally) a "winter flow-er" (a stream which flows during the

---

229 Literally, "was gathered."
230 I D; see Vol. I; pp. 40, 41.

winter-season). The name *Kedron* itself (according to what is probably the best reading) means dark, turbid.

It was here that devout king Asa had burned the abominable image which his wicked mother had set up (I Kings 15:13). At the command of another pious ruler, Josiah, idolatrous vessels had been burned in this vicinity (II Kings 23:4). And under King Hezekiah the Levites had carried to this valley the unclean things that had been left in the temple by the former administration (II Chron. 29:16; cf. 30:14). This was "the valley of the dead bodies and of the ashes" (Jer. 31:40).

But the one outstanding event which had occurred here was David's passing over this same brook, while fleeing before his rebellious son Absolom (II Sam. 15:23). Was he not, in this act of humiliation and suffering, a type of Christ?

Now just east of this brook there was a garden which is elsewhere called *Gethsemane* (oil-press). It seems to have been a grove of olive-trees, furnished with a press for the purpose of squeezing oil from the fruit. It was at the foot of the Mount of Olives. The site which is pointed out to travelers today is slightly east of the bridge by which the road from the gate of St. Stephen crosses the Kedron.[231]

It must, however, be stressed that no one knows the *exact* location of the grove which Jesus entered that night. Something similar is true with respect to many of the sites where Jesus taught and performed his miracles. The general vicinity is often rather well established; the *exact* place is another matter! Deeply rooted within the heart of many people is the desire to know the precise spot! Others are glad to satisfy this yearning, usually "for a consideration."

The record of the agony which Jesus suffered in this garden is found in the other Gospels. John takes it for granted that the readers are not in need of any further information with respect to that subject. All he says is, ". . . where was a garden, into which he went, *he and his disciples.*" The leisurely addition of the words in italics serves to picture the scene and to show its pathos. While John is writing this, he vividly recalls what happened that night. He (and Peter and James) had seen more than some of the others (Mark 14:33).

2. Now also Judas, who was betraying him, knew this place; for Jesus often met there with his disciples.

It must be considered within the realm of possibility (cf. Luke 21:37; 22:39) that Jesus and his disciples had spent Tuesday-night and Wednesday-night in Gethsemane. Was there, perhaps, a grotto here or a small house, sleeping-quarters of some kind, and was the owner of the grove a follower

---

[231] See W.H.A.B., p. 100; also *Viewmaster Travelogue,* Reel Number 4001, Gethsemane to Calvary, Scene 1.

of Jesus? Gethsemane was, in any event, a customary gathering-place (note the verb: *met*; literally: *was gathered*) for the Master and his disciples. It was a quiet place of prayer and probably of teaching.

And Judas knew this! He had been there with Jesus. It was, therefore, relatively easy for him to lead a detachment of soldiers and a squad of temple-guards to the place where they could find Jesus. At this very moment Judas was on his way. The evangelist pictures this in vivid colors: Judas *was betraying* him. See on verse 3.

Not only did Judas know the place, but Jesus knew that Judas knew it! *Nevertheless* (shall we not rather say, "*Because* of that very fact"?), Jesus went there! The good shepherd is not going to be "caught." No, he is going to "lay down his life" as a willing sacrifice (see on 10:11).[232]

3. So Judas took the cohort and some officers from the chief priests and the Pharisees, and went there with torches and lanterns and weapons.

At the request of the Sanhedrin (cf. Matt. 27:62-66) a *cohort* had been secured, probably from the tower of Antonio. This fortress was situated at the north-west corner of the temple-area. It had been repaired and strengthened by Herod the Great. In this castle the Roman government kept a number of soldiers. During the Jewish festivals, when Jewish patriots streamed to Jerusalem in great numbers and enthusiasm ran high, the garrison was enlarged, in order to be ready for all emergencies (see Josephus, *Antiquities* XVIII, iv, 3).

The exact number of soldiers in *this* detachment is not known. Though a cohort ordinarily consisted of six hundred men (the tenth of a legion), it would seem that the term is used in a less restricted sense here, as is often the case with respect to such terms (even today). At any rate the band must have been rather large. It seems well-nigh certain that permission for its use had been obtained *from Pilate*, the governor (cf. Matt. 27:62). Matt. 27:18, 19 clearly proves that he knew about the "case" of Jesus before the accused was actually brought to him. The Synoptics make no mention of *the soldiers* in this connection.

In addition to these *soldiers* there were *temple-guards* sent by the Sanhedrin, which counted among its members many *chief priests* — the acting highpriest, ex-highpriests, and members of highpriestly families (but this is not certain; another interpretation of the term is given by A. Sizoo, *Uit*

---

232 Calvin has seen this point. His comment here is beautiful: Consilium Evangelistae praecipue spectandum est in loci indicatione: nam ostendere voluit Christum sponte ad mortem prodiisse. Venit in locum, quem Iudae familiariter notum sciebat. Quorsum id nisi ut sponte se offerat proditori et hostibus? Nec eum fallebat incogitantia, quum omnium quae instabant praescius esset. Postea etiam subiicit Ioannes eum obviam progressum esse. Mortem ergo non coactus, sed ultro subiit, ut voluntarium esset sacrificium: nam sine obedientia nobis expiatio parta non esset (*op. cit.*, p. 326).

de Wereld v.h. N.T., pp. 70-72) — and *Pharisees.* As the chief priests were *mostly Sadducees* (cf. on 1:24), the *Pharisees* are mentioned separately. — According to Luke 22:52 there were also *members of the Sanhedrin.* Had they postponed the eating of the Passover-supper? See on 18:28.

The soldiers and the policemen from the temple were fully armed. They were equipped with *torches* and with *lanterns.* With respect to the latter, think of the oil-fed "lamps" carried by the ten virgins of the well-known parable (Matt. 25:1-3). John mentions *weapons.* He refers probably to the *swords* carried by the soldiers, as well as to the *cudgels* in the hands of the policemen (cf. Matt. 26:47).

Torches and lanterns . . . to search for *the Light of the world!* And it was full moon! Swords and cudgels . . . to subdue *the Prince of peace!* This was a cruel insult. It proved how thoroughly his mission had been misinterpreted. For the Man of Sorrows, the very sight of this band of ruffians, which considered him their quarry, meant indescribable suffering. They had come out against him as if he were a criminal, a robber for instance. This was agony. He felt the bitter insult, as is clear from the words he spoke (Matt. 26:55). He saw the approach of the power of darkness (Luke 22:53).

In describing what the soldiers did, how the guards treated him, in speaking about Judas, Peter, Caiaphas, Annas, Pilate, and others, the main purpose must ever be to show what each contributed to *his* suffering!

Judas *took* this detachment of soldiers and this posse of temple-police. The meaning is that he served as *guide,* for he was thoroughly acquainted with the object of the search and with the latter's familiar haunts. See on 13:27.

4. Then Jesus, knowing all that was going to happen to him, came out and said to them, For whom are y o u looking?

From the mind of Jesus nothing was hid. For this knowledge of Jesus see on 1:42, 47, 48; 2:24, 25; 5:6; 6:64; 13:1, 3; 21:17. The agony of Gethsemane (the prayer that the cup might be taken away, the bloody sweat, etc.) was past. Now there is nothing but calm resolution, sublime majesty. So Jesus *came out.* Out of what? The answer is not given; hence, certainty is lacking. Some say "out of the garden-gate"; "out of the grotto"; or "out of the house." To others (and we are inclined to agree with them) the meaning is "out from among the trees in this grove"; that is, out of relative darkness he stepped into the light, into the open, striding forward until he stood right in front of the band.

Just as he did this (or was it at some other juncture; but if so, when?), Judas performed that act which has caused all later generations to recoil with horror at the mere mention of his name. Embracing Jesus, he kissed him repeatedly, while he said, "Hail, Rabbi!" See Matt. 26:49 (the orig-

378

inal). That was the pre-arranged sign. How mean, how devilish! For the foulest deed that was ever committed Judas selected the most sacred night (that of the Passover), the most sacred place (the sanctuary of the Master's devotions), and the most sacred symbol, a kiss! And also, how utterly ridiculous! As if Jesus would have failed to identify himself!

Finished with Judas, Jesus demanded of the band (particularly, of its leaders): "For whom are y o u looking?" He was standing in full view of everyone. He was giving his soul as a ransom in exchange for many. The Master of winds and waves was also fully *in control* of the present situation.

5. They answered him, For Jesus, the Nazarene. The answer was given by several (not only by the commander — verse 12 —; the verb is plural). It was probably stated in the exact language of the official order which the band had received from the authorities. "Jesus, the man from Nazareth" was to be the object of the search.[233]

He said to them, I am he. Unnecessary were all the kisses given by Judas! See on verse 4 (above). Here we see Jesus as the great Prophet, making himself known. In verse 6 we see him as the King of kings. In verses 7 and 8, as the sympathetic Highpriest, who lovingly provides for his own. **Now Judas also, the one who was betraying him, was standing (there) with them.** Why does not John record the kissing-episode? Was it merely because he knew that the readers were already sufficiently acquainted with this, having read it in the Synoptics? Or was it also because he shuddered to dwell on this black deed? Yes, Judas, the treasurer (shall we say *ex*-treasurer?), the man in whom the others had put their trust, he too was now standing with the powers of the prince of darkness. Hence, it is but natural to include also him in the event which is described in the next verse:

6. Then when he said to them, I am he, they lurched backward and fell to the ground. What a spectacle is presented now! Suddenly (note the aorists), at the word of Jesus ("I am he"), the would-be captors lose their footing. They lurch backward and fall to the ground. The unexpectedness of Christ's behavior (the fact that of his own accord he strode forward), the manner in which he had taken the entire situation into his own hands, the majesty of his voice and of the look in his eyes, all this may have helped to produce the effect that is here pictured. Nevertheless, these factors cannot account for it. Here is another *sign* (see on 2:11). Here is Christ Jesus, the King!

---

[233] For the form of the term *the Nazarene* (in the original), and also for the historicity of Nazareth see W. F. Albright, "The Names *Nazareth* and *Nazoraean*" in *JBL* LXV (December, 1946), 397-401.

**7, 8. So he again requested of them, For whom are y o u looking? And
they said, For Jesus, the Nazarene. Jesus answered, I told y o u that I am
he. Therefore, if y o u are looking for me, let these men go their way.**

Note the striking contrast. Their most undignified behavior was followed by his very dignified question: "he *requested* of them." See on 11:22.
He interrogates these stricken warriors. The question was the same as before. And so was the answer.[234] But now Jesus brings home the purpose
of his inquiry. Having twice compelled them to repeat their *orders,* he by
the sound of *their own* voice and by the contents of *their own* answers, has
impressed upon them the fact that Jesus, the Nazarene, he *indeed,* but also
he *alone,* must be led away. "If y o u are looking for me — as, of course,
y o u are — then let these men (the disciples) go their way" (or: *withdraw
themselves*). The Highpriest lovingly protects his own.

**9. (This happened) in order that the word which he had spoken might
be fulfilled, Of those whom thou hast given me, I have lost none.**

At first glance, this passage seems very strange. The word which Jesus
had spoken is found (in one form or another) in 6:39; 10:28; and 17:12.
See on these passages. But in all of them it refers to that act of Jesus
whereby he stands guard over the *spiritual* welfare of his own, *keeping*
them, with a view to everlasting life in the mansions above. How then can
this saying be suddenly robbed of its precious import and seemingly "de-
graded" into a reference to the manner in which Jesus provided for *the
physical* escape of his disciples? [235] The only answer which satisfies us is the
one given by Calvin, Luther, Stalker, Evans, Lenski, and others. It amounts
to this: had the disciples at this time been captured by these soldiers and
temple-guards, it would have been too severe a test for their faith. They
were not ready for this extreme ordeal, this torture. Jesus knew this. Hence,
he sees to it that they are not arrested.

Note also that here the same formula "that the word . . . might be fulfilled" is employed with respect to a saying of Jesus which elsewhere is

---

[234] The question has been asked, "How is it to be explained that these men, who
had just a moment ago received such a striking proof of Christ's infinite power,
are bold enough to return the same answer as before?" The answer has been given
that this simply shows how hardened were their hearts. No doubt, there is truth
in that solution. But is it psychologically so strange that they repeated what they
had just said? Must we not suppose that the shock produced by Christ's miracle —
for it was a miracle! — was so great that for a little while their minds were dazed?
In their bewilderment, almost the only thing which at the spur of the moment
they *could* answer was that which they had uttered *last*. Besides, that phrase "Jesus,
the Nazarene" had been embedded deeply in their consciousness, probably because
of its prominent place in the official orders which they had received. Hence, it
would occur first of all.
[235] When W. F. Howard, *The Interpreter's Bible*, p. 758, does nothing more than
to write that the statement found in 18:9 hardly does justice to the thought of 6:39
and 10:28, he is hardly doing justice to the statement.

used with reference to the inspired authors of the Old Testament. The legitimate inference is certainly this, that John regarded the sayings of Jesus as being, in their infallible character, on a par with those of the prophets of old.

10. In his pride and arrogance Peter chooses not to avail himself immediately of the opportunity for physical safety which Jesus had provided. We have here the over-confident Simon of 13:37; see on that passage. What John tells in the next few verses has its parallel in the Synoptics (Matt. 26:51-54; Mark 14:47; Luke 22:50, 51). **Then Simon Peter, who had a short sword, drew it and struck the servant of the highpriest, and cut off his right ear. Now the servant's name was Malchus.**

Although this incident is related in all four Gospels, only John mentions the names of the two persons who (in addition to Jesus himself) figure most prominently in it. When John published his Gospels, it was no longer possible to punish the assailant. Hence, his name, and also the name of the person assailed can now be mentioned.

The assailant was *Peter,* who is mentioned here (and frequently in the Fourth Gospel) by his full name: Simon Peter. See on 1:40-42. Emboldened perhaps by the marvelous triumph of Jesus over the men who had come to capture him, greatly encouraged by the spectacle of these soldiers and policemen who just a moment ago lay sprawled all over the ground and by his own previous boast which he had to make good, Simon drew from its scabbard his *short sword* (μάχαιραν).[236] Was this a knife, with a blade five or six inches in length, for gutting fish (as some suggest), or perhaps one that had been used in connection with the Passover-meal? More probably it was actually a kind of dagger, the kind of weapon the soldiers also carried. It is hard to believe that in Matt. 26:47 the term would have one meaning (sword), and in 26:51 another meaning (knife).

The armor of the disciples, here in the olive-grove, consisted of two of these swords (Luke 22:38). *Naturally,* Peter carried one of them! See on 13:9 and on 13:37. How could it have been different? The disciples had asked, "Shall we smite with the sword?" (Luke 22:49). Impulsive Simon could not wait for the answer.

Peter, then, having *drawn* this sword (for the verb see on 6:44), sprang at the (specially commissioned) servant of the highpriest, and — probably because the servant quickly jumped to the side — cut off his *ear.*[237] Both John and Luke inform us that it was the right ear.

---

[236] For a discussion of this term and its synonym (ρομφαία) see W. Hendriksen, *More Than Conquerors,* Grand Rapids, Mich., sixth edition, 1952, pp. 122, 126.
[237] The diminutive used in the original has lost some of its original diminutive force. The resultant meaning, at least, is not the little lobe or lobule at the bottom of the ear, but the ear itself. For the same diminutive see Mark 14:47; for another form see Matt. 26:51; Luke 22:51.

The servant's name was Malchus. Here is the touch of an eye-witness. The Fourth Gospel is full of such details. See Vol. I, pp. 18, 19. In this connection it must also be borne in mind that the author was acquainted with the highpriest (18:15). It is, therefore, not surprising that he also knows the name of his servant.

11. Jesus, however, said to Peter, Put the sword into the sheath. The cup which the Father has given me, shall I not drink it?

Luke (*Doctor* Luke, remember!) mentions the fact that Jesus touched the servant's ear and healed it (Luke 22:51). Jesus sharply reprimands his wilful disciple, and tells him to sheathe his sword (cf. Jer. 47:6). The reasons for this command may be summarized as follows:

(1) The one given here, "The cup which the Father has given me, shall I not drink it?" The struggle in Gethsemane is over. Jesus no longer prays that the cup *of most bitter suffering and eternal death on the cross* may pass from him (cf. Matt. 26:39). He is fully determined to drink it (that is, naturally, *its contents*). It is the cup which *the Father* (see on 1:14) has given him. Hence, the enemy must not be put to flight by means of the sword. The good shepherd must lay down his life. He must voluntarily offer himself. Simon's deed is at variance with this determination. Cf. also Matt. 26:54.

(2) Jesus must be able to say to Pilate: "My kingship is not of this world. If my kingship were of this world, my attendants would have been fighting in order to keep me from being handed over to the Jews; but now my kingship does not spring from that source" (18:36).

(3) If it had been the wish of Jesus to defend himself, he had other means at his disposal, for example, more than twelve legions of angels (Matt. 26:53). Peter's rash and awkward act was entirely unnecessary and uncalled for.

(4) "All they that take the sword will perish with the sword" (Matt. 26:52).

Before Jesus surrenders himself to this band, he first avails himself of the opportunity to point out the cowardly character of this base onslaught upon him, far away from the public eye, and in the middle of the night. He also emphasizes that his surrender is "according to plan." It was in order that the scriptures might be fulfilled (Matt. 26:55, 56). Hence, this yielding was, in reality, no *surrender* at all. It was *victory!*

As Jesus is being (or *is about to be*) taken and bound, the disciples scamper away. One of the Master's followers — *not* one of the twelve — , a man who had quickly thrown a linen cloth about himself, was seized. However, he left the linen cloth in the hand of his pursuer, and fled away naked. For these details see Matt. 25:56; Mark. 14:51, 52.

Synthesis of 18:1-11

See the Outline on p. 374. *The Son of God Dying as a Substitute for His People. The Arrest.*

Having left the house, Jesus, in the company of eleven disciples crossed the Kedron. This reminds one of David's flight before Absolom, but there is this great difference: Jesus was in complete control of the situation. *He was not fleeing. His entire procedure was voluntary.* He knew that Judas would meet him there. So he went there!

The company of captors consisted of the following:

a. Judas, the guide
b. The military tribune (chiliarch)
c. The soldiers from the Tower of Antonia (probably in front)
d. The temple-police (behind the soldiers, perhaps)
e. Chief priests and elders (members of the Sanhedrin, perhaps many of them). See Luke 22:52. These probably held themselves somewhat in the background.

Soldiers carried swords, police cudgels. There were torches and lanterns.

As prophet Jesus, stepping into the light, declared himself; as king he ruled, causing the band to fall to the ground; as priest he protected his own. When Peter showed by an act of rashness (cutting off the ear of the highpriest's servant) that he did not understand the nature of Christ's kingdom, Jesus by word and deed revealed its spiritual character.

Jesus then permitted himself to be seized and bound (see the next section).

---

12 Then the cohort and its commander [238] and the officers of the Jews seized Jesus and bound him, 13 and they led him to Annas first; for he was father-in-law of Caiaphas, who was highpriest of that year. 14 Now Caiaphas was the one who had advised the Jews that it was expedient that one man die for the people.

15 Now Simon Peter was following Jesus, and so was another disciple. Now that disciple was known to the highpriest, and he entered with Jesus into the court of the highpriest. 16 But Peter was standing outside, in front of the gate. So the other disciple, the one known to the highpriest, stepped out and spoke to the girl who kept the gate, and brought Peter inside. 17 Then the girl who kept the gate said to Peter, "You surely are not also one of this man's disciples, are you?" He said, "I am not." 18 Now the servants and the officers had made a charcoal fire because it was cold, and they were standing and warming themselves. And there with them was also Peter, standing and warming himself.

19 Then the highpriest questioned Jesus concerning his disciples and concerning his teaching. 20 Jesus answered him, "*I have spoken openly to the world. I always taught at synagogue and in the temple, where all the Jews are in the habit of congregating, and in secret I said nothing. 21 Why are you questioning me?* Question

---

[238] Literally: "and the chiliarch."

those who heard what I said to them. Of course [239] they know what I said." 22 Now when he had said these things, one of the officers who was standing by slapped Jesus in the face,[240] saying, "Is this the way you answer the highpriest?" 23 Jesus answered him, "If I spoke wrongly, testify with reference to the wrong, but if rightly, why do you strike me?" [241] 24 Then Annas sent him bound to Caiaphas the highpriest.

25 Now Simon Peter was standing and warming himself. So they said to him, "You surely are not also one of his disciples, are you?" He denied it and said, "I am not." 26 One of the servants of the highpriest, a relative of the man whose ear Peter had cut off, said, "Did I not see you in the garden with him?" 27 Peter, however, again denied, and instantly, a rooster crowed.

28 Then they led Jesus Christ from Caiaphas to the governor's residence. It was early; and in order that they might not be defiled but might eat the Passover, they themselves did not enter the governor's residence. 29 Pilate then went out to them and said, "What charge do you prefer against this man?" 30 They answered and said to him, "If this man were not an evil-doer, we would not have handed him over to you." [242] 31 Pilate said to them, "Take him yourselves, and judge him in accordance with y o u r own law." The Jews said to him, "We have no right to execute anyone." 32 (This happened) in order that the word of Jesus might be fulfilled which he had spoken, signifying by what death he was about to die.

33 Then Pilate again entered the governor's residence, and he summoned Jesus and said to him, "Are *you* the king of the Jews?" Jesus answered, "Are you saying this of your own accord, or have others said it to you about me?" 35 Pilate answered, "Surely I am not a Jew, am I? Your own nation and the chief priests have handed you over to me. What have you done?" 36 Jesus answered, "My kingship is not of this world. If my kingdom were of this world, my attendants would have been fighting [243] in order to keep me from being handed over to the Jews; [244] but now my kingship does not spring from that source." 37 Then Pilate said to him, "So you are a king?" Jesus answered, "You say that I am a king. For this purpose was I born, and for this purpose have I come into the world, in order that I might testify to the truth. Whoever is of the truth listens to my voice." 38 Pilate said, "What is truth?" And having said this, he went out to the Jews again, and said to them, "No crime whatever do I find in him. 39 But y o u have a custom that [245] I release a man for y o u at the Passover. So, do y o u wish that I release for y o u the king of the Jews?" 40 Then they cried out once more, saying, "Not this man but Barabbas." Now Barabbas was a robber.

18:12-40

18:12. Then the cohort and its commander and the officers of the Jews seized Jesus and bound him.

---

[239] Literally, "look!"
[240] Literally, "gave Jesus a blow."
[241] I D, I B; see Vol. I, pp. 40, 41.
[242] II C; see Vol. I, pp. 41, 42.
[243] Or: "would fight."
[244] II A; see Vol. I, p. 41.
[245] On ἵνα see Vol. I, pp. 45, 53.

Finally, the band of soldiers and temple-guards (Gentiles and Jews; cf. Acts 4:27) goes into action. The man who in all likelihood was in command of the entire band (not only of the soldiers) is now mentioned for the first time. He was a *chiliarch*, literally: "commander of a thousand"; but the term is used here in a secondary sense, to indicate the Roman military tribune who was the leader of the cohort (cf. Acts 21:31-33, 37; 22:24-29; 23:10, 15, 17-19, 22; 24:7, 22; 25:23; see, however, also Mark 6:21; Rev. 6:15; 9:18).

At his order some of the soldiers now *seized Jesus*. The verb employed is the technical term for making an official arrest (cf. Matt. 26:55; Mark 14:48). In doing so, they actually took hold of him, and then bound him. He, the One who had come into the world to bring freedom, and apart from whom freedom is absolutely impossible (see on 8:31-36), was himself bound. He was bound, however, in order that we might be loosed from our sins.

The fact that the cohort and its commander are mentioned first probably indicates that they took the leading part in this action of arresting and binding Jesus. This is also what we would have expected.

13. And they led him to Annas first; for he was father-in-law of Caiaphas, who was highpriest of that year.

The soldiers and temple-police lead Jesus, bound, to Annas. The rather common opinion (also among commentators) is that Jesus was led to Annas *for preliminary examination*. However, no less an authority than Dr. F. W. Grosheide, the author of one of the best works on the Fourth Gospel, is among those who challenge this conclusion. He presents his arguments in *Kommentaar op het Nieuwe Testament*, Vol. II, p. 449 (also p. 454, footnote 1). As he sees it, there was no such a thing as a preliminary hearing before Annas. The trial recorded in 18:19-23 took place before Caiaphas; it was not a preliminary examination before Annas. This is also the position of A. Edersheim, *The Life and Times of Jesus, the Messiah*, Volume II, p. 548.

The most formidable argument in favor of this position is the one derived from a comparison between verses 13, 14 (together), and then 19:

"And they led him to Annas first; for he was father-in-law of *Caiaphas, who was highpriest of that year*. Now Caiaphas was the one who had advised the Jews that it was expedient that one man die for the people" (verses 13, 14). What follows concerns Simon Peter, his first denial (verses 15-18). Verse 19 states:

"*Then the highpriest questioned Jesus* concerning his disciples and concerning his teaching." Cf. also verses 15 and 16: "the highpriest."

Who, then was this highpriest by whom Jesus was examined? The answer would certainly *seem* to be, "Caiaphas, of course, for he is the only one who is distinctly called *highpriest* in the preceding verses."

It is, therefore, not at all surprising that for this reason (and for other reasons, which are not as strong, as we see it), the theory that there was no preliminary hearing before Annas is favored by certain commentators.

When we, nevertheless, respectfully disagree, it is because *we consider 18:24 to be an insuperable obstacle to its acceptance.* (In passing, it should be remarked that there is no evidence at all to support the idea, held by some, that there has been a displacement of the text, either here at verse 24 — which some place immediately after verse 14 — or anywhere else in the chapter.)

Assuming, for the sake of argument, that the highpriest (before whom the trial recorded in verses 19-23 was held) was *Caiaphas,* what intelligible meaning can anyone ascribe to verse 24, which records what happened at the *end* of this trial? We read:

"Then Annas sent him bound to Caiaphas the highpriest." Surely, a prisoner who has been standing in front of Caiaphas all through verses 19-23 *cannot now be sent to Caiaphas! Verse 24, according to the clear meaning of the words, takes for granted that the trial of verses 19-23 has been before Annas, and that it is this Annas who now sends the prisoner to Caiaphas.*

We do not see how it is possible to escape this conclusion. Yet, attempts are made to escape it. For example, there is the translation found in the A.V.: *"Now* Annas *had sent* him bound to Caiaphas the highpriest." It is true, of course, that in the original the aorist tense (sent) is used at times where we would employ the pluperfect (had sent), but in the present situation this is improbable, as will be explained in a footnote.[246]

This, however, still leaves us with the riddle of explaining how (in view

---

[246] The original has ἀπέστειλεν οὖν αὐτόν. The textual evidence is strong in favor of οὖν. That would seem to deprive Edersheim's argument of some of its strength. Just what is the meaning of οὖν here? Dr. J. R. Mantey wrote his doctor's thesis on this conjunction: "The Meaning of οὖν in John's writings." He distinguishes four meanings: a. inferential *(therefore, consequently);* b. continuative *(now, then);* c. emphatic *(to be sure, indeed, above all);* and d. adversative *(however).* It is clear from the very context, that only a. and b. are possible here, and that of the two, b. is the most natural.

But even so, cannot the conjunction be taken in the sense of *now* (which is one of the continuative possibilities) followed by the past perfect, as if introducing a kind of parenthetical idea, a belated remark? Hence, could not the A.V. rendering *("Now* Annas *had sent* him . . .") be right after all? May not John have meant this: "There is something which I have not yet made clear. I must state it now" (cf. Grosheide, *op. cit.,* p. 457). But such belated remarks in the Fourth Gospel either lack a particle altogether, or have δε, as in the following: 1:38; 6:71; 11:2; 11:51; 18:2b; 18:10b; 18:14; 18:18 (four instances right here in chapter 18); cf. also 4:54.

Hence, the only reasonable translation, it would appear to us, is the one which is favored by the author of the doctoral thesis to which we referred a moment ago.

of verses 13, 14) *the highpriest* to which verse 19 refers can be Annas? The solution is probably not too difficult. In the four New Testament references to Annas *he is twice called highpriest,* and this name is applied to him even though it was well-known to the inspired author that he was no longer the *actual* highpriest. Note:

Luke 3:2: "In *the highpriesthood of Annas and Caiaphas,* the word of God came to John."

Acts 4:6: "And *Annas, the highpriest* was there, and Caiaphas . . .'"

The only other New Testament references to Annas are right in this chapter: John 18:13, 24. John, who probably assumes that the readers have read the earlier Gospels (see Vol. I, pp. 31-33), takes for granted that they know that Annas *was still* called highpriest. His *main* thought, here in verse 13, is that *the band led Jesus to Annas.* The rest (in verse 13 and all of verse 14) is *secondary.* It is important, to be sure, but not of *primary* significance. It simply gives the reason why Jesus was led before Annas, namely, because he was father-in-law to (stood in close connection with) the titular highpriest of that year. This is followed by a parenthetical remark about the son-in-law of Annas. The main idea is still that Jesus was brought *to Annas first!* Let not the reader begin to think that the trial about which he has read in the other Gospels, namely, the trial before Caiaphas, was the *only* one. No, *first,* says John, Jesus was brought before Annas! *Hence, the reader has been led to expect that John will say something about this trial. And he does in verses 19-23.*

Who was this Annas? The chief sources which one should read in order to form an opinion of the man are the following: Luke 3:2; Acts 4:6; John 2:14-16 (cf. Matt. 21:12, 13); 18:13, 24; Josephus, *Antiquities of the Jews,* XVIII, ii, 2; XX, ix, 1, 2; *Talmud,* Pes. 57a. Combining all of this information, one arrives at the following picture:

Annas (or Ananus, as Josephus calls him; the name is from the Hebrew Hananiah, meaning *Jehovah is gracious*) had been appointed highpriest by Quirinius in the year 6 A. D., and was deposed by Valerius Gratus, about 15 A. D. Though deposed, he remained for a long time the ruling spirit of the Sanhedrin. He was the dominant member of the Jewish hierarchical machine. There have been somewhat similar "machines" since that day. It generally takes a clever manipulator to be the virtual head of one. Annas was just such a man. Five sons (Eleazer, Jonathan, Theophilus, Matthias, and Ananus), one son-in-law (Caiaphas), and a grandson fol-

---

Dr. Mantey offers the translation: "*Then* Annas sent him bound to Caiaphas, the highpriest." See also H. E. Dana and J. R. Mantey, *A Manual Grammar of the Greek New Testament,* New York, 1950, p. 254. Similar is the translation found in R.S.V.; and also the one in the new Dutch version: "Annas dan zond Hem geboeid naar Kajafas, den hogepriester." And the difference between this and the translation found in the A.R.V. is not great: "Annas therefore sent him bound unto Caiaphas the highpriest."

lowed him in the highpriesthood. When Annas had been deposed, someone not of his family had succeeded him, but almost immediately afterward a son of Annas had been appointed. After another intermission, Annas' son-in-law (Caiaphas) had been given the title. He was the highpriest *now*. Next the highpriesthood would go to a second son of Annas; then to a third; after still another brief intermission, to a fourth; and then after several others would have been tried out, to the fifth son. Thus, during the entire period of Christ's ministry and for a long time afterward, Annas was the man who was responsible, to a large extent, for the actions of the Jewish Sanhedrin. Someone else might be the presiding officer of the Sanhedrin, Annas was the man to consult. One can imagine how, whenever a priest would come up with a plan or idea, and would broach it, another would immediately reply, "Have you cleared this with Annas?"

He was very proud, exceedingly ambitious, and fabulously wealthy. His family was notorious for its greed. The main source of his wealth seems to have been a goodly share of the proceeds from the price of sacrificial animals, which were sold in the Court of the Gentiles. See on 2:14. By him the house of prayer had been turned into a den of robbers. Even the Talmud declares: "Woe to the family of Annas! Woe to the serpent-like *hisses*" (probably *the whisperings* of Annas and the members of his family, seeking to bribe and influence the judges).

John adds that Annas was father-in-law of Caiaphas! And in character these two were twins. See on 11:49, 50 for a description of the character of Caiaphas. Hence, from Annas, Jesus could expect the same treatment as from his son-in-law. Let Annas get some preliminary evidence in the case of Jesus. He will probably be able to give some good (?) advice to his son-in-law. Meanwhile, there will be an opportunity to gather the members of the Sanhedrin, as many as can be assembled at this hour of the night!

14. Now Caiaphas was the one who had advised the Jews that it was expedient that one man die for the people. The intent of this parenthetical remark is this: Caiaphas had been plotting Christ's death for a long time. His father-in-law, the real power behind the throne, would cooperate heartily. In fact, he may even have been the instigator. With respect to Caiaphas see also on 11:49, 50.

Here the account leaves Jesus for a while, as he is brought before Annas, and returns to Peter (see on 13:36-38).

15. Now Simon Peter was following Jesus, and so was another disciple. Now that disciple was known to the highpriest, and he entered with Jesus into the court of the highpriest.

The story of Peter's denial is told in all four Gospels. It is important to see *how* these various accounts, which differ in so many details but never clash, harmonize. One fact must be well understood: not only Matthew (26:34), and Mark (14:30), and Luke (22:34), but also John (13:38) definitely expects *three* denials. Hence, when it appears that John has nothing that corresponds with that denial which by the others is counted as the second one, we are led to conclude, either:

1. That he reports only on what he also considers the first and the third denials, and simply assumes that the readers (already acquainted with the account of the denials in the Synoptics) need no further information about the second denial; or,

2. That he also reports on three denials, but counts differently, splitting up into two denials that which by the others is considered the third denial. In the latter case, what by the others is presented as the third denial is by John counted as the second and the third.

Something can be said in favor of either of these theories. The first is favored by Lenski.[247] It may be correct. We simply do not know. Yet, if a choice must be made, we would feel inclined to favor the second of these alternatives, and this for the following reasons:

a. John has recorded the fact that Jesus predicted *three* denials (13:38). Hence, he has caused the reader to expect that *three* denials will be described, in fulfilment of the prediction.

b. In this expectation the reader is not disappointed. Note *how* the Fourth Gospel reports on the denials:

"He said, *I am not*" (18:17).

"He denied it and said, *I am not*" (18:25).

"Peter, however, again denied" (18:27). This means, of course, that Peter again said, "I am not," or something similar.

Will it not be natural, then, for the reader to see in these *three* — not *two* nor *four* — "I am not"-statements the fulfilment of the prediction with reference to the *three* denials?

Though admitting that the first theory may be the correct one, we shall, for the reasons given, proceed on the assumption that the second is right. As to *the material,* there is no clash here of any kind. All the accounts (whether in John or in the Synoptics) are fully inspired and without error.

We suggest the following harmony:

First Denial:
Matt. 26:58, 69, 70; Mark 14:54, 66-68; Luke 22:54-57; and John 18:15-18.

Second Denial (according to Matthew, Mark, Luke):
Matt. 26:71, 72; Mark 14:69, 70a; Luke 22:58; *not in John*

---

[247] See his Commentary, p. 1184.

Third Denial (according to Matthew, Mark, and Luke):
Matt. 26:73-75; Mark 14:70b-72; Luke 22:59-62; John 18:25 (the second
denial, as counted by
John); 18:26, 27 (the
third denial, as counted
by John).

When Jesus predicted that Peter was going to deny him three times, he
surely did not mean that exactly three times (and no more) Simon would
say, "I know not the man," or something similar. There were, indeed,
three separate situations in connection with which Peter was going to deny
the Master, *three and no more*. But the last time, while several are speaking, *one* accuser, namely, a relative of Malchus, attracts special attention.
Hence, the author of the Fourth Gospel singles him out for separate mention, thus dividing the *third* denial (of the other Gospels) into *two* denials.

The question may be asked, "Why is it that John gives such a detailed
account of the denials, though these had already been related by the earlier
Gospel-writers?" The answer is probably:

(1) His Gospel is going to contain an account of Peter's restoration.
Hence, the reason for the necessity of this restoration must be fully re-
corded. Besides, no one must be able to say, "This Gospel covers up
Peter's *sin*."

(2) The beloved disciple probably felt that he himself was partly responsible for Peter's fall. It was he who brought Peter inside the courtyard!
Being a very humble man, John wants his readers to know this, sothat the
blame may not be placed *entirely* on Peter.

(3) Of all the apostles only *John* had returned with Peter to the highpriest's palace. Hence, he was able to supply certain details which the
others had not furnished.

Though all the disciples had fled, two soon rallied, and began to follow
the band which was leading Jesus to the highpriest's palace. Still fearful,
Peter *was following* (imperfect tense) from a considerable distance (Matthew, Mark, Luke). With him was someone who is simply called *another
disciple*. That this unnamed person was no one else than the author of
the Fourth Gospel we have tried to prove (Vol. I, pp. 3-31).

The "other disciple" (John) *was known* — though not of necessity inti-
mately — to the highpriest. How it was that Annas (see on verse 13) —
hence, probably also his son-in-law — knew John remains a mystery.
Theories — such as, that John was a distant relative, or that his father's
firm delivered fish to the highpriest's palace (the view of Nonnus, an
Egyptian scholar, about 400 A. D.) — are nothing but guesses. It is important, nevertheless, to bear in mind *the fact* as such (that John was
known to the highpriest). See also on 18:10. This explains why, without

difficulty, John — who, having by this time regained courage, had shortened the distance between himself and the band — entered with Jesus into the court of the highpriest.

It is not certain whether the term αὐλή, as here used (see also on 10:1, 16), indicates *the entire palace* (a meaning which, according to J. H. Moulton and G. Milligan, *op. cit.*, p. 92, lacks papyri support) or refers to *the open courtyard* around which the Oriental house or palace was built. It is, however, clear that at least in Matt. 26:69; Mark 14:66; and Luke 22:55 it must refer to the open courtyard.

But where was this courtyard? That it was in the house or palace of *Caiaphas* is clearly implied in Matt. 26:57, 59. That it was, nevertheless, also in the palace occupied by *Annas* seems clear by comparing with this passage from Matthew, John 18:13, 15, 24. The reader should see this for himself, in order to appreciate the problem. Hence, we print the two references in parallel columns:

Matt. 26:57, 58:	John 18:13, 15, 24:
"And those who had seized Jesus led him away to Caiaphas the highpriest, where the scribes and the elders had assembled. But Peter followed him at a considerable distrance, to the court (or *courtyard*) of the highpriest . . ."	"And they led him to Annas first; for he was father-in-law of Caiaphas, who was highpriest of that year . . . Now Simon Peter was following Jesus, and so was another disciple. Now that disciple was known to the highpriest, and he entered with Jesus into the court (or *courtyard*) of the highpriest . . . Then Annas sent him bound to Caiaphas the highpriest."

Is it not *very natural* (cf. M. Dods, *op. cit.*, p. 848) to assume that these two very close relatives (Annas and his son-in-law), who, besides, were kindred souls — they were two of a kind! — lived in the same palace? In spite of all the objections that have been urged against this view, we still believe it to be the most natural solution. Probably one wing of the palace was occupied by Annas; another by Caiaphas. This is also the conclusion reached by A. Sizoo, *Uit De Wereld van het Nieuwe Testament*, pp. 81, 82. That in such a palace, occupied by the most *important* persons in all Judea, there would, indeed, be a room or hall big enough to accommodate a large assembly may be taken for granted. A prisoner could easily *be sent* from one wing to another, across the courtyard.

16. But Peter was standing outside, in front of the gate. So the other disciple, the one known to the highpriest, stepped out and spoke to the girl who kept the gate, and brought Peter inside.

It seems that Peter was not known either to the highpriest or to his servants. So, he is waiting outside, though John has already been admitted. What follows cannot be understood apart from a knowledge of the construction of an Oriental palace or house of the well-to-do. Such a house looks into its own interior; that is, its rooms are built around an open courtyard. An arched passage leads from the heavy outside *door* or (better) *gate* into this inner court. In this passage there is a place (in some houses a little room) for the gate-keeper. Sometimes, as also in the present instance, the court was lower than the rooms which ranged around it (see Mark 14:66: "Peter was *beneath* in the court"). It is not entirely impossible that the room to which Jesus had been led was a kind of gallery, from which what happened in the court could be seen and heard.[248] This theory has its objections, however. One might ask, "Would not the loud conversations of the men who stood in the open court-yard have been a cause of annoyance to the priests who conducted the trial?"

When John had been admitted by the gate-keeper, he secured admission for Peter also. John "spoke to the girl who kept the gate." Apparently, not only the highpriest but also his servants (this girl and Malchus) knew John and were known by him. Hence, they must have known that he was a follower of Jesus (see on verse 17). But it seems that in John's case there had been no strict enforcement of the rule mentioned in 9:22. Probably the Sanhedrin had relaxed somewhat, thinking, "Once Jesus is out of the way, his disciples will no longer adhere to his teachings." We know from the book of Acts that when this proved to be an erroneous assumption, the persecution was resumed with undiminished vigor.

John, in securing Peter's admittance, made a tragic error, as is shown by the verses which follow:

17. Then the girl who kept the gate said to Peter, You surely are not also one of this man's disciples, are you? He said, I am not.

What happened to John is not related. He probably crossed the court-yard and entered the room (or "hearing" hall) to which Jesus had been led. By this time the men who had taken Jesus into the palace of the highpriest and into the "hearing" hall had finished their task. For them (probably with a few exceptions, cf. 18:22) it was no longer necessary to remain in the immediate presence of the prisoner, in order to prevent his escape (as if this had ever been necessary!). Most of *the soldiers* had probably returned to the fortress of Antonia. As to *the palace-servants* and *the*

---

[248] This is suggested by A. Sizoo, *Uit De Wereld van het Nieuwe Testament*, Kampen, (second edition) 1948, p. 82. He refers to Luke 22:61, which indicates that Jesus, *having heard* the words of Peter's third denial, *turned and looked at him.* (One might add Matt. 26:58.) — But it is possible that just at this moment Jesus was being led across the court-yard, and that for this reason he was able to hear (and look at) Peter.

temple-guards (policemen), these had by this time entered (or re-entered) the large courtyard, where, because it was cold, they had made a charcoal fire (18:18; cf. Mark 14:54; Luke 22:55).

Peter, having entered the passage-way which led from the gate into the courtyard, was ill at ease. It must be borne in mind that it was he who had struck the servant of the highpriest, cutting off his right ear! See on 18:10. It may have been for this reason that he did not dare to proceed as far as John. Or it may have been for other reasons. So he entered the courtyard, and sat down in the midst of the servants and officers (Luke 22:55).

It would seem that the very moment when Peter entered, the portress had her suspicions. The very fact that she had admitted him *at the request of John* seemed to indicate that Peter too must be a disciple of Jesus. His failure to enter the *"hearing" hall* with John, and the general uneasiness which characterized all his movements and which could be read on his countenance, confirmed her suspicions. So, about to be relieved by another gate-keeper, she stepped a little closer and fixed her eyes on Peter, studying him a long time (Luke 22:56). Then, stepping right up to him and giving him that piercing look, she said, "You surely are not also one of this man's disciples, are you?" There must have been a bit of malice in her voice, as the very form of the question seems to indicate. The question was put in such a way that a *negative* answer was expected.[249] But this is irony: she *knew* better. In her heart she was fully convinced that Peter was, indeed, a disciple of Jesus.

Peter, shocked by the suddenness and the boldness of the question, to which he must give an immediate reply, is caught off guard. In spite of all his loud boasts of a few hours ago (see on 13:37), he is now thoroughly frightened. "I am not," he blurts out. Had he failed to take to heart the admonition recorded in Matt. 26:41 (cf. Mark 14:38)?

18. Now the servants and the officers had made a charcoal fire because it was cold, and they were standing and warming themselves. And there with them was also Peter, standing and warming himself.

Most of this has been explained in connection with verse 17; see on that passage. See also on 18:13, footnote 245. It is true that Matt. 26:69 (Mark 14:54; Luke 22:55) pictures Peter as *sitting* with the officers, while John says that he was *standing* with them. This surely need not be a contradic-

---

[249] Lenski states that the question expects a *positive* answer, *op. cit.*, p. 1173. But this in contrary to the rule which applies to cases in which the particle μή is used. C. B. Williams, *The New Testament, A Translation in the Language of the People*, Chicago, 1949, translates correctly. This is also in harmony with A. T. Robertson, *Word Pictures*, Volume V, p. 287; F. W. Grosheide, *op. cit.*, p. 453. The new Dutch version translates very neatly: "Gij behoort toch ook niet tot de discipelen van dezen mens?"

tion. Is it not reasonable to assume that after sitting down a little while, he had arisen? Perhaps, at the moment when the portress from her place in the archway was looking him over, he was sitting down; but when she started to address him, he — man of action that he was — had arisen. We may also safely assume that after the first denial he remained standing a while, looking for an avenue of escape. Then he started for the archway. What happened there (as counted by the Synoptics, the *second* denial) is related in Matt. 26:71, 72 and parallels. When John resumes the story of Peter's denial, he is back in the courtyard, standing and warming himself, just like before (see on 18:25).

19. Then the highpriest questioned Jesus concerning his disciples and concerning his teaching. The highpriest here is probably Annas (see on verse 13). By combining the Gospel-accounts it becomes clear that Jesus had to undergo two trials. The first has been called the *ecclesiastical;* the second the *civil.*[250] The first contained three stages, and so did the second. We may distinguish as follows:

1. *"Ecclesiastical" Trial*

a. *Preliminary hearing before Annas,* while Peter "in the court of the highpriest" denied the Master. For the hearing see John 18:19-24 (the present paragraph); for this denial see 18:15-18. The second denial — *second,* as the Synoptics count them — is not recorded in the Fourth Gospel, but (as well as the first) must have occurred during Christ's trial before Annas. Between the first and the second denial *a little while* elapsed (Luke 22:58); between the second and the third (as the Synoptics count them), about an hour elapsed (Luke 22:59).

b. *Trial before Caiaphas and "all the chief priests and the elders and the scribes"* (Mark 14:53). It took place "in the highpriest's house" (Luke 22:54). This trial is recorded in Matt. 26:57-68; Mark 14:53-65 (cf. Luke 22:54, 63, 64). During this trial what is regarded by the Synoptics as the third (by John as the second and the third) denial took place. The place was, as in the first denial, "the court of the highpriest" (as is clear by comparing 18:15, 18 with 18:25). For this denial see Matt. 26:73-75; Mark 14:70b-72; Luke 22:59-62; John 18:25 (as John counts, the second denial); 18:26, 27 (as John counts, the third denial). This trial before Caiaphas and the members of the Sanhedrin over which he presided must have ended about (or shortly before) 3 A. M., Friday.

---

250 This is the terminology employed by several authors, among whom is J. Stalker, *The Trial and Death of Jesus Christ,* New York, 1894, p. 16. Others: "Tried by the Jews, Tried by the Gentiles"; or "Before Caiaphas, Before Pilate." Objections can be advanced against each of these captions.

c. *Trial before Caiaphas and the Sanhedrin* (hence, the same body as b. above) just after day-break (Luke 22:66). It is recorded in Luke 22:66-71; cf. Matt. 27:1; Mark 15:1.[251]

2. *"Civil" Trial*

a. *Trial before Pilate*
b. *Jesus before Herod* (Luke 23:6-12)
c. *Trial before Pilate resumed*

In the Fourth Gospel the trial before Pilate is found in the section 18:28-19:16.

Returning now to the first stage of the trial before the Jews, to which stage we assign the name *Preliminary Hearing before Annas,* it must not escape our attention that John purposely jumps from the story of the denial to that of the trial, and then back again to the denial. He does this in order to show that in connection with both of these Jesus suffered intensely. He suffered by being denied. He suffered also by being tried, as if he were a criminal. Between the two (denial and trial) there was this contrast: while Peter *denied,* Jesus *confessed* the truth!

For the absolutely sinless One to be subjected to a trial conducted by sinful men was in itself a deep humiliation. To be tried by *such* men, under *such* circumstances made it infinitely worse. Greedy, serpent-like, vindictive Annas (see on 18:13), rude, sly, hypocritical Caiaphas (see on 11:49, 50), crafty, superstitious, self-seeking Pilate (see on 18:29); and immoral, ambitious, superficial Herod Antipas; these were his judges!

In reality, the entire trial was a farce. It was a mis-trial. There was no intention at all of giving Jesus a fair hearing in order that it might be discovered, in strict conformity with the laws of evidence, whether or not the charges against him were just or unfounded. In the annals of jurisprudence no travesty of justice ever took place that was more shocking than this one. Moreover, in order to reach this conclusion it is not at all necessary to make a close study of all the technical points with reference to Jewish law of that day. It has been emphasized by various authors that the trial of Jesus was illegal on several technical grounds, such as the following: a. No trial for life was allowed during the night. Yet, Jesus was tried and condemned during the hours of 1-3 A. M. Friday. b. The arrest of Jesus was effected as a result of a bribe, namely, the blood-money which Judas received. c. Jesus was asked to incriminate himself. d. In cases of

---

[251] The *place* where it was held is disputed. See S. Greydanus, *Het Heilig Evangelie naar de Beschrijving van Lukas* (in Kommentaar op het Nieuwe Testament), Amsterdam, 1941, Volume II, p. 1106.

capital punishment, Jewish law did not permit the sentence to be pronounced until the day after the accused had been convicted.

Such and similar points of law have been mentioned again and again and used as arguments to prove the illegality of the entire procedure against Jesus of Nazareth. Attempts have also been made to refute them, one by one.[252]

But to any fair-minded individual it must be evident at once that all these technicalities are but so many details. They do not touch the heart of the matter. The main point is nothing less than this: *it had been decided long ago that Jesus must be put to death* (see on 11:49, 50). *And the motive behind this decision was envy.* The Jewish leaders just could not "take" it that they were beginning to lose their hold upon the people and that Jesus of Nazareth had denounced and exposed them publicly. They were filled with rage because the new prophet had laid bare their hidden motives, and had called the temple-court from which they derived much of their profit *a den of thieves.* On the surface, the dignified chief priests, elders, and scribes might try to put on an act by the seeming imperviousness of their demeanor; underneath they were vengefully nettled, convulsively agitated. They were thirsting for blood!

Hence, this is not a trial but a plot, and the entire plot is *their own.* *They* have devised it, and *they* see to it that it is carried out. *Their* officers take part in the arrest of Jesus. They themselves were present! *They* seek the witnesses — *false* witnesses, of course! — against Jesus, in order that *they* may put him to death (Matt. 26:59). *They* all condemn him as being deserving of death (Mark 4:64). "They (by means of *their* underlings) bind him and lead him away" (Mark 15:1). *They* deliver him to Pilate (John 18:28). Before Pilate *they* stir up the people to get Barabbas released in order that Jesus may be destroyed (Matt. 27:20). *They* intimidate Pilate, until at last the latter delivers Jesus up, to be crucified (John 19:12, 16). And even when he hangs upon the cross, *they* mock him, saying, "He saved others, himself he cannot save" (Mark 15:31).

Hence, this in reality is no *trial* at all. *It is murder!* Church History offers other sad examples of leaders who were cast out by judges who were filled with envy, and who themselves instigated the witnesses (*false* witnesses, of course!), in order that certain men whom *they* (the leaders) hated might be thrown out. The day of judgment will reveal some startling matters! But among all the travesties of justice, none even begins to compare with the one in which the *heavenly* Highpriest, Jesus Christ, stood before the

---

[252] See in this connection J. J. Maclaren, "Jesus Christ, Arrest and Trial of," in I.S.B.E., Vol. III, pp. 1168-1673; W. Evans, *From the Upper Room to the Empty Tomb,* Grand Rapids, Mich., 1934, pp. 149-154; A. C. Bisek, *The Trial of Jesus Christ,* Chicago, 1925. The last-named author tries to refute the arguments which by others are used in order to prove the illegality of the trial.

earthly highpriests, Annas and Caiaphas. For the spotlessly Holy One to be arrayed before such wicked scoundrels, *that* was suffering! — And in the courtyard stood a man for whom he suffered all this. And that man — Simon Peter — was saying again and again that he had never heard of Jesus!

It is not at all surprising that Annas questioned Jesus *first* of all concerning *his disciples,* and *then* concerning *his teaching.* At least, the disciples are mentioned before the teaching. That is exactly what one can expect from Annas! He was far more interested in the "success" of Jesus — how large was his following? — than in the truthfulness or untruthfulness of that which he had been teaching. That is ever the way of the world.

20, 21. Jesus answered him, *I* have spoken openly to the world. *I* al-ways taught at synagogue and in the temple, where all the Jews are in the habit of congregating, and in secret *I* said nothing. Why are you questioning *me*? Question those who heard what I said to them. Of course, *they* know what *I* said.

Though Annas had placed the emphasis where it did not belong, namely, on the outward success ("the disciples") of Christ's ministry, Jesus says not a word about this. *He* places the emphasis where it does belong, namely, on the teaching; for if the teaching is right, the teacher has the right to gather disciples!

The words in verses 20, 21 which have been placed in italics are those which receive emphasis in the original. At synagogue (especially in *Galilee*) and in the temple (located at Jerusalem, in *Judea*) Jesus has always taught *openly.* Even though his teaching had often been cast in the form of parables and paroimias (see on 16:25), nevertheless, he had kept back no central truth. His speaking had been open and non-secretive. Whoever wanted to listen, whether at synagogue or in the temple, was welcome. What a contrast between his *open* teaching and *the strictly executive sessions* and *secret plottings* of the Sanhedrin! For the meaning of the adverb *openly* see also on 7:26. Jesus had spoken to *the world* (the general public; cf. the use of the word in 7:4 and in 14:22; and see Vol. I, p. 79, footnote 26, probably meaning 3). Of course, though attendance at the meetings in the court of the Gentiles of the temple was not entirely restricted to the Jews, yet Jesus is thinking especially *of them;* note: "where all the Jews are in the habit of congregating."

Jesus demands that information with reference to his teaching should be obtained from those who heard it. It is as if today someone under investigation would answer: "I decline to be a witness against myself, and I demand that y o u produce honest witnesses as the law requires."

22. Now when he had said these things, one of the officers who was

standing by slapped Jesus in the face, saying, Is this the way you answer the highpriest?

While Jesus, as a prisoner, was standing with his hands bound before Annas, a certain miserable underling, who belonged to the temple-guards (see on 18:3), sought to exploit the situation for his own petty advantage. The man may have been dreaming about a promotion! So, he gave Jesus a blow in the face (cf. Mic. 5:1). As he did this he said in a tone of scornful rebuke, "Is this the way you answer the highpriest?" Had Jesus been an ordinary man, and had he been guilty of a crime, he would not have deserved such treatment. After all, even a guilty person has his rights. By Hebrew law he was not compelled to testify against himself. Here, however, is no ordinary man, but the Son of God, the *real* Highpriest. And *he* was *not* guilty, but completely innocent. He was more than merely *innocent;* he was *holy.* The underling had had ample opportunity to discover this. Hence, his deed was thoroughly despicable. He was the kind of man who, in a controversy, likes to "get on the band-wagon." He has had his followers.

23. Jesus answered him, If I have spoken wrongly, testify with reference to the wrong, but if rightly, why do you strike me? One is especially impressed with the dignity and majesty of this reply. Had Jesus given an answer similar to that which Paul returned in a somewhat analogous situation (Acts 23:1-5), no fault could have been found. The deed of the officer was completely unjustified. He had not even been *ordered* to strike Jesus. It is exactly as the Lord points out: if he had spoken wrongly, this should have been proved by adequate testimony. Now that he had spoken rightly, the blow in the face was all the more reprehensible.

The verb which refers to the officer's base deed probably has the ordinary, colloquial sense: *to beat* or *to strike* (rather than *to bruise* or *to flay.*)[253]

24. Then Annas sent him bound to Caiaphas the highpriest.

From the point of view of Annas the preliminary investigation had been unsuccessful. No incriminating evidence had been presented. The investigation had merely served the purpose of allowing time for the members of the Sanhedrin to hurry to the palace of the highpriest.

In complete consistency with the verses which precede, we now read that Annas sends Jesus, still bound, to Caiaphas; not, of course, to him as an individual but to him as president of the Sanhedrin, which by this time is ready to receive him. For further explanation of verse 24 and for comment on the problem which arises already in connection with verse 13, see on 18:13, especially footnote 245. For the place where this Sanhedrin-meeting was held see on 18:15.

---

[253] Cf. J. H. Moulton and G. Milligan, *op. cit.,* p. 142.

**25. Now Simon Peter was standing and warming himself. So they said
to him, You surely are not also one of his disciples, are you?**

While Jesus was being tried before Caiaphas (see on 18:19), and proclaimed himself to be the Son of God, a declaration which was called blasphemy by those who heard it, and while he, as a result, was being subjected
to insult and injury, his suffering was aggravated by Peter's wicked behavior. This was the third situation in connection with which Peter denied
his Lord. The first was recorded in 18:15-18. John says nothing with reference to the second. According to Matthew, Mark, and Luke, when the
erring disciple had been ensnared in his first denial, he tried to get out of
the building. He got as far as the arch-way. Here both of the portresses —
the one who was going off duty and the one who had come to relieve her
— said to those who were standing around, "This man was also with Jesus
the Nazarene. He is one of them." At least one male-bystander chimed in,
and addressing Peter directly, said, "You also are one of them." This time
Simon was beside himself with rage. He did something which he had not
done during the *first* denial. *With an oath* (Matt. 26:72) he denied, saying
very forcefully, "I do not know the man."

When John takes up the story again, Peter is back in the courtyard,
standing and warming himself, just as before (during the first denial; see
on 18:18). It seems that his attempt to escape from the palace had not succeeded. During the hour which had elapsed since the second denial the
suspicion which had been aroused regarding him had probably spread.
By this time everybody has heard about it. So "they" said to him . . . But
who are meant by *they?* Evidently the servants and the officers, the men
who were standing around the fire with Peter (cf. 18:18, 25; Matt. 26:73;
Mark 14:70b).

So, they said to him, "You surely are not also one of his disciples, are
you?" Some grew even bolder, and confidently affirmed, "Certainly, you
are also one of them, for your brogue gives you away. You are a Galilean"
(Matt. 26:73; Mark 14:70b). Some were talking *to* Peter (cf. the account
in Matthew and the one in Mark); others were talking *about* him (cf. the
account in Luke). This was enough to get anyone excited, especially a very
excitable person like Simon!

He denied it and said, I am not. "Man, I don't know what you're talking about," said Peter to one of them (Luke 22:60). He stood there invok-
ing upon himself one curse after another. As the author of the Fourth
Gospel counts, this was the second denial. See, however, on 18:15. How it
must have grieved the Master, much more even than the hypocritical behavior of Caiaphas and the blows which he received from the guards.

26, 27. One of the servants of the highpriest, a relative of the man

whose ear Peter had cut off, said, Did I not see you in the garden with him? Peter, however, again denied, and instantly a rooster crowed.

The third denial (as John seems to count) was an outgrowth of the second. The two belong together, and pertain to the same situation, namely, to the time after Simon had returned from the archway and was again standing with the guards and servants, warming himself. The particular incident recorded now is found only in John's Gospel. It must be borne in mind that the beloved disciple was acquainted with the highpriest, and apparently also with his servant, whose very name he knew (Malchus), and with the portress (or portresses). See on 18:10, 15, 16. So it is not surprising that he also knew a certain individual who happened to be a relative of Malchus. That relative had been in the garden during the arrest. He had seen what Peter had done to Malchus. At least, he was *almost sure* that it was Peter. Almost, but not quite sure. So he said to Peter, "Did I not see you in the garden with him (that is, with Jesus)?" The question is put in such a form that an affirmative answer is expected. One might also render it, "I saw you in the garden with him, did I not?" [254]

Again Peter denied. At that very instant a rooster crowed. To be sure, there had been rooster-crowing once before, namely, after the first denial (Mark 14:68). Then, however, it had not registered. This time, however, it was different, for at this very moment Peter noticed that someone was looking into his eyes (Luke 22:61).[255] That look, so full of pain and yet also so full of love, rang a bell in Peter's memory. Suddenly he recalled the words which Jesus had spoken in predicting the three denials (see on 13:38). He went out and wept as one would expect Peter to weep, *bitterly, intensely* (Luke 22:62). Full of deep feeling is also the way Mark puts it: "And when he thought thereon he wept" (Mark 14:72).

28. Then they led Jesus from Caiaphas to the governor's residence.

From three o'clock until day-break Jesus must have been held in imprisonment. Then, at that very early hour (see Mark 15:1) the Sanhedrin was convened. The intention was *to rush* Jesus off to Pilate, before the multitudes in Jerusalem would be aware of what was going on. Besides, *everything* must be over before sabbath! The dawn-session — a few minutes sufficed! — was probably held in order to give a semblance of legality to the corrupt proceedings that had marked the night-session. See on 18:19. It stands to reason that once the verdict of the Sanhedrin had been officially pronounced Jesus had to be taken to Pontius Pilate, the Roman governor.

---

[254] Note: *in* the garden. This lends support to our explanation of 18:4. It shows that the arrest did not take place *outside* the garden-gate but *inside*. Those who have explained 18:4 as if it meant that Jesus went out of the gate to meet the band get into difficulty in explaining the present passage.

[255] How this was possible has been discussed in connection with 18:16; see specially footnote.

The Sanhedrin had the right *to decree* death, but did not have the right *to execute* such a decree. If it was to be carried out, the Romans must make that decision.

At this point John resumes the story. He states that Jesus was led from Caiaphas (the president of the Sanhedrin) to *the governor's residence*. The language used in Luke 23:7 makes it well-nigh impossible to believe that here in 18:28 Herod's palace is meant. John has in mind the fortress of Antonia, situated at the northwest corner of the temple-area. See on 18:3. Pilate had rooms in this fortress, in close proximity to the garrison, as is also indicated by Mark 15:16. **It was early.** The earliness of the hour is emphasized. This should be borne in mind. If that is not done, 19:14 will present an insuperable difficulty. See on that passage. **And in order that they might not be defiled but might eat the Passover they themselves did not enter the governor's residence.**

Rising at (or very soon after) dawn, and being ready for business at such an early hour, was not unusual in the ancient world, not even on the part of important officials, such as Pilate. At the gate of the Praetorium Jesus was handed over to the soldiers of the governor; for the "venerable" members of the Sanhedrin who were in the procession which delivered up their prisoner had religious scruples against entering the dwelling-place of a heathen! They did not desire *to be defiled*. They apparently regarded *ceremonial* defilement to be a much more serious matter than *moral* defilement. That was typical of them. Cf. Luke 11:39. They wanted to be able "to eat the Passover."

But how must we explain this last clause? We reject immediately any answer which would bring John into conflict with the Synoptics. See the discussion in connection with 13:1. There is no *disturbing* problem of any kind here. Here let me be very specific: a. The Fourth Gospel, *in complete harmony with the Synoptics,* teaches that on Thursday-evening Jesus partook of the Passover-supper with his disciples. b. The Fourth Gospel, *in complete harmony with the Synoptics,* teaches that Jesus was crucified on (what we would call) the next day, that is, on Friday. So far many will agree. They will say, "That does not touch the real issue." Hence, we now add: c. The Fourth Gospel, *in complete harmony with the Synoptics,* regards the day of Christ's crucifixion to be the fifteenth of Nisan!

It simply is not true that the Fourth Gospel defends the view that when Jesus was about to be crucified the Passover-Supper still had to be eaten by all the people or by a large section of the people. What does 18:28 actually state? Only this: "And in order that they might not be defiled but might eat the Passover they themselves did not enter the governor's residence." Who are those people that are referred to by the pronoun *they?* Everybody? All the Sadducees? Such things are simply read into the text. They are not there. All the text says is that they, namely, *the members of the Sanhedrin and their temple-police* did not enter the governor's palace. If they had entered, they might have defiled themselves. How? By the vessels within that house? See on 4:9. By too close a contact with an idolator? By contact with leaven? Or by contact with a dead body? We simply do not know, but surely in a pagan Praetorium there must have been ever so many possibilities for defilement, such as would make the worshipper ceremonially unclean sothat he would not be able to "eat the Passover."

But, again, just what does that last clause mean? Passover, to be sure, was *over* for practically everybody. But these Sanhedrists and their servants are afraid of entering the Praetorium, lest they become defiled; for in that case they would not be able to "eat the Passover." There is here a little problem. In explaining the meaning of "eating the Passover" one can go in either of two directions. Either of them is far better than the assumption of a contradiction. Such an assumption is not only doctrinally unsound but is in direct conflict with the entire setting in John which so clearly harmonizes with the setting in the Synoptics (as has been shown in connection with 13:1).

The first conservative attempt at a solution is the one according to which the term *Passover* refers here to the entire seven-day feast, together with the festal offerings that were enjoyed in connection with it. The expression, "that they might eat the Passover," would simply mean, "that they might keep (or celebrate) the feast." In this connection such a passage as II Chron. 30:22 (cf. also Ex. 12:3-5) is often referred to. "To eat the festival" means, then, *to keep it,* eating its festive meals. The special reference here in 18:28, according to the advocates of this theory, is to the Chagigah (sacrificial meal) that was enjoyed on (what we would call) the day after the Passover Supper.

Among the many arguments that are urged in favor of this theory are also these:

1. It does not arbitrarily create a conflict between John and the Synoptics.

2. The term Passover elsewhere in John refers to the entire seven-day feast; if elsewhere, why not here? See also Luke 22:1.

3. This theory does justice to the statement about ceremonial defilement: "in order that they might not be defiled." The Passover-meal proper was eaten *in the evening.* By evening the period of defilement would ordinarily have ended. Why then should the Sanhedrists hesitate to enter the Praetorium early in the morning, for fear of defilement, *if they were thinking about eating the Passover-lamb?* Those are the arguments.

A detailed defence of this theory may be found in the following sources:
A. Edersheim, *op. cit.,* Vol. II, pp. 565-568.

R. C. H. Lenski, *op. cit.*, on 18:28.

And especially, N. Geldenhuys, *Commentary on the Gospel of Luke,* Grand Rapids, 1951, pp. 649-670. This is, perhaps, the most recent, detailed defence.

Whatever one may think of this view, so much is clear at least that *"whatever be its merits,* it commends itself as being at least *more reasonable"* than the views which set up a conflict where there is no conflict. See Vol. I, pp. 16, 17.

The reader who studied that statement in Vol. I of this Commentary has noticed its guarded character. We purposely used the expression "whatever be its merits," and "more reasonable than . . ." Though this interpretation is far better than those which assume a conflict, *it has its drawbacks.*

The chief of these is that, after all, the expression "to eat the Passover" refers elsewhere in the Gospels to the eating of the Passover Supper with its Passover-lamb. See Matt. 26:17; Mark 14:12, 14; Luke 22:8, 11, and 15. If it has that meaning everywhere else in the New Testament, why not here, in 18:28? Besides, we have very little information with respect to the Chagigah.

Is there not an explanation of 18:28 that is more simple? We refer here to the theory which has been defended *in a masterly manner* by Dr. H. Mulder.[256]

Briefly, according to Dr. Mulder, the text simply means that the members of the Sanhedrin had been so thoroughly pre-occupied with the arrest and trial of Jesus that *they* had not had time for their Passover-meal. Thursday-evening these men had been awaiting Judas. They did not know just when he would come. (Even Judas did not know in advance just where Jesus would keep the Last Supper with his disciples.) The Sanhedrists had to be ready. They also wanted to take part in the arrest, even though it be merely as spectators (see Luke 22:53). Then there was the night-trial. All this took time, much time. Hence, they were convinced that *in the interest of the one really important assignment, namely, to get rid of Jesus* — see on 11:50 — all else, even the Passover Supper, could afford to wait. Hence, when very early in the morning they brought Jesus before Pilate, they had not yet partaken of the Passover-meal. They must not defile themselves by entering the house of a heathen. See Acts 10:28; 11:3. Hence, these hypocrites who regard ceremonial defilement to be so much worse than moral defilement (cf. Luke 11:39) cannot enter the Praetorium. Once Jesus is actually hanging on the cross (mocked by them!), they can go home and eat the lamb!

Objections will also be presented against this theory; for example, "Must

---

[256] H. Mulder, *GThT* (1951). The articles of Dr. Mulder should be translated into English. *I have not found a better defence of this particular view anywhere else.*

we really believe that these legalists would dare to postpone their Passover-supper?" "Would they dare to bring a curse upon themselves this night by engaging in all manner of activity which had nothing to do with the Passover Supper?" "After all, could they not have eaten the Passover first, and then have gone to the garden in order to join in the arrest of Jesus?"

As we said at the beginning, the problem has not been solved sothat all is now clear. The *main* point, however, is this: there is absolutely nothing here which even remotely suggests *contradiction* between John and the Synoptics.

29, 30. Pilate then went out to them and said, What charge do y o u prefer against this man? They answered and said to him, If this man were not an evildoer, we would not have handed him over to you.

Pontius Pilate was the fifth governor of the southern half of Palestine. See Vol. I, p. 180. He was "governor" in the sense of being *procurator*, ruling over an imperial province, and as such directly responsible to the emperor. Although he had been endowed with civil, criminal, and military jurisdiction, he was under the authority of the legate of Syria.

From the sources that have come down to us [257] we may conclude that he was *not* a *very tactful* person. Once he caused soldiers who were under his command to bring with them ensigns with their images of the emperor. To the Jew this was sacrilege. When he threatened with death those who had come to petition him for the removal of these idolatrous standards, they called his bluff, and he yielded. At another time he used the temple-treasure to pay for an aqueduct. When a crowd complained and rioted, he ordered his soldiers to club them into submission. The incident which finally led to his removal from office was his interference with a multitude of fanatics who, under the leadership of a false prophet, were at the point of ascending Mt. Gerizim in order to find the sacred vessels which, as they thought, Moses had hidden there. Pilate's cavalry attacked them, killing many of them. Upon complaint by the Samaritans, Pilate was then removed from office. He started out for Rome in order to answer the charges that had been leveled against him. Before he reached Rome, the emperor (Tiberius) had died. An unconfirmed story, related by Eusebius, states that Pilate "was forced to become his own slayer."

From the Gospels we gather that he was *proud* (see on 19:10); and *cruel* (Luke 13:1). He was probably just as *superstitious* as his wife (19:8; cf. Matt. 27:19). Above all, as all the accounts of the trial of Jesus before him

---

[257] These sources are, first of all, *The Gospels;* then Philo, *De Legationem ad Caium* XXXVIII; Josephus, *Antiquities* XVIII, iii, iv; same author, *The Jewish War* II, ix; Tacitus, *Annals* XV, xliv; and Eusebius, *Ecclesiastical History,* I, ix, x; II, ii, vii. See also G. A. Müller, *Pontius Pilatus der fünfte Prokurator von Judäa,* Stuttgart, 1888.

indicate, he was *a self-seeker,* wishing to stand well with the emperor. He thoroughly hated the Jews who, as he saw it, were always causing him trouble upon trouble. That he was *utterly* devoid of any remnant of human sympathy and any sense of justice cannot be proved. In fact, there are passages which seem to point in the opposite direction. At any rate, though his guilt was great, it was not as great as that of Annas and Caiaphas (19:11).

Comparing all the Gospel-accounts with reference to this trial, one gains the impression — which is strengthened as the story proceeds — that Pilate *did everything in his power to get rid of this case.* He had no love for the Jews; hence, hated to please them and to grant their request regarding Jesus. And on the other hand, deep down in his heart he was afraid of them and of the possibility that they might use their influence against him. Up to a point he was willing to do what justice demanded, especially if by doing so he could vex his enemies, the Jews. But only up to a point. When his position is threatened, he surrenders!

Jesus, then, was brought before this governor. The latter, having probably been informed by the soldiers on guard-duty that a prisoner had been brought by a Sanhedrin-delegation which refused to enter the Praetorium, went out to them. Standing on a gallery or porch over the pavement in front of his residence (see on 19:13), he asked the Jewish rulers to present the indictment. "What charge do y o u prefer against this man?" said he. The question was, of course, entirely proper. The answer, however, was impudent. They replied, "If this man were not an evil-doer, we would not have handed him over to you." This was a broad hint. It meant, "Governor, if you know what is good for you, stop asking such questions. You know very well that in nearly all matters we constitute the highest court in Israel. You should confirm our decision and do what we are about to ask you to do."

31. Pilate said to them, Take him yourselves, and judge him in accordance with y o u r own law. The Jews said to him, We have no right to execute anyone.

Pilate was not yet aware of the fact that the Jewish leaders were determined on *the death* of Jesus. Thinking that they intended to inflict a lesser punishment, he is at a loss to understand why they should bother *him* with this prisoner. And if they are not even willing to present an indictment, then he wants to have nothing to do with the case. So, when he now blurts out, "Take him yourselves, and judge him in accordance with y o u r own law," he does not imply that the prisoner has not even had a trial. No, what he means is: "Dispose of the case yourselves." The verb used in the original has many shades of meaning (see on 3:17), and can certainly indicate (as it seems to do here), *to adjudge, pass and execute sentence, condemn.*

That the Sanhedrists so understood it is clear from their reply: "We have no right to execute anyone." By means of this answer they showed what kind of punishment they desired to inflict, nothing less than *capital* punishment. Though, under Roman law, they had the right to pass such a sentence, they did not have the right actually to put anyone to death. (In the case of Stephen, they simply took the law into their own hands, Acts 7:58.) They also knew, of course, that if Pilate, the Roman, would yield to their wishes, Jesus would be *crucified* (not stoned or strangled); he would be "lifted up from the earth" (12:32; cf. 3:14). And *that* was exactly what they wanted. *That* was also exactly what — for totally different reasons — Jesus himself wanted! Hence, there follows:

32. (This happened) in order that the word of Jesus might be fulfilled which he had spoken, signifying by what death he was about to die. See on 3:14 and on 12:32. Cf. Matt. 20:19. Jesus, according to his own prophecy and *in order* (see Vol. I, p. 46) that it might be fulfilled, must die the death of *an accursed one* (Deut. 21:23; Gal. 3:13). Such was the plan of God for our salvation.

33. Then Pilate re-entered the governor's residence, and he summoned Jesus and said to him, Are *you* the king of the Jews?
At this point John seems to assume that the readers are acquainted with the earlier Gospels, particularly with the Gospel according to Luke. See Vol. I, pp. 31, 32. From Luke 23:2 it appears that when Pilate had refused to sentence Jesus without due process of law, and had by his refusal forced the Sanhedrists to present charges, they had presented three: 1. He perverts our nation. 2. He forbids us to pay tribute to the emperor. 3. He says that he himself is Christ a king.

In reality the three charges were *one*. It amounted to saying: "This man is a politically dangerous individual. He is guilty of high treason." Note also that they said that they had actually *found* this to be the true state of affairs. They had reached this conclusion upon due investigation!

How grievously he, who is about to declare himself king in the realm of the truth (18:37), suffered here from the lie! What the Jewish authorities here declared was *the very opposite* of the truth. For proof see on 6:15 and on 12:14, 15. Pilate, moreover, was not fooled. He knew very well what was the *real* reason why the Jews had delivered Jesus to him (namely, *envy*, Matt. 27:19).

But, of course, the governor simply could not afford to ignore such charges, not with suspicious Tiberius in the saddle at Rome! So, re-entering the residence (that is, going *back* to the place from which he had come when the soldiers on guard had reported to him the arrival of the Jews and of their prisoner), he now summoned Jesus — ordering his soldiers to take him out of the hands of the Jewish officers and to bring him inside — , and said to him, "Are *you* the king of the Jews" (with all the emphasis on the pronoun).

There may have been a touch of ridicule in this question, ridicule not directed at Jesus but at those who had brought *such* charges against *such* a prisoner. It is as if Pilate is saying, as he looks intently upon *this* prisoner: "Are *you* the king of the Jews? How utterly ridiculous such a charge!" But at the same time, he asked the question, and it required an answer. However, before it could be *answered*, it would have to be *explained*.

34. Jesus answered, Are you saying this of your own accord, or have others said it to you about me? This question was altogether in place, for as asked by Pilate, neither a pure and simple "Yes," nor a pure and simple "No" would have sufficed. "Yes," would have been interpreted as meaning, "Yes, I am, *in a political sense,* the king of the Jews." "No," might have been construed as indicating, "No, I am not the king of the Jews *in any sense whatever.*" If Pilate's question is based merely upon what *others* (the Jewish leaders) have said, in their accusation, then, of course, the answer must be "No." But if, *apart from* any charges that have been preferred against Jesus, Pilate, *of his own accord* is asking whether Jesus is, indeed, the king of the Jews, and if Jesus may be permitted to put *his own* meaning into this question (as he certainly does by implication in the parallel verse 37), then the answer will be, "Yes, indeed!" Jesus is the *real* king of the *real* Jews. See on 18:37.

Is Pilate speaking like a carnally-minded Jew, who concentrates on nothing higher than an earthly kingdom? Or is he not speaking in that vein?

35. Pilate answered, I surely am not a Jew, am I? Your own nation and the chief priests have handed you over to me. What have you done? With a gesture of disdain and in a tone of contempt Pilate brushes aside the suggestion that he might possibly have asked the question as a Jew would have asked it. "I surely am not a Jew, am I?" he asks. No, Pilate himself did not see a revolutionist in this meek-looking person standing before him. Not such a fool was the governor. But, so Pilate continues, the question — "Are you the king of the Jews?" — *had to be asked* because "Your own nation, the people to which you belong, and specifically *the chief priests* (representing the entire Sanhedrin) have handed you over to me. It is *they* who have brought the charges. What is your answer? What have you done?" — Although Pilate knew very well that *envy* (on the part of the Jewish leaders) was the power which had brought Jesus to his residence for judgment, he was not certain that this explained *everything.* Had the prisoner committed any crime at all? And if so, *what* was it?

Thus, the way was paved for Christ's explanation of the nature of his kingship:

36. Jesus answered, My kingship is not of this world. If my kingship were of this world, my attendants would have been fighting in order to keep me from being handed over to the Jews, but now my kingship does not spring from that source.

The question, "What have you done?" Jesus does not answer. Let Pilate enter into *the charges* that have been preferred against this prisoner. Anything in addition to this is surely "out of order."

In his answer, therefore, Jesus goes back to Pilate's question recorded in verse 33: "Are you the king of the Jews?" The way has been paved sothat all is now clear for the answer to this question. Pilate has indicated that not he but the Jewish nation and the Sanhedrin charged Jesus with *political conspiracy*. It is now up to Jesus to explain the nature of his kingship.

The answer which Jesus gives is threefold:

First, he shows that he realizes that back of the question, "Are you the king of the Jews?" there lies another, still more fundamental, namely, "Are you a king *in any sense whatever?*" The answer to this question is *implied* in verse 36, for when Jesus now says, *"My kingship* is not of this world," he implies, of course, that he is a king! The same answer is *expressed* in verse 37: "You say that I am a king."

Secondly, Jesus indicates what his kingship *is not,* namely, it is not of this world (verse 36).

Thirdly, he shows what his kingship *is,* namely, it is a kingship in the hearts and lives of all those who listen to the truth (verse 37).

To begin with the first: "My kingship," says Jesus, with emphasis on *my.* He *is* a king, then. That the term here means *kingship,* not kingdom, is clear from the fact that according to verse 37 it consists of Christ's rule in the hearts of those who obey him. We are dealing, therefore, with a *spiritual-dominion* concept. For the use of the word in that "abstract" sense see also Luke 1:33; 22:29; Rev. 12:10. The term in the sense of kingship, rule, has its root in the Old Testament (Ps. 103:19; 145:13; Dan. 4:3, 25; also — a different word — Ps. 22:28; Obad. 21; and again a different term in I Chron. 29:11).[258]

However, here in 18:36, 37 it does not have reference to God's dominion (hence, also the dominion of the second person of the Trinity) over all his creatures, but distinctly to *Christ's spiritual kingship* in the hearts and lives of his followers.

Secondly, then, the kingship of Jesus is not like an earthly kingship. It does not spring from the earth: it was not given to him by any earthly

---

[258] On this entire subject see especially L. Berkhof, *Systematic Theology,* Grand Rapids, Mich., fourth edition, 1949, pp. 406-412, 569, 710, 713-716; G. Vos, *The Teaching of Jesus concerning the Kingdom of God and the Church,* N. Y., 1903, pp. 25-37; and H. Ridderbos, *De Komst van het Koninkrijk,* Kampen, 1950 (in the present connection especially p. 25).

power, and it is totally different in character. Thus, for example, it does not employ earthly means. If Christ's kingship had been earthly in origin and character, he would have had officers ("underlings") — just like the Sanhedrin, for instance, which had its police-force, and just like Pilate, who had his Roman guards —, and these would have been fighting, sothat he would not have been handed over to . . . here we probably expect "the Romans," but Jesus says, *"the Jews!"* Far from trying to lead the Jews in a revolt against the Romans, Jesus considers these Jews his opponents. Have they not delivered him up to Pilate? Had Christ's kingship been of an earthly kind, his attendants would have been fighting, *under his own command,* sothat in Gethsemane he would not have been handed over to the Jews and their wicked Sanhedrin! But instead of ordering them to fight in his defence, he had done the exact opposite (see on 18:10, 11).

37. Then Pilate said to him, So you are a king? Jesus answered, You say that I am a king. For this purpose was I born, and for this purpose have I come into the world, in order that I might testify to the truth. Whoever is of the truth listens to my voice.

And now *thirdly,* what, then, is this kingship? Pilate wants to know. Although the charge against Jesus, representing him as a seditionist, had not arisen in the heart of *Pilate,* nevertheless he cannot understand how a man can talk about his kingship, if he be not an earthly king. Pilate, therefore, wishes to know whether this prisoner is really a king.

Jesus answers by saying, "You say that I am a king." Cf. also Matt. 27:11; 26:64; Mark 15:2; Luke 23:3. In the present connection it is very clear that with this answer Jesus is not trying to remain non-committal. The reply cannot mean, "That is what *you* are saying, but I have never said that." The immediately following context leaves room for only one interpretation, namely, that Jesus in replying, "You say that I am a king," definitely meant that Pilate was correct in inferring that the prisoner possessed and claimed royal authority! Note what follows: "For this purpose was I born," etc. Hence, the meaning is "I am, indeed, a king; I was born for this very purpose."

The words, "You say it (namely, that I am a king)," should not sound strange to people who so often use the very similar expression, *"You said it!"* This, of course, means, "Yes, indeed; it is even as you have just now affirmed."

Jesus, however, was not a person who, as a result of certain circumstances — say, the death of a predecessor, or the successful revolution of a people against its rulers — had become a king. No, he was *a born king;* in fact, he was born for the very purpose of being a king! "Born" not only, as any other person might be born, but "come into the world" *from* another realm, namely, from heaven. From the ivory palaces of heaven he had descended into this sin-cursed world in order there to take upon himself his mediatorial task, his saving ministry. See on 1:9.

He came, moreover, in order to give competent testimony concerning that which he had himself heard from the Father respecting man's salvation. For *testimony* and to *testify* see on 1:7, 8. For the idea that Jesus came to testify to the things which he had seen and heard while in the Father's presence see 3:11, 32; 8:28, 38; 12:49; 14:10; cf. also 17:8.

He had come, therefore, to testify to *the truth* with respect to man's salvation unto the glory of God. See on 14:6. He had come to destroy the realm of *the lie* (see on 8:44). Very significantly Jesus adds, "Whoever is of the truth listens to my voice." This was, of course, an implied invitation that Pilate, too, might listen! Now, *every one,* whether Jew or Gentile does not matter at all — see also on 1:29; 3:16, 17; 4:42; 6:33, 51; 8:12; 9:5; 10:16; 11:52; 12:32 — who owes his spiritual origin to him who is *the* truth, is eager *to listen* to this voice of the truth. For the verb *to listen* (not merely *to hear*) see on 10:3.

38. Pilate said, What is truth? And having said this, he went out to the Jews again, and said to them, No crime whatever do I find in him.

When Pilate hears this remark about the truth, he shrugs his shoulders. Skeptic that he is, this subject no longer holds any interest for him. It must be borne in mind, in this connection, that many leading Romans had by this time given up all the traditional pagan beliefs with respect to the gods. O surely, the gods *might* exist after all, and might take revenge if one should offend them. Hence, many of these people, including those of the family of Pilate (see Matt. 19:7-9; Matt. 27:9), were filled with superstitious fears; but as to any settled conviction or deeply rooted faith with respect to God or basic realities it just did not exist for them.

It is in that spirit of extreme skepticism and cynicism that Pilate blurts out: "What is truth," not realizing that *the answer* was standing in front of him (see on 14:6).

Having said this, Pilate returns to the porch, and definitely tells the Jews — the multitude is steadily increasing in front of the Praetorium —, "No crime whatever do I find in him." No crime, no cause of indictment! This man Jesus, who, as Pilate saw it, speculated in spiritual vagaries, was not a dangerous individual. From him the state had nothing to fear. Had the governor been an honest man, had he been willing to serve the cause of justice, he would at this juncture have released the prisoner. But Pilate was not such a man. For the character of Pilate see on 18:29, 30.

When the Jews — we think especially of the leaders, the Sanhedrists — heard Pilate's verdict ("no cause of indictment"), they immediately accused Jesus of continuous sedition, which, so they claimed, had had its beginning in Galilee and had continued right into Jerusalem. The result was that

Pilate — who, of course, realized very well that he had full jurisdiction in this case, for according to the charge the attempted insurrection had continued to the very gates of Jerusalem! — sent him to Herod. It was a polite gesture. At the same time (and this was uppermost in Pilate's mind), just in case Herod should be willing to adjudicate this matter, he (Pilate) would be rid of it. And *to be rid of it* was Pilate's yearning desire! The story of Jesus' appearance before Herod is told in Luke 23:5-12. The trick failed. Herod returned the prisoner, arrayed in a mock-garment. So, Pilate again addresses the members of the Sanhedrin, telling them that neither he himself nor Herod has found a cause of indictment. But again he compromises. Superstitious fear, and perhaps a very small remnant of a sense of justice, keeps Pilate from sentencing Jesus to be crucified. He is not ready for this . . . that is, not yet! On the other hand, fear of what the Jews might do to him if he should add one more offence to all the previous ones restrains him from releasing Jesus. Thus his wretched heart is being torn between these two fears. Hence, he now proposes to please *the Jews* by having Jesus scourged; and to placate *the voice of his own conscience and the gods* (*if* they existed!) by not issuing the order that the prisoner be crucified. See Luke 23:13-16.

The Jews, however, have other ideas. At this very juncture the multitude — by this time a *multitude* has gathered! — demands of Pilate that he do what he is in the habit of doing at Passover-time, namely, release a prisoner, whom they would (probably, as a symbol and reminder of the release of the ancestors from the prison-house of Egypt). See Mark 15:6-8. And here the Fourth Gospel resumes the story:

39. But y o u have a custom that I release a man for y o u at the Passover. Now do y o u wish that I release to y o u the king of the Jews?

Pilate, for once, is most willing to grant the privilege demanded by the Jews. He sees in this another opportunity to get Jesus off his hands. So, on the nomination for release he places two candidates: Barabbas and Jesus. See Matt. 27:15-18.

This too was suffering for Jesus. By implication he was treated as one who had already been found guilty by the Roman government, functioning through Pilate. Yet Pilate had declared, only a moment ago, "*I myself do not find in him any cause of indictment . . . neither does Herod!*" The suffering which Jesus endured was intensified by the fact that he was placed on the nomination with, of all people, *Barabbas!* See on 18:40.

It seems altogether probable that Pilate expected the multitude to choose *Jesus.* After all, the echoes of their hosanna's in honor of the prophet from Galilee had scarcely died. If five days ago "the whole world" applauded him — and Pilate was not completely ignorant of this; cf. Matt. 27:18; Mark 15:9, 10 —, would they now turn against him? (It is *not* true that the

411

Hosanna-shouters consisted *exclusively* of people from Galilee, and the crowds that exclaimed "Crucify him!" *exclusively* of Jerusalemites; see on ch. 12.) It is clear that the governor himself *suggested* that the people choose Jesus in preference to Barabbas. He said, "Now do y o u wish that I release to y o u the king of the Jews?" From the point of view of strategy that last phrase was a mistake. Even in his desperate attempt to escape his responsibility with respect to Jesus, Pilate still could not resist mingling a bit of mockery with his earnest appeal. This prisoner, bound, helpless (for so it seemed) . . . the *king* of the Jews, the only king the Jews had been able to produce, a king on whose destruction their own leaders were bent. How ridiculous!

40. Then they cried out once more, saying, Not this man but Barabbas. Now Barabbas was a robber.

In order to understand the greatly abbreviated account as given in the Fourth Gospel, particularly the words of verse 40, it is necessary to consult Matt. 27:19-21. From this it appears that at this very critical moment a messenger arrived to inform Pilate about a dream which had caused intense suffering to his wife. While Pilate was busy with this message from his wife, "the chief priests and the elders persuaded the multitudes that they should ask for Barabbas and destroy Jesus" (Matt. 27:20). Did these wretched leaders remind the people that by choosing Jesus they would be playing into the hands of their deadly enemy Pilate? Did they make much of the fact that just a moment ago Pilate had mocked them by calling Jesus *the king of the Jews?* Did they recount all the crimes which Pilate had previously committed against the Jewish nation? And did they intimidate those who at first were inclined to choose Jesus (cf. 7:13; 9:22; 19:38; 20:19)? At any rate, when Pilate reappears and asks the people for their decision, they cry, "Release Barabbas." They must have shouted this more than once. John probably assumes that the readers have learned about the first shout from the Synoptics (see Vol. I, pp. 31, 32), for he writes, "They cried out *once more.*"

What they roared was, "Not this man (or "Not this *fellow*") but Barabbas." Barabbas — meaning, *son of the father,* which probably indicates that he was the son of a rabbi — was a notorious *robber,* a *brigand* (cf. 10:1, 8; Matt. 21:13; 26:55; 27:38, 44; Mark 11:17; 14:48; 15:27; Luke 10:30, 36; 19:46; 22:52; II Cor. 11:26). He was a man who for a certain insurrection made in the city *and for murder* had been imprisoned (Luke 23:19). Him the people chose. And this choice, though entirely unjustified and-wicked beyond words, was in accordance with the kind decree and providence of God. Barabbas must go free in order that Jesus may be crucified, his people saved, and God glorified!

For Synthesis see pp. 422, 423.

CHAPTER XIX

19 1 Then Pilate therefore took Jesus and scourged him. 2 And the soldiers plaited a crown of thorns, and put it on his head, and threw a purple robe around him; 3 and they kept on marching up to him and saying, "Hail, King of the Jews!" and they kept on slapping him in the face.[259]

4 And Pilate went out again and said to them, "See here, I am bringing him out to y o u in order that y o u may know that I find no crime in him." 5 So Jesus came outside, still wearing the thorny crown and the purple robe. And he said to them, "Look! The man!" 6 Then when the chief priests and the officers saw him, they cried out, saying, "Crucify (him), crucify (him)!" Pilate said to them, "Take him yourselves and crucify (him); for I, on my part, do not find any crime in him." 7 The Jews answered him, "We have a law, and according to that law he ought to die, because he made himself the Son of God."

8 Now when Pilate heard this word, he was the more afraid, 9 and he entered into the governor's residence again, and said to Jesus, "Where are you from?" But Jesus gave him no answer. 10 So Pilate said to him, "To *me* you do not speak? Don't you know that I have the authority [260] to release you and that I have the authority [260] to crucify you?" 11 Jesus answered, "You would have no authority [260] at all over me if it had not been given to you from above.[261] Therefore the one who delivered me up to you has the greater sin."

12 As a result of this, Pilate was making efforts to release him. But the Jews cried out, saying, "If you release this man, you are no friend of the emperor.[262] Whoever makes himself king rebels against the emperor."

13 Then Pilate, on hearing these words, led Jesus out, and sat down on the judgment-seat, in a place called The Stone Pavement, in Aramaic: Gabbatha. 14 Now it was the Preparation of the Passover.[263] The hour was about the sixth. And he said to the Jews, "Look! Y o u r king!" 15 Then they cried out, "Away with him, away with him, crucify him!" Pilate said to them, "Y o u r *king* shall I crucify?" Answered the chief priests, "We have no king but the emperor." 16 So he then handed him over to them in order to be crucified.

19:1-16

19:1. Then Pilate therefore took Jesus and scourged him. Once more Pilate, foiled in his previous attempts to evade his clear duty, seeks to com-

---

[259] Literally: "giving him blows."
[260] Or: *right.*
[261] II C; see Vol. I, pp. 41, 42.
[262] IIIA2; see Vol. I, pp. 42, 43.
[263] Or simply, "Passover-Friday."

promise. He orders Jesus to be taken and scourged (for both verbs are, of course, causative). Such scourging was hideous torture.[264]

The Roman scourge consisted of a short wooden handle to which several thongs were attached, the ends equipped with pieces of lead or brass and with sharply pointed bits of bone. The stripes were laid especially (not always exclusively) on the victim's back, bared and bent. The body was at times torn and lacerated to such an extent that deep-seated veins and arteries — sometimes even entrails and inner organs — were exposed. Such flogging, from which Roman citizens were exempt, often resulted in death. Or it preceded execution, and was ordered as a sign to indicate that the person to whom it was administered was about to be crucified.

It seems, however, that in the present case Pilate ordered this scourging not as a signal for crucifixion, but in order to avoid the necessity of sentencing Jesus to be crucified. We arrive at this conclusion upon the following grounds:

1. The passage 19:12 clearly shows that even after the scourging Pilate was still trying desperately to release Jesus.

2. Another passage, 19:5, seems to indicate that the governor was trying to arouse pity for the prisoner. See on that verse.

3. The interpretation which we favor is in harmony with the requirements of consistent character-portrayal, which has been mentioned before. See Vol. I, p. 165. *Pilate was consistently trying to evade the issue. He desired to get Jesus off his hands.* He was trying hard, very hard, to find a way by which he could, on the one hand, avoid ordering Jesus to be crucified, and yet, on the other hand, escape the revenge of Annas, Caiaphas, and company.

One can picture Jesus after the scourging, covered with horrible bruises and lacerations, by wales and welts. We are not surprised to read that Simon of Cyrene was compelled to bear the cross after Jesus had carried it a little while (19:16, 17; cf. Luke 23:26). It must, however, be borne in mind that the suffering of the Man of Sorrows was not only intense but also vicarious; cf. Is. 53:5.

"But he was wounded for our transgressions, he was bruised for our iniquities; the chastisement of our peace was upon him; and *with his stripes we are healed.*"

2, 3. And the soldiers plaited a crown of thorns, and put it on his head, and threw a purple robe around him; and they kept marching up to him and saying, Hail, king of the Jews! and they kept on slapping him in the face.

The flagellation was followed by mock-coronation and mock-salutation

---

[264] Consult the following sources: Josephus, *The Jewish War* II, xiv, 8, 9; V, xi, 1; Eusebius, *Ecclesiastical History* IV, xv, 4. See also in W.D.B., p. 538.

in the courtyard of the Praetorium (Mark 15:16). Somewhere in the vicinity the soldiers found some thorny twigs. Many commentators, in agreement with the opinion of the crusaders, mention as the plant from which the torture crown was plaited the *Spina Christi* or *Palinrus Shrub,* whose branches have ugly spikes and whose leaves resemble the ivy which was used in crowning emperors and generals. This plant still thrives in Judea. However, it has been pointed out by several archaeologists that few countries of the size of Palestine have so many varieties of prickly plants. See also such biblical passages as Judg. 8:7, Ps. 58:9; Hos. 9:6; Mic. 7:4. Hence, the identity of the species which was used by the soldiers cannot be established. It is of little importance. More significant is the fact that thorns and thistles are mentioned in Gen. 3:18 in connection with Adam's fall. Hence, here in 19:2, 3 Jesus is pictured as bearing the curse that lies upon nature. He bears it in order to deliver nature (and us) from it (Rom. 8:20, 21).

With fiendish cruelty the soldiers pressed down this crown upon his head, causing rivulets of blood to run down his face, neck, and body (still aching sorely from the scourging). They wanted to *torture* him. They also wanted to *mock* him. The crown of thorns satisfied both ambitions. They aggravated the bitter insult and the ignominious suffering by another bit of contemptuous mimicry: they threw around Jesus what was probably a discarded and faded soldier's mantle, of a hue resembling the royal purple. In his hand they placed a reed, as a mock-scepter (this last item is not recorded by John, but see Matt. 27:29). Then they kept marching up to him, probably filing past him, in order to give him their mock-salute: "Hail, king of the Jews." As they did so, they kept on giving him blows.

To say that also this mockery *had been ordered by Pilate* [265] is hardly warranted, it would seem to us. The record before us does not sustain this interpretation. It is Pilate who *orders the scourging* (19:1). He does not seem to have been responsible *in the same degree* (though certainly to *some* extent, for he might have prevented it!) for the mockery. Where was Pilate while all this was going on? Evidently inside his residence. See the next verse:

4, 5. And Pilate went out again and said to them, See here, I am bringing him out to y o u in order that y o u may know that I find no crime in him. So Jesus came outside, still wearing the thorny crown and the purple robe. And he said to them, "Look! The man!"
When Pilate appears before the public once more, he states the reason why he is bringing Jesus before them, namely, "in order that y o u may know that I find no crime in him" (see also 18:38; 19:6 for a similar

---

[265] So, for example, Lenski, *op. cit.,* pp. 1226-1228.

verdict). Of course, he should have immediately released his prisoner. But again he dilly-dallies. This time, in complete harmony with all his previous attempts to get rid of the case, he tries to work on the sympathy of the people. He exposes to their view a pathetic spectacle: Jesus, covered with gashing wounds, blood streaking down his face, neck, back; the horrible "crown" still upon his head; the purple robe still around him. Then Pilate exclaims, "Look! The man!" Has he not suffered enough? Is it really necessary to inflict more punishment upon him? And does *he* look like a dangerous rebel?

That this was actually what Pilate had in mind when he uttered these words would seem to follow from the reply given by the chief priests and the officers. They seem to have been of the opinion that what the governor meant was this, "Is any further action necessary against this person in whom I have found no guilt, who has suffered so much already, and who does not at all look like an insurrectionist? Is not this enough?"

6. Then when the chief priests and the officers saw him, they cried out, saying, Crucify (him), crucify (him)! Pilate said to them, Take him yourselves and crucify (him), for I, on my part, do not find any crime in him.

Hardly has Pilate's dramatic appeal ended, when the most hardened individuals of all, (note: *not* the mob, but) the chief priests and their officers, upon seeing the object of their ghoulish envy, begin to shriek, "Crucify, Crucify!" Over and over again these terrible words are yelled until they become a monotonous refrain, an eery, ominous chant: "Crucify . . . crucify . . . crucify . . . crucify . . ."

In thorough exasperation the governor answers, "Take him yourselves and crucify (him), for I, on my part, do not find any crime (any cause of indictment) in him." Of course, Pilate knows very well that without his order *they cannot* crucify Jesus! In a veiled manner he is reminding them of their political impotence. He *hates* these Jews, who have caused him so much trouble. And at the same time he *fears* them. Otherwise he would have released the prisoner long ago. Moreover, they know that he is afraid of them!

It is rewarding to count the number of times the governor uttered the words, "I do not find any crime in him." In the Fourth Gospel it is found in 18:38; 19:4; 19:6. But to this should be added: Matt. 27:23; 27:24; Mark 15:14; Luke 23:4; 23:13-15; 23:22. Even when due allowance is made for parallel (duplicate) passages, the fact remains that Pilate stresses and constantly re-iterates the truth that in Jesus there is no cause of indictment. And by means of Pilate, it was God himself who declared his Son's perfect innocence. Nevertheless, in a few more moments this same Pilate is going to succumb to the persistent clamor of the Jews, and is going to sentence Jesus to die the accursed death of crucifixion. "No guilt in him . . . no guilt in him . . . no guilt in him . . . no guilt in him . . . So then he handed him over in order to be crucified." Thus reads the sacred record. But how could a righteous God permit this? There is only *one* solution. It is found in Is. 53:6, 8, "Jehovah has laid on him the iniquity of us all . . . He was cut off out of the land of the living for the transgression of my people to whom the stroke was due." Cf. Gal. 3:13.

7. The Jews answered him, We have a law, and according to that law he ought to die, because he made himself the Son of God.

Full well do *the Jews* (probably especially the leaders) realize that Pilate is trying to evade the issue, and is attempting to return Jesus to them. This, of course, they do not want. Hence, the gist of what they now say is this: "After careful examination *we* have found him guilty, that is, guilty when judged by the standard of *our own law.* In fact, we have found him to be deserving the death-penalty because he is a blasphemer (cf. Lev. 24: 16). Again and again he, though merely a man, has called himself the Son of God (cf. 3:16; 5:18; 8:53; 10:30, 33, 36; Matt. 26:63). Hence, *you,* Pilate, are now duty-bound to sentence him to death."

It was true — as the references given clearly indicate — that Jesus had again and again declared himself to be God's Son, his *only-begotten* Son, his Son in a very unique sense. See on 1:14. This was either the most horrible blasphemy, or else it was the most glorious truth. Sin-hardened Sanhedrists wickedly chose the first alternative. On this ground their council had condemned him (Matt. 26:63-66). The issue was becoming very clear at last. But why *at last?* Why had they not advanced this accusation immediately, that is, at the very beginning of the trial before the governor? Probably, because they had felt that such a purely religious charge might make very little impression upon a pagan. But *now,* when every other method has failed, and Pilate is once more saying, "I find no guilt in him," they present the one and only charge which was official. Perhaps at *this* juncture they spoke so boastfully about *their law* ("We have a law") because Pilate had reminded them of the fact that they were a subjugated people (see on verse 6). It is as if in reply they now wish to say, "But has not the Roman government left us a considerable measure of freedom to regulate our own affairs? Do we not enjoy Home Rule? And is it not *your* duty, Pilate, to respect *our laws* anent such matters? *We* have a law, and according to *that law* he ought to die, because he made himself the 'Son of God."

8, 9. Now when Pilate heard this word, he was the more afraid, and he entered into the governor's residence again, and said to Jesus, Where are you from? But Jesus gave him no answer.

Pilate was more afraid than ever. This new fear was caused not so much by the dogged determination of the Jews to have things their own way as

417

by the item of information which he had received just now. What! This mysterious prisoner a son of the gods? Was that, perhaps, the reason why Pilate's wife had endured such agonies when she dreamed about him? See Matt. 27:19.

So, shaken to the bottom of his soul by these superstitious uncertainties, the judge, with Jesus, re-enters the residence. "Where are you from?" he asks anxiously. He received no answer, and he *deserved* none. Surely, a man who was so utterly corrupt that he had ordered Jesus to be scourged almost to death, even though he knew (and declared again and again) that this prisoner was innocent, was not worthy of a reply. Besides, if Pilate had paid more attention to the words of Jesus spoken previously (18:36, 37), he could have discovered the answer to his question!

10. So Pilate said to him, To *me* you do not speak? Don't you know that I have the authority to release you and that I have the authority to crucify you? What Pilate does now is altogether natural in cases of this kind. It must be borne in mind that he is trembling all over (see on 19:8, 9). Hence, in order to conceal his fear he begins to boast! Indignantly he fumes, "To *me* (note the position of this pronoun at the very beginning of the question) you do not speak?" How dare you? Don't you realize who I am? And don't you understand that "I have the *authority* (see on 1:12; 10:18) to release you and I have the authority to crucify you?" Pilate speaks of *releasing* before he mentions *crucifying*, probably because *releasing* Jesus was uppermost in his mind, that is, *if* it could be done without injury to Pilate; otherwise not, of course!

11. Jesus answered, You would have no authority at all over [266] me if it had not been given to you from above. Jesus impresses upon Pilate the fact that the latter's vaunted authority had been *delegated* to him. It was a sacred trust, a responsibility for the discharge of which Pilate was answerable to God.

Jesus continues, **"Therefore the one who delivered me to you has greater sin."** Pilate, indeed, had been given authority to pronounce sentence in this case. Failure to realize that this authority had been *given* to him and that he was accountable to God for the manner in which he exercised it, rendered him culpable. But Caiaphas who, as ruling highpriest, had wickedly condemned the Righteous One and had delivered him up to Pilate with the request that he be sentenced to die the accursed death on the cross, had not received any authority from God to commit such baseness. Besides, Pilate, though thoroughly corrupt, did not fully realize what he was

---

[266] The translation *over* is probably correct. It has not been proved that the preposition used in the original must mean *against* in such a context. See Gramm. N.T., p. 607.

doing. But Caiaphas acted with knowledge and grim determination (see on 11:49, 50). Therefore the sin of Caiaphas was greater than the sin of Pilate. There are gradations in sin (Luke 12:47, 58). Unto whom much is given, from him much will be required!

12. As a result of this, Pilate was making efforts to release him. But the Jews cried out, saying, If you release this man, you are no friend of the emperor. Whoever makes himself king rebels against the emperor.

From the answer of Jesus (verse 11) *one* fact was clear to Pilate: *this* prisoner was no rebel. Of course, the governor had *felt* this right along; he *was certain* about it now. This man had regard for Pilate's *authority* (see verse 11). Hence, having gone outside once more where the people could see and *hear* him, Pilate intensified his efforts to release Jesus. That he did not succeed in these repeated attempts was due to his own moral weakness, his unwillingness to do the right no matter what the cost. When the Jews finally began to scream, "If you release this man (or *this fellow*), you are no friend of the emperor," Pilate capitulated to their wishes. It was this outcry that floored the governor. In his feverish imagination he saw how he was about to lose his prestige, his position, his possessions, his freedom, even his very life perhaps. The *manner* in which the Jews delivered this final blow must have done as much as anything else to discomfit Pilate. They merely said, "If you release this man, you are no *friend of the emperor*." [267] But Pilate understood immediately that such a statement *implied* much more than it actually *expressed*. It implied: "You will then be *the enemy* of that very suspicious emperor Tiberias. We will, of course, lodge a complaint against you. We will tell the emperor that you condone high treason against the government; that you have released a man who was guilty of continuous sedition, and who allowed himself to be called 'king of Israel' (12:13; cf. Mark 11:10; Luke 19:38). We will accuse you of 'softness toward rebels.' Then where will *you* be?"

This was the last straw. One can imagine the rage which these words kindled in the heart of Pilate! He knew that these Jews were liars, and that they had no love whatever for the Roman government or its emperor. He was thoroughly convinced of the fact that deep down in their hearts they themselves were most unloyal. Yet, here they were, apparently deeply disturbed about the political loyalty of One who had never so much as spoken a single word against the Roman government. Despicable hypocrites they were, but they had him cornered.

13. Then Pilate, on hearing these words, led Jesus out, and sat down

---

[267] Whether or not "friend of the emperor" (amicus Caesaris) — for which see A. Deissmann, *op. cit.*, pp. 377, 378 — is used here as an official title (as later, in the days of Vespasian) makes little difference. The context would seem to point in the direction of non-technical use.

on the judgment-seat, in a place called The Stone Platform, in Aramaic: Gabbatha.

The moment for which the entire history of redemption had been waiting has now arrived. Pilate has made up his mind to deliver Jesus over to be crucified. John, who in his account of Christ's passion had frequently abbreviated, becomes very circumstantial in his description of what *now* occurred. He led Jesus out (or: caused him to be led out). Then he, Pilate, *sat down*. The meaning is not that he *seated* Jesus (or "had him sit") on the judge's seat, adding to the mockery. Though that translation is favored by eminent authorities (Moffatt, Goodspeed, Montgomery), the verb used does not need to have that meaning. Moreover, it is very improbable that Pilate would thus degrade himself and his official tribunal.[268]

This time Pilate sits down with the purpose of passing sentence. He sat down on his official chair which was standing on a platform reached by steps (the noun *tribunal* or *judgment-seat* — see especially its original sense in Acts 7:5 — is related to the verb *to step, walk*). For the noun see also Matt. 27:19; Acts 12:21; 18:12, 16, 17; 25:6, 10, 17; Rom. 14:10 (tribunal of God); II Cor. 5:10 (tribunal of Christ). The place of the tribunal was *The Stone Pavement* (in Aramaic *Gabbatha*). This may be the one that was recently excavated in the neighborhood of the Tower of Antonia.[269] See also on 18:28 (the location of the Praetorium).

14. Now it was the Preparation of the Passover. This does not mean, "It was the Preparation *for* the Passover," as if John wanted to indicate that Jesus was sentenced before the day of the Passover. Such a day of *preparation* (cooking the food to be used on that day, etc.) preceded *sabbaths*, not feasts. The expression simply means that it was the Friday of the Passover-week. See also on 13:1 and on 18:28. One finds a very clear commentary in Luke 23:54, "And it was the day of the Preparation, *and the sabbath drew on*"; and in Mark 15:42, "the Preparation, that is, *the day before the sabbath*." John, in complete harmony with the other Gospels, teaches that Jesus was sentenced and crucified on Friday, which was the day of Preparation *for* the sabbath. In this particular case it was the day of Preparation *of* (belonging to) Passover-week.

The hour was about the sixth. Much has been written with reference to this brief note of time. Bible-critics cite this passage as proof-positive that Scripture contains errors and contradictions. Does not Mark 15:25 state that Jesus was crucified at "the third hour," that is, at nine o'clock

---

[268] See F. M. Derwacter, "The Modern Translators and John 19:13: Is It *Sat* or *Seated?*" *Classical Journal*, XL (1944-1945), 24-28. This is a very good article.
[269] L. H. Vincent, "L'Antonia et le Prétoire," *Revue Biblique*, XLII (1933), 83-113.

in the morning? Surely, he was *sentenced* before he was *crucified.* Yet, according to John (say the critics), the sentencing took place *at noon* ("the sixth hour"). — But it has been shown that in other passages the author of the Fourth Gospel in all probability used *the Roman civil day time-computation.* See on 1:39; 4:6; 4:52. If there, why not here?

Now the two statements — the one from John, namely, that Jesus was sentenced at *about six o'clock* in the morning; and the one from Mark, that he was actually nailed to the cross at *nine o'clock in the morning,* can hardly be said to be in hopeless conflict with each other.[270] It must be borne in mind that John does not say *six o'clock* but *about* six o'clock. Let us suppose that it was actually half past six. We grant that even this leaves a difficulty, but the difficulty is not great. It is difficult for us to understand how the trial before Pilate (in reality the Pilate-Herod-Pilate trial) was so speedy, how everything transpired so rapidly. On the other hand, does it not seem probable that the Sanhedrin had been doing all in its power to *rush* Pilate to a decision? Is it not true that this august body had been rushing the case from the very moment when Jesus was captured? The morning-meeting of the Sanhedrin may have been *very* early, indeed! It may have taken only a few minutes. After all, everyone knew in advance what was going to be decided. The real decision had been agreed on long before.

Once the sentence had been pronounced by Pilate, the heat was off. So, three hours intervened between the sentencing and the crucifixion; or, let us say two hours and a half (in case the sentence was pronounced at 6:30 A. M., *"about* six o'clock"). Why so much time elapsed between the two events we do not know.

And he said to the Jews, Look! Y o u r king! This exclamation must have been uttered with stinging ridicule. It was born of sullen resentment. Such is y o u r king, O Jews, shackled, weak, defenceless, bloody, sentenced to a horrible death, *at y o u r own request!* Pilate "rubs it in." How he hates these people!

15, 16. Then they cried out, Away with him, away with him, crucify him! — Pilate said to them, Y o u r *king* shall I crucify? — Answered the chief priests, We have no king but the emperor. — So he then handed him over to them in order to be crucified.

The priests and the priest-ridden mob felt the sting of Pilate's plaguing question. So in answer to his spitefully nettling remark they scream back:

---

[270] It seems to me that the language which Lenski uses in this connection is too strong. We admit that a difficulty remains, but surely not a hopeless conflict. See R. C. H. Lenski, *op. cit.,* pp. 1249, 1250.

"Away with him, away with him, crucify him." The governor jabs them once more with, "Y o u r *king* shall I crucify?" (note the order of the words, which is true to the original.) With unabashed, but all too transparent, hypocrisy *the chief priests* answer, "We have no king but the emperor."

In a way, they were right! Having rejected their Messianic hope when they said, "Away with him, away with him, crucify him," (a hope which in the case of *the chief priests,* mostly Sadducees, had never been fervent) they surely have no right to claim Jesus as king (spiritual ruler, in the sense of 18:36, 37). The only one whom they now recognize as king is Tiberius. And even *that* recognition is definitely faked. They forget, however, that God, as king of the universe, is not through with them. In a certain, terrible sense, he is still their king. Indescribable punishments were not far away. They have continued ever since. See Rom. 11:25.

While avowing their unswerving loyalty to the emperor, they at the same time hinted at the governor's possible disloyalty. It was as if they said, *"We have no king but the emperor. What about you, Pilate? Where is your loyalty?"* That this was in their mind can hardly be doubted (see on 19:12).

So Pilate then handed him over to them; not as if *they* — the Jews — were now going to crucify him, but in the sense that he surrendered to their wishes. Humanly speaking, *jealousy had won the day, the jealousy of the leaders.* Since that time, envy has often triumphed; yet, what happened here is unique. Here it succeeded in casting out the Righteous One. But in (seemingly!) winning this battle, it lost the war.

In connection with 19:15, 16 the following stirring passages should now be read: Luke 23:24, 25 and Matt. 27:24, 25.

Synthesis of 18:12 — 19:16

See the Outline on p. 374. *The Son of God Dying as a Substitute for His People. The Trial and the Denial.*

The rather detailed *Outline* which we have given on p. 374 is in itself of the nature of a Synthesis. In addition, note the following:

A. Before Annas, trial and denial

The real Highpriest, Jesus Christ, is led before the corrupt highpriests, Annas and (a little later) his son-in-law Caiaphas. The former, though no longer the official highpriest and Sanhedrin-chairman, was still the ruling spirit. He was proud, ambitious, wealthy.

While Jesus was given a preliminary hearing before him, Peter, having been brought into the palace by John, aroused the suspicions of the portress. Stepping right up to him, she said (with malice in her voice), "You surely are not also one of this man's disciples, are you?" Shocked by the suddenness and boldness of the question, Peter was caught off guard and in spite of all his previous promises of loyalty, he answered bluntly, "I am not."

Thus, as if the humiliation which Jesus was experiencing before Annas were not sufficient, this affliction was added to his bitter suffering, that one of his leading disciples disavowed him. The preliminary hearing itself was a farce, as was the entire trial before the Jews. It was a farce in the sense that no serious attempt was made of getting at the truth. Christ's death had been decided on long ago. *The verdict was a foregone conclusion!* Annas, moreover, was more interested to discover the size of Christ's following than to know about his teaching, except only in so far as this teaching might serve the purpose of providing material for formulating the terms of an unfavorable verdict. Jesus was asked to testify with reference to himself. When he refused to do this and asked that witnesses be produced, a miserable underling slapped him, and asked him an impudent question. With majesty the Lord defended his own request that witnesses be heard. Still bound, Jesus was then sent to Caiaphas.

While, before Caiaphas and the Sanhedrin, Jesus made his good confession, which resulted in insult and injury to himself; Peter, having returned to the courtyard from which he had sought escape, was again pelted with questions, such as, "You surely are not also one of his disciples, are you?" "I am not," he answered, lying again. A relative of Malchus then asked, "Did I not see you in the garden with Jesus?" Again Peter denied, and instantly the rooster crowed!

B. Before Pilate, trial

For the synthesis of this section we refer to the Outline. A clarifying remark is necessary, however. In the Outline we have called the gesture of Pilate that in connection with a Passover-custom a prisoner be released, and that in the present case that prisoner be Jesus, the governor's *second* attempt to rid himself of responsibility. It was indeed the *second* attempt as far as the Gospel of John is concerned. As a matter of actual history, it was the third, for it was preceded by the attempt on Pilate's part to have Herod assume responsibility for the case. But that is not recorded in the Fourth Gospel.

The chief lesson to be learned with respect to the trial before Pilate is that one can never be neutral with respect to Jesus. One always sides either for him or against him. Pilate's "neutrality" failed completely. He succumbed at last to intimidation, and handed Jesus over to be crucified.

Again and again Pilate proclaimed Christ's innocence. Then he sentenced him! It is clear that Jesus suffered punishment not for his own but for our sins (he had none), and that he suffered all this willingly. In discussing the details of the Passion the eye should remain fixed upon *him, his* suffering, *his* love!

423

17 Then they took Jesus along; and carrying the cross by himself he went out to (a place) called The Place of The Skull, which in Aramaic is called Golgotha; 18 where they crucified him, and with him two others, on this side and on that, and in the middle Jesus.

19 Now Pilate also had a title written, and had it put on the cross. There was written, "Jesus of Nazareth, the King of the Jews." 20 Now this title many of the Jews read, because the place where Jesus was crucified was near the city; and it was written in Aramaic, Latin, and Greek. 21 Then the chief priests of the Jews were saying to Pilate, "Do not write, 'The King of the Jews,' but that he said, 'I am king of the Jews.'" 22 Pilate answered, "What I have written I have written."

23 Then, when the soldiers had crucified Jesus, they took his garments and made four parts, for each soldier a part, and (they took) the tunic. Now the tunic was seamless, woven all the way from top to bottom. 24 So they said to each other, "Let us not tear it, but cast lots for it (to see) whose it shall be." (This was) in order that the scripture might be fulfilled,

"They divided my garments among themselves,
And for my vestment they cast lot."

These things, indeed, the soldiers did.

25 Now there were standing near the cross of Jesus his mother, and his mother's sister, Mary the (wife) of Clopas, and Mary Magdalene. 26 Then when Jesus saw his mother and the disciple whom he loved standing there, he said to his mother, "Woman, look! Your son!" 27 Then he said to that disciple, "Look! Your mother!" And from that hour the disciple took her to his own home.

28 After this, since Jesus knew that everything was now finished, he said, in order that the scripture might be accomplished, "I am thirsty." 29 A vessel full of vinegar was lying there. So they stuck a sponge full of vinegar around a hyssop-stick and brought it to his mouth. 30 Then when Jesus had received the vinegar, he said, "It is finished." And he bowed his head and gave up his spirit.

31 Then the Jews, since it was the Preparation, in order that on the sabbath the bodies might not remain on the cross — for great was the day of that sabbath — asked Pilate that their legs might be broken and that they might be removed. 32 So the soldiers came and broke the legs of the first and of the other who had been crucified with him. 33 But when they came to Jesus and saw that he was dead already, they did not break his legs, 34 but one of the soldiers with a spear pierced his side, and immediately there came out blood and water. 35 And he who has seen it has testified, and genuine is his testimony, and he knows that he is telling the truth, in order that y o u also may come to believe. 36 For these things took place in order that the scripture might be fulfilled,

"Not a bone of him shall be broken."

37 And again another scripture says,

"They shall look upon him whom they pierced."

19:17-37

19:17, 18. Then they took Jesus along; and carrying the cross by himself he went out to (a place) called The Place of The Skull, which in Aramaic is called Golgotha; where they crucified him, and with him two others, on this side and on that, and in the middle Jesus.

Verse 17 contains all that John has to say about what happened on The Sorrowful Way. For a much more complete account see Luke 23:26-32.

The soldiers took Jesus and, though his back was torn by many a gaping wound as a result of the scourging to which he had been subjected, they made him carry his own cross. He carried it as long as he was physically able to do so. Then Simon of Cyrene was requisitioned to take over the arduous task (Luke 23:26; cf. Matt. 27:32; Mark 15:21).

Much has been written about the form of the cross. Did it resemble the letter X (the St. Andrew's cross), the letter T (the St. Anthony's cross), or the dagger (the Latin cross)? In the light of the fact that *the title* (see on verse 19) was written *above* Christ's head (Matt. 27:37; Luke 23:38) it is well-nigh certain that artists are correct when they adopt the last of these three possibilities, the so-called dagger-type or Latin cross.

It would seem that the entire cross (upright post and cross-beam) was laid upon Christ's back. At least, there is nothing in the text that suggests otherwise. The idea of the intended victim carrying the cross on which he himself will be suspended reminds one of Isaac, carrying the wood of the burnt-offering (Gen. 22:6). The words, "And carrying the cross by himself he went out," imply a fourfold curse:

1. Death by crucifixion was in itself regarded as a curse (Gal. 3:13); "he that is hanged is accursed of God" (Deut. 21:23, true even if it applies merely to the hanging of the dead body; how much more so when it has reference to the living person). That the cross was a term of horror is also clear from verse 31 of the present chapter; from I Cor. 1:23; and from Phil. 2:8.

2. Compelling the sentenced person, in this case Jesus, *to carry the cross* added to the shame.

3. Carrying it *by himself,* meaning: carrying it all alone although it was heavy and although his body had already been subjected to terrible punishment, stresses the fact that the Suffering Servant was being led into complete isolation.

4. *Going outside the city* to be crucified ("he went out") adds still another element to the curse, as is clearly taught in Heb. 13:12, 13, on the basis of Ex. 29:14; Lev. 4:12, 21; 9:11; 16:27; Num. 19:3.

The spot where the crucifixion occurred was called *The Place of the Skull.* To remain as close as possible to the sound (as well as the meaning) of the original one might give as the English equivalent: *The Place of the Cranium.* The Greek-from-Aramaic term *Golgotha* means *the skull.* The Latin *Calvaria* (from which we derive our *Calvary*) also means *skull.* It is related to *calvus, calva* (cf. German *kahl,* Dutch *kaal,* meaning *bald;* hence, *calva:* the scalp without hair).[271]

---

[271] Cf. Harper's *Latin Dictionary*, New York, 1907; entries *calvaria, calvus,* p. 273.

But why was this spot called The Place of the Skull? Various answers have been given: a. because it resembled a skull; b. because according to a widely accepted legend (found in the writings of Origen, Athanasius, and Epiphanius) the skull of Adam had been discovered there; c. because it was a place of execution; and (closely related) d. because it was a place where skulls could be seen lying about. Some of these theories are objectionable on the very surface. Even a. (cranium-like shape) is by no means certain. Epiphanius, writing in the fourth century, already rejected this view, saying that the place did not resemble a skull at all. (But Cyril of Jerusalem seems to indicate that there was a resemblance, *Catechetical Lectures* XIII, 39.) The best answer is that we do not know why the spot was called *The Place of the Skull.*

Where was Calvary? Some who have made a trip to Palestine locate it about 250 yards n.e. of the Damascus gate. This is *Gordon's Calvary.* The hill really resembles a skull. It is outside the gate, near a highway. In its neighborhood are rock-hewn tombs and gardens. As some see it, this just about settles the matter. Other interpreters, however, object to this theory, for the following reasons:

1. The skull-like shape of the place (eye-holes, rounded top) may be due to artificial excavation since the time of Christ. And even if not, how do we know whether the name *Place of the Skull* means *skull-like place?*

2. This place lacks the support of tradition.

About a third of a mile to the s.w. of Gordon's Calvary, and inside the walls of the modern city, is the Church of the Holy Sepulcher. This is the site supported by early tradition. If any credence is to be given to this tradition, it must first be proved a. that this site was actually "outside the gate" in the days of Jesus' ministry on earth (19:17, 18; Heb. 13:12, 13); b. that it was, nevertheless, near to the city-wall (19:20); c. that it was near a road or highway (Matt. 27:39); and d. that in its immediate vicinity there was a garden (John 19:41). To this moment these things have not all been proved with respect to *any* site (whether the traditional site, or Gordon's Calvary, or any other). Because of the general physiography of Jerusalem and its surroundings, it is, however, well-nigh certain that neither of the two most favored sites can be very far away from the actual spot where the Lord was crucified.[272]

Here, then, *they* crucified him. The pronoun refers to *the soldiers,* as is clear from 19:23. In the original the most glorious fact in the history of redemption is expressed in just three words (literally *"where him they-crucified"*). This mode of execution existed in many ancient nations; such as Macedonia, Persia, Syria, Egypt, the Roman Empire. (The Jews used

---

[272] See also the discussion in I.S.B.E., article "Golgotha" by E. W. G. Masterman; W.D.B., p. 99, and Plate XVII C; and *Viewmaster Travelogue,* Reel Number 4001, Gethsemane to Calvary, Scenes 2-7.

other methods, especially stoning.) Rome generally (not always!) reserved this form of punishment for slaves and those who had been convicted of the grossest crimes.

Just what it was that led Pilate to crucify two others with Jesus, one on either side, has not been revealed. It may have been in order to insult the Jews, as if he wanted to say, "Such is y o u r king, on the level with other gross criminals." But, from the divine point of view, this was a place of honor, for Jesus had come "into the world, sinners to save." More-over, in this crucifixion between two malefactors (Luke 23:33) prophecy was being fulfilled, Is. 53:12: "He was numbered with the transgressors."

It has been well said that the person who was crucified "died a thousand deaths." Large nails were driven through hands and feet (20:25; cf. Luke 24:40). Among the horrors which one suffered while thus suspended (with the feet resting upon a little tablet, not very far away from the ground) were the following: severe inflammation, the swelling of the wounds in the region of the nails, unbearable pain from torn tendons, fearful dis-comfort from the strained position of the body, throbbing headache, and burning thirst (19:28).

In the case of Jesus the emphasis, however, should not be placed on this physical torture which he endured. It has been said that only the damned in hell know what Jesus suffered when he died on the cross. In a sense this is true, for they, too, suffer eternal death. One should add, however, that *they* have never been in heaven. The Son of God, on the other hand, descended from the regions of infinite delight in the closest possible fellow-ship with his Father (1:1; 17:5) to the abysmal depths of hell. On the cross he cried out, "My God, my God, why hast thou forsaken me?" (Matt. 27:46).

19, 20. Now Pilate also had a title written, and had it put on the cross. There was written, Jesus of Nazareth, the King of the Jews. Now this title many of the Jews read, because the place where Jesus was crucified was near the city; and it was written in Aramaic, Latin, and Greek.

Above the head of Jesus Pilate caused a *title* (Matt. 27:37: *accusation;* Mark 15:26 and Luke 23:38: *superscription*) to be written. With respect to this title (a *title,* indeed, for in the case of Jesus no *crime* was recorded!) critics have found another contradiction in the Bible. They point to the fact that the words of which it was composed differ in all four Gospels. But this argument is rather easy to refute. It certainly was not necessary for each Gospel-writer to write down *all* of the words. Each gives the gist, as he sees it. The full title must have been about as follows: THIS IS JESUS OF NAZARETH THE KING OF THE JEWS. So Matthew says that the accusation written over the head of Jesus read: THIS IS JESUS THE KING OF THE JEWS (Matt. 27:37). Mark states that the super-

427

scription was: THE KING OF THE JEWS (Mark 15:26). Luke's version of the superscription reads: THIS IS THE KING OF THE JEWS (Luke 23:38). And according to John, who was himself present and must have seen it, the title was: JESUS OF NAZARETH THE KING OF THE JEWS.

Where, just where, is the discrepancy? Is a person who has witnessed an accident a liar because he does not report *everything* that occurred?

Now because the place where Jesus was crucified was near the city (and there were so many Jews in and just outside the city, having streamed to Jerusalem from every direction in order to attend the Passover feast) this title was read by many. Moreover, even those who had come from far away places and had forgotten their Aramaic but were able to read Greek could interpret the title. It was written in Aramaic, which was the language spoken by the Jews of Palestine (and by some others besides!), in Latin, the official language of the government, and in Greek, the world-language of commerce and culture.

The king of the Jews crucified at the request of the Jews; let the whole world know this. By rejecting him they have rejected themselves. And that latter rejection means "the reconciliation of the world" (God's elect from every tribe and nation). See Rom. 11:15. Hence, the whole world must be able to read this title! Here is a Savior who has international significance.

21, 22. Then the chief priests and the Jews were saying to Pilate, Do not write, The King of the Jews, but that he said, I am king of the Jews. — Pilate answered, What I have written I have written.

It was God himself who in his wonderful providence had directed the hand of Pilate. This does not in any way make God responsible for Pilate's *motives* in writing the superscription. Nor does it mean that God interpreted the title as the governor interpreted it. But *the words,* as such, were, nevertheless, true. They were true in this sense that the king *of the Jews* is crucified in order that he may be the king *of a spiritual kingdom* (see on 18:36, 37) *which recognizes no national or racial distinctions,* a kingdom in which the Aramaic-speaking Jew, the Roman, and the Greek — yes, the elect from *every* "tribe, tongue, people, and nation" (Rev. 5:9) — are the citizens. See on 1:29; 3:16, 17; 4:42; 6:33, 51; 8:12; 9:5; 10:16; 11:52; 12:32.

To the chief priests this title is an insult. In all probability Pilate had intended it as such. These Jewish dignitaries contact the governor with the demand, "Do not write, 'The King of the Jews,' but that he said, 'I am king of the Jews.'" For the chief priests (and perhaps even more so for the Pharisaic members of the Sanhedrin) the idea that "The King of the Jews, The Hope of Israel," was being crucified, was a bitter pill to swallow. It became even more bitter when they reflected on the fact that this curse had been pronounced upon him *at their own request!* This must not be. Pilate must by all means change *the title* into a *description of the crime* which Jesus had committed. Had he not committed the crime of claiming to be king of the Jews?

But this time Pilate refuses to yield. Still filled with wrath because of the major defeat which he had suffered, he will at least achieve a minor victory. Curt and crisp is his answer "What I have written I have written." It remains!

And it seems as if we hear the voice of God confirming this terse statement. He too is saying, "What *I* have written *I* have written."

23, 24. Then, when the soldiers had crucified Jesus, they took his garments and made four parts, for each soldier a part, and (they took) the tunic. Now the tunic was seamless, woven all the way from top to bottom. So they said to each other, Let us not tear it, but cast lots for it (to see) whose it shall be. — (This was) in order that the scripture might be fulfilled,

> **They divided my garments among themselves,**
> **And for my vestment they cast lot.**

As was customary, the garments that had been worn by the condemned man were divided among those who carried out the sentence. Cf. Matt. 27:35; Mark 15:24; Luke 23:34. Especially in the light of Mark 15:24 ("casting lots upon them, *what each should take*") it would seem that the idea is not that one garment was torn or cut into four parts (or that several garments were cut into equal parts) — in that case why cast lots at all? — but rather that there were four pieces of apparel, and that each of the soldiers received one of these. These garments were of unequal value; hence the soldiers (as is clear from the Synoptics) cast lots (throwing dice, perhaps). It has been suggested that these four pieces were: head gear, sandals, belt, and outer garment.

But there was also a fifth garment, namely, the seamless tunic, "woven all the way from top to bottom." This was the garment worn next to the skin. Had there been only *four garments,* there would have been no problem, for there were four soldiers; hence, one for each. But what to do with the fifth? That was the problem. To tear this garment and give each soldier a piece would have served no useful purpose. One could do very little with a torn-off piece. So they decide not to do this. Instead they decide that the inner garment, all of one piece (not sewed together but woven all the way from top to bottom), must also be put into the lottery even though this may mean that thus one man will receive more in value that the others.[273]

---

[273] Josephus singles out for special mention the fact that the high priest's long robe

Now, in all this, a prophecy was being fulfilled, the prophecy found in Ps. 22:18 (quoted exactly from the LXX, Ps. 21:19). It is a well-known fact that David endured much suffering for the sake of God's kingdom. This however, does not necessarily mean that all the passages of this moving Psalm refer *directly* to what he had himself literally experienced, and only *indirectly* to the cross and its agonies. If the reference is throughout to David's own suffering, one will have to conclude that full use was made of the figure of speech called *hyperbole;* see especially verses 12-18. A more reasonable view would seem to be this, that the woes that are described in these verses have reference directly to Christ, and were fulfilled in him alone, though in the life of David they were dimly foreshadowed.

It is clear that the prophecy of Ps. 22 refers both to the division of the garments and to the casting of the lot. Some commentators believe that the singular noun in the second line (vestment) refers exclusively to the seamless tunic. However, owing to the parallelism, it is probably better to look upon this singular as a collective synonym for garments. The fulfilment of the prophecy in connection with the distribution of Christ's clothing excites our wonder even without introducing any over-refinements in exegesis.

Dr. J. P. Free in his excellent book *Archaeology and Bible History*, p. 284, calls attention to the fact that *according to Canon Liddon* there are three hundred thirty-two distinct prophecies in the Old Testament which have been literally fulfilled in Christ, and to the additional fact that the mathematical probability of all these prophecies being fulfilled in *one* man is represented by the fraction:

$$\frac{1}{840000000000000000000\,00000000000000000000\,00000000000000000000\,00000000000000000000\,00000000000000000}$$

The clear implication of the passage which we are studying must not escape us. It is this: Jesus bore for us the curse of nakedness in order to deliver us from it! Cf. Gen. 3:9-11, 21; then II Cor. 5:4; Rev. 7:13, 14. Surely if what Ham did to his father Noah is singled out for special mention because of its reprehensible character, what the soldiers did when they disrobed Jesus and then divided his garments among themselves, casting lots, should cause us to pause with horror. Such a pause is suggested by the words: **These things, indeed, the soldiers did.** They did that which was shameful. Yet, by means of that shameful deed God's eternal plan

---

was not sewed together but was one long vestment. It is clear, therefore, that such garments, so woven, were considered very precious. See *Antiquities of the Jews,* III, vii, 4.

(hence, also prophecy) was fulfilled. Hence, we pause in abhorrence . . . and adoration!

25. Now there were standing near the cross of Jesus his mother, and his mother's sister, Mary the (wife) of Clopas, and Mary Magdalene.

From among the *many* women (Matt. 27:55) that were standing *near* (see on 14:23, footnote 168) — but not too near (see Matt. 27:55; Mark 15:40; Luke 23:49: "afar off") [274] — the cross of Jesus, John selects *four* for special consideration.

It is interesting to compare John's list with similar lists in Matthew and Mark:

Matthew 27:56	Mark 15:40	John 19:25
1. Mary Magdalene	1. Mary Magdalene	1. His mother
2. Mary the mother of James and Joses	2. Mary the mother of James the Less and of Joses	2. His mother's sister
3. The mother of the sons of Zebedee	3. Salome	3. Mary the (*wife* probably) of Clopas
		4. Mary Magdalene

Why just these four are mentioned here in 19:25 has not been revealed. It is not improbable that they stood in closer relation to the Lord than other women. Thus, for example, the mother of Jesus is mentioned, and also the mother of the sons of Zebedee (who were disciples of Jesus, belonging to the inner *three*). A comparison between Matthew's list and that of Mark would seem to indicate that the name of the mother of James and John was Salome.

We cannot accept the theory [275] according to which John mentions only *three* women. If that were true, two sisters (Jesus' mother and his aunt) would have the same first name (Mary). Besides, in that case John, though not mentioning by name *the mother* of Jesus, would not only mention by name her sister but would also inform the readers that she stood in some relation to Clopas (being probably his wife). This is not at all reasonable. Far more likely to be correct is the view that "the mother of the sons of Zebedee" and "Salome" and "his mother's sister" were the same person.[276]

It may even be that the three lists are identical, with the one exception,

---

[274] Did they, perhaps, stand far off at first, and did they draw closer later on when they were convinced that the soldiers would not harm them?

[275] For the arguments in favor of this theory see Lenski, *op. cit.*, pp. 1266-1270.

[276] In accepting the *four women* theory I am in complete agreement with F. W. Grosheide, *op. cit.*, pp. 499-501; G. T. Purves, art. "Mary" in W.D.B.; and many others.

namely, that John adds the mother of Jesus (without mentioning her *by name*). *If* this be true, we get the following harmony:

The mother of Jesus

Her sister, who according to Mark was Salome, the mother of James and of the author of the Fourth Gospel (see Vol. I, p. 28, last paragraph, continued on p. 29)

Mary, the wife of Clopas. She — if this harmony be correct — is the mother of James the Less and of Joses

Mary Magdalene.

It must be stressed, however, that this harmony, though not improbable, cannot be proved.

Taking these four in the order named, and assuming the harmony given to be correct, the New Testament references to them are as follows:

(1) The mother of Jesus. Her name was Mary. She was the wife of Joseph. Other references to her are found in the following passages: Matt. 1:16, 18, 20; 2:11; 13:55; Mark 6:3; Luke 1:27, 30, 34, 38, 39, 41, 46, 56; 2:5, 16, 19, 34; John 2:1, 3, 5, 12; 6:42; 19:25, 26, 27; Acts 1:14. See also Vol. I, pp. 113-121, 238.

(2) Salome. See Matt. 27:56; Mark 15:40; 16:1; John 19:25.

(3) Mary, the wife of Clopas. See Matt. 27:56, 61; 28:1; Mark 15:40, 47; 16:1; Luke 24:10; John 19:25.

(4) Mary Magdalene. See Matt. 27:56, 61; 28:1; Mark 15:40, 47; 16:1, 9; Luke 8:2; 24:10; John 19:25; 20:1, 2, 11-18.

While hardly anything is known about Salome and Mary, the wife of Clopas, more has been recorded with reference to Mary Magdalene. She resided at Magdala, located on the s.w. coast of the Sea of Galilee. Jesus had performed a wonderful act of mercy, having cast seven demons out of her. Hence, it is not surprising that she became a most grateful disciple of the Lord. (Incidentally, she was *not* the woman of ill repute, whose story is recorded in Luke 7:36-50. The identification does her an injustice.) She was one of those women who, having once become a follower of Jesus, helped him in his ministry by giving him of her substance. We are not surprised to find her at the cross, at the tomb when Jesus was buried (together with Mary, the wife of Clopas), and again at the tomb on the third day (together with Mary, the wife of Clopas, and with Salome). For further information concerning her see on John 20:1, 2, 11-18.

Although the *faith* of these women was not what it should have been, their *love* for the Lord is certainly evident throughout. It would seem that of the entire circle of eleven *men* only *one* was at the cross. That one was the apostle John. But there were several *women*. All honor to them, to their courage, and to their love.

26, 27. Then when Jesus saw his mother and the disciple whom he loved standing (there), he said to his mother, Woman, look! Your son! Then he said to that disciple, Look! Your mother! And from that hour the disciple took her to his own home.

Of the seven words from the cross John records three. The seven with their references are as follows:

(1) "Father, forgive them: for they do not know what they are doing" (Luke 23:34)
(2) "Today you will be with me in Paradise" (Luke 23:43)
(3) "Woman, look! Your son! . . . Look! Your mother!" (John 19: 26, 27)
(4) "My God, my God, why hast thou forsaken me?" (Matt. 27:46; Mark 15:34)
(5) "I am thirsty" (John 19:28)
(6) "It is finished" (John 19:30)
(7) "Father, into thy hands I commend my spirit" (Luke 23:46).

Hence, what we have here in 19:26, 27 is *the third word from the cross*. It was suffering for Jesus to see his mother among those who stood near the cross. He suffered because of her suffering. Standing at her side was the apostle John. The participle *standing* is masculine, and refers to John alone. Hence, one might paraphrase the sentence as follows: "Then when Jesus saw his mother, and when he saw the disciple whom he loved standing (by her side), he said to his mother," etc. On the phrase "the disciple whom he loved" see Vol. I, pp. 3-31; also on 13:23; and for the verb in distinction from its synonym see 21:15-17. No one understood Jesus better than did John. Moreover, the Lord's love for him evoked the response of love. Hence, we see him here at the cross.

Jesus, then, taking note of these two said to his mother, "Woman, look! Your son!" It was very kind of him to say, "Woman," and not, "Mother." The word "Mother" would have driven the sword even more deeply into the soul of Mary, that sharp and painful sword of which Simeon had spoken (Luke 2:35). Here at the cross, exactly as at Cana's wedding (see Vol. I, p. 115), it was very kind of Jesus to emphasize by the use of the word *woman* that Mary must no longer think of him as being merely her son; for, the more she conceives of him as her son, the more also will she suffer when he suffers. Mary must begin to look upon Jesus as her *Lord*. Yes, even then she will suffer, but this suffering will be of a different nature. She will then know that though indescribably terrible, his agony is, nevertheless, glorious because of its purpose. She will then begin to concentrate on its redemptive meaning. Hence, not *mother* but *woman*. Mary's merely emotional suffering — as any mother would suffer for her son who was being crucified — must be replaced by something higher and nobler, that is, by adoration!

433

By saying, "Woman, look! Your son!" Jesus is committing Mary to the care of John, who, as has been shown (see on 19:25), may well have been her own nephew, the son of her sister Salome. It seems that John had a lodging in Jerusalem (so did Peter; see on 20:2), though his real home was in Galilee. The question might be raised, "But why was not Mary committed to the care of one of her other children?" The answer is: probably because they as yet had not received him by a living faith (see on 7:5). And besides, who could be expected to take better care of Mary than the disciple whom Jesus loved?

To that disciple Jesus said, "Look! Your mother!" John immediately understood, and from that hour took her to his own home.

That a lesson in the responsibility of children (think of Jesus) toward their parents (think of Mary) is implied here is true. But certainly that is not the main lesson. The *suffering* of Jesus in seeing Mary suffer, and especially *his wonderful love* — a *Savior's* concern for one of *his own*, far more than a *son's* concern for his *mother* — these are the things on which the emphasis should be placed.

28. After this, since Jesus knew that everything was now finished, he said, in order that the scripture might be accomplished, I am thirsty.

Having spoken words (1) — (4), Jesus knew that his work for others had now been completely accomplished. Throughout his earthly sojourn and especially on the cross he had suffered the wrath of God against sin so as to deliver his people from it and to merit for them everlasting salvation. The task had been brought to completion. Jesus knew this, for he knew all things both in their totality and one by one. For the knowledge of Jesus see also on 1:42, 47, 48; 2:24, 25; 5:6; 6:64; 16:30; 21:17.

Hence, turning now to his own need, he said, "I am thirsty." He said this in order that also with respect to his thirst prophecy might be fulfilled. Scripture was constantly being accomplished in the life and death of the Lord. See on 19:23, 24. In the present instance the prophecy of Ps. 22:15 and of Ps. 69:21b was being fulfilled. For Ps. 22 as a Messianic Psalm see on 19:23, 24; for Ps. 69 similarly see on 2:17 and on 15:25.

It has been suggested that Jesus desired to slake his agonizing thirst in order to be able to utter the loud cry recorded in Luke 23:46 (the seventh word; see on 19:26, 27). It is possible, but the text does not say anything to this effect.

Here also, as before, the emphasis is on the infinite love of the Lord, revealed in being willing to suffer burning *thirst* in order that for his people he might be the everlasting fountain of *living water*. For the physical suffering of Jesus see also on 19:18. For Jesus as the source of living water see on 4:10-15; and on 7:37-39.

29, 30. A vessel full of vinegar was lying there. So they stuck a sponge full of vinegar around a hyssop-stick and brought it to his mouth. And when Jesus had received the vinegar, he said, It is finished. And he bowed his head and gave up his spirit.

The vessel full of vinegar, sour wine such as soldiers drank, was the source by means of which the thirst of Jesus was assuaged. Even in the process of satisfying, in a small way, this raving physical need, Jesus was mocked. But John does not tell that part of the story. See Matt. 27:48, 49. He does, however, make mention of the fact that *they* (probably referring to the centurion and one of the soldiers, the latter acting as ordered by the former), having dipped a sponge into the vinegar-vessel (this is clearly implied), stuck it "around a hyssop-stick and brought it to his mouth," so that this liquid might bring some relief to his parched lips and throat.

Much has been written about this *hyssup*. Some see an error and would substitute a shorter and very similar term for the one that is translated *hyssup*. (Instead of ὑσσώπῳ they prefer ὑσσῷ.)[277] They point to the fact that hyssup is an herb which does not provide a long enough stalk to serve as a *reed* (Matt. 27:48) on which to affix a sponge. Hence, they "correct" the text and use the shorter Greek term, which means *pike*. But this is certainly not necessary. The hyssup or hyssup-stick to which John refers may have been the *marjoram* (Origanum maru), whose woody stalks are sufficiently sturdy and sufficient in length to satisfy all the requirements. It did not have to be very lengthy to reach the lips of Jesus, for the cross was probably not very high above the ground.

Having received the vinegar Jesus said, "It is finished" (or *consummated*). As Jesus saw it, the entire work of redemption (both active and passive obedience, fulfilling the law and bearing its curse) had been brought to completion. And if someone should object that the burial had not yet taken place and that this too (as well as the repose in the tomb until the moment of the resurrection) was part of Christ's humiliation, the answer would be very simple: in the mind of Christ the burial is so certain that he can speak as if that too had already been accomplished. See also, in this connection, on 17:4 and on 17:11.

Having said this, Jesus bowed his head — just before doing so, speaking one more word, Luke 23:46 — and gave up his spirit. He *gave* it. No one took it away from him. He laid down his life. See on 10:11; also on 19:34-37. For the meaning of the term *spirit* see on 13:21, especially footnote 139.

---

[277] So, for example, E. J. Goodspeed, *Problems of New Testament Translation*, Chicago, 1945, pp. 115, 116. Thus also Joachim Camerarius, Sylburg, Beza, Boisius, Cobet, Dalman, Howard. See also F. Field, *Notes on the Translation of the New Testament*, Cambridge, 1899, pp. 106 ff.

31-33. Then the Jews, since it was the Preparation, in order that on the sabbath the bodies might not remain on the cross — for great was the day of that sabbath — asked Pilate that their legs might be broken and that they might be removed. So the soldiers came and broke the legs of the first and of the other who had been crucified with him. But when they came to Jesus and saw that he was dead already, they did not break his legs.

At times the Sanhedrists could be very scrupulous in observing the details of the ceremonial law. Was it not true that the land would be defiled if a body was hanging all night upon a tree? See Deut. 21:23. Such defilement would be even worse if bodies remained on the cross on the sabbath. It was getting later in the afternoon (the afternoon of the Preparation, that is, of Friday; see on 19:14, 42); it was going toward sun-set, that is, toward sabbath. Moreover, this particular sabbath was "very great," for it was the sabbath of the Passover-feast, a feast of seven days.

So the Jews (probably the chief priests) asked Pilate that the legs of the crucified persons might be broken, in order that death might result immediately. Then the bodies could be removed and everything could be over before sabbath.

Such breaking of the bones (*crurifragium,* as it is called) by means of the heavy blows of a hammer or iron was frightfully inhuman. It caused death, which otherwise might be delayed by several hours or even days. Says Dr. S. Bergsma in an article to which I shall refer more in detail a little later (see on verses 34-37): "The shock attending such cruel injury to bones can be the coup de grace causing death."

Pilate readily granted permission. John saw how the soldiers crushed the bones of the two malefactors. He also saw that upon noticing that Jesus had already died, they did not break his bones. It is altogether probable that they refrained from doing so upon orders from the centurion, on whom the central Sufferer had made such a deep impression (Luke 23:47). Does it not seem probable also that Joseph of Arimathea (see on verse 38) had already made known to the centurion that he was going to ask Pilate for permission to take down the body of Jesus?

34-37. But one of the soldiers with a spear pierced his side, and immediately there came out blood and water. And he who has seen it has testified and genuine is his testimony, and he knows that he is telling the truth, in order that y o u also may continue to believe. For these things took place in order that the scripture might be fulfilled:

> **Not a bone of him shall be broken.**
> **And again another scripture says:**
> **They shall look upon him whom they pierced.**

In order to insure that not the slightest possibility would exist that any life had remained in the body of Jesus, one of the soldiers with his lance or spear pierces the side of Jesus. If the spear was held in the right hand, as is probable, it was in all likelihood the left side of Jesus that was pierced. *Immediately there came out blood and water.*

John enlarges upon this fact, devoting no less than four verses to it. He must have had a purpose in doing so. It is altogether probable that he was trying to tell his readers that Christ, the Son of God, *actually died* (according to his human nature). The death of Jesus was not a mere semblance; it was *real*. The apostle had been there himself, and had seen the blood and the water flowing from the side of the Lord. Let all docetics take notice! See also Vol. I, p. 33.

But what caused this *blood and water* to issue from the opening made by the spear? Much has been written about this. Consult the various commentaries; also the article *Blood and Water* in I.S.B.E. According to that article the physiological explanation might be this, that the death of Jesus resulted from rupture of the heart in consequence of great mental agony and sorrow. Such a death would be almost instantaneous, and the blood flowing into the pericardium would coagulate into the red clot (blood) and the limpid serum (water). This blood and water would then be released by the spear-thrust. The article mentions the names of several distinguished physicians who have accepted this theory.

Very recently Dr. Stuart Bergsma, prominent physician in Grand Rapids, Mich. (formerly missionary-doctor in Ethiopia — Surgeon of the Tafari Makonnen Hospital, George Memorial Building, Addis Ababa —; later missionary-doctor in India; author of *Rainbow Empire*, Grand Rapids, Mich., 1932; and of *Sons of Sheba*, Grand Rapids, Mich., 1933) wrote an excellent article on this subject. It appeared in the March, 1948 issue of *Calvin Forum*. Dr. Bergsma has kindly permitted me to quote from his article.

He wisely refrains from drawing a definite conclusion. The matter is too uncertain, and specialists on heart-diseases (and particularly on the rupture of the heart) do not seem to be in complete agreement. Nevertheless, it is clear from the article that Dr. Bergsma leans somewhat toward the ruptured-heart theory as an explanation of the blood and water issuing from the side of Jesus. He went about his task with characteristic thoroughness and consulted several specialists in the field of the heart and its rupture. In his article he quotes the sources (published books and articles and private correspondence).

Before we enter into this subject more fully, some erroneous ideas should be swept away:

1. The proposition "Jesus died of a broken heart," generally evokes immediate opposition. We are so used to interpreting such phraseology meta-

phorically. Thus, with reference to a person who has been sorely wounded in his affections, we are apt to say, "That broke his heart." Now it is certainly true that Jesus did not die of disappointment. He died a victor. When we speak about the possibility that the blood and the water issuing from the side of the Lord indicate previous heart-rupture, we are using the term heart-rupture in a purely physiological sense.

2. Another error which needs to be removed is this, that if Jesus died of a broken heart, he did not *lay down* his life. His death, then, was not a voluntary sacrifice. — Such a conclusion is, of course, entirely erroneous! *Jesus most surely laid down his life in voluntary sacrifice.* That is the clear teaching of Scripture throughout, especially 10:11; see on that passage. But let us imagine, for a moment, that Jesus, while knowing full well that taking upon himself the wrath of God will break his heart, decides to do so anyway, would we then be able to say that his death was not voluntary? The voluntary character of our Lord's death would certainly not be diminished in any way whatever.

3. One more error must be removed, namely, that the *spear-thrust* caused the death. That is absolutely erroneous; for, the inspired writer, before saying anything about the piercing of Christ's side, has already written, "And when Jesus had received the vinegar, he said, 'It is finished.' And he bowed his head and gave up his spirit." *What John writes with reference to the spear-thrust was not written in order to describe what caused Christ's death, but in order to show that Jesus had actually died!* Besides, as Dr. S. Bergsma says in his article, "To presuppose, as some do, that the spear pierced the still living heart, and thus to account for the blood and water is contrary . . . to science, for pure blood would have issued forth. It was in the crucifixion itself that his death was to be accomplished, not in a spear-thrust by a soldier."

Having disposed of these errors we shall now state the position of Dr. Bergsma, quoting his words:

"In my own opinion, which I humbly maintain unsupported by the first four authorities quoted, but certainly supported by the last two quoted, the presence of any considerable quantity of serum and blood clot, issuing after a spear wound as described above, could only come from the heart or the pericardial sac. We must agree from the outset that no pre-existing disease affected Christ's body. He was a perfect lamb of God. It is extremely rare, well-nigh impossible, authorities say, for the normal heart-muscle to rupture. Christ, however, suffered as no man before or since has suffered. Ps. 69:20 says prophetically, 'Reproach has broken my heart.' The next verse continues, 'They gave me gall for my food; and in my thirst they gave me vinegar to drink.' We take the second prophecy as literally fulfilled, but many consider it fantastic to take verse 20 also literally. If Christ's heart did not rupture, it is difficult to explain any accumulation of *blood and water* as described by John. The normal pericardial effusion of an ounce or less would be a mere trickle unobserved by anyone."

John writes that he has seen this. He is giving authoritative testimony of that which with his own eyes he has witnessed. For the verb *to testify* see on 1:7, 8. This testimony is genuine. "He" — probably referring to Christ — knows that John is telling the truth. He is telling the truth with reference to the blood and water (proving both that Christ had actually taken upon himself the human nature, and that in his human nature he actually died) in order that the readers may not be swept off their feet by docetic heresies, but may *continue to* believe. See also on 20:30, 31.

It is not at all impossible that the highly symbolical Gospel of John intends to link this *blood* and *water* with the effects of Christ's atonement; somewhat as we do to-day when we sing:

"Let the water and the blood,
From thy wounded side which flowed,
Be of sin the double cure,
Cleanse me from its guilt and power."

I John 5:6 may point in that direction. Cf. John 3:5; 7:37-39.

When John saw how the soldiers were restrained from breaking the bones of Christ, he saw in this a fulfilment of the words recorded in Ex. 12:46; Num. 9:12. No bone of the paschal lamb was to be broken. Christ was the true paschal lamb. See on 1:29; read also I Cor. 5:7.

When the apostle observed the piercing of Christ's side, he saw in this the fulfilment of the prophecy of Zech. 12:10. For the general import of Zechariah's prophecies see on 12:14, 15. The words of the prophet are quoted here not according to the LXX but more nearly according to the original Hebrew. The same prophecy, in slightly modified form, is found in Rev. 1:7. For the present — here in 19:37 — all that is meant is that the spear-thrust fulfilled the prophecy.

Synthesis of 19:17-37

See the Outline on p. 374. *The Son of God Dying as a Substitute for His People. The Crucifixion*

A. Jesus carrying the cross; nailed to the cross between two criminals.

The King of the Jews crucified between two criminals. By the governor this arrangement was probably ordered as an insult to the Jews. But now the other side: the Savior crucified between two sinners, one of whom was going to be saved. By God (and in fulfilment of prophecy) this arrangement was providentially effected in order to depict the glorious purpose of the cross.

B. The dispute about the superscription.

Though Pilate did not know it, this superscription was inspired! God himself really wrote it. It was inspired in what was omitted: there was no mention at all of any sin. It was also inspired in what it expressed: the King of the Jews crucified in order that the King of both Jew and Gentile, — elect from every nation — might be made manifest.

C. The division of the garments.

A marvelous fulfilment of prophecy this, and a bearing of the curse in order to free us from it. As to the fraction printed in the explanation on verse 24, I do not vouch for its accuracy. I wrote it down, nevertheless, because I am convinced that it points in the direction of the truth, namely, the truly astonishing fulfilment of prophecy in connection with Christ. Who can listen to a rendition of the Messiah and not be impressed by this?

D. The Word to Mary and to John.

The most loving heart (that of John) stood closest to Jesus. To him alone the care of Mary was entrusted. That also reveals the "character" of Jesus.

E. Jesus' thirst; his death.

The very Gospel which loudly proclaims Christ's deity also most strikingly reveals his humanity. It was in his human nature — and in his human nature *only* — that he suffered. The divine nature cannot suffer. Between the cry, "I thirst" and the cry, "It is finished," very little time intervened. Then he *gave up* his spirit. *The voluntary character of this deed cannot be emphasized too strongly.* Of course, this does not in any way rule out the idea of *a physical cause* which brought about his physical death. But that physical cause, too, was completely in his power.

F. The piercing of his side.

In addition to what has already been said, note the following:

1. The theory of the ruptured heart (previous to the spear-thrust!) has the following points in its favor:

a. It takes very seriously the prophecy of Ps. 69:20 ("Reproach has broken my heart"), and it accepts the same literal fulfilment of this prophecy as is commonly accepted with reference to the next verse ("They gave me also gall for my food; And in my thirst they gave me vinegar to drink").

b. It is argued that this theory gives a reasonable explanation for the issuance of blood and water, which other theories fail to do.

c. This theory emphasizes the greatness of Christ's mental and spiritual agony. Ordinarily death by crucifixion might not cause the heart to rupture, but this was no ordinary death. This Sufferer bore the wrath of God against sin. He suffered eternal death, the pangs of hell!

2. This theory has the following weaknesses:

a. It is no more than a possibility. To raise it to the rank of probability we would have to have more information than has been furnished in the

440

Gospel. So, for example, we cannot even prove that the side which was pierced was the left side.

b. Post-mortem findings with reference to individuals who died by crucifixion are lacking. Even if we had them, they still would not be able to show what could have happened in the case of *this* unique Sufferer.

c. A miracle may have occurred, or there may be another non-miraculous way to account for the issuance of blood and water. We simply do not know.

As has been pointed out, Dr. Bergsma has expressed himself with great and commendable caution. His article is worthy of careful study.

One point, already stressed in the exegesis, should be emphasized once more:

The inspired record is not interested in showing us how it was that blood and water issued from the side of Jesus. It is only interested in revealing the fact as such. Hence, our own attention should be mainly fixed upon that point. Blood and water actually came forth from the side of Jesus. Hence, he was most certainly human, having a real human body. He had most certainly died. His blood and his Spirit will most certainly cleanse from sin. Prophecy most certainly was fulfilled, both in the omission of the crurifragium in his case and in the issuance of blood and water.

---

38 Now after these things Joseph of Arimathea, being a disciple of Jesus but because of fear for the Jews a secret one, requested Pilate that he might take away the body of Jesus; and Pilate gave permission. So he came and took away his body. 39 And there came also Nicodemus, who at an earlier occasion had come to him by night, bringing a mixture of myrrh and aloes, about a hundred pounds. 40 Then they took the body of Jesus, and bound it in linen bandages, along with the aromatics, as is the burial custom of the Jews.
41 Now in the place where he was crucified there was a garden, and in that garden a new tomb, in which no one had ever yet been laid. 42 There, accordingly, because of the Jews' (day of) Preparation, since the tomb was nearby, they laid Jesus.

19:38-42

19:38, 39, 40. Now after these things Joseph of Arimathea, being a disciple of Jesus but because of fear for the Jews a secret one, requested Pilate that he might take away the body of Jesus; and Pilate gave permission. So he came and took away his body. And there came also Nicodemus, who at an earlier occasion had come to him by night, bringing a mixture of myrrh and aloes, about a hundred pounds. Then they took the body of Jesus, and bound it in linen bandages, along with the aromatics, as is the burial custom of the Jews.

We print these three verses together because Joseph and Nicodemus acted in concert. They must have agreed together beforehand as to what each would do. Hence, they came thoroughly prepared. That some women were also present is clear from the other Gospels. See, for example, Luke 23:55.

After everything had been accomplished and it had been definitely established that Jesus was actually dead, Joseph of Arimathea appeared upon the scene. He was a rich man (Matt. 27:57), devout (Mark 15:43), and a member of the Sanhedrin (Luke 23:51), one who had not consented (by being absent during the balloting?) to the plot to condemn Jesus and to have him crucified (Luke 23:51). The Arimathea from which he came was probably the ancient Ramathaim-zophim, situated a little way over twenty miles north-west of Jerusalem, or fifteen miles straight east from Joppa.

Only *secretly* had he been a disciple of Jesus. He had been filled with sinful fear; thinking, perhaps, that if he should do anything for Jesus, the other members of the Sanhedrin would dismiss him from their council, and not only from their council but even from the synagogue. See on 7:13; 9:22; and 20:19. But now, as a fruit of Christ's atoning death and love for him, this man has suddenly become very courageous. He goes to Pilate and requests the body of Jesus. Mark 15:43 stresses the boldness of the act. The boldness appears especially in this, that he acted in spite of the fact that he knew that his fellow-Sanhedrists would hear about it!

Pilate, having ascertained that Jesus had really died (Mark 15:44), granted the request. So Joseph returned to Calvary and, with the help of others, took the body from the cross. Just how this was done has not been revealed. We shall leave it to the artists to fill in this gap.

What we do know is that Joseph had the willing cooperation of Nicodemus. For Nicodemus see also on 3:1-21 and on 7:50-52. While Joseph furnished the linen bandages and his own new tomb (Matt. 27:60), Nicodemus provided the spices or aromatics. He brought a mixture of myrrh and aloes. The *myrrh* had probably been derived from a small tree with odoriferous wood, namely, the Balsamodendron of Arabia; the *aloes* from a large tree, the Agallocha, whose wood contains resin and furnishes powdered perfume. Nicodemus had bought a mixture of these two, not less than one hundred *pounds* by weight. For this weight-measure see also on 12:3. One hundred of these pounds amounted to about seventy-two of our pounds avdp., surely no insignificant contribution.

As the linen bandages were wound around the body, limb by limb, the mixture of myrrh and aloes was strewn in. That was the manner in which the Jews prepared their dead for burial. They did not *embalm* like the Egyptians, who removed brain and entrails.

41, 42. Now in the place where he was crucified there was a garden, and in that garden a new tomb, in which no one had yet been laid.

442

There, accordingly, because of the Jews' (day of) Preparation, since the tomb was nearby, they laid Jesus.

The body of Jesus was carried to a tomb. As this tomb figures prominently in the account of the resurrection, it is necessary to bestow more than merely passing attention upon it. We shall itemize the points of information which Scripture (and to a small measure Archaeology) furnishes with respect to this tomb. From a list of recent archaeological material we select a few titles; see the footnote.[278]

(1) *Its location.* The tomb was located in the immediate proximity of Calvary: "In the place where he was crucified there was a garden." Since we do not know where Calvary was, we do not know either where this tomb was. See on 19:17. Some travelers who have seen the "Garden Tomb," in a secluded spot beneath a hill that has the shape of a human skull, are convinced that this tomb, with its ante-chamber and roomy tomb-chamber, with only one place finished where a body can rest, is the one to which the Gospel-account refers. It must be admitted that in many respects the description of this tomb fits the information which one can glean from the Gospel-accounts. Others who have also seen and investigated the site, are not at all convinced, and claim that the Garden tomb is probably of far more recent date than the first century A. D. It is probably impossible to reach any definite conclusion with respect to the identity of the sepulchre in which the body of Jesus was laid. And why should this be considered deplorable?

Kind providence provided a *near-by* tomb. It was the Jews' day of Preparation. See on 19:14, 31. In other words, it was Friday. Sunset was approaching. Hence, in order that everything might be finished before sabbath, no time must be lost. The body of Jesus could not be buried in a distant tomb. Time would not allow.

(2) *Its newness.* This tomb was *new.* See also on 13:34. It was new in the sense that it had never been used. Decay and decomposition had never entered it. This was a fit resting-place for the body of the Lord. Cf. Ps. 16:10.

(3) *Its owner.* According to Matt. 27:60 it was Joseph's own tomb. And Joseph was a rich man. Hence, Is. 53:9 occurs to the mind immediately, "And (he was) with a rich man in his death."

---

[278] George W. Elderkin, *Archaeological Paper, VII: Golgotha, Kraneion and the Holy Sepulchre,* Springfield, Mass., 1945; W.H.A.B., p. 99; A. Van Deursen, *Bijbels Beeld Woordenboek,* Kampen, 1947, pp. 72, 73; E. L. Sukenik, *The Earliest Records of Christianity,* A Special Abstract from *The American Journal of Archaeology,* Menasha, Wis., October-December, 1947. This is a description of a family-tomb near Jerusalem. The tomb was in use from the first century B. C. to the first half of the first century A. D. The description of this tomb should be compared with the biblical information regarding Christ's tomb. There are certain points of resemblance; also certain differences.

(4) *Its general appearance.* This tomb was not a natural cave. It had been hewn out of a solid cliff or rock (Mark 15:46). After depositing the body of Jesus, Joseph (with the help of others, of course) rolled a great stone in front of the entrance of the tomb-chamber (Matt. 27:60). This particular stone was *very heavy* (or *very large*) (Mark 16:4). The entrance to the tomb-chamber was low, as is evident from the fact that Mary had to stoop to look into the tomb (20:11). So did Peter (20:5; Luke 24:12). At the foot-end and at the head-end of the place where the body was laid the rock was left thick enough to form a kind of seat (20:12).

It is clear that the tomb-chamber of Joseph's sepulchre did not contain a shaft or niche (kôk) into which the body of Jesus was shoved endwise. In Palestine there are many graves of this character, but *this* was not one of them, for in that case the angels could not have been sitting at the foot-end and at the head-end!

It would seem that the tomb-chamber of Joseph's sepulchre was provided (not with a shelf or bench but) with a declivity — a place where the floor had been hewn out a little lower — in which the body of Jesus could rest.

Picture, therefore, the tomb of Joseph. It has: a. *low entrance* to the tomb-chamber; b. a *very heavy stone* (probably round, and rolling in a groove) in front of this entrance; c. a *seal* affixed to the stone (at the request of the Sanhedrists, Matt. 27:66), that is, a cord covered with clay or wax, on which a seal has been impressed; see article "Seal" in I.S.B.E.; d. a *tomb-chamber* with elevations where persons could sit, and between these: f. a *declivity* in which the body of Jesus rested.

Some assume that there was a roofless courtyard or ante-chamber, formed by a low semi-circular wall, in front of the tomb-chamber. Others deny this. It make no essential difference in the interpretation.

We see the exceedingly heavy stone, the seal, the guard. "Have a guard; go, make it as sure as y o u can," Pilate said to the Sanhedrists who came to bother him Saturday-morning. "He that sits in the heavens shall laugh. The Lord will have them in derision" (Ps. 2:4). See the next (resurrection) chapter, John 20.

Synthesis of 19:38-42

See the Outline on p. 374. *The Son of God Dying as a Substitute for His People. The Entombment*

The burial of Jesus was a necessary element in his humiliation. By means of it he sanctified the grave for all his followers. In the entombment prophecy was fulfilled. (See the exegesis.) The chief actors were Joseph of Arimathea and Nicodemus, whose courage must be admired. The tomb was located in Joseph's garden, in the immediate vicinity of the cross. The exact spot cannot be pointed out today. This is something for which we may well thank God. Had it been known, *the place* would probably have received more honor than *the Christ*. (Some of that spirit, in fact, prevails even today, in connection with those places which are advertised as being authentic.) The tomb was equipped with what was probably a low entrance, in front of which was rolled a very heavy stone, to which a seal was affixed by order of Pilate at the request of the Sanhedrin; lastly, there was the roomy tomb-chamber with probably a declivity for the body of Jesus. In this tomb, because of its nearness, and because sabbath was approaching, the body of Jesus was placed.

Although the entombment is an element in Christ's humiliation, nevertheless it affords a foreglimpse of his exaltation: it is a *new* tomb. Decay has never entered it. The body of Jesus did not suffer corruption. God took care of that. The tomb belonged to a rich man. It was a tomb fit for a king! Here everything points to exaltation.

Outline of Chapters 20, 21

Theme: *Jesus, the Christ, the Son of God*
During His Private Ministry Triumphing Gloriously: Resurrection
and Appearances

I. 20:1-10 The Visit of Peter and John to the Tomb. Within the Tomb the Evidences of the Resurrection

II. 20:11-18 Appearance to Mary Magdalene

III. 20:19-23 Appearance to the Disciples except Thomas

IV. 20:24-31 Appearance to the Disciples, Thomas Also Present; Conclusion: Statement of the Purpose of the Gospel

V. ch. 21 Appearance at the Sea of Tiberias
  A. The Miraculous Catch of Fishes and the Breakfast on the Beach (verses 1-14)
  B. Peter's "Reinstatement"; Prediction concerning Peter; Correction of a Misunderstanding regarding Jesus' Statement about John; Concluding Testimonial (verses 15-25)

CHAPTER XX

20 1 Now on the first day of the week Mary Magdalene came to the tomb early, while it was still dark, and noticed the stone removed from the tomb. 2 So she ran and came to Simon Peter and to the other disciple, the one whom Jesus loved, and she said to them, "They have taken the Lord out of the tomb, and we do not know where they have laid him." 3 Then Peter came out and that other disciple, and they were coming toward the tomb. Now these two came running side by side. 4 But that other disciple started to run ahead, faster than Peter, and arrived at the tomb first. 5 And as he stooped, he noticed the linen bandages lying (there); however, he did not go inside. 6 Then Simon Peter also came, following him, and went into the tomb; and he observed the linen bandages lying (there), 7 and the sweat-band, which had been around his head, not lying with the linen bandages but folded up in a place by itself. 8 So then the other disciple, who had arrived at the tomb first, also went inside, and he saw and believed; 9 for they had not previously understood the Scripture, that he must rise from the dead. 10 Then the disciples went back again to their homes.

20:1-10

20:1. Now on the first day of the week Mary Magdalene came to the tomb early, while it was still dark, and noticed the stone removed from the tomb.

It is Sunday-morning, the first day *of the week.*[279] While it is still dark some women leave their homes (or temporary lodgings) "bringing the spices which they had prepared" (Luke 24:1). They came in order that they might anoint the corpse (Mark 16:1). Compare 12:1-8; contrast 19:38-40.

Who were these women? Mary Magdalene and Mary the mother of James (or simply "the other Mary") are mentioned by name in the other Gospels (Matt. 28:1; Mark 16:1; Luke 24:10). Mark adds Salome (Mark

---

[279] It makes little difference whether one conceives of the Greek plural for *sabbath* as referring to *the day* or to an entire *week* (the time from one day of rest to another). If the first is meant, then the idea is that this was the first day counting from the sabbath-day; hence, the first day after the sabbath-day. If the second is meant, the result is still the same: the day indicated is then not the last of the week but the first. In either case Sunday is meant. The plural noun used in the original may mean either *sabbath-day* or *week.*

16:1). Luke adds Joanna, and seems to indicate that there were others (Luke 24:10; cf. also Luke 23:55 and 24:1). See on 19:25.

John probably assumes that the readers are acquainted with the other Gospels and confines his story to Mary Magdalene. See Vol. I, pp. 31, 32. However, he implies that other women had accompanied Mary (20:2: *"we do not know"*).

Although it was still dark when the women started out, the sun had risen when they arrived at the tomb.

As they trudged sorrowfully out of Jerusalem's gate, they were worried about the huge stone (Mark 16:3) which had been placed at the tomb's entrance. For the appearance and location of the tomb see on 19:41, 42. But suddenly they saw — probably at a turn in the path — that the heavy slab had been turned away already; no, not merely turned away but actually removed (*lifted* out of its groove), sothat it was lying flat on the ground!

Nowhere is it stated that this stone had to be removed in order that Jesus might arise from the grave. That the resurrection-body of the Lord was such that he was able to leave the tomb even though the stone was not removed seems to be clearly implied in 20:26; see on that verse. Nevertheless, the stone had to be removed. This was necessary for two reasons: 1. In order to indicate that the grave had been conquered, that the victory had been achieved. 2. In order that Peter and John might be able to enter (see on 20:6, 8), and that everyone might be able to see that the tomb was empty!

While the mother of James the Less, the mother of James and John, Joanna, and the other women entered the tomb but did not find the body of the Lord Jesus (Luke 24:3), Mary Magdalene started to run away in order to get help in this terrible situation. She was convinced that the tomb had been rifled by enemies. For Mary Magdalene see on 19:25.

2. So she ran and came to Simon Peter and to the other disciple, the one whom Jesus loved, and she said to them, They have taken the Lord out of the tomb, and we do not know where they have laid him.

It is not at all surprising that Mary, greatly alarmed (cf. Mark 16:8), ran to Peter and to John. These two were probably regarded as the chief apostles. They were often seen together (see on 21:7). Nevertheless, although it is grammatically possible that they were lodging at the same address, the more natural interpretation of the original is that each had *his own* home in Jerusalem. See also 19:27 and 20:10. Both would be deeply concerned about Mary's baffling report. John was, moreover, *the disciple whom Jesus loved.* For the meaning of this expression see on 13:23, 24; for the identity of this apostle see Vol. I, pp. 3-31; and for the verb (*loved;* here in 20:2 the original employs the less usual verb, as is indicated in the Chart on p. 498) see on 21:15-17, especially footnote 306.

In terrified distress Mary exclaims, "They have taken the Lord out of the tomb, and we do not know where they have laid him." For Mary's state of mind see p. 470. The opened tomb was to Mary a reason for alarmed dismay. She thinks, "The enemies have been busy again. Having murdered the Lord, they have added to their crimes by rifling the tomb. *Now* not even the body of Jesus is left." It is interesting, nevertheless, that Mary is still calling Jesus "the Lord." See on 1:38 and on 12:21. This indicates *at least* that she had learned to regard him as her great Benefactor. This is not surprising; see on 19:25.

3, 4. Then Peter came out and that other disciple, and they were coming toward the tomb. Now these two came running side by side. But that other disciple started to run ahead, faster than Peter, and arrived at the tomb first.

Peter and John, perplexed by Mary's report, start out at once toward the tomb. At first they are pictured as merely *walking;* then as *running* side by side; finally, as still running, but now John is outdistancing Peter and therefore arrives at the tomb first. John in his old age recalls the scene as if it had happened yesterday. That is why the description is so lively.

Two questions are asked. The first is, "What caused these two men to change from *walking* to *running?* Was it, perhaps, a message of the women who by this time had left the tomb and had something very startling to say to the apostles?" See Matt. 28:1, 5-8 and parallels. We do not know.

The next question is, "What caused John to outrun Peter?" The answer could be: he has youth in his favor. But again, we do not know. It is useless to speculate.

5. And as he stooped, he noticed the linen bandages lying (there); however, he did not go inside.

Some prefer a different translation here. But the rendering "Having glanced he saw," sounds awkward. It may be granted that the verb employed in the original does not always and necessarily mean *to stoop.* Nevertheless, when it is used in connection with *saw* (or *noticed*), this is surely the most natural meaning. The entrance, as in many similar Oriental tombs today, was probably low. Hence, two actions were necessary: first, one had *to stoop.* Having stooped, one was able *to look* inside. It is not true that stooping would have made it impossible to see the linen bands in the declivity in which the body of Jesus had been placed. That would have been true only if the place for the body had been very deep.

As John stooped and looked, he saw *the linen bandages.* See on 19:40; also on 11:44 (where a synonym is used). The significance of these bandages lying there is discussed in connection with verses 6 and 7.

John did not go inside. He was filled with alarm. Any idea of a resurrection is completely absent from his mind.

6, 7. Then Simon Peter also came, following him, and went into the tomb; and he observed the linen bandages lying (there), and the sweat-band, which had been around his head, not lying with the linen bandages but folded up in a place by itself.

It is entirely in line with Peter's usual conduct that although he has been outdistanced by John, once at the tomb he enters before John does. See on 13:9. What John, from the outside looking in, had merely *noticed*, Peter, once inside, *observed*. He naturally saw *more* than John, and saw *more clearly*. And what he saw was truly marvelous. Here were the linen bandages lying very orderly, and the sweat-band, which had been around Christ's head, lying in a place by itself. For the bandages see on 19:40; also on 11:44 (the synonym). For the sweat-band see on 11:44. (In countries where the climate is hot even a handkerchief used by the living is called a *sweat-band*.)

Just what did all this mean? It is necessary to stress at this point that not more must be read into the text than is actually there. Ideas such as these, namely, that the headband was lying there as if it had not been removed from the head, and that the bandages were lying there just as if the limbs of Jesus were still enclosed by them, or as if the body had been abstracted from them, are foreign to the text. We do not even know exactly *where* the linen bandages and the sweat-band were lying. Neither John nor Luke (in his Gospel, 24:12) says anything about such matters. What Luke emphasizes is that the bandages were lying there *by themselves*, which, again, does not mean that they were being held in position mysteriously and in violation of the laws of gravity; but simply indicates that they were lying there *without the body*.

The facts which are actually related are wonderful enough without exegetical (?) embellishments. What they indicate is this: everything was orderly in the tomb. The body of the Lord was no longer there. No disciple had been there to remove it, nor had any enemy visited the tomb in order to pillage it. In either case the bandages would no longer have been present. Could it be that the Lord had himself removed the bandages and the sweat-band, had provided for himself a garment such as is worn by the living, had calmly and majestically "put everything in its place" in the tomb, putting the bandages *here* and the sweat-band *there* (neatly folded or rolled up in a place by itself), and had then departed from the tomb, gloriously alive?

It is not stated in so many words that *Peter* immediately drew this conclusion, namely, that Jesus was risen from the grave. It would seem, nevertheless, that he did soon reach this level of faith. He reached it a little later than John, perhaps after the two had discussed the matter together. See verse 9.

8, 9. So then the other disciple, who had arrived at the tomb first, also went inside, and he saw and believed; for they had not previously understood the Scripture, that he must rise from the dead.

John now also enters the tomb. For a description of the tomb see on 19:41, 42. He saw and believed. What did he see? Exactly what Peter had seen. What did he believe? That Jesus was actually risen from the dead, and was the real Messiah, the Lord of Glory, the Son of God in the most exalted sense. This is nothing less than living faith in the act of embracing the truth of the resurrection.

At this point some commentators seem to think that the purpose of the text is to emphasize the *weakness* of the apostles' faith, as if the meaning were on this order: the faith of these men was but a step removed from unbelief, for they needed *to see* before they were willing to believe. — However, that is probably not the sense of the words. What is meant is this: they *now* saw and believed. They *saw* the things which the Lord had arranged in such a manner as to arouse and strengthen faith. *Scripture* also began to take on a new meaning now. *Previously* such beautiful passages as Ps. 16:10, 11; Ps. 110:1, 4; Ps. 118:22-24; and Is. 53:11, 12 — passages which referred to Christ's resurrection — had meant very little to them. *Now* these same passages were beginning to assume significance! They now understood that Christ's glorious resurrection was a divine *must*. Cf. Luke 24:26. On and after Pentecost all this would become even clearer.

10. Then the disciples went back again to their homes. The climax has been reached. In the heart of John there is rejoicing, and this is (or *is soon to be*) true also with respect to Peter, as he himself testifies (I Pet. 1:3). So each goes to his respective lodging-place. At the home of John there is someone who must have been overjoyed to hear the story. That "someone" was the apostle's aunt, namely, Mary, the mother of Jesus. See on 19:27; then on 19:25.

---

11 But Mary was standing outside the tomb weeping. Then as she was weeping, she stooped to look into the tomb, 12 and she saw two angels sitting (there) in white garments, one at the head and one at the feet, where the body of Jesus had been lying. 13 And they said to her, "Woman, why are you weeping?" She said to them, "They have taken away my Lord, and I do not know where they have laid him." 14 On saying this, she turned around and saw Jesus standing (there), but she did not know that it was Jesus. 15 Jesus said to her, "Woman, why are you weeping, for whom are you looking?" Thinking that he was the gardener, she said to him, "Sir, if you have carried him away, tell me where you have laid him, and I will remove him." [280] 16 Jesus said to her, "Miriam." She turned and said to him in Aramaic, "Rabboni" (which means "Teacher"). 17 Jesus said to her, "Do not keep clinging to me, for I have not yet ascended to the Father. But

---

[280] I D; see Vol. I, pp. 40, 41.

go to my brothers and say to them, 'I ascend to my Father and y o u r Father, and
to my God and y o u r God.' " 18 Mary Magdalene went and announced to the
disciples, "I have seen the Lord," and (she told them) that he had said these
things to her.

20:11-18

**20:11, 12. But Mary was standing outside the tomb weeping. Then as she
was weeping, she stooped to look into the tomb and she saw two angels
sitting (there) in white garments, one at the head and one at the feet,
where the body of Jeus had been lying.**

The story now returns to Mary Magdalene. See on 19:25 and on 20:1, 2.
It is reasonable to suppose that she was a little slower in arriving at the
tomb than were Peter and John. There are those who think that on her
way back to Joseph's garden Mary met the two apostles, who related to her
what they had seen in the tomb; and that, as a result, Mary's fear that
robbers had stolen the body of Jesus vanished, sothat she now imagined
that friendly hands had removed it. However, if such a meeting took place,
we would be forced to conclude that the thrilling conviction, which had
been instilled in the hearts of Peter and John as a result of what they had
seen, had made little impression on Mary. This, of course, is possible.
Nevertheless, since nothing in the record suggests a conversation between
the apostles, on the one hand, *after* they had been in the tomb, and Mary,
on the other hand, it is better to abandon this theory entirely. It is probably safe to state that Mary returned to the tomb all alone, and that on the
way she did not stop to engage in conversation with anyone.

So Mary was standing outside the tomb *weeping*. For the meaning of this
verb see on 11:31, 32 (and compare with the verb used in 11:35; see also
on that verse). Her poignant grief expressed itself in constant, unrestrained
sobbing. While she was giving vent to her bitter sorrow, she stooped to
peer into the tomb (see on verse 5). She saw two angels sitting, one at the
head and the other at the feet, where the body of Jesus had been lying.

It must be deemed probable that these two angels appeared in the form
of young men (cf. Mark 16:5). Their white garments indicated holiness
(perhaps also joy and victory). They symbolized the triumph of life over
death, of light over darkness, of grace over sin. For the general appearance
of the tomb and the place where the angels sat see on 19:41, 42.

But why did these angels appear to the women and not to Peter and
John? Was it because the faith of the women was so much weaker than
that of the men that it was in need of the extra support of the ministry of
angels? This answer has been suggested, but we find nothing in the record
to prove it. One might, in fact, go in the opposite direction and say that
the appearance of these angels and the message which they brought (first

to the other women, Matt. 28:5-7; then, to Mary, John 20:13) was a special reward for the singular ministry of love in which these women, including Mary, had been engaged. But the best answer is the simple admission that we do not know why the angels appeared to the women (in the present instance, to Mary) and not to the men.

Heaven takes a vital interest in Christ's resurrection. The *absence* of angels would have been surprising.

13. And they said to her, Woman, why are you weeping? Implied in the question which the angels ask is a message: "This is the time for joy, not for weeping." May we not add that the question is a tenderly-phrased expression of disapproval, as if the angels meant to say, "Has the Lord's teaching with respect to his approaching death and resurrection been entirely in vain? Mary, are you not ashamed of your unbelief?"

But so completely has sorrow and grief captured the soul of Mary that she is not frightened, no, not even startled by these angels or by their question. She seems to be even more at ease in their presence than, for example, in a recent book [281] "Jacobus" is in the presence of "Gabriel."

In the tempest-tossed mind of Mary there is room for only *one* thought which she expresses by answering, **They have taken away my Lord, and I do not know where they have laid him.**

One might also render this, "My Lord has been taken away," etc. Note: Mary still speaks of Jesus as her *Lord* (see on 20:2). Oh, if she only knew where the body was, she could carry out the purpose for which she had come to the tomb. Besides, just to be near him — even if it means no more than being near his dead body — will give a measure of satisfaction.

14. On saying this, she turned around and saw Jesus standing (there), but she did not know that it was Jesus. Mary has been peering into the tomb (20:11, 12). Now she turns around and looks in the opposite direction. Why? Here again there is room for theorizing. A few samples are: a. because Jesus had suddenly made his appearance, and the angels who saw him from their position in the tomb bowed in adoration, causing Mary to turn around in order to see why the angels did this; b. because the angels, beholding Jesus, pointed to him, hinting that Mary should look away from the tomb; c. because Mary heard someone approaching; d. because the angels suddenly vanished out of sight; etc. It has not pleased the Lord to answer. The one important fact is that Mary is now facing a person whom she does not recognize. See on the next verse:

15. Jesus said to her, Woman, why are you weeping, for whom are you looking? Again Mary hears *the same question* as was asked her a moment

---

[281] Arjen Miedema, *Talks With Gabriel* (translated from the Dutch by Henry Zylstra), Grand Rapids, Mich., 1950.

ago: "Woman, why are you weeping?" See on verse 13. Notice a very similar correspondence between the words of *the angel* to the women (Matt. 28:5, 7) and the words which they heard from the lips of *the Lord himself* a little later (Matt. 28:10). In the perfect kingdom there is perfect harmony. The angels say what their Lord says. And the question was most timely and appropriate, for surely *this* was not the proper time for weeping! The Stranger adds, "For whom are you looking?" Notice *whom*, not *what*. Although in her reply to the angels Mary had spoken about her *Lord*, she had not been looking for *him* but for his *corpse*. She had been looking for some*thing*, not for some*one*. When the One who addresses Mary now asks, "For *whom* are you looking," he is beginning to turn her thoughts in another and better direction. She must begin to look for a person, not a thing.

Thinking that he was the gardener she said to him, Sir, if you have carried him away, tell me where you have laid him, and I will remove him.
Why did Mary think that this person who addressed her was the man who took care of Joseph's garden? We answer:

1. Because, due to her unbelief, she was not looking for the resurrected Savior.

2. Perhaps, because Jesus looked different than before (see Mark 16:12; cf. 9:3). Yet, the fact that she took him to be the gardener proves that he had the common human form.

3. Because in the garden she expected to see a gardener or care-taker.

To this supposed gardener Mary says, "Sir, if you have carried him away, tell me where you have laid him, and I will remove him."

"Sir" is here the correct translation of the original; not "Lord." See Vol. I, p. 103, footnote 44. Mary now asks this person a favor: if he, for reasons of his own, has transferred the corpse, will he please tell Mary where he has laid it, sothat she may have it removed to some convenient place where she can bestow further care upon it? It is true that Mary actually says, "him," not "it," but it is clear that she is thinking of Christ's *body*. In connection with funerals similar language (personal instead of impersonal) is used even today.

Verse 16 probably implies that having said this, Mary, despairing perhaps of a satisfactory reply, turned around, sothat she was again looking toward the open tomb. This, after all, in a despondent woman, would not be strange. This interpretation of what happened is probably better than to assign a rather unusual meaning to the participle στραφεῖσα (for example, *having leaned forward*) as used in that verse.

16. Jesus said to her, Miriam. With infinite tenderness and warmth, in a tone which resembled that of former days, Jesus now addresses Mary by using just *one* word, "Miriam." [282] The original Aramaic name by which her parents and friends must have addressed her many a time, the name which Jesus had always used in speaking to her, is employed also in this instance. Jesus addresses her by her native name, in her native tongue!

She turned and said to him in Aramaic, Rabboni (which means Teacher). When Mary hears this word — her own name in her own language — spoken in that familiar way as only One person could ever pronounce it, she quickly turns away from the tomb and toward the speaker (see on verse 15) and with a word of dramatic surprise, glad recognition, and humble reverence exclaims, "Rabboni." Though this word (which originally meant *my master* or *my teacher*) has a *meaning* which closely approaches (and may even be identical with) that of "Rabbi," and is so translated by John ("Teacher") for the benefit of his non-Aramaic speaking readers in Asia Minor, in actual *usage* it was far less common than Rabbi. For the use of *Rabbi* see Vol. I, p. 103, footnote 44. The title *Rabboni* was given to only a few rabbis, for example, to Gamaliel I and Gamaliel II. It was often used with reference to God.

17. Jesus said to her, Do not keep clinging to me, for I have not yet ascended to the Father. What Jesus probably means is this: "Do not think, Mary, that by grasping hold of me so firmly (cf. Matt. 28:9), you can keep me always with you. That uninterruptible fellowship for which you yearn must wait until I have ascended to be forever with the Father." Jesus did not object to being *touched*. Otherwise, how can we explain his word to Thomas? See on 20:27. What he condemned was Mary's mistaken notion that the former mode of fellowship was going to be resumed, in other words, that Jesus would once again live in daily visible association with his disciples, both men and women. The fellowship, to be sure, would be resumed; but it would be far richer and more blessed. It would be the communion of the ascended Lord in the Spirit with his Church.[283]

But go to my brothers and say to them, I ascend to my Father and y o u r Father, and to my God and y o u r God.

---

[282] The Aramaic form is better attested than is the Greek here in 20:16.
[283] This rather common interpretation which is found in several of the commentaries is better, it seems to me, than the one according to which Jesus is telling Mary, "Do not stop me, for I'm in a hurry; I am on my way to heaven." Somewhat related ideas, for example, that John means to convey the thought that Jesus ascended that very day, or that only one week intervened between resurrection and ascension, hardly deserve discussion. John's Gospel clearly teaches three subsequent appearances; one that very evening (20:19-23); another, a week later (20:24-29); and a third "after these things," how long afterward we are not told (chapter 21). On the entire subject of Christ's ascension see also C. Stam, *De Hemelvaart Des Heren* (doctoral dissertation submitted to the Free University at Amsterdam), Kampen, 1950.

Both Mary Magdalene and the other women receive a message to be conveyed to the eleven. But while the other women must tell the men *what has happened* ("He is risen from the dead") and *where Jesus will meet them* ("He is going before y o u to Galilee; there y o u will see him"), Mary must announce to them what great event in the history of redemption is about to take place ("I ascend to my Father," etc.).

Jesus now calls his disciples by a new name: "brothers." (Cf. Ps. 22:23; 122:8; Heb. 2:11.) *A new relationship* — fellowship in the Spirit, about to be poured out — requires *a new name*, a name even more intimate than the very beautiful name "friends."

Brothers belong to one and the same family. They possess much in common. They share in the same inheritance. Thus every true believer is a joint-heir with Christ (Rom. 8:17). Thus, also, in the spiritual sense, God is not the Father of all men but only of those who, having been chosen from eternity, have embraced the Son by a living faith. These — these *all*, these *alone* — are Christ's brothers.

When we reflect on the fact that just a few days previously all these men had "left him and fled," it is all the more striking that Jesus, in tender mercy, is willing to call them his *brothers*.

What Mary must say to them as Christ's message for them is this, "I ascend (it is *about* to happen; it is *certain* to happen; hence present tense) to my Father and y o u r Father, and to my God and y o u r God." Jesus makes a distinction here, and at the same time emphasizes the closeness of fellowship between himself, his Father, and the disciples. *The distinction* is clearly evident from this, that he does not say, "I am ascending to *our* Father." *His* sonship differs from *theirs;* hence, he says, "to *my* Father and to y o u r Father." See on 1:14 for this distinction. *He* is Son by nature; *they* are sons by adoption. Hence, also "and to *my* God and y o u r God." Nevertheless, *the closeness* of fellowship is also stressed: the same God who is the Father of Jesus is also the Father of the disciples!

It is to this God and Father that Jesus is ascending. That is the message which must be transmitted to the disciples. It is at the same time the lesson which Mary needs to learn.

18. Mary Magdalene went and announced to the disciples, I have seen the Lord, and (she told them) that he had said these things to her.

Where the Lord went after appearing to Mary has not been recorded. Moreover, it is even a question whether, had it been recorded, we would have been able to grasp it, for it must be borne in mind that the period of his day-by-day visible association with his disciples is over. He simply *appears*, now to this one, then to that one; and we must not ask, "Where was he in the time which intervened between any two appearances?" We know very little about the character of the resurrection-body and about its coming and going.

With Mary the case is different. We learn that she did as she had been told. Mary must have been a deeply emotional woman. In a way, she reminds us of Peter. One moment you see her weeping profusely. Her whole heart is in these tears, so much so that even the presence of angels hardly registers. But the next moment — the moment of joyful recognition, when the resurrected Lord pronounced her name — all has changed. "Rabboni," she exclaims; and, arrived in the company of the disciples, she can hardly wait to shout, "I have seen the Lord." (For *Lord* see on 20:2, 13). No longer was she thinking about a corpse now. No, this was the living Lord, gloriously risen from the grave! — Mary conveyed her message, word for word, exactly as the Lord had told her to do. And these *words* must have been like apples of gold in a framework of silver.

---

19 Now when it was evening on that day, the first of the week, and out of fear for the Jews the doors were locked where the disciples were, there came Jesus, and he stood in their midst and said to them, "Peace to y o u." 20 And on saying this, he showed them his hands and his side. The disciples therefore rejoiced over seeing their Lord.
21 Then Jesus said to them again, "Peace to y o u. Just as the Father commissioned me, so I am sending y o u." 22 And on saying this, he blew and said to them, "Receive the Holy Spirit." 23 If y o u forgive the sins of any, they are forgiven them; [284] if y o u retain (those) of any, they are retained." [285]

20:19-23

20:19. Now when it was evening on that day, the first of the week, and out of fear for the Jews the doors were locked where the disciples were, there came Jesus, and he stood in their midst and said to them, Peace to y o u.

Note the stress that is laid on the specific day when Jesus appeared to the disciples with the exception of Thomas. John might have written, "Now when it was the evening of the first day." But he is far more definite. It is clear that he wants to emphasize that this was none other than the first day of the week. So he begins by saying, "Now when it was evening of *that* day." That already marks the day as the first day, in the light of the context (20:1). But he is not satisfied with this. So he continues, "that day, *the first of the week.*"

The New Testament everywhere singles out the day of Christ's resurrection as chief among the days of the week. See Matt. 28:1; Mark 16:2; Luke 24:1; John 20:1, 19, 26; Acts 20:7; I Cor. 16:2; Rev. 1:10.

---

[284] IIIA3; see Vol. I, pp. 42, 43.
[285] IIIB3; see Vol. I, p. 44.

For the meaning of "the first of the week" see on 20:1. It was evening. In the light of Luke 24:29, 33, 36 we have a right to conclude that it was no longer *early* in the evening when the great event recorded in the present paragraph took place. As the Jews compute the days it was no longer the first day of the week. But John, though a Jew, is writing much later than Matthew and Mark, and does not seem to concern himself with Jewish time-reckoning. See on 1:39.

Out of fear for the Jews (or *for fear of the Jews*) the disciples had locked the doors. For this fear inspired by the Jewish authorities (we think especially of the Sanhedrin) see on 7:13; 9:22; 14:27; 19:38. The rulers had brought about the death of *Jesus.* Were the apostles going to be next on the program of destruction? The exact place where the disciples gathered is not indicated. See, however, Acts 12:12.

It is not difficult to understand what had brought them together. There had been so many strange happenings and marvelous experiences that day that a meeting was in order. Jesus had already appeared to Mary Magdalene, to the women, to Cleopas and his companion, and to Peter. See on 21:1. Peter and John and also the women had been inside the tomb. What they had seen was just too wonderful for words. Indeed, it is not surprising that the disciples found each other's company this Sunday-evening.

Of a sudden, there came Jesus, and he stood in their midst! But how was that possible, with the doors locked? (The *doors* — plural — refers, perhaps, to *the gate of the house and the door of the room* in which they were; but may also indicate the two folding doors which formed the gate.)

To the question how this sudden appearance of Jesus was possible all kinds of answers have been given. Some of these answers must be rejected immediately; for example, Jesus had been hiding in the room; he "sneaked in" with the men of Emmaus; he entered through the (Oriental substitute for our) window; he descended from the roof; etc. Those who believe that the *human* nature of Christ was now in possession of the qualities of the *divine* nature answer that this human nature had now become omnipresent.[286] We have high respect for the faith and the scholarship of those who are inclined to accept this last view. Along with us they worship Jesus as the Son of God, and along with us they accept his Word as being infallible. In the battle against liberalism of every description they put many to shame. Nevertheless, we cannot accept this solution. We believe that neither in the state of humiliation nor in that of exaltation are the two natures ever confused or blended, sothat one partakes of the qualities of the other. We believe that our Lord Jesus Christ is to be acknowledged "in two natures *inconfusedly* and *unchangeably,* as well as indivisibly and inseparably" (Symbol of Chalcedon).

---

[286] So, for example, R. C. H. Lenski, *op. cit.*, p. 1340.

Moreover, we believe that the words "There *came* Jesus" are best interpreted literally. He not only suddenly *stood* in their midst, but he actually *came* and stood! Had his human nature been omnipresent, he would not have to *come* (unless this coming be taken in a metaphorical sense). To the question, "But how was it possible for Jesus, who was not a mere phantom but had a real body (though a resurrection-body) to come and stand, when the doors were locked?" Scripture gives no answer. Some day we'll understand. Stating it differently, one might also say, "The resurrection-body has different qualities than the pre-resurrection body" (I Cor. 15:42-44; cf. Phil. 3:21). But that is not really answering the question.

Jesus speaks peace to the surprised disciples. He said, "Peace to y o u." For explanation see on 14:27; 16:33; 20:21, 26. He said it now as the One who has actually merited this peace for them.

20. And on saying this, he showed them his hands and his side.

Much, very much, is implied in this statement:

1. The person standing in the midst of the little circle is really Jesus. He is not someone else. The marks in his hands (where the nails have been) and the wound in his side identify him.

2. This person has a real body. He has hands. He shows his side (probably the left side). He is not a phantom. Let all docetics take note. In John's day there were many.

3. It was not only *the spirit* of Christ that had arisen from the grave — as the liberals teach — but *the body* also! This was really a *bodily* resurrection.

4. The peace pronounced on the disciples — *pronounced* not only but actually *given* — was real; it had been bought at such a price! Let the disciples look at his hands and at his side. Then let them meditate and adore.

The disciples therefore rejoiced over seeing their Lord. Luke supplies the best commentary on this passage in John. Not immediately did the disciples rejoice. First, when they saw him standing there so suddenly, they were frightened. They thought that they were looking at a spirit or ghost. Then Jesus, in tender love, said, "Why are y o u troubled? And why do questionings arise in y o u r hearts? See my hands and my feet, that it is I myself; handle me and see; for a spirit does not have flesh and bones as y o u see me having." They rejoiced. Nevertheless, "they still disbelieved for joy." Jesus then said, "Do y o u have anything to eat here?" They gave him a piece of broiled fish. He took it and ate in their presence. Jesus then repeated words which he had formerly spoken. See Luke 24:36-49. When they finally believed without doubting any longer, it was because they could not do anything else. Note that according to John here in 20:20 — and bear in mind that John was there when it happened! — the disciples at

459

last saw in Jesus their exalted *Lord.* For the term see on 1:38; 12:21; cf. also 20:2, 13, 18.

21. Then Jesus said to them again, Peace to y o u. Just as the Father commissioned me, so I am sending y o u.

To all those present (the ten, the men from Emmaus, and others) Jesus repeats, "Peace to y o u." For the meaning see on 20:19. It is not strange that he repeated this word. His sudden appearance had caused instant alarm. Even though that fear had been largely allayed, and rejoicing had taken its place, the gracious words, bestowing peace on those present, could stand repetition.

By adding, "Just as the Father," etc., Jesus says in substance what he had said before. Hence, see on 17:18 for the explanation. There is, however, one important difference. In the former passage these words were addressed to *the Father* ("Just as *thou* didst send me into the world, so have I also sent them into the world"); now they are addressed to *the disciples* themselves (with a change of verb, which is, however, not very important): "Just as the Father commissioned (one might also translate *sent*) me, so I am sending y o u."

From the fact that there were others in the room besides the ten (Luke 24:33) — the ten had some welcome visitors who were *with them* (Luke 24:33) — some have concluded that there is nothing *official* about this *sending*. But though the words were meant for the entire Church, is it not true that the task of proclaiming the Gospel to the world is, nevertheless, carried out chiefly by means of those who were specially chosen? *Through them the entire Church brings God's message to the world.* Needless to say, *every believer* also has an important duty, namely, the duty of bearing witness joyfully and incessantly.

That Jesus has the *ten* (and in a sense also the absent apostle, Thomas; hence, the *eleven*) in mind follows also from the very similar or parallel passage in 17:18, 20. Note: "Just as thou didst send me into the world, so have I also sent them into the world . . . Neither concerning these only do I make request, but concerning those also who believe in me through their word." One might paraphrase this: "Just as thou didst send me into the world, so have I also sent *these eleven men* into the world . . . Neither concerning *these eleven men* only do I make request, but concerning those also who believe in me through their word."

The analogy between the sending of the Son as Mediator and the sending of the apostles has been explained in connection with 17:18. *The commissioning authority* is the same; *the message* is the same (nevertheless, there is this difference: Jesus through his atonement makes the message possible; the apostles simply proclaim it!); and *the men to whom it is proclaimed* are the same. Hence, "just as . . . so."

22, 23. And having said this, he blew, and said to them, Receive the Holy Spirit. If y o u forgive the sins of any, they are forgiven them; if y o u retain (those) of any, they are retained.

Having reminded his disciples of the fact that his resurrection in no sense relieved them of their divinely ordained task, Jesus *blew*. The best text does not read, "He blew *upon them*," but simply "He blew." This blowing (cf. on 3:8) had symbolic significance. It symbolized a particular gift of the Holy Spirit. In a sense, that gift is given to the entire Church. Nevertheless — see also on verse 21 — it is to be exercised by the officers, by them alone, by them corporately. This particular gift which is here indicated is that of forgiving or retaining sins, which in this connection must mean, *declaring* that someone's sins are either forgiven or retained (unforgiven).

That the apostles cannot act independently, that is, apart from the Spirit who speaks in the Word, is already evident from the fact that the gift is linked with the Spirit! "Receive the Holy Spirit . . . If y o u forgive the sins of any, they are forgiven," etc. Absolutions pronounced arbitrarily have no standing in heaven. Only then has the Church, acting through its officers, the right to declare sins forgiven or retained when it acts in harmony with the Spirit-inspired Word.

But when its actions are in conformity with the Word (which demands that discipline be exercised in the spirit of love), then this power is very real, and has reference to *anyone* (whoever he may be) whose sins are declared to be either forgiven or retained.

But since the Church can only *declare* that which God *has already done* (cf. Mark 2:7), we read, "If y o u forgive the sins of any, they *have been* (and continue to be; hence, *are*) forgiven them; if y o u retain (those) of any, they *have been* (and continue to be; hence, *are*) retained." [287]

This passage certainly suggests Matt. 16:19; 18:18. It is clear that the Matthew passages refer to the authority which the Church exercises by means of the apostolic office. It would, therefore, seem logical that here in John 20:33 the meaning is the same. But by many writers any notion of *office* is being rejected vigorously.[288]

---

[287] Much has been written, especially during the last few years, concerning the exact meaning of the perfect tense in the case of both of these verbs which appear in the apodoses; for example, W. T. Dayton, *Greek Perfect Tense in Relation to John 20:23, Matt. 16:19, and Matt. 18:18* (unpublished Th.D. dissertation submitted to the Faculty of Northern Baptist Theological Seminary, Chicago, Ill. 1945); R. A. Baker, "The Forgiveness of Sin: An Interpretation of Matt. 16:19; 18:18; and John 20:23, *"Review and Expositor,* 41 (1944), 224-235; see also H. J. Cadbury's article on this subject in *JBL* 58 (Sept., 1939).

[288] We read such statements as the following: "The rise of ecclesiastical law and the constitution of the Church is an apostasy from the conditions intended by Jesus himself and originally realized" (Sohm's statement quoted with approval by A. Harnack, *The Constitution and Law of the Church,* New York, 1910, p. 5); "There is no

Office implies a divinely appointed task with authority (given to certain men and not to others) to carry it out. This authority has reference to *life* and *doctrine*. That it was established by Christ and exercised by the apostles is clear from such passages as Matt. 16:18, 19 (does not the very idea of a *key* — to open and to close — imply authority? and does not binding and loosening — whatever be its meaning — do the same?) 18:18; 28:18; I Cor. 5:3, 4; II Cor. 10:8. That this authority was through their mediation laid upon ministers and elders sothat these also have an office and are clothed with authority is clear from the following: Acts 14:23; 20:28; I Tim. 1:18; 3:1, 5; 4:14; 5:17; II Tim. 4:1, 2; Tit. 1:5-9; 3:10; Rev. 2:20.

This authority — which according to John 20:23 implies the right of expelling from the Church and of restoring the sinner to its fellowship — must ever be exercised in the spirit of love. It has as its purpose "the perfecting of the saints, the work of ministering, the building up of the body of Christ" (Eph. 4:12); and its ultimate goal may be expressed in these beautiful words: "until we all attain to the unity of the faith, and of the knowledge of the Son of God, to a fullgrown man, to the measure of the stature of the fulness of Christ" (Eph. 4:13).

The apostles who were gathered in this room on this glorious Easter day needed this comfort. In themselves they were weak and sinful. This had been demonstrated again and again, also during the last few days. Did they still have the right to call themselves *apostles,* Christ's official representatives, chosen to bring his message to the children of men and to exercise authority in the company of believers? The risen Savior speaks this word of encouragement. Without authority, chaos reigns supreme!

---

24 But Thomas, one of the Twelve, the one called the Twin, was not with them when Jesus came. 25 So the other disciples were saying to him, "We have seen the Lord." He, however, said to them, "Unless I see in his hands the mark of the nails and put my finger into the place of the nails, and put my hands into his side, I definitely will not believe." [289]

---

trace in Scripture of a formal commission of authority for government from Christ himself" (F. J. A. Hort, *The Christian Ecclesia,* London, 1897, p. 84); "The apostolate was founded by Jesus himself, not as an ecclesiastical office, but as a preaching ministry" (Carl von Weiszäcker, *The Apostolic Age of the Christian Church,* London, 1894); and "The authority of the apostolate was of a spiritual, ethical, or personal kind. It was not official" (J. C. Lambert, art. "Apostle" I.S.B.E.).

O. Linton, who defends the idea of the apostolic office, summarizes the views of those who oppose it as follows: "Alles amtliche wird ängstlichst vermieden. Diese Lehr ist der gerade Gegenpol zu der Katholischen Ansicht. Nach dieser war der Apostel der von Jesus selbst zur Regierung der Kirche Bevollmachtigte." And again: "Jesus habe die Apostel nur zum Predigen und zum Dienst an der Gemeinde bestellt, nicht zum Regieren über die Kirche." Similarly C. B. Bavinck, another defender of the reality and originality of the apostolic office, states, "Van een ambt moet men maar niet spreken" (art. "Apostel" *Christelijke Encyclopaedie*).
[289] IIIA1; see Vol. I, pp. 42, 43.

26 And eight days later his disciples were again inside, and Thomas with them. Jesus came, though the doors had been locked, and he stood in the midst and said, "Peace to y o u." 27 Then he said to Thomas, "Bring here your finger, and see my hands; and bring your hand, and put it into my side; and no longer be unbelieving but believing." 28 Thomas answered and said to him, "My Lord and my God." 29 Jesus said to him, "Because you have seen me, you have believed; blessed are they who, though not seeing, are yet believing."

30 Now Jesus, to be sure [290] in the presence of the disciples also performed many other signs, which are not written in this book. 31 But these are written in order that y o u may continue to believe that Jesus is the Christ, the Son of God, and in order that believing y o u may continue to have life in his name.

20:24-31

20:24, 25. But Thomas, one of the Twelve, the one called the Twin, was not with them when Jesus came. So the other disciples were saying to him, We have seen the Lord. — He, however, said to them, Unless I see in his hands the mark of the nails, and put my finger into the place of the nails, and put my hand into his side, I definitely will not believe.

For Thomas, his name, and his character see on 11:16; 14:5. There had been a meeting of "the Twelve." Actually only *ten* had been present (plus some welcome visitors), but the little company is still technically called "the Twelve," just as among us when fifteen of the seventeen consistory-members are present, we still speak of those who are present as "the consistory." Moreover, Thomas was one of the twelve apostles as originally chosen. He should have been there. By not being present he had missed the joy of seeing the risen Lord, and of hearing him speak words of peace. Indeed, he had missed the peace itself. It is evident from verse 25 that he had no peace. He was wretched, nervous, restless.

But the other disciples took pity on him. Besides, when the heart is full, the mouth will speak. So the other disciples — the ten (and probably also the two from Emmaus and others who had been present) — kept saying to him, "We have seen the Lord." See on 20:18. Although the immediate reference here is to the apostles who had been present in the room on Easter-evening, it is entirely probable that also others (who may or may not have been present), for example, Mary Magdalene and the other women, kept on giving gladsome testimony of that which they had seen. There had been several "appearances" before Easter evening. See on 21:1.

Thomas, however, remained stubborn. He was a very devoted disciple. He was also very despondent. Hence, for him the universe collapsed when Jesus was crucified. He was "of all men most pitiable" (I Cor. 15:19).

---

[290] See H. E. Dana and J. R. Mantey, *A Manual Grammar of the Greek New Testament,* New York, 1950, p. 255; and cf. Dr. Mantey's doctor's thesis "The Meaning of οὖν in John's Writings."

When the others continued to din their wonderful story into his ears, he finally protested, "Unless I see in his hands the mark of the nails and put my finger into the place of the nails, I definitely will not believe," that is, "I definitely will not believe that Jesus is the risen Lord."

Thomas is willing to believe . . . that is, *on certain conditions!* And he himself will lay down these conditions. The mysterious person about whom the others have been saying so much must measure up to certain standards which Thomas will establish; he must submit to certain tests which Thomas will apply. *Hearing* about him, (even from those who have both seen and heard him) is not enough. Thomas has heard too much already. Thomas wants *to see.* He also wants *to feel!* He wants to see *the mark* of the nails, and he wants to put his finger into *the place* of the nails. In the original there is an interesting alliteration here: the words for *mark* and *place* are almost identical (τύπος and τόπος), somewhat like our *imprint* and *impress.* Thomas will not be satisfied if he merely *sees* the marks which the nails have left on the surface of the hands of the One who had been crucified; no, he must also actually run his finger into the nail-holes! And even that will not be sufficient. Thomas must be permitted to put his hand into the horrible gash left by the spear. Now, *if* the mysterious character about whom Thomas has heard so much will satisfy all these demands, then . . . and not until then . . . Thomas will believe; but *if not,* he will *definitely not* (οὐ μή) believe. For discussion of nails and spear-thrust see on 19:23, 24.

26, 27, 28. And eight days later his disciples were again inside, and Thomas with them. Jesus came, though the doors had been locked, and he stood in the midst and said, Peace to y o u. Then he said to Thomas, Bring here your finger, and see my hands; and bring your hand, and put it into my side; and no longer be unbelieving but believing. Thomas answered and said to him, My Lord and my God.

For the expression "eight days later" see also on 12:1. Employing the inclusive method of time-computation — the method according to which, for example, Tuesday would be *three* days later than Sunday — John states that *eight days later* the event of the preceding Sunday-evening was repeated. The time and the place were, in all probability, the same. Did the Lord wait until Sunday-evening in order to encourage his disciples to observe *that* day — and not some other day — as the day of rest and worship? That would seem probable.

This time Thomas is present. It is probably correct to say that his presence at this occasion was the result of the work of witnessing in which the others had been engaged. Of course, this is not certain. It is also possible that Thomas rejoined the group for the simple reason that he had no other friends, no other place to go.

The rest of verse 26 is almost a word-for-word repetition of verse 19. See on that verse. Again, though the doors are locked, Jesus suddenly appears. He comes. He stands in the midst of the group. He speaks peace to (and bestows peace upon) them. Then he addresses Thomas. In the spirit of gentle condescension to the conditions laid down by Thomas, Jesus admonishes his erring disciple. In order to see how precisely and fully the demands of Thomas are met, we must place the words of Thomas and those of Jesus next to each other. Notice:

The Demands of Thomas	*The Commands of Jesus*
1. Unless I see in his hands the mark of the nails,	2. See my hands
2. And put my finger into the place of the nails,	1. Bring here your finger.
3. And put my hand into his side,	3. And bring your hand, and put it into my side.
4. I definitely will not believe	4. And no longer be unbelieving but believing.

For each demand of Thomas there is a command of Christ, though the order in which the commands are uttered is not exactly the same as that in which the demands were made.

The condescending manner in which Jesus dealt with Thomas certainly indicates that he is still the same Jesus. His love has not lessened. He might have rebuked Thomas sharply, but he deals very gently with him.

The question has been asked, "Did Thomas actually do as Christ commanded him?" Though the answer is not specifically stated, it is probable that he did. In fact, the question might be asked, "Did he have any choice in the matter?" Was he not obliged to do as instructed? Besides, there is Luke 24:39 and especially I John 1:1.

Having *heard* the words of Jesus — those words which were so wonderful because they corresponded in every detail with the words of Thomas —, having probably also *seen* his hands, and *felt* his wounds, Thomas exclaims, "My Lord and my God." This confession must be understood in the light of Thomas' immediately preceding *experience;* better still, it must be understood in the light of the immediately preceding *self-disclosure of Jesus.* Jesus had revealed himself as being (with respect to his divine nature) the Omniscient One. It is in that exalted sense that Thomas now calls Jesus his Lord and his God. He who a little while ago was trying "to lord it over the Lord" (laying down conditions for him to meet), has become submissive. No longer does Thomas wish to rule supreme. In Jesus he recognizes his sovereign, yes even his God! For a Jew that was a remarkable confession.

465

29. Jesus said to him, Because you have seen me, you have believed; blessed are they who, though not seeing, are yet believing. There was nothing wrong with the words of the confession which Thomas uttered. There was something wrong with the manner in which he reached this level of faith. He should have believed even apart from sight. For the benefit of those who would come to believe in him in the years that were to follow, Jesus now says, "Blessed are they who, though not seeing, are yet believing." Faith which results from seeing is good; but faith which results from hearing is more excellent. This is the clear lesson of Scripture throughout; see, for example, Matt. 8:5-10; John 4:48; Rom. 10:14; and I Peter 1:8.

30. Now Jesus, to be sure, in the presence of the disciples, also performed many other signs, which are not written in this book. But these are written in order that y o u may continue to believe that Jesus is the Christ, the Son of God, and in order that believing y o u may continue to have life in his name.

With the glorious confession of Thomas, "My Lord and my God," the author has achieved his purpose. One should compare this confession with the sublime declaration in 1:1: "In the beginning was the Word, and the Word was face to face with God, and the Word was God." The purpose of the evangelist has all along been this: to show that Jesus is really God (or, if one prefers, the Son of God; hence, of the very essence of God). The resurrection and particularly *the appearance* to the disciples, *including Thomas,* has had the effect of eliciting this confession from the heart and mouth of "the despondent and devoted one."

The resurrection was the greatest *sign* of all. For the meaning of the term *sign* see Vol. I, p. 117. There had been many signs. They were performed *in the presence of the disciples,* sothat these men might be qualified witnesses, that is, sothat they might be able to give competent testimony concerning that which they themselves had seen, heard, or experienced. See on 1:7, 8. It is true that no one actually saw the resurrection. But the disciples saw the resurrected Christ, and that certainly implied the reality of the resurrection. John does not "demythologize." (Contrast R. Bultmann.)

In addition to the great sign of the resurrection, those signs which are recorded in the Fourth Gospel are: the changing of the water into wine, the healing of the courtier's son, the cure of the "withered" man at the pool of Bethzatha, the miraculous feeding of the five thousand, the opening of the eyes of the man born blind,. and the resurrection of Lazarus. But that is by no means all. One might ask, "Was not the cleansing of the temple a sign? Was not the triumphal entrance into Jerusalem another sign?" Besides, as has been pointed out in connection with 2:11, the *sign never* stands alone. It is not only a work of power. There is always a *plus:* the miracle introduces teaching with reference to Christ. Sometimes

466

that teaching is implied; often it is expressed, at times in lengthy discourses. Hence, we arrive at the conclusion that from start to finish the Fourth Gospel is a book of signs. It records Christ's wonderful deeds *and their meaning!*

Now John has not recorded *all* the deeds and teachings of Christ. He has been selective. He probably took for granted that the readers had already studied the earlier Gospels; see Vol. I, pp. 31, 32. Besides, in some of these deeds the full deity of Christ was not as clearly revealed as in others. And finally, to record *all* significant deeds and words would have been impossible. But this last point is brought out not here in 20:30, 31 but in 21:25. See on that passage.

What then was John's purpose in recording the signs which he did record? The answer is expressed in these words, "But these are written in order that y o u may continue to believe . . ." Note: *continue to believe.* Remember Cerinthus, who was trying to undermine the faith of the Church in the deity of Christ! That faith must be strengthened. The enemy must be repulsed. For a further commentary on this aspect of John's purpose we refer to Vol. I, pp. 33-35. For Jesus as *the Son of God* see also on 1:1, 14.

When the Church continues to accept Jesus as the divinely appointed and qualified (hence, as the divinely *anointed*) One, that is, as *the Christ,* the fulfilment of all the Old Testament hopes and promises; when it continues to recognize him as *the Son of God,* in the most exalted sense of the term, it will continue to have life — everlasting life; see on 1:4; 3:16 — in his name, that is, in and by means of the blessed acceptance of his revelation in the sphere of redemption.

Synthesis of Chapter 20

See the Outline on p. 446. *The Son of God Triumphing Gloriously. Resurrection and Appearances*

1. The Visit of Peter and John to the Tomb.

When Mary Magdalene, greatly alarmed because the stone had been removed from the tomb's entrance, rushed to Peter and to John for help, these men responded immediately. In order to get the real picture of Peter and John's walking and then running to the tomb, one should study Burnand's famous painting. Artists so often disregard the data of Scripture, but here is a picture which, as far as I can judge, is faithful to Scripture in every respect. Note how in this picture (the original is in the Luxembourg Museum, Paris) the illusion of motion is produced by John's hair rippling backward, the forward bending of the body, Peter's long locks flaring in the wind, etc. It is evident that "the other disciple" is even now beginning to outrun Peter.

Though John arrived first, Peter first entered the tomb. Then entered John also. The orderly arrangement of everything within the tomb, the absence of the body, the recalling of Old Testament passages which they now saw in a new light, caused these men (first John, then Peter also) to believe that Jesus was actually risen.

II. The Appearance to Mary Magdalene.

Mary's weeping, her distraught behavior even in the presence of angels (so great was her grief), her conversation with the angels, and finally her conversation with the person whom she considered to be the care-taker, are described very vividly. One word "Miriam" pronounced in the most "familiar" and tenderly loving manner, changed everything for Mary. She replied, "Rabboni." Jesus then gave her a lesson in the manner in which continued fellowship with him could be attained. She reported her experience to the disciples.

III. The Appearance to the Disciples Except Thomas.

This sudden appearance of Jesus when the doors were closed cannot be explained in such a manner that human minds will be able to grasp it. Not only did the Lord prove his resurrection (even showing the disciples his side and his hands), but he also gave them a much-needed blessing, that of peace, a peace obtained by means of the cross. He further comforted them by informing them that their task, as his official representatives, would continue. Though they had all left him and fled, he still considers them to be his apostles with authority to rule the Church.

IV. The Appearance to the Disciples, Thomas Being Also Present.

The beauty of this story becomes evident especially in this particular, that Jesus meets all of the demands of his erring (but devoted) disciple. Thomas is permitted (*commanded* even!) to see and to feel the wounds in the body of Christ. The loving treatment which Thomas received evoked from his lips the glorious exclamation (a confession which would have been even more glorious had Thomas not laid down his conditions), "My Lord and my God."

With this the Gospel has returned to its starting point, namely, the deity of Christ (see on 1:1). Hence, here (with the exception of a Supplement, chapter 21) it closes. Its purpose is stated in verses 30, 31 (see the exegesis).

Reflection on Christ's Resurrection

Darkness at Noontime

A darkness that smothered sun and moon. *A darker day there never was.* Jesus of Nazareth is hanging on the cross between two thieves. Hear his cry:

"It is finished . . . Father into thy hands I commend my spirit."

Out, out are the lights, out all! Just take a look at the little band of followers.

The Eleven.

Their Master . . . gone. Their friend — and what a Friend! — departed. Their plans wrecked. Their hopes shattered. They are perplexed, baffled. They despair. Like men whose none too sturdy vessel is frozen solid in the Arctic ice-pack, with ice, ice, ice, cold bleak, barren stretching in every direction for hundreds of miles. Ice, screeching, roaring, grinding. Will they ever see their dear ones again? Abandon hope, all ye who enter here! Or — to change the figure — they resemble individuals who have been condemned to die and are pining away in some gloomy, dreadful prison-hole, knowing that the "best" they can expect is the arrival of the executioner. See John 20:19, their "doors were shut for fear of the Jews." Jesus of Nazareth . . . Crucified . . . that was the Farewell to Hope!

Am I exaggerating? Was there not so much as a ray of hope shining through the clouds of gloom and despair? A half-conscious expectation that somehow light would arise out of darkness, that the night would make room for the dawn, that . . . perhaps . . . the Master might even . . . rise again? Read the account for yourself:

"And they, when they heard that he was alive, and had been seen of her, *disbelieved.*" Mark 16:11.

"And they went away and told it unto the rest. *Neither believed they them.*" Mark 16:13.

"And the . . . women . . . told these things unto the apostles. And these words appeared in their sight as *idle talk;* and they *disbelieved* them." Luke 24:10, 11.

"And he upbraided them with their unbelief and hardness of heart, because they *believed not* them which had seen him after he was risen." Mark 16:14.

"The other disciples therefore said unto him (Thomas), We have seen the Lord. But he said unto them, Except I shall see in his hands the print of the nails, and put my finger into the print of the nails and put my hand into his side, I will not believe."

Not one of the Eleven expected Jesus to arise from the grave. That thought was farthest removed from their minds. Jesus was *dead.* He was *gone!* These happy days of close fellowship and intimate association with the Great Prophet of Nazareth would never return.

Cleopas and His Companion.

These two friends of Jesus are returning to Emmaus. It is Spring-time. Yet they hear not the singing of birds. They see not the awakening of Nature. With lagging feet, under leaden skies they continue on their way home . . . home from a funeral! A dear one has been buried. Jesus of Nazareth. "Yes, stranger, we hoped that he was the One who would redeem Israel." "We hoped — past tense — but now all hope is gone. The Cross and the Grave have blasted every last remnant of hope. Eternal despair reigns supreme in our hearts."

Mary, the Mother of the Lord.

She, too, was in the grip of cold winter. A sword was piercing through her own soul, Luke 2:35, as she saw her own son, her first-born, dying the death of a condemned criminal. A feeling of overwhelming sadness takes possession of me whenever I read the lines of that ancient hymn, describing Mary's tears:

> "Stabat mater dolorosa
> juxta crucem lacrimosa . . ."

For her, too, the Cross was the Farewell to Hope.

The Women.

See these women trudging sorrowfully through the streets of Jerusalem very early, Sunday morning. While the Eleven are in deep mourning and despair, Thomas resembling a man who is caught in the midst of an earthquake, the very ground under his feet caving in; Peter overwhelmed with remorse; John tenderly caring for the woman with the tempest-tossed soul (Mary); while night has settled upon these Eleven men, what are these women going to do? Is it their design to welcome the Risen Lord? Not in the least. The cross has blasted their hopes. The grave has buried them forever. They come . . . to anoint a dead body, the corpse of Jesus of Nazareth, their Friend and Helper.

Never was there a more dejected, disappointed, crushed group of men and women! Their own experience is, perhaps, best described in that well-known poem:

> "Now he is dead, far hence he lies
> In that lorn Syrian town;
> And on his grave with shining eyes
> The Syrian stars look down."

When the Master died, the disciples, too, died. Their hopes, their aspirations, their deepest affections and fondest anticipations were buried with their Lord. If ever hope was to be revived in their hearts, their souls would have to be rescued from the grip of death. There would have to be a new beginning . . . and that . . . by all the laws of human logic . . . was impossible!

470

And then . . . the Glorious Easter Message

A new beginning! Light in the darkness! Life conquering death! The Lord is risen indeed! Here all changes. The Cross, the very instrument of despair, becomes an object of glory. The resurrection of Jesus Christ from the dead is the source of a living hope. Listen to the message of exuberant joy, praise, and thanksgiving. Hear it from the lips of one who experienced the deepest darkness of despair and remorse. Says Peter:

"Blessed be the God and Father of our Lord Jesus Christ, who according to his great mercy begat us again unto a living hope by the resurrection of Jesus Christ from the dead."

"Begat us again unto a living hope." Now Peter can smile again. We can all be happy once more. A living hope, living, real, a desire plus expectation plus conviction that our lives here are not in vain. A hope not based upon legend or fancy but upon the immovable Rock of Christ's resurrection from the grave. The apostles proclaim the resurrection because they cannot do anything else. The proof was too clear!

He *lives*. Hence, life is worth living. Hence, all things work together for good to them that love God. Hence, we too shall live. Hence, the curse is going to be removed from the universe and we expect a new heaven and a new earth. All the darkness is dispelled. Hope lives again.

A stream of light descends from veiled skies: an angel mighty and terrible arrives. His appearance is as lightning and his garments white as snow. And the angel says:

"Fear not ye. I know that ye seek Jesus, the crucified. He is not here. He is risen as he told you." *He is risen . . . and hope is revived.*

471

CHAPTER XXI

21 1 After these things Jesus manifested himself again to the disciples at the Sea of Tiberias; now he manifested himself as follows. 2 There were together Simon Peter, and Thomas, the one called the Twin, and Nathaniel, the one from Cana in Galilee, and the (sons) of Zebedee, and two others of his disciples.

3 Simon Peter said to them, "I am going fishing." They said to him, "We will go with you." They went out and got into the boat, but that night they caught nothing.

4 Now when day was already breaking, Jesus stood on the beach, but the disciples were unaware that it was Jesus. 5 Jesus then said to them, "Lads, y o u haven't anything to eat, have y o u?" 6 They answered, "No." So he said to them, "Cast y o u r net on the right side of the boat, and y o u will catch." [291] Then they cast (it), and now they were no longer able to haul it in because of the great number of fishes. 7 Then the disciple whom Jesus loved said to Peter, "It is the Lord!" Then Simon Peter, when he heard that it was the Lord, belted his fisherman's jacket about him, for he was stripped, and flung himself into the sea. 8 But the other disciples came with the boat — for they were not far from the land, only about a hundred yards away — dragging the net full of fish. 9 Then when they stepped ashore, they saw a charcoal fire all made and a fish lying on it, also a bread-cake.[292] 10 Jesus said to them, "Bring some of the fish which y o u just caught." 11 Simon Peter went aboard and hauled the net ashore, full of large fish, a hundred fifty-three; and although there were so many, the net was not torn. 12 Jesus said to them, "Come, have breakfast." None of the disciples was venturing to ask him, "Who art thou?" for they knew that it was the Lord. 13 Jesus came and took the bread-cake and gave to them, and the fish similarly. 14 This was now the third time that Jesus was manifested to the disciples after having risen from the dead.

Preliminary Remarks on Chapter 21

I. *Authorship*

Who wrote this chapter? See what has already been said with reference to this in Vol. I, on p. 28. Absolute certainty is probably not attainable. If a person chooses to believe that John himself with his own hand wrote (or at least that he dictated) chapter 21 in its entirety (or with the exception

---

[291] Literally: "and y o u will find."
[292] Or "fish and bread."

of verses 24 and 25), he will find nothing in its grammar or vocabulary which prevents him from doing this.[293]

That we, nevertheless, favor the theory that another leader at Ephesus (probably a disciple of John), under the guidance of the Holy Spirit, and with the full approval of John, wrote 21:1-23 (and probably also verse 24 *in the name of the elders* — note the pronoun "we" — , and again personally verse 25; note how the "we" of verse 24 changes to "I" in verse 25) is due to the following considerations:

1. The conclusion of chapter 20 (verses 30 and 31) leaves the impression that the account (chapters 1-20) ends there.

2. The author of chapters 1-20 never mentions himself or the members of his immediate family by name (cf. 1:35-41; 13:23; 18:15; 19:25-27, 35;

---

[293] *Grammatical dissimilarity* of sufficient importance to prove difference in authorship has not been shown by anyone, though attempts have been made. The fact, for example, that in the entire chapter the particle ἵνα, which abounds in the Fourth Gospel (in chapter 17 it is found no less than 19 times!) does not occur even once means very little. If this point should be pressed, Chapter II would present a real obstacle, for in that chapter the particle in question makes its appearance only a single time!

Vocabulary also does not decide the issue. It leaves room for either theory: a. that the author was John himself; or b. that the author was someone else who stood in very close relation to John. Of the more than fifty *different verbs* (and verbals) found in verses 1-23 of this twenty-first chapter of John's Gospel a dozen occur nowhere in the first twenty chapters. (However, four of these twelve are found in another work by the same author, the book of Revelation.) The verbs to which we refer are: *to fish* (verse 3), *to be able* (verse 6), *to ask* (verse 12), *to have breakfast* (verses 12 and 15), *to feed* (verses 15 and 17), *to gird* (verse 18), *to become old* (verse 18), *to stretch out* (verse 18); also the following (John 21 and book of Revelation): *to drag* (verse 8), *to venture* (verse 12), *to shepherd* (verse 16), and *to turn* (verse 20).

Also, within this Gospel, of approximately thirty *nouns* that occur in 21:1-23 only eight are peculiar to this section (occurring nowhere else *in the Fourth Gospel)*, namely, *day-break* (verse 4), *beach* (verse 4), *something to eat* (verse 5), *net* (verse 6), *fish* (verse 6), *fisherman's jacket* (verse 7), *cubit* (verse 8: "two hundred cubits," which equals a hundred yards), and *lamb* (verse 15). Naturally, when new subject-matter is introduced (John's one and only fishing-miracle), new words will present themselves. A few others may be expected anyway. And sometimes a word may occur in a new sense; e.g., *brothers* (21:23).

Note also the following *resemblances* between the contents of chapters 1-20, on the one hand, and 21:1-23, on the other: 1. Chapter 21 begins with the familiar phrase, "After these things" (see on 5:1). 2. The Sea of Galilee is called "the Sea of Tiberias" (21:1) just as in 6:1. 3. The three disciples whose names are mentioned in 21:2 have been named before. See footnote 295. However, here for the first time we learn that Nathanael was from Cana in Galilee. 4. There is mention here of "the disciple whom Jesus loved" (21:7, 20) just as in 13:23; 19:26 (cf. 20:2). 5. There is here the same transition from πλοῖον (21:6) to πλοιάριον (21:8) as in chapter 6 (cf. 6:17-20 with 6:22). 6. The words, "Jesus came and took the bread-cake . . . and the fish similarly" (21:13) recall 6:11. 7. Verse 14 — "This was now the *third time* that Jesus manifested himself to his disciples" — has no meaning aside from 20:19, 26. 8. We meet the familiar double *Amen* in 21:18. See on 1:51.

20:2-10), but whoever wrote 21:2 mentions, "the sons of *Zebedee*" (the father of James and John).

3. The lengthy descriptive clause which is used here in 21:20 to indicate "the disciple whom Jesus loved," namely, "who also at the supper had leaned back on his breast and had said 'Lord, who is it that is going to betray thee?' " — stands in rather sharp contrast to the veiled manner in which the author of chapters 1-20 constantly refers to himself (1:35; cf. 1:40; 13:23; 19:26; 20:2).

II. *Purpose*

Chapter 21 has always been a part of this Gospel. Why was it added after the beautiful conclusion found in 20:30, 31? Various reasons have been offered. Since there must have been some practical considerations which occasioned the addition of this Supplement, there is probably more than merely an element of truth in the following purposes which have been suggested:

1. To prove that the risen Christ still takes an interest in his Church, and that his marvelous power and tender love have not diminished in any way. See 21:1-14; especially verses 5, 6, and 12. — However, does not 20: 19-29 prove the same fact? It does, but chapter 21 may be considered *additional* evidence in this direction.

2. To remind the disciples of the fact that they must be *fishers,* and this not only in the usual sense of the term (21:3) but also, and especially, of *men* (21:15-17). — However, in this connection it must be borne in mind that those to which reference is made in verses 15-17 are already in the Church; also, that the figure employed there is not that of a fisherman but that of a shepherd who cares for his sheep. Nevertheless, the suggested purpose may well be correct; for would not reflection upon the miracle recorded in 21:6 recall the earlier one recorded in Luke 5, and also the moral (or prophecy) appended to it in Luke 5:10 (that the disciples were going to catch *men*)? *Kingdom-work must be resumed with vigor!*

3. To emphasize to the Church that Peter had been fully re-instated. It is possible that doubt had arisen with respect to the question whether a man who had sinned so grievously could still be entrusted with the important and responsible task of shepherding the flock of Jesus Christ. This chapter strives to remove that doubt. See 21:15-17.

4. To stress *once again* the comforting truth of predestination, namely, that whatever happens in our lives has been wisely ordained by the Lord, just as the very manner of Peter's glorious death had been foreseen and predicted. See 21:18, 19.

5. To remove a misunderstanding with respect to a saying of Jesus regarding "the disciple whom Jesus loved," that is, to banish the rumor that Jesus had meant, "Said disciple is not going to die." See 21:20-23.

6. To give an opportunity to the elders at Ephesus to present an official and united testimony with respect to the reliability of the things recorded in the Fourth Gospel. See 21:24. And finally,

7. To explain why ever so many other events that had transpired during Christ's earthly sojourn were not recorded. It is possible that otherwise some would have been asking, "Why was not *this* recorded? Why was not *that* included?" See 21:25.

21:1-14

21:1. After these things Jesus manifested himself again to the disciples at the Sea of Tiberias; now he manifested himself as follows.

For the meaning of "after these things," see on 5:1. Jesus *manifested* himself, that is, he displayed his glory. He not only made a sudden physical appearance, sothat his disciples could see him, but he proved his continuing power and love, his *divine* majesty and tender *divine* and *human* sympathy, as these qualities expressed themselves in his words and deeds at this occasion.[294]

---

[294] John is fond of this verb *to manifest*. I count 18 instances of its use in the Fourth Gospel and First Epistle (Lenski counts 17, *op. cit.*, p. 1376): 1:31; 2:11; 3:21; 7:4; 9:3; 17:6; 21:1 (twice); 21:14; I John 1:2 (twice); 2:19; 2:28; 3:2 (twice); 3:5; 3:8; 4:9.
These 18 instances may be classified as follows:
a. first person singular aorist indicative active: 17:6 (I manifested thy name).
b. third person singular aorist indicative active: 2:11 (Jesus manifested his glory); 21:1 (twice: Jesus manifested himself).
c. third person singular aorist indicative passive: 21:14 (Jesus was manifested, was made manifest); I John 1:2 (twice: the life was manifested); I John 3:2 a (it was not yet made manifest what we shall be); I John 3:5 (he was manifested to take away sins); I John 3:8 (to this end was the Son of God manifested in order that he might destroy the works of the devil); I John 3:8 (the love of God was manifested for this purpose, that he might destroy the works of the devil); I John 4:9 (in this the love of God was manifested in us that God sent his only-begotten Son into the world).
d. second person singular aorist imperative active: 7:4 (make yourself manifest — or simply: "show yourself" — to the world).
e. third person singular aorist subjunctive passive: 1:31 (but in order that he might be made manifest to Israel); 3:21 (in order that it might become manifest — or evident — that his deeds were wrought in God); 9:3 (this happened in order that the works of God should be manifested — or: displayed — in him); I John 2:28 (if he shall be manifested . . . at his coming); I John 3:2b (when he will be manifested, we shall be like him).
f. third person plural aorist subjunctive passive: I John 2:19 (that they may be made manifest that they all are not of us). Cf. also Rev. 3:18; 15:4.
It is clear from this that the verb is used in connection with: a. the display of God's glory in the words and works of Jesus at his *first* coming; b. the same, at his *second* coming; and c. more specifically, in connection with his *post-resurrection appearances*. It is also employed d. in a more general way, to indicate the coming to light of that which was hidden, the revelation of a person in his true character (whether good or bad) (I John 2:19; 3:2).
The attempt (sometimes made) to distinguish between φανερόω and ἀποκαλύπτω

In view of the context it is probable that the expression "manifested himself" must here (and in 21:14) be qualified even further. It refers here specifically to *the self-disclosure of the Lord Jesus Christ to his disciples when he presented himself alive after his passion by many proofs during a period of forty days* (Acts 1:3).

What we have here (21:1-23) is a record of one of Christ's post-resurrection "appearances." It is Number 7 in the list (see also on 21:14).

Appearances

1. To Mary Magdalene (Mark 16:9; John 20:11-18).
2. To the women (Matt. 28:9, 10).
3. To Cleopas and his companion (Luke 24:13-35).
4. To Simon (Luke 24:34; I Cor. 15:15).
5. To the disciples except Thomas (John 20:19-23).
6. To the disciples, Thomas being present (John 20:24-29).

All of these occurred in Jerusalem. After the disciples have gone to Galilee, in obedience to the instructions which they had received from the Lord, Jesus appears again:

7. To the seven at the Sea of Tiberias (21:1-14).
8. To the disciples on a "mountain" in Galilee, where Jesus made a great claim, gave the great commission, and proclaimed the great presence (Matt. 28:16-20). By many commentators this appearance is identified with Number 9.
9. To the five hundred (I Cor. 15:6).
10. To James, the Lord's brother (I Cor. 15:7). Whether this took place in Galilee or in Judea is not stated.

The disciples having returned to Jerusalem:

11. To the eleven on Olivet, near Jerusalem (Acts 1:4-11; cf. Luke 24: 50, 51).

The next appearance *that is specifically recorded* is by the Lord from heaven:

12. To Paul, when he was on his way to Damascus (Acts 9:3-7; 22:6-10; 26:12-18; I Cor. 9:1; 15:8).

There may have been several others. How many there were we do not know (cf. Acts 1:3).

With respect to these "manifestations" or "appearances" the following should be noted:

---

in such a manner that φανερόω would mean *public display* (showing oneself *to men in general*) while ἀποκαλύπτω would indicate *internal disclosure* (to *believers only*) requires considerable modification in the light of the references given above (in which the verb φανερόω is used). In the light of these references we prefer the definition which we have given in this footnote and in the text.

a. We are not dealing here with the universe of unreality, with a phantom, apparition, hallucination, merely subjective dream or vision. On the contrary, in every instance it is the Lord himself in person who *manifests* himself.

b. The expression *manifested himself* is used here in 21:1, 14 in order to stress the idea that Jesus is no longer dwelling with men as he had done before. He suddenly appears upon the scene. Just as suddenly he disappears again. But while he is with them, they see him (though not always immediately) as their resurrected and glorious Lord.

The words, "Now he manifested himself as follows," are probably added because the account of this particular "appearance" is rather lengthy and circumstantial.

2. There were together Simon Peter, and Thomas, the one called the Twin, and Nathaniel, the one from Cana in Galilee, and the (sons) of Zebedee, and two others of his disciples.

To find these men together here in Galilee is not surprising. The Lord had promised to meet his disciples there (Matt. 28:7, 10; Mark 16:7). Besides, four of the five here indicated were also together at the very beginning of Christ's ministry. We refer to Simon Peter, Nathaniel, and the sons of Zebedee (John and James). See on 1:35-51. At that time Andrew and Philip were also among those mentioned. Were these the "two others of his disciples" who now reappear at the close of the Gospel? But we just do not know who these two others may have been. That they belonged to the Twelve is well-nigh certain (see 21:1, "to *the* disciples"). That here in 21:2 the reason why the two are not mentioned by name is "because they had not yet been introduced in the main body of the book (chapters 1-20)," is rather improbable and would limit the possibilities to *two* out of the following *three* men: Matthew, James the Less, and Simon the Zealot.[295]

---

[295] *All* the others (i.e., *all* except Matthew, James the Less, and Simon the Zealot) have been introduced before. See our comments on the following passages with references to the disciples whose names are mentioned or implied in the Fourth Gospel:
A. Mentioned by name:
Simon Peter: 1:40, 41, 42, 44; 6:8, 68; 13:6, 8, 9, 24, 36, 37; 18:10, 11, 15, 16, 17, 18, 25, 26, 27; 20:2, 3, 6; 21:11, 15, 16, 17, 20, 21.
Andrew: 1:40, 44; 6:8; 12:22.
Philip: 1:43, 44, 45, 46; 6:5, 7; 12:21, 22; 14:8, 9.
Nathaniel (called Bartholomew in the Synoptics): 1:45, 46, 47, 48, 49; 21:2.
Thomas: 11:16; 14:5; 20:24, 26, 27, 28, 29; 21:2.
Judas the Greater: 14:22.
Judas the Traitor: 6:71; 12:4; 13:2, 26, 29; 18:2, 35.
B. By Indirect or Veiled Reference:
James, the brother of the author: 1:41.
John: 1:35, 37, 38, 39; 13:23, 24, 25; 18:15, 16; 19:26, 27; 20:2, 3, 4, 8; 21:7, 20, 23, 24.

For the inference to be derived from the mention of "the sons of Zebedee," see p. 474, 475.

3. Simon Peter said to them, I am going fishing. They said to him, We will go with you. Peter is the man of action. He generally *acts* before John does. John generally *understands* before Peter does. So Peter says, "I'm off to fish" (literally). Does this mean that Peter turns his back (or: has already turned his back) upon preaching, considering it to be no longer worth-while, saying (or: having said) farewell to it, and returning (or: having returned) to his former occupation? Some of the best commentators (including F. W. Grosheide) are of this opinion, while others (e.g., R. C. H. Lenski) seem to ridicule the very idea. *Compelling proof* in either direction is lacking. It is true that these men had to gain a livelihood, and at least some of those mentioned were (or had been) fishermen by trade (Matt. 4:18, 21). On the other hand, it is also true that by and by Jesus is going to emphasize and re-emphasize that Peter must be a shepherd *of men*. See, moreover, what was said on p. 475 above, under item 2. Besides, even though Jesus after his resurrection had already manifested himself to Peter, it may not have been entirely clear to the mind of the latter that he, who had basely denied his Master three times, had the right to resume his spiritual activities whether as a missionary or as a minister. Accordingly, the idea that Peter, for the time being at least, had given up his kingdom-activities and had returned to his former occupation cannot be entirely dismissed. And does not 16:32 imply that in this decision to resume the former occupations on a full-time basis, and to give up the idea of vigorous Kingdom-endeavor, he had been joined by the others? See on that verse.

The other six disciples are ready to follow where Peter leads. In fact, when he said, "I am off to fish," he may have implied "Who will go with me?"

They went out and got into the boat, but that night they caught nothing. Though these men, having gone on board "the" vessel (probably Peter's), chose the most appropriate time to fish, and though at least some of them were experienced fishermen, they toiled and struggled all night long but caught nothing. History was repeating itself. Did they recall their former experience, the one recorded in Luke 5? And was their night-long failure a revelation of God's displeasure with them for having neglected Kingdom-work? But God still loved them! Hence, in his loving providence their complete failure must serve the purpose of bringing into sharp relief the greatness of the gift which he was going to provide.

4. Now when day was already breaking, Jesus stood on the beach, but the disciples were unaware that it was Jesus. The expression, "Early morning *already* arriving" stresses the frustration which these men had experienced through the long, the seemingly endless, night. At last, it was *already* dawn, and still they had caught nothing. Looking toward the beach they see a man. It was Jesus, but they did not recognize him. Why not? Because unbelief had closed their eyes? Because supernaturally their eyes were being prevented from recognizing him (cf. Luke 24:16)? Because of the nature and appearance of his body? The reason is not given. It can hardly have been that they were too far away from the shore. After all, they were only about a hundred yards off (21:8), within shouting distance (21:5). Perhaps in this case, where nothing is mentioned that would indicate any supernatural factor, the most natural explanation is the best, namely, that a mist or morning-haze made it impossible for them to identify the person on the beach. Certainty is, however, lacking.

5. Jesus then said to them, Lads, y o u haven't anything to eat, have y o u? Very lovingly the Lord of glory addresses these men as, "Lads," or "Boys." See Vol. I, p. 181. See also I John 2:13, 18, where the aged John uses the same expression. When Jesus added, "Y o u haven't anything to eat, have y o u?," expecting a negative answer, he did not mean, "Have y o u something *for me* to eat? *I* would like to buy some fish." Rather, he asks this question in order to rivet their attention on the fact that their return to the former occupation has been a complete failure. They had failed to reckon sufficiently with *God's* plan for their lives. It is as if he were saying, *"Y o u* have caught nothing at all, now have y o u? Without *me* y o u can do nothing. Please learn that lesson once and for all. And now *I* will show y o u where y o u should cast the net in order to catch fish (cf. verse 6). *Y o u* haven't anything to eat,[296] have y o u? So *I* have prepared breakfast for y o u" (cf. verse 9).

This explanation, as has been indicated, has the advantage of being in harmony with the context.

6. They answered, No. So he said to them, Cast y o u r net on the right side of the boat, and y o u will catch. The tired disciples answer the stranger's question ("Lads, y o u haven't anything to eat, have y o u?") with a single word, "No." — "Cast y o u r net *on the right side* (literally, "on the right parts," but that is simply an idiom) of the boat, and y o u will *find* (in the sense of *catch*)," says the man on the beach. Was it this command which first opened John's eyes, sothat he began to surmise who the stranger might be? Did he recall a somewhat similar instruction earlier in Christ's ministry (cf. Luke 5:4)? Was there something about this

---

[296] προσφάγιον, a staple article of food of the genus *fish*, rather than a mere relish with the food. Compare the term used below in verse 9 and also in 6:9; see Vol. I, p. 221. On the two nouns προσφάγιον and ὀψάριον see J. H. Moulton and G. Milligan, *op. cit.*, pp. 470 and 551.

stranger's voice — calmness, majesty, certainty, authority — which impressed these weary fishermen? At any rate, they immediately obeyed:

Then they cast (it), and now they were no longer able to haul it in because of the great number of fishes.
Experienced fishermen usually do not permit a perfect stranger to give them directions. Conceivably they might have said, "Do *you,* standing there upon the shore, a hundred yards away from us, mean to tell *us* where to cast the net? It is surely far easier for *us* to observe what is happening in the water on both sides of the boat than it is for *you* to see this from such a distance! Besides, *we* are fishermen. We know what we are doing. So, stranger, do not give us any unsolicited advice." But they did nothing of the kind. They do not even *begin* to offer an objection and then change over to the course of obedience. They do not even say, "We toiled all night and caught nothing . . . *but* at thy word we will lower the nets" (cf. Luke 5:5). None of this! Instead — so deeply impressed were they by the compelling tone of the stranger's voice — they obey with soldierly promptness. They cast the net on the right side, and at once it enclosed so many fishes that though these fishermen kept on exerting themselves (note force of the imperfect), they were unable to pull the net up into the boat.
It was a miracle. Jesus did not suddenly create all these fishes, but he had seen to it that at the proper moment this shoal was at the right spot to be caught. And the purpose of the miracle was to open the eyes of these men, to make them see that by themselves they could accomplish nothing, and to strengthen their faith in *him!*

7. Then the disciple whom Jesus loved said to Peter, It is the Lord.
What we said in connection with 21:3 — "Peter generally *acts* before John does. John generally *understands* before Peter does" — is illustrated also in this case. He who had been the first to grasp the significance of the linen bandages and of the sweat-band (20:8) was also the first to discern that the stranger on the beach was the Lord. He immediately acquainted Peter with his startling discovery. John and Peter are here together again, as so often (see on 1:35-41 — where John's presence is implied — ; 13:23, 24; 18: 15, 16; 20:1-10; after 21:2, 7 also verses 20-22 of this chapter; then Acts 3:1-4; 22; 8:14-17; and Gal. 2:9). In the kingdom of God the man of action and the man of vision complement each other. For the meaning of "the disciple whom Jesus loved" see on 13:23. For the verb (*loved*) see footnote 306.

Then Simon when he heard that it was the Lord, belted his fisherman's jacket about him, for he was stripped, and flung himself into the sea.
Characteristically Peter acts at once. The idea that he was already wear-

481

ing his fisherman's jacket and that he now merely fastens a belt around it (R. C. H. Lenski, *op. cit.,* p. 1381) is in conflict with the clause which follows immediately, namely, *"for* he was stripped." By putting on his jacket and fastening the belt Peter prepared himself for stepping ashore and meeting his Lord! Before this, in order to facilitate his movements during the busy but fruitless night, he (and perhaps the others also) was working stripped to his undergarment (or perhaps loin-cloth). Impetuously Peter flings himself into the sea, which, however, at this distance from the shore was probably not very deep. He is on his way to welcome his Lord. We do not meet him again until he steps off the beach again and into the boat (21:11).

8. But the other disciples came with the boat — for they were not far from the land, only about a hundred yards away — dragging the net full of fish.

The other disciples, being less impulsive than Peter, were somewhat slower in arriving, for they had remained in *the boat.*[297] So *by means of* the boat, which must have landed very soon after Peter stepped on the beach — for the distance was only about [298] "two hundred cubits" [299] or

---

[297] Literally, "the little boat," or "the small sea-going vessel." However, when a man becomes very familiar with a certain object through constant use, he may refer to it by means of a diminutive, without necessarily *stressing* its limited size. Cf. Dutch: "het bootje." The same boat is meant in verse 8 as in verse 6. See further, p. 474 above.

[298] Note ὡς, just like in 11:18, where this idiom is explained.

[299] In creating the human body and its proportions the Lord provided us with a convenient standard for measurement, which was used by the ancients and to a certain extent has remained in use to this very day. The cubit, mentioned here in 21:8, belongs to this system of measurements. Thus we have:

a. The *thumb* (cf. "rule of thumb"), Dutch: *duim,* the distance across this inner digit being about one inch.

b. The *finger* or *digit,* the distance across being about ¾ inch (Jer. 52:21).

c. The *four fingers held together* or *handbreadth,* a distance of four times ¾ of an inch, that is, three inches (II Chron. 4:5).

d. The *span,* the longest possible distance covered by the *expanded* hand, a distance of three handbreadths; hence, nine inches (Ex. 28:16).

e. The *cubit,* the length of the forearm. The word used here in 21:8 originally meant *forearm,* and acquired the secondary connotation *length of the forearm.* This equals two spans or eighteen inches (½ yard).

f. The *fathom,* the length of the *outstretched* arms. This equals four cubits or six feet. Both the English and the Greek term (ὀργυιά) are derived from a root meaning *to stretch out* (Acts 27:28).

g. The *furlong* (furrow-long) — Greek στάδιον — equals one hundred fathoms or 600 feet or ⅛ of a Roman mile. (6:19; 11:18; Rev. 14:20; 21:16). It was the length of the Olympic course. Hence, the term means *race-course* in I Cor. 9:24.

h. The *Sabbath Day's Journey* equals two thousand cubits or one thousand yards (Acts 1:12).

i. The foot originally indicated the length of the human foot. The present English or American foot (length-measure) is longer than the average foot of the a hundred yards — they got on land. The net full of fishes had been dragged along behind the boat.

9. Then when they stepped ashore, they saw a charcoal fire all made and a fish lying on it, also a bread-cake.
It was a wonderful scene which greeted the eyes of these disciples upon reaching the beach. In sharp contrast with their inability to provide food for themselves there was here a charcoal fire on which the One on the shore had prepared a simple meal of bread and fish (ὀψάριον, here as in 6:9, 11, a relish to go with the bread; see also footnote 296 above).

A good argument can be presented for the idea that here in verse 9 we should translate *a* fish and *a* bread-cake instead of the indefinite "fish and bread," which rendering — it must be admitted — is also possible. Verse 13 seems to indicate that there was only *one* bread-cake (note the definite article) and only *one* fish. Besides, the striking similarity between 21:13 and 6:11 seems to imply that in both cases we are dealing with a miracle of multiplication.

10. Jesus said to them, Bring some of the fish which y o u have just caught. Jesus did not mean, "Bring some of y o u r fishes because otherwise there will not be enough to eat." On the contrary, he simply wanted them to dispose of the small fry and to save the big fishes, taking those out of the net and feasting their eyes on them, sothat they could meditate on the greatness of the miracle and its spiritual implications.

11. Simon Peter went aboard and hauled the net ashore, full of large fish, a hundred and fifty-three; and although there were so many, the net was not torn. From the edge of the boat Peter loosens the top of the net and through the water he drags it toward the beach, where, in all probability with the help of the others (for it was very heavy; see on verse 6 above), it was lugged ashore. When the large fish were taken out of the net, they were counted. They totaled one hundred fifty-three! [300] Surely,

---

adult male. When no ruler or yardstick is handy, this common length-measure can be approximated by adding a span and a handbreadth.

j. The *mile* — Greek μίλιον, from the Latin *milia passuum:* a thousand paces — , the distance covered by taking *one thousand* double strides (Matt. 5:41).

As the measurements of the human body are not constant, and also for other reasons, these distances are not exact and allow for variation in different periods of history and in different countries.

[300] Among the strange and, for the most part, allegorical interpretations of this item of information I have found the following:

a. The fish were not counted until the shore had been reached, in order to teach us that the exact number of the elect remains unknown until they have reached the shore of heaven.

b. The ancients counted one hundred fifty-three varieties of fish!

c. There is here a veiled reference to Matt. 13:47, 48, and an indication that all kinds of people are going to be saved.

a most remarkable catch! Such a heavy load of fishes might easily have caused the net to tear (as in Luke 5:6), but in the present case the Lord had seen to it that this did not happen.

12. Jesus said to them, Come, have breakfast. From one miracle the account now proceeds to the next one, though in purpose the two are essentially one. As the men were tired and hungry, Jesus now invited them to have breakfast.

None of the disciples was venturing (note the force of the imperfect here: they never arrived at the point of doing this) **to ask him, Who art thou? for they knew that it was the Lord.** They were too filled with reverence in his presence and also too thoroughly convinced in their minds with reference to the identity of the man on the beach to make any attempt by means of questioning to *extract* [301] information from him regarding this subject. They *knew* that it was *the Lord,* the risen and glorious Master.

13. Jesus came and took the bread-cake and gave to them, and the fish similarly. The significance of this statement has been suggested above on pp. 480. It is important to bear in mind that what the Lord gives to these men does not come from the fish which *they* had caught! He himself has prepared a breakfast for them, which mysteriously is multiplied so that the *one* bread-cake and the *one* fish (in both cases the original has the definite article) becomes a breakfast for all these men. That it is the intention of the author to convey this fact is easy to see when one compares 6:11 (the miracle of the five bread-cakes and the two fishes) with the present passage (21:13):

6:11	21:13
"Jesus, therefore, took the bread-cakes, and when he had given thanks, he distributed them among those who were seated; similarly the fishes as much as they wanted.	"Jesus came and took the bread-cake and gave to them, and the fish similarly."

Much has been written about the fact that here in 21:13 we do not read, "And when he had given thanks." But was it necessary for the evangelist to write down everything that transpired?

---

d. The reference is to an important date in Church History, namely, 153 A. D.

e. The total represents the sum of all the numbers from 1 to 17. Well, what of it?

f. In Hebrew characters the numerical equivalent of *Simon Iona* is one hundred fifty-three.

g. The number one hundred fifty-three represents 100 for the Gentiles, 50 for the Jews, and 3 for the Trinity.

[301] Note the prefix in this verb, similar to the one in our *extract, examine.* Literally the verb means *to ask* (in order to find) *out;* to enquire carefully; cf. the Dutch verb *uitvragen.*

14. This was now the third time that Jesus was manifested to the disciples after having risen from the dead.

For the meaning of the verb *was manifested* see on 21:1 and also footnote 294. Jesus did not manifest himself to his enemies (Acts 10:41), but to his friends. Although the present appearance is mentioned as Number 7 on the list given in connection with verse 1, nevertheless, if we exclude from our count those in which the Lord revealed himself to the women and to individuals, and count only those in which he appeared to the inner circle of his disciples considered as a group (though not necessarily with every member present), we arrive at the conclusion that this was the *third* manifestation. That John has this in mind is clear from the phrase "to the disciples." The first is recorded in 20:19-23; the second in 20:24-29.

For Synthesis see on p. 475.

---

15 Now when they had finished breakfast, Jesus said to Simon Peter, "Simon (son) of John, do you love me more than these?" He said to him, "Indeed, Lord, thou knowest that I have affection for thee." He said to him, "Feed my lambs." 16 He said to him again a second time, "Simon (son) of John, do you love me?" He said to him, "Indeed, Lord, thou knowest that I have affection for thee." He said to him, "Shepherd my sheep." 17 He said to him the third time, "Simon, (son) of John, do you have affection for me?" Peter was grieved because he said to him this third time, "Do you have affection for me?" And he said to him, "Lord, all things thou knowest, thou dost realize that I do have affection for thee." Jesus said to him, "Feed my dear sheep. 18 I most solemnly assure you, when you were younger, you used to gird yourself and to walk where you wished (to walk); but when you will have become old, you will stretch out your hands, and another will gird you and bring you where you do not wish (to go)." 19 (This he said to signify by what kind of death he was to glorify God.) And having said this to him, he added, "Follow me."

20 Peter turned and saw following (them) the disciple whom Jesus loved, who also at the supper had leaned back on his breast and had said, "Lord, who is it that is going to betray thee?" 21 So when Peter saw him, he said to Jesus, "Lord, what about him?" 22 Jesus said to him, "If I will that he remain until I come, what is that to you? [302] *You* follow me!" 23 The word then got out among the brothers that said disciple was not to die; yet Jesus did not say to him that he was not to die; yet Jesus did not say to him that he was not to die, but, "If I will that he remain until I come, what is that to you?" [303]

24 This is the disciple who is testifying concerning these things and who has written these things, and we know that *true* is his testimony. 25 Now there are many other things which Jesus did, which if they were written one by one, I suppose that the world itself could not contain the written volumes.[304]

---

[302] IIIB1; see Vol. I, p. 44.
[303] IIIB1; see Vol. I, p. 44.
[304] IIIB1; see Vol. I, p. 44.

21:15-23

21:15. Now when they had finished breakfast, Jesus said to Simon Peter, Simon (son) of John, do you love me more than these?

Breakfast finished, the Lord now turns to Peter in order publicly to re-instate him into his office or at least to make known to the entire Church that he has been forgiven and that he, as well as the others, has been entrusted with the care of the flock of Jesus Christ.

The circumstances must have reminded Peter of the scene of his denial. And if *the circumstances* as such did not remind him of this, what was about to happen was bound to do so. Note the following resemblances:

1. It was at *a charcoal fire* that Peter denied his Master (18:18). It is here at another *charcoal fire* (21:9) that he is asked to confess (his love for) his Master.

2. *Three times* Peter had denied his Master (18:17, 25, 27). *Three times* he must now own him as his Lord, whom he loves (21:15-17).

3. The prediction with reference to the denial had been introduced with *the solemn double Amen* (13:38; see on 1:51). The prediction which immediately followed Peter's confession was introduced similarly (21:18).

But it has been shown [305] that the resemblance is even more pointed. In reverse order the same three ideas — 1. *following,* 2. *a cross,* 3. *denying* — occur here in 21:15-19 as in 13:36-38. At that other occasion Jesus had said, "Where I am going you cannot *follow* me now." With reference to Peter's death on a *cross* Jesus had predicted, "But you will follow me afterward." Then the Master had foretold the denial in these words, "I most solemnly assure you, the rooster will certainly not crow until you have *denied* me three times."

Over against 3., the three *denials,* stand the three affirmations which Jesus requires of Peter in answer to these questions: "Do you love me more than these? . . . Do you love me? . . . Do you have affection for me?" The prediction with reference to 2., Peter's death on a *cross,* followed a little later in these words, "You will stretch out your hands, and another will gird you and bring you where you do not wish to go." And as to 1. *following,* the command, "Follow me . . . *you* follow me," occurs toward the close of the story of Peter's re-instatement. Cf. also Mark 8:34 for these same three concepts.

There is, moreover, another striking trait of resemblance to which the passage now under study (21:15) calls attention. Jesus said to Peter, *"Simon* (the name which this disciple had even before he was found by Jesus; hence, very fitting here, to remind him of his behavior so like a person who does not know Jesus!), son of John, do you love me more than these?" The

---

[305] See John Foster's article, "Denying Oneself," *ExT,* 54 (1943), 331.

words, "than these" do not refer to such things as this boat, this net, these fishes, but to *these men,* standing here (see on 21:2).

The question was very appropriate, for Peter had boasted, "Even though *all* be ensnared because of thee, yet will I never be ensnared" (Matt. 26:33). In thoroughly unjustifiable self-esteem he had placed himself above the others. This trusting in self had brought about his discomfiture. Hence, in the presence of *these men* he must now make his confession.

He said to him, Indeed, Lord, thou knowest that I have affection for thee.
In two respects Simon's answer differs from the Lord's question: 1. He no longer compares himself with his fellow-disciples, to their disadvantage. His "Indeed" (ναί, not "Yes," in the sense of, "Yes, I love thee more than the others do") has reference to the fact that he feels sure that he has in his heart something similar to that about which Jesus is enquiring; something *similar,* but *not the same;* hence, 2. He uses *another* verb, a verb with a slightly different meaning.[306]

With becoming modesty and pleasing diffidence Peter, humbled by the memory of his fall, refuses to use the higher term for love, the verb which Jesus had used. For the love of intelligence and purpose, the love of whole-hearted devotion, about which Jesus was asking, Peter substitutes the more subjective *affection.* At the same time, instead of boasting, as if he were thoroughly acquainted with the state of his own heart, he casts himself upon (and appeals to) the penetrating knowledge of his Lord. Peter says, *"Thou knowest* that I have affection for thee." With respect to the knowledge possessed by the Lord see on 2:25; cf. II Cor. 11:31; Gal. 1:20.

Attachment to Jesus is an absolute prerequisite for rendering service in his kingdom. And in tender mercy Jesus is willing to bestow this great privilege upon one who lays claim to nothing better than the humbler (though still very precious) type of love. So

He (Jesus) said to him, Feed my lambs. For the meaning of this expression in comparison with the similar commands in verses 16 and 17 see on verse 17.

16. He said to him a second time, Simon, son of John, do you love me? The second question differs from the first. It probes deeper and is more painful. It is as if Jesus were saying, "Simon, by your silence with reference to *these others* you have indicated that you no longer believe that you love me *more than* they do. But now, dropping all comparison, *do you really love me?"* Jesus again uses the same verb which *he* had used before. He is again asking whether Simon loves him with thorough-going devotion

[306] See this footnote at close of this chapter, where it has been placed because of its length.

and with his entire person (not only the emotions but also the mind and the will).

He said to him, Indeed, Lord, thou knowest that I have affection for thee. Peter gives the same answer as before. He still does not dare to affirm that he possesses the higher kind of love.

He said to him, Shepherd my sheep.[307] See on verse 17.

17. He said to him the third time, Simon (son of) John, do you have affection for me? This time Jesus descends to Peter's own level, using the very term for *love* which Peter had used. The Lord *seems* to doubt whether Simon really had even such humble affection as he was claiming.

Peter was grieved because he said to him this third time, Do you have affection for me? And he said to him, Lord, all things thou knowest, thou dost realize that I do have affection for thee.

The fact that Jesus had now asked the question *in this form* grieved Peter. This is understandable. Anyone who mentally places himself in a similar situation can enter into this at once. How should Peter not be grieved when Jesus seems to call in question even his subjective attachment, his *affection* for the Lord? Within his heart Peter is convinced that he possesses this humbler love. But he has learned his lesson. He does not dare to appeal to anything within himself. So he appeals once more, and now more emphatically than ever, to his Lord's omniscience. Says he, "Lord, *all things* thou knowest." And because Jesus *knows* all things, he must be able to *realize* that Peter has affection for Jesus. (The first verb is οἶδας; the second is γινώσκεις; see on 1:10, 31; 3:11; 8:28.)

Jesus said to him, Feed my dear sheep.

Just what does Jesus mean by this threefold charge which he gives to Peter? It is hardly probable that in speaking of *lambs* (verse 15), *sheep* (verse 16), and *dear sheep* (or *dear little sheep;* note the diminutive, but this may not have reference to *age* or physical *size,* but may be due to Christ's *tender affection* for his own)·he had in mind three different groups within the Church; for example, little children, adults, and young people. The notion that Jesus refers to age-groups is no more reasonable than the belief that in the allegory of the Good Shepherd (chapter 10) three different groups of people are indicated by the thieves, the strangers, and the hirelings.

---

[307] The choice between πρόβατα and προβάτια in verse 16 is about even. N.N. has προβάτια in the text, but its critical apparatus does not show that it is better attested than πρόβατα. Since Jesus changed his question every time, something can be said in favor of the theory that he also changed the form of his command every time, though *basically* the charge to Peter remains the same.

Rather, while all three terms refer to the same flock of the Good Shepherd, Jesus Christ, this flock is viewed from three different aspects. Believers and their children are looked upon, first of all, as *lambs,* for they are weak and immature; hence, in need of the strengthening food of the Word; secondly, as *sheep,* prone to wander and dependent in everything; hence, in need of being shepherded (see on chapter 10); and finally, as *dear sheep,* immature and in need of the tender and loving nourishment of the Word.

It is as if the Master says to Peter: "Simon, you were weak like a lamb, wandering like a sheep, yet, throughout it all, you, like a dear ("little") sheep, were the object of my tender and loving solicitude. Now, having profited by your experiences (because of your sincere sorrow), consider the members of my Church to be your lambs, and feed them; your sheep, and shepherd them; yes, your *dear* sheep, and in feeding them love them! *Do not neglect the work among the flock, Simon. That is your real assignment! Go back to it!"*

Thus was Peter fully and publicly restored. With reference to *shepherding* the sheep and all that this implies, see on chapter 10. The metaphorical meaning of *feeding* — especially, as far as the character of the food is concerned — is explained in the following passages: Deut. 8:3; Job 23:12; Ps. 119:103; Is. 55:1, 2; Jer. 3:15; 15:16; John 6:33-35, 51, 58; I Cor. 3:2; 10:3, 4; I Peter 2:2; and Rev. 2:7, 17.

18. I most solemnly assure you, when you were younger, you used to gird yourself and to walk where you wished (to walk); but when you will have become old, you will stretch out your hands, and another will gird you, and bring you where you do not wish (to go).

For the words of solemn introduction see on 1:51; also above, on 21:15. Note: "When you *were younger* . . . when you will have become old." This (together with the fact that Peter died during Nero's reign, and was then already "old") seems to indicate that in the year 30 A. D. Peter was middle-aged; older than John but not yet old. Now Jesus says, as it were, "In your younger days, whenever you wished to go out, you used to *gird yourself* (literally, "you used to put on your belt," but here probably somewhat broader: "You used to get dressed for travel") and would walk wherever you desired to walk." The implication is that, on the whole, Peter did much as he pleased when he was younger. He did not always do the right thing either. Mercifully Jesus is not saying that this more or less free and undisciplined behavior was still characteristic of the man. We may believe that his experience of recent days had taught him a lesson.

This description of Peter's past uninhibited conduct is in sharp contrast with the prediction which immediately follows: "But when you will have become old, you will stretch out your hands, and another will gird you, and bring you where you do not wish (to go)." In his old age the moment would arrive when, far from enjoying freedom of movement, Peter would have to raise his arms, sothat a rope could be tied around him (or possibly: sothat he could be fastened to a cross; thus Tertullian). Contrary to the wish of the flesh, he would then be brought to the place of execution. In this connection it is interesting to note that the expression "to stretch out the hands" is often used by Greek authors and by the early fathers to indicate crucifixion.[308]

19. (This he said to signify by what kind of death he was to glorify God.)

The passage clearly indicates that when it was written Peter had already passed from the scene of history. In his death God had been glorified (an expression also used with reference to Christ's own passion and death, 13:31, 32), for in this apostle's willingness to suffer martyrdom for the cause of Christ God's grace was magnified.

The *manner* of Peter's death is related by the church-fathers, as follows:

Eusebius: "But Peter seems to have preached in Pontus and Galatia and Bithynia and Cappadocia and Asia, to the Jews of the Dispersion, and at last, having come to Rome, he was crucified head downward, for so he himself had asked to suffer" (The *Ecclesiastical History* III, i).

Tertullian: "At Rome Nero was the first who stained with blood this rising faith. Then is Peter girt by another when he is made fast to the cross" (*Antidote for the Scorpion's Sting* XV). Cf. also Origen, *Against Celsus* II, xlv).

And having said this to him, he added, Follow me. The command, "Follow me," was not meant literally, as if from now on Peter were again to accompany Jesus step by step. It must be borne in mind that the Lord's former former visible, day-by-day association with his disciples had ceased. Accordingly, what Jesus meant was, "Be my disciple and apostle, and as such follow me in service, in suffering, and in death (by being willing to endure affliction and even martyrdom for my sake)." It was a renewed call to discipleship and to the duties of the apostolic office (cf. Matt. 4:19, 20).

20. Peter turned and saw following (them) the disciple whom Jesus loved, who also at the supper had leaned back on his breast and had said, Lord, who is it that is going to betray thee?

Jesus walks away from the group, in order that presently he may vanish as suddenly from view as he had appeared. But as he walks away, Peter seems to have walked along with him. Some surmise that Peter did this because he had taken *literally* (see on 2:19) what Jesus had intended to be

---

[308] See J. H. Bernard, *op. cit.*, pp. 708-710.

understood *metaphorically* ("Follow me"). Of this we have no definite proof. The suggestion cannot be lightly dismissed, however. The fact that Jesus is going to repeat his command ("Follow me") may mean that Peter *had failed* to comprehend its meaning (see 21:22).

Having walked a few steps by the side of Jesus, Peter, turning, notices someone following them. That someone was "the disciple whom Jesus loved, who also at the supper had leaned back on his breast and had said, 'Lord, who is it that is going to betray thee?'" For this descriptive clause see on 13:23-25, also footnote 306; for the light which this clause sheds on the authorship of this chapter see p. 475.

To see John following Peter is not strange. Very often the two are together, as has been indicated (see on 21:7). They were intimate friends. Where the one is, the other also wishes to be.

21. So when Peter saw him, he said to Jesus, Lord, what about him? Being an intimate friend of John, Peter naturally is deeply concerned about his colleague's future. A moment ago Jesus had predicted how *Peter* was going to glorify God in his death as a martyr. Was *John* going to accompany him in this experience? Peter wanted to know.

But though to us, had we been present, the question might have seemed altogether commendable — proof of Peter's friendly interest in his junior partner —, the penetrating eyes of the Lord probed deeper into the heart and mind of the oft-faltering disciple. Jesus knew that the sudden turn which Simon had given to the conversation indicated that the command, "Follow me," had not registered, at least not sufficiently. Hence,

22. Jesus said to him, If I will that he remain until I come, what is that to you? *You* **follow me!** By means of these words the Lord impresses upon Peter's mind the fact that *curiosity* about John's future must make way for *obedience* to the Lord's all-important command, "Follow me . . . Feed my lambs . . . Shepherd my sheep . . . Feed my dear sheep." *Peter must not be so deeply interested in God's secret counsel* (regarding John) *that he fails to pay attention to God's revealed will!* It is a lesson which every believer in every age should take to heart.

There is work to be done. There are souls to be reached. There is a task to be accomplished. Let Peter rivet all his attention upon this! Some people are always asking questions. They are asking so many questions that their real mission in life fails to receive the proper amount of interest and energy. There are times when questions are out of order. It has been well said that a man who has been wounded by a feathered, poisoned arrow should not begin to ask, "Of what wood is this arrow made? Of what bird did these feathers come? Is the person who shot it dark or fair, short or tall?" Let him *do* something first of all!

23. The word then got out among the brothers that said disciple was not to die.

Here we are introduced to the early Christian *brotherhood*. The term *brothers* is used here in a sense different from that which it has in 2:12; 7:3, 5, 10 (and even somewhat different from its connotation in 20:17); see on these passages. The members of the early Church are indicated here. They constituted a Christian family, and as such regarded themselves as brothers. Cf. Acts 1:16; 2:29, 37; 6:3; 7:2; 9:30, etc.

These "brothers" misinterpreted the words of Jesus with reference to John. They also placed the emphasis where Jesus had not placed it. In the remark of Jesus to Peter the main thing by far was the positive directive: *"You* follow me!" The rest ("If I will that he remain until I come, what is that to you?") was secondary. To be sure, it was a necessary rebuke, but its intention was to turn Peter's mind from his curiosity to his calling. That calling was, after all, the one important issue! By the brethren, however, what had been secondary was made the main thing, and misinterpreted besides!

Although verse 23 would still be able to stand even if John had already died, nevertheless, it certainly conveys the most intelligible sense if it be construed as having been written *while John was still alive!* After John's death the practical necessity for reporting this misunderstanding on the part of the Church with reference to a word of the Master regarding the beloved disciple would probably have vanished. The error would have corrected itself by the very fact of the apostle's departure from this earthly scene. *With John still alive* the error must be corrected, in order that believers may again place the emphasis where it belonged, and may not be shocked in their faith when John dies. Hence, we read: **Yet Jesus did not say to him that he was not to die, but, If I will that he remain until I come, what is that to you?** For the meaning of this see on verse 22. Note that the passage just quoted indicates three persons: *Jesus . . . Peter* ("him") *. . . John* ("he"); and again, *Jesus* ("I") *. . . John* ("he") *. . . Jesus* ("I") *. . . Peter* ("you").

The question now is, To whom does the word *this* in the next clause refer?

24. This is the disciple who is testifying concerning these things and who has written these things. "This" cannot refer to Jesus, for he was no disciple. It must indicate either Peter or John. But Peter was no longer bearing witness (except indirectly through his epistles and through the testimony of those whom he had taught), as has already become clear, on the basis of 21:18, 19. Neither is it possible to introduce a new personality at this point. The pronoun "this" clearly refers to someone who has just been mentioned. Only John is left. That person must, therefore, be John. Accordingly, the passage must mean: "This disciple (John) is still bearing witness (the *present* participle is used: μαρτυρῶν) and, in addition, he is the one who has written (the *aorist* participle is used: γράψας; the definite article is probably authentic in both cases) these things." The two ideas are distinct; hence, *not:* "By means of his Gospel John is still bearing witness," but, "This disciple, John, is the one who is still bearing witness orally; *and* he recently recorded these things."

Verse 25 clearly shows that the expression "these things" does not refer to the contents of just one chapter. It refers to the very many things which the apostle related in chapters 1-20. Indirectly it refers even to the facts recorded in chapter 21, for this story *about* John and Peter and other disciples must have been obtained *from* (out of the very mouth of) the disciple whom Jesus loved. The manner in which it was finally recorded must have had his full approval.

Nevertheless, it is also clear that *others* had a hand in writing chapter 21 (whether as a whole or in part), for the next sentence reads: **And** *we* **know that true is his testimony.**

The Fourth Gospel is here called a *testimony.* It is the official proclamation, by an apostle and eye-witness, of the good news concerning Jesus, the Son of God. See also on 1:7, 8.

Now what verse 24 offers is a statement of confidence, a *testimonial regarding a testimony.* The authors of this testimonial express themselves in very positive language. All the emphasis is on the adjective *true.* Notice its forward position in the sentence: "We know that *true* is his testimony." Having known John for a long time, having lived with him from day to day, having heard the story from him and from others, having read about it in the Synoptics, above all: having experienced the testimony of the Holy Spirit in their own hearts with reference to the truthfulness and excellence of the contents of this Gospel, these men write as they do.

The persons who present this testimony have not identified themselves by name. In all probability they were the elders of the church at Ephesus (or: the elders of the churches in Ephesus and surroundings).

To be sure, the Fourth Gospel is not in need of this testimonial. It can stand on its own merits. It carries within itself the hallmark of its genuineness. But though *this Gospel* does not need this testimonial, *the Cerinthus-circle* needed it! See Vol. I, p. 33. By means of denying Christ's deity it was destroying the significance of his atonement and undermining the faith of the Church. And that Cerinthus-circle is still with us. It has persisted throughout the centuries, appearing now in this form, then in that. It is the duty of the Church to bid defiance to Satan and to testify both officially and unofficially (both as an institution and as an organism).

25. Now there are many other things which Jesus did, which if they were written one by one, I suppose that the world itself could not contain the written volumes.

For the reason why this passage was added see on 20:30. This closing verse has been called *hyperbole* (rhetorical overstatement). Its importance has been minimized. It has been characterized as the subjective opinion of one scribe. But in reality what is presented here is a very fitting conclusion. Many, very many facts pertaining to the sojourn of Christ on earth had been recorded in this book. All of them served to strengthen the faith of the Church in the deity and all-sufficiency of Jesus. But, now that the book is finished, no one must begin to think that the story is *complete* in the sense that everything that Jesus did has been recorded. How could it ever be possible for anyone to deposit in writing the full significance of all that Jesus did, enumerating the facts *one by one*, and bringing out the significance of each word and deed in which his love (and all the other divine virtues) was so gloriously displayed? It is literally true that were one to attempt this he would discover that "the world itself could not contain the written volumes," and this for the simple reason that no finite number can ever record the deeds performed by Infinite Love.

Pencilled on the wall of a narrow room of an asylum were these familiar words:

"Could we with ink the ocean fill,
And were the skies of parchment made;
Were every stalk on earth a quill,
And every man a scribe by trade;
To write the love of God above
Would drain the ocean dry;
Nor could the scroll contain the whole,
Though stretched from sky to sky."

Synthesis of Chapter 21

See the Outline on p. 446. *The Son of God Triumphing Gloriously. Resurrection and Appearances. Appearance at the Sea of Tiberias*

See *Preliminary Remarks*, II. *Purpose* (pp. 475, 476), which at the same time gives a Summary or Synthesis of the contents and meaning of this entire chapter.

---

³⁰⁶ 1. *The Question Formulated*

The *question* should be carefully formulated. It is not: "Are ἀγαπάω and φιλέω at times used interchangeably? Is there an area of agreement between them?" That the verbs have much in common and that ἀγαπάω is more and more encroaching upon the territory of φιλέω is well-known. We do not agree with those who

494

believe that there is "a great distinction" (R. C. H. Lenski, *op. cit.*, p. 1393) in meaning between the two verbs. But though the area of agreement may be very wide, this still leaves room for the question, "Is there *any* distinction, at least in certain contexts?"

Nor is the question this: "Was it possible for these two men (Jesus and Peter), who conversed with each other *in Aramaic*, to choose synonyms with delicate distinction, in such a manner that the exact shade of meaning for each verb could be preserved when the story was translated into Greek; and have the precise Aramaic equivalents for ἀγαπάω and φιλέω been found?" We simply do not have the Aramaic written text, if there ever was one. And we do not know enough to be able to affirm categorically that in no possible way could such fine distinctions have been conveyed by means of the Aramaic of that day. We are compelled to proceed on the basis of *the Greek text as it lies before us,* in the conviction that it is fully inspired; hence, accurate in every way.

The question, then, is this: "Here in 21:15-17 are the two verbs ἀγαπάω and φιλέω *identical* in meaning, sothat the variation in their use is merely stylistic; or do the two verbs as here employed convey meanings which *differ* to a certain extent, and does the point of the story hinge on this difference?"

II. *Those Who Accept the Former Alternative (Identity in Meaning)*

Among the translators who see no difference and therefore use the same verb seven times in their translation of 21:15-17 are the following:

Wycliffe (1380), Tyndale (1534), "Cranmer" (The Great Bible, 1539), Geneva (1557), Rheims (1582), and A.V. (1611). For these six, in parallel columns, see *The English Hexapla*, London, 1841. Other English renderings that do not bring out any difference are: Coverdale (1535), John Rogers (1537), Taverner (1539), Bishops (1568), Al. Campbell (1826), Norton (1855), Anderson (1864), Noyes (1869), English Revised (1881), A.R.V. (1901) — see, however, its footnote —, Moffatt (1913), Ballantine (1923), Torrey (1933), Spencer (1937), New Catholic Authorized (1941), and R.S.V. (1946) without even a footnote to indicate that the original uses two different verbs.

To this list should be added such translations into other languages as Syriac Peshitta (see the edition published by the American Bible Society, 1932, and also the one published by the British and Foreign Bible Society, 1950), Dutch (Statenvertaling, 1619), French (D' Ostervald, 1917), German (e.g., Luther 1522, and later translations), Danish (see the Danish-English New Testament published by the American Bible Society, 1914), etc.

Among commentators, to mention only a few, M. Dods (in *Expositor's Greek Testament,* on this verse) believes that the verbs were interchanged merely for the sake of euphony; W. F. Howard (in *Interpreters Bible*) sees no distinction; *The Westminster Study Edition of the Holy Bible,* in its comments, sees only stylistic variation, and a good many of the older commentators (including Calvin) are either entirely silent on this point or express it as their opinion that the two words are identical in meaning.

G. Abbott-Smith, *Manual Greek Lexicon of the New Testament,* entry ἀγαπάω, leaves the matter undecided ("If this distinction holds," etc.); "Bauer and Kittel in their lexicons have thrown no fresh light upon the problem" (thus, E. G. Goodspeed, *Problems of New Testament Translation.* Chicago, 1945, pp. 117, 118; I agree.)

John A. Scott, in an article, "The Words for *Love* in John xxi.15 ff.," *CLW*, 39 (1945-1946), 71, 72, defends the position that there is no distinction whatever between the two verbs, and that the author "regarded them as the very same word."

III. *Those Who Accept the Latter Alternative (Difference in Meaning)*

The list of names on the other side is just as formidable. Jerome (383 A.D.) detected a distinction here, and he has had his followers throughout the centuries, even to the present. A few of these will now be listed, together with the rendering which they propose:

"Diligis? . . . Amo" (Jerome in Vulgate, 383).

"Do you love me? . . . you are dear to me" (Weymouth, 1903, and Montgomery, 1923).

"Do you love me? . . . I am your friend" (The Twentieth Century, 1940).

"Are you my friend? . . . I love you" (Ferrar Fenton, 1905).

"Are you devoted to me? . . . I love you" (Goodspeed, 1923; again, 1945).

"Dost thou love me? . . . I am fond of thee" (Concordant, 1927).

"Dost thou love me? . . . I have affection for thee" (Lenski, 1931).

"Dost thou care for me? . . . I love thee" (Ronald Knox, 1944).

"Do you prize me dearly? . . . I love thee" (Verkuyl, Berkeley Version, 1945).

"Are you devoted to me? . . . I tenderly love you" (Williams, 1949).

"Hebt gij mij waarlijk lief? . . . (Gij weet dat) ik u liefheb" (Dutch, 1951, Nieuwe Vertaling).

"Hastu my ljeaf? . . . (jo witte dat) ik fen jo hald" (Frisian, 1946).

"Alskar du mig? . . . (du vet, att), jag har dig kär (Swedish, 1917).

In support of this position there is a long list of commentators; e.g., C. Bouma, C. R. Erdman, F. W. Grosheide (though with commendable caution), R. C. H. Lenski, A. T. Robertson, Th. Zahn, etc.

J. H. Moulton and G. Milligan in their *Vocabulary of the Greek New Testament Illustrated From the Papyri and Other Non-Literary Sources*, Grand Rapids, Mich., 1952 (reprint of the 1930 edition), state (on p. 2), "In so severely simple a writer as John it is extremely hard to reconcile ourselves to the meaningless use of synonyms, where the point would seem to lie in the identity of the word employed." R. C. Trench, *Synonyms of the New Testament*, Grand Rapids, 1948 (reprint of the 1880 edition) devotes a section to these two words, and is clearly on the side of those who see a distinction in meaning here (see pp. 42, 43). L. Berkhof, *Principles of Biblical Interpretation*, Grand Rapids, Mich., 1950, defends the same view (pp. 72, 73), as does also Thayer's *Greek-English Lexicon of the New Testament*, New York, 1889, p. 653.

One of the most scholarly and comprehensive articles written in favor of the distinction is that by B. B. Warfield, in *PThR*, XVI (1918), 153-203. He states: *"That anyone should doubt that the words are used here (in John 21:15-17) in distinctive senses would seem incredible prior to experience."*

With such a manifest division of opinion on this subject we deem it proper to present the pertinent facts, in order that the reader may get a clear picture of the manner in which the two verbs in question are used in the Four Gospels. Hence, we now present

IV. *A Chart Indicating the Meaning of* ἀγαπάω *and* φιλέω *in the Gospels.*

The meaning of ἀγαπάω and φιλέω in The Gospels.

References printed in italics indicate that φιλέω is used. The others have ἀγαπάω.

	MATTHEW	MARK	LUKE	JOHN
Quotation from Deut. 6:6 "love God"	22:37	12:30; 12:33a	10:27a	
Quotation from Lev. 19:18 "love your neighbor."	5:34; 19:19; 22:39	12:31; 12:33b	10:27b (implied)	
The Father loving the Son				3:35; 10:17; 15:9a; 17:23b; 17:24; 17:26; *5:20*
The Father loving the disciples				14:21c; 14:23b; 17:23a; *16:27a*
God loving the world				3:16
Jesus loving the Father				14:31
Jesus loving his disciples (& loving the r.y. ruler)		10:21		11:5; 13:1a; 13:1b; 13:34b; 14:21d; 15:9b; 15:12b; *11:3; 11:36*
The disciple whom Jesus loved				13:23; 19:26; 21:7; 21:20; *20:2*
Jesus issuing the precept: Love one another				13:34a; 13:34c; 15:12a; 15:17

	MATTHEW	MARK	LUKE	JOHN
Jesus issuing the precept: Love your enemies	5:44		6:27; 6:35	
The disciples loving Jesus				14:15; 14:21a; 14:21b; 14:23a; 21:15; 21:16 *16:27b*; *21:15*; *21:16*; *21:17a*; *21:17b*; *21:17c*
Sinful or very imperfect love; lack of love	5:46a; 5:46b	7:6	6:32a; 6:32b; 6:32c; 6:32d	3:19; 8:42; 12:43; 14:24; 14:28 *12:25; 15:19*
The Pharisees loving honor	*6:5; 23:6*		11:43 *20:46*	
Loving "our nation"			7:5	
Loving father, mother, son, daughter	*10:37a; 10:37b*			
Loving the money-lender who cancels the debt			7:42	
Loving much and loving little			7:47a; 7:47b	
Loving one's master	6:24		16:13	
Kissing	*26:48*	*14:44*	*22:47*	

V. Results of the Study of the Chart

From a close study of the Chart the following becomes clear:

(1) By far the most prevalent word for love is ἀγαπάω. It is used in order to indicate almost every shade or variety of love.

(2) *Both* verbs are used with respect to:

a. The love of the Father for the Son.

b. The love of the Father for his disciples.

c. The love of Jesus for his disciples (the verb φιλέω being reserved for the love of Jesus toward Lazarus; while the verb ἀγαπάω is employed with respect to the love of Jesus for Martha, Mary, and Lazarus and for the Twelve).

d. The love of Jesus for the apostle John.

e. The love of the disciples for Jesus.

f. Sinful love.

g. The love of the Pharisees for honor and public display.

Though this does not necessarily prove that the two verbs have *identical* meanings, it does indicate that the meanings in such contexts approach each other very closely. *The verb* ἀγαπάω *is pushing out the verb* φιλέω.

(3) That there is, nevertheless, a difference — however slight and fading — between the two verbs (at least, in certain contexts) is evident from the following considerations:

a. Whenever a command or precept is issued (whether it be an Old Testament command or a New Testament precept makes no difference in this connection), the verb is always ἀγαπάω; never φιλέω. Thus "Love God," "Love your neighbor," "Love one another," and "Love y o u r enemies," all require the verb ἀγαπάω (e.g., ἀγαπᾶτε ἀλλήλους).

b. Love within the family-circle is indicated by φιλέω.

c. Kissing (an outward sign of love) requires the verb φιλέω.

All this certainly points in the direction of the conclusion that although the two verbs are very close together in meaning, so close that in certain connections they may be used interchangeably, a difference can still be detected. There are contexts in which ἀγαπάω is the right word, and φιλέω will not do; others where the opposite is true.

Moreover, the area in which this difference in meaning must be sought is also clear from a study of the Chart. I can be ordered *to seek* (what I consider) *someone's good,* and to do so from a high and idealistic motive, or/and out of devotion to a principle (whether good or bad). I cannot be ordered *to have affection* for a person. *Devotion* and *emotion* are not the same. Emotions do not permit themselves to be "ordered around." Also, since φιλέω is the verb used in connection with *family-ties* and *kissing* it would seem that it implies and brings into prominence an element of subjective feeling which is not (at least not necessarily) stressed by the verb ἀγαπάω.

The conclusions to which we have arrived on the basis of a study of the use of these two verbs in the Gospels (conclusions both as to *closeness* in meaning and as to probable *difference* in certain contexts) are fully confirmed by the rest of the New Testament. Paul uses φιλέω only twice (I Cor. 16:22 and Titus 3:15). Revelation has it twice (3:19; 22:15). For the rest it disappears completely.

On the other hand, the noun *kiss* (φίλημα cf. φιλέω) occurs frequently (Rom. 16:16; I Cor. 16:20; II Cor. 13:12; I Thess. 5:26; I Peter 5:14 and also in Luke 7:45; 22:48). Note also "lovers of pleasure" (φιλήδονοι) rather than "lovers of God" (φιλόθεοι) in II Tim. 3:4. The verb ἀγαπάω is employed more than thirty times by Paul; about the same number of times by John in his epistles; and about half as many times in the other New Testament books.

In present-day Greek φιλῶ is defined as meaning: "to kiss, to love"; ἀγαπῶ: "to love, to like, to be fond of." Note that today ἀγαπῶ is very wide in meaning; yet the outward expression of affection in kissing is still φίλημα. Used widely is φίλος and φιλ— in combinations; cf. N.T.

VI. Reasons Why We Agree With Those Who See A Distinction in The Meaning of These Two Verbs Here in 21:15-17

(1) It has *not* been shown that these two verbs are *completely identical in meaning everywhere else* in the Gospels. Then why *must* they be completely identical here? The *possibility* of a distinction should, at least, be granted.

(2) Would an author who usually carefully distinguishes between one verb and another verb for *praying,* cf. 11:22; 14:16; between one verb and another verb for *knowing,* 1:10, 31; 3:11; 8:28; and between several verbs for *seeing,* cf. 20:5-8, place next to each other two verbs for *loving* without *any* distinction in meaning, and would he do that in *this* context? This seems hardly probable.

(3) Verse 17 does not say that Peter was grieved because Jesus had asked *the very same question* three times (or *the same* question for the third time), which, as a matter of fact, would not have been true even if we disregard the disputed difference in meaning between the two verbs, but that he was grieved because *the third time* (note the definite article here, and its absence in verse 16: "*a* second time") he asked: φιλεῖς με;

(4) By translating the two verbs exactly alike, the conversation is reduced to mere repetition. There is then no progress between questions two and three. Jesus once again asks the question which Peter has just answered. We grant that a reason can be suggested for this procedure, but it is hard to believe that Jesus would do this.

(5) The very fact that Peter in his answer chooses a different word than the one employed by Jesus in his question, *and that he does this not once but twice in succession,* points in the direction of a difference in meaning (be it ever so small) between the two words. It would be difficult — and perhaps impossible — to give an up-to-date illustration of the use of two synonyms thus employed, and not produce the same effect, namely, that of difference in meaning. For example:

Q. "You have recommended this person, but do you actually know him?"
A. "Yes, I am acquainted with him."
Q. "Do you know him?"
A. "I am acquainted with him."
Q. "*Are* you acquainted with him?"

The man frowned when this third time he was asked, "Are you acquainted with him?" He answered, "Now, listen! You know us well enough to realize that he and I are really acquainted with each other."

To really know a person is one thing; *to be acquainted with* that person is not quite so strong, does not necessarily imply such a high degree of intimacy or familiarity. *Synonyms are hardly ever (if ever!) exactly alike in meaning in every context.* Hence also ἀγαπάω and φιλέω are not "the same word."

For the reasons indicated we believe that ἀγαπάω *in this story* (and generally throughout the Gospels, though *with varying degree of distinctness in meaning*) indicates love, deep-seated, thorough-going, intelligent and purposeful, a love in which the entire personality (not only the emotions, but also the mind and the will) plays a prominent part, which is based on esteem for the object loved or else on reasons which lie wholly outside of this object; while φιλέω indicates (or at least tends in the direction of) spontaneous natural affection, in which the emotions play a more prominent role than either the intellect or the will.

Note on John 3:13b: "Who is in heaven."

By some this phrase is retained (Zahn, Lenski, Burgon, etc.). Impassioned pleas are made for its retention. Whether these arguments will convince even the majority of conservative scholars who have made a special study of textual criticism is doubtful.

The following should be consulted: N.N., textual apparatus, A. T. Robertson, *Introduction to the Textual Criticism of the New Testament,* New York, 1925, p. 111 (but cf. his remark with textual app. in N.N.); A. W. Argyle, "The Elements of

New Testament Textual Criticism" in *Bible Translator,* July, 1953, p. 23; Grosheide, *op. cit.,* Vol. I, p. 226, footnote 1; R.S.V. on this passage; the Dutch translation (Nieuwe Vertaling).

A. T. Robertson states as his opinion that the phrase is "probably a gloss" (Word
Pictures, Vol. V, p. 49). Grosheide adheres to Nestle's text, and omits the phrase in
his comments. Argyle states that the combined attestation of B,S,L is so strong
that the words should probably be rejected.

Dr. B. M. Metzger of Princeton Seminary, who is known as an expert in textual
criticism and has performed much valuable work in this field, has kindly furnished
me with information to some of which at the moment I did not have access. He
has also stated his own definite conclusion, which is that the phrase is not to be
considered as authentic.

From his letter I quote the following:

"The clause is lacking in the following witnesses: Aleph B L W 083 33 1241
1293 and 1010; sahidic, some mss. of the bohairic, and the subachmimic Coptic
(according to Sir Herbert Thompson . . .); Tatian (according to Ephraim and the
medieval Italian Harmony in the Venetian Dialect); Didymus and Cyril of Alexandria. In the editions of Westcott and Hort, B. Weiss, H. von Soden, and A. Merk
the clause is not printed as part of the original text; it is doubtless to be understood as interpretive gloss which crept into various types of N.T. text at an early
date, the Neutral . . . text alone remaining without accepting this fundamentally
'Western' reading."

Further Dr. Metzger points out that in the set of *Tischendorf's 8th ed. of the N.T.*
which Hort owned and on which the latter (together with Westcott) worked in
preparation of his own text, Hort has added various patristic evidences for the
shorter text of John 3:13, and has corrected two errors in Tischendorf's apparatus
(where the latter cited patristic evidence in favor of the addition). Dr. Metzger
accordingly states, "Thus there is less evidence in its favor and more evidence
against the reading than the ordinary user of Tischendorf would surmise."

It is my own opinion that stronger internal-evidence arguments will have to be
presented than have been presented thus far, before the majority of experts in the
field of Textual Criticism will be convinced that these arguments are of sufficient
weight to offset the textual evidence.

I am also of the opinion that if the words be retained, the example of the A.S.V.
should be followed; that is, a note should indicate the fact that "many ancient
authorities omit *who is in heaven.*" In fact, in that case, it might even be better,
if space allows, to state precisely which texts retain and which omit these words.

With respect to the question, "Does 3:13b express a truth?" the answer is very
easy. It certainly does give expression to a sublime and most glorious Scriptural
truth: Jesus Christ, the only begotten, is ever in the bosom of the Father (1:18).
Jesus Christ (according to his divine nature) is present in heaven even while (according to his divine and human nature) he is present on earth.

SELECT BIBLIOGRAPHY

An attempt has been made to make this list *as small as possible*. Those commentaries that are entirely or predominantly conservative in character have been marked with an asterisk (*).

Bernard, J. H., *A Critical and Exegetical Commentary on the Gospel according to St. John*. two volumes, in International Critical Commentary, New York, 1929.

*Calvin, John, *In Evangelium Ioannis Commentarii*, Berolini (apud Guilelmum Thome), 1553; English translation, in Calvin's Commentaries, Grand Rapids, 1948.

*Godet, F., *Commentaire sur l'Evangile de Saint Jean*, two volumes, Paris, 1864, 1865; English translation, two volumes, New York, 1886.

*Grosheide, F. W., *Het Heilig Evangelie Volgens Johannes*, two volumes, in Kommentaar op het Nieuwe Testament, Amsterdam, 1950.

Howard, W. F. and Gossip, A. J., *The Gospel According to St. John*, in The Interpreter's Bible, New York & Nashville, 1952.

*Lenski, R. C. H., *The Interpretation Of St. John's Gospel*, Columbus, Ohio, 1931.

*Robertson, A. T., *The Fourth Gospel*, in Word Pictures in the New Testament, Nashville, 1932.

*Tenney, M. C., *John: The Gospel of Belief*, Grand Rapids, 1948.

*Zahn, Th., *Das Evangelium des Johannes* in Kommentar zum Neuen Testament, Leipzig, 1908.

GENERAL BIBLIOGRAPHY

Only those books, dissertations, and articles are listed to which reference has been made in the two volumes on John. Many more books have been used, but these are not listed.

Aalders, G. Ch., *Daniel* (in Korte Verklaring der Heilige Schrift), Kampen, 1928.

Abbott, E. A., *Johannine Grammar*, London, 1906.

Abbott-Smith, G., *A Manual Greek Lexicon of the New Testament*, London, third edition, 1937.

Albright, W. F., *From the Stone Age to Christianity*, Baltimore, 1940.

Albright, W. F., "Some Observations Favoring the Palestinian Origin of the Gospel of John," *HThR*, April, 1924.

Albright, W. F., "The Names *Nazareth* and *Nazoraean*," *JBL*, 65 (December, 1946).

Allis, O. T., "The Alleged Aramaic Origin of the Gospels," *PThR* 26 (1928), 531 ff.

Andrews, Mary E., "The Authorship and Significance of the Gospel of John," *JBL* 64 (June, 1945).

Bacon, B. W., *The Fourth Gospel in Research and Debate*, New York, 1910.

Bavinck, H., *The Doctrine of God* (translated by William Hendriksen), Grand Rapids, Mich., 1951.

Bavinck, H., *Gereformeerde Dogmatiek*, four volumes, (third edition) Kampen, 1918.

Bergsma, S. (M.D.), "Did Jesus Die Of A Broken Heart?," *Calvin Forum*, March, 1948.

Berkhof, L. *Systematic Theology*, Grand Rapids, Mich., 1949.

Berkhof, L., *Principles of Biblical Interpretation*, Grand Rapids, Mich., 1950.

Berkhof, L., *Vicarious Atonement Through Christ*, Grand Rapids, Mich., 1936.

Bernard, J. H., *A Critical and Exegetical Commentary on the Gospel according to St. John*, two volumes, in International Critical Commentary, New York, 1929.

Bible, Holy, The, In addition to the original for both Testaments, various New Testament translations have been consulted (the familiar English modern-language translations; also translations in Dutch, both old and new, French, German, Latin, Swedish, and Syriac).

Bisek, A. S., *The Trial of Jesus Christ*, Chicago, 1925.

Bouma, C., *Het Evangelie Naar Johannes* (in Korte Verklaring der Heilige Schrift), Kampen, 1927.

Bouma, C., *Geen Algemeene Verzoening*, Kampen, 1928.

Bouman, J., "Son of Man," *ExT* 59 (1948).

Bultmann, R., *Das Evangelium des Johannes*, Göttingen, rev. ed., 1950.

Burney, C. F., *The Aramaic Origin of the Fourth Gospel*, Oxford, 1922, especially pp. 126-152.

Brown, F., Driver, S. R., and Briggs, C. A., *A Hebrew and English Lexicon of the Old Testament*, New York, 1906.

Calvin, John, *In Evangelium Ioannis Commentarii*, Berolini (apud Guilelmum Thome), 1553; English translation, in Calvin's Commentaries, Grand Rapids, 1948.

JOHN

Casey, R. P., "Prof. Goodenough and the Fourth Gospel," *JBL* 64 (December, 1945).

Chamberlain, W. D., *An Exegetical Grammar of the Greek New Testament*, New York, 1941.

Christelijke Encyclopaedia, De, six volumes, Kampen, 1925. The articles which have been consulted are not listed separately in this Bibliography.

Colwell, E. C., *The Greek of the Fourth Gospel*, Chicago, 1931.

Dana, H. E., and Mantey, J. L., *A Manual Grammar of the Greek New Testament*, New York, 1950.

Dalman, G. D., *Jesus-Jeshua, Studies in the Gospels* (translated by P. P. Levertoff), New York, 1929.

Dayton, W. T., *Greek Perfect Tense in Relation to John 20:23, Matt. 16:19, and Matt. 18:18* (unpublished Th.D. dissertation presented to Northern Baptist Theol. Seminary), Chicago, 1945.

Daube, David, "Jesus and the Samaritan Woman," *JBL* 69 (June, 1950), 137-147.

Deissmann, A., *Light From the Ancient East* (translated by L. R. M. Strachan), New York, 1922.

Derwacter, F. M., "The Modern Translation on John 19:13: Is It *Sat* or *Seated? Classical Journal* 40 (1944-1945).

De Zwaan, J., "John Wrote Aramaic," *JBL*, 57 (1938).

Dods, M., "The Gospel of St. John" (in *The Expositor's Greek Testament*), Reprint Grand Rapids, Michigan (no date).

Edersheim, A., *The Life and Times of Jesus the Messiah*, two volumes, New York, 1897.

Edersheim, A., *The Temple*, London (no date).

Elderkin, G. W., *Archaeological Paper VII: Golgotha, Kraneion, and the Holy Sepulchre*, Springfield, Mass., 1945.

Eusebius, *Ecclesiastical History*. The volumes in *The Loeb Classical Library* were consulted.

Evans, W., *From the Upper Room to the Empty Tomb*, Grand Rapids, Mich., 1934.

Field, F., *Notes on the Translation of the New Testament*, Cambridge, 1899.

Filson, F. W., *One Lord — One Faith*, Philadelphia, 1943.

Filson, F. W., "Who Was the Beloved Disciple?" *JBL* 68 (June, 1949).

Finkelstein, L., *The Pharisees*, two volumes, Philadelphia, 1938.

Finkelstein, L., and other authors, *The Jews, Their History, Culture, and Religion*, two volumes, New York, 1945.

Free, J. P., *Archaeology and Bible History*, Wheaton, Ill., 1950.

Gallus, T., "Quid mihi et tibi, mulier? Nondum venit hora mea (Joh. 2:4)," V.D., 22 (1942).

Gardner-Smith, Percival, *St. John and the Synoptic Gospels*, Cambridge, 1938.

Ginrich, F. W., "The Gospel of John and Modern Greek," *CIW*, 36 (1942-1943).

Ginrich, F. W., "Ambiguity of Word Meaning in John's Gospel," *CIW* 37 (1943-1944).

Godet, F., *Commentaire sur l'Évangile de Saint Jean*, two volumes, Paris, 1864, 1865; English translation, two volumes, New York, 1886.

Goguel, M., *Le Quatrième Évangile*, Paris, 1924.

Goodenough, E. R., "John A Primitive Gospel," *JBL* 64 (1945), 145-182.

Goodspeed, E. J., *New Chapters in New Testament Study*, New York, 1937.

Goodspeed, E. J., *Problems of New Testament Translation*, Chicago, 1945.

Greijdanus, S., *Het Evangelie naar de Beschrijving van Lukas*, two volumes (in Kommentaar op het Nieuwe Testament), Amsterdam, 1940.

Grosheide, F. W., *Het Heilig Evangelie Volgens Johannes*, two volumes (in Kommentaar op het Nieuwe Testament), Amsterdam, 1950.

Harnack, A., *The Constitution and Law of the Church*, New York, 1910.

Harper-Lewis and Short *Latin Dictionary*, New York, 1907.

Harris, E. N., "Why John Wrote His Gospel," *WE* 32 (1944), 250, 251.

Harris, R., The Origin of the Prologue to St. John's Gospel, Cambridge, 1917.

Hastings, *Dictionary of Christ and the Gospels.*

Henderson, W. Griffen, "The Ethical Idea of the World in John's Gospel" (unpublished Ph.D. dissertation submitted to Southern Baptist Theological Seminary), Louisville, Kentucky, 1945.

Hendriksen, W., *The Meaning of the Preposition ANTI in the New Testament* (unpublished doctoral dissertation submitted to Princeton Seminary), 1948.

Hendriksen, W., *Lectures on the Last Things,* Grand Rapids, Mich., 1951.

Hendriksen, W., *Bible Survey,* Grand Rapids, Mich., third edition, 1953.

Hendriksen, W., *More Than Conquerors,* Grand Rapids, Mich., sixth edition, 1952.

Hodge, A. A., *The Atonement,* Philadelphia, 1867.

Hoeksema, H., *The Amazing Cross,* Grand Rapids, Mich, 1944.

Hort, F. J. A., *The Christian Ecclesia,* London, 1897.

Hoskyns, E. C., *The Fourth Gospel,* 2 vols., London, 1940.

Howard, W. F., *The Fourth Gospel in Recent Criticism and Interpretation,* London, 1945.

Howard, W. F., *Christianity According to St. John,* Philadelphia, 1946, especially pp. 11-33; also his review of Hoskyns, The Fourth Gospel, *JThS* 42 (1941), 75-81.

Howard, W. F., *The Gospel According to St. John* (in The Interpreter's Bible, Vol. 8), New York, 1952.

Howard, W. F., and Gossip, A. J., *The Gospel According to St. John* (in The Interpreter's Bible), New York & Nashville, 1952.

Hurlbut, J. L., *A Bible Atlas,* New York, Chicago, San Francisco, 1940.

Hutton, W. R., "Spring and Well in John 4:6, 11, 12," *ExT,* 56 (1945).

Ignatius, *Epistles of. The Loeb Classical Library* has been consulted.

International Standard Bible Encyclopaedia, five volumes, edition published in Grand Rapids, 1943. The articles which have been consulted are not listed separately in this Bibliography.

Irenaeus, *Against Heresies. The Ante-Nicene Fathers,* Volume I, Grand Rapids, 1950, has been consulted.

Jeremias, J., *Die Wiederontdeckung von Bethesda,* Göttingen, 1949.

Josephus, Works of. *The Loeb Classical Library* has been consulted.

Justin Martyr, Works of. *The Loeb Classical Library* has been consulted.

Koehler, L., *A Dictionary of the Hebrew Old Testament in English and German,* Leiden, The Netherlands, and Grand Rapids, Mich., 1951

Kopp, Ch., *Das Kana des Evangeliums,* Cologne, 1940.

Lange, J. P., *John* (in Commentary on the Holy Scriptures), edition Grand Rapids, Mich. (no date).

Lenski, R. C. H., *The Interpretation Of St. John's Gospel,* Columbus, Ohio, 1931.

Luthardt, C. E., *St. John The Author of the Fourth Gospel,* Edinburgh, 1875.

Macartney, C. E., *Of Them He Chose Twelve,* Philadelphia, 1927.

Machen, G. J., *The Origin of Paul's Religion,* edition Grand Rapids, Mich., 1947.

Machen, G. J., *The Virgin Birth of Christ,* New York, 1924.

Meeter, H. H., *The Heavenly Highpriesthood of Christ* (doctoral dissertation submitted to the Free University at Amsterdam), Grand Rapids, Mich., (no date).

Menoud, P. H., *L'évangile de Jean d'après les recherches recentés,* Neuchatel and Paris, 1943.

Miedema, A., *Talks With Gabriel* (translated by H. Zylstra), Grand Rapids, Mich., 1950.

Miller, M. S., and J. L., *Encyclopedia of Bible Life*, New York and London, 1944.

Moulton, W. F., and Geden, A. S., *A Concordance To The Greek Testament*, Edinburgh, third edition, 1950.

Moulton, J. H., and Milligan, G., *The Vocabulary of the Greek New Testament*, New York, 1945.

Mulder, H., "De Datum Der Kruisiging," *GThT* (1951).

Müller, G. A., *Pontius Pilatus der fünfte Prokurator von Judäa*, Stuttgart, 1888.

Nestle, E., "Abraham Rejoiced," *ExT*, 20 (1909).

Nicklin, T., "A Suggested Dislocation in the Text of St. John XIV-XVI," *ExT*, 44 (May, 1933).

Novum Testamentum Graece, edited by Nestle, D. Eberhard and D. Erwin, twentieth edition, Stuttgart, 1950.

Nunn, H. P. V., "The Fourth Gospel in the Early Church," *EQ* 16 (1944), 173-191.

Nunn, H. P. V., *The Fourth Gospel, An Outline of the Problem and Evidence*, London, 1946.

Ogg, G., "The Jerusalem Visit of John 2:13-3:21," *ExT* 56 (1944).

Orr, J., *The Virgin Birth of Christ*, New York, 1924.

Oursler, F., *The Greatest Story Ever Told*, Garden City, N. Y., edition 1949.

Philo, Works of. *The Loeb Classical Library* has been consulted.

Phythian-Adams, W. P., "The Logos Doctrine of the Fourth Gospel," *CQR*, 139 (1944).

Redlich, E. B., *An Introduction to the Fourth Gospel*, London, 1939.

Redlich, E. B., "St. John 1-3: A Study in Dislocation," *ExT* 55 (1944).

Ridderbos, H. N., *Zelfopenbaring En Zelfverberging*, Kampen, 1946.

Ridderbos, H., *De Komst van het Koninkrijk*, Kampen, 1950.

Riddle, D. W., and Hutson, H. H., *New Testament Life and Literature*, Chicago, Ill., 1946.

Riddle-Torrey Debate, ChrC, July 18-Oct. 31, 1934.

Roberts, C. H., *An Unpublished Fragment of the Fourth Gospel*, Manchester, 1935.

Robertson, A. T., *The Fourth Gospel* (in Word Pictures in the New Testament), Nashville, 1932.

Robertson, A. T., *Grammar of the Greek New Testament in the Light of Historical Research*, New York, 1923.

Robertson, A. T., *The Pharisees and Jesus*, New York, 1920.

Robertson, A. T., *An Introduction to the Textual Criticism of the New Testament*, New York, 1925.

Robertson, A. T., *A Harmony of the Gospels*, New York, 1922.

Robinson, J. A., *The Historical Character of St. John's Gospel*, London and New York, 1908.

Sanday, W., *The Authorship and Historical Character of the Fourth Gospel*, London, 1872.

Sanday, W., *The Criticism of the Fourth Gospel*, Oxford, 1905.

Sasse, H., "Der Paraklet in John. Evang," *ZNTW*, 24 (1925).

Schaff-Herzog Encyclopedia of Religious Knowledge, The New, thirteen volumes, edition Grand Rapids, Mich., 1950. The articles which have been consulted are not listed separately, in this Bibliography.

Schaff, P., *Creeds of Christendom*, three volumes, New York and London, edition 1919.

Scott, W., E. F., *The Fourth Gospel, Its Purpose and Theology*, Edinburgh, 1906.

Scott, E. F., *The Literature of the New Testament*, New York, 1940.

Strachan, R. H., *The Fourth Evangelist, Dramatist or Historian?*, London, 1925.

Streeter, B. H., *The Four Gospels*, New York, 1925.

Septuaginta (Ed. A. Rahlfs), two volumes, Stuttgart and New York, third edition, 1949.

Sickenberger, J., "Das in die Welt Kommende Licht," *ThG*, 33 (1941).

Sizoo, A., *Uit De Wereld van het Nieuwe Testament*, Kampen, 1946.

Smilde, E., *Leven In De Johanneische Geschriften* (a doctoral dissertation submitted to the Free University at Amsterdam), Kampen, 1943.

Smith, M., "Notes on Goodspeed's *Problems of New Testament Translation*," *JBL*, Dec., 1945.

Snaith, H., "The Meaning of 'The Paraclete,'" *ExT*, 57 (Nov. 1945).

Spencer, W. H., "John 9:3" *ExT*, 55 (1944).

Stagg, F., "ΣΗΜΕΙΟΝ in the Fourth Gospel," (unpublished dissertation submitted to Southern Baptist Theological Seminary), Louisville, Kentucky, 1943.

Stalker, J., *The Trial and Death of Jesus Christ*, New York, 1894.

Stam, *De Hemelvaart des Heren* (doctoral dissertation submitted to the Free University at Amsterdam), Kampen, 1950.

Stevens G. B., *The Theology of the New Testament*, New York, 1925.

Strack und Billerbeck, *Das Evangelium nach Johannes* (in Kommentar zum Neuen Testament aus Talmud und Midrasch), München, 1924.

Sukemik, E. L., *The Earliest Records of Christianity*, Menasha, Wis., 1947.

Tacitus, The Works of. For these *The Loeb Classical Library* was consulted.

Talmud, The Babylonian (translated by M. L. Rodkinson), Boston, 1918.

Taylor, Vincent, "The Fourth Gospel and Some Recent Criticism," in *Contemporary Thinking About Jesus* (edited by T. S. Kepler), New York, Nashville, 1944, pp. 99-106.

Tenney, M. C., *John: The Gospel of Belief*, Grand Rapids, 1948.

Tertullian, *Against Marcion*

Theological Word Book of the Bible, A. (edited by A. Richardson), New York, 1952.

Theologisches Wörterbuch zum Neuen Testament (edited by G. Kittel), Stuttgart, 1933-.

Titus, E. L., "The Identity of the Beloved Disciple," *JBL* 69 (Dec. 1950).

Torry, C. C., *The Four Gospels, A New Translation*, New York and London, 1933.

Torrey, C. C., *Our Translated Gospels*, New York and London, 1936.

Torrey, C. C., *Documents of the Primitive Church*, New York and London, 1941.

Trench, R. C., *Synonyms of the New Testament*, edition Grand Rapids, 1948.

Van Deursen, A., *Bijbels Beeld Woordenboek*, Kampen, 1947.

Vincent, L. H., "L'Antonia et le Prétoire," *Revue Biblique*, 42 (1933).

Vos, G., *The Self-disclosure of Jesus*, New York, 1926.

Vos, G., *The Teaching of Jesus Concerning the Kingdom of God and the Church*, Kampen, 1950.

Walker, T., *Jewish Views of Jesus*, New York, 1931.

Werner, Eric, "Hosanna in the Gospels," *JBL* 65 (June, 1946).

Weiszäcker, C., *The Apostolic Age of the Christian Church*, London, 1894.

Westminster Dictionary Of The Bible, The, by J. D. Davis, revised and rewritten by H. S. Gehman, Philadelphia, 1944.

Westminster Historical Atlas To The Bible, edited by G. E. Wright and F. V. Filson, Philadelphia, 1945.

Young, E. J., *The Prophecy of Daniel*, Grand Rapids, Mich., 1949.

Zahn, Th., *Das Evangelium des Johannes*, in Kommentar zum Neuen Testament, Leipzig, 1908.